The High-Yield Mod
For NAPLEX Success

The High-Yield Approach

Don't just memorize, learn to understand! When you understand the concept and why it matters, you can answer any exam question. More importantly, you will be equipped to provide the best care to your patients as you begin your career as a pharmacist.

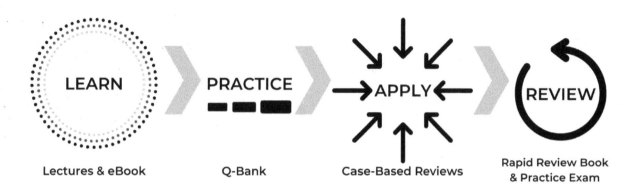

LEARN	PRACTICE	APPLY	REVIEW
Lectures & eBook	Q-Bank	Case-Based Reviews	Rapid Review Book & Practice Exam

The NAPLEX Rapid Review Book

You are going to love this product! It is the FINAL step in NAPLEX Review, providing the must-know content in an easy to study format. It fits into the High-Yield model for success as the "Review" component after you have taken the time to Learn, Practice, and Apply the core concepts.

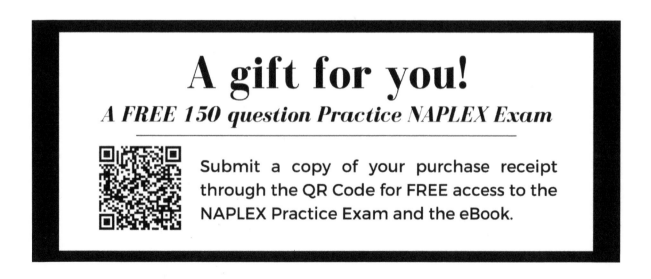

A gift for you!

A FREE 150 question Practice NAPLEX Exam

Submit a copy of your purchase receipt through the QR Code for FREE access to the NAPLEX Practice Exam and the eBook.

Need a more complete review?

Upgrade to the full Premium Package so you can have the Lectures, Q-Bank practice questions and Case-Based Reviews to complete your learning! Email customerservice@highyieldmedreviews.com today and we'll apply the cost of your book towards a full Premium Course!

HIGH-YIELD
MED REVIEWS

2022

NAPLEX

A COMPREHENSIVE
RAPID REVIEW

Editor-in-Chief:

Anthony J. Busti, MD, PharmD, MSc, FNLA, FAHA

Associate Editor:

Craig Cocchio, PharmD, BCPS, DABAT

Co-Authors:

Cassie L. Boland, PharmD, BCACP, CDCES
Shawn Riser Taylor, PharmD, CPP, CDCES
Elizabeth Travers, PharmD, BCOP
Erika Heffner, PharmD, MBA, BCPS
Christine Vo, PharmD, BCPS

Table of Contents

NAPLEX Comprehensive Rapid Review

PART 3: DISEASE STATE RAPID REVIEWS

Disclaimer for Educational Material and other Publications:

All rights reserved. MedEducation LLC, (dba, High-Yield MED Reviews) and EBM Consult, LLC are Texas corporations, advised by healthcare providers who provide unbiased education in generally accepted practices. No part of this material may be reproduced, stored, or transmitted in any way whatsoever without written permission from the President of MedEducation, LLC and EBM Consult, LLC. The editors rely primarily on peer-reviewed, published medical information and on the opinions of the editorial staff and independent peer-reviewers.

All education and recommendations are considered to be educational and not meant to apply to specific patients. The information provided should be used appropriately in the context of the provider's legal role as a healthcare provider in their respective state or country.

MedEducation, LLC and EBM Consult, LLC do not accept responsibility for the application of this information in direct or indirect patient care. It is the responsibility of the healthcare provider to ascertain the Food and Drug Administration status of each drug and to check the product information provided by the manufacturer of each drug for any changes. The editors and authors have made every effort to provide accurate and complete information and shall not be held responsible for any damage from any error, possible omission, or inaccuracy.

For additional information, please refer to our policies online.

PART 1

INTRODUCTORY TOPICS
RAPID REVIEW

GENERAL CONCEPTS

- Pharmacokinetics has to do with the movement of drugs throughout the body
  - ADME, Cmax, Cmin, Half-life, Duration of Action, Protein Binding, Vd
- Pharmacodynamics has to do with what drugs do once they are inside (i.e., mechanism of action or biologic effect)
  - Parameters: ED50% (reflects potency), LD50%, TI
- General principles:
  - Load doses (LD) achieve steady state concentrations (Css)

PHARMACOKINETICS

- **Absorption**
  - The bioavailability (F) is the fraction of drug administered that actually made it into the body.
    - Drugs given by mouth are usually < 100% or have a F that is < 1.0
  - Drugs needing an acidic environment to be absorbed = itraconazole capsules (not solution), posaconazole, atazanavir, erlotinib, dasatinib
  - Gut edema and loop diuretics → furosemide (most impacted) vs. bumetanide or torsemide (least impacted)
- **Distribution**
  - Protein binding:
    - The free fraction (or unbound) of drug exerts the pharmacologic effect
    - Clinical Example of Relevance:
      - Methimazole 0% vs propylthiouracil (PTU) 80% where PTU is less likely to get into breastmilk and possibly safer in post-partum period
      - Phenytoin risk of toxicity can occur with low albumin levels → requires the "free phenytoin" level to be checked for accuracy
  - Volume of distribution (Vd) = does NOT determine which tissue it goes just tells you the drug is leaving the central or vascular compartment and going into "tissue". The tissue it distributes into is influenced by the drug itself (molecular size, shape, etc).
    - E.g., Drug with large Vd that goes into muscle = Digoxin → selective for cardiac muscle → clinical relevance = dosed based on lean body mass
    - E.g., Drug with large Vd that goes into fat = benzodiazepines → lipophilic molecules → clinical relevance = can deposit into fat, pass through BBB to get into CNS
    - E.g., Dosing variations based on Vd = vancomycin (Vd 0.7 L/kg) use actual BW vs. gentamicin (Vd = 0.25 L/kg) use ideal or adjusted BW
    - E.g., Differences in dosing of gentamicin in pediatrics vs adult …. Why would a pediatric patient receive more per kg/dose
    - Site of action → prostate infection → must get into the prostate → clinical example: fluoroquinolones and trimethoprim/sulfamethoxazole both penetrate the prostate and cover organisms that cause prostatitis, thus they are the drugs of choice
  - Transporters:
    - Influx cell membrane transporters (e.g., OATP) help drugs to come inside of the cell
    - Efflux cell membrane transporters remove drug from inside of the cell. The most common is P-glycoprotein (P-gp) which is also prone to drug-drug interactions.
      - Clinical Example of Relevance: Amiodarone use with digoxin → must reduce dose by 50%
- **Metabolism**
  - Phase I – Oxidation / reduction reactions mainly by CYP450 enzymes located in liver (most common location), GI tract, kidney.
    - Metabolic reactions can active or inactivate drugs
    - Prodrugs (drugs that need to be activated by CYP450) = clopidogrel, codeine, cyclophosphamide, hydrocodone, iphosphamide, nabumetone, prasugrel
      - Drugs that need to be activated further for a greater effect: Loratadine, losartan, tramadol
  - Phase II – Conjugation by non-microsomal enzymes to aid increasing water solubility and elimination

- Most common pathway involves glucuronidation (UGT). Others are sulfation, acetylation, glutathione, methylation
- **Elimination**
  - Most drugs follow first-order kinetics. This is preferred and considered safer over zero-order.
  - Zero-order elimination
    - Rate of elimination is "independent" of drug concentration (i.e., the same "amount" of drug is eliminated per hour regardless of how much drug is in the body).
    - Plasma concentrations decrease in a linear fashion with time
    - E.g., aspirin, ETOH, higher doses of phenytoin (for adults this is usually over 300 mg/d)
  - First-order elimination
    - Rate of elimination is "dependent" of drug concentration (i.e., the more drug in the body the more eliminated per hour). Each half-life 50% of the concentration is gone.
    - Plasma concentrations decrease exponentially with time (i.e., curved line).
  - Renal elimination:
    - Drugs can filter or secreted and even reabsorbed by the nephron
      - E.g., thiazides are secreted into the renal tubule and must do that to work
      - E.g., SGLT-2 inhibitors block the tubular reabsorption of glucose by the nephron to treat diabetes
      - E.g., Probenecid inhibits the renal tubular secretion of penicillin into the tubule to prolong the duration of action of penicillin present in the body. This reduces dosing frequency. Probenecid can also inhibit the renal tubular secretion of uric acid thus aid in its removal from the body.
    - Drugs can be eliminated by changing the pH of urine filtrate
      - E.g., Sodium bicarbonate alkalinizes the urine to facilitate the ionization of aspirin which makes it more water soluble and able to be removed from the body in the context of toxicity

PHARMACODYNAMICS

- The ED50 reflects the potency of a drug. Note: potency does NOT mean "better" → it simply means you need LESS drug (smaller doses) to achieve the same pharmacologic effect
  - E.g., NSAIDs = Meloxicam as 5, 7.5, or 10 mg tablets vs ibuprofen as 200, 400, 600, 800 mg tablets
  - E.g., Thiazide diuretics = Metolazone 2.5, 5, 10 mg tablets vs. hydrochlorothiazide 12.5, 25, 50 mg tablets
  - E.g., Statins = Atorvastatin 10 mg being equivalent to simvastatin 20 mg
- Therapeutic index (TI) = LD50/ED50
  - We desire LARGE LD50s and SMALL ED50s → larger TI → safer to use
  - The smaller the TI the smaller the window of safe use (or the more toxic the drug can be if overdose)
  - From smallest or worst TI to greatest → Lithium < Digoxin < Carbamazepine < Phenytoin ~ Theophylline ~ Vancomycin > valproic acid

Pathophysiology
- Pharmacogenomics describes the impact on genetic factors that interact with drugs to influence efficacy and/or safety.
- From known genetic-drug relationships, appropriate selection, dosing, and monitoring can be accomplished to improve outcomes that would otherwise be unobtainable or observed inaccurately as idiosyncratic.
- Polymorphisms are a key factor in pharmacogenomics and describe the genetic variations that impact drug efficacy, metabolism, or other effects.
- Single-nucleotide polymorphisms (SNP) are most commonly associated with drug response and occur due to single base-pair substitution that can typically exist between individuals and produces two possible alleles; normal/wild type, or the variant allele.

Classic Presenting Features
- Polymorphisms in cytochrome P450 enzymes are frequently encountered in clinical practice, and among of the best described applications of pharmacogenomics.
    - Alterations in enzymatic function from genetic polymorphisms have been described for CYP2A6, CYP2B6, CYP2C9, CYP2C19, CYP2D6, AND CYP3A4/5.
    - Phase II metabolism polymorphisms have been described for glucuronidation (UGT), dihydropyrimidine dehydrogenase (DPD) thiopurine S-methyltransferase (TPMT) enzymes.
    - Drug transporter mechanisms including P-glycoprotein may be affected by genetic polymorphisms.
- A specific drug target may also be subject to genetic polymorphisms that can either render the medication ineffective or improve drug response.
    - The VKORC1 gene is responsible for encoding the vitamin K oxidoreductase enzyme, which is the specific target of warfarin. Mutations in the gene encoding VKORC1 result in resistance to warfarin.
    - The response to beta-1 antagonist therapy for blood pressure reduction has been associated with beta-1 receptor gene functional differences.
        - Genetic modifications in the beta-adrenergic G-protein coupled receptor kinase gene confers improved survival in heart failure without taking beta-blocker therapy.
- Human leukocyte antigen (HLA) genes have been linked to potentially fatal adverse reactions to specific drugs, including abacavir (HLA-B*5701), carbamazepine, or phenytoin (HLA-B*1502), and carbamazepine (HLA-B*3101).
- Genetic mutations also influence QT-interval prolongation and risk of Torsade De Pointes in genes for the pore-forming channels governing potassium and sodium transport in the cardiac cell.
- Therapeutic advantages of pharmacogenomics have led to the development of patient-specific targeted treatments for cancer, including the human epidermal growth factor receptor 2 (HER2) related to breast cancer (trastuzumab).

Primary Labs & Imaging
- Genotype / Phenotypic screening

Diagnostic Criteria
- Clinical diagnosis based on patient history, known factors, or laboratory evidence of altered drug metabolism/response.

Primary Treatment(s)
- Disease and patient-specific drug and dose selection as well as monitoring.

High-Yield Clinical Knowledge
- The efficacy of clopidogrel is influenced by polymorphisms of CYP2C19, with the CYP2C19*1 allele conferring fully functional metabolism, but the CYP2C19*2 and CYP2C19*3 alleles correspond to poor metabolism and are commonly found in Caucasian and Asian patients.
- Patients with UGT1A1*28 allele are known to be at significant risk of neutropenia due to irinotecan.

- Identification of HLA-B*5801 predicts a significantly increased risk of allopurinol hypersensitivity syndrome that may lead to Stevens-Johnson syndrome/toxic epidermal necrolysis.

HIGH-YIELD BOARD EXAM ESSENTIALS
- **PATHO:** Impact on genetic factors that interact with drugs to influence efficacy and/or safety.
- **CLASSIC PRESENTATION:** Genotype / Phenotypic screening, drug therapeutic monitoring.
- **CLASSIC FINDINGS:** Patient history, known factors, or laboratory evidence of altered drug metabolism/response.
- **TREATMENT:** Disease and patient-specific drug and dose selection as well as monitoring.

Pathophysiology
- Beta-lactam antibiotics possess similar core beta-lactam ring structures and thiazolidine rings but differ in their spectrum of activity based on sidechain substitutions.
- The core ring structure and the R1 sidechain component have been associated with hypersensitivity and antigenic reactions.
    - Beta-lactam ring structures are metabolized into major and minor antigenic determinates that may result in IgE-mediated mast cell degranulation.
    - R1 chain components have also been identified to possess antigenic properties, resulting in IgE-mediated mast cell degranulation.
- Delayed hypersensitivity reactions including Type 2 IgG and IgM antibody-mediated cell destruction (hemolytic anemia, thrombocytopenia, agranulocytosis), Type 3 immune complex-mediated reactions (glomerulonephritis, necrotizing vasculitis, rheumatoid arthritis, serum sickness, SLE), or Type 4 delayed cell-mediated hypersensitivity reactions (SJS/TEN).

Classic Presenting Features
- Type 1 – Anaphylaxis (immediate onset of angioedema, bronchospasm, hives, hypotension, wheezing, shock).
- Type 2 – Delayed onset (3 days to weeks after exposure) hemolytic anemia, thrombocytopenia, agranulocytosis, myasthenia gravis, Goodpasture syndrome, Graves' disease.
- Type 3 – Delayed onset (3 days to weeks after exposure) glomerulonephritis, necrotizing vasculitis, rheumatoid arthritis, serum sickness, SLE
- Type 4 – Subdivided to IVa through IVd based on mechanism and onset, between 3 days to weeks after exposure.
    - IVa – Contact dermatitis, tuberculin reaction (PPD)
    - IVb – Eosinophilic maculopapular rash
    - IVc – Bullous exanthems, fixed drug eruptions
    - IVd – Acute generalized exanthematous pustulosis

Primary Labs & Imaging
- No immediate labs. Beta-lactam skin testing

Diagnostic Criteria
- Beta-lactam skin testing positive reaction. Clinical evidence of hypersensitivity after exposure to beta-lactam.

Primary Treatment(s)
- Non-pharmacologic interventions include airway management (non-invasive or invasive ventilation), breathing support, discontinuation, or allergen removal.
- Epinephrine IM 0.3 to 0.5 mg q5-15minutes
- Additional supportive medications – Diphenhydramine IV 25 to 50 mg, famotidine IV 20 to 40 mg, methylprednisolone IV 125 mg, albuterol nebulized 2.5 to 5 mg, sodium chloride 0.9% IV 20 to 30 mL/kg

Alternative Treatment(s)
- Epinephrine IV 0.01 to 3 mcg/kg/minute infusion

High-Yield Clinical Knowledge
- IgE antibodies to beta-lactams decrease by approximately 10% per year without repeated exposure to where patients may no longer manifest Type 1 reactions after approximately 10 years.
- Amoxicillin or penicillin administration during EBV infection may result in a non-allergic generalized rash that is often misattributed to a beta-lactam allergy.
- Allergy cross-reactivity to beta-lactams is believed to be related to the specific R1 sidechain components of the beta-lactam structure.

- Beta-lactam agents with similar R1 sidechains represent a high risk of cross-reactivity, but the overall cross-reactivity rate between beta-lactams is approximately 1 to 2.5%.

HIGH-YIELD BOARD EXAM ESSENTIALS
- **PATHO:** Beta-lactam core ring structure and the R1 sidechain component are associated with hypersensitivity and antigenic reactions.
- **CLASSIC PRESENTATION:** Allergic reaction, all Gell-Coombs types.
- **CLASSIC FINDINGS:** Clinical evidence of hypersensitivity after exposure to beta-lactam.
- **TREATMENT:** Epinephrine, airway management (non-invasive or invasive ventilation), breathing support, discontinuation, or allergen removal.

Pathophysiology

- Drug interactions may be broadly classified as pharmacokinetic interactions or pharmacodynamic interactions.
- Pharmacokinetic interactions affect absorption, distribution, metabolism, and/or elimination of a given drug.
    - For example, trimethoprim/sulfamethoxazole and warfarin interaction possess two pharmacokinetic mechanisms – displacement of warfarin from albumin and decreased hepatic metabolism (CYP2C9 inhibition).
- Pharmacodynamic interactions occur as a result of the physiologic and biochemical effects of drugs on the body.
    - For example, ACE-inhibitors and potassium-sparing diuretics resulting in hyperkalemia or the combination of SSRIs and triptan agents may result in additive serotonergic activity.

Classic Presenting Features

- May result in failure of drug therapy or increased risk of toxicity.
    - For example, lamotrigine used in combination with valproic acid results in an increased risk of rash and Steven-Johnson Syndrome due to valproate's inhibition of phase II glucuronidation (UGT2B7).
    - Conversely, the combination of atazanavir and pantoprazole may result in clinical failure of the protease inhibitor due to significantly reduced absorption.

Primary Labs & Imaging

- Drug-specific therapeutic drug monitoring.

Diagnostic Criteria

- Clinical diagnosis aided by clinical history and known/identified drug interaction.

Primary Treatment(s)

- Identification of harmful drug interactions should prompt evaluation of the patient to determine whether immediate interventions are needed to treat the interaction's sequelae and to evaluate alternative therapeutic strategies once the interacting xenobiotic is removed.

High-Yield Clinical Knowledge

- Commonly clinically encountered drug interactions include inhibition of hepatic CYP450 inhibition, with specific isoenzyme inhibition of CYP3A4, 2C9, 2C19, 2D6, 2E1, and 1A2 accounting for more than 90% of drug interactions.
- CYP450 isoenzymes 2A*, 2B*, 2C*, 2E*, and 3A* are inducible, but this induction occurs over time as new proteins are synthesized, compared to inhibition of isoenzymes, which is immediate.
- Non-oxidation hepatic metabolic pathways subject to inhibition or induction include glucuronidation (UGT) and sulfation (TPST, SULT).
- Drug interactions involving drug transporters are also possible, altering their normal function as either influx or efflux transporters, and are commonly located in the brain, GI, kidneys, and placenta.
    - ATP binding cassette (ABC) and solute linked carriers/transporters (SLC) are transport families that are subject to drug interactions.
    - P-glycoprotein is a member of the ABC transporter family and is involved in numerous drug interactions, including cyclosporine, digoxin, quinidine, and ritonavir.
    - SLC transporters are involved in numerous physiologic processes and are also subject to drug interactions, such as inhibition of carnitine transport by valproic acid or probenecid inhibition of organic anion transporter, reducing nephrotoxicity of cidofovir, or renal elimination of beta-lactams.

Pathophysiology
- Drug allergies to sulfonamide xenobiotics can be classified as either immediate anaphylaxis or delayed hypersensitivity reaction.
- Type 1 allergy to sulfonamides is attributed to the heterocyclic ring at the N1 position, not the sulfonamide-defining moiety.
- Three separate mechanisms of non-type 1 sulfonamide reactions have been described, including the drug or metabolite acting as haptens, stimulation of a cellular or humoral immune response, or direct cytotoxicity and T-cell stimulation.
- As a result of their N4-hydroxylated metabolite oxidization to a reactive nitroso compound, sulfonamide antibiotics elicit non-type 1 hypersensitivity, which may be increased in patients who are slow-acetylators or depletion of glutathione.

Classic Presenting Features
- Sulfonamide antibiotic reactions – maculopapular rash, fever within 7-14 days of initiation.
  - May also manifest as SJS/TEN.

Primary Labs & Imaging
- Skin testing
- Suspected SJS/TEN – CBC, chest x-ray, CMP, C-reactive protein, Erythrocyte sedimentation rate

Diagnostic Criteria
- Skin testing positive reaction. Clinical evidence of hypersensitivity after exposure to sulfonamide.
- SJS – BSA less than 10%; SJS/TEN overlap – BSA 10-30%; TEN – BSA greater than 30%

Primary Treatment(s)
- For SJS/TEN – Treat similar to a thermal burn.
- Non-pharmacologic interventions include wound cleansing, debridement, nutrition (higher caloric demands), temperature management (normothermia) synthetic occlusive dressings.
- Fluid resuscitation (first 24 hours after injury) Lactated ringers, other balanced electrolyte solution.
  - Parkland formula = 4 mL x weight in kg x % TBSA with 50% administered within the first 8 hours; Brooke formula = 2 mL/kg / %TBSA
    - Modified parkland = 4 mL x weight in kg x % TBSA over 24 hours
- Fluid resuscitation (beyond 24 hours) – Albumin 5% IV (0.3 to 1 mL/kg/%TBSA)/16 per hour, urine output of 0.5-1 mL/kg/hr in adults and 1-2 mL/kg/hr in children
- Analgesia – Cooling with cold water, opioids, acetaminophen, lidocaine
- GI prophylaxis – Esomeprazole, famotidine, pantoprazole
- Tetanus immunization

Alternative Treatment(s)
- Cyclosporine, IVIG IV 1 to 1.5 g x 3 days, plasmapheresis

High-Yield Clinical Knowledge
- Patients with HIV experience a higher incidence of delayed onset hypersensitivity to trimethoprim/sulfamethoxazole than the general population.
- There is no evidence to suggest there exists true cross-reactivity between sulfonamide antibiotics (i.e., sulfamethoxazole) and non-antibiotic sulfonamides (sulfonylureas, loop diuretics, hydrochlorothiazide, etc.)
- Sulfonamides are also associated with hemolysis, methemoglobinemia, thrombocytopenia, pneumonitis, aseptic meningitis, hepatotoxicity, renal injury, and CNS toxicity.
- Sulfate and sulfite salts are not considered to have potential cross-reactivity to patients with sulfonamide allergy.

HIGH-YIELD BOARD EXAM ESSENTIALS

- **PATHO:** Immediate anaphylaxis or delayed hypersensitivity reaction (N4-hydroylated metabolite oxidization to a reactive nitroso compound).
- **CLASSIC PRESENTATION:** Maculopapular rash, fever within 7-14 days of initiation, SJS/TEN.
- **CLASSIC FINDINGS:** SJS – BSA less than 10%; SJS/TEN overlap – BSA 10-30%; TEN – BSA greater than 30%.
- **TREATMENT:** Removal of offending sulfonamide, treat similar to a thermal burn.

1. **Unit conversions**
    a. Imperial
        i. Weight (Pound, ounce, dram, scruple, grain)
        ii. Volume (gallon, quart, pint, fluidounce, fluidram, minim)
    b. Metric (International System of Units)
        i. Weight
        ii. Volume
    c. Household System
        i. Tablespoon, teaspoon, cup
    d. Temperature
        i. Fahrenheit, Celsius, Kelvin
2. **Abbreviations and Related Numbers**
    a. ss = 0.5
    b. I = 1
    c. V = 5
    d. X = 10
    e. L = 50
    f. C = 100
    g. D = 500
    h. M = 1000
3. **Percent and Ratio**
    a. W/W = grams of ingredient in 100 grams of the product; assumed for mixtures of solids and semisolids
    b. V/V = milliliters of ingredient in 100 milliliters of the product; assumed for solutions of liquids in liquids
    c. W/V = grams of ingredient in 100 milliliters of the product; assumed for solutions or suspensions of solids in liquids or gases in liquids
4. **Reconstitution**
5. **IV Drip rates, infusion, or flow rates**
6. **Ionization**

All Healthcare Professionals Play a Fundamental role in the safe and effective use of medications.
- Knowledge must extend beyond drug information.
    - Must include skills required to transform medication into appropriate dosage forms for administration.
- Specific pharmaceutical skills, including:
    - Calculating individual drug doses
    - Accurate conversion between units of measurement
- Using dimensional analysis and ratio-proportion methods of calculation is how drugs are dispensed at appropriate doses for each patient.

- Without units of measure, numbers and digits in a formula would be meaningless to practical application.
- Four systems of measure:
  - **Apothecaries' system**
    - Still found in modern pharmaceutical applications
    - Employs **minims** for liquids and **grains** for solids.
      - Phenobarbital, which can be ordered or prescribed in grains.
    - Volume = 1 pint is equivalent to 16 fluid ounces.
    - Weight = pounds (lb.), ounces.
  - **Avoirdupois system**
    - With this system, 1 pound (lb.) is 16 ounces (as opposed to 1 pound = 12 ounces in the apothecary system).
  - **International System of Units (SI), formerly known as the metric system**
    - The most logical to recognize as each unit of measure is a factor or power of 10.
      - For example, when converting from a milliliter to a liter, as 1000 mL of normal saline is equivalent to 1 L of normal saline, the decimal had moved three spaces.
  - **Household system**
    - Commonly used measurement system.
    - Teaspoons, tablespoons, cups, pints, quarts, and gallons are used to describe volume.

Apothecary - Weight

Pound (lb.)	Ounce (oz)	Dram	Scruple	Grain
1	12	96	288	5760
	1	8	24	480
		1	3	60
			1	20
				1

Apothecary - Volume

Gallon (gal)	Quart (qt)	Pint (pt.)	Fluid Ounce (fl. oz)	Fluidram	Minim
1	4	8	128	1024	61440
	1	2	32	256	15360
		1	16	128	7680
			1	8	480
				1	60

Avoirdupois

Pound (lb.)	Ounce (oz)	Grain (gr)
1	16	7000
	1	437.5

Temperature

- **Fahrenheit, Celsius, and kelvin.**
    - Describing the difference between these units, using the freezing and boiling points of water can help provide context.
    - Water freezes at zero degrees Celsius, which is 32 degrees Fahrenheit, and 273 degrees Kelvin.
    - Water boils at 100-degree degrees Celsius, 212 degrees Fahrenheit, and 273 degrees Kelvin 373.1 Kelvin.
    - Fever in Fahrenheit is 100.4 degrees, which is 38 degrees Celsius.

Number Systems

- Calculations are accomplished using two numbering systems:
    - Arabic
    - Roman

Roman Numeral	Meaning
ss	0.5
I or i	1
V or v	5
X or x	10
L or l	50
C or c	100
D or d	500
M or m	1000

- **Roman**
  - Written prescriptions frequently contain Roman numeral representation of the desired quantity of a given dosage form to be taken.
    - For example, the prescription sig "i tab PO daily" instructs the dispensing pharmacist to dispense sufficient quantity to provide the patient one tablet by mouth daily.
  - When Roman numerals are grouped, they are interpreted using addition or subtraction.
    - Super Bowl LI, or Super Bowl 51, where L = 50 and I = 1 are added together.
    - Prescription with a quantity of IV tablets, subtraction is necessary (5 minus 1 = 4).

- **Arabic**
  - Often referred to as a decimal system, the decimal itself acts as an anchor.
  - Each place to the left of the decimal identifies an increase of 10x, where each place to the right denotes a 10x decrease.

Percent and Ratio

- When a given medication is administered, its dosage form likely contains active components and inactive ingredients.
- To appropriately describe the amount of each active ingredient, there are several methods to select from:
  1. **Percent**
     a. Describes the number of a given part per 100 parts.
        i. W/W, which describes the grams of ingredients in 100 grams of the product. Assumes for mixtures of solids and semisolids (g/100 g)
        ii. V/V, describing milliliters of ingredients in 100 milliliters of the product, assumed for solutions of liquids in liquids (mL/100 mL)
        iii. W/V, where grams of ingredients in 100 milliliters of the product are assumed for solutions or suspensions of solids in liquids or gases in liquids (g/100 mL)
     b. The percentages representing these measures can be written or expressed as a decimal or using the percent symbol (%).
        i. Converting from the decimal digit to % requires dividing or multiplying by 100, depending on the conversion.
           1. For example, a lidocaine 2% can also be represented as lidocaine 2 g/100mL.
              a. 2g/100mL x 1000 mg/1g = 2000 mg/100mL (cancelling two zeros in the numerator 2000 and two zeros in the denominator 100) we get 20 mg/mL.
              b. So we now in order to give 100 mg, we arrange the following calculation: 100 mg / x mL = 20 mg / 1 mL; rearranging to solve for "x" we know that x = 1 mL x 100 mg / 20 mg; x = 5 mL.
  2. **Ratio strength**
     a. How much epinephrine in milligrams a patient would receive from a 0.5 mL intramuscular injection of epinephrine 1:1000?

        i. A 1:1000 ratio can be expressed as 1 part epinephrine per 1,000 parts of solution; in other words, 0.1 parts epinephrine per 100 parts solution can be represented using a percentage proportion as described above (W/V%) where 0.1 g of epinephrine per 100 mL solution.

           1. 0.1 g / 100 mL x 1000 mg / 1 g = 100 mg / 100 mL; (canceling two zeros in the numerator and denominator) we know now that there is 1 mg of epinephrine in 1 mL solution.

3. Parts per million, parts per billion, or parts per trillion

    a. Parts per million (ppm), parts per billion (ppb), or parts per trillion (ppt) are unique cases of ratio strength used to describe very dilute concentrations.

        i. There are few medications and doses using ppm, ppb, or ppt, but occupational exposures to potentially toxic substances are frequently described using these measures.

           1. According to OSHA, the permissible exposure limit (or PEL) to ammonia in the workplace is 50 ppm, where the potentially dangerous threshold is 300 ppm.

           2. We could express this ppm as 50 parts per 1,000,000 parts of the solution.

Reconstitution and IV Infusion Rates

- A 21-year-old patient is treated for a sexually transmitted disease (Neisseria gonorrhoeae) with ceftriaxone 500 mg administered as a single intramuscular injection.
    - After finding the reconstitution instructions in the prescribing information, you are to add 1.0 mL of sterile water to the 500 mg vial yielding a final concentration of 350 mg/mL (note that the concentration changed!).
    - To give the prescribed dose of 500 mg, what is the volume of ceftriaxone solution to be administered?
        - Arranging the proportion relationship:
            - x mL / 500 mg = 1 mL / 350 mg
            - Solving for x, x mL = 500 mg x 1 mL / 350 mg = 1.4 mL.

- In practice, you could not quickly and accurately measure 1.42857143 mL.
    - Using a 3mL syringe, the sensitivity is only a single decimal point, so we must round up or down, following the principles of rounding rules:
        - If the digit to be eliminated is less than 5, round down to eliminate it though changing the preceding digit. (4.54 to 4.5)
        - If the digit to be eliminated is 5 or greater, round up by increasing the preceding digit by 1 (4.55 to 4.6)
    - Round at the end of multiple-step calculations, not at the beginning or middle.
    - Knowing how many decimals to include depends on the clinical scenario.

- Reconstruction of Crotalidae polyvalent immune fab (CroFab).
    - For the initial treatment of a North American Pit Viper envenomation, the dose is 4 vials diluted in a final volume of 250 mL normal saline and administered over 1 hour.
        - First, reconstitution of each vial with 18 mL of normal saline, yielding a final volume of 20 mL per vial (CroFab is dosed in the number of vials, not a SI based unit of measure).
        - The total volume to add to be further diluted is
            - x mL / 4 vials = 20 mL / 1 vial
            - solving for x mL = 20 mL x 4 vials / 1 vial
            - x mL = 80 mL.
        - To correctly dilute this volume of 80 mL to a final total volume of 250 mL of normal saline, we first must withdraw volume from the normal saline.
            - Normal saline IV bag, there is 25 mL of overfill in the 250 mL product
                - (275 mL + 80 mL) - x mL = 250 mL
                - Solving for x mL = (275 mL + 80 mL) - 250 mL = x mL
                - x mL = 105 mL.
                    - Therefore, before adding the drug, we must FIRST remove 105 mL and then add the 80 mL of CroFab.
            - With the final product appropriately labeled, the 250 mL total volume is administered over 1 hour.
            - We must now determine the IV infusion rate in mL per minute to program the IV pump
                - 250 mL / 1 hour x 1 hour / 60 minutes = 4.2 mL/minute.

IV Drip Rates by Drop

- No IV pump available in the scenario; infusion rates are calculated using IV drip counters.
    - IV infusion using a drip counter
    - Between 10 to 60 drops equals 1 mL.
        - By counting the number of drops per minute, an infusion rate in mL/minute can be determined.
- A provider in an acute care hospital and receive a call from an EMS paramedic, transferring a critically ill patient to your facility.
    - They need assistance determining the appropriate infusion rate for an epinephrine drip they compounded using 1 mg of epinephrine in 1000 mL normal saline.
    - Agreeing that the desired dose is 5 mcg/minute, how many drops per minute should the paramedic observe using a 20 gtt/mL infusion set?
        - 1 mg / 1000mL x 1000 mcg / 1 mg = 1000 mcg / 1000 mL,
        - Final concentration of 1 mcg / 1 mL.
        - The desired dose is 5 mcg/minute in volume is x mL / 5 mcg = 1 mcg / 1 mL
        - x = 5 mL, or 5 mL/minute
        - Finally determining the number of drops per minute:
            - x drops / 5 mL = 20 drops / 1 mL
            - x drops = 20 drops x 5 mL / 1 mL
            - x = 100 drops per minute.
                - Therefore, you instruct the paramedic to adjust the drip rate to count 100 drops per minute.

pH and PKA

- Pharmacokinetics of medicines (absorption, distribution, metabolism, and elimination) involves the transfer of these medications across cell membranes.
- To understand and predict how a given medication will behave in this manner, an understanding of the drug's lipid solubility, molecular size and shape, and the degree of ionization.

Ionization

- Most medications are either weak acids or weak bases that, in solution, exist in both ionized and unionized forms.
  - Only the unionized molecules can penetrate lipid membranes and, in most cases, exert the desired response.
- The transmembrane distribution of either a weak acid or weak base is determined by its pKa
  - Relates to the pH at which ionized and unionized forms of medication are equal, and the pH gradient across the membrane.
- Henderson-Hasselbalch equations (describes the relative ratio to ionized to the unionized drug in a set pH of solution):
  - For a medication that is a weak acid:
    - $pH = pKa + \log(A^-/HA)$
      - Where A- (the conjugate base) is the ionized drug and HA the unionized drug.
  - For a medication that is a weak base:
    - $pH = pKa + \log(B/HB^+)$
      - Where B is the unionized drug and HB+ (the conjugate acid) is the ionized drug.
- Considering when the given environment's pH is equal to the medication's pKa, the medicine will exist as 50% ionized and 50% unionized.
- Determining the percent ionization of the given medication, the following formulas are used:
  - For weak acids, the percent ionized (%) = $100 / (1+10^{[pKa-pH]})$
  - For a weak base, the percent ionized (%) = $100 / (1+10^{[pH-pKa]})$
- When the pH is higher than the pKa (i.e., a basic environment), there will be a low concentration of hydrogen (H+) relative to a higher concentration of OH- resulting in more than 50% of the medication in its ionized state.
  - Aspirin pKa 3.5 means that at a pH of 3.5, aspirin exists equally in 50% in the ionized and unionized state.
    - In the gastric pH of about 1.5, aspirin primarily (more than 50%) lives in its unionized form permitting absorption into the blood (pH ~7.4).
    - This unionized aspirin can cross membranes and be absorbed into the blood.
    - In the blood, a more basic environment, aspirin donates its proton and exists in an ionized state (currently unable to cross membranes) where it provides its therapeutic benefits.
    - In overdose, where the blood's pH can become acidic (pH 7.0 to 7.2), aspirin can now cross other membranes like the blood-brain barrier (normal pH of CNS is 7.2) and

become ionized or trapped in the CNS, leading to toxic metabolic effects and even death.
- To correct this, clinically, we give large doses of sodium bicarbonate to increase the urine pH (targeting a pH of 8) to create a gradient where aspirin would be more unionized in the CNS relative to urine subsequently be safely eliminated from the brain.
  - In the gastric environment with a pH of 1.5 and pKa of aspirin 3.5, we can create the following relationship:
    - pH = pKa + log (A-/HA)
    - 1.5 = 3.5 + log (aspirin-/aspirin-H)
    - 1.5-3.5 = log (aspirin-/aspirin-H)
    - 10^{-2} = (aspirin-/aspirin-H)
    - 0.01= (aspirin-/aspirin-H)
    - 0.01 (aspirin-H)= aspirin-
      - There is 100x more aspirin in its unionized form (the lipid-soluble, thus cross membranes).
  - But in the physiologic blood pH of 7.4
    - pH = pKa + log (A-/HA)
    - 7.4 = 3.5 + log (aspirin-/aspirin-H)
    - 7.4-3.5 = log (aspirin-/aspirin-H)
    - $10^{3.9}$ = (aspirin-/aspirin-H)
    - 7943.2 (aspirin-H)=aspirin-
      - In this case there is 7943.2 times more ionized aspirin than unionized.

In the scenario above, where we intend to enhance the elimination of aspirin in the urine, we can see that at a normal urine pH of 5.4 compared to a urine pH of 8.0; we can substantially increase the amount of ionized aspirin in this compartment, thus enhancing elimination.

- Normal urine pH 5.4
  - pH = pKa + log (A-/HA)
  - 5.4 = 3.5 + log (aspirin-/aspirin-H)
  - 5.4-3.5 = log (aspirin-/aspirin-H)
  - $10^{1.9}$ = (aspirin-/aspirin-H)
  - 79.4 (aspirin-H)=aspirin-
  - In this case there is 79.4 times more ionized aspirin than unionized.

- But increasing the urine pH to 8.0
  - pH = pKa + log (A-/HA)
  - 8.0 = 3.5 + log (aspirin-/aspirin-H)
  - 8.0-3.5 = log (aspirin-/aspirin-H)
  - $10^{4.5}$ = (aspirin-/aspirin-H)
  - 31,622.7 (aspirin-H)=aspirin-
  - In this case there is 31,622.7 times more ionized aspirin than unionized.
    - *(Note here that although then environments pH changed to 8.0 or alkaline, we did not change the equation to the "weak base" format - the acid/base orientation of the equation refers to the pKa of the drug, not the environment)*

1. **Patient Weight**
   a. Ideal Body Weight
      i. Female
      ii. Male
   b. Adjusted Body Weight
   c. BMI
   d. BSA
      i. Gehan and George Method
      ii. Du Bois Method
      iii. Mosteller Method
2. **Nutrition**
   a. Kcal
      i. Carbohydrate
      ii. Lipid
      iii. Protein

Ideal body weight (IBW)

- **Devine formula:**
  - Male = 50 + 2.3 (every inch over 60 inches)
  - Female = 45.5 + 2.3 (every inch over 60 inches)
- In patients shorter than 60 inches (5 feet), the formula cannot function.
  - Male = 50 + 2.3 (every inch under 60 inches)
  - Female = 45.5 + 2.3 (every inch under 60 inches)
- A common application using IBW is calculating creatinine clearance using the Cockroft-Gault equation:
  - Creatinine Clearance (Cockroft-Gault) = (140 - Age) / (72 x Serum creatinine) x weight (x 0.85 if female)
    - Actual body weight is commonly used for patients with weights below their IBW.
      - In patients who are obese, adjusted body weight (AdjBW) in calculating CrCl.
        - The commonly accepted threshold is if TBW is greater than 130% IBW, use AdjBW with the following formula:
      - AdjBW = IBW + [0.4(TBW - IBW)]
- **Example – Application:** 70-year-old female patient who is admitted for community-acquired pneumonia.
  - The admitting provider places an order for enoxaparin 30 mg subcutaneously daily based on the computer calculated CrCl of 29 mL/minute.
  - Determine the appropriate dose of enoxaparin for this patient (TBW 110 kg, Height 74 inches, Serum creatinine 1.3 mg/dL).
    - IBW = 45.5 - (2.3 x [62-60])
    - IBW = 50.1
    - CrCl = (140 - Age) / (72 x Serum creatinine) x IBW (x 0.85 if female)
    - CrCl = (140 - 70) / (72 x 1.4) x 50.1 x 0.85
    - CrCl= 29.6 mL/minute
      - Based on this calculation, the dose of enoxaparin is appropriate. However, we did not consider that her TBW is significantly higher than her IBW (more than 130%). Therefore, we must re-calculate CrCl using the AdjBW.
    - AdjBW = IBW + [0.4(TBW - IBW)]

- AdjBW = 50.1 + [0.4(110-50.1)]
- AdjBW = 74.1 kg
- CrCl = (140 - Age) / (72 x Serum creatinine) x AdjBW (x 0.85 if female)
- CrCl = (140 - 70) / (72 x 1.4) x 74.1 x 0.85
- CrCl= 43.7 mL/minute

- Now that we've used the patient's adjusted body weight, we can see that perhaps enoxaparin 30 mg is not appropriate, and we should be using enoxaparin 40 mg.

Body Mass Index (BMI)

- Another method to describe a patient mass for drug dosing purposes is using BMI.
- BMI can be calculated using either SI (metric) or Apothecary units:
  - BMI = weight in kg / height in m^2
  - BMI = [weight in lb / height in inches^2] x 703
- Less than 18.5 = Under weight
- Between 18.5 to 24.9 = Normal weight
- Between 25 and 29.9 = Overweight
- Between 30 and 24.9 = Obese
- Over 35 = Extremely or morbidly obese

- BMI may not necessarily be used for drug dosing, but it is considered a limited dosing metric as comparable BMIs often can be misleading to body composition.
- For example, a patient with a BMI of 25.6 kg/m^2 would be considered overweight.
  - Patient A is 6'4" and 210 lb, and muscular (picture a football player).
  - Patient B is 5'0" and 135.3 lbs patient.
    - Using the same dose based on BMI for these patients would likely lead to different clinical outcomes if one never went to look at the patient.

Body surface area (BSA)

- Body surface area, on the other hand, is used often in dosing certain chemotherapeutic agents.
- With these characteristically toxic agents, particularly cytotoxic chemotherapeutics, their low therapeutic index and significant variability in therapeutic effect or narrow therapeutic/toxic window.
- BSA can be used as a method to reduce this variability.

- BSA in meter squared (m^2) = $\sqrt{[(\text{height in cm x weight in kg})/3600]}$

- High dose methotrexate, doses at or above 500 mg/m^2, is dosed based on BSA.
  - This methotrexate, used for various hematologic and solid tumor malignancies, is considered otherwise lethal unless appropriately reversed by leucovorin or glucarpidase promptly.

- Example: You receive the following medication order methotrexate 876.61 mg IV infusion but no accompanying orders for leucovorin or glucarpidase. The patient for which this order was received is 66 years old, weighing 66 kg, and is 66 inches tall. Is this dose above or below 500 mg/m^2?
  - To solve this question, we need to determine the patient's BSA and then divide the ordered methotrexate dose by BSA.

- BSA = √[(height in cm x weight in kg)/3600]
- We first need to convert the patients' height to centimeters:
  - X cm / 66 inches = 2.52 cm / 1 inch
  - X = 166.3 cm
  - BSA = √[(height in cm x weight in kg)/3600]
  - BSA = √[(166.3 cm x 66 kg)/3600]
  - BSA = 1.75 m^2

- Now that we know the BSA, we can determine the dose of methotrexate in mg/m^2.
  - = 876.61 mg / 1.75 m^2
  - = 500.92 m^2

- Similar to CrCl and BMI calculations, BSA can be calculated using several different formulas.
  - DuBois method, was used in this example
  - Gehan and George method, as well as the Mosteller method (less common)

Nutrition

- Enteral versus parenteral nutrition
  - Parenteral nutrition is the administration of IV nutrition to patients with an otherwise inaccessible or nonfunctional GI tract where it's anticipated that the patient will not be fed enterally (orally) for at least 7 days.
  - Enteral nutrition is a specific nutritional intervention in patients at risk of malnutrition from conventional oral feeding.
    - Enteral nutrition is often administered via orogastric, nasogastric, or percutaneous endoscopic gastrostomy tubes.

- Medication administration considerations with EN
  - Liquid dosage forms are preferred.
  - The liquid forms should be further diluted 2 to 3 times the medication volume with water, and crushed tables/capsule contents diluted with 15 mL water.
  - Before administration, flush enteral access with 20 mL of water and also after medication administration.
  - Don't crush dosage forms that shouldn't be crushed (SR or EC dosage forms, but there are many others - check to prescribe information)
  - Hold tube feeding before and after drug administration temporarily.
- Consider a patient you're following in the critical care unit receiving daily PN with dextrose 300 g, 250 mL of lipid emulsion 10%, and protein content of 105 g. What is the total caloric quantity the patient is receiving?

  - For each nutritional element, we must determine its caloric contribution. Starting with amino acids (protein), we recall that this nutritional component delivers 4 kcal/g.
    - In a total content of 105 g per the information provided, we can see that 105 g x 4 kcal/g = 420 kcal.
    - Dextrose, which provides 3.4 kcal/g, we see 300 g x 3.4 kcal/g = 1,020 kcal.

- Lipids, a 10% lipid emulsion provides 1.1 kcal/mL, a 250 mL volume would give 275 kcal (250 mL x 1.1 kcal/mL).
    - Adding the three together, we find that the patient is receiving 420 kcal +1,020 kcal + 275 kcal = 1715 kcal/day.

PN Component	Osmolarity	Kcal
Amino acids (Protein)	10 mOsm/g	4 kcal/g
Dextrose	5 mOsm/g	3.4 kcal/g
Lipid emulsion 10%	1.2 mOsm/g	9 kcal/g (EN) or 1.1 kcal/mL (PN)
Lipid emulsion 20%	1.5 mOsm/g	9 kcal/g (EN) or 2 kcal/mL (PN)
Sodium	2 mOsm/mEq	None
Potassium	2 mOsm/mEq	None
Calcium gluconate	1.4 mOsm/mEq	None
Magnesium sulfate	1 mOsm/mEq	None

- Using IBW for obese patients, where the true nutritional requirements may be underestimated.
- Using TBW may overestimate caloric requirements.
    - A commonly encountered clinical too uses correction adjustment of 25%:
        - Nutritional weight = IBW+0.25x(TBW−IBW)
            - Note that this is similar to the AdjBW formula discussed previously.

1. Preparation of solutions (Dilution, concentration, alligation)
2. Density, (D= mass / volume)
3. Milliequivalents
4. Moles and Millimoles
5. Milliosmoles

Preparation of solutions (Dilution, concentration, powder volume, and alligation)

- **Concentration**
  - Concentration is simply the quantity of solute divided by the quantity of preparation. Some examples include:
    - Normal saline, which is 0.9% sodium chloride solution, means there are 0.9 parts of the drug in 100 parts of the solution. In this case (recalling W/V), 0.9g / 100 mL
    - A ratio can also be used to describe the solution, as in epinephrine 1:1000, where there is 1 part per 1000 parts solution, or 1 g in 1000 mL (otherwise described as 1mg / 1mL).

- **Dilution**
  - Dilution refers to the addition of volume to a given drug, reducing its concentration.
    - Intravenous potassium chloride, which is commercially available as a 2 mEq/mL solution.
      - This is far too concentrated for safe administration to any patient and requires further dilution.
      - To achieve the desired final concentration of 20 mEq / 100 mL normal saline, how much potassium chloride 2 mEq/mL should be added to the 100 mL normal saline bag?
        - X mL / 20 mEq = 1 mL / 2 mEq
        - X mL = 20 mEq x 1 mL / 2 mEq
        - X = 10 mL
          - For this desired final concentration of 20 mEq / 100 mL normal saline, you must dilute 10 mL of potassium chloride 2 mEq/mL in 100 mL normal saline.

- **Powder Volume**
  - A 21-year-old patient is treated for a sexually transmitted disease (Neisseria gonorrhoeae) with ceftriaxone 500 mg administered as a single intramuscular injection. After finding the reconstitution instructions in the prescribing information, you are to add 1.0 mL of sterile water to the 500 mg vial yielding a final concentration of 350 mg/mL (note that the concentration changed!). To give the prescribed dose of 500 mg, what is the volume of ceftriaxone solution to be administered?
    - x mL / 500 mg = 1 mL / 350 mg
    - x mL = 500 mg x 1 mL / 350 mg = 1.4 mL.
      - In this case, we add 1.0 mL but can withdraw 1.4 mL! This is a result of the volume taken by the powdered drug itself.
      - This consideration does not necessarily need to be accounted for with each drug that exists in a powdered form.
      - However, until the practice of which common ones do require this consideration, careful analysis of the prescribing information is necessary.

- **Alligation**
  - Alligation is the mixing of solutions or solids possessing different percentages of strengths to get a given final concentration or percentage strength.
    - Alligation involves changing the percentages to parts and using ratio and proportion, solving each initial product's unknown amount.
      - A patient with a traumatic brain injury; they were shot in the head but are still alive. To attempt to intervene neurosurgically, their initial resuscitation requires a hypertonic sodium chloride infusion to reduce intracranial pressure.
      - The neurosurgeon requests an infusion of 100 mL of sodium chloride 7.5%.
        - You rapidly recognize that you do not carry a commercially available product with that concentration, and it must be prepared.
        - In searching options, you find one vial of 23.4% sodium chloride and an intravenous bag of 3% sodium chloride.
        - How much of each is required to make 100 mL 7.5% sodium chloride?
    - The first step to solve this problem requires us to subtract the target final concentration from the larger starting concentration and subtract the desired concentration's lesser concentration. Setting up this classic "X" pattern relationship for alligation.

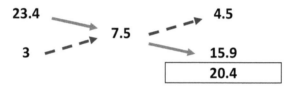

  - Based on the above calculation, we require 4.5 "parts" of 23.4% sodium chloride and 15.9 "parts" of sodium chloride 3%.
  - Adding the two together, 20.4 parts is the total final addition requirement. To determine the actual volumes to make approximately 100 mL final volume, we can make the following calculation:
    - 100 mL / 20.4 parts = x mL 23.4% sodium chloride / 4.5 parts
    - X 23.4% sodium chloride = 100 mL x 4.5 parts / 20.4 parts
    - X = 22.05 mL of 23.4% sodium chloride
      - 100 mL / 20.4 parts = X mL 3% sodium chloride / 15.9 parts
      - X mL 3% sodium chloride = 100 mL x 15.9 parts / 20.1 parts
      - X = 79.1 mL of 3% sodium chloride
        - Therefore, we must add 22.05 mL of 23.4% sodium chloride to 79.1 mL 3% sodium chloride to make the final desired concentration of 7.5%, with a volume of 101.15 (within a 10% acceptable range).

- **Density**
  - Density is the relationship between the mass of a substance and the volume it occupies and uses the formula: D= mass / volume
    - The role of density is in converting a given weight to a volume (or volume to weight).
    - As the equation above would lead you to predict, the typical units to describe density are a mass over a volume, for example, g/mL.
- **Specific gravity**
  - Specific gravity is a similar description of the ratio of a given medication's weight to the same volume of standard material (water is often the standard material for liquids).
    - There are no specific units to describe specific gravity since the mathematics cancel out the units used in its calculation.
    - Specific gravity (weight of a substance/weight of an equal volume of water)

- **Milliequivalent**
  - Milliequivalent (mEq) is a unit of measuring an electrolyte's chemical activity according to its valence.
  - It also refers to an inorganic molecule's ability to dissociate in a liquid.
  - mEq is used routinely to describe the quantity, or dose, of many electrolytes such as potassium chloride.
  - To convert the provided dose to milligrams or milliequivalents, the following equation can be used:
    - mEq = mg x valence / molecular weight
    - In the case of calcium, which has a molecular weight of 40.078 and valence of 2, we can determine the dose in mEq from 500 mg of calcium.
      - mEq = 500 mg x 2 / 40.078
      - mEq = 24.95 mEq

- **Moles and Millimoles**
  - The measurement mole is the molecular weight of a substance in grams
  - Millimole is the same weight in milligrams.
    - Avogadro's number, which is the number of particles in 1 mole (or 1 gram of molecular weight) per liter of solution.
    - Calcium has an atomic weight of 40.078, and you need to find out the weight of 5 millimoles of calcium.
    - 1 mole of calcium = atomic weight in g; 40.078 g
    - 5 moles = atomic weight in g x 5
    - 5 moles = 200.39

- **Milliosmoles**
    - In the previously discussed example where a patient required sodium chloride 7.5%, we would have to ensure it can be safely given before administering this product.
    - Namely, concerning the osmotic concentration, determining if the drug can be given through a peripheral IV (limit of 900 mOsmol/L) or requires a central IV due to the risk of serious harm if extravasation occurs.
        - This osmotic concentration is the total number of particles in solution and is expressed in milliosmoles (mOsmol).
            - mOsmol/L = weight of a substance (g/L) x number of species x 1000 / molecular weight (g)
            - Sodium chloride 7.5% = 7.5 g / 100 mL or 75g / 1L
            - Number of species for NaCl = 2
            - Molecular weight of Na = 22.9
            - Molecular weight of Cl = 35.45
            - mOsmol/L = 75 g/L x 2 x 1000 / (22.9 + 35.45)
            - mOsmol/L = 2566.7 mOsmol/L
                - Therefore, NaCl 7.5%'s osmolarity is certainly hypertonic at 2566.7 mOsmol/L and should be administered via central IV.

a. **Acid/Base**
   i. Anion Gap
   ii. Henderson-Hasselbalch Equation
   iii. Osmolal Gap
       1. Osmolal Gap (SI Units)
       2. Osmolality Estimator (serum)
b. **Electrolytes**
   i. Calcium Correction in Hypoalbuminemia
   ii. Sodium Correction in Hyperglycemia or hypertriglyceridemia
   iii. Potassium correction in acidemia
   iv. Fractional Excretion of Sodium
   v. Sodium Deficit in Hyponatremia
   vi. Water Deficit in Hypernatremia

Acid/Base Basics

- AcidEMIA is simply the measurement of a pH less than 7.35.
  - AcidOSIS is a specific physiologic process can be tied to it.
    - For example, a pH of less than 7.35 and decreased bicarbonate ($\downarrow$ HCO3) is a metabolic acidOSIS.
- A pH greater than 7.45, is an alkalEMIA.
  - It only becomes an alkalOSIS when the pH of greater than 7.45 is attributed to either a metabolic cause (increase in bicarbonate) or a respiratory cause (decrease in carbon dioxide).

- Yet another factor is the presence of a counterregulatory process to offset, or compensate, for the given "OSIS."
  - For example, a pH less than 7.35 and $\downarrow$ HCO$_3$ AND $\downarrow$ CO$_2$ is a metabolic acidOSIS with respiratory compensation.
    - pH less than 7.35 = acidEMIA
    - pH greater than 7.45 = alkalEMIA
    - pH less than 7.35 and $\downarrow$ HCO$_3$ = metabolic acidOSIS
    - pH less than 7.35 and $\downarrow$ HCO$_3$ AND $\downarrow$ CO$_2$ = metabolic acidOSIS with respiratory compensation
    - pH less than 7.35 and $\uparrow$ CO$_2$ = respiratory acidOSIS
    - pH less than 7.35 and $\uparrow$ CO$_2$ AND $\uparrow$ HCO$_3$ = respiratory acidOSIS with metabolic compensation

- **Henderson-Hasselbalch Equation** when examining the effect of different physiologic pH on the distribution of aspirin.
  - Weak acid: pH = PKA + log S/A
  - Weak base: pH = PKA + log B/S

Anion Gap (AG)

- Another concept used to describe a given acidosis is the anion gap. The anion gap a measure of the difference of charged particles, and is represented in the following formula:
- $AG = NA - (Cl + HCO_3)$
- Typically, a normal anion gap is between 8 and 16, however, the range may be slightly different from one lab to another.
- There exists a corrected anion gap calculation that accounts for the presence of albumin, which is an anion and should be corrected for if outside its normal range.
    - The corrected AG equation is:
        - $AG(corrected) = AG + [(2.5 \times \{4-albumin\})]$
    - The AG can be further corrected for lactate (which was at the time the AG equation developed, not able to be measured).
        - $AG(corrected) = AG + [(2.5 \times \{4-albumin\})-(lactate)]$
- In patients with an anion gap above 16 with evidence of metabolic acidosis from an arterial or venous blood gas, we then must identify the likely causes of the "effective anions" that are contributing to this acid/base disorder.
    - A commonly used acronym to recall the common causes of a metabolic anion gap acidosis is CAT MUDPILES:

C	Carbon monoxide Cyanide CHF
A	Alcoholic keto acidosis
T	Toluene
M	Metformin Methanol
U	Uremia
D	DKA
P	Paraldehyde Phenformin Propylene glycol Paracetamol (Acetaminophen)
I	Iron Isoniazid Inborn errors of metabolism
L	Lactate
E	Ethanol Ethylene glycol
S	Salicylates

- Some important causes of NEGATIVE anion gap acidosis include
  - Bromide, lithium carbonate, polymyxin b, hypoalbuminemia, hypercalcemia, hyperkalemia, hypermagnesemia, and multiple myelomas.

Osmolar Gap

- Osmolar gap calculation is intended to identify unmeasured osmols and appropriately intervene to resolve the underlying insult.
  - One essential difference between an anion gap is that for an osmolar gap you must measure the serum osmolarity and compare it to a calculated osmolarity.
- Osmolar Gap = calculated osmolarity - measured osmolarity
- Calculated osmolarity = 2(serum Na) + (glucose/18) + (BUN/2.3) + (ethanol/4.6)
- Normal is approximate +/- 10.
  - Common clinical scenarios where an osmolar gap is necessary to include:
    - Toxic alcohol ingestions (ethanol, ethylene glycol, methanol, isopropyl alcohol, propylene glycol).
- The osmolar gap is a dynamic finding, in that, it changes with the course of the pathophysiology.

- A 20-year-old female ingested an unknown quantity of ethanol and is now in the emergency department for altered mental status (brought in by friends). Upon initial laboratory examination, we observe the following labs: Na: 132 mg/dL, glucose 222 mg/dL, BUN 28 mg/dL, serum ethanol 332 mg/dL, and a measured serum osmolarity of 282 mOsmol/kg.
  - Using the previously mentioned equations we observe that:
    - Osmolar Gap = calculated osmolarity - measured osmolarity
    - Calculated osmolarity = 2(serum Na) + (glucose/18) + (BUN/2.3) + (ethanol/4.6)
    - Calculated osmolarity = 2(132) + (222/18) + (28/2.3) + (332/4.6)
    - Calculated osmolarity = 264 + 12.3 + 12.17 + 72.17
    - Calculated osmolarity = 360.64
    - Osmolar gap = 360.64 - 282
    - Osmolar gap = 78.64
      - This patient has a positive osmolar gap, and appropriate therapeutic interventions should be taken (in this case, intravenous volume resuscitation, thiamine and pyridoxine administration, and alcohol withdrawal precautions).

Corrected Electrolyte Calculations

- Corrected calcium = Measured Ca + (0.8[4.0-Albumin g/dL])
- Corrected sodium = Measured Na + ({1.6[measured glucose -100]}/100)
- Corrected sodium = Measured Na + (0.2 x triglyceride level)
- Corrected potassium = Measured K - (0.6[{7.4 - measured pH}/0.1])
- Corrected calcium = Measured Ca + (0.8[4.0-Albumin g/dL])

- A 48-year-old male with liver failure has a measured calcium of 6.9 mg/dL(normal 8.6 to 10.3 mg/dL), and serum albumin of 1.8 g/dL. Calculate the corrected calcium.
    - Corrected calcium = Measured Ca + (0.8[4.0-Albumin g/dL])
    - Corrected calcium = 6.7 + (0.8[4.0-1.8 g/dL])
    - Corrected calcium = 8.66 mg/dL
        - So instead of beginning calcium replacement, you inform the team that this patient's calcium is actually normal.

- A 22-year-old female, presenting with DKA and the following labs: Serum sodium 128 mEq/L, glucose 883 mg/dL. What is the corrected sodium?
    - Corrected sodium = Measured Na + ({1.6[measured glucose -100]}/100)
    - Corrected sodium = 128 + ({1.6[883 -100]}/100)
    - Corrected sodium = 140.5 mEq/L
        - So instead of beginning hyponatremia interventions, you inform the team that this patient's sodium is actually normal.
- In the same patient, an arterial blood gas provides the following data: pH 6.98, HCO3 12 CO2 28; some additional electrolytes were also provided on the ABG including a potassium measurement of 4.8 mEq/mL.
    - The team is beginning an insulin drip on the patient and decide to not include the potassium replacement component of the order. To verify this is the best intervention, calculate the corrected potassium.
        - Corrected potassium = Measured K - (0.6[{7.4 - measured pH}/0.1])
        - Corrected potassium = 4.8 - (0.6[{7.4 - 6.98}/0.1])
        - Corrected potassium = 2.28 mEq/L
            - You inform the team that in addition to initial volume resuscitation, potassium replacement should take place with careful observation of the pH and glucose before beginning insulin (which may further worsen hypokalemia).

Sodium Deficit in Hyponatremia

- Estimates the total amount of sodium that needs to be replaced in hyponatremia patients.
- Hyponatremia is a very dangerous clinical scenario that can induce seizures that are very difficult to treat, potentially leading to neurologic injury without intervention.
- Furthermore, if hyponatremia is corrected too quickly can also cause neurologic injury, potentially leading to death.
- Calculating the sodium deficit is the first step in determining how much to replace serum sodium.

- An 82-year-old female (65 kg) presents with altered mental status and serum sodium of 118 mEq/mL (the albumin was 4.0 g/dL). What is the sodium deficit if we want to correct 12 mEq/mL in the first 24 hours?
    - Sodium deficit = 0.6 x weight in kg x (desired sodium - actual sodium)
    - Sodium deficit = 0.6 x 65 kg x ([118+12] - 118)
    - Sodium deficit = 468 mEq
        - Therefore, this patient requires 468 mEq of sodium in the first 24 hours to increase the serum sodium by 12 mEq/mL.
            - From our previous discussions, we can calculate how much sodium chloride 3% IV solution is required to do this. We know that sodium chloride 3% has 513 mEq of sodium per liter solution.
            - 1000 mL / 513 mEq = x mL / 468 mEq
            - X mL = 1000 mL x 468 mEq / 513 mEq
            - X = 912.3 mL
                - This patient requires 912.3 mL of sodium chloride 3% IV over the next 24 hours to increase the serum sodium by 12 mEq/mL.
        - But because this patient is exhibiting neurologic sequela of hyponatremia, we would want to correct 50% of the deficit in the first 4 hours, then the remainder over the next 20 hours.
            - NaCl 3% dose of 912.3 mL in 24 hours to increase sodium by 12, so in other words, 76 mL of NaCl increases serum sodium by 1 mEq/L.
            - If we want 50% of the sodium corrected in 4 hours, then 1 mEq/L / 76 mL = 6 mEq/L / x mL
            - X mL = 76 mL x 6 mEq/L / 1 mEq/L
            - X = 456 mL
        - So in the first 4 hours, we must infuse 456 mL (or a rate of 114 mL/hour), with the remainder (912.3 mL - 456 mL) of 456.3 over the next 20 hours (rate of 22.82 mL/hour).

Water Deficit in Hypernatremia

- Water deficit = 0.6 x weight in kg x [(Serum sodium/140) -1]
    - The water deficit is a similar concept to what we've been discussing but applies to patients with high serum sodiums, typically dehydrated patients.
    - In this scenario, we would like to determine their water, or "free-water" deficit to be administered over 24 hours.

Fractional Excretion of Sodium (FENa)

- In some patients where the cause of oliguria and/or acute kidney injury are unclear, calculating their fractional excretion of sodium can help identify common causes to add to the differential diagnosis.
- However, the FENa should only be used in patients where the oliguric AKI occurs without any of the following: diuretic use, chronic kidney disease (CKD), urinary tract obstruction, or acute glomerular disease.
- To calculate FENa, we use the following formula:
    - Fractional Excretion of Sodium = [(Urine NA / Serum NA) / (Urine Cr / Serum Cr)]x100

- For a patient with the following findings, calculate their FENa: Serum sodium 135 mEq/L, serum creatinine 1 mg/dL, urine sodium 222 mEq/L, urine creatinine 55 mg/dL.
    - FENa = [(Urine Na / Serum Na) / (Urine Cr / Serum Cr)]x100
    - FENa = [(222 mEq/L/ 135mEq/L) / (55 mg/dL / 1 mg/dL)]x100
    - FENa = 3.0%
        - This suggests the patient may have "intrinsic" renal injury because the FENa is between 1 to 4%
        - Above 4% would suggest post-renal injury and below 1% would suggest a pre-renal injury.

- Absolute Neutrophil Count
- Child-Pugh Classification
- MELD
- Renal Function
   a. Creatinine Clearance
      i. Creatinine Clearance by Cockcroft-Gault
      ii. Creatinine Clearance by Jelliffe
      iii. Creatinine Clearance by Sanaka
      iv. Creatinine Clearance by Schwartz
   b. Glomerular Filtration Rate Estimate
      i. Glomerular Filtration Rate by MDRD

Absolute Neutrophil Count (ANC)

- In immunocompromised patients, a rapid and straightforward assessment of their risk of developing opportunistic infections can be accomplished by calculating the ANC.
- This tool can help clinical teams determine if there is an ongoing myelosuppressive clinical picture and identify a coexistence of a fever.
- Rapid broad-spectrum antimicrobials upon the identification of neutropenia is a crucial intervention to avoid excess mortality.

- ANC = white blood cells (WBC) x (segmented neutrophils% + segmented bands%) / 100

- A 54-year-old male patient with lymphoma who last received chemotherapy ten days ago presents to the ED with malaise and subjective fever. In the ED, the following labs are available: WBC 0.1 segmented neutrophils x and bands y. What is this patient's ANC?
   - ANC = white blood cells (WBC) x (segmented neutrophils% + segmented bands%) / 100
   - ANC = 0.1 (x+y)/100
      - This patient is neutropenic and requires immediate intervention.

Child-Pugh Classification

- Renal function calculations are routine to practice, but assessments o hepatic function are less commonly used.
- One such measure is the Child-Pugh Classification.
   - It is a calculation based on several liver function assessments, placing patients into three categories: A, B, or C, with C being severe hepatic impairment.

- The Child-Pugh Classification is the sum of 5 different liver function assessment risk categories:
   - Serum albumin: >3.5 1 point; 2.8-3.5 2 points; <2.8 3 points.
   - Total bilirubin: <2 1 point; 2-3 2 points; >3 3points
   - INR: <1.7 1 point; 1.71-2.20 2 points; > 2.2 3 points
   - As cites: present? No 1 point, yes 2 points, tense 3 points

	1 Point	2 Points	3 Points
Serum albumin (g/L)	Over 3.5	2.8 to 3.5	Less than 2.8
Total bilirubin (mg/dL)	Less than 2	2 to 3	More than 3
INR	1.7 or less	1.71 to 2.20	More than 2.2
Ascites (Present?)	No	Yes	Tense
Encephalopathy	No	Grade I or II	Grade III or higher

Encephalopathy: no 1 point, grade I or I 2 points; grade 3 or higher 3 points

- Child-Pugh Classification A is 5-6
- Child-Pugh Classification B is 7-9
- Child-Pugh Classification C is 10-15

MELD Score

- Another method to determine hepatic function is the model of end-stage liver disease or MELD score. The MELD score is calculated with the following formula:
  - MELD = 3.78×ln[serum bilirubin (mg/dL)] + 11.2×ln[INR] + 9.57×ln[serum creatinine (mg/dL)] + 6.43
    - A meld score of less than 9 indicates 3-month mortality of 1.9-3.7%
    - A meld score of less than 10-19 indicates a 3-month mortality of 6-20%
    - A meld score of less than 20-29 indicates a 3-month mortality of 19.6-45.5%
    - A meld score of less than 30-39 indicates a 3-month mortality of 52.6-74.5%
    - A meld score of less than >40 indicates a 3-month mortality of 71-100%

Renal Function

- We calculated an estimated glomerular filtration rate using the Creatinine Clearance by Cockcroft-Gault formula in examples from previous modules.
  - In this example, we used different weights (IBW, TBW, and AdjBW) and the Cockroft-Gault method of calculation:
    - Creatinine Clearance = (140 - Age) / (72 x Serum creatinine) x weight (x 0.85 if female)

- In this formula, the patient's actual body weight is commonly used for patients with weights at, or below, their IBW.
  - However, in patients who are obese, a correction is applied to prevent overestimation of CrCl.
  - That correction is using the adjusted body weight (AdjBW) in calculating CrCl.
  - The commonly accepted threshold is if TBW is greater than 130% IBW, use AdjBW with the following formula:
    - AdjBW = IBW + [0.4(TBW - IBW)]

- A 45-year-old male patient with a skin and soft tissue infection (cellulitis) on his right foot and will be started to vancomycin empirically. To determine the appropriate dose of vancomycin for this patient (TBW 90 kg, Height 70 inches, Serum creatinine 1.8 mg/dL), we must first determine his renal function.
    - IBW = 50 + (2.3 x [70-60])
    - IBW = 73
    - CrCl = (140 - Age) / (72 x Serum creatinine) x IBW (x 0.85 if female)
    - CrCl = (140 - 45) / (72 x 1.8) x 73
    - CrCl= 53.5 mL/minute
- According to the Cockroft-Gault formula, this patient's creatinine clearance is 53.5 mL/minute. But if we used an alternative method of calculating his renal function, would we observe the same result?
    - Creatinine Clearance by Jelliffe is an alternative formula occasionally used clinically. The result is the same units as the Cockroft-Gault formula, but its contents are slightly different:
        - CrCl (Jelliffe) = [98- 0.8 x (Age-20)] x 0.9 if female / SCr
            - For the patient mentioned above, let's use the Jelliffe formula to determine the creatinine clearance (TBW 90 kg, Height 70 inches, Serum creatinine 1.8 mg/dL):
                - CrCl (Jelliffe) = [98-0.8 x (Age-20)] x 0.9 if female / SCr
                - CrCl (Jelliffe) = [98-0.8 x (45-20)] / 1.8
                - CrCl (Jelliffe) = 43.33 mL/minute

- So when using Cockroft-Gault, this patient's CrCl was 53.5 mL/minute, but with Jelliffe, it is 43.33 mL/minute.

- Creatinine Clearance by Sanaka is yet another equation but is seldom used. **Its role is to estimate renal function in older patients (60 to 92 years) with low muscle mass (weight 24 to 61kg).**
    - For males: CrCl = (weight x [19 x plasma albumin + 32]) / 100 x SCr
    - For females: CrCl = (weight x [19 x plasma albumin + 29]) / 100 x SCr

- Lastly, for **pediatric patients, Schwartz's creatinine clearance calculation is used** since the previous equations do not account for the smaller body sizes associated with children.
    - CrCl = k x height (cm) / SCr
    - K is a proportionality constant specific to the age of the patient:
    - Infants (less than 1 years of age) = 0.45
    - Children and adolescent females = 0.55
    - Adolescent males = 0.7

Modified Diet in Renal Disease Study equation (MDRD)

- The MDRD is yet another estimate of renal function, which estimates GFR adjusted for body surface area.
  - It was designed to be used with laboratory creatinine values that are standardized.
  - It is primarily regarded as more accurate than creatinine clearance measured from 24-hour urine collections or estimated by the Cockcroft-Gault formula.
- Estimated Glomerular Filtration Rate (eGFR) = $175 \times (Scr)^{-1.154} \times (Age)^{-0.203} \times 0.742$ [if female] $\times 1.212$ [if Black]
  - For the above patient again, let's determine the eGFR using MDRD:
  - eGFR = $175 \times (Scr)^{-1.154} \times (Age)^{-0.203} \times 0.742$ [if female] $\times 1.212$ [if Black]
  - eGFR = $175 \times (1.8)^{-1.154} \times (45)^{-0.203}$
  - eGFR = $175 \times (0.4) \times (0.46)$
  - eGFR = 32.6 mL/min/$1.73m^2$
- So from three different equations, we found three different renal function estimates for the same patient: 53.5 mL/minute, 43.3 mL/minute, and 32.6 32.6 mL/min/$1.73m^2$. Which one is right?
  - This is a complicated question that requires an understanding of the methods and populations in which these estimates were validated, as well as your clinical judgment.

1. **General PK (Pharmacokinetic) formulas**
   a. Bioavailability
   b. Volume of distribution = clearance / Ke
   c. Clearance = FxDose / AUC or = KeV
   d. Half-life = 0.693/Ke
   e. Loading dose: C = Dose / Vd OR = $(D/V)e^{-Ket}$
2. **Aminoglycosides**
3. **Phenytoin**
   a. Albumin corrected phenytoin level
   b. Phenytoin Total Drug Level/Free

Medications Requiring TDM

	Side effects or ADR	Narrow Therapeutic index	Efficacy	Compliance
Aminoglycosides	x		x	
Carbamazepine	x	x	x	x
Cyclosporine	x		+/-	x
Digoxin	x	x		x
Flucytosine	x		+/-	
Fosphenytoin and Phenytoin	x		x	x
Itraconazole			x	x
Lithium	x	x	+/-	x
Phenobarbital	x		x	x
Protease inhibitors			x	x
Procainamide	x			x
Valproic acid	x		x	x
Vancomycin	x		x	

Bioavailability (F) = 100% x [(PO AUC / IV AUC)] x [(IV Dose / PO Dose)]

- The amount of drug that is absorbed when taken orally (or subcutaneously/intramuscularly, topically, or via inhalation) compared to an equivalent intravenous dose is the bioavailability.

- We consider intravenous drug administration to be devoid of any factors that would limit absorption, where no drug is lost in the administration itself.
  - The same cannot be said for orally administered drugs (or subcutaneously/intramuscularly, topically, or via inhalation).
- Certain factors that affect the oral bioavailability include the salt formulation, dosage form, and stability of the agent in the gastrointestinal tract.

Volume of distribution = clearance / Ke

- The volume of distribution is the amount of drug in the body to the plasma concentration.
  - Another way of considering this is tissue penetration.
  - Several assumptions are made for this formula of volume of distribution that is generally accepted:
    - Single-compartment model and no elimination.
- Medications that are distributed only to the plasma typically have a Vd of approximately 4% of the patient's weight, but medications that are protein-bound or have larger distributions even exceeding the total physical volume of the patient.
  - For example, amiodarone has a large Vd of 66 L/kg body weight, much larger than the average adult blood volume of 5 L, or even a physical body volume of 70 L.

Half-life = 0.693/Ke

- Half-life describes the time required for the concentration of a given medication to fall to half of its original value.
  - We use the formula Half-life = 0.693/Ke or = (0.693 x Vd) / Cl - to determine this parameter.

Clearance = FxDose / AUC or = KeV

- Clearance represents the rate of elimination of the plasma concentration.
- With most medications following first-order kinetics, clearance is constant.
  - However, in some situations, like in zero-order kinetics (phenytoin), clearance is not constant.
    - Other factors affecting clearance include blood flow to the organ eliminating the drug (kidney, liver, lung, blood) and the elimination system's working condition.

- A 64-year-old female is treated for hospital-acquired pneumonia with a combination of cefepime, gentamicin, and vancomycin. Determine an appropriate loading dose strategy for gentamicin based on the following patient data (SCR 1.0, TBW 60 kg, Ht 64 inches).
  - There are three commonly used loading dose formulas:
  - LD = Vd x Cp/S x F
  - LD = Vd(Cp desired - Cp observed) / S x F
  - LD = Cp desired x Vd

- For this specific case, we do not need to consider S or salt factor and F (bioavailability) since gentamicin is administered IV in this case.
  - The appropriate calculation to use in this specific case is LD = Cp desired x Vd.
    - For gentamicin, we know the once-daily dosing target peak level is 20 to 25 mcg/mL, so that we will select 20 as our target Cp.
    - Also, we reference drug information to learn that the Vd of gentamicin is empirically 0.25 to 0.3 L/kg, so we shall select 0.25 L/kg.
      - LD = Cp desired x Vd
      - LD = 20 mcg/mL x 0.25 L/kg
    - There's a problem; our units are not consistent.

- 20 mcg/mL x 1 mg / 1000 mcg x 1000 mL / 1 L = 20 mg/L
    - LD = 20 mg/L x 0.25 L/kg
    - LD = 5 mg/kg
  - So our initial loading dose is 5 mg/kg IV of gentamicin. This patient's weight is 60 kg, therefore
    - LD = 5 mg/kg x 60 kg
    - LD = 300 mg
  - After this initial dose of 300 mg IV is continued q24h for three days, the gentamicin 8-hour random level returned at 8.9 mg/L and another level 22-hours after the dose was 0.7 mg/L.
    - Calculate the half-life and elimination rate constant for this patient's gentamicin.
      - To solve this problem, we need to determine the elimination rate constant (Ke) first.
      - Ke= [(ln C1-lnC2)/(t2-t1)]
      - Ke= [ln(8.9 mg/L)-ln(0.7 mg/L)] / [22-8]
      - Ke = [2.19- (-0.36)] / [14]
      - Ke = 0.182
- With this new Ke, we can now determine the half-life using the equation:
  - T ½ = 0.693/Ke
  - T ½ = 0.693/0.182
  - T ½ = 3.8
    - We now know that the patient-specific Ke is 0.182 and t ½ of 3.8 hours.

Phenytoin

- Phenytoin pharmacokinetics is described as Zero-Order, non-linear, or Michaelis-Menten.
  - The unique pharmacokinetic characteristics of phenytoin extend to the observation and correction of therapeutic drug monitoring levels.
- Albumin-corrected phenytoin levels are relevant to total serum phenytoin therapeutic drug monitoring.

- A 23-year-old female patient is in the clinic for phenytoin monitoring.
  - Calculate the corrected phenytoin level considering the following available data: CrCl of 120 mL/minute, measured total phenytoin level 8.0 mg/L, serum albumin 2.8 g/L.
    - Using the phenytoin (Winter-Tozer) calculation, we can determine the corrected phenytoin level.
      - Corrected phenytoin = Phenytoin observed / [(albumin x 0.2) +0.1]
      - Corrected phenytoin = 8.0 mg/L / [(2.8 g/L x 0.2) +0.1]
      - Corrected phenytoin = 12.12 mg/L
    - Therefore, although initially, this patient's phenytoin level appeared subtherapeutic (normal range 10 to 20 mg/L), it is, in fact, an appropriate level, and no further adjustments are needed.
- Using the same scenario, but now the patient has a history of ESRD and a CrCl of 8 mL/minute, we have to use an adjusted phenytoin calculation:
  - Corrected phenytoin (revised for renal disease) = Phenytoin observed / [(albumin x 0.1) +0.1]
  - Corrected phenytoin (revised for renal disease) = 8.0 / [(2.8 x 0.1) +0.1]
  - Corrected phenytoin (revised for renal disease) = 21.1 mg/L
- In this case, the patient's phenytoin level is now supratherapeutic, and her dose should be either adjusted or remain the same with more frequent monitoring.

- Phenytoin, as described above, is more commonly measured using the free drug level rather than the total drug level.
  - The free drug phenytoin therapeutic window is 10% (accounting for 90% albumin binding) of the total window: 1 to 2 mg/L.
  - With these levels, calculating the correction for albumin binding changes is unnecessary since taking the free level already accounts for a higher free fraction of the drug.

- General Information:
  - Technically is considered a paradigm shift in the how we teach her trained physicians to think and rely on factors that guide decision making and medical practice.
    - The original publication of the EBM working group was in JAMA 1992
  - Most consider EBM as the equal and strategic contribution of:
    - Best available evidence
    - Clinical experience or expertise
    - Patient factors or preferences

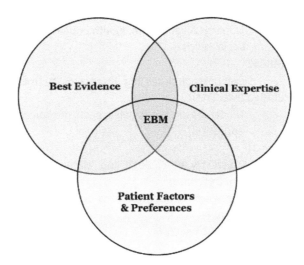

- The 5-A's or Steps of Implementing EBM
  - Ask a clinical question
  - Acquire the best evidence
  - Appraise the evidence
  - Apply the evidence
  - Assess the impact on your clinical practice

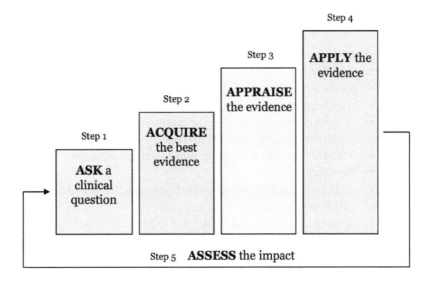

- **Asking a Clinical Question**
  - Create a structured question using the PICO or PICOTS format:
    - P = Patient or population
    - I = intervention
    - C = Comparison
    - O = Outcome
    - +/- T = Timing of the Outcome Being Assessed
    - +/- S = Setting (i.e., clinical environment applicable)
- **Acquire the Evidence**
  - Search sources of evidence:
    - **Primary Literature Databases:**
      - Represents the original studies published.
      - CINHAL
        - Nursing, Allied health, health education, occupational and physiotherapy, and social services
      - EMBASE
        - Emphasis on drugs and pharmacology (the European's version of Medline)
      - PubMed (Medline)
        - US database covering all aspects of clinical medicine, biologic sciences, and education.
      - PsychLIT
        - Psychiatry, psychology, and related disciplines
    - **Secondary Literature Databases**
      - Typically represent summaries of the original evidence or studies published
      - Examples include:
        - ACP Journal Club
        - AHRQ
        - Clinical Evidence
        - Cochrane Library
        - UK Nice
    - **Tertiary Literature**
      - Typically represents general reviews and summaries of other summaries. Sometimes covers the original evidence but is not consistent.
      - Examples include:
        - Dynamed
        - eMedicine
        - FOAMED
        - Medscape
        - UptoDate
  - Search Strategies:
    - **Search "Sensitivity"**
      - GOAL = expand search to avoid missing key articles
      - Use keywords or key phrases only in search
      - If using bili in language use "or" between text words so that you are more inclusive
      - Consider applying wild card for spelling variations (e.g., hematology vs. haematology)
      - OVERALL IMPACT = a greater number of search result
    - **Search "Specificity"**
      - GOAL = narrow the search to find more specific headings
      - Use text words that are more specific
      - If using bili and language use " and" and "not" to be less inclusive
      - Set limits on search to date range, type of study, type of subjects
      - OVERALL IMPACT = a smaller number of search results

- **Appraise the Evidence:**
  - Utilization of tools or systematic approaches to the review and critique of the published literature to determine if the published paper have results that are trustworthy, valid and relevant.
  - A number of tools have been validated and published in the literature and are discussed within this rapid review in the section on literature evaluation.
- **Applying and Assessing the Evidence:**
  - Have to do with the application of the evidence found in the literature to a clinicians practice specifically to an individual patient or series of patients with similar characteristics.

High-Yield General Concepts

- **Why does study design matter?**
  - The study design influences the likelihood or degree of potential bias which may impact the internal validity.
    - Well-designed randomized control trials have the least potential for bias followed by cohort studies, then case-controlled studies, cross-sectional studies and then case reports and qualitative studies being at the spectrum where the potential for biases highest.

	Study Design	Best Use for Design	Ability
"Potential" for Bias	**Experimental**		
Lower	Clinical Trial	• Evaluating a treatment or intervention	• Causality
	Observational		
	Cohort Study	• Determine the incidence or natural history of a disease	• Associations
	Case-Control	• Ideal for rare diseases	
	Cross-Sectional	• Determining the prevalence • Useful at assessing need	
	Case-Reports or Case-Series	• Generating awareness and/or hypotheses	• Hypothesis Generating
Higher	Qualitative Study	• When concerned about understanding human behavior & their experience	• Human reasoning

  - The overall desired endpoint or patient population to be studied may be influenced by the study design to be best utilized.
    - **RCTs**
      - Best utilized when evaluating a treatment or intervention that wants to determine causality with a high level of internal validity and low risk for bias.
        - RCTs offer her the greatest control confounders that are known to compromise internal validity.
    - **Cohort Study Designs:**
      - Are best utilized for determining the incidence of her natural history of a disease to look for associations.
    - **Case-Control Studies**
      - Are ideal for rare diseases looking for associations.
    - **Cross-Sectional studies**
      - Are best in helping to determine the prevalence while looking for associations.
    - **Case Reports & Case Series**
      - Are generally to increase awareness about something and are usually utilized for generating hypothesis that can lead to additional studies.
    - **Qualitative Studies**
      - Are mostly concerned about understanding human behavior and experiences that lead to assessments on human reasoning.
- **Study design factors that contribute to bias or compromises and internal validity:**
  - Prospective vs. retrospective
  - Randomization

- Blinding of the intervention
  - Double blinding is preferred to reduce changes in behavior by the patient and the researcher
- Utilization of a double dummy intervention
  - Useful at preventing the disclosure of study group assignment in a blinded study
- Single versus multicenter involvement
  - Multicenter involvement helps to dilute any potential bias from a single center that might occur from local or geographic practice patterns or clinician bias
- Active or placebo-controlled arms
- Control of appropriate confounders
- Influenced by the sponsor
  - More likely to be an issue with any subjective data being collected
- Conflicts of interest by the investigators themselves

Descriptive Study Designs
- **Description:**
  - Documents a clinical experience that highlights something observed in 1 or a few cases
  - Can generate hypothesis and begin the search for explanations for further study
- **Types of Publications:**
  - Case reports
  - Case series
  - Cross-sectional (surveys or nonanalytical)
  - Qualitative studies
- **Disadvantages:**
  - Cannot provide data for determining an association or causality
  - Usually do not change clinical practice
  - High risk for potential bias

Observational Study Designs

Case-Control Study

- **Description:**
  - A study design where the investigator identifies and selects patients who have the endpoint or outcome of interest (i.e., "cases") and also patients without the endpoint or outcome of interest (i.e., "controls") and looks back in time to identify exposures or characteristics that are linked to the cases.
  - Case-control studies are retrospective.

- **Study Diagram:**

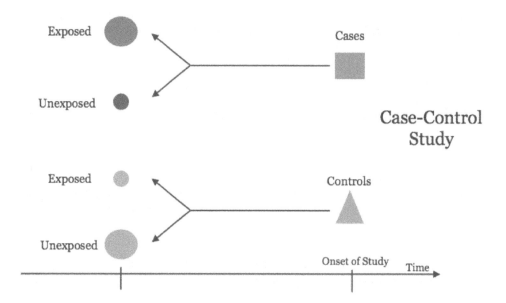

Case-Control Study

- **Advantages:**
  - Less expensive
  - Easier to do and take less time compared to most prospective studies
  - Can be useful when obtaining follow-up data that is difficult to obtain due to the nature of population being studied.
  - When disease being studies is either rare or when there is a long period of time between exposure to the time of manifesting the outcome, this study design can be more efficient.
  - Depending on the exposure and outcome of interest, this design may be the only ethical way to evaluate something.
- **Disadvantages:**
  - Potential recall bias
  - Subject to selection bias
  - Generally, do not allow investigators to calculate an incidence or absolute risk
- **Application:**
  - A case-control study may be able to show an association between an exposure and outcome, but it cannot explain causation.
- **High-Yield Board Exam Secrets:**
  - Test questions will utilize words or terminology's that include:
    - "Back in time", "retrospectively" evaluated for "risk factors"
    - Went back to look for "exposure"
    - Evaluation of a "rare event" or "rare disease"
  - **Question Secret:**
    - Question will NOT ask for prevalence or incidence because time and endpoints have already occurred.

Cohort Study

- **Description:**
  - A study design that identifies and selects two groups of patients out of a population of interest and places them into one of two cohorts, one cohort who are exposed to an intervention and another cohort have not been exposed that intervention. They are then followed over time to see if they develop the outcome of interest at various time points.

- – Cohort studies are almost always prospective, but some can be retrospective cohort studies.
  - ▪ Retrospective cohort studies are also called historical cohort studies and can evaluate a medical event from a time point in the past that then evaluates data up to the present.
- ▪ **Study Diagram:**

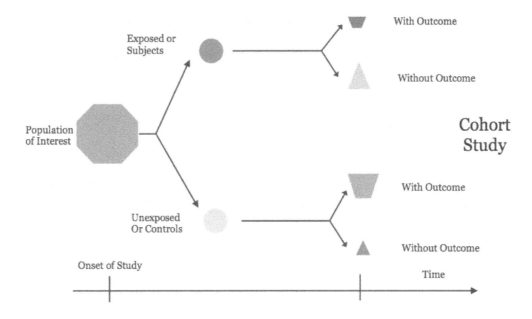

- ▪ **Advantages:**
  - – Can more clearly show the time of exposure and development of the outcome because the subjects are without the disease at baseline.
  - – Allows for evaluation of more than one outcome as it relates to an exposure
  - – Allows for the calculation of the incidence
  - – Helpful when needing to evaluate rare exposures
- ▪ **Disadvantages:**
  - – Can expensive and time consuming because of needing to follow a large number of people
  - – Loss of follow up can begin to introduce bias
  - – May not be good for rare diseases
  - – For retrospective cohort studies: recall bias due to reliance on memory of the subjects and the quality of data collected or available from the past.
- ▪ **Application:**
  - – There are many well-known cohort studies that have contributed to medicine and include:
    - ▪ British Doctors' Cohort Study
    - ▪ Framingham Heart Study
    - ▪ Nurses' Health Study
    - ▪ Physicians' Health Study
    - ▪ Women's Health Initiative
- ▪ **High-Yield Board Exam Secrets:**
  - – Test questions will utilize words or terminology's that include:
    - ▪ "Following" a large sample of people "forward" in time
    - ▪ Evaluates or assesses a large number of variables or data from my group at various "time intervals"
  - – Question Secrets:
    - ▪ A study desiring to evaluate the "natural history" or the "incidents" of something
    - ▪ Questions will not ask you to do a cohort for something about a very rare disease
    - ▪ Also, no interventions are being made by the researcher in the study design

Cross-Sectional Study

- **Description:**
  - Commonly referred to as a prevalence study since it assesses a question at a specific single point in time.
- **Study Diagram:**

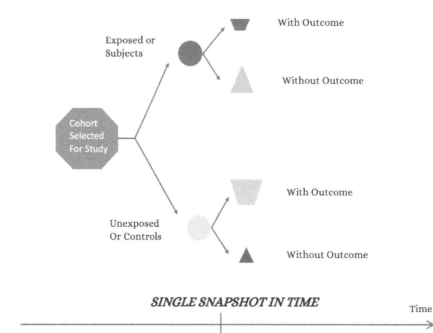

- **Advantages:**
  - Useful in assessing healthcare needs at a moment
  - Easy, fast, and relatively cheap to do
  - No lost to follow-up
  - Repeated measures can elucidate trends
  - Generates hypotheses for additional research
  - Best utilized to determine the prevalence of a disease or situation
- **Disadvantages:**
  - Risk for bias is higher compared to other study designs
  - Unable to determine the cause for an outcome
  - Cannot be utilized to determine the incidence of a disease or problem since there is no time interval
- **High-Yield Board Exam Secrets:**
  - Test questions will utilize words or terminology's that include:
    - "Snapshot" or "one–point" in time
    - Determined that "current prevalence of X"
  - Question Secrets:
    - The question will not have a "time interval" associated with it and thus the question will not be asking you to determine the "incidence".
    - Usually wanting to determine "prevalence"

Experimental Study Designs

- **High-Yield General Considerations:**
  - Offers the greatest study design for controlling for potential bias
  - The only study design that allows for the determination of causality (i.e., their intervention was the result of the desired outcome measured)

Cross-Over Study

- **Description:**
  - A study design where all patients from a population of interest are initially assigned to one of two groups, one group who gets exposed to the intervention or a second group that does not get exposed to the intervention.
  - After a period of time, an evaluation of the outcome is done and the patients from both groups undergo a period of washout so that the effect from the initial group intervention has been removed. Once this occurs, the subjects will then cross-over into the other group where the process starts over.
  - This study design provides the advantage of reducing the variability in outcome measures from outside confounders because each patient will serve as his or her own control.
- **Study Diagram:**

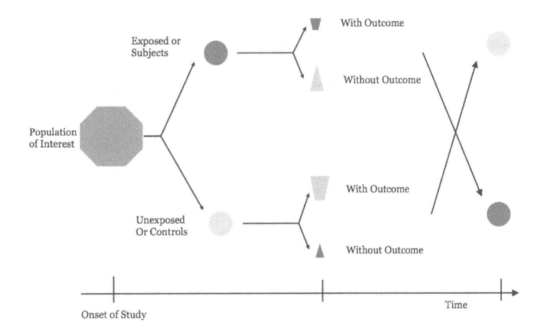

- **Advantages:**
  - Reduced influence by confounders since patients serve as their own controls
  - Reduced variability in the outcome(s) being measured, thus increasing the precision of estimation
  - Smaller sample sizes required
  - Having the opportunity to receive both treatments can sometimes be attractive for subjects
- **Disadvantages:**
  - Cannot be done when the subjects can only receive one treatment
  - Assumption of no carryover effects (from washout period) is difficult to sometimes accurately test
  - May take longer than a randomized clinical trial since patients have to cross over into each arm after an appropriate washout period

- Can be subject to period effects where differences in the effectiveness of an intervention can occur due to the passage of time. For example:
    - Development of tolerance
    - Resistance
    - Dropouts
    - Changes in the disease process being evaluated or treated
- **High-Yield Board Exam Secrets:**
    - Test questions will utilize words or terminology's that include:
        - A "washed out period" will be mentioned in the study design
    - Additional secrets:
        - A prospective study done in 2 separate phases
        - The question may mention having limited number of available patients to service subjects in the study while wanting to maximize or maintain power

Randomized Controlled Trial (RCT)

- **Description:**
    - A prospective study where patients from a population of interest are randomly assigned to either a experimental (treatment) or a control group and then are followed up a specific time intervals to collect data on the outcomes of interest.
    - Patients in the control group usually receive a placebo or comparative treatment generally considered already part of the standard of care.
- **Study Diagram:**

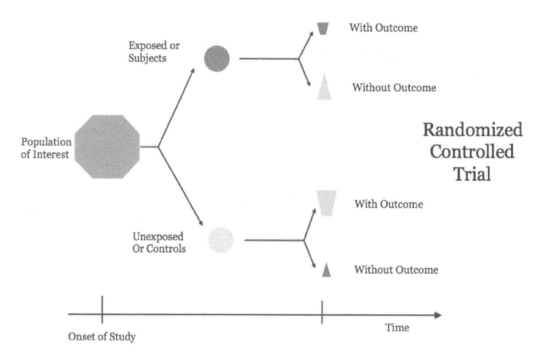

- **Advantages:**
    - Considered the gold standard for helping to explain an effect
    - When appropriate randomization has occurred, this design allows for washout of most population bias
    - Reduced influence by confounders because they can be controlled for by the investigators
    - Reduced variability in the outcome(s) being measured, thus increasing the precision of estimation (assumes proper control of confounders)
    - Is easier to blind patients than observational studies

- **Disadvantages:**
  - Generally, more time consuming
  - Tend to be more expensive

Types of Study Groups / Samples

- **Questions to Ask About Who Was Studied**
  - How many study groups or study arms are there?
    - If two or more then will need consider statistical analysis for multiple groups
  - Are the patients in the study in one or more group or is this a cross-over study?
    - If yes, then the study is dealing with patients with "related groups"
      - This means the patients will serve as their own controls
    - If no, then you have "independent groups" which means the patients in each study group are technically different patients
  - Once the type of study groups being studied is known, then determine the type of data that is reflected in the endpoint of the study or outcome in question:
    - Nominal, ordinal, or continuous (see more below for details)
  - Knowing the type of groups and data helps to govern the choice of statistical analysis that should be done (see table below)
- **Summary of Group Types:**
  - **Related Groups**
    - Reflect the same patients in ALL study groups or study arms
    - Examples:
      - Cross-over studies
      - Retrospective Study of all patients at the start and end of the study
      - Studies using the same person but topical application in two locations (e.g., left vs right eye)
  - **Independent Groups**
    - The study groups or study arms are made up of different patients (biologically different individuals that do *NOT* cross-over).
    - Examples:
      - RCT
      - Cohort Study
      - Case-Controlled Study

Distribution of Sample Data

Nonparametric Statistical Analysis

- **Definition:**
  - Refers to the use of statistical tests or methods when the data being studied comes from a sample or population of people that does not follow a normal distributed.
- **Characteristics:**
  - Assumes patient population being studied is not normally distributed (i.e., as seen with outliers)
  - Type of data: Nominal or Ordinal.
    - *Nominal*:
      - When numbers are assigned to characteristics for the purpose of data classification. Do not have a sense of order or rank.
    - *Ordinal*:
      - When numbers are assigned to data that a sense of rank or order, but the magnitude of difference between those numbers is not known.
  - The usual central measure is a median
- **Example Nonparametric Statistical Tests:**
  - Mann-Whitney test (assumes 2 independent groups (i.e., not related) being studied)

- Kruskal-Wallis test (assumes > 2 independent groups being studied/compared)
- Spearman (correlation test)

Parametric Statistical Analysis

- **Definition:**
  - Refers to the use of statistical tests or methods when the data being studied comes from a sample or population of people that is normally distributed.
- **Characteristics:**
  - Assumes patient population being studied is normally distributed
  - Assumes the variance is homogeneous
  - Type of data: interval or ratio. Sometimes referred to as continuous variables/data.
    - *Interval scale data*:
      - When numbers have units that are of equal magnitude as well as rank order on a scale *without* an absolute zero
    - *Ratio scale data*:
      - When numbers have units that are of equal magnitude as well as rank order on a scale *with* an absolute zero
  - The usual central measure is a mean
- **Example Parametric Statistical Tests:**
  - T-test (assumes 2 independent groups (i.e., not related) being studied)
  - One-way ANOVA (assumes > 2 independent groups being studied/compared)
  - Pearson (correlation test)

Type of Data

Nominal Data

- **Definition:**
  - When numbers are assigned to characteristics for the purpose of data classification arbitrarily and without any regard to order.
- **Characteristics:**
  - The numbers selected or assigned to a variable are arbitrary.
    - Thus, the data descriptors are considered "categorical" or "dichotomous."
  - Data endpoints are assigned these arbitrary numbers without any regard to order or rank.
  - Data follows a binomial distribution in many cases because the endpoint is treated as a "yes or no" or "either did or did not..."
    - As such there cannot be an average or a mean value/result
- **Applicable Measure of Data Variability:**
  - Mode
  - Frequency
  - Note: There is no mean, median, standard deviation.
    - Example: If the endpoint or main outcome is mortality then at the end of the study the patient/subject in the study is either dead or alive. The patient cannot be in between or almost dead or possibly dead.
      - It is a categorical designation of being one or the other, thus you cannot have an average or mean or even a median.
- **Examples of Nominal Data:**
  - *Achievement of a desired clinical goal (e.g., a blood pressure of < 130/80)*:
    - Yes, the patient goal was achieved is assigned the number 1
    - No, the patient goal was NOT achieved is assigned the number 2

- *Mortality*:
  - Being alive at the end of a study is assigned the number 1
  - Being dead at the end of a study is assigned the number 2
  - Note: There cannot be an in-between

Ordinal Data

- **Definition:**
  - When numbers are purposefully assigned to data that have a sense of rank or order, but the magnitude of difference between those numbers is not known or cannot be measured.
- **Characteristics:**
  - Ordinal scale data can be in specific "order" (i.e., "ORDinal data reflects an "order" or "ordering" of the endpoint options.
  - Unlike with nominal data, the assigned numbers are NOT arbitrary.
  - This type of data scale does NOT allow for the calculation of an average or mean since the magnitude of difference between each assigned number is NOT the same.
    - *Example*: An average of the degree of heart failure a group of patients have cannot be described with a mean. A patient cannot have Class 2.5 heart failure, because we do not really know what that means clinically.
- **Applicable Measure of Data Variability:**
  - Mode
  - Median
  - Frequency
  - Range or +/- Interquartile Range (IQR)
  - Note: You cannot determine an "average" or mean value since the magnitude of difference between data designations are not the same. This is also why a standard deviation cannot be representative of ordinal data, but rather a median +/- IQR
    - Example: There is no such thing as a patient with heart failure class 2.6. What does that mean? You don't know and can't tell with ordinal data.
- **Examples of Nominal Data:**
  - In both of the following examples there is a sense or ranking to condition of the patient. However, the magnitude of difference between each assigned level is not the same.
  - *New York Heart Association (NYHA) Heart Failure Classification*:
    - There are 4 classifications (Class I, II, III, & IV)
    - There is a sense of order or rank, where a patient with NYHA Class III heart failure has more symptoms and complications than a patient with NYHA Class I heart failure.
  - *Glasgow Coma Scale*:
    - Score can range from as low as 3 and as high as 15.
    - A trauma patient with a score of 8 is considered more unstable than a trauma patient whose GCS is 14.

Continuous (Interval or Ratio) Scale Data

- **Definition:**
  - Data points where there is a "sense of order" and "rank". In addition, the magnitude of difference between each number is the same and measurable.
  - Made up of two types of scales of data, interval scale and ratio scale.
  - The only difference between interval and ratio scale data is whether or not the scale being referred to has an absolute zero.
    - *Interval scale data*:
      - When numbers have units that are of equal magnitude as well as rank order on a scale *without* an absolute zero
      - Scales of this type can have an arbitrarily assigned "zero", but it will not correspond to an absence of the measured variable. For example, temperature in Fahrenheit scale.

- *Ratio scale data*:
  - When numbers have units that are of equal magnitude as well as rank order on a scale *with* an absolute zero
  - Examples include:
    - o Pulse (heart rate)
    - o Blood pressure
    - o Temperature
    - o Distance or length of something measured
- **Characteristics:**
  - For interval and ratio data can be converted into ordinal data, but ordinal data cannot be converted into continuous data.
  - Can be described as a mean or median.
- **Applicable Measure of Data Variability:**
  - Mode
  - Median
  - Mean
  - Frequency
  - Range or +/- Interquartile Range
  - Standard Deviation
  - Note: The only time you might report this data as a median instead of a mean would be in the presence of data endpoints that are serving as "outliers" which can skew the data.
    - If the data is skewed (right or left) due to outliers, then the data analysis should be done using non-parametric statistical test since the data is not normally distributed.

Summary Table – Statistical Tests

Type of Data	Two Independent Samples/Groups	Related or Paired Samples/Groups	Three or More Independent Groups	Three or More Related Samples/Groups	Measures of Correlation
Nominal	Chi Square Fisher's Exact	McNemar Test	Chi-Square for K Independent Samples	Cochran Q	Contingency Coefficient
Ordinal	Mann-Whitney U Wilcoxon Rank Sum	Sign Test Wilcoxon Signed Rank	Kruskal-Wallis	Freidman	Spearman Kendal Rank Kendal Coe
Continuous	Student's t-test Mann-Whitney U	Paired t-test	ANOVA	ANOVA	Pearson's Correlation

Other Statistical Considerations & Findings

Alpha (α) Value

- **Definition:**
  - α ("Alpha") is the probability of concluding that there is a difference between the groups studied, but in reality, there is no difference (also known as making a "type I error").
  - α is usually set *a-priori* to be 0.05.
  - A finding is considered to be statistically significant if the p-value obtained is < 0.05.
- **Interpretation:**
  - Simplistically, α is the chance of making a type I error.
  - The smaller the α value the lower the risk of making a type I error. Note: doing this also usually means the investigator will need a larger sample size to a difference if it exists.

- **Considerations:**
  - The alpha value and sample size are the two most common contributors to the power of a study.
  - Setting the alpha to be smaller (e.g., going from an $\alpha < 0.05$ to an $\alpha < 0.025$) prior to starting a study will make it harder for investigators to find a difference if in fact a difference is to be found.
  - However, if a difference is found when doing this, the risk of making a type I error is lower.

Beta (β)

- **Definition:**
  - The probability of saying or concluding that a study found no difference between groups when in reality there is a difference.
  - This is also known as the chance of making a type II error or false negative rate
- **Application:**
  - β ("Beta") is an important part of power, which is defined as being $1 - \beta$.
  - Most clinicians accept a power of 0.8 (or 80%), which means β has to be 0.2 (or 20%)
  - Reducing β will decrease the chance of making a type I error and at the same time increase the power of the study.
    - Note: As β is decreased, the sample size will increase in order to find a difference if one exists. This will clearly add to the cost and time to complete a study.

Power Analysis

- **Definition:**
  - Power = $1 - \beta$
  - Where β ("Beta") is the chance of making a type II error or false negative rate
  - A type II error occurs when you fail to reject the null hypothesis and in fact, the alternative hypothesis is true.
- **Interpretation:**
  - Simplistically, power is the chance of NOT making a type II error (β).
  - As beta (β) gets smaller so does the likelihood that you will not make a type II error and find a difference if there is in fact a difference to be found.
    - Another way of saying this is "the probability you will say there is no difference between two interventions, when in fact a difference does exist between them."
  - Most accept an adequate study power to be 0.8 (80%), which would make β or chance of making a type II error to be 0.2 (20%). Therefore, as power increases, beta or chance of making a type II error will decrease.
- **Influencing Factors:**
  - The two factors contributing to the power of study include:
    - Sample size
    - Alpha value (α)
      - α ("Alpha") is the probability of concluding that there is a difference between the groups/interventions studied, but in reality there is no difference (also known as making a "type I error")
      - α is usually set to be 0.05 and a finding is considered to be statistically significant if the p-value is < 0.05 or the chance of making a type I error is < 5%
  - *Clinical Application*:
    - If a study or clinical trial fails to find a difference or fails to reject the null hypothesis, one of the most common factors contributing to this is having an insufficient sample size (n). If this occurs, you should recognize that a type II error may have occurred.
      - A study with too small of a sample size is often said to be "under-powered" for this reason.

P-Values

- **Definition:**
  - The level at which a statistically significant finding occurs.
  - It reflects the strength of the results found and determines the likelihood the results were due to chance.
- **Interpretation:**
  - A p-value < 0.05 simply means that the probability of the results was due to chance or random error is less than 1 in 20 or less than 5%.
  - The smaller the p-value the lower the likelihood that the results found in a study was due to chance or random error or said another way, "the smaller the p-value the more likely the results found are real."
    - This is why researchers hope to have small p-values.
  - It is important to know that the p-value **does _NOT_** tell you anything about the:
    - Clinical significance of the findings
      - This is determined by the clinician reading the study
    - Size of an effect found
- **Example:**
  - If a study was done and found that the two interventions being evaluated were statistically different due to a p-value of 0.01, then we can say that there is a 1% change that the results found in this study are either due to chance or random error.

95% Confidence Intervals

- **Definition:**
  - It is an attempt to try to quantify the greatest likelihood of where the true population finding or result falls within an interval since the entire population is not being studied but rather a sample pulled from the general population is being studied.
    - As such, the subjects included in his study for closer you will move to the true population result.
- **Interpretation:**
  - In general, the closer a result or point lies in the middle of the night 5% confidence interval the more likely it will represent the true population result.
  - A 95% CI for a result that is a mean value can be rejected if it contains and/or pass through "0.00" within its interval.
  - A 95% CI for a hazard ratio, risk ratio, or relative risk can be rejected if the interval contains and passes through "1.00"
- **Example:**
  - Study endpoint result = RR 0.65 (95% CI, 0.45 – 0.76)
    - The p-value is < 0.05 or "statistically significant" because the interval does not include or passed through 1.00.
    - To interpret appropriately you must subtract this relative risk from 1
      - 1 – 0.65 = 0.35, therefore 35% of the risk of the outcome was removed or prevented by being exposed to the intervention

Relative Risk & Odds Ratio

- **Background:**
  - **Relative Risk (RR)**
    - The risk of an event after the experimental treatment as a percentage of the original risk
    - Relative Risk = Risk Ratio = RR
  - **Odds Ratio (RR)**
    - Most commonly, the Odds Ratio (OR) is an estimate of the RR but within a retrospective or case-controlled study

- When the incidence of disease is < 10% in a population, the OR = RR
- The incidence cannot be calculated since the number of patients at risk is not known
- Formulas:
  - OR = (A/C)/(B/D) = (A/B)/(C/D) = (AD)/(BC)

Treatment	Disease Present	Disease Absent
Exposed	A	B
Unexposed	C	D

- **Interpretation:**
  - RR = (incidence rate and expose group)/(incidence rate and nonexposed group)
  - RR = 1
    - The incidence is the same for both groups, thus no difference.
  - RR > 1
    - The incidence in the exposed group is greater or higher.
    - This results in an Attributable Risk (AR)
  - RR < 1
    - The incidence in the exposed group is less or lower.
    - This results in a Relative Risk Reduction (RRR)
      - Note: This is different than Absolute Risk Reduction (ARR) which is the difference between the incidence of 2 groups (i.e., difference being subtraction of the two incidence to calculate the absolute number).
- **Example:**
  - A randomized controlled study is done where patients were randomly assigned to receive a new drug versus placebo to determine a difference in the endpoint after 4 years of treatment.
    - Incidence of Group A (Treatment Exposed Group) = 4.5%
    - Incidence of Group B (Placebo or Unexposed Group) = 7.5%
    - How to calculate:
      - RR = 0.045/0.075 = 0.60
    - Interpretation = 1 – 0.60 = 0.40 (40% of the risk of the outcome was removed or prevented with the new treatment)

Number Needed to Treat (NNT)

- **Background:**
  - How many patients have to be treated (or expose) for 1 patient to benefit.
  - Must be put into the proper context of the study (duration, doses used, etc) for which the NNT was obtained.
  - NNT = 1/ARR
- **Interpretation:**
  - Determined by taking the absolute risk reduction where the difference in the incidence of the outcomes
  - In most cases we desire a small or low NNT
- **Example:**
  - Drug X versus placebo for 4 weeks in a randomized control trial to assess the risk of developing the outcome (MI)
    - Group A (Treated with Drug X) = 5%
    - Group B (Treated with Placebo) = 15%
    - How to Calculate:
      - Calculate the ARR = 0.15 – 0.05 = 0.10
      - NNT = 1/ARR = 1/0.10 = 10

- Interpretation: We must treat 10 patients for 4 weeks with drug acts to prevent 1 AMI

Number Needed to Harm (NNH)

- **Background:**
  - Similar to the NNT but is a measure or reflection of harm as result of treatment or exposure
  - Must also be put in the proper context of the study duration.
- **Interpretation:**
  - Determined by calculating the attributable risk which is the difference in the incidence of the groups
  - Most cases we desire a large or high NNH
- **Example:**
  - A study was done over 9 months to assess the risk of bleeding between 2 regimens.
    - Group A (treated with aspirin) = 2.7%
    - Group B (treated with aspirin + clopidogrel) = 3.7%
    - How to Calculate:
      - Attributable Risk = $0.37 - 0.027 = 0.01$
      - NNH = $1/AR = 1/0.01 = 100$
    - Interpretation: For every 100 patient is treated with aspirin + clopidogrel over 9 months, 1 patient would develop a major bleed

Validity of the Results

- **High-Yield Core Knowledge**
  - There are 2 levels of validity that need to be considered by the clinician.
    - Internal validity
      - Being able to conclude that the independent variable (usually the treatment) was in fact responsible for the change seen in the deep end and variable (usually the outcome)
      - Studies with high risk for potential bias or bias highly suspected have compromised internal validity thereby inherently compromising external validity.
    - External validity
      - Concerned with the "generalizability" of the results to and across populations of subjects or settings.
      - Requires that the study demonstrate appropriate internal validity.
        - A study that is not internally valid cannot be externally valid or have the results of the study to be generalized to the population.

Considerations for Internal Validity

Observational Bias

- **Background:**
  - Observational bias is a common type of systematic error that occurs in studies where there is inaccurate:
    - Classification of disease
    - Measurement of disease
    - Exposure
- **Common Reasons for Observational Bias:**
  - **Detection Bias:**
    - Increased monitoring of a group of exposed patients due to a known risk factor compared to an unexposed group that leads to a higher probability of detecting the disease.
  - **Observer Bias:**

- Misclassification of date because of differences in observer interpretation or expectations regarding the study
  - **Recall Bias:**
    - Relies on the subject to remember certain information accurately.
    - Subjects who have a negative outcome may be more likely to report certain exposures compared to subjects who had a positive outcome.
  - **Reporter Bias:**
    - The subject either over or under report exposures due to perceived social stigmatization or based on what that subject believes to be important.
  - **Considerations:**
    - Recall bias is most commonly seen in retrospective studies.

Selection Bias

- **Background:**
  - This is a common type of systematic error that occurs in studies where there is:
  - Inappropriate selection of patients
  - Unrepresentative sample of the target population
  - Insufficient retention of subjects
- **Common Types of Selection Bias:**
  - **Attrition Bias:**
    - Occurs when there is a high loss of study subjects within a study (eg., lost to follow up) and the remaining sample now differs from the original sample being studied that was supposed to be representative of the target population.
  - **Berkson Bias:**
    - The disease being studied is only being done from patients in the hospital that may not lead to results representative of the target population.
  - **Neyman Bias:**
    - Occurs when the exposure occurs before the assessment of the disease resulting in missed cases that die early or happen to recover.
  - **Nonresponse Bias:**
    - Occurs when this is a poor response rate of the desired sample population where the responders now are different from the nonresponders.
  - **Sampling Bias:**
    - Occurs when a study does not randomize patients at all or does not appropriately randomize subjects to where there the study population does not represent the target population.
- **Considerations:**
  - If selection bias is present it can lead to differences in the measure of association between the sample versus target population.
    - For example, differences can occur with the incidence rate or odds ratio and thus is not reflective of the true difference between the groups studied and the target population.
  - This type of bias occurs often with surveys where a high nonresponse rate leading to a possible difference between those who fill out the survey from the majority who did not.

- **General Information:**
  - Studies or tests done for the purposes of helping to guide a specific diagnosis have been evaluated in clinical practice to provide analytical and quantitative data about how well the test performs in aiding the clinician to determine the presence or absence of a disease.
  - What we desire in a diagnostic test are the presence of true positives (TP) and true negatives (TN) when appropriate.
    - What is not desired and impacts the utility of a diagnostic test is the presence of false positives (FP) and false negatives (FN)

Disease Diagnosed by the Gold Standard

	+	-
+	TP	FP
-	FN	TN

(vertical axis label: Disease Diagnosed by New Test)

  - New diagnostic tests are always compared to a gold standard or reference tests where the following characteristics of a diagnostic test can be reported:
    - Sensitivity (SN)
    - Specificity (SP)
    - Positive Predictive Value (PPV)
    - Negative Predictive Value (NPV)
    - Likelihood Ratio (LR)
    - Receiver Operator Characteristic (ROC) Curve

Sensitivity (SN)

- **Background:**
  - Determines the ability of a test to detect the presence of a disease when it is actually present in the patient. Said another way:
    - Proportion of all patients with the disease who also test positive.
  - Used for ruling out disease
    - Pearl = SeNsitivity rules OUT = "SNOUT"
- **Interpretation:**
  - SN = (TP)/(TP + FN)
  - The closer to 1 (or 100%) the better because it means there are less false negatives.
- **Example:**
  - If a study has a sensitivity of 100% and you get a negative result then this helps you to "rule out" the presence of that disease since at 100% sensitivity there are no false negatives.

Specificity (SP)

- **Background:**
  - Determines the ability of a test to reliably detect the absence of a disease when it is actually not present in the patient. Said another way:
    - Proportion of all patients without the disease who also test negative.
  - Used for ruling out disease
    - Pearl = SPecificity rules IN = "SPIN"
- **Interpretation:**
  - SN = (TN)/(TN + FP)
  - The closer to 1 (or 100%) the better because it means there are less false positives.
- **Example:**
  - If a test has 100% specificity and you get a positive test on a patient then you can "rule in that disease" since at 100% specificity there are no false positive results.

Positive Predictive Value (PPV)

- **Background:**
  - Proportion of patients with a positive result that actually have the disease. Said another way:
    - Probability that a patient with a positive result actually has the disease.
- **Interpretation:**
  - PPV = (TP)/(TP + FP)
  - The closer to 1 (or 100%) the better because it means there are less false positives.
- **Note:**
  - If the disease has a low prevalence and a test has a high sensitivity and specificity, it will still have a low PPV.

Negative Predictive Value (PPV)

- **Background:**
  - Proportion of patients with a negative test result that actually do not have the disease. Said another way:
    - Probability the patient has a negative result that actually does not have the disease.
- **Interpretation:**
  - NPV = (TN)/(TN + FN)
  - The closer to 1 (or 100%) the better because it means there are less false negatives.
- **Note:**
  - If the disease has a low prevalence and a test has a high sensitivity and specificity, it will still have a low PPV.

Likelihood Ratio (LR)

- **Background:**
  - It is used to assess how good diagnostic test is in which test you might choose and or in what order to use them.
  - With a particular test, it will help you consider the "odds" that a person has for the disease.
  - It is calculated based on utilizing the sensitivity and specificity of a diagnostic test.
- **Application and Interpretation:**
  - Relies on some awareness to her knowledge of what is called a "pretest probability" which can be the prevalence of the condition in question so that you can determine the posttest probability.
    - Basically will this diagnostic test help increase the probability of a diagnosis if performed?

- • If a diagnostic test will not improve the posttest probability it is pointless to order and try to use in the patient evaluation
  - − The LARGER the LR (i.e., > 10) the greater value in impact it has on the posttest probability and usefulness of the test and helping to guide the "presence" of a diagnosis.
    - ▪ At the same time having a SMALL LR (i.e., < 1) can be useful in helping to "rule out" the presence of a disease and may also sometimes be useful.
    - ▪ LR+ = TP% / FP%   or   = (Sensitivity) / (1 − Specificity)
    - ▪ LR- = FN% / TN%   or   = (1-Sensitivity) / (Specificity)
    - ▪ Pre-Test Odds = (Pre-test probability)/(1-pre-test probability)
    - ▪ Post-Test Odds = Pre-Test Odds x LR
    - ▪ Post-Test Probability = Post-Test Odds / (Post-Test Odds + 1)
    - ▪ Use of the Fagen Nomogram is easier and helpful

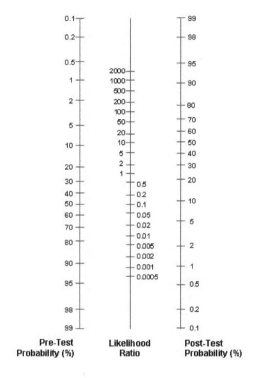

Receiver Operator Characteristic (ROC) Curves

- ▪ **Background:**
  - − Used to select the cut off value so that we can get the most accuracy from a diagnostic test that we are using when the following are present:
    - ▪ The test result is a continuous variable
    - ▪ When there is no clear cut value that makes the presence of a disease presence "positive"
    - ▪ Making adjustments on the "cut off" value can influence the sensitivity and specificity to identify a threshold point
  - − This is done or considered with many diagnostic tests because if we increase the sensitivity of a test we likely see a decrease in the specificity.
  - − The ROC curve represents an area under the curve that can be used as a graphical summary of the sensitivity and specificity to help us figure out the most acceptable cut off.

- **Summary:**

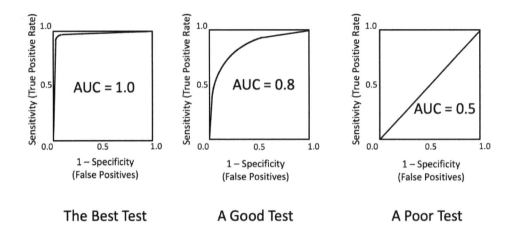

The Best Test   A Good Test   A Poor Test

- **Systematic Reviews**
  - In overview of studies about a specific topic that is done in a manner that is systematic and reproducible.
    - The studies being reviewed have inclusion and exclusion criteria similar to a research protocol for study thereby making it more objective and transparent.
    - Different from a review article that may include published literature that are not clinical studies or trials.
  - The process by which is set of studies are used is usually evidence-based and is a "QUALITATIVE" summary.
  - **Limitations:**
    - Potential bias by the authors
    - Denies NOT provide an estimation of the "magnitude of effect"
- **Meta-Analysis**
  - Utilizes the data from the clinical studies most commonly included in a systematic review and does statistical analysis in an effort to "QUANTITATIVELY" combined the data to provided overall estimate of the magnitude of affect (i.e., the "pooled estimate").
  - A Cochran Review represents a systematic review and meta-analysis done according to a very strict set of guidelines and criteria that is very systematic and transparent.
    - Not all reported systematic reviews of meta-analysis in the published literature needs the same quality of reporting which is why the Cochrane reviews are so valuable and respected.
  - **Potential Advantages:**
    - Increases the overall sample size
    - Increases power, which decreases the chance of making a type II error
    - Can reveal clinically important differences in treatments that smaller studies are unable to detect
    - Can investigate the degree of heterogeneity between studies
      - Typically heterogeneity considered to be greater than 50% is considered high and of concern
    - Can generate a hypothesis for supporting the development of a randomized control trial (RCT)
  - **Potential Criticisms:**
    - Heterogeneity in combining data from different studies (if done)
    - Selection bias of studies included
    - Existence of publication bias (look for funnel plots)
  - **Reporting of Data:**
    - The quantitative assessment is summarized in a "forest plot"
    - Each study is represented by a blob (which is a small square whose size is influenced by the sample size of that study and its overall influence on the pooled estimate
      - The lines extending from each side of the blob representing 95% confidence interval in most cases
    - The pooled estimate is in the shape of a diamond
      - The middle of the diamond at the top is called the point estimate
      - The 2 points on the sides represent the confidence interval
    - Sensitivity analyses are sometimes considered when there is concern for degree of heterogeneity in the potential influence on a final pole statistic.

Reporting Guidelines for Publishing

- Published standards and criteria for how a particular publication type is to be submitted for publication and ultimately reported in a journal.
- **The desired goals include:**
  - Improvement in the quality of reporting
  - Improving the transparency of information
  - Standardize the format of a particular publication type to be more effective and efficient when being appraised by readers.

Publication Type	Guideline	Reference
Randomized control trial	CONSORT	BMJ 2010;340:c332.
Observational study	STROBE	BMJ 2007;335:806-8.
Systematic review	PRISMA	BMJ 2009;339;b2535
Cochrane review	Cochrane Handbook	Cochrane-org
Case reports	CARE	J Clin Epi 2014;67:46-51.
Qualitative research	SRQR; COREQ	Acad Med 2014;89:1245.
Diagnostic–prognostic studies	STARD TRIPOD	BMJ 2015;351:h5527.
Quality improvement studies	SQUIRE	MID: 26369893
Economic evaluations	CHEERS	BMJ 2013;346:f1049
Animal preclinical studies	ARRIVE	PLoS Biol 2010;8:e1000412.
Study protocols	SPIRIT PRISMA-P	PMID: 23295957 PMID: 25554246

Critical Appraisal Tools

- The desired objectives for critical or "systematic" appraisal of the literature is to determine if the published paper have results that are:
  - Trustworthy or valid
  - Relevant
- **Tools to assess for risk of bias:**
  - GRADE is now used for assessing guidelines and RCTs in a systematic review/meta-analysis
  - For Non-RCTs = ACROBAT-NRIS (A Cochrane Risk of Bias Assessment Tool
  - Free online tools: Critical Appraisal Skills Programme (CASP)

Publication Type	Guideline
Guidelines	GRADE AGREE
Systematic review	PRIMSA AMSTAR
Randomized control trial	CASP
Cohort study	CASP
Diagnostic study	QAUDAS-2 QAREL
Qualitative research	CASP
Clinical prediction rule	CASP

Publication Bias

- Most commonly assessed using a funnel plot which is an inverted final and helps to assess the distribution of findings of reports in the literature
- The distribution of those reports gives a visualization for the possibility of potential bias
- Example for the potential presence of publication bias (see image)

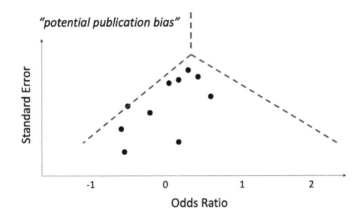

- **Cost minimization**
  - Used when outcomes or consequences of 2 or more interventions are considered to be equal.
    - In which case pick the cheapest option.
  - Easiest analysis and useful when used correctly
  - If there is any doubt, then cost effectiveness or cost benefit analysis should be implemented
- **Cost effectiveness**
  - Most common analysis used
  - Useful interventions are not considered to be equal based on clinical effectiveness
  - Measures cost $10 and the outcomes and natural health units
  - May suggest that you choose the treatment that cost more
- **Cost benefit**
  - Outcomes are expressed as a benefit:cost ratio or as a total net benefit or total neck cost
  - Pick the 1 with the greatest benefit
  - Have to be able to convert outcomes to some meaningful dollar value
- **Cost utility**
  - Applicability to clinical practice is still questionable and is not largely excepted
  - Does take into account measurements of health consequences
  - Usually reports things as quality of life adjustments

Overview of Regulatory Bodies

- **Food & Drug Administration (FDA):**
  - Enforces the federal Food, Drug, and Cosmetic Act
    - Also enforces the Drug Quality and Security Act (DQSA) which includes:
      - The Compounding Quality Act that defines outsourcing compounders and creates a registration program that is voluntary
      - The Drug Supply Chain Security Act (DSCSA) that helps track products throughout distribution using a nationalmayb electronic system
  - Sets labeling requirement for:
    - Food
    - Prescription medications
    - Over-the-counter drugs and cosmetics
    - Sets standards for investigational drug studies and product approval
    - Regulates and oversees the manufacturing and marketing of drugs
- **Drug Enforcement Administration (DEA):**
  - Enforces federal laws related to controlled substances act (CSA)
  - Relates to:
    - Manufacturing
    - Distribution
    - Dispensing of legal products
  - Investigates and prepares prosecution of activities that violate the CSA
- **Occupational Safety and Health Administration (OSHA):**
  - Formed from the Occupational Safety and Health Act of 1970
  - Ensures working environment and conditions are safe by setting the standards and then ensuring they are being met
  - Conducts period work site inspections
- **National Institute for Occupational Safety & Health (NIOSH):**
  - Responsible for "conducting research" and making recommendations for the "prevention" of work-related injury and illness
  - Comes from the same legislation as OSHA
- **Centers for Disease Control and Prevention:**
  - This is the U.S. health protection agency whose purpose is to save lives and protect people from health, safety, and security threats within the U.S., and abroad.
  - Examples of guidelines:
    - Infection control
    - Hand-hygiene
    - Standard or universal precautions
    - Safe injection practices

Other Standards – USP

- **United States Pharmacopeia:**
  - A non-governmental organization
  - Sets standards for drugs, dietary supplements, and other healthcare products
    - Published in the United States Pharmacopeia and National Formulary
      - Example, USP Chapter 795 set standards for nonsterile compounding, USP Chapter 797 sets standards for pharmaceutical compounding of sterile productions, and USP Chapter 800 sets standards for handling hazardous drugs
  - Goals:

- Advance public health by ensuring the quality of medications, ingredients in foods, and other products
- Promote safe and proper use of medications
- Verifying ingredients in dietary supplements

Summary

- The U.S. healthcare system has a number of regulatory bodies formed by federal laws that are intended to improve the safety and quality of the environments and delivery of services to the public.
- Healthcare organizations and participants involved in the provision of healthcare related services must comply and ensure standards are being met in order to operate and receive funding.

- **Health-System Practice:**
  - Governed and regulated by a number of organizations and accrediting bodies
  - Also includes professional organizations that help set standards of practice (i.e., within pharmacy, nursing, etc).
  - Benefits:
    - Participation in programs paying for healthcare such as:
      - Insurance companies
      - Government agencies
    - Attract good healthcare staff
    - May be exempt from other inspections
  - Government & Non-government agencies look for these accreditations and compliance to allow an institution to participate in government programs.
    - These are called "Conditions of Participation (CoPs)"
    - Government agencies include Medicare and Medicaid
    - Nongovernment agencies include Kaiser

- **Accrediting Bodies:**
  - **Joint Commission (JCAHO)**
    - The primary accrediting organization for the operation of hospitals
    - Set Standards for hospitals and healthcare organizations
      - Performance expectations
        - Provide details for healthcare professionals to make decisions on to best accomplish any standard but not a "cook-book" approach
    - Also developed National Patient Safety Goals (NPSG)
    - Example standards:
      - Medication management
      - Infection control
      - Patient care
      - Medical records
      - Safety and security
      - Education
      - Performance improvement
      - Environment of care
    - The Joint Commission visit and preparation:
      - The Joint Commission's Accreditation Survey Activity Guide for Healthcare Organizations
      - Comprehensive Accreditation Manual for Hospitals: The Official Handbook (CAMH)
  - **Center for Improvement in Healthcare (CIHQ)**
    - An accrediting organization for the operation of hospitals.
  - **Healthcare Facilities Accreditation Program (HFAP)**
    - An accreditation for the operation of hospitals set by the accrediting organization from American Osteopathy Associations (AOA).
- **Summary:**
  - Healthcare systems have a number of accreditations and/or certifications that it must obtain and maintain in order to not only operate but to ensure a certain level of quality and safety is being provided while also being able to receive payment for services rendered.
  - We have accreditations, certifications and then regulatory agencies that enforce various laws to help regulate healthcare activities.

Background

- **General Information:**
  - Medicare and Medicaid are the two major healthcare coverage programs in the United States that is supervised by the Centers for Medicare and Medicaid Services (CMS)
    - Medicare is regulated and controlled by the federal government
    - Medicaid has some involvement by the federal government but is regulated mostly by the states
  - The Medicare Prescription Drug Improvements and Modernization Act (MMA) created 4 programs in Medicare (Parts A – D)

Medicare Parts A – D

Part	Purpose
A	Provides insurance for hospitalization
B	Provides insurance for physician services
C	Medicare managed care or Medicare Advantage
D	Provides prescription coverage for drugs

Medicare Part D

- **Medicare Part D:**
  - Medicare patients have the option to enroll into the prescription drug plan (PDP)
    - Medicare contracts with private insurance companies who then provide drug-only coverage or through the Medicare Advantage local plans
    - Applies only to one person so married couples must each have their own
    - The cost is income dependent
      - If not low-income, then they may have a monthly premium, annual deductible and co-payments just like regular insurance
    - Co-payments are tier based
  - Tiered co-payments:
    - Tier 1 = Lease expensive generic drug
    - Tier 2 = Preferred brand name drug
    - Tier 3 = Non-preferred brand name drug
    - Tier 4 = Rare, high cost drugs
- **Medicare formulary requirements:**
  - All standard plans must include options within all USP therapeutic categories
  - Developed by a P&T Committee that is made up of physicians and pharmacists
  - Not required to have all drug options with a class but for certain classes have to include most options:
    - Anticonvulsants
    - Antidepressants
    - Antineoplastics

- Antipsychotics
- Antiretrovirals
- Immunosuppressants

Features of the Programs

- Additional features of the medicare program include:
    - All prescription benefit programs must accept participation from any pharmacy agreeing to their drug plan
    - Sponsors cannot force the patient to obtain drugs through mail-order pharmacies
    - 90-day supplies for chronic medications allowed
    - If a brand name drug is dispensed, the patient must be informed of availability of lower cost options
    - Pharmacists are eligible to get paid for providing MTM for patients enrolled in Part D
    - Drug plans must establish MTM programs for patients to enroll into especially those with chronic, expensive drugs
    - Allow generic drug companies of a product to have 180 days exclusivity if they file on first day of eligibility

Summary

- CMS oversees Medicare and Medicaid which are the two main health coverage programs in the U.S. and has 4 main parts.
    - Part A covers hospitalization
    - Part B covers doctor visits
    - Part C is a managed care program
    - Part D provides options for prescription drug coverage

Background Information

- **Controlled Substance:**
  - A drug or substance included in schedule I, II, III, IV, or V of the Controlled Substances Act (CSA)
  - Does not include alcohol-based beverages or tobacco
- **Classification of medications per the CSA:**
  - Enforced by the Drug Enforcement Administration (DEA)
    - The DEA is under the supervision of the Attorney General of U.S.
- Who can possess or handle controlled substances?
  - Researchers, manufacturers, distributors, labs, exporters, narcotic treatment programs, and pharmacies that are registered with the DEA
  - Must complete appropriate forms:
    - Pharmacies = Form 224
    - Manufacturers, distributors, importers/exporters, or researchers = Form 225
    - Narcotic treatment programs = Form 363
    - A DEA registration is good for 36 months
      - Renewals are sent to registrants 60 days prior to expiration
    - Note: Pharmacists working at a pharmacy with a DEA license do not have register with the DEA themselves

Controlled Substances Designations

- **Schedule I Substances:**
  - High risk of abuse
  - No currently acceptable medical use in the treatment of a condition with the U.S.
  - Does not have accepted information related to the safety of their use
  - Can only be purchased using a DEA 222 form
  - Drugs:
    - Diethylamide
    - Heroin
    - LSD
    - Mescaline
    - Methaqualone
    - Peyote
    - Note: marijuana but this likely to change
- **Schedule II Substances:**
  - High potential for abuse and dependence
  - Has currently accepted uses in the U.S. but under tight restrictions
  - Can only be purchased with a DEA Form 222
  - Example Drugs:
    - Amphetamine
    - Cocaine
    - Codeine
    - Diphenoxylate
    - Fentanyl
    - Hydrocodone
    - Hydromorphone
    - Methadone
    - Methamphetamine
    - Methylphenidate

- Oxycodone
- Pentobarbital
- PCP
- **Schedule III Substances:**
  - Has potential for abuse and dependence but less than schedule II agents
  - Has currently accepted uses in the U.S.
  - Example Drugs:
    - Acetaminophen + codeine
    - Anabolic steroids (some states make them schedule II)
    - Buprenorphine
    - Butalbital
    - Dronabinol
    - Any compound or formulation containing amobarbital, secobarbital, pentobarbital
- **Schedule IV Substances:**
  - Has low potential for abuse compared to schedule III agents
  - Has currently accepted uses in the U.S.
  - Limited risk of physical or mental dependence compared to lower schedules
  - Example Drugs:
    - Benzodiazepines
    - Butorphanol
    - Carisoprodol
    - Chlordiazepoxide
    - Eszopiclone
    - Meprobamate
    - Modafinil
    - Pentazocine
    - Phentermine
    - Tramadol
    - Triazolam
    - Zaleplon
    - Zolpidem
- **Schedule V Substances:**
  - Have a low potential for abuse compared to schedule IV agents
  - Has currently accepted uses in the U.S.
  - Limited risk of physical or mental dependence compared to lower schedules
  - Example Drugs:
    - Acetaminophen + codeine elixir
    - Promethazine + codeine
    - Diphenoxylate + atropine
    - Lacosamide
    - Pregabalin

Labeling and Controlled Substances

- All labels for controlled substances must include:
  - In addition to normal labeling it must also have the following statement:
    - "Caution: Federal law prohibits the transfer of this drug to any person other than the patient for whom it was prescribed."

Purchasing

- The purchasing of schedule I & II substances:
  - Use of a DEA Form 222
  - 3 Copies:

- Copy 1 (Brown) = Goes to the supplier
- Copy 2 (Green) = First goes to supplier which is then forwarded to the DEA
- Copy 3 (Blue) = Kept by the purchaser
- CSOS (Controlled Substances Ordering System):
  - Electronic ordering
    - Faster, more accurate, decreased costs and ordering freedom

Special Situations

- **Emergency situations:**
  - Schedule II substances:
    - An oral order by the provider to the pharmacist can be done to dispense a limited quantity
    - Within 7 days of authorization a written prescription must be delivered to the dispensing pharmacy
  - Partial fills
    - Patients cannot request a partial fill
    - May be implement if the pharmacy lacks the full supply to fill
    - Must be filled within 72 hours and if extends beyond, a new prescription is required
- **Refills:**
  - Schedule I & II: None
  - Schedule III & IV:
    - Based on the date the prescription was issued it cannot be refilled more than 5 times in a six-month period
  - Schedule V:
    - Based on prescribers' instructions unless different by state law

Summary

- The level risk for abuse, physical, and/or psychological dependence influences the schedule designation of the product.
- The CSA sets the rules for prescription products and their scheduling via the Attorney General and DEA.

General Prescription Information

- **Prescription:**
  - It is basically an order to provide a patient with a specific medication.
  - General factors:
    - Usually is not for immediate/acute use (e.g., within the hospital which is usually considered a medication order by a provider and can be verbal or in written/electronic form)
    - Presented on specific prescription pad paper or electronically submitted as a fax
    - Written and provided someone authorized to prescribe and considered to be valid
- **What is a valid prescription?**
  - Per the US Code – Title 21 829(e)(2)(A):
    - The term "valid prescription" means a prescription that is issued for a legitimate medical purpose in the usual course of professional practice by—(i)a practitioner who has conducted at least 1 in-person medical evaluation of the patient; or (ii)a covering practitioner.
- **Who is authorized to prescribe?**
  - This is state dependent
  - Some non-physician providers will have prescriptive limitations such as:
    - Nurse practitioners
    - Physician assistants
    - Pharmacists
  - Some providers can self-prescribe but is state influenced and excludes controlled substances
- **Can a pharmacist refuse to fill a prescription?**
  - Yes, but it generally needs to fall within one of the following categories or situations:
    - The person prescribing the medication is not authorized to prescribe
    - Suspicion that the prescription is forged or has been altered by someone other than the authorized prescriber
    - If the prescription is written for something that is considered illegal
    - The pharmacist does not have the medication to fill it
    - The pharmacist believes that the medication would be harmful to the patient
- **Prescription refills and rules:**
  - Controlled substances have different rules applied to them. For example:
    - CII drugs cannot have refills
  - The pharmacist is usually restricted to refill based on the number of refills authorized by the prescriber
  - Pharmacists must have a reliable way to track the refills
  - Emergency refills of a limited are allowed in most cases especially if failing to provide the medication could harm the patient
- **Prescription management:**
  - Once the prescription has been filled, it is own by that pharmacy
  - Prescriptions must be kept and stored.
    - The duration can vary be state
    - The FDA states they can ask for data going back 5 years
    - The 2003 Medicare Modernization Act states prescriptions need to be stored for 10 years

Prescription Labels and Packaging

- **Standards for prescription label:**
  - Determined by USP 36-NF31
  - Priority elements of the label:

- Specify the patient's name
- Prescription number
- Full generic and brand name
- Strength
- Clear instructions in simple language
- **Other elements of the label:**
  - Date filled
  - Expiration date
  - Quantity
  - Prescribers name
  - Pharmacy name, address and phone number
  - Remaining refills
- **Font style and size:**
  - Times New Roman 12 point
  - Arial 11 point
- **Spell out names of medications:**
  - Do not use abbreviations
- **Other considerations:**
  - Indication or the purpose (unless the patient does not want it)
  - Use patient preferred language when possible, but the drug name must be in English for emergency personnel to be able to read
- **Packaging Considerations:**
  - Prescription medications come in small or larger bulk quantities for day to dispensing
  - To help reduce medication errors medication identification the FDA and the Institute for Safe Medication Practices (ISMP) instituted and published a list of look-alike medications utilizing a technique called Tall Man Lettering.
- **Labeling Considerations:**
  - **Tall Man Lettering examples:**
    - acetaZOLAMIDE vs. acetoHEXAMIDE
    - buPROPion vs. busPIRone
    - cycloSERINE vs. cycloSPORINE
    - hydrALAZINE vs. hydroxyzine
    - vinBLAStine vs. vinCRIStine
- **Packaging to protect children from accidental poisoning:**
  - Prescription products
    - Child resistant containers
      - Providers can provide a waiver but for each individual prescription
      - Patients can provider a waiver to cover more than one prescription
    - Poison Prevention Packaging Act (PPPA)
      - Under the supervision of the Consumer Product Safety Commission (CPSC)
      - Goal: Protect children < 5 years of age from accidental ingestion
      - Example drugs under the rule:
        - All prescription and especially controlled substances
        - Acetaminophen
        - Aspirin
        - Diphenhydramine
        - Fluoride
        - Ibuprofen and naproxen
        - Iron
        - Loperamide
        - Methyl salicylate
        - Minoxidil

Patient Counseling

- **Drug utilization review (DUR):**
  - States:
    - They have them in place per CMS rules for participating in the Medicaid program
    - They must have prospective and retrospective DUR programs in place
  - Pharmacists:
    - Are supposed to do a prospective DUR of the patient's written medical record before the prescription is dispensed to the patient
    - Evaluate:
      - Name, address, age or DOB, gender, presence of disease states, allergies, list of prior medications filled, and any comments
      - Evaluate for over or under utilization of a medication
      - Look for duplication of therapy
      - Evaluate the doses and instructions
      - Offer to talk to the patient anything relevant
        - OBRA 90 has the requirement to offer counseling
- **OBRA 90:**
  - Mandates the requirement of offering to counsel the patient
  - Since this is part of the Medicaid program which are run by the states, they have to show support for this being done to participate
  - The federal law does not dictate what must be said, so use professional judgement

Summary

- While the prescription is a provider's order for a medication, the pharmacist plays an important role between the provider and the patient.
- This level of checks and balance helps to protect the patient from any bad outcomes or from inappropriate use of a treatment.

- **HIPAA:**
  - "Health Insurance Portability and Accountability Act"
  - Established 1996
  - By the US Dept of Health & Human Services
  - Purpose:
    - Protect Individual Privacy
    - Protect Individual Security
  - With the HHS, the Office of Civil Rights (OCR) is responsible for enforcing
  - Why?
    - Prior to HIPAA there was no generally accepted set of security standards or requirements for protecting health information while at the same time technology was changing from paper charts to electronic creating potential security risks
- **The Privacy Rule:**
  - *Standards for Privacy of Individually Identified Health Information*
  - National standards that regulate the use of disclosures of health information, called "protected health information" to "covered entities" without the patient's permission
  - Also establish standards for patient's privacy rights to understand and control "how" their health info is used
  - Attempts a balance to assure the patients' health information is properly protected while also allowing for the flow of health information needed to provide & promote high quality health care
  - The privacy rule applies to any of the below who transmit health info in electronic form in connection with a transaction:
    - Health plans
    - Health care clearinghouses
    - Any healthcare provider
    - Business associates
  - **Individually Identifiable Health Information:**
    - Individual's past, present or future physical or mental health or condition
    - The provision of health care to the individual (or)
    - The past, present, or future payment for the provision of health care to the individual
    - Includes related demographic data that could be used to identify the person
  - **De-identified Health Information:**
    - Neither identifies nor provides a reasonable basis to identify an individual
    - There are no restrictions on the use or disclosure
    - 2 ways to de-identify Info:
      - A formal determination by a qualified statistician (or)
      - Removal of specified identifiers of individual and of the individual's relatives, household members, and employers
  - **Required Disclosures: A covered entity must disclose PHI in only 2 situations:**
    - To individuals (or their personal representative)
    - To HHS when undertaking a compliance investigation or review or enforcement action
  - **Uses and Disclosures of Protected Health Information by a covered entity may occur without the persons authorization for the following:**
    - To the individual
    - Treatment, payment, and healthcare operations
    - Opportunity to agree or object
    - Incident to an otherwise permitted use and disclosure
    - Public interest and benefit activities
    - Limited data set for the purposes of research, public health, or healthcare operations
  - **Authorization must be obtained by the covered entity if disclosure is not for treatment**

- **The Security Rule:**
  - *Security Standards for the Protection of Electronic Protected Health Information*
  - Set national regulations that protect health information that is held or electronically transmitted
  - It operationalizes the protections contained in the Privacy Rule by addressing the technical and non-technical safeguards that organizations call "covered entities"
  - Goal: Protect the privacy of PHI while allowing covered entities to adopt new technologies to improve the quality and efficiency of patient care
  - Requirements of covered entities:
    - Ensure the confidentiality, integrity, and availability of all e-PHI they create, receive, maintain or transmit
    - Identify and protect against reasonably anticipated threats to the security or integrity of info
    - Protect against reasonably anticipated, impermissible uses or disclosures
    - Ensure compliance by their workforce

Summary

- HIPAA was created as a set of security standards and general requirements for protecting health information (PHI), while at the same time allowing adjustments and changes in technology
- The US Dept of HHS facilitates this with rules outlined in the:
  - Standards for Privacy of PHI (and)
  - Security Standards for the Protection of ePHI

Federal Criteria for NTI Drugs

- Narrow Therapeutic Index (NTI) Drugs:
  - The safe and effective use of these drugs requires specific dosing and close monitoring of the patient
  - FDA sets the criteria and determines this list of drugs
  - Described as drugs with narrow therapeutic ratios as described by:
    - The difference between the median lethal dose (LD50) and the median effective dose (ED50) is < 2-fold
    - The difference between the minimum toxic concentration (MTC) and the minimum effective concentration (MEC) in the blood is < 2-fold
    - The FDA allows most drugs to have a variability limit of 90 to 110% of the claim on the label

Calculating the Therapeutic Index

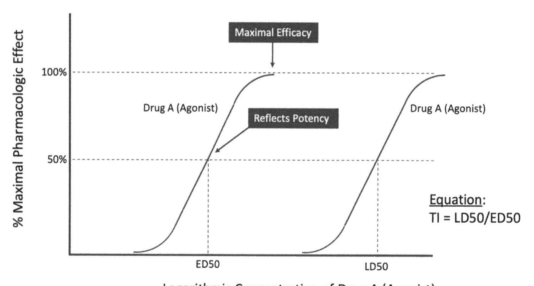

- The higher the TI the "safer" the drug
- Inversely, the smaller the TI or ratio the greater the risk of toxicity

FDA's List of NTI Drugs

FDA List of NTI Drugs	
Carbamazepine	Phenytoin
Cyclosporine	Procainamide
Digoxin	Phenytoin
Ethosuximide	Tacrolimus
Levothyroxine	Theophylline
Lithium	Warfarin

Drugs Needing Therapeutic Drug Monitoring

Drugs Requiring Therapeutic Drug Monitoring				
Drug	**SE / ADRs**	**Narrow TI**	**Efficacy**	**Compliance**
Aminoglycosides	✓		✓	
Carbamazepine	✓	✓	✓	✓
Cyclosporine	✓		±	✓
Digoxin	✓	✓		✓
Dilantin (phenytoin)	✓		✓	✓
Flucytosine	✓		±	
Itraconazole			✓	✓
Lithium	✓	✓	±	✓
Phenobarbital	✓		✓	✓
Protease Inhibitors			✓	✓
Procainamide	✓	✓		✓
Valproic Acid	✓		✓	✓
Vancomycin	✓		✓	
Warfarin	✓	✓		

Summary

- Narrow therapeutic index (NTI) drugs have a narrow margin for their safe and effective use in clinical practice.
- They also have smaller therapeutic indexes (TI).
- This creates dosing that must be implemented more carefully and with closer monitoring of the patient.

General Information

- **General Description:**
  - Over-the-counter (OTC) or nonprescription medications are considered safe or suitable for use without the supervision of a physician and that:
    - Used for self-diagnosed conditions
    - Contain labeling with adequate directions for self-use

Labeling

- **Information and Contents:**
  - Contains a *Drug Facts* section
  - The goal is to aid the consumer to choose the proper product for the condition and to have enough information to self-manage
  - Must contain certain information in the same format so that consumers for consistency
  - Failing to include all components is considered to be "misbranding"

Section	Description
Active Ingredients	- Amount per unit dose
Uses	- Based on disease or symptoms to prevent or treat
Warnings	- When to not use or consult with a physician - Possible side effects and drug-interactions - When to stop and consult with a physician
Inactive Ingredients	- List all substances (including coloring or flavors)
Purpose	- Provides a general action of the drug (e.g., decongestant)
Directions for Use	- How to take - How often to take per day - Duration of treatment
Other Info	- Proper storage - If the product contains calcium potassium, or sodium - Lot number and expiration date - Net quantities of packaged product - What to do in an overdose

- **General Messages:**
  - **Special Populations (Pregnancy & Nursing Mothers)**
    - If OTC product will be for systemic use and if the product is not already intended to benefit the fetus or nursing infant, then the label must state the following:
      - "As with any drug, if you are pregnant or nursing a baby, seek the advice of a health professional before using this product."
    - If the OTC product is to be taken by mouth or rectally then it must also contain the following:
      - "It is especially important not to use this product during the last three months of pregnancy unless specifically directed to do so by a doctor."

Packaging Considerations

- **General Considerations**
  - **Tamper-Resistant Packaging Act**
    - Now called Tamper-evident Packaging
    - Several cases of deliberate poisonings
    - Goal: To prevent intentional contamination of OTC products
    - Exceptions to the rule:
      - Aerosol products
      - Products not available to the public (e.g., clinics only)
      - Lozenges
      - First aid kits

Practice Considerations

- **Potential issues related to drug interactions**
  - Antacids
    - pH changes and bioavailability
      - Atazanavir
      - Dasatinib
      - Erlotinib
      - Levothyroxine
  - CYP450 Interactions
    - Cimetidine → weak inhibitor of CYP1A2, 2C19, 3A4
    - Lansoprazole and omeprazole → inhibits clopidogrel activation
- **Potential issues related to topical application**
  - Topical steroids
    - Avoid around the eyes
    - Avoid placement to face or genitals
    - Avoid use between the fingers and toes → maceration of tissue
- **Special populations:**
  - Pediatric patients
    - Age:
      - If < 6 months → no NSAIDs
      - If < 2 years old → no Benadryl
      - Dosing requirements
      - Avoid aspirin → risk of Reye's syndrome
  - Pregnant patients & nursing mothers
    - Watch out for → NSAIDs
  - Patients with kidney disease
  - Patients on anticoagulants or on antiplatelets
  - Patient with hypertension
  - Patient with risks for small bowel obstruction
    - Watch out for → laxatives

Summary

- OTC / Nonprescription medications are still medications that do require some degree of federal and clinical awareness.
- Complete a medication use evaluation at each visit that includes OTC medications.
- As appropriate educate and counsel the patient.

Basic Terminology

- **Parenteral Therapy:**
  - Medications in dosage forms that are meant to be injected through the skin and into a tissue compartment or vascular space instead of being administered by mouth or alimentary canal.
- **Rationale for Parenteral Therapy:**
  - Patient is unable to swallow
  - Alimentary (enteral) canal is unable to be used or not functioning correctly
  - To by-pass first pass metabolism
  - Lack of oral bioavailability
  - Time-sensitive onset of drug action needed
  - Compliance or adherence

Dosage Formulations

- **Parenteral Dosage Formulation Terminology:**
  - **Ampul**
    - A glass container containing a single-use of medication
    - The glass container is gently broken at one end and may require the use of a needle filter to extract contents to avoid glass particles being pulled into injection device.
  - **Vial**
    - A plastic (usually) or glass container with a rubber gromet sealed closure at the top surrounded by a metal ring
    - Can be a single-use or multi-dose vial
  - **Vehicle**
    - The liquid that contains the medication that is dissolved, suspended or emulsified
    - The most common liquid is sterile water for injection (USP) but can also sometimes include:
      - Ethanol
      - Oils
  - **Total Parenteral Nutrition (TPN)**
    - Also referred to as hyperalimentation
    - Used for patients unable to consume nutrients and calories enterally

Administration Considerations

- **Considerations for preparation and dispensing:**
  - Try to dispense or have admixtures that are ready-to-use
  - Have a standardized process for compounding medications in sterile manner and free of distractions
  - Label IV admixtures in a standard format
  - Ensure competency of those preparing the medication
- Special considerations "prior to" administration of parenteral therapy:
  - Double checks in place
  - Have standardized IV medication administration recommendations to minimize distractions or interruptions
  - Personnel competency to administer the IV medications
  - Limit number of steps to prepare IV medications
  - Establish plans for antidotes and on-going monitoring procedures
  - Standard Precautions

- Guidelines that are meant to protect the healthcare worker who has occupational exposure to blood borne pathogens or bodily fluids.
- All bodily fluids should generally be considered infectious

Routes of Administration

- **Epidural:**
  - This is the space just above the dura matter of the brain and spinal cord but inferior to the ligamentum flavum
  - This where the CSF fluid is located
  - Should be administered by strict aseptic technique given access to the CNS
- **Intra-arterial (IA):**
  - Generally, this route is NOT advised and can lead to serious complications to the end organ of that artery
  - Examples
    - Directly administered tPA for clots for conditions such as:
      - STEMI
      - Acute ischemic stroke
      - Submassive or massive PE with hemodynamic instability
      - Acute peripheral arterial occlusion
- **Intra-articular:**
  - Administration of the medication directly into the joint space
  - Strict aseptic technique should be following to avoid risk of introducing bacterial into the joint which can lead to a septic joint
  - In some cases, extraction of some fluid may be required to avoid inserting too much fluid into the space
    - May also have a volume limitation based on the size of the joint space available
- **Intradermal:**
  - Administration of the medication directly into the superficial layer of the skin between the dermis and epidermis
  - Absorption is slower than SubQ or IM
  - Limited volume of administration to ~ 0.1 mL
  - Examples for use:
    - Tuberculin skin test for TB evaluation
    - Vaccines or IgG (e.g., rabies)
- **Intraosseous (IO):**
  - Administration of the medication directly into the bone marrow
  - Easy to insert and set up
  - Absorption is rapid and similar to IV
  - No significant limitation of volume of administration
  - Can be painful. Consider premedication with IO lidocaine
  - Examples for use:
    - ACLS / Codes
    - Unable to obtain IV access and emergency treatment needed
  - Note:
    - Avoid use of a bone that is injured
    - Apply infusions under a pressure bag
- **Intrathecal:**
  - Administration of the medication directly into the spinal canal or subarachnoid space
  - Difficult to do and more invasive
  - Requires strict aspect technique
  - Examples:
    - Anesthesia
    - Chemotherapy

- **Intramuscular (IM):**
  - Administration of the medication directly into the muscle
  - One-time medication administration
  - Locations of administration:
    - Upper arm (in adults)
    - Thigh (especially in pediatric patients)
    - Gluteal muscles (in adults)
  - Volume limitation of 2-3 mL to the upper arm and no more than 5 mL in the gluteal muscle of an adult
  - Absorption rate is less than IV, but faster than SubQ and intradermal
- **Intravenous (IV):**
  - Administration of the medication directly into the vascular space and is the most common route in the hospital
  - Provides 100% bioavailability and a rapid onset of action (when needed)
  - Volume of fluid can be small or large depending on the vessel cannulated with an IV
  - Duration of IV placement:
    - Short, peripheral: replace every 72-96 hrs
    - Midline, peripheral: replace every 7 – 30 days
    - Central lines: last weeks up to 1 year
  - Central line vs Peripheral IVs:
    - Central lines can receive chemotherapy, irritants, TPN, medications with pH < 5 or > 9 or osmolarity > 600 mOsm
    - Peripheral IV lines can receive moderate pH 5 to 9 and parenteral nutrition up to 900 mOsm/L.
      - Generally, avoid vesicants or irritating drugs (dopamine, chemo)
    - Risks:
      - Pain and venous irritation
      - Infiltration or extravasation of infusion into the tissue
      - Line infection
      - Most medication suspensions cannot be given this route
- **Subcutaneous (SubQ):**
  - Administration of the medication directly into the tissue beneath the skin and above the muscle
  - Locations of administration:
    - Upper arm
    - Thigh
    - Abdomen
  - Absorption rate is less than IM or IV, but faster than intradermal
  - Usually one-time medication administration but a few options for continuous infusions though less common
- **Special considerations for administration of parenteral therapy:**
  - **Duration of stability once mixed or prepared**
  - Protection from light
  - Need for an IV pump
  - Concentration of the parenteral mixture
  - Suspension or solution
  - Ability or need to titrate
  - Need for a filter (0.22, 0.45, or 5-micron filters) to capture particular matter
  - Binding of drug to plastic tubing
  - Latex allergies
  - Size of the blood vessel in relation to the medication being administered (i.e., IV access)
    - Ability to cause phlebitis
    - Risk of infiltration (e.g., under pressure) or extravasation

Disposal

- Disposal of parenteral drug therapy:
    - All blood or bodily fluid containing needles or syringes should NOT be recapped
    - Placed in a "sharps" container which is a nonpermeable, puncture resistant, tamper proof biohazard container

Summary

- Parenteral drug therapy is a method of medication administration that avoids the alimentary canal.
- There are a number of factors that go into which route of administration is utilized.

Terminology

- **Basic Terminology and Descriptions:**
  - **Pharmaceutical Equivalents:**
    - Drug products that are considered to be identical dosage forms, route(s) of administration, and contain an identical active drug ingredient
    - Products can vary or differ in the inactive ingredients, shape of dosage form, scoring set up, mechanism of release, packaging, excipients used, expiration date and labeling.
  - **Pharmaceutical Alternatives:**
    - Drug product that contain an identical therapeutic moiety or its precursor, but may not be the same dosage amount, dosage form, or the salt or ester
      - Example: A single manufacturer that have a product line with different dosage forms and strength
  - **Bioequivalence:**
    - When drug products are administered under the same molar dose and under similar conditions in a controlled study environment, there is no presence of significant differences in the rate and extent of which the drug is available at the site of action.
  - **Biosimilars:**
    - Unique biologic drugs derived from living organisms by recombinant technology and is highly similar to the reference product.
  - **Therapeutic Equivalents:**
    - Products that have been approved by the FDA that are pharmaceutical equivalents where bioequivalence has been documented and expected to have the same clinical effect and safety profile when used in the same medical conditions.
    - Therapeutically equivalent drug products meet the following general criteria:
      - Approved as safe and effective
      - Are pharmaceutical equivalents
      - Are bioequivalent
      - Adequately labeled
      - Manufactured in compliance with GMP regulations

The Orange Book

- **Determining therapeutic equivalence:**
  - Historically it was the "Orange Book" which is printed in book format
    - The purpose was to find and evaluate for therapeutic equivalence codes for various pharmaceutical products
  - Now replaced with "Electronic Orange Book" (EOB)
    - Living electronic document (continuously updated)
- **Electronic Orange Book (EOB) Content Areas:**
  - Applicant Number
    - Basic information about the manufacturer, date of approval, etc
  - Therapeutic Equivalence Evaluations (TE) Bioequivalence Code
    - The bioequivalence status of each drug product
  - Reference Listed Drug (RLD)
    - Usually the innovators product considered to be the "reference standard" set by the FDA by which new applicants apply for ANDA
  - Active Ingredient
  - Dosage formulation
  - Route of administration

- Strength
- Propriety Name
- Applicant

Bioequivalence Codes

Code	Interpretation
AA	No bioequivalence problems for conventional dosage forms
AB	Meets necessary bioequivalence requirements
AB1	Meets bioequivalence requirement to AB1 rated reference drug
AB2	Meets bioequivalence requirement to AB2 rated reference drug
AB3	Meets bioequivalence requirement to AB3 rated reference drug
AB4	Meets bioequivalence requirement to AB4 rated reference drug

Generic Substitution of Biosimilars

- **Basic definition:**
  - Unique biologic drugs derived from living organisms by recombinant technology and is highly similar to the reference product.
- **Federal Law:**
  - Biologics Price Competition and Innovation Act (BPCIA) of 2009
    - Includes a process of approving generic small-molecule drugs under the Hatch-Waxman Act
    - Application of generic products:
      - Apply utilizing a Biologic License Application (BLA) for full evaluation of purity, potency, and safety
      - Apply utilizing a Biosimilar Application which is an abbreviated evaluation.
- **Basic Criteria for Approval of a Generic Product:**
  - All generic substitutes must also be compared to a reference product and demonstrate:
    - Same mechanism of action
    - Same route of administration
    - Same dosage form
    - Same dosage strength
    - No difference in purity, potency, and/or safety to reference drug
  - Published in the FDA's "Purple Book"
- **Examples of Biosimilars for generic substitution can include:**
  - Blood or blood component
  - Gene therapy
  - Proteins
  - Tissue
  - Vaccines

Summary

- The Orange Book is now the Electronic Orange Book which is used by pharmacists to determine of one drug product is considered therapeutically equivalent enough allow for generic substitution.
- Given the growing number of biologic agents now on the market, there are also rules or generic substitution in what is now called biosimilars.

PART 2

DRUG CLASS
RAPID REVIEW

High-Yield Basic Pharmacology

- **Mechanism of Action**
  - Sodium channel blockers - slows cardiac conduction, decreases cardiac automaticity, and increases refractory periods.
  - By depressing conduction and prolong refractoriness, class 1a agents can convert a reentry arrhythmia to normal conduction by blocking both directions of electrical flow.
    - Orthodromic conduction is antegrade conduction through the AV node.
    - Antidromic conduction is retrograde conduction through the AV node.

Primary Net Benefit

- Disopyramide and quinidine are rarely used clinically, but procainamide still has a role in the acute management of supraventricular arrhythmias and ventricular arrhythmias.

Vaughan Williams Class Ia - Drug Class Review			
High-Yield Med Reviews			
Mechanism of Action: *Sodium channel blockers - slows cardiac conduction, decreases cardiac automaticity, and increases refractory periods.*			
Class Effects: *Terminates or slows pathologic conduction contributing to arrhythmias*			
Generic Name	**Brand Name**	**Indication(s) or Uses**	**Notes**

Disopyramide	Norpace	• Ventricular arrhythmias	• **Dosing (Adult):**
			  - Patients weight less than 50 kg:
			    • Oral loading dose 200 mg
			    • Maintenance dose 100 mg q6h (IR), or 200 mg q12h (CR)
			  - Patients weight 50 kg or greater
			    • Oral loading dose 300 mg
			    • Maintenance dose 150 to 200 mg q6h (IR), or 300 mg q12h (CR).
			    • Maximum dose of 400mg q6h)
			• **Dosing (Peds):** Immediate release only
			  - IR 1.5 to 7.5 mg/kg/dose q6h
			    • Maximum 1,600 mg/day
			• **CYP450 Interactions:** Substrate CYP 3A4
			• **Renal or Hepatic Dose Adjustments:**
			  - Controlled release
			    • Not recommended if GFR less than 40 mL/minute
			  - Immediate release
			    • GFR 10 to 50 mL/minute 100 to 200 mg every 12 to 24 hours
			    • GFR less than 10 mL/minute 100 to 200 mg every 24 to 48 hours
			• **Dosage Forms:** Oral (IR capsule, ER capsule)

Vaughan Williams Class Ia - Drug Class Review
High-Yield Med Reviews

Generic Name	Brand Name	Indication(s) or Uses	Notes

Procainamide	Pronestyl	• Supraventricular arrhythmias
		• Ventricular arrhythmias
			• **Dosing (Adult):**
			  – IV loading dose of 10 to 17 mg/kg infusion at 20 to 50 mg/minute (maximum 1g)
			  – IV 100 mg bolus every 5 minutes (maximum 1g)
			    • Administration endpoints
			      – QRS interval widening by 50% of its original width
			      – Maximum dose of 1 g
			      – Hypotension
			  – IV continuous infusion 1 to 4 mg/minute
			• **Dosing (Peds):**
			  – IV loading dose 10 to 15 mg/kg over 30 to 60 minutes.
			  – IV infusion of 20 to 80 mcg/kg/minute (maximum 2,000 mg/24 hours)
			• **CYP450 Interactions:** Substrate of CYP 2D6
			• **Renal or Hepatic Dose Adjustments:**
			• For continuous infusion only
			  – Reduce total dose by 25% to 50%
			    • GFR 10 to 50 mL/minute
			    • Dialysis
			    • Child-Pugh score of 8-10
			  – Reduce total dose by 50% to 75% and follow NAPA levels.
			    • GFR less than 10 mL/minutes
			    • Child-Pugh score greater than 10
			• **Dosage Forms:** IV solution

Quinidine	Quinaglute, Quinidex	• Supraventricular arrhythmias
		• Ventricular arrhythmias
			• **Dosing (Adult):**
			  – Quinidine sulfate- initial dose 200 to 400 mg/q6h.
			  – Quinidine gluconate- initial dose 324 to 648 mg q8h
			• **Dosing (Peds):** Quinidine sulfate- 7.5 mg/kg q6h
			• **CYP450 Interactions:** Substrate of CYP 3A4, 2C9, 2E1, P-gp. Inhibits CYP 2D6, 3A4, P-gp.
			• **Renal or Hepatic Dose Adjustments:**
			  – Reduce to 75% of normal dose if GFR less than 10 mL/minute
			• **Dosage Forms:** Oral tablet (IR and ER)

High-Yield Clinical Knowledge

- **Conduction and Refractoriness**
  - By depressing conduction and prolong refractoriness, class 1a agents can convert a reentry arrhythmia to normal conduction by blocking both directions of electrical flow.
    - Orthodromic conduction is antegrade conduction through the AV node.
    - Antidromic conduction is retrograde conduction through the AV node.

- **Disopyramide**
  - Due to calcium channel blocking properties, disopyramide produces the most negative inotropic effects among the Class 1a agents.
    - Disopyramide, more specifically its active metabolite, produces the most anticholinergic effects among the Class 1a agents, as well as possessing calcium channel blocking effects.
    - Its active metabolite (N-despropyldisopyramide) is produced by hepatic mono-N-dealkylation.
  - R-disopyramide possesses a sodium channel blocking effect, whereas S-disopyramide has pharmacologic actions similar to quinidine.
  - Should not be used in HFrEF patients
    - Produces more negative inotropy than either procainamide or quinidine
- **Procainamide**
  - Least likely to cause hypotension among the Class 1a agents since procainamide lacks alpha-adrenergic blocking properties.
  - Procainamide therapy can be monitored using serum concentrations, with a normal therapeutic range of 4 to 12 mcg/mL.
    - Additionally, NAPA concentrations (normal range of 10 to 20 mcg/mL) should be followed, particularly in acute overdoses/toxicity and CKD patients
    - NAPA is eliminated renally, with an elimination half-life of 6 to 10 hours, much longer than the parent procainamide half-life of 3 to 4 hours.
- **Quinidine**
  - Anticholinergic adverse events are expected, including dry mucous membranes and flushed skin.
  - Rarely used due to cardiotoxicities, including syncope, QT prolongation, and Torsade de Pointes can occur at normal therapeutic doses.
    - Cinchonism, occurring from acute or chronic quinidine overdose, consists of abdominal pain, diarrhea, tinnitus, and altered mental status
- **Disopyramide And Quinidine Induced Hypoglycemia**
  - Can induce insulin release from pancreatic islet cells via potassium channel blockade.
- **Slow Acetylators And Procainamide**
  - Patients who are "slow acetylators" are at higher risk of early development of procainamide-induced lupus syndrome.
    - The parent compound, not NAPA, causes this syndrome.
      - Subjects with procainamide-induced lupus who were exposed to NAPA alone had their lupus-like symptoms resolve.
- **Procainamide Dosing Regimens**
  - Drug references list various loading doses for procainamide and titration parameters.
    - Acceptable dosing, including infusion loading doses of 10 to 17 mg/kg infusion at 20 to 50 mg/minute, 100 mg IV bolus every 5 minutes.
    - The therapeutic endpoint for these doses includes QRS interval widening by 50% of its original width, a maximum dose of 1 g is reached, or hypotension occurs.

HIGH-YIELD BOARD EXAM ESSENTIALS
- **CLASSIC AGENTS:** Disopyramide, procainamide, quinidine
- **DRUG CLASS:** VW Class 1a
- **INDICATIONS:** Supraventricular arrhythmias, ventricular arrhythmias
- **MECHANISM:** Slows cardiac conduction decreases cardiac automaticity and increases refractory periods primarily by blocking the opening of sodium channels with intermediate recovery from the blockade.
- **SIDE EFFECTS:** Negative inotropy (disopyramide), ANA antibody (procainamide), cardiotoxicity (quinidine)
- **CLINICAL PEARLS:** Disopyramide and quinidine are rarely used clinically, but procainamide still has a role in the acute management of supraventricular arrhythmias and ventricular arrhythmias.

High-Yield Basic Pharmacology

- **Mechanism of Action**
  - Block inward sodium current by blocking inactivated sodium channels, preventing myocardial reentry and subsequent dysrhythmias.

Primary Net Benefit

- Lidocaine may be as effective as amiodarone for shock-refractory ventricular fibrillation or pulseless ventricular tachycardia, avoiding numerous potential drug interactions and adverse events.

Vaughan Williams Class Ib - Drug Class Review			
High-Yield Med Reviews			
Mechanism of Action: *Block inward sodium current by blocking inactivated sodium channels, preventing myocardial reentry and subsequent dysrhythmias.*			
Class Effects: *Increases the effective refractory period and prolongs the action potential.*			
Generic Name	**Brand Name**	**Indication(s) or Uses**	**Notes**

Lidocaine	Xylocaine	- Ventricular arrhythmias	- **Dosing (Adult):**
			  - IV or IO (intraosseous) 1 to 1.5 mg/kg bolus.
			    - Maximum 3 mg/kg
			  - IV continuous infusion 1 to 4 mg/minute
			- **Dosing (Peds):**
			  - IV or IO (intraosseous) 1 to 1.5 mg/kg bolus.
			    - Maximum 3 mg/kg
			  - IV continuous infusion 20 to 50 mg/kg/minute
			- **CYP450 Interactions:** Substrate of CYP 1A2, 2A6, 2B6, 2C9, 3A4
			- **Renal or Hepatic Dose Adjustments:** No specific dose adjustment but follow GX/MEGX concentrations.
			- **Dosage Forms:** Solution for injection. Numerous other dosage forms exist, but not for antiarrhythmic indications.

Vaughan Williams Class Ib - Drug Class Review
High-Yield Med Reviews

Generic Name	Brand Name	Indication(s) or Uses	Notes

Mexiletine	Mexitil	• Ventricular arrhythmias	• **Dosing (Adult):**
			  - Oral loading dose 400 mg (optional)
			  - Oral maintenance dose 150 to 200 mg q8h to q12h
			    ▪ Maximum dose 1.2 g/day
			• **Dosing (Peds):**
			  - Initial oral dose of 6 to 8 mg/kg/day in 2 or 3 divided doses
			    ▪ Maximum dose 15 mg/kg/day or 1.2 g/day, whichever is less
			• **CYP450 Interactions:** Substrate of CYP 1A2, 2D6. Inhibits CYP 1A2
			• **Renal or Hepatic Dose Adjustments:**
			  - None recommended, but elimination half-life is doubled in the setting of hepatic failure.
			• **Dosage Forms:** Oral (capsule)

High-Yield Clinical Knowledge

- **Lidocaine**
  - Lidocaine undergoes significant first-pass metabolism, resulting in oral bioavailability of 3%.
    - While this absorption prevents oral use for antiarrhythmic or analgesic effects, it is sufficient to precipitate toxicity, particularly in children.
      - Therapeutic monitoring of lidocaine consists of following the plasma lidocaine concentration and the toxic and active metabolite monoethylglycinexylidide (MEGX).
  - **Mexiletine**
    - Developed as an analog of lidocaine, but with the desire to permit oral therapy. By specifically reducing first-pass hepatic metabolism, mexiletine can be thought of as orally available lidocaine.
      - It is used clinically in combination with other antiarrhythmics such as sotalol, which can improve efficacy while limiting dose-related toxicities of either agent.
- **Mexiletine Tremors**
  - A common complaint that may affect compliance is the development of tremors in patients taking mexiletine. However, this effect may be minimized by simply having the patient take mexiletine with food.
- **Neuropathic Pain Management and Opioid-sparing**
  - To reduce chronic opioid use, numerous agents have been investigated for their potential opioid-sparing effects. Mexiletine has been proposed as an agent for chronic neuropathic pain management in patients where opioid-sparing therapies may be useful.
- **Lidocaine Therapeutic Monitoring**
  - CYP3A4 metabolizes lidocaine to two metabolites, glycine xylidide (GX) and the aforementioned MEGX.
  - MEGX is less potent of a sodium channel blocker but has a much longer half-life.
    - Target lidocaine levels are 1.5 to 5.0 mcg/mL
      - Heart failure, hepatic impairment, beta-blockers, and patients receiving prolonged infusions of lidocaine should be kept at the lower end of the therapeutic range to prevent toxicity.

HIGH-YIELD BOARD EXAM ESSENTIALS

- **CLASSIC AGENTS:** Lidocaine, mexiletine
- **DRUG CLASS:** VW Class 1b
- **INDICATIONS:** Chronic treatment to prevent ventricular tachycardia (VT) and ventricular fibrillation (VF), Acute treatment of VF or pulseless VT
- **MECHANISM:** Block inward sodium current by blocking inactivated sodium channels with rapid kinetics, preventing myocardial reentry and subsequent dysrhythmias.
- **SIDE EFFECTS:** Tremors, headache, seizures
- **CLINICAL PEARLS:**
  - Due to the sodium channel blockade within the ventricular myocyte there is QRS widening on the ECG with higher doses.
  - Lidocaine is not absorbed when taken by mouth, thus mexiletine is the pro-drug of lidocaine and can be given by mouth.
  - Patients on IV lidocaine infusions can be transitioned to mexiletine by administering 200 mg of mexiletine when the lidocaine infusion is stopped.

High-Yield Basic Pharmacology

- **Mechanism of Action**
  - Prevent reentry pathways by slowing conduction via blocking fast inward sodium current.
    - Flecainide and propafenone are inhibitors of the ryanodine receptor 2 (RyR2) calcium channel in cardiac cells. This effect leads to the suppression of delayed afterdepolarizations.
      - This should not be confused with the RyR1 calcium channel, which is better known for its role in malignant hyperthermia.
    - Flecainide, like propafenone, possesses sodium channel blocking properties as well as potassium rectifier current blocking and calcium channel blocking properties.

Primary Net Benefit

- Unique role in outpatient oral cardioversion for patients with paroxysmal atrial fibrillation.

Vaughan Williams Class Ic - Drug Class Review High-Yield Med Reviews			
Mechanism of Action: *Prevent reentry pathways by slowing conduction via blocking fast inward sodium current*			
Class Effects: *Prolonging refractoriness in all areas of the heart and reducing spontaneous depolarizations.*			
Generic Name	**Brand Name**	**Main Indication(s) or Uses**	**Notes**
Flecainide	Tambocor	<ul><li>Pharmacological cardioversion</li><li>Paroxysmal Afib, Aflutter, or PSVT</li></ul>	<ul><li>**Dosing (Adult):**<ul><li>Oral 50 mg q12h<ul><li>Maximum 300 mg/day</li></ul></li><li>Cardioversion<ul><li>Weight less than 70 kg - 200 mg</li><li>Weight 70 kg or greater - 300 mg</li></ul></li></ul></li><li>**Dosing (Peds):**<ul><li>Oral 50 to 100 mg/m^2/day divided q8 to 12h<ul><li>Maximum 200 mg/m^2/day</li></ul></li></ul></li><li>**CYP450 Interactions:** Substrate CYP2D6, CYP1A2</li><li>**Renal or Hepatic Dose Adjustments:**<ul><li>GFR less than or equal to 35 mL/minute - 100 mg q24h</li></ul></li><li>**Dosage Forms:** Oral (tablet)</li></ul>
Propafenone	Rythmol	<ul><li>Pharmacological cardioversion</li><li>Paroxysmal Afib, Aflutter, or PSVT</li></ul>	<ul><li>**Dosing (Adult):**<ul><li>Extended-release - 225 mg q12h<ul><li>Maximum 425 mg q12h</li></ul></li><li>Immediate-release - 150 mg q8h (300 mg every 8 hours)</li><li>Cardioversion (IR tablet)<ul><li>Weight less than 70 kg - 450 mg</li><li>Weight 70 kg or greater - 600 mg</li></ul></li></ul></li><li>**Dosing (Peds):** Not routinely used</li><li>**CYP450 Interactions:** Substrate CYP3A4, CYP2D6, CYP1A2. Inhibits CYP1A2, CYP2D6, P-gp</li><li>**Renal or Hepatic Dose Adjustments:**<ul><li>No specific recommendations</li></ul></li><li>**Dosage Forms:** Oral (ER capsule, IR tablet)</li></ul>

High-Yield Clinical Knowledge

- **Flecainide**
    - Each of the class 1c agents carries a warning that there is increased mortality in patients with structural heart disease receiving these agents. This warning originated from the results of the CAST trials, described further below.
        - The specific warning pertains to patients receiving these agents for asymptomatic, non-life-threatening ventricular arrhythmias who had a recent myocardial infarction.
            - This stipulation is often omitted, preventing patients without these specific risk factors from potentially receiving these agents for atrial arrhythmias or as a bridge to ablation therapy.
- **Propafenone**
    - In addition to its class 1c sodium channel effects, propafenone acts as a weak beta-adrenergic blocker and is an L-type calcium channel blocker and potassium channel blocker.
        - Propafenone is a structural analog of propranolol. It is hypothesized this similarity gives rise to its beta-blocking properties.
- **Flecainide Toxicities**
    - Patients with impaired renal function, low urine pH, concomitant CYP2D6 inhibitors, HFrEF have reduced flecainide clearance.
- **Visual Disturbances**
    - Patients taking flecainide commonly complain of visual disturbances and dose-related blurred vision.
- **Propafenone and CYP2D6**
    - The metabolism of propafenone by CYP2D6 is saturable, leading to unpredictable and abrupt increases in plasma levels.
        - In patients with low or absent CYP2D6 (from drug interactions or poor metabolizer patients), the first-pass effect is significantly diminished and will lead to much higher plasma propafenone levels and toxicity.

HIGH-YIELD BOARD EXAM ESSENTIALS
- **CLASSIC AGENTS:** Flecainide, propafenone
- **DRUG CLASS:** VW Class Ic
- **INDICATIONS:** Pharmacological cardioversion of paroxysmal Afib, Prevention of paroxysmal Afib/flutter and paroxysmal SVT, ventricular arrhythmias
- **MECHANISM:** Prevent reentry pathways by slowing conduction via blocking fast inward sodium current
- **SIDE EFFECTS:** Decreased inotropy, blurry vision, arrhythmias
- **CLINICAL PEARLS:** Each of the class 1c agents carries a warning that there is increased mortality in patients with structural heart disease receiving these agents. This warning originated from the results of the CAST trials.

High-Yield Basic Pharmacology

- **Mechanism of Action**
  - Competitive inhibitors of catecholamines on beta-adrenergic receptors and blunt the chronotropic and inotropic response to catecholamines.
  - The antiarrhythmic action of beta-blockers is mediated via beta-blockade in the AV node. This is observed on the ECG as PR interval prolongation.

Primary Net Benefit

- Beta-blockers exert numerous beneficial effects, including reduction of the heart rate and blood pressure, as well as having anti-arrhythmic and anti-ischemic properties, and inhibit ACE release from the juxtaglomerular apparatus.
  - In heart failure, beta-blockers confer benefits by inhibiting cardiac remodeling that puts patients increased risk of sudden cardiac death.

Vaughn Williams Class II (Beta-antagonists) - Drug Class Review High-Yield Med Reviews			
Mechanism of Action: *Competitive inhibitors of catecholamines on beta-adrenergic receptors and blunt the chronotropic and inotropic response to catecholamines*			
Class Effects: *Slows the rate of SA node discharge, prevent ectopic pacemakers, and decrease conduction through the atrial and the AV node*			
Generic Name	**Brand Name**	**Indication(s) or Uses**	**Notes**

Acebutolol	Sectral	▪ Hypertension
		 ▪ Premature ventricular contractions
			▪ **Dosing (Adult):**
			   – Oral 200 to 400 mg once daily
			     ▪ Maximum 1200 mg daily
			 ▪ **Dosing (Peds):** Not commonly used
			 ▪ **CYP450 Interactions:** none
			 ▪ **Renal or Hepatic Dose Adjustments:**
			   – GFR 25 to 49 mL/minute: Reduce dose by 50%
			   – GFR less than 25 mL/minute: Reduce dose by 75%
			 ▪ **Dosage Forms:** Oral (capsule, tablet)

Atenolol	Tenormin	▪ Hypertension
		 ▪ Premature ventricular contractions
			▪ **Dosing (Adult):**
			   – Oral 25 to 100 mg once daily
			     ▪ Maximum 100 mg daily
			 ▪ **Dosing (Peds):**
			   – Oral 0.3 to 1 mcg/kg/day once daily or in divided doses q12h
			 ▪ **CYP450 Interactions:** none
			 ▪ **Renal or Hepatic Dose Adjustments:**
			   – GFR 15 to 35 mL/minute: Maximum daily dose of 50 mg
			   – GFR less than 15: Maximum daily dose of 25 mg
			   – Hemodialysis: Administer after dialysis
			 ▪ **Dosage Forms:** Oral (tablet)

Vaughn Williams Class II (Beta-antagonists) - Drug Class Review
High-Yield Med Reviews

Generic Name	Brand Name	Indication(s) or Uses	Notes

Carvedilol	Coreg	• HFrEF
		• Hypertension
			• **Dosing (Adult):**
			  – IR: 3.125 mg to 25 mg BID
			    • If over 85 kg, maximum 50 mg BID
			  – ER 20 mg daily
			    • Maximum 80 mg/day
			• **Dosing (Peds):**
			  – Oral 0.075-0.08 mg/kg/dose BID
			    • Maximum 50 mg BID.
			• **CYP450 Interactions:** Inhibits P-gp. Substrate of P-gp, CYP 2C9, 2D6, 3A4, 1A2
			• **Renal or Hepatic Dose Adjustments:** None
			• **Dosage Forms:** Oral (tablet, capsule)

Betaxolol	Kerlone	• Hypertension	• **Dosing (Adult):** – Oral 5 to 20 mg once daily • **Dosing (Peds):** Not used • **CYP450 Interactions:** Minor substrate of CYP1A2, 2D6 • **Renal or Hepatic Dose Adjustments:** None • **Dosage Forms:** Oral (tablet)

Bisoprolol	Zebeta	• Hypertension	• **Dosing (Adult):**
			  – Oral 1.25 to 10 mg daily
			    • Maximum 10 mg/day
			• **Dosing (Peds):** None
			• **CYP450 Interactions:** Substrate of CYP2D6, and CYP3A4
			• **Renal or Hepatic Dose Adjustments:**
			  – GFR less than 40 mL/minute, initial dose no more than 2.5 mg daily
			• **Dosage Forms:** Oral (tablet)

Esmolol	Brevibloc	• Atrial fibrillation/flutter
		• Intraoperative and/or postoperative tachycardia and/or hypertension
		• Sinus tachycardia
		• Supraventricular tachycardia
			• **Dosing (Adult):**
			  – IV bolus 500 to 1000 mcg/kg over 30 to 60 seconds
			  – IV infusion 50 to 300 mcg/kg/min
			• **Dosing (Peds):**
			  – IV bolus 100 to 500 mcg/kg over 30 to 60 seconds
			  – IV infusion 50 to 300 mcg/kg/min
			• **CYP450 Interactions:** None
			• **Renal or Hepatic Dose Adjustments:** None
			• **Dosage Forms:** IV solution

Vaughn Williams Class II (Beta-antagonists) - Drug Class Review
High-Yield Med Reviews

Generic Name	Brand Name	Indication(s) or Uses	Notes

Labetalol	Trandate	• Acute aortic dissection
		• Acute ischemic stroke
		• Acute hemorrhagic stroke
		• Hypertension
		• Preeclampsia/eclampsia
			• **Dosing (Adult):**
			  – Oral 100 mg twice daily up to
			    • Maximum 400 mg twice daily
			  – IV 10-20 mg IV push every 10 minutes
			• **Dosing (Peds):**
			  – Oral 1 to 3 mg/kg/day in 2 divided doses
			    • Maximum 10 to 12 mg/kg/day, or 1,200 mg/day
			  – IV 0.2 to 1 mg/kg/dose
			    • Maximum 40 mg/dose
			• **CYP450 Interactions:** Extensive first pass, hepatic glucuronidation
			• **Renal or Hepatic Dose Adjustments:** None
			• **Dosage Forms:** Oral (tablet), IV solution

Metoprolol	Lopressor
	Toprol
		• Angina
		• HFrEF
		• Hypertension
		• Myocardial infarction
			• **Dosing (Adult):**
			  – Oral IR 12.5 to 200 mg BID
			    • Maximum 400 mg daily
			  – Oral ER 50 to 200 mg
			    • Maximum 400 mg daily
			  – IV 2.5 to 5 mg IV push q5minutes as needed
			    • Maximum total dose 15 mg
			• **Dosing (Peds):**
			  – Oral 0.1 to 0.2 mg/kg/dose BID
			    • Maximum 2 mg/kg/day, or 200 mg/day
			  – IV 0.1 to 0.2 mg/kg
			    • Maximum 10 mg/dose
			• **CYP450 Interactions:**
			  – Substrate CYP 2D6, and CYP 2C19
			• **Renal or Hepatic Dose Adjustments:** None
			• **Dosage Forms:** Oral (tablet [IR and ER], capsule [IR and ER]), IV solution

Nebivolol	Bystolic	• Hypertension	• **Dosing (Adult):**
			  – Oral 5 mg once daily
			    • Maximum 40 mg daily
			• **Dosing (Peds):** Not used
			• **CYP450 Interactions:** Extensive first pass, hepatic glucuronidation
			• **Renal or Hepatic Dose Adjustments:**
			  – GFR less than 30 mL/minute: Initial dose of 2.5 mg once daily
			• **Dosage Forms:** Oral (tablet)

Vaughn Williams Class II (Beta-antagonists) - Drug Class Review
High-Yield Med Reviews

Generic Name	Brand Name	Indication(s) or Uses	Notes

Nadolol	Corgard	• Angina
		• Hypertension
			• **Dosing (Adult):**
			  - Oral 10 to 240 mg once daily
			• **Dosing (Peds):**
			  - Oral for SVT - Initial dose of 0.5 to 1 mg/kg/day
			    • Maximum 2.5 mg/kg/day
			• **CYP450 Interactions:**
			  - None, but major P-gp substrate
			• **Renal or Hepatic Dose Adjustments:**
			  - GFR greater than 50 mL/minute, every 24 hours.
			  - GFR 31 to 50 mL/minute, every 24 to 36 hours
			  - GFR 10 to 30 mL/minute, every 24 to 48 hours
			  - GFR <10 mL/minute, every 40 to 60 hours
			  - HD - administer post-dialysis
			• **Dosage Forms:** Oral (tablet)

Pindolol	Visken	• Hypertension	• **Dosing (Adult):**
			  - Oral 2.5 to 30 mg BID
			    • Maximum 60 mg daily
			• **Dosing (Peds):** Not routinely used
			• **CYP450 Interactions:** Substrate of CYP2D6
			• **Renal or Hepatic Dose Adjustments:** No specific recommendations.
			• **Dosage Forms:** Oral (tablet)

Vaughn Williams Class II (Beta-antagonists) - Drug Class Review			
High-Yield Med Reviews			
Generic Name	**Brand Name**	**Indication(s) or Uses**	**Notes**
Propranolol	Inderal	<ul><li>Angina</li><li>Cardiac arrhythmias</li><li>Essential tremor</li><li>Hypertension</li><li>Migraine prophylaxis</li><li>MI</li><li>Obstructive hypertrophic cardiomyopathy</li><li>Pheochromocytoma</li><li>Proliferating infantile hemangioma</li></ul>	<ul><li>**Dosing (Adult):**<ul><li>Oral IR 10 to 320 mg once to four times daily<ul><li>Maximum 320 mg daily</li></ul></li><li>Oral ER 80 to 320 mg daily<ul><li>Maximum 320 mg daily</li></ul></li><li>IV solution 1 mg IV q2minutes<ul><li>Maximum 3 doses</li></ul></li></ul></li><li>**Dosing (Peds):**<ul><li>Oral IR 0.5 to 1 mg/kg/day in 3 divided doses<ul><li>Maximum 4 mg/kg/day</li></ul></li><li>IV 0.01 to 0.15 mg/kg/dose q6 to 8 hours</li><li>Age-dependent maximum of 1 mg/dose for infants, and 3 mg/dose for children and adolescents</li></ul></li><li>**CYP450 Interactions:** Extensive first pass, oxidation via CYP1A2, CYP2C19, CYP2D6, and CYP3A4. Inhibits CYP 1A2</li><li>**Renal or Hepatic Dose Adjustments:** None</li><li>**Dosage Forms:** Oral (tablet, capsule [ER], solution), IV solution</li></ul>

High-Yield Clinical Knowledge

- **Cardiac Effect from Sympathetic Stimuli**
    - Beta receptor antagonists slow the heart rate and decrease myocardial contractility if there are sympathetic stimuli to antagonize.
    - These agents have the most pronounced effect when the sympathetic nervous system stimulates cardiac activity.
        - Acute administration of beta-antagonists may temporarily increase peripheral vascular resistance (PVR) as a response to decreased cardiac output. But over time, PVR returns to baseline values or may even lower in patients with hypertension by inhibiting catecholamine activation of renin in renal juxtaglomerular cells.
- **IV to PO Conversion Errors**
    - When converting propranolol from IV to PO (or vice versa), careful attention must be given to avoid significant drug errors.
    - The oral bioavailability of propranolol is ~25% due to extensive first-pass metabolism. There are no empiric dose conversion recommendations because of patient variation, drug interactions, and clinical indication.
        - But considering the use of propranolol in acute indications such as thyroid storm where both dosage forms are recommended, a general concept of the difference in bioavailability can be inferred: 0.5 to 1 mg IV over 10 minutes versus 60 to 80 mg by mouth.
- **Hypoglycemic Masking**
    - Beta-antagonists diminish sympathetic-mediated responses to hypoglycemia (tachycardia, tremor, and hunger)

- During the acute hypoglycemic stress response, sweating is not diminished as this response is mediated by nicotinic activation by acetylcholine.
- **Rate Control for AF**
  - For acute control rate control in AF, beta-1 selective agents are potentially less effective compared to non-dihydropyridine calcium channel blockers (evidence described below)
    - However, in AF precipitated by increased sympathetic tone such as surgery, or thyrotoxicosis, rapid-acting beta-blockers can be highly effective and should be considered first-line therapy.
- **Paroxysmal Supraventricular Tachycardia (PSVT)**
  - Beta-blockers can be used in the management of acute PSVT. Specifically, beta-1 selective agents act on the AV nodal portion of the reentrant circuit to slow the antegrade electrical flow.
    - Beta-blockers may also benefit PSVT by limiting conduction through slow, calcium-dependent tissues.
- **Bronchoconstriction and Bronchospasm**
  - Non-selective beta-blocking agents and selective beta-1 antagonists used at high doses may cause bronchoconstriction and bronchospasm in some patients.
    - Although selective beta-1 antagonists are less likely to cause these effects, at doses in the high-end of normal or above, selectivity is lost, and beta-2 effects can be observed.
    - Agents with ISA activity may be less likely to cause adverse respiratory effects, but if the risk of bronchospasm or bronchoconstriction is a concern, alternative rate control agents such as calcium channel blockers should be used.

HIGH-YIELD BOARD EXAM ESSENTIALS

- **CLASSIC AGENTS:** Acebutolol, atenolol, carvedilol, bisoprolol, betaxolol, esmolol, metoprolol, nadolol, nebivolol, penbutolol, pindolol
- **DRUG CLASS:** VW Class 2
- **INDICATIONS:** Angina, atrial fibrillation/flutter, HFrEF, hypertension, hypertensive emergency, myocardial infarction, variceal hemorrhage prophylaxis (propranolol).
- **MECHANISM:** Competitive inhibitors of catecholamines on beta-adrenergic receptors and blunt the chronotropic and inotropic response to catecholamines
- **SIDE EFFECTS:** Bradycardia, fatigue, hypotension, poor exercise performance, bronchospasm in asthmatics.
- **CLINICAL PEARLS:**
  - Historically indicated for hypertension but are not the best antihypertensive agents as monotherapy.
  - They can reduce remodeling in heart failure which reduces risk of sudden cardiac death.
  - Beta-antagonists diminish sympathetic-mediated responses to hypoglycemia (tachycardia, tremor, and hunger), during the acute hypoglycemic stress response, sweating is not diminished as this response is mediated by nicotinic activation by acetylcholine.
  - Risk of bronchospasm in asthmatics and some COPD patients.

High-Yield Basic Pharmacology

- **Mechanism of Action**
  - Potassium channel antagonists block the delayed rectifier potassium current and prolong refractoriness in atrial and ventricular tissues.
  - The agents utilize reverse use-dependence which describes the class effect of preferentially prolonging the cardiac action potential at slow heart rates and a diminished effect at fast heart rates.
    - This causes both decreased efficacy at controlling tachyarrhythmias and increasing the risk of torsades de pointes at slow heart rates.

Primary Net Benefit

- Acute and chronic management of atrial and ventricular arrhythmias. Several agents have significant toxicities and may only be initiated in acute care settings.

Vaughan Williams Class 3 - Drug Class Review			
High-Yield Med Reviews			
Mechanism of Action: *Potassium channel antagonists block the delayed rectifier potassium current and prolong refractoriness in atrial and ventricular tissues.*			
Class Effects: *Prevent and terminate reentry dysrhythmias.*			
Generic Name	**Brand Name**	**Indication(s) or Uses**	**Notes**

Amiodarone	Nexterone, Pacerone	• Ventricular arrhythmia	• **Dosing (Adult):**
			  - IV (with pulses) 150 mg over 10 minutes, then 1 mg/minute for 6 hours, then 0.5 mg/minute for 18 hours.
			  - IV (pulseless) 300 mg bolus, may be followed by an additional 150 mg
			  - Oral 400 to 600 mg daily in divided doses for 2 to 4 weeks, adjusting to doses range from 100 to 400 mg once daily.
			• **Dosing (Peds):**
			  - IV 5 mg/kg
			• Maximum 3 doses or 15 mg/kg
			  - Oral 10 to 15 mg/kg/day in 1 to 2 divided doses, adjusting to 2.5 to 5 mg/kg/day
			• **CYP450 Interactions:** Substrate of CYP1A2, CYP2C19, CYP2C8, CYP2D6, CYP3A4, P-gp. Inhibits CYP2C9, CYP2D6, CYP3A4, P-gp
			• **Renal or Hepatic Dose Adjustments:**
			  - No specific recommendations, but reduced doses in hepatic failure should be considered.
			• **Dosage Forms:** IV solution, oral (tablet)

Vaughan Williams Class III - Drug Class Review
High-Yield Med Reviews

Generic Name	Brand Name	Indication(s) or Uses	Notes
Bretylium	Bretylol	• Ventricular arrhythmia	• **Dosing (Adult):** – IV bolus 5 mg/kg • Repeat 10 mg/kg q15 to 30 minutes, as necessary • **Dosing (Peds):** Not routinely used • **CYP450 Interactions:** None known • **Renal or Hepatic Dose Adjustments:** No specific adjustments • **Dosage Forms:** IV (solution)

Dofetilide	Tikosyn	• Atrial fibrillation/atrial flutter	• **Dosing (Adult):**
			  – Oral 500 mcg BID
			• **Dosing (Peds):** Not routinely used
			• **CYP450 Interactions:** Substrate of CYP3A4
			• **Renal or Hepatic Dose Adjustments:**
			  – GFR between 40 to 60 mL/minute reduce initial dose to 250 mcg twice daily
			  – GFR between 20 to 39 mL/minute reduce initial dose to 125 mcg twice daily
			  – Do not use if GFR is less than 20 mL/minute
			  – Child-Pugh class C - use caution
			• **Dosage Forms:** Oral (capsule)

Dronedarone	Multaq	• Paroxysmal or persistent atrial fibrillation	• **Dosing (Adult):**
			  – Oral 400 mg BID with meals.
			• **Dosing (Peds):** Not routinely used
			• **CYP450 Interactions:** Substrate of CYP3A4. Inhibits CYP2D6, CYP3A4, P-gp
			• **Renal or Hepatic Dose Adjustments:**
			  – Contraindicated in severe hepatic impairment
			• **Dosage Forms:** Oral (tablet)

Ibutilide	Corvert	• Atrial fibrillation/flutter	• **Dosing (Adult):**
			  – Patients less than 60 kg - IV 0.01 mg/kg over 10 minutes
			  – Patients 60 kg or greater - IV 1 mg over 10 minutes
			• **Dosing (Peds):** Not routinely used
			• **CYP450 Interactions:** None known
			• **Renal or Hepatic Dose Adjustments:** No specific adjustments
			• **Dosage Forms:** IV (solution)

Vaughan Williams Class III - Drug Class Review
High-Yield Med Reviews

Generic Name	Brand Name	Indication(s) or Uses	Notes

Sotalol	Betapace, Sorine, Sotylize	• Atrial fibrillation/flutter, symptomatic
		• Ventricular arrhythmias
			• **Dosing (Adult):**
			  - Oral 40 to 160 mg BID
			• Maximum 480 mg/day
			  - IV 75 mg over 5 hours q12h
			• **Dosing (Peds):**
			  - 30 mg/m^2/dose q8h
			• Dose adjustment based on age-related factor graph
			• **CYP450 Interactions:** None known
			• **Renal or Hepatic Dose Adjustments:**
			  - GFR 30 to 60 mL/minute reduce frequency to every 24 hours.
			  - GFR 10 to 29 mL/minute reduce frequency to every 36 to 48 hours.
			  - GFR less than 10 mL/minute use not recommended
			• **Dosage Forms:** IV (solution), Oral (solution, tablet)

High-Yield Clinical Knowledge

- **Amiodarone pharmacokinetics, toxicities, drug interactions**
  - Amiodarone possesses antiarrhythmic properties of each Vaughn Williams class: Sodium channel antagonist, beta-antagonist, potassium channel antagonist, and calcium channel antagonist.
    - Amiodarone is known to cause dose-limiting toxicities in all tissues, except for the kidneys.
    - However, acute renal failure can occur as an indirect result of cardiovascular, hepatic, hematologic, or endocrine-related toxicities.
  - The hepatic metabolism and impact on hepatic oxidation by amiodarone are extensive. Amiodarone is a substrate of CYP1A2, CYP2C19, CYP2C8, CYP2D6, CYP3A4, and P-gp. It also inhibits CYP2C9, CYP2D6, CYP3A4, and P-gp.
    - Although amiodarone prolongs the PR, QRS, and QT interval, the incidence of torsades de pointes associated with amiodarone is extremely rare.
- **Dronedarone warnings**
  - There are specific patient populations uniquely unable to receive dronedarone due to an increased risk of morbidity or mortality.
    - The use of dronedarone is contraindicated in patients with permanent atrial fibrillation, those with symptomatic heart failure and/or a recent decompensation requiring hospitalization or NYHA Class III or IV symptoms, liver, or lung toxicity related to previous amiodarone use.
      - Other contraindications include patients with pre-existing second-degree or third-degree AV block or sick sinus syndrome without a functioning pacemaker, concomitant use of potent CYP3A4 inhibitors, other QT-interval prolonging drugs, severe hepatic impairment, or if the patient is pregnant or breastfeeding.
- **Dofetilide FDA warning**
  - Dofetilide initiation is associated with a relatively high risk of Torsade De Pointes of approximately 3%. Therefore, initiation or dose adjustments must be in an acute care setting where the patient can be observed for a minimum of 3 days.

- Facilities must have the capacity to conduct continuous cardiac monitoring, renal function assessments, and the ability to perform cardiac resuscitation.

High-Yield Fast-Facts

- **Benzyl Alcohol and Polysorbate 80**
  - Amiodarone is poorly soluble in water; therefore, it is commercially available as an IV solution in benzyl alcohol and polysorbate 80. As a result, when further diluted with D5W, there is a high risk of precipitation, requiring administration with a 5-micron in-line filter.
    - Rapid administration of amiodarone is associated with hypotension. However, this effect is hypothesized to be due to polysorbate 80 induced vasodilation.
      - Polysorbate and benzyl alcohol-free "aqueous" amiodarone preparation was commercially available and did reduce the incidence of hypotension. However, due to the increased cost, and lack of patient-oriented benefit of this agent, it is not commonly available.
- **Weight-based Vs. Fixed Amiodarone Doses**
  - The commonly used IV doses of amiodarone (300mg or 150 mg IV bolus followed by 1mg/min for 6 hours, then 0.5 mg/min for 16 hours) is not appropriate for all indications.
    - For pharmacologic cardioversion of adult patients with atrial tachyarrhythmias, the appropriate dose is 5 mg/kg IV over 30 minutes followed by an infusion of 10 mg/kg over 20 hours.
      - Many patients do not tolerate this 5 mg/kg loading dose due to hypotension and fail this pharmacologic strategy.

HIGH-YIELD BOARD EXAM ESSENTIALS
- **CLASSIC AGENTS:** Amiodarone, bretylium, dronedarone, dofetilide, ibutilide, sotalol
- **DRUG CLASS:** VW Class III
- **INDICATIONS:** Atrial fibrillation/atrial flutter, ventricular arrhythmias
- **MECHANISM:** Potassium channel antagonists block the delayed rectifier potassium current and prolong refractoriness in atrial and ventricular tissues. The QRS can widen and QT interval can be prolonged. It also has a half-life of about 58 days.
- **SIDE EFFECTS:** Arrhythmias, amiodarone (hyper/hypothyroid, hepatotoxicity, pulmonary toxicity, skin discoloration)
- **CLINICAL PEARLS:**
  - Amiodarone is a well-known inhibitor of CYP2C9, 3A4 and P-gp and causes a lot of drug interactions (warfarin, diltiazem, verapamil, simvastatin, and many other drugs). Amiodarone possesses antiarrhythmic properties of each Vaughn Williams class:
  - Sodium channel antagonist, beta-antagonist, potassium channel antagonist, and calcium channel antagonist. Sotalol is renally eliminated and thus requires dose adjustments to avoid bradycardia or heart block.

High-Yield Basic Pharmacology

- **Mechanism of Action**
  - Slows heart rate and rate of recovery in nodal tissue by decreasing calcium flow into cardiac nodal cells.

Primary Net Benefit

- Routinely used for acute control of ventricular rate in patients with atrial fibrillation with a rapid ventricular response.

Vaughan Williams Class IV - Drug Class Review			
High-Yield Med Reviews			
Mechanism of Action: *Myocardial muscle and smooth muscle* *-L-type calcium channel inhibition, ultimately leading to vasodilation, negative inotropy.* *SA and AV nodal tissue* *-Slows heart rate and rate of recovery in nodal tissue by decreasing calcium flow into cardiac nodal cells.*			
Class Effects: *Vasodilation, decreased chronotropic and inotropic effect*			
Generic Name	**Brand Name**	**Main Indication(s) or Uses**	**Notes**
Diltiazem	Cardizem, Cartia, Matzim, Taztia, Tiadylt, Tiazac	<ul><li>Angina</li><li>Atrial fibrillation or atrial flutter</li><li>Hypertension</li><li>Ventricular tachycardia</li><li>SVT</li></ul>	<ul><li>**Dosing (Adult):**<ul><li>IR: 30 mg 4 times daily<ul><li>Maximum 240 to 360 mg/day</li></ul></li><li>12-hour (twice-daily) formulations: 60 mg twice daily<ul><li>Maximum 240 to 360 mg/day</li></ul></li><li>24-hour (once-daily) formulations: 120 to 180 mg once daily<ul><li>Maximum 240 to 360 mg/day</li></ul></li><li>IV 0.25 or 0.35 mg IV push<ul><li>Alternatively 10 mg IV push</li></ul></li><li>IV infusion 5 to 15 mg/hour</li></ul></li><li>**Dosing (Peds):**<ul><li>IR: 1.5 to 2 mg/kg/day in 3 to 4 divided doses<ul><li>Maximum 6 mg/kg/day or 360 mg/day, whichever is less</li></ul></li><li>IV 0.25 or 0.35 mg IV push</li></ul></li><li>**CYP450 Interactions:** Major substrate of CYP3A4, P-gp</li><li>**Renal or Hepatic Dose Adjustments:** None</li><li>**Dosage Forms:** Oral (solution, capsule or tablet), IV solution</li></ul>

Vaughan Williams Class IV - Drug Class Review			
High-Yield Med Reviews			
Generic Name	**Brand Name**	**Indication(s) or Uses**	**Notes**

Verapamil	Calan, Verelan	• Angina
		• Atrial fibrillation or atrial flutter
		• Hypertension
		• Ventricular tachycardia
		• SVT
			• **Dosing (Adult):**
			  - IR 80 to 120 mg 3 times daily.
			  - ER: 180 mg once daily
			• Maximum 480 mg/day
			  - IV bolus 2.5 to 10 mg IV push
			• **Dosing (Peds):**
			  - IR 2 to 8 mg/kg/day in 3 divided doses
			• Maximum 480 mg/day
			  - IV 0.1 to 0.3 mg/kg/dose
			• Maximum 5 mg/dose
			• **CYP450 Interactions:** Major substrate of CYP3A4
			• **Renal or Hepatic Dose Adjustments:**
			  - Cirrhosis, reduce oral dose to 20-30% of normal, IV dose 50% reduction
			• **Dosage Forms:** Oral (capsule or tablet), IV solution

High-Yield Clinical Knowledge

- **Myocardial Muscle and Smooth Muscle Calcium Channel Block**
  - Bind to and prevent calcium entry through "long-type" or L-type calcium channels on myocardial and smooth muscle.
    - The reduction in calcium influx intracellularly prevents the calcium-calmodulin complex from stimulating myosin light chain kinase phosphorylation and ultimately activating actin-myosin interaction and a resulting contraction.
- **Verapamil Racemate**
  - Knowledge of verapamil being a racemic mixture is clinically relevant. This is because of L-verapamil's significant first-pass metabolism, which is the more potent calcium channel blocker.
  - Therefore, when administered intravenously, verapamil has a more pronounced effect on the PR interval than when taken orally.
    - Since this first-pass effect results from several CYP450 isoenzymes, this effect can also be observed if drug-interactions inhibit the first-pass metabolism.
    - Diltiazem also undergoes first-pass metabolism but does not appear to have appreciable differences in action between routes of ingestion.
- **Atrial Fibrillation with Rapid Ventricular Response**
  - Diltiazem or verapamil can be used for rapid control of ventricular rates in patients with atrial fibrillation. In these patients, diltiazem is commonly used in a fixed-dose (10 mg IV) or weight-based dose regimen (0.25 mg/kg IV followed by 0.35 mg/kg if inadequate response). An infusion of diltiazem can follow successful rate control at a rate of 5 to 15 mg/hr.
    - Avoid in patients who also have Wolff-Parkinson-White (WPW) syndrome as this can worsen the tachycardia
- **Supraventricular Tachycardia (SVT)**
  - Verapamil can be used as an alternative to adenosine. As a result of the significant first-pass metabolism of oral verapamil, the intravenous dose is 5 to 10 mg. Whereas the oral dose for atrial fibrillation rate control is up to 480 mg/day.
- **Atrial Fibrillation Rate Control**

- Non-dihydropyridine calcium channel blockers can be used for rate control of patients with atrial fibrillation.
- However, these agents should be avoided in patients with HFrEF and atrial fibrillation.
- **Constipation**
  - Non-dihydropyridine calcium channel blockers are associated with constipation.
    - This is no trivial adverse event, which can lead to GI obstruction and potentially perforation.

High-Yield Fast-Facts

- **Not Just L-Type**
  - Cardiac calcium channels are predominantly L-type; however, T-type calcium channels are present as well. Mibefradil was a T-type cardiac calcium channel blocker but has been withdrawn from the market.
- **Non-Cardiac Indications**
  - Verapamil can be used for numerous non-cardiac indications, including cluster headaches, migraines, and cocaine-induced chest pain.
- **Overdose**
  - Non-dihydropyridine calcium channel blocker overdose can be treated with high dose insulin therapy (insulin regular 1 unit/kg)

HIGH-YIELD BOARD EXAM ESSENTIALS
- **CLASSIC AGENTS:** Diltiazem, verapamil
- **DRUG CLASS:** VW Class IV
- **INDICATIONS:** Atrial fibrillation or atrial flutter rate control, SVT, chronic stable angina, hypertension, vasospastic angina
- **MECHANISM:** L-type calcium channels inhibition, ultimately leading to vasodilation, negative inotropy (myocardial muscle and smooth muscle); slows heart rate and rate of recovery in nodal tissue by decreasing calcium flow into cardiac nodal cells (SA and AV nodal tissue)
- **SIDE EFFECTS:** Bradycardia, hypotension, constipation
- **CLINICAL PEARLS:**
  - Avoid both agents in patients with WPW along with AFib with RVR.
  - Verapamil can be used as an alternative to adenosine for SVT.
  - As a result of the significant first-pass metabolism of oral verapamil, the intravenous dose is 5 to 10 mg. Whereas the oral dose for atrial fibrillation rate control is up to 480 mg/day.

High-Yield Basic Pharmacology

- **Adenosine**
  - Activates inward rectifier potassium current and inhibition of calcium current in the SA and AV nodes.
    - This shortens the action potential duration, hyperpolarization, and slowing of normal automaticity
- **Digoxin**
  - Antiarrhythmic properties from increasing parasympathetic tone thereby decreasing the rate of depolarization of the SA node and decreasing the rate of conduction through the AV node
    - Also inhibits the sodium-potassium ATPase pump resulting in increased myocardial cell calcium concentration and causing a positive inotropic effect.
      - Inhibition of this pump causes increased sodium within the cell, permitting exchange for calcium via calcium-sodium antiporter. This enhances the calcium release from the sarcoplasmic reticulum during systole which increases the force of contraction of the cardiac muscle.
- **Magnesium sulfate**
  - May cause a decrease in the rate of calcium entry, thereby limiting the rate of initial depolarizations of early after depolarizations associated with torsade de pointes.
  - Magnesium is also a cofactor of the Na+,-K+-ATPase exchange, with enhanced function associated with magnesium administration, and therefore decreased calcium entry to cardiac cells

Primary Net Benefit

- Adenosine has a key role in acute management of supraventricular arrhythmias, and magnesium sulfate is a safe and effective adjunct to therapy in ventricular arrhythmias.
- The role of digoxin continues to become limited due to safety of the drug and more advanced electrophysiologic cardiac interventions.

Vaughan Williams Misc/Unclassified - Drug Class Review			
High-Yield Med Reviews			
Mechanism of Action: *See above.*			
Class Effects: *Slows conduction through cardiac tissue.*			
Generic Name	**Brand Name**	**Indication(s) or Uses**	**Notes**

Adenosine	Adenocard	• Paroxysmal SVT	• **Dosing (Adult):**
			  - IV bolus 6 mg
			  - May repeat 12 mg twice
			• **Dosing (Peds):**
			  - IV bolus of 0.1 mg/kg (maximum 6 mg)
			  - May repeat 0.2 mg/kg (maximum 12 mg) twice
			• **CYP450 Interactions:** None known
			• **Renal or Hepatic Dose Adjustments:** None
			• **Dosage Forms:** IV (solution)

Vaughan Williams Misc/Unclassified - Drug Class Review
High-Yield Med Reviews

Generic Name	Brand Name	Indication(s) or Uses	Notes

Digoxin	Digitek, Digox, Lanoxin	• Atrial fibrillation or atrial flutter
		• HFrEF
			• **Dosing (Adult):**
			  – IV LD 0.25 to 0.5 mg, followed by 0.25 mg IV q6h
			• Maximum 1 to 1.5 mg/24 hours
			  – Oral LD 0.5 mg, followed by 0.125 to 0.25 mg q6h
			• Maintenance 0.125 to 0.25 mg daily
			• **Dosing (Peds):**
			  – Complex dosing exists for pediatrics.
			  – Initial IV loading dose of 10 to 12 mcg/kg/dose q8h x 3 doses
			  – Oral loading dose of 13 to 17 mcg/kg/dose q8h x 3 doses
			  – Maintenance dose 8 to 10 mcg/kg/day by mouth divided once or twice daily
			• **CYP450 Interactions:** Substrate of CYP3A4, P-gp
			• **Renal or Hepatic Dose Adjustments:**
			  – Loading dose: GFR 15 mL/minute or less, administer 50% of normal dose.
			  – Maintenance dose: GFR 45 to 60 mL/minute, reduce to 0.0625 to 0.125 mg once daily.
			  – GFR 30 to less than 45 mL/minute 0.0625 mg once daily.
			  – GFR less than 30 mL/minute 0.0625 mg every 48
			• **Dosage Forms:** IV (solution), Oral (tablet)

Magnesium sulfate	N/A	• Torsades de Pointes:
		• Polymorphic VT with QT prolongation, with pulse
		• Ventricular fibrillation/ Pulseless VT
			• **Dosing (Adult):**
			  – IV bolus 1 to 4.5 g over 1 to 5 minutes.
			  – IV infusion 0.5 to 1g hour (initial rate).
			• **Dosing (Peds):**
			  – IV bolus 25 to 50 mg/kg/dose
			    • Maximum 2g/dose
			• **CYP450 Interactions:** None
			• **Renal or Hepatic Dose Adjustments:** None
			• **Dosage Forms:** IV (solution)

High-Yield Clinical Knowledge

- **Rapid administration of adenosine**
  - The conventional method of rapidly pushing adenosine through a proximal Y-site on IV tubing, followed by a fluid bolus from a more distal Y-site, may not be the most effective method of administration.
    - Adenosine can be administered through the same IV Y-site as the subsequent fluid bolus using a device known as a 3-way stopcock.
    - Adenosine may also be diluted into the 20 mL sodium chloride 0.9% flush without compromising activity.
- **Digoxin for atrial fibrillation rate control**

- Digoxin is widely used in patients with atrial fibrillation, however, intravenous diltiazem is safe and more effective in achieving ventricular rate control and leads to a shorter hospital stay in patients with acute atrial fibrillation. (Crit Care Med. 2009 Jul;37(7):2174-9)
- **Magnesium sulfate rate of administration**
  - For use as an antiarrhythmic, magnesium sulfate 1 to 4.5g must be administered rapidly to achieve the rate and rhythm control effects.
    - Many hospitals computerized order entry systems default magnesium sulfate infusions to run over 1 hour. For use as an antiarrhythmic, 4.5g must be administered over approximately 10 minutes or faster if hemodynamically unstable.
- **Digoxin Loading Doses Onset**
  - Digoxin has a relatively slow onset of action in its ability to control the ventricular rate.
    - Initial rate control can be achieved within 1 hour of the first component of a loading dose, maximum benefit isn't achieved for 24 to 48 hours.
- **Adenosine Alternative Administration**
  - Adenosine may be administered via a central intravenous catheter, however, the dose must be lowered to 3 mg followed by 6 mg twice, if the desired response is not achieved.
- **Digifab**
  - Digifab is the digoxin immune antigen-binding fragment that binds to and eliminates digoxin renally.
    - Can be used for other non-digoxin cardiac glycosides.
- **Digoxin Drug Interactions - Amiodarone or Dronedarone**
  - By inhibiting P-gp, amiodarone can potentially double digoxin concentrations, therefore, digoxin dose should be empirically lowered by 50% when amiodarone is started.
    - Similar to amiodarone, dronedarone also inhibits P-gp and can increase digoxin concentrations by about 2.5-fold. The same empiric digoxin dose reduction of 50%.

HIGH-YIELD BOARD EXAM ESSENTIALS

- **CLASSIC AGENTS:** Adenosine, digoxin, magnesium sulfate
- **DRUG CLASS:** VW unclassified
- **INDICATIONS:** Paroxysmal SVT (adenosine), Vfib/Vtach (magnesium), Afib/flutter, HFrEF (digoxin), seizures in severe eclampsia (magnesium)
- **MECHANISM:** Activates inward rectifier potassium current and inhibition of calcium current in the SA and AV nodes (adenosine); increases parasympathetic tone, decreases rate of depolarization of the SA node and decreasing the rate of conduction through the AV node (digoxin); may decrease in the rate of calcium entry, thereby limiting the rate of initial depolarizations of early after depolarizations associated with torsade de pointes (magnesium).
- **SIDE EFFECTS:** Bradycardia, hyperkalemia, paralysis (magnesium)
- **CLINICAL PEARLS:**
  - Digoxin is widely used in patients with atrial fibrillation, however, intravenous diltiazem is safe and more effective in achieving ventricular rate control and leads to a shorter hospital stay in patients with acute atrial fibrillation.
  - Digoxin is a major substrate of P-gp and thus is prone to drug interactions.
  - Adenosine is the drug of choice for SVT but must be given by rapid IV push due to its very short half-life.

High-Yield Basic Pharmacology

- **Mechanism of Action**
  - Prevent the conversion of angiotensin I to angiotensin II which is known to increase vascular resistance and stimulate the release aldosterone that can lead to increases in plasma volume.
- **Remodeling:**
  - These agents are known to prevent cardiac remodeling after myocardial infarction, improve renal perfusion and reduce the risk of renal complications particularly in diabetic patients, improve mortality in patients with left ventricular systolic dysfunction.

Primary Net Benefit

- ACE-inhibitors are first-line disease-modifying agents for hypertension. All patients, unless contraindicated should be prescribed an ACE-inhibitor, or ARB if intolerant.

<table>
<tr><td colspan="4">ACE-Inhibitors - Drug Class Review
High-Yield Med Reviews</td></tr>
<tr><td colspan="4">Mechanism of Action: ACE-inhibitors reduce the actions of Angiotensin II and lower blood pressure</td></tr>
<tr><td colspan="4">Class Effects: Blood pressure lowering, decreased cardiac remodeling, improved renal perfusion, and other microvascular complications</td></tr>
<tr><td>Generic Name</td><td>Brand Name</td><td>Indication(s) or Uses</td><td>Notes</td></tr>
<tr>
<td>Benazepril</td>
<td>Lotensin</td>
<td>• Hypertension</td>
<td>
• Dosing (Adult):
  – Oral 5 to 10 mg once daily, maximum 40 mg/day in 1 or 2 divided doses
• Dosing (Peds):
  – 6 years or older, oral initial dose of 0.2 mg/kg/dose once daily titrate to 0.1 to 0.6 mg/kg/dose, max daily dose of 40 mg.
• CYP450 Interactions: No CYP interactions
• Renal or Hepatic Dose Adjustments:
  – GFR less than 30 mL/min or hemodialysis, use initial dose of 5 mg initially then titrate to maximum tolerated dose.
• Dosage Forms: Oral (tablet)
</td>
</tr>
<tr>
<td>Captopril</td>
<td>Capoten</td>
<td>
• Diabetic nephropathy
• Heart failure with reduced ejection fraction
• Hypertension
• Myocardial infarction with left ventricular dysfunction
</td>
<td>
• Dosing (Adult):
  – Oral 6.25 mg 3 times daily, titrate to 50 mg 3 times daily, as tolerated
• Dosing (Peds):
  – Starting dose of 0.1 to 0.3 mg/kg/dose every 6 to 24 hours, titrate to target dose of 0.3 to 3.5 mg/kg/day divided every 6 to 12 hours. Maximum daily dose of 6 mg/kg/day.
• CYP450 Interactions: None
• Renal or Hepatic Dose Adjustments:
  – GFR 10 to 50 mL/min, use initial dose of 75% of normal dose every 12 hours.
  – GFR less than 10 mL/min, use 50% of normal dose, every 24 hours
• Dosage Forms: Oral (tablet)
</td>
</tr>
</table>

ACE-Inhibitors - Drug Class Review
High-Yield Med Reviews

Generic Name	Brand Name	Indication(s) or Uses	Notes

Enalapril	Vasotec	• Heart failure
		• Hypertension
			• **Dosing (Adult):**
			  – Oral starting dose of 2.5 mg twice daily, target dose of 10 to 20 mg twice daily.
			    • Maximum 40 mg/day.
			  – IV (enalaprilat) 0.625 to 1.25 mg IV every 6 hours
			• **Dosing (Peds):**
			  – Oral initial dose of 0.1 mg/kg/day in 1 to 2 divided doses, maximum of 0.5 mg/kg/day.
			  – IV (enalaprilat) 5 to 10 mcg/kg/dose every 8 to 24
			• **CYP450 Interactions:** None
			• **Renal or Hepatic Dose Adjustments:**
			  – GFR < 30 mL/min, or in heart failure patients with serum creatinine >1.6 mg/dL start with 2.5 mg *once* daily.
			  – Hemodialysis, administer 50% of normal dose after dialysis
			• **Dosage Forms:** Oral (solution, tablet), IV (enalaprilat)

Fosinopril	Monopril	• Heart failure
		• Hypertension
			• **Dosing (Adult):**
			  – Initial dose of 10 mg once daily, increasing dose as tolerated to target range 20 to 40 mg once daily with maximum dose of 40 mg/day.
			• **Dosing (Peds):**
			  – Initial dose of 0.1 mg/kg/dose once daily, titrate to a maximum daily dose of 0.6 mg/kg/day, or 40 mg/day, whichever is less.
			• **CYP450 Interactions:** None
			• **Renal or Hepatic Dose Adjustments:**
			  – GFR < 30 mL/min initial dose of 5 mg initially then titrate to maximum tolerated dose
			• **Dosage Forms:** Oral (tablet)

Lisinopril	Zestril	• Heart failure
		• Hypertension
		• ST-elevation myocardial infarction
			• **Dosing (Adult):**
			  – Initial dose of 2.5 to 10 mg once daily, increasing dose as tolerated to target range 40 mg once daily
			• **Dosing (Peds):**
			  – Initial dose of 0.07 mg/kg/dose once daily, titrate to a maximum daily dose of 0.6 mg/kg/day, or 40 mg/day, whichever is less.
			• **CYP450 Interactions:** None
			• **Renal or Hepatic Dose Adjustments:**
			  – GFR < 30 mL/min initial dose of 2.5 mg once daily initially then titrate to maximum tolerated dose.
			• **Dosage Forms:** Oral (solution or tablet)

ACE-Inhibitors - Drug Class Review
High-Yield Med Reviews

Generic Name	Brand Name	Indication(s) or Uses	Notes

Perindopril	Aceon	• Heart failure
		• Stable coronary artery disease
			• **Dosing (Adult):**
			  − Initial dose of 2 mg once daily, target dose of 8 to 16 mg once daily
			• **Dosing (Peds):**
			  − Not routinely used
			• **CYP450 Interactions:** None
			• **Renal or Hepatic Dose Adjustments:**
			  − GFR between 30 and 80 mL/min, maximum dose of 8 mg/day.
			  − GFR less than 30 mL/min, 2.5 mg every other day initially
			  − HD - administer on dialysis days
			• **Dosage Forms:** Oral (tablet)

Moexipril	Univasc	• Hypertension	• **Dosing (Adult):**
			  − Initial dose of 3.75 to 7.5 mg once daily, target maximum dose of 30 mg/day in 1 or 2 divided doses.
			• **Dosing (Peds):**
			  − Not routinely used
			• **CYP450 Interactions:** None
			• **Renal or Hepatic Dose Adjustments:**
			  − GFR less than 40 mL/min, 2.5 mg daily, maximum 15 mg/day.
			• **Dosage Forms:** Oral (tablet)

Quinapril	Accupril	• Heart failure
		• Hypertension
			• **Dosing (Adult):**
			  − Initial dose of 5 mg twice daily, target maximum tolerated dose of 80 mg/day in divided doses.
			• **Dosing (Peds):**
			  − Initial dose of 0.2 mg/kg.
			• **CYP450 Interactions:** None
			• **Renal or Hepatic Dose Adjustments:**
			  − GFR less than 30 mL/min, start with 2.5 mg daily.
			• **Dosage Forms:** Oral (tablet)

Ramipril	Altace	• Heart failure
		• Hypertension
			• **Dosing (Adult):**
			  − Initial dose of 1.25 to 2.5 mg once daily, titrate to a target maximum of 10 mg once daily
			• **Dosing (Peds):**
			  − Not routinely used
			• **CYP450 Interactions:** None
			• **Renal or Hepatic Dose Adjustments:**
			  − GFR less than 40 mL/min use 25% of normal dose initially then titrate to maximum tolerated dose or 10 mg per day, whichever is less.
			• **Dosage Forms:** Oral (capsule or tablet)

ACE-Inhibitors - Drug Class Review
High-Yield Med Reviews

Generic Name	Brand Name	Indication(s) or Uses	Notes

Trandolapril	Mavik	• Hypertension
		• Post-myocardial infarction heart failure or left-ventricular dysfunction
			• **Dosing (Adult):**
			  – Initial dose of 1 mg once daily, to a maximum dose of 4 mg once daily
			• **Dosing (Peds):**
			  – Not routinely used
			• **CYP450 Interactions:** None
			• **Renal or Hepatic Dose Adjustments:**
			  – GFR less than 30 mL/min use initial dose of 0.5 mg once daily, and titrate to maximum tolerated dose, or 4 mg whichever is less.
			• **Dosage Forms:** Oral (capsule or tablet)

High-Yield Clinical Knowledge

- **ACE Vasodilation**
  - ACE-inhibitors all produce vasodilation but their use in the acute setting is limited as these actions are delayed in nature.
  - This includes enalaprilat (an IV dosage form) whose onset is around 15 minutes - much longer than other vasodilators such as nitroglycerin whose onset is less than 1 minute.
- **Hypertension**
  - ACE-inhibitors are first-line disease-modifying agents for hypertension.
  - All patients, unless contraindicated should be prescribed an ACE-inhibitor, or ARB if intolerant.
  - There are numerous compelling indications for ACE-inhibitor therapy in patients with hypertension, post-myocardial infarction, diabetes, and CKD.
- **Congestive heart failure**
  - When starting ACE-inhibitor therapy, the initial dose should be low.
  - In specific instances, a half normal dose is appropriate, including patients with a history of or increased risk of orthostatic hypotension, the elderly, CKD, sodium or volume-depleted, acute HF exacerbation, or taking concomitant vasodilators/thiazide diuretics.
  - However, titration to the maximum tolerated dose and to specific hemodynamic targets should be sought.
- **Enalaprilat IV**
  - Enalaprilat exists as an intravenous preparation but despite a relatively short onset of approximately 15 minutes, there exists a dose-dependent duration of action of approximately 6 hours.
  - Thus, one should consider the onset and caution against rapid administration of several boluses as well as prepare to manage prolonged hemodynamic effects.
- **Captopril Use**
  - Captopril can be used as an oral agent for acute hypertension, not requiring intravenous interventions.
- **Diabetic nephropathy**
  - ACE-inhibitors or ARBs should be used in patients with diabetes to reduce the risk of the development of nephropathy. However, their use in combination with each other is not recommended. Instead combining either agent with an SGLT-2 inhibitor is preferred.

HIGH-YIELD BOARD EXAM ESSENTIALS

- **CLASSIC AGENTS:** Benazepril, captopril, enalapril, fosinopril, lisinopril, ramipril
- **DRUG CLASS:** ACE-inhibitors
- **INDICATIONS:** Acute Hypertension, acute myocardial infarction, acute decompensated heart failure (captopril, enalaprilat), hypertension, congestive heart failure diabetic nephropathy (captopril, lisinopril, enalapril, benazepril, quinapril, ramipril, moexipril, fosinopril, trandolapril, perindopril)
- **MECHANISM:** Reduce the actions of angiotensin II (ATII) and lower blood pressure. Also inhibit ATII mediated vascular remodeling.
- **SIDE EFFECTS:** Cough (dry), hyperkalemia, angioedema
- **CLINICAL PEARLS:**
  - A first line, monotherapy agent for most patients with hypertension, unless contraindicated should be prescribed an ACE-inhibitor, or ARB if intolerant. This is especially true if patients have diabetes for their renal protective and prevention of vascular remodeling effects.
  - African American/Black patients may not benefit as much from monotherapy with ACEi but work well as part of a 2 or 3 drug regimen.
  - All ACE-inhibitors can cause hyperkalemia and AKI in patients with "bilateral" renal artery stenosis.
  - Counsel to avoid use of potassium containing salt substitutes to avoid hyperkalemia.
  - All ACE-inhibitors are contraindicated in pregnancy.

High-Yield Basic Pharmacology

- Nonselective alpha-1 antagonism leads to vasodilation via inhibition of Gq-protein coupled receptors in the systemic vasculature.
  - Inhibition of these Gq receptors inhibits the IP3 pathway and ultimately inhibits SR release of calcium.
- Additional Consideration:
  - Phenoxybenzamine is unique among alpha-1 antagonists in that it causes an irreversible blockade.
  - This is due to a reactive ethylenediammonium intermediate which covalently binds to these receptors and causes an irreversible blockade.

Primary Net Benefit

- Potent vasodilation in many patients that results in reflex tachycardia and risk of orthostasis in older patients.

Alpha-1 Antagonists (Nonselective) - Drug Class Review			
High-Yield Med Reviews			
Mechanism of Action: *Vasodilation systemic vasculature to result in a lowering of the blood pressure.*			
Class Effects: *Vasodilation, reflex tachycardia, risk of orthostasis in older patients*			
Generic Name	**Brand Name**	**Indication(s) or Uses**	**Notes**

Doxazosin	Cardura, Cardura XL	• Benign prostatic hyperplasia
		• Hypertension
		• Ureteral calculi expulsion
			• **Dosing (Adult):**
			  – IR: 1 mg once daily, maximum 16 mg/day.
			  – Extended release: 4 mg once daily, maximum 16 mg/day
			• **Dosing (Peds):**
			  – IR 0.5 mg once daily at bedtime, maximum 2 mg/day
			• **CYP450 Interactions:** Substrate of CYP3A4, 2C19, 2D6
			• **Renal or Hepatic Dose Adjustments:**
			  – Contraindicated for patients with moderate or severe hepatic impairment (Child-Pugh class B/C)
			• **Dosage Forms:** Oral tablet (immediate-release and extended-release)

Phenoxybenzamine	Dibenzyline	• Pheochromocytoma treatment	• **Dosing (Adult):**
			  – Oral 10 mg twice daily, maximum 240 mg/day
			• **Dosing (Peds):**
			  – Oral 0.2 to 0.25 mg/kg/dose once or twice daily; maximum dose: 40 mg/dose
			• **CYP450 Interactions:** None
			• **Renal or Hepatic Dose Adjustments:** None
			• **Dosage Forms:** Oral (capsule)

Alpha-1 Antagonists (Nonselective) - Drug Class Review
High-Yield Med Reviews

Generic Name	Brand Name	Indication(s) or Uses	Notes

Phentolamine	OraVerse, Rogitine	• Extravasation of sympathomimetic vasopressors
		• Pheochromocytoma diagnosis
			• **Dosing (Adult):**
			  – Local infiltration: Inject 5 to 10 mg (diluted in 10 mL 0.9% sodium chloride) into extravasation area.
			• **Dosing (Peds):**
			  – Infiltrate area of extravasation with a small amount of 0.5 to 1 mg/mL.
			• **CYP450 Interactions:** None
			• **Renal or Hepatic Dose Adjustments:** None
			• **Dosage Forms:** IV solution

Prazosin	Minipress	• Hypertension
		• PTSD-related nightmares and sleep disruption
		• Raynaud syndrome (off-label)
			• **Dosing (Adult):**
			  – Oral 1 mg 2 to 3 times daily, maximum 40 mg/day.
			• **Dosing (Peds):**
			  – Oral 0.05 to 0.1 mg/kg/day in divided doses every 8 hours, maximum 20 mg/day
			• **CYP450 Interactions:** None
			• **Renal or Hepatic Dose Adjustments:** None
			• **Dosage Forms:** Oral (capsule)

Terazosin	Hytrin	• Benign prostatic hyperplasia
		• Hypertension
		• Ureteral calculi expulsion
			• **Dosing (Adult):**
			  – Oral 1 mg at bedtime, maximum 20 mg/day.
			• **Dosing (Peds):**
			  – Oral 1 mg at bedtime, maximum 20 mg/day.
			• **CYP450 Interactions:** None
			• **Renal or Hepatic Dose Adjustments:** None
			• **Dosage Forms:** Oral (capsule)

High-Yield Clinical Knowledge

- **Extravasation of a Sympathomimetic Vasopressor:**
  - Phentolamine (when available) should be considered as an agent to prevent tissue necrosis of the affected tissue.
    - The administration of phentolamine should be as a subcutaneous injection of phentolamine using 25 gauge or smaller needles.
  - Phentolamine should be prepared as a 5 mg in NS to a final total volume of 10 mL.
  - Then, incremental doses of up to 10 mg should be injected through the catheter and subcutaneously around the site.
  - There should be an immediate response to the tissue, and if not, consider additional dose(s).
  - However, additional doses should be used with caution since phentolamine may cause systemic hypotension, and given the patient was already on a vasopressor, this may be clinically relevant.
- **Ureteral Calculi Expulsion:**
  - Tamsulosin is commonly used to enhance the passage of ureteral stones in both male and female patients.
  - However, the efficacy of this treatment is questionable.

- **Hypertension and Dyslipidemia:**
  - In patients with uncontrolled hypertension and uncontrolled lipids, alpha-1 antagonists exert a pleiotropic effect on lipids.
  - Alpha-1 antagonists can help lower LDL and triglycerides and increase concentrations of HDL.
- **Urethral Underactivity:**
  - Alpha-1 antagonists may be useful in patients with urethral underactivity since they are capable of relaxing the internal bladder sphincter.
- **Adverse Effects (Floppy Iris Syndrome):**
  - Tamsulosin is associated with floppy iris syndrome. Although it has been reported with doxazosin and silodosin, it is more prevalent with tamsulosin.
  - This adverse effect occurs due to the alpha-1a antagonist effects in iris dilator muscles which increases the likelihood of post-ophthalmologic operative complications, including posterior capsular rupture, retinal detachment, residual retained lens material, or endophthalmitis. Permanent loss of vision can result.
- **Erectile Dysfunction:**
  - Since phentolamine can reduce peripheral adrenergic tone and enhance cholinergic tone, it can be used to improve cavernosal filling. This use as an erectogenic agent has fallen out of favor given the availability of PDE-5 inhibitors but can still be occasionally seen in practice. To avoid excessive hypotension, phentolamine is combined with papaverine.

HIGH-YIELD BOARD EXAM ESSENTIALS

- **CLASSIC AGENTS:** Doxazosin, phenoxybenzamine, phentolamine, prazosin, terazosin
- **DRUG CLASS:** Alpha-1 blockers (nonselective)
- **INDICATIONS:** Extravasation of sympathomimetic vasopressors (phentolamine); pheochromocytoma treatment (phenoxybenzamine); Benign prostatic hyperplasia, ureteral calculi expulsion (doxazosin, terazosin)
- Hypertension (doxazosin, prazosin, terazosin), PTSD-related nightmares and sleep disruption, Raynaud syndrome (prazosin).
- **MECHANISM:** Vasodilation via inhibition of Gq-protein coupled receptors in the systemic vasculature.
- **SIDE EFFECTS:** Hypotension, reflex tachycardia, headache
- **CLINICAL PEARLS:**
  - Contrary to nitrates, nonselective alpha-1 blockers may cause vasodilation in arteriolar resistance vessels and veins at normal therapeutic dosing. Nitrates need larger doses to achieve both.
  - None of these agents are recommended as monotherapy for the treatment of hypertension. They are most commonly used for secondary causes of elevated BP and/or as adjunct to other treatments.

High-Yield Basic Pharmacology

- **Mechanism of Action**
  - These agents exert an agonist effect on the presynaptic alpha-2 receptors in the central nervous system (CNS), thereby enhancing the activity of inhibitory neurons in the vasoregulatory regions of the CNS.
  - This ultimately leads to a *decrease* in the release of norepinephrine.
- **Methyldopa is Unique:**
  - Methyldopa is a prodrug that is converted to α-methylnorepinephrine in the brain, which ultimately activates central alpha-2 receptors similar to clonidine.
    - However, chronic use can result in sodium and water retention, complicating comorbidities such as heart failure.

Primary Net Benefit

- Potent vasodilators with a wide range of indications, including hypertension, Attention-Deficit/Hyperactivity Disorder, muscle spasms, and spasticity.

Alpha-2 Agonists - Drug Class Review			
High-Yield Med Reviews			
Mechanism of Action: Central alpha-2 agonist, enhancing the activity of inhibitory neurons in the vasoregulatory regions of the central nervous system. Imidazoline receptor agonism (clonidine).			
Class Effects: *Vasodilation, potential sedating effects*			
Generic Name	**Brand Name**	**Indication(s) or Uses**	**Notes**

Clonidine	Catapres Kapvay	- Hypertension	- **Dosing (Adult):**
			  - Oral: Initial: 0.1 mg twice daily, > 0.6 mg/day not recommended.
			  - TD Patch: 0.1 mg/24-hour patch once every 7 days
			- **Dosing (Peds):**
			  - Weight 45 kg or less: Initial: 0.05 mg at bedtime
			  - Weight more than 45 kg: Initial: 0.1 mg at bedtime.
			    - Max is based on patient weight: 27 to 40.5 kg: 0.2 mg/day; 40.5 to 45 kg: 0.3 mg/day; > 45 kg: 0.4 mg/day
			- **CYP450 Interactions:** No CYP interactions
			- **Renal or Hepatic Dose Adjustments:** None
			- **Dosage Forms:** Topical (transdermal patch), Oral (tablet, IR and ER (Kapvay))

Dexmedetomidine	Precedex	- ICU Sedation	- **Dosing (Adult):**
			  - D 1 mcg/kg x 10 min IV, then 0.2-0.7 mcg/kg/hr.
			- **Dosing (Peds):**
			  - LD 0.5-1 mcg/kg x 10 min IV, then 0.2-0.5 mcg/kg/hr.
			- **CYP450 Interactions:** Substrate of CYP2A6
			- **Renal or Hepatic Dose Adjustments:** None
			- **Dosage Forms:** Solution for IV injection

Alpha-2 Agonists - Drug Class Review
High-Yield Med Reviews

Generic Name	Brand Name	Indication(s) or Uses	Notes

Guanfacine	Intuniv	• Hypertension
		• Attention-deficit/hyperactivity disorder
			• **Dosing (Adult):**
			  – Oral 0.5 to 1 mg once daily at bedtime, maximum 3 mg.
			• **Dosing (Peds):**
			  – Oral 0.5 to 1 mg once daily at bedtime, maximum is based on patient weight: 27 to 40.5 kg: 2 mg/day; 40.5 to 45 kg: 3 mg/day; > 45 kg: 4 mg/day.
			• **CYP450 Interactions:** Major substrate of CYP3A4
			• **Renal or Hepatic Dose Adjustments:** None
			• **Dosage Forms:** Oral (tablet IR and ER (Intuniv))

Methyldopa	Aldomet	• Hypertension	• **Dosing (Adult):**
			  – Oral 250 mg 2 to 3 times daily, maximum 3000 mg/day.
			• **Dosing (Peds):**
			  – Oral 10 mg/kg/day in 2 to 4 divided doses, max 65 mg/kg/day or 3000 mg
			• **CYP450 Interactions:** Major substrate of COMT
			• **Renal or Hepatic Dose Adjustments:** Every 12 or 24 hours if CrCl <10 mL/minute. Give after HD
			• **Dosage Forms:** Oral (tablet)

Tizanidine	Zanaflex	• Muscle spasm and/or musculoskeletal pain
		• Spasticity
			• **Dosing (Adult):**
			  – Oral 2 to 4 mg every 6 to 12 hours as needed and/or at bedtime, maximum 24 mg/day
			• **Dosing (Peds):**
			  – Oral 1 mg at bedtime, titrate as needed
			• **CYP450 Interactions:** Major substrate of CYP1A2
			• **Renal or Hepatic Dose Adjustments:**
			  – Use with caution in patients with CrCl <25 mL/minute
			• **Dosage Forms:** Oral (capsule or tablet)

High-Yield Clinical Knowledge

- **Hypertension**
    - Clonidine is an oral agent with a rapid onset that can facilitate blood pressure lowering in patients with hypertensive urgency. In these patients, where oral antihypertensive agent interventions are appropriate, clonidine can be titrated and reduced as blood pressure goals are assessed.
- **Pre-eclampsia/Eclampsia**
    - Many drug references and textbooks continue to list methyldopa as a potential first-line agent for pre-eclampsia. However, since safer and agents with more predictable pharmacokinetics and clinical effects are available (i.e., labetalol), methyldopa is seldom used for this indication any longer.
- **Opioid Withdrawal**
    - Clonidine has been used as an adjunct agent in the management of opioid withdrawal.
        - However, it is essential to note that despite its I2 agonist properties, clonidine primarily acts via its central alpha-2 agonist effects and masks the sympathetic effects of opioid withdrawal.

- **Attention-Deficit/Hyperactivity Disorder (ADHD)**
  - Only the extended-release dosage formulations are indicated for this indication in pediatric patients.
    - Those formulations include extended-release clonidine (Kapvay) and extended-release guanfacine (Intuniv).
- **Hypertension**
  - If one of these agents is to be discontinued, abrupt cessation must be avoided.
    - This is because of rebound hypertension and a withdrawal-like syndrome.
    - This effect is thought to be a result of a compensatory increase in norepinephrine release, as well as CNS manifestations of nervousness, agitation, headache, and tremor.
  - As described above, although methyldopa is seldom used anymore, it can also cause hepatitis or hemolytic anemia, which should prompt rapid discontinuation.
- **Muscle spasm and/or musculoskeletal pain**
  - Although tizanidine shares similar pharmacology with clonidine, in that they are both central alpha-2 agonists.
  - Tizanidine largely lacks any antihypertensive effects at normal therapeutic dosing and is primarily used as a skeletal muscle relaxant.
  - However, if combined with clonidine, there could be additional antihypertensive responses observed.

HIGH-YIELD BOARD EXAM ESSENTIALS

- **CLASSIC AGENTS:** Clonidine, dexmedetomidine, guanfacine, methyldopa, tizanidine
- **DRUG CLASS:** Alpha-2 agonists
- **INDICATIONS:** Hypertension, ICU Sedation (dexmedetomidine), ADHD (extended-release formulations of clonidine and guanfacine)
- **MECHANISM:** Central alpha-2 agonist, enhancing the activity of inhibitory neurons in the vasoregulatory regions of the central nervous system. Imidazoline receptor agonism (clonidine).
- **SIDE EFFECTS:** Hypotension, reflex tachycardia
- **CLINICAL PEARLS:**
  - Clonidine should not be used as monotherapy for the treatment of chronic HTN but can be used as monotherapy for ADHD. It is rather used as an adjunct or for the short-term use in acute hypertension. Abrupt discontinuation of chronic clonidine will result in tachycardia and elevated BP.
  - Dexmedetomidine can be used to aid in weaning patients off the vent in ICU (does not suppress respiratory drive).
  - Guanfacine is available in a sustained-release form that is FDA approved for treating ADHD in children aged 6–17 years. Extreme caution should be used if the patient is in the same household as children younger than two since guanfacine can potentially cause fatal toxicity from a single tablet/capsule ingestion in children.

High-Yield Basic Pharmacology

- **Mechanism of Action**
  - ARB antagonists ultimately yield a similar clinical response but do so by directly inhibiting the angiotensin 1 preferentially
- **Remodeling**
  - Similar to ACE inhibitors, this class of drugs can prevent remodeling.

Primary Net Benefit

- Angiotensin receptor blockers (ARBs) are often used in place of an ACE-inhibitor and deliver similar survival benefits. However, these agents should not be used together for hypertension, given an increased risk of renal injury, hyperkalemia, and hypotension.

Angiotensin Receptor Blocker - Drug Class Review			
High-Yield Med Reviews			
Mechanism of Action: *ARBs ultimately reduce the actions of AngII and lower blood pressure*			
Class Effects: *Vasodilation, blood pressure-lowering, decreased cardiac remodeling, improved renal perfusion, and other microvascular complications*			
Generic Name	**Brand Name**	**Indication(s) or Uses**	**Notes**
Azilsartan	Edarbi	• Hypertension	• **Dosing (Adult):** – Oral 40 mg once daily as tolerated to a maximum dose of 80 mg daily. • **Dosing (Peds):** Not used • **CYP450 Interactions:** Substrate of CYP2C9 • **Renal or Hepatic Dose Adjustments:** None • **Dosage Forms:** Oral (tablet)

Candesartan	Atacand	• Heart failure with reduced ejection fraction
		• Hypertension
			• **Dosing (Adult):**
			  – Initial starting dose of 4 to 8 mg once daily, titrated to a target maximum dose of 32 mg once daily
			• **Dosing (Peds):**
			  – Starting initial dose of 0.2 mg/kg/day once daily, adjusted to target range of 0.05 to 0.4 mg/kg/day divided once or twice daily. Maximum daily dose 0.4 mg/kg/day, or 32 mg, whichever is less.
			• **CYP450 Interactions:** Substrate of CYP2C9
			• **Renal or Hepatic Dose Adjustments:** Child-Pugh class C, reduce initial starting dose
			• **Dosage Forms:** Oral (tablet)

Eprosartan	Teveten	• Secondary prevention after acute coronary syndrome • Stable coronary artery disease	• **Dosing (Adult):** – Oral initial starting dose of 600 mg once daily, titrate to a maximum dose of 800 mg/day in 1 to 2 divided doses • **Dosing (Peds):** Not used • **CYP450 Interactions:** None • **Renal or Hepatic Dose Adjustments:** None • **Dosage Forms:** Oral (tablet)

Angiotensin Receptor Blocker - Drug Class Review
High-Yield Med Reviews

Generic Name	Brand Name	Indication(s) or Uses	Notes

Irbesartan	Avapro	▪ Diabetic nephropathy
		▪ Hypertension
			▪ **Dosing (Adult):**
			  – Initial starting dose of 150 mg once daily, titrated to maximum of 300 mg once daily.
			▪ **Dosing (Peds):**
			  – Fixed dosing based on weight: 10 to 20 kg, initial dose of 37.5 mg once daily; 21 to 40 kg, initial dose of 75 mg once daily; >40 kg, initial dose of 150 mg once daily.
			▪ **CYP450 Interactions:** Substrate of CYP2C9
			▪ **Renal or Hepatic Dose Adjustments:** None
			▪ **Dosage Forms:** Oral (tablet)

Telmisartan	Micardis	▪ Cardiovascular risk reduction ▪ Hypertension	▪ **Dosing (Adult):** – Initial dose of 20 to 40 mg once daily, target maximum daily dose of 80 mg. ▪ **Dosing (Peds):** Not used. ▪ **CYP450 Interactions:** None ▪ **Renal or Hepatic Dose Adjustments:** None ▪ **Dosage Forms:** Oral (tablet)

Olmesartan	Benicar	▪ Hypertension	▪ **Dosing (Adult):**
			  – Initial dose of 20 mg once daily, titrated to maximum 40 mg once daily.
			▪ **Dosing (Peds):**
			  – 5 to 20 kg: Oral starting dose of 0.3 mg/kg/dose once daily, maximum dose of 0.6 mg/kg/dose.
			  – 20 to 35 kg: Initial dose of 10 mg once daily, maximum daily dose of 20 mg/day.
			  – Greater than 35 kg, see adult dosing.
			▪ **CYP450 Interactions:** None, substrate of OATP1B1/1B3
			▪ **Renal or Hepatic Dose Adjustments:**
			  – GFR less than 20 mL/min, maximum daily dose of 20 mg.
			▪ **Dosage Forms:** Oral (tablet)

Losartan	Cozaar	▪ Hypertension
		▪ Proteinuric chronic kidney disease
			▪ **Dosing (Adult):**
			  – Oral initial dose of 25 to 50 mg once daily, maximum 100 mg/day.
			▪ **Dosing (Peds):**
			  – Children older than 6 years of age, 0.7 mg/kg once daily, to a maximum initial dose of 50 mg/dose, and titrated to a maximum daily dose of 1.4 mg/kg/day or 100 mg/day.
			▪ **CYP450 Interactions:** Substrate of CYP2C9, CYP3A4
			▪ **Renal or Hepatic Dose Adjustments:**
			  – Mild to moderate hepatic impairment, initial dose of 25 mg once daily
			▪ **Dosage Forms:** Oral (tablet)

		Angiotensin Receptor Blocker - Drug Class Review	
		High-Yield Med Reviews	
Generic Name	**Brand Name**	**Indication(s) or Uses**	**Notes**
Valsartan	Diovan	▪ Hypertension	▪ **Dosing (Adult):** – Oral initial dose of 20 mg twice daily, titrated up to a maximum dose of 160 mg twice daily. ▪ **Dosing (Peds):** – Starting dose of 0.25 to 4 mg/kg/dose once daily, up to a maximum of 1.35 mg/kg/dose twice daily, or 160 mg/day, whichever is less. ▪ **CYP450 Interactions:** Substrate of OATP1B1/1B3 ▪ **Renal or Hepatic Dose Adjustments:** none ▪ **Dosage Forms:** Oral (tablet)

High-Yield Clinical Knowledge

▪ **Hypertension**
  – In patients with type 2 diabetes, ARB therapy significantly lowers the risk of developing chronic kidney disease.

▪ **Congestive Heart Failure**
  – In patients who cannot tolerate ACE-inhibitors, ARBs maintain the beneficial effects of preventing hospitalizations in patients with HFrEF.

▪ **Post-Ischemic Stroke**
  – Patients receiving ARBs as a component of their secondary stroke prevention have a lower risk of recurrent stroke than patients receiving a calcium channel blocker.

▪ **CKD With Proteinuria**
  – ARBs and ACE-inhibitors are interchangeable in terms of their beneficial effects of doubling serum creatinine and preventing albuminuria progression in patients with CKD.
  – Furthermore, any ARB can be selected since this is considered a class effect.

▪ **ACE-inhibitor Plus ARB**
  – The combination of ACE-inhibitor with an ARB for lack of response to improving proteinuria is no longer recommended. Instead, either agent should be combined with an SGLT-2 inhibitor.
  – This combination can reduce the risk of renal events, cardiovascular mortality, and hospitalization for heart failure.

HIGH-YIELD BOARD EXAM ESSENTIALS
- **CLASSIC AGENTS:** Azilsartan, candesartan, eprosartan. irbesartan, losartan, olmesartan, telmisartan, valsartan
- **DRUG CLASS:** ARB
- **INDICATIONS:** Hypertension, congestive heart failure, CKD with proteinuria
- **MECHANISM:** Reduce the actions of Angiotensin II and lower blood pressure.
- **SIDE EFFECTS:** Cough, hyperkalemia, angioedema
- **CLINICAL PEARLS:**
  – In patients who cannot tolerate ACE-inhibitors, ARBs maintain the beneficial effects of preventing hospitalizations in patients with HFrEF.
  – African American/Black patients may not benefit as much from monotherapy with ACEi but work well as part of a 2 or 3 drug regimen.
  – All ARBs can cause hyperkalemia and AKI in patients with "bilateral" renal artery stenosis.
  – Counsel to avoid use of potassium containing salt substitutes to avoid hyperkalemia.
  – All ARBs are contraindicated in pregnancy.

High-Yield Basic Pharmacology

- **Mechanism of Action**
    - Antagonists of beta-1 decrease calcium-dependent calcium release from the sarcoplasmic reticulum and limit the actin-myosin interaction in cardiac tissue which decrease chronotropy (pulse) and inotropy (force of contraction) that can both lead to a reduction in cardiac output and thus blood pressure.
    - Beta-2 receptors exist primarily in bronchioles, skeletal muscle, and arteries.
        - Activation or stimulation of these Gs- or Gi-protein coupled receptors ultimately leads to increased actin-myosin activity and muscle contraction.
        - Thus, antagonist activity on these receptors causes bronchoconstriction, skeletal muscle vasculature contraction, and arterial contraction
    - Alpha-1 antagonists lead to vasodilation via inhibition of Gq-protein coupled receptors. Inhibition of these Gq receptors inhibits the IP3 pathway and ultimately inhibits SR release of calcium.
    - This class of drugs also have remodeling benefits in patients with heart failure.
- **Clinical Classifications**
    - Beta-blockers are also commonly pharmacologically categorized as:
        - Selective (i.e., beta-1 selective antagonists)
        - Non-selective (beta-1 and beta-2 nonselective antagonists)
        - Non-selective beta and alpha-1 antagonists (beta-1, beta-2, and alpha-1 antagonists)
        - Intrinsic sympathomimetic activity (Can have beta-agonist or antagonist properties)
        - Membrane stabilizing activity (Sodium channel blocking properties)
        - Class II antiarrhythmics (Vaughan Williams Classification)

Primary Net Benefit

- Lowers blood pressure with minimal or no change in heart rate also contributes to the prevention of cardiac remodeling post-myocardial infarction.

	Beta-Blockers - Drug Class Review High-Yield Med Reviews		
Mechanism of Action: *See above*			
Class Effects: Lowers blood pressure with minimal or no change in heart rate			
Generic Name	**Brand Name**	**Indication(s) or Uses**	**Notes**

Atenolol	Tenormin	• Acute MI
		• Angina pectoris
		• Hypertension
			• **Dosing (Adult):**
			  – Oral 25 to 100 mg once daily, maximum 100 mg daily
			• **Dosing (Peds):**
			  – Oral 0.3 to 1 mcg/kg/day once daily or in divided doses q12h.
			• **CYP450 Interactions:** none
			• **Renal or Hepatic Dose Adjustments:**
			  – GFR 15 to 35 mL/minute - Maximum daily dose of 50 mg
			  – GFR less than 15 - Maximum daily dose of 25 mg
			  – Hemodialysis: moderately dialyzable, normal dosing range 25 to 50 mg/day administered after dialysis.
			• **Dosage Forms:** Oral (tablet)

Beta-Blockers - Drug Class Review
High-Yield Med Reviews

Generic Name	Brand Name	Indication(s) or Uses	Notes

Betaxolol	Kerlone	▪ Hypertension	▪ **Dosing (Adult):**
			  – Oral 5 to 20 mg once daily
			▪ **Dosing (Peds):**
			  – Not routinely used
			▪ **CYP450 Interactions:** Minor substrate of CYP1A2, 2D6
			▪ **Renal or Hepatic Dose Adjustments:** None
			▪ **Dosage Forms:** Oral (tablet)

Bisoprolol	Zebeta	▪ Hypertension	▪ **Dosing (Adult):**
			  – Oral 1.25 to 10 mg once daily up to a maximum 10 mg/day.
			▪ **Dosing (Peds):**
			  – Not routinely used
			▪ **CYP450 Interactions:** Substrate of CYP2D6, and CYP3A4
			▪ **Renal or Hepatic Dose Adjustments:**
			  – GFR less than 40 mL/minute use initial dose of 2.5 mg daily with very slow titration
			▪ **Dosage Forms:** Oral (tablet)

Esmolol	Brevibloc	▪ Intraoperative and postoperative tachycardia and/or hypertension
		▪ Sinus tachycardia
		▪ Supraventricular tachycardia and atrial fibrillation/flutter
			▪ **Dosing (Adult):**
			  – IV bolus 500 to 1000 mcg/kg over 30 to 60 seconds followed by 50 to 300 mcg/kg/min
			▪ **Dosing (Peds):**
			  – IV bolus 100 to 500 mcg/kg over 30 to 60 seconds followed by 50 to 300 mcg/kg/min
			▪ **CYP450 Interactions:** None
			▪ **Renal or Hepatic Dose Adjustments:** None
			▪ **Dosage Forms:** IV solution

Labetalol	Trandate	▪ Hypertension
		▪ Acute aortic syndromes/Acute aortic dissection
		▪ Acute ischemic stroke
		▪ Acute hemorrhagic stroke
		▪ Preeclampsia/eclampsia
			▪ **Dosing (Adult):**
			  – Oral 100 mg twice daily up to maximum 400 mg twice daily
			  – IV 10-20 mg IV push every 10 minutes
			▪ **Dosing (Peds):**
			  – Oral: 1 to 3 mg/kg/day in 2 divided doses, maximum daily dose of 10 to 12 mg/kg/day, or 1,200 mg/day
			  – IV: 0.2 to 1 mg/kg/dose, maximum dose: 40 mg/dose
			▪ **CYP450 Interactions:** Extensive first pass, hepatic glucuronidation
			▪ **Renal or Hepatic Dose Adjustments:** None
			▪ **Dosage Forms:** Oral (tablet), IV solution

Beta-Blockers - Drug Class Review
High-Yield Med Reviews

Generic Name	Brand Name	Indication(s) or Uses	Notes
Metoprolol	Lopressor Toprol	<ul><li>Angina</li><li>Heart failure with reduced ejection fraction (ER oral formulation)</li><li>Hypertension</li><li>Myocardial infarction</li></ul>	<ul><li>**Dosing (Adult):**<ul><li>Oral IR 12.5 to 200 mg twice daily up to maximum 400 mg daily; Oral ER 50 to 200 mg, up to maximum 400 mg daily;</li><li>IV 2.5 to 5 mg IV push over 2 minutes and repeat every 5 minutes as needed. Maximum total dose of 15 mg.</li></ul></li><li>**Dosing (Peds):**<ul><li>Oral initial dose of 0.1 to 0.2 mg/kg/dose twice daily, titrating up to 1 to 2 mg/kg/day. Maximum daily dose of 2 mg/kg/day or 200 mg/day</li><li>IV: 0.1 to 0.2 mg/kg; maximum dose: 10 mg/dose</li></ul></li><li>**CYP450 Interactions:** Substrate CYP 2D6, and CYP 2C19</li><li>**Renal or Hepatic Dose Adjustments:** None</li><li>**Dosage Forms:** Oral (tablet [IR and ER], capsule [IR and ER]), IV solution</li></ul>
Nebivolol	Bystolic	<ul><li>Hypertension</li></ul>	<ul><li>**Dosing (Adult):**<ul><li>Oral 5 mg once daily, maximum 40 mg daily</li></ul></li><li>**Dosing (Peds):**<ul><li>Not routinely used</li></ul></li><li>**CYP450 Interactions:** Extensive first pass, hepatic glucuronidation</li><li>**Renal or Hepatic Dose Adjustments:**<ul><li>GFR <30 mL/minute: Initial dose of 2.5 mg once daily</li></ul></li><li>**Dosage Forms:** Oral (tablet)</li></ul>
Nadolol	Corgard	<ul><li>Angina</li><li>Hypertension</li></ul>	<ul><li>**Dosing (Adult):**<ul><li>Oral 10 to 240 mg once daily</li></ul></li><li>**Dosing (Peds):**<ul><li>Oral for SVT - Initial dose of 0.5 to 1 mg/kg/day once daily or in 2 divided doses. Maximum 2.5 mg/kg/day</li></ul></li><li>**CYP450 Interactions:** None, but major P-gp substrate</li><li>**Renal or Hepatic Dose Adjustments:**<ul><li>GFR greater than 50 mL/minute, every 24 hours.</li><li>GFR 31 to 50 mL/minute, every 24 to 36 hours</li><li>GFR 10 to 30 mL/minute, every 24 to 48 hours</li><li>GFR <10 mL/minute, every 40 to 60 hours</li><li>HD - administer post-dialysis</li></ul></li><li>**Dosage Forms:** Oral (tablet)</li></ul>

Beta-Blockers - Drug Class Review High-Yield Med Reviews			
Generic Name	**Brand Name**	**Indication(s) or Uses**	**Notes**

Propranolol	Inderal	▪ Angina, chronic stable
		▪ Cardiac arrhythmias
		▪ Essential tremor
		▪ Hypertension
		▪ Migraine headache prophylaxis
		▪ Myocardial infarction, early treatment and secondary prevention
		▪ Obstructive hypertrophic cardiomyopathy
		▪ Pheochromocytoma
		▪ Proliferating infantile hemangioma
			▪ **Dosing (Adult):**
			  – Oral IR 10 to 320 mg 1-4 times daily
			  – Oral ER 80 to 320 mg daily, max 320 mg/d
			  – IV solution 1 mg IV every 2 minutes as needed, maximum 3 doses.
			▪ **Dosing (Peds):**
			  – Oral immediate release initial dose of 0.5 to 1 mg/kg/day in 3 divided doses. Maximum daily dose of 4 mg/kg/day
			  – IV solution 0.01 to 0.15 mg/kg/dose slow IV over 10 minutes every 6 to 8 hours as needed. The max dose is age-dependent with maximum of 1 mg/dose for infants, and 3 mg/dose for children and adolescents
			▪ **CYP450 Interactions:** Extensive first pass, oxidation via CYP1A2, CYP2C19, CYP2D6, and CYP3A4. Inhibits CYP 1A2
			▪ **Renal or Hepatic Dose Adjustments:** None
			▪ **Dosage Forms:** Oral (tablet, capsule [ER], solution), IV solution

High-Yield Clinical Knowledge

- **Vasodilatory Properties**
  - Most beta-blockers do not possess vasodilatory properties at normal therapeutic dosing.
  - Beta-1 selective agents work primarily in the heart, where approximately 80% of beta receptors are beta-1.
  - Beta-2 antagonist activity in the vasculature leads to vasoconstriction (consider beta-2 agonists like albuterol cause bronchodilation, and also how non-selective beta-blockers precipitate bronchospasm).
  - Only beta-blockers with alpha-1 antagonist effects and some with intrinsic sympathomimetic activity can cause vasodilation.
    - The former was used for this action; the latter was not used as vasodilators.
  - The vasodilatory properties of carvedilol and labetalol are a function of the ratio of alpha to beta antagonist activity. The ratio for carvedilol is 1:10 (alpha: beta), whereas labetalol's ratio changes depending on the route of administration (oral - 1:3; IV - 1:7).
- **Antihypertensive Actions**
  - Beta-1 antagonists exert their antihypertensive effect mainly through the RAAS system (beta-1 inhibition of renin release from the juxtaglomerular cells), not through decreased cardiac output (which would cause a reflex increase in MAP).
- **Acute Blood Pressure Lowering**
  - In patients with acute ischemic stroke who are eligible for fibrinolysis with rt-PA, their blood pressure must be less than 185 mmHg systolic and less than 110 mmHg diastolic.
  - Labetalol is a first-line agent to manage blood pressure in this scenario and should be given as an IV bolus at a dose of 20 mg.
  - While patients are receiving rt-PA and for the next 24 hours, blood pressure should be maintained less than 180/105 mmHg.
  - These patients can be managed with labetalol as an IV agent or transitioned to oral dosage forms.

- **Esophageal Varices**
  - Carvedilol's mixed beta-blocking and alpha-1 antagonist activity yield a beneficial effect in patients with esophageal varices and primary variceal bleeding prophylaxis.
  - These benefits from carvedilol result from downregulation of intrahepatic resistance and an additional decrease in hepatic venous pressure gradient.
- **Non-Selective Beta Effects**
  - Non-selective inhibits vasodilation and can increase vascular tone.
  - This action is why in patients with pheochromocytoma, non-selective beta-blockers are contraindicated.
  - If these patients receive a beta-blocker, there would be an uncompensated alpha receptor-mediated vasoconstriction caused by epinephrine secreted from the tumor.

HIGH-YIELD BOARD EXAM ESSENTIALS

- **CLASSIC AGENTS:** Atenolol, carvedilol, betaxolol, bisoprolol, labetalol, propranolol, metoprolol, nebivolol
- **DRUG CLASS:** Beta-blockers
- **INDICATIONS:** Angina, atrial fibrillation/flutter, HFrEF, hypertension, hypertensive emergency, myocardial infarction, variceal hemorrhage prophylaxis (propranolol).
- **MECHANISM:** Reduces pulse (negative chronotropy), decreases cardiac output (due to negative inotropy), reduces renin release to lower BP via indirect inhibition of ATII levels. Improves remodeling in HF.
- **SIDE EFFECTS:** Bradycardia, fatigue, hypotension, poor exercise performance.
- **CLINICAL PEARLS:**
  - Beta-1 antagonists exert their antihypertensive effect mainly through the RAAS system (beta-1 inhibition of renin release from the juxtaglomerular cells), not through decreased cardiac output (which would cause a reflex increase in MAP).
  - Beta-blockers can reduce remodeling seen in HF which can reduce the risk of sudden cardiac death. Only metoprolol succinate and carvedilol are approved for HF.
  - In most cases can be safely used in pregnancy (e.g., labetalol). T
  - his class may mask the effects of hypoglycemia in diabetics (though they can still sweat).
  - Use in patients with moderate to severe asthma or COPD can experience SOB due to bronchospasm.

High-Yield Basic Pharmacology

- **Mechanism of Action**
  - They bind to and prevent calcium entry through "long-type" or L-type calcium channels on myocardial and smooth muscle. The reduction in calcium influx intracellularly prevents the calcium-calmodulin complex from stimulating myosin light chain kinase phosphorylation and ultimately activating actin-myosin interaction and a resulting contraction.
  - Slows rate of phase 4 recovery of nodal tissue by decreasing calcium flow into cardiac nodal cells. In nodal tissue, calcium influx initiates depolarization instead of sodium which initiates depolarization in other cardiac tissues
- **Cardiac Calcium Channels**
  - In cardiac tissue, the inhibition of calcium entry into cells limits the activation of the ryanodine receptor on the sarcoplasmic reticulum, limiting calcium-dependent calcium release.
  - Without this massive efflux of calcium from the sarcoplasmic reticulum, there will be insufficient quantities of calcium to bind with troponin C, essential for displacing troponin and tropomyosin from actin, freeing actin to bind with myosin.

Primary Net Benefit

- Calcium channel blockers provide a wide range of cardiovascular and neurologic benefits, and depending on the agent, provide vasodilation, decreased chronotropy, and inotropy. However, do not inhibit remodeling.

Calcium Channel Blockers - Drug Class Review			
High-Yield Med Reviews			
Mechanism of Action: -L-type calcium channels inhibition, ultimately leading to vasodilation, negative inotropy. SA and AV nodal tissue -Slows heart rate and rate of recovery in nodal tissue by decreasing calcium flow into cardiac nodal cells.			
Class Effects: Vasodilation, decreased chronotropy, and inotropy			
Generic Name	**Brand Name**	**Indication(s) or Uses**	**Notes**

Amlodipine	Katerzia, Norvasc	• Angina
		 • Hypertension
		 • Raynaud phenomenon
			• **Dosing (Adult):**
			   – Oral 2.5 to 5 mg once daily, maximum 10 mg/day
			 • **Dosing (Peds):**
			   – Oral 0.1 mg/kg/dose once daily up to 5 mg for < 6 yrs and up to 10 mg for ≥ 6 yrs old
			 • **CYP450 Interactions:** Major CYP 3A4 substrate
			 • **Renal or Hepatic Dose Adjustments:** None
			 • **Dosage Forms:** Oral tablet, oral suspension

Clevidipine	Cleviprex	• Hypertension	• **Dosing (Adult):**
			   – IV: Initial: 1 to 2 mg/hour, doubled every 5 to 10 min to a maximum of 21 mg/hour
			 • **Dosing (Peds):**
			   – Not routinely used
			 • **CYP450 Interactions:** No CYP interactions
			 • **Renal or Hepatic Dose Adjustments:** None
			 • **Dosage Forms:** IV solution (20% emulsion)

Calcium Channel Blockers - Drug Class Review
High-Yield Med Reviews

Generic Name	Brand Name	Indication(s) or Uses	Notes

Diltiazem	Cardizem, Cartia, Maztim, Taztia, Tiadilt, Tiazac	▪ Angina
		▪ Atrial fibrillation or atrial flutter, rate control
		▪ Hypertension
		▪ Nonsustained ventricular tachycardia or ventricular premature beats, symptomatic
		▪ Supraventricular tachycardia
			▪ **Dosing (Adult):**
			  – IR: 30 mg 4 times daily (maximum 240 to 360 mg/day);
			  – 12-hour (twice-daily) formulations: 60 mg twice daily (maximum 240 to 360 mg/day,
			  – 24-hour (once-daily) formulations: 120 to 180 mg once daily (maximum 240 to 360 mg/day)
			  – IV 0.25 or 0.35 mg IV push, alternatively 10 mg IV push. Continuous infusion 5 to 15 mg/hour.
			▪ **Dosing (Peds):**
			  – IR: initial 1.5 to 2 mg/kg/day in 3 to 4 divided doses to maximum 6 mg/kg/day or to 360 mg/day whichever is less
			  – IV 0.25 or 0.35 mg IV push
			▪ **CYP450 Interactions:** Major substrate of CYP3A4, P-gp
			▪ **Renal or Hepatic Dose Adjustments:** None
			▪ **Dosage Forms:** Oral (solution, capsule or tablet), IV solution

Isradipine	DynaCirc	▪ Hypertension	▪ **Dosing (Adult):**
			  – Oral 2.5 mg twice daily, maximum 5 mg twice daily.
			▪ **Dosing (Peds):**
			  – Oral 0.05 to 0.1 mg/kg/dose 2 to 3 times daily, up to 0.6 mg/kg/dose or 10 mg/day (lesser of the two)
			▪ **CYP450 Interactions:** Major substrate of CYP3A4
			▪ **Renal or Hepatic Dose Adjustments:** None
			▪ **Dosage Forms:** Oral (capsule)

Nicardipine	Cardene	▪ Angina
		▪ Hypertension
			▪ **Dosing (Adult):**
			  – Oral: 20 to 40 mg 3 times daily
			  – IV: 5 mg/hour titrate by 2.5 mg/hour every 5-10 minutes, maximum dose 15 mg/hour
			▪ **Dosing (Peds):**
			  – Oral 0.5 to 1 mcg/kg/minute, maximum dose 4 to 5 mcg/kg/minute
			▪ **CYP450 Interactions:** Major substrate of CYP3A4, inhibits 2D6
			▪ **Renal or Hepatic Dose Adjustments:**
			  – Oral: Initial: 20 mg 3 times daily
			▪ **Dosage Forms:** Oral (capsule), IV solution

Calcium Channel Blockers - Drug Class Review
High-Yield Med Reviews

Generic Name	Brand Name	Indication(s) or Uses	Notes

Nifedipine	Procardia; Procardia XL	• Angina, Hypertension, Pre-eclampsia, Pulmonary arterial hypertension (group 1)	• **Dosing (Adult):**
			  − ER 30 to 90 mg once daily; maximum: 120 mg/day
			• **Dosing (Peds):**
			  − ER: 0.25 to 0.5 mg/kg/day once daily or divided in 2 doses; maximum daily dose of 3 mg/kg/day (or 120 mg/day)
			• **CYP450 Interactions:** Major substrate of CYP3A4
			• **Renal or Hepatic Dose Adjustments:** None
			• **Dosage Forms:** Oral immediate or extended-release (capsule or tablet)

Nimodipine	Nimotop, Nymalize	• Subarachnoid hemorrhage	• **Dosing (Adult):**
			  − Oral 60 mg every 4 hours for 21 consecutive days
			• **Dosing (Peds):**
			  − Not routinely used
			• **CYP450 Interactions:** Major substrate of CYP3A4
			• **Renal or Hepatic Dose Adjustments:**
			  − Cirrhosis - 30 mg every 4 hours
			• **Dosage Forms:** Oral (capsule), oral solution

Nisoldipine	Sular	• Hypertension	• **Dosing (Adult):**
			  − Geomatrix delivery system (brand name Sular) Initial: 17 mg once daily, maximum 34 mg per day; ER oral tablet 20 mg once daily, maximum 60 mg/day
			• **Dosing (Peds):**
			  − Not routinely used
			• **CYP450 Interactions:** Major substrate of CYP3A4
			• **Renal or Hepatic Dose Adjustments:**
			  − Hepatic impairment, no more than 8.5 mg/day (Sular), or no more than 10 mg/day ER dosage form
			• **Dosage Forms:** Oral (tablet)

Verapamil	Calan, Verelan	• Angina pectoris (IR form only)	• **Dosing (Adult):**
			  − IR form: 80 to 120 mg 3 times daily.
			  − Extended-release: Initial: 180 mg once daily. Maximum 480 mg/day
			  − IV bolus 2.5 to 10 mg IV push (2 minutes)
			• **Dosing (Peds):**
			  − IR: 2 to 8 mg/kg/day in 3 divided doses; maximum daily dose: 480 mg/day
			  − IV 0.1 to 0.3 mg/kg/dose, maximum 5 mg/dose
			• **CYP450 Interactions:** Major substrate of CYP3A4
			• **Renal or Hepatic Dose Adjustments:**
			  − Cirrhosis, reduce oral dose to 20-30% of normal, IV dose 50% reduction.
			• **Dosage Forms:** Oral (capsule or tablet), IV solution

High-Yield Clinical Knowledge

- **Dihydropyridines**
  - Dihydropyridine calcium channel blockers are more selective for smooth muscle calcium channels at normal therapeutic doses.
  - This specificity yields vasodilation and little to no effect on heart rate or contractility.
  - The specificity of dihydropyridines is owed to their preference for less negative resting potentials of calcium-binding site tissues. Since the typical resting potential of smooth muscle is -70mV, dihydropyridines preferentially bind there and not to the more negative myocardial tissue (-90mV).
  - At normal therapeutic dosing, dihydropyridines do not have a measurable effect on the SA node. However, isradipine is the exception to this rule as it has a significant depressant effect on the SA node at therapeutic dosing sufficient to blunt any reflex tachycardia from its vasodilation.
- **Hypertension**
  - The JNC 8 guidelines include dihydropyridine and non-dihydropyridine calcium channel blockers as first-line options for managing hypertension.
- **High-Risk Drug-Interactions:**
  - All undergo the first-pass metabolism
  - Diltiazem/Verapamil inhibits 2C9, 2D6, 3A4 and P-glycoprotein; 3A4 substrates
  - Dihydropyridines substrates of 3A4, 2D6 and 2C9, inhibit 3A4
  - Clevidipine - red blood cell hydrolysis (no known pharmacokinetic interactions)
- **Atrial Fibrillation with Rapid Ventricular Response**
  - Diltiazem or verapamil can be used for rapid control of ventricular rates in patients with atrial fibrillation. In these patients, diltiazem is commonly used in a fixed-dose (10 mg IV) or weight-based dose regimen (0.25 mg/kg IV followed by 0.35 mg/kg if inadequate response). An infusion of diltiazem can follow successful rate control at a rate of 5 to 15 mg/hr.
- **Supraventricular Tachycardia**
  - Verapamil can be used as an alternative to adenosine. As a result of the significant first-pass metabolism of oral verapamil, the intravenous dose is 5 to 10 mg. Simultaneously, the oral dose for atrial fibrillation rate control is up to 480 mg/day.
- **Subarachnoid hemorrhage**
  - Nimodipine is used almost exclusively for this indication and only exists as an oral dosage form.

HIGH-YIELD BOARD EXAM ESSENTIALS

- **CLASSIC AGENTS:** Amlodipine, clevidipine, diltiazem, nicardipine, nifedipine, verapamil.
- **DRUG CLASS:** Calcium channel blockers
- **INDICATIONS:** Acute ischemic stroke, angina / ACS, AFib +/- RVR, SVT, preeclampsia/eclampsia, subarachnoid hemorrhage, ventricular arrhythmias, migraine/cluster headache (verapamil), hypertension, pulmonary artery hypertension, Raynaud phenomenon
- **MECHANISM:** L-type calcium channels inhibition, ultimately leading to vasodilation. Diltiazem and verapamil exhibit additional negative inotropy (myocardial muscle and smooth muscle) which slows heart rate and rate of recovery in nodal tissue by decreasing calcium flow into cardiac nodal cells (SA and AV nodal tissue).
- **SIDE EFFECTS:** Bradycardia, hypotension, constipation; case reports of gingival hyperplasia
- **CLINICAL PEARLS:**
  - The non-DHP CCB (diltiazem & verapamil) can be useful when rate control needed in AFib with RVR, but they do prevent cardiac remodeling or protect patients from sudden cardiac death (like beta-blockers). These two agents are also known to inhibit CYP3A4 and P-gp causing drug-interactions.
  - Nimodipine is used almost exclusively for subarachnoid hemorrhage indication and only exists as an oral dosage form.
  - CCB can be used in pregnancy for treatment of hypertension.

High-Yield Basic Pharmacology

- **Mechanism of Action**
  - Direct renin inhibitor, of which only aliskiren exists, directly inhibits renin which mediates the conversion of AngI to angiotensinogen mediated.
  - Specifically, aliskiren is a potent competitive inhibitor of renin.
  - It binds the active site of renin to block the conversion of angiotensinogen to AngI, thus reducing the consequent production of AngII.

Primary Net Benefit

- Aliskiren carries the same safety concerns as other agents working on the RAAS. These include hyperkalemia, elevations in serum creatinine, teratogenicity (do not use in pregnancy), and angioedema.

Direct Renin Inhibitor - Drug Class Review High-Yield Med Reviews			
Mechanism of Action: *Direct renin inhibitors reduce the actions of AngII and lower blood pressure*			
Class Effects: *Vasodilation, blood pressure lowering.*			
Generic Name	**Brand Name**	**Indication(s) or Uses**	**Notes**

Aliskiren	Tekturna	• Hypertension	• **Dosing (Adult):**
			  – Oral initial dose of 150 mg once daily, maximum dose of 300 mg once daily
			• **Dosing (Peds):**
			  – For children > 6 with weight 20 to 50 kg initial dose of 75 mg once daily, and maximum daily dose of 150 mg/day.
			• **CYP450 Interactions:** Substrate of CYP3A4, and P-glycoprotein
			• **Renal or Hepatic Dose Adjustments:** None
			• **Dosage Forms:** Oral (tablet)

High-Yield Clinical Knowledge

- **Hypertension**
  - The use of aliskiren in combination with an ACE-inhibitor or ARB is not recommended by the European Society of Hypertension (Eur Heart J, 2013, 34:2159-2219.).
- **Monotherapy**
  - Aliskiren should not be used as monotherapy for any indication and has only demonstrated a clinical role combined with standard hypertension therapy.
- **NSAIDs and RAAS Agents**
  - Opioid reduction initiatives often promote NSAIDs for routine use of pain control. In patients taking aliskiren (or any other RAAS agent for that matter), these NSAIDs could eliminate the clinical benefit and response to RAAS agents. Other alternative analgesics should be considered.
- **ACE/ARB Effects**
  - Aliskiren has similar end-organ effects as the ACE-inhibitors or ARBs
  - In addition to the effects mentioned above on AngI and AngII, it down-regulates sympathetic discharge, promotes natriuresis and diuresis, and inhibits cardiac and vascular remodeling.
- **CK Elevations**
  - In rare instances (less than 1%), aliskiren is associated with 300% increases in creatine phosphokinase.
- **Drug Interactions**

- Aliskiren is a CYP 3A4 substrate as well as a P-glycoprotein substrate.
- Since it must be used in combination with other antihypertensive agents, drug interactions are a fundamental consideration when choosing appropriate drug therapy.
- Notable drugs that are contraindicated in combination with aliskiren include itraconazole and cyclosporine.

HIGH-YIELD BOARD EXAM ESSENTIALS
- **CLASSIC AGENTS:** Aliskiren
- **DRUG CLASS:** Direct renin inhibitor
- **INDICATIONS:** Hypertension
- **MECHANISM:** Directly inhibits renin which mediates the conversion of angiotensinogen to angiotensin I.
- **SIDE EFFECTS:** Elevations in CK, angioedema
- **CLINICAL PEARLS:** Aliskiren has little value or use in clinical practice due better alternatives. Aliskiren is a CYP 3A4 substrate as well as a P-glycoprotein substrate, notable drugs that are contraindicated in combination with aliskiren include itraconazole and cyclosporine.

High-Yield Basic Pharmacology

- **Mechanism of Action**
  - Sacubitril inhibits neprilysin (aka neutral endopeptidase), preventing the breakdown of natriuretic peptides, bradykinin, and other vasodilators.
  - Valsartan is an angiotensin receptor blocker that directly inhibits angiotensin 1, ultimately reducing the actions of AngII and lowering blood pressure
- **ARB Component Effects**
  - Sacubitril alone is not commercially available in the US; it is always co-formulated with valsartan.
  - Much of the monitoring and safety pertains to the ARB component
    - ARBs are associated with an increase in serum creatinine and hyperkalemia.

Primary Net Benefit

- In HFrEF, the combination of sacubitril-valsartan significantly improves cardiovascular-related morbidity and mortality when compared to ACE-inhibitor therapy alone.

Neprilysin Inhibitor - Drug Class Review			
High-Yield Med Reviews			
Mechanism of Action: *Inhibits neprilysin and prevents the breakdown of natriuretic peptides, bradykinin, and other vasodilators* *Valsartan reduces the actions of AngII and lowers blood pressure*			
Class Effects: *Vasodilation, blood pressure-lowering, decreased cardiac remodeling, improved renal perfusion, and other microvascular complications*			
Generic Name	**Brand Name**	**Indication(s) or Uses**	**Notes**

Sacubitril-valsartan	Entresto	• Heart failure	• **Dosing (Adult):**
			  – Oral sacubitril-valsartan 24mg/26mg BID
			  – Titrate to target sacubitril-valsartan 97mg/103mg BID
			• **Dosing (Peds):**
			  – Oral 1.6 mg/kg/dose BID (based on the combined dose of sacubitril-valsartan)
			    • Target dose of 2.3 mg/kg/dose
			• **CYP450 Interactions:** None known
			• **Renal or Hepatic Dose Adjustments:**
			  – GFR less than 30 mL/minute - initial dose 24mg/26mg BID
			  – Severe hepatic impairment (Child-Pugh C) - not recommended
			• **Dosage Forms:** Oral (tablet)

High-Yield Clinical Knowledge

- **HFrEF and NYHA Class II-III**
  - The AHA currently recommends replacing ACE-inhibitor or ARB with sacubitril-valsartan in patients with HFrEF and NYHA class II-III symptoms to reduce morbidity and mortality further.
- **Sacubitril and ACE-Inhibitors**
  - When switching therapy from ACE-inhibitor to sacubitril-valsartan, the ACE-inhibitor must be discontinued 36 hours before initiating sacubitril.

- The risk of angioedema is very high with the combination of sacubitril and an ACE-inhibitor.
  - The initial clinical investigation of omapatrilat (neprilysin inhibitor) was combined with ACE-inhibitors, which caused a 3.2-fold increase in the risk of angioedema. (Am J Hypertens. 2004 Feb;17(2):103-11)
- **HFpEF Uncertain**
  - In the PARAGON-HF trial, which examined HFpEF patients, sacubitril-valsartan failed to show improvement in CV outcomes compared to valsartan alone.
- **Use in Pregnancy**
  - Similar to ACE-inhibitors, direct-renin inhibitors, sacubitril should not be used in pregnancy due to the risk of fetal toxicity.

HIGH-YIELD BOARD EXAM ESSENTIALS
- **CLASSIC AGENTS:** Sacubitril
- **DRUG CLASS:** Neprilysin inhibitor
- **INDICATIONS:** HFrEF
- **MECHANISM:** Inhibits neprilysin, preventing the breakdown of natriuretic peptides, bradykinin, and other vasodilators.
- **SIDE EFFECTS:** Cough, hyperkalemia (due to valsartan), angioedema
- **CLINICAL PEARLS:** In an RCT sacubitril-valsartan was superior to enalapril in reducing the risks of death and hospitalization for heart failure. When switching therapy from ACE-inhibitor to sacubitril-valsartan, the ACE-inhibitor must be discontinued 36 hours before initiating sacubitril.

High-Yield Basic Pharmacology

- **Mechanism of Action**
  - Acts as a nitric oxide (NO) donor, replacing NO that would normally be produced by endothelial cells that leads to vasodilation.

Primary Net Benefit

- At standard doses reduces preload and offers a reduction in preload and vasodilation of coronary vasculature. At higher doses can also reduce afterload. It also comes in different dosage forms allowing for broad use.

Nitrates - Drug Class Review **High-Yield Med Reviews**			
Mechanism of Action: *Acts as a nitric oxide (NO) donor, replacing NO that would normally be produced by endothelial cells..*			
Class Effects: Vasodilation, but the degree of venodilation and arterial dilation differ by agent and dose used.			
Generic Name	**Brand Name**	**Indication(s) or Uses**	**Notes**
Nitroglycerin	Nitro-Bid Nitro-Dur NitroMist Nitrostat Tridil	• Acute decompensated heart failure • Angina • Acute coronary syndrome • Anal fissures, chronic (topical) • Esophageal spasm • Extravasation of vasopressors	• **Dosing (Adult): IV:** — Initial: 10 to 20 mcg/minute, with subsequent titration (eg, 10 to 20 mcg/minute every 5 to 15 minutes) up to 200 mcg/minute • **Dosing (Peds):** — 0.25 to 0.5 mcg/kg/minute; titrate by 1 mcg/kg/minute every 15 to 20 minutes • **CYP450 Interactions:** — No CYP interactions but important interactions with PDE5 inhibitors • **Renal or Hepatic Dose Adjustments:** None • **Dosage Forms:** — IV solution, Oral (sublingual, capsule, translingual), topical (patch, ointment)

		Nitrates - Drug Class Review	
		High-Yield Med Reviews	
Generic Name	**Brand Name**	**Indication(s) or Uses**	**Notes**

Nitroprusside	Nipride RTU Nitropress	• Acute decompensated heart failure
		• Acute hypertension
		• Aortic dissection (in combination with esmolol most cases)
		▪
			• **Dosing (Adult):**
			  – 0.3 to 0.5 mcg/kg/minute; may be titrated by 0.5 mcg/kg/minute every few minutes (max 2 mcg/kg/min)
			• **Dosing (Peds):**
			  – Initial: 0.3 to 0.5 mcg/kg/minute, titrate every 5 minutes to desired effect; usual dose: 3 to 4 mcg/kg/minute; maximum dose: 10 mcg/kg/minute
			▪ **CYP450 Interactions:**
			  – No CYP interactions, but contraindicated with PDE5 inhibitors.
			▪ **Renal or Hepatic Dose Adjustments:**
			  – GFR < 30 ml/min increases the risk of cyanide toxicity. Limit mean infusion rate to <3 mcg/kg/minute.
			▪ **Dosage Forms:** IV solution
			▪

Isosorbide dinitrate	Dilatrate-SR Isordil, Titradose, BiDil (with hydralazine)	Angina pectoris, prevention	• **Dosing (Adult):**
			  – IR form: 5 to 80 mg BID or TID, SR form: 40 to 160 mg/day
			• **Dosing (Peds):** not used
			▪ **CYP450 Interactions:**
			  – Major substrate of CYP3A4
			▪ **Renal or Hepatic Dose Adjustments:** None
			▪ **Dosage Forms:**
			• Oral (capsule or tablet)

Isosorbide mononitrate	Imdur	• Angina pectoris (IR form only)
		▪
			• **Dosing (Adult):**
			  – IR: 5 to 20 mg BID. ER 30 to 60 mg QD, max 240 mg.
			• **Dosing (Peds):** not used
			▪ **CYP450 Interactions:**
			  – Major substrate of CYP3A4
			▪ **Renal or Hepatic Dose Adjustments:** None
			▪ **Dosage Forms:**
			• Oral (capsule or tablet)

High-Yield Clinical Knowledge

- **Acute Care**
  - **Acute Ischemic Stroke with Hypertensive Crisis:**
    - The use of nitroprusside to control blood pressure (i.e., > 185 mm Hg systolic or > 110 mm Hg diastolic) in patients with acute ischemic stroke is a relative contraindication for fibrinolysis with rt-PA.
      - Since it is the last line agent, other therapies such as labetalol and nicardipine should have been attempted, optimized, but then failed.
    - Such a degree of hypertension that is difficult to control could increase the risk of hemorrhagic conversion of the ischemic stroke, which would be made worse in the presence of rt-PA.
  - **Acute Pulmonary Edema in Heart Failure:**

- Consider the use of sublingual nitroglycerin with a short course (~20 min) of BiPap to reduce reload and reduce afterload to encourage forward flow that will relieve vascular congestion.
- Given 0.4 mg or 400 mcg sublingually every 5 minutes until desired effect can offer an estimated equivalent of about 80 mcg/min (400 mcg / 5 minutes = ~80 mcg/min). While a SL tab does not function as a controlled release drug, this convenient and readily available treatment can be similar to the IV doses up to 200 mcg/min.
  - **Angina / Acute Coronary Syndrome:**
    - Although nitroglycerin is a common component in the acute management of myocardial infarction, it's clinical impact is minimal, if any is present. While the use of a nitroglycerin dosage form in this scenario may relieve chest pain or discomfort, it has not demonstrated a patient-oriented clinical benefit with no change in morbidity or mortality.
  - **Cyanide Toxicity from Nitroprusside Infusions:**
    - To reduce the risk of cyanide toxicity from nitroprusside infusions, it can be formulated with sodium thiosulfate, one of the antidotes of cyanide.
    - Also, preventing exposure to UV light (not fluorescent lighting in most pharmacy departments) can limit the risk of cyanide toxicity.
  - **Extravasation of a Vasopressor:**
    - In the event of extravasation of a vasopressor, phentolamine is often cited as the ideal agent to treat the surrounding tissue. However, it is rarely available, often on shortage.
    - An acceptable alternative can be the use of nitroglycerin in its topical ointment dosage form. Although, patients may have systemic hypotensive effects due to the absorption of the topical nitroglycerin.
  - **High-Risk Drug-Interactions:**
    - It is critically important to avoid the use of nitrates in patients taking type 5 phosphodiesterase inhibitors within 24 hours or up to 48 hours if tadalafil due to the risk of severe hypotension.
- **Chronic Care**
  - With long term use of nitrates, tolerance or tachyphylaxis can occur.
    - This diminishing effect is thought to be due to counterregulatory neurohumoral mechanisms opposing nitric oxide.
    - This is thought to occur because of an impairment in the bioconversion of nitrates, thus limiting NO release or an increase in NO clearance due to the generation of superoxide.
    - Nitroglycerin exists in numerous dosage forms: sublingual tablet, sublingual packet, translingual aerosol, extended-release capsule, transdermal ointment, transrectal ointment, transdermal patch, and an intravenous solution.

High-Yield Fast-Facts

- **Nitroglycerin Exploding:**
  - While it can spontaneously explode, in its commonly available dosage forms, the concentration of nitroglycerin is well below the threshold for this risk.
- **NitRITE vs. Nitrate:**
  - Amyl nitrite is a nitRITE, not a nitRATE. It was once used as an inhaled vasodilator but is no longer used for this indication. Instead, it's role is as a cauterizing agent for certain types of hemorrhages.
- **Anesthesia:**
  - Nitric oxide used as an anesthetic gas can induce methemoglobin

HIGH-YIELD BOARD EXAM ESSENTIALS

- **CLASSIC AGENTS:** Isosorbide dinitrate, Isosorbide mononitrate, Nitroglycerin, Nitroprusside
- **DRUG CLASS:** Nitrates, Vasodilators
- **INDICATIONS:** Hypertensive emergency, Angina, Esophageal Spasms, Extravasation of Vasopressors (Topical), Anal Fissures (topical use)
- **MECHANISM:** Acts as a nitric oxide (NO) donor, replacing NO that would normally be produced by endothelial cells that leads to vasodilation.
- **SIDE EFFECTS:** Hypotension, reflex tachycardia, headache
- **CLINICAL PEARLS:**
  - At standard doses reduces preload and offers a reduction in preload and vasodilation of coronary vasculature. At higher doses can also reduce afterload. It also comes in different dosage forms allowing for broad use.
  - Avoid with the co-administration of type 5 PDE inhibitors (i.e., sildenafil) due to risk of hypotension.
  - Nitroprusside is formulated with cyanide (CN) and prolonged infusions can result in accumulation with toxicity. It also must be protected from the light.
  - With chronic use, tachyphylaxis can occur which may warrant a "nitrate free interval".

High-Yield Basic Pharmacology

- **Hydralazine**
    - The vasodilation caused by hydralazine often leads to baroreceptor reflex activation.
        - This results in tachycardia due to increased sympathetic outflow to the heart, increasing rate, and contractility.
- **Ivabradine**
    - Ivabradine's actions are specific to the SA node.
        - As a result, there are no direct actions affecting blood pressure, cardiac contractility, or AV nodal conduction.
- **Phenoxybenzamine**
    - In addition to its unique, irreversible alpha-1 blocking properties, phenoxybenzamine has also been described as a serotonin receptor antagonist and H1 antagonist effects.
- **Fenoldopam**
    - It is primarily a D1 receptor agonist but has also been described as possessing antagonist effects on prejunctional alpha-2 autoreceptors at postganglionic sympathetic axons.

Primary Net Benefit

- Vasodilation, but the degree of vasodilation and arterial dilation differ by agent and dose used.

Miscellaneous Vasodilators - Drug Class Review			
High-Yield Med Reviews			
Mechanism of Action: *See Agents Above.*			
Class Effects: *Vasodilation, but the degree of vasodilation and arterial dilation differ by agent and dose used.*			
Generic Name	**Brand Name**	**Indication(s) or Uses**	**Notes**

Fenoldopam	Corlopam	- Short-term treatment of severe hypertension	- **Dosing (Adult):**
			  - IV infusion 0.01 to 0.3 mcg/kg/minute, titrate by 0.05 to 0.1 mcg/kg/minute q15min to target blood pressure
			    - Maximum 1.6 mcg/kg/minute for 48 hours.
			- **Dosing (Peds):**
			  - IV infusion 0.2 mcg/kg/minute, titrate by 0.3 to 0.5 mcg/kg/minute q20 to 30min
			    - Maximum 0.8 mcg/kg/minute
			- **CYP450 Interactions:** None
			- **Renal or Hepatic Dose Adjustments:** None
			- **Dosage Forms:** IV solution

Miscellaneous Vasodilators - Drug Class Review
High-Yield Med Reviews

Generic Name	Brand Name	Indication(s) or Uses	Notes

Hydralazine	Apresoline	▪ Hypertension
		▪ Hypertensive emergency in pregnancy or postpartum
			▪ **Dosing (Adult):**
			  − Oral initial dose 10 to 25 mg q6h
			    ▪ Maximum 100 to 200 mg/day
			  − IM or IV 5 to 20 mg q4-6hours
			    ▪ Maximum 20-40 mg/dose
			▪ **Dosing (Peds):**
			  − Oral initial dose 0.75 to 3 mg/kg/day divided q6-12h
			    ▪ Maximum 7 mg/kg/day or 200 mg/day, whichever is less
			▪ **CYP450 Interactions:** None
			▪ **Renal or Hepatic Dose Adjustments:**
			  − CrCl greater than or equal to 10 mL/minute- frequency of q8h
			  − CrCl <10 mL/minute- frequency of q8-16h.
			  − Intermittent hemodialysis: Dose after dialysis
			▪ **Dosage Forms:** IV solution, Oral (tablet)

Ivabradine	Corlanor	▪ Hospitalization risk reduction in patients with symptomatic heart failure and an ejection fraction of 35% or less.	▪ **Dosing (Adult):**
			  − Oral initial dose of 2.5 to 5 mg twice daily
			▪ **Dosing (Peds):**
			  − Less than 40 kg- initial dose of 0.05 mg/kg/dose twice daily
			    ▪ Maximum 7.5 mg twice daily
			  − Greater than or equal to 40 kg, see adult dosing
			▪ **CYP450 Interactions:** Major substrate of CYP3A4
			▪ **Renal or Hepatic Dose Adjustments:**
			  − Child-Pugh class C, contraindicated
			▪ **Dosage Forms:** Oral (capsule or tablet)

Minoxidil	Loniten	▪ Management of hypertension
		▪ Hair growth (topical only)
			▪ **Dosing (Adult):**
			  − Oral initial dose of 5 mg daily
			    ▪ Maximum dose of 100 mg/day
			▪ **Dosing (Peds):**
			  − Oral initial dose 0.2 mg/kg/dose once
			    ▪ Maximum dose 5 mg/dose
			▪ **CYP450 Interactions:** None known
			▪ **Renal or Hepatic Dose Adjustments:** None known
			▪ **Dosage Forms:** Oral (tablet)

Phenoxybenzamine	Dibenzyline	▪ Management of pheochromocytoma
		▪ Hair growth (topical only)
			▪ **Dosing (Adult):**
			  − Oral initial 10 mg twice daily
			    ▪ Maximum dose of 240 mg daily
			▪ **Dosing (Peds):**
			  − Oral initial 0.2 to 0.25 mg/kg/dose once or twice daily
			    ▪ Maximum 10 mg/dose
			▪ **CYP450 Interactions:** None
			▪ **Renal or Hepatic Dose Adjustments:** None
			▪ **Dosage Forms:** Oral (capsule)

Miscellaneous Vasodilators - Drug Class Review
High-Yield Med Reviews

Generic Name	Brand Name	Indication(s) or Uses	Notes

Phentolamine	Rogitine OraVerse	• Diagnosis & management of pheochromocytoma
		• Extravasation management
			• **Dosing (Adult):**
			  – IV or IM 5 mg once
			  – Local infiltration of 5 to 10 mg
			• **Dosing (Peds):**
			  – IV 1 mg bolus or IM 3 mg once
			  – Local infiltration of 0.5 to 1 mg/mL solution
			• **CYP450 Interactions:** None
			• **Renal or Hepatic Dose Adjustments:** None
			• **Dosage Forms:** IV (solution)

Ranolazine	Ranexa	• Chronic angina	• **Dosing (Adult):**
			  – Oral initial dose of 500 mg twice daily
			    • Maximum 1,000 mg twice daily
			• **Dosing (Peds):** Not used
			• **CYP450 Interactions:** Substrate and inhibitor of CYP3A4, CPY2D6, and P-gp
			• **Renal or Hepatic Dose Adjustments:** None
			• **Dosage Forms:** Oral (tablet)

High-Yield Clinical Knowledge

- **Fenoldopam**
  - Limited use in clinical practice but may be a reasonable alternative to nitroprusside in patients where the risk of cyanide/thiocyanate toxicity is high (high dose, prolonged use, renal impairment).
- **Hydralazine**
  - Despite being frequently used for acute hypertension, it has an unpredictable clinical response, onset, and duration of action. Alternative agents should be recommended.
- **Ivabradine**
  - Narrow spectrum of HFrEF patients due to FDA-approved indication. With greater clinical experience, these indications may change over time.
- **Phenoxybenzamine**
  - Uniquely used for the management of the sequelae of pheochromocytoma.
- **Phentolamine**
  - Use limited to management of extravasation or pheochromocytoma.
- **Minoxidil**
  - Not used clinically for acute hypertension but use during other indications may affect blood pressure.
- **Ranolazine**
  - It is still commonly used, despite numerous drug interactions (CYP3A4, P-gp, and metformin) and lack of established benefit.
- **Hydralazine and NSAIDs**
  - Hydralazine should not be used concomitantly with NSAIDs.
    - Hydralazine is thought to augment the arachidonic acid, COX, and prostacyclin pathways.
      - The administration of NSAIDs could blunt these vasodilatory effects of hydralazine.
- **Acute Care Use of Phentolamine**
  - Limited to the management of extravasation of norepinephrine and other sympathomimetic vasopressors.
    - Administered directly into the extravasation area.

- The dose is typically between 5 and 10 mg but first diluted to a final volume of 10 mL with normal saline.
- **Pheochromocytoma Diagnosis Vs. Management**
  - Both phentolamine and phenoxybenzamine are used for pheochromocytoma.
    - Phentolamine is used primarily in the diagnosis of pheochromocytoma via the phentolamine-blocking test.
    - Phenoxybenzamine is used in the treatment, or more specifically, the management of the sequelae of pheochromocytoma such as hypertension and sweating.

HIGH-YIELD BOARD EXAM ESSENTIALS

- **CLASSIC AGENTS:** Fenoldopam, hydralazine, ivabradine, phenoxybenzamine, phentolamine, minoxidil, ranolazine
- **DRUG CLASS:** CV agents and vasodilators
- **INDICATIONS:** Acute hypertension (fenoldopam, hydralazine), pheochromocytoma treatment (phenoxybenzamine), pheochromocytoma diagnosis, prevention (phentolamine), extravasation management (phentolamine), chronic angina (ranolazine), hypertension (minoxidil), risk reduction of hospitalization for worsening heart failure (ivabradine)
- **MECHANISM:**
  - Fenoldopam: D1 receptor agonist, causing arterial dilation
  - Ivabradine: Vasodilation from stimulation of nitric oxide release and reduction of intracellular calcium concentrations (hydralazine), decreases spontaneous depolarization of the SA node
  - Minoxidil: Opening of potassium channels, hyperpolarizing, and relaxing vascular smooth muscle
  - Phenoxybenzamine: Nonselective, irreversible alpha-1 receptor antagonists
  - Phentolamine: Competitive, reversible alpha-1 and alpha-2 receptor antagonist
  - Ranolazine: Decreases inward sodium current during repolarization, enhancing relaxation of ventricular tension and decreases myocardial oxygen consumption
- **SIDE EFFECTS:** Hypotension, reflex tachycardia, headache
- **CLINICAL PEARLS:** Hydralazine/isosorbide dinitrate should be used in patients who can't tolerate an ACE inhibitor, ARB, or angiotensin II-neprilysin inhibitor.

High-Yield Basic Pharmacology

- **Mechanism of Action**
  - Direct thrombin inhibitors (DTI), as their name suggests, inhibit thrombin by directly binding to its active site. In other words, these agents do not require antithrombin it exerts this action.
- **Thrombin Binding Sites**
  - DTIs bind to one or two binding sites on thrombin, relevant to DTIs as there are two subcategories.
  - The bivalent DTI (bivalirudin) binds to the thrombin's active site and at the substrate recognition site.
  - Conversely, the monovalent DTIs (argatroban and dabigatran) are smaller molecules and bind exclusively to thrombin's active site.

Primary Net Benefit

- DTIs play an essential role in managing thromboembolic disease states where heparin or other anticoagulants cannot be used or may be preferred in some circumstances.

Direct Thrombin Inhibitors - Drug Class Review			
High-Yield Med Reviews			
Mechanism of Action: *Direct thrombin inhibitors (DTI), as their name suggests, inhibit thrombin by directly binding to its active site. In other words, these agents do not require antithrombin it exerts this action.*			
Class Effects: *Decreased thrombin generation, increase risk of bleeding*			
Generic Name	**Brand Name**	**Indication(s) or Uses**	**Notes**

Argatroban	Acova	• Heparin-induced thrombocytopenia (HIT)
		• Percutaneous coronary intervention
			• **Dosing (Adult):**
			  – **STEMI:** Initial dose of 2 mcg/kg/minute IV infusion then adjusted until the steady-state aPTT is 1.5 to 3 times
			  – **HIT:** IV infusion of 0.1 to 1.5 mcg/kg/minute
			• **Dosing (Peds):**
			  – HIT: IV infusion initial rate of 0.75 mcg/kg/minute
			• **CYP450 Interactions:**
			  – No CYP interactions
			• **Renal or Hepatic Dose Adjustments:**
			  – Child-Pugh B or C - start continuous IV infusion at 0.5 mcg/kg/minute and adjust to target aPTT.
			• **Dosage Forms:** IV solution

Direct Thrombin Inhibitors - Drug Class Review
High-Yield Med Reviews

Generic Name	Brand Name	Indication(s) or Uses	Notes

Bivalirudin	Angiomax	• Percutaneous coronary intervention	• **Dosing (Adult):**
			  – During PCI: IV 0.75 mg/kg bolus immediately prior to the procedure, then 1.75 mg/kg/hour for the remainder of the procedure adjusted to ACT target.
			    ▪ Can continue at 1.75 mg/kg/hour for up to 4 hours post-procedure.
			  – Prior to PCI: 0.1 mg/kg bolus, then 0.25 mg/kg/hour continued until PCI.
			• **CYP450 Interactions:** None
			• **Renal or Hepatic Dose Adjustments:**
			  – PCI: CrCl less than 30 mL/minute no bolus adjustment, but start infusion at 1 mg/kg/hour. If on hemodialysis, the initial rate should be 0.25 mg/kg/hour.
			  – PCI: CrCl less than 30 mL/min or on HD initial infusion rate of 0.04 to 0.07 mg/kg/hour.
			• **Dosage Forms:** IV solution

Dabigatran	Pradaxa	• Deep venous thrombosis and pulmonary embolism treatment and prophylaxis
		• Nonvalvular atrial fibrillation
		• Venous thromboembolism prophylaxis in total hip arthroplasty
			• **Dosing (Adult):**
			  – Oral 150 mg twice daily
			• **Dosing (Peds):**
			  – Not routinely used
			• **CYP450 Interactions:** None, P-glycoprotein substrate
			• **Renal or Hepatic Dose Adjustments:**
			  – CrCl between 30 and 50 mL/minute AND receiving concomitant dronedarone or ketoconazole, 75 mg twice daily.
			  – CrCl between 15 and 30 mL/min adjust to 75 mg twice daily. CrCl less than 15 mL/min do not use.
			• **Dosage Forms:** Oral (capsule)

High-Yield Clinical Knowledge

- **DTI for HIT with Renal Impairment**
  - In patients with heparin-induced thrombocytopenia, there is a delicate balance between ongoing antithrombotic therapy and hemorrhage risk.
  - Therefore, careful selection of the appropriate DTI or fondaparinux is essential.
  - Argatroban is preferred for use in renal insufficiency, although bivalirudin can be used provided appropriate dosage adjustment is considered.
- **Argatroban Conversion to Warfarin**
  - Argatroban prolongs the INR. Therefore, when transitioning to warfarin, bridging requires consideration of both the dose of argatroban and a longer INR than typically encountered in practice.
    - For patients on argatroban at more than 2 mcg/kg/minute, argatroban should be lowered to 2 mcg/kg/minute with a repeated measure INR 4 to 6 hours after the dose.
    - For patients on argatroban at 2 mcg/kg/minute or less, it can be stopped when the INR is greater than 4 on combined warfarin and argatroban therapy. If argatroban is stopped, remeasure the INR 4 to 6 hours after, and restart argatroban if the INR is below 2.

- **Dabigatran Dyspepsia**
  - Many patients who begin dabigatran therapy cannot tolerate the associated dyspepsia and require conversion to an alternative antithrombotic strategy. If patients experience dyspepsia, suggest taking with meals, but remind patients that the capsules cannot be opened. Other interventions such as PPIs, H2RA, or antacids may play a role but require consideration for drug-drug or drug-disease interactions.
- **STEMI DTI Strategy**
  - Only bivalirudin currently has a role in the management of STEMI.
  - Depending on clinical practice, either a GPIIb/IIIa receptor antagonist plus anticoagulation (heparin or LMWH) or bivalirudin alone are acceptable strategies for adjuncts to primary PCI.
  - However, while head-to-head clinical trials have suggested these strategies are interchangeable in preventing secondary major cardiac events, there is significantly less bleeding observed in patients receiving bivalirudin.
- **Therapeutic Monitoring**
  - While either argatroban or bivalirudin can be therapeutically monitored using the aPTT, dabigatran does not reliably prolong this test and should not be used clinically for this purpose.
  - For dabigatran, less commonly available coagulation assays, including the dilute thrombin time (dTT), thrombin time (TT), and the ecarin clotting time (ECT), are hypothetically more accurate reflections of the anticoagulation effect.
  - However, these tests are neither commonly available nor are they FDA approved.
- **Prodrug**
  - Dabigatran etexilate is a prodrug that is converted by serum esterase to active dabigatran.
  - Similar to other DOACs, after an appropriate therapeutic dose, peak concentrations occur in 2 hours.
  - But despite being 85% eliminated renally (85%), dose adjustments are not generally recommended except for patients receiving dabigatran for non-valvular atrial fibrillation and a CrCl less between 15 - 30 mL/minute.

HIGH-YIELD BOARD EXAM ESSENTIALS
- **CLASSIC AGENTS:** Argatroban, bivalirudin, dabigatran
- **DRUG CLASS:** Direct thrombin inhibitors
- **INDICATIONS:** HIT, STEMI, DVT/PE, Afib
- **MECHANISM:** Inhibit thrombin by directly binding to its active site. In other words, these agents do not require antithrombin to exert this action.
- **SIDE EFFECTS:** Hemorrhage, dyspepsia (dabigatran)
- **CLINICAL PEARLS:**
  - Dabigatran is the only oral DTI and is used for the prevention of cardioembolic stroke on-valvular atrial fibrillation. It can be revered with idarucizumab.
  - Argatroban and bivalirudin are commonly the drugs of choice for HIT on board exams.
  - Argatroban prolongs the INR. Therefore, when transitioning to warfarin, bridging requires consideration of both the dose of argatroban and a longer INR than typically encountered in practice.

High-Yield Basic Pharmacology

- **Mechanism of Action**
  - Indirect anticoagulants that activate antithrombin, which then exerts antithrombotic effect by inhibiting coagulation factors.
- **Unfractionated vs. Fractionated**
  - As the name suggests, unfractionated heparin is a long polysaccharide chain with a therapeutically active pentasaccharide component.
  - The larger amount of sufficiently sized polysaccharide chains of heparin gives it a ratio of its anti-factor-Xa capacity to the anti-factor-IIa capacity of 1:1.
  - Conversely, that ratio anti-factor-Xa capacity to anti-factor-IIa for LMWHs is approximately 3 to 4:1.
  - With fondaparinux, it does not possess pentasaccharide chains sufficiently long to bridge antithrombin to thrombin.

Primary Net Benefit

- Heparin, LMWH, and fondaparinux are used extensively for anticoagulant indications, and each possesses unique pharmacokinetics that can be used to help guide the selection of the appropriate therapy.

Heparin and Low Molecular Weight Heparins - Drug Class Review			
High-Yield Med Reviews			
Mechanism of Action: *Indirect anticoagulants that activate antithrombin, which then exerts antithrombotic effect by inhibiting coagulation factors.*			
Class Effects: Heparin, LMWH, and fondaparinux are used extensively for anticoagulant indications, and each possesses unique pharmacokinetics that can be used to help guide the selection of the appropriate therapy.			
Generic Name	**Brand Name**	**Indication(s) or Uses**	**Notes**
Dalteparin	Fragmin	<ul><li>Non-ST elevation acute coronary syndromes</li><li>Venous thromboembolism prophylaxis</li><li>Venous thromboembolism treatment in patients with active cancer</li><li>Venous thromboembolism treatment in pediatric patients</li></ul>	<ul><li>**Dosing (Adult):**<ul><li>NSTEMI with non-invasive intervention- 120 units/kg sq every 12 hours for 5 to 8 days (maximum 10,000 units).</li><li>VTE prophylaxis- 5,000 units sq daily</li></ul></li><li>**Dosing (Peds):**<ul><li>VTE prophylaxis: <50 kg, 100 units/kg/dose sq q24h (target anti-Xa 0.2 to 0.4 units/mL) (maximum 5,000 units)</li><li>VTE treatment: Age under 2 years 150 units/kg/dose sq q12h.</li><li>2 years to 8 years, 125 units/kg/dose sq q12h.</li><li>8 years or older 100 units/kg/dose sq q12h.</li></ul></li><li>**CYP450 Interactions:** No CYP interactions</li><li>**Renal or Hepatic Dose Adjustments:**<ul><li>CrCl less than 30 mL/minute is not recommended, although this is controversial.</li></ul></li><li>**Dosage Forms:** Subcutaneous solution</li></ul>

Heparin and Low Molecular Weight Heparins - Drug Class Review
High-Yield Med Reviews

Generic Name	Brand Name	Indication(s) or Uses	Notes

Enoxaparin	Lovenox	▪ Acute coronary syndromes
		▪ Deep vein thrombosis treatment (acute)
		▪ Venous thromboembolism prophylaxis
			▪ **Dosing (Adult):**
			  – ACS or VTE treatment- 1 mg/kg SQ q12h.
			  – STEMI with PCI- Younger than 75 years- IV bolus of 30 mg plus 1 mg/kg SQ q12h (maximum of 100 mg). No IV bolus for patients 75 years or older.
			  – VTE prophylaxis: 40 mg SQ daily, or 30 mg SQ q12h.
			▪ **Dosing (Peds):**
			  – VTE Prophylaxis: 1 to 2 months, 0.75 mg/kg/dose SQ q12h. Two months or older, 0.5 mg/kg/dose SQ q12h.
			  – Therapeutic dosing: 1 to 2 months, 1.5 mg/kg/dose SQ q12h
			▪ **CYP450 Interactions:** No CYP interactions
			▪ **Renal or Hepatic Dose Adjustments:**
			  – VTE prophylaxis- 30 mg SQ daily
			  – ACS or VTE treatment- 1 mg/kg SQ daily
			▪ **Dosage Forms:** Injection solution, subcutaneous solution

Fondaparinux	Arixtra	▪ Deep vein thrombosis
		▪ Pulmonary embolism
		▪ Venous thromboembolism prophylaxis in surgical patients
			▪ **Dosing (Adult):**
			  – VTE treatment for patients less than 50 kg: 5 mg SQ daily; patients between 50 to 100 kg: 7.5 mg SQ daily; greater than 100 kg: 10 mg SQ daily.
			  – VTE prophylaxis- 2.5 mg SQ daily
			▪ **Dosing (Peds):**
			  – VTE treatment- 0.1 mg/kg/dose SQ daily
			▪ **CYP450 Interactions:** None
			▪ **Renal or Hepatic Dose Adjustments:**
			  – Contraindicated in patients with CrCl less than 30 mL/minute
			▪ **Dosage Forms:** Subcutaneous solution

Heparin and Low Molecular Weight Heparins - Drug Class Review
High-Yield Med Reviews

Generic Name	Brand Name	Indication(s) or Uses	Notes

Heparin	N/A	▪ Anticoagulation	▪ **Dosing (Adult):**
			  – ACS: 60 units/kg IV bolus followed by 12 units/kg/hour IV infusion. If using fibrinolytic strategy, maximum bolus dose of 4000 units, and maximum infusion rate of 1000 units/hour.
			  – VTE treatment: 80 units/kg IV bolus followed by 18 units/kg/hour IV infusion.
			  – VTE prophylaxis: 5000 units SQ q8h.
			▪ **Dosing (Peds):**
			  – Systemic heparinization:
			    ▪ Age 0 to 1 year: 75 units/kg IV bolus (over 10 minutes) followed by 28 units/kg/hour
			    ▪ Age over 1 year: 75 units/kg IV bolus (over 10 minutes) followed by 20 units/kg/hour
			▪ **CYP450 Interactions:** None
			▪ **Renal or Hepatic Dose Adjustments:**
			  – None, adjust doses to target aPTT or anti-Xa
			▪ **Dosage Forms:** Injection solution

High-Yield Clinical Knowledge

- **Antithrombin**
  - Heparin, LWMH, and fondaparinux bind to antithrombin, creating a conformational change that exposes the active site more readily to target coagulation factors (in addition to other proteases).
  - Antithrombin bound to heparin, LWMH, and fondaparinux accelerates the factor Xa inhibition.
  - For factor IIa (thrombin) inhibition, only heparin and LMWHs (but not fondaparinux) with sufficient polysaccharide chains (ones longer than 18 saccharide units) to bridge both antithrombin and thrombin.
  - After antithrombin binds to either factor, the anticoagulant dissociates from the complex and catalyzes other antithrombin molecules.
- **Body Weight Dosing**
  - Weight-based doses of enoxaparin of 1 mg/kg subcutaneously every 12 hours have been reliably used in patients up to 150 kg.
  - In morbidly obese patients weighing more than 150 mg/kg, there is observational literature to guide dosing, but in general, dosing enoxaparin on actual body weight in morbidly obese patients over-exposes patients to enoxaparin, and should be dosed on ideal or adjust body weight and titrated to target anti-Xa level.
- **Reversal of Anticoagulation**
  - The anticoagulant effects of heparin, LMWH, and (potentially) fondaparinux may be reversed with protamine sulfate.
  - Protamine sulfate rapidly reverses heparin's anticoagulant effect by binding directly to heparin, thereby reversing its anticoagulant effect.
  - Protamine should be dosed as a function of the remaining therapeutic heparin, with an empiric dose of 1 mg of protamine for every 100 units of heparin remaining in the patient.
  - However, caution should be taken to estimate the remaining heparin (based on t1/2 of 1.5 hours) since excessive protamine sulfate can exert an anticoagulant effect of its own.
  - It's also important to note that protamine only partially reverses the anticoagulant activity of LMWH and has no effect on that fondaparinux.

- **ACT vs. aPTT**
  - In patients undergoing percutaneous coronary intervention (PCI), or cardiac bypass, large doses of heparin are generally used as a means to prevent early clotting.
  - However, the doses used in this scenario are often much higher than those used elsewhere clinically.
  - These doses are sufficiently high to prolong the aPTT.
  - Therefore, an alternative, less-sensitive coagulation test, the ACT, is utilized to monitor therapy in this situation.

HIGH-YIELD BOARD EXAM ESSENTIALS

- **CLASSIC AGENTS:** Dalteparin, enoxaparin, fondaparinux, heparin
- **DRUG CLASS:** Heparin and LMWH
- **INDICATIONS:** Acute MI, DVT/PE treatment and prophylaxis
- **MECHANISM:** Activate antithrombin and enhance its ability to inactivate coagulation factors along the coagulation pathway.
- **SIDE EFFECTS:** Hemorrhage, HIT
- **CLINICAL PEARLS:**
  - All agents require antithrombin to be present to provide anticoagulation. Thus, patients with AT deficiency may not receive a therapeutics effect.
  - Only unfractionated heparin can be monitored with aPTT or ACT.
  - The risk of HIT is greatest with heparin > LMWH > fondaparinux.
  - Heparin, LMWH, and (potentially) fondaparinux may be reversed with protamine sulfate, which rapidly reverses heparin's anticoagulant effect by binding directly to heparin, thereby reversing its anticoagulant effect.

High-Yield Basic Pharmacology

- Inhibition of FXa affects the coagulation pathways in both the common pathway and the extrinsic pathway.
- By preventing the activation of FXa, the prothrombinase complex (FXa-Va), oral Factor Xa inhibitors prevent the cleavage of FII to FIIa in the extrinsic pathway/initiation phase of coagulation.
  - Without this generation of small amounts of FIIa, the intrinsic pathway/amplification phase cannot become initiated, and thus impairs the generation of physiologic concentrations of FIIa
- Peak plasma levels of apixaban and rivaroxaban are achieved within 2 hours, which is comparable to the initiation of parenteral heparin.
  - This rapid and reliable onset of action permits patients to be discharged from emergency departments on apixaban or rivaroxaban for the treatment of VTE to follow up in an out-patient setting.

Primary Net Benefit

- Antithrombotic therapeutic benefits as good as warfarin (rivaroxaban), and superior to warfarin (apixaban), with less routine monitoring, and drug interactions.

Oral Factor Xa Inhibitors - Drug Class Review			
High-Yield Med Reviews			
Mechanism of Action: Oral Factor Xa Inhibitors (apixaban, edoxaban, rivaroxaban) - Direct factor Xa inhibitor, preventing the conversion of prothrombin to thrombin.			
Class Effects: _Increases clotting time, decreasing the risk of thrombosis._			
Generic Name	**Brand Name**	**Indication(s) or Uses**	**Notes**
Apixaban	Eliquis	<ul><li>Atrial fibrillation</li><li>Treatment of VTE</li></ul>	<ul><li>**Dosing (Adult):**<ul><li>Afib - Oral 5 mg twice daily</li><li>DVT/PE - 10 mg twice daily for 7 days followed by 5 mg twice daily</li></ul></li><li>**Dosing (Peds):** No specific recommendations</li><li>**CYP450 Interactions:** Substrate of CYP1A2, CYP2C19, CYP2C8, CYP2C9, CYP3A4, and P-gp</li><li>**Renal or Hepatic Dose Adjustments:**<ul><li>Afib: Reduce to 2.5 mg BID if:</li><li>Age 80 years or older</li><li>Bodyweight 60 kg or less</li><li>Serum creatinine 1.5 mg/dL or higher</li><li>Child-Pugh C - Not recommended</li></ul></li><li>**Dosage Forms:** Oral (tablet)</li></ul>

Oral Factor Xa Inhibitors - Drug Class Review
High-Yield Med Reviews

Generic Name	Brand Name	Indication(s) or Uses	Notes

Edoxaban	Savaysa	• Atrial fibrillation
		• Treatment of VTE
			• **Dosing (Adult):**
			  - Afib - Oral 60 mg once daily
			  - DVT/PE
			    ▪ Patient weight greater than 60 kg, 60 mg once daily.
			    ▪ Patient weight 60 kg or less, 30 mg once daily
			• **Dosing (Peds):** No specific recommendations
			• **CYP450 Interactions:** Substrate P-gp
			• **Renal or Hepatic Dose Adjustments:**
			  - CrCl greater than 95 mL/minute OR less than 15 mL/minute - use not recommended
			  - CrCl 15 to 50 mL/minute - 30 mg daily
			  - Child-Pugh B or C - Not recommended
			• **Dosage Forms:** Oral (tablet)

Rivaroxaban	Xarelto	• Atrial fibrillation
		• Treatment of VTE
			• **Dosing (Adult):**
			  - Afib - Oral 20 mg once daily with food
			  - DVT/PE - 15 mg twice daily with food for 21 days followed by 20 mg once daily with food
			• **Dosing (Peds):** No specific recommendations
			• **CYP450 Interactions:** Substrate of CYP2J2, CYP3A4, P-gp
			• **Renal or Hepatic Dose Adjustments:**
			  - Afib - 15 mg daily with food if CrCl between 15 to 50 mL/minute.
			  - Avoid use if CrCl less than 15 mL/minute
			• **Dosage Forms:** Oral (tablet)

High-Yield Clinical Knowledge

- **Apixaban Dose Adjustments**
  - Patients receiving apixaban for nonvalvular atrial fibrillation should receive a reduced dose of 2.5 mg twice daily if they have at least two of the following:
    - Age 80 years or older, bodyweight 60 kg or less, or serum creatinine 1.5 mg/dL or higher.
  - The current prescribing information does not provide support for using apixaban in patients on hemodialysis.
- **Edoxaban And Normal Renal Function**
  - Uniquely, edoxaban should not be used in patients that have either normal renal function (CrCl above 95 mL/min) or severely impaired renal function (CrCl less than 15 mL/min).
- **Rivaroxaban Once or Twice Daily**
  - Apixaban requires twice-daily dosing compared to rivaroxaban which can be administered once daily.
    - This is, in part, due to apixaban's 50% smaller volume of distribution compared to rivaroxaban.
- **Reversal of Oral Factor Xa Inhibitors**
  - Prothrombin complex concentrate (PCC) can be used to reverse the antithrombotic effects of warfarin in patients with acute major hemorrhage, require emergent surgical intervention, and/or have supratherapeutic INRs.

- The initial variable, weight-based dosing for Kcentra (PCC) has been replaced by a lower, fixed-dose regimen.
- Patients achieve a similar reduction of the INR and hemostasis with a lower incidence of thrombosis.
    - Andexanet alfa
        - Directly binds and sequesters apixaban and rivaroxaban, halting their antithrombotic actions, in addition to inhibition of tissue factor pathway inhibitors.
- **Obesity and Oral FXa Inhibitors**
    - Patients who weigh more than 120 kg have not been adequately prospectively studied to develop strong recommendations regarding the use of oral Factor Xa inhibitors.
- **Edoxaban Restrictions**
    - Unlike the other available oral FXa inhibitors and warfarin, the use of edoxaban for VTE and atrial fibrillation is limited to specific populations.
        - Treatment of venous thromboembolism with edoxaban is permitted after 5 to 10 days of initial therapy with a parenteral anticoagulant.
        - For edoxaban use in patients with nonvalvular atrial fibrillation, patients must have a CrCl less than or equal to 95 mL/minute.

HIGH-YIELD BOARD EXAM ESSENTIALS

- **CLASSIC AGENTS:** Apixaban, edoxaban, rivaroxaban
- **DRUG CLASS:** Oral Factor Xa inhibitors
- **INDICATIONS:** Nonvalvular atrial fibrillation, VTE (treatment and prophylaxis)
- **MECHANISM:** Prevent the conversion of prothrombin to thrombin by direct selective and reversible inhibition of free and clot-bound factor Xa (FXa).
- **SIDE EFFECTS:** Bleeding
- **CLINICAL PEARLS:**
    - Many of these agents are considered alternatives to warfarin in most cases.
    - Unlike fondaparinux, these agents are all oral and do not require the presence of antithrombin to work.
    - Edoxaban should not be used in patients that have either normal renal function (CrCl above 95 mL/min) or severely impaired renal function (CrCl less than 15 mL/min).
    - Andexanet alfa can reverse these agents.

High-Yield Basic Pharmacology

- **Mechanism of Action**
  - Inhibits the activation of the coagulation factors II, VII, IX, and X as well as proteins C and S.
- **Racemic Mixture**
  - Warfarin is a racemic mixture of R- and S-warfarin. S-warfarin is the more active component and is metabolized by CYP2C9.
    - R-warfarin is metabolized specifically by CYP1A2 and CYP3A4.
- **Polymorphisms**
  - Patients with polymorphisms in CYP2C9 and/or in VKORC1 gene expression can have substantially different responses to warfarin.
    - In poor metabolizer CYP2C9 subtypes (increased risk of bleeding), there is no evidence to suggest there are measurable differences in clinically relevant bleeding or thromboembolic outcomes.
- **Clotting Factor Concentration**
  - A typical target therapeutic INR of 2 to 3 for warfarin therapy requires vitamin K-dependent factor concentrations to decline to approximately 25% to 30% of normal values.

Primary Overall Net Benefit

- Antithrombotic with an extensive history of preventing thromboembolism (stroke and VTE) but higher risk of clinically relevant bleeding than oral Factor-Xa inhibitors.

Vitamin K Antagonist - Drug Class Review			
High-Yield Med Reviews			
Mechanism of Action: *Vitamin K Antagonists (Warfarin) - Inhibits the activation of the coagulation factors II, VII, IX, and X as well as proteins C and S.*			
Class Effects: *Increases clotting time, decreasing the risk of thrombosis.*			
Generic Name	**Brand Name**	**Main Indication(s) or Uses**	**Notes**

Warfarin	Coumadin
	Jantoven
		• Treatment of VTE
		• Atrial fibrillation
		• Stroke
		• Post-myocardial infarction
			• **Dosing (Adult):** Dosing ranges depending on target INR
			  – Oral initial doses of 2.5 to 10 mg once daily
			• **Dosing (Peds):** Dosing ranges depending on target INR
			  – Oral initial dose of 0.2 mg/kg once daily (Maximum 10 mg)
			• **CYP450 Interactions:** Substrate of CYP2C19, CYP2C9, CYP3A4, CYP1A2
			• **Renal or Hepatic Dose Adjustments:**
			  – No specific empiric adjustments, but hepatic failure patients likely more sensitive to warfarin.
			• **Dosage Forms:** Oral (tablet)

High-Yield Clinical Knowledge

- **Warfarin Pharmacology**
  - Although warfarin rapidly achieves peak concentrations and inhibits vitamin k regeneration (within 3 hours), its therapeutic onset for initiation of therapy is days.
  - This delayed effect is because the existing stores of vitamin K must be depleted, and the active coagulation factors are removed from circulation in accordance with the duration of their half-life.
    - The factor half-life for each vitamin K dependent clotting factor is:
      - Factor VII, 5 hours
      - Factor IX, 24 hours
      - Factor X, 48 hours
      - Factor II, 60 hours
      - Protein C/S, 7 hours
- **Meaningful Pharmacokinetics**
  - The half-life of warfarin is approximately 35 hours.
    - While the half-lives of the coagulation factors are often associated with the onset of therapy, the half-life of warfarin itself is also relevant to its duration of action, which can be days after the drug has been discontinued.
  - Warfarin is extensively bound to plasma albumin (90%).
    - Drug-interactions that displace or compete with warfarin for albumin, or disease states causing hypoalbuminemia, patients will be exposed to a higher proportion of active (free) drugs.
- **Vitamin K Reversal**
  - Whenever vitamin K is used to reverse the antithrombotic effect of warfarin, the underlying thrombotic risk returns.
    - In patients with a high thromboembolism risk, the most cautious method to correct hemorrhaging should be considered and use appropriately dosed vitamin K (phytonadione) of INR overcorrection.
- **Effect on Existing Thrombi**
  - At therapeutic INRs, warfarin may prevent existing thrombi from expanding but has no direct effect on previously circulating clotting factors or previously formed thrombus.
- **Dosing and Monitoring**
  - Warfarin therapy is adjusted to target INR, typically 2 to 3, but varies depending on the indication.
    - Dose adjustments should be calculated, in most patients, with dose adjustments of 5 to 25% (up or down) based on the average weekly dose.
  - Once target INR is achieved, the interval of monitoring can increase (up to 12 weeks), with acute adjustments for surgical procedures, new or discontinued drugs, or changes in clinical status.

HIGH-YIELD BOARD EXAM ESSENTIALS

- **CLASSIC AGENTS:** Warfarin
- **DRUG CLASS:** Vitamin K antagonist
- **INDICATIONS:** Atrial fibrillation, myocardial infarction, secondary prevention, VTE (treatment and prophylaxis)
- **MECHANISM:** Inhibits the activation of the coagulation factors II, VII, IX, and X as well as proteins C and S.
- **SIDE EFFECTS:** Bleeding, contraindicated in pregnancy
- **CLINICAL PEARLS:**
  - Although warfarin rapidly achieves peak concentrations and inhibits vitamin k regeneration (within 3 hours), its therapeutic onset for initiation of therapy is days. This delayed effect is because the existing stores of vitamin K must be depleted, and the active coagulation factors are removed from circulation in accordance with the duration of their half-life.
  - Reversal agent is vitamin K.

High-Yield Basic Pharmacology

- **Mechanism of Action**
  - Reversibly inhibits platelet aggregation by binding to the GPIIb/IIIa receptor on the platelet surface and prevents fibrin binding.
- **Reversibility and Receptor Affinity**
  - Abciximab is a relatively nonspecific chimeric monoclonal antibody (MAB) that irreversibly inhibits platelet aggregation with a receptor binding ratio of approximately 2:1.
  - Conversely, both eptifibatide and tirofiban are highly specific, reversible inhibitors of platelet aggregation. In therapeutic terms, the latter agents are associated with a higher degree of acute inhibition of platelet activity in a ratio of approximately 1000:1.

Primary Net Benefit

- These agents are potent inhibitors of platelet aggregation, but all require the coadministration of anticoagulation with heparin or low molecular weight heparins.

Glycoprotein IIb/IIIa inhibitor - Drug Class Review High-Yield Med Reviews			
Mechanism of Action: *Reversibly inhibits platelet aggregation by binding to the GPIIb/IIIa receptor on the platelet surface and prevents fibrin binding.*			
Class Effects: *Prevents early thrombosis of coronary artery and stenting devices. Increases risk of hemorrhage.*			
Generic Name	**Brand Name**	**Indication(s) or Uses**	**Notes**

Abciximab	ReoPro	• Percutaneous coronary intervention
		• Unstable angina/non-ST-elevation myocardial infarction
			• **Dosing (Adult):**
			  – IV bolus of 0.25 mg/kg 10 to 60 minutes prior PCI. Can continue 0.125 mcg/kg/minute (maximum: 10 mcg/minute) for 12 hours.
			  – For NSTEMI use an initial bolus of 0.25 mg/kg followed by infusion at 10 mcg/minute until 1 hour after PCI.
			• **Dosing (Peds):** Not used
			• **CYP450 Interactions:** No CYP interactions
			• **Renal or Hepatic Dose Adjustments:** None
			• **Dosage Forms:** IV solution

Eptifibatide	Integrilin	• Percutaneous coronary intervention with or without coronary stenting	• **Dosing (Adult):**
			  – IV bolus of 180 mcg/kg q10minutes for 2 doses.
			    • Start continuous infusion of 2 mcg/kg/minute after the first bolus. (Maximum bolus: 22.6 mg; maximum infusion: 15 mg/hr)
			• **Dosing (Peds):** Not used
			• **CYP450 Interactions:** No CYP interactions
			• **Renal or Hepatic Dose Adjustments:**
			  – CrCl less than 50 mL/minute lower continuous infusion starting dose of 1 mcg/kg/minute (maximum 7.5 mg/hour).
			  – Should not be used in ESRD patients on HD.
			• **Dosage Forms:** IV solution

Glycoprotein IIb/IIIa inhibitor - Drug Class Review			
High-Yield Med Reviews			
Generic Name	**Brand Name**	**Indication(s) or Uses**	**Notes**
Tirofiban	Aggrastat	▪ Unstable angina/non-ST-elevation myocardial infarction	▪ **Dosing (Adult):** − IV bolus 25 mcg/kg over 5 minutes followed by 0.15 mcg/kg/minute continued for up to 18 hours. ▪ **Dosing (Peds):** Not used ▪ **CYP450 Interactions:** None ▪ **Renal or Hepatic Dose Adjustments:** − CrCl less than or equal to 60 mL/minute, no change in bolus, but a lower infusion of 0.075 mcg/kg/minute continued for up to 18 hours. ▪ **Dosage Forms:** IV solution

High-Yield Clinical Knowledge

- **Abciximab Antibodies**
  - Abciximab use can induce the formation of human antichimeric antibodies, leading to acute hypersensitivity reactions.
  - Patients receiving abciximab for the first time have a risk of reaction of approximately 6%, but with repeated exposure after the second administration increases to 27%.
  - If patients receive abciximab four or more times, their risk of acute hypersensitivity is as high as 44%.
- **Contraindications**
  - The contraindications to using a GPIIb/IIIa inhibitor are analogous to the contraindications to fibrinolytics (i.e., alteplase).
  - These contraindications include any patient with a history of hypersensitivity to any product component, active internal bleeding or a history of bleeding diathesis, major surgical procedure, or severe physical trauma within the previous 4 to 6 weeks.
  - There are additional agent-specific contraindications, including the presence of abciximab antibodies or previous exposure.
- **Acute Myocardial Infarction**
  - Thrombocytopenia due to GPIIb/IIIa inhibitors may be difficult to distinguish from heparin-induced thrombocytopenia since these agents are given concomitantly.
    - However, thrombocytopenia due to GPIIb/IIIa inhibitors is more likely to cause rapid thrombocytopenia within hours of administration and a greater absolute reduction in platelet level.
- **Antithrombotic Strategy**
  - There is clinical equipoise with regards to adjunct antithrombotic strategy during PCI.
  - Depending on clinical practice, either a GPIIb/IIIa receptor antagonist plus anticoagulation (heparin or LMWH) or bivalirudin alone are acceptable practices.
  - While head-to-head clinical trials have suggested these strategies are interchangeable in preventing secondary major cardiac events, there is significantly less bleeding observed in patients receiving bivalirudin.
  - Patients receiving fibrinolytic therapy for STEMI should not receive a GPIIb/IIIa receptor antagonist due to the significantly higher risk of hemorrhage.
- **Acute Stroke**
  - Eptifibatide was investigated as an adjunct to alteplase for acute ischemic stroke. However, the results of the CLEAR-ER study did not demonstrate a therapeutic benefit.

HIGH-YIELD BOARD EXAM ESSENTIALS

- **CLASSIC AGENTS:** Abciximab, eptifibatide, tirofiban
- **DRUG CLASS:** GP IIb/IIIa inhibitors
- **INDICATIONS:** Acute myocardial infarction, adjunct to percutaneous coronary intervention
- **MECHANISM:** Inhibit fibrinogen from binding to the platelet glycoprotein IIb/IIIa receptors.
- **SIDE EFFECTS:** Acute hypersensitivity (abciximab), hemorrhage
- **CLINICAL PEARLS:**
  - These agents are potent inhibitors of platelet aggregation, but all require the coadministration of anticoagulation with heparin or low molecular weight heparins.
  - Abciximab is the only agent that is a monoclonal antibody (MAB) that irreversibly inhibits platelet aggregation whereas the agents are not MABs and are reversible.

High-Yield Basic Pharmacology

- **Mechanism of Action**
  - Irreversible (clopidogrel, prasugrel) or reversible (cangrelor, and ticagrelor) inhibitor of platelet P2Y12 receptor, preventing ADP from binding and activating the glycoprotein GPIIb/IIIa complex, thereby inhibiting platelet aggregation.
- **Reversibility**
  - The reversible inhibitors of P2Y12 are reversible in the sense that they disassociate from their binding site, which permits restoration of normal platelet aggregation.
    - This is one of the reasons that ticagrelor must be dosed twice daily.
- **Bradycardia**
  - Ticagrelor's unique mechanism increases the risk of symptomatic bradycardia and shortness of breath in some patients.
    - This results from ticagrelor's effect on the inhibition of adenosine degradation and inhibition of adenosine uptake by erythrocytes.
    - This interaction produces an increase in adenosine exposure that likely explains these unique adverse effects.

Primary Net Benefit

- First-line antiplatelet agents for patient's post-myocardial infarction, stroke, or in peripheral arterial disease.

Thienopyridines - Drug Class Review			
High-Yield Med Reviews			
Mechanism of Action: *Irreversible (clopidogrel, prasugrel) or reversible (cangrelor, and ticagrelor) inhibitor of platelet P2Y12 receptor, preventing ADP from binding and activating the glycoprotein GPIIb/IIIa complex, thereby inhibiting platelet aggregation*			
Class Effects: First-line antiplatelet agents for patients who are post-myocardial infarction, stroke, or in peripheral arterial disease.			
Generic Name	**Brand Name**	**Indication(s) or Uses**	**Notes**
Cangrelor	Kengreal	• Adjunct to PCI	• **Dosing (Adult):** – IV bolus 30 mcg/kg prior to PCI, 4 mcg/kg/minute for at least 2 hours or for the duration of the PCI, whichever is longer. • **Dosing (Peds):** Not used • **CYP450 Interactions:** None • **Renal or Hepatic Dose Adjustments:** None • **Dosage Forms:** IV solution

Clopidogrel	Plavix	• Acute coronary syndrome
		• Secondary prevention of MI, stroke, or PAD
			• **Dosing (Adult):**
			  – Oral LD 300 to 600 mg, then 75 mg once daily
			• **Dosing (Peds):**
			  – Oral 0.2 to 1 mg/kg once daily
			• **CYP450 Interactions:** Inhibits CYP2B6, CYP2C8, substrate of CYP3A4, and CYP2C19
			• **Renal or Hepatic Dose Adjustments:** None
			• **Dosage Forms:** Oral (tablet)

Thienopyridines - Drug Class Review
High-Yield Med Reviews

Generic Name	Brand Name	Indication(s) or Uses	Notes

Prasugrel	Effient	• Acute coronary syndrome	• **Dosing (Adult):**
			  – Oral LD 60 mg before PCI, followed by 5 to 10 mg daily
			    • Over 60 kg, 10 mg once daily
			    • Less than 60 kg, 5 mg once daily
			• **Dosing (Peds):** Not used
			• **CYP450 Interactions:** Substrate of CYP2B6, CYP3A4
			• **Renal or Hepatic Dose Adjustments:** None
			• **Dosage Forms:** Oral (tablet)

Ticagrelor	Brilinta	• Acute coronary syndrome
		• CAD primary prevention
			• **Dosing (Adult):**
			  – Oral LD 180 mg once, followed by 90 mg BID for 12 months.
			    • After 12 months, reduce dose to 60 mg BID.
			• **Dosing (Peds):** Not used
			• **CYP450 Interactions:** Substrate of CYP3A4
			• **Renal or Hepatic Dose Adjustments:** None
			• **Dosage Forms:** Oral (tablet)

Ticlopidine	Ticlid (Not available in USA)	• Stroke primary and secondary prevention	• **Dosing (Adult):** – Oral 250 mg twice daily • **Dosing (Peds):** Not used • **CYP450 Interactions:** Substrate of CYP3A4, CYP1A2, CYP2B6, CYP2C19, CYP2D6 • **Renal or Hepatic Dose Adjustments:** None • **Dosage Forms:** Oral (tablet)

High-Yield Clinical Knowledge

- **Clopidogrel 300 mg vs 600 mg**
  - Clopidogrel loading doses of 600 mg should be administered to patients with STEMI undergoing emergent PCI, PCI at least 24 hours after fibrinolytic therapy, and NSTEMI patients undergoing an early invasive approach.
    - The lower 300 mg loading dose should be used in STEMI if PCI occurs after a fibrinolytic strategy is chosen.
    - NSTEMI patients can receive either 300 mg or 600 mg loading dose if using an ischemia-guided approach.
- **Continuing Beyond 12 Months**
  - The AHA guidelines recommend dual antiplatelet therapy (DAPT) for at least 12 months in patients after PCI with drug-eluting stents.
    - However, continuing DAPT beyond 12 months is an area of uncertainty regarding the ideal duration and patient characteristics where the benefit outweighs the risk.
- **P2Y12 Prodrugs**
  - Clopidogrel and prasugrel are prodrugs that require CYP2C19 (clopidogrel) or CYP3A4 and CYP2B6 (prasugrel) for activation.
    - However, ticagrelor and its metabolite are active. Therefore, the risk of decreased absorption from PPI agents, strong CYP2B6 or 2C19, inhibitors does not exist with ticagrelor.

- But since CYP3A4 metabolizes ticagrelor, inhibitors of CYP3A4 would increase the exposure and risk of bleeding.

- **Parenteral Agent**
  - Cangrelor is the only thienopyridine that is available in the US as a parenteral dosage form.
  - After the loading dose, it can achieve platelet inhibition within 2 minutes, and once the infusion is stopped, restoration of normal platelet reactivity occurs within 1 to 2 hours.
    - In the CHAMPION trials, cangrelor may be as effective as a GP IIb/IIIa based strategy but is associated with less bleeding risk.
    - However, it is still yet to be determined whether cangrelor maintains similar efficacy and benefits compared to a bivalirudin-based PCI strategy since only 19% of the population of the CHAMPION-PHOENIX received this PCI strategy.

- **Aspirin and Ticagrelor**
  - In the PLATO study, there seemed to be an increased risk of stent thrombosis in patients receiving aspirin plus ticagrelor.
  - While this contradictory finding led to an FDA warning and limiting aspirin's dose in patients receiving ticagrelor, this finding was later linked to a small subgroup of patients in the United States (it was a multinational study) with other significant differences in baseline characteristics and clinical outcomes.
    - Therefore, while the warning to not exceed 100mg of aspirin daily with ticagrelor, analysis, and evaluation in additional patients established there is no actual clinically relevant interaction causing the combination to increase the risk of thrombosis.

- **Prasugrel Lower Dose 5 Mg Vs 10 Mg**
  - The TRITON-TIMI 38 study described below established the role of prasugrel in managing acute coronary syndromes where PCI is planned.
    - In this study, patients who are elderly (75 years or older), low body weight (less than 60 kg) had a higher risk of bleeding.

HIGH-YIELD BOARD EXAM ESSENTIALS

- **CLASSIC AGENTS:** Cangrelor, clopidogrel, prasugrel, ticagrelor
- **DRUG CLASS:** P2Y12 inhibitors
- **INDICATIONS:** Acute coronary syndrome, primary and secondary prevention of MI, stroke, or PAD
- **MECHANISM:** Irreversible (clopidogrel, prasugrel) or reversible (cangrelor, and ticagrelor) inhibitor of platelet P2Y12 receptor, preventing ADP from binding and activating the glycoprotein GPIIb/IIIa complex, thereby inhibiting platelet aggregation.
- **SIDE EFFECTS:** Bleeding, bradycardia (ticagrelor)
- **CLINICAL PEARLS:**
  - The reversible inhibitors of P2Y12 are reversible in the sense that they disassociate from their binding site, which permits restoration of normal platelet aggregation.
  - Traditionally, clopidogrel and prasugrel are considered to be irreversible inhibitors of platelet activation.
  - Cangrelor is a parenterally administered option for those going to the cath lab.

High-Yield Basic Pharmacology

- **Dipyridamole**
  - Causes inhibition of platelet aggregation by inhibiting adenosine deaminase and phosphodiesterase and thus preventing the degradation of cyclic AMP to 5'-AMP, which leads to intraplatelet accumulation of cyclic AMP.
  - It can also cause an increase in the release of prostacyclin or prostaglandin D2 and causes coronary vasodilation.
- **Cilostazol**
  - Inhibits phosphodiesterase III, thus preventing the degradation of cyclic AMP, causing a reversible inhibition of platelet aggregation, vasodilation, and inhibition of vascular smooth muscle cell proliferation.
- **Vorapaxar**
  - Leads to inhibition of platelet aggregation by inhibiting protease-activated receptor-1 (PAR-1), thrombin-induced, and thrombin receptor agonist peptide (TRAP)-induced platelet aggregation
    - Vorapaxar results in prolonged, irreversible inhibition of platelet activity within one week and persist for up to 4 weeks.
    - Consequently, vorapaxar is contraindicated in patients with active bleeding and patients with a history of stroke, transient ischemic attacks, or intracranial hemorrhage.

Primary Net Benefit

- Antiplatelet agents have fallen out of favor for the thienopyridine antiplatelet agents but remain used for unique indications, including diagnostic aids in CAD.

Other Antiplatelet - Drug Class Review			
High-Yield Med Reviews			
Mechanism of Action: *See above.*			
Class Effects: *Antithrombotic, antiplatelet effect*			
Generic Name	**Brand Name**	**Indication(s) or Uses**	**Notes**

Cilostazol	Pletal	• Intermittent claudication	• **Dosing (Adult):** Oral 100 mg twice daily
			• **Dosing (Peds):** Not used
			• **CYP450 Interactions:**
			  – Inhibitor of CYP3A4.
			  – Substrate of CYP 3A4, 2CYP C19, CYP 2D6, and CYP1A2
			• **Renal or Hepatic Dose Adjustments:** None
			• **Dosage Forms:** Oral (tablet, capsule)

Dipyridamole	Persantine
	Aggrenox
		• Secondary stroke and CV prevention
		• Diagnostic agent in CAD
			• **Dosing (Adult):**
			  – IV bolus of 0.56 mg/kg over 4 minutes (maximum dose 70 mg)
			  – Oral - aspirin 25 mg/dipyridamole ER 200 mg twice daily
			• **Dosing (Peds):**
			  – IV bolus of 0.56 mg/kg over 4 minutes (maximum dose 70 mg)
			  – Oral 2 to 5 mg/kg/day in divided doses
			• **CYP450 Interactions:** None
			• **Renal or Hepatic Dose Adjustments:** None
			• **Dosage Forms:** IV solution, Oral (tablet, capsule)

Other Antiplatelet - Drug Class Review
High-Yield Med Reviews

Generic Name	Brand Name	Indication(s) or Uses	Notes
Vorapaxar	Zontivity	• Thrombotic risk reduction with history of MI or PAD	• **Dosing (Adult):** – Oral 2.08 mg once daily in combination with aspirin and/or clopidogrel • **Dosing (Peds):** Not used • **CYP450 Interactions:** Substrate of CYP3A4, CYP2J2 • **Renal or Hepatic Dose Adjustments:** None • **Dosage Forms:** Oral (tablet)

High-Yield Clinical Knowledge

- **Dipyridamole and Cardiac Stress Testing**
  - Although used orally as an antiplatelet agent, dipyridamole also is used parenterally in pharmacologically-based cardiac nuclear stress tests.
    - This diagnostic procedure involves the injection of radioactive tracer, administered in conjunction with dipyridamole (or adenosine, or regadenoson), utilizing its coronary vasodilation properties.

- **Cilostazol, Milrinone and FDA Warnings**
  - As a phosphodiesterase III inhibitor, cilostazol exists in the same medication class as milrinone.
    - In the past, milrinone had been used orally as an agent to improve cardiac output in heart failure patients.
    - Still, it was found to increase mortality and subsequently removed from the market (oral dosage form only).
    - As a result of being in the same class, cilostazol also now carries an FDA warning stating its use is contraindicated with patients with heart failure of any severity.

- **Symptomatic Bradycardia and Exacerbation of Angina**
  - Dipyridamole, through its actions on adenosine deaminase as described previously, can increase the concentration of adenosine.
    - As a result, although platelet function is affected, the risk of adenosine exerting an effect on cardiac conduction increases.
    - Thus the high incidence of chest pain and bradycardia can be linked to this known effect, and its use should be limited in patients taking agents or food that can further prevent the metabolism of adenosine, including methylxanthines (caffeine, theobromine, or theophylline).

- **Secondary Stroke Prevention**
  - The American Stroke Association guidelines for secondary stroke prevention recommend either clopidogrel or the combination of aspirin-dipyridamole as antiplatelet therapy.
    - Many patients cannot tolerate the bradycardic and or angina-related adverse events that accompany dipyridamole therapy, and thus clopidogrel is often used as the primary agent.

HIGH-YIELD BOARD EXAM ESSENTIALS

- **CLASSIC AGENTS:** Cilostazol, dipyridamole, vorapaxar
- **DRUG CLASS:** Antiplatelet
- **INDICATIONS:** Stroke prevention, thrombotic risk reduction (post-MI or PAD)
- **MECHANISM:**
  - Cilostazol inhibits phosphodiesterase III, thus preventing the degradation of cyclic AMP, causing a reversible inhibition of platelet aggregation, vasodilation, and inhibition of vascular smooth muscle cell proliferation.
  - Dipyridamole inhibits adenosine deaminase and phosphodiesterase, preventing the degradation of cyclic AMP to 5'-AMP, which leads to intraplatelet accumulation of cyclic AMP.
  - Vorapaxar leads to inhibition of platelet aggregation by inhibiting protease-activated receptor-1 (PAR-1), thrombin-induced, and thrombin receptor agonist peptide (TRAP)-induced platelet aggregation.
- **SIDE EFFECTS:** Bleeding, bradycardia (dipyridamole), angina (dipyridamole)
- **CLINICAL PEARLS:** Dipyridamole, through its actions on adenosine deaminase as described previously, can increase the concentration of adenosine.

High-Yield Basic Pharmacology

- **Mechanism of Action**
  - Fibrinolytics break susceptible fibrin via activation of plasmin from plasminogen.
    - Specifically, these agents promote the initiation of fibrinolysis by producing plasmin from fibrin-bound plasminogen.

Primary Net Benefit

- Fibrinolytics are often referred to as thrombolytics. While these drugs work to dissolve a thrombus (a clot), they do so by ultimately breaking down fibrin.
  - To prevent confusion and an erroneous assumption that they have a direct effect on thrombin, these drugs will be referred to hereafter as fibrinolytics.

Thrombolytics - Drug Class Review			
High-Yield Med Reviews			
Mechanism of Action: Fibrinolytics break susceptible fibrin via activation of plasmin from plasminogen. Defibrotide achieves fibrinolysis via increases in endogenous t-PA, increasing thrombomodulin expression, decreasing von Willebrand factor, and plasminogen activator inhibitor-1.			
Class Effects: *Fibrin cross-link degradation and dissolution of a fibrin-based thrombus.*			
Generic Name	**Brand Name**	**Indication(s) or Uses**	**Notes**

Alteplase	Activase Cathflo Activase	• Acute ischemic stroke (AIS)
		 • Pulmonary embolism (PE)
		 • ST-elevation myocardial infarction (STEMI)
			• **Dosing (Adult):**
			   – AIS: 0.9 mg/kg with 10% (0.09 mg/kg) as IV bolus over 1 minute, followed immediately by 90% (0.81 mg/kg) over 1 hour. Maximum 90 mg total dose.
			   – PE: 100mg IV over 2 hours; 50 mg IV over OR 50 mg IV bolus repeated 15 minutes later by another 50 mg IV bolus (for massive PE cardiac arrest)
			   – STEMI: Patients over 67 kg receive 100 mg over 1.5 hours; administered as a 15 mg IV bolus over 1 to 2 minutes followed by infusions of 50 mg over 30 minutes, then 35 mg over 1 hour. Patients less than or equal to 67 kg receive 15 mg IV bolus over 1 to 2 minutes followed by infusions of 0.75 mg/kg (maximum of 50 mg) over 30 minutes, then 0.5 mg/kg (maximum 35 mg) over 1 hour. Maximum total dose of 100 mg
			 • **Dosing (Peds):**
			   – Same weight-based dose as adults. Additional off-label uses exist with varied specific doses.
			 • **CYP450 Interactions:** No CYP interactions
			 • **Renal or Hepatic Dose Adjustments:** None
			 • **Dosage Forms:** IV solution

Thrombolytics - Drug Class Review
High-Yield Med Reviews

Generic Name	Brand Name	Indication(s) or Uses	Notes

Defibrotide	Defitelio	• Sinusoidal obstruction syndrome (SOS)	• **Dosing (Adult):**
			  – IV solution 6.25 mg/kg over 2 hours, q6h for at least 21 days (maximum of 60 days). Must be infused with a 0.2-micron in-line filter.
			• **Dosing (Peds):**
			  – IV solution 6.25 mg/kg over 2 hours, q6h for at least 21 days (maximum of 60 days). Must be infused with a 0.2-micron in-line filter.
			• **CYP450 Interactions:** No CYP interactions
			• **Renal or Hepatic Dose Adjustments:** None
			• **Dosage Forms:** IV solution

Reteplase	Retavase	• ST-elevation myocardial infarction (STEMI)	• **Dosing (Adult):** – Initial dose of 10 mg once daily, increasing dose as tolerated to target range 20 to 40 mg once daily with maximum dose of 40 mg/day. • **Dosing (Peds):** Not used • **CYP450 Interactions:** None • **Renal or Hepatic Dose Adjustments:** None • **Dosage Forms:** IV solution
Tenecteplase	TNKase	• ST-elevation myocardial infarction (STEMI)	• **Dosing (Adult):** – Scaled weight based dosing. Less than 60 kg: 30 mg; ≥60 to <70 kg: 35 mg, ≥70 to <80 kg: 40 mg; ≥80 to <90 kg: 45 mg; ≥90 kg: 50 mg. Maximum dose of 50 mg • **Dosing (Peds):** Not used • **CYP450 Interactions:** None • **Renal or Hepatic Dose Adjustments: None** • **Dosage Forms:** IV solution

High-Yield Clinical Knowledge

- **Contraindications to Fibrinolysis**
  - Absolute Contraindications
    - Prior intracranial hemorrhage
    - Known structural cerebral vascular lesion
    - Known malignant intracranial neoplasm
    - Ischemic stroke within three months
    - Suspected aortic dissection
    - Active bleeding or bleeding diathesis (excluding menses)
    - Significant closed-head trauma or facial trauma within three months
  - Relative contraindications
    - Uncontrolled hypertension (systolic blood pressure > 180 mm Hg or diastolic blood pressure > 110 mm Hg)
    - Traumatic or prolonged CPR or major surgery within three weeks
    - Recent (within 2–4 weeks) internal bleeding
    - Noncompressible vascular punctures

- Current use of warfarin and INR > 1.7
- **Acute Ischemic Stroke Caveats to Contraindications**
  - Recent changes in recommendations have relaxed contraindications to alteplase for acute ischemic stroke. The specific contraindications that have been revised include:
    - Patients may receive alteplase in the setting of a historic intracranial hemorrhage, but not an acute hemorrhage.
    - Patients currently taking a DOAC and have taken a dose within 48 hours should not receive alteplase.
- **Hemorrhage and Angioedema**
  - Complications of fibrinolytics include bleeding, which is intuitive.
  - However, angioedema is a relatively prevalent adverse event occurring in 1% of patients.
    - To put this in context, angioedema occurs in approximately 0.8% of patients on ACE-inhibitors.

High-Yield Fast-Facts

- Some agents like tenecteplase are referred to as more 'fibrin specific.' This translates to less likely to activate counterregulatory enzymes such as PAI-1 (plasminogen activator inhibitor 1). However, the clinical benefit of this action has not always translated into patient-oriented benefits.
- Low doses of alteplase can be used to assist catheter clearance from thrombosed access sites. Under the brand name Cathflo, alteplase given at a dose of 2 mg can assist in catheter recanalization

---

HIGH-YIELD BOARD EXAM ESSENTIALS
- **CLASSIC AGENTS:** Alteplase, reteplase, tenecteplase, defibrotide
- **DRUG CLASS:** Fibrinolytics
- **INDICATIONS:** Acute ischemic stroke, acute myocardial infarction, acute pulmonary embolism, hepatic sinusoidal obstruction syndrome
- **MECHANISM:** Break susceptible fibrin via activation of plasmin from plasminogen. Specifically, these agents promote the initiation of fibrinolysis by producing plasmin from fibrin-bound plasminogen.
- **SIDE EFFECTS:** Hemorrhage, angioedema
- **CLINICAL PEARLS:**
  - Fibrinolytics are often referred to as thrombolytics. While these drugs work to dissolve a thrombus (a clot), they do so by ultimately breaking down fibrin.
  - Alteplase is indicated for acute ischemic stroke within 3 hrs of onset, submassive & massive PE, and STEMI within 12 hrs of onset.
  - Tenecteplase has the longest half-life and thus can be given as a single IVP dose for STEMI.

High-Yield Basic Pharmacology

- **Mechanism of Action**
  - Prevents potassium secretion by inhibiting sodium influx in the luminal membrane (amiloride, triamterene) or via inhibition of aldosterone on mineralocorticoid receptors in collecting tubules.

Primary Net Benefit

- Potassium-sparing diuretics are weak diuretics on their own but can be added to loop diuretic therapy with synergistic effects. Aldosterone antagonists reduce cardiac remodeling in heart failure with a mortality benefit.

Potassium-Sparing Diuretics - Drug Class Review			
High-Yield Med Reviews			
Mechanism of Action: *Prevents potassium secretion by inhibiting sodium influx in the luminal membrane (amiloride, triamterene) or via inhibition of aldosterone on mineralocorticoid receptors in collecting tubules.*			
Class Effects: *Diuresis, aldosterone antagonism reducing cardiac remodeling. Risk of hyperkalemia especially with salt-substitutes.*			
Generic Name	**Brand Name**	**Indication(s) or Uses**	**Notes**

Amiloride	Midamor	• Heart failure
		• Hypertension
			• **Dosing (Adult):**
			  - Oral 5 mg daily
			    • Maximum 40 mg/day
			• **Dosing (Peds):**
			  - Oral 0.3 to 0.625 mg/kg/day
			    • Maximum 20 mg/day
			• **CYP450 Interactions:** None
			• **Renal or Hepatic Dose Adjustments:**
			  - GFR between 10 and 50 mL/minute - reduce dose by 50%
			  - GFR less than 10 mL/minute - avoid use
			• **Dosage Forms:** Oral (tablet)

Eplerenone	Inspra	• Heart failure, post-MI
		• Hypertension
			• **Dosing (Adult):**
			  - Oral 25 mg daily
			    • Maximum 50 mg/day
			• **Dosing (Peds):**
			  - Not routinely used
			• **CYP450 Interactions:** Substrate of CYP 3A4
			• **Renal or Hepatic Dose Adjustments:**
			  - GFR between 31 and 50 mL/minute - an initial dose of 25 mg every other day, maximum 25 mg/day
			  - GFR 30 mL/minute or less - Not recommended
			• **Dosage Forms:** Oral (tablet)

Potassium-Sparing Diuretics - Drug Class Review
High-Yield Med Reviews

Generic Name	Brand Name	Indication(s) or Uses	Notes

Spironolactone	Aldactone	▪ Ascites
		▪ Heart failure
		▪ Hypertension
		▪ Primary hyperaldosteronism
			▪ **Dosing (Adult):**
			  – Oral 12.5 mg daily
			    ▪ Maximum 200 mg/day
			▪ **Dosing (Peds):**
			  – Oral 1 to 3 mg/kg/day
			    ▪ Maximum 3 mg/kg/day or 100 mg/day
			▪ **CYP450 Interactions:** None
			▪ **Renal or Hepatic Dose Adjustments:**
			  – GFR between 31 and 50 mL/minute - an initial dose of 12.5 mg every other day, maximum 25 mg/day
			  – GFR 30 mL/minute or less - Not recommended
			▪ **Dosage Forms:** Oral (solution, tablet)

Triamterene	Dyrenium	▪ Edema
		▪ Hypertension
			▪ **Dosing (Adult):**
			  – Oral 50 mg daily
			    ▪ Maximum 300 mg/day
			▪ **Dosing (Peds):**
			  – Oral 1 to 4 mg/kg/day divided into 1 to 2 doses
			    ▪ Maximum 6 mg/kg/day or 300 mg/day
			▪ **CYP450 Interactions:** None
			▪ **Renal or Hepatic Dose Adjustments:**
			  – GFR 50 mL/minute or less - Not recommended
			  – Severe hepatic impairment - contraindicated
			▪ **Dosage Forms:** Oral (capsule)

High-Yield Clinical Knowledge

- **Hyperkalemia Risk**
  - These agents pose a risk of hyperkalemia that can be minimized by avoiding use in specific patient populations.
    - Aldosterone antagonists should be avoided in patients with:
      - Serum creatinine concentration above 2.0 mg/dL in women or above 2.5 mg/dL in men or a creatinine clearance of less than 30 mL/minute.
      - Serum potassium concentration is greater than 5.0 mEq/L.
      - Taking potassium supplements or reduce the dose of potassium supplementation.
      - Concomitant NSAIDs or COX-2 inhibitors.
      - Concomitant high-dose ACE inhibitors or ARBs.
    - When starting eplerenone or spironolactone, potassium concentrations and kidney function should be checked 3 and 7 days after the initial dose.
- **Cardiac Remodeling**
  - Spironolactone or eplerenone should be used in HFrEF, specifically in patients NYHA class II to IV and in patients with acute HF or diabetes early after MI.

- Eplerenone and spironolactone exert a specific aldosterone antagonist effect in cardiac tissue that ultimately inhibits collagen deposition in the cardiac extracellular matrix and reduces cardiac fibrosis and ventricular remodeling.

- **Ascites**
  - Spironolactone and furosemide are used in combination in patients with ascites.
    - This combination has a specific ratio of spironolactone to furosemide of 100:40 (spironolactone 100 mg and furosemide 40 mg).
    - The maximum dose for this combination is spironolactone 400 mg and furosemide 160.

- **Heart Failure**
  - According to the current AHA guidelines, low-dose aldosterone antagonists should be added to standard therapy to improve heart failure symptoms, reduce the risk of heart failure hospitalizations, and increase survival in select patients.

- **Resistant Hypertension**
  - In patients with treatment-resistant hypertension (on ACE-inhibitor or ARB, CCB, and diuretic), spironolactone significantly improved the likelihood of achieving blood pressure targets than bisoprolol, doxazosin, or placebo. (PATHWAY-2. Lancet. 2015 Nov 21;386(10008):2059-2068.)

HIGH-YIELD BOARD EXAM ESSENTIALS

- **CLASSIC AGENTS:** Amiloride, eplerenone, spironolactone, triamterene
- **DRUG CLASS:** Aldosterone Antagonists; Potassium sparing diuretics
- **INDICATIONS:** Ascites (spironolactone), heart failure (eplerenone, spironolactone), hypertension (amiloride, eplerenone, spironolactone, triamterene), primary hyperaldosteronism (spironolactone)
- **MECHANISM:** Prevents potassium secretion by inhibiting sodium influx in the luminal membrane (amiloride, triamterene) or via inhibition of aldosterone on mineralocorticoid receptors in collecting tubules.
- **SIDE EFFECTS:** Gynecomastia (mainly spironolactone), impotence, and menstrual irregularities (spironolactone), dose-dependent hyperkalemia.
- **CLINICAL PEARLS:**
  - Aldosterone antagonists can prevent remodeling in patients with HF which is why they are recommended by the guidelines (supported by evidence from RALES trial and Ephesus Trial). They can elicit acidemia because the same process that prevents potassium elimination also prevents the elimination of hydrogen in the collecting tubule's intercalated cells, similar to a type IV renal tubular acidosis.
  - Spironolactone is commonly used in the chronic management of ascites from cirrhosis in high doses with a small dose of furosemide (dose ratio is 100:40) to prevent hyperkalemia.

High-Yield Basic Pharmacology

- **Mechanism of Action**
  - Inhibition of carbonic anhydrase blunts the reabsorption of sodium bicarbonate, promoting diuresis.
    - Carbonic anhydrase is responsible for converting carbonic acid to carbon dioxide at the renal luminal membrane and rehydration of carbon dioxide to the carbonic acid in the cytoplasm.
    - By blocking these processes, carbonic anhydrase inhibitors promote a reduction of hydrogen secretion, increased renal excretion of sodium, potassium, bicarbonate, and water
  - Mannitol is a solute that cannot be reabsorbed and increases the glomerulus' osmotic pressure, causing inhibition of tubular reabsorption of water and nearly all electrolytes.
- **Carbonic anhydrase inhibitors are sulfonamide derivatives**
  - There is a theoretical risk of cross-reactivity in patients with a history of sulfonamide hypersensitivity.
    - As a result of its sulfonamide structure, carbonic anhydrase inhibitors carry a risk of bone marrow depression, Stevens-Johnson Syndrome, and sulfonamide-like kidney injury.

Primary Net Benefit

- **Carbonic Anhydrase Inhibitors**
  - The limited diuretic effect, and clinically used for other indications where carbonic anhydrase inhibitors may be beneficial.
- **Osmotic Diuretics**
  - Used to decrease elevated intracranial pressure, with osmotic diuresis a notable sequela for this agent. As a result, hypertonic saline is becoming preferred since it maintains hemodynamic effects but does not induce osmotic diuresis.

Carbonic Anhydrase Inhibitors & Osmotic Diuretics - Drug Class Review			
High-Yield Med Reviews			
Mechanism of Action: *Carbonic anhydrase inhibitor - inhibits the reabsorption of sodium bicarbonate, promoting diuresis.* *Osmotic diuretic - Increases osmotic pressure of the glomerulus and inhibition of tubular reabsorption of water and electrolytes.*			
Class Effects: *Diuresis, intravascular volume decreases, electrolyte abnormalities.*			
Generic Name	**Brand Name**	**Indication(s) or Uses**	**Notes**
Acetazolamide	Diamox	<ul><li>Acute altitude/mountain sickness</li><li>Glaucoma/Elevated intraocular pressure</li><li>Edema</li><li>Epilepsy</li></ul>	<ul><li>**Dosing (Adult):**<ul><li>Oral 125 to 500 mg once to four times per day<ul><li>Maximum 30 mg/kg/day</li></ul></li><li>IV 500 mg once</li></ul></li><li>**Dosing (Peds):**<ul><li>Oral 2.5 to 30 mg/kg/dose q12h<ul><li>Maximum 1000 mg/day</li></ul></li></ul></li><li>**CYP450 Interactions:** None</li><li>**Renal or Hepatic Dose Adjustments:**<ul><li>Contraindicated in severe renal impairment</li><li>Contraindicated in patients with cirrhosis or marked liver disease</li></ul></li><li>**Dosage Forms:** IV solution, oral (extended-release capsule, immediate-release tablet)</li></ul>

Carbonic Anhydrase Inhibitors & Osmotic Diuretics - Drug Class Review
High-Yield Med Reviews

Generic Name	Brand Name	Indication(s) or Uses	Notes

Mannitol	Osmitrol	• Elevated intracranial pressure
		• Elevated intraocular pressure
			• **Dosing (Adult):**
			  – IV 0.25 to 2 g/kg/dose
			    • May repeat every 6 to 8 hours
			• **Dosing (Peds):**
			  – IV 0.25 to 2 g/kg/dose
			    • May repeat every 6 to 8 hours
			• **CYP450 Interactions:** None
			• **Renal or Hepatic Dose Adjustments:**
			  – PI states contraindicated in severe renal impairment, but this may not be observed clinically for these indications.
			• **Dosage Forms:** IV solution

Methazolamide	Neptazane	• Glaucoma/Elevated intraocular pressure	• **Dosing (Adult):**
			  – Oral 50 to 100 mg 2 to 3 times/day
			• **Dosing (Peds):**
			  – Not routinely used
			• **CYP450 Interactions:** None
			• **Renal or Hepatic Dose Adjustments:**
			  – Contraindicated in severe renal impairment
			  – Contraindicated in patients with cirrhosis or marked liver disease
			• **Dosage Forms:** Oral (tablet)

High-Yield Clinical Knowledge

- **Hyperchloremic Metabolic Acidosis**
  - Carbonic anhydrase inhibitors block the excretion of hydrogen ions accumulating in the plasma.
    - In normal healthy kidneys reabsorb bicarbonate and offsets the accumulation of hydrogen and ensuing acidosis.
    - With impaired renal function, high doses, or otherwise altered metabolic function, renal tubules' capacity to reabsorb bicarbonate is impaired, which ultimately leads to an increasing acidosis.
      - The acidosis typically resolves upon discontinuation of the carbonic anhydrase inhibitor.
- **Reflection coefficient**
  - The reflection coefficient is the relative impermeability of a given agent concerning the blood-brain barrier, where a reflection coefficient of zero suggests a free permeability molecule. At the same time, a value of 1 represents a completely impermeable molecule.
    - The reflection coefficient for mannitol is 0.9, and with a high dose and prolonged use, it can cross the blood-brain barrier.
    - With repeated dosing, mannitol crosses the blood-brain barrier, diminishing the osmotic gradient and the response to elevated intracranial.
- **Mannitol Administration**
  - Mannitol must be administered with a 5-micron in-line filter.
    - Mannitol is poorly soluble in water, frequently precipitates, and could cause vascular trauma and decreased therapeutic response to mannitol.
  - Mannitol may be stored in a warm environment to reduce the risk of crystallization. However, even after visual inspection, it is still required to be administered with an in-line filter.

- **Mannitol and Hypernatremia**
  - Although mannitol promotes water and sodium elimination, the proportion of natriuresis is relatively lower than free water diuresis.
  - With prolonged use, this effect can produce hypernatremia.
- **Starling Forces and Intracranial Pressure**
  - In addition to diuresis, mannitol promotes a shift in Starling forces and promotes water movement out of cells, reducing intracellular volume.
    - This effect is used as one method to reduce intracranial pressure or intraocular pressure.
- **Limited Carbonic Anhydrase Inhibitor Use as a Diuretic**
  - The use of carbonic anhydrase inhibitors as diuretics is rare, given the likelihood of developing metabolic acidosis with long-term use.

HIGH-YIELD BOARD EXAM ESSENTIALS

- **CLASSIC AGENTS:** Acetazolamide, mannitol, methazolamide
- **DRUG CLASS:** Osmotic diuretics (mannitol), carbonic anhydrase inhibitors (acetazolamide, methazolamide)
- **INDICATIONS:** Acute altitude/mountain sickness, edema, epilepsy (acetazolamide), elevated intraocular or intracranial pressure (mannitol),
- **MECHANISM:** Inhibits the reabsorption of sodium bicarbonate, promoting diuresis (carbonic anhydrase inhibitor). Increases osmotic pressure of the glomerulus and inhibition of tubular reabsorption of water and electrolytes (osmotic diuretic).
- **SIDE EFFECTS:** Hyperkalemic metabolic acidosis, hypernatremia, acute kidney injury.
- **CLINICAL PEARLS:** The use of carbonic anhydrase inhibitors as diuretics is rare, given the likelihood of developing metabolic acidosis with long-term use; carbonic anhydrase inhibitors are primarily used for open-angle glaucoma (brinzolamide and dorzolamide). However, acetazolamide is probably most commonly used in pseudotumor cerebri.

High-Yield Basic Pharmacology

- **Mechanism of Action**
  - Prevent the kidney's ability to concentrate urine by inhibiting the activity of the sodium-potassium-2-chloride symporter in the thick ascending limb of the loop of Henle.
    - The primary effect is the increased urinary elimination of sodium and chloride; however, numerous other solutes are also eliminated (bicarbonate, hydrogen, magnesium, phosphate, potassium, and uric acid)
  - Acute administration of loop diuretics increases uric acid excretion, but with chronic administration, uric acid excretion is inhibited.
    - This effect may result from enhanced proximal tubule transport or competition between uric acid and the loop diuretic for organic acid secretion in the proximal tubule.

Primary Net Benefit

- Loop diuretics produce acute and sustained diuresis, but long-term effects may be net-negative to therapeutic outcomes if the counterregulatory neurohormonal response is not accounted for.

Loop Diuretics - Drug Class Review			
High-Yield Med Reviews			
Mechanism of Action: *Inhibits the sodium-potassium-2-chloride symporter in the thick ascending limb of the loop of Henle.*			
Class Effects: *Prevents the kidney's ability to concentrate urine.*			
Generic Name	**Brand Name**	**Indication(s) or Uses**	**Notes**

Bumetanide	Bumex	• Edema
		• Heart failure
		• Hypertension
			• **Dosing (Adult):**
			  – Oral 0.5 to 2 mg divided once to TID
			  – IV bolus 0.5 to 1 mg, or 1 to 2.5 times total daily dose
			  – IV infusion 0.5 to 2 mg/hour
			• **Dosing (Peds):**
			  – All routes (oral, IM, IV) 0.01 to 0.1 mg/kg/dose every 6 to 24 hours.
			    • Maximum 10 mg/day
			  – IV infusion 1 to 10 mcg/kg/hour
			• **CYP450 Interactions:** None
			• **Renal or Hepatic Dose Adjustments:** None
			• **Dosage Forms:** IV solution, oral (tablet)

Ethacrynic acid	Edecrin	• Edema
		• Heart failure
			• **Dosing (Adult):**
			  – Oral 50 mg daily
			    • Maximum 400 mg daily
			  – IV 0.5 to 1 mg/kg/dose or fixed 50 mg
			    • Maximum 100 mg/dose
			• **Dosing (Peds):**
			  – Oral 1 mg/kg/dose Q24H
			    • Maximum 3 mg/kg/day
			  – IV 0.5 mg/kg/dose q8 to 24h or IV infusion of 0.1 mg/kg/hour
			• **CYP450 Interactions:** None
			• **Renal or Hepatic Dose Adjustments:** None
			• **Dosage Forms:** IV solution, oral (tablet)

Loop Diuretics - Drug Class Review			
High-Yield Med Reviews			
Generic Name	Brand Name	Indication(s) or Uses	Notes

Furosemide	Lasix	• Edema
		• Heart failure
		• Hypertension
			• **Dosing (Adult):**
			  - Oral 20 to 40 mg daily
			    • Maximum 160 mg daily
			  - IV 20 to 40 mg or 1 to 2.5 times the total daily dose
			    • Maximum 100 mg/dose
			  - IV infusion of 5 to 20 mg/hour
			    • Maximum 600 mg/day
			• **Dosing (Peds):**
			  - IM or IV 0.5 to 2 mg/kg/dose q6 to 12h
			    • Maximum 6 mg/kg/day
			• **CYP450 Interactions:** None
			• **Renal or Hepatic Dose Adjustments:**
			  - Acute renal failure - may need to increase the dose to total daily dose of 1 to 3 g
			• **Dosage Forms:** IV solution, oral (tablet)

Torsemide	Demadex	• Edema
		• Heart failure
		• Hypertension
			• **Dosing (Adult):**
			  - Oral 10 to 20 mg once daily
			    • Maximum 200 mg/day
			• **Dosing (Peds):**
			  - Not routinely used
			• **CYP450 Interactions:** Substrate of CYP2C8, CYP2C9
			• **Renal or Hepatic Dose Adjustments:** None
			• **Dosage Forms:** Oral (tablet)

High-Yield Clinical Knowledge

- **Not for All Heart Failure Patients**
  - In patients with AHA Stage C or higher HFrEF or HFpEF, loop diuretics may be added for patients with persistent peripheral or pulmonary edema.
    - Early use of loop diuretics without appropriate RAAS inhibition (ACE-inhibitor/ARB/neprilysin-ARB, and beta-blocker) and sympathetic nervous system inhibition (beta-blocker) can potentially worsen heart failure due to activation of these neurohormonal responses.
- **Acute Decompensated Heart Failure**
  - The benefit of loop diuretics in acute decompensated heart failure is more relevant to their vasodilatory effects than diuretic effects.
  - Some ADHF patients may be intravascularly volume depleted, and loop diuretic administration alone can worsen their clinical condition.
- **Dose equivalents**
  - Changing between loop diuretic agents can be accomplished using accepted approximate oral dose equivalencies.
  - These should only be used in patients with normal renal function.
    - Furosemide 40 mg = bumetanide 1 mg = torsemide 20 mg
- **Non-CYP450 Drug Interactions**
  - Aminoglycosides
    - Loop diuretic-associated ototoxicity manifests as tinnitus, hearing impairment, deafness, vertigo, and a sense of fullness in the ears.

- Different from aminoglycoside ototoxicity, loop diuretic hearing impairment is usually reversible upon discontinuation or dose adjustment.
    - Ototoxicity can also occur with concomitant amphotericin B, carboplatin, and paclitaxel.
- Digoxin
    - Loop diuretics promote potassium and magnesium clearance, which may predispose patients to digoxin toxicity, even if there are therapeutic levels before initiation.
        - Hypokalemia reduces the sodium-potassium-ATPase pump activity and enhances pump inhibition induced by digoxin, which increases the risk of dysrhythmias.
        - Hypomagnesemia increases the risk of dysrhythmias from digoxin toxicity due to decreased sodium-potassium-ATPase pump exchange activity.
- Lithium
    - Loop diuretics increase urinary sodium loss and decrease lithium excretion.
- Insulin & Sulfonylureas
    - Loop diuretics may increase insulin resistance and decrease insulin release.
- NSAIDs
    - Blunted diuretic effect by preventing prostaglandin-mediated increases in renal blood flow and increasing risk of nephrotoxicity.
    - Increase RAAS activation, blunting diuretic response, and increased risk of hyperkalemia.
- **Sulfa Allergy**
    - The loop diuretics bumetanide and furosemide contain a sulfonamide moiety, and torsemide is a sulfonylurea. This often raises the concern of sulfonamide allergy and cross-sensitivity to other "sulfa" containing drugs.

High-Yield Fast-Facts

- **Oral Diuretic and Food**
    - When bumetanide or furosemide are administered with food, bioavailability can significantly decrease. There is no effect from food on the bioavailability of torsemide.
- **Oral or IV for ADHF**
    - While oral loop diuretic dosing regimens exist, the true bioavailability in this scenario may be lower or unpredictable due to decreased gut perfusion.
- **Limited primary literature**
    - Despite loop diuretics being a component of cardiovascular and renal therapeutics for decades, there is limited high-quality prospective evidence to support their use in this setting.

HIGH-YIELD BOARD EXAM ESSENTIALS
- **CLASSIC AGENTS:** Bumetanide, ethacrynic acid, furosemide, torsemide
- **DRUG CLASS:** Loop diuretics
- **INDICATIONS:** Edema, hypertension, heart failure
- **MECHANISM:** Prevent the kidney's ability to concentrate urine by inhibiting the activity of the sodium-potassium-2-chloride symporter in the thick ascending limb of the loop of Henle.
- **SIDE EFFECTS:** Volume depletion, hypokalemia, hyponatremia, ototoxicity
- **CLINICAL PEARLS:**
    - In patients with AHA Stage C or higher HFrEF or HFpEF, loop diuretics may be added for patients with persistent peripheral or pulmonary edema, but early use of loop diuretics without appropriate RAAS inhibition and sympathetic nervous system inhibition can potentially worsen heart failure due to activation of these neurohormonal responses.
    - Low dose loops are usually added to high dose spironolactone for the management of ascites.
    - Loop diuretics are commonly associated with causing hypokalemia and hypomagnesemia.

High-Yield Basic Pharmacology

- **Mechanism of Action**
  - Inhibit sodium and chloride transport in the early segment of the distal convoluted tubule.
    - This promotes the excretion of primarily sodium and water.
- **Chlorthalidone CV Benefits**
  - Chlorthalidone may possess greater cardiovascular benefits owing to its ability to inhibit carbonic anhydrase relative to other thiazide agents.
    - Hydrochlorothiazide and chlorthalidone both contain a sulfonamide moiety, which has been proposed to exert this carbonic anhydrase activity, but chlorthalidone possesses additional carbonic anhydrase properties.

Primary Net Benefit

- Long-standing history of clinical benefit in patients with hypertension from a mechanism other than diuresis.

<table>
<tr><td colspan="4">Thiazide Diuretics - Drug Class Review
High-Yield Med Reviews</td></tr>
<tr><td colspan="4">Mechanism of Action: Inhibit sodium and chloride transport in the early segment of the distal convoluted tubule.</td></tr>
<tr><td colspan="4">Class Effects: Moderate sodium and chloride diuresis.</td></tr>
<tr><td>Generic Name</td><td>Brand Name</td><td>Indication(s) or Uses</td><td>Notes</td></tr>
<tr>
<td>Chlorthalidone</td>
<td>Chlorthalid, Thalitone</td>
<td>• Edema
• Hypertension</td>
<td>• Dosing (Adult):
  - Oral 12.5 to 25 mg once daily
    • Maximum 100 mg/day
• Dosing (Peds):
  - Oral 0.3 mg/kg/dose once daily
    • Maximum 2 mg/kg/day or 50 mg/day
• CYP450 Interactions: None
• Renal or Hepatic Dose Adjustments:
  - GFR less than 10 mL/minute - avoid use
• Dosage Forms: Oral (tablet)</td>
</tr>
<tr>
<td>Chlorothiazide</td>
<td>Diuril</td>
<td>• Edema
• Hypertension</td>
<td>• Dosing (Adult):
  - Oral 250 to 2,000 mg daily divided into 1 to 2 doses
  - IV 500 to 1000 mg daily
• Dosing (Peds):
  - Oral 10 to 40 mg/kg/day in 1 or 2 divided doses
    • Maximum 375 mg/day (children under 2).
  - IV 5 to 10 mg/kg/day in divided doses
    • Maximum 20 mg/kg/day
• CYP450 Interactions: None
• Renal or Hepatic Dose Adjustments:
  - GFR 10 to 30 mL/minutes - Diuretic response significantly diminished but no specific dose adjustment
  - GFR less than 10 mL/minute - avoid use
• Dosage Forms: IV solution, oral (tablet)</td>
</tr>
</table>

Thiazide Diuretics - Drug Class Review
High-Yield Med Reviews

Generic Name	Brand Name	Indication(s) or Uses	Notes

Hydro-chlorothiazide (HCTZ)	Microzide	• Edema
		• Hypertension
			• **Dosing (Adult):**
			  - Oral 12.5 to 25 mg once daily
			    • Maximum 50 mg/day
			• **Dosing (Peds):**
			  - Oral 1 to 2 mg/kg/day in 1 to 2 divided doses
			    • Maximum 37.5 mg/day
			• **CYP450 Interactions:** None
			• **Renal or Hepatic Dose Adjustments:**
			  - GFR 10 to 30 mL/minutes - Diuretic response significantly diminished but no specific dose adjustment
			  - GFR less than 10 mL/minute - avoid use
			• **Dosage Forms:** Oral (capsule, tablet)

Indapamide	Indipam	• Heart failure
		• Hypertension
			• **Dosing (Adult):**
			  - Oral 1.25 mg daily
			    • Maximum 5 mg/day
			• **Dosing (Peds):**
			  - Not routinely used
			• **CYP450 Interactions:** None
			• **Renal or Hepatic Dose Adjustments:**
			  - GFR less than 50 mL/min - Maximum 2.5 mg/day
			• **Dosage Forms:** IV solution, oral (tablet)

Methyclothiazide	Aquatensen Enduron	• Edema
		• Hypertension
			• **Dosing (Adult):**
			  - Oral 2.5 to 10 mg/day
			• **Dosing (Peds):**
			  - Not routinely used
			• **CYP450 Interactions:** None
			• **Renal or Hepatic Dose Adjustments:**
			  - GFR less than 30 mL/minutes - Diuretic response significantly diminished but no specific dose adjustment
			• **Dosage Forms:** Oral (tablet)

Metolazone	Zaroxolyn	• Edema
		• Hypertension
			• **Dosing (Adult):**
			  - Oral 2.5 mg oral
			    • Maximum 20 mg/day
			• **Dosing (Peds):**
			  - Oral 0.2 to 0.4 mg/kg/day
			    • Usually in combination with furosemide
			    • Maximum 20 mg/day
			• **CYP450 Interactions:** None
			• **Renal or Hepatic Dose Adjustments:**
			  - Diuretic response significantly diminished, but no specific dose adjustment
			• **Dosage Forms:** Oral (tablet)

- **Mechanism of Antihypertensive Effect**
  - Thiazide diuretics do not appear to exert their antihypertensive effect from their diuretic action as plasma, and extracellular volumes return to baseline values within 4–6 weeks of initiation.
    - Thiazide-induced volume loss leads to decreased venous return, RAAS activation, sympathetic nervous system activation, reduced cardiac output, and decreased blood pressure.
- **Lipids and Glucose**
  - Thiazide diuretics may increase total cholesterol, LDL, and triglycerides, as well as causing hyperglycemia via three proposed mechanisms (insulin resistance, decreased insulin release, and inhibition of glucose uptake).
    - There is speculation that thiazide-induced hyperglycemia may result from the effect of these agents on potassium.
      - Additional theories of thiazide induced hyperglycemia involve hyperuricemia, changes in fat distribution, and PPAR-gamma downregulation.
    - Thiazide diuretics may also increase serum calcium by increasing calcium reabsorption in the distal convoluted tubule.
    - Similar to loop diuretics, thiazide agents may cause hyperuricemia.
- **Nephrogenic Diabetes Insipidus (DI)**
  - Thiazide diuretics are a key component in treating nephrogenic DI since they can reduce urine volume by half.
    - This action is mediated by thiazide-induced increased proximal tubular water reabsorption and the prevention of the distal convoluted tubule's ability to form dilute urine and increases urine osmolality.
- **Dosing Target**
  - Unlike other antihypertensive agents, thiazide diuretics do not need to be titrated to the maximum tolerated dose.
  - Most patients respond with a clinically relevant effect at initial doses and do not benefit from aggressive titration.

HIGH-YIELD BOARD EXAM ESSENTIALS

- **CLASSIC AGENTS:** Chlorthalidone, chlorothiazide, hydrochlorothiazide, indapamide, methyclothiazide, metolazone
- **DRUG CLASS:** Thiazide diuretics
- **INDICATIONS:** Edema, hypertension
- **MECHANISM:** Inhibit sodium and chloride transport in the early segment of the distal convoluted tubule.
- **SIDE EFFECTS:** Volume depletion, electrolyte abnormalities, increased total cholesterol, triglycerides, elevations in glucose.
- **CLINICAL PEARLS:** Thiazide diuretics do not appear to exert their antihypertensive effect from their diuretic action as plasma, and extracellular volumes return to baseline values within 4–6 weeks of initiation.

High-Yield Basic Pharmacology

- **Mechanism of Action**
  - Dobutamine, isoproterenol, and milrinone share a common pathway in their action: increasing the heart's contractility by increasing cAMP, which allows for increased phospholipase activity, and enhanced calcium influx to cardiac cells during systole.
    - Dobutamine is a beta-1 and beta-2 agonist and alpha-1 agonist (dose-dependent).
    - Isoproterenol is a beta-1 and beta-2 agonist.
    - Milrinone is a phosphodiesterase-3 (PDE3) inhibitor
- **Catecholamines Vs. Pressor/Inotropes**
  - The clinical classification of agents as vasopressors and inotropes describes the physiologic action of these drugs.
  - However, it is worth noting that these agents also differ in chemical classification.
    - The common term "catecholamine" refers to the drugs that share a beta-phenylethylamine core structure with hydroxyl groups substituted at positions 3 and 4 of the benzene ring.
    - Substitution of different groups to this basic platform manipulates alpha and beta-receptor activities and susceptibility to monoamine oxidase metabolism.

Primary Net Benefit

- Inotropes increase contractility and heart rate to improve cardiac output but often are accompanied by vasodilation with escalating doses.

Inotropes - Drug Class Review			
High-Yield Med Reviews			
Mechanism of Action: *Dobutamine is a beta-1 and beta-2 agonist and alpha-1 agonist (dose-dependent). Isoproterenol is a beta-1 and beta-2 agonist. Milrinone is a phosphodiesterase-3 (PDE3) inhibitor.*			
Class Effects: Inotropes increase contractility and heart rate to improve cardiac output but often are accompanied by vasodilation with escalating doses.			
Generic Name	**Brand Name**	**Indication(s) or Uses**	**Notes**

Dobutamine	Dobutrex	• Cardiac decompensation	• **Dosing (Adult):**
			  – 2 to 20 mcg/kg/minute IV infusion
			• **Dosing (Peds):**
			  – 2 to 20 mcg/kg/minute IV infusion
			• **CYP450 Interactions:** Non-CYP (Linezolid- may enhance the hypertensive effect)
			• **Renal or Hepatic Dose Adjustments:** None
			• **Dosage Forms:** IV (solution)

Isoproterenol	Isuprel	Mild or transient episodes of heart block	• **Dosing (Adult):**
			  – 2 to 20 mcg/minute IV infusion
			• **Dosing (Peds):**
			  – 0.05 to 0.5 mcg/kg/minute IV
			• **CYP450 Interactions:** Non-CYP (Riociguat coadministration contraindicated)
			• **Renal or Hepatic Dose Adjustments:** None
			• **Dosage Forms:** IV (solution)

Generic Name	Brand Name	Indication(s) or Uses	Notes

Milrinone	Primacor	▪ Heart failure with a reduced ejection fraction	▪ **Dosing (Adult):**
			  – Initial dose 0.375 mcg/kg/min (0.125 to 0.75 mcg/kg/minute) IV infusion
			▪ **Dosing (Peds):**
			  – 0.25 to 0.75 mcg/kg/minute IV infusion
			▪ **CYP450 Interactions:** Non-CYP (Linezolid- may enhance the hypertensive effect)
			▪ **Renal or Hepatic Dose Adjustments:**
			  – GFR 41-50 mL/minute - initial dose 0.25 mcg/kg/min
			  – GFR 31-40 mL/minute - 0.125 mcg/kg/min
			  – GFR 21-30 mL/minute - 0.0625 mcg/kg/min
			  – GFR less than 20 mL/minute - avoid use.
			▪ **Dosage Forms:** IV (solution)

High-Yield Clinical Knowledge

- **Dobutamine Dose Response**
  - When the dose of dobutamine exceeds 20 mcg/kg/min, the proportional selectivity of beta-1 is lost, and beta-2 effects increase.
  - This change's net effect will likely lead to vasodilation and decreases in mean arterial pressure; this may be detrimental to cardiac perfusion and venous return.
  - Alternative agents and re-evaluation of the clinical strategy are needed if doses are approaching this threshold.
- **Ino-DILATORS**
  - While dobutamine, isoproterenol, and milrinone can increase cardiac output, they can also decrease peripheral vascular resistance.
  - In some scenarios, this can be beneficial by reducing preload and improving venous return but can lead to hypotension and hypoperfusion if not closely titrated.
- **Milrinone Warning**
  - Milrinone carries a black boxed warning that it should not be used for long-term management of heart failure.
  - However, many patients with end-stage heart failure or awaiting heart transplant may be on continuous/chronic outpatient infusions of milrinone.
  - This use is intended to prolong life until definitive care (i.e., a heart transplant or perhaps an LVAD) can be arranged.
- **Dobutamine/Isoproterenol Use**
  - Dobutamine may be used in clinical scenarios where there is preserved mean arterial pressure but a decreased cardiac output.
    - The use of isoproterenol is narrower, as it is used in patients with decreased cardiac output who are hypertensive.
  - As dopamine levels extend towards and beyond its upper limit of 20 mcg/kg/minute, heart rate will continue to increase, systemic vascular resistance will decrease, and stroke volume will decline due to impaired diastole leading to decreases in cardiac output.
- **Milrinone Use**
  - Milrinone is not often considered first-line due to a higher propensity to decrease vascular resistance and cause hypotension.
  - This decrease in vascular resistance extends to the pulmonary vasculature, making milrinone preferable in specific patient populations, such as pulmonary hypertension.

- Since milrinone can bypass beta-blockade to exert its inodilatory effects when compared to dobutamine, milrinone may be beneficial to support cardiac output in patients exposed to beta-blockers.
- However, due to the prolonged onset of action (as a result of foregoing the bolus dose to avoid excessive hypotension), a four to six-hour half-life, and medication accumulation in renal failure patients, the clinical use of this drug is limited.

HIGH-YIELD BOARD EXAM ESSENTIALS

- **CLASSIC AGENTS:** Dobutamine, isoproterenol, milrinone
- **DRUG CLASS:** Inotropes
- **INDICATIONS:** Cardiac decompensation (dobutamine), heart failure with a reduced ejection fraction (milrinone), mild or transient episodes of heart block (Isoproterenol)
- **MECHANISM:** Increasing the heart's contractility by increasing cAMP, which allows for increased phospholipase activity, and enhanced calcium influx to cardiac cells during systole.
- **SIDE EFFECTS:** Tachycardia, vasodilation
- **CLINICAL PEARLS:** Dobutamine can also stimulate the beta-2 receptor. When the dose of dobutamine exceeds 20 mcg/kg/min, the proportional selectivity of beta-1 is lost, and beta-2 effects increase; this change's net effect will likely lead to vasodilation and decreases in mean arterial pressure; this may be detrimental to cardiac perfusion and venous return. Due to this effect, sometimes a vasopressor may need to be added.

High-Yield Basic Pharmacology

- **Dopamine, Epinephrine, Norepinephrine, Phenylephrine**
  - Activation of numerous intracellular secondary signaling activation that ultimately causes a muscle contraction (in the case of alpha-1, beta-1) or relaxation (alpha-2, beta-2).
- **Vasopressin**
  - Vasopressin stimulates V1 via activation of PLC-beta producing IP3 and DAG and ultimately calcium-dependent calcium release.
- **Angiotensin II**
  - Angiotensin II causes a rapid increase in peripheral resistance through the stimulation of AT1 receptors.

Primary Net Benefit

- Essential medications for hemodynamic support in emergency medicine and critical care. Vasopressors generally increase mean arterial pressure, improving perfusion to essential organs during resuscitation.

<table>
<tr><td colspan="4">VASOPRESSOR - Drug Class Review
High-Yield Med Reviews</td></tr>
<tr><td colspan="4">Mechanism of Action: Increases vascular resistance and perfusion via alpha and/or beta-agonist activity, V1 agonist activity or AT1 agonist activity.</td></tr>
<tr><td colspan="4">Class Effects: Vasoconstriction, increase in mean arterial pressure</td></tr>
<tr><th>Generic Name</th><th>Brand Name</th><th>Indication(s) or Uses</th><th>Notes</th></tr>
<tr>
<td>Epinephrine</td>
<td>Adrenalin</td>
<td>• Hypotension/shock</td>
<td>

- **Dosing (Adult):**
  - IV 0.1 to 3 mcg/kg/min continuous
  - IV push 1 mg (cardiac arrest)
  - IV push 10 to 100 mcg (push-dose)
- **Dosing (Peds):**
  - IV 0.1 to 3 mcg/kg/min continuous
- **CYP450 Interactions:** None, but metabolized by COMT and MAO
- **Renal or Hepatic Dose Adjustments:** None
- **Dosage Forms:** IV solution
</td>
</tr>
<tr>
<td>Norepinephrine</td>
<td>Levophed</td>
<td>• Hypotension/shock</td>
<td>

- **Dosing (Adult):**
  - IV 0.1 to 3 mcg/kg/min continuous IV
- **Dosing (Peds):**
  - IV 0.1 to 3 mcg/kg/min continuous IV
- **CYP450 Interactions:** None, but metabolized by COMT and MAO
- **Renal or Hepatic Dose Adjustments:** None
- **Dosage Forms:** IV solution
</td>
</tr>
<tr>
<td>Phenylephrine</td>
<td>Neo-Synephrine</td>
<td>• Hypotension/shock</td>
<td>

- **Dosing (Adult):**
  - IV 0.5 to 10 mcg/kg/min continuous
  - IV 40 to 250 mcg bolus q1-2minutes
  - Intercavernous 100 to 500 mcg
- **Dosing (Peds):**
  - IV 0.5 to 10 mcg/kg/min continuous
  - IV 40 to 250 mcg bolus q1-2minutes
- **CYP450 Interactions:** None, but metabolized by COMT and MAO
- **Renal or Hepatic Dose Adjustments:** None
- **Dosage Forms:** IV solution
</td>
</tr>
</table>

VASOPRESSOR - Drug Class Review
High-Yield Med Reviews

Generic Name	Brand Name	Indication(s) or Uses	Notes

Dopamine	None	• Hypotension/shock	• **Dosing (Adult):**
			  – IV 1 to 20 mcg/kg/min continuous
			• **Dosing (Peds):**
			  – IV 1 to 20 mcg/kg/min continuous
			• **CYP450 Interactions:** None, but metabolized by COMT and MAO
			• **Renal or Hepatic Dose Adjustments:** None
			• **Dosage Forms:** IV solution

Vasopressin	Vasostrict	• Hypotension/shock	• **Dosing (Adult):**
			  – IV 0.03 or 0.04 units/minute continuous
			  – IV 40 units push
			• **Dosing (Peds):**
			  – IV 0.5 to 10 milliunits/kg/hour
			• **CYP450 Interactions:** None
			• **Renal or Hepatic Dose Adjustments:** None
			• **Dosage Forms:** IV solution

Angiotensin II	Giapreza	• Hypotension/shock	• **Dosing (Adult):**
			  – IV 10 to 20 nanogram/kg/min continuous
			• **Dosing (Peds):**
			  – Not routinely used
			• **CYP450 Interactions:** None
			• **Renal or Hepatic Dose Adjustments:** None
			• **Dosage Forms:** IV solution

High-Yield Clinical Knowledge

- **Inopressors Vs. Pure Vasopressors**
  - Although commonly referred to as vasopressors or inotropes, reclassifying these drugs differently better matches their clinical effects.
  - The "*inopressors*" (norepinephrine, epinephrine) deliver both increases in vascular resistance as well as provide inotropic effects.
  - Whereas the "pure vasopressors" (vasopressin, phenylephrine, angiotensin II) provide almost exclusively vasoconstriction without effect on inotropic or chronotropic effects.
    - There also exist "inodilators" such as dobutamine or milrinone which cause increases in cardiac output but can cause vasodilation.
- **Catecholamine Resistance**
  - In critically ill patients, there is evidence to suggest that there can be resistance to exogenous catecholamine via receptor desensitization, downregulation of receptors from exogenous catecholamine infusions, overproduction of NO via iNOS, and promotion of inflammatory cytokines such as IL-1 and TNF-alpha.
  - These patients may require higher dosing, use of non-catecholamine pressors (for example, vasopressin or angiotensin II), corticosteroids, or a combination of these therapies.
- **Dopamine Dose**
  - Dopamine is often quoted in pharmacology teaching as having discrete receptor activity at specific doses: D1 agonism 0-3 mcg/kg/min, beta agonism 3-10mcg/kg/min and alpha agonist activity > 10 mcg/kg/min.
  - However, these effects have significant (10 to 75-fold) interpatient variability, meaning each patient may respond differently to different doses.
- **Epinephrine Lab Changes**
  - Epinephrine can potentially produce numerous laboratory changes relevant to patient care.

- Hyperlactatemia secondary to epinephrine is caused by the inhibition of pyruvate dehydrogenase, causing a pyruvate shunt towards lactate production.
  - Thus, while not a result of tissue hypoperfusion, and no impact on clinical outcome, it may limit the usefulness of tracking lactate clearance as a marker of resuscitation.
- Hyperglycemia is another common effect, which is caused by increased liver glycogenolysis, reduced tissue uptake of glucose, and inhibition of pancreatic secretion of insulin.
- Finally, hypokalemia is as a result of an intracellular shift of potassium due to epinephrine.

- **IV Push**
  - Vasopressors can be used in an IV push format, in addition to the conventional IV infusion.
  - "Push-dose pressors" using phenylephrine or epinephrine are used as temporary measures to maintain perfusion in critically ill patient care scenarios.
  - Temporary measures such as push doses, rather than continuous IV infusions could augment perfusion while other definitive therapies are prepared (i.e., pressor drips, central lines, various procedures).

- **Drug of Choice**
  - The vast majority of clinical scenarios where a vasopressor is indicated, norepinephrine will be the drug of choice.
  - While the initial dosing should be weight-based, and adjusted body weight used for morbidly obese patients, guideline statements do not provide any recommendations on which dosing strategy is preferred.

HIGH-YIELD BOARD EXAM ESSENTIALS

- **CLASSIC AGENTS:** Angiotensin II, dopamine, epinephrine, norepinephrine, phenylephrine, vasopressin
- **DRUG CLASS:** Vasopressors
- **INDICATIONS:** Hypotension, septic shock
- **MECHANISM:** Increases vascular resistance and perfusion via alpha and/or beta-agonist activity, V1 agonist activity or AT1 agonist activity.
- **SIDE EFFECTS:** Arrythmias (tachycardia), decreased lactate clearance, extravasation
- **CLINICAL PEARLS:** Dopamine is often quoted in pharmacology teaching as having discrete receptor activity at specific doses: D1 agonism 0-3 mcg/kg/min, beta agonism 3-10mcg/kg/min and alpha agonist activity > 10 mcg/kg/min. However, these effects have significant (10 to 75-fold) interpatient variability, meaning each patient may respond differently to different doses. Dopamine is known to be associated with tachydysrhythmias when compared to norepinephrine and thus is not the vasopressor of choice in septic shock.

High-Yield Basic Pharmacology

- **Mechanism of Action**
  - Positively charged molecules that bind to negatively charged bile acids in the intestinal lumen, decreasing enterohepatic circulation of bile acids, thereby stimulating the hepatic synthesis of bile acids from cholesterol.
- **Increased LDL Receptors**
  - As bile acids sequestrants increase the excretion of bile acids in the stool and deplete the hepatic pool of cholesterol, induces the synthesis and number of available LDL receptors on hepatocytes.
    - Other lipid-lowering agents also increase LDL receptors, including PCSK9 inhibitors, and statins.
      - With statins, and hypothetically with bile acid sequestrants as well, the sterol regulatory element-binding protein (SREBP) which increases the expression of genes promoting LDL receptors also promotes the production of PCSK9, causing a decrease in LDL receptor recycling.
- **Increased Triglycerides**
  - The decreased hepatic concentration of cholesterol from bile acid sequestrant therapy causes a subsequent increase in hepatic cholesterol and triglyceride synthesis.
  - These agents should not be used in patients with triglyceride levels above 300 mg/dL.

Primary Net Benefit

- These agents achieve a modest LDL reduction of up to 20% but have a limited place in therapy for LDL reduction during pregnancy, as they are not systemically absorbed.

Bile Acid Sequestrants - Drug Class Review			
High-Yield Med Reviews			
Mechanism of Action: *Bind to bile acids in the intestinal lumen, increasing hepatic consumption of cholesterol to increase bile acids production.*			
Class Effects: *LDL reduction, small ASCVD risk improvement but less so than available, better-tolerated alternatives.*			
Generic Name	**Brand Name**	**Indication(s) or Uses**	**Notes**

Cholestyramine resin	Prevalite Questran	• Dyslipidemia
		• Pruritus associated with cholestasis
			• **Dosing (Adult):**
			  – Oral 4 g once to twice/day, increase to target 8 to 16 g/day
			    • Maximum 24 g/day
			• **Dosing (Peds):**
			  – Oral 2 to 4 g per day in divided doses (or 240 mg/kg/day), increase to target 8 g/day
			• **CYP450 Interactions:** None, but other clinically relevant interactions (absorption) exist.
			• **Renal or Hepatic Dose Adjustments:** None
			• **Dosage Forms:** Oral (packet, powder)

Colesevelam	Welchol	• Dyslipidemia
		• Diabetes mellitus, type 2
			• **Dosing (Adult):**
			  – Oral 3.75 g/day in 1 or 2 divided doses
			• **Dosing (Peds):**
			  – Oral 3.75 g/day in 1 or 2 divided doses
			• **CYP450 Interactions:** None, but other clinically relevant interactions (absorption) exist.
			• **Renal or Hepatic Dose Adjustments:** None
			• **Dosage Forms:** Oral (packet, tablet)

Bile Acid Sequestrants - Drug Class Review
High-Yield Med Reviews

Generic Name	Brand Name	Indication(s) or Uses	Notes
Colestipol	Colestid	▪ Dyslipidemia	▪ **Dosing (Adult):** – Oral granules 5 g once to twice/day, increase to target 30 g/day – Oral tablets 2 g once to twice/day, increase to target 16 g/day ▪ **Dosing (Peds):** – Oral 2 to 12 g per day in divided doses (or 125 to 250 mg/kg/day), increase to target 10 g/day ▪ **CYP450 Interactions:** None, but other clinically relevant interactions (absorption) exist. ▪ **Renal or Hepatic Dose Adjustments:** None ▪ **Dosage Forms:** Oral (granules, packet, tablet)

High-Yield Clinical Knowledge

- **Oral Administration**
  - Cholestyramine and colestipol are available in powdered resin dosage forms that require admixture with water or juice for oral administration.
    - These are notoriously poor-tasting and are accompanied by dose-dependent GI adverse events including constipation, bloating, epigastric fullness, nausea, and flatulence.
  - Colesevelam and colestipol are available as tablets which eliminated the aversion to the powdered resin formulations but maintain the GI intolerances.
  - Patients rarely tolerate titration to target doses (to achieve maximum LDL reduction) because of these GI adverse events.
- **Fat-soluble Vitamin Depletion**
  - Decreased GI absorption of bile acids also has the deleterious effect of decreasing fat-soluble vitamin absorption.
    - Appropriate spacing of cholestyramine and colestipol can permit sufficient absorption of necessary fat-soluble vitamins.
    - Colesevelam does not appear to affect fat-soluble vitamin absorption.
- **Drug-Interactions**
  - Cholestyramine and colestipol may also decrease the absorption of many orally administered drugs including aspirin, ascorbic acid, digoxin, diuretics (thiazides, loop diuretics), iron, levothyroxine, propranolol, phenytoin, tetracycline, and warfarin.
    - Other medications should be spaced by 1 hour before or 4 hours after bile acid sequestrant administration.
  - Fluvastatin, ezetimibe, and pravastatin absorption may also be decreased, therefore if used in combination with a statin, an alternative agent should be used.
  - Colesevelam does not appear to interfere with the absorption of digoxin, lovastatin, metoprolol, valproic acid, and warfarin.
- **Pediatric Use**
  - Cholestyramine and colestipol have a relatively large degree of clinical experience in pediatric patients (older than 10 years), compared to statins, ezetimibe, and PCSK9 inhibitors.
- **Combination with Statins**
  - As described above, the action of bile acid sequestrants causes an increase in hepatic cholesterol synthesis by upregulating HMG-CoA reductase.
    - The combination of statin therapy can substantially increase the effectiveness of bile acid sequestrants.
- **Diverticulitis**

– In patients diagnosed with diverticulitis, bile acid sequestrants should be avoided.

HIGH-YIELD BOARD EXAM ESSENTIALS

- **CLASSIC AGENTS:** Cholestyramine resin, colesevelam, colestipol
- **DRUG CLASS:** Bile acid sequestrants
- **INDICATIONS:** Dyslipidemia (cholestyramine resin, colesevelam, colestipol) Pruritus associated with cholestasis (cholestyramine resin), diabetes mellitus, type 2 (colesevelam)
- **MECHANISM:** Positively charged molecules that bind to negatively charged bile acids in the intestinal lumen, decreasing enterohepatic circulation of bile acids, thereby stimulating the hepatic synthesis of bile acids from cholesterol.
- **SIDE EFFECTS:** Decreased absorption of fat-soluble vitamins, elevated triglycerides, GI intolerance.
- **CLINICAL PEARLS:**
  - Can reduce LDL-c but must be taken with each meal to capture the bile.
  - Avoid using these agents if the patient has elevated TGs at baseline as they can worsen the risk of developing TG-induced pancreatitis.
  - Cholestyramine and colestipol may also decrease the absorption of many orally administered drugs including aspirin, ascorbic acid, digoxin, diuretics (thiazides, loop diuretics), iron, levothyroxine, propranolol, phenytoin, tetracycline, and warfarin.
  - The most common side effects are GI related and impact compliance.

High-Yield Basic Pharmacology

- **Mechanism of Action**
  - Ezetimibe undergoes glucuronide conjugation in the small intestine and liver to an active metabolite.
  - Inhibits Niemann-Pick C1-Like-1, a sterol transport protein in the brush border of the small intestine, ultimately decreasing hepatic cholesterol delivery, hepatic cholesterol storage, and increased clearance from the blood.
    - Effects on lipids include decreasing total cholesterol, LDL, apolipoprotein-B, triglycerides, and increased HDL
- **Duration of action**
  - The long duration of action of ezetimibe is related to its enterohepatic recirculation.
    - Once ezetimibe is metabolized (via glucuronide conjugation) in the small intestine and liver, it's excreted in the bile back into the intestinal lumen (a primary site of action).
      - This pathway also partially accounts for the risk of cholelithiasis.

Primary Net Benefit

- While ezetimibe can be used alone for the management of dyslipidemia it should be reserved as an adjunct to statin therapy.
  - Ezetimibe is a moderately potent lowering agent of LDL but has a controversial history with evidence communicating this to patient-oriented outcomes in improved cardiovascular mortality.

Ezetimibe - Drug Class Review			
High-Yield Med Reviews			
Mechanism of Action: *Inhibits absorption of cholesterol in the small intestine.*			
Class Effects: Decreases: total cholesterol, LDL, apolipoprotein-B, triglycerides. Increases HDL. Easy daily dosing with no significant side effects for most patients.			
Generic Name	**Brand Name**	**Indication(s) or Uses**	**Notes**
Ezetimibe	Zetia	<ul><li>Homozygous familial hypercholesterolemia</li><li>Homozygous sitosterolemia</li><li>Primary hyperlipidemia</li></ul>	<ul><li>**Dosing (Adult):**<ul><li>Oral 10 mg once daily</li></ul></li><li>**Dosing (Peds):**<ul><li>Oral 10 mg once daily<ul><li>Children aged 5 to 9, limited data</li></ul></li></ul></li><li>**CYP450 Interactions:** None</li><li>**Renal or Hepatic Dose Adjustments:**<ul><li>Child-Pugh class B or C - Not recommended</li></ul></li><li>**Dosage Forms:** Oral (tablet)</li></ul>

High-Yield Clinical Knowledge

- **Severe Primary Hypercholesterolemia**
  - In patients with severe primary hypercholesterolemia, if high dose statin is started and LDL is still above 100 mg/dL or does not achieve a 50% reduction, ezetimibe may be added to target LDL below this threshold.
- **Very High-Risk Patients**
  - Ezetimibe may be used in combination with a statin in patients at very high-risk ASCVD to target an LDL of 70 mg/dL.
    - After the addition of ezetimibe to high-dose statin therapy and LDL is still above 70 mg/dL, a PCSK9 inhibitor is reasonable to add to treatment.

- **Drug interactions**
  - Ezetimibe has few drug interactions relative to other lipid-lowering drug classes; however, there is a clinically relevant interaction with cyclosporine and fibrates.
    - Coadministration of cyclosporine and ezetimibe increases ezetimibe AUC 2.5 times and nearly triples peak concentration.
    - Cyclosporine peak concentrations are also increased by 15%, and AUC increased by 10%.
  - Fibrates may also increase the risk of ezetimibe's risk of myopathy and cholelithiasis.
- **Use Without A Statin**
  - In patients whose statin therapy is contraindicated, ezetimibe may be used in combination with other lipid-lowering interventions.
- **Add-On Therapy**
  - Ezetimibe can be a key add-on therapy to statins that provides additional LDL lowering and a potential 2% absolute risk reduction in cardiovascular mortality and morbidity (number needed to treat (NNT) of 50).

High-Yield Fast-Facts

- **NPC1L1 Polymorphisms**
  - Individuals with polymorphisms of Niemann-Pick C1-Like1 generally have lower LDL-C levels and decreased ASCVD risk than individuals without these polymorphisms.
- **No Increased Risk of Cancer**
  - In preliminary clinical evidence with ezetimibe, there appeared a small increased risk of cancer. However, these concerns have been resolved from the IMPROVE-IT study (described elsewhere) did not show an increased risk of cancer.

HIGH-YIELD BOARD EXAM ESSENTIALS
- **CLASSIC AGENTS:** Ezetimibe
- **DRUG CLASS:** Antilipemic
- **INDICATIONS:** Homozygous familial hypercholesterolemia, homozygous sitosterolemia, primary hyperlipidemia
- **MECHANISM:** Inhibits Niemann-Pick C1-Like-1, a sterol transport protein in the brush border of the small intestine, ultimately decreasing hepatic cholesterol delivery, hepatic cholesterol storage, and increased clearance from the blood.
- **SIDE EFFECTS:** Well tolerated, sinusitis
- **CLINICAL PEARLS:**
  - Dosed once-a-day due to enterohepatic recirculation.
  - Very well tolerated and no major drug interactions.
  - In patients with severe primary hypercholesterolemia, if high dose statin is started and LDL is still above 100 mg/dL or does not achieve a 50% reduction, ezetimibe may be added to target LDL below this threshold.

High-Yield Basic Pharmacology

- **Mechanism of Action**
  - Fibrates activate peroxisome proliferator-activated receptor type alpha (PPAR-alpha), facilitating PPAR-alpha mediated stimulation of fatty acid oxidation, increased lipoprotein lipase synthesis, and decreasing apolipoprotein C-III production.
    - Enhancing the clearance of triglyceride-rich lipoproteins, VLDLs, and LDL.
    - PPAR-alpha stimulation increases HDL from activation of apolipoprotein A-I and A-II.

Primary Net Benefit

- Fibrate therapy has fallen out of favor, with the guidelines preferring initiating statin therapy or intensifying statin therapy in patients with severe hypertriglyceridemia and ASCVD risk of 7.5% or higher.
  - If triglycerides are greater than 1000 mg/dL, fibrate therapy could be considered to avoid pancreatitis AFTER addressing the following: a very low-fat diet, avoidance of refined carbohydrates and alcohol, consumption of omega-3 fatty acids.

<table>
<tr><td colspan="4">Fibrates - Drug Class Review
High-Yield Med Reviews</td></tr>
<tr><td colspan="4">Mechanism of Action: Activate PPAR-alpha causing fatty acid oxidation, increased lipoprotein lipase synthesis, decreased apolipoprotein C-III production, and activation of apolipoprotein A-I and A-II.</td></tr>
<tr><td colspan="4">Class Effects: Decreasing TG, VLDL, LDL, increasing HDL</td></tr>
<tr><td>Generic Name</td><td>Brand Name</td><td>Indication(s) or Uses</td><td>Notes</td></tr>
<tr>
<td>Fenofibrate</td>
<td>Antara
Fenoglide
Fibricor
Lipofen
Tricor
Trilipix</td>
<td>• Hypertriglyceridemia</td>
<td>

- **Dosing (Adult):** Various, depending on dosage form:
  - Tablets of 48 and 145 mg
  - Capsules of 67, 134, and 200 mg
  - As fenofibric acid 45 mg and 135 mg
    - 135 mg = 145 mg tablet = 200 mg capsule
- **Dosing (Peds):** Not routinely used
- **CYP450 Interactions:** Inhibits CYP2C9
- **Renal or Hepatic Dose Adjustments:**
  - GFR less than 30 mL/minute - contraindicated
  - Hepatic impairment - contraindicated
- **Dosage Forms:** Oral (capsule, tablet)

</td>
</tr>
<tr>
<td>Gemfibrozil</td>
<td>Lopid</td>
<td>• Hypertriglyceridemia</td>
<td>

- **Dosing (Adult):**
  - Oral 600 mg BID, 30 minutes before food
- **Dosing (Peds):** Not routinely used
- CYP450 Interactions: Substrate of CYP3A4. Inhibits CYP2C8
- **Renal or Hepatic Dose Adjustments:**
  - GFR 10 to 50 mL/minute - reduce dose by 25%
  - GFR less than 10 mL/minute - reduce dose by 50%
  - Hepatic impairment - contraindicated
- **Dosage Forms:** Oral (tablet)

</td>
</tr>
</table>

High-Yield Clinical Knowledge

- **Renal Dose Adjustment**
  - Different from statins, fibrates should not be used in patients with renal impairment.
    - With gemfibrozil, dose adjustments should begin when the patient's GFR is below 50 mL/minute, whereas use with fenofibrate is contraindicated in patients with a GFR of less than 30 mL/minute.
      - Some statins do require renal dose adjustment, but none are contraindicated in renally impaired patients.

- **Increase LDL**
  - When used for hypertriglyceridemia, fibrates may lead to modest reciprocal rises in LDL, mainly when baseline triglycerides are greater than 1000 mg/dL.
    - Although the LDL concentration increases, this effect is still considered to be beneficial as the morphology of the LDL changes, preserving a potential cardiovascular benefit.

- **Drug Interactions**
  - Gemfibrozil should not be used combined with statins due to the significant risk of enhanced toxicity and limited clinical benefit.
    - Specifically, gemfibrozil should not be used with lovastatin, pravastatin, and simvastatin.
      - However, experts suggest use can be considered in combination with atorvastatin, pitavastatin, and rosuvastatin, provided that lower doses are used, and the patient is followed closely.
      - Fluvastatin may be used in combination with gemfibrozil without any specific dose adjustments.

- **ATP4 & Place in Therapy**
  - According to the ATP4 guidelines, due to the lack of patient-oriented clinical benefit, and the effectiveness of statins at lowering triglycerides, fibrates are considered the last line for the management of hypertriglyceridemia.
    - There are patient-specific indications where use may still be reasonable, including

- **Fibrates and Protease Inhibitors**
  - Protease inhibitors (used for HIV) are known to cause metabolic abnormalities, including hypercholesterolemia and hypertriglyceridemia.
    - Fenofibrate can be used to manage this effect, but consideration should be made to ensure the patient is not taking raltegravir (an integrase inhibitor) since the risk of myopathy is increased.

High-Yield Fast-Fact

- **Gallstone Risk**
  - Fibrates lower cholesterol, in part by enhancing its elimination in bile and thus increasing the cholesterol content of bile.
  - In some patients, this can increase the risk of cholesterol-based gallstones. However, they are fine to use if a patient has had a cholecystectomy.

HIGH-YIELD BOARD EXAM ESSENTIALS
- **CLASSIC AGENTS:** Fenofibrate, gemfibrozil
- **DRUG CLASS:** Fibrates
- **INDICATIONS:** Hyperlipidemia, hypertriglyceridemia
- **MECHANISM:** Activate PPAR-alpha, facilitating PPAR-alpha mediated stimulation of fatty acid oxidation, increased lipoprotein lipase synthesis, and decreasing apolipoprotein C-III production.
- **SIDE EFFECTS:** Increased LDL, gallstones, dyspepsia, diarrhea
- **CLINICAL PEARLS:** According to the guidelines, due to the lack of patient-oriented clinical benefit, and the effectiveness of statins at lowering triglycerides, fibrates are considered the last line for the management of hypertriglyceridemia.

High-Yield Basic Pharmacology

- **Mechanism of Action**
    - Niacin decreases plasma and adipose free fatty acids, increases lipolysis of triglycerides, and hepatic esterification of triglycerides, promoting chylomicron triglyceride removal from plasma.
    - Increases HDL by reversing cholesterol transport in hepatocytes by apolipoprotein A1
    - Niacin improves dyslipidemia by decreasing free fatty acids, increases clearance and hepatic utilization of triglycerides, as well as increasing HDL by reversing hepatic cholesterol transport.
    - However, this effect has not been demonstrated to be sustained and may explain the absence of ASCVD risk reduction in modern dyslipidemia management.

Primary Net Benefit

- The current guidelines do not support the use of niacin for LDL lowering, as clinical evidence does not suggest additional patient-oriented benefit when added to statin therapy.

Niacin - Drug Class Review High-Yield Med Reviews			
Mechanism of Action: *Decreases free fatty acids, increases lipolysis of triglycerides, and hepatic esterification of triglycerides, promoting chylomicron triglyceride removal from plasma.*			
Class Effects: Can improve LDL, but with no decrease in cardiovascular morbidity or mortality.			
Generic Name	**Brand Name**	**Indication(s) or Uses**	**Notes**

Niacin	Niacor
	Niaspan
		• Dyslipidemia	• **Dosing (Adult):**
			  – Oral (regular release) 250 mg daily
			    • Maximum 6 g total daily
			  – Oral (sustained or controlled release) 250 to 750 mg daily.
			  – Oral (extended-release) 500 mg at bedtime
			    • Maximum 2 g daily
			• **Dosing (Peds):** Age over 10 years
			  – Oral (regular release) 100 to 250 mg daily
			    • Maximum 10 mg/kg/day
			  – Oral (sustained or controlled release) 500 to 1500 mg daily
			    • Maximum 10 mg/kg/day
			• **CYP450 Interactions:** None known
			• **Renal or Hepatic Dose Adjustments:** None
			• **Dosage Forms:** Oral (ER capsule, powder, IR tablet, SR tablet, ER tablet)

High-Yield Clinical Knowledge

- **Niacin Vs Niacinamide**
    - At appropriate therapeutic doses, niacin is capable of lowering LDL, however, niacinamide has no lipid-lowering effect.
        - Niacinamide is the amide derivative of niacin.
- **Increasing HDL**
    - Niacin is primarily considered to be an add on agent to increase HDL.

- The clinical impact of this augmentation has not been significant, and niacin is not generally recommended to be added to lipid pharmacotherapy.
- **Flushing**
  - The most notorious adverse event with niacin is flushing or the sensation of warmth after each dose.
    - This effect is dose-dependent, with target doses required for lipid-lowering effects promoting flushing symptoms.
    - Taking niacin with warm beverages (i.e., coffee or tea) or with alcohol can increase the likelihood and severity of flushing.
  - Tachyphylaxis may occur within 3 consecutive days of therapy, but aspirin can be added to blunt this prostaglandin-mediated response.
- **Hypothetical Physiologic Benefits**
  - Niacin has been associated with a potential benefit early in the acute phase of myocardial infarction by lowering cytosolic redox stats in ischemia-reperfusion.
    - Another proposed mechanism of niacin in acute myocardial infarction is the stimulation of anaerobic glycolysis in ischemia-reperfusion states.
  - The proposed mechanism for these benefits is due to enhanced tissue NADP, and enhanced activity of G-protein linked receptors.
    - These benefits may occur from normal dietary intake of niacin, not therapeutic dosing ranges for dyslipidemia.
- **Dose-Dependent Hepatic Risk**
  - Niacin use in patients with acute hepatic failure is contraindicated, and there is a dose-dependent risk of hepatotoxicity in patients taking niacin.
  - However, doses less than 3 g per day are generally well tolerated, and not associated with sustained changes in liver enzymes or liver function.

High-Yield Fast-Fact

- **Pellagra**
  - Niacin can be used to cure primary pellagra, as the cause of this disease is insufficient dietary intake of niacin.

HIGH-YIELD BOARD EXAM ESSENTIALS
- **CLASSIC AGENTS:** Niacin
- **DRUG CLASS:** Lipid-Lowering Agents
- **INDICATIONS:** Dyslipidemia
- **MECHANISM:** Decreases plasma and adipose free fatty acids, increases lipolysis of triglycerides, and hepatic esterification of triglycerides, promoting chylomicron triglyceride removal from plasma.
- **SIDE EFFECTS:** Flushing, hepatic injury, hyperuricemia, increases in glucose
- **CLINICAL PEARLS:** At appropriate therapeutic doses, niacin is capable of lowering LDL, however, niacinamide has no lipid-lowering effect. Patients must be titrated to appropriate doses over time to avoid worsening side effects and risk of liver toxicity.

High-Yield Basic Pharmacology

- **Mechanism of Action**
  - Reduce the hepatic synthesis of triglyceride-rich VLDL by increasing hepatic oxidation of free fatty acids and increasing LDL hydrolysis from activation of PPAR-alpha and inhibition of apoprotein C-III.
- **EPA/DHA vs. EPA**
  - EPA-only icosapent may hypothetically derive its benefit from a lack of DHA, preventing its effect on increasing LDL in patients with severe hypertriglyceridemia.

Primary Net Benefit

- Omega-3 fatty acids containing only EPA (icosapent) are associated with a significant reduction in the rate of ischemic cardiac events, an effect that the former omega-3 fatty acids with EPA/DHA did not demonstrate.

Omega-3 Polyunsaturated Fatty Acid - Drug Class Review High-Yield Med Reviews			
Mechanism of Action: *Increasing hepatic oxidation of free fatty acids, increasing LDL hydrolysis from activation of PPAR-alpha, and inhibiting apoprotein C-III.*			
Class Effects: *Reduction in triglycerides, increase HDL. Possible increase in LDL.*			
Generic Name	**Brand Name**	**Indication(s) or Uses**	**Notes**
Icosapent ethyl (Omega-3-acid ethyl ester of EPA)	Vascepa	• Hypertriglyceridemia	• **Dosing (Adult):** – Oral 2 g BID with meals • **Dosing (Peds):** Not routinely used • **CYP450 Interactions:** None known • **Renal or Hepatic Dose Adjustments:** None • **Dosage Forms:** Oral (capsule)
Omega-3-acid ethyl ester of EPA/DHA	Lovaza	• Hypertriglyceridemia	• **Dosing (Adult):** – Oral 2 g BID or 4 g daily • **Dosing (Peds):** Not routinely used • **CYP450 Interactions:** None known • **Renal or Hepatic Dose Adjustments:** None • **Dosage Forms:** Oral (capsule)

High-Yield Clinical Knowledge

- **Cardiovascular Benefit**
  - The proposed mechanism for reduced cardiovascular disease events is inhibiting platelet aggregation due to an increase in EPA/arachidonic acid ratio.
- **Bleeding Risk**
  - Omega-3 agents independently may prolong bleeding time by impairing platelet function and reducing several coagulation factors (antithrombin, thrombin, fibrinogen, factor V, factor VII, and von Willebrand factor).
  - The combination of omega-3 agents and warfarin may increase INR in patients with an otherwise stable INR.
  - Although more challenging to quantify clinically, omega-3 agents may also increase the risk of bleeding from dabigatran, oral factor Xa inhibitors (apixaban, edoxaban, rivaroxaban), salicylates, thienopyridines (clopidogrel, cangrelor, prasugrel, ticagrelor), SSRIs, ibrutinib, and NSAIDs.

- **Fishy Burps**
  - A common complaint of omega-3 products (OTC and the EPA/DHA combination) is abdominal bloating, dyspepsia, and "fishy burps."
    - These effects can be minimized by keeping the capsules refrigerated.
- **Fish or Shellfish Allergies**
  - Patients with known hypersensitivity to fish or shellfish should not take omega-3 products, including icosapent.
    - Of note, fish or shellfish allergies should not preclude patients from receiving iodinated contrast agents, as shellfish allergies are not a result of iodine (true iodine allergies are incompatible with life).
- **OTC vs. Rx**
  - As opposed to niacin products, the various omega-3 EPA/DHA OTC products are generally similar to the prescription version (Lovaza).
  - The main difference is that the relative dose of omega-3 EPA/DHA is much higher than available OTC formulations.
    - A 4 g dose of Lovaza (4 capsules) is roughly equivalent to 6 to 8 capsules of OTC omega-3.

High-Yield Fast-Fact

- **Dietary Omega-3**
  - The AHA recommends we all eat various fish at least twice per week to maintain healthy omega-3 acquisition from a diet with omega-3 supplementation reserved for those with cardiovascular disease or high triglycerides.

HIGH-YIELD BOARD EXAM ESSENTIALS
- **CLASSIC AGENTS:** Omega-3-acid ethyl ester of EPA/DHA, icosapent ethyl (Omega-3-acid ethyl ester of EPA)
- **DRUG CLASS:** Omega-3 polyunsaturated fatty acid
- **INDICATIONS:** Hypertriglyceridemia
- **MECHANISM:** Reduce the hepatic synthesis of triglyceride-rich VLDL by increasing hepatic oxidation of free fatty acids and increasing LDL hydrolysis from activation of PPAR-alpha and inhibition of apoprotein C-III.
- **SIDE EFFECTS:** Increased risk of bleeding (very small risk), fishy breath/burps
- **CLINICAL PEARLS:**
  - These agents are effective at decreasing triglycerides especially in doses of 2,000 mg or more per day. The risk of drug interactions is very low. Overall well tolerated.
  - Omega-3 agents independently may prolong bleeding time by impairing platelet function and reducing several coagulation factors. The clinical relevance of this is unknown but appears to be minimal.

High-Yield Basic Pharmacology

- **Mechanism of Action**
  - Inhibition of proprotein convertase subtilisin/kexin type 9 (PCSK-9) permits the recycling of the LDL receptor on hepatocytes and lowers plasma LDL by enhancing the hepatic clearance of LDL.
- **Statins and PCSK9 Expression**
  - Although statins are a cornerstone of lipid pharmacotherapy, their inhibition of HMG-CoA reductase activates sterol regulatory element-binding protein (SREBP), which increases the expression of genes promoting the production of PCSK9 and LDL receptors.
  - Although LDL receptor density increases, these receptors are not recycled because of the increased expression of PCSK9 and its digestion of the LDL receptor.

Primary Net Benefit

- PCSK9 inhibitors are potent reducers of LDL by as much as 60% in patients already taking maximally tolerated statin therapy.
  - These LDL reductions can be as low as 20 mg/dL, with supporting evidence suggesting cardiovascular morbidity reduction.

PCSK-9 Inhibitors - Drug Class Review			
High-Yield Med Reviews			
Mechanism of Action: *Inhibits PCSK-9, promoting LDL receptor recycling and lowering plasma LDL.*			
Class Effects: *ASCVD morbidity reduction; expensive agents.*			
Generic Name	**Brand Name**	**Main Indication(s) or Uses**	**Notes**

Alirocumab	Praluent	• Hyperlipidemia (primary and secondary prevention)	• **Dosing (Adult):**
			  – SubQ 75 mg q2weeks
			  – SubQ 300 mg q4weeks
			    • Maximum 150 mg q2weeks
			• **Dosing (Peds):** Not routinely used
			• **CYP450 Interactions:** None known
			• **Renal or Hepatic Dose Adjustments:** None
			• **Dosage Forms:** Solution for subcutaneous injection

Evolocumab	Repatha	• Hyperlipidemia (primary and secondary prevention)
		• Homozygous familial hypercholesterolemia
			• **Dosing (Adult):**
			  – SubQ 140 mg q2weeks
			  – SubQ 420 mg q4weeks
			    • Maximum 420 mg q2weeks
			• **Dosing (Peds):**
			  – Children 12 years and older - SubQ 420 mg q4weeks
			    • Maximum 420 mg q2weeks
			• **CYP450 Interactions:** None known
			• **Renal or Hepatic Dose Adjustments:** None
			• **Dosage Forms:** Solution for subcutaneous injection

High-Yield Clinical Knowledge

- **Alirocumab Administration**
    - The administration of alirocumab is not a straightforward subcutaneous injection, but specific administration methods must be followed to ensure the full clinical benefit is realized.
        - The solution for injection must stand at room temperature (not aided by heat or hot water) for at least 30 to 45 minutes prior to use.
        - Appropriate administration sites include the abdomen, at least 2 inches from the navel, the thigh, or upper arm.
        - The administration itself may take up to 20 seconds, and if the patient is prescribed the 300 mg dose, administer two 150 mg injections consecutively at two different injection sites (i.e., two 20 second injections).
- **Evolocumab Administration**
    - Similar to alirocumab, the administration of evolocumab is not a straightforward subcutaneous injection, but specific administration methods must be followed to ensure the full clinical benefit is realized.
        - The solution for injection must stand at room temperature (not aided by heat or hot water) for at least 30 to 45 minutes prior to use.
        - Appropriate administration sites include the abdomen, at least 2 inches from the navel, the thigh, or upper arm.
        - If patients are taking a once-monthly dose, the subcutaneous injection is over 9 minutes!
            - If the patient doesn't use the single-use infusor, they must take three consecutive individual subcutaneous 140 mg injections, all within a 30-minute.
- **Influenza and UTIs**
    - Aside from a 15% incidence of injection site reactions, the PCSK9 inhibitors are associated with a relatively high incidence of bacterial infections (UTI and respiratory infection), and influenza of 5-6% and up to 9%, respectively.
- **Dose Adjustments**
    - For dose changes (i.e., changing from every two weeks to every four weeks, or vice versa), the first dose of the new regimen should be administered at the time of the next scheduled day of the prior regimen.
- **Missed Doses**
    - Missed doses for the every 2-week regimen; if the dose is not administered within seven days of the missed date, skip the missed dose and resume the normal dosing schedule, or if dosage is monthly, start a new schedule based on this date.
    - For missed doses for the every 4-week regimen, the target the missed dose within seven days from the missed dose, then resume the original schedule.
        - If not administered within seven days, still administer the dose, begin a new schedule from this date.
- **PCSK9 Inhibitor or Ezetimibe?**
    - Although the addition of a PCSK9 inhibitor to statin therapy is associated with a 60% further reduction in LDL, the evidence supporting their effect on mortality is similar to that of ezetimibe (i.e, none).
        - Clinical experts encourage weighing the cost-effectiveness difference between PCSK9 inhibitors to ezetimibe until head-to-head data is available.

HIGH-YIELD BOARD EXAM ESSENTIALS

- **CLASSIC AGENTS:** Alirocumab, evolocumab
- **DRUG CLASS:** PCSK9 inhibitors
- **INDICATIONS:** Hyperlipidemia (mainly heterozygous and homozygous familial HLD), secondary prevention of cardiovascular events
- **MECHANISM:** Inhibition of PCSK-9 permits the recycling of the LDL receptor on hepatocytes and lowers plasma LDL by enhancing the hepatic clearance of LDL.
- **SIDE EFFECTS:** Injection site reactions, increased risk of infection (UTI, respiratory, influenza).
- **CLINICAL PEARLS:**
    - The drugs in this care monoclonal antibodies (MABs) which must be given parenterally.
    - As with most MABs their long half-lives allow for longer durations between injections. If the dose is not administered within seven days of the missed date, skip the missed dose and resume the normal dosing schedule, or if dosage is monthly, start a new schedule based on this date.

High-Yield Basic Pharmacology

- **Hepatic Cholesterol Synthesis**
  - In response to the inhibition of HMG-CoA reductase by statins, hepatic cholesterol synthesis is decreased which induces upregulation of surface LDL receptors, and decreased breakdown of LDL receptors.
    - As a result, LDL is increasingly removed from the plasma, limiting its effect on atherosclerosis.
    - Triglycerides are also removed from the plasma by this mechanism.

Primary Net Benefit

- Statins reduce the incidence of cardiovascular events, cardiovascular mortality, and all-cause mortality.

Statins (HMG-CoA Reductase Inhibitors) - Drug Class Review High-Yield Med Reviews			
Mechanism of Action: *Inhibit HMG-CoA reductase, reducing the conversion of HMG-CoA to mevalonic acid, the rate-limiting enzyme in cholesterol synthesis.*			
Class Effects: Lowers LDL (up to 50-60% from baseline), VLDL, triglycerides, total cholesterol. Increase HDL			
Generic Name	**Brand Name**	**Indication(s) or Uses**	**Notes**
Atorvastatin	Lipitor	<ul><li>Atherosclerotic cardiovascular disease</li><li>Heterozygous familial hypercholesterolemia</li><li>Homozygous familial hypercholesterolemia</li></ul>	<ul><li>**Dosing (Adult):**<ul><li>Oral 10 to 80 mg daily</li></ul></li><li>**Dosing (Peds):**<ul><li>Oral 2.5 to 80 mg daily</li></ul></li><li>**CYP450 Interactions:** Substrate CYP3A4, Pgp</li><li>**Renal or Hepatic Dose Adjustments:**<ul><li>Active liver disease - contraindicated</li></ul></li><li>**Dosage Forms:** Oral (tablet)</li></ul>
Fluvastatin	Lescol	<ul><li>Atherosclerotic cardiovascular disease</li><li>Heterozygous familial hypercholesterolemia</li><li>Homozygous familial hypercholesterolemia</li></ul>	<ul><li>**Dosing (Adult):**<ul><li>Oral 40 to 80 mg twice daily</li></ul></li><li>**Dosing (Peds):**<ul><li>Oral 20 mg daily<ul><li>Maximum 40 mg BID</li></ul></li></ul></li><li>**CYP450 Interactions:** Substrate CYP2C8, CYP2C9, CYP 2D6, CYP3A4</li><li>**Renal or Hepatic Dose Adjustments:**<ul><li>Active liver disease - contraindicated</li><li>Severe renal impairment - Max 40 mg/day</li></ul></li><li>**Dosage Forms:** Oral (tablet)</li></ul>
Lovastatin	Altoprev Mevacor	<ul><li>Atherosclerotic cardiovascular disease</li><li>Heterozygous familial hypercholesterolemia</li><li>Homozygous familial hypercholesterolemia</li></ul>	<ul><li>**Dosing (Adult):**<ul><li>Oral 20 to 60 mg daily</li></ul></li><li>**Dosing (Peds):**<ul><li>Oral 20 to 60 mg daily</li></ul></li><li>**CYP450 Interactions:** Substrate CYP3A4</li><li>**Renal or Hepatic Dose Adjustments:**<ul><li>GFR less than 30 mL/min - Maximum 20 mg/day</li></ul></li><li>**Dosage Forms:** Oral (tablet)</li></ul>

Statins (HMG-CoA Reductase Inhibitors) - Drug Class Review
High-Yield Med Reviews

Generic Name	Brand Name	Indication(s) or Uses	Notes

Pitavastatin	Livalo Zypitamag	▪ Atherosclerotic cardiovascular disease
		▪ Heterozygous familial hypercholesterolemia
			▪ **Dosing (Adult):**
			  – Oral 1 to 4 mg daily
			▪ **Dosing (Peds):**
			  – Oral 1 to 4 mg daily
			▪ **CYP450 Interactions:** Substrate CYP2C8, CYP2C9
			▪ **Renal or Hepatic Dose Adjustments:**
			  – GFR 15 to 59 mL/min - maximum 2 mg/day
			  – Active liver disease - contraindicated
			▪ **Dosage Forms:** Oral (tablet)

Pravastatin	Pravachol	▪ Atherosclerotic cardiovascular disease
		▪ Heterozygous familial hypercholesterolemia
		▪ Homozygous familial hypercholesterolemia
			▪ **Dosing (Adult):**
			  – Oral 20 to 80 mg daily
			▪ **Dosing (Peds):**
			  – Oral 5 to 80 mg daily
			▪ **CYP450 Interactions:** Substrate CYP3A4, Pgp
			▪ **Renal or Hepatic Dose Adjustments:**
			  – Active liver disease - contraindicated
			  – Severe renal impairment - Maximum 10 mg daily
			▪ **Dosage Forms:** Oral (tablet)

Rosuvastatin	Crestor	▪ Atherosclerotic cardiovascular disease
		▪ Familial hypercholesterolemia
			▪ **Dosing (Adult):**
			  – Oral 5 to 40 mg daily
			▪ **Dosing (Peds):**
			  – Oral 5 to 40 mg daily
			▪ **CYP450 Interactions:** CYP2C9, CYP3A4
			▪ **Renal or Hepatic Dose Adjustments:**
			  – GFR less than 30 mL/min - maximum 10 mg daily
			▪ **Dosage Forms:** Oral (table)

Simvastatin	Zocor	▪ Atherosclerotic cardiovascular disease
		▪ Heterozygous familial hypercholesterolemia
		▪ Homozygous familial hypercholesterolemia
			▪ **Dosing (Adult):**
			  – Oral 20 to 40 mg daily
			▪ **Dosing (Peds):**
			  – Oral 10 to 40 mg daily
			▪ **CYP450 Interactions:** Substrate CYP3A4
			▪ **Renal or Hepatic Dose Adjustments:**
			  – Active liver disease - contraindicated
			  – Severe renal impairment - initial 5 mg daily
			▪ **Dosage Forms:** Oral (tablet)

High-Yield Clinical Knowledge

▪ **Statin Intensity**
  – Statins are subdivided into high-intensity, moderate-intensity, and low-intensity agents and dosage ranges.
    – High-intensity: Atorvastatin 40-80 mg, rosuvastatin 20-40mg
    – Moderate-intensity: Atorvastatin 10-20 mg, fluvastatin 40 mg BID (or XL 80mg), lovastatin 40 mg, pitavastatin 2-4 mg, pravastatin 40-80 mg, rosuvastatin 5-10 mg, simvastatin 20-40 mg

- Low-intensity: Fluvastatin 20-40 mg BID, lovastatin 20 mg, pitavastatin 1 mg, pravastatin 10-20 mg, simvastatin 10 mg
- **Lipid-Lowering Effects**
    - In general, statins lower LDL by 20-55%, with the high-intensity agents having the most potent effects.
        - Once established on therapy, the doubling of the statin dose further decreases LDL by 6%.
- **Pleiotropic Effects**
    - Statins are used not just for their lipid-lowering effects, but also for additional benefits known as pleiotropic effects that are not specific to the HMG-CoA reductase inhibition.
    - These include anti-inflammatory effects, stabilization of coronary plaque, prevents endothelial dysfunction, reduces blood viscosity, reduces fibrinogen levels, reduces platelet aggregation, decreases tissue factor release, and activates nitric oxide synthase.
- **Hepatotoxicity (Dose- or Concentration-Dependent)**
    - All statins are associated with a dose or concentration dependent risk of causing liver damage.
    - According to updated FDA guidance, statin therapy does no longer requires routine hepatic monitoring.
        - This is based on observations that suggest traditional routine monitoring does not appear to be effective in either detecting or preventing serious liver injury.
        - Hepatic enzymes should be measured only if there is clinical suspicion suggestive of liver injury following initiation or changes in statin treatment.
- **Myopathy**
    - Similar to hepatic enzyme monitoring, routine screening for myopathy (CPK), is not recommended, unless there is clinical suspicion of statin-induced myopathy.
        - Patients who are at higher risk of myopathies from statins include patients who are over 80 years of age, pre-existing hepatic or renal dysfunction, post-surgical or perioperative use of statins, low BMI, and untreated or undiagnosed hypothyroidism.
        - Drug interactions that increase the risk of statin-induced myopathy include fibrates (particularly gemfibrozil), niacin, protease inhibitors, amiodarone, digoxin, cyclosporine, warfarin, macrolide antibiotics, and azole antifungals.
- **Diabetes**
    - Statin therapy is associated with a slightly increased risk of diabetes primarily from decreased insulin release from pancreatic beta-cells.
    - The reduction in the risk of major adverse coronary events greatly outweighs this small increased risk of developing diabetes.
        - Potential alternative mechanisms include inhibition of glucose uptake by pancreatic beta cells, beta-cell apoptosis from nitric oxide production, glucokinase inhibition due to increased hepatic LDL uptake.

HIGH-YIELD BOARD EXAM ESSENTIALS

- **CLASSIC AGENTS:** Atorvastatin, fluvastatin, lovastatin, pitavastatin, pravastatin, rosuvastatin, simvastatin
- **DRUG CLASS:** Statins; HMG-CoA reductase Inhibitors
- **INDICATIONS:** Atherosclerotic cardiovascular disease, hypercholesterolemia
- **MECHANISM:** Inhibit HMG-CoA reductase, reducing the conversion of HMG-CoA to mevalonic acid, the rate-limiting enzyme in cholesterol synthesis.
- **SIDE EFFECTS:** Myalgia, rhabdomyolysis (rare)
- **CLINICAL PEARLS:**
    - Statins have good evidence in both primary and secondary prevention of CVD.
    - Statins are used not just for their lipid-lowering effects, but also for additional benefits known as pleiotropic effects that are not specific to the HMG-CoA reductase inhibition.
    - The risk of muscle and liver damage is a dose or concentration dependent problem.

High-Yield Basic Pharmacology

- **Benzoyl Peroxide**
  - Penetrates the stratum corneum and follicular openings where it is converted to benzoic acid, exerting an antimicrobial activity against propionibacterium acnes.
- **Retinoic Acid Derivatives**
  - Expulsion of open comedones and transformation of closed to open comedones by decreasing cohesion between epidermal cells and increased epidermal cell turnover.
  - The effect of retinoic acid and derivatives on epithelial tissue is varied, including stabilizing lysosomes, increasing RNA polymerase activity, and increasing PGE2, cAMP, and cGMP.
  - The acid form of vitamin A, tretinoin, is an effective topical treatment for acne.
  - Isotretinoin is the 13-cis-retinoic acid analog of vitamin A
- **Azelaic Acid, Clindamycin, Erythromycin, Minocycline, Sarecycline**
  - Antimicrobial action against Cutibacterium acnes, Propionibacterium acnes, and Staphylococcus epidermidis.

Primary Net Benefit

- Topical and systemic interventions for the treatment of acne. Serious teratogenic effects due to retinoids and isotretinoin are core knowledge for health care providers.

Acne - Drug Class Review			
High-Yield Med Reviews			
Mechanism of Action: *See above.*			
Class Effects: Topical and systemic interventions for the treatment of acne. Serious teratogenic effects due to retinoids and isotretinoin are core knowledge for health care providers.			
Generic Name	**Brand Name**	**Indication(s) or Uses**	**Notes**

Azelaic Acid	Azelex, Finacea	▪ Acne vulgaris
		▪ Acne rosacea
			▪ **Dosing (Adult):**
			  – Topical twice daily
			▪ **Dosing (Peds):**
			  – Topical twice daily
			▪ **CYP450 Interactions:** None
			▪ **Renal or Hepatic Dose Adjustments:** None
			▪ **Dosage Forms:** Topical (cream, foam, gel)

Adapalene	Differin	▪ Acne vulgaris	▪ **Dosing (Adult):**
			  – Topical once daily in the evening before bedtime
			▪ **Dosing (Peds):**
			  – Topical once daily in the evening before bedtime
			▪ **CYP450 Interactions:** None
			▪ **Renal or Hepatic Dose Adjustments:** None
			▪ **Dosage Forms:** Topical (cream, gel, lotion, pad, solution)

Acne - Drug Class Review
High-Yield Med Reviews

Generic Name	Brand Name	Indication(s) or Uses	Notes

Adapalene, benzoyl peroxide	Epiduo	▪ Acne vulgaris	▪ **Dosing (Adult):**
			  – Topical once daily in the evening before bedtime
			▪ **Dosing (Peds):**
			  – Topical once daily in the evening before bedtime
			▪ **CYP450 Interactions:** None
			▪ **Renal or Hepatic Dose Adjustments:** None
			▪ **Dosage Forms:** Topical (gel, pad)

Benzoyl peroxide	Numerous names including: Acne Medication, Benzac, BenzEFoam, Benzoyl Peroxide, Clearplex, Clearskin, Desquam, and others	▪ Acne vulgaris	▪ **Dosing (Adult):**
			  – Topical once daily in the evening before bedtime
			    ▪ Up to 2-3 times daily
			▪ **Dosing (Peds):**
			  – Topical once daily in the evening before bedtime
			    ▪ Up to 2-3 times daily
			▪ **CYP450 Interactions:** None
			▪ **Renal or Hepatic Dose Adjustments:** None
			▪ **Dosage Forms:** Topical (cream, foam, gel, kit, liquid, lotion, pad, solution)

Benzoyl peroxide, hydrocortisone	Vanoxide-HC	▪ Acne vulgaris	▪ **Dosing (Adult):**
			  – Topical 1 to 3 times daily
			▪ **Dosing (Peds):**
			  – Topical 1 to 3 times daily
			▪ **CYP450 Interactions:** None
			▪ **Renal or Hepatic Dose Adjustments:** None
			▪ **Dosage Forms:** Topical (lotion)

Benzoyl peroxide, clindamycin	Acanya, BenzaClin, Duac, Neuac, Onexton	▪ Acne vulgaris	▪ **Dosing (Adult):**
			  – Topical 1 to 2 times daily
			▪ **Dosing (Peds):**
			  – Topical 1 to 2 times daily
			▪ **CYP450 Interactions:** None
			▪ **Renal or Hepatic Dose Adjustments:** None
			▪ **Dosage Forms:** Topical (gel, kit)

Benzoyl peroxide, erythromycin	Aktipak, Benzamycin	▪ Acne vulgaris	▪ **Dosing (Adult):**
			  – Topical 1 to 2 times daily
			▪ **Dosing (Peds):**
			  – Topical 1 to 2 times daily
			▪ **CYP450 Interactions:** None
			▪ **Renal or Hepatic Dose Adjustments:** None
			▪ **Dosage Forms:** Topical (gel, kit)

Acne - Drug Class Review
High-Yield Med Reviews

Generic Name	Brand Name	Indication(s) or Uses	Notes

Clindamycin, tretinoin	Veltin, Ziana	• Acne vulgaris	• **Dosing (Adult):**
			  – Topical once daily in the evening before bedtime
			• **Dosing (Peds):**
			  – Topical once daily in the evening before bedtime
			• **CYP450 Interactions:** None
			• **Renal or Hepatic Dose Adjustments:** None
			• **Dosage Forms:** Topical (gel)

Erythromycin	Ery, Erygel	• Acne vulgaris	• **Dosing (Adult):**
			  – Topical 1 to 2 times daily
			• **Dosing (Peds):**
			  – Topical 1 to 2 times daily
			• **CYP450 Interactions:** None
			• **Renal or Hepatic Dose Adjustments:** None
			• **Dosage Forms:** Topical (gel, pad, solution)

Isotretinoin	Absorica, Accutane, Amnesteem, Claravis, Myorisan, Zenatane	• Acne vulgaris	• **Dosing (Adult):**
			  – Oral 0.5 mg/kg/day x 1 month, then 1 mg/kg/day in 2 divided doses
			  – Oral (micronized) 0.4 to 0.8 mg/kg/day in 2 divided doses
			• **Dosing (Peds):**
			  – Children over 12 years, use adult dosing
			• **CYP450 Interactions:** None
			• **Renal or Hepatic Dose Adjustments:** None
			• **Dosage Forms:** Oral (capsule)

Minocycline	Amzeeq, Zilxi	• Acne vulgaris	• **Dosing (Adult):**
			  – Topical once daily in the evening before bedtime
			• **Dosing (Peds):**
			  – Topical once daily in the evening before bedtime
			• **CYP450 Interactions:** None
			• **Renal or Hepatic Dose Adjustments:** None
			• **Dosage Forms:** Topical (Foam)

Salicylic acid	Numerous brand names	• Acne vulgaris	• **Dosing (Adult):**
			  – Topical 1 to 3 times daily
			• **Dosing (Peds):**
			  – Topical 1 to 3 times daily
			• **CYP450 Interactions:** None
			• **Renal or Hepatic Dose Adjustments:** None
			• **Dosage Forms:** Topical (cream, foam, gel, kit, liquid, lotion, ointment, pad, shampoo, solution)

Acne - Drug Class Review
High-Yield Med Reviews

Generic Name	Brand Name	Indication(s) or Uses	Notes
Sarecycline	Seysara	▪ Acne vulgaris	▪ **Dosing (Adult):** – Oral 60 to 150 mg daily ▪ **Dosing (Peds):** – Oral 60 to 150 mg daily ▪ **CYP450 Interactions:** None ▪ **Renal or Hepatic Dose Adjustments:** None ▪ **Dosage Forms:** Oral (tablet)
Sulfacetamide	Klaron, Ovace, Seb-Prev	▪ Acne vulgaris	▪ **Dosing (Adult):** – Topical 1 to 3 times daily ▪ **Dosing (Peds):** – Topical 1 to 3 times daily ▪ **CYP450 Interactions:** None ▪ **Renal or Hepatic Dose Adjustments:** None ▪ **Dosage Forms:** Topical (cream, gel, liquid, shampoo)
Sulfacetamide and sulfur	Avar, Clarifoam, Clenia, Plexion, Prascion, Rosanil, Rosula, SulfaCleanse, Sumadan, Sumaxin, Zencia	▪ Acne vulgaris	▪ **Dosing (Adult):** – Topical 1 to 3 times daily ▪ **Dosing (Peds):** – Topical 1 to 3 times daily ▪ **CYP450 Interactions:** None ▪ **Renal or Hepatic Dose Adjustments:** – Renal impairment - contraindicated ▪ **Dosage Forms:** Topical (cream, gel, lotion, pad, solution, wash)
Tazarotene	Arazlo, Avage, Fabior, Tazorac	▪ Acne vulgaris	▪ **Dosing (Adult):** – Topical once daily in the evening before bedtime ▪ **Dosing (Peds):** – Topical once daily in the evening before bedtime ▪ **CYP450 Interactions:** None ▪ **Renal or Hepatic Dose Adjustments:** None ▪ **Dosage Forms:** Topical (cream, foam, gel, lotion)
Tretinoin	Altreno, Atralin, Avita, Refissa, Renova, Retin-A, Tretin-X	▪ Acne vulgaris	▪ **Dosing (Adult):** – Topical once daily in the evening before bedtime ▪ **Dosing (Peds):** – Topical once daily in the evening before bedtime ▪ **CYP450 Interactions:** None ▪ **Renal or Hepatic Dose Adjustments:** None ▪ **Dosage Forms:** Topical (cream, gel, lotion)

Acne - Drug Class Review
High-Yield Med Reviews

Generic Name	Brand Name	Indication(s) or Uses	Notes

Trifarotene	Aklief	• Acne vulgaris	• **Dosing (Adult):**
			  – Topical once daily in the evening before bedtime
			• **Dosing (Peds):**
			  – Topical once daily in the evening before bedtime
			• **CYP450 Interactions:** None
			• **Renal or Hepatic Dose Adjustments:** None
			• **Dosage Forms:** Topical (cream)

High-Yield Clinical Knowledge

- **Isotretinoin**
  - The use of isotretinoin in women of childbearing potential must utilize the iPLEDGE registration and follow-up system to ensure the risk of teratogenic effects is eliminated.
  - Before initiation of isotretinoin, women must have a negative serum pregnancy test within two weeks of starting isotretinoin.
  - Women who will begin isotretinoin must use an effective means of contraception for at least one month before isotretinoin therapy and continuously throughout isotretinoin therapy.
    - Effective birth control must also be continued for two menstrual cycles following discontinuation of isotretinoin.
  - Isotretinoin therapy must be started on the second or third day of the next normal menstrual period cycle.
  - Patients may experience an acne flair shortly after starting oral isotretinoin therapy, an effect similar to topical retinoid therapy.
- **Acne Management Approach**
  - Retinoids are considered the first-line treatment of inflammatory acne and should be used in combination with benzoyl peroxide.
  - Isotretinoin can be used as a first-line agent for cystic and conglobate acne and continued until complete clearance of acne is achieved.
  - Topical or systemic antibiotics must not be used empirically as monotherapy to treat acne.
  - For pregnant women, azelaic acid topical therapy can be used as retinoids are contraindicated.
- **Application of Retinoic Acids**
  - For the topical application of retinoic acids, the initial concentration should be sufficient to induce mild erythema and peeling.
    - Dose titration is required if too much irritation or too little irritation occurs.
- **Onset of Retinoic Acid Effect**
  - The full onset of the effect of retinoic acid on acne lesions takes approximately 8 to 12 weeks.
  - Patients may be discouraged by the appearance of worsening acne lesions during the first 4 to 6 weeks of treatment, but these lesions will clear with continued therapy.
- **Photosensitivity**
  - Patients using topical tretinoin are at increased susceptibility to UV light and sunburns.
  - It's recommended to use a daily sunscreen and other protective measures while taking topical tretinoin agents.
  - Caution is also warranted in patients with a personal or family history of skin cancer, as UV exposure with retinoid therapy may increase cancer risk.
- **Benzoyl Acid Combinations**
  - Benzoyl acid has a concentration-dependent irritant effect on the skin and is often co-formulated with other anti-acne antibiotics or retinoids to reduce irritation while maintaining efficacy.

High-Yield Fast-Facts

- **Oral Contraceptives**
    - As isotretinoin requires some contraception format, estrogen-containing oral contraceptives can also help treat acne in some women.
- **Spironolactone**
    - Although there is insufficient data to support its use routinely, some dermatologist specialists reserve spironolactone for acne treatment in some women.

HIGH-YIELD BOARD EXAM ESSENTIALS
- **CLASSIC AGENTS:** Azelaic acid, adapalene, benzoyl peroxide, erythromycin, isotretinoin, minocycline, salicylic acid, sarecycline, sulfacetamide, tazarotene, tretinoin, trifarotene
- **DRUG CLASS:** Anti-acne
- **INDICATIONS:** Acne
- **MECHANISM:** Penetrates the stratum corneum and follicular openings where it is converted to benzoic acid, exerting an antimicrobial activity against propionibacterium acnes (benzoyl peroxide). Expulsion of open comedones and transformation of closed to open comedones by decreasing cohesion between epidermal cells and increased epidermal cell turnover (retinoic acid derivatives). Antimicrobial action against Cutibacterium acnes, Propionibacterium acnes, and Staphylococcus epidermidis (azelaic acid, clindamycin, erythromycin, minocycline, sarecycline)
- **SIDE EFFECTS:** Dry skin, erythema, teratogen (isotretinoin)
- **CLINICAL PEARLS:** Retinoids are considered the first-line treatment of inflammatory acne and should be used in combination with benzoyl peroxide.

High-Yield Basic Pharmacology

- **Mechanism of Action**
  - Bind to cyclophilin (cyclosporine) or FKBP12 (tacrolimus), which inhibits calcineurin, halting the transcription of numerous key cytokines (specifically IL-2) necessary for T-cell activation
  - Calcineurin usually is responsible for the dephosphorylation and then the movement of a component of the nuclear factor of activated T lymphocytes, which induces cytokine genes for IL-2.
    - Thus, blocking calcineurin activity (calcineurin inhibitor) or its secondary downstream effects (everolimus, sirolimus) prevents the activation of IL-2.

Primary Net Benefit

- Topical calcineurin inhibitors are second-line agents for the temporary and intermittent treatment of atopic dermatitis.

Calcineurin Inhibitors - Drug Class Review			
High-Yield Med Reviews			
Mechanism of Action: *Bind to cyclophilin (cyclosporine) or FKBP12 (tacrolimus), which inhibits calcineurin, halting the transcription of numerous key cytokines (specifically IL-2) necessary for T-cell activation.*			
Class Effects: Topical calcineurin inhibitors are second-line agents for the temporary and intermittent treatment of atopic dermatitis.			
Generic Name	**Brand Name**	**Indication(s) or Uses**	**Notes**

Pimecrolimus	Elidel	• Atopic dermatitis	• **Dosing (Adult):**
			  – Topical application twice daily
			• **Dosing (Peds):**
			  – Topical application twice daily
			• **CYP450 Interactions:** Substrate CYP3A4
			• **Renal or Hepatic Dose Adjustments:** None
			• **Dosage Forms:** Topical (cream)

Tacrolimus	Protopic	• Atopic dermatitis	• **Dosing (Adult):**
			  – Topical application twice daily
			• **Dosing (Peds):**
			  – Topical application twice daily
			• **CYP450 Interactions:** Substrate CYP3A4
			• **Renal or Hepatic Dose Adjustments:** None
			• **Dosage Forms:** Topical (ointment)

High-Yield Clinical Knowledge

- **Malignancy Warning**
  - Tacrolimus and pimecrolimus are associated with the rare development of lymphoma or skin malignancies and should be avoided in patients with premalignant dermatologic disorders.
  - The FDA issued a black-boxed warning specific to this effect for topical tacrolimus and pimecrolimus.
- **Warts**
  - New skin papillomas, otherwise known as warts, are associated with topical tacrolimus and pimecrolimus therapy.
  - Treatment with tacrolimus or pimecrolimus may continue if warts occur; however, it's recommended to discontinue calcineurin inhibitor therapy if warts do not respond to conventional therapies.
- **Alcohol Consumption**

- Systemic calcineurin inhibitors inhibit aldehyde dehydrogenase and prevent the metabolism of ethanol, producing a disulfiram-like effect.
    - Topical tacrolimus or pimecrolimus are minimally absorbed and will not likely cause this effect; however, the warning exists in the prescribing information.
- **Netherton Syndrome**
    - Topical calcineurin inhibitors should not be used in patients with Netherton syndrome where systemic absorption of tacrolimus or pimecrolimus occurs.
    - Netherton syndrome is an autosomal recessive genetic disorder characterized by an increased incidence of atopic eczema, scaling skin, and hair abnormalities.

HIGH-YIELD BOARD EXAM ESSENTIALS
- **CLASSIC AGENTS:** Pimecrolimus, tacrolimus
- **DRUG CLASS:** Topical calcineurin Inhibitors
- **INDICATIONS:** Atopic dermatitis
- **MECHANISM:** Bind to FKBP12, which inhibits calcineurin, halting the transcription of numerous key cytokines (specifically IL-2) necessary for T-cell activation.
- **SIDE EFFECTS:** New skin papillomas
- **CLINICAL PEARLS:** Tacrolimus and pimecrolimus are associated with the rare development of lymphoma or skin malignancies and should be avoided in patients with premalignant dermatologic disorders.

High-Yield Basic Pharmacology

- **Aluminum Acetate, Calamine, Lanolin**
  - Topical soothing effect on the skin.
- **Capsaicin**
  - Agonist of the transient receptor potential vanilloid (TRPV1) receptor modulating noxious stimulation and the sensation of heat.
- **Coal Tar**
  - Anti-inflammatory, antimicrobial, and antipruritic activity as a result of suppression of DNA synthesis.
- **Selenium sulfide**
  - Slows the production of corneocytes and skin flaking on the epidermis and epithelium through a cytostatic activity.
- **Silver sulfadiazine**
  - Silver ions complex with chloride in tissues to form silver chloride, causing cellular protein coagulation and the formation of an eschar.
- **Urea**
  - Dissolves intracellular matrix, disrupting the horny layer of skin or debriding of the nail plate.
- **Zinc oxide**
  - Mild astringent and antiseptic activity

Primary Net Benefit

- Commonly available over-the-counter topical skin products that can be used with or without concomitant topical corticosteroids.

Miscellaneous Agents - Drug Class Review			
High-Yield Med Reviews			
Mechanism of Action: *see above*			
Class Effects: Commonly available over-the-counter topical skin products that can be used with or without concomitant topical corticosteroids.			
Generic Name	**Brand Name**	**Indication(s) or Uses**	**Notes**

Aluminum acetate	Boro-Packs, Pedi-Boro Soak	• Skin irritation	• **Dosing (Adult):**
			  – Soak affected area in solution for 15-30 minutes as needed
			• **Dosing (Peds):**
			  – Soak affected area in solution for 15-30 minutes as needed
			• **CYP450 Interactions:** None
			• **Renal or Hepatic Dose Adjustments:** None
			• **Dosage Forms:** Topical (packet, solution)

Calamine	Caladryl, Calagesic	• Skin irritation	• **Dosing (Adult):**
			  – Topical application as often as needed
			• **Dosing (Peds):**
			  – Topical application as often as needed
			• **CYP450 Interactions:** None
			• **Renal or Hepatic Dose Adjustments:** None
			• **Dosage Forms:** Topical (lotion, suspension)

Miscellaneous Agents - Drug Class Review
High-Yield Med Reviews

Generic Name	Brand Name	Indication(s) or Uses	Notes

Capsaicin	Numerous brand products, including Capzasin, Flexin, Neuvaxin, Releevia, Salonpas Trixaicin, Zostrix	▪ Analgesia	▪ **Dosing (Adult):**
			  – Topical application 3 to 4 times daily, as needed
			  – Topical 1 to 4 patches to affected area for up to 8 hours
			▪ **Dosing (Peds):**
			  – Topical application 3 to 4 times daily, as needed
			  – Topical 1 to 4 patches to affected area for up to 8 hours
			▪ **CYP450 Interactions:** Substrate CYP2E1
			▪ **Renal or Hepatic Dose Adjustments:** None
			▪ **Dosage Forms:** Topical (cream, gel, liquid, lotion, patch)

Coal Tar	Beta Care Betatar, DHS Tar, Ionil-T, PC-Tar, Scytera, TeraGel, Theraplex, X-Seb	▪ Seborrhea
		▪ Dandruff
		▪ Psoriasis
			▪ **Dosing (Adult):**
			  – Topical application 1 to 4 times daily
			  – Bath - add 60 to 90mL to bathwater
			▪ **Dosing (Peds):**
			  – Topical application 1 to 4 times daily
			▪ **CYP450 Interactions:** None
			▪ **Renal or Hepatic Dose Adjustments:** None
			▪ **Dosage Forms:** Topical (foam, ointment, shampoo, solution)

Lanolin	HPA Lanolin, Lan-O-Soothe	▪ Skin protectant	▪ **Dosing (Adult):**
			  – Topical application as needed several times daily
			▪ **Dosing (Peds):**
			  – Topical application as needed several times daily
			▪ **CYP450 Interactions:** None
			▪ **Renal or Hepatic Dose Adjustments:** None
			▪ **Dosage Forms:** Topical (cream)

Selenium Sulfide	Anti-Dandruff, SelRx, Tersi	▪ Dandruff	▪ **Dosing (Adult):**
			  – Topical application to wet scalp and leave for 2-3 minutes, then rinse scalp thoroughly
			▪ **Dosing (Peds):**
			  – Topical application to wet scalp and leave for 2-3 minutes, then rinse scalp thoroughly
			▪ **CYP450 Interactions:** None
			▪ **Renal or Hepatic Dose Adjustments:** None
			▪ **Dosage Forms:** Topical (foam, lotion, shampoo)

Miscellaneous Agents - Drug Class Review
High-Yield Med Reviews

Generic Name	Brand Name	Indication(s) or Uses	Notes
Silver sulfadiazine	Silvadene, SSD	▪ Burn treatment	▪ **Dosing (Adult):** – Topical apply to a thickness of 1/16th inch once or twice daily, until healing has occurred ▪ **Dosing (Peds):** – Topical apply to a thickness of 1/16th inch once or twice daily, until healing has occurred ▪ **CYP450 Interactions:** None ▪ **Renal or Hepatic Dose Adjustments:** None ▪ **Dosage Forms:** Topical (cream))
Urea	Numerous brand products, including Aquaphilic, Beta Care, Carb-O-Lac, Carmol, Gordons Urea, Rea Lo, Rynoderm, Umecta	▪ Hyperkeratotic conditions	▪ **Dosing (Adult):** – Topical application 1-3 times daily ▪ **Dosing (Peds):** – Not routinely used ▪ **CYP450 Interactions:** None ▪ **Renal or Hepatic Dose Adjustments:** None ▪ **Dosage Forms:** Topical (cream, emulsion, foam, gel, kit, lotion, ointment, shampoo, solution, stick, suspension)
Zinc oxide	Numerous brand products, including: AmeriDerm, Ammens, Balmex, Boudreaux's Butt Paste, Desitin, Dr. Smith's Diaper Rash, Triple paste	▪ Protective coating for skin irritations	▪ **Dosing (Adult):** – Topical application as needed several times daily ▪ **Dosing (Peds):** – Topical application as needed several times daily ▪ **CYP450 Interactions:** None ▪ **Renal or Hepatic Dose Adjustments:** None ▪ **Dosage Forms:** Topical (cream, paste, stick, powder)

High-Yield Clinical Knowledge

▪ **Butt Paste**
  – Diaper dermatitis is a common skin irritation due to infrequent diaper changes, poor cleansing techniques, among other causes.
  – Barriers such as zinc oxide 40% ointment (commercially available under the brand name Butt Paste, among others) can be used to manage diaper dermatitis.
  – Once diaper dermatitis is resolved, a lower concentration of zinc oxide can be used with each diaper change to prevent a recurrence.
▪ **Washing Hands**
  – Patients must be instructed to wash their hands before and after applying topical skin products to avoid oral ingestion.

– This is particularly important after applying capsaicin, as accidental exposure to mucous membranes and the eyes can lead to severe burns.

High-Yield Fast-Facts

- **Corn Starch**
    – Over the counter, cornstarch-based powders are recommended instead of the formerly available talc powders, which have been removed from the market.
- **Alcohol Content**
    – Parents should be encouraged to avoid diaper wipes containing fragrance or alcohol to prevent diaper dermatitis's recurrence.

HIGH-YIELD BOARD EXAM ESSENTIALS

- **CLASSIC AGENTS:** Aluminum acetate (Burow Solution), calamine, capsaicin, coal tar, lanolin, selenium sulfide, silver sulfadiazine, urea, zinc oxide
- **DRUG CLASS:** Miscellaneous Agents
- **INDICATIONS:** Analgesia (capsaicin), dandruff (coal tar, selenium sulfide), seborrhea (coal tar), skin irritation (aluminum acetate, calamine), protective coating for skin irritations (zinc oxide), psoriasis (coal tar)
- **MECHANISM:**
    – Aluminum Acetate, Calamine, Lanolin - Topical soothing effect on the skin.
    – Capsaicin - Agonist of the transient receptor potential vanilloid (TRPV1) receptor modulating noxious stimulation and the sensation of heat.
    – Coal Tar - Anti-inflammatory, antimicrobial, and antipruritic activity as a result of suppression of DNA synthesis.
    – Selenium sulfide - Slows the production of corneocytes and skin flaking on the epidermis and epithelium through a cytostatic activity.
    – Silver sulfadiazine - Silver ions complex with chloride in tissues to form silver chloride, causing cellular protein coagulation and an eschar's formation.
    – Zinc oxide - Mild astringent and antiseptic activity.
- **SIDE EFFECTS:** Dry skin, skin discoloration, burning sensation (capsaicin)
- **CLINICAL PEARLS:** Patients must be instructed to wash their hands before and after applying topical skin products to avoid oral ingestion. This is particularly important after applying capsaicin, as accidental exposure to mucous membranes and the eyes can lead to severe burns.

High-Yield Basic Pharmacology

- **Prostaglandin Products**
  - NSAID inhibition of cyclooxygenase decreases the production of not just prostaglandins but also thromboxane and prostacyclin.
    - Prostaglandin H2 typically produces prostacyclins, Prostaglandin D, E, and F, as well as thromboxanes.
  - Thromboxanes stimulate platelet aggregation and decrease renal blood flow.
    - Thus, inhibition of thromboxane (typically TXA2) by NSAIDs decreases platelet aggregation and may augment renal blood flow.
  - Prostaglandin inhibition may also produce vasoconstriction and bronchoconstriction.

Primary Net Benefit

- NSAIDs produce dose-dependent analgesia, anti-inflammatory, and antiplatelet effects, which are devoid of CNS effects but are associated with GI bleeding, adverse cardiac effects (other than aspirin), and may be nephrotoxic.

NSAIDs - Drug Class Review			
High-Yield Med Reviews			
Mechanism of Action: *Inhibit the conversion of arachidonic acid to prostaglandins by inhibition of COX-1 and/or COX-2 either reversibly (NSAIDs) or irreversibly (aspirin).*			
Class Effects: NSAIDs produce dose-dependent analgesia, anti-inflammatory, and antiplatelet effects, which are devoid of CNS effects but are associated with GI bleeding, adverse cardiac effects (other than aspirin), and may be nephrotoxic.			
Generic Name	**Brand Name**	**Indication(s) or Uses**	**Notes**
Diclofenac	Diclo Gel, Diclozor, EnovaRX, Flector, Klofensaid, Licart, Pennsaid, Rexaphenac, Solaraze, Venn Gel, Voltaren, Xrylix	<ul><li>Actinic keratosis</li><li>Analgesia</li></ul>	<ul><li>**Dosing (Adult):**<ul><li>Patch - apply 1 patch twice daily to the painful area</li><li>Gel - apply 2 to 4 g to the painful area 3 to 4 times daily for up to 7 days</li></ul></li><li>**Dosing (Peds):**<ul><li>Patch - apply 1 patch twice daily to the painful area</li><li>Gel - apply 2 to 4 g to the painful area 3 to 4 times daily for up to 7 days</li></ul></li><li>**CYP450 Interactions:** Substrate CYP1A2, 2B6, 2C19, 2C9, 2D6, 3A4; Inhibits UGT 1A6</li><li>**Renal or Hepatic Dose Adjustments:** None (for topical use)</li><li>**Dosage Forms:** Topical (cream, gel, kit, patch, solution, therapy pack)</li></ul>

High-Yield Clinical Knowledge

- **Cardiovascular Risk**
  - Inhibition of COX-2 by NSAIDs produces an inhibition of endothelial-derived prostacyclin I2 and lack of potent TXA2 inhibitory effect on platelets, leading to an increased risk of cardiovascular adverse events.
  - COX-2 selective inhibitors were developed to reduce the risk of GI and cardiac adverse events, but rofecoxib and valdecoxib were removed from the market due to their association with increased cardiac events.

- Celecoxib remains in the market but carries a black boxed warning concerning this cardiovascular risk.
  - Aspirin is the exception to this class effect, as it has a net clinical benefit in reducing cardiovascular morbidity and mortality.
- **GI Bleeds**
  - Inhibition of COX-1 by NSAIDs prevents PGE2 and PGI2, which leads to a decline in the production of the protective mucous lining in the GI mucosal lining, exposing the underlying tissue to gastric acid.
    - Normal coagulation may be impaired due to NSAIDs due to their inhibition of TXA2 and direct cytotoxic and irritating effects.
  - The most common ulcers formed by NSAIDs are located in the duodenum.
- **Kidney Injury**
  - Renal perfusion and glomerular filtration rate are partially regulated by COX-1 and PGI2, PGE2, and PGD2.
  - Inhibition of COX-1 can decrease renal blood flow and counteract renal hemodynamics by causing increased sodium reabsorption and decreased renin synthesis.
- **Closing Patent Ductus Arteriosus**
  - Ibuprofen and indomethacin can be used intravenously in preterm infants for the closure of patent ductus arteriosus.
    - Other parenteral NSAIDs include ketorolac and meloxicam, although these are only used in adult patients.
- **NSAIDs in Pregnancy**
  - The use of NSAIDs during pregnancy is associated with premature closure of the ductus arteriosus, which impairs fetal circulation in utero.
    - This was observed among patients who were given indomethacin to terminate preterm labor.

HIGH-YIELD BOARD EXAM ESSENTIALS
- **CLASSIC AGENTS:** Diclofenac
- **DRUG CLASS:** NSAIDs (Topical)
- **INDICATIONS:** Analgesia
- **MECHANISM:** Inhibit the conversion of arachidonic acid to prostaglandins by inhibition of COX-1 and/or COX-2 either reversibly (NSAIDs) or irreversibly (aspirin).
- **SIDE EFFECTS:** Dry skin, red skin, scaling or hardening of skin
- **CLINICAL PEARLS:** Although patients with Rheumatoid Arthritis may take both, NSAIDs may increase the serum levels of methotrexate, potentially leading to toxicity. NSAIDs are believed to decrease the renal excretion of methotrexate by inhibiting its renal transport and a decreased renal perfusion.

High-Yield Basic Pharmacology

- **Mechanism of Action**
  - Essential element involved in basic cellular functions, protein synthesis, cardiac and skeletal muscle contractility, neurotransmission, and parathyroid secretion.
- **Smooth Muscle Relaxation and Cardiac Contractility**
  - Magnesium produces smooth muscle relaxation by displacing calcium from actin/myosin and also as by blocking calcium entry into synaptic terminals.

Primary Net Benefit

- Distributed primarily in bone and muscle tissue, magnesium is the second most abundant intracellular cation supporting a wide range of physiologic functions.

Magnesium - Drug Class Review			
High-Yield Med Reviews			
Mechanism of Action: *Essential element involved in basic cellular functions, protein synthesis, cardiac and skeletal muscle contractility, neurotransmission, and parathyroid secretion.*			
Class Effects: Increase serum Mg, risk for smooth muscle relaxation/paralysis (at high doses) and diarrhea.			
Generic Name	**Brand Name**	**Indication(s) or Uses**	**Notes**

Magnesium carbonate	Magonate	• Dietary supplementation	• **Dosing (Adult):**
			  – Oral 5 mL 3 times daily
			• **Dosing (Peds):**
			  – Oral (elemental magnesium) 10 to 20 mg/kg/dose q6-24h
			• **CYP450 Interactions:** None
			• **Renal or Hepatic Dose Adjustments:**
			  – Should be avoided in PEDIATRICS with renal impairment
			• **Dosage Forms:** Oral (liquid, powder)

Magnesium chloride	Chloromag
	Magdelay
	Nu-Mag
	Slow-Mag
		• Dietary supplementation	• **Dosing (Adult):**
			  – Oral 2 tablets daily
			  – IV 8 to 20 mEq/day
			• **Dosing (Peds):**
			  – IV (elemental magnesium) 2.5 to 5 mg/kg/dose q6h
			  – Oral (elemental magnesium) 10 to 20 mg/kg/dose q6-24h
			• **CYP450 Interactions:** None
			• **Renal or Hepatic Dose Adjustments:**
			  – Should be avoided in PEDIATRICS with renal impairment
			• **Dosage Forms:** Oral (tablet), IV (solution)

Magnesium - Drug Class Review
High-Yield Med Reviews

Generic Name	Brand Name	Indication(s) or Uses	Notes
Magnesium citrate	Citroma	▪ Laxative	▪ **Dosing (Adult):** – 1 to 1.5 bottles (300 to 450 mL) 8 hours prior to procedure ▪ **Dosing (Peds):** – Age 2 to 6 years: 60 to 90 mL once or in divided doses – Age 6 to less than 12 years: 100 to 150 mL once or in divided doses ▪ **CYP450 Interactions:** None ▪ **Renal or Hepatic Dose Adjustments:** – Should be avoided in PEDIATRICS with renal impairment ▪ **Dosage Forms:** Oral (solution, tablet)
Magnesium gluconate	Mag-G Magonate	▪ Dietary supplement	▪ **Dosing (Adult):** – Oral 550 mg once or twice daily ▪ **Dosing (Peds):** – Oral (elemental magnesium) 10 to 20 mg/kg/dose q6-24h ▪ **CYP450 Interactions:** None ▪ **Renal or Hepatic Dose Adjustments:** – Should be avoided in PEDIATRICS with renal impairment ▪ **Dosage Forms:** Oral (tablet)

Magnesium hydroxide	Milk of Magnesia
	Pedia-Lax
	Phillips Milk of Magnesia
		▪ Antacid
		▪ Laxative
			▪ **Dosing (Adult):**
			– Oral 400 to 1,200 mg as needed up to 4 times daily
			  ▪ Maximum 4,800 mg/day
			▪ **Dosing (Peds):**
			– Oral 400 to 1,200 mg as needed up to 4 times daily
			  ▪ Age 2 to 6 years maximum 1,200 mg/day
			  ▪ Age 6 to less than 12 years: maximum 2,400 mg/day
			▪ **CYP450 Interactions:** None
			▪ **Renal or Hepatic Dose Adjustments:**
			– Should be avoided in PEDIATRICS with renal impairment
			▪ **Dosage Forms:** Oral (suspension, tablet)

Magnesium - Drug Class Review
High-Yield Med Reviews

Generic Name	Brand Name	Indication(s) or Uses	Notes

Magnesium L-aspartate hydrochloride	Maginex	• Dietary supplementation	• **Dosing (Adult):**
			  – Oral 2 tablets daily
			  – Oral 1 packet up to three times daily
			• **Dosing (Peds):**
			  – Oral (elemental magnesium) 10 to 20 mg/kg/dose q6-24h
			• **CYP450 Interactions:** None
			• **Renal or Hepatic Dose Adjustments:**
			  – Should be avoided in PEDIATRICS with renal impairment
			• **Dosage Forms:** Oral (granules, tablet)

Magnesium L-lactate	Mag-Tab SR	• Dietary supplementation	• **Dosing (Adult):**
			  – Oral 1 to 2 caplets q12h
			• **Dosing (Peds):**
			  – Oral (elemental magnesium) 10 to 20 mg/kg/dose q6-24h
			• **CYP450 Interactions:** None
			• **Renal or Hepatic Dose Adjustments:**
			  – GFR less than 30 mL/minute - use with caution
			• **Dosage Forms:** Oral (tablet)

Magnesium oxide	Mag-Oxide
	Magox
	Uro-Mag
		• Antacid
		• Dietary supplementation
			• **Dosing (Adult):**
			  – Oral 400 mg twice daily
			• **Dosing (Peds):**
			  – Extra info if needed
			    • Extra info if needed
			• **CYP450 Interactions:** None
			• **Renal or Hepatic Dose Adjustments:**
			  – Should be avoided in PEDIATRICS with renal impairment
			• **Dosage Forms:** Oral (capsule, packet, tablet)

Magnesium - Drug Class Review
High-Yield Med Reviews

Generic Name	Brand Name	Indication(s) or Uses	Notes
Magnesium sulfate	Epsom Salt Magnacaps	▪ Asthma ▪ Constipation ▪ Eclampsia/preeclampsia ▪ Hypomagnesemia ▪ Torsades de pointes	▪ **Dosing (Adult):** – Oral 10 to 20 g dissolved in 240 mL water, maximum 2 doses/day – IV 1 to 2 g IV push over 1-2 minutes – IV 1 to 6 g IV over 1-30 minutes, followed by 1 to 4 g/hour infusion (if necessary) – IM 10 g (2x 5g in each buttock) at onset of labor, followed by 5 g q4h ▪ **Dosing (Peds):** – IV (elemental magnesium) 2.5 to 5 mg/kg/dose q6h – Oral (elemental magnesium) 10 to 20 mg/kg/dose q6-24h ▪ **CYP450 Interactions:** None ▪ **Renal or Hepatic Dose Adjustments:** – Severe renal impairment ▪ IV 4-6 g loading dose over 15-30 min, then 1 g/hour infusion (maximum 10 g/24h) ▪ **Dosage Forms:** Oral (capsule, granules), IV (solution)

High-Yield Clinical Knowledge

- **Hypomagnesemia Risk Factors**
  - Patients with a history of GI disease involving small bowel (where magnesium is absorbed) or who have an increased renal elimination of magnesium (due to diuretic therapy) are at risk of hypomagnesemia.
- **Acute Care Uses**
  - Magnesium sulfate is used acutely for acute severe asthma (in combination with bronchodilators and steroids), for the treatment of cardiac arrhythmias (primarily ventricular tachycardia/fibrillation and QT interval prolongation), and in the management of eclampsia and preeclampsia.
- **Hypermagnesemia**
  - Although rare, hypermagnesemia can occur during the use of high-dose magnesium sulfate infusions in pregnant women with eclampsia or preeclampsia.
  - While serum magnesium levels are kept below 4 mEq/L, signs of hypermagnesemia, primarily loss of deep tendon reflexes, may be more rapidly recognized.
  - Without rapid correction (with calcium and decreased magnesium doses), loss of deep tendon reflexes can extend to loss of skeletal and smooth muscle activity.

High-Yield Fast-Facts

- **Nutritional Intake**
  - The normal recommended daily intake of magnesium ranges from 310 mg/day for healthy women to 400 mg/day for healthy men.
- **Diarrhea**
  - Excessive magnesium supplementation or doses above 800 mg/dose, are associated with diarrhea.
  - In fact, magnesium citrate is used primarily as a laxative, and these dose ranges should be considered when determining a magnesium supplementation regimen.

HIGH-YIELD BOARD EXAM ESSENTIALS

- **CLASSIC AGENTS:** Magnesium carbonate, magnesium chloride, magnesium citrate, magnesium gluconate, magnesium hydroxide, magnesium l-aspartate hydrochloride, magnesium l-lactate, magnesium sulfate, magnesium oxide
- **DRUG CLASS:** Magnesium salts
- **INDICATIONS:** Acute severe asthma, cardiac arrest/ventricular arrhythmias/QT prolongation, dietary supplement, eclampsia.
- **MECHANISM:** Essential element involved in basic cellular functions, protein synthesis, cardiac and skeletal muscle contractility, neurotransmission, and parathyroid secretion. It is a divalent cation (like calcium) and thus competes with calcium to result in a decreased muscle contraction.
- **SIDE EFFECTS:** Smooth muscle relaxation/paralysis, diarrhea
- **CLINICAL PEARLS:**
  - Patients with a history of GI disease involving small bowel (where magnesium is absorbed) or who have an increased renal elimination of magnesium (due to diuretic therapy) are at risk of hypomagnesemia.
  - Magnesium works like a calcium-antagonist to cause bronchodilation of small airways and reduce neurotransmitter release in pre-eclampsia or eclampsia.

High-Yield Basic Pharmacology

- **Normal Serum Potassium**
  - Normal serum concentrations of potassium typically range from 3.5 to 5.5 mEq/L.
  - It is the principal intracellular cation with approximately 98% of its total body load existing intracellularly, with 2% in the extracellular space.
  - Approximately 75% of intracellular potassium is found in muscle cells.
- **Potassium acetate, potassium bicarbonate, potassium chloride, potassium gluconate**
  - Replaces potassium for necessary physiologic functions.
- **Potassium citrate**
  - Undergoes hepatic metabolism to produce bicarbonate, contributing to establishing alkalemia
- **Potassium iodide**
  - Specific and competitive inhibitor of iodine uptake into the thyroid and inhibit thyroglobulin proteolysis, inhibiting thyroid hormone release.
- **Potassium phosphate**
  - Supplements and replaces phosphate.
- **Potassium P-aminobenzoate**
- P-aminobenzoate is a B vitamin complex, providing dietary supplementation

Primary Net Benefit

- Potassium is the principal intracellular cation responsible for numerous physiologic functions. Potassium salts provide supplementation but are limited in dose GI adverse events, tolerability of IV infusion, and cardiac conduction effects.

Potassium - Drug Class Review			
High-Yield Med Reviews			
Mechanism of Action: *See agents above.*			
Class Effects: Infusion reactions, diarrhea, cardiac toxicity.			
Generic Name	**Brand Name**	**Indication(s) or Uses**	**Notes**

Potassium acetate	Brand Name (if available)	• Hypokalemia	• **Dosing (Adult):**
			  – IV 10 mEq/hour up to 400 mEq/24 hours
			• **Dosing (Peds):**
			  – IV 1 to 4 mEq/kg/day, maximum 40 mEq/dose
			• **CYP450 Interactions:** None
			• **Renal or Hepatic Dose Adjustments:** None
			• **Dosage Forms:** IV (solution)

Potassium bicarbonate	Effer-K, K-Prime, K-Vescent, Klor-Con/EF	• Hypokalemia	• **Dosing (Adult):**
			  – Oral 20 to 100 mEq/day in 1 to 4 divided doses
			• **Dosing (Peds):**
			  – Not routinely used
			• **CYP450 Interactions:** None
			• **Renal or Hepatic Dose Adjustments:** None
			• **Dosage Forms:** Oral (tablet)

Potassium - Drug Class Review
High-Yield Med Reviews

Generic Name	Brand Name	Indication(s) or Uses	Notes

Potassium chloride	K-tab, Klor-Con, K-Dur	• Hypokalemia	• **Dosing (Adult):**
			  – Oral 10 to 40 mEq 3-4 times daily
			  – IV 10 to 20 mEq/hour
			• **Dosing (Peds):**
			  – Oral 2 to 5 mEq/kg/day, maximum 2 mEq/kg/dose
			  – IV 2 to 4 mEq/kg/day, maximum 0.5 mEq/kg/hour
			• **CYP450 Interactions:** None
			• **Renal or Hepatic Dose Adjustments:** None
			• **Dosage Forms:** Oral (capsule, packet, solution, tablet), IV (solution)

Potassium citrate	Urocit-K	• Alkalinization	• **Dosing (Adult):**
			  – Oral 10 to 30 mEq 2-3 times daily
			• **Dosing (Peds):**
			  – Not routinely used
			• **CYP450 Interactions:** None
			• **Renal or Hepatic Dose Adjustments:**
			  – GFR less than 0.7 mL/kg/minute - Contraindicated
			• **Dosage Forms:** Oral (tablet)

Potassium gluconate	K-99	• Dietary supplement	• **Dosing (Adult):**
			  – Oral one capsule daily
			• **Dosing (Peds):**
			  – Oral 2 to 5 mEq/kg/day, maximum 2 mEq/kg/dose
			• **CYP450 Interactions:** None
			• **Renal or Hepatic Dose Adjustments:** None
			• **Dosage Forms:** Oral (capsule, tablet)

Potassium iodide	iOSTAT, SSKI, ThyroSafe	• Antidote
		• Expectorant
			• **Dosing (Adult):**
			  – Antidote - Oral 130 mg daily for 10-14 days
			  – Expectorant - Oral 300 to 600 mg 3-4 times daily
			  – Thyrotoxicosis (SSKI) 250 mg q6h
			• **Dosing (Peds):**
			  – Infants and children younger than 3 years, 32.5 mg daily
			  – Age 3 to 12 years, oral 65 mg daily
			• **CYP450 Interactions:** None
			• **Renal or Hepatic Dose Adjustments:** None
			• **Dosage Forms:** Oral (solution, tablet)

Potassium - Drug Class Review
High-Yield Med Reviews

Generic Name	Brand Name	Indication(s) or Uses	Notes

Potassium Phosphate	K-Phos	• Hypophosphatemia
		• Urine acidification
			• **Dosing (Adult):**
			  – IV 0.16 to 1 mmol/kg over 4 to 12 hours
			  – Oral 1,000 mg q6h
			• **Dosing (Peds):**
			  – IV 0.16 to 1 mmol/kg over 4 to 12 hours
			• **CYP450 Interactions:** None
			• **Renal or Hepatic Dose Adjustments:**
			  – GFR less than 30 mL/minute - ORAL contraindicated
			• **Dosage Forms:** Oral (tablet), IV (solution)

Potassium P-aminobenzoate	Potaba	• Scleroderma	• **Dosing (Adult):**
			  – Oral 12 g/day divided 4-6 doses
			• **Dosing (Peds):**
			  – Oral 1 g/4.54 kg body weight per day
			• **CYP450 Interactions:** None
			• **Renal or Hepatic Dose Adjustments:** None
			• **Dosage Forms:** Oral (capsule, packet)

High-Yield Clinical Knowledge

- **Potassium Replacement**
  - For every 0.3 mEq decrease in serum potassium, there is approximately 100 mEq total body deficit.
  - For each 10 mEq of potassium that is replaced, the serum potassium should increase by 0.1 mEq/L.
  - Before replacing potassium, reversible or modifiable causes should be addressed to avoid continued potassium loss.
    - Magnesium should be considered, as failure to correct hypomagnesemia can fail to restore potassium.
    - This is a result of a failure of the sodium-potassium-ATPase pump function.
- **Potassium Administration**
  - For mild to moderate hypokalemia (2.5 to 3.5 mEq/L), oral potassium replacement should be considered.
  - For most patients, the maximum tolerated oral dose of potassium chloride is 40 mEq every 4 hours.
  - In contrast, the maximum concentration for administering potassium chloride via peripheral IV access is 10 mEq/100 mL per 1 hour.
    - A typical administration cocktail for select patients is administering 40 mEq oral while beginning an infusion of 10 mEq/100 mL per 1 hour for four doses.
- **Regulation**
  - The potassium gradient that exists across cell membranes is maintained by the sodium-potassium-ATPase pump and also regulated by renal handling of potassium.
    - Other systems that contribute to potassium regulation include the renin-angiotensin-aldosterone system, pH, certain medications (ACE inhibitors, diuretics, catecholamines), and the GI tract.
- **Organ Systems**
  - Cardiac tissue is sensitive to potassium concentration changes as conduction abnormalities will occur in hyper or hypokalemia scenarios.
  - Skeletal muscle is also dependent on potassium for normal function and can lead to weakness, paresthesias, paralysis, among other symptoms, if concentrations are above or below normal reference ranges.

- **Hypokalemia**
  - Hypokalemia is very common in clinical practice, existing in approximately 20% of hospitalized patients and patients taking diuretics (thiazide and loop).
  - Other causes of hypokalemia include osmotic diuresis, increased mineralocorticoid activity, kidney injury, GI losses from vomiting or diarrhea, skin loss through perspiration or burns, inadequate dietary intake, transcellular shifts, and certain genetic disorders.

High-Yield Fast-Fact

- **Sialadenitis**
  - Supplementation with potassium iodide is associated with sialadenitis, otherwise known as iodide mumps.
  - Other common adverse effects include acneiform rash, mucous membrane ulceration, conjunctivitis, and bleeding disorders.

HIGH-YIELD BOARD EXAM ESSENTIALS

- **CLASSIC AGENTS:** Potassium acetate, potassium bicarbonate, potassium chloride, potassium citrate, potassium gluconate, potassium iodide, potassium phosphate, potassium p-aminobenzoate
- **DRUG CLASS:** Potassium
- **INDICATIONS:** Antidote (potassium iodide), Alkalinization (potassium citrate), Dietary supplement (potassium gluconate), Expectorant (potassium iodide), Hypokalemia (potassium acetate, potassium bicarbonate, potassium chloride), Hypophosphatemia (potassium phosphate), Urine acidification (potassium phosphate)
- **MECHANISM:**
  - **Potassium acetate, potassium bicarbonate, potassium chloride, potassium gluconate** - Replaces potassium for necessary physiologic functions.
  - **Potassium citrate** - Undergoes hepatic metabolism to produce bicarbonate, contributing to establishing alkalemia.
  - **Potassium iodide** – Specific and competitive inhibitor of iodine uptake into the thyroid and inhibit thyroglobulin proteolysis, inhibiting thyroid hormone release.
  - **Potassium phosphate** - Supplements and replaces phosphate.
  - **Potassium P-aminobenzoate** - P-aminobenzoate is a B vitamin complex, providing dietary supplementation.
- **SIDE EFFECTS:** Infusion reactions, diarrhea, cardiac toxicity (SA node depression)
- **CLINICAL PEARLS:** Potassium is the principal intracellular cation responsible for numerous physiologic functions. Potassium salts provide supplementation but are limited in dose due to GI adverse events, tolerability of IV infusion, and cardiac conduction effects.

High-Yield Basic Pharmacology

- **Sodium bicarbonate**
  - Increases plasma and urine bicarbonate, buffering excess hydrogen ions. Increases sodium and changes the proportion of sodium channel blocking xenobiotic that is ionized, displacing it from binding sites.
- **Sodium citrate**
  - Citrate chelates free ionized calcium, preventing its use in the coagulation cascade, thereby causing an anticoagulation effect.
- **Sodium chloride**
  - Supports numerous physiologic functions, including volume regulation, osmotic pressure control, and electrolyte balance.
- **Sodium phosphate**
  - Produces osmotic effect in the small intestine, stimulating distention and peristalsis.
- **Sodium nitrate**
  - Induces the formation of methemoglobin.
- **Sodium stibogluconate**
  - Converted to trivalent antimony, which affects glucose homeostasis, fatty acid beta-oxidation, and ATP formation.

Primary Overall Net Benefit

- Sodium is an essential element, with numerous salt preparations that possess unique indications and pharmacologic actions.

Sodium - Drug Class Review			
High-Yield Med Reviews			
Mechanism of Action: *See agents above*			
Class Effects: Sodium is an essential element, with numerous salt preparations that possess unique indications and pharmacologic actions.			
Generic Name	**Brand Name**	**Indication(s) or Uses**	**Notes**

Sodium Bicarbonate	Neut	• Management of metabolic acidosis
		• Sodium channel blocker toxicity
		• Urine alkalinization
			• **Dosing (Adult):**
			  – IV/IO 1 mEq/kg/dose repeated as necessary with or without 0.5 to 1 mEq/kg/hour infusion
			• **Dosing (Peds):**
			  – IV/IO 1 mEq/kg/dose repeated as necessary with or without 0.5 to 1 mEq/kg/hour infusion
			• **CYP450 Interactions:** None
			• **Renal or Hepatic Dose Adjustments:** None
			• **Dosage Forms:** IV (solution), Oral (powder, tablet)

Sodium citrate (with citric acid, and/or potassium citrate)	Cytra-2, Oracit, Cytra-3	• Systemic alkalization	• **Dosing (Adult):**
			  – Oral 10 to 30 mL four times daily
			• **Dosing (Peds):**
			  – Oral 2 to 4 mL/kg/day
			• **CYP450 Interactions:** None
			• **Renal or Hepatic Dose Adjustments:** None
			• **Dosage Forms:** Oral (solution)

Sodium - Drug Class Review
High-Yield Med Reviews

Generic Name	Brand Name	Indication(s) or Uses	Notes
Sodium chloride	Normal Saline	• Restores sodium and volume	• **Dosing (Adult):** – Inhalation/nebulized 1 to 4 mL 2 to 4 times daily – Irrigation 1 to 3 L/day – IV 10 to 20 mL/kg bolus (0.9% NaCl) – Ophthalmic 1-2 drops in affected eyes q3-4h • **Dosing (Peds):** – See adult dosing • **CYP450 Interactions:** None • **Renal or Hepatic Dose Adjustments:** None • **Dosage Forms:** Nasal (aerosol, gel), IV (solution), Inhalation (solution), Oral (tablet), Ophthalmic (solution)
Sodium phosphate	Fleet enema, OsmoPrep	• Constipation • Bowel cleansing • Hypophosphatemia	• **Dosing (Adult):** – IV 0.16 to 1 mmol/kg over 4 to 12 hours – Parenteral nutrition 10 to 15 mmol/1,000 kcal – Rectal 4.5 ounces once – Oral 15 to 45 mL once • **Dosing (Peds):** – IV 0.16 to 1 mmol/kg over 4 to 12 hours – Parenteral nutrition 0.5 to 2 mmol/kg/day Rectal 4.5 ounces once – Oral 7.5 to 45 mL once • **CYP450 Interactions:** None • **Renal or Hepatic Dose Adjustments:** – GFR less than 30 mL/minute - avoid oral solution • **Dosage Forms:** IV (solution), Oral (solution, tablet), Rectal (solution)
Sodium nitrite	Cyanide antidote kit	• Cyanide poisoning	• **Dosing (Adult):** – IV 300 mg, or 0.19 to 0.39 mL/kg of 3% solution • **Dosing (Peds):** – IV 6 mg/kg, maximum 300 mg • **CYP450 Interactions:** None • **Renal or Hepatic Dose Adjustments:** None • **Dosage Forms:** IV (solution)
Sodium stibogluconate	Pentostam	• Leishmaniasis	• **Dosing (Adult):** – IM/IV 20 mg/kg/day for 28 days • **Dosing (Peds):** – IM/IV 20 mg/kg/day for 28 days • **CYP450 Interactions:** None • **Renal or Hepatic Dose Adjustments:** None • **Dosage Forms:** IV (solution)

High-Yield Clinical Knowledge

- **Osmolarity**
  - Under most circumstances, the maximum osmolarity of intravenous fluid for peripheral administration is 900 mOsmol.
  - Sodium bicarbonate is commonly available 8.4% solution has an osmolarity of 2,000 mOsmol but is routinely administered via peripheral IV access.
  - "Normal Saline," which is sodium chloride 0.9%, has a serum osmolarity of 308 mOsmol, and sodium chloride 3%'s osmolarity is 1028 mOsmol

- **Corrected Sodium Formula**
  - Among patients with hyperglycemia, serum sodium concentrations may be falsely low on basic or complete metabolic panels.
  - To correct for hyperglycemia, the observed serum sodium should be increased by 1.6 mEq/L for every 100 mg/dL of glucose over 100 to 400 mg/dL.
    - For glucose above 400 mg/dL, the observed serum sodium should be increased by 4.0 for every 100 mg/dL over 400 mg/dL.

- **Clinical Presentation of Hyponatremia**
  - The clinical manifestations of hyponatremia depend on how rapid the change in serum sodium, not just how low serum sodium levels reach.
  - Nonspecific symptoms of hyponatremia include anorexia, nausea and vomiting, and weakness.
  - Severe acute reductions in serum sodium can cause altered mental status, seizures, coma, cerebral edema, and brainstem herniation.

- **Treatment Strategies of Hyponatremia**
  - The management of hyponatremia depends on the presenting symptoms, the onset of hyponatremia, and the degree of hyponatremia.
  - Euvolemic hyponatremia likely attributed to SIADH, can be managed with free water restriction and treatment of the underlying disease or with "vaptans," otherwise known as vasopressin V2 receptor antagonists (conivaptan, tolvaptan)
  - Hypervolemic hyponatremia is managed with water restriction and treatment of the underlying cause, often excess free water intake.
  - Hypovolemic hyponatremia is treated with sodium replacement, but depending on the clinical sequelae, the concentration and rate of administration of sodium changes.

- **Antimony**
  - Sodium stibogluconate is a pentavalent antimony preparation that is used for the treatment of cutaneous or visceral leishmaniasis.
  - Upon absorption, antimony is converted to trivalent antimony, affecting glucose homeostasis, fatty acid beta-oxidation, and ATP formation.

- **Hyponatremia Types**
  - Hyponatremia can be described as hypovolemic, euvolemic, hypervolemic or pseudohyponatremia.

- **Emergent Sodium Correction**
  - In hyponatremic patients presenting with seizures or severe mental status changes, hypertonic saline (typically NaCl 3%) is rapidly administered to increase serum sodium by 4 to 6 mEq/L within 6 hours until seizures stop.
  - Once symptoms have been controlled, sodium chloride is administered at 1-2 mEq/L/hour with the goal of 10 to 12 mEq/24hour replacement.

- **Rapid Sodium Correction Consequences**
  - Osmotic demyelination results from correcting serum sodium too rapidly, as fluid is pulled from the neurons into extracellular space, causing paralysis and death.
  - Risk factors of osmotic demyelination include overcorrection of sodium (more than 12 mEq/24 hours or 18 mEq/48 hours), patients with a history of alcoholism, malnourishment, and the elderly.

HIGH-YIELD BOARD EXAM ESSENTIALS

- **CLASSIC AGENTS:** Sodium (bicarbonate, citrate, chloride, phosphate, nitrite, stibogluconate)
- **DRUG CLASS:** Sodium
- **INDICATIONS:** Sodium replacement, management of metabolic acidosis, sodium channel blocker toxicity, urine alkalinization
- **MECHANISM:**
  - **Sodium bicarbonate** - Sodium channel blocker toxicity, salicylate overdose, phenobarbital overdose, methotrexate overdose.
  - **Sodium citrate** – Alkalization. Sodium chloride – Restores sodium and volume.
  - **Sodium phosphate** - Hypophosphatemia, Parenteral nutrition, Laxative.
  - **Sodium nitrate** - Cyanide poisoning. Sodium stibogluconate - Leishmaniasis
- **SIDE EFFECTS:** Hypernatremia, volume overload, diarrhea
- **CLINICAL PEARLS:** In hyponatremic patients presenting with seizures or severe mental status changes, hypertonic saline (typically NaCl 3%) is rapidly administered to increase serum sodium by 4 to 6 mEq/L within 6 hours until seizures stop.

High-Yield Basic Pharmacology

- **Therapy Considerations**
  - Oral testosterone has a low bioavailability; non-oral dosage forms are generally preferred
  - Hepatic metabolism
  - Highly protein-bound

Primary Net Benefit

- Replacement of androgen to achieve adequate testosterone level

Androgen Replacement Therapy Drug Class Review			
High-Yield Med Reviews			
Mechanism of Action: Androgens are responsible for male sexual organ growth and development.			
Class Effects: Replacement of androgen to achieve adequate testosterone level.			
Generic Name	**Brand Name**	**Indication(s) or Uses**	**Notes**
Testosterone Intramuscular Injection	Depo-Testosterone ® Aveed®	• Hypogonadism (testosterone deficiency), female-to-male hormone therapy	• **Dosing (Adult):** – Testosterone enanthate, cypionate: 75-100mg once weekly or 150-200mg every 2 weeks – Testosterone undecanoate: 750mg every 4 weeks x 2, then 750mg every 10 weeks after that • **Dosing (Peds):** various regimens – Testosterone enanthate, cypionate: approved $\geq$12 years of age • **CYP450 Interactions:** minor substrate of CYP2B6, CYP2C19, CYP2C9, CYP3A4 • **Renal or Hepatic Dose Adjustments:** Testosterone cypionate contraindicated in hepatic failure • **Dosage forms:** Injection (solution)

Androgen Replacement Therapy Drug Class Review
High-Yield Med Reviews

Generic Name	Brand Name	Indication(s) or Uses	Notes
Testosterone Subcutaneous Injection	Xyosted®	▪ Hypogonadism (testosterone deficiency), female-to-male hormone therapy	▪ **Dosing (Adult):** – 75mg once weekly ▪ **Dosing (Peds):** not approved ▪ **CYP450 Interactions:** minor substrate of CYP2B6, CYP2C19, CYP2C9, CYP3A4 ▪ **Renal or Hepatic Dose Adjustments:** Testosterone cypionate contraindicated in hepatic failure ▪ **Dosage forms:** Injection (subcutaneous solution)
Testosterone Oral	Jatenzo®	▪ Hypogonadism (testosterone deficiency), female-to-male hormone therapy	▪ **Dosing (Adult):** – Testosterone enanthate, cypionate: 75-100mg once weekly or 150-200mg every 2 weeks – Testosterone undecanoate: 750mg every 4 weeks x 2, then 750mg every 10 weeks after that ▪ **Dosing (Peds):** various regimens – Testosterone enanthate, cypionate: approved $\geq$12 years of age ▪ **CYP450 Interactions:** minor substrate of CYP2B6, CYP2C19, CYP2C9, CYP3A4 ▪ **Renal or Hepatic Dose Adjustments:** Testosterone cypionate contraindicated in hepatic failure ▪ **Dosage forms:** Oral (capsule)
Testosterone Nasal	Natesto®	▪ Hypogonadism (testosterone deficiency), female-to-male hormone therapy	▪ **Dosing (Adult):** 11mg (2 pumps) three times daily ▪ **Dosing (Peds):** not approved ▪ **CYP450 Interactions:** minor substrate of CYP2B6, CYP2C19, CYP2C9, CYP3A4 ▪ **Renal or Hepatic Dose Adjustments:** Testosterone cypionate contraindicated in hepatic failure ▪ **Dosage forms:** Intranasal (gel)
Testosterone Pellet	Testopel®	▪ Hypogonadism (testosterone deficiency), female-to-male hormone therapy	▪ **Dosing (Adult):** 150 to 450 mg implanted every 3 to 6 months ▪ **Dosing (Peds):** approved $\geq$12 years of age, various regimens, consider weight-based dosing ▪ **CYP450 Interactions:** minor substrate of CYP2B6, CYP2C19, CYP2C9, CYP3A4 ▪ **Renal or Hepatic Dose Adjustments:** Testosterone cypionate contraindicated in hepatic failure ▪ **Dosage forms:** Pellet (non-oral)

Androgen Replacement Therapy Drug Class Review
High-Yield Med Reviews

Generic Name	Brand Name	Indication(s) or Uses	Notes
Testosterone Transdermal Gel and Solution	AndroGel® Fortesta® Vogelxo® Axiron®	• Hypogonadism (testosterone deficiency), female-to-male hormone therapy	• **Dosing (Adult):** variable doses depending on the product selected, approximately 40mg – 60mg once daily • **Dosing (Peds):** not approved • **CYP450 Interactions:** minor substrate of CYP2B6, CYP2C19, CYP2C9, CYP3A4 • **Renal or Hepatic Dose Adjustments:** Testosterone cypionate contraindicated in hepatic failure • **Dosage forms:** Topical (gel solution)
Testosterone Transdermal Patch	Androderm®	• Hypogonadism (testosterone deficiency), female-to-male hormone therapy	• **Dosing (Adult):** 4mg patch once daily • **Dosing (Peds):** not approved • **CYP450 Interactions:** minor substrate of CYP2B6, CYP2C19, CYP2C9, CYP3A4 • **Renal or Hepatic Dose Adjustments:** Testosterone cypionate contraindicated in hepatic failure • **Dosage forms:** Topical (patch)

High-Yield Clinical Knowledge

- **Androgen Therapy Initiation**
    - Total testosterone of <200 – 300 ng/dL is consistently considered androgen deficient
    - Present symptoms
    - Patient understanding of risks and benefits
- **Androgen Therapy Contraindications**
    - The upcoming desire for fertility
    - Breast or prostate cancer
    - PSA >4 ng/mL (>3 ng/mL with high-risk prostate cancer)
    - Untreated severe obstructive sleep apnea
    - Elevated hematocrit, thrombophilia
    - Uncontrolled heart failure or stroke or myocardial infarction within 6 months
- **Differentiation from Erectile Dysfunction**
    - Androgen deficiency symptoms: fatigue, muscle wasting, low libido
        - The patient does not have an adequate response to stimulation
    - Erectile dysfunction symptoms: inadequate erection (quality, quantity)
        - The patient has a response to stimulation, but the inability to achieve an adequate erection
- **Hypogonadism**
    - Screening should be completed for me with symptoms of hypogonadism
    - Total testosterone level must be drawn fasting x 2 separate days due to influencing variables
- **Dosage Form Selection Considerations**
    - Injectable therapies are generally the most cost-effective
    - Topical preparation caution for pets, children, females
- Many Adverse Reactions
    - Sodium retention, polycythemia (hematocrit >55%), hepatotoxicity
    - Data regarding the increased risk of prostate cancer is controversial

HIGH-YIELD BOARD EXAM ESSENTIALS

- **CLASSIC AGENTS:** Testosterone
- **DRUG CLASS:** Androgen replacement therapy
- **INDICATIONS:** Hypogonadism (testosterone deficiency), female-to-male hormone therapy
- **MECHANISM:** Responsible for male sexual organ growth and development.
- **SIDE EFFECTS:** Hepatotoxicity, hypernatremia, polycythemia, possibly increased risk of prostate cancer.
- **CLINICAL PEARLS:** Routine screening of total testosterone for hypogonadism for cisgender males is not recommended.

High-Yield Basic Pharmacology

- **Mechanism of Action**
  - Replaces endogenous insulin due to pancreatic beta-cell deficiency or insufficiency; insulin normally regulates carbohydrate, protein, and fat metabolism, stimulates hepatic glycogen synthesis, decreases lipolysis, and increases uptake of triglycerides.

Primary Net Benefit

- Improves glycemic control by replacing insulin and reducing post-prandial glucose.

<table>
<tr><td colspan="4" align="center">Prandial Insulin Drug Class Review
High-Yield Med Reviews</td></tr>
<tr><td colspan="4">Mechanism of Action: Replaces endogenous insulin due to pancreatic beta-cell deficiency or insufficiency.</td></tr>
<tr><td colspan="4">Class Effects: Decrease A1c 0.5-1%, hypoglycemia, weight gain/edema, injection site reactions</td></tr>
<tr><td>Generic Name</td><td>Brand Name</td><td>Indication(s) or Uses</td><td>Notes</td></tr>
<tr>
<td>Insulin Aspart</td>
<td>Fiasp (
Novolog</td>
<td>
<ul>
<li>Treatment of T1DM and T2DM in adult and pediatric patients</li>
<li>Off-label: Gestational DM, DKA, HHS, hyperglycemia in critical illness, hyperkalemia</li>
</ul>
</td>
<td>
<ul>
<li>Dosing (Adult): Approx. 50-60% total daily dose in prandial insulin; dosing should be patient specific.
  <ul>
  <li>T1DM: 0.4-1 units/kg/d total daily insulin dose</li>
  <li>T2DM: 4-5 units or 10% of basal dose daily prior to largest meal; add to other meals as needed</li>
  </ul>
</li>
<li>Dosing (Peds): Approx. 50-60% total daily dose in prandial insulin; dosing should be patient specific.
  <ul>
  <li>T1DM: 0.4-1 units/kg/d total daily insulin dose</li>
  <li>T2DM: 4-5 units or 10% of basal dose daily prior to largest meal; add to other meals as needed</li>
  </ul>
</li>
<li>CYP450 Interactions: N/A</li>
<li>Renal or Hepatic Dose Adjustments: N/A</li>
<li>Dosage Forms: U-100 pen, vial</li>
</ul>
</td>
</tr>
</table>

Prandial Insulin Drug Class Review
High-Yield Med Reviews

Generic Name	Brand Name	Indication(s) or Uses	Notes

Insulin Glulisine	Apidra	▪ Treatment of T1DM and T2DM in adult and pediatric patients
		▪ Off-label: Gestational DM, DKA, HHS, hyperglycemia in critical illness, hyperkalemia
			▪ **Dosing (Adult):** Approx. 50-60% total daily dose in prandial insulin; dosing should be patient specific.
			   − T1DM: 0.4-1 units/kg/d total daily insulin dose
			   − T2DM: 4-5 units or 10% of basal dose daily prior to largest meal; add to other meals as needed
			▪ **Dosing (Peds):** Approx. 50-60% total daily dose in prandial insulin; dosing should be patient specific.
			   − T1DM: 0.4-1 units/kg/d total daily insulin dose
			   − T2DM: 4-5 units or 10% of basal dose daily prior to largest meal; add to other meals as needed
			▪ **CYP450 Interactions:** N/A
			▪ **Renal or Hepatic Dose Adjustments:** N/A
			▪ **Dosage Forms:** U-100 pen, vial

Insulin Lispro	Admelog
	Humalog
		▪ Treatment of T1DM and T2DM in adult and pediatric patients
		▪ Off-label: Gestational DM, DKA, HHS, hyperglycemia in critical illness, hyperkalemia
			▪ **Dosing (Adult):** Approx. 50-60% total daily dose in prandial insulin; dosing should be patient specific.
			   − T1DM: 0.4-1 units/kg/d total daily insulin dose
			   − T2DM: 4-5 units or 10% of basal dose daily prior to largest meal; add to other meals as needed
			▪ **Dosing (Peds):** Approx. 50-60% total daily dose in prandial insulin; dosing should be patient specific.
			   − T1DM: 0.4-1 units/kg/d total daily insulin dose
			   − T2DM: 4-5 units or 10% of basal dose daily prior to largest meal; add to other meals as needed
			▪ **CYP450 Interactions:** N/A
			▪ **Renal or Hepatic Dose Adjustments:** N/A
			▪ **Dosage Forms:** Admelog (U-100 pen, vial); Humalog (U-100 pen, vial; U-200 pen)

Prandial Insulin Drug Class Review
High-Yield Med Reviews

Generic Name	Brand Name	Indication(s) or Uses	Notes

Insulin Lispro-aabc	Lyumjev	▪ Treatment of T1DM and T2DM in adult and pediatric patients
		▪ Off-label: Gestational DM, DKA, HHS, hyperglycemia in critical illness, hyperkalemia
			▪ **Dosing (Adult):** Approx. 50-60% total daily dose in prandial insulin; dosing should be patient specific.
			  – T1DM: 0.4-1 units/kg/d total daily insulin dose
			  – T2DM: 4-5 units or 10% of basal dose daily prior to largest meal; add to other meals as needed
			▪ **Dosing (Peds):** Approx. 50-60% total daily dose in prandial insulin; dosing should be patient specific.
			  – T1DM: 0.4-1 units/kg/d total daily insulin dose
			  – T2DM: 4-5 units or 10% of basal dose daily prior to largest meal; add to other meals as needed
			▪ **CYP450 Interactions:** N/A
			▪ **Renal or Hepatic Dose Adjustments:** N/A
			▪ **Dosage Forms:** U-100 pen, vial

Insulin Regular	Humulin R
	Novolin R
		▪ Treatment of T1DM and T2DM in adult and pediatric patients
		▪ Off-label: Gestational DM, DKA, HHS, hyperglycemia in critical illness, hyperkalemia
			▪ **Dosing (Adult):** Approx. 50-60% total daily dose in prandial insulin; dosing should be patient specific.
			  – T1DM: 0.4-1 units/kg/d total daily insulin dose
			  – T2DM: 4-5 units or 10% of basal dose daily prior to largest meal; add to other meals as needed
			  – DKA: Bolus: 0.1 units/kg (optional)
			    – Infusion:
			      - Bolus – 0.1 units/kg/h
			      - No Bolus – 0.14 units/kg/h
			▪ **Dosing (Peds):** Approx. 50-60% total daily dose in prandial insulin; dosing should be patient specific.
			  – T1DM: 0.4-1 units/kg/d total daily insulin dose
			  – T2DM: 4-5 units or 10% of basal dose daily prior to largest meal; add to other meals as needed
			▪ **CYP450 Interactions:** N/A
			▪ **Renal or Hepatic Dose Adjustments:** N/A
			▪ **Dosage Forms:** Humulin R (vial); Novolin R (U-100 pen, vial)

High-Yield Clinical Knowledge

▪ **Prandial Insulin Dosing**
  – Insulin pens should be primed with 2 units before use.
  – Basal/Bolus is usually divided in approximately a 50/50% ratio.

- T1DM
  - Dosing is initially weight-based, but should be adjusted in a patient-specific manner.
  - 0.4-1 units/kg/d total daily insulin dose
- T2DM
  - Dosing should be patient specific.
  - Start 4-5 units or 10% of basal dose daily prior to largest meal. Add to other meals as needed.
- Adjust prandial insulin by 1-2 units every 3-4 days depending on patient goals and response.
- Decrease dose for hypoglycemia by 10-40% depending on severity.
- Doses should be empirically reduced when adding other DM medications and/or those that predispose to hypoglycemia depending on current glycemic control and/or goals.

- **DKA Dosing**
  - Insulin regular preferred; insulin glulisine also has off-label use.
  - Bolus: 0.1 units/kg (optional)
  - Infusion:
    - Bolus – 0.1 units/kg/h
    - No Bolus – 0.14 units/kg/h
  - When glucose is <200 mg/dL, decrease infusion to 0.02-0.05 units/kg/h or switch to SC rapid-acting 0.1 units/kg every 2 hours.
  - Administer dextrose-containing fluids with a goal glucose 150-200 mg/dL until resolution.
  - Resolution considered when glucose <200 mg/dL and 2 of the following: bicarbonate $\geq$15, venous pH >7.3, anion gap $\leq$12. Monitor K^+.

- **Administration**
  - Dose timing depends on the type of prandial insulin.
    - Rapid
      - Admelog, Humalog, or Novolog – 5-15 min prior to meal start or immediately after meal
      - Apidra – 15 min prior to meal start or within 20 min after starting meal
      - Fiasp, Lyumjev – at start of meal or within 20 min after starting meal
    - Regular
      - Insulin regular – 30 min prior to meals
  - May inject SC only into back of the arm, outer thigh, buttocks, or abdomen.
    - Site rotation should be advised to avoid lipodystrophy.
  - Clean site; do not pinch, unless the patient is very thin; inject at a 90° angle; hold needle in skin for a count of 5-10 to ensure insulin does not leak out of injection site.
  - Insulin should be clear, except insulin containing NPH, which is cloudy.
  - Do not draw insulin out of pen devices.
  - Do not mix insulin glulisine.

- **IV Insulin**
  - May cause hypokalemia and should be monitored during therapy as it can cause significant complications.
  - IV insulin infusion is preferred in critically ill patients; basal-bolus therapy is preferred in non-critically ill.
  - Flush IV tubing with priming solution of 20 mL from the insulin infusion to minimize insulin adsorption to IV tubing whenever a new tubing set is added.

- **Storage and Expiration**
  - Insulin expires according to the package date if refrigerated.
  - Insulin expires at varying times once at room temperature and/or used for the first time.
    - Typically, expiration is 28 days once used/at room temperature.

- **Inhaled Insulin (Afrezza)**
  - Short-acting inhaled dosage form available in 4, 8, or 12 units cartridges.
  - Contraindicated in chronic lung disease, such as COPD and asthma, as well as patients who smoke or recently quit.
  - Spirometry should be performed prior to and after starting therapy to assess for lung disease.

HIGH-YIELD BOARD EXAM ESSENTIALS

- **CLASSIC AGENTS:** Insulin regular, Insulin aspart (Fiasp, Novolog), glulisine, lispro, lispro-aabc
- **DRUG CLASS:** Prandial insulin
- **INDICATIONS:** Treatment of T1DM and T2DM in adult and pediatric patients
- **MECHANISM:** Replaces endogenous insulin due to pancreatic beta-cell deficiency or insufficiency.
- **SIDE EFFECTS:** Hypoglycemia, weight gain, injection site pain
- **CLINICAL PEARLS:** Rapid insulins are considered to cause less risk of hypoglycemia than regular insulin because of their shorter duration of action.

High-Yield Basic Pharmacology

- **Mechanism of Action**
  - Replaces endogenous insulin due to pancreatic beta-cell deficiency or insufficiency; insulin normally regulates carbohydrate, protein, and fat metabolism, stimulates hepatic glycogen synthesis, decreases lipolysis, and increases uptake of triglycerides.

Primary Net Benefit

- Improves glycemic control by replacing insulin and reducing fasting glucose.

Basal Insulin Drug Class Review			
High-Yield Med Reviews			
Mechanism of Action: *Replaces endogenous insulin due to pancreatic beta-cell deficiency or insufficiency.*			
Class Effects: Decrease A1c 1.5-2%, hypoglycemia, weight gain/edema, injection site reactions			
Generic Name	**Brand Name**	**Indication(s) or Uses**	**Notes**

Insulin Degludec	Tresiba (U-100, U-200)	• Treatment of T1DM and T2DM in adult and pediatric patients	• **Dosing:** Approx. 1/3-1/2 total daily dose in basal insulin; dosing should be patient specific.
			  – T1DM: 0.4-1 units/kg/d total daily insulin dose
			  – T2DM: 0.1-0.2 units/kg/d total daily insulin or 10 units daily
			• **Dosing (Peds):** 0.4-1 units/kg/d in insulin-naïve depending on developmental stage and history
			  • Start 80% of current basal dose when converting to degludec
			• **CYP450 Interactions:** N/A
			• **Renal or Hepatic Dose Adjustments:** N/A
			• **Dosage Forms:** U-100 pen, U-200 pen, U-100 vial

Insulin Detemir	Levemir	• Treatment of T1DM and T2DM in adult and pediatric patients	• **Dosing (Adult):** Approx. 1/3-1/2 total daily dose in basal insulin; dosing should be patient specific.
			  – T1DM: 0.4-1 units/kg/d total daily insulin dose
			  – T2DM: 0.1-0.2 units/kg/d total daily insulin or 10 units daily
			• **Dosing (Peds):** ≥2 yo – 0.4-1 units/kg/d depending on developmental stage and history
			• **CYP450 Interactions:** N/A
			• **Renal or Hepatic Dose Adjustments:** N/A
			• **Dosage Forms:** U-100 pen, U-100 vial

Basal Insulin Drug Class Review
High-Yield Med Reviews

Generic Name	Brand Name	Indication(s) or Uses	Notes

Insulin Glargine	Basaglar (U-100)
	Lantus (U-100)
	Semglee (U-100)
	Toujeo (U-300)
		▪ Treatment of T1DM and T2DM in adult and pediatric patients	▪ **Dosing (Adult):** Approx. 1/3-1/2 total daily dose in basal insulin; dosing should be patient specific.
			  – T1DM: 0.4-1 units/kg/d total daily insulin dose
			  – T2DM: 0.1-0.2 units/kg/d total daily insulin or 10 units daily
			▪ **Dosing (Peds):** ≥6 yo – 0.4-1 units/kg/d total daily dose depending on developmental stage and history
			▪ **CYP450 Interactions:** N/A
			▪ **Renal or Hepatic Dose Adjustments:** N/A
			▪ **Dosage Forms:** U-100 pen (Basaglar, Lantus, Semglee), U-300 pen (Toujeo, Toujeo Max), U-100 vial (Lantus, Semglee)

Insulin NPH	Humulin N
	Novolin N
		▪ Treatment of T1DM and T2DM in adult and pediatric patients	▪ **Dosing (Adult):** Approx. 1/3-1/2 total daily dose in basal insulin; give 2/3 NPH in AM, 1/3 in PM; dosing should be patient specific.
			  – T1DM: 0.4-1 units/kg/d total daily insulin dose
			    ▪ May consider lower to avoid hypoglycemia
			  – T2DM: 0.1-0.2 units/kg/d total daily insulin or 10 units daily or divided BID
			▪ **Dosing (Peds):** 0.4-1 units/kg/d total daily dose depending on developmental stage and history
			▪ **CYP450 Interactions:** N/A
			▪ **Renal or Hepatic Dose Adjustments:** N/A
			▪ **Dosage Forms:** U-100 pen, U-100 vial

High-Yield Clinical Knowledge

▪ **Adverse Events**
- Causes hypoglycemia, weight gain and/or edema, and injection-site reactions.
  - Patients with renal or hepatic disease may be more susceptible to hypoglycemia.
  - Beta-blockers can mask hypoglycemic effects.

▪ **Basal Insulin Dosing**
- Insulin pens should be primed with 2-4 units before use.
- Basal/Bolus is usually divided in approximately a 50/50% ratio, but can vary from 30-50% of each insulin type.
- T1DM
  - Dosing is initially weight-based, but should be adjusted in a patient-specific manner.
  - 0.4-1 units/kg/d total daily insulin dose
- T2DM
  - Dosing should be patient specific.
  - Start 10 units daily or 0.1-0.2 units/kg/d in insulin-naïve, or 1:1 if converting from another basal insulin for most.

▪ **Administration**
- May inject SC only into back of the arm, outer thigh, buttocks, or abdomen.

- Abdomen results in most consistent absorption.
- Site rotation should be advised to avoid lipodystrophy.
- Insulin should be clear, except insulin containing NPH, which is cloudy.
  - Need to invert or roll NPH in hands to re-suspend.
- **U-500**
  - U-500 regular insulin is utilized in patients (mostly T2DM) requiring >200 units daily to improve absorption by decreasing the injected volume.
    - U-500 is the only concentrated insulin that accomplishes this effect.
- **Storage and Expiration**
  - Insulin expires according to the package date if refrigerated.
  - Insulin expires at varying times once at room temperature and/or used for the first time.
    - Typically, expiration is 28 days once used/at room temperature.
      - Insulin detemir and insulin glargine U-300 expires after 42 days.
      - Insulin degludec expires after 52 days.

HIGH-YIELD BOARD EXAM ESSENTIALS

- **CLASSIC AGENTS:** NPH, U-500, insulin degludec (U-100, U-200), detemir, glargine (U-100, U-300)
- **DRUG CLASS:** Basal insulin
- **INDICATIONS:** Treatment of T1DM and T2DM in adult and pediatric patients
- **MECHANISM:** Replaces endogenous insulin due to pancreatic beta-cell deficiency or insufficiency.
- **SIDE EFFECTS:** Hypoglycemia, weight gain, edema, injection site pain
- **CLINICAL PEARLS:**
  - Insulin degludec and glargine are typically better basal insulins that can be administered once a day whereas detemir typically requires twice a day dosing and can result in dose increases over time.
  - The basal agents should not be mixed with other insulins (e.g., glargine is acidic).
  - U-500 regular insulin is utilized in patients (mostly T2DM) requiring >200 units daily to improve absorption by decreasing the injected volume.

High-Yield Basic Pharmacology

- **Mechanism**
  - Pancreatic alpha-amylase and intestinal brush border alpha-glucosidase inhibitor which delays hydrolysis of complex carbohydrates and disaccharides and glucose absorption
  - These agents act locally in GI tract, with pharmacokinetic peaks within 1 hour, and a half-life of 2 hours.

Primary Net Benefit

- Delays absorption of glucose that results in post-prandial glucose reductions.

Alpha-Glucosidase Inhibitors Drug Class Review High-Yield Med Reviews			
Mechanism of Action: *delays absorption of carbohydrates from the small intestine.*			
Class Effects: Decrease A1c 0.6-0.8%, CV neutral, no beneficial effect on weight, high rate of GI adverse effects.			
Generic Name	**Brand Name**	**Indication(s) or Uses**	**Notes**

Acarbose	Precose	▪ Type 2 diabetes as adjunct to diet and exercise	▪ **Dosing (Adult):** 25 mg TID with first bite of each meal
			  – Increase every 4 weeks to 50-100 mg TID as tolerated.
			  – Max dose ≤60 kg = 50 mg TID; >60 kg = 100 mg TID.
			▪ **Dosing (Peds):** ≥10 yo 25 mg TID with first bite of each meal
			  – Increase every 4 weeks to 50-100 mg TID as tolerated.
			  – Max dose ≤60 kg = 50 mg TID; >60 kg = 100 mg TID.
			▪ **CYP450 Interactions:** N/A
			▪ **Renal Dose Adjustments:** SCr>2 mg/dL or CrCl<25 mL/min not recommended
			▪ **Dosage Forms:** 25 mg, 50 mg, 100 mg tablets

Miglitol	Glyset	▪ Type 2 diabetes as adjunct to diet and exercise	▪ **Dosing (Adult):** 25 mg TID with first bite of each meal – Increase in 4 weeks to 50 mg TID, then 100 mg TID in 3 months. ▪ **Dosing (Peds):** None ▪ **CYP450 Interactions:** N/A ▪ **Renal or Hepatic Dose Adjustments:** SCr>2 mg/dL or CrCl<25 mL/min not recommended ▪ **Dosage Forms:** 25 mg, 50 mg, 100 mg tablets

High-Yield Clinical Knowledge

- **Doses Should Be Titrated Slowly Over 4-8 Weeks.**
  - May start with 1 meal and increase to other meals, then increase the dose, or start with low doses at all 3 meals.
  - Max dose for ≤60 kg = 50 mg TID; >60 kg = 100 mg TID.

- **GI Adverse Effects**
  - Most prominently flatulence, diarrhea, bloating, and/or abdominal pain, occur frequently and limit use, although transient if tolerated.
  - Avoid diet high in sugar because of increased risk of significant GI effects.
  - If GI effects occur despite a low carbohydrate diet, reduce dose and consider whether titration can be retried.
- **Hypoglycemic Risk**
  - These agents have a low risk of hypoglycemia.
    - Use dextrose instead of sucrose (cane sugar) to treat hypoglycemia since hydrolysis of sucrose to glucose/fructose is inhibited.
- **Contraindications and Warnings**
  - Contraindicated in cirrhosis, IBD, and other GI diseases.
  - Discontinue therapy with LFT elevations.

High-Yield Fast-Facts

- Has off-label use for postprandial hyperinsulinemic hypoglycemia post-gastric bypass surgery.
- Patients do not favor this class of medications because of the social implications of the adverse effects.

HIGH-YIELD BOARD EXAM ESSENTIALS
- **CLASSIC AGENTS:** Acarbose, miglitol
- **DRUG CLASS:** Alpha-glucosidase inhibitors
- **INDICATIONS:** Type 2 diabetes (T2DM) management as adjunct to diet and exercise
- **MECHANISM:** Delays absorption of carbohydrates from the small intestine.
- **SIDE EFFECTS:** High rate of GI adverse effects (flatulence, diarrhea, bloating, and/or abdominal pain)
- **CLINICAL PEARLS:** Has low risk of hypoglycemia. Use dextrose instead of sucrose (cane sugar) to treat hypoglycemia since hydrolysis of sucrose to glucose/fructose is inhibited.

High-Yield Basic Pharmacology

- **Mechanism of Action**
  - Amylin analogue that is secreted with insulin from pancreatic beta cells
    - Delays gastric emptying, decreases post-prandial glucagon secretion, and reduces appetite through centrally-mediated mechanism.

Primary Overall Net Benefit

- Decreases post-prandial glucose while promoting weight loss.

Amylin Mimetic Drug Class Review			
High-Yield Med Reviews			
Mechanism of Action: *Decreases post-prandial glucose by delaying gastric emptying, decreasing post-prandial glucagon secretion, and centrally-mediated appetite suppression.*			
Class Effects: Decreases A1c 0.2-0.7% by post-prandial glucose control, weight loss, hypoglycemia, nausea, injection site reactions			
Generic Name	**Brand Name**	**Indication(s) or Uses**	**Notes**

Pramlintide	SymlinPen	▪ Type 1 and 2 diabetes adjunct therapy with prandial insulin use	▪ **Dosing (Adult):** decrease prandial/mixed insulin 50% when initiating
			  – Type 1 DM
			    ▪ 15 mcg immediately prior to major meals
			    ▪ Titrate by 15 mcg every 3 days to 30-60 mcg
			    ▪ Consider DC if intolerant to $\geq$30 mcg
			  – Type 2 DM
			    ▪ 60 mcg immediately prior to major meals
			    ▪ Titrate to 120 mcg in 3 days if nausea is insignificant
			▪ **Dosing (Peds):** None
			▪ **CYP450 Interactions:** None
			▪ **Renal or Hepatic Dose Adjustments:** None
			▪ **Dosage Forms:** 60 pen (1500 mcg/1.5 mL), 120 pen (2700 mcg/2.7 mL)

High-Yield Clinical Knowledge

- **Adverse Events and Precautions**
  - Causes nausea (transient), weight loss (1-2 kg), hypoglycemia, and injection site reactions.
    - Severe hypoglycemia may occur within 3 hours when administered with insulin.
  - Avoid with gastroparesis and hypoglycemia unawareness.
  - Must reduce prandial and mixed insulin 50% when initiating pramlintide.
- **Administration**
  - Administer SC into abdomen or thigh; do not inject in the arm due to erratic absorption.
  - If rapid absorption of other medications is needed, administer them 1 h before or 2 h after pramlintide.
- **Injection temperature**
  - Room temperature injections may decrease injection site reactions; injections are stable at room temperature or refrigeration for 30 days after initial use

High-Yield Fast-Facts

- Cannot be mixed with insulin; requires additional injections.
- Some providers utilize pramlintide in combination with basal insulin as an alternative to basal plus prandial insulin to promote improved post-prandial glucose control and weight loss.

HIGH-YIELD BOARD EXAM ESSENTIALS
- **CLASSIC AGENTS:** Pramlintide
- **DRUG CLASS:** Amylin mimetic
- **INDICATIONS:** Type 1 and 2 diabetes adjunct therapy with prandial insulin use
- **MECHANISM:** Decreases post-prandial glucose by delaying gastric emptying, decreasing post-prandial glucagon secretion, and centrally-mediated appetite suppression.
- **SIDE EFFECTS:** Causes nausea, weight loss, hypoglycemia, and injection site reactions.
- **CLINICAL PEARLS:** If rapid absorption of other medications is needed, administer them 1 h before or 2 h after pramlintide.

High-Yield Basic Pharmacology

- **Mechanism**
  - Decreases insulin resistance, hepatic glucose production, and intestinal absorption of glucose.
- **Renal dose adjustments are recommended based on eGFR**
  - eGFR 46-60 mL/min/1.73m^2 – none, or may consider max 1500 mg/daily
  - eGFR 30-45 mL/min/1.73m^2 – initiate only at 500 mg BID if started; if already taking metformin, decrease to 500 mg BID
  - eGFR <30 mL/min/1.73m^2 – contraindicated

Primary Net Benefit

- Lowers Hgb A1C up to 2% without causing beta-cell burnout while also offering weight loss and limited risk for drug interactions.

Biguanide Drug Class Review			
High-Yield Med Reviews			
Mechanism of Action: *Decreases insulin resistance, hepatic glucose production, and intestinal absorption of glucose.*			
Class Effects: decreases A1c, promotes weight neutrality or loss, causes low hypoglycemic risk, causes GI adverse effects			
Generic Name	**Brand Name**	**Main Indication(s) or Uses**	**Notes**
Metformin	Glucophage	▪ Type 2 diabetes as adjunct to diet and exercise ▪ Off-label: PCOS, GDM, antipsychotic-induced weight gain	▪ A1c reduction: 0.7-1.6% ▪ Dosing (Adult): 500 mg PO daily with food; increase by 500 mg weekly up to 2000 mg daily ▪ Dosing (Peds): ≥6 years (obesity) and ≥10 years (DM) same as adult ▪ CYP450 Interactions: None ▪ Renal or Hepatic Dose Adjustments: 45-60 mL/min/1.73m^2 increase monitoring; 30-45 mL/min/1.73m^2 500 mg BID with close monitoring; 30 mL/min/1.73m^2 not recommended ▪ Dosage Forms: 500 mg, 750 mg, 850 mg, 1000 mg tablets (IR and ER, except 850 mg IR only); 500 mg/5mL solution and ER suspension

High-Yield Clinical Knowledge

- **Side Effects**
  - Diarrhea and other GI adverse effects are most common.
    - GI adverse effects may be mitigated by utilizing metformin ER formulations, taking metformin with food, and slowly titrating doses (i.e. increase 500 mg weekly).
  - Metformin is minimally weight neutral and may promote weight loss.
  - No hypoglycemia risk with monotherapy.
  - Peripheral neuropathy and anemia may indicate vitamin B12 deficiency.
- **Formulations**
  - May see ER tablet shells in stools.
  - Use metformin IR post-bariatric surgery due to reduction in absorption with ER formulations
- **Hypoglycemic Risk**

- This agent has a low risk of hypoglycemia.
- **Special Population or Clinical Situations**
    - May increase the risk of lactic acidosis in patients with renal or hepatic dysfunction, taking other drugs causing lactic acidosis, $\geq$65 years old, undergoing radiologic study with contrast dye, having surgery or other procedures, with excessive alcohol use, and with hypoxic states (acute HF).
    - Hold metformin at or before iodinated contrast imaging procedures if patients have eGFR 30-60 mL/min/1.73m^2, history of hepatic disease, alcoholism, heart failure, or intra-arterial iodinated contrast use; reevaluate eGFR 48 hours post-procedure and restart if renal function is stable.
    - Hold metformin on day of surgery and restart when stable post-op due to risk of hypotension or blood loss that may decrease renal perfusion as a result of the surgery.

High-Yield Fast-Facts

- **Type 1 Diabetics**
    - Is utilized off-label in type 1 diabetes, especially if overweight or obese.
- **CVD and Events**
    - Metformin may improve CV risk and mortality in T2DM.
- **Dosage Formulations for Special Populations**
    - Metformin is available in liquid form for pediatric patients

---

HIGH-YIELD BOARD EXAM ESSENTIALS
- **CLASSIC AGENTS:** Acarbose, miglitol
- **DRUG CLASS:** Alpha-glucosidase inhibitors
- **INDICATIONS:** Type 2 diabetes (T2DM) management as adjunct to diet and exercise
- **MECHANISM:** Delays absorption of carbohydrates from the small intestine.
- **SIDE EFFECTS:** High rate of GI adverse effects (flatulence, diarrhea, bloating, and/or abdominal pain)
- **CLINICAL PEARLS:** Has low risk of hypoglycemia. Use dextrose instead of sucrose (cane sugar) to treat hypoglycemia since hydrolysis of sucrose to glucose/fructose is inhibited.

High-Yield Basic Pharmacology

- **Mechanism of Action**
  - Inhibits the dipeptidyl peptidase-4 enzyme that is responsible for the inactivation of incretin hormones, allowing greater availability of native hormones.

Primary Net Benefit

- Increases availability of GLP-1 approximately 2-fold, but does not increase the concentration of GLP-1.

Dipeptidyl Peptidase-4 Inhibitors Drug Class Review			
High-Yield Med Reviews			
Mechanism of Action: *Inhibits the dipeptidyl peptidase-4 enzyme that is responsible for the inactivation of incretin hormones, allowing greater availability of native hormones.*			
Class Effects: Decrease A1c 0.5-0.9%, low hypoglycemia risk, neutral regarding weight and CV/renal benefits			
Generic Name	**Brand Name**	**Indication(s) or Uses**	**Notes**
Alogliptin	Nesina	▪ Type 2 diabetes (T2DM) management as adjunct to diet and exercise	▪ **Dosing (Adult):** 25 mg daily ▪ **Dosing (Peds):** None ▪ **CYP450 Interactions:** text ▪ **Renal or Hepatic Dose Adjustments:** CrCl$\geq$30-60 mL/min 12.5 mg daily; CrCl$\geq$15-30 mL/min 6.25 mg daily; CrCl<15 mL/min or HD 6.25 mg daily; if persistent or worsening LFTs without alternative etiology, discontinue. ▪ **Dosage Forms:** 6.25 mg, 12.5 mg, 25 mg
Linagliptin	Tradjenta	▪ Type 2 diabetes (T2DM) management as adjunct to diet and exercise]	▪ **Dosing (Adult):** 5 mg daily – Check drug interactions for required dose reductions to 2.5 mg. ▪ **Dosing (Peds):** None ▪ **CYP450 Interactions:** CYP3A4 inducers, P-glycoprotein/ABCB1 inducers ▪ **Renal or Hepatic Dose Adjustments:** text ▪ **Dosage Forms:** 5 mg
Saxagliptin	Onglyza	▪ Type 2 diabetes (T2DM) management as adjunct to diet and exercise	▪ **Dosing (Adult):** 2.5-5 mg daily – Check drug interactions for required dose reductions to 2.5 mg. ▪ **Dosing (Peds):** None ▪ **CYP450 Interactions:** CYP3A4 inhibitors, P-glycoprotein/ABCB1 inhibitors ▪ **Renal or Hepatic Dose Adjustments:** eGFR<45 mL/min/1.73m^2 2.5 mg daily; HD 2.5 mg daily post-dialysis ▪ **Dosage Forms:** 2.5 mg, 5 mg
Sitagliptin	Januvia	▪ Type 2 diabetes (T2DM) management as adjunct to diet and exercise	▪ **Dosing (Adult):** 100 mg daily ▪ **Dosing (Peds):** None ▪ **CYP450 Interactions:** text ▪ **Renal or Hepatic Dose Adjustments:** eGFR$\geq$30-45 mL/min/1.73m^2 50 mg daily; eGFR<30 mL/min/1.73m^2 or intermittent HD 25 mg daily ▪ **Dosage Forms:** 25 mg, 50 mg, 100 mg

High-Yield Clinical Knowledge

- **Weight Gain/Loss**
  - Have neutral weight effects.
- **Adverse Events**
  - Cause low risk of hypoglycemia due to glucose-dependent effects.
  - Class is neutral regarding CV and renal benefits.
  - Generally, are well-tolerated; most common clinical adverse effect may be transient nasopharyngitis.
  - May cause reversible arthralgias at any point in therapy. Discontinue and evaluate pain, then restart to determine if DPP-4s are the etiology.
  - May cause pancreatitis; caution in patients with a history of or risk factors for pancreatitis.
  - May cause bullous pemphigoid; patients should report blisters or erosions, discontinue therapy, and seek referral to dermatologist.
    - Cases normally resolve with discontinuation of DPP-4 inhibitor and topical or systemic immunosuppressive therapy.
- **Drug Interactions with Saxagliptin and Linagliptin**
  - Linagliptin and saxagliptin may have significant drug interactions due to being major substrates of CYP 3A4 and p-glycoprotein/ABCB1; check drug interactions to assess
- **Hospitalization Risk**
  - Saxagliptin and alogliptin may increase risk of hospitalizations for HF. Others have not been implicated.
- **Hepatotoxicity**
  - Alogliptin may cause hepatotoxicity; monitor LFTs prior to initiation and if signs/symptoms of hepatic injury occur.
    - If LFTs elevated at baseline, consider alternative agent in class.
    - If LFT elevations are clinically significant or worsening, discontinue until alternative etiology determined.

HIGH-YIELD BOARD EXAM ESSENTIALS

- **CLASSIC AGENTS:** Sitagliptin, saxagliptin, linagliptin, alogliptin
- **DRUG CLASS:** Dipeptidyl peptidase-4 inhibitors
- **INDICATIONS:** Type 2 diabetes (T2DM) management as adjunct to diet and exercise
- **MECHANISM:** Inhibits the dipeptidyl peptidase-4 enzyme that is responsible for the inactivation of incretin hormones, allowing greater availability of native hormones.
- **SIDE EFFECTS:** Low hypoglycemia risk, neutral regarding weight and CV/renal benefits
- **CLINICAL PEARLS:** May cause reversible arthralgias at any point in therapy. Discontinue and evaluate pain, then restart to determine if DPP-4s are the etiology.

High-Yield Basic Pharmacology

- **Mechanism of Action**
  - Mimics human GLP-1 hormone to increase glucose-dependent insulin secretion, decrease glucagon secretion, increase satiety, and delay gastric emptying.
  - Consider the half-life and dose titration of once weekly agents to determine appropriate timing for rechecking A1c and follow-up.
    - Approximate time to efficacy:
    - Dulaglutide – 2 weeks
    - Exenatide ER – 6-10 weeks
    - Semaglutide SC – 4-5 weeks
    - Drug interactions may exist with slowing of gastric emptying

Primary Net Benefit

- GLP-1 agonists promote weight loss and should be considered in obese patients with T2DM.

GLP-1 Agonist Drug Class Review High-Yield Med Reviews			
Mechanism of Action: *Mimics glucagon-like peptide-1 and increases glucose-dependent insulin secretion, decreases glucagon secretion, increases satiety, and delays gastric emptying.*			
Class Effects: decreases A1c, promotes weight loss, cause low hypoglycemic risk, cause GI adverse effects			
Generic Name	**Brand Name**	**Indication(s) or Uses**	**Notes**
Dulaglutide	Trulicity	▪ Type 2 diabetes as adjunct to diet and exercise ▪ Risk reduction of major CV events in type 2 diabetes and established CVD or multiple CVD risk factors	▪ **A1c reduction:** 0.7-1.6% ▪ **Dosing (Adult):** 0.75 mg SC weekly; may increase to 1.5 mg weekly if needed after 4 weeks ▪ **Dosing (Peds):** N/A ▪ **CYP450 Interactions:** None ▪ **Renal or Hepatic Dose Adjustments:** None ▪ **Dosage Forms:** 0.75 mg pen, 1.5 mg pen
Exenatide	Byetta	▪ Type 2 diabetes as adjunct to diet and exercise	▪ **A1c reduction:** 0.5-0.9% (>1% with insulin) ▪ **Dosing (Adult):** 5 mcg SC BID within 60 min before 2 main meals; may increase to 10 mcg if needed after 4 weeks ▪ **Dosing (Peds):** N/A ▪ **CYP450 Interactions:** None ▪ **Renal or Hepatic Dose Adjustments:** Caution when initiating/increasing at CrCl 30-50 mL/min; Not recommended CrCl<30 mL/min ▪ **Dosage Forms:** 5 mcg pen, 10 mcg pen
Exenatide ER	Bydureon, Bydureon BCise	▪ Type 2 diabetes as adjunct to diet and exercise	▪ **A1c reduction:** 0.9-1.6% ▪ **Dosing (Adult):** 2 mg SC weekly ▪ **Dosing (Peds):** N/A ▪ **CYP450 Interactions:** None ▪ **Renal or Hepatic Dose Adjustments:** Not recommended eGFR<45 mL/min/1.73m^2 ▪ **Dosage Forms:** 2 mg (different devices)

GLP-1 Agonist Drug Class Review
High-Yield Med Reviews

Generic Name	Brand Name	Indication(s) or Uses	Notes
Liraglutide	Victoza	• Type 2 diabetes as adjunct to diet and exercise • Risk reduction of major CV events in type 2 diabetes and established CVD	• **A1c reduction:** 0.8-1.5% • **Dosing (Adult):** 0.6 mg SC daily x 7 days, then 1.2 mg daily x 7 days; may increase to 1.8 mg daily if needed • **Dosing (Peds):** $\geq$10 years same as adult • **CYP450 Interactions:** None • **Renal or Hepatic Dose Adjustments:** None, but use caution when initiating or titrating • **Dosage Forms:** 18 mg/3mL pen
Liraglutide/insulin degludec	Xultophy	• Type 2 diabetes as adjunct to diet and exercise • Risk reduction of major CV events in type 2 diabetes and established CVD	• **Dosing (Adult):** Naïve to GLP-1 agonist or basal – 10 units SC daily; Current GLP-1 agonist or basal – 16 units daily; titrate by 2 units q3-4 days with max dose 50 units • **Dosage Forms:** 100 units/3.6 mg/mL
Lixisenatide	Adlyxin	• Type 2 diabetes as adjunct to diet and exercise	• **A1c reduction:** 0.5-0.9% • **Dosing (Adult):** 10 mcg SC daily x 14 days, then increase to 20 mcg daily • **Dosing (Peds):** N/A • **CYP450 Interactions:** None • **Renal or Hepatic Dose Adjustments:** No dose adjustment eGFR 15-89 mL/min/1.73m^2 but monitor for favorable conditions for dehydration; levels increased from eGFR 15-29 mL/min/1.73m^2; recommended eGFR<15 mL/min/1.73m^2 • **Dosage Forms:** Starter Kit 10 mcg/0.2 mL & 20 mcg/0.2 mL; 20 mcg/0.2 mL pen
Lixisenatide/insulin glargine	Soliqua	• Type 2 diabetes as adjunct to diet and exercise	• **Dosing (Adult):** Naïve, current GLP-1, or current insulin users at <30 units - 15 units SC daily; titrate by 2-4 units weekly with max dose 60 units • **Dosage Forms:** 100 units/33 mcg/mL
Semaglutide PO	Rybelsus	• Type 2 diabetes as adjunct to diet and exercise	• **A1c reduction:** 0.9-1.4% • **Dosing (Adult):** 3 mg PO daily x 30 days, then 7 mg daily x 30 days; may increase to 14 mg daily if needed; MUST be taken with $\leq$4 oz WATER AND 30-60 min BEFORE ANY food, drink, or medication. • **Dosing (Peds):** N/A • **CYP450 Interactions:** None • **Renal or Hepatic Dose Adjustments:** None • **Dosage Forms:** 3 mg, 7 mg, 14 mg
Semaglutide SC	Ozempic	• Type 2 diabetes as adjunct to diet and exercise • Risk reduction of major CV events in type 2 diabetes and established CVD	• **A1c reduction:** 1.2-1.7% • **Dosing (Adult):** 0.25 mg SC weekly x 4 weeks, then 0.5 mg weekly; may increase to 1 mg weekly if needed • **Dosing (Peds):** N/A • **CYP450 Interactions:** None • **Renal or Hepatic Dose Adjustments:** None • **Dosage Forms:** 0.25 mg/0.5 mg/DOSE pen, 1 mg/DOSE pen

High-Yield Clinical Knowledge

- **Cardiovascular Disease Benefit**
  - Liraglutide, semaglutide SC, and dulaglutide should be considered when a patient has CVD.
  - GLP-1 agonists promote weight loss and should be considered in obese patients with T2DM
- **GI Effects**
  - Nausea, vomiting, and other GI adverse effects (diarrhea, constipation, reflux) are the most common adverse effects. Headaches and injection site reactions may also occur.
  - Liraglutide, lixisenatide, and semaglutide PO/SC have a titration schedule to manage transient GI adverse effects in which the lowest dose is not therapeutic. Exenatide and dulaglutide should also be started with the lower dose and increased to avoid GI adverse effects. Exenatide ER is the only GLP-1 agonist without potential for dose titration or escalation.
- **Hypoglycemic Risk**
  - Hypoglycemia risk is low due to glucose-dependent insulin secretion, unless administered with insulin or SUs.
- **Antibody Development**
  - Antibodies can develop with exenatide (Byetta), liraglutide and lixisenatide, but ONLY exenatide and lixisenatide antibodies may affect therapeutic efficacy that requires therapy modification.
- **Pancreatitis**
  - May increase the risk of pancreatitis. Use caution if the patient has a history of pancreatitis and if other conditions may predispose to pancreatitis (obesity, TG$\geq$500 mg/dL, excessive alcohol consumption).
- **Pediatric Use**
  - Liraglutide is approved for use in pediatric patients. Monitor closely for hypoglycemia regardless of concomitant therapies.
- **Combination use**
  - Lixisenatide (Adlyxin) is not typically prescribed as monotherapy, but may be utilized in lixisenatide/insulin glargine (Soliqua®).

High-Yield Fast-Facts

- Liraglutide and semaglutide can be dosed by "clicks" to further mitigate GI adverse effects by slowing titration.
- Exenatide is a synthetic form of a protein that mimics GLP-1 from a Gila monster.
- Liraglutide is also marketed for obesity as Saxenda® and dosed up to 3 mg daily.
- Semaglutide (Ozempic®) comes with pen needles. No additional prescription for needles is needed.
- Consider dulaglutide for a patient with visual disabilities due to its ease of dosing and administration with its device.

HIGH-YIELD BOARD EXAM ESSENTIALS

- **CLASSIC AGENTS:** Dulaglutide, exenatide, exenatide ER, liraglutide, lixisenatide, semaglutide
- **DRUG CLASS:** Glucagon-like peptide-1 agonists (GLP-1 agonists)
- **INDICATIONS:** Type 2 diabetes (T2DM) management as adjunct to diet and exercise; risk reduction of major CV events in T2DM and established CVD (liraglutide, semaglutide SC); risk reduction of major CV events in T2DM and established CVD or multiple CV risk factors (dulaglutide)
- **MECHANISM:** Mimics glucagon-like peptide-1 and increases glucose-dependent insulin secretion, decreases glucagon secretion, increases satiety, and delays gastric emptying.
- **SIDE EFFECTS:** Nausea, vomiting, GI intolerance, weight loss.
- **CLINICAL PEARLS:** Liraglutide, lixisenatide, and semaglutide PO/SC have a titration schedule to manage transient GI adverse effects in which the lowest dose is not therapeutic. Exenatide and dulaglutide should also be started with the lower dose and increased to avoid GI adverse effects. Exenatide ER is the only GLP-1 agonist without potential for dose titration or escalation.

High-Yield Basic Pharmacology

- **Mechanism of Action**
  - Blocks ATP-dependent K^+ channels, which depolarizes the membrane and causes Ca^{2+} influx that stimulates insulin release.

Primary Net Benefit

- Stimulates insulin release in a glucose-dependent manner.

Meglitinides Drug Class Review			
High-Yield Med Reviews			
Mechanism of Action: *Stimulates insulin release in a glucose-dependent manner through influx of Ca^{2+}.*			
Class Effects: Decreases A1c 0.4-0.9%, CV neutral, weigh gain, low risk hypoglycemia			
Generic Name	**Brand Name**	**Indication(s) or Uses**	**Notes**
Nateglinide	Starlix	▪ Type 2 diabetes (T2DM) management as adjunct to diet and exercise	▪ **Dosing (Adult):** 60-120 mg TID 30 min prior to meals ▪ **Dosing (Peds):** N/A ▪ **CYP450 Interactions:** CYP3A4 and CYP2C9 substrate ▪ **Renal Dose Adjustments:** eGFR<30 mL/min/1.73m² start at 60 mg TIDAC ▪ **Hepatic Dose Adjustments:** None, but Child Pugh B/C may increase risk of hypoglycemia ▪ **Dosage Forms:** 60 mg, 120 mg tablets

Repaglinide	Prandin	▪ Type 2 diabetes (T2DM) management as adjunct to diet and exercise	▪ **Dosing (Adult):** 0.5-2 mg TID 30 min prior to meals
			  – Titrate weekly.
			  – Start 0.5 mg if close to goal.
			  – 16 mg/d max.
			▪ **Dosing (Peds):** N/A
			▪ **CYP450 Interactions:** CYP3A4 and CYP2C8 inhibitors/inducers
			▪ **Renal Dose Adjustments:** CrCl 20-40 mL/min start 0.5 mg and titrate; CrCl<20 mL/min not studied
			▪ **Dosage Forms:** 0.5 mg, 1 mg, 2 mg tablets

High-Yield Clinical Knowledge

- **Class Benefits**
  - Low cost, oral option to target post-prandial glucose.
    - Should only take if eating a meal.
    - May take with each meal, which can vary between patients (typically 2-4 meals daily).
- **Adverse Events**
  - May result in weight gain (1-3 kg) and upper respiratory infections.
  - Has low risk of hypoglycemia due to glucose-dependent effects when utilized with non-insulin modulating agents.

- Adrenal or pituitary disease may predispose to hypoglycemia.

High-Yield Fast-Facts

- **Therapeutic Role**
  - Due to the availability of other options with additional benefits beyond glycemia and compliance, this class is rarely utilized.

HIGH-YIELD BOARD EXAM ESSENTIALS
- **CLASSIC AGENTS:** Nateglinide, repaglinide
- **DRUG CLASS:** Meglitinides
- **INDICATIONS:** Type 2 diabetes (T2DM) management as adjunct to diet and exercise
- **MECHANISM:** Stimulates insulin release in a glucose-dependent manner through influx of Ca^{2+}.
- **SIDE EFFECTS:** Weight gain, upper respiratory tract infection, hypoglycemia
- **CLINICAL PEARLS:** Has low risk of hypoglycemia due to glucose-dependent effects when utilized with non-insulin modulating agents.

High-Yield Basic Pharmacology

- **Mechanism of Action**
  - Inhibits reabsorption of filtered glucose in the proximal renal tubules by blocking SGLT2 receptors (~90% reabsorption), causing increased urinary glucose elimination and decreasing the renal threshold for glucose.

Primary Net Benefit

- Decreases renal glucose reabsorption in a glucose-dependent manner.

SGLT2-Inhibitors Drug Class Review			
High-Yield Med Reviews			
Mechanism of Action: *inhibits glucose reabsorption in the proximal renal tubule by blocking SGLT2 receptors.*			
Class Effects: Decreases A1c 1%, weight loss 1-2 kg, low hypoglycemia risk, GU infections, CV and renal benefits (various drugs), orthostatic hypotension, DKA, amputations, fracture risk, Fournier's gangrene, AKI, elevated LDL			
Generic Name	**Brand Name**	**Indication(s) or Uses**	**Notes**
Canagliflozin	Invokana	▪ Type 2 diabetes as adjunct to diet and exercise ▪ Risk reduction of major CV events in T2DM and established CVD or multiple CVD risk factors ▪ Risk reduction of ESRD, doubling SCr, CV death, and hospitalization for HF in T2DM and DM nephropathy with UAE>300 mg/d	▪ **Dosing (Adult):** 100 mg daily prior to first meal – Increase to 300 mg daily after 4-12 weeks if needed ▪ **Dosing (Peds):** N/A ▪ **CYP450 Interactions:** N/A ▪ **Renal or Hepatic Dose Adjustments:** eGFR 30-60 mL/min/1.73m^2 100 mg daily; eGFR<30 mL/min/1.73m^2 do not initiate, but if established, may continue 100 mg daily ▪ **Dosage Forms:** 100 mg, 300 mg

Dapagliflozin	Farxiga	▪ Type 2 diabetes as adjunct to diet and exercise
		▪ Risk reduction of hospitalization for HF in T2DM and established CVD or multiple CV risk factors
		▪ HFrEF (NYHA Class II-IV) to reduce CV death and hospitalization for HF
			▪ **Dosing (Adult):** 5 mg daily in AM
			  – Increase to 10 mg daily after 4-12 weeks if needed
			  – HF: 10 mg daily
			▪ **Dosing (Peds):** N/A
			▪ **CYP450 Interactions:** N/A
			▪ **Renal or Hepatic Dose Adjustments:** Not recommended eGFR <45 mL/min/1.73m^2; HF with eGFR 30-45 mL/min/1.73m^2 no adjustment
			▪ **Dosage Forms:** 5 mg, 10 mg

Empagliflozin	Jardiance	▪ Type 2 diabetes as adjunct to diet and exercise ▪ Risk reduction of CV mortality in T2DM and established CVD	▪ **Dosing (Adult):** 10 mg daily in AM – Increase to 25 mg daily after 4-12 weeks if needed. ▪ **Dosing (Peds):** N/A ▪ **CYP450 Interactions:** N/A ▪ **Renal or Hepatic Dose Adjustments:** Not recommended eGFR <45 mL/min/1.73m^2 ▪ **Dosage Forms:** 10 mg, 25 mg

		SGLT2-Inhibitors Drug Class Review	
		High-Yield Med Reviews	
Generic Name	**Brand Name**	**Indication(s) or Uses**	**Notes**
Ertugliflozin	Steglatro	▪ Type 2 diabetes as adjunct to diet and exercise	▪ **Dosing (Adult):** 5 mg daily in AM – Increase to 15 mg daily if needed ▪ **Dosing (Peds):** N/A ▪ **CYP450 Interactions:** N/A ▪ **Renal or Hepatic Dose Adjustments:** Not recommended in preexisting impairment or when continuously between 30-60 mL/min/1.73m^2; contraindicated eGFR<30 mL/min/1.73m^2 ▪ **Dosage Forms:** 5 mg, 15 mg

High-Yield Clinical Knowledge

- **Recommended Populations for Use**
  - Independent of metformin or A1c target, patients with the following comorbidities can be considered candidates for SGLT2 inhibitor therapy
    - CVD - canagliflozin or empagliflozin
    - DKD with albuminuria – canagliflozin
    - HF - dapagliflozin
- **Renal Considerations**
  - Initial decreases in eGFR can occur in weeks, but decreased eGFR over time is slowed.
  - Contraindicated with eGFR<30 mL/min/1.73m^2, ESRD, and dialysis.
    - Canagliflozin can be used except in patients on dialysis.
  - AKI may occur; caution with loop diuretics, ACEIs, ARBs, NSAIDs, and other drugs that can precipitate AKI.
  - Consider reducing loop diuretic dose when starting (up to 50%).
- **DKA**
  - DKA can occur in T1DM and T2DM, although more common in T1DM patients, and may be euglycemic.
    - Do not abruptly discontinue insulin when initiating or while on SGLT2 inhibitor. Adjust insulin doses slowly to avoid DKA.
    - Caution if patients may not be able to maintain hydration to avoid DKA.
      - Discontinue 3-5 days prior to surgery and with acute illness that may predispose to dehydration (GI illness, influenza).
- **Weight Loss/Gain**
  - Weight loss of 1-2 kg is a potential beneficial effect.
- **Adverse Events**
  - Consider as low risk for hypoglycemia when given as monotherapy or combination therapy with drugs that do not modulate insulin release.
  - May cause genital mycotic infections or UTIs, mainly in patients with a history of GU infections, females or uncircumcised males.
  - Monitor for signs/symptoms of orthostatic hypotension, especially in those predisposed (i.e. elderly).
  - Increased risk of fracture has been demonstrated.
    - Consider risk factors of prior amputation, PVD, neuropathy, and DM foot ulcers due to potential increased risk of amputation.

HIGH-YIELD BOARD EXAM ESSENTIALS

- **CLASSIC AGENTS:** Canagliflozin, dapagliflozin, empagliflozin, ertugliflozin
- **DRUG CLASS:** SGLT2 Inhibitors
- **INDICATIONS:** Type 2 DM, HFrEF
- **MECHANISM:** Inhibits reabsorption of filtered glucose in the proximal renal tubules by blocking SGLT2 receptors (~90% reabsorption), causing increased urinary glucose elimination and decreasing the renal threshold for glucose.
- **SIDE EFFECTS:** GU/UTI infections, normoglycemic ketoacidosis, increased fracture risk
- **CLINICAL PEARLS:**
  - The weight loss manifested is a loss in "water weight" due to increased diuresis, not fat. This may be helpful to a patient also with HFrEF and evidence of fluid overload.
  - The increase in glucose in the urine can increase the risk of UTIs and yeast infections.
  - May elevate LDL but have not demonstrated increased CV risk due to this potential.
  - Effect may be due to reduced clearance of LDL. Has been associated with euglycemic DKA.

High-Yield Basic Pharmacology

- **Mechanism of Action**
  - Stimulates pancreatic insulin secretion (primary); also reduces hepatic glucose output and improves peripheral insulin sensitivity (to a lesser degree).

Primary Net Benefit

- Increases insulin secretion to lower A1c.

Sulfonylureas Drug Class Review			
High-Yield Med Reviews			
Mechanism of Action: *stimulates pancreatic insulin secretion (primary); also reduces hepatic glucose output and improves peripheral insulin sensitivity.*			
Class Effects: Decreases A1c 1-2%, weight gain, high hypoglycemic risk			
Generic Name	**Brand Name**	**Indication(s) or Uses**	**Notes**
Glimepiride	Amaryl	▪ Type 2 diabetes as adjunct to diet and exercise	▪ **Dosing (Adult):** 1-2 mg daily – Titrate weekly up to 8 mg daily ▪ **Dosing (Peds):** None ▪ **CYP450 Interactions:** None ▪ **Renal or Hepatic Dose Adjustments:** Start 1 mg daily; consider alternative if eGFR<15 mL/min/1.73m^2 ▪ **Dosage Forms:** 1 mg, 2 mg, 4 mg
Glipizide	Glucotrol, Glucotrol XL	▪ Type 2 diabetes as adjunct to diet and exercise	▪ **Dosing (Adult):** 2.5 mg daily – Titrate weekly by 2.5-5 mg up to 20 mg daily ▪ **Dosing (Peds):** None ▪ **CYP450 Interactions:** None ▪ **Renal or Hepatic Dose Adjustments:** Start 2.5 mg daily ▪ **Dosage Forms:** 5 mg, 10 mg; ER 2.5 mg, 5 mg, 10 mg

Glyburide	Glynase	▪ Type 2 diabetes as adjunct to diet and exercise	▪ **Dosing (Adult):**
			  – Conventional: 2.5-5 mg daily
			    ▪ Titrate weekly by 2.5 mg up to 20 mg daily
			  – Micronized: 1.5-3 mg daily
			    ▪ Titrate weekly by 1.5 mg up to 12 mg daily
			▪ **Dosing (Peds):** None
			▪ **CYP450 Interactions:** None
			▪ **Renal or Hepatic Dose Adjustments:** Avoid in CKD
			▪ **Dosage Forms:** 1.25 mg, 1.5 mg, 2.5 mg, 3 mg, 5 mg, 6 mg

High-Yield Clinical Knowledge

- **Special Considerations for Glyburide**
  - Glyburide has active metabolites, increasing the risk of hypoglycemia.
  - Avoid glyburide in CKD
- **Administration Considerations**
  - Take with the first meal daily. Morning administration will also assist in avoiding nocturnal hypoglycemia.
  - Titrate weekly to the next dose until control achieved.
  - May split doses BID when at highest doses for improved control.
  - Micronized glyburide is not bioequivalent to conventional glyburide. Reiterate if changing formulation.
  - Glimepiride 8 mg may offer little benefit compared to 4 mg daily. Can divide dose.
- **Warnings**
  - Secondary failure may occur due to decreased beta cell function with T2DM progression.
  - Avoid glyburide in elderly due to active metabolite that may increase risk of hypoglycemia (Beers List).
  - Consider potential CV risk; glimepiride may be preferred.
    - Evidence on CV safety or risk with SUs is controversial. Some data demonstrate least risk with glimepiride and greatest risk with glyburide.
  - Glyburide may have efficacy in pregnancy but crosses the placenta and increases risk of neonatal hypoglycemia.
  - Caution is advised with sulfonamide allergies, although cross-reactivity is unlikely.
  - Consider alternatives in patients with G6PD deficiency due to increased risk of hemolytic anemia

High-Yield Fast-Facts

- **Beers List**
  - Avoid glyburide in elderly due to active metabolite that may increase risk of hypoglycemia (Beers List).
- **Pregnancy Use**
  - Glyburide may have efficacy in pregnancy but increases neonatal hypoglycemia.
- **Bioequivalence**
  - Micronized glyburide is not bioequivalent to conventional glyburide. Reiterate if changing formulation.

HIGH-YIELD BOARD EXAM ESSENTIALS
- **CLASSIC AGENTS:** Glimepiride, glipizide, glyburide
- **DRUG CLASS:** Sulfonylureas
- **INDICATIONS:** Type 2 diabetes (T2DM) management as adjunct to diet and exercise
- **MECHANISM:** Stimulates pancreatic insulin secretion (primary); also reduces hepatic glucose output and improves peripheral insulin sensitivity (to a lesser degree).
- **SIDE EFFECTS:** Weight gain, high hypoglycemic risk
- **CLINICAL PEARLS:**
  - Can lower HgbA1c by up to 2% from baseline but unfortunately is not sustained.
  - This class of drugs are initially cost-effective but also cause beta-islet cell burn out which progresses the disease.
  - Just like any drug class that increases insulin secretion, eight gain can be a problem.
  - Avoid glyburide in elderly due to active metabolite that may increase risk of hypoglycemia (Beers List).

High-Yield Basic Pharmacology

- **Mechanism of Action**
  - Decreases insulin resistance as a peroxisome proliferator-activated receptor-gamma (PPARgamma) agonist, affecting genetic production in glucose metabolism.

Primary Net Benefit

- Decreases insulin resistance to lower A1c by 1 – 1.5%

Thiazolidinediones Drug Class Review			
High-Yield Med Reviews			
Mechanism of Action: *Decreases insulin resistance as a peroxisome proliferator-activated receptor-gamma (PPARgamma) agonist.*			
Class Effects: Decreases A1c 1-1.5%, edema, weight gain, low hypoglycemic risk			
Generic Name	**Brand Name**	**Indication(s) or Uses**	**Notes**
Pioglitazone	Actos	• Type 2 diabetes as adjunct to diet and exercise	• **Dosing (Adult):** 15-45 mg daily – Limit to lower dose if NYHA Class I/II HF • **Dosing (Peds):** None • **CYP450 Interactions:** Strong CYP2C8 inhibitors • **Renal or Hepatic Dose Adjustments:** If LFTs >3xULN after initiating therapy and pioglitazone is suspected, do not restart. • **Dosage Forms:** 15 mg, 30 mg, 45 mg
Rosiglitazone	Avandia	• Type 2 diabetes as adjunct to diet and exercise	• **Dosing (Adult):** 4-8 mg daily – May divide BID • **Dosing (Peds):** None • **CYP450 Interactions:** Strong CYP2C8 inhibitors • **Renal or Hepatic Dose Adjustments:** DC if ALT consistently >3xULN • **Dosage Forms:** 2 mg, 4 mg

High-Yield Clinical Knowledge

- **Warnings**
  - Contraindicated in patients with NYHA Class III/IV HF.
    - Caution with NYHA Class I/II HF, or in patients on insulin due to increase in edema.
    - May cause new HF.
  - May cause hepatic failure; LFT monitoring required.
  - May increase risk of fractures.
  - Avoid use in patients with bladder cancer, and caution with a history of bladder cancer
    - Formal dosing limitations have been removed due to controversial evidence.
- **Special Populations**
  - May improve insulin resistance in NAFLD and fibrosis in NASH.
- **Edema and Weight Gain**
  - Edema and weight gain are common as a result of visceral fat being converted to SC fat.
- **Vision Changes**
  - Monitor any vision changes due to potential macular edema and refer to ophthalmologist.
- **Lipid Effects**
  - Decrease TG and raise HDL, but data has been inconsistent with the class.

- Rosiglitazone demonstrated potential CV risk and was under a REMS program, but this barrier has been removed; however, most clinicians now utilize pioglitazone as a result.
- Pioglitazone may provide CV benefit, although this is not a common reason for utilizing in practice.

High-Yield Fast-Fact

- Anecdotally, TZDs have been used short-term (8-12 weeks) to reduce visceral fat and improve insulin resistance in patients on insulin therapy, with the hope of improving the response to insulin even after discontinuation.

HIGH-YIELD BOARD EXAM ESSENTIALS
- **CLASSIC AGENTS:** Pioglitazone, rosiglitazone
- **DRUG CLASS:** Thiazolidinediones (TZDs)
- **INDICATIONS:** Type 2 diabetes (T2DM) management as adjunct to diet and exercise
- **MECHANISM:** Decreases insulin resistance as a PPAR-gamma agonist.
- **SIDE EFFECTS:** Edema, weight gain, low hypoglycemic risk
- **CLINICAL PEARLS:** Contraindicated in patients with NYHA Class III/IV HF. Caution with NYHA Class I/II HF, or in patients on insulin due to increase in edema. May cause new HF.

High-Yield Basic Pharmacology

- **Colchicine**
    - Inhibits polymerization of intracellular tubulin into microtubules, inhibiting leukocyte migration and phagocytosis.
- **Pegloticase, Rasburicase**
    - A recombinant form of uricase converts uric acid to the more water-soluble allantoin.
- **Probenecid**
    - Enhances uric acid elimination by reducing net reabsorption via inhibition of its active reabsorption transport as well as secretion on the proximal tubule

Primary Net Benefit

- Colchicine aids in relieving acute gouty attacks and has recently been developed as an adjunct post-myocardial infarction and chronic CAD. Pegloticase is reserved for severe cases where patients can't tolerate alternative agents.

Antigout Agents - Drug Class Review			
High-Yield Med Reviews			
Mechanism of Action: *Colchicine - Inhibits microtubules, leukocyte migration and phagocytosis.* *Pegloticase, Rasburicase - A recombinant form of uricase converts uric acid to the more water-soluble allantoin.* *Probenecid - Reduces net reabsorption via inhibition of its active reabsorption transport and secretion on the proximal tubule.*			
Class Effects: Improvement in inflammation; chronic colchicine use or overdoses can cause BMS.			
Generic Name	**Brand Name**	**Indication(s) or Uses**	**Notes**

Colchicine	Colcrys, Gloperba, Mitigare	• Familial Mediterranean fever
		• Gout
			• **Dosing (Adult):**
			  – Oral 0.6 mg once or twice daily
			    • Maximum 1.2 mg/day
			  – Oral 1.2 mg at first sign of flare, followed in 1 hour by 0.6 mg x 1 or for 3 doses for 1 day OR 0.6 mg TID on first day of flare; then 0.6 mg BID until flare resolves
			    • Maximum 1.8 mg/day
			• **Dosing (Peds):**
			  – Not routinely used
			• **CYP450 Interactions:** Substrate CYP3A4, P-gp
			• **Renal or Hepatic Dose Adjustments:**
			  – GFR less than 30 mL/minute - consider alternate therapy or 0.3 mg/day
			  – Hepatic impairment - use with caution
			• **Dosage Forms:** Oral (capsule, solution, tablet)

Pegloticase	Krystexxa	• Gout	• **Dosing (Adult):**
			  – IV 8 mg q2weeks
			• **Dosing (Peds):**
			  – Not routinely used
			• **CYP450 Interactions:** None
			• **Renal or Hepatic Dose Adjustments:** None
			• **Dosage Forms:** IV (solution)

Antigout Agents - Drug Class Review
High-Yield Med Reviews

Generic Name	Brand Name	Indication(s) or Uses	Notes

Probenecid	Benemid, Probalan	• Gout	• **Dosing (Adult):**
			  – Oral 250 to 500 mg q6-12h
			    • Maximum 2,000 mg/day
			• **Dosing (Peds):**
			  – Oral 25 to 40 mg/kg/day divided q6-12h
			    • Maximum 500 mg/dose
			• **CYP450 Interactions:** None
			• **Renal or Hepatic Dose Adjustments:**
			  – GFR less than 30 mL/minute - avoid use
			• **Dosage Forms:** Oral (tablet)

Rasburicase	Elitek	• Hyperuricemia associated with malignancy	• **Dosing (Adult):**
			  – IV 0.05 mg to 0.2 mg/kg once daily for up to 7 days
			• **Dosing (Peds):**
			  – IV 0.2 mg/kg/dose once daily for up to 5 days
			• **CYP450 Interactions:** None
			• **Renal or Hepatic Dose Adjustments:** None
			• **Dosage Forms:** IV (solution)

High-Yield Clinical Knowledge

- **Colchicine Drug Interactions**
  - Colchicine is a substrate of CYP3A4 and requires dose adjustment for patients taking inhibitors of CYP3A4 (amiodarone, clarithromycin, diltiazem, protease inhibitors, statins, verapamil, and others) or P-glycoprotein inhibitors (amiodarone, cyclosporine, tacrolimus, among others).
  - Pharmacodynamic interactions with NSAIDs and ACE-inhibitors
- **Colchicine Toxicity**
  - Colchicine is a narrow therapeutic agent with the potential for fatal drug overdoses.
  - Toxic and potentially lethal doses are between 0.5 to 0.8 mg/kg, so for small children, a single tablet of 0.6 mg can be fatal.
  - Patients on concomitant potent CYP3A4 inhibitors or P-glycoprotein inhibitors, or in those with renal dysfunction, can experience toxic effects at much lower doses.
  - Colchicine poisoning presents in three phases:
    - Early GI distress and severe volume distribution persisting 12-24 after ingestion.
    - Multiorgan dysfunction and failure, including bone marrow suppression, begins 24 hours after ingestion and lasts for several days.
    - Death or recovery occurs within one week of ingestion or exposure.
- **Uricosuric Therapy**
  - Probenecid is indicated in gout patients where allopurinol or febuxostat are contraindicated or if tophaceous gout is present.
  - Alternatively, probenecid can be added to either allopurinol or febuxostat, but patients must be educated to maintain adequate hydration to avoid the development of uric acid renal stones.
    - Urine pH should also be maintained above 6.0 while taking probenecid, which can be achieved by administering agents such as sodium bicarbonate.
- **GABA Effects**
  - Colchicine is a competitive GABA-A receptor antagonist, which can potentiate seizures.

- **Rasburicase and Plasma Uric Acid**
  - Patients receiving rasburicase must have blood samples of uric acid transported to the lab with special handling to prevent falsely low plasma uric acid levels due to ex-vivo enzymatic degradation of uric acid.
- **Colchicine Myopathy, Neuropathy, and Myoneuropathy**
  - Although colchicine can produce myopathy (made worse by concomitant statin therapy) and neuropathies, myoneuropathies are frequent sequelae of chronic colchicine therapy.

HIGH-YIELD BOARD EXAM ESSENTIALS

- **CLASSIC AGENTS:** Colchicine, pegloticase, probenecid, rasburicase
- **DRUG CLASS:** Anti-gout agents
- **INDICATIONS:** Hyperuricemia associated with malignancy (rasburicase), gout (colchicine, pegloticase, probenecid,
- **MECHANISM:** *Inhibits microtubules, leukocyte migration and phagocytosis (colchicine). A recombinant form of uricase converts uric acid to the more water-soluble allantoin (pegloticase, rasburicase). Reduces net reabsorption via inhibition of its active reabsorption transport and secretion on the proximal tubule (probenecid).*
- **SIDE EFFECTS:** Myopathy, neuropathy, and myoneuropathy (colchicine), anaphylaxis (pegloticase)
- **CLINICAL PEARLS:**
  - Colchicine is most commonly used for acute gout flares. On rare occasions colchicine can be used for chronic gout but carries a small risk of bone marrow suppression.
  - Colchicine aids in relieving acute gouty attacks and has recently been developed as an adjunct post-myocardial infarction and chronic CAD.
  - Pegloticase is reserved for severe cases of gout where patients can't tolerate alternative agents but should be avoided in patients with G6PD deficiency. Rasburicase is indicated for hyperuricemia of malignancy, not gout.

High-Yield Basic Pharmacology

- **Mechanism of Action**
  - Prevent the conversion of hypoxanthine to uric acid by inhibiting xanthine oxidase.
- **Allopurinol and Alloxanthine**
  - Allopurinol is metabolized to oxypurinol (alloxanthine), which is also active and inhibits xanthine oxidase.

Primary Net Benefit

- Allopurinol is a first-line treatment for chronic gout but can precipitate gout during the initiation of therapy. Febuxostat also inhibits xanthine oxidase but carries an increased risk of cardiovascular death in some patients.

Xanthine Oxidase Inhibitors - Drug Class Review			
High-Yield Med Reviews			
Mechanism of Action: *Prevent the conversion of hypoxanthine to uric acid by inhibiting xanthine oxidase.*			
Class Effects: Can worsen acute gouty arthritis if used in acute phase, rash, allopurinol requires renal dosing.			
Generic Name	**Brand Name**	**Indication(s) or Uses**	**Notes**

Allopurinol	Aloprim, Zyloprim	• Gout
		• Nephrolithiasis prophylaxis
		• Tumor Lysis Syndrome
			• **Dosing (Adult):**
			  − Oral 100 to 800 mg daily
			  − Oral (for TLS) 10 mg/kg/day or 300 mg/m2/day divided q8h (maximum 800 mg/day)
			  − IV 200 to 400 mg/m2/day, maximum 600 mg/day
			• **Dosing (Peds):**
			  − Oral (for TLS) 10 mg/kg/day or 300 mg/m2/day divided q8h (maximum 800 mg/day)
			  − IV 200 to 400 mg/m2/day, maximum 600 mg/day
			• **CYP450 Interactions:** None
			• **Renal or Hepatic Dose Adjustments:**
			  − GFR 30 to 60 mL/minute - 50 mg daily
			  − GFR 15 to 30 ml/minute - 50 mg q48h
			  − GFR 5 to 15 mL/minute - 50 mg twice weekly
			  − GFR less than 5 mL/minute - 50 mg weekly
			• **Dosage Forms:** IV (solution), Oral (tablet)

Febuxostat	Uloric	• Gout	• **Dosing (Adult):**
			  − Oral 40 to 120 mg daily
			• **Dosing (Peds):**
			  − Not routinely used
			• **CYP450 Interactions:** Substrate CYP1A2, 2C8, 2C9
			• **Renal or Hepatic Dose Adjustments:**
			  − GFR less than 30 mL/minute - Maximum 40 mg/day
			• **Dosage Forms:** Oral (tablet)

High-Yield Clinical Knowledge

- **Allopurinol Vs. Febuxostat**
  - Allopurinol inhibits xanthine oxidase and may also inhibit purine nucleoside phosphorylase (PNP) and orotidine-5'-monophosphate decarboxylase (OMPDC).
    - PNP and OMPDC are necessary for the synthesis of pyrimidines required for RNA and DNA synthesis.
  - Febuxostat is only inhibits xanthine oxidase.
- **Allopurinol Hypersensitivity Syndrome (AHS)**
  - AHS is a potentially fatal reaction to allopurinol characterized by reactions ranging from Stevens-Johnson syndrome to toxic epidermal necrolysis, as well as multiorgan injury (liver, renal, bone marrow).
  - The highest risk of AHS occurs within 2 to 4 weeks of starting allopurinol.
    - Other risk factors include HLA-B*5801 genotype (prevalent among Han Chinese, Korean, or Thai patients), concomitant diuretic, amoxicillin, or ampicillin use.
  - Allopurinol should immediately be discontinued if a rash occurs during this timeframe.
- **Tumor Lysis Syndrome**
  - Allopurinol is a therapy component for tumor lysis syndrome as its xanthine oxidase inhibition reduces purine conversion to uric acid.
  - As tumors rapidly lyse, large quantities of purines are released, which can precipitate urate nephropathy or calcium-phosphate nephropathy.
  - Alternatively, rasburicase can be used to promote uric acid metabolism to allantoin.
- **Allopurinol Toxicity**
  - Aside from a risk of precipitating gout early in treatment, allopurinol is associated with peripheral neuritis, necrotizing vasculitis, hematologic toxicities (bone marrow suppression, aplastic anemia), hepatotoxicity, renal injury, and skin reactions.
- **Drug Interactions**
  - Allopurinol inhibition of xanthine oxidase can lead to increased azathioprine exposure due to reduced xanthine oxidase activity, which is partially responsible for inactivating 6-mercaptopurine.
    - Allopurinol may also inhibit a secondary metabolic pathway of 6-MP, thiopurine methyltransferase.
  - Without appropriate dose reduction of allopurinol (reduce by 75%), life-threatening bone marrow suppression may occur.
- **Initiating Allopurinol**
  - If initiating allopurinol therapy in proximity to an acute gout flare, either colchicine, NSAIDs, or corticosteroids must be given with allopurinol to avoid acutely worsening gout flare or initiating a new flare.
  - NSAIDs or colchicine should also be started with febuxostat to reduce the risk of gout flares.
- **Cardiovascular Death Risk**
  - Febuxostat has been associated with an increased risk of cardiovascular death among patients with preexisting cardiovascular disease.
  - Allopurinol does not impact cardiovascular death risk.
- **Renal Adjustment**
  - Allopurinol dose must be reduced in patients with GFR less than 60 mL/minute, which may significantly limit effectiveness.
  - Febuxostat does not typically require renal dose adjustment

HIGH-YIELD BOARD EXAM ESSENTIALS

- **CLASSIC AGENTS:** Allopurinol, febuxostat
- **DRUG CLASS:** Xanthine oxidase inhibitors
- **INDICATIONS:** Tumor lysis syndrome, gout, nephrolithiasis prophylaxis
- **MECHANISM:** Prevent the conversion of hypoxanthine to uric acid by inhibiting xanthine oxidase.
- **SIDE EFFECTS:** CV death risk (febuxostat), AHS, precipitating gout (allopurinol)
- **CLINICAL PEARLS:**
  - Febuxostat is a "cleaner" xanthine oxidase inhibitor compared to allopurinol thereby causing less side effects.
  - Aside from a risk of precipitating gout early in acute treatment, allopurinol is associated with peripheral neuritis, necrotizing vasculitis, hematologic toxicities (bone marrow suppression, aplastic anemia), hepatotoxicity, renal injury, and skin reactions.
  - Avoid allopurinol in patients with HLA-B*5801 genotype due to risk of hypersensitivity reaction.
  - Both agents should be avoided in almost every scenario with the co-administration of azathioprine or 6-mercaptopurine due to risk of BMS.

High-Yield Basic Pharmacology

- **Mechanism of Action**
  - Corticosteroids possess numerous mechanisms of action, including regulation of gene expression, modulation of carbohydrate, fat, and protein metabolism, fluid and electrolyte homeostasis.
- **Mineralocorticoid Vs Glucocorticoid**
  - Corticosteroids are either mineralocorticoid or glucocorticoid, depending on their relative potency, sodium and water retention, and carbohydrate metabolism.
  - The anti-inflammatory of a given steroid mirrors its impact on glucose metabolism.

Primary Net Benefit

- Glucocorticoids have a wide range of therapeutic uses that require specific dosing targeting the desired physiological effects these agents can wield, including regulation of intermediary metabolism, cardiovascular function, growth, and immunity.

Long-Acting Corticosteroids - Drug Class Review			
High-Yield Med Reviews			
Mechanism of Action: *Corticosteroids possess numerous mechanisms of action, including regulation of gene expression, modulation of carbohydrate, fat, and protein metabolism, fluid and electrolyte homeostasis.*			
Class Effects: Reductions in inflammation, accumulation of fluid/edema, elevation of glucose, CNS stimulation, decreased bone mineral density with chronic use, increases in gastric acid production.			
Generic Name	**Brand Name**	**Indication(s) or Uses**	**Notes**

Betamethasone	BSP 0820, Celestone Soluspan, Pod-Care, ReadySharp	• Antenatal fetal maturation
		• Bursitis
		• Dermatologic conditions
		• Foot disorders
		• Multiple sclerosis
		• Rheumatoid and osteoarthritis
		• Tenosynovitis
			• **Dosing (Adult):**
			  – IM 0.25 to 12 mg/day
			  – Intra-articular 3 to 12 mg once
			• **Dosing (Peds):**
			  – IM 0.02 to 0.3 mg/kg/day
			• **CYP450 Interactions:** Substrate of CYP3A4
			• **Renal or Hepatic Dose Adjustments:** None
			• **Dosage Forms:** Injection suspension

Deflazacort	Emflaza	• Duchenne muscular dystrophy	• **Dosing (Adult):**
			  – Oral 0.9 mg/kg once daily
			• **Dosing (Peds):**
			  – Oral 0.9 mg/kg once daily
			• **CYP450 Interactions:** Substrate of CYP3A4
			• **Renal or Hepatic Dose Adjustments:** None
			• **Dosage Forms:** Oral (suspension, tablet)

Dexamethasone	Decadron	• Allergic states
		• Dermatologic diseases
		• Endocrine disorders
		• GI diseases
		• Hematologic disorders
		• Neoplastic diseases
		• Ophthalmic diseases
		• Renal diseases
		• Respiratory diseases
		• Rheumatic disorders
			• **Dosing (Adult):**
			  – Oral/IV/IM 4 to 20 mg/day divided q6-24h
			• **Dosing (Peds):**
			  – Oral/IV/IM 0.02 to 0.3 mg/kg/day divided q6-24h
			• **CYP450 Interactions:** Substrate of CYP3A4
			• **Renal or Hepatic Dose Adjustments:** None
			• **Dosage Forms:** Oral (concentrate, elixir, solution, tablet), IV (solution)

Long-Acting Corticosteroids - Drug Class Review
High-Yield Med Reviews

Generic Name	Brand Name	Indication(s) or Uses	Notes

Fludrocortisone	Florinef	• Addison disease (primary adrenal insufficiency)
		• Congenital adrenal hyperplasia
			Dosing (Adult):
			  – Oral 0.05 to 0.1 mg daily
			Dosing (Peds):
			  – Oral 0.05 to 0.2 mg daily
			    • Maximum 0.3 mg/day
			CYP450 Interactions: Substrate of CYP3A4
			Renal or Hepatic Dose Adjustments: None
			Dosage Forms: Oral (tablet)

High-Yield Clinical Knowledge

- **Withdrawal**
  - Abrupt discontinuation of corticosteroid therapy can cause acute withdrawal syndrome and an acute worsening of the underlying disease for which corticosteroids were indicated.
  - Acute adrenal insufficiency is concerning complication of acute corticosteroid withdrawal as a result of the suppression of the hypothalamic-pituitary-adrenal (HPA) axis suppression.
  - For discontinuation of corticosteroids, a gradual decrease in dose over days to weeks reduces the risk of withdrawal syndromes for discontinuation of corticosteroids.

- **Taper**
  - Typically, courses of 5-7 days or less do not require tapering.
  - Individualized patient evaluation as to the exact dose reduction and schedule depends mainly on the duration of steroid therapy and the steroid dose.
  - However, despite tapering, the recovery of the HPA axis may require several months, and underlying minor but potentially clinically relevant HPA axis suppression may be present for as long as several months after a course of as few as 10-14 days duration.

- **Equivalent**
  - Dosing of glucocorticoids is often expressed in prednisone dosing, where clinical guidance can select an alternative agent, using a dose conversion to deliver the same glucocorticoid effect.
  - Prednisone 5 mg is equivalent to:
    - Betamethasone 0.6 mg
    - Cortisone 25 mg
    - Dexamethasone 0.75 mg
    - Fludrocortisone 2 mg
    - Hydrocortisone 20 mg
    - Methylprednisolone 4 mg
    - Prednisolone 5mg
    - Triamcinolone 4 mg

- **Lung Maturation**
  - Betamethasone is administered to mothers where delivery is anticipated before 34 weeks gestation and is used to promote lung maturation by stimulation of fetal secretion of cortisol.
  - As a result of lower proportional maternal protein binding and decreased placental metabolism compared to other steroids, betamethasone is the preferred agent.

- **Croup**
  - Dexamethasone is administered as a single dose therapy for croup treatment, an acute upper airway infection causing inflammation and characteristic barking cough.
  - A single dose of 0.15 to 0.6 mg/kg of dexamethasone is appropriate, and the parenteral dosage form is often administered orally as tablets are difficult to swallow as a result of the characteristic upper airway swelling of croup.

- **Mineralocorticoid**
  - Although it possesses glucocorticoid properties, fludrocortisone is used primarily for its mineralocorticoid effects.
  - Fludrocortisone is primarily used in the management of primary adrenal insufficiency and congenital adrenal hyperplasia.

HIGH-YIELD BOARD EXAM ESSENTIALS

- **CLASSIC AGENTS:** Betamethasone, deflazacort, dexamethasone, fludrocortisone
- **DRUG CLASS:** Long-acting corticosteroids (glucocorticoids)
- **INDICATIONS:** Antenatal fetal maturation, acne vulgaris, acute hypersensitivity/allergy, asthma, atopic dermatitis. bronchiolitis, cancer (hematologic malignancies, prostate cancer), cluster headache, COPD, gout and hyperuricemia, immunosuppression after solid organ transplant, meningitis, nausea and vomiting, osteoarthritis, systemic lupus erythematosus, tuberculosis
- **MECHANISM:** Corticosteroids possess numerous mechanisms of action, including regulation of gene expression, modulation of carbohydrate, fat, and protein metabolism, fluid and electrolyte homeostasis.
- **SIDE EFFECTS:** Electrolyte abnormalities, volume overload, hyperglycemia
- **CLINICAL PEARLS:** Although it possesses glucocorticoid properties, fludrocortisone is used primarily for its mineralocorticoid effects. Fludrocortisone is primarily used in the management of primary adrenal insufficiency and congenital adrenal hyperplasia.

High-Yield Basic Pharmacology

- **Mechanism of Action**
  - Corticosteroids possess numerous mechanisms of action, including regulation of gene expression, modulation of carbohydrate, fat, and protein metabolism, fluid and electrolyte homeostasis.

Primary Net Benefit

- Glucocorticoids have a wide range of therapeutic uses that require specific dosing targeting the desired physiological effects these agents can wield, including regulation of intermediary metabolism, cardiovascular function, growth, and immunity.

Short To Medium Acting Corticosteroids - Drug Class Review			
High-Yield Med Reviews			
Mechanism of Action: *Corticosteroids possess numerous mechanisms of action, including regulation of gene expression, modulation of carbohydrate, fat, and protein metabolism, fluid and electrolyte homeostasis.*			
Class Effects: Reductions in inflammation, accumulation of fluid/edema, elevation of glucose, CNS stimulation, decreased bone mineral density with chronic use, increases in gastric acid production.			
Generic Name	**Brand Name**	**Indication(s) or Uses**	**Notes**
Cortisone	Brand Name (if available)	<ul><li>Allergic states</li><li>Dermatologic diseases</li><li>Endocrine disorders</li><li>GI diseases</li><li>Hematologic disorders</li><li>Neoplastic diseases</li><li>Ophthalmic diseases</li><li>Renal diseases</li><li>Respiratory diseases</li><li>Rheumatic disorders</li></ul>	<ul><li>**Dosing (Adult):**<ul><li>Oral 25 to 300 mg/day</li></ul></li><li>**Dosing (Peds):**<ul><li>Oral 0.7 to 10 mg/kg/day</li><li>Usual range 25 to 300 mg/day</li></ul></li><li>**CYP450 Interactions:** Substrate CYP3A4</li><li>**Renal or Hepatic Dose Adjustments:** None</li><li>**Dosage Forms:** Oral (tablet)</li></ul>
Hydrocortisone	Solu-Cortef	<ul><li>Allergic states</li><li>Dermatologic diseases</li><li>Endocrine disorders</li><li>GI diseases</li><li>Hematologic disorders</li><li>Neoplastic diseases</li><li>Ophthalmic diseases</li><li>Renal diseases</li><li>Respiratory diseases</li><li>Rheumatic disorders</li></ul>	<ul><li>**Dosing (Adult):**<ul><li>IV 50 to 100 mg q6-8h</li><li>Oral 10 to 240 mg/day divided q8-12h</li><li>IM/SQ 100 to 500 mg q6-12h</li></ul></li><li>**Dosing (Peds):**<ul><li>IV 50 to 100 mg/m2/day q6-8h</li><li>Oral 2.5 to 10 mg/kg/day divided q6-8h</li><li>IM/SQ 20 to 240 mg/m2/day q6-8h</li></ul></li><li>**CYP450 Interactions:** Substrate CYP3A4, P-gp</li><li>**Renal or Hepatic Dose Adjustments:** None</li><li>**Dosage Forms:** Oral (capsule, tablet), IV solution</li></ul>

Short To Medium Acting Corticosteroids - Drug Class Review
High-Yield Med Reviews

Generic Name	Brand Name	Indication(s) or Uses	Notes

Methylprednisol one	Solu-Medrol	▪ Allergic states
		▪ Dermatologic diseases
		▪ Endocrine disorders
		▪ GI diseases
		▪ Hematologic disorders
		▪ Neoplastic diseases
		▪ Ophthalmic diseases
		▪ Renal diseases
		▪ Respiratory diseases
		▪ Rheumatic disorders
			▪ **Dosing (Adult):**
			  – IV 1 to 2 mg/kg/day
			  – Oral 16 to 64 mg/day
			  – IM 40 to 60 mg/dose
			  – Intra-articular 10 to 80 mg
			▪ **Dosing (Peds):**
			  – IV/Oral 1 to 2 mg/kg/day
			    ▪ Maximum 60 mg/day
			  – IM 7.5 mg/kg/day
			    ▪ Maximum 240 mg/day
			▪ **CYP450 Interactions:** Substrate CYP3A4
			▪ **Renal or Hepatic Dose Adjustments:** None
			▪ **Dosage Forms:** Oral (tablet), Injection (solution, suspension)

Prednisone	Brand Name (if available)	▪ Allergic states
		▪ Dermatologic diseases
		▪ Endocrine disorders
		▪ GI diseases
		▪ Hematologic disorders
		▪ Neoplastic diseases
		▪ Ophthalmic diseases
		▪ Renal diseases
		▪ Respiratory diseases
		▪ Rheumatic disorders
			▪ **Dosing (Adult):**
			  – Oral 2.5 to 80 mg/day once or divided q6-12h
			▪ **Dosing (Peds):**
			  – Oral 0.25 to 2 mg/kg/day divided 1 to 2 times daily
			    ▪ Maximum 60 mg/day
			▪ **CYP450 Interactions:** Substrate CYP3A4
			▪ **Renal or Hepatic Dose Adjustments:** None
			▪ **Dosage Forms:** Oral (concentrate, solution, tablet)

Prednisolone	Omnipred, Pred Forte, Pred Mild	▪ Allergic states
		▪ Dermatologic diseases
		▪ Endocrine disorders
		▪ GI diseases
		▪ Hematologic disorders
		▪ Neoplastic diseases
		▪ Ophthalmic diseases
		▪ Renal diseases
		▪ Respiratory diseases
		▪ Rheumatic disorders
			▪ **Dosing (Adult):**
			  – Oral 5 to 60 mg/day
			  – Ophthalmic - instill 1 to 2 drops to affected eye(s) 2 to 4 times daily
			▪ **Dosing (Peds):**
			  – Oral 0.25 to 2 mg/kg/day divided 1 to 2 times daily
			    ▪ Maximum 60 mg/day
			  – Ophthalmic - instill 1 to 2 drops to affected eye(s) 2 to 4 times daily
			▪ **CYP450 Interactions:** Substrate CYP3A4
			▪ **Renal or Hepatic Dose Adjustments:** None
			▪ **Dosage Forms:** Oral (solution, syrup, tablet), Ophthalmic ointment

Triamcinolone	Kenalog	▪ Allergic states
		▪ Dermatologic diseases
		▪ Endocrine disorders
		▪ GI diseases
		▪ Hematologic disorders
		▪ Neoplastic diseases
		▪ Ophthalmic diseases
		▪ Renal diseases
		▪ Respiratory diseases
		▪ Rheumatic disorders
			▪ **Dosing (Adult):**
			  – IM 40 to 160 mg once
			  – Intra-articular 2.5 to 80 mg once
			  – Intravitreal 1 to 4 mg once
			▪ **Dosing (Peds):**
			  – Intra-articular 0.5 to 2 mg/kg/dose
			▪ **CYP450 Interactions:** Substrate CYP3A4
			▪ **Renal or Hepatic Dose Adjustments:** None
			▪ **Dosage Forms:** Injection suspension

High-Yield Clinical Knowledge

- **Inflammation**
  - Glucocorticoids effectively counteract inflammation caused by a wide range of clinical scenarios by preventing extravasation and infiltration of leukocytes into the affected tissue.
  - Suppress polymorphonuclear leukocytes migration, and decrease capillary permeability, thereby reducing inflammation.
  - Inflammation is also inhibited through phospholipase A2 inhibition, reducing the synthesis of arachidonic acid and reducing the release of cyclooxygenase 2 and inducible nitric oxide synthase.
  - The long-term suppression of prostaglandin synthesis may also impact GI epithelial function, leading to peptic ulcers.
- **Immunosuppression**
  - The immunosuppressive effects of glucocorticoids are similar in mechanism to the anti-inflammatory effects.
  - Although there may be increases in the circulating number of neutrophils due to increased influx from the bone and decreased migration from blood vessels, there is ultimately a reduced number at the active sites.
    - Increases in white blood cell counts are approximately 4,000/mm3 and can exceed levels of 20,000/mm3 in some patients.
    - The demargination of neutrophils from the endovascular lining largely attributes this increase and delayed migration of polymorphonuclear leukocytes.
  - Other antigen-presenting cells are also inhibited, including dendritic cells and macrophages, which cannot kill microorganisms and produce TNF-alfa, IL-1, IL-12, interferon-gamma, T-helper cells metalloproteinases, and plasminogen activator.
- **Glucose**
  - The effect of glucocorticoids on glucose homeostasis is clinically significant and varied.
  - Glucocorticoids are known to increase glucose levels by stimulating hepatic gluconeogenesis and glycogen synthesis and storage and inhibit the uptake of glucose by muscle cells despite insulin release and increase the synthesis of glutamine and increase lipolysis.
    - This insulin release also stimulates lipogenesis, inhibits lipolysis, increasing fat deposition in addition to increased release of fatty acids and glycerol.
- **Lipid Metabolism**
  - Chronic glucocorticoids may cause a redistribution of adipose tissue manifesting as decreased fat in the extremities but increased fat deposition on the back of the neck and around the face, causing the characteristic buffalo hump, or moon face, respectively.
- **Renal**
  - Sodium and water retention are a characteristic effect of mineralocorticoids due to their actions on the renal distal tubules and collecting ducts.
  - Mineralocorticoids also increase the urinary excretion of both hydrogen and potassium.
  - Glucocorticoids cause excess retention of free water due to increased secretion of arginine vasopressin (antidiuretic hormone), causing the kidney to reabsorb water.
- **Cardiovascular**
  - Mineralocorticoid-induced primary aldosteronism causing decreased sodium elimination may cause hypertension, but other mineralocorticoid effects include interstitial cardiac fibrosis and enhanced vascular response to vasoactive substances.
- **Anabolic and Catabolic Effects**
  - Glucocorticoids cause an anabolic and catabolic effect in connective tissue, skin, fat, and muscle.
  - As a result, clinical sequelae associated with high-dose glucocorticoids include decreased muscle mass, weakness, thinning of the skin, osteoporosis, and reduced growth in children.
- **CNS/Psychiatric**
  - Glucocorticoids may impair sleep quality causing insomnia, as well as other behavioral disturbances or psychosis.
  - These agents also produce Cushing's syndrome, dose-dependent suppression of ACTH, growth hormone, thyroid-stimulating hormone, and luteinizing hormone.

- **Bone and Skeletal Muscle**
  - Hypokalemia due to mineralocorticoids may cause a depressive effect on skeletal muscle function.
  - Steroid myopathy is an effect of chronic glucocorticoid excess leading to muscle weakness and muscle wasting.
  - Acute vascular necrosis is associated with high-dose glucocorticoid therapy, generally with therapies exceeding prednisone 20 mg per day for extended periods.
    - Risk factors for acute vascular necrosis include patients with underlying systemic lupus erythematosus, renal transplant, and disproportionately occurring post total hip arthroplasties.

HIGH-YIELD BOARD EXAM ESSENTIALS

- **CLASSIC AGENTS:** Cortisone, hydrocortisone, methylprednisolone, prednisone, prednisolone
- **DRUG CLASS:** Short to medium acting corticosteroids
- **INDICATIONS:** Acne vulgaris, acute hypersensitivity/allergy, asthma, atopic dermatitis. bronchiolitis, cancer (hematologic malignancies, prostate cancer), cluster headache, COPD, gout and hyperuricemia, immunosuppression after solid organ transplant, meningitis, nausea and vomiting, osteoarthritis, systemic lupus erythematosus, tuberculosis
- **MECHANISM:** Corticosteroids possess numerous mechanisms of action, including regulation of gene expression, modulation of carbohydrate, fat, and protein metabolism, fluid and electrolyte homeostasis.
- **SIDE EFFECTS:** Electrolyte abnormalities, volume overload, hyperglycemia, avascular necrosis of hip (rare; more common with high doses)
- **CLINICAL PEARLS:** The effect of glucocorticoids on glucose homeostasis is clinically significant and varied. Glucocorticoids are known to increase glucose levels by stimulating hepatic gluconeogenesis and glycogen synthesis and storage and inhibit the uptake of glucose by muscle cells despite insulin release and increase the synthesis of glutamine and increase lipolysis.

High-Yield Basic Pharmacology

- **Mechanism of Action**
  - Increases hepatic glycogenolysis and gluconeogenesis, causing an increase in blood glucose.
- **Recombinant Glucagon**
  - The pharmacologic glucagon product is a recombinant form of the single-chain 29 amino acid polypeptide.
- **Hepatic Glycogen**
  - The effect of glucagon on increasing blood glucose requires sufficient existing hepatic glycogen stores.
- **Hepatocyte Action**
  - Glucagon increases intracellular cAMP via the Gs-cAMP-PKA pathway and binds to a specific glucagon binding site (GTP-Gs).

Primary Net Benefit

- Glucagon may rapidly increase blood glucose in patients who cannot take oral glucose, or intravenous access has not yet been established.

Glucagon - Drug Class Review *High-Yield Med Reviews*			
Mechanism of Action: *Increases hepatic glycogenolysis and gluconeogenesis causing an increase in blood glucose.*			
Class Effects: Rapid increase in glucose; causes nausea/vomiting in a dose-dependent fashion.			
Generic Name	**Brand Name**	**Indication(s) or Uses**	**Notes**

Glucagon	Baqsimi, GlucaGen, Gvoke	• Anaphylaxis
		• BB or CCB overdose
		• Hypoglycemia
			• **Dosing (Adult):**
			  – IV Initial dose of 50 mcg/kg (3-5 mg)
			    • Continuous infusion of 2-5 mg/hr is if positive clinical response.
			  – IM/SQ 1 mg once, may repeat in 15 minutes.
			  – Intranasal 3 mg once, may repeat in 15 minutes.
			• **Dosing (Peds):**
			  – IV Initial dose of 50 mcg/kg (3-5 mg)
			    • Continuous infusion of 0.05 to 0.1 mg/kg/hr is if positive clinical response.
			  – IM/SQ 0.5 mg once, may repeat in 15 minutes.
			• **CYP450 Interactions:** None
			• **Renal or Hepatic Dose Adjustments:** None
			• **Dosage Forms:** IV (solution), Nasal powder

High-Yield Clinical Knowledge

- **Glucagon Rescue**
  - Glucagon should be prescribed to all patients who take insulin, have a history of severe hypoglycemia, or are at a high risk of hypoglycemia.
  - Additionally, the family members or caretakers should be educated on the preparation and administration of glucagon since the patient will unlikely be able to self-administer the dose.

- **Onset**
  - The increasing glucose effect of glucagon is delayed and may take up to 15 minutes.
  - This is a result of the action of glucagon in mobilizing hepatic glucose stores.
- **Nausea and Vomiting**
  - Glucagon is associated with a dose-dependent effect of nausea and vomiting.
  - Patients, caretakers, and family members should be educated to position the patient on their side with the head tilted downwards to avoid aspiration should vomiting occur.
- **Glucagon Uses**
  - Glucagon has a wide range of acute uses, including hypoglycemia, anaphylaxis refractory to epinephrine, TCA overdose refractory to sodium bicarbonate, and BB overdose.
  - In beta-blocker toxicity, glucagon can improve both chronotropy, inotropy, and coronary blood flow.
  - The initial dose of 50 mcg/kg (3-5 mg) is recommended via slow IV push over 10 minutes.
    - Lower doses can paradoxically worsen bradycardia and hypotension.
    - The slow administration is essential to avoid dose and rate-dependent nausea and vomiting, which may compromise the patient's airway leading to aspiration and require advanced airway support.
  - Continuous infusion of 2-5 mg/hr is used if a positive clinical response is observed.
  - Tachyphylaxis can occur; increasing the infusion rate may be necessary.
  - Administration: Slow IV administration over 10 minutes
- **Preferred Route**
  - Although glucagon may be administered via IV, SQ, or IM injection, the IM route is preferred for hypoglycemic patients as the onset of effect is similar but associated with a lower risk of nausea and vomiting.

HIGH-YIELD BOARD EXAM ESSENTIALS
- **CLASSIC AGENTS:** Glucagon
- **DRUG CLASS:** Glucagon
- **INDICATIONS:** Acute beta-blocker or calcium channel blocker toxicity, hypoglycemia
- **MECHANISM:** Increases hepatic glycogenolysis and gluconeogenesis causing an increase in blood glucose.
- **SIDE EFFECTS:** Nausea and vomiting (dose-dependent)
- **CLINICAL PEARLS:** Although glucagon may be administered via IV, SQ, or IM injection, the IM route is preferred for hypoglycemic patients as the onset of effect is similar but associated with a lower risk of nausea and vomiting.

High-Yield Basic Pharmacology

- **Mechanism of Action**
  - A recombinant form of IGF-1, circumventing a lack of growth hormone (GH), stimulated hepatic IGF-1 secretion.
- **Glucose Effects.**
  - IGF-1 suppresses hepatic glucose production, promotes peripheral glucose utilization, and inhibits pancreatic insulin secretion.

Primary Net Benefit

- Increases growth velocity in children with short stature due to severe primary IGF-1 deficiency.

Insulin-Like Growth Factor - Drug Class Review High-Yield Med Reviews			
Mechanism of Action: *A recombinant form of IGF-1, circumventing a lack of growth hormone (GH), stimulated hepatic IGF-1 secretion.*			
Class Effects: Growth or improvement in stature.			
Generic Name	**Brand Name**	**Indication(s) or Uses**	**Notes**

Mecasermin	Increlex	• Primary insulin-like growth factor 1 deficiency	• **Dosing (Adult):**
			  – Not routinely used
			• **Dosing (Peds):**
			  – SQ 0.04 to 0.08 mg/kg/dose BID, increasing by 0.04 mg/kg/dose q7days to maximum 0.12 mg/kg/dose
			• **CYP450 Interactions:** None
			• **Renal or Hepatic Dose Adjustments:** None
			• **Dosage Forms:** Subcutaneous solution

High-Yield Clinical Knowledge

- **Growth Effects**
  - Congenital or acquired IGF-1 deficiency causes defects in growth hormone function, causing short stature.
    - Treatment alone with GH may not improve growth.
  - Mecasermin is a recombinant IGF-1, bypassing the role of GH in stimulating IGF-1 release.
    - In addition to improving growth, mecasermin is also associated with adenoidal hypertrophy, lymphoid hypertrophy, and coarsening facial features.
- **With Meals**
  - Mecasermin must be administered within 20 minutes of a meal or snack.
  - If the patient cannot eat, the dose should be skipped.
  - If hypoglycemia occurs despite adequate food intake, the next dose should be reduced.
- **Open Epiphyses**
  - Mecasermin is contraindicated in patients with close epiphyses.
  - It is also contraindicated in patients with suspected or active cancer and should be stopped if cancer is found.
- **Adverse Events**
  - Severe adverse reactions associated with mecasermin include intracranial hypertension and anaphylaxis.

- **Alternative Indications**
  - Mecasermin can also be used in some patients with severe insulin resistance, including patients with muscular dystrophy and HIV-related fat redistribution syndrome.

HIGH-YIELD BOARD EXAM ESSENTIALS
- **CLASSIC AGENTS:** Mecasermin
- **DRUG CLASS:** Insulin-Like Growth Factor
- **INDICATIONS:** Primary insulin-like growth factor 1 (IGF-1) deficiency
- **MECHANISM:** A recombinant form of IGF-1, circumventing a lack of growth hormone (GH), stimulated hepatic IGF-1 secretion.
- **SIDE EFFECTS:** Intracranial hypertension and anaphylaxis.
- **CLINICAL PEARLS:** Mecasermin has been used for bodybuilding as a growth agent but is generally avoided due to its hypoglycemic effects.

High-Yield Basic Pharmacology

- **Mechanism of Action**
  - Supplements pancreatic activity through supplementation of pancreatic enzymes amylase, lipase, and protease.
- **Pancreatic Enzyme Supplement**
  - Pancreatin is an over-the-counter pancreatic enzyme supplement derived from porcine pancreas and has relatively low concentrations of lipase and proteolytic enzymes.
  - Pancrelipase is an enriched preparation of pancreatic enzymes and is the pharmacologically relevant pancreatic enzyme supplement.

Primary Net Benefit

- Pancrelipase prompts weight maintenance or weight gain by aiding the absorption of fat, protein, fat-soluble vitamin absorption and reduces the incidence of steatorrhea, azotorrhea, and weight loss.

Pancreatic Enzymes - Drug Class Review **High-Yield Med Reviews**			
Mechanism of Action: *Supplements pancreatic activity through supplementation of pancreatic enzymes amylase, lipase, and protease.*			
Class Effects: Weight maintenance or weight gain (when deficient in enzymes)			
Generic Name	**Brand Name**	**Indication(s) or Uses**	**Notes**

Pancrelipase	Creon, Pancreaze, Pancrelipase, Pertzye, Viokace, Zenpep	• Pancreatic insufficiency	• **Dosing (Adult):**
			  – Oral 500 to 2,500 units/kg/meal
			• **Dosing (Peds):**
			  – Infants: Oral 2,000 to 5,000 units per feeding
			    • Maximum 10,000 units/kg/day
			  – Ages 1 to 4 year: Oral 1,000 to 2,5000 units/kg/meal
			    • Maximum 10,000 units/kg/day
			  – Ages 4 and older: Oral 500 to 2,500 units/kg/meal
			• **CYP450 Interactions:** None
			• **Renal or Hepatic Dose Adjustments:** None
			• **Dosage Forms:** Oral (capsule, tablet)

High-Yield Clinical Knowledge

- **Band Names**
  - Pancrelipase is available in numerous different dosage forms under a wide range of brand names.
  - Depending on the formulation, different amylase, lipase, and protease concentrations are present but are not always reflected by the clinical enzymatic activity of a given product.
  - Products are not equivalent, and one product's substitution for another should prompt close monitoring, including patients admitted where formularies may not contain their particular dosage form.
- **Dosage Forms**
  - Available oral dosage forms include conventional tablets, bicarbonate-buffered enteric-coated tablets, enteric-coated tablets, beads, minitablets, or microtablets.

- **Administration Schedule**
  - Pancrelipase must be administered with each meal or snack, but dosing is individualized to patient-specific factors, including age, weight, pancreatic insufficiency, and dietary fat intake.
- **Do Not Chew**
  - Decreased clinical responses to enteric-coated agents may be a result of inadequate mixing of the granules with food.
  - Patients must be instructed that capsules must be swallowed, not chewed, which increases the risk of mucositis.
- **NPO Administration**
  - For patients who cannot swallow or have feeding tubes, pancrelipase microspheres can be mixed with enteral feeding formula products for administration.
  - However, these microspheres must be administered with food or solutions with a pH of 4.5 or less.
- **Long Term Use**
  - In patients with cystic fibrosis who require long-term pancrelipase therapy are at risk of fibrosing colonopathy leading to colon strictures.

HIGH-YIELD BOARD EXAM ESSENTIALS

- **CLASSIC AGENTS:** Pancrelipase
- **DRUG CLASS:** Pancreatic Enzymes
- **INDICATIONS:** Exocrine pancreatic insufficiency
- **MECHANISM:** Supplements pancreatic activity through supplementation of pancreatic enzymes amylase, lipase, and protease.
- **SIDE EFFECTS:** Abdominal pain, diarrhea, itching, headache
- **CLINICAL PEARLS:** Decreased clinical responses to enteric-coated agents may be a result of inadequate mixing of the granules with food. Patients must be instructed that capsules must be swallowed, not chewed, which increases the risk of mucositis.

High-Yield Basic Pharmacology

- **Mechanism of Action**
  - Form insoluble compounds with phosphate in the GI by binding to dietary phosphorus.
- **Calcium Carbonate or Acetate**
  - Although calcium carbonate contains more elemental calcium, calcium acetate is preferred in patients with CKD due to the lower elemental calcium content.
    - For every 1 g of calcium acetate, 45 mg of phosphorus is bound.
    - Calcium carbonate 1 g binds approximately 39 mg of phosphorus.

Primary Net Benefit

- Oral calcium phosphate binders are first-line agents, followed by sevelamer, which may reduce the risk of coronary artery calcification associated with long-term calcium use. Lanthanum is an alternative with a lower hypercalcemia risk, and more recent iron-based binders lower phosphorus with a lower pill burden.

Phosphate Binding Agents - Drug Class Review **High-Yield Med Reviews**			
Mechanism of Action: *Form insoluble compounds with phosphate in the GI by binding to dietary phosphorus*			
Class Effects: Decrease serum phosphate levels; Calcium-based binders can precipitate with phosphorus at high concentrations.			
Generic Name	**Brand Name**	**Indication(s) or Uses**	**Notes**

Aluminum hydroxide	AlternaGel	• Hyperphosphatemia	• **Dosing (Adult):**
			  – Oral 300 to 600 mg qmeal
			• **Dosing (Peds):**
			  – Oral 150 to 300 mg qmeal
			• **CYP450 Interactions:** None
			• **Renal or Hepatic Dose Adjustments:** None
			• **Dosage Forms:** Oral (capsule, solution, tablet)

Calcium acetate	Calphron
	Eliphos
	PhosLo
	Phoslyra
		• Hyperphosphatemia	• **Dosing (Adult):**
			  – Oral 1,334 to 2,668 mg qmeal
			• **Dosing (Peds):**
			  – Oral 667 to 1,000 mg qmeal
			• **CYP450 Interactions:** None
			• **Renal or Hepatic Dose Adjustments:** None
			• **Dosage Forms:** Oral (capsule, solution, tablet)

Calcium carbonate	Antacid
	Cal-Carb
	Caltrate
	Florical
	Maalox
	Oysco
	Tums
		• Antacid
		• Calcium supplementation
		• Hyperphosphatemia
		• Hypoparathyroidism
			• **Dosing (Adult):**
			  – Oral 500 to 8,000 mg per day
			    • Maximum for CKD 2,000 mg/day
			• **Dosing (Peds):**
			  – Oral 375 to 7,500 mg/day
			    • Maximum for CKD 2,000 mg/day
			• **CYP450 Interactions:** None
			• **Renal or Hepatic Dose Adjustments:** None
			• **Dosage Forms:** Oral (capsule, powder, suspension, tablet)

Phosphate Binding Agents - Drug Class Review
High-Yield Med Reviews

Generic Name	Brand Name	Indication(s) or Uses	Notes

Ferric citrate	Auryxia	▪ Hyperphosphatemia
		▪ Iron deficiency anemia
			▪ **Dosing (Adult):**
			  – Oral 210 to 420 mg TID
			    ▪ Maximum 2,520 mg/day
			▪ **Dosing (Peds):**
			  – Not routinely used
			▪ **CYP450 Interactions:** None
			▪ **Renal or Hepatic Dose Adjustments:** None
			▪ **Dosage Forms:** Oral (tablet)

Lanthanum	Fosrenol	▪ Hyperphosphatemia	▪ **Dosing (Adult):**
			  – Oral 1,500 to 4,500 mg daily
			▪ **Dosing (Peds):**
			  – Not routinely used
			▪ **CYP450 Interactions:** None
			▪ **Renal or Hepatic Dose Adjustments:** None
			▪ **Dosage Forms:** Oral (packet, tablet)

Magnesium carbonate	Magonate	▪ Dietary supplementation	▪ **Dosing (Adult):**
			  – Oral 5 mL 3 times daily
			▪ **Dosing (Peds):**
			  – Oral (elemental magnesium) 10 to 20 mg/kg/dose q6-24h
			▪ **CYP450 Interactions:** None
			▪ **Renal or Hepatic Dose Adjustments:**
			  – Should be avoided in PEDIATRICS with renal impairment
			▪ **Dosage Forms:** Oral (liquid, powder)

Sevelamer	Renagel, Renvela	▪ Hyperphosphatemia	▪ **Dosing (Adult):**
			  – Oral 600 to 1,600 mg TID with meals
			▪ **Dosing (Peds):**
			  – Oral 400 to 800 mg TID with meals
			▪ **CYP450 Interactions:** None
			▪ **Renal or Hepatic Dose Adjustments:** None
			▪ **Dosage Forms:** Oral (packet, tablet)

Sucroferric oxyhydroxide	Velphoro	▪ Hyperphosphatemia	▪ **Dosing (Adult):**
			  – Oral 500 to 2,000 mg TID with meals
			▪ **Dosing (Peds):**
			  – Not routinely used
			▪ **CYP450 Interactions:** None
			▪ **Renal or Hepatic Dose Adjustments:** None
			▪ **Dosage Forms:** Oral (tablet)

High-Yield Clinical Knowledge

▪ **Relevant Interactions**
  – Numerous interactions exist with oral phosphate binders, and patients must be counseled to separate other medications by at least 1-2 hours before or 3 hours after phosphate binder administration.

- Sevelamer may reduce the absorption of fluoroquinolones and mycophenolate resulting in the risk of clinical failure.
- Lanthanum may reduce the absorption of fluoroquinolones, tetracyclines, and levothyroxine.
- Iron-based binding agents may result in the chelation of numerous medications due to their iron content.

- **Phosphate Binding Equivalence**
  - Dosing equivalents are compared to the phosphate binding capacity of calcium carbonate 1g:
    - Aluminum hydroxide 500 mg = 0.75
    - Calcium carbonate 1,000 mg = 1
    - Calcium acetate 667 mg = 0.67
    - Ferric citrate 210 mg = 0.64
    - Lanthanum 500 mg = 1.0
    - Sevelamer carbonate 800 mg = 0.6
    - Sucroferric oxyhydroxide 500 mg = 1.6

- **Hyperphosphatemia**
  - Hyperphosphatemia occurs in patients with chronic kidney disease due to decreased phosphorus elimination and may cause secondary hyperparathyroidism and increased osteoclast activity.

- **Serum Iron**
  - Iron-based phosphate binders may increase serum iron, ferritin, and iron saturation, thus increasing iron overload risk.

- **Aluminum and HD**
  - Aluminum hydroxide used as a phosphate binder has diminished due to the availability of suitable alternatives and aluminum toxicity risk.
  - Aluminum may inhibit delta-aminolaevulinic acid dehydrogenase leading to the accumulation of erythrocyte protoporphyrin, which manifests as microcytic hypochromic anemia resistant to iron.

- **Vascular Calcifications**
  - Chronic use of calcium-based phosphate binders contributes to increased vascular calcification in patients with chronic kidney disease.

HIGH-YIELD BOARD EXAM ESSENTIALS
- **CLASSIC AGENTS:** Aluminum hydroxide, calcium acetate, calcium carbonate, ferric citrate, magnesium carbonate, lanthanum, sevelamer, sucroferric oxyhydroxide
- **DRUG CLASS:** Phosphate Binding Agents
- **INDICATIONS:** Antacid (calcium acetate), calcium supplementation (calcium acetate, calcium carbonate), hyperphosphatemia (calcium acetate, calcium carbonate, ferric citrate, lanthanum, sevelamer, sucroferric oxyhydroxide), hypoparathyroidism (calcium carbonate), iron deficiency anemia (ferric citrate)
- **MECHANISM:** Form insoluble compounds with phosphate in the GI by binding to dietary phosphorus
- **SIDE EFFECTS:** Metallic taste, constipation, diarrhea
- **CLINICAL PEARLS:**
  - Chronic use of calcium-based phosphate binders contributes to increased vascular calcification in patients with chronic kidney disease.
  - Aluminum-based phosphate binders are very effective at binding phosphate, but aluminum can accumulate with chronic use and lead to bone disease.

High-Yield Basic Pharmacology

- **Sorbitol Suspension**
    - SPS is a suspension in sorbitol to promote excretion of the bound potassium but frequently is associated with diarrhea.
    - Patiromer also contains sorbitol but a significantly lower quantity than in SPS.

Primary Net Benefit

- Potassium lowering agents that are used for chronic management of hyperkalemia in patients with chronic kidney disease.

<table>
<tr><td colspan="4" align="center">Potassium Binding Agents - Drug Class Review
High-Yield Med Reviews</td></tr>
<tr><td colspan="4">Mechanism of Action: Cation exchange resins that reduce potassium absorption from the gut.</td></tr>
<tr><td colspan="4">Class Effects: Potassium lowering agents used for chronic management of hyperkalemia in patients with chronic kidney disease.</td></tr>
<tr><td>Generic Name</td><td>Brand Name</td><td>Indication(s) or Uses</td><td>Notes</td></tr>
<tr>
<td>Patiromer</td>
<td>Veltassa</td>
<td>- Hyperkalemia</td>
<td>
- Dosing (Adult):
    - Oral 8.4 to 25.2 g once daily
- Dosing (Peds):
    - Not routinely used
- CYP450 Interactions: None
- Renal or Hepatic Dose Adjustments: None
- Dosage Forms: Oral (packet)
</td>
</tr>
<tr>
<td>Sodium Polystyrene Sulfonate</td>
<td>Kayexalate, Kionex</td>
<td>- Hyperkalemia</td>
<td>
- Dosing (Adult):
    - Oral 15 to 60 g 1 to 4 times daily
    - Rectal 30 to 50 g q6h
- Dosing (Peds):
    - Oral 1g/kg/dose q6h
        - Maximum 15 g/dose
    - Rectal 1 g/kg/dose retained for 15-60 minutes q2-6h
        - Maximum 50 g/dose
- CYP450 Interactions: None
- Renal or Hepatic Dose Adjustments: None
- Dosage Forms: Oral (powder, suspension), Rectal (suspension)
</td>
</tr>
<tr>
<td>Sodium Zirconium Cyclosilicate</td>
<td>Lokelma</td>
<td>- Hyperkalemia</td>
<td>
- Dosing (Adult):
    - Oral 5 to 15 g TID for up to 48 hours
- Dosing (Peds):
    - Not routinely used
- CYP450 Interactions: None
- Renal or Hepatic Dose Adjustments: None
- Dosage Forms: Oral (packet)
</td>
</tr>
</table>

High-Yield Clinical Knowledge

- **Sodium Content**
  - SPS also contains a considerable amount of sodium, 100 mg per 1 g of SPS.
    - For a given dose of 15 to 60 g, patients may be exposed to 1,500 to 6,000 mg of sodium, and when administered q4h, this can significantly exceed the recommended daily intake of sodium.
  - Each 10 g dose of sodium zirconium cyclosilicate contains 800 mg of sodium, for a total daily intake of 2,400 mg of sodium from this drug alone.
- **Colonic Necrosis**
  - Sorbitol has also been associated with colonic necrosis, particularly in preparations with 70% sorbitol.
  - There is a lower risk of colonic necrosis with the 33% sorbitol SPS formulation.
- **SPS Potassium Lowering**
  - Although 1 mEq of SPS will exchange 1 mEq of potassium, this exchange occurs in the intestines and does not equate to SPS's plasma potassium lowering effect.
  - SPS may lower plasma potassium by approximately 0.5 mEq/L and may do so within 3 to 4 hours of an oral or rectal dose.
    - Therefore, SPS should not be used to rapidly lower potassium in patients with severe or symptomatic hyperkalemia.
  - Patiromer is not appropriate for rapid potassium lowering effect.
  - Sodium zirconium cyclosilicate has a much more rapid onset within 1 hour after administration; however, clinical experience lacks and more clinically important interventions in hyperkalemia should be prioritized (calcium, insulin, diuresis/dialysis, beta-agonists).
- **Chronic SPS Vs. Alternatives**
  - Patients with chronic kidney disease receiving RAAS inhibitor therapy can receive SPS to maintain normal serum potassium.
  - However, due to the significant sodium content, associated diarrhea, and risk of colonic necrosis, alternative cation exchange resins (patiromer, sodium zirconium cyclosilicate) can be used.
- **Drug Interactions**
  - Any of these cation exchange agents will bind numerous oral medications and are required to be administered at least 3 hours before or after any other medication.
- **Potassium Exchange Location**
  - SPS and sodium zirconium cyclosilicate exchange sodium for potassium across the length of the intestinal tract.
  - Conversely, patiromer only exchanges calcium for potassium in the distal colon.

HIGH-YIELD BOARD EXAM ESSENTIALS

- **CLASSIC AGENTS:** Patiromer, sodium polystyrene sulfonate, sodium zirconium cyclosilicate
- **DRUG CLASS:** Potassium binding agents
- **INDICATIONS:** Hyperkalemia
- **MECHANISM:** Cation exchange resins that reduce potassium absorption from the gut.
- **SIDE EFFECTS:** Hypernatremia, edema, diarrhea
- **CLINICAL PEARLS:** Patients with chronic kidney disease receiving RAAS inhibitor therapy can receive SPS to maintain normal serum potassium. However, due to the significant sodium content, associated diarrhea, and risk of colonic necrosis, alternative cation exchange resins (patiromer, sodium zirconium cyclosilicate) can be used.

High-Yield Basic Pharmacology

- **Mechanism of Action**
    - Specific and competitive inhibitor of iodine uptake into the thyroid.
    - Inhibit thyroglobulin proteolysis, inhibiting thyroid hormone release.
- **Iodine Vs. Iodide**
    - Iodine is the chemical element and is caustic.
    - Iodide refers to the negatively charged state, forming inorganic compounds such as sodium and potassium iodide.

Primary Net Benefit

- Iodide dietary supplements but more importantly used for thyroid protection after radiologic exposure or rapid establishment of the euthyroid state in thyrotoxicosis or before thyroid surgery.

Iodides - Drug Class Review High-Yield Med Reviews			
Mechanism of Action: *Specific and competitive inhibitor of iodine uptake into the thyroid. Inhibit thyroglobulin proteolysis, inhibiting thyroid hormone release.*			
Class Effects: Reduced thyroid function by inhibiting release and also blood flow to the thyroid gland.			
Generic Name	**Brand Name**	**Indication(s) or Uses**	**Notes**

Potassium iodide	iOSTAT, SSKI, Thyrosafe	• Antidote
		• Expectorant
			• **Dosing (Adult):**
			  – Antidote - Oral 130 mg daily for 10-14 days
			  – Expectorant - Oral 300 to 600 mg 3-4 times daily
			  – Thyrotoxicosis (SSKI) 250 mg q6h
			• **Dosing (Peds):**
			  – Infants and children younger than 3 years, 32.5 mg daily
			  – Age 3 to 12 years, oral 65 mg daily
			• **CYP450 Interactions:** None
			• **Renal or Hepatic Dose Adjustments:** None
			• **Dosage Forms:** Oral (solution, tablet)

Sodium iodide	Iodopen	• Iodine supplement	• **Dosing (Adult):**
			  – IV 1 to 3 mcg/kg/day administered in parenteral nutrition
			• **Dosing (Peds):**
			  – IV 1 to 3 mcg/kg/day administered in parenteral nutrition
			• **CYP450 Interactions:** None
			• **Renal or Hepatic Dose Adjustments:** None
			• **Dosage Forms:** IV (solution)

High-Yield Clinical Knowledge

- **Pregnant Women and Children**
    - Children and pregnant women are at high risk of radioactive iodine's toxic effects than men and adult women.

- However, pregnant women must only receive a single dose as the risk of the Wolff-Chaikoff effect where iodine inhibits the synthesis of thyroid hormones may be catastrophic in fetal neurologic development.

- **Physiologic Function**
  - Iodine is an essential element required to synthesize thyroid hormones triiodothyronine (T3) and thyroxine (T4).
    - If the synthesis of T3 or T4 is absent, supplementation is necessary for life.

- **Iodine Allergy**
  - A true iodine allergy is incompatible with life.
  - There has been no evidence to suggest IgE antibody development to small molecules, including either iodine or iodide.
    - Radiocontrast media, which often contains iodine, is associated with anaphylactoid reactions due to osmolarity or other high-molecular-weight components but is not a result of its iodine content.
  - Patients who experience allergic responses to povidone-iodine do not exhibit adverse reactions to potassium iodide.

- **Thyroid Effects**
  - Iodides inhibit organification and hormone release from thyroid tissue and can also decrease its size and vascularity.
  - Iodides can precipitate either hyperthyroidism or hypothyroidism.

- **SSKI, Lugol's, or Tablets**
  - Potassium iodide is available as either a supersaturated potassium iodide (SSKI) containing 38 mg iodide/drop, a less concentrated solution (Lugol's) of 6.3 mg/drop of potassium iodide, and tablets which are available as 130 mg.

- **Radiologic Exposure**
  - Potassium iodide is used for post-exposure prophylaxis after radiation exposures to competitively inhibit radioactive iodine uptake into the thyroid.
    - Exposure usually occurs from inhalation of radioactive iodine or ingestion of contaminated food.
  - It has been used in Pacific Islanders exposed to nuclear weapon testing in the 1950s to reduce thyroid exposure to radioactive iodine.
  - More recently, nuclear incidents in Ukraine (Chernobyl) and Japan (Fukushima) have prompted the public at risk of exposure to take potassium iodine.
    - Among children with radiologic exposure from Chernobyl, children in Poland who had access to potassium iodine have a significantly lower risk of thyroid cancer than Ukrainian children who were largely not given potassium iodine.

HIGH-YIELD BOARD EXAM ESSENTIALS
- **CLASSIC AGENTS:** Sodium iodide, potassium iodide
- **DRUG CLASS:** Iodides
- **INDICATIONS:** Antidote (radioactive iodine), expectorant, iodine supplement
- **MECHANISM:** Specific and competitive inhibitor of iodine uptake into the thyroid. inhibit thyroglobulin proteolysis, inhibiting thyroid hormone release.
- **SIDE EFFECTS:** Sialadenitis, acneiform rash, mucous membrane ulceration, conjunctivitis, and bleeding disorders.
- **CLINICAL PEARLS:**
  - Since these agents in higher doses can not only suppress thyroid hormone release, it can also reduce blood flow to the thyroid gland and thereby inhibit the delivery of other drugs to the thyroid gland. Thus, the order of drug administration in certain conditions can be relevant.
  - Children and pregnant women are at high risk of radioactive iodine's toxic effects than men and adult women. However, pregnant women must only receive a single dose as the risk of the Wolff-Chaikoff effect where iodine inhibits the synthesis of thyroid hormones may be catastrophic in fetal neurologic development.

High-Yield Basic Pharmacology

- **Mechanism of Action**
  - Block thyroid hormone synthesis by inhibiting thyroid peroxidase; does not inactivate existing T3 or T4.
  - Propylthiouracil: also, inhibits peripheral conversion of T4 to T3.
  - Do not interfere with orally or parenterally administered thyroid hormones.

Primary Net Benefit

- Acutely prevent thyroid hormone production, interrupting physiologic process resulting from hyperthyroidism. Generally, serve as a bridge to definitive care (surgery or irradiation), and not necessarily used for chronic care.

Thyroid Replacements Drug Class Review			
High-Yield Med Reviews			
Mechanism of Action: *blocks thyroid hormone synthesis. Propylthiouracil also inhibits conversion of peripheral T4 to T3.*			
Class Effects: Hepatotoxicity (propylthiouracil>methimazole), bone marrow suppression, hypothyroidism			
Generic Name	**Brand Name**	**Indication(s) or Uses**	**Notes**

Methimazole	Tapazole	• Hyperthyroidism
		• Thyroid storm
		• Iodine and amiodarone-induced thyrotoxicosis
			• **Dosing (Adult):** 5-40 mg daily
			  – Free T4 1-1.5x ULN: 5-10 mg; 1.5-2x ULN: 10-20 mg; 2-3x ULN: 30-40 mg.
			  – May divide in 2-3 doses >30 mg daily; may mitigate GI effects.
			  – Adjust dose and duration based on definitive therapy and thyroid function tests.
			• **Dosing (Peds):** 0.4 mg/kg/d divided Q8h, then 0.2 mg/kg/d divided Q8h
			  – Can also follow fixed dosing by age
			• **CYP450 Interactions:** N/A
			• **Renal or Hepatic Dose Adjustments:** None
			• **Dosage Forms:** 5 mg, 10 mg

Propylthiouracil		• Hyperthyroidism
		• Thyroid storm (preferred)
			• **Dosing (Adult):** 300 mg daily divided Q8h
			  – Doses up to 900 mg daily may be given.
			  – Thyroid storm: 500-1000 mg, then 250 mg Q4h, then reduce to maintenance dosage.
			• **Dosing (Peds):** Initial 6-10 yo: 50-150 mg/d divided Q8h; >10 yo 150-300 mg/d divided Q8h
			  – Maintenance 50 mg BID
			• **CYP450 Interactions:** N/A
			• **Renal or Hepatic Dose Adjustments:** None
			• **Dosage Forms:** 50 mg

High-Yield Clinical Knowledge

- **Bone Marrow Suppression**
  - May cause bone marrow suppression, including agranulocytosis, thrombocytopenia, and aplastic anemia.
  - Methimazole
    - Risk increases with doses ≥40 mg daily.

- **Hepatic Toxicity**
  - May cause acute and/or fatal liver failure.
  - Propylthiouracil demonstrates greater risk than methimazole. Recommended only in patients intolerant to methimazole or who are not candidates for surgery and radioactive iodine.
- **Other Warnings**
  - Bleeding, fever, dermatologic toxicities, pneumonitis, nephritis, lupus-like syndrome, and vasculitis may occur.
- **Pediatric Patients**
  - Methimazole is preferred; propylthiouracil should be used only in patients who have experienced adverse effects with methimazole or are not candidates for surgery or radioactive iodine treatment due to hematologic and hepatic toxicities.
- **Pregnancy**
  - 1st Trimester
    - Avoid methimazole in 1st trimester due to teratogenesis.
    - Use propylthiouracil.
  - 2nd/3rd Trimester
    - Methimazole is preferred due to increased risk of adverse effects with propylthiouracil to the mother.
  - Monitor and adjust doses as pregnancy progresses to maintain response.
    - Thyroid function can improve with pregnancy progression, leading to potential discontinuation 2-3 months prior to birth with careful monitoring.
- **Lactation**
  - Thioamides are compatible with breastfeeding.
    - Methimazole recommended at 20-30 mg daily in divided doses taken after breastfeeding sessions.
    - Propylthiouracil is acceptable at $\leq$450 mg daily.
  - Monitor infant's thyroid function, growth, and development.

HIGH-YIELD BOARD EXAM ESSENTIALS

- **CLASSIC AGENTS:** Methimazole, propylthiouracil
- **DRUG CLASS:** Thioamide
- **INDICATIONS:** Hyperthyroidism/thyrotoxicosis
- **MECHANISM:** Blocks thyroid hormone synthesis. Propylthiouracil also inhibits conversion of peripheral T4 to T3.
- **SIDE EFFECTS:** Hepatotoxicity (propylthiouracil>methimazole), bone marrow suppression, hypothyroidism
- **CLINICAL PEARLS:** Propylthiouracil may be preferred in thyroid storm because it inhibits peripheral conversion of T4 to T3, unless the patient has liver disease or is in the 2nd/3rd trimester of pregnancy.

High-Yield Basic Pharmacology

- **Mechanism of Action**
  - Ultimately, agents result in thyroid replacement.
  - Desiccated thyroid: primarily T3, but also contains T4 and iodine.
  - Levothyroxine: synthetic T4 (thyroxine) that is converted to its active metabolite T3 (triiodothyronine).
  - Liothyronine: T3 hormone as replacement.

Primary Net Benefit

- Utilized to replace thyroid hormone in a hypothyroid state.

Thyroid Replacements Drug Class Review			
High-Yield Med Reviews			
Mechanism of Action: *replaces thyroid hormone in hypothyroid state.*			
Class Effects: cardiac toxicities, BMD changes, monitor dosage forms for bioequivalence, T4 preferred			
Generic Name	**Brand Name**	**Indication(s) or Uses**	**Notes**

Desiccated thyroid	Armour Thyroid Nature-Thyroid NP Thyroid Westhroid WP Thyroid	• Hypothyroidism	• **Dosing (Adult):** 30-32.5 mg/d
			  – Increase 15-16.25 mg/d every 2-3 weeks
			  – With CVD: 15-16.25 mg/d
			• **Dosing (Peds):** 1.2-6 mg/kg/dose based on age from 1 month-17 years; higher doses at younger ages
			• **CYP450 Interactions:** None
			• **Renal or Hepatic Dose Adjustments:** None
			• **Dosage Forms:** Armour Thyroid (15, 30, 60, 90, 120, 180, 240, 300 mg); Nature-Throid (48.75, 65, 81.25, 97.5, 113.75, 130, 146.25, 162.5, 195, 260, 325 mg); NP Thyroid (15, 30, 60, 90, 120 mg); Westhroid (32.5, 65, 97.5, 130, 195 mg); WP Thyroid (16.25, 32.5, 48.75, 65, 81.25, 97.5, 113.75, 130 mg)

Levothyroxine	Euthyrox Levoxyl Synthroid Tirosint Tirosint-SOL Unithroid	• Hypothyroidism
		• Pituitary TSH suppression
		• Myxedema coma (IV)
			• **Dosing (Adult):** 1.6 mcg/kg/d, including new diagnosis in pregnancy
			  – >60 yo or with CVD: 12.5-50 mcg/d
			  – Increase by 12.5 mcg-25 mcg every 4-6 weeks
			  – Myxedema coma (concomitant glucocorticoid +/-liothyronine): 200-400 mcg IV slow bolus, then 50-100 mcg daily
			• **Dosing (Peds):** 4-15 mcg/kg/dose based on age from 1 month-12 years; higher doses at younger ages; >12 yo use adult dosing
			• **CYP450 Interactions:** None
			• **Renal or Hepatic Dose Adjustments:** None
			• **Dosage Forms:** Capsules & PO solution (13, 25, 50, 75, 88, 100, 112, 125, 137, 150, 175, 200 mcg); IV (100 mcg/5mL, 200 mcg/5mL, 500 mcg/5mL); Tablets (25, 50, 75, 88, 100, 112, 125, 137 150, 175, 200, 300 mcg)

Thyroid Replacements Drug Class Review
High-Yield Med Reviews

Generic Name	Brand Name	Indication(s) or Uses	Notes

Liothyronine	Cytomel
	Triostat
		• Hypothyroidism	• **Dosing (Adult):** 25 mcg daily; increase by 25 mcg every 1-2 weeks
			  – CVD: 5 mcg daily, then increase by 5 mcg every 2 weeks
			  – Myxedema coma in combination with levothyroxine: 5-20 mcg LD, then 2.5-10 mcg Q8H
			  – Changing from desiccated thyroid or levothyroxine: stop other agent; start low dose liothyronine and increase slowly.
			• **Dosing (Peds):** 20-75 mcg daily based on age from infant-17 yo; doses increase with age.
			• **CYP450 Interactions:** None
			• **Renal or Hepatic Dose Adjustments:** None
			• **Dosage Forms:** IV (10 mcg/mL); Tablet (5, 25, 50 mcg)

Liotrix	Thyrolar	• Hypothyroidism	• **Dosing (Adult):** levothyroxine 25 mcg/liothyronine 6.25 mcg daily
			  – CVD: 12.5 mcg/3.1 mcg daily
			  – Increase 12.5 mcg/3.1 mcg every 2-3 weeks
			• **Dosing (Peds):** levothyroxine 12.5-75 mcg/ liothyronine 3.1-18.75 mcg daily from under 6 months-17 years; doses increase with age
			• **CYP450 Interactions:** None
			• **Renal or Hepatic Dose Adjustments:** None
			• **Dosage Forms:** Tablet (levothyroxine mcg/liothyronine mcg) [1/4 (12.5/3.1), 1/2 (25/6.25), 1 (50/12.5), 2 (100/25), 3 (150/37.5)]

High-Yield Clinical Knowledge

- **Levothyroxine First Line**
  - Levothyroxine is recommended as first-line therapy for hypothyroidism and in other hypothyroid states.
- **Drug Interactions**
  - Sucralfate, bile acid sequestrants, raloxifene, and calcium- or iron-containing products may reduce thyroid absorption and decrease effect of replacement. Consider separating by 4 hours.
  - Amiodarone, iodine-containing medications, estrogen derivatives, and lithium may decrease the effect of thyroid hormone replacement.
  - Rifampin, phenobarbital, phenytoin, and carbamazepine can increase the metabolism of thyroxine.
  - Furosemide, mefenamic acid, and salicylates can displace thyroid hormone from protein binding.
  - Warfarin effects may be increased (elevated INR).
  - Cardiac glycoside and theophylline concentrations may be reduced.
  - Sodium iodide I131 effects may be decreased by thyroid replacement; discontinue T3 2 weeks before and T4 4 weeks before administration.
- **Desiccated Thyroid**
  - Contains variable amounts of T4, T3, and other compounds more likely to cause cardiac toxicities.
  - Is porcine-derived, so there is a low potential risk for contamination with viruses.

- **Cardiovascular Disease**
  - Dosage forms containing active T3 increase potential for cardiac toxicities.
  - Initiate reduced doses and increase doses cautiously. Overtreatment can increase risk of adverse cardiac events in all patient populations.
  - Reduce dose or hold for 7 days if signs or symptoms occur.
- **Diabetes**
  - May worsen glycemic control with treatment.
- **Osteoporosis**
  - Long-term treatment may reduce BMD and is likely dose-related. Use caution especially in postmenopausal women.

HIGH-YIELD BOARD EXAM ESSENTIALS

- **CLASSIC AGENTS:** Desiccated thyroid, levothyroxine, liothyronine, liotrix
- **DRUG CLASS:** Thyroid Replacements
- **INDICATIONS:** Hypothyroidism, myxedema coma, pituitary thyrotropin-stimulating hormone suppression
- **MECHANISM:** Replaces thyroid hormone in hypothyroid state.
- **SIDE EFFECTS:** Cardiac toxicity, glucose intolerance, BMD changes
- **CLINICAL PEARLS:**
  - Synthetic T4 hormone replacement is the drug of choice in hypothyroidism. Upon starting, change in dosage, or change in manufacturer, a TSH lab check will be needed in 6-7 weeks to discern level of control.
  - Dosage forms containing active T3 increase potential for cardiac toxicities. Initiate reduced doses and increase doses cautiously. Overtreatment can increase risk of adverse cardiac events (e.g., atrial fibrillation or high output heart failure) in some patient populations.
  - Pregnant patients will need much higher doses of levothyroxine very early on to avoid risk of miscarriage, pre-term delivery, poor CNS development of the baby.

High-Yield Basic Pharmacology

- **Demeclocycline**
  - Tetracycline antibiotic, but inhibits renal tubular arginine vasopressin activity, increasing free water excretion.
- **Conivaptan and Tolvaptan**
  - Vasopressin 2 (aquaporin 2) receptor antagonists
- **Vasopressin Receptor Selectivity**
  - Vasopressin receptor antagonism produces free-water loss (aquaresis) and increases serum sodium concentrations.
  - Conivaptan is a nonselective V1a and V2 receptor antagonist.
  - Tolvaptan is a selective V2 receptor antagonist.

Primary Net Benefit

- AVP receptor antagonists are effective means of correcting hyponatremia, but their effects are short-lived and present safety concerns related to rapid sodium correction, hepatic injury, and drug interactions.

Demeclocycline and Vasopressin Receptor Antagonists - Drug Class Review			
High-Yield Med Reviews			
Mechanism of Action: *Demeclocycline - inhibits renal tubular arginine vasopressin activity, increasing free water excretion.* *Conivaptan and Tolvaptan - Vasopressin 2 (aquaporin-2) receptor antagonists.*			
Class Effects: Increases in serum sodium concentrations; risk of dehydration, volume depletion, hypotension, as well as pyrexia and xerostomia.			
Generic Name	**Brand Name**	**Indication(s) or Uses**	**Notes**

Demeclocycline	Detravis, Meciclin, Mexocine, Clortetrin	• SIADH	• **Dosing (Adult):**
			   – Oral 600 to 1,200 mg/day divided q6h
			 • **Dosing (Peds):**
			   – Oral 7 to 13 mg/kg/day divided q6-12h
			 • **CYP450 Interactions:** None
			 • **Renal or Hepatic Dose Adjustments:** None
			 • **Dosage Forms:** Oral (tablet)

Conivaptan	Vaprisol	• Euvolemic or hypervolemic hyponatremia	• **Dosing (Adult):**
			   – IV 20 mg over 30 minutes, then 0.83 to 1.7 mg/hour for 2-4 days
			     • Maximum 40 mg/24hours
			 • **Dosing (Peds):**
			   – Not routinely used
			 • **CYP450 Interactions:** Substrate CYP3A4; Inhibits CYP3A4
			 • **Renal or Hepatic Dose Adjustments:**
			   – GFR less than 30 mL/minute - not recommended
			   – Anuria - Contraindicated
			   – Child-Pugh class C - Use with caution
			 • **Dosage Forms:** IV (solution)

Demeclocycline and Vasopressin Receptor Antagonists - Drug Class Review			
High-Yield Med Reviews			
Generic Name	Brand Name	Indication(s) or Uses	Notes

Tolvaptan	Jynarque Samsca	• Autosomal dominant polycystic kidney disease
		• Euvolemic or hypervolemic hyponatremia
			• **Dosing (Adult):**
			  – Oral 60 mg/day in divided doses, titrated to 120 mg/day in divided doses to urine osmolality less than 300 mOsm/kg
			  – Oral 15 to 60 mg daily for maximum 30 days
			• **Dosing (Peds):**
			  – Not routinely used
			• **CYP450 Interactions:** Substrate CYP3A4, P-gp
			• **Renal or Hepatic Dose Adjustments:**
			  – GFR less than 10 mL/minute - not recommended
			  – AST/ALT greater than 3x upper limit of normal, or underlying liver disease - not recommended
			• **Dosage Forms:** Oral (tablet)

High-Yield Clinical Knowledge

- **Chronic Management**
    - Demeclocycline, conivaptan, and tolvaptan should not be used in the immediate management of acute hyponatremia.
    - Tolvaptan's onset of action is up to 4 hours and has not been evaluated thoroughly in serum sodium concentrations below 120 mEq/L.
- **Limited Duration and Effects**
    - Tolvaptan and conivaptan are effective interventions to correct hyponatremia in euvolemic or hypovolemic scenarios.
    - Furthermore, their effects are short-lived as tolvaptan is limited to 30 days of therapy, and hyponatremia returns with drug discontinuation.
    - Conivaptan is only available as an IV dosage form and should not be used for more than four days.
    - Vaptan therapy is limited due to the increased risk of liver injury with continued therapy beyond the recommended time.
- **Gradual Sodium Replacement**
    - Correction of sodium levels in patients with hyponatremia should not exceed 10 to 12 mEq/L in a given 24-hour period.
- **Demeclocycline Induced DI**
    - The action of demeclocycline on the inhibition of renal tubular vasopressin activity is essentially a drug-induced nephrogenic diabetes insipidus used to treat SIADH.
    - Other causes of drug-induced nephrogenic diabetes insipidus include cisplatin, clozapine, colchicine, foscarnet, and lithium.
- **Anuric Patients**
    - Conivaptan and tolvaptan are contraindicated in patients with stage 4 or 5 chronic kidney disease.
- **Adverse Events**
    - As a result of the potent free-water losses, patients on conivaptan or tolvaptan therapy are at risk of dehydration, volume depletion, hypotension, as well as pyrexia and xerostomia.
    - Conivaptan and tolvaptan have also been associated with hyperkalemia, hyperglycemia as a result of free-water losses.

HIGH-YIELD BOARD EXAM ESSENTIALS

- **CLASSIC AGENTS:** Demeclocycline, conivaptan, tolvaptan
- **DRUG CLASS:** Demeclocycline and Vasopressin Receptor Antagonists
- **INDICATIONS:** Autosomal dominant polycystic kidney disease, euvolemic or hypervolemic hyponatremia, SIADH
- **MECHANISM:** Demeclocycline - inhibits renal tubular arginine vasopressin activity, increasing free water excretion. Conivaptan and Tolvaptan - Vasopressin 2 (aquaporin-2) receptor antagonists.
- **SIDE EFFECTS:** Hyperkalemia, hyperglycemia, dehydration, volume depletion, hypotension, pyrexia, xerostomia
- **CLINICAL PEARLS:**
    - These agents should only be considered in patients who have failed free water restriction when managing SIADH.
    - The action of demeclocycline (an old tetracycline antibiotic) on the inhibition of renal tubular vasopressin activity is essentially a drug-induced nephrogenic diabetes insipidus used to treat SIADH.

High-Yield Basic Pharmacology

- 5-ASA has localized or targeted anti-inflammatory effects within the colonic mucosa within the lumen of the GI tract by modulating the formation of pro-inflammatory mediators derived from arachidonic acid
- The location and severity of intestinal inflammation may influence which dosage forms a patient can take. Location of lesions is typically determined by EGD, pill endoscopy, and/or colonoscopy.
  - Oral dosage forms:
    - Administered by mouth but are formulated with coatings to affect the release of 5-ASA to a specific target or location within the intestine.
  - Enema dosage formulations:
    - Administered rectally (lying in lateral position), which can provide treatment up to the splenic flexure.
  - Suppositories:
    - Administered rectally and can provide topical treatment to the rectum only.
- The azo-bonded prodrugs must have the azo bond cleaved so that the 5-ASA (active product) can provide an anti-inflammatory effect. The breaking or cleavage of this bond can occur by bacteria specifically located in the colon.
  - Olsalazine consists of two 5-ASA moieties linked by an azo bond, whereas balsalazide has an inert carrier molecule linked to 5-ASA.
  - Sulfasalazine is 5-ASA linked to sulfapyridine but not by an azo-bond.

Primary Net Benefit

- Reduce the symptoms of inflammatory bowel disorder with significant systemic effects by providing localized topical effects within the GI tract.

5-Aminosalicylic Acid (5-ASA) Drug Class Review			
High-Yield Med Reviews			
Mechanism of Action: *intestinal mucosal inflammation by reducing the release of pro-inflammatory mediators.*			
Class Effects: *The dosage formulation used in part influenced by the location of intestinal inflammation.*			
Active Drugs of 5-ASA			
Generic Name	**Brand Name**	**Main Indication(s) or Uses**	**Notes**

Mesalamine	Apriso
	Asacol HD
	Canasa
	Delzicol
	Lialda
	Pentasa
	Rowasa
		▪ Crohn's Disease
		▪ Ulcerative Colitis
			▪ **Note:** No carrier or linked molecule. Active form only.
			▪ **Dosing (Adult):**
			  − Dose depends on dosage formulation used, but doses up to 4.8 g/day
			▪ **Dosing (Peds):**
			  − Dose depends on dosage formulation.
			▪ **CYP450 Interactions:** None
			▪ **Renal or Hepatic Dose Adjustments:** None
			▪ **Dosage Forms:**
			  − Capsule (Delayed & Extended Release), Enema, Rectal Kit, Suppository, Tablets

Prodrugs Converted to 5-ASA			
Azo Bonded (also called "diazo-bonded" to allow for release in the colon)			

Balsalazide	Colazal	▪ Ulcerative Colitis	▪ **Note:**
			  − Inert carrier molecule azo-bound to 5-ASA
			▪ **Dosing (Adult):**
			  − 1.5 to 3.3 g twice a day
			▪ **Dosing (Peds):**
			  − 2.25 g three times per day or 750 mg three times per day.
			▪ **CYP450 Interactions:** None
			▪ **Renal or Hepatic Dose Adjustments:** None
			▪ **Dosage Forms:** Capsule, Tablets

Olsalazine	Dipentum	▪ Ulcerative Colitis	▪ **Note:**
			  − Two 5-ASA moieties linked by an azo bond
			▪ **Dosing (Adult):**
			  − 1 to 3 g per day in 2-4 divided doses
			▪ **Dosing (Peds):** None
			▪ **CYP450 Interactions:** None
			▪ **Renal or Hepatic Dose Adjustments:** None
			▪ **Dosage Forms:** Capsule

Non-Azo Bonded			

Sulfasalazine	Azulfidine	▪ Crohn's Disease
		▪ Ulcerative Colitis
		▪ Rheumatoid Arthritis
		▪ Psoriasis / Psoriatic Arthritis
			▪ **Note:**
			  − Sulfapyridine linked to 5-ASA without an azo-bond.
			  − Avoid in patients allergic to sulfa
			▪ **Classic Side Effects:**
			  − Infertility in men, reduction in folate absorption, and GI intolerance.
			▪ **Dosing (Adult):**
			  − 2-4 g/d in 3-4 divided doses. If GI intolerance, decrease dose by 50%.
			▪ **Dosing (Peds):**
			  − 30-70 mg/kg/day in 3-6 divided doses
			▪ **CYP450 Interactions:** None
			▪ **Renal or Hepatic Dose Adjustments:** None
			▪ **Dosage Forms:**
			  − Tablet (Regular & Delayed Release)

High-Yield Clinical Knowledge

▪ **Which IBD Benefits More?**
  − 5-ASA derivatives are considered first-line therapy for mild Crohn's disease or mild to moderate UC traditionally defined as fewer than 4-6 bowel movements per day, mild-moderate rectal bleeding, absence of systemic symptoms, and low overall inflammatory burden.
    − They can help with active flares as well as inducing remission for UC. Compliance with 5-ASA products during remission is essential for preventing flares (i.e., this is a chronic treatment, not intermittent use).
  − Most patients with mild to moderate UC respond to 5-ASA products and gain clinical remission with their use. The remaining are more complicated cases warranting other immunomodulating treatments.

- 5-ASA derivatives that have azo-bonds (i.e., balsalazide and olsalazine) work primarily in the colon or large intestine, which is why they are more effective and approved for the treatment of UC and not Crohn's disease.

- **Side Effects of 5-ASA Products**
  - The sulfapyridine carrier molecule of sulfasalazine has no therapeutic benefit in IBD and instead contributes to most of the side effects experienced by patients. Common side effects include GI intolerance, male infertility due to a reversible decrease in sperm production and interference of folate absorption. Furthermore, patients with "sulfa" allergies should avoid this drug.
    - For this reason, mesalamine does not contain a sulfa group and is the active drug only (i.e., 5-ASA) and more commonly used.
    - Women of child-bearing age who want to get pregnant and are also taking sulfasalazine should take 2 mg of folate per day.
    - If GI side effects result in intolerance, consider reducing the dose of sulfasalazine by 50%.

- **Dosage Formulations and UC**
  - Enemas and suppository dosage formulations are primarily useful for UC, given the dosage forms ability to get to the site of inflammation. Since the inflammation in UC starts at the rectum and moves proximally in the large intestine, they can be helpful. In contrast, Crohn's disease occurs as skip lesions anywhere from the oropharynx to the rectum.
    - Formulations of mesalamine include Canasa (rectal suppositories) and Rowasa (rectal suspension).

- **Rheumatoid Arthritis**
  - Only sulfasalazine is used in the treatment of Rheumatoid arthritis. Ironically it may be the sulfapyridine component that exerts the therapeutic effect, which may be why the other 5-ASA products are not used.

High-Yield Core Evidence

- One of the original articles aiding in the severity definition of UC was the Truelove and Witt's criteria.
  - Br Med J 1955;2:1041-8.

High-Yield Fast-Facts

- The underlying cause of IBD is not fully known. What is known is that immunomodulating drugs help control the disease. What is causing the immune system to be overly aggravated in the colonic mucosa is not known.
- Patients with UC are at risk of toxic megacolon, whereas Crohn's disease is only associated with the formation of fistulas.
- Patients with UC are at increased risk of colon cancer and need colonoscopies sooner than patients without UC.

HIGH-YIELD BOARD EXAM ESSENTIALS
- **CLASSIC AGENTS:** Balsalazide, mesalamine, olsalazine
- **DRUG CLASS:** 5-ASA Derivatives
- **INDICATIONS:** Crohn's Disease, Ulcerative Colitis
- **MECHANISM:** Intestinal mucosal inflammation by reducing the release of pro-inflammatory mediators.
- **SIDE EFFECTS:** GI side effects, infertility due to reversible reduced sperm production (sulfasalazine only)
- **CLINICAL PEARLS:**
  - These agents have greater efficacy at lower doses in ulcerative colitis because of how these drugs work to provide targeted topical therapy. With Crohn's disease having skip lesions and involvement outside of the large intestine where these agents work, the overall efficacy is less.
  - Several agents come in multiple dosage formulations that allow for patient specific use based on the extent of disease, especially in patients with ulcerative colitis.

High-Yield Basic Pharmacology

- **Bismuth Compounds**
  - Bismuth counteracts pepsin and gastric acid's effects on ulcers and erosions by increasing bicarbonate (increasing pH) and stimulating prostaglandin and mucus production.
  - Salicylate, although it inhibits intestinal and gastric prostaglandin secretion, also increases chloride secretion.
- **Crofelemer**
  - Inhibitor of cystic fibrosis transmembrane conductance regulator (CFTR) causing inhibition of chloride-rich secretion into the GI tract and a slowing of intestinal transit.
- **Methylcellulose, Polycarbophil, Psyllium**
  - Forms of soluble fiber that absorbs water into the intestine, promoting peristalsis.

Primary Net Benefit

- Over-the-counter products are used for a range of GI disorders, including constipation and diarrhea.

Adsorbents and Antisecretory Agents - Drug Class Review
High-Yield Med Reviews

Mechanism of Action:
See above for each agent.

Class Effects: Over-the-counter products are used for a range of GI disorders, including constipation and diarrhea.

Generic Name	Brand Name	Indication(s) or Uses	Notes

Bismuth subsalicylate	Bismatrol Diotame Pepto-Bismol	• Diarrhea
		• Dyspepsia
		• Helicobacter pylori eradication
			• **Dosing (Adult):**
			  – Oral 300 to 1,050 mg q30-60 minutes
			    • Maximum 4,200 mg/day
			• **Dosing (Peds):**
			  – Oral 87 to 262 mg q30-60 minutes up to 1,050 mg/dose (age and weight dependant)
			    • Maximum 8 doses/day
			• **CYP450 Interactions:** None
			• **Renal or Hepatic Dose Adjustments:** None
			• **Dosage Forms:** Oral (suspension, tablet)

Bismuth subcitrate	Pylera (bismuth subcitrate, metronidazole, tetracycline)	H. pylori-associated duodenal ulcer	**Dosing (Adult):**
			  – Oral 3 capsules 4 times daily after meals and at bedtime x 10 days
			Dosing (Peds):
			  – Not routinely used
			CYP450 Interactions: None
			Renal or Hepatic Dose Adjustments:
			  – Child-Pugh class C - Not recommended
			Dosage Forms: Oral (suspension, tablet)

Adsorbents and Antisecretory Agents - Drug Class Review
High-Yield Med Reviews

Generic Name	Brand Name	Indication(s) or Uses	Notes

Crofelemer	Mytesi	• HIV related diarrhea	• **Dosing (Adult):**
			  – Oral 125 mg BID
			• **Dosing (Peds):**
			  – Not routinely used
			• **CYP450 Interactions:** None
			• **Renal or Hepatic Dose Adjustments:** None
			• **Dosage Forms:** Oral (tablet)

Methylcellulose	Citrucel	Constipation	**Dosing (Adult):**
			  – Oral 2 g in 240 mL water as needed up to 3 times daily
			Dosing (Peds):
			  – Oral 1 g in 240 mL water as needed up to 3 times daily
			CYP450 Interactions: None
			Renal or Hepatic Dose Adjustments: None
			Dosage Forms: Oral (powder, tablet)

Polycarbophil	Fiber Laxative FiberCon	• Constipation or Diarrhea	• **Dosing (Adult):**
			  – Oral 1,250 mg q6-24h
			• **Dosing (Peds):**
			  – Oral 625 mg q6-24h
			• **CYP450 Interactions:** None
			• **Renal or Hepatic Dose Adjustments:** None
			• **Dosage Forms:** Oral (tablet)

Psyllium	Konsyl Metamucil Mucilin Natural Fiber	• Constipation or Diarrhea	• **Dosing (Adult):**
			  – Oral 2.5 to 30 g per day in divided doses
			• **Dosing (Peds):**
			  – Oral 1.25 to 30 g per day in divided doses
			• **CYP450 Interactions:** None
			• **Renal or Hepatic Dose Adjustments:** None
			• **Dosage Forms:** Oral (capsule, packet, powder, wafer)

High-Yield Clinical Knowledge

- **Stool Discoloration**
  - Bismuth compounds cause a darkening of stools, including blackening of the stool.
  - This discoloration may be confused with GI (melena), but patients on anticoagulants should be educated on other signs and symptoms of GI bleeding.
  - A similar discoloration of the tongue can also occur.
- **Cardiovascular Risk Reduction**
  - Psyllium dietary supplementation may reduce cardiovascular disease risk and can be added to most patients concerning for primary or secondary cardiac disease.
  - The target daily dose is 30 g of soluble fiber, challenging to ingest and tolerate if initial slow titration is not followed.
  - Dietary supplementation of psyllium fiber products does not affect the absorption of most medications.

- **Antimicrobial Action**
  - Bismuth possesses direct antimicrobial activity, particularly against Helicobacter pylori, and binding effectively to enterotoxins associated with traveler's diarrhea pathogens.
- **Helicobacter pylori Treatment**
  - Bismuth-containing compounds are a component of triple or quadruple therapy for H. pylori infection.
    - Prolonged therapy with excessive doses may result in salicylate toxicity and rarely in encephalopathy.

High-Yield Fast-Facts

- **Psyllium Origin**
  - Psyllium was once derived from the Plantago herb's seed, where most modern products contain a component of the Plantago herb.
- **Erythema of the 9th Day**
  - Bismuth has been associated with the so-called "Erythema of the 9th day," a self-resolving rash first attributed to arsphenamine used to treat syphilis in the early 1910s.

HIGH-YIELD BOARD EXAM ESSENTIALS
- **CLASSIC AGENTS:** Bismuth subsalicylate, bismuth subcitrate, crofelemer, methylcellulose, polycarbophil, psyllium
- **DRUG CLASS:** Adsorbents and antisecretory agents
- **INDICATIONS:** Constipation, diarrhea, dyspepsia, Helicobacter pylori eradication, HIV related diarrhea, soluble fiber supplementation
- **MECHANISM:** Bismuth increases bicarbonate (thus increasing pH) and stimulating prostaglandin and mucus production. Crofelemer - Inhibitor of CFTR and a slowing of intestinal transit. Methylcellulose, Polycarbophil, Psyllium - Absorbs water into the intestine, promoting peristalsis.
- **SIDE EFFECTS:** Stool discoloration, constipation, flatulence
- **CLINICAL PEARLS:** Bismuth compounds cause a darkening of stools, including blackening of the stool. This discoloration may be confused with GI (melena), but patients on anticoagulants should be educated or other signs and symptoms of GI bleeding. A similar, reversible, discoloration of the tongue can also occur.

High-Yield Basic Pharmacology

- **H2 Blockade**
  - H2RAs are highly selective and competitive inhibitors of parietal cell histamine-2 receptors, both basal and meal-stimulated acid secretion.
- **Gastric Acid Suppression**
  - All H2RAs reduce gastric acid secretion by between 60 and 70% in a given 24-hour period.
    - However, nocturnal gastric acid secretion is inhibited to a more considerable degree since this gastric acid secretion is dependent on histamine.

Primary Net Benefit

- Cornerstone therapy for gastroesophageal reflux disease and available as over-the-counter agents for dyspepsia.

Histamine H2 Receptor Antagonists - Drug Class Review High-Yield Med Reviews			
Mechanism of Action: *Competitive inhibition of the parietal cell histamine-2 receptor, preventing gastric acid secretion.*			
Class Effects: Reduction in dyspepsia, reflux, risk of gastritis; drug interactions with medications requiring an acid environment (e.g., atazanazir); all need to be renally dose adjusted; tachyphylaxis is common with chronic use			
Generic Name	**Brand Name**	**Indication(s) or Uses**	**Notes**

Cimetidine	Tagamet	• Dyspepsia
		• Gastroesophageal reflux disease
			• **Dosing (Adult):**
			  – Oral 200 to 400 mg q6h or 800 mg q12h
			• **Dosing (Peds):**
			  – Oral 20 to 40 mg/kg/day in 3-4 divided doses
			    • Maximum 2,400 mg/day
			• **CYP450 Interactions:** Substrate P-gp; Inhibits CYP 1A2, 2C19, 2D6, 3A4
			• **Renal or Hepatic Dose Adjustments:**
			  – GFR 10 to 50 mL/minute - Administer 50% of normal dose
			  – GFR less than 10 mL/minute - 300 mg q12h
			• **Dosage Forms:** Oral (solution, tablet)

Famotidine	Pepcid	• Dyspepsia
		• Gastroesophageal reflux disease
		• Helicobacter pylori
		• Peptic ulcer disease
			• **Dosing (Adult):**
			  – IV 20 to 40 mg q12h
			  – Oral 10 to 20 mg q12h
			• **Dosing (Peds):**
			  – Oral 0.5 to 1 mg/kg/dose
			    • Maximum 40 mg/dose
			  – IV 0.25 mg/kg/dose q12-24h
			    • Maximum 40 mg/day
			• **CYP450 Interactions:** None
			• **Renal or Hepatic Dose Adjustments:**
			  – GFR 30 to 60 mL/minute - administer q24h
			  – GFR less than 30 mg - 10 mg q24-48h
			• **Dosage Forms:** Oral (suspension, tablet), IV (solution)

Histamine H2 Receptor Antagonists - Drug Class Review			
High-Yield Med Reviews			
Generic Name	**Brand Name**	**Indication(s) or Uses**	**Notes**

Nizatidine	Axid	• Dyspepsia
		• Gastroesophageal reflux disease
		• Peptic ulcer disease
			• **Dosing (Adult):**
			  – Oral 150 to 300 mg q12-24h, maximum 8 weeks
			• **Dosing (Peds):**
			  – Oral 5 mg/kg/dose q12h
			    • Maximum 300 mg/day
			• **CYP450 Interactions:** text
			• **Renal or Hepatic Dose Adjustments:**
			  – GFR 20 to 50 mL/minute - 150 mg q24h
			  – GFR less than 20 mL/minute - 150 mg q48h
			• **Dosage Forms:** Oral (capsule, solution)

High-Yield Clinical Knowledge

- **Renal Dose Adjustment**
    - All available H2RAs require dose adjustments in the setting of renal impairment.
        - Independent of renal function, elderly patients (over the age of 65 years) also have a decrease in H2RA drug clearance by as much as 50%.
    - These patients may be at increased risk of Clostridoides difficile infection and CNS effects (confusion).
- **Cimetidine Drug Interactions**
    - Cimetidine is a potent inhibitor of P-glycoprotein and an inhibitor of CYP 1A2, 2C19, 2D6, 3A4.
    - Numerous clinically relevant interactions exist, including narrow therapeutic agents such as theophylline, phenytoin, warfarin, phenytoin, calcium channel blockers, and beta-blockers.
    - Furthermore, cimetidine, as with all H2RAs, can decrease the absorption of protease inhibitors, necessitating appropriate spacing to facilitate adequate absorption.
- **Common Indications**
    - H2RAs are used for a wide range of indications that span both prescription use indications and over-the-counter use.
        - OTC indications - Dyspepsia
        - Rx indications - H. pylori infection/Peptic ulcer disease, GERD, stress ulcer prophylaxis.
- **Alcohol Dehydrogenase Inhibition**
    - Cimetidine inhibits alcohol dehydrogenase and can significantly decrease the rate of elimination of alcohol.
    - In the case of ethanol, alternative metabolic pathways via CYP2E1 are limited in capacity, and patients can quickly experience the toxic and inebriating effects of ethanol at much lower doses/volumes than their average perceived tolerance level.
- **Duration of Therapy**
    - For GERD treatment, H2RAs may be continued for a prolonged duration of therapy, whereas for duodenal ulcer treatment, treatment is limited to 6 weeks.
    - For patients taking over-the-counter products for extended periods or at excessive doses should be referred to primary care for a re-evaluation of their dyspepsia.
- **Serum Creatinine Changes**
    - Cimetidine is associated with an increase in serum creatinine (thus also decrease in calculated GFR) due to the competitive inhibition of cimetidine with creatinine for active tubular secretion.
    - The actual underlying renal function is not changed, and serum creatinine elevations return to baseline after cimetidine discontinuation.

HIGH-YIELD BOARD EXAM ESSENTIALS

- **CLASSIC AGENTS:** Cimetidine, famotidine, nizatidine
- **DRUG CLASS:** Histamine H2 receptor antagonists
- **INDICATIONS:** Dyspepsia, gastroesophageal reflux disease, Helicobacter pylori, peptic ulcer disease
- **MECHANISM:** Competitive inhibition of the parietal cell histamine-2 receptor, preventing gastric acid secretion
- **SIDE EFFECTS:** Confusion, C. difficile infection
- **CLINICAL PEARLS:**
  - Available OTC. This could be a problem if patients are taking medications that require an acidic environment for absorption and do not consult with you or their prescribing provider.
  - Due to other pathways of acid production, many patients will experience escape acid production (gastritis) and also tolerance over time both of which do not occur with PPIs.
  - All available H2RAs require dose adjustments in the setting of renal impairment. Independent of renal function, elderly patients (over the age of 65 years) also have a decrease in H2RA drug clearance by as much as 50%.

High-Yield Basic Pharmacology

- **Mechanism of Action**
  - Inhibit acid secretion by binding covalently to sulfhydryl groups of the H, K-ATPase (aka proton pump), causing an irreversible inhibition of the pump molecule.
- **Prodrugs**
  - All PPIs are prodrugs that are converted to their active form in the acidic secretory canaliculi of the parietal cell.
- **Irreversible Inhibition**
  - As a result of their covalent binding to sulfhydryl groups of the proton pump, PPIs irreversibly inhibit its activity.
  - New proton pumps are formed in the interstitial gastric membrane, then moved to the luminal membrane after 24-48 hours.

Primary Net Benefit

- PPIs are associated with the most meaningful GI symptom improvement, improved gastric ulcer healing rates, and low risk of clinically relevant adverse events.

Proton Pump Inhibitors Drug Class Review **High-Yield Med Reviews**			
Mechanism of Action: *Inhibit acid secretion by binding covalently to sulfhydryl groups of the H, K-ATPase (aka proton pump), causing an irreversible inhibition of the pump molecule.*			
Class Effects: Reduction in dyspepsia, reflux, risk of gastritis; drug interactions with medications requiring an acid environment (e.g., atazanavir); tachyphylaxis is <u>NOT</u> common with chronic use.			
Generic Name	**Brand Name**	**Indication(s) or Uses**	**Notes**
Dexlansoprazole	Dexilant	<ul><li>Erosive esophagitis</li><li>Gastroesophageal reflux disease</li></ul>	<ul><li>**Dosing (Adult):**<ul><li>Oral 60 mg daily for up to 8 weeks</li><li>Oral 30 mg daily<ul><li>Maximum 4 weeks for GERD</li></ul></li></ul></li><li>**Dosing (Peds):**<ul><li>Oral 30 to 60 mg daily for 8 weeks<ul><li>Maximum 4 weeks for GERD</li></ul></li></ul></li><li>**CYP450 Interactions:** Substrate CYP2C19</li><li>**Renal or Hepatic Dose Adjustments:**<ul><li>Child-Pugh class C - not recommended</li></ul></li><li>**Dosage Forms:** Oral (capsule)</li></ul>

Proton Pump Inhibitors Drug Class Review
High-Yield Med Reviews

Generic Name	Brand Name	Indication(s) or Uses	Notes

Esomeprazole	Nexium	• Gastroesophageal reflux disease
		• Helicobacter pylori eradication
		• Peptic ulcer disease
			• **Dosing (Adult):**
			  – Oral/IV 20 to 40 mg q12-24h
			  – IV 80 mg bolus followed by 8 mg/hour infusion
			• **Dosing (Peds):**
			  – Oral 2.5 to 10 mg daily for up to 6 weeks
			  – IV 0.5 to 3.3 mg/kg/dose daily, maximum 40 mg/dose
			• **CYP450 Interactions:** Substrate CYP2C19, 3A4; Inhibits CYP2C19
			• **Renal or Hepatic Dose Adjustments:**
			  – Child-Pugh class B - Lower infusion rate to 6 mg/hour
			  – Child-Pugh class C - Maximum 20 mg/day; Lower infusion rate to 4 mg/hour
			• **Dosage Forms:** Oral (capsule, kit, packet, tablet), IV (solution)

Lansoprazole	Prevacid	• Gastroesophageal reflux disease
		• Hypersecretory conditions
		• Peptic ulcer disease
			• **Dosing (Adult):**
			  – Oral 15 to 60 mg daily
			  – Oral 30 mg up to TID (H. pylori)
			• **Dosing (Peds):**
			  – Oral 0.7 to 3 mg/kg/day
			    • Maximum 30 mg/day
			• **CYP450 Interactions:** Substrate CYP2C19, 2C9, 3A4
			• **Renal or Hepatic Dose Adjustments:**
			  – Child-Pugh class C - Maximum 30 mg/day
			• **Dosage Forms:** Oral (capsule, tablet)

Omeprazole	Prilosec	• Gastroesophageal reflux disease
		• Helicobacter pylori eradication
		• Peptic ulcer disease
		• Zollinger-Ellison Syndrome
			• **Dosing (Adult):**
			  – Oral 10 to 40 mg q12-24h
			• **Dosing (Peds):**
			  – Oral 2.5 to 10 mg daily for up to 6 weeks
			    • Maximum 20 mg/day
			• **CYP450 Interactions:** Substrate CYP2A6, 2C19, 2D6, 3A4; Inhibits CYP2C19
			• **Renal or Hepatic Dose Adjustments:**
			  – Child-Pugh class A-C - Maximum 20 mg/day
			• **Dosage Forms:** Oral (capsule, packet, tablet)

Proton Pump Inhibitors Drug Class Review
High-Yield Med Reviews

Generic Name	Brand Name	Indication(s) or Uses	Notes

Pantoprazole	Protonix	• Gastroesophageal reflux disease
		• Helicobacter pylori eradication
		• Peptic ulcer disease
		• Zollinger-Ellison Syndrome
			• **Dosing (Adult):**
			  – Oral/IV 20 to 40 mg q12-24h
			  – IV 80 mg bolus followed by 8 mg/hour infusion
			• **Dosing (Peds):**
			  – Oral 2.5 to 10 mg daily for up to 6 weeks
			  – IV 0.5 to 3.3 mg/kg/dose daily, maximum 40 mg/dose
			• **CYP450 Interactions:** Substrate CYP2C19, 2D6, 3A4
			• **Renal or Hepatic Dose Adjustments:** None
			• **Dosage Forms:** Oral (packet, tablet), IV (solution)

Rabeprazole	Aciphex	• Duodenal ulcers
		• Gastroesophageal reflux disease
		• Helicobacter pylori eradication
			• **Dosing (Adult):**
			  – Oral 20 to 40 mg q12-24h
			• **Dosing (Peds):**
			  – Oral 2.5 to 10 mg daily for up to 6 weeks
			    • Maximum 20 mg/day
			• **CYP450 Interactions:** Substrate 2C19, 3A4
			• **Renal or Hepatic Dose Adjustments:**
			  – Child-Pugh class C - Avoid use
			• **Dosage Forms:** Oral (capsule, packet, tablet)

High-Yield Clinical Knowledge

- **Drug Interactions**
    - PPIs have numerous clinically relevant pharmacokinetic and pharmacodynamic interactions.
    - Omeprazole and esomeprazole inhibit CYP2C19 and can induce CYP1A2.
        - Induction of CYP1A2 can increase the clearance of numerous antipsychotic agents, imipramine and theophylline.
        - Inhibition of CYP2C19 can prevent the activation of clopidogrel from its prodrug to the active compound.
            - Pantoprazole is the least likely to cause changes in clopidogrel activation.
    - PPIs compete for elimination with methotrexate, and therefore, increase the risk of methotrexate toxicity.
    - Medications such as atazanavir, itraconazole capsules, erlotinib require an acidic environment for adequate absorption
- **Chronic Use Adverse Events**
    - PPIs are associated with an increased risk of pneumonia, including hospital-acquired pneumonia and Clostridoides difficile infection.
    - In patients with underlying hepatic disease and ascites, PPIs increase the risk for spontaneous bacterial peritonitis.
    - Bone fractures have also been associated with long-term use of PPIs, attributed to decreased absorption of calcium and magnesium.
- **Enteric Coatings**
    - All PPIs are susceptible to degradation in acidic environments, such as the stomach, necessitating formulation in delayed-release capsules or tablets.
    - Importantly, patients must be instructed not to split, crush or chew tablets and not open capsules.
    - In patients unable to swallow oral dosage forms whole, capsules may be opened and taken with sodium bicarbonate (omeprazole), water (esomeprazole), applesauce (rabeprazole).

- Dexlansoprazole and lansoprazole are available as an orally disintegrating tablet.
- **Time to Maximum Onset**
  - PPIs will only inhibit active proton pumps' activity, requiring repetitive dosing (when given once per day) over approximately 2 to 5 days.
  - More frequent dosing intervals, including every 12-hours, or give as an IV infusion, can reduce this time to maximum onset.
- **Vitamin B12**
  - Omeprazole, when used chronically, is associated with decreased absorption of vitamin B12.
- **Acute GI Bleeding**
  - In patients with acute gastric bleeding or undifferentiated upper gastrointestinal bleeding, an IV bolus of esomeprazole or pantoprazole 80 mg is followed by an infusion of 8 mg/hour to target a gastric pH of 6-7, continued for 72 hours.
  - Alternative dosing of 80 mg IV q12h achieves similar gastric pH and may be a reasonable alternative to continuous infusions.

HIGH-YIELD BOARD EXAM ESSENTIALS

- **CLASSIC AGENTS:** Dexlansoprazole, esomeprazole, lansoprazole, omeprazole, pantoprazole, rabeprazole
- **DRUG CLASS:** Proton pump inhibitors
- **INDICATIONS:** Acute gastrointestinal bleeding, duodenal ulcer, erosive esophagitis, gastroesophageal reflux disease, Helicobacter pylori eradication, peptic ulcer disease, Zollinger-Ellison syndrome
- **MECHANISM:** Inhibit acid secretion by binding covalently to sulfhydryl groups of the H, K-ATPase (aka proton pump), causing an irreversible inhibition of the pump molecule.
- **SIDE EFFECTS:** Infections (pneumonia, spontaneous bacterial peritonitis, C. difficile), B12 deficiency
- **CLINICAL PEARLS:**
  - Unlike H2RA, there is no development of tolerance to gastric acid suppression and PPIs can maintain the gastric pH > 4 for a longer duration thereby conferring a greater ability of gastric ulcers to heal.
  - All PPIs are susceptible to degradation in acidic environments, such as the stomach, necessitating formulation in delayed-release capsules or tablets. Importantly, patients must be instructed not to split, crush or chew tablets and not open capsules.
  - Pantoprazole may be less likely to interfere with clopidogrel activation and overall activity, whereas lansoprazole and omeprazole are more likely to inhibit the functional activation of clopidogrel.

High-Yield Basic Pharmacology

- **Mechanism of Action**
  - Block dopamine receptors in the chemoreceptor trigger zone (CTZ).
- **Grouped by Chemical Structure**
  - Butyrophenone Antipsychotics
    - Includes droperidol and haloperidol.
  - Phenothiazine Antipsychotics
    - Includes chlorpromazine, perphenazine, prochlorperazine, and promethazine.
  - Substituted Benzamides
    - Includes metoclopramide and trimethobenzamide.

Primary Net Benefit

- Provide relief for nausea and/or vomiting

Dopamine Antagonist Antiemetics - Drug Class Review High-Yield Med Reviews			
Mechanism of Action: *Block dopamine receptors in the chemoreceptor trigger zone (CTZ)*			
Class Effects: Provide relief for nausea and/or vomiting; risk of dystonic reactions or Parkinson's-like features; small risk of QT prolongation			
Generic Name	**Brand Name**	**Indication(s) or Uses**	**Notes**

Chlorpromazine	Compazine (DSC)	• Nausea and/or vomiting	• **Dosing (Adult):**
			  – PO: 10 to 25 mg Q4-8H PRN
			  – IM, IV: 25 to 50 mg once PRN
			• **Dosing (Peds), >2 years:**
			  – IM, IV: 0.01 to 0.015 mg/kg/dose (Max dose = 1.25 mg/dose)
			• **CYP450 Interactions:** Substrate of CYP1A2, CYP2D6, CYP3A4
			• **Renal or Hepatic Dose Adjustments:** None
			• **Dosage Forms:** PO (tablet), Injectable

Droperidol	Brand Name (if available)	• Nausea and/or vomiting	• **Dosing (Adult):**
			  – IM, IV: 0.625 to 2.5 mg
			• **Dosing (Peds), >2 years:**
			  – IM, IV: 0.01 to 0.015 mg/kg/dose (Max dose = 1.25 mg/dose)
			• **CYP450 Interactions:** None
			• **Renal or Hepatic Dose Adjustments:** None
			• **Dosage Forms:** Injectable

Haloperidol	Haldol	• Nausea and/or vomiting	• **Dosing (Adult):**
			  – PO, IV: 0.5 to 2 mg q6hr
			  – Cont SubQ: 1 to 5 mg per 24 hours
			• **Dosing (Peds):** Not routinely used for this indication
			• **CYP450 Interactions:** Substrate of CYP1A2, CYP2D6, CYP3A4
			• **Renal or Hepatic Dose Adjustments:** None
			• **Dosage Forms:** PO (tablet, solution), Injectable

Dopamine Antagonist Antiemetics - Drug Class Review
High-Yield Med Reviews

Generic Name	Brand Name	Indication(s) or Uses	Notes

Metoclopramide	Reglan
	
	Gimoti
	(nasal)
		• Nausea and/or vomiting	• **Dosing (Adult):**
			  – PO: 10 mg Q4-6H PRN
			  – IV: 10 to 20 mg PRN
			• **Dosing (Peds):**
			  – IV: 0.1 to 0.25 mg/kg/dose q6-8hr (Max dose= 10 mg)
			• **CYP450 Interactions:** Substrate of CYP1A2, CYP2D6
			• **Renal or Hepatic Dose Adjustments:**
			  – CrCl 10-60 mL/min: Reduce dose by 50%
			  – Child-Pugh Class C or D: Use not recommended
			• **Dosage Forms:** PO (tablet, ODT, solution), Nasal, Injectable

Perphenazine	N/A	• Nausea and/or vomiting	• **Dosing (Adult):** – PO: 8-24 mg/day • **Dosing (Peds):** Not used • **CYP450 Interactions:** Substrate of CYP2D6 • **Renal or Hepatic Dose Adjustments:** None • **Dosage Forms:** Oral (tablet, concentrate)

Prochlorperazine	Compazine,
	Compro
	(rectal)
		• Nausea and/or vomiting	• **Dosing (Adult):**
			  – PO/IM/IV: 2.5-10 mg Q6H PRN
			    • Max daily dose: 40 mg
			  – PR: 25 mg BID
			• **Dosing (Peds), >2 yrs and >9 kg:**
			  – PO: 2.5 mg Q6-24H PRN
			  – Frequency and maximum daily doses vary by weight
			  – IM/IV: 0.1-0.15 mg/kg/dose
			  – Maximum single dose: 10 mg/dose
			• **CYP450 Interactions:** None
			• **Renal or Hepatic Dose Adjustments:** None
			• **Dosage Forms:** Oral (tablet), Injectable, Rectal

Promethazine	Phenergan	• Nausea and/or vomiting	• **Dosing (Adult):**
			  – PO/IM/IV/PR: 12.5-25 mg Q4-6H PRN
			Dosing (Peds), >2 yrs:
			  – PO/IM/IV/PR: 0.25-1 mg/kg/dose Q4-6H PRN
			    • Maximum dose: 25 mg/dose
			• **CYP450 Interactions:** None
			• **Renal or Hepatic Dose Adjustments:** text
			• **Dosage Forms:** Oral (tablet, solution, syrup), Injectable, Rectal

Dopamine Antagonist Antiemetics - Drug Class Review
High-Yield Med Reviews

Generic Name	Brand Name	Indication(s) or Uses	Notes

Trimethobenza mide	Tigan	• Nausea and/or vomiting	• **Dosing (Adult):**
			  – PO: 300 mg TID-QID
			  – IM: 300 mg TID-QID
			    • Extra info if needed
			• **Dosing (Peds):**
			  – PO: 100-200 mg Q6H PRN
			    • Use is strongly discouraged due to risk of EPS
			• **CYP450 Interactions:** None
			• **Renal or Hepatic Dose Adjustments:** CrCl < 70 mL/min: reduce dose or increase interval
			• **Dosage Forms:** Oral (capsule), Injection

High-Yield Clinical Knowledge

- **Antipsychotic Agents as Antiemetics**
  - Chlorpromazine, droperidol, haloperidol, and prochlorperazine are all considered first-generation antipsychotic agents and can be utilized for other indications. Antiemetic effects of these agents are attributed to the blockade of dopamine subtype 2 receptors in the CTZ.
- **Extrapyramidal Side Effects**
  - Extrapyramidal symptoms (EPS) is an umbrella term used to describe antipsychotic-induced movement side effects due to excess dopamine blockade in the nigrostriatal pathway. Symptoms include dystonia, akathisia, pseudoparkinsonism, and tardive dyskinesia.
  - Extrapyramidal effects appear to occur more commonly in children and young adults and at higher doses.
  - Prochlorperazine can cause EPS after a one-time dose. Metoclopramide has a lower risk of EPS compared to prochlorperazine.
- **QT Interval Prolongation**
  - Many antipsychotic agents can also block potassium currents in the myocardium, leading to a prolonged QT interval. The smaller doses of antipsychotic agents utilized for their antiemetic effects decrease the clinical risk of QT prolongation.
- **Patient Population Considerations**
  - Avoid in Patients with Parkinson Disease
    - Dopamine antagonism can reduce levodopa's efficacy due to direct dopamine antagonism and exacerbate symptoms of Parkinson's disease. These agents should be avoided in this patient population. Parkinson's disease is a contraindication to haloperidol therapy.
  - Pediatric Considerations
    - Dopamine receptor antagonists are not considered the preferred agents for treating nausea and/or vomiting in pediatric patients due to the side effect profile and risk of EPS. Use has generally been replaced by agents that are more effective with fewer adverse events. If used, employ extreme caution and utilize the lowest effective dose.
    - Promethazine should not be used in pediatric patients younger than two years because of the potential for fatal respiratory depression. It carries a black box warning for this reason.
    - Droperidol and prochlorperazine lack black box warnings for use in pediatric populations but should not be utilized for patients younger than two years of age.

HIGH-YIELD BOARD EXAM ESSENTIALS

- **CLASSIC AGENTS:** Droperidol, haloperidol, metoclopramide, trimethobenzamide, chlorpromazine, perphenazine, prochlorperazine, promethazine
- **DRUG CLASS:** Dopamine antagonist antiemetics
- **INDICATIONS:** Nausea and/or vomiting
- **MECHANISM:** Block dopamine receptors in the chemoreceptor trigger zone (CTZ)
- **SIDE EFFECTS:** QT prolongation, dystonia, akathisia, pseudoparkinsonism, and tardive dyskinesia.
- **CLINICAL PEARLS:** Chlorpromazine, droperidol, haloperidol, and prochlorperazine are all considered first-generation antipsychotic agents and can be utilized for other indications. Antiemetic effects of these agents are attributed to the blockade of dopamine subtype 2 receptors in the CTZ.

High-Yield Basic Pharmacology

- **Anticholinergics**
  - The anticholinergics included in this class act as antagonists at muscarinic subtype-1 (M_1) receptors.
  - These receptors are found on the central nervous system (CNS) neurons, many presynaptic sites, and gastric and salivary glands.
- **H_1-antihistamines**
  - Inverse agonists
    - Although antihistamines are commonly called histamine antagonists, they act as inverse agonists. Inverse agonists preferentially bind to and stabilize the inactivated conformation of receptors and produce the opposite pharmacological effect of an activating ligand.

Primary Net Benefit

- Provide relief for nausea and/or vomiting

Miscellaneous Antiemetics - Drug Class Review			
High-Yield Med Reviews			
Mechanism of Action: *Antihistamines*: Inverse agonist at H_1-receptors; *Anticholinergics*: M_1-antagonists; *Cannabinoids*: CB-1 agonists			
Class Effects: Provide relief for nausea and/or vomiting			
Generic Name	**Brand Name**	**Indication(s) or Uses**	**Notes**

Dronabinol	Marinol (capsules)
	
	Syndros (solution)
		• Nausea and/or vomiting
		• Anorexia in patients with AIDS
			• **Dosing (Adult):**
			  – PO, capsules: 2.5 to 10 mg TID-QID *or* 5 to 15 mg/m² up to 6 doses/day
			  – PO, solution: 4.2 to 12.6 mg/m² up to 6 doses/day
			• **Dosing (Peds):** Same as adults
			• **CYP450 Interactions:** Substrate of CYP2C9, CYP3A4
			• **Renal or Hepatic Dose Adjustments:** None
			• **Dosage Forms:** PO (capsules, solution)

Nabilone	N/A	• Nausea and/or vomiting	• **Dosing (Adult):**
			  – PO: 1 to 2 mg BID-TID
			    • Max daily dose=6 mg/day
			• **Dosing (Peds, ≥ 3 yrs):**
			  – PO: 0.5 to 1 mg BID
			    • Weight-based adjustments
			• **CYP450 Interactions:** None
			• **Renal or Hepatic Dose Adjustments:** None
			• **Dosage Forms:** PO (capsules)

Miscellaneous Antiemetics - Drug Class Review
High-Yield Med Reviews

Generic Name	Brand Name	Indication(s) or Uses	Notes

Dimenhydrinate	Driminate (OTC), GoodSense Motion SIckness (OTC)	▪ Nausea and/or vomiting associated with motion sickness	▪ **Dosing (Adult):**
			  – PO: 50 to 100 mg Q4-6H PRN
			    ▪ Max daily dose= 400 mg/day
			  – IM/IV: 50 to 100 mg Q4H PRN
			▪ **Dosing (Peds, ≥ 2 yrs):**
			  – PO: 12.5 to 25 mg Q6-8H *or* 1 to 1.5 mg/kg/dose Q6H
			    ▪ Max daily dose varies by age group
			  – IM: 1.25 mg/kg/dose QID
			    ▪ Max daily dose=300 mg/day
			▪ **CYP450 Interactions:** None
			▪ **Renal or Hepatic Dose Adjustments:** text
			▪ **Dosage Forms:** PO (tablets, chewable), Injectable

Diphenhydramine	Benedryl
	
	*Multiple OTC brand names
		▪ Nausea and/or vomiting
		▪ Nausea and/or vomiting associated with motion sickness
			▪ **Dosing (Adult):**
			  – PO: 25 to 50 mg Q4-8H PRN
			  – IM/IV: 10 to 50 mg Q6H PRN
			▪ **Dosing (Peds):**
			  – PO: 5 mg/kg/day divided into 3 or 4 doses
			  – IM/IV: 1.25 mg/kg/dose Q6H
			▪ **CYP450 Interactions:** Substrate of CYP1A2, CYP2C9, CYP2D6; Inhibits CYP2D6
			▪ **Renal or Hepatic Dose Adjustments:** None
			▪ **Dosage Forms:** PO (capsules, tablets, chewable, elixir, solution, syrup), Injectable

Meclizine	Bonine (OTC), Dramamine Less Drowsy (OTC), Motion-Time (OTC), Travel-Ease (OTC)	▪ Nausea and/or vomiting associated with motion sickness ▪ Vertigo	▪ **Dosing (Adult):** – PO, PR: 25 mg prn ▪ **Dosing (Peds, ≥ 12 yrs):** Same as adults ▪ **CYP450 Interactions:** Substrate of CYP2D6 ▪ **Renal or Hepatic Dose Adjustments:** text ▪ **Dosage Forms:** PO (tablets, chewable)

Scopolamine	Transderm-Scop	▪ Nausea and/or vomiting associated with motion sickness
		▪ Nausea and/or vomiting associated with preoperative anesthesia
			▪ **Dosing (Adult):**
			  – Topical: 1 patch every 3 days PRN
			▪ **Dosing (Peds):**
			  – Topical: ¼ to 1 patch PRN (varies by age)
			▪ **CYP450 Interactions:** None
			▪ **Renal or Hepatic Dose Adjustments:** None
			▪ **Dosage Forms:** Topical (72 hr-patch) [Injectable formulation available in Canada]

High-Yield Clinical Knowledge

- **Cannabinoids**
  - The term cannabinoids encompass a wide variety of compounds. They can be endogenous, derived from plants, or synthetically produced. Dronabinol and nabilone are FDA-approved, synthetically produced analogs of delta-9-tetrahydrocannabinol (THC), a naturally occurring component of *Cannabis sativa* (marijuana).

- To date, two endogenous cannabinoid receptors have been identified, CB-1 and CB-2. The pharmacological effects of cannabinoids have been attributed to the activation of the CB-1 receptor.
- **Adverse Effects**
  - Anticholinergic Toxidrome:
    - The classic anticholinergic toxidrome can be remembered with the phrase "mad as a hatter" (altered mental status), "blind as a bat" (mydriasis), "red as a beet" (flushed skin), "hot as a hare" (dry skin), "dry as a bone" (dry mucous membranes), and "full as a flask" (urinary retention).
  - CNS effects
    - Euphoria: Cannabinoids
    - Sedation: Anticholinergics, first-generation H_1-antihistamines, and cannabinoids
- **Antiemetic Selection and Patient Considerations**
  - Avoid anticholinergics and antihistamines in elderly patients, and those with benign prostatic hypertrophy (BPH), gastrointestinal motility disorders, and narrow or closed-angle glaucoma as these comorbidities can be exacerbated by the side effect profile of anticholinergics.
  - Antihistamines may be beneficial as antiemetics in patients with Parkinson's Disease who are at an increased risk of extrapyramidal symptoms associated with dopaminergic antiemetics.
  - Cannabinoids may be useful in patients with chemotherapy-induced nausea/vomiting or other indications which cause appetite suppression due to their stimulating effect.
- **Antiemetic Selection and Situational Emesis**
  - Postoperative: Scopolamine
  - Motion sickness: Antihistamines, scopolamine
  - Pregnancy: Antihistamines
  - Chemotherapy-induced: Cannabinoids
- **Nonpharmacological Antiemetic Options**
  - Ginger: Studies have shown that constituents of ginger have inhibitory effects at neurokinin-1 (NK-1), serotonin ($5-HT_3$), and muscarinic receptors. The predominant effect of ginger is located in the gastrointestinal tract, but some evidence has shown that some constituents may have CNS effects.
  - Acupressure wristbands: These wristbands are sold as an over-the-counter product under various brand names. The antiemetic effect is attributed to stimulation of the pericardium 6 (P6) meridian point.

HIGH-YIELD BOARD EXAM ESSENTIALS
- **CLASSIC AGENTS:** Hyoscyamine, scopolamine, dimenhydrinate, diphenhydramine, meclizine, dronabinol, nabilone
- **DRUG CLASS:** Miscellaneous antiemetics
- **INDICATIONS:** Nausea and/or vomiting
- **MECHANISM:** Inverse agonist at H1-receptors (antihistamines), M1-antagonists (anticholinergics), CB-1 agonists (cannabinoids)
- **SIDE EFFECTS:** Anticholinergic effects, euphoria, sedation
- **CLINICAL PEARLS:** Avoid anticholinergics and antihistamines in elderly patients, and those with benign prostatic hypertrophy (BPH), gastrointestinal motility disorders, and narrow or closed-angle glaucoma as these comorbidities can be exacerbated by the side effect profile of anticholinergics.

High-Yield Basic Pharmacology

- **Mechanism of Action**
  - Selective serotonin antagonists (5-HT$_3$-RA) selectively block serotonin subtype 3 receptors (5-HT$_3$) both centrally in the chemotherapy trigger and peripherally in the gastrointestinal tract resulting in antiemetic effects.
- **Serotonin receptor subtypes**
  - Several serotoninergic receptor subtypes have been identified (5-HT1 (5-HT1A, 5-HT1B, 5-HTID, 5-HTIE, and 5-HT1F), 5-HT2 (5-HT2A, 5-HT2B and 5-HT2C), 5-HT3, 5-HT4, 5-HT5 (5-HT5A, 5-HT5B), 5-HT6 and 5-HT7.
    - 5-HT3 receptors are located in the vomiting center of the brain and the gastrointestinal system
      - Peripheral 5-HT3 receptor antagonism in the gut prevents ACh release, decreasing gut motility and vagal nerve excitation.
      - Central 5-HT3 receptor antagonism reduced chemotherapy trigger zone stimulation.

Primary Net Benefit

- Provide supportive care for nausea and emesis

Serotonin Antagonists - Drug Class Review			
High-Yield Med Reviews			
Mechanism of Action: *Selectively block 5-HT$_3$ serotonin receptors, both peripherally and centrally, resulting in antiemetic effects*			
Class Effects: Reduction in nausea and vomiting; small risk for dose-dependent increases in QT prolongation			
Generic Name	**Brand Name**	**Indication(s) or Uses**	**Notes**

Alosetron	Lotronex	• Women with diarrhea-predominant irritable bowel syndrome (IBS)	• **Dosing (Women):**
			  – PO: 0.5 to 1 mg BID
			• **Dosing (Peds):** Not used
			• **CYP450 Interactions:** Substrate of CYP1A2, CYP2C9, CYP3A4
			• **Renal or Hepatic Dose Adjustments:**
			  – Child-Pugh C: Contraindicated
			• **Dosage Forms:** Oral (tablets)

Dolasetron	Anzemet	• Nausea and/or vomiting	• **Dosing (Adult):**
			  – PO: 100 mg
			• **Dosing (Peds):**
			  – PO: 1.8 mg/kg
			• **CYP450 Interactions:** Substrate of CYP2C9, CYP3A4
			• **Renal or Hepatic Dose Adjustments:** None
			• **Dosage Forms:** Oral (tablets)

Serotonin Antagonists - Drug Class Review
High-Yield Med Reviews

Generic Name	Brand Name	Indication(s) or Uses	Notes

Granisetron	Sancuso (transdermal patch)
	
	Sustol (SubQ)
		• Nausea and/or vomiting	• **Dosing (Adult):**
			  – PO: 1-2 mg daily
			  – IV: 10 **mcg**/kg or 1 mg
			  – SC: 10 mg
			  – Transdermal: 3.1 mg/24hr patch, may be worn for up to 7 days
			• **Dosing (Peds):**
			  – PO: 40 mcg/kg/dose every 12 hours on chemotherapy days
			  – IV: 40 mcg/kg as a single dose prior to chemotherapy
			• **CYP450 Interactions:** Substrate of CYP3A4
			• **Renal or Hepatic Dose Adjustments:**
			  – IV, Oral, Transdermal: No dosage adjustment necessary
			  – SC:
			    ▪ CrCl 30-59 mL/min: 10 mg NMT once every 14 days
			    ▪ CrCl <30: Avoid use
			• **Dosage Forms:** Oral (tablets), subcutaneous, injectable, transdermal

Ondansetron	Zofran
	
	Zuplenz (oral film)
		• Nausea and/or vomiting	• **Dosing (Adult):**
			  – Oral: 4 to 16 mg/day, divided doses
			  – IV, IM: 4 to 8 mg as a single dose
			• **Dosing (Peds):**
			  – Oral: 2 to 8 mg
			  – IV: 0.15 to 0.4 mg/kg/dose (maximum dose: 16 mg/dose)
			• **CYP450 Interactions:** Substrate of CYP1A2, CYP2C9, CYP2D6, CYP2E1, CYP3A4
			• **Renal or Hepatic Dose Adjustments:**
			  – Child-Pugh C: Maximum daily dose 8 mg
			• **Dosage Forms:** Oral (tablet, disintegrating tablet, film, solution), Injectable

Palonosetron	Aloxi (IV)	• Nausea and/or vomiting	• **Dosing (Adult):**
			  – IV: 0.25 mg
			• **Dosing (Peds):**
			  – IV: 20 **mcg**/kg (maximum dose: 1500 **mcg**/dose)
			• **CYP450 Interactions:** Substrate of CYP1A2, CYP2D6, CYP3A4
			• **Renal or Hepatic Dose Adjustments:** None
			• **Dosage Forms:** Injectable (also available as a combo product)

Serotonin Antagonists - Drug Class Review			
High-Yield Med Reviews			
Generic Name	**Brand Name**	**Indication(s) or Uses**	**Notes**

Fosnetupitant/**palonosetron**	Akynzeo (IV)	• Nausea/vomiting	• **Dosing (Adult):**
			  – IV: 235/0.25 mg on day 1 of chemo only
			• **Dosing (Peds):** Not used
			• **CYP450 Interactions:** None
			• **Renal or Hepatic Dose Adjustments:**
			  – CrCl < 30: Avoid
			  – Child-Pugh C: Avoid
			• **Dosage Forms:** Injectable

Netupitant/**palonsetron**	Akynzeo (PO)	• Nausea/vomiting	• **Dosing (Adult):**
			  – PO: 300/0.5 mg on day 1 of chemo
			• **Dosing (Peds):** Not used
			• **CYP450 Interactions:** Substrate of CYP3A4; Inhibits CYP3A4
			• **Renal or Hepatic Dose Adjustments:**
			  – CrCl < 30: Avoid
			  – Child-Pugh C: Avoid
			• **Dosage Forms:** Oral (capsule)

High-Yield Clinical Knowledge

- **Class Naming Convention**
  - The 5-HT$_3$-RA can be identified by their shared suffix, -*setron*
- **Use and efficacy**
  - Useful as a single-agent or combination therapy for prophylaxis of chemotherapy-induced nausea/vomiting (CINV) or postoperative nausea/vomiting (PONV)
  - These agents (except for alosetron) are equally efficacious at equivalent doses; thus, agent selection is usually dictated by cost and availability
  - Alosetron (Lotronex) is only indicated for use in women with irritable bowel syndrome; it should not be utilized as an antiemetic agent
- **Contraindications**
  - 5-HT$_3$-RAs are contraindicated with concurrent apomorphine administration due to their ability to cause profound hypotension
- **Alosetron**
  - Alosetron is only approved for women with severe diarrhea-predominant irritable bowel syndrome (IBS)
  - It was briefly withdrawn from the US market due to the high incidence of ischemic colitis, leading to surgery and even death. However, it was reapproved for diarrhea-predominant IBS under a limited distribution system.
  - It may only be dispensed upon presenting a prescription for Alosetron with a sticker for the Prescribing Program for Alosetron attached. No telephone, facsimile, or computerized prescriptions are permitted with this program. Refills are allowed to be written on prescriptions.
- **Serotonin syndrome**
  - Characterized by alterations in mentation and cognition, autonomic nervous system dysfunction, and neuromuscular abnormalities
- **Chemotherapy-induced nausea/vomiting (CINV)**
  - While useful for preventing acute CINV, when 5-HT$_3$-RA are used as monotherapy they have little efficacy for preventing delayed CINV.
  - 5-HT$_3$-RA may be used in combination with other antiemetic classes to prevent CINV depending on the emetogenic potential of the chemotherapeutic regimen being utilized.

- **QT Interval Prolongation**
  - Dolasetron, granisetron, and ondansetron cause a dose-dependent prolongation of the QT interval and are associated with a risk of ventricular arrhythmias.
  - Palonosetron has not been observed to prolong the QT interval, whereas dolasetron carries the highest QT interval prolongation risk.
    - Historical use of ondansetron for chemotherapy-induced nausea prophylaxis used single doses of 16 and 32 mg and is the setting in which most QT interval prolongation has been observed.

HIGH-YIELD BOARD EXAM ESSENTIALS

- **CLASSIC AGENTS:** Alosetron, dolasetron, granisetron, ondansetron, palonosetron
- **DRUG CLASS:** Serotonin Antagonists
- **INDICATIONS:** Nausea/vomiting, chemotherapy-induced nausea and vomiting prophylaxis, postoperative nausea and vomiting, women with diarrhea-predominant - irritable bowel syndrome
- **MECHANISM:** Selective inhibition of 5-HT3 both centrally in the chemotherapy trigger and peripherally in the gastrointestinal tract resulting in antiemetic effects.
- **SIDE EFFECTS:** QT prolongation, serotonin syndrome
- **CLINICAL PEARLS:** Alosetron is only approved for women with severe diarrhea-predominant IBS. It was briefly withdrawn from the US market due to the high incidence of ischemic colitis, leading to surgery and even death. However, it was reapproved for diarrhea-predominant IBS under a limited distribution system.

High-Yield Basic Pharmacology

- **Mechanism of Action**
  - Selectively inhibit substance P/neurokinin-1 (NK-1) receptors distributed peripherally and centrally to inhibit substance P-mediated responses.
- **Prodrugs**
  - Fosaprepitant is rapidly (within 30 minutes of the end of the infusion) converted into aprepitant.
  - Fosnetupiant is rapidly converted into netupitant via hydrolysis.
- **Hepatic Metabolism**
  - All agents are extensively metabolized via the CYP3A4 pathway and are therefore subject to many drug-drug interactions. Aprepitant and fosaprepitant undergo minor metabolism via CYP1A2 and CYP2C19.

Primary Net Benefit

- Prevents acute and delayed phase CINV

Substance P/Neurokinin 1 Receptor Antagonist - Drug Class Review			
High-Yield Med Reviews			
Mechanism of Action: *Selectively inhibit substance P/neurokinin-1 (NK-1) receptors distributed peripherally and centrally to inhibit substance P-mediated responses*			
Class Effects: Prevents acute and delayed phase CINV			
Generic Name	**Brand Name**	**Indication(s) or Uses**	**Notes**

Aprepitant	Cinvanti	• Nausea/vomiting	• **Dosing (Adult):**
			  – PO: 40-125 mg or 3 mg/kg
			  – IV: 100-300 mg
			• **Dosing (Peds):**
			  – PO: 2-3 mg/kg/dose
			• **CYP450 Interactions:** Substrate of CYP1A2, CYP2C19, CYP3A4; Inhibits CYP3A4; Induces CYP2c9
			• **Renal or Hepatic Dose Adjustments:** None
			• **Dosage Forms:** Oral (capsule, suspension), injectable

Fosaprepitant	Emend	• Nausea/vomiting	• **Dosing (Adult):**
			  – IV: 150 mg on day 1 of chemo only
			    • Infused over 20-30 min
			• **Dosing (Peds):**
			  – IV: 3-5 mg/kg on day 1 of chemo only
			• **CYP450 Interactions:** Substrate of CYP1A2, CYP2C19, CYP3A4; Inhibits CYP3A4; Induces CYP2C9
			• **Renal or Hepatic Dose Adjustments:** None
			• **Dosage Forms:** Injectable

Substance P/Neurokinin 1 Receptor Antagonist - Drug Class Review
High-Yield Med Reviews

Generic Name	Brand Name	Indication(s) or Uses	Notes

Rolapitant	Varubi	• Nausea/vomiting	• **Dosing (Adult):**
			  – PO: 180 mg on day 1 of chemo only
			  – IV: 166.5 mg on day 1 of chemo only
			• **Dosing (Peds):** Not used
			• **CYP450 Interactions:** Substrate of CYP1A2, CYP2C19, CYP3A4; Inhibits CYP2B6, CYP2D6, PGP
			• **Renal or Hepatic Dose Adjustments:** None
			• **Dosage Forms:** Oral (tablet), injectable (discontinued in the US)

Fosnetupitant/ palonosetron	Akynzeo (IV)	• Nausea/vomiting	• **Dosing (Adult):**
			  – IV: 235/0.25 mg on day 1 of chemo only
			• **Dosing (Peds):** Not used
			• **CYP450 Interactions:** None
			• **Renal or Hepatic Dose Adjustments:**
			  – CrCl < 30: Avoid
			  – Child-Pugh C: Avoid
			• **Dosage Forms:** Injectable

Netupitant/palonsetron	Akynzeo (PO)	• Nausea/vomiting	• **Dosing (Adult):**
			  – PO: 300/0.5 mg on day 1 of chemo
			• **Dosing (Peds):** Not used
			• **CYP450 Interactions:** Substrate of CYP3A4; Inhibits CYP3A4
			• **Renal or Hepatic Dose Adjustments:**
			  – CrCl < 30: Avoid
			  – Child-Pugh C: Avoid
			• **Dosage Forms:** Oral (capsule)

High-Yield Clinical Knowledge

- **Naming convention**
  - Can be identified by the suffix *-prepitant*
- **Chemotherapy-induced nausea/vomiting (CINV)**
  - Substance P/NK-1 receptor antagonists are considered to be effective in the prevention of acute and delayed phase CINV.
  - They are used as part of a three- or four-drug combination to prevent CINV, depending on the emetogenic potential of the chemotherapeutic regimen being utilized.

High-Yield Fast-Facts

- **Dosing schedule**
  - All substance P/NK-1 antagonists are single-dose regimens administered on day 1 of chemotherapy only, except for aprepitant, which can be utilized as a three-day regimen.
- **Oral contraceptives**
  - The efficacy of hormonal contraceptives may be reduced during and for 28 days following the last dose of aprepitant or fosaprepitant. Clinicians should recommend alternative or additional contraceptive methods during treatment and at least one month following treatment.

HIGH-YIELD BOARD EXAM ESSENTIALS

- **CLASSIC AGENTS:** Aprepitant, fosaprepitant (± palonsetron), netupitant (± palonsetron), rolapitant
- **DRUG CLASS:** Substance P/neurokinin 1 receptor antagonist
- **INDICATIONS:** CNIV, PONV
- **MECHANISM:** Selectively inhibit substance P/neurokinin-1 (NK-1) receptors distributed peripherally and centrally to inhibit substance P-mediated responses.
- **SIDE EFFECTS:** Fatigue, neutropenia, hypotension, bradycardia, headache, constipation
- **CLINICAL PEARLS:** All substance P/NK-1 antagonists are single-dose regimens administered on day 1 of chemotherapy only, except for aprepitant, which can be utilized as a three-day regimen.

High-Yield Basic Pharmacology

- **Mechanism of Action**
  - Mu and delta-opioid receptor agonists decreasing gastrointestinal motility and secretion.
  - **Opioid Receptors**
    - The three primary opioid receptors relevant to pharmacotherapy are the delta, kappa, and mu-opioid receptors.
  - **Mu Receptor Subtype**
    - Mu-2 opioid receptors, although responsible for the diminished ventilatory response to hypoxia, are also located in the GI wall.
    - Agonist activity on GI mu-2 receptors is responsible for constipation from chronic systemic opioid use and the target for opioid-antidiarrheal agents.

Primary Net Benefit

- Over-the-counter and prescription relief for non-infectious diarrhea formulated in abuse-deterrent combinations or limited sale to prevent acute toxicity.

Antimotility Agents - Drug Class Review			
High-Yield Med Reviews			
Mechanism of Action: *Mu and delta-opioid receptor agonists decreasing gastrointestinal motility and secretion.*			
Class Effects: Constipation, nausea; small risk of abuse due structures similar to opioids.			
Generic Name	**Brand Name**	**Indication(s) or Uses**	**Notes**

Diphenoxylate-Atropine	Lomotil (C-V)	• Diarrhea	• **Dosing (Adult):**
			  – Oral 5 mg q6h until control achieved
			    • Maximum 20 mg/day
			• **Dosing (Peds):**
			  – Oral 0.3 to 0.4 mg/kg/day divided q6h
			    • Maximum 10 mg/day
			• **CYP450 Interactions:** None
			• **Renal or Hepatic Dose Adjustments:** None
			• **Dosage Forms:** Oral (liquid, tablet)

Difenoxin-Atropine	Motofen (C-IV)	• Diarrhea	• **Dosing (Adult):**
			  – Oral 2 tablets x 1, then 1 tablet after each loose stool or q3-4h
			    • Maximum 8 tablets/day
			• **Dosing (Peds):**
			  – For children 12 years and older only
			    • Use adult dosing
			• **CYP450 Interactions:** None
			• **Renal or Hepatic Dose Adjustments:**
			  – No specific adjustments
			  – Use with caution in patients with renal or hepatic dysfunction
			• **Dosage Forms:** Oral (tablet)

Antimotility Agents - Drug Class Review
High-Yield Med Reviews

Generic Name	Brand Name	Indication(s) or Uses	Notes

Loperamide	Immodium A-D (OTC)	▪ Diarrhea	▪ **Dosing (Adult):**
			  – Oral 4 mg followed by 2 mg after each loose stool
			    ▪ Maximum 16 mg/day
			▪ **Dosing (Peds):**
			  – Oral 0.08 to 0.25 mg/kg/day q6-12h as needed after each loose stool
			    ▪ Maximum: age-dependent 3 to 8 mg/day
			▪ **CYP450 Interactions:** Substrate of CYP2B6, 2C8, 2D6, 3A4, P-gp
			▪ **Renal or Hepatic Dose Adjustments:** None
			▪ **Dosage Forms:** Oral (capsule, liquid, solution, suspension, tablet)

Opium tincture	N/A (C-II)	▪ Diarrhea	▪ **Dosing (Adult):**
			  – Oral 6 mg q6h
			▪ **Dosing (Peds):**
			  – Not routinely used
			▪ **CYP450 Interactions:** None
			▪ **Renal or Hepatic Dose Adjustments:** None
			▪ **Dosage Forms:** Oral tincture

Paregoric	N/A (C-III)	▪ Diarrhea	▪ **Dosing (Adult):**
			  – Oral 5 to 10 mL q6-24h
			    ▪ 1 mL = 0.4 mg morphine
			▪ **Dosing (Peds):**
			  – Oral 0.25 to 0.5 mL/kg/dose q6-24h
			    ▪ Maximum 10 mL/dose
			▪ **CYP450 Interactions:** None
			▪ **Renal or Hepatic Dose Adjustments:** None
			▪ **Dosage Forms:** Oral tincture

High-Yield Clinical Knowledge

▪ **Atropine**
  – Although diphenoxylate and difenoxin are co-formulated with atropine, its role is primarily abuse-deterrent rather than therapeutic.
  – If patients surreptitiously administer diphenoxylate or difenoxin in massive quantities orally or parenterally, atropine creates an unpleasant anticholinergic response to offset any opioid-related euphoria.
    – Anticholinergic antidiarrheal effects are minimal and not likely contributory to the action of these agents.

▪ **Inflammatory Bowel Disease**
  – Loperamide should be avoided in patients with IBD that involves the colon due to the high risk of developing toxic megacolon.

▪ **Opioid Tinctures**
  – Opium tincture contains significantly more morphine than paregoric, which can lead to significant dosing errors if dosing in drops is miscalculated.

- Opium tincture contains morphine 10 mg/mL, whereas paregoric contains 0.4 mg/mL of morphine.
- Both preparations pose a high risk of abuse, diversion, or misuse and have fallen out of favor.
- Although largely abandoned in clinical practice, updates regarding opium tincture dosing expression have included representing it in terms of morphine dosing units.
- The concentration of morphine in opium tincture is 10 mg/mL.
- Significant dosing errors are possible when converting between doses expressed as drops, milligrams, or units.

- **Opioid Antagonists**
  - Conversely, the opioid antagonist methylnaltrexone or naloxone can be used to treat opioid-induced constipation.
    - Oral naloxone doses between 2-6 mg are often ideal for this indication and doses greater than 6 mg should be avoided due to systemic absorption and potential precipitation of acute systemic opioid withdrawal.

- **Infectious Diarrhea**
  - Infectious causes of diarrhea, particularly diarrhea caused by Clostridoides difficile, should be ruled out before initiating one of these agents.
    - Some infectious diarrhea may be treated using antimotility agents but should be done under an appropriate provider's observation.

HIGH-YIELD BOARD EXAM ESSENTIALS

- **CLASSIC AGENTS:** Diphenoxylate-atropine, difenoxin-atropine, loperamide, opium tincture, paregoric
- **DRUG CLASS:** Antimotility agents
- **INDICATIONS:** Diarrhea
- **MECHANISM:** Mu and delta-opioid receptor agonists decreasing gastrointestinal motility and secretion.
- **SIDE EFFECTS:** Constipation, GI obstruction
- **CLINICAL PEARLS:** Although diphenoxylate and difenoxin are co-formulated with atropine, its role is primarily abuse-deterrent rather than therapeutic since these agents can stimulate the mu opioid receptors and increase risk of possible abuse. Avoid their use in patients with ulcerative colitis and evidence or risk for toxic megacolon because this could result in bowel perforation.

High-Yield Basic Pharmacology

- **Bulk-forming agents (methylcellulose, polycarbophil, psyllium)**
  - Increase water content of stool, thereby increasing the bulk and weight of the stool.
- **Emollient laxatives (docusate)**
  - Facilitates mixing of aqueous and fatty materials in the GI tract.
- **Lubricant laxative (castor oil, mineral oil)**
  - Improves water content in stool and lubricates the intestine.
- **Osmolar laxatives**
  - Lactulose, sorbitol
    - Colonic bacteria metabolize these agents to low-molecular-weight acids that increase fluid retention in the colon.
  - Glycerin, Polyethylene glycol
    - Creates a hyperosmotic environment without metabolism, different from lactulose or sorbitol.
- **Saline cathartics (Sodium Picosulfate, Sodium Sulfate, Magnesium Hydroxide, Magnesium Oxide, Magnesium Sulfate, Potassium Chloride, Potassium Sulfate)**
  - Promotes osmotic retention of fluid, distending the colon and stimulating peristaltic activity.
- **Stimulant Laxative (bisacodyl, senna)**
  - Stimulates the nerve plexus of the colon to stimulate peristalsis and increases interstitial fluid secretion.

Primary Net Benefit

- Over-the-counter agents for self-care of constipation, as well as bowel preparatory agents, to facilitate endoscopy.

Laxatives (Emollient, Lubricant, Osmotic, Saline, Stimulant) - Drug Class Review			
High-Yield Med Reviews			
Mechanism of Action: *See above for each agent*			
Class Effects: Diarrhea, cramping, abdominal pain (degree varies by agent)			
Generic Name	**Brand Name**	**Indication(s) or Uses**	**Notes**

Bisacodyl	Biscolax Ducodyl Dulcolax Fleet Bisacodyl	• Constipation	• **Dosing (Adult):**
			  – Rectal 10 mg once
			  – Oral 5 to 15 mg once daily
			• **Dosing (Peds):**
			  – Rectal 10 mg once
			  – Oral 5 to 15 mg once daily
			• **CYP450 Interactions:** None
			• **Renal or Hepatic Dose Adjustments:** None
			• **Dosage Forms:** Oral (tablet), Rectal (enema, suppository)

Castor oil	GoodSense Castor Oil	• Constipation	• **Dosing (Adult):**
			  – Oral 15 to 60 mL as a single dose
			• **Dosing (Peds):**
			  – Oral 5 to 60 mL as a single dose
			• **CYP450 Interactions:** None
			• **Renal or Hepatic Dose Adjustments:** None
			• **Dosage Forms:** Oral (oil)

Laxatives (Emollient, Lubricant, Osmotic, Saline, Stimulant) - Drug Class Review
High-Yield Med Reviews

Generic Name	Brand Name	Indication(s) or Uses	Notes

Docusate	Colace
	Stool softener
		• Constipation
		• Ear wax removal (off-label; OTC as a Ceruminolytic)
			• **Dosing (Adult):**
			  – Oral (sodium salt) 50 to 360 mg daily
			  – Oral (calcium salt) 240 mg daily
			  – Rectal 283 mg 1 to 3 times daily
			• **Dosing (Peds):**
			  – Oral (sodium salt) 5 mg/kg/day in 1-4 divided doses
			  – Rectal 100 to 283 mg daily
			• **CYP450 Interactions:** None
			• **Renal or Hepatic Dose Adjustments:** None
			• **Dosage Forms:** Oral (capsule, liquid, syrup, tablet), Rectal (enema)

Glycerin	Fleet Liquid Glycerin	• Constipation	• **Dosing (Adult):**
			  – Rectal enema or suppository daily as needed
			• **Dosing (Peds):**
			  – Rectal enema or suppository daily as needed
			• **CYP450 Interactions:** None
			• **Renal or Hepatic Dose Adjustments:** None
			• **Dosage Forms:** Rectal (enema, suppository)

Lactulose	Constulose
	Enulose
	Generlac
	Kristalose
		• Constipation
		• Hepatic encephalopathy
			• **Dosing (Adult):**
			  – Oral 10 to 30 g q1-8h as needed
			  – Rectal 200 g
			• **Dosing (Peds):**
			  – Extra info if needed
			    • Extra info if needed
			• **CYP450 Interactions:** text
			• **Renal or Hepatic Dose Adjustments:** text
			• **Dosage Forms:** [e.g., basic info]

Magnesium citrate	Citroma	• Bowel preparation prior to colonoscopy	• **Dosing (Adult):**
			  – 1 to 1.5 bottles (300 to 450 mL) 8 hours prior to procedure
			• **Dosing (Peds):**
			  – Age 2 to 6 years : 60 to 90 mL once or in divided doses
			  – Age 6 to less than 12 years : 100 to 150 mL once or in divided doses
			• **CYP450 Interactions:** None
			• **Renal or Hepatic Dose Adjustments:**
			  – Should be avoided in PEDIATRICS with renal impairment
			• **Dosage Forms:** Oral (solution, tablet)

Laxatives (Emollient, Lubricant, Osmotic, Saline, Stimulant) - Drug Class Review
High-Yield Med Reviews

Generic Name	Brand Name	Indication(s) or Uses	Notes

Magnesium hydroxide	Milk of Magnesia Pedia-Lax Phillips Milk of Magnesia	▪ Antacid
		▪ Laxative
			▪ **Dosing (Adult):**
			  – Oral 400 to 1,200 mg as needed up to 4 times daily
			    ▪ Maximum 4,800 mg/day
			▪ **Dosing (Peds):**
			  – Oral 400 to 1,200 mg as needed up to 4 times daily
			    ▪ Age 2 to 6 years maximum 1,200 mg/day
			    ▪ Age 6 to less than 12 years: maximum 2,400 mg/day
			▪ **CYP450 Interactions:** None
			▪ **Renal or Hepatic Dose Adjustments:**
			  – Should be avoided in PEDIATRICS with renal impairment
			▪ **Dosage Forms:** Oral (suspension, tablet)

Magnesium sulfate	Epsom Salt MagNA caps	▪ Asthma
		▪ Constipation
		▪ Eclampsia/preeclampsia
		▪ Hypomagnesemia
		▪ Torsades de pointes
			▪ **Dosing (Adult):**
			  – Oral 10 to 20 g dissolved in 240 mL water, maximum 2 doses/day
			  – IV 1 to 2 g IV push over 1-2 minutes
			  – IV 1 to 6 g IV over 1-30 minutes, followed by 1 to 4 g/hour infusion (if necessary)
			  – IM 10 g (2x 5g in each buttock) at onset of labor, followed by 5 g q4h
			▪ **Dosing (Peds):**
			  – IV (elemental magnesium) 2.5 to 5 mg/kg/dose q6h
			  – Oral (elemental magnesium) 10 to 20 mg/kg/dose q6-24h
			▪ **CYP450 Interactions:** None
			▪ **Renal or Hepatic Dose Adjustments:**
			  – Severe renal impairment
			    ▪ IV 4-6 g loading dose over 15-30 min, then 1 g/hour infusion (maximum 10 g/24h)
			▪ **Dosage Forms:** Oral (capsule, granules), IV (solution)

Methylcellulose	Citrucel	▪ Constipation	▪ **Dosing (Adult):**
			  – Oral 2 caplets 6 times per day, up to 12 caplets/day
			▪ **Dosing (Peds):**
			  – Oral 1 caplets 6 times per day, up to 6 caplets/day
			▪ **CYP450 Interactions:** None
			▪ **Renal or Hepatic Dose Adjustments:** None
			▪ **Dosage Forms:** Oral (powder, tablet)

Laxatives (Emollient, Lubricant, Osmotic, Saline, Stimulant) - Drug Class Review
High-Yield Med Reviews

Generic Name	Brand Name	Indication(s) or Uses	Notes

Mineral oil	Fleet oil	• Constipation	• **Dosing (Adult):**
			  – Oral 15 to 45 mL/day (plain) or 30 to 90 mL/day (suspension)
			  – Rectal 118 mL once
			• **Dosing (Peds):**
			  – Oral 5 to 15 mL/day (plain) or 10 to 30 mL/day (suspension)
			  – Rectal 59 to 118 mL once
			• **CYP450 Interactions:** None
			• **Renal or Hepatic Dose Adjustments:** None
			• **Dosage Forms:** Oral (oil), Rectal (enema)

Polycarbophil	Fiber Laxative, Fiber-Caps, Fiber-Lax, FiberCon	• Constipation	• **Dosing (Adult):**
			  – Oral 1250 mg q6-24h
			• **Dosing (Peds):**
			  – Oral 625 mg q6-24h
			• **CYP450 Interactions:** None
			• **Renal or Hepatic Dose Adjustments:** None
			• **Dosage Forms:** Oral (tablet)

Polyethylene glycol 3350	Gavilax, Gialax, Glycolax, Healthylax, MiraLAX, PEGylax	• Bowel preparation prior to colonoscopy	• **Dosing (Adult):**
			  – Oral 17 g in 240 mL q10minutes until 2,000 mL consumed.
			  – Oral 17g in 240 mL once daily, as needed
			• **Dosing (Peds):**
			  – Oral 1.5 g/kg/day for 4 days
			    • Maximum 100 g/day
			  – Oral 0.2 to 1 g/kg once daily
			    • Maximum 17 g/day
			• **CYP450 Interactions:** None
			• **Renal or Hepatic Dose Adjustments:** None
			• **Dosage Forms:** Oral (kit, packet, powder)

Psyllium	Evac, Knsyl, Metamucil, Mucilin, Natural Fiber Therapy, Sorbulax	• Constipation
		• CHD risk reduction
			• **Dosing (Adult):**
			  – Oral 2.5 to 30 g per day in divided doses
			• **Dosing (Peds):**
			  – Oral 2.5 to 30 g per day in divided doses
			• **CYP450 Interactions:** None
			• **Renal or Hepatic Dose Adjustments:** None
			• **Dosage Forms:** Oral (capsule, packet, powder)

Senna	Ex-Lax, Geri-kot, Senexon, Senna Lax, Senna-tabs, Senokot	• Constipation	• **Dosing (Adult):**
			  – Oral 8.6 to 50 mg (of sennosides) 1-2 times/day
			• **Dosing (Peds):**
			  – Oral 4.4 to 50 mg (of sennosides) 1-2 times/day
			• **CYP450 Interactions:** None
			• **Renal or Hepatic Dose Adjustments:** None
			• **Dosage Forms:** Oral (leaves, liquid, syrup, tablet)

Laxatives (Emollient, Lubricant, Osmotic, Saline, Stimulant) - Drug Class Review
High-Yield Med Reviews

Generic Name	Brand Name	Indication(s) or Uses	Notes
Sodium Picosulfate, Magnesium Oxide, and Citric Acid	Clenpiq Prepopik	• Bowel preparation prior to colonoscopy	• **Dosing (Adult):** – Oral 150 to 160 mL 12 hours prior to colonoscopy. • **Dosing (Peds):** – Extra info if needed • Extra info if needed • **CYP450 Interactions:** None • **Renal or Hepatic Dose Adjustments:** – GFR less than 30 mL/minute - Contraindicated • **Dosage Forms:** Oral (powder, solution)
Sodium Sulfate, Magnesium Sulfate, and Potassium Chloride	Sutab	• Bowel preparation prior to colonoscopy	• **Dosing (Adult):** – Night before procedure: Take 12 tablets with 16 ounces of water over a 15-20 minute period, followed in 1 hour by an additional 16 oz of water every 30 minutes, twice. – Morning of procedure: repeat the above process, starting 8 hours before the procedure. • **Dosing (Peds):** – Not routinely used • **CYP450 Interactions:** None • **Renal or Hepatic Dose Adjustments:** None • **Dosage Forms:** Oral (tablet)
Sodium Sulfate, Potassium Sulfate, and Magnesium Sulfate	Suprep Bowel Prep Kit	• Bowel preparation prior to colonoscopy	• **Dosing (Adult):** – Oral 2,888 mL in divided doses prior to the procedure. • **Dosing (Peds):** – Oral 2,128 mL in divided doses prior to the procedure. • **CYP450 Interactions:** None • **Renal or Hepatic Dose Adjustments:** None • **Dosage Forms:** Oral (solution)
Sorbitol	N/A	• Laxative	• **Dosing (Adult):** – Oral 30 to 45 mL as 70% solution – Rectal 120 mL as 25 to 35% solution • **Dosing (Peds):** – Oral 1 to 3 mL/kg/day in divided doses – Rectal 30 to 120 mL as needed • **CYP450 Interactions:** None • **Renal or Hepatic Dose Adjustments:** None • **Dosage Forms:** Oral (solution), Rectal (solution)

High-Yield Clinical Knowledge

- **Cardiovascular Benefits**
  - Fiber supplementation has been associated with improved cardiovascular outcomes and is recommended to consume approximately 30 g of fiber daily for most adults.
  - The typical American diet does not contain sufficient fiber, and supplementation using bulk-forming laxatives can consume the target fiber intake.
- **Prevention of Opioid Associated Constipation**
  - Patients receiving acute or chronic opioids should maintain bowel health to avoid intestinal obstructions, which increase the risk of perforation.
  - Combining docusate plus senna is a commonly recommended bowel regimen for patients in acute care facilities receiving opioids.
  - In patients presenting with constipation related to opioid use, GI obstruction must be ruled out before using stimulant laxatives, as they are associated with an increased risk of perforation.
- **Stimulant Laxative Duration**
  - Stimulant laxatives, namely bisacodyl, should not be used for more than ten consecutive days.
  - If relief has not been achieved, referral to primary care or GI specialists is required.
- **Dietary Supplement Product**
  - Senna leaf extract syrup is considered a dietary supplement and is not interchangeable with other sennoside containing products.
- **Docusate Ear Wax Removal**
  - Docusate has been used in some cases to aid in disimpaction of cerumen in the outer ear.
  - The gel capsules can be opened, with the contents administered in the outer ear.
- **Mineral Oil Ingestion**
  - Mineral oil, taken by mouth to relieve constipation, must be used with caution in patients with difficulty swallowing or altered mental status as the risk of aspiration is very high.
  - If inhaled, lipoid pneumonia can result, which can lead to unnecessary increased morbidity and mortality.

HIGH-YIELD BOARD EXAM ESSENTIALS

- **CLASSIC AGENTS:** Bisacodyl, castor oil, docusate, glycerin, lactulose, magnesium salts, methylcellulose, mineral oil, polyethylene glycol, senna, sorbitol
- **DRUG CLASS:** Laxatives
- **INDICATIONS:** Constipation
- **MECHANISM:** Bulk-forming agents (methylcellulose, polycarbophil, psyllium), emollient laxatives (docusate), lubricant laxative (castor oil, mineral oil), osmolar laxatives (glycerin, lactulose, polyethylene glycol, sorbitol), saline cathartics (sodium picosulfate, sodium sulfate, magnesium hydroxide, magnesium oxide, magnesium sulfate, potassium chloride, potassium sulfate), stimulant laxative (bisacodyl, senna)
- **SIDE EFFECTS:** Flatulence, diarrhea
- **CLINICAL PEARLS:**
  - Fiber supplementation has been associated with improved cardiovascular outcomes and is recommended to consume approximately 30 g of fiber daily for most adults.
  - The typical American diet does not contain sufficient fiber, and supplementation using bulk-forming laxatives can consume the target fiber intake.
  - Stool softeners (e.g., docusate) alone are not sufficient for preventing opioid induced constipation.

High-Yield Basic Pharmacology

- **Erythromycin**
  - Direct agonist effect on motilin receptors in GI smooth muscle.
- **Eluxadoline**
  - Mu-opioid receptor agonist, delta-opioid receptor agonist, and kappa-opioid receptor agonist acting locally on GI epithelium.
- **Metoclopramide**
  - Dopamine (D-2) receptor antagonists in the GI and chemoreceptor trigger zone, aiding cholinergic smooth muscle stimulation.
- **Lubiprostone**
  - Activates chloride channels on GI luminal epithelium by binding to the prostanoid receptor (EP4) for prostaglandin E2, stimulating chloride-rich fluid secretion in the intestinal lumen, increasing intraluminal fluid secretion softening the stool, and accelerating GI transit.
- **Linaclotide, Plecanatide**
  - Activates the intestinal epithelial guanylate cyclase C receptor, increasing intestinal fluid secretion.
- **Prucalopride**
  - Selective serotonin (5-HT4) receptor agonist

Primary Net Benefit

- Stimulate GI motility, aiding in resolving constipation from various underlying causes.

Prokinetic Agents - Drug Class Review			
High-Yield Med Reviews			
Mechanism of Action: *See above for each agent*			
Class Effects: Improvement in bowel movements, cramping, diarrhea (agent specific).			
Generic Name	**Brand Name**	**Indication(s) or Uses**	**Notes**

Eluxadoline	Viberzi	- Irritable bowel syndrome	- **Dosing (Adult):**
			  - Oral 75 to 100 mg BID
			- **Dosing (Peds):**
			  - Not routinely used
			- **CYP450 Interactions:** None
			- **Renal or Hepatic Dose Adjustments:**
			  - GFR less than 60 mL/minute - 75 mg BID
			  - Child-Pugh class A or B - 75 mg BID
			  - Child-Pugh class C - Contraindicated
			- **Dosage Forms:** Oral (Tablet)

Erythromycin	Erythrocin	- Bacterial infections
		- Pre-endoscopy prokinetic adjunct
			- **Dosing (Adult):**
			  - IV 3 mg/kg or 250 mg as a single dose over 30 minutes, 1 hour prior to endoscopy
			- **Dosing (Peds):**
			  - Not used for GI indication
			- **CYP450 Interactions:** Substrate CYP2B6, 3A4, P-gp; Inhibits CYP3A4, P-gp
			- **Renal or Hepatic Dose Adjustments:** None
			- **Dosage Forms:** Oral (capsule, tablet, solution), IV (solution)

Prokinetic Agents - Drug Class Review
High-Yield Med Reviews

Generic Name	Brand Name	Indication(s) or Uses	Notes

Metoclopramide	Reglan	▪ Chemotherapy-induced nausea and vomiting prophylaxis
		▪ Gastroparesis
		▪ Nausea and Vomiting
			▪ **Dosing (Adult):**
			  – Oral/IV/SQ 10 mg q4-6h
			▪ **Dosing (Peds):**
			  – IV 0.5 to 2 mg/kg/dose q6-8h
			  – Oral 0.1 to 0.2 mg/kg/dose q6-8h
			    ▪ Maximum 10 mg/dose
			▪ **CYP450 Interactions:** Substrate CYP1A2
			▪ **Renal or Hepatic Dose Adjustments:**
			  – GFR 10 to 60 mL/minute - Administer 50% of total daily dose
			  – GFR less than 10 mL/minute - Administer 33% of total daily dose
			  – Child-Pugh class B or C - Use not recommended
			▪ **Dosage Forms:** Oral (solution, tablet), IV (solution), Nasal solution

Linaclotide	Linzess	▪ Chronic idiopathic constipation
		▪ Irritable bowel syndrome
			▪ **Dosing (Adult):**
			  – Oral 72 to 290 mcg daily
			▪ **Dosing (Peds):**
			  – Not routinely used
			▪ **CYP450 Interactions:** None
			▪ **Renal or Hepatic Dose Adjustments:** None
			▪ **Dosage Forms:** Oral (capsule)

Lubiprostone	Amitiza	▪ Chronic idiopathic constipation
		▪ Irritable bowel syndrome
		▪ Opioid-induced constipation
			▪ **Dosing (Adult):**
			  – Oral 8 to 24 mcg BID
			▪ **Dosing (Peds):**
			  – Not routinely used
			▪ **CYP450 Interactions:** None
			▪ **Renal or Hepatic Dose Adjustments:**
			  – Child-Pugh class B - 16 mcg BID
			  – Child-Pugh class C - 8 mcg BID
			▪ **Dosage Forms:** Oral (capsule)

Plecanatide	Trulance	▪ Chronic idiopathic constipation
		▪ Irritable bowel syndrome
			▪ **Dosing (Adult):**
			  – Oral 3 mg daily
			▪ **Dosing (Peds):**
			  – Not routinely used
			▪ **CYP450 Interactions:** None
			▪ **Renal or Hepatic Dose Adjustments:** None
			▪ **Dosage Forms:** Oral (tablet)

Prucalopride	Motegrity	▪ Chronic idiopathic constipation	▪ **Dosing (Adult):**
			  – Oral 2 mg daily
			▪ **Dosing (Peds):**
			  – Not routinely used
			▪ **CYP450 Interactions:** Substrate of P-gp
			▪ **Renal or Hepatic Dose Adjustments:**
			  – GFR less than 30 mL/minute - 1 mg daily
			▪ **Dosage Forms:** Oral (tablet)

High-Yield Clinical Knowledge

- **Nausea**
  - Lubiprostone, linaclotide, and plecanatide are associated with a high incidence of drug-induced nausea in up to 30% of patients.
- **Pancreatitis**
  - The use of eluxadoline is associated with a dose-dependent increased risk of pancreatitis.
  - The risk of pancreatitis is significantly higher in patients who have had their gallbladder removed, sphincter of Oddi disease, or dysfunction.
    - Other risk independent factors that increase pancreatitis risk include pancreatic duct obstruction, alcohol abuse, severe hepatic impairment.
- **QT Prolongation**
  - This group of medications, except for prucalopride, is associated with QT prolongation.
    - Inhibition of Human Ether-a-go-go-related Gene (hERG) potassium channels is a known cause of QT interval prolongation.
  - Cisapride and tegaserod were GI prokinetic agents used commonly but have been removed from the US market due to the risk of QT prolongation and adverse cardiovascular events.
- **Endoscopy Adjunct Therapy**
  - In patients with acute GI bleeding who require emergent endoscopy, the presence of clots in the stomach makes effective visualization on emergency endoscopy difficult.
  - Erythromycin and metoclopramide have been used for their prokinetic effects to stimulate GI motility, aiding in the clearance of obstructions from the GI and improving visualization on an endoscopic exam.
    - As the dose of erythromycin used for this indication is lower than an otherwise therapeutic dose, the safety (QT prolongation, nausea/vomiting) is likely better than metoclopramide, which is dosed at normal therapeutic doses, increasing the risk of extrapyramidal symptoms.
- **Metoclopramide EPS**
  - As a result of its dopamine antagonist properties, metoclopramide is associated with extrapyramidal effects, including akathisia, dystonias, and parkinsonism.
    - With chronic use, metoclopramide is also associated with galactorrhea, gynecomastia, impotence, and menstrual disorders.

HIGH-YIELD BOARD EXAM ESSENTIALS
- **CLASSIC AGENTS:** Erythromycin, metoclopramide, eluxadoline, linaclotide, lubiprostone, plecanatide, prucalopride
- **DRUG CLASS:** Prokinetic agents
- **INDICATIONS:** Pre-endoscopy prokinetic adjunct (erythromycin), gastroparesis (metoclopramide), nausea and vomiting (metoclopramide), chronic idiopathic constipation (linaclotide, lubiprostone, plecanatide, prucalopride), irritable bowel syndrome (eluxadoline, linaclotide, lubiprostone, plecanatide), opioid-induced constipation (lubiprostone)
- **MECHANISM:**
  - Direct agonist effect on motilin receptors in GI smooth muscle (erythromycin)
  - Opioid receptor agonist acting locally on GI epithelium (eluxadoline)
  - D-2 receptor antagonists in the GI and chemoreceptor trigger zone (metoclopramide)
  - Activates GI chloride channels increasing intraluminal fluid secretion (lubiprostone)
  - Intestinal epithelial guanylate cyclase c receptor agonists, increasing intestinal fluid secretion (linaclotide, plecanatide)
  - Selective 5-ht4 receptor agonist (prucalopride)
- **SIDE EFFECTS:** Nausea, pancreatitis, QT prolongation
- **CLINICAL PEARLS:** Lubiprostone, linaclotide, and plecanatide are associated with a high incidence of drug-induced nausea in up to 30% of patients.

High-Yield Basic Pharmacology

- **Mechanism of Action**
  - Inhibit 5-alpha-reductase mediated conversion of testosterone to dihydrotestosterone which can reduce the growth and size of the prostate gland.
- **Type 1 and 2 5-Alpha-Reductase**
  - Dutasteride and finasteride differ slightly in their mechanism as dutasteride inhibits type 1 and 2 5-alpha-reductase, whereas finasteride inhibits type 2 only.

Primary Net Benefit

- 5-alpha-reductase inhibitor therapy decreases prostate size and prostate-specific antigen (PSA), but combination therapy with tamsulosin, mirabegron, or a PDE5 inhibitor may be added to improve time to relieve BPH symptoms but do not impact disease progression.

5-Alpha Reductase Inhibitors - Drug Class Review High-Yield Med Reviews			
Mechanism of Action: *Inhibit 5-alpha-reductase mediated conversion of testosterone to dihydrotestosterone.*			
Class Effects: Improvement in urine flow, bladder emptying; effect is delayed by several months; teratogenic for pregnant patients; small risk in causing sexual dysfunction due to reduced DHT.			
Generic Name	**Brand Name**	**Indication(s) or Uses**	**Notes**

Dutasteride	Avodart	• Benign prostatic hyperplasia	• **Dosing (Adult):**
			  – Oral 0.5 mg daily
			• **Dosing (Peds):**
			  – Not routinely used
			• **CYP450 Interactions:** Substrate CYP3A4
			• **Renal or Hepatic Dose Adjustments:** None
			• **Dosage Forms:** Oral (capsule)

Dutasteride and tamsulosin	Jalyn	• Benign prostatic hyperplasia	• **Dosing (Adult):**
			  – Oral one capsule (0.5 mg / 0.4 mg) daily
			• **Dosing (Peds):**
			  – Not routinely used
			• **CYP450 Interactions:** Substrate CYP2D6, 3A4
			• **Renal or Hepatic Dose Adjustments:** None
			• **Dosage Forms:** Oral (capsule)

Finasteride	Propecia, Proscar	• Androgenetic alopecia
		• Benign prostatic hyperplasia
			• **Dosing (Adult):**
			  – Oral 1 to 5 mg daily
			• **Dosing (Peds):**
			  – Not routinely used
			• **CYP450 Interactions:** Substrate CYP3A4
			• **Renal or Hepatic Dose Adjustments:** None
			• **Dosage Forms:** Oral (tablet)

High-Yield Clinical Knowledge

- **Pre-Treatment PSA**
  - As a result of decreased prostate-specific antigen (PSA) levels from dutasteride or finasteride treatment, a baseline level must be drawn for prostate cancer screening.

- While taking dutasteride and finasteride, measured PSA levels should be doubled as a means of prostate cancer screening.
- **Category X**
  - Both dutasteride and finasteride are contraindicated in pregnancy or women of child-bearing age.
  - Furthermore, pregnant women or women of child-bearing age should not handle either medication without appropriate personal protective equipment.
- **Combination Treatment**
  - Among patients with moderate to severe BPH with enlarged prostates greater than 40 g may benefit from combination therapy of dutasteride and tamsulosin to improve urinary flow rate and BPH progression.
- **Onset of Benefit**
  - Dutasteride and finasteride may take days to achieve clinical benefit and provide relief to patients.
  - 5-alpha-reductase inhibitor therapy should continue for 6 to 12 months before determining clinical response.
  - Combination therapy with tamsulosin, mirabegron, or a PDE5 inhibitor may be added to improve time to relieve BPH symptoms but do not impact disease progression.
- **Sexual Dysfunction**
  - 5-alpha-reductase inhibitor therapy is associated with sexual dysfunction, including decreased libido, impotence as well as gynecomastia.
- **Baldness**
  - Finasteride is also commonly used to treat androgenetic alopecia or male pattern baldness but may also be used to treat hirsutism.

HIGH-YIELD BOARD EXAM ESSENTIALS

- **CLASSIC AGENTS:** Dutasteride, finasteride
- **DRUG CLASS:** 5-alpha reductase inhibitors
- **INDICATIONS:** Androgenetic alopecia (finasteride), benign prostatic hyperplasia (dutasteride, finasteride)
- **MECHANISM:** Inhibit 5-alpha-reductase mediated conversion of testosterone to dihydrotestosterone.
- **SIDE EFFECTS:** Teratogenic effects, sexual dysfunction
- **CLINICAL PEARLS:**
  - Finasteride is also commonly used to treat androgenetic alopecia or male pattern baldness but may also be used to treat hirsutism.
  - Pregnant patients should avoid physical contact with these agents to include handling the dosage forms or coming in contact with fluids containing these agents due to the very rare risk of absorbing the drugs that could impact the developing baby.

High-Yield Basic Pharmacology

- Knowing that about 75% of the alpha receptors in the bladder are alpha 1a subtype receptors allows for a better localized effect specific to the bladder and prostate.
    - This means fewer alpha 1 receptors located in the systemic vasculature will likely be antagonized thereby leading to less vasodilation (or changes in blood pressure when it is not desired).

Primary Net Benefit

- In the context of BPH, they improve urinary flow rates, greater emptying of the bladder, and overall symptoms of BPH without causing as much orthosis stasis in older patients. In kidney stone expulsion, these agents "may" help relax the ureters to facilitate the expulsion or elimination of a renal stone.

Selective Alpha-1a Blockers - Drug Class Review			
High-Yield Med Reviews			
Mechanism of Action: *Selectively inhibit alpha-1a receptors primarily located in the prostate and bladder thereby causing a relaxation of the smooth muscle of the bladder neck and prostate to improve the flow of urine and a reduction in the symptoms of BPH.*			
Class Effects: *Improved urine flow, lower residuals in the bladder; less orthostasis compared to non-selective agents*			
Generic Name	**Brand Name**	**Main Indication(s) or Uses**	**Notes**
Alfuzosin	Uroxatral	• Benign prostatic hyperplasia • Ureteral calculi expulsion	• **Dosing (Adult):** PO: 10 mg once daily • **Dosing (Peds):** Not used in pediatrics • **CYP450 Interactions:** Substrate of CYP3A4 • **Renal or Hepatic Dose Adjustments:** Contraindicated for patients with moderate or severe hepatic impairment (Child-Pugh class B or C) • **Dosage Forms:** Extended release tablet
Silodosin	Rapaflo	• Benign prostatic hyperplasia • Ureteral calculi expulsion	• **Dosing (Adult):** 8 mg once daily • **Dosing (Peds):** Not recommended • **CYP450 Interactions:** Substrate of CYP3A4, P-gp • **Renal or Hepatic Dose Adjustments:** CrCl 30-50 mL/minute: 4 mg once daily; CrCl <30 mL/minute: Contraindicated. • Contraindicated for patients with moderate or severe hepatic impairment (Child-Pugh class B or C) • **Dosage Forms:** Oral (capsule)
Tamsulosin	Flomax	• Benign prostatic hyperplasia • Ureteral calculi expulsion	• **Dosing (Adult):** 0.4 to 0.8 mg once daily • **Dosing (Peds):** 0.2 or 0.4 mg once daily at bedtime • **CYP450 Interactions:** Substrate of CYP3A4, 2D6 • **Renal or Hepatic Dose Adjustments:** None • **Dosage Forms:** Oral (capsule)

High-Yield Clinical Knowledge

- **Acute Care**
  - Ureteral calculi (renal stones located in the ureter) expulsion may be facilitated by the smooth relaxation in the bladder specifically in the area where the ureter empties into the bladder (e.g., at the ureterovesical junction (UVJ))
- **Chronic Care**
  - Selective alpha 1a blockers are not indicated for the management of hypertension like the non-selective alpha 1 blockers (e.g., doxazosin, prazosin) due to their focused mechanisms for alpha 1a receptors that reside mainly in the prostate and bladder.
  - Tamsulosin is associated with floppy iris syndrome. Although it has been reported with doxazosin and silodosin, it is more prevalent with tamsulosin.
    - This adverse effect occurs due to the alpha-1a antagonist effects in iris dilator muscles which increases the likelihood of post-ophthalmologic operative complications, including posterior capsular rupture, retinal detachment, residual retained lens material, or endophthalmitis. Permanent loss of vision can result.

HIGH-YIELD BOARD EXAM ESSENTIALS

- **CLASSIC AGENTS:** Alfuzosin, silodosin, tamsulosin
- **DRUG CLASS:** Alpha-1A Selective Blockers
- **INDICATIONS:** Benign Prostatic Hyperplasia, Ureteral Calculi Expulsion)
- **MECHANISM:** Selectively inhibit alpha-1a receptors located in the prostate and bladder thereby causing a relaxation of the smooth muscle of the bladder neck and prostate to improve the flow of urine and a reduction in the symptoms.
- **SIDE EFFECTS:** Minimal, fairly well tolerated
- **CLINICAL PEARLS:**
  - The primary value of these agents in older patients with BPH is in causing less side effects (mainly less orthostasis). However, they cost more than non-selective alpha-1 blockers.
  - While tamsulosin may be helpful to some patients trying to pass a kidney stone, the evidence supporting this indication is not significant.

High-Yield Basic Pharmacology

- **Mechanism of Action**
  - Competitive antagonists of acetylcholine on muscarinic receptors.
    - M2 and M3 receptors are primarily expressed in the bladder, but the M3 is responsible for direct activation and contraction.
    - Selective M3 antagonists include oxybutynin, and the newer agents trospium, darifenacin, and solifenacin. Tolterodine is selective for M2 and M3
  - Mirabegron
    - Beta-3 adrenergic receptor activator, relaxing detrusor muscle during the urinary bladder-fill-void cycle

Primary Net Benefit

- Second-line treatment for overactive bladder provides symptomatic relief of urinary urgency, but older agents' nonspecific antimuscarinic properties may lead to concerning adverse events, particularly in the elderly.

Antimuscarinics - Drug Class Review			
High-Yield Med Reviews			
Mechanism of Action: *Competitive antagonists of acetylcholine on muscarinic receptors.* *Mirabegron is a beta-3 adrenergic receptor activator, relaxing detrusor muscle during the urinary bladder-fill-void cycle.*			
Class Effects: Urinary retention.			
Generic Name	**Brand Name**	**Indication(s) or Uses**	**Notes**

Darifenacin	Enablex	• Overactive bladder	• **Dosing (Adult):**
			  – Oral 7.5 to 15 mg daily
			• **Dosing (Peds):** Not routinely used
			• **CYP450 Interactions:** Substrate CYP2D6, 3A4; Inhibits CYP2D6
			• **Renal or Hepatic Dose Adjustments:**
			  – Child-Pugh class B - Maximum 7.5 mg/day
			  – Child-Pugh class C - Not recommended
			• **Dosage Forms:** Oral (tablet)

Fesoterodine	Toviaz	• Overactive bladder	• **Dosing (Adult):**
			  – Oral 4 to 8 mg daily
			• **Dosing (Peds):** Not routinely used
			• **CYP450 Interactions:** Substrate 2D6, 3A4
			• **Renal or Hepatic Dose Adjustments:**
			  – Child-Pugh class C - Not recommended
			  – GFR less than 30 mL/minute - 4 mg/day
			• **Dosage Forms:** Oral (tablet)

Methscopolamine	Pamine	• Peptic ulcer	• **Dosing (Adult):**
			  – Oral 2.5 mg 30 min before meals and 2.5 to 5 mg at bedtime
			    • Maximum 30 mg/day
			• **Dosing (Peds):** Not routinely used
			• **CYP450 Interactions:** None
			• **Renal or Hepatic Dose Adjustments:** None
			• **Dosage Forms:** Oral (tablet)

Antimuscarinics - Drug Class Review
High-Yield Med Reviews

Generic Name	Brand Name	Indication(s) or Uses	Notes

Mirabegron	Myrbetriq	▪ Overactive bladder	▪ **Dosing (Adult):**
			  – Oral 25 to 50 mg daily
			▪ **Dosing (Peds):**
			  – Not routinely used
			▪ **CYP450 Interactions:** Substrate CYP2D6, 3A4, P-gp
			▪ **Renal or Hepatic Dose Adjustments:**
			  – GFR 15 to 29 mL/minute - Maximum 25 mg/day
			  – GFR less than 15 mL/minute - not recommended
			  – Child-Pugh class B - Maximum 25 mg/day
			  – Child-Pugh class C - Not recommended
			▪ **Dosage Forms:** Oral (tablet)

Oxybutynin	Ditropan
	Gelnique
	Oxytrol
		▪ Overactive bladder	▪ **Dosing (Adult):**
			  – Oral ER 5 to 30 mg daily
			  – Oral IR 2.5 to 5 mg q8-12h, maximum 5 mg 4 times daily
			  – Topical gel apply 1 sachet or 1 actuation of pump once daily
			  – Transdermal 3.9 mg/day patch q3-4days
			▪ **Dosing (Peds):**
			  – Oral 0.1 to 0.2 mg/kg/dose q8-12h
			    ▪ Maximum 5 mg/dose
			  – Oral ER 5 mg daily
			▪ **CYP450 Interactions:** Substrate CYP3A4
			▪ **Renal or Hepatic Dose Adjustments:** None
			▪ **Dosage Forms:** Oral (syrup, tablet), Transdermal (gel, patch)

Propantheline	Brand Name (if available)	▪ Peptic ulcer	▪ **Dosing (Adult):**
			  – Oral 15 mg TID and 30 mg QHS
			▪ **Dosing (Peds):**
			  – Oral 1.5 to 3 mg/kg/day divided q4-6h
			    ▪ Maximum 75 mg/day
			▪ **CYP450 Interactions:** None
			▪ **Renal or Hepatic Dose Adjustments:** None
			▪ **Dosage Forms:** Oral (tablet)

Scopolamine	Transderm Scop	▪ Nausea and vomiting from motion sickness	▪ **Dosing (Adult):**
			  – Topical apply 1 patch behind ear at least 4 hours prior to exposure q3days as needed
			▪ **Dosing (Peds):**
			  – Oral apply 0.25 to 1 patch q3-7days as needed
			▪ **CYP450 Interactions:** text
			▪ **Renal or Hepatic Dose Adjustments:** text
			▪ **Dosage Forms:** [e.g., basic info]

Antimuscarinics - Drug Class Review
High-Yield Med Reviews

Generic Name	Brand Name	Indication(s) or Uses	Notes
Solifenacin	Vesicare	▪ Overactive bladder	▪ **Dosing (Adult):** – Oral 5 to 10 mg daily ▪ **Dosing (Peds):** – Not routinely used ▪ **CYP450 Interactions:** Substrate CYP2A4 ▪ **Renal or Hepatic Dose Adjustments:** – Child-Pugh class B - Maximum 5 mg/day – Child-Pugh class C - Not recommended – GFR less than 30 mL/minute - 5 mg/day ▪ **Dosage Forms:** Oral (suspension, tablet)
Tolterodine	Detrol, Detrol LA	▪ Overactive bladder	▪ **Dosing (Adult):** – Oral IR 1 to 2 mg BID – Oral ER 2 to 4 mg daily ▪ **Dosing (Peds):** – Not routinely used ▪ **CYP450 Interactions:** Substrate CYP2C9, 2C19, 2D6, 3A4 ▪ **Renal or Hepatic Dose Adjustments:** – Child-Pugh class B - Maximum 2 mg/day – Child-Pugh class C - Not recommended – GFR 10 to 30 mL/minute - 2 mg/day – GFR less than 10 mL/minute - Not recommended ▪ **Dosage Forms:** Oral (capsule, tablet)
Trospium	Trosec	▪ Overactive bladder	▪ **Dosing (Adult):** – Oral IR 20 mg BID – Oral ER 60 mg daily ▪ **Dosing (Peds):** – Not routinely used ▪ **CYP450 Interactions:** None ▪ **Renal or Hepatic Dose Adjustments:** – GFR less than 30 mL/minute - IR 20 mg daily; ER not recommended – Child-Pugh class B or C - not recommended ▪ **Dosage Forms:** Oral (capsule, tablet)

High-Yield Clinical Knowledge

- **Antimuscarinic (Anticholinergic)**
  - Antimuscarinic adverse events associated with this class include dry mouth, altered mental status, hyperpyrexia, vision disturbances, and flushing.
  - These adverse events are particularly concerning in elderly patients, as antimuscarinic agents increase the risk of falls.
  - Newer generation antimuscarinics that are more specific for M2 and M3 receptors decrease the risk of these adverse events.
- **Contraindications**
  - Antimuscarinic agents are contraindicated in patients with a history of narrow-angle glaucoma, urinary or gastric retention, or ileus.

- **Drug Interactions**
  - Although some antimuscarinic agents may possess pharmacokinetic interactions mediated via CYP 450 inhibition, other pharmacodynamic interactions are important.
    - The combination of tolterodine with potent CYP3A4 inhibitors may significantly increase tolterodine exposure.
  - Additive antimuscarinic effects can be observed when these agents are combined with antipsychotics, antidepressants, antiparkinsonian agents, or over-the-counter antihistamines.
- **BPH**
  - Although not explicitly contraindicated, these agents should be used with caution in patients with benign prostatic hyperplasia due to the risk of acute urinary retention, particularly in patients with poor detrusor contractility.
- **Maximum Benefit**
  - For patients to receive maximal benefit from these agents, the highest tolerable dose should be targeted.
  - Still, the maximal benefit's onset may be up to 8 weeks after initiation or dose titration.
- **Quaternary Ammonium**
  - Quaternary ammonium antimuscarinics do not readily cross the blood-brain barrier and carry a lower risk of CNS-related anticholinergic adverse events (confusion, altered mental status.
    - Trospium, methscopolamine, and propantheline are quaternary ammonium compounds.

HIGH-YIELD BOARD EXAM ESSENTIALS
- **CLASSIC AGENTS:** Darifenacin, fesoterodine, methscopolamine, mirabegron, oxybutynin, propantheline, scopolamine, solifenacin, tolterodine, trospium
- **DRUG CLASS:** Antimuscarinics
- **INDICATIONS:** Overactive bladder (darifenacin, fesoterodine, oxybutynin, scopolamine, solifenacin, tolterodine, trospium), peptic ulcer (methscopolamine, propantheline), nausea and vomiting from motion sickness (scopolamine)
- **MECHANISM:** Competitive antagonists of acetylcholine on muscarinic receptors. Mirabegron specifically is a beta-3 adrenergic receptor activator, relaxing detrusor muscle during the urinary bladder-fill-void cycle.
- **SIDE EFFECTS:** Dry mouth, altered mental status, hyperpyrexia, vision disturbances, and flushing.
- **CLINICAL PEARLS:** Antimuscarinic agents are contraindicated in patients with a history of narrow-angle glaucoma, urinary or gastric retention, or ileus.

High-Yield Basic Pharmacology

- **Mechanism of Action**
  - Inhibit the phosphodiesterase-5 inhibitor which is responsible for degrading cGMP
    - cGMP allows for smooth muscle relaxation and penile blood-filling

Primary Net Benefit

- Achievement and maintenance of an erection
  - Note: does not affect libido, a male must have adequate libido/sexual desire

PDE5 - Inhibitors Drug Class Review			
High-Yield Med Reviews			
Mechanism of Action: inhibition of PDE5 enzyme results in smooth muscle relaxation and subsequently increased blood flow into the penis			
Class effects: alpha blockers should be used cautiously, nitrates are contraindicated within 24 hours of taking avanafil, sildenafil and vardenafil and within 48 hours of taking tadalafil			
Generic Name	**Brand Name**	**Indication(s) or Uses**	**Notes**
Avanafil	Stendra	• Erectile dysfunction	• **Dosing (Adult):** 50 to 200 mg • **Renal or Hepatic Dose Adjustments:** – Severe hepatic impairment: avoid use
Sildenafil	Viagra	• Erectile dysfunction • Pulmonary arterial hypertension	• **Dosing (Adult):** 50 to 100 mg • **Renal or Hepatic Dose Adjustments:** – Severe hepatic impairment: starting dose 25 mg

Tadalafil	Cialis	• Erectile dysfunction
		• Pulmonary arterial hypertension
		• Benign prostatic hyperplasia
			• **Dosing:**
			  – As needed: 5 to 20 mg
			  – Daily: 2.5mg
			• **Renal or Hepatic Dose Adjustments:**
			  – Severe hepatic impairment: avoid use
			  – CrCl 30-50 mL/min: max dose 5mg
			  – CrCl <30 mL/min: avoid use

Vardenafil	Levitra
	Staxyn
		• Erectile dysfunction	• **Dosing:**
			  – Oral tablet (Levitra®): 5 to 20 mg
			  – Oral disintegrating tablet (Staxyn®): 10mg
			• **Renal or Hepatic Dose Adjustments:**
			  – Severe hepatic impairment: avoid use

High-Yield Clinical Knowledge

- **Efficacy**
  - Up to 40% of patients prescribed a PDE5-i report it to be ineffective
    - Strategies to mitigate perceived and real ineffectiveness of PDE5-i
      - Counsel on timing and interactions that may delay onset
      - Educate on need for sexual stimulation
      - Use at least five times before deemed failed intervention
      - Increase dosage
      - Trial another medication in same class
- **Ethanol Use**
  - Caution against alcohol use

- Efficacy: contributes to erectile dysfunction
- Safety: increases risk of orthostasis
- **Vasodilators**
  - Strong caution/contraindication in combination with other vasodilators
    - Increased risk of orthostasis

High-Yield Fast-Facts

- Prior to the 1980s, erectile dysfunction was considered by most clinicians to be of mental etiology. Dr. Giles Brindley, a British physiologist, shocked the audience at the 1983 American Urological Association Meeting when he revealed his full erection while speaking. Dr. Brindley had injected a vasodilator into his penis prior to taking the stage as a showcase that erectile dysfunction was not solely a psychiatric diagnosis.
- PDE5-i were discovered accidentally. In a clinical trial investigating sildenafil for angina and hypertension, the adverse effect of erections was identified. Subsequently, Pfizer decided to study the medication for erectile dysfunction. Sildenafil gained FDA approval as the first oral therapy to treat the disease in 1998.

HIGH-YIELD BOARD EXAM ESSENTIALS

- **CLASSIC AGENTS:** Avanafil, sildenafil, tadalafil, vardenafil
- **DRUG CLASS:** Phosphodiesterase-5 inhibitors
- **INDICATIONS:** Erectile dysfunction (avanafil, sildenafil, tadalafil, vardenafil), pulmonary arterial hypertension (sildenafil, tadalafil), benign prostatic hyperplasia (tadalafil)
- **MECHANISM:** Inhibit the phosphodiesterase-5 inhibitor which is responsible for degrading cGMP
- **SIDE EFFECTS:** Hypotension (in combination with nitrates/vasodilators)
- **CLINICAL PEARLS:**
  - The agents in this class are subject to drug interactions when used with other medications that inhibit CYP3A4.
  - Avoid co-administration with nitrates within 24 hrs of each other due to risk of hypotension.
  - High fat meals delay onset of sildenafil and vardenafil, alcohol increases risk of orthostasis and can contribute to erectile dysfunction.

High-Yield Basic Pharmacology

- **Mechanism of Action**
  - Synthetic erythropoietin interacts with red cell progenitor erythropoietin receptors to stimulate erythroid proliferation and differentiation.
- **Endogenous Erythropoietin**
  - Most of the body's erythropoietin is usually produced in the kidney and is stimulated in response to tissue hypoxia through an increased rate of erythropoietin gene transcription.
  - In chronic kidney disease, endogenous erythropoietin levels are suppressed as the erythropoietin growth factor production is limited.

Primary Net Benefit

- ESAs stimulate red blood cell production, and in combination with appropriate iron intake, are effective for a wide range of anemias but must be balanced with the risk of thromboembolic events and hypertension.

<table>
<tr><td colspan="4" align="center">Erythropoiesis Stimulating Agents - Drug Class Review
High-Yield Med Reviews</td></tr>
<tr><td colspan="4">Mechanism of Action: Synthetic erythropoietin interacts with red cell progenitor erythropoietin receptors to stimulate erythroid proliferation and differentiation.</td></tr>
<tr><td colspan="4">Class Effects: Increases in RBC concentrations, plasma volume, blood pressure.</td></tr>
<tr><td>Generic Name</td><td>Brand Name</td><td>Indication(s) or Uses</td><td>Notes</td></tr>
<tr>
<td>Darbepoetin alfa</td>
<td>Aranesp</td>
<td>• Anemia (chemotherapy, chronic kidney disease, zidovudine)</td>
<td>• Dosing (Adult):
  – IV/SQ 0.45 to 0.75 mcg/kg q1-4weeks, adjusted to hemoglobin
• Dosing (Peds):
  – IV/SQ 0.45 to 0.75 mcg/kg q1-4weeks, adjusted to hemoglobin
• CYP450 Interactions: None
• Renal or Hepatic Dose Adjustments: None
• Dosage Forms: Injection solution</td>
</tr>
<tr>
<td>Epoetin alfa</td>
<td>Epogen, Procrit, Retacrit</td>
<td>• Anemia (chemotherapy, chronic kidney disease, zidovudine)
• Reduction of allogeneic RBC transfusion</td>
<td>• Dosing (Adult):
  – IV/SQ 50 to 100 mcg/kg three times weekly or q1-2weeks adjusted to hemoglobin
• Dosing (Peds):
  – IV/SQ 50 to 100 mcg/kg three times weekly or q1-2weeks adjusted to hemoglobin
• CYP450 Interactions: None
• Renal or Hepatic Dose Adjustments: None
• Dosage Forms: Injection solution</td>
</tr>
<tr>
<td>Methoxy polyethylene glycol-epoetin beta</td>
<td>Mircera</td>
<td>• Anemia</td>
<td>• Dosing (Adult):
  – IV 0.6 mcg/kg q2weeks, adjusted to hemoglobin
• Dosing (Peds):
  – IV 0.6 mcg/kg q2weeks, adjusted to hemoglobin
• CYP450 Interactions: None
• Renal or Hepatic Dose Adjustments: None
• Dosage Forms: Injection solution</td>
</tr>
</table>

High-Yield Clinical Knowledge

- **Thrombosis Risk**
  - The risk of cardiovascular, stroke, thromboembolic events, and mortality are all increased with the use of ESAs when hemoglobin levels are above 11 g/dL.
  - Rapid increases in hemoglobin, faster than 0.5 g/dL per week, may also contribute to this risk.
    - Hemoglobin levels among patients with chronic kidney disease receiving ESAs should not increase above 11 g/dL.
  - However, in cancer patients, ESAs are associated with an increased rate of all-cause mortality and venous thromboembolism.
    - ESAs should be used in cancer patients to avoid transfusion when hemoglobin levels are below 10 g/dL.
    - In cancers where therapeutic interventions are considered to be curative, ESAs are not recommended.
- **Hypertension**
  - Increases in blood pressure among patients receiving ESAs are expected and correlate with rapid increases in hematocrit.
  - ESAs should be avoided in patients with uncontrolled hypertension but can be used in patients receiving antihypertensive drug therapy.
- **Iron Intake**
  - Iron is a crucial component of heme and essential during erythropoietin therapy among patients with serum ferritin levels less than 100 mcg/L or transferrin saturation is below 20%.
  - Iron supplementation can be accomplished using oral iron dosage forms targeting 200 mg elemental iron per day or parenteral iron supplementation.
- **ESA in Oncology**
  - ESAs are less commonly used in oncologic applications and reserved for select patients where conservation of blood transfusions are desired.
  - However, methoxy polyethylene glycol-epoetin beta must be avoided in this patient population due to an association with increased mortality in cancer patients.
- **Hypoxia-Inducible Factor (HIF)**
  - HIF is a DNA-regulating factor that becomes activated in hypoxic conditions, resulting in erythropoiesis.
  - HIF is regulated and inactivated by prolyl hydroxylases (PHD) at normal oxygen levels, which has become a new drug therapy target and the action of the oral agent roxadustat.
- **ESAs Vs. Roxadustat**
  - In phase 3 studies (below), roxadustat achieved similar increases in hemoglobin than epoetin alfa in CKD patients on dialysis but is associated with a roughly 30% lower risk of major adverse cardiac events.

HIGH-YIELD BOARD EXAM ESSENTIALS

- **CLASSIC AGENTS:** Darbepoetin alfa, epoetin alfa, methoxy polyethylene glycol-epoetin beta
- **DRUG CLASS:** Erythropoiesis stimulating agents
- **INDICATIONS:** Anemia, reduction of allogeneic RBC transfusion
- **MECHANISM:** Synthetic erythropoietin interacts with red cell progenitor erythropoietin receptors to stimulate erythroid proliferation and differentiation.
- **SIDE EFFECTS:** Thrombosis, hypertension
- **CLINICAL PEARLS:** The risk of cardiovascular, stroke, thromboembolic events, and mortality are all increased with the use of ESAs when hemoglobin levels are above 11 g/dL. Rapid increases in hemoglobin, faster than 0.5 g/dL per week, may also contribute to this risk.

High-Yield Basic Pharmacology

- **G-CSF (Filgrastim/tbo-filgrastim, pegfilgrastim)**
  - Stimulates the proliferation, differentiation, and function of neutrophils.
- **GM-CSF (sargramostim)**
  - Stimulates the proliferation, differentiation, and function of numerous myeloid cells, including basophils, eosinophils, granulocytes, and monocytes.

Primary Net Benefit

- Reduces neutropenic nadirs and shortens the duration of neutropenia caused by myelosuppressive chemotherapy.

Granulocyte Colony Stimulating Factor - Drug Class Review			
High-Yield Med Reviews			
Mechanism of Action: *G-CSF - Stimulates the proliferation, differentiation, and function of neutrophils.* *GM-CSF - Stimulates the proliferation, differentiation, and function of numerous myeloid cells, including basophils, eosinophils, granulocytes, and monocytes.*			
Class Effects: increases in cell count seen in CBC; mobilization of stem cells into vascular.			
Generic Name	**Brand Name**	**Indication(s) or Uses**	**Notes**

Filgrastim; TBO-filgrastim	Granix, Neupogen, Nivestym, Zarxio	- Acute myeloid leukemia
		 - Chemotherapy-induced myelosuppression
		 - Bone marrow transplant
		 - Hematopoietic radiation injury syndrome
		 - Peripheral blood progenitor cell collection and therapy
		 - Severe chronic neutropenia
			- **Dosing (Adult):**
			   – IV/SQ 5 to 10 mcg/kg/day
			   – SQ 75 to 300 mcg three times weekly
			 - **Dosing (Peds):**
			   – IV/SQ 5 to 10 mcg/kg/day
			   – SQ 1 to 20 mcg/kg/day mcg three times weekly
			 - **CYP450 Interactions:** None
			 - **Renal or Hepatic Dose Adjustments:** None
			 - **Dosage Forms:** Injection solution, Subcutaneous solution

Sargramostim	Leukine	- Acute myeloid leukemia
		 - Chemotherapy-induced myelosuppression
		 - Bone marrow transplant
		 - Hematopoietic radiation injury syndrome
		 - Peripheral blood progenitor cell collection, therapy, and transplantation
			- **Dosing (Adult):**
			   – IV/SQ 250 mcg/m2/day
			     ▪ IV over 2 hours
			     ▪ SQ immediately following infusion of progenitor cells
			 - **Dosing (Peds):**
			   – IV/SQ 250 mcg/m2/day
			     ▪ IV over 2 hours
			     ▪ SQ immediately following infusion of progenitor cells
			 - **CYP450 Interactions:** None
			 - **Renal or Hepatic Dose Adjustments:** None
			 - **Dosage Forms:** Injection solution

Granulocyte Colony Stimulating Factor - Drug Class Review
High-Yield Med Reviews

Generic Name	Brand Name	Indication(s) or Uses	Notes

Pegfilgrastim	Fulphila, Neulasta, Udenyca, Ziextenzo	• Acute myeloid leukemia
		• Chemotherapy-induced myelosuppression
		• Bone marrow transplant
		• Hematopoietic radiation injury syndrome
		• Peripheral blood progenitor cell collection and therapy
		• Severe chronic neutropenia
			• **Dosing (Adult):**
			  – SQ 6 mg once per chemotherapy cycle
			• **Dosing (Peds):**
			  – SQ 0.1 mg/kg or 1.5 to 6 mg once per chemotherapy cycle
			• **CYP450 Interactions:** None
			• **Renal or Hepatic Dose Adjustments:** None
			• **Dosage Forms:** Injection solution, Subcutaneous solution

High-Yield Clinical Knowledge

- **Adverse Events**
    - G-CSF/GM-CSF agents are commonly associated with bone pain, flu-like symptoms, rash, diarrhea, dyspnea, supraventricular arrhythmias, and elevations in serum creatinine, bilirubin, and hepatic enzymes.
- **Sargramostim Fever**
    - GM-CSF (sargramostim) is more often associated with acute fever, limiting its use in preventing febrile neutropenia.
    - Acute first dose reactions to sargramostim may also occur, consisting of flushing, hypotension, dyspnea, nausea, and vomiting.
        - Oxygen saturation may also decrease acutely as a result of pulmonary sequestration of granulocytes.
- **Acute Myeloid Leukemia**
    - G-CSF agents were historically avoided in acute myeloid leukemia (AML), as leukemic cells arose from progenitors that were regulated, in part, by G-CSF and GM-CSF.
    - New evidence suggests these agents are safe following induction and consolidation treatment of AML and acute lymphoblastic leukemia and lead to FDA approvals for these indications.
- **Neutropenia**
    - Absolute neutrophil counts (ANC) of less than 500 cells/mL is associated with significant morbidity and mortality among patients receiving myelosuppressive chemotherapy.
    - The ANC is calculated using the formula = (segmented neutrophils + banded neutrophils)/WBC.
    - G-CSF/GM-CSF agents reduce the incidence, magnitude, and duration of neutropenia and are recommended if the risk of febrile neutropenia of a given chemotherapy regimen is at least 20%.
    - However, these interventions do not impact mortality among cancer patients.
- **Stem Cell Transplant Adjunct**
    - Due to the benefit of G-CSF or GM-CSF-induced mobilization of peripheral hematopoietic stem cells from the marrow to the peripheral blood, these agents have become a common method to enhance donor stem cell products.
- **Alternative Indications**
    - G-CSF/GM-CSF agents may also play a role in neutropenia in patients with congenital neutropenia, cyclic neutropenia, myelodysplasia, and aplastic anemia.

HIGH-YIELD BOARD EXAM ESSENTIALS

- **CLASSIC AGENTS:** Filgrastim and Tbo-filgrastim, sargramostim, pegfilgrastim
- **DRUG CLASS:** Granulocyte colony stimulating factor
- **INDICATIONS:** AML, chemotherapy-induced myelosuppression, bone marrow transplant, hematopoietic radiation injury syndrome, peripheral blood progenitor cell collection and therapy, severe chronic neutropenia
- **MECHANISM:** G-CSF (Filgrastim/tbo-filgrastim, pegfilgrastim) stimulates the proliferation, differentiation, and function of neutrophils. GM-CSF (sargramostim) stimulates the proliferation, differentiation, and function of numerous myeloid cells, including basophils, eosinophils, granulocytes, and monocytes.
- **SIDE EFFECTS:** Bone pain, flu-like symptoms, rash, diarrhea, dyspnea, supraventricular arrhythmias, and elevations in serum creatinine, bilirubin, and hepatic enzymes.
- **CLINICAL PEARLS:**
  - ANC of less than 500 cells/mL is associated with significant morbidity and mortality among patients receiving myelosuppressive chemotherapy.
  - G-CSF/GM-CSF agents reduce the incidence, magnitude, and duration of neutropenia and are recommended if the risk of febrile neutropenia of a given chemotherapy regimen is at least 20%.

High-Yield Basic Pharmacology

- **Thrombopoietin Receptor Agonists (avatrombopag, eltrombopag, lusutrombopag)**
  - Thrombopoietin receptor agonists increased platelet production through the stimulation of proliferation and differentiation of megakaryocytes from bone marrow progenitor cells.
- **Thrombopoietin (TPO) Mimic (romiplostim)**
  - Binds with high affinity to the thrombopoietin receptor and mimicking the thrombopoietic effect of TPO
  - Romiplostim is administered via subcutaneous injection and is a very small volume for the typical dose.
  - The administration must be accomplished using a syringe with 0.01 mL graduations.

Primary Net Benefit

- Novel agents for the management of thrombocytopenia that may reduce the need for platelet transfusions.

Megakaryocyte Growth Factor - Drug Class Review			
High-Yield Med Reviews			
Mechanism of Action: *Avatrombopag, eltrombopag, lusutrombopag - Thrombopoietin receptor agonists increased platelet production by stimulating proliferation and differentiation of megakaryocytes bone marrow progenitor cells.* *Romiplostim - Binds with high affinity to the thrombopoietin receptor and mimicking the thrombopoietic effect of TPO.*			
Class Effects: Increase in platelet count.			
Generic Name	**Brand Name**	**Indication(s) or Uses**	**Notes**

Avatrombopag	Doptelet	• Chronic immune thrombocytopenia
		• Chronic liver disease-associated thrombocytopenia
			• **Dosing (Adult):**
			  – Oral 20 mg daily adjusted to "dose-level 1 to 6"
			• **Dosing (Peds):**
			  – Not routinely used
			• **CYP450 Interactions:** Substrate CYP2C9, 3A4, P-gp
			• **Renal or Hepatic Dose Adjustments:** None
			• **Dosage Forms:** Oral (tablet)

Eltrombopag	Promacta	• Aplastic anemia
		• Chronic hepatitis C infection-associated thrombocytopenia
		• Immune thrombocytopenia
			• **Dosing (Adult):**
			  – Oral 25 to 100 mg daily
			• **Dosing (Peds):**
			  – Oral 2.5 mg/kg/dose
			    • Maximum 37.5 mg/dose
			• **CYP450 Interactions:** Substrate CYP1A2, 2C8
			• **Renal or Hepatic Dose Adjustments:**
			  – Child-Pugh class A, B, or C - 12.5 mg daily
			• **Dosage Forms:** Oral (packet, tablet)

Lusutrombopag	Mulpleta	• Chronic liver disease-associated thrombocytopenia	• **Dosing (Adult):**
			  – Oral 3 mg daily for 7 days
			• **Dosing (Peds):**
			  – Not routinely used
			• **CYP450 Interactions:** None
			• **Renal or Hepatic Dose Adjustments:** None
			• **Dosage Forms:** Oral (tablet)

Megakaryocyte Growth Factor - Drug Class Review
High-Yield Med Reviews

Generic Name	Brand Name	Indication(s) or Uses	Notes

Romiplostim	Nplate	▪ Hematopoietic syndrome of acute radiation syndrome
		▪ Immune thrombocytopenia
			▪ **Dosing (Adult):**
			  – SQ 10 mcg/kg once
			  – SQ 1 to 10 mcg/kg q1week
			▪ **Dosing (Peds):**
			  – SQ 10 mcg/kg once
			  – SQ 1 to 10 mcg/kg q1week
			▪ **CYP450 Interactions:** None
			▪ **Renal or Hepatic Dose Adjustments:** None
			▪ **Dosage Forms:** Injection solution

High-Yield Clinical Knowledge

- **Thromboembolic Complications**
  - Avatrombopag, eltrombopag, lusutrombopag, and romiplostim have been associated with thromboembolic complications.
  - Among patients receiving these agents with concomitant chronic liver disease, portal vein thrombosis may be prevalent.
- **Myelodysplastic Syndromes**
  - With romiplostim, there is a risk of progression from an existing myelodysplastic syndrome to acute myeloid leukemia.
- **Hepatic Decompensation**
  - Eltrombopag is associated with an increased risk of severe, life-threatening hepatotoxicity.
  - There is an increased risk of hepatic decompensation in patients with chronic hepatitis C receiving eltrombopag with concomitant interferon and ribavirin.
    - The current recommendations are to discontinue eltrombopag should hepatic decompensation occur.

HIGH-YIELD BOARD EXAM ESSENTIALS
- **CLASSIC AGENTS:** Avatrombopag, eltrombopag, lusutrombopag, romiplostim
- **DRUG CLASS:** Megakaryocyte growth factor
- **INDICATIONS:** Aplastic anemia (eltrombopag), chronic hepatitis C infection-associated thrombocytopenia (eltrombopag), chronic liver disease-associated thrombocytopenia (avatrombopag, lusutrombopag), hematopoietic syndrome of acute radiation syndrome (romiplostim), immune thrombocytopenia (eltrombopag, romiplostim)
- **MECHANISM:** Thrombopoietin receptor agonists increased platelet production through the stimulation of proliferation and differentiation of megakaryocytes from bone marrow progenitor cells (avatrombopag, eltrombopag, lusutrombopag). Binds with high affinity to the thrombopoietin receptor and mimicking the thrombopoietic effect of TPO (romiplostim)
- **SIDE EFFECTS:** Thrombosis, progression of myelodysplastic syndrome
- **CLINICAL PEARLS:** Among patients receiving these agents with concomitant chronic liver disease, portal vein thrombosis may be prevalent.

High-Yield Basic Pharmacology

- **Mechanism of Action**
  - Replace physiologic iron stores which promote appropriate erythropoiesis and erythrocyte maturation.
- **Iron Content**
  - Elemental iron content varies between the different iron salts.
  - Among the available oral iron preparations, the polysaccharide-iron complex contains 46% elemental iron, the highest elemental iron content, and ferrous gluconate contains the least at 12%.
  - Parenteral iron salts contain considerably lower elemental iron with iron dextran and iron sucrose containing 5%, and 2%, respectively.

Primary Net Benefit

- Iron deficiency anemia is the most common cause of chronic anemia but can be treated with available oral or parenteral iron products.

		Iron - Drug Class Review	
		High-Yield Med Reviews	
Mechanism of Action: *Replace physiologic iron stores which promote appropriate erythropoiesis and erythrocyte maturation.*			
Class Effects: Increases in RBC production (delayed effect), when taken orally (GI upset, dark stools, drug interactions.)			
Generic Name	**Brand Name**	**Indication(s) or Uses**	**Notes**

Ferric carboxymaltose	Injectafer	• Iron-deficiency anemia	• **Dosing (Adult):**
			  – IV 15 mg/kg for two doses separated by 7 days
			    • Maximum 750 mg/dose
			  – IV 1,000 mg, followed by 500 mg 7 days later
			• **Dosing (Peds):**
			  – Not routinely used
			• **CYP450 Interactions:** None
			• **Renal or Hepatic Dose Adjustments:** None
			• **Dosage Forms:** Intravenous (solution)

Ferric citrate	Auryxia	• Hyperphosphatemia
		• Iron-deficiency anemia
			• **Dosing (Adult):**
			  – Oral 1 to 12 tablets TID
			• **Dosing (Peds):**
			  – Not routinely used
			• **CYP450 Interactions:** None
			• **Renal or Hepatic Dose Adjustments:** None
			• **Dosage Forms:** Oral tablet

Ferric derisomaltose	Monoferric	• Iron-deficiency anemia	• **Dosing (Adult):**
			  – IV 20 mg/kg once
			  – IV 1,000 mg
			• **Dosing (Peds):**
			  – Not routinely used
			• **CYP450 Interactions:** None
			• **Renal or Hepatic Dose Adjustments:** None
			• **Dosage Forms:** Intravenous (solution)

Iron - Drug Class Review
High-Yield Med Reviews

Generic Name	Brand Name	Indication(s) or Uses	Notes

Ferric gluconate	Ferrlecit	▪ Iron-deficiency anemia	▪ **Dosing (Adult):**
			  – IV 125 to 250 mg per dialysis session
			▪ **Dosing (Peds):**
			  – IV 1.5 mg/kg/dose per dialysis sessions for 8 sequential sessions
			    ▪ Maximum 125 mg/dose
			▪ **CYP450 Interactions:** None
			▪ **Renal or Hepatic Dose Adjustments:** None
			▪ **Dosage Forms:** Intravenous (solution)

Ferric maltol	Accrufer	▪ Iron-deficiency anemia	▪ **Dosing (Adult):**
			  – Oral 30 mg BID
			▪ **Dosing (Peds):**
			  – Not routinely used
			▪ **CYP450 Interactions:** None
			▪ **Renal or Hepatic Dose Adjustments:** None
			▪ **Dosage Forms:** Oral

Ferric pyrophosphate citrate	Triferic	▪ Iron-deficiency anemia	▪ **Dosing (Adult):**
			  – Intradialytic admixture into bicarbonate concentrate dialysate for use at each dialysis session
			▪ **Dosing (Peds):**
			  – Not routinely used
			▪ **CYP450 Interactions:** None
			▪ **Renal or Hepatic Dose Adjustments:** None
			▪ **Dosage Forms:** Solution for dialysate

Ferrous fumarate	Ferretts, Ferrimin, Hemocyte	▪ Iron-deficiency anemia	▪ **Dosing (Adult):**
			  – Oral 30 to 200 mg elemental iron/day in three divided doses
			▪ **Dosing (Peds):**
			  – Oral 3 to 6 mg/kg/day in 3 divided doses
			    ▪ Maximum 200 mg/day
			▪ **CYP450 Interactions:** None
			▪ **Renal or Hepatic Dose Adjustments:** None
			▪ **Dosage Forms:** Oral (tablet)

Ferrous gluconate	Ferate	▪ Iron-deficiency anemia	▪ **Dosing (Adult):**
			  – Oral 65 to 200 mg elemental iron/day in three divided doses
			▪ **Dosing (Peds):**
			  – Oral 3 to 6 mg/kg/day in 3 divided doses
			    ▪ Maximum 200 mg/day
			▪ **CYP450 Interactions:** None
			▪ **Renal or Hepatic Dose Adjustments:** None
			▪ **Dosage Forms:** Oral (tablet)

Iron - Drug Class Review
High-Yield Med Reviews

Generic Name	Brand Name	Indication(s) or Uses	Notes

Ferrous sulfate	Fe-Vite, Fer-In-Sol, Fer-Iron, FeroSul, Slow Fe, Slow Iron	• Iron-deficiency anemia	• **Dosing (Adult):**
			  – Oral 65 to 200 mg elemental iron/day in three divided doses
			• **Dosing (Peds):**
			  – Oral 3 to 6 mg/kg/day in 3 divided doses
			    • Maximum 200 mg/day
			• **CYP450 Interactions:** None
			• **Renal or Hepatic Dose Adjustments:** None
			• **Dosage Forms:** Oral (elixir, liquid, solution, syrup, tablet)

Ferumoxytol	Feraheme	• Iron-deficiency anemia	• **Dosing (Adult):**
			  – IV 510 mg over 15 minutes, repeated after 3-8 days later
			  – IV 1,020 mg over 30 minutes once
			• **Dosing (Peds):**
			  – Not routinely used
			• **CYP450 Interactions:** None
			• **Renal or Hepatic Dose Adjustments:** None
			• **Dosage Forms:** Intravenous (solution)

Iron dextran	Infed	• Iron-deficiency anemia	• **Dosing (Adult):**
			  – IV 25 mg test dose followed by 75 mg q1week for 2 weeks, then 100 mg per week
			  – IM/IV Dose (in mL) = 0.0442 (desired hemoglobin - observed hemoglobin) x Lean body weight in kg + (0.26 x LBW)
			• **Dosing (Peds):**
			  – IM/IV Dose (in mL) = 0.0442 (desired hemoglobin - observed hemoglobin) x Lean body weight in kg + (0.26 x LBW)
			• **CYP450 Interactions:** None
			• **Renal or Hepatic Dose Adjustments:** None
			• **Dosage Forms:** Intravenous (solution)

Iron sucrose	Venofer	• Iron-deficiency anemia	• **Dosing (Adult):**
			  – IV 100 to 300 mg/dose during dialysis to a total cumulative dose of 1,000 mg
			  – IV 200 mg once every 3 weeks for 5 doses
			• **Dosing (Peds):**
			  – IV 0.5 mg/kg/dose every 2-4 weeks for 12 weeks
			    • Maximum 100 mg/dose
			  – IV 5 to 7 mg/kg/dose q1-7days
			    • Maximum 300 mg/dose
			• **CYP450 Interactions:** None
			• **Renal or Hepatic Dose Adjustments:** None
			• **Dosage Forms:** Intravenous (solution)

Iron - Drug Class Review			
High-Yield Med Reviews			
Generic Name	**Brand Name**	**Indication(s) or Uses**	**Notes**

Polysaccharide iron complex	EZFE, Ferrex, IFerex, Myferon, NovaFerrum, Nu-Iron, Poly-Iron	▪ Iron-deficiency anemia	▪ **Dosing (Adult):**
			  – Oral 65 to 200 mg elemental iron/day in three divided doses
			▪ **Dosing (Peds):**
			  – Oral 3 to 6 mg/kg/day in 3 divided doses
			    ▪ Maximum 200 mg/day
			▪ **CYP450 Interactions:** None
			▪ **Renal or Hepatic Dose Adjustments:** None
			▪ **Dosage Forms:** Oral (capsule, liquid)

High-Yield Clinical Knowledge

- **Iron Deficiency Anemia**
  - Severe iron deficiency anemia manifests as microcytic, hypochromic anemia, affecting the oxygen-carrying capacity of hemoglobin, myoglobin synthesis, heme enzyme synthesis, and function, as well as other enzymatic processes, including xanthine oxidase.
- **Oral Vs. Parenteral Iron**
  - Oral iron supplementation is preferred, with a target dose of 200 mg of elemental iron daily, which should be taken on an empty stomach (if tolerated).
  - For patients who cannot tolerate oral iron, are non-compliant or have identified oral iron malabsorption, parenteral iron therapy should be used.
- **Test Doses**
  - Before administering the first dose of iron dextran, a test dose is required as the risk of hypersensitivity and anaphylaxis is high, specifically with this dosage form.
  - While other iron products suggest test doses, they are not required before administration.
- **IV Complications**
  - Common adverse events associated with parenteral iron products include arthralgias, hypotension, flushing, pruritus, and arrhythmias.
- **Iron Chelation**
  - If serum iron concentrations are above 500 mcg/dL, patients are at high risk of hemodynamic collapse and shock.
  - This toxic iron level is an indication for iron chelation therapy with deferoxamine.
    - Other indications for deferoxamine in iron toxicity include:
      - Repetitive vomiting, toxic appearance, lethargy, hypotension with metabolic acidosis, shock.
  - For each 100 mg of deferoxamine will bind 8.5 mg of ferric ion.
- **Chelation of Other Medications**
  - Oral iron therapy will bind to numerous medications, including fluoroquinolones, tetracyclines, and phenytoin.
  - Proton pump inhibitors cause a decreased absorption of oral iron products by increasing the duodenum's pH, causing oxidation of ferrous iron to ferric iron, which is not readily absorbed.

HIGH-YIELD BOARD EXAM ESSENTIALS

- **CLASSIC AGENTS:** Ferric carboxymaltose, ferric citrate, ferric derisomaltose, ferric gluconate, ferric maltol, ferric pyrophosphate citrate, ferrous fumarate, ferrous gluconate, ferrous sulfate, ferumoxytol, iron dextran, iron sucrose, polysaccharide-iron complex
- **DRUG CLASS:** Iron
- **INDICATIONS:** Iron-deficiency anemia
- **MECHANISM:** Replace physiologic iron stores which promote appropriate erythropoiesis and erythrocyte maturation.
- **SIDE EFFECTS:** Constipation, infusion reactions (IV only), chelation
- **CLINICAL PEARLS:** Severe iron deficiency anemia manifests as microcytic, hypochromic anemia, affecting the oxygen-carrying capacity of hemoglobin, myoglobin synthesis, heme enzyme synthesis, and function, as well as other enzymatic processes, including xanthine oxidase.

High-Yield Basic Pharmacology

- **Mechanism of Action**
  - The pharmacologic effects of aminocaproic acid and TXA are similar to the plasmin activator inhibitor-1 (PAI-1) (which inhibits tissue plasminogen activator), PAI-2 (which inhibits urokinase plasminogen activator), and thrombin activatable fibrinolysis inhibitor (TAFI).
  - Alpha-2-antiplasmin has a similar role, however, it prevents the activation of prothrombin to thrombin by inhibiting plasmin.

Primary Net Benefit

- Analogs of lysine analogs occupy lysing binding sites in plasminogen, thus interfering with the fibrinolysis process and promoting hemostasis.

<table>
<tr><td colspan="4">Antifibrinolytics - Drug Class Review
High-Yield Med Reviews</td></tr>
<tr><td colspan="4">Mechanism of Action: Analogs of lysine analogs occupy lysing binding sites in plasminogen, thus interfering with the fibrinolysis process.</td></tr>
<tr><td colspan="4">Class Effects: Hemostasis, hemorrhage control.</td></tr>
<tr><td>Generic Name</td><td>Brand Name</td><td>Indication(s) or Uses</td><td>Notes</td></tr>
<tr>
<td>Epsilon-aminocaproic acid</td>
<td>Amicar</td>
<td>

- Acute hemorrhage from surgery
- Postpartum hemorrhage

</td>
<td>

- **Dosing (Adult):**
  - Loading dose oral or IV, 4 to 5 g
    - IV infusion 1 g IV per hour
  - Oral 1.25 g q1h for 8 hours or until bleeding controlled
    - Maximum daily dose of 30 g
- **Dosing (Peds):**
  - Loading dose (oral or IV) 50-100 mg/kg/dose every 6 hours
    - Maximum daily dose 24 g/day
- **CYP450 Interactions:** None
- **Renal or Hepatic Dose Adjustments:**
  - Cardiac surgery in anephric patients, reduce infusion to 5 mg/kg/hour
- **Dosage Forms:** IV solution, oral (tablet)

</td>
</tr>
<tr>
<td>Tranexamic acid</td>
<td>Cyklokapron
Lysteda</td>
<td>

- Acute hemorrhage from surgery
- Acute trauma
- Postpartum hemorrhage
- Menstrual bleeding, heavy
- Tooth extraction

</td>
<td>

- **Dosing (Adult):**
  - Loading dose oral or IV, 4 to 5 g
    - IV infusion 1 g IV per hour
  - Oral 1.25 g q1h for 8 hours or until bleeding controlled
    - Maximum daily dose of 30 g
- **Dosing (Peds):**
  - Loading dose (oral or IV) 50-100 mg/kg/dose every 6 hours
    - Maximum daily dose 24 g/day
- **CYP450 Interactions:** None
- **Renal or Hepatic Dose Adjustments:**
  - Cardiac surgery in anephric patients, reduce infusion to 5 mg/kg/hour
- **Dosage Forms:** IV solution, oral (tablet)

</td>
</tr>
</table>

- **Stabilization of Fibrin**
  - The antifibrinolytics promote the stabilization of fibrin already existing in clots, not a true procoagulant effect.
    - This occurs from the preservation of the lysine residues on fibrin and can promote clot maturity via the actions of factor XIIIa and TAFI.
      - After fibrin polymerizes to form protofibrils and is subsequently stabilized by XIIIa, these fibrin protofibrils create a mesh linking platelets via the GPIIb/IIIa receptor (which was mobilized to the surface via P2Y12 receptor activation).
      - TAFI, activated by the thrombin-thrombomodulin complex removes the C-terminal lysine residues from fibrin, thus slowing the rate of fibrin degradation and ultimately yielding fibrin resistant to lysis.
- **Adult Women with Heavy Menstrual Bleeding**
  - The specific branded product of TXA, Lysteda, is approved for use in adult women with heavy menstrual bleeding. It should be reserved for patients who decline or should not use hormonal therapy. The specific branded product allows for the evidence-supported dosing of 1.3 g three times daily for up to 5 days during monthly menstruation (see evidence summary below).
- **TXA For Angioedema**
  - TXA may play a role in the management of angioedema, either from a RAAS agent (ACE-inhibitor, ARB, DRI) or hereditary angioedema.
    - TXA can prevent the consumption of C1-esterase and reduce the activation of the complement pathway by limiting the production of plasmin.
      - C1-esterase inhibition acts to limit the production of kallikrein, bradykinin, and thus the generation of angioedema.
- **Dose-dependent Risk of Seizures**
  - Aminocaproic acid and TXA have been associated with generalized tonic-clonic seizures in up to 7.6% of patients.
    - This data is based on the historical application of these agents in cardiac surgery where doses greater than 50 mg/kg (ie, 4000 mg in an 80 kg patient).
      - In the CRASH-2 trial, CRASH-3, and the WOMAN trial, there was no increase in the risk of seizures in patients receiving TXA compared to those who received a placebo.

HIGH-YIELD BOARD EXAM ESSENTIALS

- **CLASSIC AGENTS:** Epsilon-aminocaproic acid (aminocaproic acid), tranexamic acid (TXA)
- **DRUG CLASS:** Antifibrinolytics
- **INDICATIONS:** Adjunct to cardiac surgery, acute major hemorrhage, acute trauma, postpartum hemorrhage, menstrual bleeding, tooth extraction in patients with hemostatic defects.
- **MECHANISM:** Analogs of lysine analogs occupy lysing binding sites in plasminogen, thus interfering with the fibrinolysis process.
- **SIDE EFFECTS:** Thrombosis, seizures
- **CLINICAL PEARLS:**
  - TXA may help reduce the risk of death in major trauma with high risk or already with severe bleeding.
  - In addition, TXA may play a role in the management of angioedema, by preventing the consumption of C1-esterase and reduce the activation of the complement pathway by limiting the production of plasmin.

High-Yield Basic Pharmacology

- **Protamine**
  - Provides exogenous vitamin K to allow gamma-carboxylation (activation) of coagulation factors (II, VII, IX, X).
  - Patients with prior exposure to protamine in insulin, vasectomy, or fish allergy are at higher risk for protamine-induced adverse reactions.
- **Phytonadione**
  - Rapidly reverses heparin's anticoagulant effect by binding directly to heparin, thereby reversing its anticoagulant effect.
  - Parenteral phytonadione is an aqueous colloidal suspension of a castor oil derivative, dextrose, and benzyl alcohol.
    - These excipients have been attributed to the risk of anaphylactoid reactions associated with phytonadione use.

Primary Net Benefit

- Protamine rapidly reverses the antithrombotic effects of heparin and may partially reverse low-molecular-weight heparins. Phytonadione is a key component to warfarin reversal, regardless of acute strategies, including FFP or PCC.

Anticoagulant Reversal - Drug Class Review			
High-Yield Med Reviews			
Mechanism of Action: *Phytonadione - Provides exogenous vitamin K to allow gamma-carboxylation (activation) of coagulation factors (II, VII, IX, X).* *Protamine Sulfate - Rapidly reverses heparin's anticoagulant effect by binding directly to heparin, thereby reversing its anticoagulant effect.*			
Class Effects: Protamine rapidly reverses the antithrombotic effects of heparin and may partially reverse low-molecular-weight heparins. Phytonadione is a key component to warfarin reversal, regardless of acute strategies, including FFP or PCC.			
Generic Name	**Brand Name**	**Indication(s) or Uses**	**Notes**

Phytonadione	Mephyton	• Warfarin-associated INR elevation or hemorrhage (phytonadione)	• **Dosing (Adult):**
			  – IV/Oral/SQ/IM 1 to 10 mg once
			• **Dosing (Peds):**
			  – IV/Oral/SQ/IM 0.5 to 10 mg once
			• **CYP450 Interactions:** None
			• **Renal or Hepatic Dose Adjustments:** None
			• **Dosage Forms:** Injection (aqueous colloidal), Oral (tablet)

Anticoagulant Reversal - Drug Class Review
High-Yield Med Reviews

Generic Name	Brand Name	Indication(s) or Uses	Notes
Protamine	Prosulf	• Reversal of heparin or low molecular weight heparin (protamine)	• **Dosing (Adult):** – IV dose determined based on heparin administration where 1 mg of protamine neutralizes approximately 100 units of heparin. – Enoxaparin within 8 hours - dosed 1mg to 1 mg of protamine, maximum 50 mg/dose – Enoxaparin 8 to 12 hours ago - 0.5 mg protamine for every 1 mg enoxaparin – Dalteparin, nadroparin, tinzaparin - 1 mg for every 100 anti-factor Xa units • **Dosing (Peds):** – IV dose determined based on heparin administration where 1 mg of protamine neutralizes approximately 100 units of heparin. • **CYP450 Interactions:** None • **Renal or Hepatic Dose Adjustments:** None • **Dosage Forms:** IV (solution)

High-Yield Clinical Knowledge

- **Warfarin Reversal**
  - Phytonadione reverses INR to normal values between 8 to 24 hours, depending on the dosage form.
  - For patients with no acute hemorrhage, there is no difference in efficacy between oral and IV.
  - In settings of acute hemorrhage, IV phytonadione is more appropriate than oral, as the onset of action is significantly faster (1-2 hours vs. 6 hours).
- **Phytonadione IV Administration**
  - Phytonadione must be diluted and administered slowly over 1 hour.
  - Slow IV infusion is required to reduce the risk of an anaphylactoid reaction.
  - Subcutaneous administration should be limited to use when IV administration is unnecessary, but patients cannot tolerate oral phytonadione.
  - IM should be avoided in patients with coagulopathies due to the risk of hematoma and bleeding.
- **Protamine Reversal of Anticoagulation**
  - The anticoagulant effects of heparin, LMWH, and (potentially) fondaparinux may be reversed with protamine sulfate.
  - It's also important to note that protamine only partially reverses the anticoagulant activity of LMWH and has no effect on that fondaparinux.
- **Protamine Dosing**
  - Protamine should be dosed as a function of the remaining therapeutic heparin, with an empiric dose of 1 mg of protamine for every 100 units of heparin remaining in the patient.
  - However, caution should be taken to estimate the remaining heparin (based on t1/2 of 1.5 hours) since excessive protamine sulfate can exert an anticoagulant effect of its own.
- **Protamine Maximum Dose**
  - The maximum single dose of protamine is 50mg.
  - Higher doses can cause paradoxical anticoagulant effects.
- **Other Anticoagulants**
  - Protamine sulfate is not effective for the reversal of fondaparinux, direct thrombin inhibitors, or any direct oral anticoagulant.

- ▪ **Thrombosis Risk**
  - – Whenever vitamin K is used to reverse the antithrombotic effect of warfarin, the underlying thrombotic risk returns.
  - – In patients with a high thromboembolism risk, the most cautious method to correct hemorrhaging should be considered and use appropriately dosed vitamin K (phytonadione) of INR overcorrection.

HIGH-YIELD BOARD EXAM ESSENTIALS

- **CLASSIC AGENTS:** Phytonadione, protamine
- **DRUG CLASS:** Anticoagulant reversal
- **INDICATIONS:** Reversal of heparin or low molecular weight heparin (protamine), warfarin-associated INR elevation or hemorrhage (phytonadione)
- **MECHANISM:**
  - – Phytonadione (vitamin K) provides exogenous vitamin K to allow gamma-carboxylation (activation) of coagulation factors.
  - – Protamine rapidly reverses heparin's anticoagulant effect by binding directly to heparin, thereby reversing its anticoagulant effect.
- **SIDE EFFECTS:** Anaphylaxis, infusion reaction (phytonadione), thrombosis, hemorrhage (protamine).
- **CLINICAL PEARLS:**
  - – Phytonadione (vitamin K) reverse warfarin but its onset is delayed.
  - – Protamine should be dosed as a function of the remaining therapeutic heparin, with an empiric dose of 1 mg of protamine for every 100 units of heparin remaining in the patient (max dose is considered 50 mg because it can start act like an anticoagulant in higher doses).

High-Yield Basic Pharmacology

- **Mechanism of Action**
  - Idarucizumab binds to free, and thrombin bound dabigatran, neutralizing its anticoagulant effect.
  - Activated prothrombin complex concentrate replaces factors II, IX, X, and activated factor VII (VIIa).
  - Four-factor prothrombin complex concentrate replaces the vitamin K-dependent coagulation factors II, VII, IX, and X in addition to protein C and protein S.
- **Reversal, Not Procoagulant**
  - Idarucizumab does not intrinsically possess procoagulant activity, which differs from andexanet alfa, aPCC, and PCC.
- **Procoagulants**
  - Andexanet alfa is thought to exert a procoagulant effect by inhibiting TFPI (a double-negative statement, inhibits and inhibitor of tissue factor, thus allowing tissue factor activity) and activation of the extrinsic coagulation pathway.
    - Since there is no more anti-Xa activity, the initial thrombin burst from extrinsic pathway activation allows for intrinsic pathway activation and clot formation.
  - Both aPCC and PCC contribute to supraphysiologic concentrations of vitamin-K-dependent clotting factors and promote coagulation.

Primary Net Benefit

- PCC products provide a concentrated, rapid means of replacing vitamin K-dependent clotting factors, where andexanet alfa presents an inactive factor Xa to bind circulating oral FXa inhibitors, and idarucizumab is a specific monoclonal antibody directed against dabigatran.

Reversal Agents - Drug Class Review			
High-Yield Med Reviews			
Mechanism of Action: *Andexanet Alfa directly binds and sequestered apixaban and rivaroxaban, halting their antithrombotic actions, in addition to inhibition of tissue factor pathway inhibitor (TFPI)* *Idarucizumab binds to free, and thrombin bound dabigatran, neutralizing its anticoagulant effect.* *Activated prothrombin complex concentrate replaces factors II, IX, and X, as well as activated factor VII (VIIa)* *Four-factor prothrombin complex concentrate replaces the vitamin K-dependent coagulation factors II, VII, IX, and X in addition to protein C and protein S.*			
Class Effects: *Reversal of therapeutic anticoagulation*			
Generic Name	**Brand Name**	**Indication(s) or Uses**	**Notes**

Andexanet Alfa	Andexxa	• Life-threatening bleeding associated with apixaban or rivaroxaban	• **Dosing (Adult):**
			   – Dose-dependent on dose and time since the last dose.
			   – IV 400 mg (low dose) bolus, followed immediately by 4 mg/minute IV infusion for up to 120 minutes.
			   – High dose: 800 mg (low dose) bolus, followed immediately by 8 mg/minute IV infusion for up to 120 minutes.
			 • **Dosing (Peds):** Not used
			 • **CYP450 Interactions:** None
			 • **Renal or Hepatic Dose Adjustments:** None
			 • **Dosage Forms:** IV solution

Reversal Agents - Drug Class Review
High-Yield Med Reviews

Generic Name	Brand Name	Indication(s) or Uses	Notes

Activated prothrombin complex concentrate	FEIBA	• Control and prevention of bleeding episodes in patients with hemophilia
		• Life-threatening bleeding associated with oral anticoagulants
			• **Dosing (Adult):**
			  – IV 50 to 100 units/kg/dose
			• **Dosing (Peds):**
			  – IV 50 to 100 units/kg/dose
			• **CYP450 Interactions:** None
			• **Renal or Hepatic Dose Adjustments:** None
			• **Dosage Forms:** IV lyophilized powder for reconstitution. Also known as Anti-inhibitor Coagulant Complex

Four-Factor prothrombin complex concentrate	Kcentra	• Control and prevention of bleeding episodes in patients with hemophilia
		• Life-threatening bleeding associated with oral anticoagulants
			• **Dosing (Adult):**
			  – For warfarin-associated hemorrhage - INR 2 to <4: 25 units/kg (max 2,500 units); INR 4 to 6: 35 units/kg (max 3,500 units), INR >6: 50 units/kg (max 5,000 units).
			  – DOAC associated hemorrhage- IV 2,000 units once or 25-50 units/kg once
			• **Dosing (Peds):** use adult dosing
			• **CYP450 Interactions:** None
			• **Renal or Hepatic Dose Adjustments:** None
			• **Dosage Forms:** IV lyophilized powder for reconstitution

Idarucizumab	Praxbind	• Life-threatening hemorrhage due to dabigatran	• **Dosing (Adult):** – IV infusion of 5 g • **Dosing (Peds):** Not routinely used • **CYP450 Interactions:** None • **Renal or Hepatic Dose Adjustments:** None • **Dosage Forms:** IV solution

High-Yield Clinical Knowledge

- **Fixed-dose vs. variable weight-based dosing PCC**
    - Upon initial FDA approval, PCC was dosed in a variable dose based on both the INR and the patient's weight.
    - This dosing was based on presumed factor deficiencies and was tested in a small group of patients in the study described below.
    - However, when clinicians gained experience with the drug, fixed dosing schedules of 1000 to 2000 units were widely adopted.
    - After the publication of numerous single centers and some multicentered studies, fixed-dose PCC was suggested to be as effective at achieving target INRs and reducing the risk of thrombosis and overall drug cost.
        - With more advanced coagulation assays such as thromboelastography, these doses may yet change further and become more patient-specific.
- **Andexanet vs PCC or Andexanet plus PCC for DOAC**
    - The initial phase 3 and phase 4 evidence with andexanet alfa was not compared to any other therapy.
    - This made a comparison between the currently used interventions of DOAC reversal (PCC and aPCC) difficult to assess.
    - However, there is a rationale that andexanet alfa may not replace the need for PCC or aPCC but rather act as an adjunct.
    - Since andexanet alfa does not have strong intrinsic procoagulant activity (other than inhibition of TFPI), it primarily sequesters the DOAC molecule preventing further anticoagulant effect.

- While this is certainly a desirable clinical outcome, in acute major hemorrhage in the setting of a DOAC, there may also be an acute need for procoagulant activity.
- It's currently unknown what dose of aPCC or PCC is relevant to andexanet alfa function and whether the increased risk of thrombosis would offset any potential benefit.
- **Clinical Considerations**
  - Kcentra (PCC) also contains heparin and carries a small but present risk of thrombocytopenia in patients with heparin-induced thrombocytopenia.

HIGH-YIELD BOARD EXAM ESSENTIALS

- **CLASSIC AGENTS:** aPCC, andexanet alfa, PCC, idarucizumab
- **DRUG CLASS:** Reversal agents
- **INDICATIONS:** Life-threatening bleeding associated with: apixaban or rivaroxaban (andexanet alfa), apixaban, rivaroxaban, edoxaban, warfarin (aPCC, PCC), dabigatran (idarucizumab), urgent reversal warfarin therapy in patients with acute major bleeding or a need for an urgent surgery/invasive procedure (PCC), hemorrhage in patients with hemophilia (aPCC).
- **MECHANISM:**
  - aPCC: Replaces factors II, IX, and X, as well as VIIa.
  - PCC: Replaces the vitamin K-dependent coagulation factors II, VII, IX, and X in addition to protein C and protein S (PCC).
  - Andexanet alfa: Directly binds and sequestered apixaban and rivaroxaban, halting their antithrombotic actions, in addition to inhibition of TFPI.
  - PCC: Replaces the vitamin K-dependent coagulation factors II, VII, IX, and X in addition to protein C and protein S (PCC).
  - Idarucizumab: Humanized monoclonal antibody fragment specific to free and thrombin bound dabigatran, neutralizing its anticoagulant.
- **SIDE EFFECTS:** Thrombosis, HIT (Kcentra)
- **CLINICAL PEARLS:** PCC and aPCC use has departed from the prescribing information recommended dosing, and commonly use fixed dosing schedules of 1000 to 2000 units are widely accepted.

High-Yield Basic Pharmacology

- **Histamine-1 Receptor Inverse agonists**
  - Inverse agonists at H1 receptors that compete with histamine for binding sites and stabilizes the receptor's inactive state.
  - This is a distinction from H1 antagonists, which are competitive antagonists of histamine at the H1 receptor

Primary Net Benefit

- Over-the-counter agents for the management of common allergy-related complaints and acute care use of specific agents for numerous indications that are extensions of their central and peripheral antihistamine effect.

Antihistamines (Oral and Parenteral) - Drug Class Review			
High-Yield Med Reviews			
Mechanism of Action: *Inverse agonist at H1 receptors that compete with histamine for binding sites and stabilizes the receptor's inactive state.*			
Class Effects: Reduction in allergies, dry mouth, constipation, sedation (older agents).			
Generic Name	**Brand Name**	**Indication(s) or Uses**	**Notes**

Brompheniramine	With phenylephrine: Brohist, Dimaphen, Dimetapp, Triaminic
	
	With pseudoephedrine: Brotapp, Lodrane, Rynex
	
	With Dextromethorphan and phenylephrine; Dimetapp DM
	
	With pseudoephedrine and dextromethorphan: Brotapp-DM
		• Cough and upper respiratory symptoms	• **Dosing (Adult):**
			  – Oral 1 to 4 mg q4h as needed
			• **Dosing (Peds):**
			  – Oral 1 to 4 mg q4h as needed
			• **CYP450 Interactions:** None
			• **Renal or Hepatic Dose Adjustments:** None
			• **Dosage Forms:** Oral (capsule, liquid, syrup)

Antihistamines (Oral and Parenteral) - Drug Class Review
High-Yield Med Reviews

Generic Name	Brand Name	Indication(s) or Uses	Notes

Carbinoxamine	Karbinal ER, Ryvent	• Allergic rhinitis	• **Dosing (Adult):**
			  – Oral IR 4 to 8 mg q6-8h
			  – Oral ER 6 to 16 mg q12h
			• **Dosing (Peds):**
			  – Oral 0.2 to 0.4 mg/kg/day divided q6-8h
			    • Maximum 16 mg/dose
			• **CYP450 Interactions:** None
			• **Renal or Hepatic Dose Adjustments:** None
			• **Dosage Forms:** Oral (extended-release suspension, tablet)

Cetirizine	Zyrtec, Zyrtec-D (with pseudoephedrine), Zerviate, Quzyttir	• Allergic rhinitis	• **Dosing (Adult):**
			  – Oral 5 to 10 mg daily
			  – Ophthalmic 1 drop in affected eye(s) twice daily
			  – IV 10 mg q12-24h
			• **Dosing (Peds):**
			  – Oral 2.5 to 10 mg daily
			  – Ophthalmic 1 drop in affected eye(s) twice daily
			• **CYP450 Interactions:** Substrate CYP3A4, P-gp
			• **Renal or Hepatic Dose Adjustments:**
			  – GFR 11 to 30 mL/minute - 5 mg daily
			  – GFR less than 10 mL/minute - not recommended
			  – Child-Pugh class A, B or C - 5 mg daily
			• **Dosage Forms:** Oral (liquid, tablet), Ophthalmic solution, IV (solution)

Chlophedianol	Chlo Hist, Chlo Tuss	• Cough and upper respiratory symptoms	• **Dosing (Adult):**
			  – Oral 12.5 to 25 mg q6h
			• **Dosing (Peds):**
			  – Oral 12.5 to 25 mg q6h
			• **CYP450 Interactions:** None
			• **Renal or Hepatic Dose Adjustments:** None
			• **Dosage Forms:** Oral (solution)

Chlorpheniramine	Chlor-Trimeton (available in numerous combinations under various brand names)	• Allergic pruritus, rhinitis, urticaria	• **Dosing (Adult):**
			  – Oral IR 4 mg q4-6h
			  – Oral ER 12 mg q12h
			    • Maximum 24 mg/day
			• **Dosing (Peds):**
			  – Oral IR 1 to 4 mg q4-6h
			    • Maximum 6 to 24 mg/day
			  – Oral ER - Children older than 12, use adult dosing
			• **CYP450 Interactions:** Substrate of CYP2D6, 3A4
			• **Renal or Hepatic Dose Adjustments:** None
			• **Dosage Forms:** Oral (liquid, syrup, tablet)

Antihistamines (Oral and Parenteral) - Drug Class Review
High-Yield Med Reviews

Generic Name	Brand Name	Indication(s) or Uses	Notes

Clemastine	Dayhist, Tavist	• Allergic rhinitis	• **Dosing (Adult):**
			  – Oral 1.34 mg BID to 2.68 mg TID
			    • Maximum 8.04 mg/day
			• **Dosing (Peds):**
			  – Children younger than 12 years
			    • Oral 0.67 mg BID; Maximum 4.02 mg/day
			• **CYP450 Interactions:** None
			• **Renal or Hepatic Dose Adjustments:** None
			• **Dosage Forms:** Oral (tablet)

Cyproheptadine	Periactin	• Allergic conditions
		• Serotonin syndrome
		• Spasticity due to spinal cord damage
			• **Dosing (Adult):**
			  – Oral 4 to 20 mg divided q8h
			    • Maximum 32 mg/day
			  – Oral 12 mg then 2 mg q2h or 4 to 8 mg q6h
			• **Dosing (Peds):**
			  – Oral 2 to 4 mg q8-12h
			    • Maximum 12 to 16 mg/day
			• **CYP450 Interactions:** None
			• **Renal or Hepatic Dose Adjustments:** None
			• **Dosage Forms:** Oral (syrup, tablet)

Desloratadine	Clarinex, Clarinex-D	• Chronic idiopathic urticaria	• **Dosing (Adult):**
			  – Oral 5 mg daily, up to 10 mg BID
			• **Dosing (Peds):**
			  – Oral 1 to 5 mg daily
			• **CYP450 Interactions:** Substrate:CYP2C8, P-gp
			• **Renal or Hepatic Dose Adjustments:** None
			• **Dosage Forms:** Oral (syrup, tablet)

Dexbrompheniramine	RyClora	• Allergic rhinitis	• **Dosing (Adult):**
			  – Oral 2 mg q4-6h
			• **Dosing (Peds):**
			  – Oral 0.5 to 2 mg q4-6h
			• **CYP450 Interactions:** None
			• **Renal or Hepatic Dose Adjustments:** None
			• **Dosage Forms:** Oral (solution)

Dimenhydrinate	Dramamine Dramanate	• Motion sickness	• **Dosing (Adult):**
			  – Oral 50 to 100 mg q4-6h
			    • Maximum 400 mg/day
			  – IM/IV 50 to 100 mg q4h
			• **Dosing (Peds):**
			  – Oral 12.5 to 100 mg q4-8h
			    • Maximum 75 to 400 mg/day
			  – IM 1.25 mg/kg/dose q6h
			    • Maximum 300 mg/day
			• **CYP450 Interactions:** None
			• **Renal or Hepatic Dose Adjustments:** None
			• **Dosage Forms:** Oral (tablet), IV (solution)

Antihistamines (Oral and Parenteral) - Drug Class Review
High-Yield Med Reviews

Generic Name	Brand Name	Indication(s) or Uses	Notes
Diphenhydramine	Benadryl, (numerous other brand names)	<ul><li>Allergies</li><li>Anaphylaxis</li><li>Angioedema</li><li>Extrapyramidal symptoms</li><li>Insomnia</li><li>Motion sickness</li><li>Nausea and vomiting</li><li>Pruritus</li><li>Vertigo</li></ul>	<ul><li>**Dosing (Adult):**<ul><li>Oral 12.5 to 50 mg q4-6h as needed</li><li>IV/IM 10 to 50 mg q6h as needed</li><li>Topical apply 1% to 2% to affected area up to 3-4 times daily</li></ul></li><li>**Dosing (Peds):**<ul><li>IV/IM/Oral 0.5 to 2 mg/kg/dose q6h</li><li>Topical apply 1% to 2% to affected area up to 3-4 times daily</li></ul></li><li>**CYP450 Interactions:** Substrate of CYP1A2, 2C19, 2C9, 2D6; Inhibits CYP2D6</li><li>**Renal or Hepatic Dose Adjustments:** None</li><li>**Dosage Forms:** Oral (capsule, elixir, liquid, strip, syrup, tablet), IV (solution), Topical cream</li></ul>
Doxylamine	Sleep Aid With pyridoxine: Bonjesta, Diclegis	<ul><li>Nausea and vomiting associated with pregnancy</li><li>Insomnia</li></ul>	<ul><li>**Dosing (Adult):**<ul><li>Oral 10 to 25 daily</li></ul></li><li>**Dosing (Peds):**<ul><li>Oral 25 mg at bedtime</li></ul></li><li>**CYP450 Interactions:** None</li><li>**Renal or Hepatic Dose Adjustments:** None</li><li>**Dosage Forms:** Oral (tablet)</li></ul>
Fexofenadine	Allegra	<ul><li>Allergies</li><li>Chronic idiopathic urticaria</li></ul>	<ul><li>**Dosing (Adult):**<ul><li>Once daily formulations<ul><li>Oral 60 mg q12h</li></ul></li><li>Twice daily formulations<ul><li>Oral 180 mg daily</li></ul></li></ul></li><li>**Dosing (Peds):**<ul><li>Oral 15 to 30 mg q12h<ul><li>Maximum 60 mg/day</li></ul></li></ul></li><li>**CYP450 Interactions:** Substrate CYP3A4, P-gp</li><li>**Renal or Hepatic Dose Adjustments:**<ul><li>GFR less than 10 mL/minute - IR q24h, do not use 24 hour formulation</li></ul></li><li>**Dosage Forms:** Oral (suspension, tablet)</li></ul>
Hydroxyzine	Vistaril	<ul><li>Anxiety</li><li>Pruritus/Urticaria</li></ul>	<ul><li>**Dosing (Adult):**<ul><li>Oral 10 to 50 mg up to 4 times daily<ul><li>Maximum 400 mg/day</li></ul></li><li>IM 25 to 50 mg q4-6h as needed</li></ul></li><li>**Dosing (Peds):**<ul><li>Oral 0.5 to 2 mg/kg/day q6-8h<ul><li>Maximum 25 mg/dose</li></ul></li></ul></li><li>**CYP450 Interactions:** None</li><li>**Renal or Hepatic Dose Adjustments:**<ul><li>GFR less than 50 mL/minute - Reduce dose by 50%</li></ul></li><li>**Dosage Forms:** Oral (capsule, syrup, tablet), IV solution</li></ul>

Antihistamines (Oral and Parenteral) - Drug Class Review
High-Yield Med Reviews

Generic Name	Brand Name	Indication(s) or Uses	Notes

Levocetirizine	Xyzal	• Allergic rhinitis
		• Chronic idiopathic urticaria
			• **Dosing (Adult):**
			  – Oral 2.5 to 5 mg daily
			• **Dosing (Peds):**
			  – Oral 1.25 to 5 mg daily
			• **CYP450 Interactions:** None
			• **Renal or Hepatic Dose Adjustments:**
			  – GFR 50 to 80 mL/minute - 2.5 mg daily
			  – GFR 30 to 50 mL/minute - 2.5 mg q48h
			  – GFR 10 to 30 mL/minute - 2.5 mg twice weekly
			  – GFR less than 10 mL/minute - contraindicated
			• **Dosage Forms:** Oral (solution, tablet)

Loratadine	Alavert, Alavert-D Claritin, Claritin-D	• Allergic rhinitis	• **Dosing (Adult):**
			  – Oral 10 mg daily or 5 mg BID
			• **Dosing (Peds):**
			  – Children younger than 6 years
			    • Oral 5 mg daily
			• **CYP450 Interactions:** Substrate CYP2D6, 3A4, P-gp
			• **Renal or Hepatic Dose Adjustments:**
			  – GFR 10 to 50 mL/minute - q24-48h
			  – GFR less than 10 mL/minute - q48h
			• **Dosage Forms:** Oral (capsule, solution, syrup, tablet)

Meclizine	Bonine, Travel-Ease	• Motion sickness
		• Vertigo
			• **Dosing (Adult):**
			  – Oral 25 to 50 mg 1 hour before travel
			  – Oral 25 to 100 mg daily in divided doses
			• **Dosing (Peds):**
			  – Oral 25 to 50 mg 1 hour before travel
			  – Oral 25 to 100 mg daily in 3 to 4 divided doses
			• **CYP450 Interactions:** Substrate CYP2D6
			• **Renal or Hepatic Dose Adjustments:** None
			• **Dosage Forms:** Oral (tablet)

Promethazine	Phenadoz, Phenergan, Promethegan	• Allergies
		• Motion sickness
		• Nausea and vomiting
		• Sedation
			• **Dosing (Adult):**
			  – IM/IV/Rectal/Oral 6.25 to 25 mg q4-8h as needed
			• **Dosing (Peds):**
			  – IM/IV/Rectal/Oral 0.25 to 1.1 mg/kg q4-6h as needed
			    • Maximum 25 mg/dose
			• **CYP450 Interactions:** Substrate CYP2B6, 2D6
			• **Renal or Hepatic Dose Adjustments:** None
			• **Dosage Forms:** IV solution, Oral (solution, syrup, tablet), Rectal suppository

Copyright: High-Yield Med Reviews

highyieldmedreviews.com

Antihistamines (Oral and Parenteral) - Drug Class Review			
High-Yield Med Reviews			
Generic Name	Brand Name	Indication(s) or Uses	Notes

Triprolidine	Dr Manzanilla Antihistamine, Histex	• Allergies	• **Dosing (Adult):**
			  – Oral 2.5 mg q4-6h
			    • Maximum 10 mg/day
			• **Dosing (Peds):**
			  – Oral 0.313 to 1.25 mg q4-6h as needed
			    • Maximum 4 doses/24 hours
			• **CYP450 Interactions:** text
			• **Renal or Hepatic Dose Adjustments:** text
			• **Dosage Forms:** Oral (liquid, syrup, tablet)

High-Yield Basic Pharmacology

- **Generational Antihistamines**
  - First-generation antihistamines are non-selective histamine antagonists and are associated with sedation, anticholinergic effects.
    - First-generation antihistamines include brompheniramine, carbinoxamine, chlophedianol, chlorpheniramine, clemastine, dexbrompheniramine, dimenhydrinate, diphenhydramine, doxylamine, hydroxyzine, meclizine, and promethazine.
  - Second-generation antihistamines are more H1 selective and preferred as first-line agents for most indications.
    - Second-generation antihistamines include cetirizine, desloratadine, fexofenadine, levocetirizine, loratadine, and triprolidine.
- **Cyproheptadine**
  - Cyproheptadine is a nonselective antihistamine and possesses 5-HT2A receptor blocking properties, improving autonomic instability observed in serotonin syndrome.
  - For serotonin syndrome, cyproheptadine must be used in combination with benzodiazepines, removal of serotonergic agents, and extravascular/intravascular cooling.
- **Fexofenadine and Terfenadine**
  - Fexofenadine is the active metabolite of the first-generation antihistamine, terfenadine.

High-Yield Clinical Knowledge

- **Angioedema**
  - Parenteral diphenhydramine can be used as a component of the management of angioedema.
  - However, diphenhydramine alone is unlikely to be beneficial, as angioedema must be aggressively managed with epinephrine, corticosteroids, and airway support, including endotracheal intubation.
- **Anticholinergic Toxicity**
  - First-generation antihistamines may cause excessive sedation in supratherapeutic doses or when combined with other sedative agents.
  - There is also a risk of potentially fatal anticholinergic toxicity in an overdose of first-generation antihistamines with characteristic anticholinergic toxidrome.
  - Classic antimuscarinic toxidrome: "Blind as a bat, Dry as a bone, Hot as a hare, Mad as a hatter, Red as a beet."
  - The anticholinergic toxidrome presents in three phases:
    - Induction phase: peripheral anticholinergic effects
    - Stupor phase: somnolence, restlessness, ataxia hyperthermia, hypertension.
    - Delirium phase: amnesia, confusion, hallucinations, incoherent speech.

- **Second-Generation Sedation**
  - Although the likelihood of sedative effects due to second-generation antihistamines may be lower than from first-generation agents, there is wide interpatient variability.
  - As the first-generation agents are similarly effective to second-generation agents for the treatment of allergies as over-the-counter agents, patient-specific response and cost play into selecting the appropriate agent.
- **Sleep Aids**
  - As a result of their sedative properties, some first-generation antihistamines are used as over-the-counter night-time sleep-aids.
  - Doxylamine, diphenhydramine, and doxylamine are commonly used for their sedative properties.
  - Some children, particularly those younger than 2, may experience paradoxical stimulant properties to first-generation antihistamines.
- **Urticaria**
  - The underlying pathophysiologic mechanism of urticaria is histamine, and specifically, H1 receptor-mediated, first-generation antihistamines are preferred for acute management, and second-generation agents can be used for pre-exposure prevention.
- **Nausea and Vomiting in Pregnancy**
  - Doxylamine is commonly used for the treatment of nausea and vomiting in pregnancy.
  - It is coformulated with pyridoxine (brand name Bonjesta or Diclegis), which also may have antiemetic properties, but is only available as a prescription agent.
    - Compared to 5-HT3 antagonists (ondansetron), doxylamine plus pyridoxine is similarly effective and does not carry the small (and questionable) risk of birth defects.
- **Drug Interactions**
  - Cetirizine, chlorpheniramine, fexofenadine, and loratadine are CYP3A4 substrates and should be avoided with potent CYP3A4 inhibitors including macrolide antibiotics, erythromycin, ketoconazole, and itraconazole.
  - Diphenhydramine is a substrate of CYP1A2, 2C19, 2C9, 2D6, it inhibits CYP2D6, leading to potentially numerous pharmacokinetic interactions, and in the case of antidepressants (fluoxetine, sertraline, TCAs), it can also have additive anticholinergic effects.
- **Pregnancy Risks**
  - Hydroxyzine and fexofenadine have been associated with teratogenic effects in animal models.
  - The antihistamines chlorpheniramine, cetirizine, diphenhydramine, and loratadine have not been associated with this risk.

HIGH-YIELD BOARD EXAM ESSENTIALS
- **CLASSIC AGENTS:** Brompheniramine, carbinoxamine, cetirizine, chlophedianol, chlorpheniramine, clemastine, cyproheptadine, desloratadine, dexbrompheniramine, dimenhydrinate, diphenhydramine, doxylamine, fexofenadine, hydroxyzine, levocetirizine, loratadine, meclizine, promethazine, triprolidine
- **DRUG CLASS:** Antihistamines
- **INDICATIONS:** Allergies, anaphylaxis, angioedema, extrapyramidal symptoms, insomnia, motion sickness, nausea and vomiting, pruritus
- **MECHANISM:** Inverse agonist at H1 receptors that compete with histamine for binding sites and stabilizes the receptor's inactive state.
- **SIDE EFFECTS:** Dry mucous membranes, somnolence, restlessness, ataxia hyperthermia, hypertension
- **CLINICAL PEARLS:**
  - Although the likelihood of sedative effects due to second-generation antihistamines may be lower than from first-generation agents, there is wide interpatient variability.
  - Cyproheptadine is more commonly used for appetite stimulant for weight gain and is one of the historical "antidotes" for the treatment of serotonin syndrome.
  - At high doses or toxicology cases, diphenhydramine can inhibit Na+ channels in the heart and cause QRS widening.

High-Yield Basic Pharmacology

- **Mechanism of Action**
  - Removes both B and T lymphocytes from the blood, bone marrow, and organs by binding to the CD52 surface antigen and inducing antibody-dependent cell lysis.
- **Alemtuzumab or Antithymocyte Globulins**
  - Alemtuzumab has been compared with antithymocyte globulins for induction of immunosuppression therapy.
  - The long-term immunosuppression observed with alemtuzumab is weighed against the safety and tolerability of antithymocyte globulins in the acute phase of transplant care.

Primary Net Benefit

- Used for induction of immunosuppression for an organ transplant as an alternative to antithymocyte globulins.

Anti-CD52 Monoclonal Antibody - Drug Class Review High-Yield Med Reviews			
Mechanism of Action: *Removes both B and T lymphocytes from the blood, bone marrow, and organs by binding to the CD52 surface antigen and inducing antibody-dependent cell lysis.*			
Class Effects: *Infusion reactions, need for PJP prophylaxis*			
Generic Name	**Brand Name**	**Indication(s) or Uses**	**Notes**

Alemtuzumab	Campath
	Lemtrada
		• Acute graft-versus-host disease
		• B-cell chronic lymphocytic leukemia
		• Relapsing Multiple sclerosis
			• **Dosing (Adult):**
			  – B-CLL:
			    • Initial IV 3 mg q24h, increasing to 30 mg IV/SQ three times weekly
			  – Transplant:
			    • IV 10 mg daily x 5 days, then 10 mg weekly until symptom resolution
			    • IV/SQ 30 mg immediately before transplant, then repeated for 1-2 doses q24h
			  – MS:
			    • IV 12 mg daily x 5 days, then 12 months later 12 mg daily for 3 days
			• **Dosing (Peds):**
			  – IV 0.2 mg/kg/dose x 10 days
			    • Maximum 10 mg/dose
			• **CYP450 Interactions:** None
			• **Renal or Hepatic Dose Adjustments:** None
			• **Dosage Forms:** IV (solution)

High-Yield Clinical Knowledge

- **Infusion Reactions**
  - Alemtuzumab must be administered as an IV infusion over 2 hours, not via IV push.
  - Rare infusion-related reactions include rigors, hypotension, fever, shortness of breath, bronchospasms, and chills.
    - The risk of these adverse events can be minimized by using premedications such as acetaminophen, corticosteroids, and diphenhydramine.

- **Pneumocystis Jiroveci Prophylaxis**
  - PJP prophylaxis is recommended for at least two months after the last dose of alemtuzumab or until the patient's CD4+ count is 200 cells/microL or higher.
  - Prophylaxis for herpes is recommended for as long as PJP prophylaxis is administered.
- **Deceiving Half-life**
  - Despite a half-life of 11 hours to 6 days after 12 weeks of therapy, the duration of effect of alemtuzumab is profound.
  - After one to two doses, alemtuzumab causes complete lymphocyte depletion, which persists for more than one year.
    - The extent of alemtuzumab's effect is due to the presence of CD52 surface antigen found on eosinophils, macrophages, monocytes.
- **B/T-Cell Action**
  - The precise mechanism of alemtuzumab is unknown, but leading hypotheses point towards induction of complement and antibody-dependent cytotoxicity.

High-Yield Fast-Fact

- **Free Drug**
  - The manufacturer provided alemtuzumab at a very small or no cost through its US Campath Distribution program for a short period.

HIGH-YIELD BOARD EXAM ESSENTIALS
- **CLASSIC AGENTS:** Alemtuzumab
- **DRUG CLASS:** Anti-CD52 monoclonal antibody
- **INDICATIONS:** Acute graft-versus-host disease, B-cell chronic lymphocytic leukemia, relapsing Multiple sclerosis
- **MECHANISM:** Removes both B and T lymphocytes from the blood, bone marrow, and organs by binding to the CD52 surface antigen and inducing antibody-dependent cell lysis.
- **SIDE EFFECTS:** Infusion-related reactions (rigors, hypotension, fever, shortness of breath, bronchospasms, and chills)
- **CLINICAL PEARLS:** PJP prophylaxis is recommended for at least two months after the last dose of alemtuzumab or until the patient's CD4+ count is 200 cells/microL or higher.

High-Yield Basic Pharmacology

- **Mechanism of Action**
  - Antithymocyte globulins bind to CD2, CD3, CD4, CD8, CD 11a, CD18, CD25, CD 44, CD45 receptors, and HLA class I and II molecules on the surface of lymphocytes, causing complement-mediated lymphocyte lysis leading to lymphocyte depletion (including B-cells, T-cells, and leukocytes) and blocking lymphocyte function.
- **Antiequine Antibodies**
  - Antibody development to anti-thymocyte globulin frequently occurs in 78% of patients receiving equine and up to 68% of patients receiving rabbit formulations.
    - The clinical impact is not fully understood; however, many patients who begin therapy with equine formulations ultimately are converted to the rabbit formulation due to intolerances or adverse events.

Primary Net Benefit

- Induction of immunosuppression agents for transplant recipients with significant toxicities related to immunosuppression/myelosuppression and infusion reactions.

Antithymocyte Globulin – Drug Class Review **High-Yield Med Reviews**			
Mechanism of Action: *Bind to numerous CD* receptors and HLA class I and II molecules on lymphocytes, causing complement-mediated lymphocyte lysis leading to lymphocyte depletion and blocking lymphocyte function.*			
Class Effects: Infusion reactions (give diphenhydramine, acetaminophen and steroids)			
Generic Name	**Brand Name**	**Indication(s) or Uses**	**Notes**
Antithymocyte Globulin (Equine)	Atgam	<ul><li>Aplastic anemia</li><li>Transplant induction therapy</li><li>Transplant rejection</li></ul>	<ul><li>**Dosing (Adult):** – IV 5 to 40 mg/kg q24h x 3 to 14 days</li><li>**Dosing (Peds):** – IV 5 to 40 mg/kg q24h x 3 to 14 days</li><li>**CYP450 Interactions:** None</li><li>**Renal or Hepatic Dose Adjustments:** None</li><li>**Dosage Forms:** IV (solution)</li></ul>
Antithymocyte Globulin (Rabbit)	Thymoglobulin	<ul><li>Renal transplant rejection</li><li>Transplant induction therapy</li></ul>	<ul><li>**Dosing (Adult):** – IV 0.5 to 2.5 mg/kg q24h for 5 to 7 days</li><li>**Dosing (Peds):** – IV 0.5 to 3.5 mg/kg q24h for 5 to 7 days</li><li>**CYP450 Interactions:** None</li><li>**Renal or Hepatic Dose Adjustments:** None</li><li>**Dosage Forms:** IV (solution)</li></ul>

High-Yield Clinical Knowledge

- **Administration & Pre-Medication**
  - Infusion-related febrile events frequently occur with the administration of either antithymocyte globulin preparation.
    - This is otherwise known as the "cytokine release syndrome," causing a range of events including fever, headache, chills, rigors, dyspnea, hyper OR hypotension, rash, and nausea/vomiting/diarrhea.

- All patients should receive acetaminophen, diphenhydramine, and corticosteroids before administration of either antithymocyte product.
- Administration via central IV catheters and/or slowing the infusion to be administered over 4-6 hours can also reduce these reactions.

- **Delayed Calcineurin Inhibitor**
  - In renal transplant recipients, antithymocyte globulins are administered to recover from ischemic reperfusion injuries and avoid early therapy with the nephrotoxic calcineurin inhibitors (cyclosporin and tacrolimus).

- **Atgam Test Dose**
  - Before administering antithymocyte globulin (equine), a test dose is recommended to screen for anaphylaxis reactions.
    - Testing may be accomplished using an escalating technique of exposure from epicutaneous prick to an intradermal injection of the dilute drug with saline control.
    - Positive tests, although they predict an increased risk of anaphylaxis, are not a contraindication; but additional precautions should be taken (crash cart, airway support, epinephrine, close by).

- **CMV Screening**
  - Screening for CMV before transplant and for patients in whom CMV screening is seropositive at the time of transplant should receive antiviral prophylaxis.
    - CMV-seronegative, but receiving organ tissue from a CMV-seropositive donor should also receive antiviral prophylaxis.

High-Yield Fast-Fact

- **Malignancy Risk**
  - Both antithymocyte globulins are associated with an increased risk of malignancies.

HIGH-YIELD BOARD EXAM ESSENTIALS
- **CLASSIC AGENTS:** Antithymocyte globulin (equine), antithymocyte globulin (rabbit)
- **DRUG CLASS:** Antithymocyte globulin
- **INDICATIONS:** Acute/chronic graft-versus-host disease, aplastic anemia, transplant induction therapy, transplant rejection
- **MECHANISM:** Bind to numerous CD* receptors and HLA class I and II molecules on lymphocytes, causing complement-mediated lymphocyte lysis leading to lymphocyte depletion and blocking lymphocyte function.
- **SIDE EFFECTS:** Infusion-related fever, cytokine release syndrome, anaphylaxis
- **CLINICAL PEARLS:** In renal transplant recipients, antithymocyte globulins are administered to recover from ischemic reperfusion injuries and avoid early therapy with the nephrotoxic calcineurin inhibitors (cyclosporin and tacrolimus).

High-Yield Basic Pharmacology

- **Mechanism of Action**
  - Bind to cyclophilin (cyclosporine) or FKBP12 (tacrolimus), which inhibits calcineurin, halting the transcription of numerous key cytokines (specifically IL-2) necessary for T-cell activity.
- **Cyclosporine Modified Vs. Non-Modified**
  - Oral dosage forms of cyclosporine exist in either a "modified" or "non-modified" format, which are not bioequivalent.
    - To convert between dosage forms that are not bioequivalent, patients should have a trough concentration drawn 7 days before conversion, then every 5-7 days afterward with appropriate adjustments made at that time.
  - The FDA has deemed the generic formulations of both Neoral and Sandimmune bioequivalent.

Primary Net Benefit

- A core component of immunosuppression post-transplant with clinically relevant drug interactions, therapeutic drug level monitoring, and nephrotoxicity.

Calcineurin Inhibitors – Drug Class Review			
High-Yield Med Reviews			
Mechanism of Action: *Bind to cyclophilin (cyclosporine) or FKBP12 (tacrolimus), which inhibits calcineurin, halting the transcription of numerous key cytokines (specifically IL-2) necessary for T-cell activity.*			
Class Effects: *Risk of drug interactions, elevations in glucose, renal toxicity, elevations in lipids and blood pressure.*			
Generic Name	**Brand Name**	**Indication(s) or Uses**	**Notes**

Cyclosporine	Gengraf Neoral Sandimmune	• Psoriasis
		• Rheumatoid arthritis
		• Transplant rejection prophylaxis
			• **Dosing (Adult):**
			  – Modified - Oral 4 to 12 mg/kg/day in two divided doses
			  – Non-modified - IV 3 to 7.5 mg/kg/day continuous or intermittent infusion
			• **Dosing (Peds):**
			  – Modified - Oral 4 to 12 mg/kg/day in two divided doses
			  – Non-modified - IV 3 to 7.5 mg/kg/day continuous or intermittent infusion
			• **CYP450 Interactions:** Substrate of CYP3A4, P-gp; Inhibits CYP2C9, CYP3A4, P-gp
			• **Renal or Hepatic Dose Adjustments:**
			  – Dose adjustments for non-transplant indications (psoriasis, rheumatoid arthritis, and nephritic syndrome)
			    • Reduce dose by 25 to 50% for serum creatinine levels more than 25-30% above baseline
			• **Dosage Forms:**
			  – Modified (capsule, oral solution)
			  – Non-modified (capsule, oral solution)
			  – IV (solution)

Calcineurin Inhibitors – Drug Class Review
High-Yield Med Reviews

Generic Name	Brand Name	Indication(s) or Uses	Notes

Tacrolimus	Astagraf XL, Envarsus, Prograf	• Transplant rejection prophylaxis	• **Dosing (Adult):**
			  – Oral 0.1 to 0.2 mg/kg/day in 2 divided doses
			  – IV 0.03 to 0.05 mg/kg/day continuous infusion
			• **Dosing (Peds):**
			  – Extra info if needed
			    • Extra info if needed
			• **CYP450 Interactions:** Substrate of CYP3A4, P-gp
			• **Renal or Hepatic Dose Adjustments:** No empiric adjustments
			• **Dosage Forms:** Oral (capsule, packet, tablet), IV (solution)

High-Yield Clinical Knowledge

- **Glucose Intolerance**
  - New-onset diabetes after transplantation is observed frequently with tacrolimus as it impairs pancreatic beta-cell response to glucose.
  - However, the combination of cyclosporine plus corticosteroids may cause diabetes more frequently.
- **Nephrotoxicity**
  - Dose-dependent nephrotoxicity complicates the use of calcineurin inhibitors, particularly after renal transplants.
    - This effect is dose/concentration-dependent; therefore, close therapeutic drug monitoring may limit the degree of nephrotoxicity.
    - Also, reducing exposure to other nephrotoxins (aminoglycosides, loop diuretics, NSAIDs, etc.) can control the risk of nephrotoxicity.
- **Cardiovascular Adverse Events**
  - Cyclosporine is associated with a high incidence of hyperlipidemia, hypertension, which could increase cardiovascular events.
  - Tacrolimus is not associated with hyperlipidemia and may be more ideal in patients where cardiovascular disease risk is high and/or continuing high-intensity statin therapy.
- **Tacrolimus Dosing**
  - Tacrolimus therapeutic drug monitoring should use trough concentrations to guide acute and post-transplant therapy.
  - Target tacrolimus trough concentrations in the acute post-transplant phase range from 10 to 15 ng/mL and increase to 100 to 200 ng/mL 3 months post-transplant.
- **Oral Tacrolimus Formulations**
  - Like cyclosporine, the modified release preparations of tacrolimus are not interchangeable with any other immediate or modified release dosage form.
  - If conversions are clinically necessary, increased drug level monitoring should occur until troughs are maintained in the therapeutic range.
- **Cyclosporine Absorption and Monitoring**
  - The gold standard cyclosporine drug level is drawn two hours after dose administration, known as C2 levels.

HIGH-YIELD BOARD EXAM ESSENTIALS

- **CLASSIC AGENTS:** Cyclosporine, tacrolimus
- **DRUG CLASS:** Calcineurin inhibitors
- **INDICATIONS:** Psoriasis, rheumatoid arthritis, transplant rejection prophylaxis
- **MECHANISM:** Bind to cyclophilin (cyclosporine) or FKBP12 (tacrolimus), which inhibits calcineurin, halting the transcription of numerous key cytokines (specifically IL-2) necessary for T-cell activity.
- **SIDE EFFECTS:** Nephrotoxicity, hyperlipidemia, hypertension, glucose intolerance
- **CLINICAL PEARLS:** New-onset diabetes after transplantation is observed frequently with tacrolimus as it impairs pancreatic beta-cell response to glucose. However, the combination of cyclosporine plus corticosteroids may cause diabetes more frequently.

High-Yield Basic Pharmacology

- **Tyle 1 Interferons**
  - Interferon-Alfa and interferon-Beta
    - Produce intracellular antimicrobial effects by producing interferon-stimulated genes in hepatitis B or C infected cells and neighboring cells.
    - Enhance adaptive immune responses by amplifying antigen presentation, macrophage, NK cell, and cytotoxic T-lymphocyte activation by innate immune cells.
- **Type 2 Interferons**
  - Interferon-gamma
    - Exerts an immune-enhancing effect by augmenting antigen presentation and macrophage, NK cell, and cytotoxic T-lymphocyte activation.
  - Enhances increased expression of class II MHC molecules on cell surfaces
- **Pegylation**
  - Several interferon products exist as conventional or pegylated products.
  - The addition of a PEG (polyethylene glycol) polymer chain to the interferon drug molecule enhances pharmacokinetic half-life, permitting less frequent dosing.
  - However, toxicities are not necessarily improved with the PEG modification of the interferon product.

Primary Net Benefit

- Conveys antiviral, antiproliferative, and immunomodulatory functions onto target cells yet comes with significant toxicities and intolerances that preclude completion of the full course of treatment.

Interferon - Drug Class Review High-Yield Med Reviews			
Mechanism of Action: *See above.*			
Class Effects: *Antiviral activity, flu-like symptoms, thrombocytopenia, neutropenia.*			
Generic Name	**Brand Name**	**Indication(s) or Uses**	**Notes**

Interferon-Alfa-2b	Intron A	• AIDS-related Kaposi sarcoma
		• Chronic hepatitis B
		• Chronic hepatitis C infection
		• Condylomata acuminata
		• Follicular lymphoma
		• Hairy cell leukemia
		• Malignant melanoma
			• **Dosing (Adult):**
			  – IM/SQ 5 million units daily
			  – IM/SQ 2 to 30 million units/m² three times weekly
			  – IV 20 million units/m² daily x 5 days for 4 weeks, then SQ 10 million units/m² three times weekly x 48 weeks
			• **Dosing (Peds):**
			  – IM/SQ 3 million units/m² three times weekly for 1 week, then 6 million units/m² three times weekly
			    • Maximum 10 million units/dose
			• **CYP450 Interactions:** Inhibits CYP1A2
			• **Renal or Hepatic Dose Adjustments:**
			  – ASL/ALT 5 to 10x ULN - temporarily hold, then resume at 50% previous dose
			  – ASL/ALT greater than 10x ULN - discontinue
			• **Dosage Forms:** Injection (solution, powder for solution)

Interferon - Drug Class Review
High-Yield Med Reviews

Generic Name	Brand Name	Indication(s) or Uses	Notes

Peginterferon-Alfa-2a	Pegasys	▪ Chronic hepatitis B
		▪ Chronic hepatitis C
			▪ **Dosing (Adult):**
			  – SQ 180 mcg qweek x48 weeks
			    ▪ Extra info if needed
			▪ **Dosing (Peds):**
			  – SQ 65 to 180 mcg/dose (based on BSA)
			  – SQ 104 mcg/m^2 qweek
			    ▪ Maximum 180 mcg/dose
			▪ **CYP450 Interactions:** Inhibits CYP1A2
			▪ **Renal or Hepatic Dose Adjustments:**
			  – GFR less than 30 mL/minute - 135 mcg qweek
			  – ALT 5x ULN - temporarily hold, then resume at 135 mcg dose
			  – ALT greater than 10x ULN - discontinue
			▪ **Dosage Forms:** Injection (solution)

Peginterferon-Alfa-2b	PegIntron, Sylatron	▪ Chronic hepatitis C
		▪ Melanoma adjuvant treatment
			▪ **Dosing (Adult):**
			  – SQ 6 mcg/kg/week x8 doses, then 3 mcg/kg/week for up to 5 years
			▪ **Dosing (Peds):**
			  – SQ 60 mcg/m2 qweek
			▪ **CYP450 Interactions:** Inhibits CYP1A2
			▪ **Renal or Hepatic Dose Adjustments:**
			  – GFR 30 to 50 mL/min/1.73 m^2 - 4.5 mcg/kg/week, then 2.25 mcg/kg/week
			  – GFR less than 30 mL/min/1.73 m^2 - 3 mcg/kg/week, then 1.5 mcg/kg/week
			▪ **Dosage Forms:** IV (powder for solution)

Interferon-Alfa-n3	Alferon N	▪ Condylomata acuminata	▪ **Dosing (Adult):**
			  – Intralesional 250,000 units per wart twice weekly
			    ▪ Maximum dose per session of 2.5 million units, maximum duration 8 weeks
			▪ **Dosing (Peds):** Not routinely used
			▪ **CYP450 Interactions:** None
			▪ **Renal or Hepatic Dose Adjustments:** None
			▪ **Dosage Forms:** Injection (solution)

Interferon-Gamma-1b	Actimmune	▪ Chronic granulomatous disease
		▪ Malignant osteopetrosis
			▪ **Dosing (Adult):**
			  – SQ 50 mcg/m^2 three times weekly
			▪ **Dosing (Peds):**
			  – BSA 0.5 m^2 or less - 1.5 mcg/kg/dose three times weekly
			    ▪ Maximum 50 mcg/m^2
			▪ **CYP450 Interactions:** None
			▪ **Renal or Hepatic Dose Adjustments:** None
			▪ **Dosage Forms:** Injection (solution)

Interferon - Drug Class Review
High-Yield Med Reviews

Generic Name	Brand Name	Indication(s) or Uses	Notes

Interferon-Beta-1a	Avonex, Rebif	• Relapsing multiple sclerosis	• **Dosing (Adult):**
			  – IM 30 mcg qweek
			  – SQ 8.8 mcg three times weekly x2 weeks, then 22 mcg three times weekly x2 weeks, then 44 mcg three times weekly
			• **Dosing (Peds):** Not routinely used
			• **CYP450 Interactions:** None
			• **Renal or Hepatic Dose Adjustments:**
			  – ALT 5x ULN - temporarily hold, then resume at 50% previous dose
			• **Dosage Forms:** Injection (solution)

Interferon-Beta-1b	Betaseron, Extavia	• Relapsing multiple sclerosis	• **Dosing (Adult):**
			  – SQ 2 million units every other day, titrated up q2weeks
			    • Target dose 8 million units every other day
			• **Dosing (Peds):** Not routinely used
			• **CYP450 Interactions:** None
			• **Renal or Hepatic Dose Adjustments:** None
			• **Dosage Forms:** Injection (solution)

Peginterferon-Beta-1a	Plegridy	Relapsing multiple sclerosis	• **Dosing (Adult):** – SQ 63 mcg on day 1, 94 mcg on day 15, then 125 mcg q2weeks on day 29 • **Dosing (Peds):** Not routinely used • **CYP450 Interactions:** None • **Renal or Hepatic Dose Adjustments:** None • **Dosage Forms:** Injection (solution)

High-Yield Clinical Knowledge

- **Toxicities and Adverse Events**
  - Therapy with interferon products is complicated by common injection site reactions, flu-like syndrome (lasting up to 24 hours after injection), thrombocytopenia, neutropenia (in up to 90% of patients) hepatic injury/failure.
    - There are numerous other serious and therapy complicating adverse reactions ranging from fatigue, chills, depression to alopecia, myalgias, and insomnia.
  - Many patients cannot tolerate the adverse events therapy the duration, prompting discontinuation and selecting alternative regimens.
    - There are numerous antiviral therapeutics for hepatitis B and C that have now largely replaced interferons for this indication.
- **Pregnancy Safety**
  - Interferons have been associated with spontaneous abortion in pregnant patients and are therefore not recommended for this population.
  - Sexually active pregnant patients should be counseled to use appropriate contraception while taking interferon products.
- **Relapsing-Remitting Multiple Sclerosis**
  - Interferon-beta 1-a, interferon-beta-1b, and peginterferon-beta-1a are key medications for the management of relapsing-remitting multiple sclerosis.

- Head to head data is lacking, but these agents can be selected based on patient-specific criteria.
- **Avonex Titration**
  - During the initiation of interferon-beta-1a therapy, although the initial IM dosing is 30 mcg once weekly, most patients cannot tolerate this starting dose due to flu-like symptoms.
  - An initial lower starting dose of 7.5 mcg administered IM every week with 7.5 mcg incremental dose increases every 2-4 weeks is recommended to mitigate this adverse reaction.
- **Adaptive Immune Augmentation**
  - Interferon-gamma enhances the adaptive immune system's activity through Ig-isotype switching in B cells and T helper cell 1 differentiation.
- **Evolution in Safety and Efficacy**
  - With the development of alternative agents to treat hepatitis infections and multiple sclerosis, interferon therapy has been relegated as a non-preferred therapy, finding clinical use among patients who fail or otherwise are not candidates for these newer interventions.
  - As a result, rarer adverse events are becoming more prevalent, specifically pulmonary arterial hypertension.
  - PAH secondary to interferon therapy appears to be irreversible in nature, and its risk increases with prolonged therapy.

High-Yield Fast-Facts

- **HCV Antivirals**
  - HCV treatment with newer antiviral regimens such as ledipasvir-sofosbuvir and sofosbuvir-velpatasvir have largely replaced interferon-based therapy.
- **Cytokine Family**
  - Interferons belong to the larger group known as cytokines, including TNF-alpha, Interleukin 2, and GCSF.
- **Interferon Delta, Epsilon, And Omega**
  - Other interferons exist, including interferons delta, epsilon, and omega.
  - Interferon epsilon and omega belong to the Type 1 interferon family, whereas interferon delta is a type three interferon.

HIGH-YIELD BOARD EXAM ESSENTIALS
- **CLASSIC AGENTS:** Interferon-alfa-2b, interferon-gamma-1b, peginterferon-alfa-2a, peginterferon-alfa-2b, interferon-alfa-n3, interferon-beta-1a, interferon-beta-1b, peginterferon-beta-1a
- **DRUG CLASS:** Interferon
- **INDICATIONS:** AIDS-related Kaposi sarcoma, chronic hepatitis B, chronic hepatitis C infection, condylomata acuminata, follicular lymphoma, hairy cell leukemia, malignant melanoma, relapsing multiple sclerosis
- **MECHANISM:** Produce interferon-stimulated genes in hepatitis B or C infected cells and neighboring cells and enhances adaptive immune responses (Type 1 Interferons); Immune-enhancement by augmenting antigen presentation and macrophage, NK cell, and cytotoxic T-lymphocyte activation (Type 2 Interferons)
- **SIDE EFFECTS:** Injection site reactions, flu-like syndrome, thrombocytopenia, neutropenia, hepatic injury/failure.
- **CLINICAL PEARLS:** With the development of alternative agents to treat hepatitis infections and multiple sclerosis, interferon therapy has been relegated as a non-preferred therapy, finding clinical use among patients who fail or otherwise are not candidates for these newer interventions. As a result, rarer adverse events are becoming more prevalent, specifically pulmonary arterial hypertension.

High-Yield Basic Pharmacology

- **Azathioprine**
  - A prodrug, metabolized to 6-mercaptopurine (6-MP), then to 6-thioguanine nucleotides, ultimately disrupting de novo and salvage synthesis of DNA and RNA proteins, preventing cellular proliferation.
- **Mycophenolic acid (MPA) derivatives (mycophenolate mofetil and mycophenolate sodium)**
  - Non-competitive inhibitor of inosine monophosphate dehydrogenase (IMPDH) I and II, preventing de novo guanosine nucleotide synthesis, diminished DNA polymerase activity, and reducing lymphocyte proliferation
    - Mycophenolate mofetil is a prodrug form that MPA produced after hepatic-first pass metabolism.
    - Mycophenolate sodium uses an enteric coating to preserve MPA from gastric pH but allows for direct absorption of MPA from the small intestine.
      - Both are metabolized hepatically to the inactive metabolite MPAG, which is excreted in the bile and urine.

Primary Net Benefit

- Azathioprine is used in combination with corticosteroids for immunosuppression after organ transplant, but due to dose-limiting toxicities, it has been reserved for patients intolerant to alternative medications.
- MPA derivatives combined with calcineurin inhibitors produce targeted immunosuppression and improved tolerability and safety post-transplant with expanding roles in other diseases.

Antimetabolites - Drug Class Review
High-Yield Med Reviews

Mechanism of Action:
Azathioprine - Metabolized to 6-MP, then to 6-thioguanine nucleotides, disrupting DNA and RNA synthesis, preventing cellular proliferation.
MPA derivatives - prevent de novo guanosine nucleotide synthesis, diminished DNA polymerase activity, and reduced lymphocyte proliferation.

Class Effects: Bone marrow suppression (pancytopenia).

Generic Name	Brand Name	Indication(s) or Uses	Notes

Azathioprine	Azasan, Imuran	• Kidney transplantation
		• Rheumatoid arthritis
			• **Dosing (Adult):**
			  – IV/Oral 2 to 5 mg/kg once followed by 1 to 3 mg/kg by mouth daily
			    • Normal dose range 50 to 150mg/day
			• **Dosing (Peds):**
			  – IV/Oral 2 to 5 mg/kg once followed by 1 to 3 mg/kg by mouth daily
			• **CYP450 Interactions:** None
			• **Renal or Hepatic Dose Adjustments:**
			  – GFR 10 to 50 mL/minute - Reduce dose by 25%
			  – GFR less than 10 mL/minute - Reduce dose by 50%
			• **Dosage Forms:** IV (solution), Oral (tablet)

Antimetabolites - Drug Class Review
High-Yield Med Reviews

Generic Name	Brand Name	Indication(s) or Uses	Notes
Mycophenolate mofetil	CellCept	• Organ transplantation	• **Dosing (Adult):** – IV/Oral 1 to 1.5 g q12h • **Dosing (Peds):** – Oral 600 mg/m²/dose divided q12h • Maximum 2,000 mg/day • **CYP450 Interactions:** None • **Renal or Hepatic Dose Adjustments:** None • **Dosage Forms:** IV (solution), Oral (capsule, tablet, suspension)
Mycophenolate sodium	Myfortic	Organ transplantation	• **Dosing (Adult):** – Oral 360 to 1080 mg BID • Extra info if needed • **Dosing (Peds):** – Oral 400 mg/mg/m²/dose divided q12h • Maximum 1,440 mg/day • **CYP450 Interactions:** None • **Renal or Hepatic Dose Adjustments:** None • **Dosage Forms:** Oral (tablet)

High-Yield Clinical Knowledge

- **Azathioprine Dose Limiting Toxicity**
    - The use of azathioprine is limited by hematologic toxicities, including anemia, leukopenia, and thrombocytopenia.
    - Other common adverse events include alopecia, hepatotoxicity, and pancreatitis.
- **Xanthine-Oxidase and Its Inhibitors**
    - Coadministration of azathioprine (or 6-MP for that matter) increases 6-TGN production, resulting in an increased risk of bone marrow toxicity and pancytopenia.
    - Empiric dose reductions by 5- to 75 % are recommended when allopurinol is added to azathioprine.
- **MPA Oral Forms Not Equivalent**
    - The different MPA formulations, mycophenolate mofetil and mycophenolate sodium are not equivalent with respect to dose.
        - The approximate equivalence is mycophenolate mofetil 250 mg is equivalent to mycophenolate sodium 180 mg.
- **Pregnancy**
    - MPA derivatives should be avoided in pregnant patients due to the risk of pregnancy loss and congenital malformations.
    - In patients of childbearing potential should follow appropriate contraception during MPA treatment and for 6 weeks after.
- **Cell Phase**
    - The specific cell cycle azathioprine disrupts the G2-M phase.
- **MPA Oral dosage form**
    - In pediatric patients, mycophenolate mofetil may be preferred because of the availability of an oral suspension, where mycophenolate sodium is only available as a tablet.

HIGH-YIELD BOARD EXAM ESSENTIALS

- **CLASSIC AGENTS:** Azathioprine, mycophenolate mofetil, mycophenolate sodium
- **DRUG CLASS:** Antimetabolites
- **INDICATIONS:** Prophylaxis of organ rejection, rheumatoid arthritis, Lupus nephritis
- **MECHANISM:** Azathioprine - Metabolized to 6-MP, then to 6-thioguanine nucleotides, disrupting DNA and RNA synthesis, preventing cellular proliferation. MPA derivatives prevent de novo guanosine nucleotide synthesis, diminished DNA polymerase activity, and reduced lymphocyte proliferation.
- **SIDE EFFECTS:** Anemia, leukopenia, thrombocytopenia, alopecia, hepatotoxicity, and pancreatitis.
- **CLINICAL PEARLS:** Coadministration of azathioprine (or 6-MP for that matter) increases 6-TGN production, resulting in an increased risk of bone marrow toxicity and pancytopenia. Empiric dose reductions by 5- to 75 % are recommended when allopurinol is added to azathioprine.

High-Yield Basic Pharmacology

- **Mechanism of Action**
  - Complex with FKBP12 to form a complex that binds to and inhibits the protein kinase mTOR and thus prevents cell cycle progression at the G1 to S phase transition.
- **Everolimus Origin**
  - Everolimus is a synthetic derivative of sirolimus but carries a much shorter half-life than sirolimus (30 hours vs. 62 hours).
- **Oral Absorption**
  - A high-fat meal decreases exposure of both everolimus and sirolimus by 23-35%.
  - Patients should be instructed to keep a consistent diet, which will allow appropriate titration to therapeutic targets.

Primary Net Benefit

- Similar efficacy, but improved safety compared to calcineurin-inhibitor-based therapy post-transplant.

Antiproliferative Agents (mTOR Inhibitors) - Drug Class Review High-Yield Med Reviews			
Mechanism of Action: *Complex with FKBP12 to form a complex that binds to and inhibits the protein kinase mTOR and prevents cell cycle progression at the G1 to S phase transition.*			
Class Effects: *Prevention of organ rejection, mouth ulcers, delayed wound healing, dose-dependent BMS.*			
Generic Name	**Brand Name**	**Main Indication(s) or Uses**	**Notes**

Everolimus	Afinitor, Zortress	• Breast cancer
		• Neuroendocrine tumors
		• Liver, renal transplant
		• Renal cell carcinoma
			• **Dosing (Adult):**
			  – Oral 5 to 10 mg daily
			  – Oral 1 mg BID with tacrolimus
			• **Dosing (Peds):**
			  – Oral 0.8 to 4.5 mg/m2/dose once to twice daily. Max dose 1.5 mg/dose (transplant indication)
			• **CYP450 Interactions:** Substrate & inhibits CYP3A4
			• **Renal or Hepatic Dose Adjustments:**
			  – Child-Pugh Class A - Reduce dose by ⅓
			  – Child-Pugh Class B - Reduce dose by ½
			  – Child-Pugh Class C - Reduce dose by ½ to ¾
			• **Dosage Forms:** Oral (tablet, soluble tablet)

Sirolimus	Rapamune	• Renal transplant	• **Dosing (Adult):**
			  – Less than 40kg: 3 mg/m^2 x1 followed by 1 mg/m^2 daily
			  – 40 kg or over: 6 to 15 mg x 1 followed by 2 to 5 mg daily. Max loading dose of 40 mg
			• **Dosing (Peds):**
			  – 3 mg/m^2 x1 followed by 1 mg/m^2 daily
			    • Maximum daily dose of 40 mg
			• **CYP450 Interactions:** Substrate of CYP3A4
			• **Renal or Hepatic Dose Adjustments:**
			  – Child-Pugh Class A - Reduce dose by ⅓
			  – Child-Pugh Class B/C - Reduce dose by ½
			• **Dosage Forms:** Oral (solution, tablet)

High-Yield Clinical Knowledge

- **Delayed Wound Healing**
  - The initiation of sirolimus is delayed 3 months after transplant (or once surgical wounds are healed) due to sirolimus delayed wound healing.
  - Everolimus has a lower risk of delayed wound healing, with some providers beginning therapy before the 3-month time-frame associated with sirolimus.
- **Cholesterol and Triglycerides**
  - The mTOR inhibitors are associated with hypercholesterolemia and hypertriglyceridemia due to the overproduction of lipoproteins and lipoprotein lipase inhibition.
  - These effects are managed via dose reduction or the initiation of a statin or fibrate.
- **Mouth Ulcers**
  - Mouth ulcers are a dose-dependent adverse event associated with sirolimus and can occur in up to 60% of patients.
- **Drug Interactions**
  - Sirolimus and cyclosporine are both CYP3A4 substrates and inhibitors; thus, when combined, they cause increased AUC and trough concentrations of each.
    - The risk of neurotoxicity and nephrotoxicity is significant, without appropriate dose adjustments.
  - The combination of sirolimus tacrolimus is associated with an increased risk of nephrotoxicity.
    - Everolimus has not demonstrated this increased risk when combined with cyclosporine or tacrolimus.
  - Grapefruit and grapefruit juice may affect the absorption of sirolimus and everolimus, and its consumption should be discouraged.
- **Dose-Dependent Myelosuppression**
  - Both everolimus and sirolimus are associated with dose-dependent myelosuppression that is often transient.
  - Thrombocytopenia typically occurs within 2 weeks of sirolimus initiation and is associated with higher trough concentrations (above 15 ng/mL).
- **Combination Therapy**
  - The role of sirolimus is limited to preventing rejection in kidney transplant patients in combination with cyclosporine, tacrolimus, or mycophenolate.
  - Compared with cyclosporine or tacrolimus, the combination of sirolimus and mycophenolate can be similarly effective but reduce the risk of nephrotoxicity.

HIGH-YIELD BOARD EXAM ESSENTIALS

- **CLASSIC AGENTS:** Everolimus, sirolimus
- **DRUG CLASS:** Antiproliferative agents (mTOR inhibitors)
- **INDICATIONS:** Breast cancer, neuroendocrine tumors, liver, renal transplant, renal cell carcinoma, renal transplant
- **MECHANISM:** Complex with FKBP12 to form a complex that binds to and inhibits the protein kinase mTOR and prevents cell cycle progression at the G1 to S phase transition.
- **SIDE EFFECTS:** Delayed wound healing, mouth ulcers, hypercholesterolemia and hypertriglyceridemia
- **CLINICAL PEARLS:**
  - Impaired renal function, glucose regulation, and lipid metabolism are common with this drug class and requiring lab monitoring.
  - Sirolimus and cyclosporine are both CYP3A4 substrates and inhibitors and are associated with drug interactions.
  - Both everolimus and sirolimus are associated with dose-dependent myelosuppression that is often transient. Thrombocytopenia typically occurs within 2 weeks of sirolimus initiation and is associated with higher trough concentrations (above 15 ng/mL).

High-Yield Basic Pharmacology

- **Hydroxychloroquine**
  - Poorly understood mechanism that may include interference with antigen processing in macrophages and other antigen-presenting cells.
- **Leflunomide**
  - A prodrug converted in the GI and blood to an active metabolite (A77 1726) stops cellular growth by inhibiting dihydroorotate dehydrogenase and decreased ribonuclease synthesis.
- **Methotrexate (low-dose)**
  - Inhibits lymphocyte, macrophage, neutrophil, and dendritic cell function via amino-imidazole-carboxamide-ribonucleotide (AICAR) transformylase and thymidylate synthetase inhibition and extracellular AMP accumulation.
- **Sulfasalazine**
  - Converted to 5-aminosalicylic (5-ASA) acid and sulfapyridine, which impair B-cell and T-cell response and proliferation and inhibit the production of inflammatory cytokines including IL-1, IL-6, IL-12, and TNF-alpha.
- **Tofacitinib**
  - Selectively inhibits Janus Kinase 3 (JAK3) and JAK1, which then prevents the JAK3/JAK1 complex from activating the signal transduction and activators of transcription (STATs), impairing cytokine and growth factor-mediated gene expression and intracellular activity of B and T lymphocytes, CD- natural killer cells, and immune globulins.

Primary Net Benefit

- Recently designated conventional synthetic DMARDs (csDMARDs) impact disease severity and quality of life in autoimmune disease but carry significant toxicities and intolerances.

DMARDs – Drug Class Review			
High-Yield Med Reviews			
Mechanism of Action: *See agents above*			
Class Effects: *Recently designated conventional synthetic DMARDs (csDMARDs) impact disease severity and quality of life in autoimmune disease but carry significant toxicities and intolerances.*			
Generic Name	**Brand Name**	**Indication(s) or Uses**	**Notes**
Hydroxychloroq uine	Plaquenil	• Lupus erythematosus	• **Dosing (Adult):** Oral 200 to 400 mg daily • **Dosing (Peds):** – Oral 5 mg/kg/day in 1-2 divided doses • Maximum 400 mg/day • **CYP450 Interactions:** Substrate CYP2D6 • **Renal or Hepatic Dose Adjustments:** None • **Dosage Forms:** Oral (tablet)
Leflunomide	Arava	• Rheumatoid arthritis	• **Dosing (Adult):** – Oral 100 mg daily x 3 days, then 20 mg daily • **Dosing (Peds):** – < 20 kg - 100 mg x 1 then 10 mg every other day – 20 to 40 kg - 100 mg daily x 2, then 10 mg daily • **CYP450 Interactions:** Inhibits CYP2C8, Induces CYP1A2 • **Renal or Hepatic Dose Adjustments:** – DC if ALT elevations more than 3 times ULN • **Dosage Forms:** Oral (tablet)

DMARDs – Drug Class Review
High-Yield Med Reviews

Generic Name	Brand Name	Indication(s) or Uses	Notes

Methotrexate	Otrexup
	Rasuvo
	Trexall
	Xatmep
		• Polyarticular course juvenile idiopathic arthritis
		• Psoriatic arthritis
		• Rheumatoid arthritis
		• Ulcerative colitis
			• **Dosing (Adult): Rheumatic/DMARD Dosing only**
			  – IM/SQ/Oral 7.5 to 25 mg weekly
			• **Dosing (Peds):**
			  – Oral/SQ 10 to 30 mg/m^2
			    • Maximum 25 mg/week
			• **CYP450 Interactions:** P-gp substrate
			• **Renal or Hepatic Dose Adjustments:**
			  – GFR 10 to 50 mL/minute - Reduce dose by 50%
			  – GFR less than 10 mL/minute - avoid use
			• **Dosage Forms:** Oral (tablet, solution), Injection (solution)

Sulfasalazine	Azulfidine	• Rheumatoid arthritis
		• Ulcerative colitis
			• **Dosing (Adult):**
			  – Oral 500 to 2000 mg/day in 1-2 divided doses
			    • Maximum 3 g/day
			• **Dosing (Peds):**
			  – Oral 40 to 70 mg/kg/day in 3 to 6 divided doses
			    • Maximum 4 g/day
			• **CYP450 Interactions:** None
			• **Renal or Hepatic Dose Adjustments:** None
			• **Dosage Forms:** Oral (tablet)

Tofacitinib	Xeljanz	• Polyarticular course juvenile idiopathic arthritis
		• Psoriatic arthritis
		• Rheumatoid arthritis
		• Ulcerative colitis
			• **Dosing (Adult):**
			  – Oral IR tablet 5 to 10 mg BID
			  – Oral ER tablet 11 to 22 mg daily
			• **Dosing (Peds):** IR only
			  – 10 to less than 20 kg - Oral 3.2 mg BID
			  – 20 to less than 40 kg - Oral 4 mg BID
			• **CYP450 Interactions:** Substrate CYP2C19, CYP3A4
			• **Renal or Hepatic Dose Adjustments:**
			  – Moderate to severe impairment - reduce dose by half
			• **Dosage Forms:** Oral (tablet)

High-Yield Clinical Knowledge

- **Hepatotoxicity**
  - Leflunomide has been associated with mitochondrial toxicity, which is directly related to its mechanism inhibiting dihydroorotate dehydrogenase, which is also essential for Coenzyme Q's oxidation complex III of the electron transport chain.
    - The electron transport chain's inhibition may cause a shutdown of glycolysis, ATP production, and a shift to lipolysis, proteolysis, oxidative stress, and necrosis.
  - Liver tissue, particularly zone three hepatocytes, are at high risk of this oxidative damage, and their damage or loss can lead to hepatic injury and failure.
- **Methotrexate Dosing**
  - For rheumatoid arthritis and other autoimmune disorders, methotrexate is typically dosed on a weekly schedule.
    - Typical starting doses of methotrexate 7.5 mg weekly.

- Severe toxicity can occur through prescribing, dispensing, or administration errors that deliver the required weekly dose daily.
- **Tofacitinib Cancer Risk**
  - JAK inhibitors have been associated with an increased incidence of lymphomas and other malignancies, including breast cancer.
    - This risk is the subject of one of the Black Box Warnings for tofacitinib.
- **Gold**
  - Gold salts were used to treat RA but have fallen out of favor due to significant toxicity and unproven benefits.
- **Biologic DMARDs (bDMARDs)**
  - bDMARDs are large-molecule medications and can be further divided into the biological original (boDMARD) and biosimilar DMARDs (bsDMARDs).
- **Genomic Prediction**
  - Patients with CYP450 mutations, specific solute carrier genes, or mitochondrial aldehyde dehydrogenase genes are at higher risk of methotrexate toxicity.
- **Hydroxychloroquine and COVID**
  - The use of hydroxychloroquine for COVID-19 was the subject of much controversy, but available evidence suggested no significant improvement on the pandemic causing virus.

HIGH-YIELD BOARD EXAM ESSENTIALS
- **CLASSIC AGENTS:** Hydroxychloroquine, Leflunomide, Methotrexate, Sulfasalazine, Tofacitinib
- **DRUG CLASS:** DMARD
- **INDICATIONS:** Lupus erythematosus, polyarticular course juvenile idiopathic arthritis, psoriatic arthritis, rheumatoid arthritis, ulcerative colitis
- **MECHANISM:**
  - Interferences with antigen processing in macrophages and other antigen-presenting cells (hydroxychloroquine)
  - Its active metabolite (A77 1726) stops cellular growth by inhibiting dihydroorotate dehydrogenase and decreased ribonuclease synthesis (leflunomide)
  - Inhibits lymphocyte, macrophage, neutrophil, and dendritic cell function via AICAR transformylase and thymidylate synthetase inhibition and extracellular AMP accumulation (methotrexate)
  - Impairs B-cell and T-cell response and proliferation and inhibits inflammatory cytokines production, including IL-1, IL-6, IL-12, and TNF-alfa (sulfasalazine)
  - Selectively JAK inhibitor, impairing cytokine and growth factor-mediated gene expression and intracellular activity of B and T lymphocytes, CD- natural killer cells, and immune globulins (tofacitinib)
- **SIDE EFFECTS:** Nausea, stomatitis, anemia, leukopenia, alopecia, rash
- **CLINICAL PEARLS:** Patients with HLA-B*08-01 and HLA-A*31-01 are at high risk of neutropenia from sulfasalazine.

High-Yield Basic Pharmacology

- **Mechanism of Action**
  - IL-1 receptor antagonists competitively inhibit the proinflammatory IL-1-alpha and IL-1-beta
    - Anakinra decreases immune-inflammatory response by its actions as a recombinant version of IL-1 receptor agonists and blocks the effects of IL-1-alpha and IL-1-beta on this receptor.
    - Canakinumab and rilonacept complex with IL-1-beta, preventing its binding to IL-1 receptors
- **Bone and Joint Effects**
  - IL-1 receptor antagonism can decrease or stop cartilage degradation from loss of proteoglycans and halts bone resorption.

Primary Net Benefit

- High IL-1 levels are correlated with active inflammatory processes, sparking IL-1 receptor antagonists' development, but their use has been limited due to costs and efficacy compared to conventional DMARDs.

IL-1 Antagonists - Drug Class Review High-Yield Med Reviews			
Mechanism of Action: *Competitively inhibit proinflammatory interleukins IL-1-alpha and IL-1-beta.*			
Class Effects: *Reduction in inflammation, injection site reactions, URIs.*			
Generic Name	**Brand Name**	**Indication(s) or Uses**	**Notes**
Anakinra	Kineret	<ul><li>Deficiency of IL-1 receptor antagonist</li><li>Neonatal-onset multisystem inflammatory disease</li><li>Rheumatoid arthritis</li></ul>	<ul><li>**Dosing (Adult):**<ul><li>SQ 1 to 4 mg/kg q24h or 100 mg q24h<ul><li>Maximum 200 mg/day</li></ul></li></ul></li><li>**Dosing (Peds):**<ul><li>SQ 1 to 4 mg/kg q24h<ul><li>Maximum 200 mg/day</li></ul></li></ul></li><li>**CYP450 Interactions:** None</li><li>**Renal or Hepatic Dose Adjustments:**<ul><li>GFR less than 30 mL/minute - Administer every other day</li></ul></li><li>**Dosage Forms:** Prefilled syringe</li></ul>
Canakinumab	Ilaris	<ul><li>Adult-onset Still's disease</li><li>Periodic fever syndromes</li><li>Systemic juvenile idiopathic arthritis</li></ul>	<ul><li>**Dosing (Adult):**<ul><li>SQ 2 to 8 mg/kg every 4 weeks<ul><li>Maximum 8 mg/kg/day</li></ul></li></ul></li><li>**Dosing (Peds):**<ul><li>SQ 2 to 4 mg/kg q24h<ul><li>Maximum 8 mg/kg/day</li></ul></li></ul></li><li>**CYP450 Interactions:** None</li><li>**Renal or Hepatic Dose Adjustments:** None</li><li>**Dosage Forms:** Solution for subcutaneous injection</li></ul>

IL-1 Antagonists - Drug Class Review				
High-Yield Med Reviews				
Generic Name	Brand Name	Indication(s) or Uses	Notes

Rilonacept	Arcalyst	• Cryopyrin-associated periodic syndromes
		• Deficiency of IL-1 receptor antagonist
			• **Dosing (Adult):**
			  – Initial: SQ 320 mg as two injections at two different sites on the same day
			  – Maintenance: SQ 160 mg qweek
			• **Dosing (Peds):**
			  – Initial: SQ 4.4 mg/kg (maximum 320 mg) as two injections at two different sites on the same day
			  – Maintenance: SQ 2.2 mg/kg (maximum 160 mg) qweek
			• **CYP450 Interactions:** None
			• **Renal or Hepatic Dose Adjustments:** None
			• **Dosage Forms:** Solution for subcutaneous injection

High-Yield Clinical Knowledge

- **Antibody Vs. Recombinant Receptor**
  - Anakinra and rilonacept are recombinant forms of the IL-1 receptor and the IL-1 receptor ligand-binding domain, respectively.
  - Canakinumab is a human monoclonal antibody against IL-1-beta specifically.
- **Injection Reactions**
  - These agents are all administered via subcutaneous injection, associated with a high prevalence of injection site reactions.
  - Injection site reactions are self-limiting and do not frequently require intervention.
- **Infection Risk**
  - Upper respiratory tract infections are a frequent adverse event following IL-1 antagonist therapy, affecting 55% of patients.
  - Mycoplasma tuberculosis infection is also possible and requires TB screening before initiation of these agents.
- **Off-Label Uses**
  - Anakinra, canakinumab, and rilonacept have been used for various off-label indications, including gout, familial Mediterranean fever.
- **HIT and Recurrent Stroke**
  - Anakinra has been suggested as an alternative agent for treating heparin-induced thrombocytopenia or preventing recurrent stroke or TIA.

HIGH-YIELD BOARD EXAM ESSENTIALS
- **CLASSIC AGENTS:** Anakinra, canakinumab, rilonacept
- **DRUG CLASS:** IL-1 Antagonists
- **INDICATIONS:** Deficiency of IL-1 receptor antagonist (anakinra, rilonacept), neonatal-onset multisystem inflammatory disease, rheumatoid arthritis (anakinra), adult-onset still's disease, periodic fever syndromes, systemic juvenile idiopathic arthritis (canakinumab), cryopyrin-associated periodic syndromes (rilonacept)
- **MECHANISM:** Competitively inhibit proinflammatory interleukins IL-1-alpha and IL-1-beta.
- **SIDE EFFECTS:** Injection site reactions, upper respiratory tract infections
- **CLINICAL PEARLS:** IL-1-beta inhibition has been proposed to improve the inflammatory pathway after acute myocardial infarctions, particularly C-reactive protein and IL-6. This effect has been supported with the use of canakinumab in the CANTOS trial, further described below.

High-Yield Basic Pharmacology

- **Mechanism of Action**
  - Binds to the alpha chain of IL-2 - CD25 receptor complex on the surface of activated T-cells, preventing IL-2 activation and proliferation of T-cells.
- **IL-2 Receptor Binding**
  - The degree of IL-2 receptor binding accomplished by basiliximab is extensive, occurs rapidly, and persists for a long period of time, typically 4 to 6 weeks after administration.

Primary Net Benefit

- Compared with other immunosuppressant induction agents, antithymocyte globulins, and alemtuzumab, basiliximab has a safer adverse event profile, similar efficacy but lacks robust data to support widespread use.

<table>
<tr><td colspan="4">IL-2 Antagonist - Drug Class Review
High-Yield Med Reviews</td></tr>
<tr><td colspan="4">Mechanism of Action: Binds to the alpha chain of IL-2 - CD25 receptor complex on the surface of activated T-cells, preventing IL-2 activation and proliferation of T-cells.</td></tr>
<tr><td colspan="4">Class Effects: Less infusion reactions compared to other agents, prevention of rejection of transplanted organ.</td></tr>
<tr><td>Generic Name</td><td>Brand Name</td><td>Main Indication(s) or Uses</td><td>Notes</td></tr>
<tr>
<td>Basiliximab</td>
<td>Simulect</td>
<td>• Acute rejection prophylaxis</td>
<td>
• Dosing (Adult):
  – IV 20 mg within 2 hours before transplant surgery, then 20 mg 4 days after transplant
  – IV 20 mg on days 1 and 4
• Dosing (Peds):
  – Less than 35 kg - IV 10 mg within 6 hours before surgery, then 10 mg 4 days after surgery
• CYP450 Interactions: None
• Renal or Hepatic Dose Adjustments: None
• Dosage Forms: IV (solution)
</td>
</tr>
</table>

High-Yield Clinical Knowledge

- **Improved Safety**
  - Compared with other immunosuppression induction agents, basiliximab is not associated with infusion reactions.
    - Of course, immunosuppression is a class effect and the desired clinical outcome.
- **Antimurine Antibodies**
  - Basiliximab is not a fully human monoclonal antibody but contains approximately 20% murine monoclonal antibodies.
  - As a result, there is a risk of the development of human anti murine antibodies.
- **Renal And Liver Transplant**
  - Although approved for renal transplants, basiliximab has been used in other organ transplants, including liver, lung, and heart.
  - The use of basiliximab can delay the initiation of calcineurin inhibitor therapy and delaying their associated toxicities.

High-Yield Fast-Fact

- **Tacrolimus Interaction**
    - According to drug-interaction software programs, the concomitant use of basiliximab and tacrolimus is contraindicated.
    - Since basiliximab is used immediately around transplant and calcineurin inhibitors are typically started 1-3 months after the transplant, this interaction's clinical significance is questionable.

HIGH-YIELD BOARD EXAM ESSENTIALS

- **CLASSIC AGENTS:** Basiliximab
- **DRUG CLASS:** IL-2 Antagonists
- **INDICATIONS:** Acute rejection prophylaxis, acute graft-versus-host disease
- **MECHANISM:** Binds to the alpha chain of IL-2 - CD25 receptor complex on the surface of activated T-cells, preventing IL-2 activation and proliferation of T-cells.
- **SIDE EFFECTS:** Immunosuppression, anti-murine antibody development
- **CLINICAL PEARLS:** The use of basiliximab can delay the initiation of calcineurin inhibitor therapy and delaying their associated toxicities.

High-Yield Basic Pharmacology

- **Mechanism of Action**
  - Inhibits IL-6 mediated inflammation by binding to both soluble and membrane-bound IL-6 receptors.
- **Alternative CYP Induction**
  - IL-6 inhibition can cause an increase in activity of cytochrome P450, leading to numerous interactions.
  - Current evidence suggests IL-6 inhibitors inhibit CYP3A4, but there may also be induction of other isoenzymes, including CYP2C9, CYP2C19, and CYP2D6.

Primary Net Benefit

- Considered non-TNF biologic DMARD (bDMARD) and counteracts proinflammatory cytokines active in the pathogenesis of rheumatoid arthritis.

<table>
<tr><td colspan="4">IL-6 Receptor Antagonist - Drug Class Review
High-Yield Med Reviews</td></tr>
<tr><td colspan="4">Mechanism of Action: Inhibits IL-6 mediated inflammation by binding to both soluble and membrane-bound IL-6 receptors.</td></tr>
<tr><td colspan="4">Class Effects: Risk of infection (including TB), neutropenia, thrombocytopenia, liver enzyme elevation.</td></tr>
<tr><td>Generic Name</td><td>Brand Name</td><td>Indication(s) or Uses</td><td>Notes</td></tr>
<tr>
<td>Sarilumab</td>
<td>Kevzara</td>
<td>• Rheumatoid arthritis</td>
<td>
• Dosing (Adult):
  – SQ 200 mg q2weeks
• Dosing (Peds):
  – Not routinely used
• CYP450 Interactions: None
• Renal or Hepatic Dose Adjustments:
  – ALT elevation 3x to less than 5x ULN - interrupt therapy until ALT less than 3x ULN, then resume at 150 mg q2weeks
  – ALT more than 5x ULN - discontinue
• Dosage Forms: Solution for subcutaneous injection, prefilled syringe
</td>
</tr>
<tr>
<td>Tocilizumab</td>
<td>Actemra</td>
<td>
• Cytokine release syndrome, severe or life-threatening
• Giant cell arteritis
• Polyarticular juvenile idiopathic arthritis
• Rheumatoid arthritis
• Systemic juvenile idiopathic arthritis
</td>
<td>
• Dosing (Adult):
  – IV 4 mg/kg once, maximum 800 mg/dose
  – SQ 162 mg q1week
    • Extra info if needed
• Dosing (Peds):
  – IV 8 to 12 mg/kg/dose q1-4weeks
  – SQ 162 mg q2-3weeks
    • Extra info if needed
• CYP450 Interactions: Induces CYP3A4, possibly CYP2C9, CYP2C19, and CYP2D6
• Renal or Hepatic Dose Adjustments:
  – ALT elevation 3x to less than 5x ULN - interrupt therapy until ALT less than 3x ULN, then resume at 150 mg q2weeks
  – ALT more than 5x ULN - discontinue
• Dosage Forms: Solution for IV and subcutaneous injection, prefilled syringe
</td>
</tr>
</table>

High-Yield Clinical Knowledge

- **Antibody Development**
  - Approximately 2% of patients receiving tocilizumab, and up to 9% of patients taking sarilumab develop antibodies to the drug, causing hypersensitivity reactions and prompting drug discontinuation.
    - This observation may be counterintuitive fully human MABs are considered to have a lower risk of neutralizing antibodies and allergic reactions, but tocilizumab is a humanized anti-IL-6 receptor antibody, whereas sarilumab is a fully human monoclonal antibody.
- **Infection Risk**
  - Boxed warnings for infections exist for IL-6 antagonists, specifically tuberculosis (pulmonary or extrapulmonary) or other infections, including invasive fungal, bacterial, viral, protozoal, and other opportunistic infections.
  - Patients should have tuberculosis screening completed before initiation of IL-6 antagonist therapy and to monitor for the development of other infections continually.
- **COVID-19**
  - Sarilumab and tocilizumab were investigated early on as a possible therapeutic intervention for COVID-19 infection; however, was found not to have a significantly positive effect, but further research in the REMAP-CAP trial suggested a benefit and an NNT of 12.
- **ANC and ALT Screening**
  - IL-6 antagonists should not be initiated before drawing absolute neutrophil counts (ANC), platelets, and hepatic enzyme levels
  - IL-6 antagonists should not be initiated if ANC is less than 2,000/mm^3, platelets are less than 100,000/mm^3, or if ALT is greater than 1.5 times ULN.

High-Yield Fast-Fact

- **COVID-19**
  - Sarilumab and tocilizumab were investigated early on as a possible therapeutic intervention for COVID-19 infection; however, was found not to have a significantly positive effect, but further research in the REMAP-CAP trial suggested a benefit and an NNT of 12.

HIGH-YIELD BOARD EXAM ESSENTIALS
- **CLASSIC AGENTS:** Sarilumab, tocilizumab
- **DRUG CLASS:** IL-6 receptor antagonist
- **INDICATIONS:** Cytokine release syndrome, giant cell arteritis, polyarticular juvenile idiopathic arthritis, rheumatoid arthritis, systemic juvenile idiopathic arthritis
- **MECHANISM:** Inhibits IL-6 mediated inflammation by binding to both soluble and membrane-bound IL-6 receptors.
- **SIDE EFFECTS:** Antibody development/hypersensitivity reaction, infections
- **CLINICAL PEARLS:** IL-6 antagonists should not be initiated before drawing absolute neutrophil counts (ANC), platelets, and hepatic enzyme levels.

High-Yield Basic Pharmacology

- **Mechanism of Action**
  - Selectively binds to IL-17A and blocks its action on IL-17 receptors, thus inhibiting its release of pro-inflammatory cytokines and chemokines.
  - In patients with plaque psoriasis, the action of IL-17 antagonists can specifically bind to keratinocytes, halting their pro-inflammatory response and preventing characteristic psoriatic plaques.

Primary Net Benefit

- IL-17 antagonists prevent the inflammatory process associated with plaque psoriasis, psoriatic arthritis and appear to be superior to other bDMARDs for this indication.

IL-17 Antagonists - Drug Class Review				
High-Yield Med Reviews				
Mechanism of Action: *Selectively binds to IL-17A and blocks its action on IL-17 receptors, thus inhibiting its release of pro-inflammatory cytokines and chemokines.*				
Class Effects: *Risk of infection, could worsen pre-existing IBD, injection site reactions.*				
Generic Name	**Brand Name**	**Indication(s) or Uses**	**Notes**	
Brodalumab	Siliq	• Plaque psoriasis	• **Dosing (Adult):** – SQ 210 mg qweek for 3 weeks, then 210 mg q2weeks • **Dosing (Peds):** Not routinely used • **CYP450 Interactions:** None • **Renal or Hepatic Dose Adjustments:** None • **Dosage Forms:** Solution prefilled syringe	

Ixekizumab	Taltz	• Ankylosing spondylitis
		• Nonradiographic axial spondyloarthritis
		• Plaque psoriasis
		• Psoriatic arthritis
			• **Dosing (Adult):**
			  – SQ 160 mg once, then 80 mg q2-4weeks
			• **Dosing (Peds):**
			  – Less than 25 kg - SQ 40 mg once, then 20 mg q4weeks
			  – 25 to 50 kg - SQ 80 mg once, then 40 mg q4weeks
			• **CYP450 Interactions:** None
			• **Renal or Hepatic Dose Adjustments:** None
			• **Dosage Forms:** Solution prefilled syringe	

Secukinumab	Cosentyx	• Ankylosing spondylitis • Plaque psoriasis • Psoriatic arthritis	• **Dosing (Adult):** – SQ 150 mg qweek for 4 weeks then 150 to 300 mg q4weeks • **Dosing (Peds):** Not routinely used • **CYP450 Interactions:** None • **Renal or Hepatic Dose Adjustments:** None • **Dosage Forms:** Solution prefilled syringe	

- ▪ **Neutralizing Antibodies**
    - − Like other IL antagonists (such as the IL-6 antagonists), there is evidence of the development of neutralizing antibodies that can cause reduced serum concentrations of the biologic and reduced efficacy.
- ▪ **Infection Risk**
    - − Patients taking IL-17 antagonists are at increased risk of infection, similar to other IL antagonists.
    - − The most commonly observed infection with IL-17 antagonists is mucocutaneous Candida infections.
- ▪ **Inflammatory Bowel Disease**
    - − Patients starting IL-17 antagonists and have a history of IBD may worsen their IBD or development of Crohn's disease and ulcerative colitis.
    - − The use of these drugs in the context of IBD is discouraged.
- ▪ **Adverse Events**
    - − Other common adverse events associated with IL-17 antagonists include injection site reactions, nasopharyngitis, cellulitis, and major cardiac adverse events.
- ▪ **Brodalumab Psychiatric Risk**
    - − Suicidal ideation or behavior was observed in clinical trials, prompting a black boxed warning of this effect.
    - − Furthermore, brodalumab is contraindicated in patients with suicidal ideation, recent suicidal behavior, or a history of suicidal ideation.
    - − Brodalumab is also exclusively available through a risk evaluation and mitigation strategy program.

HIGH-YIELD BOARD EXAM ESSENTIALS
- **CLASSIC AGENTS:** Brodalumab, ixekizumab, secukinumab
- **DRUG CLASS:** IL-17 receptor antagonists
- **INDICATIONS:** Ankylosing spondylitis, nonradiographic axial spondyloarthritis, plaque psoriasis, psoriatic arthritis
- **MECHANISM:** Selectively binds to IL-17A and blocks its action on IL-17 receptors, thus inhibiting its release of pro-inflammatory cytokines and chemokines.
- **SIDE EFFECTS:** Increased risk of infection, suicide (brodalumab), injection site reactions, nasopharyngitis, cellulitis, MACE
- **CLINICAL PEARLS:** Patients taking IL-17 antagonists are at increased risk of infection, similar to other IL antagonists. The most commonly observed infection with IL-17 antagonists is mucocutaneous Candida infections.

High-Yield Basic Pharmacology

- **Guselkumab, Risankizumab, Tildrakizumab**
  - Bind to the p19 subunit of IL-23 on CD4 cells and NK cells, resulting in inhibition of proinflammatory cytokines and chemokine release.
- **Ustekinumab**
  - Inhibits IL-12 and IL-23 by preventing the binding of the p40 subunit, suppressing the formation of inflammatory T helper cells
- **IL-12 and IL-23 Blockade**
  - The inhibition of cellular signaling produced by IL-12 and IL-23 receptor antagonists block cytokine production and gene activation and inhibits T helper cell 1 and T helper cell 17 mediated responses.

Primary Net Benefit

- IL-12/IL-23 inhibitors are safe and effective options for treating plaque psoriasis that require less frequent dosing than alternative classes and carry a lower risk of candidiasis or inflammatory bowel disease.

IL-23 Receptor Antagonists Drug Class Review			
High-Yield Med Reviews			
Mechanism of Action: *Guselkumab, Risankizumab, Tildrakizumab - Bind to the p19 subunit of IL-23 on CD4 cells and NK cells, resulting in inhibiting the release of proinflammatory cytokines and chemokine.* *Ustekinumab - Inhibits IL-12 and IL-23 by preventing the binding of the p40 subunit, suppressing the formation of inflammatory T helper cells.*			
Class Effects: *Lower risk of infection compared to other agents.*			
Generic Name	**Brand Name**	**Indication(s) or Uses**	**Notes**
Guselkumab	Tremfya	• Plaque psoriasis • Psoriatic arthritis	• **Dosing (Adult):** – SQ 100 mg at weeks 0, 4, then q8weeks • **Dosing (Peds):** – Not routinely used • **CYP450 Interactions:** None • **Renal or Hepatic Dose Adjustments:** None • **Dosage Forms:** Subcutaneous prefilled syringe
Risankizumab	Skyrizi	• Plaque psoriasis	• **Dosing (Adult):** – SQ 150 mg (as 2 separate injections) at weeks 0, 4, then q12weeks • **Dosing (Peds):** – Not routinely used • **CYP450 Interactions:** None • **Renal or Hepatic Dose Adjustments:** None • **Dosage Forms:** Subcutaneous prefilled syringe
Tildrakizumab	Ilumya	• Plaque psoriasis	• **Dosing (Adult):** – SQ 100 mg at weeks 0, 4, then q12weeks • **Dosing (Peds):** – Not routinely used • **CYP450 Interactions:** None • **Renal or Hepatic Dose Adjustments:** None • **Dosage Forms:** Subcutaneous prefilled syringe

IL-23 Receptor Antagonists Drug Class Review
High-Yield Med Reviews

Generic Name	Brand Name	Indication(s) or Uses	Notes

Ustekinumab	Stelara	▪ Crohn's disease
		▪ Plaque psoriasis
		▪ Psoriatic arthritis
		▪ Ulcerative colitis
			▪ **Dosing (Adult):**
			  – Induction - IV 260 to 520 mg x 1
			  – Maintenance - SQ 80 mg q8weeks
			  – SQ 45 to 90 mg at weeks 0, 4, then q12weeks
			▪ **Dosing (Peds):**
			  – SQ 0.75 mg/kg at 0 and 4 weeks, then q12weeks
			    ▪ Maximum 90 mg/dose
			▪ **CYP450 Interactions:** None
			▪ **Renal or Hepatic Dose Adjustments:** None
			▪ **Dosage Forms:** IV (solution), Subcutaneous prefilled syringe

High-Yield Clinical Knowledge

- **Tildrakizumab Administration**
  - Although tildrakizumab has a similar administration and dosing schedule to the other IL-23 antagonists, it may only be administered by a healthcare provider.
- **bDMARD Conversion**
  - Switching between bDMARDs is possible and likely necessary with long-term treatment as neutralizing antibodies develop after 3 years of treatment.
  - Conversion between agents in the same class is acceptable.
    - Some experts suggest using a four-to-twelve-week washout period (or the dosing interval) before and the planned date of a new biologic initiation.
- **IL-23 Antagonist Comparison**
  - Although the data are emerging, guselkumab and risankizumab appear to be associated with better Psoriasis Area Severity Index and a static Physician's Global Assessment scores, compared to tildrakizumab and ustekinumab.
- **Major Adverse Cardiac Events**
  - MACE has been a subject of debate surrounding IL-12/23 antagonists; some developmental agents have failed to come to market due to excessive risk in this category, namely briakinumab.
- **Pregnancy**
  - Ustekinumab has the most data in pregnant patients and carries a pregnancy category B.

HIGH-YIELD BOARD EXAM ESSENTIALS
- **CLASSIC AGENTS:** Guselkumab, risankizumab, tildrakizumab, ustekinumab (also IL-12 antagonist)
- **DRUG CLASS:** IL-23 receptor antagonists
- **INDICATIONS:** Crohn's disease, plaque psoriasis, psoriatic arthritis, ulcerative colitis
- **MECHANISM:** Bind to the p19 subunit of IL-23 on CD4 cells and NK cells, resulting in inhibiting the release of proinflammatory cytokines and chemokine
- **SIDE EFFECTS:** Infections, injection site reactions, MACE
- **CLINICAL PEARLS:** The proposed mechanism by which IL-23 antagonists lead to a lower incidence of infections involves the conservation of T helper 1 response activation by IL-12, which preserves interferon-gamma protection against intracellular pathogens Mycobacterium species, Salmonella, Pneumocystis jirovecii, and Toxoplasmosis gondii.

High-Yield Basic Pharmacology

- **Mechanism of Action**
  - Inactivation of Janus kinase (JAK), JAK inhibitors prevent the recruitment, phosphorylation, and activation of STATs, halting the pro-inflammatory cytokine signaling from reaching the cell nucleus, thus stopping the pro-inflammatory process.
- **Baricitinib JAK Selectivity**
  - Baricitinib has demonstrated JAK selectivity by reversibly inhibiting JAK1 and JAK3 to a greater degree than JAK2.

Primary Net Benefit

- Targeted synthetic small molecule disease-modifying antirheumatic drugs (tsDMARDs) produce targeted anti-inflammatory effects and can be used in combination with other DMARDs or monotherapy.

Janus Kinase Inhibitor - Drug Class Review			
High-Yield Med Reviews			
Mechanism of Action: *Inactivation of Janus kinase (JAK), JAK inhibitors prevent the recruitment, phosphorylation, and activation of STATs, halting the pro-inflammatory cytokine signaling form reaching the cell nucleus, thus stopping the pro-inflammatory process.*			
Class Effects: *Increased risk of herpes zoster infection; need to screen for TB before starting; risk of clot formation, can worsening lipid profile.*			
Generic Name	**Brand Name**	**Indication(s) or Uses**	**Notes**

Baricitinib	Olumiant	• Rheumatoid arthritis	• **Dosing (Adult):**
			  – Oral 2 to 4 mg daily
			• **Dosing (Peds):**
			  – Oral 2 to 4 mg daily
			• **CYP450 Interactions:** Substrate of CYP3A4, P-gp
			• **Renal or Hepatic Dose Adjustments:**
			  – GFR 30 to 60 mL/min/1.73 m2 - 1 mg daily
			  – GFR less than 30 mL/min/1.73 m^2 - not recommended
			• **Dosage Forms:** Oral (tablet)

Tofacitinib	Xeljanz	• Polyarticular course juvenile idiopathic arthritis
		• Psoriatic arthritis
		• Rheumatoid arthritis
		• Ulcerative colitis
			• **Dosing (Adult):**
			  – Oral IR tablet 5 to 10 mg BID
			  – Oral ER tablet 11 to 22mg daily
			• **Dosing (Peds):**
			  – Oral solution 3.2 to 5 mg BID
			    • Extra info if needed
			• **CYP450 Interactions:** text
			• **Renal or Hepatic Dose Adjustments:**
			  – Moderate to severe renal impairment - reduce starting dose by 50%
			  – Child-Pugh class C hepatic impairment - use not recommended
			• **Dosage Forms:** Oral (IR and ER tablet)

Janus Kinase Inhibitor - Drug Class Review			
High-Yield Med Reviews			
Generic Name	Brand Name	Indication(s) or Uses	Notes

Upadacitinib	Rinvoq	▪ Rheumatoid arthritis	▪ **Dosing (Adult):**
			  – Oral 15 mg daily
			▪ **Dosing (Peds):**
			  – Not routinely used
			▪ **CYP450 Interactions:** text
			▪ **Renal or Hepatic Dose Adjustments:**
			  – Child-Pugh class C hepatic impairment - use not recommended
			▪ **Dosage Forms:** Oral (tablet)

High-Yield Clinical Knowledge

- **Viral and Mycobacterial infections**
  - The combination of baricitinib, tofacitinib, or upadacitinib plus prednisone increases the risk of herpes zoster infection, or reactivation of herpes virus infections, invasive fungal infections, or bacterial infections.
  - Similarly, these agents' use is associated with mycobacteria tuberculosis infectious, thus screening for active or latent tuberculosis is necessary before treatment.
- **Cardiovascular Mortality**
  - Patients receiving tofacitinib for rheumatoid arthritis who are 50 years of age or older with at least 1 cardiovascular risk factor have a dose-dependent risk of all-cause mortality, including sudden cardiovascular death.
- **Gastrointestinal Perforations**
  - The use of baricitinib has been associated with GI perforations in patients with a history of diverticulitis, prompting caution regarding its use in this population or selecting an alternative agent.
- **Cholesterol**
  - Tofacitinib is associated with increases in LDL, HDL, and total cholesterol.
    - This may be used to partially explain the dose-dependent increase in cardiovascular death risk associated with this agent.
- **Thrombosis Risk**
  - Venous and arterial thrombosis have been observed in patients treated with any JAK inhibitor, but the strongest evidence lies with tofacitinib.
  - Like the cardiovascular mortality risk, patients who are 50 years of age or older with at least 1 cardiovascular risk factor have a higher risk of thrombotic events.
- **Rheumatoid Arthritis**
  - tsDMARDs can be used alone or in combination with methotrexate (or other csDMARDs) to manage rheumatoid arthritis.
  - As a result of the increased risk of infection with tsDMARDs, including JAK inhibitors, they should not be used with potent immunosuppressants such as azathioprine, cyclosporine, or biologic DMARDs.

HIGH-YIELD BOARD EXAM ESSENTIALS

- **CLASSIC AGENTS:** Baricitinib, Tofacitinib, Upadacitinib
- **DRUG CLASS:** Janus Kinase Inhibitor
- **INDICATIONS:** Polyarticular course juvenile idiopathic arthritis, psoriatic arthritis, rheumatoid arthritis, ulcerative colitis
- **MECHANISM:** Prevent the recruitment, phosphorylation, and activation of STATs, halting the pro-inflammatory cytokine signaling form reaching the cell nucleus, thus stopping the pro-inflammatory process.
- **SIDE EFFECTS:** Increased CV death risk, infection risk, increased risk of VTE and arterial thrombosis, increases in LDL, HDL, and total cholesterol
- **CLINICAL PEARLS:** As a result of the increased risk of infection with tsDMARDs, including JAK inhibitors, they should not be used with potent immunosuppressants such as azathioprine, cyclosporine, or biologic DMARDs.

High-Yield Basic Pharmacology

- **Mechanism of Action**
  - Prevents activation of T-cells by binding to CD80 and CD86 on antigen-presenting cells (APC), blocking the T cell interaction with CD28 and the APCs.
- **T-Cell-CD28-APC Interaction**
  - Blocking the T-Cell-CD28-APC Interaction, abatacept and belatacept prevent activation of T-cells in synovial fluid (in the case of abatacept and rheumatoid arthritis) as well as preventing T-cell activation post-kidney transplantation from mediators of acute immunologic organ rejection.

Primary Net Benefit

- Unique therapeutic targets of abatacept and belatacept offer advantages over conventional DMARDs and prevent organ rejection, respectively.

Selective T-Cell Costimulation Blocker - Drug Class Review
High-Yield Med Reviews

Mechanism of Action: *Prevents activation of T-cells by binding to CD80 and CD86 on antigen-presenting cells (APC), blocking the T cell interaction with CD28 and the APCs.*

Class Effects: Increased risk of infections, BBW for PML; can exacerbate COPD, could be calcineurin sparing.

Generic Name	Brand Name	Indication(s) or Uses	Notes

Abatacept	Orencia	• Psoriatic arthritis
		• Rheumatoid arthritis
			• **Dosing (Adult):**
			  – IV 500 to 1000 mg at 0, 2, 4 weeks, then q4weeks
			  – SQ 125 mg once weekly
			• **Dosing (Peds):**
			  – IV 10 mg/kg at 0, 2, 4 weeks, then q4weeks
			    • Maximum 1000 mg/dose
			  – SQ 50 to 125 mg weekly
			• **CYP450 Interactions:** None
			• **Renal or Hepatic Dose Adjustments:** None
			• **Dosage Forms:** IV (solution), prefilled syringes

Belatacept	Nulojix	• Prophylaxis of organ rejection	• **Dosing (Adult):**
			  – Induction IV 10 mg/kg on day 1, 15, 29, 43, and 57 following transplant
			  – Maintenance IV 5 mg/kg q4weeks on day 1, 15, 29, 43, and 57 following transplant
			• **Dosing (Peds):** Not routinely used
			• **CYP450 Interactions:** None
			• **Renal or Hepatic Dose Adjustments:** None
			• **Dosage Forms:** IV (solution)

High-Yield Clinical Knowledge

- **Epstein Barr Virus Screening**
  - Patients who may be candidates for belatacept must undergo EBV screening and test negative to be eligible for the drug.
    - Patients with EBV had a higher incidence of posttransplant lymphoproliferative disease (PTLD), compared to no such cases in patients who were EBV negative.

- **Progressive multifocal leukoencephalopathy (PML)**
  - PML has been reported with the use of belatacept and is a black box warning.
  - A REMS program has been developed, which ensures screening and education for both PTLD and PML.
- **COPD Risk**
  - Abatacept has been associated with increased COPD exacerbations and should be used with caution in this population.
- **Abatacept/Belatacept Formation**
  - These drugs are products of recombinant fusion proteins composed of the extracellular domain of cytotoxic T-lymphocyte-associated antigen 4, then fused to the Fc domain of human IgG1.

HIGH-YIELD BOARD EXAM ESSENTIALS

- **CLASSIC AGENTS:** Abatacept, belatacept
- **DRUG CLASS:** Selective T-cell costimulation blocker
- **INDICATIONS:** Psoriatic arthritis, rheumatoid arthritis (abatacept), prophylaxis of organ rejection (belatacept)
- **MECHANISM:** Prevents activation of T-cells by binding to CD80 and CD86 on antigen-presenting cells (APC), blocking the T cell interaction with CD28 and the APCs.
- **SIDE EFFECTS:** Increased risk of infections, PML, COPD
- **CLINICAL PEARLS:** Patients receiving abatacept are at higher risk of infections, with more than 50% of patients developing an infection in some clinical trials. However, serious infections are rare but may include viral (EBV, HSV), mycobacterial, or fungal.

High-Yield Basic Pharmacology

- **Mechanism of Action**
  - Specifically isolates lymphocytes into the lymph nodes and Peyer patches, away from the circulation, preventing lesions and grafts from T-cell-mediated attacks.
- **T-Cell Sequestration**
  - In addition to its effect on T-cells in the peripheral circulation, fingolimod may also provide a neuroprotective effect by reducing T-lymphocytes' infiltration and macrophages into the CNS.

Primary Net Benefit

- Oral medications for relapsing multiple sclerosis management, with significantly improved safety profiles with newer agents in this class.

Sphingosine 1-Phosphate (S1P) Receptor Modulator - Drug Class Review			
High-Yield Med Reviews			
Mechanism of Action: *Specifically isolates lymphocytes into the lymph nodes and Peyer patches, away from the circulation, preventing lesions and grafts from T-cell-mediated attacks.*			
Class Effects: *Risk for bradycardia with first dose; QT prolongation, could worsen FEV1 and blood pressure.*			
Generic Name	**Brand Name**	**Indication(s) or Uses**	**Notes**

Fingolimod	Gilenya	• Relapsing multiple sclerosis	• **Dosing (Adult):**
			  – Oral 0.5 mg daily
			• **Dosing (Peds):**
			  – 40 kg or less - 0.25 mg daily
			• **CYP450 Interactions:** Substrate of CYP3A4, CYP4F2
			• **Renal or Hepatic Dose Adjustments:** None
			• **Dosage Forms:** Oral (capsule)

Ozanimod	Zeposia	• Relapsing multiple sclerosis	• **Dosing (Adult):**
			  – Oral 0.23 mg daily on days 1-4, then 0.46 mg daily on days 5-7, then 0.92 mg starting day 8
			• **Dosing (Peds):**
			  – Not routinely used
			• **CYP450 Interactions:** Substrate of CYP2C8, CYP3A4
			• **Renal or Hepatic Dose Adjustments:** None
			• **Dosage Forms:** Oral (capsule)

Siponimod	Mayzent	• Multiple sclerosis	• **Dosing (Adult):**
			  – Oral 0.25 mg daily x2, then 0.5 mg x1, 0.75 mg x1, then 1.25 mg daily
			    • Dosing adjusted based on CYP2C9 genotype
			• **Dosing (Peds):**
			  – Not routinely used
			• **CYP450 Interactions:** Substrate CYP2C9
			• **Renal or Hepatic Dose Adjustments:** None
			• **Dosage Forms:** Oral (tablet)

High-Yield Clinical Knowledge

- **First Dose Bradycardia**
  - Fingolimod is associated with first dose bradycardia, which may include bradyarrhythmias such as AV block.
  - Patients must be observed for at least 6 hours after the first dose and longer periods of time in patients at high risk (pre-existing cardiac disease).
    - Ozanimod does not appear to cause bradycardia or heart block in patients receiving this drug in clinical studies.
- **QT Prolongation**
  - Fingolimod has been associated with QT interval prolongation and risk of torsades de pointes.
  - Concomitant QT-prolonging drugs should be avoided, including amiodarone, dronedarone, dofetilide, ibutilide, sotalol, procainamide, quinidine, and disopyramide.
- **Pre-existing Cardiac Disease**
  - Patients with type II or III heart block, recent myocardial infarction, or heart failure should also not receive fingolimod due to excessive risk of cardiac toxicity.
    - The bradycardia associated fingolimod further increases the risk of arrhythmias due to QT interval prolongation.
- **Adverse Events**
  - Other common adverse events include infections, macular edema, decreased FEV1 in patients with respiratory disease, liver enzyme elevations, increases in blood pressure, and lymphoma.
- **Ulcerative Colitis**
  - Ozanimod may also play a role in the disease management of Ulcerative Colitis, with evidence front the TOUCHSTONE trial supporting its increased remission incidence compared to placebo.

HIGH-YIELD BOARD EXAM ESSENTIALS

- **CLASSIC AGENTS:** Fingolimod, ozanimod, siponimod
- **DRUG CLASS:** Sphingosine 1-phosphate receptor modulator
- **INDICATIONS:** Relapsing multiple sclerosis
- **MECHANISM:** Specifically isolates lymphocytes into the lymph nodes and Peyer patches, away from the circulation, preventing lesions and grafts from T-cell-mediated attacks.
- **SIDE EFFECTS:** Bradycardia (first dose), QT prolongation, infections, macular edema, decreased FEV1 in patients with respiratory disease, liver enzyme elevations, increases in blood pressure, and lymphoma
- **CLINICAL PEARLS:** Fingolimod is associated with first dose bradycardia, which may include bradyarrhythmias such as AV block. Patients must be observed for at least 6 hours after the first dose and longer periods of time in patients at high risk (pre-existing cardiac disease).

High-Yield Basic Pharmacology

- **Mechanism of Action**
    - Anti-TNF-alpha drugs that complex with TNF-alpha, preventing its interaction with the cell surface receptors p55 and/or p75 that ultimately down-regulate macrophage and T-cell function.
- **MAB Source**
    - Adalimumab, certolizumab, and golimumab are fully-humanized monoclonal antibodies, but subtle differences may confer different pharmacologic or pharmacokinetic actions.
        - Certolizumab is a humanized antibody Fab fragment that lacks the Fc region, potentially leading to decreased antibody-dependent cell-mediated cytotoxicity and reduced complement response.

Primary Net Benefit

- TNF-alpha inhibitors are primarily used for rheumatoid arthritis generally after disease activity remains moderate or high despite conventional DMARD therapy, and cost and safety may limit its use.

TNF-Alpha Inhibitors - Drug Class Review			
High-Yield Med Reviews			
Mechanism of Action: *Anti-TNF-alpha drugs that complex with TNF-alpha, preventing its interaction with the cell surface receptors p55 and/or p75 that ultimately down-regulate macrophage and T-cell function.*			
Class Effects: Worsening of class IIII or IV hear failure, risk of infection (must screen for latent TB) & skin cancer			
Generic Name	**Brand Name**	**Indication(s) or Uses**	**Notes**
Adalimumab	Humira	<ul><li>Ankylosing spondylitis</li><li>Crohn's disease</li><li>Hidradenitis suppurativa</li><li>Juvenile idiopathic arthritis</li><li>Plaque psoriasis</li><li>Psoriatic arthritis</li><li>Rheumatoid arthritis</li><li>Ulcerative colitis</li><li>Uveitis</li></ul>	<ul><li>**Dosing (Adult):**<ul><li>SQ 80 to 160 mg once, then 40 mg q1-2weeks</li></ul></li><li>**Dosing (Peds):**<ul><li>17 to less than 40 kg - SQ 80 mg once, then 20 to 40 mg q1-2weeks</li></ul></li><li>**CYP450 Interactions:** None</li><li>**Renal or Hepatic Dose Adjustments:** None</li><li>**Dosage Forms:** Prefilled syringe kit</li></ul>
Certolizumab	Cimzia	<ul><li>Ankylosing spondylitis</li><li>Axial spondyloarthritis</li><li>Crohn's disease</li><li>Plaque psoriasis</li><li>Psoriatic arthritis</li><li>Rheumatoid arthritis</li></ul>	<ul><li>**Dosing (Adult):**<ul><li>SQ 400 mg repeat dose 2 and 4 weeks after initial dose, followed by 200 mg q2weeks or 400 mg q4weeks</li></ul></li><li>**Dosing (Peds):** Not routinely used</li><li>**CYP450 Interactions:** None</li><li>**Renal or Hepatic Dose Adjustments:** None</li><li>**Dosage Forms:** Prefilled syringe kit</li></ul>
Etanercept	Enbrel	<ul><li>Ankylosing spondylitis</li><li>Juvenile idiopathic arthritis</li><li>Plaque psoriasis</li><li>Psoriatic arthritis</li><li>Rheumatoid arthritis</li></ul>	<ul><li>**Dosing (Adult):**<ul><li>SQ 25-50 mg twice weekly or 50 mg once weekly</li></ul></li><li>**Dosing (Peds):**<ul><li>Less than 63 kg - 0.8 mg/kg/dose weekly<ul><li>Maximum 50 mg/dose</li></ul></li></ul></li><li>**CYP450 Interactions:** None</li><li>**Renal or Hepatic Dose Adjustments:** None</li><li>**Dosage Forms:** Prefilled syringe kit, solution for subcutaneous injection</li></ul>

TNF-Alpha Inhibitors - Drug Class Review
High-Yield Med Reviews

Generic Name	Brand Name	Indication(s) or Uses	Notes

Golimumab	Simponi	▪ Ankylosing spondylitis
		▪ Juvenile idiopathic arthritis
		▪ Psoriatic arthritis
		▪ Rheumatoid arthritis
		▪ Ulcerative colitis
			▪ **Dosing (Adult):**
			  – IV 2 mg/kg at weeks 0, 4, then q8weeks
			  – SQ 50 mg q1month
			▪ **Dosing (Peds):**
			  – IV 80 mg/m^2/dose at week 0, 4, then q8weeks
			  – SQ 90-200 mg/m2 at week 0 then 45 mg/m2 at week 2 and q1month thereafter
			▪ **CYP450 Interactions:** None
			▪ **Renal or Hepatic Dose Adjustments:** None
			▪ **Dosage Forms:** IV (solution), Prefilled syringe kit

Infliximab	Avsola
	Inflectra
	Remicade
	Renflexis
		▪ Ankylosing spondylitis
		▪ Crohn's disease
		▪ Plaque psoriasis
		▪ Psoriatic arthritis
		▪ Rheumatoid arthritis
		▪ Ulcerative colitis
			▪ **Dosing (Adult):**
			  – IV 5 mg/kg at 0, 2 and 6 weeks, then 5 mg/kg q6weeks
			▪ **Dosing (Peds):**
			  – IV 5 mg/kg at 0, 2 and 6 weeks, then 5 mg/kg q6weeks
			▪ **CYP450 Interactions:** None
			▪ **Renal or Hepatic Dose Adjustments:** None
			▪ **Dosage Forms:** IV (solution)

High-Yield Clinical Knowledge

- **Heart Failure Warning**
  - TNF-alpha inhibitor initiation has been associated with new-onset or acute worsening of existing heart failure.
  - As a result, these agents should be avoided in patients with a history of New York Heart Association class III/IV heart failure.
- **Infliximab Infusion Reaction and Antibodies**
  - A high proportion of patients (up to 15%) receiving infliximab develop antibodies to infliximab.
  - Antibody development is associated with a higher risk of infusion reactions, more rapid infliximab clearance, and decreased efficacy.
  - The risk of antibody development can be reduced with concomitant use of methotrexate.
  - Infusion reactions can be mitigated with the use of pre-infusion antihistamines, acetaminophen, and corticosteroids.
- **Skin Cancer Risk**
  - The increased risk of skin cancer and melanoma is a class effect of the TNF-alpha inhibitor agents.
    - Patients should undergo routine skin examinations to monitor these cancer types in patients at high risk closely.
- **Infection Risk**
  - All TNF-alpha inhibitors are associated with an increased risk of infections in patients prescribed these agents.
  - Infections of concern related to TNF-alpha agents include opportunistic bacterial infections, tuberculosis, viral (hepatitis), or fungal infections.
- **TNF-Alpha Inhibitor in Pregnancy**
  - Careful selection of TNF-alpha agents for pregnant patients is necessary, but certolizumab demonstrated a safer experience in pregnancy patients.
  - Certolizumab is associated with minimal to no placental transfer to the fetus.

- Similarly, there is no to small transfer from plasma to breast milk.
- **Neutropenias and Demyelinating Disorders**
  - The TNF-alpha inhibitors are associated with an increased risk of neutropenias, leukopenia, thrombocytopenia, or pancytopenia.
  - These agents have been rarely associated with new-onset or acute worsening of demyelinating disorders (multiple sclerosis).

HIGH-YIELD BOARD EXAM ESSENTIALS

- **CLASSIC AGENTS:** Adalimumab, certolizumab, etanercept, golimumab, infliximab
- **DRUG CLASS:** TNF-alpha inhibitors
- **INDICATIONS:** Ankylosing spondylitis, axial spondyloarthritis, Crohn's disease, hidradenitis suppurativa, juvenile idiopathic arthritis, plaque psoriasis, psoriatic arthritis, rheumatoid arthritis, ulcerative colitis, uveitis
- **MECHANISM:** Complex with TNF-alpha, preventing its interaction with the cell surface receptors p55 and/or p75 that ultimately down-regulate macrophage and T-cell function.
- **SIDE EFFECTS:** Increased risk of infection, neutropenia, leukopenia, thrombocytopenia, pancytopenia, demyelinating disorders
- **CLINICAL PEARLS:**
  - TNF-alpha inhibitor initiation has been associated with new-onset or acute worsening of existing heart failure. As a result, these agents should be avoided in patients with a history of New York Heart Association class III/IV heart failure.
  - In addition, patients should be screened for the presence of latent TB and started on TB therapy prior to initiating these agents due to conversion to an active infection.

High-Yield Basic Pharmacology

- **Mechanism of Action:**
  - **Montelukast, Zafirlukast**
    - Inhibit the binding of leukotriene D4 to its receptor on target tissues.
  - **Zileuton**
    - Inhibit 5-Lipoxygenase, reducing arachidonic acid synthesis
- **Leukotriene Effects**
  - Leukotriene modifiers reduce the impact of leukotrienes on the respiratory tract by limiting bronchospasm and airway hyperresponsiveness.
  - As airway leukotrienes are also responsible for plasma exudation, mucus secretion, and eosinophilic inflammation, inhibitors of leukotrienes improve airway function by limiting their production.

Primary Net Benefit

- Improve asthma control in poorly controlled asthma and reduce the frequency of asthma exacerbations but are less effective than inhaled corticosteroids in mild asthma.

Leukotriene Modifiers - Drug Class Review			
High-Yield Med Reviews			
Mechanism of Action: *Montelukast, Zafirlukast - Inhibit the binding of leukotriene D4 to its receptor on target tissues.* *Zileuton - Inhibit 5-Lipoxygenase, reducing arachidonic acid synthesis.*			
Class Effects: Can be helpful in exercise-induced asthma; Small risk of liver toxicity (worse with zileuton), sleep disturbances			
Generic Name	**Brand Name**	**Indication(s) or Uses**	**Notes**

Zileuton	Zyflo	• Asthma	• **Dosing (Adult):**
			  – Oral IR 600 mg q6h
			  – Oral ER 1,200 mg q12h
			• **Dosing (Peds):**
			  – Oral IR 600 mg q6h
			  – Oral ER 1,200 mg q12h
			    • Maximum 2,400 mg/day
			• **CYP450 Interactions:** Substrate CYP1A2, 2C9, 3A4; Inhibits CYP1A2
			• **Renal or Hepatic Dose Adjustments:**
			  – Active liver disease or AST/ALT greater than 3x upper limit of normal - Contraindicated
			• **Dosage Forms:** Oral (Tablet)

Montelukast	Singulair	• Allergic rhinitis
		• Asthma
		• Exercise-induced bronchoconstriction
			• **Dosing (Adult):**
			  – Oral 10 mg daily
			• **Dosing (Peds):**
			  – Oral 4 to 10 mg daily
			• **CYP450 Interactions:** Substrate CYP2C8, 2C9, 3A4
			• **Renal or Hepatic Dose Adjustments:** None
			• **Dosage Forms:** Oral (packet, tablet)

		Leukotriene Modifiers - Drug Class Review	
		High-Yield Med Reviews	
Generic Name	Brand Name	Indication(s) or Uses	Notes

Zafirlukast	Accolate	▪ Asthma	▪ **Dosing (Adult):**
			  – Oral 20 mg BID
			▪ **Dosing (Peds):**
			  – Oral 10 to 20 mg BID
			▪ **CYP450 Interactions:** Substrate CYP2C9; Inhibits CYP2C9
			▪ **Renal or Hepatic Dose Adjustments:**
			  – Hepatic impairment - Contraindicated
			▪ **Dosage Forms:** Oral (tablet)

High-Yield Clinical Knowledge

- **Drug Interactions**
  - Zafirlukast is an inhibitor of CYP2C9 and, as a result, can decrease the elimination of narrow therapeutic index drugs including warfarin, or theophylline.
    - Increased INR monitoring should occur when starting or titrating zafirlukast in the presence of a CYP2C9 substrate.
- **Cardiac and Hepatic Injury**
  - Hepatic injury is a rare effect secondary to leukotriene modifiers and necessitates routine liver-enzyme monitoring.
    - Zileuton carries the highest risk of hepatic injury, which occurs within three months after starting therapy.
  - Leukotriene modifiers have been associated with new-onset eosinophilic vasculitis targeting cardiac, peripheral nerves, and renal tissue known as Churg-Strauss syndrome.
- **Taken with Food**
  - In some children with poor compliance with inhaled LABA or ICS therapy, oral leukotriene modifiers can improve asthma control.
  - Montelukast is available as a once-daily oral preparation that can be taken without regard to food but has only a modest effect on pulmonary function improvements.
  - Zafirlukast must be taken on an empty stomach, as food significantly decreases absorption.
- **Aspirin-Exacerbated Respiratory Disease (AERD)**
  - As a result of the shifting arachidonic acid metabolism in AERD to the leukotriene pathway, montelukast, zafirlukast, and zileuton have been shown to reduce this response to aspirin and improve asthma control.
    - AERD does not involve immune sensitization to aspirin, as it is not a true allergy, but it can produce severe bronchospasm due to arachidonic acid activation.
- **COPD**
  - Leukotriene modifiers should not be used in patients with COPD.
- **Neuropsychiatric Effects**
  - Children receiving montelukast are 12 times more likely to experience adverse neuropsychiatric effects compared to children receiving ICS.
    - Neuropsychiatric symptoms associated with montelukast include irritability, aggressiveness, and sleep disturbances.

High-Yield Fast-Fact

- **Exercise-Induced Bronchospasm**
  - Montelukast can be used to prevent exercise-induced bronchospasm and, for this indication, should be taken at least 2 hours before physical exertion.

HIGH-YIELD BOARD EXAM ESSENTIALS

- **CLASSIC AGENTS:** Montelukast, zafirlukast, zileuton
- **DRUG CLASS:** Leukotriene modifiers
- **INDICATIONS:** Asthma, COPD
- **MECHANISM:** Montelukast, Zafirlukast - Inhibit the binding of leukotriene D4 to its receptor on target tissues. Zileuton - Inhibit 5-Lipoxygenase, reducing arachidonic acid synthesis.
- **SIDE EFFECTS:** Irritability, aggressiveness, and sleep disturbances
- **CLINICAL PEARLS:** Hepatic injury is a rare effect secondary to leukotriene modifiers and necessitates routine liver-enzyme monitoring. Leukotriene modifiers have been associated with new-onset eosinophilic vasculitis targeting cardiac, peripheral nerves, and renal tissue known as Churg-Strauss syndrome.

High-Yield Basic Pharmacology

- **Live Attenuated Vaccines**
    - Intranasal influenza, MMR, rotavirus, varicella vaccine (Varivax), and zoster vaccine (ZVL, Zostavax) are examples of live attenuated vaccines.
    - Certain vaccines use a weakened form of a virus that contains antigens directed to stimulate an immune response.
    - Viruses used in such vaccines have been manipulated to reduce virulence but maintain immunogenic antigens capable of eliciting humoral and cellular responses sufficient for memory cell development.
    - Viruses of live attenuated vaccines can mutate in vivo and possibly become virulent, leading to disease.
    - Live attenuated viruses cannot be used in pregnant patients, immunocompromised patients, such as those with active cancer or HIV
- **Inactivated Vaccines**
    - Influenza, polio, and rabies are examples of inactivated vaccines.
    - Inactivated vaccines are developed using chemicals, heat, or radiation to inactivate pathogens that produce antigenic responses.
    - These vaccine types induce an immune response similar, although much weaker than the natural infection, and require multiple doses to sustain immunity to the pathogen.
- **Subunit Vaccines**
    - Vaccines contain components of the microorganism to elicit an antigenic response that mimics the organism's response.
    - These vaccines contain surface proteins or toxins but elicit a less-robust immune response compared to live attenuated viruses.
    - Subunit vaccines can be polysaccharide subunits, surface protein subunits, or toxoids.
        - Polysaccharide vaccines (Hib, PCV13) are often bound to carrier proteins (such as diphtheria) to elicit sustained disease protection.
        - Surface protein subunits such as acellular pertussis (DTaP, Tdap) and hepatitis B vaccines utilize purified proteins from the pathogen to induce an immune response.
        - Toxoids elicit an immune response to the toxin produced by Clostridium tetani (tetanus) or Corynebacterium diphtheria (diphtheria).
            - Toxoids are often formulated with aluminum salts that induce an inflammatory response and enhance their antigenicity.
- **DNA Vaccines**
    - DNA vaccines such as the SARS-CoV-2 vaccines (AstraZeneca Oxford or Johnson & Johnson's Janssen), or Zika virus vaccine, or CMV vaccines use encapsulated viral DNA expressing a target protein and introducing it to the host cell cytoplasm. The host nucleus then utilizes host enzymes to convert the delivered viral DNA component into RNA to produce ribosomes to develop proteins (translation) to express either MHC-1 or 2 proteins.
- **Immunoglobulins**
    - Vaccinations confer expansion and differentiation of B-cells to memory cells that maintain long-term protection.
    - Immunoglobulins provide passive immunity by providing human-derived Ig antibodies that the host does not produce.

Primary Net Benefit

- Induce an active immune response to numerous diseases that improve morbidity, mortality, and public health.

<table>
<tr><td colspan="4" align="center">**Vaccines - Drug Class Review**
High-Yield Med Reviews</td></tr>
<tr><td>**Generic Name**</td><td>**Brand Name**</td><td>**Vaccine Format**</td><td>**Notes**</td></tr>
<tr><td colspan="4">**Diphtheria**</td></tr>
<tr>
<td>**Diphtheria and tetanus toxoids adsorbed, DT**</td>
<td>TDVax</td>
<td>▪ Toxoid</td>
<td>

▪ **Dosing (Adult):**
  – IM 0.5 mL every 10 years if pertussis vaccine contraindicated
▪ **Dosing (Peds):**
  – For children at least 6 weeks old to 7 years old, or if pertussis vaccine contraindicated
  – IM 0.5 mL for 5 doses
▪ **Contraindications & Allergies:**
  – Anaphylaxis to previous DT or any other vaccine containing any similar component
▪ **Dosage Forms:** Intramuscular suspension

</td>
</tr>
<tr>
<td>**Diphtheria and tetanus toxoids and acellular pertussis vaccine adsorbed, DTaP**</td>
<td>Daptacel, Infanrix</td>
<td>▪ Toxoid
▪ Inactivated (bacterial)</td>
<td>

▪ **Dosing (Adult):**
  – Not routinely used
▪ **Dosing (Peds):**
  – For children at least 6 weeks old to 7 years old
  – IM 0.5 mL for 5 doses
▪ **Contraindications & Allergies:**
  – Anaphylaxis to previous DTaP or any other vaccine containing any similar component
  – Encephalopathy within 7 days of pertussis vaccine
▪ **Dosage Forms:** Intramuscular suspension

</td>
</tr>
<tr>
<td>**Diphtheria and tetanus toxoids and acellular pertussis adsorbed, hepatitis B and inactivated poliovirus vaccine, DTaP-HepB-IPV**</td>
<td>Pediarix</td>
<td>▪ Toxoid
▪ Inactivated (bacterial)
▪ Inactivated (viral)</td>
<td>

▪ **Dosing (Adult):**
  – Not routinely used
▪ **Dosing (Peds):**
  – For children at least 6 weeks old to 7 years old
  – IM 0.5 mL for 3 doses
▪ **Contraindications & Allergies:**
  – Anaphylaxis to any other vaccine containing any similar component
  – Encephalopathy within 7 days of pertussis vaccine
  – Progressive neurologic disorders
▪ **Dosage Forms:** Intramuscular suspension

</td>
</tr>
<tr>
<td>**Diphtheria and tetanus toxoids and acellular pertussis adsorbed and inactivated poliovirus vaccine, DTaP-IPV**</td>
<td>Kinrix, Quadracel</td>
<td>▪ Toxoid
▪ Inactivated (bacterial)
▪ Inactivated (viral)</td>
<td>

▪ **Dosing (Adult):**
  – Not routinely used
▪ **Dosing (Peds):**
  – For children at least 6 weeks old to 7 years old
  – IM 0.5 mL once
▪ **Contraindications & Allergies:**
  – Anaphylaxis to any other vaccine containing any similar component
  – Encephalopathy within 7 days of pertussis vaccine
  – Progressive neurologic disorders
▪ **Dosage Forms:** Intramuscular suspension

</td>
</tr>
</table>

Vaccines - Drug Class Review
High-Yield Med Reviews

Generic Name	Brand Name	Vaccine Format	Notes

Diphtheria and tetanus toxoids and acellular pertussis adsorbed, inactivated poliovirus and Haemophilus influenzae type b conjugate vaccine, DTaP-IPV/Hib	Pentacel	• Toxoid
		• Inactivated (bacterial)
		• Inactivated (viral)
			• **Dosing (Adult):**
			  – Not routinely used
			• **Dosing (Peds):**
			  – For children at least 6 weeks old to 7 years old
			  – IM 0.5 mL for 4 doses
			• **Contraindications & Allergies:**
			  – Anaphylaxis to any other vaccine containing any similar component
			  – Encephalopathy within 7 days of pertussis vaccine
			  – Progressive neurologic disorders
			• **Dosage Forms:** Intramuscular suspension

Haemophilus b			

Haemophilus b conjugate vaccine, Hib	PedvaxHIB, Hiberix, ActHIB	• Inactivated (bacterial)	• **Dosing (Adult):**
			  – IM 0.5 mL once
			• **Dosing (Peds):**
			  – For children at least 6 weeks old
			  – IM 0.5 mL for 3 doses (ActHIB, Hiberix); or 2 doses (PedvaxHIB)
			• **Contraindications & Allergies:**
			  – Anaphylaxis to any other vaccine containing any similar component
			• **Dosage Forms:** Injection powder for reconstitution, Injection suspension

Haemophilus influenzae type b conjugate and hepatitis B vaccine, Hib-HepB	Comvax	• Inactivated (bacterial)
		• Inactivated (viral)
			• **Dosing (Adult):**
			  – Not routinely used
			• **Dosing (Peds):**
			  – For children at least 6 weeks old to 7 years old
			  – IM 0.5 mL for 3 doses
			• **Contraindications & Allergies:**
			  – Anaphylaxis to any other vaccine containing any similar component
			  – Not intended for initial (birth) dose of HepB vaccine
			• **Dosage Forms:** Injection suspension

Hepatitis			

Hepatitis A vaccine, HepA	Havrix, Vaqta	• Inactivated (viral)	• **Dosing (Adult):**
			  – IM 1 mL for two doses
			• **Dosing (Peds):**
			  – For children 12 to 23 months
			  – IM 0.5 mL for two doses
			• **Contraindications & Allergies:**
			  – Anaphylaxis to previous HepA or any other vaccine containing any similar component including neomycin
			• **Dosage Forms:** Injection suspension

Vaccines - Drug Class Review
High-Yield Med Reviews

Generic Name	Brand Name	Vaccine Format	Notes

Hepatitis B vaccine, HepB	Engerix-B, Recombivax HB	▪ Inactivated (viral)	▪ **Dosing (Adult):**
			  – IM 1 mL for 3 doses
			▪ **Dosing (Peds):**
			  – IM 0.5 mL for 3 doses
			▪ **Contraindications & Allergies:**
			  – Anaphylaxis to previous HepB or any other vaccine containing any similar component
			▪ **Dosage Forms:** Injection suspension

Hepatitis B vaccine, HepB-CpG	HEPLISAV-B	▪ Inactivated (viral)	▪ **Dosing (Adult):**
			  – IM 0.5 mL for two doses
			▪ **Dosing (Peds):**
			  – Not routinely used
			▪ **Contraindications & Allergies:**
			  – Anaphylaxis to previous HepB-CpG or any other vaccine containing any similar component
			▪ **Dosage Forms:** Injection suspension, prefilled syringe

Hepatitis A inactivated and hepatitis B vaccine, HepA-HepB	Twinrix	▪ Inactivated (viral)	▪ **Dosing (Adult):**
			  – IM 1 mL for 3 doses
			▪ **Dosing (Peds):**
			  – Indicated for 18 years and older
			▪ **Contraindications & Allergies:**
			  – Anaphylaxis to previous HepA or HepB or any other vaccine containing any similar component
			▪ **Dosage Forms:** Injection suspension

Hepatitis B immune globulin	HepaGam B, HyperHEP B S/D, Nabi-HB	▪ Immune Globulin	▪ **Dosing (Adult):**
			  – IM 0.06 mL/kg as soon as possible after exposure, may repeat dose 28-30 days later
			▪ **Dosing (Peds):**
			  – Infants - IM 0.5 mL as soon as possible after exposure
			  – Children 12 months and older - IM 0.06 mL/kg as soon as possible after exposure, may repeat dose 28-30 days later
			▪ **Contraindications & Allergies:**
			  – Anaphylaxis to previous human globulin preparations.
			  – IgA deficiency
			▪ **Dosage Forms:** Injection solution

Vaccines - Drug Class Review
High-Yield Med Reviews

Generic Name	Brand Name	Vaccine Format	Notes
Herpes zoster			

Zoster vaccine live, ZVL	Zostavax	▪ Live (viral)	▪ **Dosing (Adult):**
			  – SQ 0.65 mL once
			▪ **Dosing (Peds):**
			  – Not routinely used
			▪ **Contraindications & Allergies:**
			  – Anaphylaxis to gelatin, neomycin, or any other vaccine component
			  – Immunosuppressed or immunodeficiency patients
			  – Pregnancy
			▪ **Dosage Forms:** Injection suspension

Zoster vaccine recombinant, RZV	Shingrix	▪ Inactivated (viral)	▪ **Dosing (Adult):**
			  – IM 0.5 mL for two doses
			▪ **Dosing (Peds):**
			  – Not routinely used
			▪ **Contraindications & Allergies:**
			  – Anaphylaxis to any vaccine component
			▪ **Dosage Forms:** Injection suspension

Human papillomavirus			

Human papillomavirus 9-valent, 9vHPV	Gardasil 9	▪ Inactivated (viral)	▪ **Dosing (Adult):**
			  – IM 0.5 mL for 3 doses
			▪ **Dosing (Peds):**
			  – For children at least 9 years old
			  – IM 0.5 mL for 2 or 3 doses
			▪ **Contraindications & Allergies:**
			  – Anaphylaxis to previous HPV vaccine or any vaccine component
			▪ **Dosage Forms:** Injection suspension

Human papillomavirus quadrivalent, 4vHPV	Gardasil	▪ Inactivated (viral)	▪ **Dosing (Adult):**
			  – IM 0.5 mL for 3 doses
			▪ **Dosing (Peds):**
			  – For children at least 9 years old
			  – IM 0.5 mL for 2 or 3 doses
			▪ **Contraindications & Allergies:**
			  – Anaphylaxis to previous HPV vaccine or any vaccine component
			▪ **Dosage Forms:** Injection suspension

Human papillomavirus bivalent, 2vHPV	Cervarix	▪ Inactivated (viral)	▪ **Dosing (Adult):**
			  – IM 0.5 mL for 3 doses
			▪ **Dosing (Peds):**
			  – For children at least 9 years old
			  – IM 0.5 mL for 2 or 3 doses
			▪ **Contraindications & Allergies:**
			  – Anaphylaxis to previous HPV vaccine or any vaccine component
			▪ **Dosage Forms:** Injection suspension

Vaccines - Drug Class Review
High-Yield Med Reviews

Generic Name	Brand Name	Vaccine Format	Notes
Influenza			

Trivalent inactivated influenza vaccine, IIV3	Afluria, Fluad, Flucelvax, FluLaval, Fluzone	▪ Inactivated (viral)	▪ **Dosing (Adult):**
			  – IM 0.5 to 0.7 mL once per flu season
			▪ **Dosing (Peds):**
			  – For children 6 months and older
			  – IM 0.25 to 0.5 mL once per flu season
			▪ **Contraindications & Allergies:**
			  – Anaphylaxis to previous influenza or any other vaccine containing any similar component including egg protein
			▪ **Dosage Forms:** Injection suspension

Quadrivalent inactivated influenza vaccine, IIV4	Fluarix	▪ Inactivated (viral)	▪ **Dosing (Adult):**
			  – IM 0.5 to 0.7 mL once per flu season
			▪ **Dosing (Peds):**
			  – For children 6 months and older
			  – IM 0.25 to 0.5 mL once per flu season
			▪ **Contraindications & Allergies:**
			  – Anaphylaxis to previous influenza or any other vaccine containing any similar component including egg protein
			▪ **Dosage Forms:** Injection suspension

Live attenuated influenza vaccine, LAIV	FluMist	▪ Live, attenuated (viral)	▪ **Dosing (Adult):**
			  – Intranasal 0.2 mL per flu season
			▪ **Dosing (Peds):**
			  – Children at least 2 years old
			  – Intranasal 0.2 mL per flu season
			▪ **Contraindications & Allergies:**
			  – Anaphylaxis to previous flu vaccine or any other vaccine containing any similar component
			  – 50 years of age or older
			▪ **Dosage Forms:** Nasal suspension

Measles, mumps, and rubella vaccine			

Measles, mumps, and rubella vaccine, MMR	MMR II	▪ Live (viral)	▪ **Dosing (Adult):**
			  – SQ 0.5 mL for 2 doses
			▪ **Dosing (Peds):**
			  – For children at least 12 months old
			  – SQ 0.5 mL for two doses
			▪ **Contraindications & Allergies:**
			  – Anaphylaxis to previous MMR or any other vaccine containing any similar component
			  – Active febrile illness
			  – Active untreated tuberculosis
			  – Immunosuppressed or immunodeficiency patients
			  – Pregnancy
			▪ **Dosage Forms:** Injection reconstituted

Vaccines - Drug Class Review
High-Yield Med Reviews

Generic Name	Brand Name	Vaccine Format	Notes

Measles, mumps, rubella, and varicella vaccine, MMRV	ProQuad	▪ Live (viral)	▪ **Dosing (Adult):**
			  – SQ 0.5 mL for 2 doses
			▪ **Dosing (Peds):**
			  – For children at least 12 months old
			  – SQ 0.5 mL for two doses
			▪ **Contraindications & Allergies:**
			  – Anaphylaxis to previous MMR or any other vaccine containing any similar component
			  – Active febrile illness
			  – Active untreated tuberculosis
			  – Immunosuppressed or immunodeficiency patients
			  – Pregnancy
			▪ **Dosage Forms:** Injection reconstituted

Meningococcal			

Quadrivalent meningococcal conjugate vaccine, MenACWY, MenACWY-D, MenACWY-CRM	Menactra, MenQuadfi Menveo	▪ Inactivated (bacterial)	▪ **Dosing (Adult):**
			  – IM 0.5 mL for one to two doses
			▪ **Dosing (Peds):**
			  – Children 11 to 12 years
			    ▪ IM 0.5 mL for one to two doses
			  – Infants at least 2 months to 2 years
			    ▪ IM 0.5 mL for 2 to 4 doses
			▪ **Contraindications & Allergies:**
			  – Anaphylaxis to previous vaccine or any vaccine containing any similar component (diphtheria)
			▪ **Dosage Forms:** Injection solution

Serogroup B meningococcal vaccines, MenB, MenB-4c, MenB-FHbp	Bexsero, Trumenba	▪ Inactivated (bacterial)	▪ **Dosing (Adult):**
			  – IM 0.5 mL for 2 to 3 doses
			▪ **Dosing (Peds):**
			  – For children at least 10 years old
			  – IM 0.5 mL for 2 to 3 doses
			▪ **Contraindications & Allergies:**
			  – Anaphylaxis to previous vaccine or any vaccine containing any similar component
			▪ **Dosage Forms:** Injection suspension

Bivalent meningococcal conjugate vaccine and Haemophilus influenza type b conjugate vaccine, Hib-MenCY	MenHibrix	▪ Inactivated (bacterial)	▪ **Dosing (Adult):**
			  – Not routinely used
			▪ **Dosing (Peds):**
			  – For children at least 6 weeks old to 18 months old
			  – IM 0.5 mL for 4 doses
			▪ **Contraindications & Allergies:**
			  – Anaphylaxis to previous vaccine or any vaccine containing any similar component
			▪ **Dosage Forms:** Injection solution

Vaccines - Drug Class Review
High-Yield Med Reviews

Generic Name	Brand Name	Vaccine Format	Notes

Meningococcal polysaccharide vaccine, MPSV4	Menomune	▪ Inactivated (bacterial)	▪ **Dosing (Adult):**
			  − IM 0.5 mL once
			▪ **Dosing (Peds):**
			  − Not routinely used
			▪ **Contraindications & Allergies:**
			  − Anaphylaxis to previous vaccine or any vaccine containing any similar component
			▪ **Dosage Forms:** Injection solution

Pneumococcal			

Pneumococcal conjugate vaccine 13 valent, PCV13	Prenvar 13	▪ Inactivated (bacterial)	▪ **Dosing (Adult):**
			  − IM 0.5 mL once
			▪ **Dosing (Peds):**
			  − For children at least 6 weeks old to 15 months old
			  − IM 0.5 mL for 4 doses
			▪ **Contraindications & Allergies:**
			  − Anaphylaxis to previous pneumococcal vaccine or any other vaccine containing any similar component (diphtheria toxoid)
			▪ **Dosage Forms:** Injection suspension

Pneumococcal polysaccharide vaccine 23 valent, PPSV23	Pneumovax 23	▪ Inactivated (bacterial)	▪ **Dosing (Adult):**
			  − IM/SQ 0.5 mL once
			▪ **Dosing (Peds):**
			  − For children at least 2 years old
			  − IM/SQ 0.5 mL once
			▪ **Contraindications & Allergies:**
			  − Anaphylaxis to previous pneumococcal vaccine or any other vaccine containing any similar component (diphtheria toxoid)
			▪ **Dosage Forms:** Injection suspension

Poliovirus			

Inactivated poliovirus vaccine, IPV	Ipol	▪ Inactivated (virus)	▪ **Dosing (Adult):**
			  − IM/SQ 0.5 mL for 3 doses
			▪ **Dosing (Peds):**
			  − For children at least 6 weeks old
			  − IM 0.5 mL for 3 doses
			▪ **Contraindications & Allergies:**
			  − Anaphylaxis to previous IPV or any other vaccine containing any similar component (neomycin, formaldehyde, 2-phenoxyethanol, streptomycin, polymyxin B)
			  − Acute, febrile illness
			▪ **Dosage Forms:** Injection suspension)

Vaccines - Drug Class Review
High-Yield Med Reviews

Generic Name	Brand Name	Vaccine Format	Notes
Rabies			

Rabies Vaccine	Imovax Rabies, RabAvert	▪ Inactivated (virus)	▪ **Dosing (Adult):**
			  – IM 1 mL for 4 doses
			▪ **Dosing (Peds):**
			  – IM 1 mL for 4 doses
			▪ **Contraindications & Allergies:**
			  – Anaphylaxis to previous human globulin preparations.
			▪ **Dosage Forms:** Injection suspension

Rabies immunoglobulin	HyperRAB, HyperRAB S/D, Imogam Rabies-HT, Kedrab	▪ Immune Globulin	▪ **Dosing (Adult):**
			  – Local infiltration or IM 20 units/kg once
			▪ **Dosing (Peds):**
			  – Local infiltration or IM 20 units/kg once
			▪ **Contraindications & Allergies:**
			  – Anaphylaxis to previous human globulin preparations (risks vs. benefits)
			▪ **Dosage Forms:** Injection solution

RhO(D)			

RhO(D)	HyperRHO S/D, MICRhoGam, Rhophylac, WinRho	▪ Immune Globulin	▪ **Dosing (Adult):**
			  – IV 25 to 60 mcg/kg once
			  – IM 300 mcg once at week 26-28 gestation, or within 72 hours of delivery
			▪ **Dosing (Peds):**
			  – Infants - IV 50 to 75 mcg/kg once
			▪ **Contraindications & Allergies:**
			  – Anaphylaxis to previous human globulin preparations.
			  – IgA deficiency
			▪ **Dosage Forms:** Injection solution

Rotavirus			

Rotavirus vaccine monovalent, RV1	Rotarix	▪ Live (virus)	▪ **Dosing (Adult):**
			  – Not routinely used
			▪ **Dosing (Peds):**
			  – For children at least 6 to 24 weeks old
			  – Oral 1 mL/dose for 2 doses
			▪ **Contraindications & Allergies:**
			  – Anaphylaxis to previous Rotavirus or any other vaccine containing any similar component
			  – History of uncorrected congenital malformation of the GI
			  – History of intussusception
			  – Severe combined immunodeficiency disease
			▪ **Dosage Forms:** Oral powder for suspension

Vaccines - Drug Class Review
High-Yield Med Reviews

Generic Name	Brand Name	Vaccine Format	Notes

Rotavirus vaccine pentavalent, RV5	RotaTeq	▪ Live (virus)	▪ **Dosing (Adult):**
			  – Not routinely used
			▪ **Dosing (Peds):**
			  – For children at least 6 to 32 weeks old
			  – Oral 2 mL/dose for 3 doses
			▪ **Contraindications & Allergies:**
			  – Anaphylaxis to previous Rotavirus or any other vaccine containing any similar component
			  – History of uncorrected congenital malformation of the GI
			  – History of intussusception
			  – Severe combined immunodeficiency disease
			▪ **Dosage Forms:** Oral solution

SARS-CoV-2			

AstraZeneca Oxford	N/A	▪ SARS-CoV-2 infection	▪ **Dosing (Adult)**:
			  – IM 0.5 mL with the first and second doses separated by 28 to 84 days.
			▪ **Dosing (Peds):**
			  – Extra info if needed
			    ▪ Extra info if needed
			▪ **Contraindications:**
			  – Anaphylaxis to first dose
			  – Allergy to polyethylene glycol
			▪ **Allergies:** No relevant concerns
			▪ **Dosage Forms:** Intramuscular suspension

Johnson & Jonson's Janssen	N/A	▪ SARS-CoV-2 infection	▪ **Dosing (Adult):**
			  – IM 0.5 mL once
			▪ **Dosing (Peds):**
			  – IM 0.5 mL once
			▪ **Contraindications:**
			  – Anaphylaxis to first dose
			  – Allergy to polyethylene glycol
			▪ **Allergies:** No relevant concerns
			▪ **Dosage Forms:** Intramuscular suspension

Moderna	N/A	▪ SARS-CoV-2 infection	▪ **Dosing (Adult):**
			  – IM 0.5 mL once, followed by a second 0.5 mL dose separated by 28 days.
			▪ **Dosing (Peds):**
			  – IM 0.5 mL once, followed by a second 0.5 mL dose separated by 28 days.
			▪ **Contraindications:**
			  – Anaphylaxis to first dose
			  – Allergy to polyethylene glycol
			▪ **Allergies:** No relevant concerns
			▪ **Dosage Forms:** Intramuscular suspension

Vaccines - Drug Class Review
High-Yield Med Reviews

Generic Name	Brand Name	Vaccine Format	Notes

Pfizer-BioNTech	N/A	▪ SARS-CoV-2 infection	▪ **Dosing (Adult):**
			  – IM 0.3 mL once, followed by a second 0.3 mL dose separated by 21 days.
			▪ **Dosing (Peds):**
			  – IM 0.3 mL once, followed by a second 0.3 mL dose separated by 21 days.
			▪ **Contraindications:**
			  – Anaphylaxis to first dose
			  – Allergy to polyethylene glycol
			▪ **Allergies:** No relevant concerns
			▪ **Dosage Forms:** Intramuscular suspension

Tetanus			

Tetanus and diphtheria toxoids adsorbed, Td	Decavac, Tenivac	▪ Toxoid	▪ **Dosing (Adult):**
			  – IM 0.5 mL every 10 years if pertussis vaccine contraindicated
			▪ **Dosing (Peds):**
			  – IM 0.5 mL once (booster) for children at least 7 years old
			▪ **Contraindications & Allergies:** Anaphylaxis to previous Td or any other vaccine containing any similar component
			▪ **Dosage Forms:** Injection suspension

Tetanus toxoid adsorbed, TT		▪ Toxoid	▪ **Dosing (Adult):**
			  – IM 0.5 mL every 10 years if pertussis vaccine contraindicated
			▪ **Dosing (Peds):**
			  – IM 0.5 mL once (booster) for children at least 7 years old
			▪ **Contraindications & Allergies:** Anaphylaxis to previous TT or any other vaccine containing any similar component
			▪ **Dosage Forms:** Injection suspension

Tetanus toxoid, reduced diphtheria toxoid, and acellular pertussis vaccine, adsorbed, Tdap	Adacel, Boostrix	▪ Toxoid
		▪ Inactivated (bacterial)
			▪ **Dosing (Adult):**
			  – IM 0.5 mL every 10 years
			▪ **Dosing (Peds):**
			  – IM 0.5 mL once (booster) for children at least 7 years old
			▪ **Contraindications & Allergies:** Anaphylaxis to previous Tdap or any other vaccine containing any similar component
			▪ **Dosage Forms:** Injection suspension

Vaccines - Drug Class Review
High-Yield Med Reviews

Generic Name	Brand Name	Vaccine Format	Notes

Tetanus immune globulin	HyperTET	▪ Immune Globulin	▪ **Dosing (Adult):**
			  – IM 250 units administered with tetanus toxoid containing vaccine
			▪ **Dosing (Peds):**
			  – IM 250 units, or 4 units/kg, administered with tetanus toxoid containing vaccine
			▪ **Contraindications & Allergies:**
			  – None
			▪ **Dosage Forms:** Injection solution

Varicella			

Varicella vaccine, VAR	Varivax	▪ Live	▪ **Dosing (Adult):**
			  – SQ 0.5 mL for two doses
			▪ **Dosing (Peds):**
			  – For children at least 12 months old
			  – SQ 0.5 mL for two doses
			▪ **Contraindications & Allergies:**
			  – Anaphylaxis to previous varicella or any other vaccine containing any similar component
			  – Active untreated tuberculosis
			  – Active febrile illness
			  – Pregnancy or planning pregnancy within the next 3 months
			  – Immunosuppressed or immunodeficient patients
			▪ **Dosage Forms:** Injection suspension

Varicella-zoster immune globulin	Varizig	▪ Immune Globulin	▪ **Dosing (Adult):**
			  – IM 625 units once
			▪ **Dosing (Peds):**
			  – IM 62.5 to 625 units once
			▪ **Contraindications & Allergies:**
			  – Anaphylaxis to previous human globulin preparations.
			  – IgA deficiency
			▪ **Dosage Forms:** Injection solution

High-Yield Clinical Knowledge

- **Administration of multiple vaccines or simultaneous administration of vaccines**
  - Live vaccines that are not administered during the same visit must be delayed for at least 30 days following the measles or MMR vaccine.
  - Inactivated and live attenuated vaccines can be administered at the same visit but must be given at separate sites.
    - If not given at the same visit, inactivated vaccines must be separated from live vaccines by at least three weeks.
    - If other live vaccines are not given together at the same visit, their administration must be separated by at least four weeks.
- **Conversion Between Vaccines**
  - mRNA vaccines (Moderna and Pfizer-BioNTech) are considered interchangeable if a patient begins one series and cannot complete that product due to shortages.

- **Acute Febrile Illnesses**
  - In patients with severe acute febrile illness, mRNA vaccine administration is not recommended.
  - For patients with mild acute illnesses, there is no reason to withhold vaccination.
- **Hepatitis B Immune Globulin**
  - Post-exposure prophylaxis to hepatitis b can be accomplished by administration of hepatitis B immune globulin.
  - Common sources of exposure include perinatal exposure of infants born to mothers who are hepatitis B surface antigen-positive, sexual exposure to hepatitis B surface antigen-positive individuals, or household exposure to individuals with active acute hepatitis B infection.
- **Rabies Immunoglobulins**
  - Rabies is a potentially fatal infection with close to a 99% mortality rate.
  - Pre-exposure prophylaxis with annual rabies vaccination occurs in individuals who routinely work with animals (veterinarians, laboratory workers, wildlife officers, etc.).
  - Post-exposure prophylaxis requires first administering rabies immune globulin around the site of exposure (bite, scratch, wound, etc.), followed by a four-dose series of rabies vaccine for most individuals.
    - Special consideration for the site of administration should occur as the gluteal tissue cannot be used as a site of administration for rabies vaccine, as this has been associated with failures of the immune response.
- **Tetanus Immunoglobulins**
  - Tetanus immunoglobulin should be given to patients with wounds who have not received tetanus immunization or have not completed tetanus toxoid immunizations.
  - The immunoglobulin must be administered in a separate site from tetanus vaccines.
- **Varicella-Zoster Immunoglobulin**
  - Post-exposure prophylaxis of varicella-zoster infection provided passive immunizations in patients not adequately immunized, immunocompromised, or otherwise at high risk of varicella infection complications.
  - Indications for post-exposure varicella-zoster immunoglobulin include:
    - Severe immunocompromised patients
    - Neonates born to mothers with varicella diagnosed within five days of delivery or two days after delivery.
    - Hospitalized premature infants born to mothers with no evidence of immunity or who weigh less than 1 kg.
- **RhO(D) Immunoglobulin**
  - Mothers who are RhO(D) negative but exposed to fetal erythrocytes expressing RhO(D) are at risk of Rh antibody development.
  - Without intervention, the maternal antibodies cause erythroblastosis fetalis, a hemolytic anemia in the fetus, leading to fetal demise.
- **Smallpox**
  - The smallpox vaccine is unique in many ways from other vaccines, as it contains live vaccinia virus, not a killed or weakened virus like many other vaccines, and it is administered after dipping the bifurcated needle into the vaccine vial then prick the skin rapidly with the needle 15 times with the pricks within an area approximately 5 mm in diameter.
- **Autism and SIDS**
  - There has been no definitive association between vaccinations and the development of autism or SIDS.
  - Furthermore, the risks of preventable diseases, both to the patient or public health, are outweighed mainly by the threats of routine vaccination complications.

HIGH-YIELD BOARD EXAM ESSENTIALS

- **CLASSIC AGENTS:** Quadrivalent inactivated influenza vaccine, IIV4 (Fluarix), Pneumococcal polysaccharide vaccine 23 valent, PPSV23 (Pneumovax 23)
- **DRUG CLASS:** CDC vaccination schedule
- **INDICATIONS:** Various indications based on CDC vaccination guidelines
- **MECHANISM:** Induce an active immune response to numerous diseases that improve morbidity, mortality, and public health.
- **SIDE EFFECTS:** Injection site reaction
- **CLINICAL PEARLS:** In patients with severe immunocompromised states, live vaccines should be avoided but may receive killed vaccines or toxoids. Among patients with cancer and planned chemotherapy, live vaccines should be given at least three months before chemotherapy if possible.

High-Yield Basic Pharmacology

- **Mechanism of Action**
  - Aminoglycosides interrupt bacterial protein synthesis by binding to the 30S ribosomal subunit, ultimately leading to the accumulation of abnormal initiation complexes, resulting in bacterial cellular death.
    - Aminoglycosides also may interfere with bacterial protein synthesis by binding to polysomes, leading to premature termination of mRNA translation and incorrect amino acid insertion into bacterial polypeptide chains.
- **Penetration To 30S**
  - For aminoglycosides to exert their inhibitory effect on the 30S ribosomal subunit, they must first enter the bacterial cell via diffusion through the outer membrane and inner membranes.
    - Inner membrane aminoglycoside transport relies on a transmembrane electrical gradient, a rate-limited process that can also be blocked or inhibited by numerous factors, including low pH, divalent cations (calcium and magnesium), hyperosmolarity, and anaerobic environments.

Primary Net Benefit

- Concentration-dependent bactericidal activity with post-antibiotic effect after concentrations fall below minimum inhibitory concentration.

Aminoglycosides - Drug Class Review			
High-Yield Med Reviews			
Mechanism of Action: *Inhibit bacterial protein synthesis at the 30S ribosomal subunit, resulting in bacterial death.*			
Class Effects: *Concentration-dependent bactericidal activity with a post-antibiotic effect, risk of nephrotoxicity and ototoxicity*			
Generic Name	**Brand Name**	**Indication(s) or Uses**	**Notes**

Amikacin	Amikin	• Bacterial Endocarditis
		• Cystic fibrosis
		• Meningitis
		• Pneumonia
		• Sepsis
		• Urinary Tract Infections
			• **Dosing (Adult):**
			  – Extended interval dosing
			    ▪ IV 15 to 20 mg/kg/day
			  – Conventional dosing
			    ▪ IV/IM 5 to 7.5 mg/kg/dose q8h
			• **Dosing (Peds):**
			  – IV/IM 15 to 30 mg/kg/*day* divided q8h
			  – IV 15 to 20 mg/kg/*dose* q24h
			• **CYP450 Interactions:** None
			• **Renal or Hepatic Dose Adjustments:**
			  – GFR less than 20 mL/minute should not receive extended interval dosing
			  – Conventional dosing
			    ▪ GFR 10 to 50 mL/minute q24-72 hours follow serum concentrations
			    ▪ GFR <10 mL/minute q48-72 follow serum concentrations.
			• **Dosage Forms:** IV solution

Aminoglycosides - Drug Class Review
High-Yield Med Reviews

Generic Name	Brand Name	Indication(s) or Uses	Notes
Gentamicin	Garamycin	▪ Bacterial Endocarditis ▪ Cystic fibrosis ▪ Meningitis ▪ Pneumonia ▪ Sepsis ▪ Urinary Tract Infections	▪ **Dosing (Adult):** 　– Extended interval dosing 　　▪ IV 15 to 20 mg/kg/day 　– Conventional dosing 　　▪ IV/IM 3 to 5 mg/kg/dose q8h ▪ **Dosing (Peds):** 　– IV/IM 2 to 2.5 mg/kg/day divided q8h 　– IV 3 to 5 mg/kg/dose q24h ▪ **CYP450 Interactions:** None ▪ **Renal or Hepatic Dose Adjustments:** 　– GFR less than 20 mL/minute should not receive extended interval dosing 　– Conventional dosing 　　▪ GFR 10 to 50 mL/minute q12-72 hours follow serum concentrations 　　▪ GFR <10 mL/minute q48-72 follow serum concentrations. ▪ **Dosage Forms:** IV (solution), Ophthalmic (solution, ointment), Topical (cream, ointment)
Tobramycin	Nebcin	▪ Bacterial Endocarditis ▪ Cystic fibrosis ▪ Meningitis ▪ Pneumonia ▪ Sepsis ▪ Urinary Tract Infections	▪ **Dosing (Adult):** 　– Extended interval dosing 　　▪ IV 15 to 20 mg/kg/day 　– Conventional dosing 　　▪ IV/IM 5 to 7.5 mg/kg/dose q8h ▪ **Dosing (Peds):** 　– IV/IM 15 to 30 mg/kg/day divided q8h 　– IV 15 to 20 mg/kg/dose q24 ▪ **CYP450 Interactions:** None ▪ **Renal or Hepatic Dose Adjustments:** 　– GFR less than 20 mL/minute should not receive extended interval dosing 　– Conventional dosing 　　▪ GFR 10 to 50 mL/minute q12-72 hours follow serum concentrations 　　▪ GFR <10 mL/minute q48-72 follow serum concentrations. ▪ **Dosage Forms:** IV (solution), Ophthalmic (solution, ointment), Topical (cream, ointment), Nebulization solution, Inhalation (capsule)
Neomycin	Mycifradin, Neosporin	▪ GI decontamination ▪ Skin and soft tissue infections	▪ **Dosing (Adult):** 　– Oral 1 g q6-8h 　– Topically applied as instructed q4-6h ▪ **Dosing (Peds):** 　– Oral 25 to 50 mg/kg/day divided in 4 doses 　　▪ Maximum 12g/day ▪ **CYP450 Interactions:** None ▪ **Renal or Hepatic Dose Adjustments:** None ▪ **Dosage Forms:** Oral (tablet), topical, urologic irrigation

Aminoglycosides - Drug Class Review
High-Yield Med Reviews

Generic Name	Brand Name	Indication(s) or Uses	Notes
Plazomicin	Zemdri	UTI (Complicated)	• **Dosing (Adult):** – 15 mg/kg IV once daily • **Dosing (Peds):** ▪ n/a • **CYP450 Interactions:** None • **Renal or Hepatic Dose Adjustments:** Reduce once CrCl < 60 mL/min to 10 mg/kg and to every 48 hrs once CrCl < 30 mL/min • **Dosage Forms:** Solution for IV injection
Streptomycin		• Brucellosis • Plague • Tuberculosis • Tularemia	• **Dosing (Adult):** – Brucellosis: 1 g IV once daily + doxycycline – Other: 15 mg/kg IV once or twice a day • **Dosing (Peds):** ▪ 20-40 mg/kg/day in 2-4 divided doses IM or IV • **CYP450 Interactions:** None • **Renal or Hepatic Dose Adjustments:** Reduce once CrCl < 50 mL/min • **Dosage Forms:** Solution for injection

High-Yield Clinical Knowledge

- **Ototoxicity**
  - Aminoglycosides may cause irreversible vestibular and cochlear toxicity.
  - These adverse effects are known to be related to high doses and/or high drug concentrations.
  - The ototoxicity from aminoglycosides differs from ototoxicity caused by loop diuretics (i.e., furosemide) as it is irreversible and causes bilateral high-frequency hearing loss and temporary vestibular dysfunction.
    - This results directly in the hair cells and neurons in the cochlea and the effect that shares similarities to the drug-drug interaction of aminoglycosides and neuromuscular blocking agents.
- **Nephrotoxicity**
  - Similar to ototoxicity, aminoglycosides may cause nephrotoxicity, which is associated with high doses, and/or high drug concentrations or concomitant nephrotoxic agents (i.e., NSAIDs).
  - Although nephrotoxicity can occur in up to 8-26% of patients receiving aminoglycosides, it is frequently reversible.
- **Traditional or Extended Interval Dosing**
  - Once-daily or extended interval dosing is the preferred dosing strategy for aminoglycosides.
  - The concentration-dependent antimicrobial effect of aminoglycosides permits maximal initial bacterial killing and relies on the postantibiotic effect to ensure optimal outcomes while maintaining, or even lowering, the risk of nephrotoxicity and ototoxicity.
- **Alternative Routes**
  - Aminoglycosides may be administered as topical skin and mucous membrane agents (neomycin), ophthalmic products (gentamicin, neomycin, and tobramycin), or as inhaled agents (amikacin, tobramycin).
- **Plague**
  - Although not limited to medieval times, treatment of plague may be relevant to central areas of the United States and can be managed with a 10-day course of gentamicin or streptomycin.
- **Oral Administration**
  - Some aminoglycosides may be ordered or prescribe via the oral route, the indication for this being bowel prep before surgical procedures or selective decontamination.

High-Yield Fast-Facts

- **Alternative Routes**
  - Aminoglycosides may be administered as topical skin and mucous membrane agents (neomycin), ophthalmic products (gentamicin, neomycin, and tobramycin), or as inhaled agents (amikacin, tobramycin).
- **Plague**
  - Although not limited to medieval times, treatment of plague may be relevant to central areas of the United States and can be managed with a 10-day course of gentamicin or streptomycin.
- **Oral Administration**
  - Some aminoglycosides may be ordered or prescribe via the oral route, the indication for this being bowel prep before surgical procedures or selective decontamination.

HIGH-YIELD BOARD EXAM ESSENTIALS

- **CLASSIC AGENTS:** Amikacin, gentamicin, tobramycin, neomycin
- **DRUG CLASS:** Aminoglycosides
- **INDICATIONS:** Bacterial endocarditis, cystic fibrosis, meningitis, pneumonia, sepsis, urinary tract infections
- **MECHANISM:** Inhibit bacterial protein synthesis at the 30S ribosomal subunit, resulting in bacterial death.
- **SIDE EFFECTS:** Acute kidney injury, ototoxicity
- **CLINICAL PEARLS:** Once-daily or extended interval dosing is the preferred dosing strategy for aminoglycosides. The concentration-dependent antimicrobial effect of aminoglycosides permits maximal initial bacterial killing and relies on the postantibiotic effect to ensure optimal outcomes while maintaining, or even lowering, the risk of nephrotoxicity and ototoxicity.

High-Yield Basic Pharmacology

- **Mechanism of Action**
  - Inhibit the final step in bacterial cell wall synthesis by binding to specific penicillin-binding proteins in the bacterial cytoplasmic membrane.
    - Beta-lactams also prevent the transpeptidation reaction and cross-linking of linear peptidoglycan chain constituents of the cell wall and activate autolytic enzymes that cause lesions in the bacterial cell wall

Primary Net Benefit

- Bactericidal to susceptible pathogens, leading to microbiologic clearance of the affecting organisms.

Aminopenicillin and Extended-Spectrum Penicillin - Drug Class Review			
High-Yield Med Reviews			
Mechanism of Action: *Inhibit the final step in bacterial cell wall synthesis by binding to specific penicillin-binding proteins in the bacterial cytoplasmic membrane.*			
Class Effects: *Cover both gram + and gram- bacteria but not MRSA or Pseudomonas (except piperacillin/tazobactam). Safe for use in pregnancy*			
Generic Name	**Brand Name**	**Indication(s) or Uses**	**Notes**

Amoxicillin	Moxatag	• GI tract infections
		• GU tract infections
		• Respiratory tract infections
		• Urinary tract infection
			• **Dosing (Adult):**
			  – Oral 250-875mg q8-12h
			• **Dosing (Peds):**
			  – Oral > 1 month and < 20 kg: 20-40 mg/kg/day in 3 divided doses
			• **CYP450 Interactions:** None
			• **Renal or Hepatic Dose Adjustments:**
			  – GFR 10 to 50 mL/minute - Decrease frequency to q12h
			  – GFR less than 10 mL/minute - Decrease frequency to q12-24h.
			• **Dosage Forms:** Oral (capsules, suspension, tablet)

Amoxicillin/ Clavulanic acid	Augmentin	• GI tract infections
		• GU tract infections
		• Respiratory tract infections
		• Skin and soft tissue infections
		• Urinary tract infection
			• **Dosing (Adult):**
			  – Oral 250-875mg q8-12h
			• **Dosing (Peds):**
			  – Oral > 1 month and < 20 kg: 20-40 mg/kg/day in 3 divided doses
			• **CYP450 Interactions:** None
			• **Renal or Hepatic Dose Adjustments:**
			  – GFR 10 to 50 mL/minute - Decrease frequency to q12h
			  – GFR less than 10 mL/minute - Decrease frequency to q12-24h.
			• **Dosage Forms:** Oral (capsules, extended-release capsule, suspension, tablet)

Aminopenicillin and Extended-Spectrum Penicillin - Drug Class Review			
High-Yield Med Reviews			
Generic Name	**Brand Name**	**Indication(s) or Uses**	**Notes**

Ampicillin	Omnipen	• Bacteremia
		• Endocarditis
		• GI tract infections
		• GU tract infections
		• Meningitis
		• Respiratory tract infections
		• Urinary tract infection
			• **Dosing (Adult):**
			  – IV 1 to 2g IV q4h
			• **Dosing (Peds):**
			  – IV/IM 50 to 200 mg/kg/day in 4-6 divided doses
			• **CYP450 Interactions:** None
			• **Renal or Hepatic Dose Adjustments:**
			  – GFR 10 to 50 mL/minute - Decrease frequency to q6-12h
			  – GFR less than 10 mL/minute - Decrease frequency to q8-24h.
			• **Dosage Forms:** Oral (capsule, solution), IV/IM (solution)

Ampicillin/ Sulbactam	Unasyn	• Bacteremia
		• Endocarditis
		• GI tract infections
		• GU tract infections
		• Meningitis
		• Respiratory tract infections
		• Skin and soft tissue infections
		• Urinary tract infection
			• **Dosing (Adult):**
			  – IV 1.5 to 3g IV q6h
			• **Dosing (Peds):**
			  – IV/IM of ampicillin 50 to 200 mg/kg/day in 4-6 divided doses
			• **CYP450 Interactions:** None
			• **Renal or Hepatic Dose Adjustments:**
			  – GFR 10 to 50 mL/minute - Decrease frequency to q6-12h
			  – GFR less than 10 mL/minute - Decrease frequency to q8-24h.
			• **Dosage Forms:** IV (solution)

Piperacillin/ Tazobactam	Zosyn	• Bacteremia
		• Endocarditis
		• GI tract infections
		• GU tract infections
		• Respiratory tract infections
		• Skin and soft tissue infections
		• Urinary tract infection
			• **Dosing (Adult):**
			  – IV 3.375 to 4.5g IV q6h
			• **Dosing (Peds):**
			  – IV of piperacillin 50 to 200 mg/kg/day in 4 divided doses
			• **CYP450 Interactions:** None
			• **Renal or Hepatic Dose Adjustments:**
			  – GFR 10 to 30 mL/minute - Decrease frequency to q12h
			  – GFR less than 10 mL/minute - Decrease frequency to q24h.
			• **Dosage Forms:** IV (solution)

High-Yield Clinical Knowledge

- **Beta-lactamase Inhibitors**
  - Clavulanic acid, sulbactam, and tazobactam are beta-lactamase inhibitors that are active against plasmid-encoded beta-lactamases but not active against beta-lactamases with AmpC chromosomal mutations frequently encountered in Pseudomonas, Citrobacter, and Enterobacter spp.
- **Double Beta-Lactam**
  - Ampicillin is often used in combination with a cephalosporin for acute bacterial meningitis empiric therapy.
    - The combination of two beta-lactam antibiotics is not a duplication of therapy since the ampicillin component is specifically targeting L. monocytogenes.

- Ampicillin should be added to patients with suspected meningitis if they are younger than 2 years of age, older than 50 years of age, or otherwise immunocompromised.

- **Allergy or Rash**
  - Many patients, approximately 10%, develop a nonpruritic, non-urticarial rash after exposure to aminopenicillins, and almost all patients taking amoxicillin while infected with Epstein-Barr virus develop a morbilliform rash.
  - These eruptions are not allergic and should not be listed as such inpatient charts as they are not associated with anaphylaxis on subsequent exposure. Instead, they should be documented as adverse events.

- **Oral Ampicillin**
  - For a localized GI tract Shigella infection, oral ampicillin has been favored for treatment because its lack of absorption is desirable.

- **Absorption differences**
  - Amoxicillin and ampicillin are very similar in pharmacologic action, but only amoxicillin is commercially available as an oral preparation in the United States.
    - Peak plasma concentrations of amoxicillin are roughly 2.5 times higher than an equal dose of ampicillin administered orally

- **Unasyn Dosing**
  - For the labeled 3 g vial of ampicillin/sulbactam, there is 2 g of ampicillin and 1 g of sulbactam, and for the 1.5 g dose vial, there is 1 g of ampicillin and 500 mg of sulbactam.
    - For weight-based dosing of ampicillin/sulbactam, the dose should be based on the ampicillin component.

- **Sulbactam for Acinetobacter**
  - The sulbactam component of ampicillin/sulbactam is uniquely active against the nosocomial pathogen Acinetobacter baumannii. That is to say, the reason for administration of ampicillin/sulbactam is strictly for the sulbactam component, as it is not commercially available alone in the United States.

- **Core Indications**
  - **Community-acquired pneumonia**
    - High-dose amoxicillin (1g q8h) or amoxicillin/clavulanate 875 mg twice daily, or ampicillin/sulbactam 3 g IV q6h in combination with azithromycin or doxycycline are recommended treatments for patients with CAP.
  - **Hospital-acquired pneumonia**
    - Piperacillin/tazobactam provides gram-negative coverage (of note, Pseudomonas aeruginosa and the Enterobacteriaceae) and increased anaerobic coverage.
  - **Intra-Abdominal infections**
    - Because of the good coverage of GI gram-negative pathogens and anaerobes found in GI flora, piperacillin/tazobactam is a first-line agent for many intra-abdominal infections.
  - **Bacterial meningitis**
    - Ampicillin is a drug of choice for meningitis caused by Listeria monocytogenes and Streptococcus agalactiae.
  - **Group B Streptococci colonization in pregnancy**
    - Antepartum administration of ampicillin may be beneficial for prophylaxis against group B streptococcal infection in infants of mothers with birth canal colonization.
      - After administration of 2g IV to the mother, bactericidal concentrations of ampicillin are achieved in the amniotic fluid within 5 minutes.
  - **Otitis Media**
    - Amoxicillin is the drug of choice for most cases of otitis media when antibiotics are indicated.
      - However, the dose is 40-45 mg/kg/dose twice a day to achieve proper penetration into the middle ear. Most max the dose at 2 g per dose.

HIGH-YIELD BOARD EXAM ESSENTIALS

- **CLASSIC AGENTS:** Amoxicillin, amoxicillin/clavulanic acid, ampicillin, ampicillin/sulbactam, piperacillin/tazobactam
- **DRUG CLASS:** Aminopenicillin and extended-spectrum penicillin
- **INDICATIONS:** Bacteremia, endocarditis, GI tract infections, GU tract infections, meningitis, respiratory tract infections, urinary tract infection
- **MECHANISM:** Inhibit the final step in bacterial cell wall synthesis by binding to specific penicillin-binding proteins in the bacterial cytoplasmic membrane.
- **SIDE EFFECTS:** Rash, diarrhea, renal injury
- **CLINICAL PEARLS:**
  - These agents are renally eliminated, cause very little drug interactions, and are consider safe in pregnancy.
  - Many patients, approximately 10%, develop a nonpruritic, non-urticarial rash after exposure to aminopenicillins, and almost all patients taking amoxicillin while infected with Epstein-Barr virus develop a morbilliform rash.
  - Only piperacillin/tazobactam in this group covers against Pseudomonas, none of the others. None of them cover against MRSA.
  - The dosing of amoxicillin is much higher for the treatment of otitis media than most people realize. The dose is 40-45 mg/kg/dose (most max the dose at 2 g/dose).

High-Yield Basic Pharmacology

- **Mechanism of Action**
  - Inhibit the final step in bacterial cell wall synthesis by binding to specific penicillin-binding proteins in the bacterial cytoplasmic membrane.

Primary Net Benefit

- Bactericidal to susceptible pathogens, leading to microbiologic clearance of the affecting organisms.

Antistaphylococcal Penicillins - Drug Class Review			
High-Yield Med Reviews			
Mechanism of Action: *Inhibit the final step in bacterial cell wall synthesis by binding to specific penicillin-binding proteins in the bacterial cytoplasmic membrane.*			
Class Effects: *Greater selectivity for gram+ bacteria (esp Staph, but not MRSA). No Pseudomonas coverage.*			
Generic Name	**Brand Name**	**Indication(s) or Uses**	**Notes**
Dicloxacillin	Diclocil	<ul><li>Endocarditis</li><li>Pneumonia</li><li>Bone and joint infections</li><li>Skin and soft tissue infections</li></ul>	<ul><li>**Dosing (Adult):**<ul><li>Oral 125 to 250 mg q6h</li></ul></li><li>**Dosing (Peds):**<ul><li>Oral 12.5 to 100 mg/kg/day divided in 4 doses</li></ul></li><li>**CYP450 Interactions:** None</li><li>**Renal or Hepatic Dose Adjustments:** None</li><li>**Dosage Forms:** Oral (capsules)</li></ul>
Nafcillin	Nallpen, Unipen	<ul><li>Endocarditis</li><li>Pneumonia</li><li>Bone and joint infections</li><li>Skin and soft tissue infections</li></ul>	<ul><li>**Dosing (Adult):**<ul><li>IV 1 to 2 g q4-6h</li></ul></li><li>**Dosing (Peds):**<ul><li>IV 50 to 200 mg/kg/day in 4-6 divided doses</li></ul></li><li>**CYP450 Interactions:** Induces CYP3A4</li><li>**Renal or Hepatic Dose Adjustments:**<ul><li>Nafcillin - 50% dose reduction may be necessary for both renal and hepatic insufficiency.</li></ul></li><li>**Dosage Forms:** IV (solution)</li></ul>
Oxacillin	Bactocill	<ul><li>Endocarditis</li><li>Pneumonia</li><li>Bone and joint infections</li><li>Skin and soft tissue infections</li></ul>	<ul><li>**Dosing (Adult):**<ul><li>IV 1 to 2 g q4-6h</li></ul></li><li>**Dosing (Peds):**<ul><li>IV 50 to 200 mg/kg/day in 4-6 divided doses</li></ul></li><li>**CYP450 Interactions:** None</li><li>**Renal or Hepatic Dose Adjustments:**<ul><li>GFR less than 10 mL/minute - Use lowest dose range initially.</li></ul></li><li>**Dosage Forms:** IV (solution)</li></ul>

- **Nafcillin Vs. Oxacillin**
  - Nafcillin treatment is associated with higher rates of adverse events and treatment discontinuation than oxacillin among hospitalized adult patients. (Antimicrob Agents Chemother. 2016 Apr 22;60(5):3090-5.)
- **Nafcillin and CYP Interactions**
  - There is some evidence to suggest that nafcillin induces CYP3A4 and possibly CYP2C9, leading to clinically relevant drug interactions. (Br J Clin Pharmacol. 2003 Jun; 55(6): 588–590.)
- **Aminoglycoside Synergy**
  - In patients with endocarditis, the combination of aminoglycosides with nafcillin or oxacillin may provide a synergistic effect and an enhanced bactericidal effect, and a more rapid resolution of fever. (J Lab Clin Med 1976;88:118-124; Ann Intern Med 1982;97:496-503.)
- **Methicillin or Oxacillin Resistant Staphylococcus Aureus?**
  - Methicillin is no longer available in the US with oxacillin taking its place in therapy.
    - Oxacillin resistant or sensitive Staphylococcus Aureus (ORSA or OSSA) would be a more accurate terminology compared to MSSA and MRSA.
- **Tissue Necrosis**
  - Nafcillin is associated with tissue necrosis if extravasation occurs during infusion. Since nafcillin is given as frequently as every 4 hours, or even as a continuous infusion, this may be a significant risk in patients.
- **Cloxacillin Availability**
  - Cloxacillin is frequently discussed in texts and primary literature; however, it is not available in the US.

HIGH-YIELD BOARD EXAM ESSENTIALS

- **CLASSIC AGENTS:** Dicloxacillin, nafcillin
- **DRUG CLASS:** Antistaphylococcal Penicillins
- **INDICATIONS:** Endocarditis, pneumonia, bone and joint infections, skin and soft tissue infections
- **MECHANISM:** Inhibit the final step in bacterial cell wall synthesis by binding to specific penicillin-binding proteins in the bacterial cytoplasmic membrane.
- **SIDE EFFECTS:** Hepatic injury (nafcillin), renal injury (dicloxacillin)
- **CLINICAL PEARLS:** These agents do NOT cover against MRSA but do cover MSSA. Nafcillin is associated with tissue necrosis if extravasation occurs during infusion. Since nafcillin is given as frequently as every 4 hours, or even as a continuous infusion, this may be a significant risk in patients.

High-Yield Basic Pharmacology

- **Mechanism of Action**
  - Inhibit the final step in bacterial cell wall synthesis by binding to specific penicillin-binding proteins in the bacterial cytoplasmic membrane.
  - Beta-lactams also prevent the transpeptidation reaction and cross-linking of linear peptidoglycan chain constituents of the cell wall as well as activate autolytic enzymes that cause lesions in the bacterial cell wall.

Primary Net Benefit

- Bactericidal to susceptible pathogens, leading to microbiologic clearance of the affecting organisms.

Carbapenem - Drug Class Review			
High-Yield Med Reviews			
Mechanism of Action: *Inhibit the final step in bacterial cell wall synthesis by binding to specific penicillin-binding proteins in the bacterial cytoplasmic membrane.*			
Class Effects: *Bactericidal to susceptible pathogens, cover Pseudomonas (except ertapenem); not coverage against MRSA. Can extend coverage for ESBL producing organisms. Risk of seizures*			
Generic Name	**Brand Name**	**Indication(s) or Uses**	**Notes**

Doripenem	Doribax	▪ Intra-abdominal infections
		▪ Urinary tract infection
			▪ **Dosing (Adult):**
			  – IV 500 mg IV q8h
			▪ **Dosing (Peds):**
			  – Not routinely used
			▪ **CYP450 Interactions:** None
			▪ **Renal or Hepatic Dose Adjustments:**
			  – GFR 30 to 50 mL/minute - 250 mg q8h
			  – GFR 11 to 29 mL/minute - 250 mg q12h
			  – GFR less than 11 mL/minutes - 250 mg q24h
			▪ **Dosage Forms:** IV (solution)

Ertapenem	Invanz	▪ Intra-abdominal infections
		▪ Pelvic infection
		▪ Pneumonia
		▪ Skin and soft tissue infection
		▪ Surgical prophylaxis
		▪ Urinary tract infection
			▪ **Dosing (Adult):**
			  – IV 1 g IV q24h
			▪ **Dosing (Peds):**
			  – IV 15 mg/kg/dose twice daily
			    ▪ Maximum 500 mg/dose
			▪ **CYP450 Interactions:** None
			▪ **Renal or Hepatic Dose Adjustments:**
			  – GFR less than 30 mL/minutes - 500 mg q24h
			▪ **Dosage Forms:** IV (solution)

Carbapenem - Drug Class Review
High-Yield Med Reviews

Generic Name	Brand Name	Indication(s) or Uses	Notes

Imipenem/ Cilastatin	Primaxin	• Bacteremia
		• Bone and joint infections
		• Gynecologic infections
		• Intra-abdominal infections
		• Pneumonia
		• Skin and soft tissue infection
		• Urinary tract infection
			• **Dosing (Adult):**
			  – IV 500 to 1000 mg q6h
			• **Dosing (Peds):**
			  – Oral 20 to 100 mg/kg/day q6-12h
			• **CYP450 Interactions:** None
			• **Renal or Hepatic Dose Adjustments:**
			  – GFR between 60 to 90 mL/minute 400 to 750 mg q6h
			  – GFR between 30 to 60 mL/minute 300 to 500 mg q6h
			  – GFR between 15 and 30 mL/minute 200 to 500 mg q6h
			  – GFR less than 15 mL/minute Not recommended
			• **Dosage Forms:** IV (solution)

Imipenem/ Cilastatin/ Relebactam	Recarbrio	• Intra-abdominal infections
		• Pneumonia
		• Urinary tract infection
			• **Dosing (Adult):**
			  – IV 1.25 g q6h
			• **Dosing (Peds):**
			  – Not routinely used
			• **CYP450 Interactions:** None
			• **Renal or Hepatic Dose Adjustments:**
			  – GFR between 60 to 90 mL/minute 1g q6h
			  – GFR between 30 to 60 mL/minute 750 mg q6h
			  – GFR between 15 and 30 mL/minute 500 q6h
			  – GFR less than 15 mL/minute Not recommended
			• **Dosage Forms:** IV (solution)

Meropenem	Merrem	• Intra-abdominal infections
		• Bacterial meningitis
		• Skin and skin structure infection
			• **Dosing (Adult):**
			  – IV 500 mg q6h or 1 to g q8h
			• **Dosing (Peds):**
			  – IV 20 mg/kg/dose q8h
			    • Maximum 2g/dose
			• **CYP450 Interactions:** None
			• **Renal or Hepatic Dose Adjustments:**
			  – GFR between 25 to 50 mL/minute 1-2g q12h
			  – GFR between 10 to 25 mL/minute 500-1000 mg q12h
			  – GFR less than 15 mL/minute 500-1000 mg q24h
			• **Dosage Forms:** IV (solution)

Carbapenem - Drug Class Review			
High-Yield Med Reviews			
Generic Name	Brand Name	Indication(s) or Uses	Notes

Meropenem/ Vaborbactam	Vabomere	▪ Urinary tract infection	▪ **Dosing (Adult):**
			  – IV 4g q8h
			▪ **Dosing (Peds):**
			  – Oral 20 to 100 mg/kg/day q6-12h
			▪ **CYP450 Interactions:** None
			▪ **Renal or Hepatic Dose Adjustments:**
			  – GFR 30 to 49 mL/minute - 2g q8h
			  – GFR 15 to 30 mL/minute - 2g q12h
			  – GFR less than 15 mL/minutes - 1 g q12h.
			▪ **Dosage Forms:** IV (solution)

High-Yield Clinical Knowledge

- **AmpC, ESBL, CRE**
  - Carbapenems can be used for susceptible ESBL positive organisms where other beta-lactams are not appropriate.
  - However, carbapenems may still be degraded by highly resistant organisms, including the emerging carbapenemase-producing gram-negative pathogens, which are referred to as carbapenem-resistant Enterobacteriaceae (CRE), and specific organisms referred to as Klebsiella producing carbapenemases (KPC).
- **Exception Ertapenem**
  - Ertapenem has a distinctly different spectrum of activity compared to other carbapenems. Notably, ertapenem does not cover Pseudomonas aeruginosa and Acinetobacter species.
- **Cilastatin And Renal Tubules**
  - Imipenem, although referred to independently in many resources, is always co-formulated with cilastatin.
  - Cilastatin prevents the inactivation of imipenem by renal tubule dehydropeptidases, thus limiting excessive elimination of the active imipenem component.

High-Yield Fast-Facts

- **Seizures Are Possible**
  - High doses, renal impairment, or a combination of the two may lead to excessive exposure to imipenem with the possibility of causing seizures.
  - The proposed mechanism is the carbapenem antagonist activity of the GABA-A receptor.
- **Penicillin Allergy**
  - Carbapenems are often used empirically in patients with a history of an allergic response to penicillin. However, many of these patients may be able to receive alternative (at times, more appropriate) beta-lactams after a thorough history of the offending allergy.
- **Extended infusion**
  - Most carbapenems are administered via extended-infusions empirically in adult patients. While the prescribing information typically suggests an infusion rate of 30 minutes, extending the infusion to 3-4 hours capitalizes on the "Time over MIC" characteristics of carbapenem agents.

HIGH-YIELD BOARD EXAM ESSENTIALS

- **CLASSIC AGENTS:** Doripenem, ertapenem, imipenem, meropenem
- **DRUG CLASS:** Carbapenem
- **INDICATIONS:** Bacteremia, bone and joint infections, gynecologic infections, intra-abdominal infections, pneumonia, skin and soft tissue infection, urinary tract infection
- **MECHANISM:** Inhibit the final step in bacterial cell wall synthesis by binding to specific penicillin-binding proteins in the bacterial cytoplasmic membrane.
- **SIDE EFFECTS:** Seizures, hypersensitivity
- **CLINICAL PEARLS:**
  - There is a small risk of cross-reaction with carbapenems in patients with reported penicillin allergy. While carbapenems are used in patients with PCN allergy, this does not negate close monitoring early on.
  - Imipenem, although referred to independently in many resources, is always co-formulated with cilastatin. Cilastatin prevents the inactivation of imipenem by renal tubule dehydropeptidases, thus limiting excessive elimination of the active imipenem component.
  - Ertapenem is the only agent in this class that does NOT cover against Pseudomonas.

High-Yield Basic Pharmacology

- **Mechanism of Action**
    - Inhibit the final step in bacterial cell wall synthesis by binding to specific penicillin-binding proteins in the bacterial cytoplasmic membrane.
        - Beta-lactams also prevent the transpeptidation reaction and cross-linking of linear peptidoglycan chain constituents of the cell wall as well as activate autolytic enzymes that cause lesions in the bacterial cell wall
- **Cephalosporins and INR**
    - The cephalosporins that contain a methylthiotetrazole group such as cefotetan, and cefoperazone, are associated with prolonged prothrombin time, leading to clinically relevant bleeding in patients receiving warfarin.

Primary Net Benefit

- Bactericidal to susceptible pathogens, leading to microbiologic clearance of the affecting organisms.

Cephalosporins - 1st Generation - Drug Class Review			
High-Yield Med Reviews			
Mechanism of Action: *Inhibit the final step in bacterial cell wall synthesis by binding to specific penicillin-binding proteins in the bacterial cytoplasmic membrane.*			
Class Effects: *Bactericidal to susceptible pathogens (gram + >> gram- coverage); no MRSA or Pseudomonas or ESBLs.*			
Generic Name	**Brand Name**	**Indication(s) or Uses**	**Notes**
Cefadroxil	Duricef	<ul><li>Pharyngitis</li><li>Skin and soft tissue infections</li><li>Urinary tract infections</li></ul>	<ul><li>**Dosing (Adult):**<ul><li>Oral 500 to 1000 mg q12-24h</li></ul></li><li>**Dosing (Peds):**<ul><li>Oral 30 mg/kg/day q12-24h</li></ul></li><li>**CYP450 Interactions:** None</li><li>**Renal or Hepatic Dose Adjustments:**<ul><li>GFR 25 to 50 mL/minute - 500 mg q12h</li><li>GFR 10 to 25 mL/minute - 500 mg q24h</li><li>GFR less than 10 mL/minutes - 500 mg q36h</li></ul></li><li>**Dosage Forms:** Oral (capsules, suspension, tablet)</li></ul>
Cefazolin	Ancef	<ul><li>Bacteremia</li><li>Bone and joint infections</li><li>Endocarditis</li><li>GI Infection</li><li>Pharyngitis</li><li>Skin and soft tissue infections</li><li>Surgical prophylaxis</li><li>Urinary tract infections</li></ul>	<ul><li>**Dosing (Adult):**<ul><li>IV/IO 1 to 2 g IV q8h</li><li>IM 250 to 1500 mg q6-8h</li></ul></li><li>**Dosing (Peds):**<ul><li>IV/IM 25 to 150 mg/kg/day in q6 to 8h</li></ul></li><li>**CYP450 Interactions:** None</li><li>**Renal or Hepatic Dose Adjustments:**<ul><li>GFR 30 to 50 mL/minute - 1 to 2 g q8-12h</li><li>GFR 10 to 30 mL/minute - 500 mg q12h</li><li>GFR less than 10 mL/minutes - 500 mg q24h</li></ul></li><li>**Dosage Forms:** IV (solution)</li></ul>

Cephalosporins - 1st Generation - Drug Class Review
High-Yield Med Reviews

Generic Name	Brand Name	Indication(s) or Uses	Notes

Cephalexin	Keflex	• Bone and joint infections
		• Endocarditis
		• Otitis media
		• Skin and soft tissue infections
		• Urinary tract infections
			• **Dosing (Adult):**
			  – Oral 250 to 1000 mg q12-24h
			• **Dosing (Peds):**
			  – Oral 20 to 100 mg/kg/day q6-12h
			• **CYP450 Interactions:** None
			• **Renal or Hepatic Dose Adjustments:**
			  – GFR 15 to 30 mL/minute - 250 to 500 mg q8-12h
			  – GFR less than 15 mL/minutes - 250 to 500 mg q24h.
			• **Dosage Forms:** Oral (capsules, suspension, tablet)

High-Yield Clinical Knowledge

- **First-Generation Uses**
  – Many oral first-generation cephalosporins are suitable for urinary tract infections and staphylococcal or streptococcal infections, including cellulitis or soft tissue abscess, but later generation agents should be selected for more serious systemic infections.
- **Culture & Sensitivity Interpretation**
  – Cefazolin is the only parenteral first-generation cephalosporin in the United States and is often listed on culture and sensitivity panels. For patients who may be eligible for oral first-generation cephalosporins, cefazolin susceptibility may be interpreted to cephalexin per CLSI.
- **Multiple Routes of Administration**
  – To ease administration, cefazolin may be administered with several different parenteral methods including intramuscular, intraosseous, intravenous infusion, or intravenous push.

High-Yield Fast-Facts

- **Oldy Moldy**
  – Cephalosporin antibiotics were derived from the mold Acremonium, which was formerly known as Cephalosporium.
- **Cephalosporin Origin**
  – Cephalosporins were first identified in 1945 by Giuseppe Brotzu from the University of Cagliari (Italy) when he isolated Cephalosporium acremonium.

HIGH-YIELD BOARD EXAM ESSENTIALS
- **CLASSIC AGENTS:** Cefadroxil, cefazolin, cephalexin
- **DRUG CLASS:** Cephalosporins 1st generation
- **INDICATIONS:** Bacteremia, bone and joint infections, endocarditis, GI infection, pharyngitis, skin and soft tissue infections, surgical prophylaxis, urinary tract infections
- **MECHANISM:** Inhibit the final step in bacterial cell wall synthesis by binding to specific penicillin-binding proteins in the bacterial cytoplasmic membrane.
- **SIDE EFFECTS:** Diarrhea, hypersensitivity, nausea
- **CLINICAL PEARLS:** None of the agents in this class cover against MRSA, Pseudomonas, or ESBL producing organisms. Many oral first-generation cephalosporins are suitable for urinary tract infections and staphylococcal or streptococcal infections, including cellulitis or soft tissue abscess, but later generation agents should be selected for more serious systemic infections. Considered generally safe in pregnancy.

High-Yield Basic Pharmacology

- **Mechanism of Action**
  - Inhibit the final step in bacterial cell wall synthesis by binding to specific penicillin-binding proteins in the bacterial cytoplasmic membrane.
    - Beta-lactams also prevent the transpeptidation reaction and cross-linking of linear peptidoglycan chain constituents of the cell wall as well as activate autolytic enzymes that cause lesions in the bacterial cell wall
- **Cephamycin Sub-Category**
  - The second-generation cephalosporins possess an additional subclass known as cephamycins, including cefoxitin and cefotetan. The primary difference with these agents is their extended-spectrum including activity against anaerobes.

Primary Net Benefit

- Bactericidal to susceptible pathogens, leading to microbiologic clearance of the affecting organisms.

Cephalosporins - 2nd Generation - Drug Class Review			
High-Yield Med Reviews			
Mechanism of Action: *Inhibit the final step in bacterial cell wall synthesis by binding to specific penicillin-binding proteins in the bacterial cytoplasmic membrane.*			
Class Effects: *Bactericidal, gained coverage to anaerobes, but no MRSA, Pseudomonas, or ESBLs*			
Generic Name	**Brand Name**	**Indication(s) or Uses**	**Notes**
Cefuroxime	Ceftin, Zinacef	<ul><li>Bone and joint infections</li><li>COPD exacerbation</li><li>Endocarditis</li><li>GI Infection</li><li>Lyme disease</li><li>Otitis media</li><li>Pharyngitis</li><li>Skin and soft tissue infections</li><li>Urinary tract infections</li></ul>	<ul><li>**Dosing (Adult):**<ul><li>IM/IV 1.5 g IV q8h</li><li>Oral 250 to 500 mg q12-24h</li></ul></li><li>**Dosing (Peds):**<ul><li>Oral 20 to 30 mg/kg/day q12-24h<ul><li>Maximum 500 mg/day</li></ul></li><li>IM/IV 100 to 200 mg/kg/day divided in 3-4 doses<ul><li>Maximum 1500 mg/dose</li></ul></li></ul></li><li>**CYP450 Interactions:** None</li><li>**Renal or Hepatic Dose Adjustments:**<ul><li>GFR 10 to 30 mL/minute - IV 750 to 1500 mg q12h; Oral 250 mg q12h or 500 mg q24h</li><li>GFR less than 10 mL/minutes - IV 750 to 1500 mg q24h; Oral 250 mg q24h or 500 mg q36h</li></ul></li><li>**Dosage Forms:** Oral (capsules, suspension, tablet), IV (solution)</li></ul>
Cefprozil	Cefzil	<ul><li>COPD exacerbation</li><li>Otitis media</li><li>Pharyngitis</li></ul>	<ul><li>**Dosing (Adult):**<ul><li>Oral 250 to 500 mg q12-24h</li></ul></li><li>**Dosing (Peds):**<ul><li>Oral 7.5 to 20 mg/kg/dose once to twice daily<ul><li>Maximum 500 mg/dose</li></ul></li></ul></li><li>**CYP450 Interactions:** None</li><li>**Renal or Hepatic Dose Adjustments:**<ul><li>GFR less than 30 mL/minutes - reduce dose by 50%</li></ul></li><li>**Dosage Forms:** Oral (suspension, tablet)</li></ul>

Cephalosporins - 2nd Generation - Drug Class Review
High-Yield Med Reviews

Generic Name	Brand Name	Indication(s) or Uses	Notes

Cefoxitin	Mefoxin	• Bacteremia
		• Bone and joint infections
		• GI/GYN Infection
		• Skin and soft tissue infections
		• Urinary tract infections
			• **Dosing (Adult):**
			  – IV 1 to 2 g IV q6-8h
			• **Dosing (Peds):**
			  – Oral 20 to 100 mg/kg/day q6-12h
			• **CYP450 Interactions:** None
			• **Renal or Hepatic Dose Adjustments:**
			  – GFR 30 to 50 mL/minute - 1 to 2 g q8-12h
			  – GFR 10 to 29 mL/minute -1 to 2 g q12-24h
			  – GFR 5 to 9 mL/minute - 500 to 1000 mg q12-24h
			  – GFR less than 5 mL/minutes - 500 to 1000 mg q24-48h
			• **Dosage Forms:** IV (solution)

Cefotetan	Cefotan	• Bone and joint infections
		• GYN infections
		• Pneumonia
		• Skin and soft tissue infections
		• Surgical prophylaxis
		• Urinary tract infections
			• **Dosing (Adult):**
			  – IM/IV 1 to 3 q12h
			• **Dosing (Peds):**
			  – IM/IV 30 mg/kg/dose q12h
			    • Maximum 3000 mg/dose
			• **CYP450 Interactions:** None
			• **Renal or Hepatic Dose Adjustments:**
			  – GFR 10 to 30 mL/minute - Adjust frequency to q24h or reduce dose by 50%
			  – GFR less than 10 mL/minutes -Adjust frequency to q48h or reduce dose by 25%
			• **Dosage Forms:** IV (solution)

High-Yield Clinical Knowledge

- **Perioperative Prophylaxis**
  - Cefoxitin and cefotetan are primarily utilized for perioperative prophylaxis in those undergoing intra-abdominal and gynecologic surgical procedures.
- **Extended Spectrum**
  - The oral second-generation cephalosporins extend their spectrum from first-generation agents by covering beta-lactamase-producing Haemophilus influenzae, and Moraxella catarrhalis and are useful to treat sinusitis, otitis, and lower respiratory tract infections.
- **NMTT Side Chain**
  - Cephalosporins containing the NMTT sidechain (cefazolin, cefotetan) have been associated with a disulfiram-like reaction if combined with ethanol.

High-Yield Fast-Facts

- **Beta-Lactamase Influence**
  - Cefuroxime may be more suitable for treatment of H. influenzae infections compared to cefazolin as a result of stability against the TEM beta-lactamase in ampicillin-resistant strains and beta-lactamase-producing Moraxella catarrhalis.
- **Third over Second-Generation**
  - Second generation cephalosporins have seen a decrease in their use, in place of either third-generation cephalosporins, or more narrow-spectrum first-generation agents.

HIGH-YIELD BOARD EXAM ESSENTIALS

- **CLASSIC AGENTS:** Cefuroxime, cefprozil, cefoxitin, cefotetan
- **DRUG CLASS:** Cephalosporins
- **INDICATIONS:** Bacteremia, bone and joint infections, endocarditis, GI infection, pharyngitis, skin and soft tissue infections, surgical prophylaxis, urinary tract infections
- **MECHANISM:** Inhibit the final step in bacterial cell wall synthesis by binding to specific penicillin-binding proteins in the bacterial cytoplasmic membrane.
- **SIDE EFFECTS:** Diarrhea, hypersensitivity, nausea
- **CLINICAL PEARLS:** None of the agents in this class cover against MRSA, Pseudomonas, or ESBL producing organisms. Cephalosporins containing the NMTT sidechain (cefazolin, cefotetan) have been associated with a disulfiram-like reaction if combined with ethanol. Generally considered safe for use in pregnancy.

High-Yield Basic Pharmacology

- **Mechanism of Action**
  - Inhibit the final step in bacterial cell wall synthesis by binding to specific penicillin-binding proteins in the bacterial cytoplasmic membrane.
    - Beta-lactams also prevent the transpeptidation reaction and cross-linking of linear peptidoglycan chain constituents of the cell wall as well as activate autolytic enzymes that cause lesions in the bacterial cell wall
- **Ceftazidime and Aztreonam**
  - Structurally, ceftazidime and aztreonam are nearly identical, except for the absence of a beta-lactam ring and accompanying side chains in the case of aztreonam.
    - As a result, their spectrum (including Pseudomonas aeruginosa), and pharmacokinetics are similar.
  - In patients with a reported Type 1 allergy to ceftazidime, aztreonam should not be used because the likelihood of cross-reactivity is high given the identical R-1 side chains which are often the contributing antigenic component of the structure.

Primary Net Benefit

- Bactericidal to susceptible pathogens, leading to microbiologic clearance of the affecting organisms.

Cephalosporins - 3rd Generation - Drug Class Review			
High-Yield Med Reviews			
Mechanism of Action: *Inhibit the final step in bacterial cell wall synthesis by binding to specific penicillin-binding proteins in the bacterial cytoplasmic membrane.*			
Class Effects: *Bactericidal; no MRSA but ceftazidime covers pseudomonas; safe in pregnancy.*			
Generic Name	**Brand Name**	**Indication(s) or Uses**	**Notes**
Cefotaxime	Claforan	<ul><li>Bacteremia</li><li>Bone and joint infections</li><li>CNS infections</li><li>GI Infection</li><li>Pharyngitis</li><li>Skin and soft tissue infections</li><li>Surgical prophylaxis</li><li>Urinary tract infections</li></ul>	<ul><li>**Dosing (Adult):**<ul><li>IV 1 to 2 g IV q6-8hours</li></ul></li><li>**Dosing (Peds):**<ul><li>IM/IV 150 to 300 mg/kg/day<ul><li>Maximum 12 g/day</li></ul></li></ul></li><li>**CYP450 Interactions:** None</li><li>**Renal or Hepatic Dose Adjustments:**<ul><li>GFR less than 10 mL/minutes - Decrease dose by 50% or administer every 24 hours</li></ul></li><li>**Dosage Forms:** IV (solution)</li></ul>
Ceftriaxone	Rocephin	<ul><li>Bacteremia</li><li>Bone and joint infections</li><li>CNS infections</li><li>GI Infection</li><li>Gonococcal infection</li><li>Pharyngitis</li><li>Pneumonia</li><li>Skin and soft tissue infections</li><li>Surgical prophylaxis</li><li>Urinary tract infections</li></ul>	<ul><li>**Dosing (Adult):**<ul><li>IV 1 to 2 g IV q12-24h</li><li>IM 250 to 2000 mg once to q12-24hours</li></ul></li><li>**Dosing (Peds):**<ul><li>IV/IM 50 to 100 mg/kg/day in q12 to 24h</li></ul></li><li>**CYP450 Interactions:** None</li><li>**Renal or Hepatic Dose Adjustments:**<ul><li>None</li></ul></li><li>**Dosage Forms:** IV (solution)</li></ul>

Cephalosporins - 3rd Generation - Drug Class Review
High-Yield Med Reviews

Generic Name	Brand Name	Indication(s) or Uses	Notes

Cefdinir	Omnicef	• Otitis media
		• Pneumonia
		• Sinusitis
		• Skin and soft tissue infections
		• Urinary tract infections
			• **Dosing (Adult):**
			  – Oral 300 mg BID or 600 mg Daily
			• **Dosing (Peds):**
			  – Oral 14 mg/kg/day divided q12-24h
			    • Maximum 600 mg/day
			• **CYP450 Interactions:** None
			• **Renal or Hepatic Dose Adjustments:**
			  – GFR less than 30 mL/minutes - 300 mg once daily
			• **Dosage Forms:** Oral (capsules, suspension)

Cefixime	Suprax	• Gonococcal infection
		• Rhinosinusitis
		• Typhoid fever
			• **Dosing (Adult):**
			  – Oral 400 mg q12-24hours
			• **Dosing (Peds):**
			  – Oral 14 mg/kg/day divided q12-24h
			    • Maximum 600 mg/day
			• **CYP450 Interactions:** None
			• **Renal or Hepatic Dose Adjustments:**
			  – GFR 21 to 59 mL/minutes - 260 mg once daily
			  – GFR less than 20 mL/minutes - 172 to 200 mg once daily
			• **Dosage Forms:** Oral (capsules, suspension)

Cefpodoxime	Vantin	• COPD exacerbation
		• Otitis media
		• Pneumonia
		• Rhinosinusitis
		• Sinusitis
		• Skin and soft tissue infections
		• Urinary tract infections
			• **Dosing (Adult):**
			  – Oral 200 to 400 mg q12-24hours
			• **Dosing (Peds):**
			  – Oral 5 mg/kg/day divided q24h
			    • Maximum 400 mg/day
			• **CYP450 Interactions:** None
			• **Renal or Hepatic Dose Adjustments:**
			  – GFR less than 30 mL/minutes - Administer q24h
			• **Dosage Forms:** Oral (capsules, suspension)

Ceftazidime	Fortaz	• Bacteremia
		• Bone and joint infections
		• CNS infections
		• GI Infection
		• Gonococcal infection
		• Pharyngitis
		• Pneumonia
		• Skin and soft tissue infections
		• Surgical prophylaxis
		• Urinary tract infections
			• **Dosing (Adult):**
			  – IV 1 to 2 g IV q8h
			• **Dosing (Peds):**
			  – Oral 14 mg/kg/day divided q12-24h
			    • Maximum 600 mg/day
			• **CYP450 Interactions:** None
			• **Renal or Hepatic Dose Adjustments:**
			  – GFR 31 to 50 mL/minutes - 1 to 2 g IV q12h
			  – GFR 16 to 30 mL/minutes - 1 to 2 g IV q24h
			  – GFR less than 15 mL/minutes - 500 to 1g IV q24h
			• **Dosage Forms:** IV (solution)

High-Yield Clinical Knowledge

- **Ceftriaxone renal adjustment**
  - In patients with renal impairment, ceftriaxone does not require dose adjustment as it has mixed hepatic and renal elimination with approximately 50% recovered from the urine, and the remainder is eliminated by biliary excretion.

- **Cefotaxime neonatal meningitis**
  - Cefotaxime must be used in neonates in place of ceftriaxone, as it is contraindicated in this population due to its ability to displace bilirubin from albumin binding sites, causing a higher free bilirubin serum concentration with subsequent accumulation of bilirubin in the tissues.
- **Ceftazidime and avibactam**
  - As cephalosporins generally have poor performance an activity against ESBL- and KPC-producing Enterobacteriaceae and AmpC β-lactamase-overexpressing Pseudomonas, but the addition of avibactam with ceftazidime extends the spectrum to include these pathogens.

High-Yield Fast-Facts

- **Cefixime Vs Ceftriaxone**
  - Cefixime may be used as an alternative to ceftriaxone for gonococcal sexually transmitted infections, particularly in circumstances where parenteral administration may not be feasible.
- **Intravitreal Route**
  - Ceftazidime can be used for endophthalmitis, but its route of administration should be intravitreal injections.
- **Lidocaine for Reconstitution**
  - When administering ceftriaxone intramuscularly, it can be reconstituted with lidocaine 1% which can decrease patient discomfort associated with the injection.

HIGH-YIELD BOARD EXAM ESSENTIALS
- **CLASSIC AGENTS:** Cefotaxime, ceftriaxone, cefdinir, cefixime, cefpodoxime, ceftazidime
- **DRUG CLASS:** Cephalosporins
- **INDICATIONS:** Bacteremia, bone and joint infections, endocarditis, GI infection, pharyngitis, skin and soft tissue infections, surgical prophylaxis, urinary tract infections
- **MECHANISM:** Inhibit the final step in bacterial cell wall synthesis by binding to specific penicillin-binding proteins in the bacterial cytoplasmic membrane.
- **SIDE EFFECTS:** Diarrhea, hypersensitivity, nausea
- **CLINICAL PEARLS:**
  - None of the agents in this class cover against MRSA or ESBL producing organisms (except ceftazidime + avibactam).
  - Ceftazidime extends coverage to Pseudomonas.
  - In patients with renal impairment, ceftriaxone does not require dose adjustment as it has mixed hepatic and renal elimination with approximately 50% recovered from the urine, and the remainder is eliminated by biliary excretion.
  - Generally considered safe for use in pregnancy.

High-Yield Basic Pharmacology

- **Mechanism of Action**
  - *Inhibit the final step in bacterial cell wall synthesis by binding to specific penicillin-binding proteins in the bacterial cytoplasmic membrane.*
- **Intermittent Vs Extended Interval**
  - Dosing for cefepime has traditionally been intermittent small volume parenteral infusions over 30 to 60 minutes. Newer evidence has supported a shift to extended infusion (4-hour infusions) with adjusted interval (q8-12h) to take advantage of beta-lactam antimicrobial kill characteristics of time over MIC.

Primary Net Benefit

- Bactericidal to susceptible pathogens, leading to microbiologic clearance of the affecting organisms.

<table>
<tr><td colspan="4">Cephalosporins - 4th Generation & Anti-MRSA - Drug Class Review
High-Yield Med Reviews</td></tr>
<tr><td colspan="4">Mechanism of Action: Inhibit the final step in bacterial cell wall synthesis by binding to specific penicillin-binding proteins in the bacterial cytoplasmic membrane.</td></tr>
<tr><td colspan="4">Class Effects: Bactericidal and greater gram- coverage with ceftaroline covering MRSA and cefepime covering Pseudomonas.</td></tr>
<tr><td>Generic Name</td><td>Brand Name</td><td>Indication(s) or Uses</td><td>Notes</td></tr>
<tr>
<td>Cefepime</td>
<td>Maxipime</td>
<td>
<ul>
<li>Intra-abdominal infection</li>
<li>Neutropenic fever</li>
<li>Pneumonia</li>
<li>Skin and soft tissue infection</li>
<li>Urinary tract infection</li>
</ul>
</td>
<td>
<ul>
<li>Dosing (Adult):
  <ul><li>IV 1 to 2 g every 8 to 12 hours</li></ul></li>
<li>Dosing (Peds):
  <ul><li>IV 50 mg/kg/dose every 12 hours
    <ul><li>Maximum 2 g/dose</li></ul></li></ul></li>
<li>CYP450 Interactions: None</li>
<li>Renal or Hepatic Dose Adjustments:
  <ul>
  <li>Various recommendations, consult local guidelines</li>
  <li>GFR 10 to 30 mL/minute - 500 to 1000 mg q12-24h; or 2000 mg q24h</li>
  <li>GFR less than 10 mL/minutes - 250 to 1000 mg q24h</li>
  </ul></li>
<li>Dosage Forms: IV (solution)</li>
</ul>
</td>
</tr>
<tr>
<td>Ceftaroline</td>
<td>Teflaro</td>
<td>
<ul>
<li>Pneumonia</li>
<li>Skin and soft tissue infection</li>
</ul>
</td>
<td>
<ul>
<li>Dosing (Adult):
  <ul><li>IV 600 mg q12hours for 5 to 14 days</li></ul></li>
<li>Dosing (Peds):
  <ul><li>IV 8 to 15 mg/kg/dose every 8 hours.
    <ul><li>Maximum 600 mg/dose</li></ul></li></ul></li>
<li>CYP450 Interactions: None</li>
<li>Renal or Hepatic Dose Adjustments:
  <ul>
  <li>GFR 30 to 50 mL/minute - 400 mg q12h</li>
  <li>GFR 15 to 30 mL/minute - 300 mg q12h</li>
  <li>GFR less than 15 mL/minutes or ESRD - 200 mg q12h</li>
  </ul></li>
<li>Dosage Forms: IV (solution)</li>
</ul>
</td>
</tr>
</table>

High-Yield Clinical Knowledge

- **ESBL Resistance**
  - Cefepime was developed to be more resistant to hydrolysis by chromosomal beta-lactamases but is hydrolyzed by extended-spectrum beta-lactamases.
- **MRSA Coverage**
  - Ceftaroline is unique and has increased binding to penicillin-binding protein 2a, which mediates methicillin resistance in staphylococci, resulting in bactericidal activity against these strains. It has some in vitro activity against enterococci and a broad gram-negative spectrum similar to ceftriaxone.
- **Empiric Coverage**
  - Cefepime is widely used in acute care settings as an empiric antibiotic when pseudomonas coverage is necessary, including in patients with febrile neutropenia.

High-Yield Fast-Facts

- **Fourth to Fifth Generation**
  - Ceftaroline can also be considered a fifth-generation cephalosporin as it can cover MRSA and emerging resistant strains including vancomycin-intermediate S. aureus (VISA), heteroresistant VISA (hVISA), and vancomycin-resistant S. aureus (VRSA).
- **Prodrug Ceftaroline**
  - In its dosage format, ceftaroline is actually a prodrug (ceftaroline fosamil) and activated after administration to ceftaroline (active).

HIGH-YIELD BOARD EXAM ESSENTIALS
- **CLASSIC AGENTS:** Cefepime, ceftaroline
- **DRUG CLASS:** Cephalosporins
- **INDICATIONS:** Bacteremia, bone and joint infections, endocarditis, GI infection, pharyngitis, skin and soft tissue infections, surgical prophylaxis, urinary tract infections
- **MECHANISM:** Inhibit the final step in bacterial cell wall synthesis by binding to specific penicillin-binding proteins in the bacterial cytoplasmic membrane.
- **SIDE EFFECTS:** Diarrhea, hypersensitivity, nausea
- **CLINICAL PEARLS:**
  - Cefepime covers Pseudomonas but not MRSA. Whereas, ceftaroline covers MRSA but not Pseudomonas.
  - Cefepime was developed to be more resistant to hydrolysis by chromosomal beta-lactamases but is hydrolyzed by extended-spectrum beta-lactamases.
  - Considered generally safe in pregnancy.

High-Yield Basic Pharmacology

- **Mechanism of Action**
  - Inhibit the final step in bacterial cell wall synthesis by binding to specific penicillin-binding proteins in the bacterial cytoplasmic membrane.
- **Penicillin-Allergic Patients**
  - Aztreonam is frequently used as an alternative agent in patients with penicillin-allergies, however, it is critical to ensure that the original allergy is not related to ceftazidime.
  - Cross-reactivity to aztreonam is likely in the case of ceftazidime allergy as these two agents share structural similarities, notably identical R1 sidechains (the antigenic component of the beta-lactam or monobactam structure).

Primary Net Benefit

- Bactericidal to susceptible pathogens, leading to microbiologic clearance of the affecting organisms.

Monobactam - Drug Class Review			
High-Yield Med Reviews			
Mechanism of Action: *Inhibit the final step in bacterial cell wall synthesis by binding to specific penicillin-binding proteins in the bacterial cytoplasmic membrane.*			
Class Effects: *Bactericidal but with mainly gram – coverage including Pseudomonas, No MRSA coverage.*			
Generic Name	**Brand Name**	**Indication(s) or Uses**	**Notes**
Aztreonam	Azactam	<ul><li>Bacterial meningitis</li><li>Osteomyelitis</li><li>Surgical prophylaxis</li></ul>	<ul><li>**Dosing (Adult):**<ul><li>IV/IM 1 to 2 g q6-8h</li><li>Neb: 75 mg TID (at least 4 hrs apart) x 28 days. Give pre-treatment bronchodilator before each dose.</li></ul></li><li>**Dosing (Peds):**<ul><li>Oral 30 mg/kg/day q12-24h</li></ul></li><li>**CYP450 Interactions:** None</li><li>**Renal or Hepatic Dose Adjustments:**<ul><li>GFR 10 to 30 mL/minute - 500 to 1000 mg q6-8h</li><li>GFR less than 10 mL/minutes - 250 to 500 mg q6-8h</li></ul></li><li>**Dosage Forms:** IV (solution)</li></ul>

High-Yield Clinical Knowledge

- **Inhaled Aztreonam**
  - Aztreonam can be administered via nebulization and is available under the brand name Cayston. It should be noted, the generic IV formulation can also be compounded for nebulization.
- **Neonatal Risk**
  - Aztreonam should be avoided in neonates, infants, and young children as the risk of hepatotoxicity is higher compared to other populations.
- **Resistance Exists**
  - Aztreonam exclusively covers gram-negative pathogens but is still susceptible to hydrolysis by AmpC beta-lactamases and extended-spectrum beta-lactamases.

High-Yield Fast-Facts

- ▪ **Rare Events**
    - – Aztreonam has been rarely associated with elevations in liver enzymes (AST, ALT), eosinophilia, and thrombocytopenia.

HIGH-YIELD BOARD EXAM ESSENTIALS
- • **CLASSIC AGENTS:** Aztreonam
- • **DRUG CLASS:** Monobactam
- • **INDICATIONS:** Bacterial meningitis, osteomyelitis, surgical prophylaxis
- • **MECHANISM:** Inhibit the final step in bacterial cell wall synthesis by binding to specific penicillin-binding proteins in the bacterial cytoplasmic membrane.
- • **SIDE EFFECTS:** Elevations in liver enzymes, eosinophilia, thrombocytopenia
- • **CLINICAL PEARLS:**
    - – The dosage formulation marketed as Cayston is administered by nebulization and indicated for cystic fibrosis.
    - – Aztreonam covers against Pseudomonas but not MRSA.
    - – Cross-reactivity to aztreonam is likely in the case of ceftazidime allergy as these two agents share structural similarities, notably identical R1 sidechains (the antigenic component of the beta-lactam or monobactam structure).

High-Yield Basic Pharmacology

- **Mechanism of Action**
    - Inhibit the final step in bacterial cell wall synthesis by binding to specific penicillin-binding proteins in the bacterial cytoplasmic membrane.
        - Beta-lactams also prevent the transpeptidation reaction and cross-linking of linear peptidoglycan chain constituents of the cell wall as well as activate autolytic enzymes that cause lesions in the bacterial cell wall.

Primary Net Benefit

- Bactericidal to susceptible pathogens, leading to microbiologic clearance of the affecting organisms.

Natural Penicillin - Drug Class Review			
High-Yield Med Reviews			
Mechanism of Action: *Inhibit the final step in bacterial cell wall synthesis by binding to specific penicillin-binding proteins in the bacterial cytoplasmic membrane.*			
Class Effects: *Bactericidal; can treat syphilis; small risk of allergies or rash.*			
Generic Name	**Brand Name**	**Indication(s) or Uses**	**Notes**
Penicillin G Aqueous	Pfizerpen	<ul><li>Botulism</li><li>Diphtheria</li><li>Endocarditis</li><li>Meningitis</li><li>Syphilis</li><li>Streptococcus (group B), maternal prophylaxis</li><li>Tetanus (Clostridium tetani infection)</li></ul>	<ul><li>**Dosing (Adult):**<ul><li>IV 4-6 million units q4h</li></ul></li><li>**Dosing (Peds):**<ul><li>IV 20,000 to 65,000 units/kg IV q6-12h</li></ul></li><li>**CYP450 Interactions:** None</li><li>**Renal or Hepatic Dose Adjustments:**<ul><li>GFR 10 to 50 mL/minute - Decrease frequency to q6-8h</li><li>GFR less than 10 mL/minute - Decrease frequency to q12h.</li></ul></li><li>**Dosage Forms:** IV solution</li></ul>
Penicillin G Benzathine	Bicillin LA	<ul><li>Syphilis</li><li>Streptococcal infection</li></ul>	<ul><li>**Dosing (Adult):**<ul><li>IM 1.2 to 2.4 million units once</li></ul></li><li>**Dosing (Peds):**<ul><li>Less than 27 kg, IM 300,000 to 600,000 units once</li></ul></li><li>**CYP450 Interactions:** None</li><li>**Renal or Hepatic Dose Adjustments:** None</li><li>**Dosage Forms:** Intramuscular suspension</li></ul>
Penicillin G Procaine	Bicillin CR, Wycillin	<ul><li>Streptococcal infection</li></ul>	<ul><li>**Dosing (Adult):**<ul><li>IM 600,000 to 1.2 million units daily for 10 days</li></ul></li><li>**Dosing (Peds):**<ul><li>IM 25,000 to 50,000 units/kg/day</li></ul></li><li>**CYP450 Interactions:** None</li><li>**Renal or Hepatic Dose Adjustments:** None</li><li>**Dosage Forms:** Intramuscular suspension</li></ul>

Natural Penicillin - Drug Class Review
High-Yield Med Reviews

Generic Name	Brand Name	Indication(s) or Uses	Notes

Penicillin V Potassium	Pen-VK	▪ Streptococcal pharyngitis
		▪ Lyme disease
			▪ **Dosing (Adult):**
			  – Oral 250 to 500 mg q6-12h for 10-30 days
			▪ **Dosing (Peds):**
			  – Oral 15 to 62.5 mg/kg/day in 3-6 divided doses for 10-30 days
			▪ **CYP450 Interactions:** None
			▪ **Renal or Hepatic Dose Adjustments:**
			  – GFR less than 10 mL/minute - decrease frequency
			▪ **Dosage Forms:** IV (solution)

High-Yield Clinical Knowledge

▪ **Ampicillin/sulbactam Dosing**
- For the labeled 3 g vial of ampicillin/sulbactam, there is 2 g of ampicillin and 1 g of sulbactam, and for the 1.5 g dose vial, there is 1 g of ampicillin and 500 mg of sulbactam.
- For weight-based dosing of ampicillin/sulbactam, the dose should be based on the ampicillin component.

▪ **Jarisch-Herxheimer Reaction**
- This reaction manifests as fever, chills, diaphoresis, tachycardia, hyperventilation, flushing, and myalgias, typically occurring within 2 hours of administration of penicillin G for treatment of syphilis.
- The Jarisch-Herxheimer reaction typically persists for about 1 day and it can be treated with aspirin or prednisone.
  - Other spirochetal infections such as leptospirosis, and Lyme disease, may also produce Jarisch-Herxheimer reactions after administration of penicillin G
- It occurs in up to 50% of patients with primary syphilis being treated with penicillin G, and up to 75% in patients with secondary syphilis.

▪ **Penicillin Allergy**
- Many patients with a penicillin allergy, report their exposure to be from penicillin VK, and typically complain of a rash. While this may be a relevant hypersensitivity, many beta-lactam alternatives can be selected that possess a dissimilar R-1 side chain, the structural element primarily responsible for type-1 hypersensitivity.

High-Yield Fast-Facts

▪ **Oral Ampicillin**
- For a localized GI tract Shigella infection, oral ampicillin has been favored for treatment because its lack of absorption is desirable.

▪ **Units, not milligrams**
- The unit of measure of the penicillin G dosage forms are 'units' where one unit is a concentration of drug that produces a given size zone of growth inhibition around an Oxford strain of Staphylococcus aureus.

▪ **The "Natural" Penicillins**
- The natural penicillin agents are produced from the fermentation of Penicillium chrysogenum.

HIGH-YIELD BOARD EXAM ESSENTIALS

- **CLASSIC AGENTS:** Penicillin G (aqueous, benzathine, procaine); penicillin V potassium
- **DRUG CLASS:** Natural penicillin
- **INDICATIONS:** Botulism, diphtheria, endocarditis, meningitis, syphilis, Streptococcus (group B), Tetanus (Clostridium tetani infection)
- **MECHANISM:** Inhibit the final step in bacterial cell wall synthesis by binding to specific penicillin-binding proteins in the bacterial cytoplasmic membrane.
- **SIDE EFFECTS:** Acute hypersensitivity, nausea, vomiting, diarrhea
- **CLINICAL PEARLS:** The unit of measure of the penicillin G dosage forms are 'units' where one unit is a concentration of drug that produces a given size zone of growth inhibition around an Oxford strain of Staphylococcus aureus.

High-Yield Basic Pharmacology

- **Mechanism of Action**
  - Binds to the 50S subunit of bacterial ribosomes and inhibits protein synthesis by interfering with the formation of initiation complexes and with aminoacyl translocation reactions.
- **Similar 50S Spectrum**
  - The spectrum of chloramphenicol activity is very similar to that of other 50S ribosomal subunit inhibitors such as macrolides and clindamycin.
    - The spectrum consists primarily of Gram-positive organisms but has activity against Haemophilus influenzae, Neisseria meningitides, and anaerobes, including Bacteroides species.

Primary Net Benefit

- Bacteriostatic protein-synthesis inhibitor with activity against susceptible strains of Gram-positive pathogens and gram-positive anaerobes, including Clostridoides species, but reserved for last line therapy due to life-threatening blood dyscrasias.

Chloramphenicol - Drug Class Review			
High-Yield Med Reviews			
Mechanism of Action: *Binds to the 50S subunit of bacterial ribosomes and inhibits protein synthesis by interfering with the formation of initiation complexes and with aminoacyl translocation reactions.*			
Class Effects: *Bacteriostatic; causes dose-dependent inhibition of RBC production, drug interactions with 2C9*			
Generic Name	**Brand Name**	**Indication(s) or Uses**	**Notes**

Chloramphenicol	Chloromycetin
	Econochlor
		• Bacteremia
		• Meningitis
		• Tickborne rickettsial diseases
			• **Dosing (Adult):**
			  – IV 50 to 100 mg/kg/day in divided q6h
			    • Maximum 4 g/day
			• **Dosing (Peds):**
			  – IV 12.5 to 25 mg/kg/dose q6h
			    • Maximum 4 g/day
			• **CYP450 Interactions:** None
			• **Renal or Hepatic Dose Adjustments:** None
			• **Dosage Forms:** IV (solution)

High-Yield Clinical Knowledge

- **Oral No More**
  - The oral dosage form of chloramphenicol is no longer available in the United States, as the IV product is the only dosage form available.
- **Aplastic Anemia**
  - Chloramphenicol exhibits a dose-dependent reversible suppression of erythrocyte production in normal therapeutic doses and increases with prolonged therapy after 1–2 weeks.
  - However, irreversible aplastic anemia due to chloramphenicol is an idiosyncratic reaction unrelated to dose but can manifest more frequently with prolonged use.
    - Salvage therapy for aplastic anemia may include bone marrow transplantation or immunosuppressive therapy.
- **Drug Interactions**
  - Clinically relevant drug interactions exist with chloramphenicol as it inhibits CYP 2C9, with clinically relevant interactions with phenytoin, rifampin, and warfarin.

High-Yield Fast-Facts

- **Gray Baby Syndrome**
  - Neonates do not possess sufficient hepatic conjugation capacity to metabolized chloramphenicol, which can lead to accumulation, toxicity, and "Gray Baby Syndrome."
    - Gray Baby Syndrome derives its name from the vasomotor collapse resulting in skin mottling ashen-gray discoloration of the skin.
      - The vasomotor collapse is preceded by abdominal distention, vomiting, hypothermia, cyanosis, and cardiovascular instability.
  - Dose reductions with a maximum of 25 mg/kg/day in this population are recommended, along with close monitoring.
- **Cross Resistance**
  - Given the similar binding sites, when resistance occurs to one of these classes, it confers others' resistance.
    - Clindamycin is active against pathogens with different resistance mechanisms to macrolides, specifically those with a macrolide efflux pump.
- **Oxidative Phosphorylation**
  - Chloramphenicol acts as an inhibitor of oxidative phosphorylation by inhibiting cytochrome c oxidase and proton-translocating ATPase.
    - This results in oxidative stress, decreased cellular ATP production, generation of free-radicals island ultimately cell death.

HIGH-YIELD BOARD EXAM ESSENTIALS
- **CLASSIC AGENTS:** Chloramphenicol
- **DRUG CLASS:** Chloramphenicol
- **INDICATIONS:** Bacteremia, cystic fibrosis exacerbations, meningitis
- **MECHANISM:** Binds to the 50S subunit of bacterial ribosomes and inhibits protein synthesis by interfering with the formation of initiation complexes and with aminoacyl translocation reactions.
- **SIDE EFFECTS:** Gray Baby Syndrome, Jarisch-Herxheimer reaction, aplastic anemia
- **CLINICAL PEARLS:** Chloramphenicol can be used as an alternative to beta-lactams in patients with severe allergies and otherwise no alternative agents available. A detailed history of the allergy is necessary to avoid suboptimal care, and consultation with experts to explore penicillin desensitization may be reasonable interventions to avoid chloramphenicol.

High-Yield Basic Pharmacology

- **Mechanism of Action**
  - Binds to the 50S subunit of bacterial ribosomes and inhibits protein synthesis by interfering with the formation of initiation complexes and with aminoacyl translocation reactions.
- **Outer Membrane Penetration**
  - The spectrum of clindamycin activity is limited to Gram-positive organisms as Gram-negative aerobic bacteria possess an outer membrane that clindamycin cannot penetrate.

Primary Net Benefit

- Bacteriostatic protein-synthesis inhibitor with activity against susceptible strains of Gram-positive pathogens and gram-positive anaerobes, including Clostridoides species.

Clindamycin - Drug Class Review			
High-Yield Med Reviews			
Mechanism of Action: *Binds to the 50S subunit of bacterial ribosomes and inhibits protein synthesis by interfering with the formation of initiation complexes and with aminoacyl translocation reactions.*			
Class Effects: Bacteriostatic; Extends coverage to anaerobes, staph and strep (including ca-MRSA); increases risk of C. diff			
Generic Name	**Brand Name**	**Indication(s) or Uses**	**Notes**
Clindamycin	Cleocin	<ul><li>Gynecological infections</li><li>Intraabdominal infection</li><li>Osteomyelitis</li><li>Pneumonia</li><li>Skin and soft tissue infection</li></ul>	<ul><li>**Dosing (Adult):**<ul><li>IV/IM 600 to 2700 mg/day divided q6-12h</li><li>Oral 600 to 1800 mg/day divided q6-12h</li></ul></li><li>**Dosing (Peds):**<ul><li>IV/IM 20 to 40 mg/kg/day divided q6-8h</li><li>Oral 8 to 40 mg/kg/day divided q6-8h</li></ul></li><li>**CYP450 Interactions:** Substrate CYP3A4</li><li>**Renal or Hepatic Dose Adjustments:** None</li><li>**Dosage Forms:** IV (solution), Oral (capsule, solution)</li></ul>

High-Yield Clinical Knowledge

- **Necrotizing Fasciitis**
  - Clindamycin can be used in combination with penicillin G to manage life-threatening skin infections, including necrotizing fasciitis.
    - Clindamycin may be used empirically, as its spectrum included Group A Streptococcus and Clostridioides perfringens or Clostridioides neoformans.
- **Pneumocystis Jiroveci**
  - Since many HIV patients cannot tolerate trimethoprim-sulfamethoxazole for moderate to moderately severe Pneumocystis jiroveci pneumonia, clindamycin with primaquine is an alternative therapy.
  - Clindamycin plus pyrimethamine and leucovorin may also be used for AIDS-related toxoplasmosis of the brain.
- **Dental Procedure Prophylaxis**
  - In patients with beta-lactam allergies, clindamycin should be used for prophylaxis of endocarditis in patients with specific valvular heart disease undergoing certain dental procedures.

High-Yield Fast-Facts

- **D-Zone Test**
  - The double-disk diffusion method (D-zone test) is recommended for testing erythromycin-resistant and clindamycin-susceptible Group-B Streptococci.
- **Bite Wound Treatment**
  - For patients allergic to penicillin, clindamycin with sulfamethoxazole-trimethoprim is an appropriate combination for bite wound prophylaxis.
- **Lincosamides**
  - Clindamycin belongs to the lincosamide class of antibiotics, but since the removal of lincosamide from the US market, it is the only member of this class.

HIGH-YIELD BOARD EXAM ESSENTIALS

- **CLASSIC AGENTS:** Clindamycin
- **DRUG CLASS:** Lincosamide
- **INDICATIONS:** Gynecological infections, intraabdominal infection, osteomyelitis, pneumonia, Skin and soft tissue infection
- **MECHANISM:** Binds to the 50S subunit of bacterial ribosomes and inhibits protein synthesis by interfering with the formation of initiation complexes and with aminoacyl translocation reactions.
- **SIDE EFFECTS:** C. difficile, rash (HIV patients)
- **CLINICAL PEARLS:** Clindamycin is associated with a high incidence of diarrhea (up to 20%), leading to discontinuation in many cases.

High-Yield Basic Pharmacology

- **Mechanism of Action**
  - Binds to the bacterial cytoplasmic membrane, causing a rapid cellular loss of potassium, membrane depolarization, and bacterial cell death.
- **Concentration Dependent**
  - Daptomycin demonstrates concentration-dependent (Cmax over MIC) bactericidal activity. As a result, some have used high doses (10-12 mg/kg) to improve the microbiologic cure.

Primary Net Benefit

- A bactericidal agent with a spectrum of activity exclusive for Gram-positive aerobic, facultative, and anaerobic bacteria.

Daptomycin - Drug Class Review			
High-Yield Med Reviews			
Mechanism of Action: *Binds to the bacterial cytoplasmic membrane, causing a rapid cellular loss of potassium, membrane depolarization, and bacterial cell death.*			
Class Effects: A bactericidal that extends coverage against MRSA; inactivated by surfactant in lung and thus not used for pneumonia; small risk of myopathy			
Generic Name	**Brand Name**	**Indication(s) or Uses**	**Notes**

Daptomycin	Cubicin	• Bacteremia
		• Skin and soft tissue infection
			• **Dosing (Adult):**
			  – IV 4 to 12 mg/kg q24h
			• **Dosing (Peds):**
			  – IV 4 to 12 mg/kg q24h
			• **CYP450 Interactions:** text
			• **Renal or Hepatic Dose Adjustments:**
			  – GFR less than 30 mL/minute - 4 to 6 mg/kg q48h
			• **Dosage Forms:** IV (solution)

High-Yield Clinical Knowledge

- **Bactericidal Not Lytic**
  - The mechanism of daptomycin does not cause lysis of the bacterial cell but rather causes an inhibition of bacterial DNA, RNA, and protein synthesis resulting in cell death.
- **Myopathy**
  - Myopathy is a common complaint with daptomycin therapy; however, this can progress to elevations in creatine phosphokinase levels, rhabdomyolysis, and renal failure in rare circumstances.
  - Patients currently taking statins.
- **Lung Penetration**
  - It is a common misconception that daptomycin does not penetrate lung tissue. In fact, daptomycin does penetrate lung tissue well; however, it is inactivated by pulmonary surfactant once it does.
- **Antibiotic Lock**
  - In patients with chronic or long-term IV catheters that become infected and removal/replacement is not possible, intra-catheter administration of daptomycin has been effective for salvaging the IV access.
    - The so-called "lock solution" is a concentrated daptomycin solution with or without heparin instilled into the lumen of the catheter and allowed to remain there for up to 72 hours.

- **Intraventricular**
  - For invasive CNS infections, rather than IV administration, daptomycin may be administered intraventricularly.
    - The intraventricular dose of daptomycin ranges from 2 to 5 mg daily and should be administered via a ventricular drain, with subsequent clamping of the drain for 15 to 60 minutes after administration.
- **Resistance**
  - Resistance to daptomycin occurs primarily via changes in bacterial cell surface charge that prevents daptomycin from binding to the cell wall.
    - Combination of daptomycin with beta-lactams may overcome resistance in scenarios where alternative therapies are not possible.

HIGH-YIELD BOARD EXAM ESSENTIALS

- **CLASSIC AGENTS:** Daptomycin
- **DRUG CLASS:** Cyclic lipopeptide
- **INDICATIONS:** Bacteremia, skin and skin structure infection
- **MECHANISM:** Binds to bacterial cytoplasmic membrane in a calcium-dependent manner, causing a rapid cellular loss of potassium, membrane depolarization, and bacterial cell death.
- **SIDE EFFECTS:** Myopathy, renal injury
- **CLINICAL PEARLS:** It is a common misconception that daptomycin does not penetrate lung tissue. In fact, daptomycin does penetrate lung tissue well; however, it is inactivated by pulmonary surfactant once it does.

High-Yield Basic Pharmacology

- **Mechanism of Action**
  - Inhibit DNA gyrase and topoisomerase IV, exerting a bactericidal effect on susceptible pathogens.
- **Peak to MIC**
  - Fluoroquinolones are bactericidal with concentration-dependent bacterial killing effects (i.e., peak:MIC effects).
    - For patients requiring renal dose adjustment, the peak:MIC effect should be maintained by preserving the dose (where possible) but prolonging the dosing interval.
  - These agents also possess a three to six-hour post-antibiotic effect on specific pathogens (staphylococci, Enterobacteriaceae, and pseudomonas aeruginosa).

Primary Net Benefit

- Fluoroquinolones are broad-spectrum antimicrobial agents with good tissue penetration, distribution, and pharmacokinetics that support once or twice daily dosing, however, are associated with increased resistance and adverse events that limit their use.

Fluoroquinolones - Drug Class Review			
High-Yield Med Reviews			
Mechanism of Action: *Inhibit DNA gyrase and topoisomerase IV, exerting a bactericidal effect on susceptible pathogens.*			
Class Effects: Bactericidal, peak to MIC dependent effect, some agents cover Pseudomonas, and delafloxacin covers MRSA; prone to drug interactions with di- or tri-valent cation co-administration; risk of tendon rupture in pediatrics or those using steroids; avoid in pregnant patients			
Generic Name	**Brand Name**	**Indication(s) or Uses**	**Notes**

Ciprofloxacin	Cipro	• Bone and joint infections
		• Infectious diarrhea
		• Intra-abdominal infections
		• Pneumonia
		• Skin and skin structure infections
		• Typhoid fever
		• Urinary tract infections
			• **Dosing (Adult):**
			  – Oral 100 to 750 mg BID to Daily
			  – IV 200 to 400 mg IV q12h
			• **Dosing (Peds):**
			  – Oral 10 to 20 mg/kg/dose BID
			    • Maximum 750 mg/dose
			  – IV 10 mg/kg/dose q8 to 12h
			• **CYP450 Interactions:** Inhibits CYP1A2, CYP3A4
			• **Renal or Hepatic Dose Adjustments:**
			  – GFR less than 30 mL/minute - oral maximum 500 mg q24h; IV 200 to 400 mg q24h
			• **Dosage Forms:** IV (solution), oral (tablet, suspension)

Delafloxacin	Baxdela	• Community-Acquired Pneumonia
		• Skin and Skin Structure Infection
			• **Dosing (Adult):**
			  – Oral: 450 mg po BID
			  – IV: 300 mg BID
			• **Dosing (Peds):**
			  – n/a
			• **CYP450 Interactions:** None
			• **Renal or Hepatic Dose Adjustments:** Once CrCl < 15 mL/min
			    Dosage Forms: IV (solution), oral (tablet)

Fluoroquinolones - Drug Class Review
High-Yield Med Reviews

Generic Name	Brand Name	Indication(s) or Uses	Notes
Levofloxacin	Levaquin	<ul><li>Bone and joint infections</li><li>Infectious diarrhea</li><li>Intra-abdominal infections</li><li>Pneumonia</li><li>Skin and skin structure infections</li><li>Urinary tract infections</li></ul>	<ul><li>**Dosing (Adult):**<ul><li>Oral/IV 250 to 750 mg Daily</li></ul></li><li>**Dosing (Peds):**<ul><li>Oral 8 to 10 mg/kg/dose q12 to 24h</li><li>Maximum 750 mg/day</li></ul></li><li>**CYP450 Interactions:** None</li><li>**Renal or Hepatic Dose Adjustments:**<ul><li>GFR 20 to 50 mL/minute - maximum 500 mg q24h</li><li>GFR less than 20 mL/minute - 250 mg q48h</li></ul></li><li>**Dosage Forms:** IV (solution), oral (tablet)</li></ul>
Moxifloxacin	Avelox	<ul><li>Pneumonia</li></ul>	<ul><li>**Dosing (Adult):**<ul><li>Oral/IV 400 mg q24h</li></ul></li><li>**Dosing (Peds):**<ul><li>Oral/IV 4 to 5 mg/kg/dose q12h, maximum 200 mg/dose</li></ul></li><li>**CYP450 Interactions:** None</li><li>**Renal or Hepatic Dose Adjustments:** None</li><li>**Dosage Forms:** IV (solution), oral (tablet)</li></ul>
Norfloxacin	Noroxin	<ul><li>Bone and joint infections</li><li>Infectious diarrhea</li><li>Intra-abdominal infections</li><li>Pneumonia</li><li>Skin and skin structure infections</li><li>Urinary tract infections</li></ul>	<ul><li>**Dosing (Adult):**<ul><li>Oral/IV 400 mg q12h</li></ul></li><li>**Dosing (Peds):**<ul><li>Not routinely used</li></ul></li><li>**CYP450 Interactions:** None</li><li>**Renal or Hepatic Dose Adjustments:**<ul><li>GFR less than 30 mL/minute - 400 mg q24h</li></ul></li><li>**Dosage Forms:** Oral (tablet)</li></ul>
Ofloxacin	Floxin	<ul><li>Bone and joint infections</li><li>Infectious diarrhea</li><li>Intra-abdominal infections</li><li>Pneumonia</li><li>Skin and skin structure infections</li><li>Urinary tract infections</li></ul>	<ul><li>**Dosing (Adult):**<ul><li>Oral/IV 200 to 400 mg q12h</li></ul></li><li>**Dosing (Peds):**<ul><li>Oral 15 mg/kg/day divided q12h</li></ul></li><li>**CYP450 Interactions:** None</li><li>**Renal or Hepatic Dose Adjustments:**<ul><li>GFR 20 to 50 mL/minute - maximum 200 to 400 mg q24h</li><li>GFR less than 20 mL/minute - 100 to 200 mg q24h</li></ul></li><li>**Dosage Forms:** Oral (tablet)</li></ul>

High-Yield Clinical Knowledge

- **Mechanism of resistance**
  - There are three primary mechanisms by which fluoroquinolones develop resistance:
    - Changes to the target sites of DNA gyrase and topoisomerase IV
    - Loss of bacterial outer membrane proteins, decreasing cell wall permeability
    - Mutations in the antibiotic efflux from the cell.
- **Drug interactions**
  - Cations

Copyright: High-Yield Med Reviews highyieldmedreviews.com

- All fluoroquinolones chelate with divalent cations (aluminum, calcium, iron, magnesium, and zinc).
  - Methylxanthines
    - Fluoroquinolones (primarily norfloxacin, ciprofloxacin, levofloxacin, and ofloxacin) can inhibit CYP1A2, and reduce the metabolism of theophylline or caffeine.
  - Tizanidine
    - The concomitant use of ciprofloxacin and tizanidine is contraindicated as ciprofloxacin inhibits the metabolism of tizanidine and can lead to a 10-fold increase in levels, and systemic toxicity including hypotension and seizures.
  - Warfarin
    - Ciprofloxacin and norfloxacin inhibit the metabolism of R-warfarin (CYP1A2 inhibition) and can lead to increased INR, bleeding, or both.

- **Ciprofloxacin and Streptococci**
  - Ciprofloxacin is not reliably active against streptococcal species including Streptococcus Pyogenes, S. Pneumoniae, Streptococci Viridans group, and enterococcus species (aka group D streptococci).
  - As a result, ciprofloxacin should not be empirically used for adult pneumonia, as it does not adequately cover this common pathogen.
    - In specific populations (i.e. children with cystic fibrosis), ciprofloxacin may be reasonable for pneumonia given its coverage of pseudomonas species, relative to other fluoroquinolones.

- **Futility for STD?**
  - The Center for Disease Control and Prevention (CDC) no longer recommends empiric use of fluoroquinolones for the treatment of gonococcal infections due to widespread resistance to these agents.
    - This pertains primarily to N. gonorrhea where there is a high level of resistance, however, for chlamydia, levofloxacin and ofloxacin have been able to achieve 90% cure rates with 7-day courses, and ciprofloxacin is effective in a 3-day course.

- **Pediatric use**
  - The use of fluoroquinolones has been discouraged in pediatric patients due to the possible higher risk of bone, cartilage, and connective tissue (tendinopathies) in this population.
    - However, emerging data from children with cystic fibrosis receiving ciprofloxacin is supporting a safer perspective on this drug class in pediatric populations.
      - So much so that the FDA has approved ciprofloxacin in patients as young as 1-year-old, but emphasizes fluoroquinolones should not be used first-line in pediatric patients.

High-Yield Fast-Facts

- **Quinolone vs Fluoroquinolones**
  - This drug class can be referred to as quinolones or fluoroquinolones. However, all modern agents used in the USA are fluoroquinolones, with Nalidixic acid the only non-fluorinated quinolone, but it is no longer clinically used.
- **Anthrax**
  - Ciprofloxacin and levofloxacin are FDA approved for the prophylaxis of inhalational Bacillus anthracis infection.
    - In the event of an act of terrorism, these agents have been strategically stockpiled for use as post-exposure prophylaxis.
    - Ciprofloxacin is preferred for inhalational and cutaneous anthrax.
- **Tuberculosis**
  - While resistance rates preclude monotherapy, the fluoroquinolones levofloxacin and moxifloxacin are used for Mycobacterium tuberculosis infections in combination with other active antimicrobial agents.

HIGH-YIELD BOARD EXAM ESSENTIALS

- **CLASSIC AGENTS:** Ciprofloxacin, levofloxacin, moxifloxacin, norfloxacin, ofloxacin
- **DRUG CLASS:** Fluoroquinolones
- **INDICATIONS:** Bone and joint infections, infectious diarrhea, intra-abdominal infections, pneumonia, skin and skin structure infections, typhoid fever, urinary tract infections
- **MECHANISM:** Inhibit DNA gyrase and topoisomerase IV, exerting a bactericidal effect on susceptible pathogens.
- **SIDE EFFECTS:** Connective Tissue Damage, QT prolongation, CNS toxicity (dizziness, confusion, headache, hallucinations, depression, psychotic reactions, and seizures)
- **CLINICAL PEARLS:**
    - Only ciprofloxacin and levofloxacin cover against Pseudomonas.
    - Only delafloxacin covered against MRSA.
    - Ciprofloxacin and norfloxacin inhibit the metabolism of R-warfarin (CYP1A2 inhibition) and can lead to increased INR, bleeding, or both.
    - Avoid administering di- and tri-valent cations at the same time as oral agents due to reduced absorption because of chelation.
    - Agents in this case are considered contraindicated in pregnancy and pediatric patients (except for unusual situations).

High-Yield Basic Pharmacology

- **Nitrofurantoin**
  - Converted by bacterial reductases to reactive intermediates, which react with bacterial ribosomal proteins causing inhibition of bacterial protein synthesis, aerobic energy metabolism, DNA, RNA, and cell wall synthesis.
- **Fosfomycin**
  - Inhibits the catalyzation of the initial step in bacterial cell wall synthesis by inactivating pyruvyl transferase

Primary Net Benefit

- Bactericidal activity for Gram-positive and Gram-negative pathogens that commonly cause urinary tract infections.

Fosfomycin and Nitrofurantoin Drug Class Review
High-Yield Med Reviews

Mechanism of Action:
Nitrofurantoin: Converted to reactive intermediates reacting with bacterial ribosomal proteins inhibiting bacterial protein synthesis, aerobic energy metabolism, DNA, RNA, and cell wall synthesis.
Fosfomycin: Inhibits the catalyzation of the initial step in bacterial cell wall synthesis by inactivating pyruvyl transferase.

Class Effects: *Bactericidal activity for Gram-positive and Gram-negative pathogens that commonly cause urinary tract infections. Not useful for pyelonephritis.*

Generic Name	Brand Name	Indication(s) or Uses	Notes

Fosfomycin	Monurol	• Urinary tract infection	• **Dosing (Adult):**]
			  – Oral 3 g once
			    • Can be given as 3 g every other day for 3 doses
			• **Dosing (Peds):**
			  – Oral 2 to 3 g once
			    • Maximum 3 g/dose
			• **CYP450 Interactions:** None
			• **Renal or Hepatic Dose Adjustments:**
			  – GFR 31 to 40 mL/minute - Give 70% of daily dose
			  – GFR 21 to 30 mL/minute - Give 60% of daily dose
			  – GFR 11 to 20 mL/minute - Give 40% of daily dose
			  – GFR less than 10 mL/minute - Give 20% of daily dose
			• **Dosage Forms:** Oral (Packet)

Nitrofurantoin	Furadantin, Macrobid, Macrodantin	• Urinary tract infection	• **Dosing (Adult):**
			  – Oral 100 mg q6-12h
			• **Dosing (Peds):**
			  – Oral 12.5 to 100 mg q6h
			    • Maximum 100 mg/dose
			• **CYP450 Interactions:** None
			• **Renal or Hepatic Dose Adjustments:**
			  – GFR less than 60 mL/minute - Use contraindicated
			• **Dosage Forms:** Oral (capsule, suspension)

- **Macrobid Vs Macrodantin**
  - Nitrofurantoin is formulated in two commonly used oral dosage forms, but the long-acting Macrobid, containing macrocrystalline nitrofurantoin, is preferred for treating urinary tract infections.
    - Clinical failure of treatment of UTI may occur with incorrect prescribing, despite supporting culture and sensitivity data
- **Cystitis Treatment**
  - Fosfomycin and nitrofurantoin are limited to treating lower urinary tract infections or cystitis in women due to lack of sufficient tissue penetration to upper urinary tract structures, including the ureters and kidneys.
- **Adverse Events**
  - Most patients tolerate fosfomycin or nitrofurantoin without complications.
    - However, peripheral neuropathy and pulmonary toxicities may occur, especially when these agents are used for long periods of time or in patients with renal impairment.
- **Nitrofurantoin in Pregnancy**
  - There is controversy regarding nitrofurantoin's role since although it is not a teratogen, there have been cases with associations with congenital anomalies.
  - The greatest risk appears when nitrofurantoin is given to the mother close to delivery leading to a risk of hemolytic anemia in newborns.
  - It is currently recommended to avoid nitrofurantoin in pregnancy in the third trimester.
- **Glucose-6-Phosphate**
  - Sensitivity testing for fosfomycin activity actually requires the supplementation of the media with glucose-6-phosphate. Interestingly, both fosfomycin and nitrofurantoin can cause hemolytic anemia can occur in patients with glucose-6-phosphate dehydrogenase deficiency.
- **Fosfomycin Oral**
  - In the US, fosfomycin is exclusively available as a powder (fosfomycin tromethamine) dissolved in water and taken orally.
- **Low Risk of C. difficile**
  - As a result of the narrow spectrum, there is a low risk of secondary C. difficile infection after treatment with either fosfomycin or nitrofurantoin.

HIGH-YIELD BOARD EXAM ESSENTIALS

- **CLASSIC AGENTS:** Fosfomycin, nitrofurantoin
- **DRUG CLASS:** Antibiotic
- **INDICATIONS:** Urinary tract infections (cystitis)
- **MECHANISM:** Converted to reactive intermediates reacting with bacterial ribosomal proteins inhibiting bacterial protein synthesis, aerobic energy metabolism, DNA, RNA, and cell wall synthesis (nitrofurantoin); Inhibits the catalyzation of the initial step in bacterial cell wall synthesis by inactivating pyruvyl transferase (fosfomycin)
- **SIDE EFFECTS:** Peripheral neuropathy and pulmonary toxicities
- **CLINICAL PEARLS:**
  - Nitrofurantoin is formulated in two commonly used oral dosage forms, but the long-acting Macrobid, containing macrocrystalline nitrofurantoin, is preferred for treating urinary tract infections and is easier to dose (twice a day; i.e., MacroBID).
  - As a result of the narrow spectrum, there is a low risk of secondary C. difficile infection after treatment with either fosfomycin or nitrofurantoin.

High-Yield Basic Pharmacology

- **Mechanism of Action**
  - Inhibition of the polymerization or transglycosylase reaction, thus preventing bacterial cell wall synthesis in sensitive bacteria by binding with high affinity to the d-alanyl-d-alanine terminus of cell wall precursor units
- **Bacterial Resistance Mechanisms**
  - Emerging vancomycin resistance, specifically, the Van A-type resistance among the Enterococcus species (E. faecium and faecalis), is caused by the expression of enzymes that modify cell wall precursors and substituting a terminal d-lactate for d-alanine, reducing affinity for vancomycin by 1000-fold.
  - Staphylococcus aureus resistance is associated with a heterogeneous phenotype, as well as plasmid gene transfer of Van A-type resistance from E. faecalis to MRSA.

Primary Net Benefit

- Bactericidal for gram-positive bacteria and gram-positive anaerobes, including C. difficile.

Glycopeptides - Drug Class Review			
High-Yield Med Reviews			
Mechanism of Action: *Inhibition of the polymerization or transglycosylase reaction, thus preventing bacterial cell wall synthesis in sensitive bacteria by binding with high affinity to the d-alanyl-d-alanine terminus of cell wall precursor units.*			
Class Effects: *Bactericidal for gram-positive bacteria and gram-positive anaerobes, including C. difficile. Covers MRSA, Risk of nephrotoxicity and infusion related reactions (being infused too fast or too large of a dose)*			
Generic Name	**Brand Name**	**Indication(s) or Uses**	**Notes**

Dalbavancin	Dalvance	• Skin and soft tissue infections	• **Dosing (Adult):**
			  – IV 1000 mg once, then 500 mg once in 7 days
			  – IV 1500 mg once
			• **Dosing (Peds):**
			  – IV 12 to 15 mg/kg once, then 6 to 7.5 mg/kg once in 7 days
			    ▪ Maximum 1000 mg/dose
			  – IV 18 to 22.5 mg/kg once
			    ▪ Maximum 1500 mg/dose
			• **CYP450 Interactions:** None
			• **Renal or Hepatic Dose Adjustments:**
			  – GFR less than 30 mL/minute - IV 750 mg once, then 375 mg once in 7 days; or IV 1125 mg once
			• **Dosage Forms:** IV (solution)

Oritavancin	Orbactiv	• Skin and soft tissue infections	• **Dosing (Adult):**
			  – IV 1200 mg once
			• **Dosing (Peds):**
			  – Not routinely used
			• **CYP450 Interactions:** None
			• **Renal or Hepatic Dose Adjustments:** None
			• **Dosage Forms:** IV (solution)

Glycopeptides - Drug Class Review
High-Yield Med Reviews

Generic Name	Brand Name	Indication(s) or Uses	Notes

Telavancin	Vibativ	• Pneumonia
		• Skin and soft tissue infections
			• **Dosing (Adult):**
			  – IV 10 mg/kg q24h
			• **Dosing (Peds):**
			  – Not routinely used
			• **CYP450 Interactions:** None
			• **Renal or Hepatic Dose Adjustments:**
			  – GFR 30 to 50 mL/minute - 7.5 mg/kg q24h
			  – GFR 10 to 30 mL/minute - 10 mg/kg q48h
			  – GFR less than 10 mL/minute - Not recommended
			• **Dosage Forms:** IV (solution)

Vancomycin	Vancocin	• Bacteremia
		• Clostridoides difficile (PO/PR only)
		• Endocarditis
		• Intra-abdominal infection
		• Meningitis
		• Osteomyelitis
		• Peritonitis
		• Pneumonia
		• Sepsis
		• Skin and soft tissue infections
		• Surgical prophylaxis
		• Urinary Tract Infections
			• **Dosing (Adult):**
			  – Oral 250 to 500 mg q6h
			  – IV 10 to 20 mg/kg IV q12h (adjusted to renal function, body weight, indication)
			• **Dosing (Peds):**
			  – Oral 10 mg/kg/dose q6h
			  – IV 5 to 60 mg/kg/day divided q6-8h
			• **CYP450 Interactions:** None
			• **Renal or Hepatic Dose Adjustments:**
			  – Renal impairment - Therapeutic drug monitoring, adjusting dose to target concentration.
			• **Dosage Forms:** IV (solution), Oral (capsule)

High-Yield Clinical Knowledge

- **Clostridoides difficile**
    - Vancomycin is a key therapy for the treatment of C. difficile infections.
    - However, the oral dosage form must be used, which takes advantage of the minimal GI absorption, permitting high gut concentrations, and effective eradication of C. difficile.
        - The IV dosage form may be used orally.
- **Key Toxicities**
    - Acute renal injury is frequently encountered with therapeutic dosing of vancomycin.
        - Appropriate weight-based dosing, and therapeutic drug monitoring, as well as limiting concomitant nephrotoxins are interventions to reduce this risk.
    - "Redman" syndrome is an infusion rate-related histamine release eliciting flushing and red skin.
        - This is often listed as an allergy in patients charts but should be further clarified and documented as an adverse event to prevent future inappropriate antibiotic selection.
- **Therapeutic Drug Monitoring**
    - Therapeutic drug monitoring of the trough concentrations allows for titration of the empiric dose to achieve ideal concentrations between 15-20 mg/dL.
        - Updated recommendations have shifted the focus away from true trough concentrations, towards the assessment of the AUC of vancomycin, which better approximates therapeutic response.
- **Empiric Cornerstone**
    - Vancomycin is a key empiric antibiotic for many infections including bacteremia, cellulitis, endocarditis, meningitis, and pneumonia.

- **Vancomycin Loading Dose**
  - Some experts have suggested administering a loading dose of 20-25 mg/kg once when initiating vancomycin therapy for serious infections.
  - Many institutions have adopted this practice and cap each dose at a maximum of 2 to 3 g.
- **Vancomycin Clinical Efficacy**
  - Vancomycin demonstrates clinical efficacy when the AUC:MIC ratio of ≥400 mg-h/L is achieved in treating staphylococcal infections.
    - There are emerging methods by which to calculate this target, however, the most widely used trough concentration is a surrogate for AUC:MIC.

HIGH-YIELD BOARD EXAM ESSENTIALS
- **CLASSIC AGENTS:** Dalbavancin, telavancin, oritavancin, vancomycin
- **DRUG CLASS:** Glycopeptides
- **INDICATIONS:** Bacteremia, Clostridoides difficile (vancomycin PO/PR only), endocarditis, intra-abdominal infection, meningitis, osteomyelitis, peritonitis, pneumonia, sepsis, skin and soft tissue infections, surgical prophylaxis, urinary tract infections
- **MECHANISM:** Inhibition of the polymerization or transglycosylase reaction, thus preventing bacterial cell wall synthesis in sensitive bacteria by binding with high affinity to the d-alanyl-d-alanine terminus of cell wall precursor units.
- **SIDE EFFECTS:** Nephrotoxicity, infusion reaction (Redman syndrome)
- **CLINICAL PEARLS:** Vancomycin demonstrates clinical efficacy when the AUC:MIC ratio of ?400 mg-h/L is achieved in treating staphylococcal infections. There are emerging methods by which to calculate this target, however, the most widely used trough concentration is a surrogate for AUC:MIC.

High-Yield Basic Pharmacology

- **Mechanism of Action**
  - Inhibit susceptible bacterial protein synthesis by binding reversibly to 50S ribosomal RNA subunits preventing peptide chain elongation and causes peptidyl-transfer RNA to become dissociated from the ribosome
- **Erythromycin Base and GI Absorption**
  - The erythromycin base is destroyed in the acidic environment of the stomach and must be enteric-coated or formulated as an ester of the base (ie, ethyl succinate).
  - The prokinetic effect of erythromycin is not affected by the dosage form, including when administered parenterally.

Primary Net Benefit

- Bacteriostatic against susceptible pathogens (mainly gram-positive bacteria).

<table>
<tr><td colspan="4">Macrolides - Drug Class Review
High-Yield Med Reviews</td></tr>
<tr><td colspan="4">Mechanism of Action: Inhibit susceptible bacterial protein synthesis by binding reversibly to 50S ribosomal.</td></tr>
<tr><td colspan="4">Class Effects: Bacteriostatic against susceptible pathogens (mainly gram-positive bacteria) with good intracellular penetration to cover against intracellular organisms. Risk of drug-interactions except with azithromycin. No coverage against MRSA or Pseudomonas.</td></tr>
<tr><td>Generic Name</td><td>Brand Name</td><td>Indication(s) or Uses</td><td>Notes</td></tr>
<tr>
<td>Azithromycin</td>
<td>Zithromax</td>
<td>
- Ophthalmic infections
- Scaling dermatoses
</td>
<td>

- **Dosing (Adult):**
  - Oral/IV 250 to 500 mg daily
- **Dosing (Peds):**
  - Oral/IV 5 to 10 mg/kg/day
    - Maximum 500 mg/dose
- **CYP450 Interactions:** Substrate CYP3A4, inhibits P-gp
- **Renal or Hepatic Dose Adjustments:** None
- **Dosage Forms:** Oral (tablet, suspension), IV (solution), Ophthalmic (solution)
</td>
</tr>
<tr>
<td>Clarithromycin</td>
<td>Biaxin</td>
<td>
- Rheumatic fever prophylaxis
- Toxoplasma gondii encephalitis
</td>
<td>

- **Dosing (Adult):**
  - Oral IR 500 mg q12h, or ER 1g q24h
- **Dosing (Peds):**
  - Oral 15 mg/kg/day divided q12h
    - Maximum 500 mg/dose
- **CYP450 Interactions:** Substrate CYP3A4, inhibits CYP3A4, P-gp
- **Renal or Hepatic Dose Adjustments:**
  - GFR less than 30 mL/minute reduce dose by 50%
- **Dosage Forms:** Oral (tablet, suspension)
</td>
</tr>
</table>

Macrolides - Drug Class Review
High-Yield Med Reviews

Generic Name	Brand Name	Indication(s) or Uses	Notes
Erythromycin	Erythrocin	<ul><li>Oral dosage form: prokinetic agent for endoscopy/ esophagogastroduodenoscopy</li><li>Topical/Ophthalmic infections</li></ul>	<ul><li>**Dosing (Adult):**<ul><li>Oral (base) 250 to 500 mg q6-12h<ul><li>Maximum 4g/day</li></ul></li><li>Oral (EES) 400 to 800 q6-12h<ul><li>Maximum 4g/day</li></ul></li><li>IV 15 to 20 mg/kg/day divided q6h<ul><li>Maximum 4g/day</li></ul></li></ul></li><li>**Dosing (Peds):**<ul><li>Oral (base or EES) 30 to 50 mg/kg/day divided q6-12h<ul><li>Maximum 4g/day</li></ul></li><li>IV 15 to 20 mg/kg/day divided q6h<ul><li>Maximum 4g/day</li></ul></li></ul></li><li>**CYP450 Interactions:** Substrate CYP2B6, CYP3A4. Inhibits CYP3A4, P-gp</li><li>**Renal or Hepatic Dose Adjustments:** None</li><li>**Dosage Forms:** Oral (capsule, tablet, suspension), IV (solution), Ophthalmic (ointment), Topical (gel, pad, solution)</li></ul>
Fidaxomicin	Dificid	<ul><li>Clostridoides difficile infection</li></ul>	<ul><li>**Dosing (Adult):**<ul><li>Oral 200 mg BID for 10 days</li></ul></li><li>**Dosing (Peds):**<ul><li>Oral 16 mg/kg/dose BID x 10 days<ul><li>Maximum 200mg/dose</li></ul></li></ul></li><li>**CYP450 Interactions:** Pgp substrate</li><li>**Renal or Hepatic Dose Adjustments:** None</li><li>**Dosage Forms:** Oral (tablet, suspension)</li></ul>

High-Yield Clinical Knowledge

- **Drug Interactions**
  - Erythromycin and clarithromycin are substrates and inhibitors of CYP3A4 leading to numerous clinically relevant drug interactions (notably, dronedarone, protease inhibitors, statins, budesonide, among others).
    - Azithromycin does not inhibit CYP3A4 at normal therapeutic dosing, but may at high concentrations.
- **Chlamydia**
  - Chlamydial infections can be treated with a single dose of azithromycin 1 g.
  - It is important that for sexually transmitted Chlamydial infections, the patient, and the patient's sexual partner must both receive treatment to avoid therapeutic failure, re-infection, or both.
- **QT Prolongation**
  - Erythromycin, clarithromycin, have been reported to cause cardiac arrhythmias, including QT prolongation with ventricular tachycardia.
  - Although azithromycin was believed to cause minimal QT prolongation, relative to other macrolides, a large database study observed that more patients receiving a macrolide (including azithromycin) developed cardiac arrhythmias compared to patients receiving fluoroquinolones. (N Engl J Med 2012; 366:1881-1890)

- **Erythromycin GI Distress**
  - Erythromycin is rarely used as an oral or IV antibiotic agent due to epigastric distress, which may be severe.
  - Erythromycin induces motilin receptors to stimulate GI motility but this can be a fortuitous effect for GI preparation to facilitate endoscopy/ esophagogastroduodenoscopy, particularly in patients with GI bleeds.
- **Rare Effects**
  - Macrolides are rarely associated with allergic reactions, however, they can manifest as fever, eosinophilia, and skin eruptions, which disappear shortly after therapy is stopped.
- **Hepatotoxicity**
  - Systemic use of erythromycin has been associated with cholestatic hepatitis, typically after 10-20 days of treatment.
  - Although the risk is much smaller with azithromycin and clarithromycin, they each still carry this warning.

HIGH-YIELD BOARD EXAM ESSENTIALS

- **CLASSIC AGENTS:** Azithromycin, clarithromycin, erythromycin, fidaxomicin
- **DRUG CLASS:** Macrolides
- **INDICATIONS:** Pneumonia, skin and soft tissue infections, chlamydial infection, helicobacter pylori infection, mycobacterial infections
- **MECHANISM:** Inhibit susceptible bacterial protein synthesis by binding reversibly to 50S ribosomal RNA subunits preventing peptide chain elongation and causes peptidyl-transfer RNA to become dissociated from the ribosome.
- **SIDE EFFECTS:** QT prolongation, hepatotoxicity, nausea/vomiting
- **CLINICAL PEARLS:**
  - Macrolide antibiotics have good intracellular penetration and coverage against intracellular organisms such as atypical bacteria, but do not cover against MRSA or Pseudomonas.
  - Erythromycin and clarithromycin are known strong inhibitors of CYP3A4 and cause drug-interactions.
  - Erythromycin, clarithromycin, have been reported to cause cardiac arrhythmias, including QT prolongation with ventricular tachycardia.
  - Erythromycin causes the most diarrhea due to its ability to stimulate bowel peristalsis.

High-Yield Basic Pharmacology

- **Mechanism of Action**
  - Nitroimidazoles are reduced in susceptible pathogens producing an active metabolite taken up into bacterial DNA, forming unstable molecules, and disrupting DNA structure and replication.
- **Disulfiram Reaction**
  - Metronidazole is associated with a disulfiram-like effect in patients who are exposed to ethanol during therapy.
    - While this is relevant for knowledge on board examinations, its clinical relevance is questionable as the incidence of clinically relevant disulfiram reactions is extremely low.

Primary Net Benefit

- Effective against most anaerobic bacteria plays a role in the treatment of Clostridoides difficile infections and some parasites.

Nitroimidazole - Drug Class Review			
High-Yield Med Reviews			
Mechanism of Action: *Reduced in susceptible pathogens to an active metabolite and taken up by bacterial DNA, forming unstable molecules and disrupting DNA structure and replication.*			
Class Effects: Bactericidal against anaerobic bacteria, including Clostridoides difficile, Trichomoniasis, as well as some parasites. Risk of disulfiram-like reaction with alcohol use; drug interactions with warfarin			
Generic Name	**Brand Name**	**Indication(s) or Uses**	**Notes**

Metronidazole	Flagyl	- Amebiasis
		- Bacterial vaginosis
		- Clostridoides difficile
		- Giardiasis
		- Helicobacter pylori
		- Trichomoniasis
			- **Dosing (Adult):**
			  - IV/Oral 500 to 750 mg q8-12h
			- **Dosing (Peds):**
			  - IV/Oral 15 to 50 mg/kg/day divided q8h
			    - Maximum 4 g/day
			- **CYP450 Interactions:** Substrate of CYP2A6, inhibits CYP2C9
			- **Renal or Hepatic Dose Adjustments:**
			  - Child-Pugh class C - reduce dose by 50%
			- **Dosage Forms:** IV (solution), Oral (capsule, tablet)

Secnidazole	Solosec	- Bacterial Vaginosis
		- Trichomoniasis
			- **Dosing (Adult):**
			  - Oral 2 g as a single dose
			- **Dosing (Peds):**
			    - n/a
			- **CYP450 Interactions:** Unknown
			- **Renal or Hepatic Dose Adjustments:** None
			- **Dosage Forms:** Oral (packet)

Tinidazole	Tindamax	- Amebiasis
		- Bacterial vaginosis
		- Clostridoides difficile
		- Giardiasis
		- Trichomoniasis
			- **Dosing (Adult):**
			  - Oral 2 g once daily
			- **Dosing (Peds):**
			  - Oral 50 mg/kg/day
			    - Maximum 2 g/dose
			- **CYP450 Interactions:** Substrate CYP3A4
			- **Renal or Hepatic Dose Adjustments:** None
			- **Dosage Forms:** Oral (tablet)

High-Yield Clinical Knowledge

- **Helicobacter pylori Infection**
  - Metronidazole is a core element to combination therapy for H. pylori infections, including bismuth quad therapy (PPI/H2RA, bismuth, metronidazole, and tetracycline), concomitant therapy (PPI, amoxicillin, clarithromycin, and metronidazole), sequential therapy (PPI and amoxicillin for 5 days, then PPI, clarithromycin, and metronidazole for 5 days).
- **C. difficile Routes**
  - Although metronidazole is no longer considered first-line therapy for C. difficile infections, it can be used in combination with oral vancomycin or fidaxomicin.
    - One advantage to metronidazole is that it can be administered orally or IV for this indication, and some propose higher colon penetration with the IV.
- **Metronidazole Pregnancy**
  - The controversy of metronidazole in pregnancy is dependent on the indication for use as it is contraindicated in the first trimester, but this specific to patients with trichomoniasis or bacterial vaginosis but acceptable for use during the second and third trimester.
  - For all other indications (C. difficile, intraabdominal infections, helicobacter infection, etc.), metronidazole is acceptable during pregnancy.
  - Despite conflicting recommendations, the available evidence suggests that metronidazole does not pose a significant risk of structural defects to the fetus.
    - The prescribing information of metronidazole from the manufacturer states For other indications, metronidazole can be used during pregnancy if there are no other alternatives with established safety profiles.

High-Yield Fast-Facts

- **Peripheral Neuropathy**
  - Metronidazole has been associated with the development of peripheral neuropathy with prolonged use, which can be seen during recurrent C. difficile infection treatment, or H. pylori treatment.
- **Possible Carcinogen**
  - Although the relevance in humans is questionable, metronidazole is considered carcinogenic by the U.S. National Toxicology Program, but this is based only on animal models and has also only been demonstrated to be mutagenic in bacterial cultures.
- **High Single Dose**
  - For the treatment of trichomoniasis, metronidazole is administered as a single 2000 mg dose orally. Although 4x the normal dose for other indications, this dose is well-tolerated and highly (greater than 90%) effective for treatment.

HIGH-YIELD BOARD EXAM ESSENTIALS
- **CLASSIC AGENTS:** Metronidazole, Tinidazole
- **DRUG CLASS:** Nitroimidazole
- **INDICATIONS:** Amebiasis, bacterial vaginosis, Clostridoides difficile, Giardiasis, Helicobacter pylori, trichomoniasis
- **MECHANISM:** Nitroimidazoles are reduced in susceptible pathogens producing an active metabolite taken up into bacterial DNA, forming unstable molecules, and disrupting DNA structure and replication.
- **SIDE EFFECTS:** Disulfiram reaction, peripheral neuropathy
- **CLINICAL PEARLS:**
  - Metronidazole can inhibit CYP2C9 which can interact with warfarin and increase the risk of bleeding.
  - Avoid alcohol when taking metronidazole due to a small risk in developing a "disulfiram-like reaction" (mainly nausea and vomiting).
  - The controversy of metronidazole in pregnancy is dependent on the indication for use as it is contraindicated in the first trimester, but this specific to patients with trichomoniasis or bacterial vaginosis but acceptable for use during the second and third trimester.

High-Yield Basic Pharmacology

- **Mechanism of Action**
  - Binds to the 23S ribosomal RNA of the 50S subunit, stopping the formation of the ribosome complex responsible for protein synthesis, ultimately inhibiting bacterial protein synthesis.
- **Unique Binding Site**
  - The unique 23S subunit binding site of linezolid results in no cross-resistance with other drug classes binding to the 50S subunit, such as clindamycin or macrolides.

Primary Overall Net Benefit

- Bacteriostatic against susceptible Gram-positive pathogens, including enterococci, staphylococci, and bactericidal against streptococci.

Oxazolidinones - Drug Class Review			
High-Yield Med Reviews			
Mechanism of Action: *Binds to the 23S RNS ribosomal RNA of the 50S subunit, inhibiting bacterial protein synthesis*			
Class Effects: *Both agents can inhibit MAO causing drug interactions. Bacteriostatic against susceptible Gram-positive pathogens, including enterococci, staphylococci, and bactericidal against streptococci*			
Generic Name	**Brand Name**	**Indication(s) or Uses**	**Notes**

Linezolid	Zyvox	• Pneumonia
		• Skin and skin structure infections
		• Vancomycin-resistant Enterococcal infection
			• **Dosing (Adult):**
			  – Oral/IV 600 mg q12h
			• **Dosing (Peds):**
			  – Oral/IV 10 mg/kg/dose q8h
			    • Maximum 600 mg/dose
			• **CYP450 Interactions:** None
			• **Renal or Hepatic Dose Adjustments:** None
			• **Dosage Forms:** Oral (tablet), IV (solution)

Tedizolid	Sivextro	• Skin and skin structure infections	• **Dosing (Adult):**
			  – Oral/IV 200 mg daily
			• **Dosing (Peds):** Children 12 years and older
			  – Oral/IV 200 mg daily
			• **CYP450 Interactions:** None
			• **Renal or Hepatic Dose Adjustments:** None
			• **Dosage Forms:** Oral (tablet), IV (solution)

High-Yield Clinical Knowledge

- **Serotonin Syndrome**
  - Linezolid is a nonspecific inhibitor of monoamine oxidase, potentially leading to excess serotonin in patients concomitantly taking SSRI, SNRI, St. John's Wort, or ingesting excessive amounts of dietary tyramine.
- **IV to PO**
  - Both linezolid and tedizolid are well absorbed after oral administration and can be converted 1:1 from IV to oral (or vice versa).

- **Mitochondrial toxicities**
  - Linezolid may directly inhibit intramitochondrial protein synthesis disrupting cellular energy production in tissues highly dependent on oxidative phosphorylation and leading to several clinically relevant adverse events: peripheral and optic neuropathy, lactic acidosis, and myelosuppression.

- **Myelosuppression**
  - Linezolid has been associated with myelosuppression (leukopenia, pancytopenia, and thrombocytopenia) and increases in incidence with prolonged therapy after 2 weeks of therapy.
    - Tedizolid also carries this risk, but this risk may be lower as clinical experience with this agent continues.
- **Vancomycin-Resistant Enterococci (VRE)**
  - The mechanism of resistance in enterococci and staphylococci results from specific point mutations of the 23S rRNA.
    - However, since most bacteria possess multiple copies of 23S rRNA genes, resistance to oxazolidinones to occur requires mutations in at least 2 copies.
- **Linezolid and Bacteremia**
  - Linezolid has excellent tissue penetration; however, blood concentrations are not adequate for reliable empiric management of bacteremia.
    - Exceptions that permit linezolid for bacteremia include VRE infections, or where alternatives otherwise do not exist.

HIGH-YIELD BOARD EXAM ESSENTIALS
- **CLASSIC AGENTS:** Linezolid, tedizolid
- **DRUG CLASS:** Oxazolidinones
- **INDICATIONS:** Pneumonia, skin and skin structure infections, vancomycin-resistant Enterococcal infection
- **MECHANISM:** Binds to the 23S RNS ribosomal RNA of the 50S subunit, inhibiting bacterial protein synthesis
- **SIDE EFFECTS:** Serotonin syndrome, myelosuppression, peripheral and optic neuropathy, lactic acidosis
- **CLINICAL PEARLS:**
  - Both agents cover MRSA and are available in both oral and IV formulations at the same dose.
  - Both agents inhibit MAO and thus used with caution with SRI, SNRI, St. John's Wort, or ingesting excessive amounts of dietary tyramine.
  - Linezolid has excellent tissue penetration; however, blood concentrations are not adequate for reliable empiric management of bacteremia. Exceptions that permit linezolid for bacteremia include VRE infections, or where alternatives otherwise do not exist.

High-Yield Basic Pharmacology

- **Mechanism of Action**
  - Act as cationic detergents that interact strongly with phospholipids and disrupt bacterial cell membranes' structure, leading to bacterial cell lysis.
  - Gram-negative bacteria sensitivity to the polymyxins is related to the phospholipids' content in the given bacterial cell wall.
    - The polymyxins' spectrum is limited to gram-negatives as their binding site to the lipopolysaccharide of the outer membrane of gram-negative bacteria inactivating it.

Primary Net Benefit

- Bactericidal, Gram-negative specific antimicrobials that have re-emerged to treat multi-drug resistant infections, despite considerable toxicity.

Polymyxins - Drug Class Review			
High-Yield Med Reviews			
Mechanism of Action: *Act as cationic detergents that interact strongly with phospholipids and disrupt bacterial cell membranes' structure, leading to bacterial cell lysis.*			
Class Effects: *Bactericidal, Gram-negative specific antimicrobials re-emerged to treat multi-drug resistant infections, despite considerable toxicity. Coverage against Pseudomonas but not MRSA.*			
Generic Name	**Brand Name**	**Indication(s) or Uses**	**Notes**

Colistimethate	Coly-Mycin M	• Bacteremia
		• Meningitis
		• Pneumonia
			• **Dosing (Adult):** Dosing based on colistin base activity (CBA)
			  – IV 300 to 360 mg CBP/day divided q12h
			• **Dosing (Peds):**
			  – IV/IM 2.5 to 5 mg CBA/kg/day divided q6-12h
			• **CYP450 Interactions:** text
			• **Renal or Hepatic Dose Adjustments:**
			  – Obese patients - dose based on adjusted body weight
			  – GFR 31 to 50 mL/minute - 183 to 250 mg CBA/day
			  – GFR 10 to 30 mL/minute - 150 to 183 mg CBA/day
			  – GFR less than 10 mL/minute - 117 mg CBA/day
			• **Dosage Forms:** IV (solution)

Polymyxin B	Polytrim	• Bacteremia
		• Meningitis
		• Pneumonia
			• **Dosing (Adult):**
			  – IV LD 20,000 to 25,000 units/kg, then 12,500 to 15,000 units/kg q12h
			• **Dosing (Peds):**
			  – IV 25,000 to 30,000 units/kg/day divided q12h
			    • Maximum 2,000,000 units/kg per day
			• **CYP450 Interactions:** None
			• **Renal or Hepatic Dose Adjustments:** None
			• **Dosage Forms:** IV (solution)

High-Yield Clinical Knowledge

- **Polymyxin B and Polymyxin E**
    - Although commonly referred to as colistin, it is otherwise known as polymyxin E.
    - It may be referred to as polymyxin E in the historical literature and is marketed either as colistimethate for intravenous administration or colistin base for topical use.
    - Polymyxin B itself not a single agent but is a mixture of polymyxins B1 and B2.
- **Nephrotoxicity**
    - The polymyxin agents are highly nephrotoxic, in a dose-dependent manner, and had fallen out of use due to this toxicity.
        - Their re-emergence into therapy is not because of increased safety but rather accepting the increased risk of renal injury to manage multi-drug resistant Gram-negative infections.
- **Pharmacokinetic Dosing**
    - As an alternative to fixed weight-based dosing, a pharmacokinetic model dosing has been proposed for colistin using the following calculation: maintenance dose = colistin steady-state target x [(1.50 x GFR)+ 30].
        - The suggested average target concentration of 2.5 mcg/mL (or 1.0 mcg/mL free-colistin).

High-Yield Fast-Facts

- **Resistance**
    - Resistance to polymyxins are acquired from bacterial exposure to polymyxins while on treatment has been documented and has become problematic among extensively drug-resistant Acinetobacter and Klebsiella.
- **Colistin**
    - Colistin is the active antimicrobial agent produced from the unstable compound colistin methane sulfonate both in vivo and in aqueous and biologic fluids ex vivo.
- **Nebulization**
    - For certain pulmonary infections or cystic fibrosis, polymyxin B or colistin may be administered via nebulization rather than intravenously or as an adjunct to IV therapy.

HIGH-YIELD BOARD EXAM ESSENTIALS
- **CLASSIC AGENTS:** Polymyxin B, colistimethate
- **DRUG CLASS:** Polymyxins
- **INDICATIONS:** Bacteremia, meningitis, pneumonia
- **MECHANISM:** Act as cationic detergents that interact strongly with phospholipids and disrupt bacterial cell membranes' structure, leading to bacterial cell lysis.
- **SIDE EFFECTS:** Nephrotoxicity, neurotoxicity
- **CLINICAL PEARLS:** For certain pulmonary infections or cystic fibrosis, polymyxin B or colistin may be administered via nebulization rather than intravenously or as an adjunct to IV therapy.

High-Yield Basic Pharmacology

- **Mechanism of Action**
  - Quinupristin and dalfopristin inhibit susceptible bacterial protein synthesis by binding reversibly to 50S ribosomal RNA subunits preventing peptide chain elongation and causes peptidyl-transfer RNA to become dissociated from the ribosome.
    - Dalfopristin possesses additional activity by enhancing quinupristin binding by binding to an adjacent location and resulting in a conformational change in the 50S ribosome
- **Early and Late Phase Inhibition**
  - The action of dalfopristin inhibits early-phase protein synthesis in bacterial cell production, whereas quinupristin inhibits late-phase inhibition of protein synthesis.

Primary Net Benefit

- Bactericidal against gram-positive cocci and organisms responsible for atypical pathogens, and bacteriostatic against Enterococcus faecium.

Quinupristin-Dalfopristin - Drug Class Review			
High-Yield Med Reviews			
Mechanism of Action: *Binds reversibly to 50S ribosomal RNA subunits inhibits susceptible bacterial protein synthesis.*			
Class Effects: *Bactericidal against gram-positive cocci and bacteriostatic against Enterococcus faecium. Covers against MRSA. Associated with infusion related reactions (hard for some patients to get).*			
Generic Name	**Brand Name**	**Indication(s) or Uses**	**Notes**
Quinupristin-dalfopristin	Synercid	<ul><li>Bacteremia</li><li>Endocarditis</li><li>Meningitis</li><li>Skin and skin structure infections</li></ul>	<ul><li>**Dosing (Adult):**<ul><li>IV 7.5 mg/kg q12h</li></ul></li><li>**Dosing (Peds):**<ul><li>IV 7.5 mg/kg q12h</li></ul></li><li>**CYP450 Interactions:** Inhibits CYP3A4</li><li>**Renal or Hepatic Dose Adjustments:** None</li><li>**Dosage Forms:** IV (solution)</li></ul>

High-Yield Clinical Knowledge

- **Interactions**
  - Quinupristin/dalfopristin is an inhibitor of CYP3A4 with clinically relevant drug interactions with warfarin, diazepam, quetiapine, simvastatin, and cyclosporine, to name a few.
- **VRE but Not Enterococcus faecalis**
  - Although quinupristin/dalfopristin is a key agent in the management of vancomycin-resistant enterococcus faecium, it is not effective against Enterococcus faecalis, as nearly all isolates are resistant to quinupristin/dalfopristin.
- **Multi-Drug Resistant Pathogens**
  - As a result of other available agents that are better tolerated, the use of quinupristin/dalfopristin has been relegated to salvage therapy for complicated skin and skin structure infections caused by methicillin-susceptible strains of S. aureus or S. pyogenes or vancomycin-resistant strains of E. faecium.
- **Problematic Adverse Reactions**
  - Administration of quinupristin/dalfopristin is frequently associated with infusion reactions, including pain, inflammation in approximately half of all patients receiving this drug.

- Administration via central IV access can reduce the incidence of infusion reactions and slow the rate of infusion.
- Hyperbilirubinemia is also highly prevalent, occurring in up to 35% of patients.

High-Yield Fast-Fact

- **Combination Ratio**
  - Quinupristin/dalfopristin is formulated in a 30:70 ratio and work synergistically in their action on the 50S ribosome as described above.

HIGH-YIELD BOARD EXAM ESSENTIALS
- **CLASSIC AGENTS:** Quinupristin/Dalfopristin
- **DRUG CLASS:** Streptogramin
- **INDICATIONS:** Bacteremia, endocarditis, meningitis, skin and skin structure infections
- **MECHANISM:** Binds reversibly to 50S ribosomal RNA subunits inhibits susceptible bacterial protein synthesis
- **SIDE EFFECTS:** Infusion reactions, hyperbilirubinemia
- **CLINICAL PEARLS:**
  - Covers against MRSA and VRE.
  - Overall, IV infusions are hard to tolerate and as a result is not commonly used first line.
  - Quinupristin/dalfopristin is an inhibitor of CYP3A4 with clinically relevant drug interactions with warfarin, diazepam, quetiapine, simvastatin, and cyclosporine, to name a few.

High-Yield Basic Pharmacology

- **Sulfonamides**
  - Competitively inhibit dihydropteroate synthase, thus preventing the incorporation of para-aminobenzoic acid (PABA) into dihydropteroic acid and production of folic acid.
- **Trimethoprim**
  - Selective inhibition of bacterial dihydrofolic acid reductase prevents the conversion of dihydrofolic acid to tetrahydrofolic acid.

Primary Net Benefit

- Bacteriostatic as independent agents but can exert bactericidal in combination with other agents.

<table>
<tr>
<td colspan="4">Sulfonamides - Drug Class Review
High-Yield Med Reviews</td>
</tr>
<tr>
<td colspan="4">Mechanism of Action:
Sulfonamides - Inhibit dihydropteroate synthase.
Trimethoprim - Inhibition of bacterial dihydrofolic acid reductase</td>
</tr>
<tr>
<td colspan="4">Class Effects: Bacteriostatic as independent agents but can exert bactericidal in combination with other agents.</td>
</tr>
<tr>
<td>Generic Name</td>
<td>Brand Name</td>
<td>Indication(s) or Uses</td>
<td>Notes</td>
</tr>
<tr>
<td>Sulfacetamide</td>
<td>Bleph-10, Klaron, Ovace</td>
<td>
• Ophthalmic infections
• Scaling dermatoses
</td>
<td>
• Dosing (Adult):
  – Ophthalmic application q2-4hours
  – Topical apply to affected areas 1 to 3 times daily
• Dosing (Peds):
  – Ophthalmic application q2-4hours
  – Topical apply to affected areas 1 to 3 times daily
• CYP450 Interactions: None
• Renal or Hepatic Dose Adjustments: None
• Dosage Forms: Ophthalmic, Topical
</td>
</tr>
<tr>
<td>Sulfadiazine</td>
<td>Lantrisul, Neotrizine, Sulfose, Terfonyl</td>
<td>
• Rheumatic fever prophylaxis
• Toxoplasma gondii encephalitis
</td>
<td>
• Dosing (Adult):
  – Oral 2 to 4 g/day in 3 to 6 divided doses
• Dosing (Peds):
  – Oral 25 to 50 mg/kg/dose q6-12h
    • Maximum 6 g/day
• CYP450 Interactions: Substrate CYP2C9, CYP2E1, CYP3A4
• Renal or Hepatic Dose Adjustments: None
• Dosage Forms: Oral (tablet)
</td>
</tr>
</table>

Sulfonamides - Drug Class Review
High-Yield Med Reviews

Generic Name	Brand Name	Indication(s) or Uses	Notes

Sulfamethoxazole/ Trimethoprim	Bactrim	▪ Toxoplasmosis
		▪ Skin and soft tissue infections
		▪ Urinary Tract Infections
			▪ **Dosing (Adult):**
			  – Oral 1 to 2 SS or DS tablet q12-24h
			  – IV 8 to 20 mg/kg/day (trimethoprim) divided q6-12h
			▪ **Dosing (Peds):**
			  – Oral 5 to 12 mg/kg/day (trimethoprim) divided q12-24h
			  – IV 8 to 20 mg/kg/day (trimethoprim) divided q6-12h
			    ▪ Maximum 320mg/day of trimethoprim
			▪ **CYP450 Interactions:** Substrate CYP2C9, CYP2E1, CYP3A4. Inhibits CYP2C9
			▪ **Renal or Hepatic Dose Adjustments:**
			  – GFR 15 to 30 mL/minute reduce dose by 50%
			  – GFR less than 15 mL/minute reduce dose by 75%
			▪ **Dosage Forms:** Oral (tablet, suspension), IV (solution)

High-Yield Clinical Knowledge

- **Drug Interactions**
  - Sulfonamides have numerous drug interactions by inhibition of CYP2C9 with common medications including warfarin, sulfonylureas, and phenytoin.
  - Sulfonamides may also displace drugs bound to albumin, increasing free-fraction drug concentrations, and potentially causing toxicities or adverse events.
    - In patients taking warfarin and being started on sulfamethoxazole/trimethoprim, empiric dose reduction of warfarin by 10-20% with close follow up and/or monitoring of signs and symptoms of bleeding must occur.
  - Trimethoprim weakly inhibits CYP2C8 but can inhibit CYP2C9 and CYP3A4 at high concentrations.
- **Hypersensitivity**
  - Sulfonamides are associated with delayed onset hypersensitivity reactions which can range from morbilliform, urticarial, purpuric, and petechial rashes, to erythema multiforme, Stevens-Johnson syndrome, or toxic epidermal necrolysis.
  - The onset of these hypersensitivities can occur after the first week of therapy but may appear earlier in patients who have been previously sensitized.
    - Patients with HIV/AIDS have a markedly higher incidence of rashes with sulfonamide treatment which can influence therapeutic selection for PJP prophylaxis or treatment of opportunistic infections.
- **Hemolytic Anemia and G6PD Deficiency**
  - Acute hemolytic anemia may occur after administration of sulfonamide antibiotics, which can be related to an erythrocytic deficiency of G6PD activity.
  - Other hematologic effects can occur, albeit less frequently, including agranulocytosis, aplastic anemia, and thrombocytopenia.
    - Similar to the increased incidence of hypersensitivity in patients with HIV/AIDS taking sulfonamides, the incidence of hematologic toxicity is also higher in this population.
- **IV or Weight Based Dosing**
  - When dosing sulfamethoxazole/trimethoprim using a weight-based format, whether it is in an adult or pediatric patient, the trimethoprim component is used to calculate the appropriate dose.

– Careful verification of the appropriate component should take place as well as confirming the dosage form, particularly if selecting the tablet format (single-strength "SS", or double-strength "DS").

High-Yield Fast-Facts

- **Selective for Bacteria**
    - The action of sulfonamides on purine synthesis is selective for bacteria and does not affect mammalian purine synthesis.
        - Mammalian cells require preformed folic acid, cannot synthesize it, and are thus insensitive to drugs acting by this mechanism.
- **Bacterial Resistance Mechanisms**
    - There are three general mechanisms by which otherwise susceptible bacteria may develop resistance to sulfonamide antibiotics:
        - The decreased target site of action affinity (dihydropteroate synthase) for sulfonamides.
        - Active efflux from the bacterial cell or decreased penetration to the site of action.
        - Bacteria have developed an alternative metabolic pathway and/or increased production of PABA.
- **Trimethoprim Distribution**
    - Sulfamethoxazole/trimethoprim is considered a preferred agent for prostatitis, in part by the ability of trimethoprim to concentrate in the more acidic environment of the prostate relative to plasma.

HIGH-YIELD BOARD EXAM ESSENTIALS
- **CLASSIC AGENTS:** Sulfacetamide, sulfadiazine, sulfamethoxazole/trimethoprim
- **DRUG CLASS:** Sulfonamides
- **INDICATIONS:** PJP prophylaxis, toxoplasmosis, skin and soft tissue infections, urinary tract infections
- **MECHANISM:** Inhibit dihydropteroate synthase (sulfonamides). Inhibition of bacterial dihydrofolic acid reductase (trimethoprim)
- **SIDE EFFECTS:** Rash, hemolytic anemia, hepatic injury
- **CLINICAL PEARLS:**
    - Sulfonamides have numerous drug interactions by inhibition of CYP2C9 with common medications including warfarin, sulfonylureas, and phenytoin.
    - Sulfonamides may also displace drugs bound to albumin, increasing free-fraction drug concentrations, and potentially causing toxicities or adverse events.

High-Yield Basic Pharmacology

- **Mechanism of Action**
  - Bind to bacterial 30S ribosome, preventing access of tRNA to the acceptor site on the mRNA-ribosome complex ultimately inhibiting protein synthesis.
- **Bacterial cellular entry**
  - Tetracyclines must enter the bacterial cell to exert their antimicrobial effect.
    - In gram-negative bacteria, this intracellular transport is accomplished by passive diffusion through channels formed by porins in the outer cell membrane and by active transport that pumps tetracyclines across the cytoplasmic membrane.

Primary Net Benefit

- Bacteriostatic antibiotics with activity against a wide range of aerobic and anaerobic gram-positive and gram-negative bacteria.

Tetracyclines - Drug Class Review			
High-Yield Med Reviews			
Mechanism of Action: *Bind to bacterial 30S ribosome, preventing access of tRNA to the acceptor site on the mRNA-ribosome complex ultimately inhibiting protein synthesis.*			
Class Effects: *Bacteriostatic antibiotics with activity against a wide range of aerobic and anaerobic gram-positive and gram-negative bacteria. No coverage against Pseudomonas, but some doxycycline and minocycline can cover MRSA-ca. Avoid in pregnancy.*			
Generic Name	**Brand Name**	**Indication(s) or Uses**	**Notes**

Demeclocycline	Declomycin, Declostatin, Ledermycin, Bioterciclin, Deganol, Deteclo	• SIADH	• **Dosing (Adult):**
			  – Oral 600 to 1200 mg/day
			• **Dosing (Peds):**
			  – Oral 7 to 13 mg/kg/day q6-12h
			    • Maximum 600 mg/day
			• **CYP450 Interactions:** None
			• **Renal or Hepatic Dose Adjustments:** None
			• **Dosage Forms:** Oral (tablet)

Doxycycline	Vibramycin	• Acne vulgaris
		• Anthrax
		• Bartonella infection
		• Brucellosis
		• Lyme disease
		• Pneumonia
		• Q-fever
		• Rocky Mountain Spotted Fever
		• Sexually transmitted disease
		• Skin and soft tissue infections
		• Tularemia
		• Urinary Tract Infections
			• **Dosing (Adult):**
			  – Oral/IV 100 mg BID
			• **Dosing (Peds):**
			  – Oral/IV 2.2 mg/kg/dose q12h
			    • Maximum 100 mg/dose
			• **CYP450 Interactions:** None
			• **Renal or Hepatic Dose Adjustments:** None
			• **Dosage Forms:** Oral (capsule, tablet, suspension, syrup), IV (solution)

Tetracyclines - Drug Class Review
High-Yield Med Reviews

Generic Name	Brand Name	Indication(s) or Uses	Notes

Eravacycline	Xerava	• Intra-abdominal infections	• **Dosing (Adult):**
			  – IV 1 mg/kg q12h
			• **Dosing (Peds):**
			  – Oral 5 to 12 mg/kg/day (trimethoprim) divided q12-24h
			  – IV 8 to 20 mg/kg/day (trimethoprim) divided q6-12h
			    • Maximum 320mg/day of trimethoprim
			• **CYP450 Interactions:** Substrate CYP3A4
			• **Renal or Hepatic Dose Adjustments:**
			  – Child-Pugh class C, 1 mg/kg q12h x 1, then 1 mg/kg q24h
			• **Dosage Forms:** IV (solution)

Minocycline	Minocin	• Acne vulgaris
		• Skin and soft tissue infections
		• Syphilis
			• **Dosing (Adult):**
			  – Oral/IV 200 mg once, then 100 mg BID
			• **Dosing (Peds):**
			  – Oral/IV 4mg/kg once, then 2 mg/kg/dose q12h
			    • Maximum 400 mg/day
			• **CYP450 Interactions:** None
			• **Renal or Hepatic Dose Adjustments:**
			  – GFR less than 80 mL/minute maximum of 200 mg/day
			• **Dosage Forms:** Oral (capsule, tablet), IV (solution)

Omadacycline	Nuzyra	• Pneumonia
		• Skin and soft tissue infections
		• Tularemia
		• Urinary Tract Infections
			• **Dosing (Adult):**
			  – Oral 300 mg daily
			  – IV 200 mg once, then 100 mg daily
			• **Dosing (Peds):**
			  – Not routinely used
			• **CYP450 Interactions:** P-gp substrate
			• **Renal or Hepatic Dose Adjustments:** None
			• **Dosage Forms:** Oral (tablet), IV (solution)

Sarecycline	Seysara	• Acne vulgaris	• **Dosing (Adult):**
			  – Ora 60 to 150 mg daily (weight based)
			    • 33 to 54 kg, 60 mg daily
			    • 55 to 84 kg, 100 mg daily
			    • 85 to 136 kg, 150 mg daily
			• **Dosing (Peds):**
			  – For children 9 and older, use weight-based dosing
			• **CYP450 Interactions:** None
			• **Renal or Hepatic Dose Adjustments:** None
			• **Dosage Forms:** Oral (tablet)

Tetracyclines - Drug Class Review			
High-Yield Med Reviews			
Generic Name	Brand Name	Indication(s) or Uses	Notes

Tetracycline	Sumycin	▪ Acne vulgaris
		▪ Helicobacter pylori
		▪ Syphilis
		▪ Tularemia
		▪ Vibrio cholerae
			▪ **Dosing (Adult):**
			  – Oral 250 to 500 mg q6-12h
			▪ **Dosing (Peds):**
			  – Oral/IV 25 to 50 mg/kg/day divided q6h
			    ▪ Maximum 250 to 500 mg/dose
			▪ **CYP450 Interactions:** Substrate of CYP 3A4
			▪ **Renal or Hepatic Dose Adjustments:**
			  – GFR 10 to 50 mL/minute - increase frequency to q8-12h)
			  – GFR less than 10 mL/minute - increase frequency to q24h
			▪ **Dosage Forms:** Oral (capsule)

Tigecycline	Tygacil	▪ Pneumonia
		▪ Intraabdominal infections
		▪ Skin and soft tissue infections
			▪ **Dosing (Adult):**
			  – IV 100 mg once followed by 50 mg q12h
			▪ **Dosing (Peds):**
			  – IV 1.5 to 3mg/kg once then 1 to 2 mg/kg/dose q12h
			    ▪ Maximum 100 mg/dose (load) or 50 mg/dose (maintenance)
			▪ **CYP450 Interactions:** None
			▪ **Renal or Hepatic Dose Adjustments:**
			  – Child-Pugh class C, 100 mg once then 25 mg q12h
			▪ **Dosage Forms:** IV (solution)

High-Yield Clinical Knowledge

- **Discoloration of Bony Structures and Teeth**
  - Tetracyclines may readily bind to calcium in newly formed bone or teeth in young children, or to fetal teeth if administered during pregnancy.
  - It must be noted, however, that the discoloration does not adversely affect bone function or growth, and the tooth discoloration is reversible.
    - Therefore, tetracyclines are not contraindicated in children but should be reserved for severe, potentially life-threatening infections, or when better alternatives are unavailable
- **Azithromycin Alternative**
  - For the treatment of community-acquired pneumonia, doxycycline may be used as an alternative to azithromycin for atypical pathogen coverage.
  - Doxycycline may also be used as an alternative to azithromycin for the treatment of sexually transmitted Chlamydial disease.
- **Photosensitivity**
  - Tetracyclines may cause photosensitivity in individuals exposed to sunlight during treatment.
  - Photosensitivity manifests in a range of symptoms from itching and burning sensations with mild erythemas, to erythematous plaques, blistering, lichenoid eruptions, and photoonycholysis.

High-Yield Fast-Facts

- **Bacterial Resistance Mechanisms**
  - There are three general mechanisms by which otherwise susceptible bacteria may develop resistance to tetracycline antibiotics including decreased antibiotic penetration into the ribosome or acquisition of an energy-dependent efflux pathway, displacement of the tetracycline from its target ribosomal site, and enzymatic inactivation.

- **Cations**
  - Concomitant oral administration of tetracyclines and di- or trivalent cations will impair absorption of both the antibiotic and the cation.
  - This interaction extends to food and dairy products high in di- and trivalent cations.

HIGH-YIELD BOARD EXAM ESSENTIALS
- **CLASSIC AGENTS:** Demeclocycline, doxycycline, eravacycline, minocycline, omadacycline, sarecycline, tetracycline, tigecycline
- **DRUG CLASS:** Tetracyclines
- **INDICATIONS:** Acne vulgaris, anthrax, Bartonella infection, Brucellosis, Lyme disease, pneumonia, Q-fever, Rocky Mountain Spotted Fever, sexually transmitted disease, skin and soft tissue infections, tularemia, urinary tract infections
- **MECHANISM:** Bind to bacterial 30S ribosome, preventing access of tRNA to the acceptor site on the mRNA-ribosome complex ultimately inhibiting protein synthesis.
- **SIDE EFFECTS:** Photosensitivity, bone/teeth discoloration
- **CLINICAL PEARLS:** Tetracyclines may readily bind to calcium in newly formed bone or teeth in young children, or to fetal teeth if administered during pregnancy. It must be noted, however, that the discoloration does not adversely affect bone function or growth, and the tooth discoloration is reversible. Regardless, for board exams this is why they are generally contraindicated.

High-Yield Basic Pharmacology

- **Mechanism of Action**
  - Amphotericin B binds to fungal cell membrane ergosterol altering the membrane permeability leading to leakage of cell components and subsequent fungal cell death.
- **Lipid Physical Form**
  - The specific physical form of the lipid of amphotericin B can impact the volume of distribution and penetration into specific tissues such as the CNS or lung.
    - Amphotericin B (lipid complex) exists in a ribbon lipid formulation, which may increase penetration through the blood-brain barrier.
    - The spherical form of amphotericin (liposomal) may limit CNS penetration given the relatively larger spherical size and ability to pass the blood-brain barrier.

Primary Net Benefit

- Fungicidal agents are used for invasive fungal infections with the broadest spectrum of activity of available antifungal drugs, despite significant toxicity.

Amphotericin B - Drug Class Review			
High-Yield Med Reviews			
Mechanism of Action: *Binds to fungal ergosterol leading to leakage of cell components and subsequent fungal cell death.*			
Class Effects: Fungicidal with a broad spectrum of coverage; associated with infusion-related reactions, renal toxicity.			
Generic Name	**Brand Name**	**Indication(s) or Uses**	**Notes**

Amphotericin B (conventional)	Fungizone IV	• Fungal infections
		• Leishmaniasis
			• **Dosing (Adult):**
			  – IV 0.3 to 1.5 mg/kg/day
			    • Typical range 0.3 to 0.7 mg/kg/day
			• **Dosing (Peds):**
			  – IV 0.25 to 1 mg/kg/dose q24h
			• **CYP450 Interactions:** None
			• **Renal or Hepatic Dose Adjustments:**
			  – Decrease dose by 50% or administer q48h if nephrotoxicity occurs.
			• **Dosage Forms:** IV (solution)

Amphotericin B (lipid complex)	Abelcet	• Cryptococcal meningitis
		• Fungal infections
			• **Dosing (Adult):**
			  – IV 3 to 5 mg/kg/dose q24h
			• **Dosing (Peds):**
			  – IV 3 to 5 mg/kg/dose q24h
			• **CYP450 Interactions:** None
			• **Renal or Hepatic Dose Adjustments:** None
			• **Dosage Forms:** IV (suspension)

Amphotericin B (liposomal)	AmBisome	• Cryptococcal meningitis
		• Fungal infections
			• **Dosing (Adult):**
			  – IV 3 to 6 mg/kg/dose q24h
			• **Dosing (Peds):**
			  – IV 3 to 6 mg/kg/dose q24h
			• **CYP450 Interactions:** None
			• **Renal or Hepatic Dose Adjustments:** None
			• **Dosage Forms:** IV (suspension)

High-Yield Clinical Knowledge

- **Infusion-Related Reactions**
  - Amphotericin B infusion-related reactions are frequent and may manifest as fever, chills, muscle spasms, vomiting, headache, and hypotension.
  - Methods to limit these reactions include premedication with antipyretics, antihistamines, or corticosteroids and slowing the rate of infusion or decreasing dose.
- **Resistance**
  - Fungi may develop resistance to amphotericin B by altering its binding to the ergosterol site via decreased membrane ergosterol concentration or modifying the sterol target molecule.
- **Dose Adjustments**
  - According to the prescribing information for patients with hepatic and/or renal impairment, no dose adjustments are recommended.
- **Lipid Delivery Vehicles**
  - Two available formulations of amphotericin B exist as lipid delivery vehicles (lipid complex and liposome), which reduce nephrotoxicity while preserving efficacy.
    - When converting between conventional and lipid amphotericin B formulations, doses are not generalizable, and close attention should be made to avoid over/underdosing.
- **Cumulative Toxicity**
  - Although renal impairment may occur early in therapy, renal function may stabilize during therapy or progress to require dialysis.
    - The general mechanisms of nephrotoxicity include a reversible, pre-renal component, which is associated with decreased renal perfusion, and an irreversible, intrinsic renal tubular injury/renal tubular acidosis.

HIGH-YIELD BOARD EXAM ESSENTIALS

- **CLASSIC AGENTS:** Amphotericin B (conventional, lipid complex, liposomal)
- **DRUG CLASS:** Antifungal
- **INDICATIONS:** Cryptococcal meningitis, fungal infections, leishmaniasis
- **MECHANISM:** Binds to fungal ergosterol leading to leakage of cell components and subsequent fungal cell death.
- **SIDE EFFECTS:** Acute kidney injury, infusion reactions (fever, chills, muscle spasms, vomiting, headache, and hypotension)
- **CLINICAL PEARLS:** Although renal impairment may occur early in therapy, renal function may stabilize during therapy or progress to require dialysis. If the patient can tolerate, giving a small 250-500 mL bolus of fluid or using one of the non-conventional formulations of amphotericin B can facilitate removal from the kidneys and help reduce the risk.

High-Yield Basic Pharmacology

- **Mechanism of Action**
  - Inhibit fungal CYP enzyme 14-α-sterol demethylase, which disrupts fungal ergosterol's biosynthesis, causing the accumulation of the toxic product 14α-methyl-3,6-diol, leading to fungal growth arrest.

Primary Net Benefit

- Broad-spectrum antifungal agents with limited adverse reactions limited to topical management of fungal infections.

Azole Topical (Imidazole) - Drug Class Review			
High-Yield Med Reviews			
Mechanism of Action: *Inhibit fungal CYP enzyme disrupting the biosynthesis of fungal ergosterol and fungal growth arrest.*			
Class Effects: *Broad-spectrum antifungal agents; associated with many CYP450 interactions, small risk of liver toxicity.*			
Generic Name	**Brand Name**	**Indication(s) or Uses**	**Notes**
Butoconazole	Gynazole-1	• Vulvovaginal candidiasis	• **Dosing (Adult):** – Intravaginal 1 applicatorful (5 g) once • **Dosing (Peds):** Not routinely used • **CYP450 Interactions:** None (not absorbed systemically) • **Renal or Hepatic Dose Adjustments:** None • **Dosage Forms:** Vaginal cream

Clotrimazole	Alevazol, Clotrimazole 3 Day, Desenex, Gyne-Lotrimin 3, Lotrimin AF, Pro-Ex Antifungal	• Topical treatment of candidiasis, tinea pedis, tinea cruris, and tinea corporis	• **Dosing (Adult):**
			  – Topical to affected area twice daily
			• **Dosing (Peds):**
			  – Topical to affected area twice daily
			• **CYP450 Interactions:** None (not absorbed systemically)
			• **Renal or Hepatic Dose Adjustments:** None
			• **Dosage Forms:** Topical (cream, vaginal cream, ointment, solution)

Econazole	Econasil, Ecoza, Zolpak	• Topical treatment of candidiasis, tinea pedis, tinea cruris, and tinea corporis	• **Dosing (Adult):**
			  – Topical to affected area twice daily
			• **Dosing (Peds):**
			  – Topical to affected area twice daily
			• **CYP450 Interactions:** None (not absorbed systemically)
			• **Renal or Hepatic Dose Adjustments:** None
			• **Dosage Forms:** Topical (cream, foam, solution)

Azole Topical (Imidazole) - Drug Class Review
High-Yield Med Reviews

Generic Name	Brand Name	Indication(s) or Uses	Notes

Ketoconazole	Extina, Ketodan, Nizoral, Xolegel	• Topical treatment of candidiasis, tinea pedis, tinea cruris, and tinea corporis	• **Dosing (Adult):**
			  – Topical application q12-24h
			• **Dosing (Peds):**
			  – Topical application q12-24h
			• **CYP450 Interactions:** Topical dosage form - none (not absorbed systemically)
			• **Renal or Hepatic Dose Adjustments:** None
			• **Dosage Forms:** Topical (cream, foam, gel, shampoo)

Luliconazole	Luzu	• Topical treatment of tinea pedis, tinea cruris, and tinea corporis]	• **Dosing (Adult):**
			  – Topical to affected area daily
			• **Dosing (Peds):**
			  – Topical to affected area daily
			• **CYP450 Interactions:** Inhibits CYP2C9 (systemic absorption minimal)
			• **Renal or Hepatic Dose Adjustments:** None
			• **Dosage Forms:** Topica (cream)

Miconazole	Desenex Lotrimin AF Micaderm Micatin Vagistat	• Topical treatment of candidiasis, tinea pedis, tinea cruris, and tinea corporis	• **Dosing (Adult):**
			  – Topical to affected area twice daily
			• **Dosing (Peds):**
			  – Topical to affected area twice daily
			• **CYP450 Interactions:** Topical dosage form - none (not absorbed systemically)
			• **Renal or Hepatic Dose Adjustments:** None
			• **Dosage Forms:** Topica (aerosol, cream, vaginal cream, ointment, powder, solution, vaginal suppository)

Oxiconazole	Oxistat	• Topical treatment of tinea pedis, tinea cruris, and tinea corporis	• **Dosing (Adult):**
			  – Topical to affected area q12-24h
			• **Dosing (Peds):**
			  – Topical to affected area q12-24h
			• **CYP450 Interactions:** Topical dosage form - none (not absorbed systemically)
			• **Renal or Hepatic Dose Adjustments:** None
			• **Dosage Forms:** Topical (cream, lotion)

Sertaconazole	Ertaczo	• Topical treatment of tinea pedis, tinea cruris, and tinea corporis	• **Dosing (Adult):**
			  – Topical to affected area q12h
			• **Dosing (Peds):**
			  – Topical to affected area q12
			• **CYP450 Interactions:** Topical dosage form - none (not absorbed systemically)
			• **Renal or Hepatic Dose Adjustments:** None
			• **Dosage Forms:** Topical (cream)

Azole Topical (Imidazole) - Drug Class Review
High-Yield Med Reviews

Generic Name	Brand Name	Indication(s) or Uses	Notes
Sulconazole	Exelderm	• Topical treatment of tinea pedis, tinea cruris, and tinea corporis	• **Dosing (Adult):** – Topical to affected area q12-24h • **Dosing (Peds):** Not routinely used • **CYP450 Interactions:** Topical dosage form - none (not absorbed systemically) • **Renal or Hepatic Dose Adjustments:** None • **Dosage Forms:** Topical (cream, solution)

Tioconazole	Vagistat-1	• Vulvovaginal candidiasis	• **Dosing (Adult):**
			  – Intravaginal 1 applicatorful q24h for 3-7 days
			• **Dosing (Peds):**
			  – Intravaginal 1 applicatorful q24h for 3-7 days
			• **CYP450 Interactions:** Topical dosage form - none (not absorbed systemically)
			• **Renal or Hepatic Dose Adjustments:** None
			• **Dosage Forms:** Topical (ointment)

High-Yield Clinical Knowledge

- **No Prescription Required**
  - Topical azole antifungals are widely available as over-the-counter products under various brand names of clotrimazole or miconazole.
- **Absorption of Topicals**
  - The topical azole antifungals can inhibit CYP450, but they are not systemically absorbed (with normal clinical use) and should not produce clinically relevant drug interactions.
- **Preferred Formulations**
  - Topical antifungal agents for cutaneous infections should be in the form of creams or solutions, as ointments are occlusive to the skin, worsening skin integrity.
    - Although convenient, antifungal powders should be reserved for lesions of the feet, groin, and similar intertriginous areas.
- **Pregnancy**
  - The topical antifungal agents are minimally absorbed but for use in pregnant patients.
  - However, rodent models have suggested teratogenicity, no adverse effects on the human fetus have been attributed to the vaginal use of imidazoles or triazoles.
- **Partner Irritation**
  - During topical vaginal azole antifungal therapies, male sexual partners of the patient may experience mild penile irritation.
- **Look-Alike-Sound-Alike**
  - Although convenient for studying, the antifungal agents' generic names are very similar, prompting many to be considered high-risk for medication errors and employ tall-man lettering to highlight differences.
  - Another potential substitution error is with metronidazole, an antibiotic, but with a similar suffix to many azole antifungals.

HIGH-YIELD BOARD EXAM ESSENTIALS

- **CLASSIC AGENTS:** Butoconazole, clotrimazole, econazole ketoconazole, luliconazole, miconazole, oxiconazole, sertaconazole, sulconazole, tioconazole
- **DRUG CLASS:** Topical azole antifungal
- **INDICATIONS:** Topical treatment of Candida albicans, Malassezia furfur, tinea pedis, tinea cruris, and tinea corporis
- **MECHANISM:** Inhibit fungal CYP enzyme 14-alpha-sterol demethylase, which disrupts fungal ergosterol's biosynthesis, causing the accumulation of the toxic product 14-alpha-methyl-3,6-diol, leading to fungal growth arrest.
- **SIDE EFFECTS:** Skin irritation
- **CLINICAL PEARLS:** The topical azole antifungals can inhibit CYP450, but they are not systemically absorbed (with normal clinical use) and should not produce clinically relevant drug interactions.

High-Yield Basic Pharmacology

- **Mechanism of Action**
  - Inhibit fungal CYP enzyme 14-α-sterol demethylase, which disrupts fungal ergosterol's biosynthesis, causing the accumulation of the toxic product 14α-methyl-3,6-diol, leading to fungal growth arrest.
  - In addition to their primary mechanism, Azole antifungal agents may disrupt phospholipid packing of acyl chains, impairing the function of membrane-bound enzyme systems, increasing the permeability of the fungal cell membrane.

Primary Net Benefit

- Broad-spectrum antifungal agents with limited adverse reactions but clinically relevant drug interactions.

<table>
<tr><th colspan="4">Azole - Drug Class Review
High-Yield Med Reviews</th></tr>
<tr><td colspan="4">Mechanism of Action: Inhibit fungal CYP enzyme disrupting the biosynthesis of fungal ergosterol and fungal growth arrest.</td></tr>
<tr><td colspan="4">Class Effects: Broad-spectrum antifungal agents with limited adverse reactions but clinically relevant drug interactions.</td></tr>
<tr><th>Generic Name</th><th>Brand Name</th><th>Indication(s) or Uses</th><th>Notes</th></tr>
<tr>
<td>Fluconazole</td>
<td>Diflucan</td>
<td>
<ul>
<li>Blastomycosis</li>
<li>Candida intertrigo</li>
<li>Candidiasis (therapy or prophylaxis)</li>
<li>Coccidioidomycosis</li>
<li>Cryptococcosis</li>
<li>Tinea</li>
</ul>
</td>
<td>
<ul>
<li>Dosing (Adult):
  <ul>
  <li>Oral 50 to 200 mg q12-24h</li>
  <li>IV 100 to 800 mg q24h
    <ul><li>Extra info if needed</li></ul>
  </li>
  </ul>
</li>
<li>Dosing (Peds):
  <ul>
  <li>IV/Oral LD 6 to 12 mg/kg/dose, then 3 to 12 mg/kg/dose q24h
    <ul><li>Maximum 600 mg/dose</li></ul>
  </li>
  </ul>
</li>
<li>CYP450 Interactions: Inhibitor CYP2C9, CYP2C19, CYP3A4</li>
<li>Renal or Hepatic Dose Adjustments:
  <ul><li>GFR less than 50 mL/minute - reduce dose by 50%</li></ul>
</li>
<li>Dosage Forms: Oral (tablet, suspension), IV (solution)</li>
</ul>
</td>
</tr>
<tr>
<td>Isavuconazole</td>
<td>Cresemba</td>
<td>
<ul>
<li>Aspergillosis</li>
<li>Mucormycosis</li>
</ul>
</td>
<td>
<ul>
<li>Dosing (Adult):
  <ul><li>IV/Oral 372 mg q8h x 6 doses, then 372 mg q24h</li></ul>
</li>
<li>Dosing (Peds): Not routinely used</li>
<li>CYP450 Interactions: Substrate and inhibits CYP3A4</li>
<li>Renal or Hepatic Dose Adjustments: None</li>
<li>Dosage Forms: IV (solution), Oral (capsule)</li>
</ul>
</td>
</tr>
</table>

Azole - Drug Class Review
High-Yield Med Reviews

Generic Name	Brand Name	Indication(s) or Uses	Notes

Itraconazole	Sporanox	▪ Aspergillosis
		▪ Histoplasmosis
		▪ Mucormycosis
		▪ Onychomycosis
			▪ **Dosing (Adult):** Oral dosage forms not interchangeable
			  – Oral (100 mg capsule or solution) 200 mg q8-12h
			  – Oral (65 mg capsule) 130 to 260 mg q24h
			▪ **Dosing (Peds):**
			  – Oral (solution) 2.5 to 5 mg/kg/dose twice daily
			    ▪ Maximum 400 mg/day
			▪ **CYP450 Interactions:** Substrate and inhibits CYP3A4, P-gp
			▪ **Renal or Hepatic Dose Adjustments:** None
			▪ **Dosage Forms:** Oral (capsule, solution)

Posaconazole	Noxafil	▪ Aspergillosis
		▪ Candidiasis
		▪ Mucormycosis
			▪ **Dosing (Adult):**
			  – IV/Oral tablet 300 mg q12h x 2 doses, then 300 mg q24h
			  – Oral suspension 200 mg q8h, or 400 mg q12h
			▪ **Dosing (Peds):**
			  – Oral 4 to 7 mg/kg/dose q8-12h
			    ▪ Maximum 400 mg/dose
			▪ **CYP450 Interactions:** Inhibits CYP3A4
			▪ **Renal or Hepatic Dose Adjustments:**
			  – IV form - GFR less than 50 mL/minute - avoid use (cyclodextrin accumulation)
			▪ **Dosage Forms:** Oral (tablet, suspension), IV (solution)

Terconazole	Terazol, Zazole	▪ Vulvovaginal candidiasis	▪ **Dosing (Adult):** – Intravaginal 1 applicatorful q24h for 3-7 days ▪ **Dosing (Peds):** Not routinely used ▪ **CYP450 Interactions:** Topical dosage form - none (not absorbed systemically) ▪ **Renal or Hepatic Dose Adjustments:** None ▪ **Dosage Forms:** Topical (vaginal cream/suppository)

Voriconazole	Vfend	▪ Aspergillosis
		▪ Candidiasis
		▪ Histoplasmosis
		▪ Mucormycosis
		▪ Onychomycosis
			▪ **Dosing (Adult):**
			  – Oral 200 to 400 mg q12h
			  – IV 6 mg/kg q12h x 2 doses, then 4 mg/kg q12h
			▪ **Dosing (Peds):**
			  – IV/Oral 6 to 9 mg/kg/dose q12h
			    ▪ Maximum 200 mg/dose
			▪ **CYP450 Interactions:** Substrate and inhibits CYP 2C9, 2C19, 3A4
			▪ **Renal or Hepatic Dose Adjustments:**
			  – Child-Pugh class A or B - Reduce maintenance dose by 50%
			▪ **Dosage Forms:** IV (solution), Oral (tablet, solution)

High-Yield Clinical Knowledge

- **Spectrum**
  - The azole antifungals are a broad-spectrum antifungal group with activity against Candida albicans, C. tropicalis, C. parapsilosis, C. neoformans, Blastomyces dermatitidis, Histoplasma capsulatum, Coccidioides spp., Paracoccidioides brasiliensis, and ringworm fungi.
    - Isavuconazole, posaconazole, and voriconazole are also active against Aspergillus species.
- **Resistance**
  - Resistance to azole antifungals is emerging among C. albicans isolates, with the primary mechanism of resistance being mutations of the gene encoding the azole target fungal binding site.
    - Other resistance mechanisms that have been described include increased azole export and decreased ergosterol content.
- **Drug Interactions**
  - Although the azoles are well tolerated, there are numerous clinically relevant drug interactions as these agents are inhibitors of CYP2D6, 2C9, 2C19, 3A4, 3A5, AND 3A7.
  - The clinical effect of these interactions may be a) decreased azole antifungal effect (CYP inducers), b) increased azole exposure/toxicity (CYP inhibitors), or c) increased drug concentrations (CYP substrates).
    - Notable interactions include decreased elimination of carbamazepine, cyclosporine, digoxin, dofetilide, eplerenone, sulfonylureas, haloperidol, statins, methadone, midazolam, omeprazole, phenytoin, risperidone, HIV protease inhibitors, sildenafil, tacrolimus, and warfarin.
  - Fluconazole is associated with the fewest clinically relevant interactions as it has the least effect of all the azoles on hepatic CYP450 enzymes.
- **Itraconazole Acidic Absorption**
  - The absorption of itraconazole is dependent on gastric pH, with more acidic environments facilitating appropriate absorption.
  - Clinical failure may occur when GI pH becomes more alkaline with PPI, H2RA, or antacid treatment due to reduced bioavailability.
  - There is also dosage form specific administration instructions:
    - Capsule and tablet absorption is best if taken with food.
    - The oral solution should be taken on an empty stomach.
      - To enhance absorption when coadministration of gastric pH increasing drugs is necessary, administration of itraconazole with cola may facilitate absorption.
- **Voriconazole Visual Disturbance**
  - A common adverse event (up to 30% of patients) that patients must be counseled regarding is the associated visual disturbances that include blurring and color vision changes or brightness.
    - These visual changes can occur immediately after a dose of voriconazole but typically resolve within 30 minutes.
- **Hepatotoxicity**
  - Azole antifungal agents have been associated with hepatotoxicity in rare circumstances.

HIGH-YIELD BOARD EXAM ESSENTIALS

- **CLASSIC AGENTS:** Fluconazole, isavuconazole, itraconazole, posaconazole, terconazole, voriconazole
- **DRUG CLASS:** Azole antifungals
- **INDICATIONS:** Fungal infections
- **MECHANISM:** Inhibit fungal CYP enzyme disrupting the biosynthesis of fungal ergosterol and fungal growth arrest.
- **SIDE EFFECTS:** Visual disturbance (voriconazole), QT prolongation (posaconazole, voriconazole), hepatotoxicity
- **CLINICAL PEARLS:** Although the azoles are well tolerated, there are numerous clinically relevant drug interactions as these agents are inhibitors of CYP2D6, 2C9, 2C19, 3A4, 3A5, AND 3A7. The clinical effect of these interactions may be a) decreased azole antifungal effect (CYP inducers), b) increased azole exposure/toxicity (CYP inhibitors), or c) increased drug concentrations (CYP substrates).

High-Yield Basic Pharmacology

- **Mechanism of Action**
  - Inhibits the synthesis of 1,3-beta-D-glucan disrupting fungal cell integrity, and ultimately cell death.
  - Unlike the azole antifungals, which target fungal CYP, which can overlap to human CYP inhibition (thus drug interactions), echinocandins are specific to fungal 1,3-beta-D-glucan, as mammalian cells do not require 1,3-beta-D-glucan.
  - Echinocandins exert the most potent antifungal effect in regions where there is active fungal cell growth.

Primary Net Benefit

- Fungicidal against Candida species, fungistatic against Aspergillus species, and plays a role for empiric therapy for febrile neutropenia.

Echinocandin - Drug Class Review High-Yield Med Reviews			
Mechanism of Action: *Inhibits the synthesis of 1,3-β-D-glucan disrupting fungal cell integrity, and ultimately cell death.*			
Class Effects: *Fungicidal against Candida species, fungistatic against Aspergillus species, and plays a role for empiric therapy for febrile neutropenia, but do NOT penetrate into CNS, drug interaction potential via CYP3A4*			
Generic Name	**Brand Name**	**Indication(s) or Uses**	**Notes**

Anidulafungin	Eraxis	• Candidemia
		• Esophageal Candidiasis
			• **Dosing (Adult):**
			  – IV 200 mg x 1, then 100 mg q24h
			• **Dosing (Peds):**
			  – IV 1.5 to 3 mg/kg/dose x 1, then 0.75 to 1.5 mg/kg/dose q24h
			    • Maximum 200 mg/dose (first dose); 100 mg/dose (subsequent doses)
			• **CYP450 Interactions:** None
			• **Renal or Hepatic Dose Adjustments:** None
			• **Dosage Forms:** IV (solution)

Caspofungin	Cancidas	• Aspergillosis
		• Candidemia
		• Esophageal Candidiasis
		• Neutropenic fever
			• **Dosing (Adult):**
			  – IV 70 mg x 1, then 50 mg q24h
			    • IV 150 mg q24h for endocarditis
			• **Dosing (Peds):**
			  – IV 70 mg/m2/dose x 1, then 50 mg/m2 q24h
			• **CYP450 Interactions:** Inhibits CYP3A4
			• **Renal or Hepatic Dose Adjustments:**
			  – Child-Pugh class B or C - IV 70 mg x 1, then 35 mg q24h
			• **Dosage Forms:** IV (solution)

Micafungin	Mycamine	• Aspergillosis
		• Candidemia
		• Esophageal Candidiasis
		• Neutropenic fever
			• **Dosing (Adult):**
			  – IV 100 to 150 mg IV q24h
			• **Dosing (Peds):**
			  – IV 2 to 4 mg/kg/dose q24h
			    • Maximum 150 mg/dose
			• **CYP450 Interactions:** Inhibits CYP3A4
			• **Renal or Hepatic Dose Adjustments:** None
			• **Dosage Forms:** IV (solution)

High-Yield Clinical Knowledge

- **Febrile Neutropenia**
  - Antifungal treatment of febrile neutropenia is not typically started at the onset of illness, where broad-spectrum antibiotics play an essential role.
  - Echinocandins may be empirically started for febrile neutropenia if clinical improvement is not observed in patients on appropriate antimicrobial therapy for 4 to 7 days without other identified indications.
- **Use in Pregnancy**
  - All available echinocandins are contraindicated in pregnancy.
    - There have been no human studies, but in animal models, echinocandins have been observed to be embryotoxic, associated with incomplete ossification of the skull and torso, and increased risk of cervical ribs.
- **Dosing in Morbid Obesity**
  - Morbidly obese patients may have decreased exposure to echinocandins and require dose adjustments.
    - However, clear clinical guidance is lacking in this area.
  - For micafungin specifically, patients weighing over 115 kg should receive increased doses of micafungin of 200 mg.
- **CNS Penetration**
  - None of the echinocandins penetrate the CNS and thus do not play a role in managing CNS fungal infections.
- **Resistance**
  - Resistance to the echinocandins emerges from mutations that cause amino acid substitutions in the Fks subunits of glucan synthase.
- **Drug Interactions**
  - Caspofungin and micafungin are substrates of CYP 3A4 and may have clinically relevant cyclosporine interactions and other strong CYP3A4 inhibitors.
    - However, three clinical observational analyses have failed to observe clinically relevant hepatotoxicity with the combination of caspofungin and cyclosporine.
  - If patients are on inducers of CYP3A4 (carbamazepine, phenytoin, rifampin, isoniazid, etc.), the caspofungin dose should be increased to 70 mg daily.

HIGH-YIELD BOARD EXAM ESSENTIALS
- **CLASSIC AGENTS:** Anidulafungin, caspofungin, micafungin
- **DRUG CLASS:** Echinocandin
- **INDICATIONS:** Disseminated and mucocutaneous Candidal infections, febrile neutropenia
- **MECHANISM:** Inhibits the synthesis of 1,3-beta-D-glucan disrupting fungal cell integrity, and ultimately cell death.
- **SIDE EFFECTS:** Peripheral edema, infusion reaction (chills, fever, phlebitis), liver enzyme elevation
- **CLINICAL PEARLS:** Caspofungin and micafungin are both hepatically metabolized; however, anidulafungin is eliminated via chemical hydrolysis.

High-Yield Basic Pharmacology

- **Mechanism of Action**
    - Flucytosine inhibits susceptible fungal DNA and RNA synthesis after conversion to its active components, 5-fluorouracil (5-FU), 5-fluorodeoxyuridine monophosphate (FdUMP), and fluorouridine triphosphate (FUTP).
- **Fungal Specific**
    - The conversion of flucytosine to 5-FU is specific to fungal cells and does not occur in human cells, protecting them from toxicity.
    - However, intestinal flora can liberate 5-FU, permitting its absorption.

Primary Net Benefit

- Fungicidal agents are used for invasive fungal infections that are converted intracellularly to 5-FU.

<table>
<tr><td colspan="4" align="center">**Flucytosine - Drug Class Review**
High-Yield Med Reviews</td></tr>
<tr><td colspan="4">**Mechanism of Action:** *Inhibits susceptible fungal DNA and RNA synthesis after conversion to 5-FU, FdUMP, and FUTP.*</td></tr>
<tr><td colspan="4">**Class Effects:** *Specific to fungus only, offers synergy to amphotericin B, monitor levels to avoid BMS with levels > 100 mcg/mL*</td></tr>
<tr><td>**Generic Name**</td><td>**Brand Name**</td><td>**Indication(s) or Uses**</td><td>**Notes**</td></tr>
<tr><td>Flucytosine</td><td>Ancobon</td><td>• Candida infections
• Cryptococcus infections</td><td>• **Dosing (Adult):**
  – Oral 25 mg/kg/dose q6h
    • Use IBW for obese patients
• **Dosing (Peds):**
  – Oral 25 mg/kg/dose q6h
    • Extra info if needed
• **CYP450 Interactions:** None
• **Renal or Hepatic Dose Adjustments:**
  – GFR 21 to 40 mL/min - 25 mg/kg/dose q12h
  – GFR 11 to 20 mL/min - 25 mg/kg/dose q24h
  – GFR less than 10 mL/min - 25 mg/kg/dose q48h
• **Dosage Forms:** Oral (capsule)</td></tr>
</table>

High-Yield Clinical Knowledge

- **Resistance**
    - Resistance to flucytosine occurs due to altered metabolism to its metabolites (5-FU, FdUMP, FUTP), which can occur in the course of flucytosine monotherapy.
- **Therapeutic Drug Monitoring**
    - The normal therapeutic target range for flucytosine is 30 to 80 mcg/mL and should be taken on day 3 of therapy and after 2 hours from administration.
    - Concentrations above 100 mcg/mL should be avoided since the risk of bone marrow toxicity, and hepatotoxicity is higher with elevated concentrations.

- **Flucytosine to Fluconazole**
  - For cryptococcal meningitis treatment, high dose fluconazole has become an alternative to flucytosine in some clinical scenarios.
- **Orally Administered**
  - Flucytosine is only available as an oral dosage form but primarily used in cryptococcal meningitis, where patients may not take oral medications.
  - Thus, it's administration frequently requires a nasogastric or orogastric tube and extemporaneous compounding from the oral capsule to an oral solution.
- **Amphotericin B Synergy**
  - When combined with amphotericin B, these agents demonstrate synergy, which has been attributed to enhanced penetration of the flucytosine through amphotericin-damaged fungal cell membranes.
- **Triple Therapy**
  - Although fluconazole may be used in place of flucytosine, it may also be used in combination along with amphotericin B as triple therapy for certain cryptococcal or candida infections.

HIGH-YIELD BOARD EXAM ESSENTIALS

- **CLASSIC AGENTS:** Flucytosine
- **DRUG CLASS:** Antifungal
- **INDICATIONS:** Candida infections, Cryptococcus infections
- **MECHANISM:** Inhibits susceptible fungal DNA and RNA synthesis after conversion to its active components, 5-FU, FdUMP, and FUTP.
- **SIDE EFFECTS:** Nephrotoxicity, hepatotoxicity, bone marrow suppression
- **CLINICAL PEARLS:**
  - For cryptococcal meningitis treatment, high dose fluconazole has become an alternative to flucytosine in some clinical scenarios.
  - Monitor blood levels (> 100 mcg/mL is associated with BMS)

High-Yield Basic Pharmacology

- **Ciclopirox**
    - Inhibits metal-dependent enzymes via chelation, causing degradation of peroxides within the fungal cell.
- **Griseofulvin**
    - Disrupts the assembly of the fungal mitotic spindle by inhibiting microtubule function, preventing fungal cell division.
    - Griseofulvin has excellent penetration to keratin precursor cells, leading to prolonged antifungal effects.
        - As keratin cells differentiate, griseofulvin persists in keratin, leading to long-term resistance to fungal invasion, including new hair or nails.
        - Terbinafine exerts a similar effect on keratin, however, it is fungicidal, where griseofulvin is fungistatic
- **Naftifine, Terbinafine**
    - Inhibits squalene-2,3-epoxidase, disrupting the synthesis of ergosterol in the fungal cell.
- **Nystatin**
- Binds to fungal cell membrane ergosterol altering the membrane permeability leading to leakage of cell components and subsequent fungal cell death

Primary Net Benefit

- Topical broad-spectrum antifungal therapy for infections where systemic agents are unnecessary or unwanted due to poor skin penetration. Griseofulvin and terbinafine are oral agents for tinea infections.

<table>
<tr><th colspan="4">Other Antifungals - Drug Class Review
High-Yield Med Reviews</th></tr>
<tr><td colspan="4">Mechanism of Action: See each agent above</td></tr>
<tr><td colspan="4">Class Effects: Topical broad-spectrum antifungal therapy for infections where systemic agents are unnecessary or unwanted due to poor skin penetration. Griseofulvin and terbinafine are oral agents for tinea infections.</td></tr>
<tr><th>Generic Name</th><th>Brand Name</th><th>Indication(s) or Uses</th><th>Notes</th></tr>
<tr>
<td>Ciclopirox</td>
<td>Ciclodan</td>
<td>
<ul>
<li>Topical treatment of tinea (pedis, corporis, cruris, versicolor), candidiasis</li>
<li>Onychomycosis</li>
<li>Seborrheic dermatitis</li>
</ul>
</td>
<td>
<ul>
<li>Dosing (Adult):
  <ul><li>Topical application twice daily</li></ul></li>
<li>Dosing (Peds):
  <ul><li>Topical application twice daily</li></ul></li>
<li>CYP450 Interactions: None</li>
<li>Renal or Hepatic Dose Adjustments: None</li>
<li>Dosage Forms: Topical (cream, gel, shampoo, solution, suspension)</li>
</ul>
</td>
</tr>
<tr>
<td>Griseofulvin</td>
<td>Gris-PEG</td>
<td>
<ul>
<li>Systemic treatment of tinea pedis, corporis, cruris, capitis, and unguium</li>
</ul>
</td>
<td>
<ul>
<li>Dosing (Adult):
  <ul>
  <li>Oral (ultramicrosize) 375 to 750 mg q24h</li>
  <li>Oral (microsize) 500 to 750 mg q24h</li>
  </ul></li>
<li>Dosing (Peds):
  <ul>
  <li>Oral (ultramicrosize) 10 to 15 mg/kg/day
    <ul><li>Maximum 750 mg/day</li></ul></li>
  <li>Oral (microsize) 20 to 25 mg/kg/day
    <ul><li>Maximum 1000 mg/day</li></ul></li>
  </ul></li>
<li>CYP450 Interactions: text</li>
<li>Renal or Hepatic Dose Adjustments: Use contraindicated in hepatic failure</li>
<li>Dosage Forms: Oral (microsize suspension, ultramicrosize tablets)</li>
</ul>
</td>
</tr>
</table>

Other Antifungals - Drug Class Review
High-Yield Med Reviews

Generic Name	Brand Name	Indication(s) or Uses	Notes

Naftifine	Naftin	• Topical treatment of tinea pedis, corporis, and cruris	• **Dosing (Adult):**
			  – Topical to affected area twice daily
			• **Dosing (Peds):**
			  – Topical to affected area twice daily
			• **CYP450 Interactions:** None
			• **Renal or Hepatic Dose Adjustments:** None
			• **Dosage Forms:** Topical (cream, gel)

Nystatin	Nystop	• Topical treatment of tinea (pedis, corporis, cruris, versicolor), candidiasis
		• Oral candidiasis
			• **Dosing (Adult):**
			  – Topical to affected area twice daily
			  – Oral 400,000 to 1,000,000 units q6-8h
			• **Dosing (Peds):**
			  – Topical to affected area twice daily
			  – Oral 200,000 to 600,000 units q6-8h
			• **CYP450 Interactions:** None
			• **Renal or Hepatic Dose Adjustments:** None
			• **Dosage Forms:** Oral (capsule, powder, suspension, tablet), topical (cream, ointment, powder)

Terbinafine	Lamisil	• Topical treatment of tinea (pedis, corporis, cruris, versicolor), candidiasis	• **Dosing (Adult):**
			  – Topical to affected area once daily
			• **Dosing (Peds):**
			  – Topical to affected area once daily
			• **CYP450 Interactions:** None
			• **Renal or Hepatic Dose Adjustments:** None
			• **Dosage Forms:** Topical (cream, gel, solution)

High-Yield Clinical Knowledge

- **Barbiturates and Griseofulvin**
  - Coadministration of oral barbiturates (ex., phenobarbital, primidone, butalbital) decreases the absorption of griseofulvin by approximately 33% to 45%.
    - The mechanism is not related to CYP interactions, and the mechanism of this interaction remains unknown. Phenobarbital does not appear to increase griseofulvin metabolism but somehow impair its absorption.
  - Griseofulvin is an inducer of CYP450 and should be used with caution in patients taking warfarin.
- **Non-CYP Ergosterol Inhibition**
  - Terbinafine inhibits ergosterol synthesis, a similar effect to azole antifungals, but terbinafine does not exert this effect through CYP450, as it inhibits the fungal enzyme squalene epoxidase.
  - Naftifine is an allylamine, similar to terbinafine, but only used as a topical antifungal agent.
- **Oral Thrush**
  - Nystatin is an optimal agent for the treatment of oral candidiasis or thrush in infants, as it is not absorbed systemically if swallowed.
    - Patients should be instructed to swish the drug around in the mouth and then swallow, but in neonates or infants, this can be difficult, if not impossible.
      - Caretakers should be instructed to paint nystatin suspension into recesses of the mouth and avoid feeding for 5 to 10 minutes.

- **Distribution to Infection**
  - Although orally administered, griseofulvin achieves good penetration to superficial sites of fungal infection due to the transfer of the drug via sweat and transepidermal fluid loss.
- **Amphotericin B and Nystatin**
  - Nystatin shares an identical mechanism of action to amphotericin B; however, it does not cause the same toxicities as nystatin is not absorbed systemically, even after oral administration.

High-Yield Fast-Facts

- **Palatability**
  - Oral nystatin is limited by its unpleasant taste, necessitating a therapeutic change to clotrimazole troches.
- **OTC vs. Rx**
  - Topical terbinafine is widely available as an OTC topical cream, but the alternative allylamine, naftifine, is only available as a prescription product.
- **Routes Not Interchangeable**
  - Topical antifungal products should not be substituted for oral, vaginal, or ocular use.

HIGH-YIELD BOARD EXAM ESSENTIALS
- **CLASSIC AGENTS:** Ciclopirox, griseofulvin, terbinafine, naftifine, nystatin
- **DRUG CLASS:** Antifungal
- **INDICATIONS:** Topical treatment of tinea (pedis, corporis, cruris, versicolor), onychomycosis (ciclopirox), oral candidiasis (griseofulvin), seborrheic dermatitis (ciclopirox).
- **MECHANISM:**
  - Inhibits metal-dependent enzymes via chelation, causing degradation of peroxides within the fungal cell (ciclopirox)
  - Disrupts the fungal mitotic spindle's assembly by inhibiting microtubule function, preventing fungal cell division (griseofulvin)
  - inhibits squalene-2,3-epoxidase, disrupting the synthesis of ergosterol in the fungal cell (naftifine, terbinafine)
  - Binds to fungal cell membrane ergosterol altering the membrane permeability leading to leakage of cell components and subsequent fungal cell death (nystatin)
- **SIDE EFFECTS:** Unpleasant taste, local irritation
- **CLINICAL PEARLS:** Topical broad-spectrum antifungal therapy for infections where systemic agents are unnecessary or unwanted due to poor skin penetration.

High-Yield Basic Pharmacology

- **Ethambutol**
  - Inhibits mycobacterial arabinosyl transferases, preventing the polymerization reaction of arabinoglycan used to form the mycobacterial cell wall.
- **Pyrazinamide**
  - Converted to pyrazinoic acid by mycobacterial pyrazinamide, disrupting the mycobacterial cell membrane metabolism and transport functions
- **Central TB**
  - In rare TB cases infecting the CNS, antimicrobial therapy with isoniazid and pyrazinamide achieve adequate CNS concentrations as they penetrate the blood-brain barrier readily.
  - Ethambutol and rifampin less readily penetrate the CNS, and alternative therapy, including fluoroquinolones, may be considered.

Primary Net Benefit

- First-line treatments for active tuberculosis are used in combination with isoniazid and rifamycins but carry risks of hepatotoxicity (pyrazinamide) and ophthalmic adverse events (ethambutol).

<table>
<tr>
<td colspan="4" align="center">Antimycobacterials - Drug Class Review
High-Yield Med Reviews</td>
</tr>
<tr>
<td colspan="4">Mechanism of Action:
Ethambutol - Inhibits mycobacterial arabinosyl transferases, preventing the polymerization reaction of arabinoglycan used to form the mycobacterial cell wall.
Pyrazinamide - Converted to pyrazinoic acid by mycobacterial pyrazinamide, disrupting the mycobacterial cell membrane metabolism and transport functions.</td>
</tr>
<tr>
<td colspan="4">Class Effects: Risks of hepatotoxicity (pyrazinamide), gout (pyrazinamide), retrobulbar neuritis (ethambutol)</td>
</tr>
<tr>
<th>Generic Name</th>
<th>Brand Name</th>
<th>Indication(s) or Uses</th>
<th>Notes</th>
</tr>
<tr>
<td>Ethambutol</td>
<td>Myambutol</td>
<td>▪ Tuberculosis</td>
<td>

- **Dosing (Adult):**
  - Oral 800 to 1,600 mg daily
  - Oral 1,200 mg to 2,400 mg three times weekly DOT
  - Oral 2,000 to 4,000 mg twice weekly DOT
- **Dosing (Peds):**
  - Oral 15 to 25 mg/kg/day or 5 times weekly DOT
  - Oral 50 mg/kg/dose two or three times weekly
- **CYP450 Interactions:** None
- **Renal or Hepatic Dose Adjustments:**
  - GFR 10 to 50 mL/minute - q24-36h
  - GFR less than 10 mL/minute - q48h
- **Dosage Forms:** Oral (tablet)
</td>
</tr>
</table>

Antimycobacterials - Drug Class Review
High-Yield Med Reviews

Generic Name	Brand Name	Indication(s) or Uses	Notes

Pyrazinamide	Macrozide, Zinamide	▪ Tuberculosis	▪ **Dosing (Adult):**
			  – Oral 1,000 to 2,000 mg daily
			  – Oral 1,500 mg to 3,000 mg three times weekly DOT
			  – Oral 2,000 to 4,000 mg twice weekly DOT
			▪ **Dosing (Peds):**
			  – Oral 30 to 40 mg/kg/day or 5 times weekly DOT
			  – Oral 50 mg/kg/dose two or three times weekly
			▪ **CYP450 Interactions:** None
			▪ **Renal or Hepatic Dose Adjustments:**
			  – GFR less than 30 mL/minute - Three times weekly after dialysis
			▪ **Dosage Forms:** Oral (tablet)

High-Yield Clinical Knowledge

- **Hepatotoxicity**
  - Pyrazinamide is associated with the development of hepatotoxicity, requiring baseline liver function tests when used in combination with rifampin or among patients with a history of liver disease.
- **Ophthalmic Injury**
  - Ethambutol has been associated with retrobulbar neuritis and is contraindicated among patients with optic neuritis.
  - Baseline visual acuity and color vision tests are required and should be monitored throughout ethambutol therapy.
    - Patients complaining of visual acuity changes or the loss of the ability to see green should prompt urgent ophthalmologic examination.
  - Therapy with ethambutol may be delayed in children who are too young to undergo visual acuity and color vision assessments.
- **Pregnant Women**
  - For the treatment of active TB in pregnant women, pyrazinamide should be avoided due to inadequate teratogenicity data.
    - However, there is growing data to support the safety of pyrazinamide in pregnancy.
- **Standard Regimen**
  - Pyrazinamide and ethambutol are used in combination with isoniazid and rifampin for two months as the standard initial regimen for TB, followed by an additional four months of isoniazid and rifampin.
  - Ethambutol can be discontinued at any point if susceptibility to isoniazid, pyrazinamide, and rifampin is known.
  - Alternatively, therapy without pyrazinamide or ethambutol can be accomplished using isoniazid and rifampin for nine months.
- **Resistance**
  - Mycobacterial resistance to pyrazinamide develops due to impaired mycobacterial uptake or mutations in the pncA gene, which prevents the conversion to pyrazinoic acid.
  - Mutations in the mycobacterial embB gene or enhanced efflux pump activity are responsible for resistance to ethambutol.
  - Both pyrazinamide and ethambutol must always be used in combination with other antimycobacterial agents to avoid resistance.

- **Gout**
  - Pyrazinamide is associated with hyperuricemia as it reduces the renal clearance of uric acid by more than 80%.
  - Other common adverse events associated with pyrazinamide include GI distress and hepatotoxicity.
  - Ethambutol has also been associated with decreased renal elimination of uric acid and may contribute to gouty attacks.

HIGH-YIELD BOARD EXAM ESSENTIALS

- **CLASSIC AGENTS:** Ethambutol, pyrazinamide
- **DRUG CLASS:** Antimycobacterials
- **INDICATIONS:** Tuberculosis
- **MECHANISM:** Inhibits mycobacterial arabinosyl transferases, preventing the polymerization reaction of arabinoglycan used to form the mycobacterial cell wall (ethambutol). Converted to pyrazinoic acid by mycobacterial pyrazinamide, disrupting the mycobacterial cell membrane metabolism and transport functions (pyrazinamide)
- **SIDE EFFECTS:** Hepatic injury, gout (pyrazinamide), retrobulbar neuritis (ethambutol)
- **CLINICAL PEARLS:**
  - Pyrazinamide and ethambutol are used in combination with isoniazid and rifampin for two months as the standard initial regimen for TB, followed by an additional four months of isoniazid and rifampin.
  - Ethambutol and pyrazinamide can both elevate uric acid levels and exacerbate gout.

High-Yield Basic Pharmacology

- **Mechanism of Action**
  - Isoniazid is activated within the mycobacterium cell by KatG to its nicotinoyl radical, which reacts spontaneously with NAD+ inhibiting cell wall enzyme synthesis and inhibiting nucleic acid synthesis by reacting with NADP+, which has bactericidal for actively growing Mycobacteria tuberculosis.
- **Collateral KatG Effects**
  - The activation of KatG by isoniazid has other effects, including superoxide production, hydrogen peroxide, nitric oxide radical, and alkyl hydroperoxides, contributing to isoniazid's mycobactericidal effects, but also its toxicity.

Primary Net Benefit

- Bactericidal for actively growing Mycobacteria tuberculosis, with less effective activity against other Mycobacteria species.

Isoniazid - Drug Class Review			
High-Yield Med Reviews			
Mechanism of Action: *Activated in mycobacterium cells by KatG to a nicotinoyl radical inhibiting cell wall enzyme synthesis and inhibiting nucleic acid synthesis.*			
Class Effects: Bactericidal for actively growing Mycobacteria tuberculosis, risk of peripheral neuropathy (provide vit B6 supplementation), seizures (with overdose), optic atrophy, optic neuritis, dizziness, ataxia, paresthesias, and encephalopathy.			
Generic Name	**Brand Name**	**Indication(s) or Uses**	**Notes**

Isoniazid		• Acute or latent tuberculosis	• **Dosing (Adult):**
			  – Oral/IM 5 mg/kg or 300 mg q24h
			    • DOT 15 mg/kg/dose or 900 mg, once-, twice-, or three-times-weekly
			• **Dosing (Peds):**
			  – Oral/IM 5 mg/kg q24h
			    • Maximum 300 mg/dose
			• **CYP450 Interactions:** Inhibits CYP2C19, 3A4, 2D6. Induces CYP2E1
			• **Renal or Hepatic Dose Adjustments:** None
			• **Dosage Forms:** Oral (tablet, syrup), IM (solution)

High-Yield Clinical Knowledge

- **Fast, Intermediate, or Slow Acetylators**
  - Phenotypic subgroups of isoniazid metabolism include fast, intermediate, or slow acetylators.
  - The patient's race can predict their phenotypic subtype with fast acetylation associated with Inuit and Japanese individuals.
    - It can be either heterozygous or homozygous expression of this autosomal dominant trait.
    - Scandinavians, Caucasians, and Jewish individuals are associated with slow acetylation.
- **Other Mycobacteria**
  - Isoniazid is most active against Mycobacterium tuberculosis but only has moderate activity to Mycobacterium bovis and Mycobacterium kansasii, and poor activity Mycobacterium Avium Complex.
- **Pharmacodynamic Anti-Mycobacteria Action**
  - Similar to other antimicrobials, isoniazid's action on mycobacteria can be described as concentration-dependent, bactericidal (or mycobactericidal)

- Isoniazid's actions can also be described as exerting peak concentration ratios over MIC or total exposure (area under the curve).
- **CYP2E1, Rifampin**
  - Isoniazid possesses alternative metabolism methods, including acetylation of isoniazid to acetylisoniazid (by NAT2), which is either excreted by the kidney or further metabolized to acetyl hydrazine and then oxidized by CYP2E1 to hepatotoxic metabolites.
  - In combination with rifampin for mycobacterium tuberculosis treatment, the risk of hepatotoxicity may be increased as it may induce CYP2E1 (in addition to the induction of 2E1 by isoniazid itself).
- **Pyridoxine Supplementation**
  - Isoniazid is frequently administered with pyridoxine to limit neurological adverse events associated with its use.
    - Without pyridoxine, the risk of the hands and feet' peripheral neuropathies' risk is approximately 2% but is much higher in patients who are slow acetylators, those with diabetes, or pre-existing anemia.
- **Neurological Adverse Events**
  - Isoniazid is frequently associated with an increased or recurrence of neurological disorders, including seizures in patients with pre-existing seizure disorders.
  - Other neurological adverse events include the development of optic atrophy, optic neuritis, dizziness, ataxia, paresthesias, and encephalopathy.

High-Yield Fast-Fact

- **IN...H?**
  - Isoniazid is commonly abbreviated INH; however, there is no H in isoniazid.
  - The H in the INH abbreviation refers to the alternative name of isoniazid, isonicotinic acid hydrazide.

HIGH-YIELD BOARD EXAM ESSENTIALS
- **CLASSIC AGENTS:** Isoniazid
- **DRUG CLASS:** Antitubercular agent
- **INDICATIONS:** Acute or latent tuberculosis
- **MECHANISM:** Activated in mycobacterium cells by KatG to a nicotinoyl radical inhibiting cell wall enzyme synthesis and inhibiting nucleic acid synthesis.
- **SIDE EFFECTS:** Seizures, optic atrophy, optic neuritis, dizziness, ataxia, paresthesias, and encephalopathy.
- **CLINICAL PEARLS:** Isoniazid is frequently administered with pyridoxine to limit neurological adverse events associated with its use. Without pyridoxine, the risk of the hands and feet' peripheral neuropathies' risk is approximately 2% but is much higher in patients who are slow acetylators, those with diabetes, or pre-existing anemia.

High-Yield Basic Pharmacology

- **Mechanism of Action**
  - Rifamycins bind to the beta subunit of bacterial DNA-dependent RNA polymerase, forming a stable drug-enzyme complex, inhibiting RNA synthesis.

Primary Net Benefit

- Bactericidal to mycobacteria, and other sensitive pathogens, particularly intracellular organisms and those sequestered in abscesses and lung cavities.

Rifamycins - Drug Class Review High-Yield Med Reviews			
Mechanism of Action: *Binds to the beta subunit of bacterial DNA-dependent RNA polymerase, inhibiting RNA synthesis.*			
Class Effects: Bactericidal to mycobacteria, orange discoloration to urine, sweat, and tears, hepatotoxicity.			
Generic Name	**Brand Name**	**Indication(s) or Uses**	**Notes**
Rifabutin	Mycobutin	<ul><li>Mycobacterium avium complex</li><li>Mycobacterium tuberculosis</li></ul>	<ul><li>**Dosing (Adult):**<ul><li>Oral 5 mg/kg/dose q24h or 300 mg q24h</li></ul></li><li>**Dosing (Peds):**<ul><li>Oral 5 to 20 mg/kg/dose q24h<ul><li>Maximum 300 mg/dose</li></ul></li></ul></li><li>**CYP450 Interactions:** Substrate CYP1A2, 3A4; Induces CYP2C9, CYP3A4</li><li>**Renal or Hepatic Dose Adjustments:** None</li><li>**Dosage Forms:** Oral (capsule)</li></ul>
Rifampin	Rifadin	<ul><li>Mycobacterium tuberculosis</li><li>Meningococcal prophylaxis</li></ul>	<ul><li>**Dosing (Adult):**<ul><li>Oral/IV 150 to 900 mg q24h<ul><li>Numerous anti-TB regimens exist.</li></ul></li></ul></li><li>**Dosing (Peds):**<ul><li>Oral/IV 10 to 20 mg/kg/dose q12-24h<ul><li>Maximum 900 mg/dose</li></ul></li></ul></li><li>**CYP450 Interactions:** Substrate Pgp; Induces CYP1A2, 2B6, 2C9, 2C19, 2C8, CYP3A4, Pgp</li><li>**Renal or Hepatic Dose Adjustments:** None</li><li>**Dosage Forms:** Oral (capsule), IV (solution)</li></ul>
Rifamycin	Aemcolo	<ul><li>Traveler's diarrhea</li></ul>	<ul><li>**Dosing (Adult):**<ul><li>Oral 388 mg BID x 3 days</li></ul></li><li>**Dosing (Peds):**<ul><li>Not routinely used</li></ul></li><li>**CYP450 Interactions:** Not systemically absorbed</li><li>**Renal or Hepatic Dose Adjustments:** None</li><li>**Dosage Forms:** Oral (tablet)</li></ul>

Rifamycins - Drug Class Review
High-Yield Med Reviews

Generic Name	Brand Name	Indication(s) or Uses	Notes

Rifapentine	Priftin	• Mycobacterium tuberculosis	• **Dosing (Adult):**
			  – Oral 600 mg BID
			    • Numerous anti-TB regimens exist
			• **Dosing (Peds):** Children 12 years and older
			  – Oral 600 mg BID
			• **CYP450 Interactions:** Induces CYP3A4
			• **Renal or Hepatic Dose Adjustments:** None
			• **Dosage Forms:** Oral (tablet)

Rifaximin	Xifaxan	• Clostridoides difficile infection
		• Hepatic encephalopathy
		• Irritable bowel syndrome
		• Traveler's diarrhea
			• **Dosing (Adult):**
			  – Oral 400 mg q8h or 550 mg q12h
			• **Dosing (Peds):**
			  – Oral 15 to 30 mg/kg/day divided q8h
			    • Maximum 400 mg/dose
			• **CYP450 Interactions:** Not systemically absorbed
			• **Renal or Hepatic Dose Adjustments:** None
			• **Dosage Forms:** Oral (tablet)

High-Yield Clinical Knowledge

- **CYP450 Inducer**
  - Rifamycins are inducers of CYP450 isoenzymes 1A2, 2C9, 2C19, 2E1, and 3A4, leading to numerous clinically relevant drug interactions.
    - Notable interactions include digoxin, prednisone, propranolol, phenytoin, sulfonylureas, warfarin, and zidovudine.
  - Not all rifamycins induce isoenzymes to the same degree.
    - Rifampin > Rifabutin > Rifapentine
    - Rifaximin and rifamycin are not absorbed to a clinically relevant degree to induce any CYP isoenzyme.
- **Red/Orange Discoloration**
  - Rifampin exerts a characteristic orange discoloration to urine, sweat, and tears.
  - However, cholestatic jaundice should be ruled out as a potential cause of skin discoloration.
- **Hepatotoxicity**
  - Systemically absorbed rifamycins may cause liver injury, hepatitis, and death.
  - Risk factors that increase the likelihood of hepatotoxicity include patients with preexisting chronic liver disease, alcoholism, old age, or concomitant hepatotoxic agents.
- **Biofilm Penetration**
  - Rifampin is not considered useful for monotherapy in susceptible isolates of S. aureus or coagulase-negative Staphylococci endocarditis. It must be used in combination with a beta-lactam and/or vancomycin.
    - The use of rifampin is useful for this indication for its ability to penetrate biofilms established by these bacteria, preventing other antimicrobial agents from penetrating the bacterial colony.
- **High-dose rifampin**
  - Although isoniazid has been proposed to be given at once-, twice-, or thrice-weekly direct observed treatment, this strategy is not recommended with high dose rifampin due to high incidence of intolerance.
  - Associated adverse events include flu-like syndrome (fever, chills, and myalgias), eosinophilia, interstitial nephritis, acute tubular necrosis, thrombocytopenia, hemolytic anemia, and shock.
    - Rare but serious events that can occur at any rifampin dose include thrombocytopenia and leukopenia.

HIGH-YIELD BOARD EXAM ESSENTIALS

- **CLASSIC AGENTS:** Rifabutin, rifampin, rifamycin, rifapentine, rifaximin
- **DRUG CLASS:** Rifamycin
- **INDICATIONS:** Mycobacteria tuberculosis (Rifabutin, Rifampin, Rifapentine), Clostridoides difficile (Rifaximin), Traveler's diarrhea prophylaxis (Rifamycin, Rifaximin), Haemophilus influenzae meningitis prophylaxis (Rifampin), Hepatic encephalopathy (Rifaximin), Staphylococcal endocarditis or osteomyelitis (Rifampin)
- **MECHANISM:** Rifamycins bind to the beta subunit of bacterial DNA-dependent RNA polymerase, forming a stable drug-enzyme complex, inhibiting RNA synthesis.
- **SIDE EFFECTS:** Orange discoloration to urine, sweat, and tears, hepatotoxicity
- **CLINICAL PEARLS:** Rifamycins are inducers of CYP450 isoenzymes 1A2, 2C9, 2C19, 2E1, and 3A4, leading to numerous clinically relevant drug interactions. Notable interactions include digoxin, prednisone, propranolol, phenytoin, sulfonylureas, warfarin, and zidovudine.

High-Yield Basic Pharmacology

- **Mechanism of Action**
  - **Cidofovir, foscarnet, ganciclovir, valganciclovir:**
    - Inhibit viral DNA synthesis by inhibiting viral DNA polymerases
  - **Letermovir:**
    - interferes with viral DNA replication by inhibiting the DNA terminase complex responsible for DNA processing and packaging

Primary Net Benefit

- Provide treatment and/or prophylaxis for CMV and several other viral infections.

<table>
<tr>
<td colspan="4">CMV Antivirals - Drug Class Review
High-Yield Med Reviews</td>
</tr>
<tr>
<td colspan="4">Mechanism of Action: Inhibit viral DNA synthesis by inhibiting viral DNA polymerases. Letermovir has a unique mechanism of inhibiting the CMV DNA terminase complex required for viral DNA processing and packaging.</td>
</tr>
<tr>
<td colspan="4">Class Effects: Nephrotoxicity, hepatotoxicity, myelosuppression, teratogen</td>
</tr>
<tr>
<td>Generic Name</td>
<td>Brand Name</td>
<td>Indication(s) or Uses</td>
<td>Notes</td>
</tr>
<tr>
<td>Cidofovir</td>
<td>N/A</td>
<td>• CMV retinitis treatment</td>
<td>
• Dosing (Adult):
  – IV 5 mg/kg once weekly for 2 consecutive weeks, then 5 mg/kg once every 2 weeks (with concomitant probenecid)
• Dosing (Peds):
  – IV 5 mg/kg once weekly for 2 consecutive weeks, then 3 to 5 mg/kg once every other week (with concomitant probenecid and IV hydration)
• CYP450 Interactions: None
• Renal or Hepatic Dose Adjustments:
  – SCr increase by 0.3 to 0.4 mg/dL reduce dose to 30 mg/kg
  – SCr increase by ≥ 0.5 mg/dL or development of ≥ 3+ proteinuria discontinue therapy
• Dosage Forms: IV (solution)
</td>
</tr>
</table>

CMV Antivirals - Drug Class Review
High-Yield Med Reviews

Generic Name	Brand Name	Indication(s) or Uses	Notes

Foscarnet	Foscavir	▪ CMV retinitis treatment
		▪ Herpes simplex virus (HSV) treatment
			▪ **Dosing (Adult):**
			  – IV 60 to 90 mg/kg every 8 to 12 hours for 14 to 21 days, then IV 90 to 120 mg/kg once daily
			  – Intravitreal 2.4 mg for 1 to 4 doses over a period of 7 to 10 days
			▪ **Dosing (Peds):**
			  – IV 120 to 180 mg/kg/day in divided doses every 8 or 12 hours for 7 to 42 days, then 90 mg/kg once daily
			  – Intravitreal 2.4 mg injection for 1 to 4 doses over a period of 7 to 10 days
			▪ **CYP450 Interactions:** None
			▪ **Renal or Hepatic Dose Adjustments:**
			  – Renal dose adjustments required when CrCl < 1.4 mL/min/kg; refer to manufacturer labeling
			▪ **Dosage Forms:** IV (solution)

Ganciclovir	Cytovene	▪ CMV retinitis treatment
		▪ CMV prophylaxis
			▪ **Dosing (Adult):**
			  – IV 5 mg/kg every 12 hours for 14 to 21 days, then 5 mg/kg every once daily
			  – Intravitreal 2 mg for 1 to 4 doses over a period of 7 to 10 days
			▪ **Dosing (Peds):**
			  – IV 5 to 7.5 mg/kg every 12 hours for 14 to 21 days, then 5 mg/kg once daily for 5 to 7 days per week
			▪ **CYP450 Interactions:** None
			▪ **Renal or Hepatic Dose Adjustments:**
			  – Renal dose adjustments required when CrCl < 70 mL/minute; refer to manufacturer labeling
			▪ **Dosage Forms:** IV (solution)

Letermovir	Prevymis	▪ CMV prophylaxis in allogeneic hematopoietic stem cell transplant (HSCT)	▪ **Dosing (Adult):**
			  – Oral/IV 480 mg once daily between day 0 and day 28 post-HSCT through day 100
			▪ **Dosing (Peds):** Not used
			▪ **CYP450 Interactions:** Substrate CYP2D6, CYP3A4, Pgp
			▪ **Renal or Hepatic Dose Adjustments:**
			  – Child-Pugh class C use not recommended
			▪ **Dosage Forms:** Oral (tablet), IV (solution)

		CMV Antivirals - Drug Class Review	
		High-Yield Med Reviews	
Generic Name	**Brand Name**	**Indication(s) or Uses**	**Notes**
Valganciclovir	Valcyte	<ul><li>CMV retinitis treatment in patients with acquired immunodeficiency syndrome (AIDS)</li><li>CMV prophylaxis in solid organ transplant recipients</li></ul>	<ul><li>**Dosing (Adult):**<ul><li>Treatment: Oral 900 mg twice daily for 14 to 21 day, then 900 mg once daily</li><li>Prophylaxis: 900 mg once daily</li></ul></li><li>**Dosing (Peds):**<ul><li>Treatment: Oral 900 mg twice daily for 14 to 21 days, then 900 mg once daily</li><li>Prophylaxis: (7 x BSA x CrCl) once daily<ul><li>CrCl calculation using modified Schwartz formula</li><li>Maximum of 900 mg/day</li></ul></li></ul></li><li>**CYP450 Interaction:** None</li><li>**Renal or Hepatic Dose Adjustments:**<ul><li>Renal dose adjustments required when CrCl < 60 mL/minute; refer to manufacturer labeling</li></ul></li><li>**Dosage Forms:** Oral (tablet, solution)</li></ul>

High-Yield Clinical Knowledge

- **Nephrotoxicity**
  - Cidofovir and foscarnet have a Black Box Warning for nephrotoxicity.
    - The nephrotoxicity of cidofovir is related to its active tubular secretion in the kidney.
    - Renal impairment may occur at any time during foscarnet therapy, commonly during the second week of induction.
    - There is an increased risk of nephrotoxicity in the elderly from ganciclovir and valganciclovir and with the use of concurrent nephrotoxic agents.
- **Myelosuppression**
  - Myelosuppression is the dose-limiting adverse effect of ganciclovir and valganciclovir.
    - Neutropenia and thrombocytopenia are the most common effects.
  - Neutropenia has been reported with cidofovir.
- **Carcinogenicity and Teratogenicity**
  - Cidofovir is carcinogenic and teratogenic and causes hypospermia in animals.
  - Ganciclovir and valganciclovir are carcinogenic and teratogenic and can impair fertility in humans.
- **Systemic and Intravitreal Administration**
  - CMV retinitis treatment with intravitreal injections should be given with concurrent systemic anti-CMV agents to prevent other end-organ diseases, including colitis, esophagitis, central nervous system disease, and pneumonitis
- **Treatment of Other CMV Infections**
  - CMV retinitis is the most common clinical manifestation of CMV infection.
  - Other manifestations include esophagitis, colitis, pneumonitis, and neurologic disease.
  - Esophagitis or colitis: IV ganciclovir followed by oral valganciclovir is the therapy of choice
  - Pneumonitis: ganciclovir or foscarnet is reasonable
  - Neurologic disease: both ganciclovir and foscarnet are recommended

HIGH-YIELD BOARD EXAM ESSENTIALS

- **CLASSIC AGENTS:** Cidofovir, foscarnet, ganciclovir, letermovir, valganciclovir
- **DRUG CLASS:** CMV antivirals
- **INDICATIONS:** CMV retinitis, HSV infection
- **MECHANISM:** Inhibit viral DNA synthesis by inhibiting viral DNA polymerases. Letermovir has a unique mechanism of inhibiting the CMV DNA terminase complex required for viral DNA processing and packaging.
- **SIDE EFFECTS:** Nephrotoxicity, hepatotoxicity, myelosuppression, teratogen
- **CLINICAL PEARLS:** CMV retinitis treatment with intravitreal injections should be given with concurrent systemic anti-CMV agents to prevent other end-organ diseases, including colitis, esophagitis, central nervous system disease, and pneumonitis.

High-Yield Basic Pharmacology

- **Mechanism of Action**
  - Competitive inhibition of HBV DNA polymerase and reverse transcriptase, causing chain termination.
- **Adefovir Prodrug**
  - Adefovir dipivoxil is a prodrug of adefovir, which is an acyclic phosphonated adenine nucleotide analog.

Primary Net Benefit

- Anti-HBV agents provide viral load suppression, although unable to establish a clinical cure.

Hepatitis B Antivirals - Drug Class Review			
High-Yield Med Reviews			
Mechanism of Action: *Competitive inhibition of HBV DNA polymerase and reverse transcriptase, causing chain termination.*			
Class Effects: HBV viral load suppression, but no cure; Myopathies, peripheral neuropathies, pancreatitis, anemias, and granulocytopenia.			
Generic Name	**Brand Name**	**Indication(s) or Uses**	**Notes**

Adefovir dipivoxil	Hepsera	- Hepatitis B	- **Dosing (Adult):**
			  - Oral 10 mg daily
			- **Dosing (Peds):**
			  - Oral 0.25 to 0.3 mg/kg/dose daily
			    - Maximum 10 mg/dose
			- **CYP450 Interactions:** None
			- **Renal or Hepatic Dose Adjustments:**
			  - GFR 30 to 49 mL/minute - 10 mg q48h
			  - GFR 10 to 29 mL/minute - 10 mg q72h
			- **Dosage Forms:** Oral (tablet)

Entecavir	Baraclude	- Hepatitis B	- **Dosing (Adult):**
			  - Oral 0.5 to 1 mg daily
			- **Dosing (Peds):**
			  - Oral 0.15 to 1 mg daily
			- **CYP450 Interactions:** text
			- **Renal or Hepatic Dose Adjustments:**
			  - GFR 30 to 49 mL/minute - 0.25 to 0.5 mg q48h
			  - GFR 10 to 29 mL/minute - 0.15 to 0.3 mg q72h
			  - GFR less than 10 - 0.05 mg to 0.1 mg daily or normal dose every 7 days
			- **Dosage Forms:** Oral (solution, tablet)

Hepatitis B Antivirals - Drug Class Review
High-Yield Med Reviews

Generic Name	Brand Name	Indication(s) or Uses	Notes

Lamivudine	Epivir, Epivir HBV	• HIV
		• Hepatitis B
			• **Dosing (Adult):**
			  – HIV
			    • Oral 300 mg daily or 150 mg BID
			  – HBV
			    • Oral 100 mg daily
			• **Dosing (Peds):**
			  – Oral 30 to 150 mg BID
			• **CYP450 Interactions:** None
			• **Renal or Hepatic Dose Adjustments:** HIV indication
			  – GFR 30 to 49 mL/minute - 150 mg daily
			  – GFR 15 to 29 mL/minute - 150 mg x1 then 100 mg daily
			  – GFR less than 15 mL/minute - 150 mg x1 then 50 mg daily
			  – GFR less than 5 - 50 mg, then 25 mg daily
			• **Dosage Forms:** Oral (solution, tablet)

Tenofovir alafenamide	Vemlidy	• Hepatitis B	• **Dosing (Adult):**
			  – HIV
			    • Only available in combination with other ART (Biktarvy, Genvoya, Odefsey, Symtuza)
			  – HBV
			    • Oral 25 mg daily
			• **Dosing (Peds):**
			  – Not routinely used
			• **CYP450 Interactions:** None
			• **Renal or Hepatic Dose Adjustments:**
			  – GFR less than 15 mL/minute - Not recommended
			  – Child-Pugh class B or C - Not recommended
			• **Dosage Forms:** Oral (tablet)

Tenofovir disoproxil	Viread	• Hepatitis B
		• HIV
			• **Dosing (Adult):**
			  – HIV
			    • Oral 300 mg daily or 150 mg BID
			  – HBV
			    • Oral 100 or 300 mg daily
			• **Dosing (Peds):**
			  – Oral 8 mg/kg/dose daily
			    • Maximum 300 mg/day
			• **CYP450 Interactions:** None
			• **Renal or Hepatic Dose Adjustments:** HIV indication
			  – GFR 30 to 49 mL/minute - 300 mg q48h
			  – GFR 10 to 29 mL/minute - 300 mg q72h
			  – GFR less than 10 mL/minute - Not recommended
			• **Dosage Forms:** Oral (solution, tablet)

High-Yield Clinical Knowledge

- **Lamivudine and Tenofovir Dosing**
  - Lamivudine and tenofovir disoproxil are used for HIV-1, HIV-2 at a dose of 300 mg daily or 150 mg twice daily and 300 or 150 mg daily, respectively.
  - For hepatitis B, lamivudine can also be used, but at a dose of 100 mg twice daily.
    - To treat coinfection with HIV and HBV, the HIV dosing (300 mg or 150 mg BID dosing).
  - Tenofovir disoproxil for HBV is used at a dose of 300 or 100 mg daily, leading to virologic failure in HIV co-infected patients.
- **Toxicities**
  - Anti-HBV antivirals may adversely affect the DNA polymerase gamma of human mitochondria, resulting in mitochondrial toxicities including myopathies, peripheral neuropathies, pancreatitis, anemias, and granulocytopenia.
  - These agents are rarely associated with lactic acidosis and hepatic steatosis.
- **HIV and HBV Coinfection**
  - Of the anti-HBV agents, tenofovir and lamivudine have clinically relevant HIV antiretroviral activity.
  - In patients with HIV and HBV coinfection, exacerbations of HBV may occur if one of these agents is discontinued.
- **Resistance and Mutations**
  - The terminology for resistance describes the target amino acid, its position, and the amino acid that has been substituted.
    - For example, an M184V mutation where methionine is substituted for valine at position 184.
  - In patients with HIV co-infection, appropriate NRTI selection should reduce the likelihood of M184V variant resistance, as observed with entecavir therapy.
- **Serum Creatinine Changes**
  - Adefovir is associated with a reversible increase in serum creatinine that is not a reflection of changes in renal function.
- **Pregnancy**
  - Adefovir should be avoided in pregnant patients as animal models have suggested this agent is embryotoxic and genotoxic.
  - Lamivudine may be suitable for therapy in pregnant patients as it has been effective in preventing vertical transmission of HBV when given for the last four weeks of gestation.

HIGH-YIELD BOARD EXAM ESSENTIALS
- **CLASSIC AGENTS:** Adefovir dipivoxil, entecavir, lamivudine, tenofovir disoproxil/alafenamide
- **DRUG CLASS:** Hepatitis B antivirals
- **INDICATIONS:** HBV infection
- **MECHANISM:** Competitive inhibition of HBV DNA polymerase and reverse transcriptase, causing chain termination.
- **SIDE EFFECTS:** Myopathies, peripheral neuropathies, pancreatitis, anemias, and granulocytopenia.
- **CLINICAL PEARLS:** Adefovir is associated with a reversible increase in serum creatinine that is not a reflection of changes in renal function.

High-Yield Basic Pharmacology

- **NS3/4A Inhibitor (Grazoprevir, Paritaprevir)**
  - Inhibition of the NS3/4A protease, responsible for cleaving the HCV polyprotein into the proteins that enable HCV RNA replication and virion assembly.
- **NS5A Inhibitors (Elbasvir, Ledipasvir, Ombitasvir, Velpatasvir)**
  - Inhibits nonstructural protein 5A (NS5A), an RNA-binding protein that is essential for HCV RNA replication, virion assembly, and modulation of host cells.
- **NS5B RNA Polymerase Inhibitors (Dasabuvir, Sofosbuvir)**
  - Bind to the catalytic site of nonstructural protein 5B (NS5B), inhibiting RNA replication by causing chain termination and increasing transcription errors.

Primary Net Benefit

- The direct-acting antivirals have transformed HCV treatment and are significantly better tolerated compared to alternatives (interferon products).

Hepatitis C Antivirals - Drug Class Review			
High-Yield Med Reviews			
Mechanism of Action: *NS3/4A Inhibitor (Grazoprevir, Paritaprevir) - Inhibition of the NS3/4A protease, responsible for cleaving the HCV polyprotein into the proteins that enable HCV RNA replication and virion assembly.* *NS5A Inhibitors (Elbasvir, Ledipasvir, Ombitasvir, Velpatasvir) - Inhibits nonstructural protein 5A (NS5A), an RNA-binding protein that is essential for HCV RNA replication, virion assembly, and modulation of host cells.* *NS5B RNA Polymerase Inhibitors (Dasabuvir, Sofosbuvir) - Bind to the catalytic site of nonstructural protein 5B (NS5B), inhibiting RNA replication by causing chain termination and increasing transcription errors.*			
Class Effects: Overall well tolerated, oral administration for ease, risk of hepatotoxicity, hemolytic anemia (ribavirin combination)			
Generic Name	**Brand Name**	**Indication(s) or Uses**	**Notes**

Elbasvir and Grazoprevir	Zepatier	• Chronic Hepatitis C	• **Dosing (Adult):**
			  – Oral 1 tablet daily for 12 to 16 weeks
			• **Dosing (Peds):**
			  – Not routinely used
			• **CYP450 Interactions:** Substrate CYP3A4, P-gp
			• **Renal or Hepatic Dose Adjustments:**
			  – Child-Pugh class B or C - contraindicated
			• **Dosage Forms:** Oral (capsule)

Glecaprevir and Pibrentasvir	Mavyret	• Chronic Hepatitis C	• **Dosing (Adult):**
			  – Oral three tablets daily for 8 to 16 weeks
			• **Dosing (Peds):**
			  – For children at least 45 kg or at least 12 years of age, use adult dosing
			• **CYP450 Interactions:** Substrate CYP3A4, P-gp; Inhibits CYP1A2, 3A4, P-gp
			• **Renal or Hepatic Dose Adjustments:**
			  – Child-Pugh class B or C - contraindicated
			• **Dosage Forms:** Oral (tablet)

Hepatitis C Antivirals - Drug Class Review
High-Yield Med Reviews

Generic Name	Brand Name	Indication(s) or Uses	Notes

Ombitasvir, Paritaprevir, and Ritonavir	Technivie	▪ Chronic Hepatitis C	▪ **Dosing (Adult):**
			  – Oral two tablets daily for 12 weeks
			▪ **Dosing (Peds):**
			  – Not routinely used
			▪ **CYP450 Interactions:** Substrate CYP2D6, 3A4, P-gp; Inhibits CYP3A4; Induces CYP1A2, 2C19
			▪ **Renal or Hepatic Dose Adjustments:**
			  – Child-Pugh class B or C - contraindicated
			▪ **Dosage Forms:** Oral (tablet)

Ombitasvir, Paritaprevir, Ritonavir, and Dasabuvir	Viekira	▪ Chronic Hepatitis C	▪ **Dosing (Adult):**
			  – Oral two to three tablets daily for 12 to 24 weeks
			▪ **Dosing (Peds):**
			  – Not routinely used
			▪ **CYP450 Interactions:** Substrate CYP2C8, 2D6, 3A4, P-gp; Inhibits CYP3A4; Induces CYP1A2, 2C19
			▪ **Renal or Hepatic Dose Adjustments:**
			  – Child-Pugh class B or C - contraindicated
			▪ **Dosage Forms:** Oral (tablet)

Sofosbuvir	Sovaldi	▪ Chronic Hepatitis C	▪ **Dosing (Adult):**
			  – Oral 400 mg daily for 12 to 16 weeks
			▪ **Dosing (Peds):**
			  – Oral 150 to 400 mg daily for 12 to 24 weeks
			▪ **CYP450 Interactions:** Substrate P-gp
			▪ **Renal or Hepatic Dose Adjustments:**
			  – Child-Pugh class B or C - contraindicated
			▪ **Dosage Forms:** Oral (tablet)

Sofosbuvir and Velpatasvir	Epclusa	▪ Chronic Hepatitis C	▪ **Dosing (Adult):**
			  – Oral one tablets daily for 12 to 24 weeks
			▪ **Dosing (Peds):**
			  – Oral sofosbuvir 200-400 mg/velpatasvir 50-100 mg daily for 12 to 24 weeks
			▪ **CYP450 Interactions:** Substrate CYP2B6, 2C8, 3A4, P-gp
			▪ **Renal or Hepatic Dose Adjustments:**
			  – Child-Pugh class B or C - contraindicated
			▪ **Dosage Forms:** Oral (tablet)

		Hepatitis C Antivirals - Drug Class Review	
		High-Yield Med Reviews	
Generic Name	Brand Name	Indication(s) or Uses	Notes

Sofosbuvir and Ledipasvir	Harvoni	• Chronic Hepatitis C	• **Dosing (Adult):**
			  – Oral sofosbuvir 400 mg/ledipasvir 90 mg daily for 12 to 24 weeks
			• **Dosing (Peds):**
			  – Oral sofosbuvir 150-400 mg/ledipasvir 33.75-90 mg daily for 12 to 24 weeks
			• **CYP450 Interactions:** Substrate P-gp
			• **Renal or Hepatic Dose Adjustments:** None
			• **Dosage Forms:** Oral (pellets, tablet)

Sofosbuvir, Velpatasvir, and Voxilaprevir	Vosevi	• Chronic Hepatitis C	• **Dosing (Adult):**
			  – Oral two tablets daily for 12 to 24 weeks
			• **Dosing (Peds):**
			  – Not routinely used
			• **CYP450 Interactions:** Substrate CYP2B6, 2C8, 3A4, P-gp
			• **Renal or Hepatic Dose Adjustments:**
			  – Child-Pugh class B or C - contraindicated
			• **Dosage Forms:** Oral (tablet)

High-Yield Clinical Knowledge

- **PPI and H2RA Spacing**
  - Patients taking HCV antivirals with concomitant H2RA or PPI require specific administration spacing considerations to avoid clinically relevant decreases in drug absorption.
  - H2RAs should not exceed doses of famotidine 40 mg twice daily, or equivalent, and may be taken at the same time as HCV antivirals or spaced by 12 hours.
  - PPIs should be administered 4 hours before velpatasvir administration.
- **P-glycoprotein and CYP3A4**
  - All of these agents are substrates of P-glycoprotein and should not be combined with inducers of P-gp, including rifampin, phenytoin, phenobarbital, or St. John's wort which could result in therapeutic failure.
  - These agents are also substrates of a relatively newly described efflux transporter, breast cancer resistance protein (BCRP).
  - All agents, except for sofosbuvir, are substrates of CYP3A4 with numerous drug interactions that may impact drug efficacy outcomes.
- **Ribavirin Combination**
  - For HCV regimens containing sofosbuvir/velpatasvir in patients without cirrhosis but have Y93 resistance identified, ribavirin can be added to avoid conversion to an alternative regimen.
  - Ribavirin may also be used with other HCV regimens among patients with increased sustained virologic response rates and other NS5A resistance-associated variants.
- **Notable Drug Interactions**
  - The combination of sofosbuvir and amiodarone should be avoided as numerous reports of symptomatic bradycardia have occurred due to this interaction.
  - This interaction's mechanism is unclear, as sofosbuvir is not a CYP 450 substrate, and a P-glycoprotein-related mechanism would increase sofosbuvir concentrations, not those of amiodarone.
  - The interaction with digoxin is more apparent as competition for P-glycoprotein leads to decreased elimination of digoxin and resulting in clinical toxicity.
    - Digoxin should also be avoided among patients receiving velpatasvir due to p-glycoprotein inhibition.

- Velpatasvir should not be used with pravastatin or rosuvastatin, as the AUC may increase by 35% or 170%, respectively.
- **Resistance Associated Variants (RAV)**
  - The emergency of resistance to HCV antiviral agents is termed resistance-associated variants (RAV).
  - The clinical consequences of RAVs are specific to the clinical outcomes of HCV drug therapy are dependent on patient treatment experience (treatment-naive vs. treatment-experienced) and the particular RAVs identified.
- **Hemolytic Anemia**
  - In regimens that include ribavirin for HCV treatment, ribavirin's addition comes with an increased risk of dose-dependent toxicities, primarily hemolytic anemia.
  - Hemolytic anemia occurs within the first two weeks of ribavirin treatment in up to 20% of patients.
  - Patients receiving ribavirin must be instructed to use two effective contraception forms by each sexual partner during treatment and six months after drug discontinuation.

HIGH-YIELD BOARD EXAM ESSENTIALS
- **CLASSIC AGENTS:** Dasabuvir, elbasvir, grazoprevir, ledipasvir, ombitasvir, paritaprevir, sofosbuvir, velpatasvir
- **DRUG CLASS:** Hepatitis C antivirals
- **INDICATIONS:** Chronic hepatitis C
- **MECHANISM:** NS3/4A Inhibitor (Grazoprevir, Paritaprevir). NS5A Inhibitors (Elbasvir, Ledipasvir, Ombitasvir, Velpatasvir). NS5B RNA Polymerase Inhibitors (Dasabuvir, Sofosbuvir)
- **SIDE EFFECTS:** Hepatotoxicity, hemolytic anemia (ribavirin combination)
- **CLINICAL PEARLS:** Most regimens can treat common strains of hepatitis C after 12 weeks of oral therapy. Patients taking HCV antivirals with concomitant H2RA or PPI require specific administration spacing considerations to avoid clinically relevant decreases in drug absorption.

High-Yield Basic Pharmacology

- **Acyclovir, famciclovir, penciclovir, trifluridine, valacyclovir**
  - Inhibit viral DNA synthesis by inhibiting viral DNA polymerases
    - Acyclovir and valacyclovir can also be incorporated into viral DNA and terminate viral DNA synthesis.
    - Valacyclovir is rapidly converted to acyclovir by intestinal mucosal cells and hepatocytes.
    - Famciclovir is rapidly deacetylated and oxidized to penciclovir by first-pass metabolism.
- **Docosanol**
  - Prevents viral entry into the cell by inhibiting fusion between the plasma membrane and viral envelope

Primary Net Benefit

- Provide acute treatment and/or suppression for HSV, VZV, and several other viral infections.

HSV and VZV Antivirals - Drug Class Review				
High-Yield Med Reviews				
Mechanism of Action: *Inhibit viral DNA synthesis by inhibiting DNA polymerases and thymidylate synthase and/or incorporating them into viral DNA. Docosanol prevents viral entry into the cell by inhibiting fusion between the plasma membrane and viral envelope.*				
Class Effects: HSV & VZV suppression, risk for neurotoxicity, nephrotoxicity				
Generic Name	**Brand Name**	**Indication(s) or Uses**	**Notes**	

Acyclovir	Zovirax	• HSV treatment
		• Herpes zoster (shingles) treatment
		• Varicella (chickenpox) treatment
			• **Dosing (Adult):**
			  – IV 5 to 10 mg/kg every 8 hours
			  – Oral 200 mg to 800 mg 2 to 5 times daily
			• **Dosing (Peds):**
			  – IV 5 to 20 mg/kg every 8 hours
			  – Oral
			    • 20 mg/kg 2 to 4 times daily
			    • 300 mg/m^2 every 8 hours
			    • 200 to 800 mg 2 to 5 times daily
			• **CYP450 Interactions:** Inhibits CYP1A2 (weak)
			• **Renal or Hepatic Dose Adjustments:**
			  – Renal dose adjustments when CrCl < 50 mL/min
			• **Dosage Forms:** Oral (capsule, tablet, suspension), IV (solution)	

Docosanol	Abreva	• Cold sore/fever blister	• **Dosing (Adult):**
			  – Topically 5 times daily to affected area of face
			• **Dosing (Peds):**
			  – Same as adult dosing for children ≥ 12 years
			• **CYP450 Interactions:** None
			• **Renal or Hepatic Dose Adjustments:** None
			• **Dosage Forms:** Topical (cream)	

Famciclovir	Famvir	• HSV treatment and suppression
		• Herpes zoster (shingles) treatment
			• **Dosing (Adult):**
			  – Oral 125 to 500 mg 2 to 3 times daily
			• **Dosing (Peds):** 250 to 1,000 mg 2 to 3 times daily
			• **CYP450 Interactions:** None
			• **Renal or Hepatic Dose Adjustments:**
			  – Renal dose when CrCl < 40 or 60 mL/min
			• **Dosage Forms:** Oral (tablet)	

HSV and VZV Antivirals - Drug Class Review
High-Yield Med Reviews

Generic Name	Brand Name	Indication(s) or Uses	Notes

Penciclovir	Denavir	• Herpes labialis (cold sores) treatment	• **Dosing (Adult):**
			  – Topical application every 2 hours during waking hours for 4 days
			• **Dosing (Peds):** [same as adult]
			  – Same as adult dosing for children ≥ 12 years and adolescents
			• **CYP450 Interactions:** None
			• **Renal or Hepatic Dose Adjustments:** None
			• **Dosage Forms:** Topical (cream)

Trifluridine	Viroptic	• Herpes keratoconjunctivitis and keratitis treatment	• **Dosing (Adult):**
			  – Ophthalmic 1 drop into affected eye(s) every 2 to 4 hours while awake
			    • Maximum of 9 drops per day
			• **Dosing (Peds):**
			  – Same as adult dosing for children ≥ 6 years and adolescents
			    • Maximum of 9 drops per day
			• **CYP450 Interactions:** None
			• **Renal or Hepatic Dose Adjustments:** None
			• **Dosage Forms:** Ophthalmic (solution)

Valacyclovir	Valtrex	• HSV treatment and suppression
		• Herpes zoster (shingles) treatment
			• **Dosing (Adult):**
			  – Oral 500 to 2,000 mg 1 to 3 times daily
			• **Dosing (Peds):**
			  – Oral
			    • 20 mg/kg 1 to 2 times daily
			      • Maximum of 1,000 mg per dose
			    • 250 to 2,000 mg 1 to 3 times daily
			• **CYP450 Interactions:** Inhibits CYP1A2 (weak)
			• **Renal or Hepatic Dose Adjustments:**
			  – Renal dose adjustments required when CrCl < 50 mL/min
			• **Dosage Forms:** Oral (tablet)

High-Yield Clinical Knowledge

- **Nephrotoxicity**
  - Acyclovir and valacyclovir cause reversible nephrotoxicity via crystalluria, interstitial nephritis (via immune reaction), and tubular necrosis (via accumulation of cytotoxic metabolite).
    - Acyclovir crystal formation is the most common cause of nephrotoxicity.
  - Nephrotoxicity can be prevented by avoiding rapid infusion and maintaining adequate hydration.
    - Acyclovir should be infused over at least 1 hour.
  - Risk factors include higher doses, rapid infusion, volume depletion, hypertension, diabetes, concurrent nephrotoxic agents, and obesity.
- **Neurotoxicity**
  - Acyclovir and valacyclovir may cause neurologic disturbances, including confusion, agitation, lethargy, hallucination, and impaired consciousness.
  - Neurotoxicity is dose-related and caused by cytotoxic metabolite accumulation.
  - Risk factors include higher doses (weight-based), renal impairment, and increased cerebrospinal fluid:albumin ratio.
- **Timing of Antiviral Initiation**
  - HSV and VZV antivirals should be initiated as soon as possible after symptom onset to be most effective.

- Specific indications and optimal timing of antiviral initiation (listed below) are generally based on what has been included in clinical trials.
    - Herpes zoster (shingles)
        - Famciclovir and valacyclovir: within 72 hours of rash
    - Herpes labialis (cold sores)
        - Famciclovir and penciclovir initiation within 1 hour of symptom onset can reduce healing time by two days and 17 hours, respectively.
        - Docosanol initiation within 12 hours of symptom onset can reduce healing time by 18 hours.
    - Genital herpes
        - Valacyclovir: within 72 hours of the first diagnosis, within 24 hours of recurrent episodes
    - Varicella (chickenpox)
        - Acyclovir and valacyclovir: within 24 hours of rash
- **Duration of Therapy**
    - HSV
        - HSV-1 and HSV-2 infections are lifelong.
        - Genital herpes can be managed with either episodic therapy to shorten the duration of lesions or daily suppressive therapy to reduce the frequency of recurrences.
    - VZV
        - The recommended duration of therapy for dermatomal lesions is 7 to 10 days.
            - Longer durations should be considered when lesions resolve slowly.
        - Acute retinal necrosis requires prolonged treatment over several months or more.
- **Selecting Topical, Intravenous, or Oral Therapy**
    - Topical antiviral therapy provides little clinical benefit for genital herpes and herpes zoster infections.
        - Systemic therapy is strongly recommended as first-line treatment.
    - Oral antiviral agents generally provide adequate systemic therapy.
        - Initial intravenous therapy may be indicated for severe mucocutaneous HSV infections, HSV complications (e.g., disseminated infection, pneumonitis, hepatitis, meningoencephalitis).
        - Intravenous agents should be used for 2 to 7 days or until regression of symptoms and can be transitioned to oral therapy to complete the total duration of therapy.

HIGH-YIELD BOARD EXAM ESSENTIALS
- **CLASSIC AGENTS:** Acyclovir, docosanol (topical), famciclovir, penciclovir (topical), trifluridine (topical), valacyclovir
- **DRUG CLASS:** HSV and VZV Antiviral
- **INDICATIONS:** HSV, VZV
- **MECHANISM:** Inhibit viral DNA synthesis by inhibiting viral DNA polymerases (• Acyclovir, famciclovir, penciclovir, trifluridine, valacyclovir); Prevents viral entry into the cell by inhibiting fusion between the plasma membrane and viral envelope (docosanol).
- **SIDE EFFECTS:** Neurotoxicity, nephrotoxicity
- **CLINICAL PEARLS:** Acyclovir and valacyclovir cause reversible nephrotoxicity via crystalluria, interstitial nephritis (via immune reaction), and tubular necrosis (via accumulation of cytotoxic metabolite). Acyclovir crystal formation is the most common cause of nephrotoxicity.

High-Yield Basic Pharmacology

- **Amantadine, Rimantadine**
  - Inhibit viral uncoating and/or viral assembly of the influenza A virus, specifically on the M2 protein, causing conformational changes in hemagglutinin transport and replication.
- **Baloxavir**
  - A selective inhibitor of influenza cap-dependent endonuclease, which interferes with viral RNA transcription and blocks virus replication.
- **Oseltamivir, Peramivir, Zanamivir**
  - A selective inhibitor of influenza A and B virus neuraminidase, leading to viral aggregation at the cell surface and reduced respiratory viral spread.

Primary Overall Net Benefit

- None of these agents cure influenza but rather reduce the duration of influenza symptoms and severity, at the cost of an offsetting increase in adverse events.

Influenza Antiviral - Drug Class Review High-Yield Med Reviews				

Mechanism of Action:
Amantadine, Rimantadine - Inhibit viral M2 protein, stopping viral transport and replication.
Baloxavir - Inhibits influenza cap-dependent endonuclease, blocking viral replication.
Oseltamivir, Peramivir, Zanamivir - Inhibits influenza A and B virus neuraminidase, and reduced respiratory viral spread.

Class Effects: Reduce the duration of influenza symptoms and severity of flu, risk for neuropsychiatric effects (oseltamivir).

Generic Name	Brand Name	Indication(s) or Uses	Notes

Amantadine	Gocovri	• Influenza A prophylaxis and treatment (no longer recommended)	• **Dosing (Adult):**
			  – Oral 100 to 200 mg q12-24h
			• **Dosing (Peds):**
			  – Oral 5 mg/kg/day divided q12h
			    • Maximum 150 mg/day
			• **CYP450 Interactions:** Substrate CYP3A4, Pgp
			• **Renal or Hepatic Dose Adjustments:**
			  – GFR 30 to 59 mL/min - 200 mg x1 then 100 mg/day
			  – GFR 15 to 29 mL/min - 200 mg x1 then 100 mg q24h
			  – GFR less than15 mL/minute - contraindicated
			• **Dosage Forms:** Oral (capsule, tablet, syrup)

Influenza Antiviral - Drug Class Review
High-Yield Med Reviews

Generic Name	Brand Name	Indication(s) or Uses	Notes

Baloxavir	Xofluza	• Influenza prophylaxis and treatment	• **Dosing (Adult):**
			  – Patients weight less than 80 kg
			    • Oral 40 mg
			  – Patients weight 80 kg or greater
			    • Oral 80 mg
			• **Dosing (Peds):**
			  – Patients weight less than 20 kg
			    • Oral 2 mg/kg
			  – Patients weight 20 kg or greater
			    • use adult dosing
			• **CYP450 Interactions:** Substrate CYP3A4, Pgp
			• **Renal or Hepatic Dose Adjustments:** None
			• **Dosage Forms:** Oral (tablet)

Oseltamivir	Tamiflu	• Influenza prophylaxis and treatment	• **Dosing (Adult):**
			  – Oral 75 mg daily (prophylaxis) or BID (treatment)
			• **Dosing (Peds):**
			  – Oral 3 to 3.5 mg/kg/dose q12-24h
			  – Less than 15 kg - Oral 30 mg q12-24h
			  – 15 to 23 kg - Oral 45 q12-24h
			  – 23 to 40 kg - Oral 60 mg q12-24h
			  – 40 kg or greater - Oral 75 mg q12-24H
			    • Treatment (q12h), prophylaxis (q24h)
			• **CYP450 Interactions:** None
			• **Renal or Hepatic Dose Adjustments:**
			  – GFR 30 to 60 mL/min - 30 mg q12-24h
			  – GFR 10 to 30 mL/min - 30 mg q24-48h
			  – GFR < 10 mL/min - not recommended
			• **Dosage Forms:** Oral (capsule, solution)

Peramivir	Rapivab	• Influenza treatment	• **Dosing (Adult):**
			  – IV 600 mg once
			    • Can be used q24h for 5-10 days
			• **Dosing (Peds):**
			  – IV 12 mg/kg once
			    • Maximum 600 mg/dose
			• **CYP450 Interactions:** None
			• **Renal or Hepatic Dose Adjustments:**
			  – GFR 31 to 49 mL/min - 150 to 200 mg
			  – GFR 10 to 29 mL/min - 100 mg
			  – GFR less than 10 mL/min - 100 mg x1 then 15 mg q24h days 2-10
			• **Dosage Forms:** IV (solution)

Influenza Antiviral - Drug Class Review
High-Yield Med Reviews

Generic Name	Brand Name	Indication(s) or Uses	Notes

Rimantadine	Flumadine	• Influenza A treatment or prophylaxis	• **Dosing (Adult):**
			  – Oral 100 mg BID x 7 days
			• **Dosing (Peds):**
			  – Oral 5 mg/kg.day
			    • Maximum 150 mg/day
			• **CYP450 Interactions:** None
			• **Renal or Hepatic Dose Adjustments:**
			  – GFR less than 30 mL/min - 100 mg daily
			• **Dosage Forms:** Oral (tablet)

Zanamivir	Relenza Diskhaler	• Influenza treatment	• **Dosing (Adult):**
			  – Inhalation - two inhalations daily for 5 to 7 days
			• **Dosing (Peds):**
			  – Children 7 and older, use adult dosing
			• **CYP450 Interactions:** None
			• **Renal or Hepatic Dose Adjustments:** None
			• **Dosage Forms:** Aerosol powder

High-Yield Clinical Knowledge

- **Neuropsychiatric Adverse Events**
  - Although rare, according to the prescribing information, prospective and retrospective evidence suggests a clinically relevant risk of neurotoxic and neuropsychiatric effects of amantadine, rimantadine, baloxavir, oseltamivir, and zanamivir.
    - Patients concomitantly taking antihistamines and psychotropic or anticholinergic drugs or with a previous psychiatric disease are at the highest risk.
- **Inhaled Zanamivir**
  - Zanamivir is only administered via inhalation and should be used with caution in patients with or without pre-existing reactive airway disease.
    - Although not a contraindication, patients with reactive airway disease, asthma, or COPD have experienced fatal bronchospasm.
- **Amantadine or Rimantadine Use**
  - The use of either amantadine or rimantadine is no longer recommended for treatment or prophylaxis of influenza A, according to the CDC, due to high resistance rates.
- **Influenza Vaccine Timing**
  - Any of the anti-influenza antivirals may diminish the efficacy of live/attenuated influenza virus vaccine administration.
- **Resistance**
  - Resistance to amantadine and rimantadine occurs readily due to a single mutation in the RNA sequence encoding for the M2 protein.
    - These resistant isolates can occur during treatment, particularly within 2 to 3 days after initiation of therapy.
  - Mutations cause resistance to zanamivir in the viral hemagglutinin or neuraminidase.
    - This resistance results in cross-resistance to other neuraminidase inhibitors.
- **Amantadine and Rimantadine Role**
  - Although they have a limited role in clinical practice, amantadine and rimantadine can be used to prophylaxis influenza A in high-risk patients in the outpatient space or as an agent for nosocomial influenza prophylaxis.

- Their role is essential in scenarios where the influenza vaccine cannot be administered or ineffective as in immunocompromised patients.

HIGH-YIELD BOARD EXAM ESSENTIALS
- **CLASSIC AGENTS:** Amantadine, baloxavir, oseltamivir, peramivir, rimantadine, zanamivir
- **DRUG CLASS:** Influenza antivirals
- **INDICATIONS:** Influenza prophylaxis and treatment
- **MECHANISM:** Inhibit viral M2 protein, stopping viral transport and replication (amantadine, rimantadine); Inhibits influenza cap-dependent endonuclease, blocking viral replication (baloxavir); Inhibits influenza A and B virus neuraminidase, and reduced respiratory viral spread (oseltamivir, peramivir, zanamivir)
- **SIDE EFFECTS:** Neuropsychiatric effects (oseltamivir)
- **CLINICAL PEARLS:**
    - Amantadine and rimantadine only cover influenza A, NOT type B. The other agents cover both strains of influenza.
    - Zanamivir is only administered via inhalation and should be used with caution in patients with or without pre-existing reactive airway disease. Although not a contraindication, patients with reactive airway disease, asthma, or COPD have experienced fatal bronchospasm.

INFECTIOUS DISEASE – ANTIVIRALS – PALIVIZUMAB

High-Yield Basic Pharmacology

- **Mechanism of Action**
  - Prevents cell entry by inhibiting the viral fusion protein.
- **Monoclonal Antibody**
  - Palivizumab is a humanized monoclonal antibody derived from that of mice using recombinant DNA technology.
  - Mouse antibodies are produced by introducing the RSV antigen to the mouse's B lymphocytes

Primary Overall Net Benefit

- Prevents RSV infection in high-risk pediatric patients, including those with a history of premature birth, bronchopulmonary dysplasia (BPD), and congenital heart disease (CHD).

Palivizumab - Drug Class Review High-Yield Med Reviews			
Mechanism of Action: *Prevents cell entry by inhibiting the viral fusion protein*			
Class Effects: *Prevents RSV infection in at-risk pediatric patients*			
Generic Name	**Brand Name**	**Indication(s) or Uses**	**Notes**

Palivizumab	Synagis	▪ Respiratory syncytial virus (RSV) prophylaxis	▪ **Dosing (Adult):** Not used
			▪ **Dosing (Peds):**
			  – IM 15 mg/kg once monthly throughout RSV season
			    ▪ Maximum 5 doses per season
			▪ **CYP450 Interactions:** None
			▪ **Renal or Hepatic Dose Adjustments:** None
			▪ **Dosage Forms:** IM (solution)

High-Yield Clinical Knowledge

- **Monoclonal Antibody**
  - Palivizumab is a humanized monoclonal antibody derived from that of mice using recombinant DNA technology.
  - Mouse antibodies are produced by introducing the RSV antigen to the mouse's B lymphocytes.
- **Resistance Mechanism**
  - Resistant RSV strains with viral fusion protein mutations have been observed in vitro.
  - These mutations currently do not significantly impact the clinical efficacy of palivizumab.

High-Yield Fast-Facts

- **Adverse Reactions**
  - Palivizumab is safe and tolerable with minimal adverse effects, including skin rash and fever.
  - Rare cases of severe thrombocytopenia and injection site reactions have been reported.
- **Duration of Efficacy**
  - Palivizumab achieves therapeutic concentrations two days after intramuscular administration.
  - The RSV season in the United States generally falls between November and March.
  - The five-dose regimen is intended to provide about 160 days of coverage during RSV season.
    - The first dose should be given just before the onset of RSV season.

- Subsequent doses accumulate to provide the highest coverage during the peak of RSV season in late December to mid-February.
- A three-dose regimen has been tested but did not provide adequate serum concentrations for seasonal coverage.

HIGH-YIELD BOARD EXAM ESSENTIALS
- **CLASSIC AGENTS:** Palivizumab
- **DRUG CLASS:** Monoclonal antibody
- **INDICATIONS:** RSV prophylaxis
- **MECHANISM:** Prevents cell entry by inhibiting the viral fusion protein
- **SIDE EFFECTS:** Rash, fever, thrombocytopenia, injection site reactions
- **CLINICAL PEARLS:** Prevents RSV infection in high-risk pediatric patients, including those with a history of premature birth, BPD, and CHD.

High-Yield Basic Pharmacology

- **Mechanism of Action**
  - Interrupts viral RNA synthesis by inhibiting the production of guanosine triphosphate.
- **Spectrum**
  - Ribavirin is effective for a wide range of DNA and RNA viruses, including influenza A and B, parainfluenza, respiratory syncytial viruses, hepatitis C, and HIV-1.

Primary Net Benefit

- Ribavirin was once a pivotal component to HCV treatment but has largely been replaced by direct-acting antiviral agents that may include ribavirin in select populations.

Ribavirin - Drug Class Review			
High-Yield Med Reviews			
Mechanism of Action: *Interrupts viral RNA synthesis by inhibiting the production of guanosine triphosphate.*			
Class Effects: Very difficult to tolerate and remain on; risk for hemolytic anemia, teratogen, embryotoxic.			
Generic Name	**Brand Name**	**Indication(s) or Uses**	**Notes**

Ribavirin	Copegus, Moderiba, Rebetol, Ribasphere, Virazole	• Hepatitis C
		• Respiratory syncytial virus
			• **Dosing (Adult):**
			  − Oral 1,000 to 1,200 mg in 2 divided doses
			  − Inhalation - continuous nebulization 6 g over 12-18 hours OR intermittent 2 g over 2-4 hours q8h
			• **Dosing (Peds):**
			  − Oral 15 mg/kg/day in 2 divided doses
			    • Maximum 1,200 mg/dose
			  − Inhalation - continuous nebulization 6 g over 12-18 hours OR intermittent 2 g over 2-4 hours q8h
			• **CYP450 Interactions:** None
			• **Renal or Hepatic Dose Adjustments:**
			  − GFR less than 50 mL/minute - contraindicated (Rebetol, Ribasphere capsules)
			  − GFR 30 to 50 mL/minute - Alternate 200 mg/400 mg every other day (Copegus, Moderiba, Ribasphere tablets)
			  − GFR less than 30 mL/minute - 200 mg daily (Copegus, Moderiba, Ribasphere tablets)
			• **Dosage Forms:** Oral (capsule, solution, tablet), Inhalation solution

High-Yield Clinical Knowledge

- **Teratogenicity**
  - Ribavirin is embryotoxic and teratogenic.
  - Patients receiving ribavirin must be instructed to use two effective forms of contraception by each sexual partner during treatment and six months after drug discontinuation.

- **Hemolytic Anemia**
  - Although high dose ribavirin is targeted for HCV treatment, this comes with an increased risk of dose-dependent toxicities, primarily hemolytic anemia.
  - Hemolytic anemia occurs within the first two weeks of ribavirin treatment in up to 20% of patients.
- **Sofosbuvir Combination**
  - For HCV regimens containing sofosbuvir/velpatasvir in patients without cirrhosis but have Y93 resistance identified, ribavirin can be added to avoid conversion to an alternative regimen.
  - Ribavirin may also be used with sofosbuvir/ledipasvir.
- **RSV Treatment**
  - A nebulized form of ribavirin is available to treat severe respiratory syncytial virus (RSV) bronchiolitis or pneumonia in children.
  - Although the concerns for teratogenic and embryotoxic effects may not be relevant to the patient, they are concerns for health care workers who may be exposed to the aerosolized ribavirin.
    - For these individuals at risk of ribavirin exposure, appropriate PPE is required.
- **Ribavirin and Didanosine**
  - The combination of ribavirin with didanosine should be avoided as ribavirin increases the risk of didanosine-induced mitochondrial toxicity.
    - This occurs as a result of the ribavirin-induced formation of a triphosphorylated form of didanosine.

HIGH-YIELD BOARD EXAM ESSENTIALS

- **CLASSIC AGENTS:** Ribavirin
- **DRUG CLASS:** Ribavirin
- **INDICATIONS:** Hepatitis C, RSV
- **MECHANISM:** Interrupts viral RNA synthesis by inhibiting the production of guanosine triphosphate.
- **SIDE EFFECTS:** Hemolytic anemia, teratogen, embryotoxic
- **CLINICAL PEARLS:** Although high dose ribavirin is targeted for HCV treatment, this comes with an increased risk of dose-dependent toxicities, primarily hemolytic anemia. Hemolytic anemia occurs within the first two weeks of ribavirin treatment in up to 20% of patients.

High-Yield Basic Pharmacology

- **Cobicistat**
  - inhibits CYP3A* enzymes.
- **Ritonavir**
  - Is an HIV-1 protease inhibitor but used clinically because of its inhibition of CYP450 enzymes
- **Relative CYP450 Inhibition**
  - Ritonavir is classically a potent CYP3A4 inhibitor, but cobicistat exhibits more selective and characteristically stronger inhibition of CYP3A4.
- **P-glycoprotein and Tenofovir**
  - Tenofovir is a substrate of P-glycoprotein, inhibited by cobicistat and ritonavir, potentially leading to increased exposure and toxicities.

Primary Net Benefit

- Improved exposure of protease inhibitor activity while limiting dose-related toxicities.

CYP450 Inhibitors - Drug Class Review			
High-Yield Med Reviews			
Mechanism of Action: *Cobicistat inhibits CYP3A* enzymes.* *Ritonavir is an HIV-1 protease inhibitor but used clinically because of its inhibition of CYP450 enzymes.*			
Class Effects: Improved exposure of protease inhibitor activity while limiting dose-related toxicities.			
Generic Name	**Brand Name**	**Indication(s) or Uses**	**Notes**

Atazanavir and cobicistat	Evotaz	▪ HIV	▪ **Dosing (Adult):**
			  – Oral 1 tablet daily
			▪ **Dosing (Peds):**
			  – For children 35 kg and over - Oral 1 tablet daily
			▪ **CYP450 Interactions:** Substrate of CYP3A4; Inhibits CYP3A4
			▪ **Renal or Hepatic Dose Adjustments:**
			  – GFR less than 70 mL/minute & tenofovir disoproxil fumarate - not recommended
			▪ **Dosage Forms:** Oral (tablet)

Cobicistat	Tybost	▪ HIV	▪ **Dosing (Adult):**
			  – Oral 150 mg daily with atazanavir or darunavir
			▪ **Dosing (Peds):**
			  – For children 35 kg and over - Oral 150 mg daily
			▪ **CYP450 Interactions:** Substrate of CYP3A4; Inhibits CYP2D6, CYP3A4, P-gp
			▪ **Renal or Hepatic Dose Adjustments:**
			  – GFR less than 70 mL/minute & tenofovir disoproxil fumarate - not recommended
			▪ **Dosage Forms:** Oral (tablet)

CYP450 Inhibitors - Drug Class Review
High-Yield Med Reviews

Generic Name	Brand Name	Indication(s) or Uses	Notes
Darunavir, Cobicistat, Emtricitabine, and Tenofovir Alafenamide	Symtuza	• HIV	• **Dosing (Adult):** 　– Oral 1 tablet daily • **Dosing (Peds):** 　– Not routinely used • **CYP450 Interactions:** Substrate of CYP3A4, P-gp; Inhibits CYP2D6, CYP3A4, P-gp • **Renal or Hepatic Dose Adjustments:** 　– GFR less than 30 mL/minute - not recommended 　– Child-Pugh class C - not recommended • **Dosage Forms:** Oral (tablet)
Elvitegravir, Cobicistat, Emtricitabine, and Tenofovir Alafenamide	Genvoya	• HIV	• **Dosing (Adult):** 　– One tablet daily • **Dosing (Peds):** 　– For children 25 kg and over - Oral 1 tablet daily • **CYP450 Interactions:** Substrate of CYP3A4; Inhibits CYP2D6, CYP3A4, P-gp • **Renal or Hepatic Dose Adjustments:** 　– GFR less than 30 mL/minute - not recommended 　– Child-Pugh class C - not recommended • **Dosage Forms:** Oral (tablet)
Elvitegravir, Cobicistat, Emtricitabine, and Tenofovir Disoproxil Fumarate	Stribild	• HIV	• **Dosing (Adult):** 　– Oral 1 tablet daily • **Dosing (Peds):** 　– For children 35 kg and over - Oral 1 tablet daily • **CYP450 Interactions:** Substrate of CYP3A4; Inhibits CYP2D6, CYP3A4, P-gp • **Renal or Hepatic Dose Adjustments:** 　– GFR less than 70 mL/minute & tenofovir disoproxil fumarate - not recommended 　– Child-Pugh class C - not recommended • **Dosage Forms:** Oral (tablet)
Ombitasvir, Paritaprevir, and Ritonavir	Technivie	• Chronic Hepatitis C, genotype 4	• **Dosing (Adult):** 　– Oral 2 tablets daily x 12 weeks with ribavirin • **Dosing (Peds):** 　– Not routinely used • **CYP450 Interactions:** Substrate of CYP2D6, CYP3A4, P-gp; Inhibits CYP3A4, P-gp; Induces CYP1A2, CYP2C19 • **Renal or Hepatic Dose Adjustments:** 　– Child-Pugh class C - contraindicated • **Dosage Forms:** Oral (tablet)

CYP450 Inhibitors - Drug Class Review
High-Yield Med Reviews

Generic Name	Brand Name	Indication(s) or Uses	Notes

Ombitasvir, Paritaprevir, Ritonavir, and Dasabuvir	Viekira XR, Viekira Pak	• Chronic Hepatitis C, genotype 1a or 1b	• **Dosing (Adult):**
			  – Oral 2 to 3 tablets daily x 12 weeks with ribavirin
			• **Dosing (Peds):**
			  – Not routinely used
			• **CYP450 Interactions:** Substrate of CYP2D6, CYP3A4, P-gp; Inhibits CYP3A4, P-gp; Induces CYP1A2, CYP2C19
			• **Renal or Hepatic Dose Adjustments:**
			  – Child-Pugh class C - contraindicated
			• **Dosage Forms:** Oral (tablet)

High-Yield Clinical Knowledge

- **Serum Creatinine Changes**
  - Cobicistat is associated with increased serum creatinine, causing a decreased calculation of GFR; however, this is not an actual change in renal function.
  - Cobicistat inhibits creatinine's renal tubular secretion, which leads to this calculated value, with no corresponding change in actual renal function.
- **Drug Interactions**
  - By definition, cobicistat and ritonavir inhibit CYP450 isoenzymes and lead to numerous clinically relevant drug interactions.
    - Statins, calcium channel blockers, certain antiarrhythmics, inhaled corticosteroids, and estrogens are commonly administered medications with HIV or HCV regimens requiring close attention to appropriate agent selection and/or dose adjustments of changes in metabolism.
  - Other strong CYP3A4 or CYP2D6 inhibitors can decrease the metabolism of cobicistat, extending its pharmacokinetic actions.
- **HIV Activity**
  - Cobicistat has no intrinsic antiretroviral activity and is not considered an active drug when treating HIV.
  - Although a protease inhibitor, ritonavir has weak antiretroviral activity and dose-limiting toxicities and is also not considered an active drug for HIV regimens.
- **Cobicistat Vs Ritonavir**
  - As cobicistat is inactive against HIV, it hypothetically reduces the likelihood of viral resistance developing to protease inhibitors.
  - Other advantages of cobicistat include specificity to CYP3A4 inhibition and the absence of lipid effects.
- **Combinations**
  - Although cobicistat is available as an independent dosage form, it's primarily used clinically in combination dosage forms with other antiretroviral medications.
  - This significantly reduces the pill burden of HIV patients and can help to improve compliance.

HIGH-YIELD BOARD EXAM ESSENTIALS
- **CLASSIC AGENTS:** Cobicistat, ritonavir
- **DRUG CLASS:** CYP450 Inhibitors
- **INDICATIONS:** HIV
- **MECHANISM:** Cobicistat inhibits CYP3A* enzymes. Ritonavir is an HIV-1 protease inhibitor but used clinically because of its inhibition of CYP450 enzymes.
- **SIDE EFFECTS:** Elevations in serum creatinine (cobicistat), hepatotoxicity (ritonavir)
- **CLINICAL PEARLS:** By definition, cobicistat and ritonavir inhibit CYP450 isoenzymes and lead to numerous clinically relevant drug interactions.

High-Yield Basic Pharmacology

- **HIV Fusion**
  - For HIV to enter human CD4 cells, it must attach to the host cell using its viral envelope glycoprotein complex.
  - This gp160 complex consists of gp120 and gp41, which anchors HIV to the host CD4 cell.
  - Chemokine receptor antagonists block gp120 (ibalizumab, maraviroc), whereas the fusion inhibitor enfuvirtide blocks gp41.
- **Ibalizumab**
  - Binds to the host CD4 receptor cell, blocking HIV from entering CD4 cells.
- **Enfuvirtide**
  - inhibits envelope fusion of HIV-1 with the target cell by binding to gp41 on the viral surface, stopping its fusion with the host cell.
- **Maraviroc**
  - Selectively binds to host CCR5 receptors, blocking HIV entry into CD4 cells

Primary Net Benefit

- By blocking HIV entry into host CD4 cells, this group of agents provides novel antiretroviral mechanisms that can complement background therapy or for salvage therapy when resistance limits regimen selection.

Entry Inhibitor - Drug Class Review				
High-Yield Med Reviews				
Mechanism of Action: *Ibalizumab - binds to the host CD4 receptor cell, blocking HIV from entering CD4 cells.* *Enfuvirtide - inhibits envelope fusion of HIV-1 with the target cell by binding to gp41 on the viral surface, stopping its fusion with the host cell.* *Maraviroc - selectively binds to host CCR5 receptors, blocking HIV entry into CD4 cells.*				
Class Effects: By blocking HIV entry into host CD4 cells, this group of agents provides novel antiretroviral mechanisms that can complement background therapy or for salvage therapy when resistance limits regimen selection.				
Generic Name	**Brand Name**	**Indication(s) or Uses**	**Notes**	

Enfuvirtide	Fuzeon	• HIV	• **Dosing (Adult):**
			   – SQ 90 mg BID
			 • **Dosing (Peds):**
			   – SQ 2 mg/kg/dose BID
			     • Maximum 90 mg/dose
			 • **CYP450 Interactions:** None
			 • **Renal or Hepatic Dose Adjustments:** None
			 • **Dosage Forms:** Subcutaneous solution	

Ibalizumab-uiyk	Trogarzo	• HIV	• **Dosing (Adult):**
			   – IV 2,000 mg once, then 800 mg q14days
			 • **Dosing (Peds):**
			   – Not routinely used
			 • **CYP450 Interactions:** None
			 • **Renal or Hepatic Dose Adjustments:** None
			 • **Dosage Forms:** IV solution	

Entry Inhibitor - Drug Class Review
High-Yield Med Reviews

Generic Name	Brand Name	Indication(s) or Uses	Notes

Maraviroc	Selzentry	• HIV	• **Dosing (Adult):**
			  – Oral 300 mg BID
			    • With CYP3A4 Inhibitors - 150 mg BID
			    • With CYP3A4 Inducers - 600 mg BID
			• **Dosing (Peds):**
			  – Weight above 30 kg - 300 mg BID
			    • With CYP3A4 Inhibitors - 50 to 150 mg BID
			    • With CYP3A4 Inducers - 600 mg BID
			• **CYP450 Interactions:** Substrate CYP3A4, P-gp
			• **Renal or Hepatic Dose Adjustments:** None
			• **Dosage Forms:** Oral (solution, tablet)

High-Yield Clinical Knowledge

- **Parenterally Administered**
  - Enfuvirtide is a twice-daily subcutaneous injection and the only parenteral antiretroviral for routine outpatient care.
  - Ibalizumab is also administered via infusion and is recommended for patients with multidrug-resistant HIV.
  - Cabotegravir plus rilpivirine is available as an injectable nanosuspension.
    - Zidovudine is also available in a parenteral dosage form but is not intended for routine outpatient care.
- **Injection Site Reactions**
  - Almost all patients taking enfuvirtide will experience injection site reactions.
  - These reactions are characterized by painful erythema and nodules at the injection site.
- **Hepatotoxicity Warning**
  - Like other antiretroviral agents, maraviroc has been associated with hepatotoxicity, necessitating baseline and periodic liver enzyme assessments.
  - Uniquely, the hepatotoxicity caused by maraviroc may be preceded by a systemic allergic response, which manifests as pruritic rash, eosinophilia, and elevated IgE.
- **Cardiovascular Disease**
  - Use of maraviroc has been associated with new or worsening myocardial ischemia or infarction and should be used with caution in patients at high cardiovascular disease risk.
- **Maraviroc Starting Doses**
  - As a result of its CYP3A4 metabolism, maraviroc is doses base on the presence or absence of potent CYP3A4 inhibitors or inducers.
    - For patients starting maraviroc and who are currently taking CYP3A4 inhibitors, the starting dose of maraviroc is 150 mg BID.
    - For patients starting maraviroc while taking a CYP3A4 inducer, the starting dose is 600 mg BID.
    - A typical starting dose without either a CYP3A4 inhibitor or inducer present is 300 mg BID.
- **Enfuvirtide Missed Doses**
  - Although enfuvirtide lacks cross-resistance to other antiretroviral classes, it has a low barrier to resistance as the viral mutation of the gp41 binding domain can occur.
  - As a result of a short half-life of approximately 4 hours, enfuvirtide must be administered twice daily.
  - If missed doses occur, there HIV viral mutation and resistance may occur.
- **Long Term CCR5 Antagonist**
  - Long-term use of maraviroc has been associated with increased susceptibility to flaviviruses, including West Nile virus and tick-borne encephalitis viruses.

High-Yield Fast-Fact

- **Exposure Prophylaxis**
  - Entry inhibitors present an option for HIV exposure prevention by preventing HIV viral entry into host cells, rather than working on viral replication once already intracellularly.

HIGH-YIELD BOARD EXAM ESSENTIALS

- **CLASSIC AGENTS:** Ibalizumab, enfuvirtide, maraviroc
- **DRUG CLASS:** Entry inhibitors
- **INDICATIONS:** HIV
- **MECHANISM:** Ibalizumab - binds to the host CD4 receptor cell, blocking HIV from entering CD4 cells (ibalizumab); inhibits envelope fusion of HIV-1 with the target cell by binding to gp41 on the viral surface, stopping its fusion with the host cell (enfuvirtide); selectively binds to host CCR5 receptors, blocking HIV entry into CD4 cells (maraviroc).
- **SIDE EFFECTS:** Hepatotoxicity, new or worsening myocardial ischemia or infarction
- **CLINICAL PEARLS:** By blocking HIV entry into host CD4 cells, this group of agents provides novel antiretroviral mechanisms that can complement background therapy or for salvage therapy when resistance limits regimen selection.

High-Yield Basic Pharmacology

- **Mechanism of Action**
  - Inhibit integration of reverse-transcribed HIV DNA into host chromosomes.
- **Elvitegravir and Cobicistat**
  - Compared to the other integrase inhibitors, elvitegravir is primarily eliminated by CYP3A4, thus providing the opportunity for combination with "boosting" agents.
  - Although ritonavir could be used, cobicistat is the only boosting agent used routinely with elvitegravir.

Primary Net Benefit

- First-line antiretroviral agents with superior tolerability and safety profile.

<table>
<tr><td colspan="4">Integrase Inhibitors - Drug Class Review
High-Yield Med Reviews</td></tr>
<tr><td colspan="4">Mechanism of Action: Inhibit integration of reverse-transcribed HIV DNA into host chromosomes.</td></tr>
<tr><td colspan="4">Class Effects: Insomnia, neural tube defects and small increases in serum creatinine (dolutegravir), avoid dolutegravir with pregnancy</td></tr>
<tr><td>Generic Name</td><td>Brand Name</td><td>Indication(s) or Uses</td><td>Notes</td></tr>
<tr>
<td>Bictegravir</td>
<td>Biktarvy</td>
<td>- HIV</td>
<td>
- Dosing (Adult):
  - Oral 1 tablet daily
- Dosing (Peds):
  - Limited to children at least 25 kg
- CYP450 Interactions: Substrate CYP3A4
- Renal or Hepatic Dose Adjustments:
  - GFR less than 30 mL/minute - Not recommended
  - Child-Pugh class C - Not recommended
- Dosage Forms: Oral (tablet)
</td>
</tr>
<tr>
<td>Cabotegravir</td>
<td>Vocabria</td>
<td>- HIV</td>
<td>
- Dosing (Adult):
  - Oral 30 mg daily with rilpivirine
  - IM 600 mg / 900 mg (cabotegravir/rilpivirine) on last day of lead-in
  - IM 400 mg / 600 mg (cabotegravir/rilpivirine) once monthly
- Dosing (Peds):
  - Not routinely used
- CYP450 Interactions: Substrate P-gp
- Renal or Hepatic Dose Adjustments: None
- Dosage Forms: Oral (tablet), SQ extended-release suspension
</td>
</tr>
</table>

Integrase Inhibitors - Drug Class Review				
High-Yield Med Reviews				
Generic Name	**Brand Name**	**Indication(s) or Uses**	**Notes**

Dolutegravir	Tivicay, Tivicay PD	▪ HIV	▪ **Dosing (Adult):**
			  – Oral 50 mg once to twice daily
			▪ **Dosing (Peds):**
			  – Children 3 to less than 14 kg
			    ▪ Oral 5 to 20 mg daily
			  – Children 14 kg and over
			    ▪ Oral 25 to 50 mg once to twice daily
			▪ **CYP450 Interactions:** Substrate CYP3A4, P-gp
			▪ **Renal or Hepatic Dose Adjustments:**
			  – Child-Pugh class C - Not recommended
			▪ **Dosage Forms:** Oral (Tablet)

Elvitegravir	Genvoya
	Stribild
		▪ HIV	▪ **Dosing (Adult):**
			  – Oral 150 mg daily (in combination with cobicistat, emtricitabine, tenofovir disoproxil fumarate/tenofovir disproxil fumurate)
			▪ **Dosing (Peds):**
			  – Limited to children at least 25 kg
			▪ **CYP450 Interactions:** Substrate CYP3A4
			▪ **Renal or Hepatic Dose Adjustments:**
			  – Child-Pugh class C - Not recommended
			  – Genvoya
			    ▪ GFR less than 30 mL/minute - Not recommended
			  – Stribild
			    ▪ GFR less than 70 mL/minute - Initial use not recommended
			    ▪ GFR less than 50 mL/minute - continued use not recommended
			▪ **Dosage Forms:** Oral (Tablet)

Integrase Inhibitors - Drug Class Review
High-Yield Med Reviews

Generic Name	Brand Name	Indication(s) or Uses	Notes

Raltegravir	Isentress, Isentress HD	▪ HIV	▪ **Dosing (Adult):**
			  – Treatment naive
			    ▪ Oral 400 mg BID or 1,200 mg daily
			  – Treatment experience
			    ▪ Oral 400 mg BID
			▪ **Dosing (Peds):**
			  – Oral suspension in children less than 20 kg
			    ▪ Oral 6 mg/kg/dose twice daily
			      ● Maximum 100 mg/dose
			  – Chewable tablets in children 11 kg and over
			    ▪ Oral 6 mg/kg/dose twice daily
			      ● Maximum 300 mg/dose
			  – Film-coated tablets
			    ▪ Limited to children at least 25 kg
			▪ **CYP450 Interactions:** None
			▪ **Renal or Hepatic Dose Adjustments:**
			  – Film-coated 600 mg tablet
			    ▪ Child-Pugh class B or C - not recommended
			▪ **Dosage Forms:** Oral (chewable tablet, solution, tablet)

High-Yield Clinical Knowledge

- **HIV Resistance**
  - Integrase inhibitors, notably bictegravir and dolutegravir, protect a high genetic barrier to HIV resistance.
  - Although patients must be counseled not to miss or skip doses, should this occur, these agents with high genetic barriers to resistance are less likely to develop resistance.
- **OCT2 Interaction**
  - Metformin should be used cautiously with bictegravir and dolutegravir as it inhibits renal organic cation transporter (OCT2) and the multidrug and toxin extrusion transporter 1.
    - Dose and exposure-dependent effects of metformin may occur (lactic acidosis) with this combination.
  - Dofetilide is a substrate of OCT2, and its use is contraindicated with bictegravir and dolutegravir.
- **Serum Creatinine Changes**
  - Dolutegravir is associated with an increase in serum creatinine that does not represent a change in renal function.
  - This occurs due to competitive inhibition of tubular secretion of creatinine, with no actual impact on GFR.
  - Cobicistat has a similar effect on serum creatinine.
- **HIV Resistance**
  - Integrase inhibitors, notably bictegravir and dolutegravir, protect a high genetic barrier to HIV resistance.
  - Although patients must be counseled not to miss or skip doses, should this occur, these agents with high genetic barriers to resistance are less likely to develop resistance.
- **OCT2 Interaction**
  - Metformin should be used cautiously with bictegravir and dolutegravir as it inhibits renal organic cation transporter (OCT2) and the multidrug and toxin extrusion transporter 1.
    - Dose and exposure-dependent effects of metformin may occur (lactic acidosis) with this combination.

- Dofetilide is a substrate of OCT2, and its use is contraindicated with bictegravir and dolutegravir.
- **Serum Creatinine Changes**
    - Dolutegravir is associated with an increase in serum creatinine that does not represent a change in renal function.
    - This occurs due to competitive inhibition of tubular secretion of creatinine, with no actual impact on GFR.
    - Cobicistat has a similar effect on serum creatinine.

High-Yield Fast-Fact

- **Raltegravir and CK**
    - Although raltegravir contains a warning for elevated creatine phosphokinase, there has been no relationship between raltegravir or CK identified in post-market research.

HIGH-YIELD BOARD EXAM ESSENTIALS
- **CLASSIC AGENTS:** Bictegravir, cabotegravir, dolutegravir, elvitegravir, raltegravir
- **DRUG CLASS:** Integrase inhibitors
- **INDICATIONS:** HIV
- **MECHANISM:** Inhibit integration of reverse-transcribed HIV DNA into host chromosomes.
- **SIDE EFFECTS:** Insomnia, neural tube defects (dolutegravir)
- **CLINICAL PEARLS:** Metformin should be used cautiously with bictegravir and dolutegravir as it inhibits renal organic cation transporter (OCT2) and the multidrug and toxin extrusion transporter 1.

High-Yield Basic Pharmacology

- **Mechanism of Action**
  - Bind directly to and inhibit HIV-1 reverse transcriptase, preventing RNA and DNA dependent DNA polymerase activity.
- **NNRTI Vs. NRTI**
  - Unlike NRTIs, the NNRTIs do not compete with nucleoside triphosphates and do not require phosphorylation for their activity.
  - In other words, NNRTIs are not incorporated into viral DNA but prevent the movement of reverse transcriptase.

Primary Net Benefit

- Antiretroviral agents with a long history of efficacy now include second-generation NNRTIs permitting once-daily dosing and improved adverse events.

<table>
<tr><td colspan="4">NNRTI - Drug Class Review
High-Yield Med Reviews</td></tr>
<tr><td colspan="4">Mechanism of Action: Bind directly to and inhibit HIV-1 reverse transcriptase, preventing RNA and DNA dependent DNA polymerase activity.</td></tr>
<tr><td colspan="4">Class Effects: GI intolerance, rash (erythema multiforme, SJS/TEN), hepatotoxicity (nevirapine), neuropsychiatric effects (efavirenz).</td></tr>
<tr><td>Generic Name</td><td>Brand Name</td><td>Indication(s) or Uses</td><td>Notes</td></tr>
<tr>
<td>Delavirdine</td>
<td>Rescriptor</td>
<td>• HIV</td>
<td>
• Dosing (Adult):
  – Oral 400 mg TID
• Dosing (Peds):
  – For children 16 years and older, use adult dosing.
• CYP450 Interactions: Substrate CYP2D6, 3A4; Inhibits CYP3A4
• Renal or Hepatic Dose Adjustments: None
• Dosage Forms: Oral (tablet)
</td>
</tr>
<tr>
<td>Doravirine</td>
<td>Pifeltro</td>
<td>• HIV</td>
<td>
• Dosing (Adult):
  – Oral 100 mg daily
• Dosing (Peds):
  – Not routinely used
• CYP450 Interactions: Substrate CYP3A4
• Renal or Hepatic Dose Adjustments:
  – GFR less than 50 mL/minute - not recommended
• Dosage Forms: Oral (tablet)
</td>
</tr>
</table>

NNRTI - Drug Class Review
High-Yield Med Reviews

Generic Name	Brand Name	Indication(s) or Uses	Notes

Efavirenz	Sustiva	▪ HIV	▪ **Dosing (Adult):**
			  – Oral 600 mg daily
			  – Oral 400 mg daily (when combined with tenofovir disoproxil fumarate and lamivudine)
			▪ **Dosing (Peds):**
			  – Children at least 3 months old and at least 3.5 kg
			    ▪ Oral 100 to 250 mg daily
			  – Children 3 years and older
			    ▪ Oral 200 to 600 mg daily
			▪ **CYP450 Interactions:** Substrate CYP2B6, 3A4; Induces CYP2B6, 2C19, 3A4
			▪ **Renal or Hepatic Dose Adjustments:**
			  – Child-Pugh class B or C - not recommended
			▪ **Dosage Forms:** Oral (capsule, tablet)

Etravirine	Intelence	▪ HIV	▪ **Dosing (Adult):**
			  – Oral 200 mg BID
			▪ **Dosing (Peds):**
			  – Children at least 10 kg and 2 years and older
			    ▪ Oral 100 to 200 mg BID
			▪ **CYP450 Interactions:** Substrate CYP2C19, 2C9, 3A4; Induces 3A4; Inhibits CYP2C19
			▪ **Renal or Hepatic Dose Adjustments:** None
			▪ **Dosage Forms:** Oral (tablet)

Nevirapine	Viramune, Viramune XR	▪ HIV	▪ **Dosing (Adult):**
			  – Oral 200 mg daily x 14 days, then IR 200 mg BID, or ER 400 mg daily
			▪ **Dosing (Peds):**
			  – Oral IR 120 to 200 mg/m2/dose daily x 14 days, then 120 to 200 mg/m2/dose BID
			    ▪ Maximum 200 mg/dose
			  – Oral ER 200 to 400 mg daily (after IR lead-in period)
			▪ **CYP450 Interactions:** Substrate CYP2B6, 2D6, 3A4; Induces CYP2B6
			▪ **Renal or Hepatic Dose Adjustments:**
			  – Child-Pugh class B or C - contraindicated
			▪ **Dosage Forms:** Oral (suspension, tablet)

NNRTI - Drug Class Review
High-Yield Med Reviews

Generic Name	Brand Name	Indication(s) or Uses	Notes

Rilpivirine	Endurant	• HIV	• **Dosing (Adult):**
			  – Oral 25 mg daily (with or without cabotegravir)
			  – IM 600 mg / 900 mg (cabotegravir/rilpivirine) on last day of lead-in
			  – IM 400 mg / 600 mg (cabotegravir/rilpivirine) once monthly
			• **Dosing (Peds):**
			  – Limited to children at least 25 kg
			• **CYP450 Interactions:** Substrate CYP3A4
			• **Renal or Hepatic Dose Adjustments:** None
			• **Dosage Forms:** Oral (tablet), SQ extended-release suspension

High-Yield Clinical Knowledge

- **Class Adverse Events**
  - NNRTIs are commonly associated with GI intolerances and skin rashes.
  - Rashes can range from mild and self-limiting to toxic epidermal necrolysis.
    - Nevirapine initiation requires slow dose titration to minimize the risk of maculopapular rash.
  - Erythema multiforme, Stevens-Johnson syndrome, and toxic epidermal necrolysis are all immune-mediated epidermal conditions that differ based on clinical presentation:
    - Erythema multiforme affects less than 10% of total body surface area, most commonly involves hands and forearms, and presents with target lesions.
    - Stevens-Johnson syndrome also affects less than 10% of total body surface area but involves at least two mucosal sites.
    - Toxic epidermal necrolysis affects more than 30% of total body surface area, has an abrupt onset, and must be treated promptly.
  - Total serum cholesterol may increase with NNRTI therapy.
    - Efavirenz is associated with a 10-20% increase in total cholesterol.
- **Efavirenz and Pregnancy**
  - Efavirenz may be avoided in pregnant women or in women planning on becoming pregnant due to a risk of neural tube defects.
  - However, as a result of this observation, but the absence of this effect in some literature, clinical guidance may permit it to be used in the population with expert advice.
  - Dolutegravir has been associated with a similar effect of neural tube defects and should be avoided in the first four weeks from conception or six weeks from the last menstrual period.
- **Hepatic Injury**
  - Nevirapine should not be used in patients with CD4 counts above 250 cells/mL (women) or greater than 400 cells/mL (men) or patients with hepatitis B or C co-infection.
  - The characteristic rash associated with nevirapine initiation is closely related to hepatotoxicity, and the development of maculopapular rash should prompt liver enzyme and function assessment.
- **Efavirenz Timing**
  - As a result of its long half-life, efavirenz may be administered once daily, but it should be taken in the evening to avoid daytime hallucinations.
    - Other CNS effects of efavirenz include dizziness, insomnia, headache, depression, mania, and psychosis.
- **Parenterally Administered**
  - Cabotegravir plus rilpivirine is available as an injectable nanosuspension.

- Other parenterally administered antiretroviral agents include:
  - Enfuvirtide is a twice-daily subcutaneous injection and the only parenteral antiretroviral for routine outpatient care.
  - Ibalizumab is also administered via infusion and is recommended for patients with multidrug-resistant HIV.
  - Zidovudine is also available in a parenteral dosage form but is not intended for routine outpatient care.

High-Yield Fast-Facts

- **Efavirenz Abuse**
  - Because of its hallucinogenic properties, some have smoked or inhaled efavirenz to achieve this effect.
- **QT Prolongation**
  - Rilpivirine has been associated with QT prolongation at high doses.

HIGH-YIELD BOARD EXAM ESSENTIALS
- **CLASSIC AGENTS:** Delavirdine, doravirine, efavirenz, etravirine, nevirapine, rilpivirine
- **DRUG CLASS:** NNRTI
- **INDICATIONS:** HIV
- **MECHANISM:** Bind directly to and inhibit HIV-1 reverse transcriptase, preventing RNA and DNA dependent DNA polymerase activity.
- **SIDE EFFECTS:** GI intolerance, rash (erythema multiforme, SJS/TEN), hepatotoxicity (nevirapine), neuropsychiatric effects (efavirenz)
- **CLINICAL PEARLS:** As a class, NNRTIs are substrates for CYP3A4 and have mixed effects as either inducer, inhibitors, or mixed inhibitors/inducers. Nevirapine induces CYP3A4, efavirenz, and etravirine both induce and inhibit CYP3A4, and delavirdine inhibits CYP3A4.

High-Yield Basic Pharmacology

- **Mechanism of Action**
  - Inhibition of HIV reverse transcription into the emerging proviral DNA.
  - After intracellular phosphorylation, nucleoside and nucleotide analogs inhibit HIV replication by competitive inhibition of native nucleotides and by the termination of elongation of nascent proviral DNA.

Primary Net Benefit

- A core component to highly-active antiretroviral regimens, but are associated with class toxicities including lactic acidosis, myopathies, peripheral neuropathies, pancreatitis, and bone marrow toxicities.

<table>
<tr><td colspan="4">NRTI - Drug Class Review
High-Yield Med Reviews</td></tr>
<tr><td colspan="4">Mechanism of Action: Inhibition of HIV reverse transcription into the emerging proviral DNA.</td></tr>
<tr><td colspan="4">Class Effects: A core component to highly-active antiretroviral regimens but are associated with class toxicities including lactic acidosis, myopathies, peripheral neuropathies, pancreatitis, bone marrow toxicities.</td></tr>
<tr><td>Generic Name</td><td>Brand Name</td><td>Indication(s) or Uses</td><td>Notes</td></tr>
<tr><td>Abacavir</td><td>Ziagen</td><td>• HIV</td><td>

- **Dosing (Adult):**
  - Oral 300 mg BID
  - Oral 600 mg daily with other antiretrovirals
- **Dosing (Peds):**
  - Oral 8 mg/kg/dose BID
    - Maximum 300 mg/dose
  - Oral 16 mg/kg/dose daily
    - Maximum 600 mg/dose
- **CYP450 Interactions:** None
- **Renal or Hepatic Dose Adjustments:**
  - Child-Pugh class A - 200 mg BID
  - Child-Pugh class B or C - contraindicated
- **Dosage Forms:** Oral (solution, tablet)

</td></tr>
<tr><td>Didanosine</td><td>Videx</td><td>• HIV</td><td>

- **Dosing (Adult):**
  - Oral 200 to 400 mg once daily
  - Oral 125 to 200 mg BID
- **Dosing (Peds):**
  - Oral 50 to 100 mg/m2/dose q12h
- **CYP450 Interactions:** None
- **Renal or Hepatic Dose Adjustments:**
  - GFR 30 to 59 mL/minute - reduce dose by 50%
  - GFR 10 to 29 mL/minute - reduce dose by approximately 62.5%
  - GFR less than 10 mL/minute - reduce dose by approximately 75 %
- **Dosage Forms:** Oral (capsule, solution)

</td></tr>
</table>

NRTI - Drug Class Review
High-Yield Med Reviews

Generic Name	Brand Name	Indication(s) or Uses	Notes

Emtricitabine	Emtriva	▪ HIV	▪ **Dosing (Adult):**
			  − Oral capsule 200 mg daily
			  − Oral solution 240 mg daily
			▪ **Dosing (Peds):**
			  − Oral solution 3 to 6 mg/kg/dose daily
			    ▪ Maximum 240 mg/day
			  − For oral capsule use, must weigh more than 33 kg
			▪ **CYP450 Interactions:** None
			▪ **Renal or Hepatic Dose Adjustments:**
			  − GFR 30 to 49 mL/minute - Capsule 200 mg q48h, solution 120 mg q24h
			  − GFR 15 to 29 mL/minute - Capsule 200 mg q72h, solution 80 mg q24h
			  − GFR less than 15 mL/minute - Capsule 200 mg q96h, solution 60 mg q24h
			▪ **Dosage Forms:** Oral (capsule, solution)

Lamivudine	Epivir, Epivir HBV	▪ HIV
		▪ Hepatitis B
			▪ **Dosing (Adult):**
			  − HIV
			    ▪ Oral 300 mg daily or 150 mg BID
			  − HBV
			    ▪ Oral 100 mg daily
			▪ **Dosing (Peds):**
			  − Oral 30 to 150 mg BID
			▪ **CYP450 Interactions:** None
			▪ **Renal or Hepatic Dose Adjustments:** HIV indication
			  − GFR 30 to 49 mL/minute - 150 mg daily
			  − GFR 15 to 29 mL/minute - 150 mg x1 then 100 mg daily
			  − GFR less than 15 mL/minute - 150 mg x1 then 50 mg daily
			  − GFR less than 5 - 50 mg, then 25 mg daily
			▪ **Dosage Forms:** Oral (solution, tablet)

Stavudine	Zerit	▪ HIV	▪ **Dosing (Adult):**
			  − Oral 30 to 40 mg q12h
			▪ **Dosing (Peds):**
			  − Oral 1 mg/kg/dose q12h
			    ▪ Maximum 30 mg/dose
			▪ **CYP450 Interactions:** None
			▪ **Renal or Hepatic Dose Adjustments:**
			  − GFR 26 to 50 mL/minute - 15 or 20 mg q12h
			  − GFR 10 to 25 mL/minute - 15 or 20 mg q24h
			▪ **Dosage Forms:** Oral (capsule, solution)

NRTI - Drug Class Review
High-Yield Med Reviews

Generic Name	Brand Name	Indication(s) or Uses	Notes

Tenofovir alafenamide	Vemlidy	• Hepatitis B	• **Dosing (Adult):**
			  – HIV
			    • Only available in combination with other ART (Biktarvy, Genvoya, Odefsey, Symtuza)
			  – HBV
			    • Oral 25 mg daily
			• **Dosing (Peds):**
			  – Not routinely used
			• **CYP450 Interactions:** None
			• **Renal or Hepatic Dose Adjustments:**
			  – GFR less than 15 mL/minute - Not recommended
			  – Child-Pugh class B or C - Not recommended
			• **Dosage Forms:** Oral (tablet)

Tenofovir disoproxil	Viread	• Hepatitis B
		• HIV
			• **Dosing (Adult):**
			  – HIV
			    • Oral 300 mg daily or 150 mg BID
			  – HBV
			    • Oral 100 or 300 mg daily
			• **Dosing (Peds):**
			  – Oral 8 mg/kg/dose daily
			    • Maximum 300 mg/day
			• **CYP450 Interactions:** None
			• **Renal or Hepatic Dose Adjustments:** HIV indication
			  – GFR 30 to 49 mL/minute - 300 mg q48h
			  – GFR 10 to 29 mL/minute - 300 mg q72h
			  – GFR less than 10 mL/minute - Not recommended
			• **Dosage Forms:** Oral (solution, tablet)

Zalcitabine	Hivid	• HIV	• **Dosing (Adult):**
			  – Oral 0.75 mg q8h
			• **Dosing (Peds):**
			  – Not routinely used
			• **CYP450 Interactions:** None
			• **Renal or Hepatic Dose Adjustments:**
			  – GFR 10 to 40 mL/minute - 0.75 mg q12h
			  – GFR less than 10 mL/minute - 0.75 mg q24h
			• **Dosage Forms:** Oral (tablet)

NRTI - Drug Class Review			
High-Yield Med Reviews			
Generic Name	**Brand Name**	**Indication(s) or Uses**	**Notes**

Zidovudine	Retrovir	• HIV	• **Dosing (Adult):**
			  – IV 2 mg/kg loading dose, then 1 mg/kg/hour
			  – Oral 300 mg BID
			• **Dosing (Peds):**
			  – Oral 9 to 12 mg/kg/dose
			    • Maximum 300 mg BID
			  – IV 120 mg/m2/dose q4-6h
			    • Maximum 160 mg/dose
			• **CYP450 Interactions:** None
			• **Renal or Hepatic Dose Adjustments:**
			  – GFR less than 15 mL/minute - oral 100 mg TID or 300 mg daily
			• **Dosage Forms:** Oral (capsule, solution, tablet), IV solution

High-Yield Clinical Knowledge

- **NRTI Toxicities**
    - NRTIs may adversely affect the DNA polymerase gamma of human mitochondria, resulting in mitochondrial toxicities including myopathies, peripheral neuropathies, pancreatitis, anemias, and granulocytopenia.
        - Zidovudine is associated with the highest risk of cytopenias and bone marrow toxicities.
    - Didanosine, stavudine, and zidovudine are associated with potentially fatal lactic acidosis and hepatic steatosis.
    - Emtricitabine, lamivudine, and tenofovir do not possess mitochondrial toxicities.
- **HLA-B*5701**
    - Before initiation of abacavir, patients must be screened for the presence of HLA-B*5701, as patients with positive HLA-B*5701 locus are at high risk of acute hypersensitivity syndrome.
- **Renal Dose Adjustment**
    - All NRTIs, except for abacavir, require renal dose adjustments when the estimated GFR is less than 60 mL/minute or less than 50 mL/minute.
    - Abacavir is often preferred in patients with chronic kidney disease who have susceptible HIV and lack HLA-B*5701 positive screening.
- **Nucleoside Vs. Nucleotide**
    - All available agents in this class, except for tenofovir, are nucleosides that must be triphosphorylated to exert their activity.
    - Tenofovir is a nucleo*tide* monophosphate that must undergo two additional phosphorylations for its antiretroviral activity.
- **Tenofovir Alafenamide Vs Disoproxil**
    - Tenofovir is formulated as two separate prodrugs, alafenamide or disoproxil.
    - The alafenamide was developed to improve oral absorption substantially and is associated with a lower risk of renal toxicity and bone marrow toxicities.
- **Lamivudine Dosing**
    - Lamivudine is used for HIV-1, HIV-2 at a dose of 300 mg daily or 150 mg twice daily.
    - For hepatitis B, lamivudine can also be used, but at a dose of 100 mg twice daily.
        - To treat coinfection with HIV and HBV, the HIV dosing (300 mg or 150 mg BID dosing).

High-Yield Fast-Fact

- **NNRTI Vs. NRTI**
  - Unlike NRTIs, the NNRTIs do not compete with nucleoside triphosphates and do not require phosphorylation for their activity.
  - In other words, NNRTIs are not incorporated into viral DNA but prevent the movement of reverse transcriptase.

HIGH-YIELD BOARD EXAM ESSENTIALS

- **CLASSIC AGENTS:** Abacavir (ABC), didanosine (ddI), emtricitabine (FTC), lamivudine (3TC), stavudine (d4T), tenofovir alafenamide (TAF), tenofovir disoproxil (TDF), zalcitabine (DDC), zidovudine (AZT)
- **DRUG CLASS:** NRTI
- **INDICATIONS:** HIV
- **MECHANISM:** Inhibition of HIV reverse transcription into the emerging proviral DNA.
- **SIDE EFFECTS:** Myopathies, peripheral neuropathies, pancreatitis, anemias, granulocytopenia; potentially fatal lactic acidosis and hepatic steatosis (didanosine, stavudine, zidovudine)
- **CLINICAL PEARLS:** Before initiation of abacavir, patients must be screened for the presence of HLA-B*5701, as patients with positive HLA-B*5701 locus are at high risk of acute hypersensitivity syndrome.

High-Yield Basic Pharmacology

- **Mechanism of Action**
  - Inhibit the processing of HIV viral proteins, forming immature, non-functional proteins incapable of infecting other cells.
- **Pharmacokinetic "Boosting"**
  - Protease inhibitors can benefit from their common hepatic oxidation pathway by causing a pharmacokinetically predictable inhibition of their metabolism using the CYP3A4 inhibitors cobicistat or ritonavir.
  - When ritonavir is used as a boosting agent, it must not be included in the count of "active" antiretroviral agents.
    - Nelfinavir is the only protease inhibitor not pharmacokinetically boosted by ritonavir.
  - Cobicistat does not possess antiretroviral activity and is only used as a pharmacokinetic boosting agent.

Primary Net Benefit

- Lopinavir and ritonavir were among the first antiretrovirals associated with high pill burden and poor tolerability, but new protease inhibitors improved efficacy and safety, permitting long-term use.

<table>
<tr><td colspan="4">Protease Inhibitor - Drug Class Review
High-Yield Med Reviews</td></tr>
<tr><td colspan="4">Mechanism of Action: Inhibit the processing of HIV viral proteins, forming immature, non-functional proteins incapable of infecting other cells.</td></tr>
<tr><td colspan="4">Class Effects: Some agents have a high pill burden, increases in glucose and lipids (especially triglycerides), jaundice (with atazanavir and indinavir), high risk for clinically relevant drug-interactions via inhibition of CYP3A4 & P-gp</td></tr>
<tr><td>Generic Name</td><td>Brand Name</td><td>Indication(s) or Uses</td><td>Notes</td></tr>
<tr>
<td>Atazanavir</td>
<td>Reyataz, Evotaz (with cobicistat)</td>
<td>• HIV</td>
<td>

- **Dosing (Adult):**
  - Oral 300 mg daily plus ritonavir or cobicistat
  - Oral 400 mg daily
- **Dosing (Peds):**
  - Boosted regimen in children 3 months or older
    - Oral 200 to 300 mg daily
  - Unboosted regimen in children 3 months or older
    - Oral 520 to 620 mg/m2/daily
- **CYP450 Interactions:** Substrate CYP3A4; Inhibits CYP3A4
- **Renal or Hepatic Dose Adjustments:**
  - ESRD - not recommended
  - Child-Pugh class C - not recommended
- **Dosage Forms:** Oral (capsule, packet)

</td>
</tr>
</table>

Protease Inhibitor - Drug Class Review
High-Yield Med Reviews

Generic Name	Brand Name	Indication(s) or Uses	Notes

Darunavir	Prezista	▪ HIV	▪ **Dosing (Adult):**
			  – Oral 800 mg once daily plus ritonavir or cobicistat
			  – Oral 600 mg twice daily plus ritonavir or cobicistat
			▪ **Dosing (Peds):**
			  – Oral 20 mg/kg BID plus ritonavir
			  – Oral 200 to 600 mg BID plus ritonavir
			▪ **CYP450 Interactions:** Substrate CYP3A4, P-gp; Inhibits CYP2D6, 3A4
			▪ **Renal or Hepatic Dose Adjustments:**
			  – Child-Pugh class C - not recommended
			▪ **Dosage Forms:** Oral (suspension, tablet)

Fosamprenavir	Lexiva	▪ HIV	▪ **Dosing (Adult):**
			  – Oral 1,400 mg BID
			  – Oral 700 mg BID plus ritonavir BID
			▪ **Dosing (Peds):**
			  – Oral 30 mg/kg/dose without ritonavir
			    ▪ Maximum 1,400 mg/day
			  – Oral 18 to 45 mg/kg/dose BID plus ritonavir 3 to 7 mg/kg BID
			▪ **CYP450 Interactions:** Substrate CYP2C9, 2D6, 3A4, P-gp; Inhibits CYP3A4
			▪ **Renal or Hepatic Dose Adjustments:**
			  – Child-Pugh class A - 700 mg BID without ritonavir or ritonavir once daily
			  – Child-Pugh class C - 700 mg BID without ritonavir or 450 mg BID with ritonavir once daily
			  – Child-Pugh class C - 350 mg BID without ritonavir or 300 mg BID with ritonavir once daily
			▪ **Dosage Forms:** Oral (suspension, tablet)

Indinavir	Crixivan	▪ HIV	▪ **Dosing (Adult):**
			  – Oral 800 mg q8h
			  – Oral 800 mg BID plus ritonavir 100 to 200 mg BID
			▪ **Dosing (Peds):**
			  – Oral 400 mg/m2/dose q12h plus ritonavir
			▪ **CYP450 Interactions:** Substrate CYP2D6, 3A4, P-gp; Inhibits CYP3A4
			▪ **Renal or Hepatic Dose Adjustments:**
			  – Child-Pugh class A or B - 600 mg q8h without ritonavir
			  – Child-Pugh class C - not recommended
			▪ **Dosage Forms:** Oral (capsule)

Protease Inhibitor - Drug Class Review
High-Yield Med Reviews

Generic Name	Brand Name	Indication(s) or Uses	Notes

Lopinavir	Kaletra (with ritonavir)	▪ HIV	▪ **Dosing (Adult):**
			  – Oral 400 mg BID with ritonavir 100 mg BID
			  – Oral 800 mg with ritonavir 200 mg daily
			▪ **Dosing (Peds):**
			  – Oral 10 to 16 mg/kg/dose or 300 mg/m2/dose BID
			  – Oral
			▪ **CYP450 Interactions:** Substrate CYP1A2, 2B6, 2D6, 3A4, P-gp; Inhibits CYP2D6, 3A4
			▪ **Renal or Hepatic Dose Adjustments:**
			  – Child-Pugh class C - use with caution
			▪ **Dosage Forms:** Oral (solution, tablet)

Nelfinavir	Viracept	▪ HIV	▪ **Dosing (Adult):**
			  – Oral 750 mg TID or 1,250 mg BID
			▪ **Dosing (Peds):**
			  – Oral 45 to 55 mg/kg/dose BID
			    ▪ Maximum 1,250 mg/dose
			  – Oral 25 to 35 mg/kg/dose TID
			    ▪ Maximum 750 mg/dose
			▪ **CYP450 Interactions:** Substrate CYP2C9, 2C19, 2D6, 3A4, P-gp; Inhibits CYP3A4; Induces CYP1A2, 2B6
			▪ **Renal or Hepatic Dose Adjustments:**
			  – Child-Pugh class C - not recommended
			▪ **Dosage Forms:** Oral (tablet)

Ritonavir	Norvir	▪ HIV	▪ **Dosing (Adult):**
			  – Oral 100 to 400 mg daily in 1-2 divided doses
			▪ **Dosing (Peds):**
			  – Oral 250 to 400 mg/m2/dose q12h
			▪ **CYP450 Interactions:** Substrate CYP1A2, 2B6, 2D6, 3A4, P-gp; Inhibits CYP2D6, 3A4; Induces CYP1A2, 2B6, 2C19, 2C9
			▪ **Renal or Hepatic Dose Adjustments:**
			  – Child-Pugh class C - not recommended
			▪ **Dosage Forms:** Oral (capsule, packet, solution, tablet)

Tipranavir	Aptivus	▪ HIV	▪ **Dosing (Adult):**
			  – Oral 500 mg BID with ritonavir 200 mg BID
			▪ **Dosing (Peds):**
			  – Oral 14 mg/kg/dose BID plus ritonavir 6 mg/kg/dose BID
			    ▪ Maximum 500 mg (tipranavir), 200 mg (ritonavir)
			▪ **CYP450 Interactions:** Substrate CYP3A4; Inhibits CYP2D6
			▪ **Renal or Hepatic Dose Adjustments:**
			  – Child-Pugh class C - contraindicated
			▪ **Dosage Forms:** Oral (capsule, packet)

High-Yield Clinical Knowledge

- **PPI Interaction**
    - Many protease inhibitors require acidic environments for adequate absorption, thus cannot be combined with proton pump inhibitors.
        - A combination of indinavir and ritonavir can permit indinavir administration with food.
    - PPI use must be avoided with atazanavir, fosamprenavir, indinavir, and nelfinavir.
- **Protease Inhibitor Class Adverse Effects**
    - Protease inhibitors are frequently associated with GI intolerance (diarrhea), central fat redistribution (buffalo hump plus peripheral fat wasting), hyperglycemia (and diabetes), hyperlipidemia, PR and QT prolongation, and numerous drug-drug interactions via cytochrome oxidation inhibition.
- **Hyperbilirubinemia**
    - Atazanavir and indinavir are associated with an increase in unconjugated bilirubin, potentially causing jaundice.
    - In the course of atazanavir therapy, scleral icterus is a surrogate for patient compliance with ART therapy and otherwise does not require drug adjustment or intervention.
    - Indinavir may also cause asymptomatic hyperbilirubinemia.
- **Oral Contraceptives**
    - Nelfinavir and ritonavir decrease oral contraceptives' concentration through induction of their hepatic metabolism (induce CYP1A2, 2B6).
- **Darunavir Rash**
    - Darunavir therapy is associated with approximately a 5% risk of rash, which can become severe due to its sulfonamide moiety.
    - Patients with a history of sulfa allergy may exhibit a higher likelihood of rash due to darunavir.
- **Ritonavir Solution**
    - The oral solution preparation of ritonavir contains ethanol and should be avoided in patients concomitantly taking metronidazole, disulfiram, NMTT side chain containing cephalosporins (cefazolin, cefotetan), or calcium carbamide.
        - A combination of ritonavir solution with amprenavir suspension should also be avoided as amprenavir suspension contains propylene glycol.
- **Indinavir Nephrolithiasis**
    - Indinavir is poorly soluble at pH above 7.5, such as in urine, which increases the risk of crystalluria and nephrolithiasis.
        - Patients must maintain adequate hydration (approximately 2,000 mL/day) to provide sufficiently dilute urine to prevent crystalluria.
    - Atazanavir has been observed to precipitate in urine, increasing the risk of kidney stones.

High-Yield Fast-Fact

- **Indinavir Effects**
    - Indinavir therapy is associated with numerous dermatologic adverse events including alopecia, and ingrown toenails.

HIGH-YIELD BOARD EXAM ESSENTIALS

- **CLASSIC AGENTS:** Atazanavir, darunavir, fosamprenavir, indinavir, lopinavir, nelfinavir, ritonavir, saquinavir, tipranavir
- **DRUG CLASS:** Protease inhibitor
- **INDICATIONS:** HIV
- **MECHANISM:** Inhibit the processing of HIV viral proteins, forming immature, non-functional proteins incapable of infecting other cells.
- **SIDE EFFECTS:** GI intolerance (diarrhea), central fat redistribution (buffalo hump plus peripheral fat wasting), hyperglycemia (and diabetes), hyperlipidemia, PR and QT prolongation, and numerous drug-drug interactions via cytochrome oxidation inhibition.
- **CLINICAL PEARLS:** Atazanavir and indinavir are associated with an increase in unconjugated bilirubin, potentially causing jaundice due to inhibition of UGT1A1. In the course of atazanavir therapy, scleral icterus is a surrogate for patient compliance with ART therapy and otherwise does not require drug adjustment or intervention.

Combination Dosage Forms - Drug Class Review
High-Yield Med Reviews

Mechanism of Action: *See drug class-specific reviews*

Class Effects: Combination dosage forms allow for highly active antiretroviral therapeutic combinations while limiting pill burden on patients.

Generic Name	Brand Name	Main Indication(s) or Uses	Notes

Efavirenz, emtricitabine, tenofovir disoproxil fumarate	Atripla	▪ HIV	▪ **Dosing (Adult):**
			  – Oral 1 tablet daily
			▪ **Dosing (Peds):**
			  – For children at least 40 kg
			▪ **CYP450 Interactions:** see individual components
			▪ **Renal or Hepatic Dose Adjustments:**
			  – GFR less than 50 mL/minute - not recommended
			  – Child-Pugh class C - not recommended
			▪ **Dosage Forms:** Oral (tablet)

Bictegravir, emtricitabine, and tenofovir alafenamide	Biktarvy	▪ HIV	▪ **Dosing (Adult):**
			  – Oral 1 tablet daily
			▪ **Dosing (Peds):**
			  – For children at least 25 kg
			▪ **CYP450 Interactions:** see individual components
			▪ **Renal or Hepatic Dose Adjustments:**
			  – GFR less than 30 mL/minute - not recommended
			  – Child-Pugh class C - not recommended
			▪ **Dosage Forms:** Oral (tablet)

Cabotegravir, relpivarine	Cabenuva	▪ HIV	▪ **Dosing (Adult):**
			  – IM 600 mg / 900 mg (cabotegravir/rilpivirine) on last day of lead-in
			  – IM 400 mg / 600 mg (cabotegravir/rilpivirine) once monthly
			▪ **Dosing (Peds):**
			  – Not routinely used
			▪ **CYP450 Interactions:** Substrate P-gp
			▪ **Renal or Hepatic Dose Adjustments:** None
			▪ **Dosage Forms:** SQ extended-release suspension

Lamivudine and tenofovir disoproxil fumarate	Cimduo, Temixys	▪ HIV	▪ **Dosing (Adult):**
			  – Oral 1 tablet daily
			▪ **Dosing (Peds):**
			  – For children at least 35 kg
			▪ **CYP450 Interactions:** see individual components
			▪ **Renal or Hepatic Dose Adjustments:**
			  – GFR less than 50 mL/minute - not recommended
			▪ **Dosage Forms:** Oral (tablet)

Combination Dosage Forms - Drug Class Review
High-Yield Med Reviews

Generic Name	Brand Name	Main Indication(s) or Uses	Notes

Lamivudine and zidovudine	Combivir	▪ HIV	▪ **Dosing (Adult):**
			  – Oral 1 tablet twice daily
			▪ **Dosing (Peds):** Not routinely used
			▪ **CYP450 Interactions:** see individual components
			▪ **Renal or Hepatic Dose Adjustments:**
			  – ESRD - not recommended
			  – Child-Pugh class A, B or C - not recommended
			▪ **Dosage Forms:** Oral (tablet)

Emtricitabine, rilpivirine, tenofovir disoproxil fumarate	Complera	▪ HIV	▪ **Dosing (Adult):**
			  – Oral 1 tablet daily
			▪ **Dosing (Peds):**
			  – For children at least 35 kg
			▪ **CYP450 Interactions:** see individual components
			▪ **Renal or Hepatic Dose Adjustments:**
			  – GFR less than 50 mL/minute - not recommended
			▪ **Dosage Forms:** Oral (tablet)

Doravirine, lamivudine, and tenofovir diproxil fumarate	Delstrigo	▪ HIV	▪ **Dosing (Adult):**
			  – Oral 1 tablet daily
			▪ **Dosing (Peds):**
			  – For children at least 35 kg
			▪ **CYP450 Interactions:** see individual components
			▪ **Renal or Hepatic Dose Adjustments:**
			  – GFR less than 50 mL/minute - not recommended
			▪ **Dosage Forms:** Oral (tablet)

Emtricidabine and tenofovir alafenamide	Descovy	▪ HIV	▪ **Dosing (Adult):**
			  – Oral 1 tablet daily
			▪ **Dosing (Peds):**
			  – For children at least 25 kg
			▪ **CYP450 Interactions:** see individual components
			▪ **Renal or Hepatic Dose Adjustments:**
			  – GFR less than 30 mL/minute - not recommended
			  – Child-Pugh class C - not recommended
			▪ **Dosage Forms:** Oral (tablet)

Dolutegravir and lamivudine	Dovato	▪ HIV	▪ **Dosing (Adult):**
			  – Oral 1 tablet daily
			▪ **Dosing (Peds):**
			  – For children at least 35 kg
			▪ **CYP450 Interactions:** see individual components
			▪ **Renal or Hepatic Dose Adjustments:**
			  – GFR less than 50 mL/minute - not recommended
			  – Child-Pugh class C - not recommended
			▪ **Dosage Forms:** Oral (tablet)

Combination Dosage Forms - Drug Class Review
High-Yield Med Reviews

Generic Name	Brand Name	Main Indication(s) or Uses	Notes

Elvitegravir, cobicistat, emtricitabine, tenofovir alafenamide	Genvoya	▪ HIV	▪ **Dosing (Adult):**
			  – Oral 1 tablet daily
			▪ **Dosing (Peds):**
			  – Not routinely used
			▪ **CYP450 Interactions:** see individual components
			▪ **Renal or Hepatic Dose Adjustments:**
			  – GFR less than 50 mL/minute - not recommended
			  – Child-Pugh class C - not recommended
			▪ **Dosage Forms:** Oral (tablet)

Abacavir, lamivudine	Epzicom	▪ HIV	▪ **Dosing (Adult):**
			  – Oral 1 tablet daily
			▪ **Dosing (Peds):**
			  – For children at least 25 kg
			▪ **CYP450 Interactions:** see individual components
			▪ **Renal or Hepatic Dose Adjustments:**
			  – GFR less than 50 mL/minute - not recommended
			▪ **Dosage Forms:** Oral (tablet)

Atazanavir with cobicistat	Evotaz	▪ HIV	▪ **Dosing (Adult):**
			  – Oral 1 tablet daily
			▪ **Dosing (Peds):**
			  – Not routinely used
			▪ **CYP450 Interactions:** see individual components
			▪ **Renal or Hepatic Dose Adjustments:**
			  – ESRD or hepatic impairment - not recommended
			▪ **Dosage Forms:** Oral (tablet)

Dolutegravir, rilpivirine	Juluca	▪ HIV	▪ **Dosing (Adult):**
			  – Oral 1 tablet daily
			▪ **Dosing (Peds):**
			  – Not routinely used
			▪ **CYP450 Interactions:** see individual components
			▪ **Renal or Hepatic Dose Adjustments:**
			  – GFR less than 30 mL/minute - not recommended
			  – Child-Pugh class C - not recommended
			▪ **Dosage Forms:** Oral (tablet)

Emtricitabine, rilpivirine, tenofovir alafenamide	Odefsey	▪ HIV	▪ **Dosing (Adult):**
			  – Oral 1 tablet daily
			▪ **Dosing (Peds):**
			  – For children at least 35 kg
			▪ **CYP450 Interactions:** see individual components
			▪ **Renal or Hepatic Dose Adjustments:**
			  – GFR less than 30 mL/minute - not recommended
			▪ **Dosage Forms:** Oral (tablet)

Combination Dosage Forms - Drug Class Review
High-Yield Med Reviews

Generic Name	Brand Name	Main Indication(s) or Uses	Notes

Darunavir and cobicistat	Prezcobix	▪ HIV	▪ **Dosing (Adult):**
			  – Oral 1 tablet daily
			▪ **Dosing (Peds):** Not routinely used
			▪ **CYP450 Interactions:** see individual components
			▪ **Renal or Hepatic Dose Adjustments:**
			  – Child-Pugh class C - not recommended
			▪ **Dosage Forms:** Oral (tablet)

Elvitegravir, cobicistat, emtricitabine, tenofovir disoproxil fumarate	Stribild	▪ HIV	▪ **Dosing (Adult):**
			  – Oral 1 tablet daily
			▪ **Dosing (Peds):**
			  – For children at least 35 kg
			▪ **CYP450 Interactions:** see individual components
			▪ **Renal or Hepatic Dose Adjustments:**
			  – GFR less than 50 mL/minute - not recommended
			▪ **Dosage Forms:** Oral (tablet)

Efavirenz, lamivudine, tenofovir dioproxil fumarate	Symfi	▪ HIV	▪ **Dosing (Adult):**
			  – Oral 1 tablet daily
			▪ **Dosing (Peds):**
			  – For children at least 35 kg
			▪ **CYP450 Interactions:** see individual components
			▪ **Renal or Hepatic Dose Adjustments:**
			  – GFR 51 to 70 mL/minute - initial use not recommended
			  – GFR < 50 mL/minute - not recommended
			  – Child-Pugh class C - not recommended
			▪ **Dosage Forms:** Oral (tablet)

Darunavir, cobicistat, emtricitabine, tenofovir alafenamide	Symtuza	▪ HIV	▪ **Dosing (Adult):**
			  – Oral 1 tablet daily
			▪ **Dosing (Peds):**
			  – Not routinely used
			▪ **CYP450 Interactions:** see individual components
			▪ **Renal or Hepatic Dose Adjustments:**
			  – GFR less than 30 mL/minute - not recommended
			  – Child-Pugh class C - not recommended
			▪ **Dosage Forms:** Oral (tablet)

Abacavir, dolutegravir, lamivudine)	Triumeq	▪ HIV	▪ **Dosing (Adult):**
			  – Oral 1 tablet daily
			▪ **Dosing (Peds):**
			  – For children at least 40 kg
			▪ **CYP450 Interactions:** see individual components
			▪ **Renal or Hepatic Dose Adjustments:**
			  – GFR less than 50 mL/minute - not recommended
			  – Child-Pugh class C - contraindicated
			▪ **Dosage Forms:** Oral (tablet)

Combination Dosage Forms - Drug Class Review
High-Yield Med Reviews

Generic Name	Brand Name	Main Indication(s) or Uses	Notes

Abacavir, lamivudine, zidovudine	Trizivir	▪ HIV	▪ **Dosing (Adult):**
			  – Oral 1 tablet twice daily
			▪ **Dosing (Peds):**
			  – For children at least 40 kg
			▪ **CYP450 Interactions:** see individual components
			▪ **Renal or Hepatic Dose Adjustments:**
			  – GFR less than 50 mL/minute - not recommended
			  – Child-Pugh class C - contraindicated
			▪ **Dosage Forms:** Oral (tablet)

Emtricitabine and tenofovir disoproxil fumarate	Truvada	▪ HIV	▪ **Dosing (Adult):**
			  – Oral 1 tablet daily
			▪ **Dosing (Peds):**
			  – For children at least 35 kg
			▪ **CYP450 Interactions:** see individual components
			▪ **Renal or Hepatic Dose Adjustments:**
			  – GFR 30 to 49 mL/minute - q48h
			  – GFR less than 30 mL/minute - not recommended
			▪ **Dosage Forms:** Oral (tablet)

High-Yield Basic Pharmacology

- **Mechanism of Action**
  - Decreases renal phosphate excretion and 1,25(OH)2-D production by inhibition of FGF23.
- **Reverses Pathophysiology**
  - In patients with FGF23 related genetic diseases, burosumab reverses the inhibition of renal uptake of phosphate and promotes 1,25(OH)2D production.

Primary Net Benefit

- Burosumab is an orphan drug approved for X-linked hypophosphatemia, a rare autosomal dominant hypophosphatemia.

Anti-FGF23 MABs - Drug Class Review High-Yield Med Reviews			
Mechanism of Action: *Decreases renal phosphate excretion and 1,25(OH)2-D production by inhibition of FGF23*			
Class Effects: Injection site reaction, hypophosphatemia			
Generic Name	**Brand Name**	**Indication(s) or Uses**	**Notes**

Burosumab	Crysvita	• Tumor-induced osteomalacia
		• X-linked Hypophosphatemia
			• **Dosing (Adult):**
			  – SQ 0.5 to 1 mg/kg q4weeks, followed by serum phosphorus-guided dosing.
			    ▪ Maximum 90 mg/dose
			• **Dosing (Peds):**
			  – SQ 0.8 to 1 mg/kg/dose q2-4weeks, followed by serum phosphorus-guided dosing.
			    ▪ Maximum 90 mg/dose
			• **CYP450 Interactions:** None
			• **Renal or Hepatic Dose Adjustments:**
			  – GFR less than 30 mL/minute - Use contraindicated
			• **Dosage Forms:** Subcutaneous solution

High-Yield Clinical Knowledge

- **Use with Oral Phosphate or Vitamin D**
  - In patients with vitamin D-dependent rickets, supplementation with standard doses of vitamin D, in combination with phosphate supplementation and calcitriol are typically considered first-line interventions.
    - However, prolonged treatment can lead to secondary hyperparathyroidism.
  - Patients diagnosed with XLH who are started on burosumab cannot receive concomitant oral phosphate or active vitamin D analogs.
- **Injection Site Reactions**
  - Burosumab is typically administered via subcutaneous injection every 2 weeks and is associated with a relatively high incidence of self-limiting local injection site reactions.

High-Yield Fast-Facts

- **Autosomal dominant hypophosphatemia**
  - This occurs as a result of FGF23 gene mutations that result in decreased proteolysis and stabilized FGF23.
- **Tumor-Induced Osteomalacia**
  - Burosumab is also indicated for tumor-induced osteomalacia, which is similar in pathophysiology to autosomal dominant hypophosphatemia where tumors increase expression of FGF23.

HIGH-YIELD BOARD EXAM ESSENTIALS

- **CLASSIC AGENTS:** Burosumab
- **DRUG CLASS:** Anti-FGF23 MAB
- **INDICATIONS:** Tumor-induced osteomalacia, X-linked Hypophosphatemia
- **MECHANISM:** Decreases renal phosphate excretion and 1,25(OH)2-D production by inhibition of FGF23
- **SIDE EFFECTS:** Injection site reaction, hypophosphatemia
- **CLINICAL PEARLS:** In patients with FGF23 related genetic diseases, burosumab reverses the inhibition of renal uptake of phosphate and promotes 1,25(OH)2D production.

High-Yield Basic Pharmacology

- **Mechanism of Action**
  - Inhibit bone resorption by interfering with the activity of osteoclasts. Overall reduce bone turn over.
- **Active Remodeling Sites**
  - Bisphosphonates concentrate in areas of bone that undergo active remodeling and remain in the bone until it is remodeled.

Primary Net Benefit

- Increase bone density and reduce the risk of hip, spine, and other fractures, but increase the risk of atypical femur fractures, particularly with long-term use.

Bisphosphonates - Drug Class Review			
High-Yield Med Reviews			
Mechanism of Action: *Inhibit bone resorption by interfering with the activity of osteoclasts.*			
Class Effects: Increase bone density, risk for dyspepsia, GI ulceration, GI perforation, increase the risk of atypical femur fractures; poor overall oral bioavailability			
Generic Name	**Brand Name**	**Indication(s) or Uses**	**Notes**

Alendronate	Binosto, Fosamax	• Osteoporosis
		• Paget disease
			• **Dosing (Adult):**
			  – Oral 35 to 70 mg once weekly or 5 to 10 mg daily
			• **Dosing (Peds):**
			  – Less than 30 kg - 5 mg daily
			  – Between 30 and 40 kg - 5 to 10 mg daily
			  – Over 40 kg - 10 mg daily
			• **CYP450 Interactions:** None
			• **Renal or Hepatic Dose Adjustments:**
			  – GFR less than 35 mL/minute - Not recommended
			• **Dosage Forms:** Oral (solution, tablet, effervescent tablet)

Ibandronate	Boniva	• Osteoporosis	• **Dosing (Adult):**
			  – IV 2 to 6 mg over 1-2 hours q3-4weeks, up to 4 years
			  – Oral 150 mg monthly
			• **Dosing (Peds):**
			  – Not routinely used
			• **CYP450 Interactions:** None
			• **Renal or Hepatic Dose Adjustments:**
			  – GFR less than 30 mL/minute - Not recommended
			• **Dosage Forms:** Oral (tablet), IV (solution)

		Bisphosphonates - Drug Class Review	
		High-Yield Med Reviews	
Generic Name	**Brand Name**	**Indication(s) or Uses**	**Notes**
Pamidronate	Aredia	<ul><li>Hypercalcemia of malignancy</li><li>Osteolytic bone metastases/lesions</li><li>Paget disease</li></ul>	<ul><li>**Dosing (Adult):**<ul><li>– IV 60 to 90 mg once or up to monthly</li></ul></li><li>**Dosing (Peds):**<ul><li>– IV 0.25 to 2 mg/kg/dose<ul><li>▪ Maximum 90 mg/dose</li></ul></li></ul></li><li>**CYP450 Interactions:** None</li><li>**Renal or Hepatic Dose Adjustments:**<ul><li>– GFR less than 30 mL/minute - Not recommended, or consider a reduced dose</li></ul></li><li>**Dosage Forms:** IV (solution)</li></ul>
Risedronate	Actonel, Atelvia	<ul><li>Osteoporosis</li><li>Paget disease</li></ul>	<ul><li>**Dosing (Adult):**<ul><li>– Oral 5 mg daily, 35 once weekly, or 150 mg once monthly</li></ul></li><li>**Dosing (Peds):**<ul><li>– Not routinely used</li></ul></li><li>**CYP450 Interactions:** None</li><li>**Renal or Hepatic Dose Adjustments:**<ul><li>– GFR less than 30 mL/minute - Not recommended</li></ul></li><li>**Dosage Forms:** Oral (tablet)</li></ul>
Zoledronic acid	Reclast, Zometa	<ul><li>Hypercalcemia of malignancy</li><li>Multiple myeloma</li><li>Osteolytic bone metastases/lesions</li><li>Osteoporosis</li><li>Paget disease</li></ul>	<ul><li>**Dosing (Adult):**<ul><li>– IV 4 mg q1-26weeks</li><li>– IV 5 mg q2years or as a single dose once</li></ul></li><li>**Dosing (Peds):**<ul><li>– IV 0.0125to 0.05 mg/kg/dose<ul><li>▪ Maximum 4 mg/dose</li></ul></li></ul></li><li>**CYP450 Interactions:** None</li><li>**Renal or Hepatic Dose Adjustments:**<ul><li>– GFR less than 35 mL/minute - Contraindicated</li></ul></li><li>**Dosage Forms:** IV (concentrate solution, solution)</li></ul>

High-Yield Clinical Knowledge

- **Oral Absorption**
  - All bisphosphonates are poorly absorbed from the intestines and have bioavailabilities of less than 1% for alendronate and risedronate.
  - Absorption can be further reduced if coadministered with divalent cations (calcium, magnesium), other antacids, or with oral iron.
- **Elimination Characteristics**
  - As a result of the large volume of distribution into bone and limited re-distribution out of bone, bisphosphonates undergo minimal hepatic elimination and are eliminated in the kidneys as unchanged molecules.
- **Esophageal Adverse Events**
  - Patients must be instructed to take oral bisphosphonates on an empty stomach with at least eight ounces of water and remain upright for 30 to 60 minutes.
    - Specific forms of risedronate, specifically the delayed-release preparation, may be taken 30 minutes after a morning meal.

  – This is to minimize GI adverse effects that range in severity from heartburn to esophageal irritation to GI ulceration, perforation, or rupture leading to critical GI bleeding.

High-Yield Fast-Facts

- **Fractures and Osteonecrosis**
  - Bisphosphonates are associated with an increased risk of osteonecrosis of the jaw (albeit rare) and an increased risk of stress fractures in the femoral shaft's lateral cortex.
  - These risks are a component of the rationale to limit bisphosphonate therapy to approximately 3-5 years (perhaps even shorter), as the risks begin to outweigh the benefits.
    - The benefits of bisphosphonates on bone mineral density persist for 4-5 years and are sustained for longer periods of time even after discontinuation.
- **Elimination Half-Life**
  - The elimination half-life of these drugs is influenced by their distribution and elimination characteristics and is profoundly long.
  - The terminal half-life of bisphosphonates is approximately 11 *years*.
- **Renal Disease**
  - Patients with an estimated creatinine clearance of less than 30 to 35 mL/minute (drug dependent) must not receive bisphosphonates.

HIGH-YIELD BOARD EXAM ESSENTIALS

- **CLASSIC AGENTS:** Alendronate, ibandronate, pamidronate, risedronate, zoledronic acid
- **DRUG CLASS:** Bisphosphonates
- **INDICATIONS:** Hypercalcemia of malignancy, multiple myeloma, osteolytic bone metastases/lesions, osteoporosis, or Paget disease
- **MECHANISM:** Inhibit bone resorption by interfering with the activity of osteoclasts.
- **SIDE EFFECTS:** Dyspepsia, GI ulceration, GI perforation, increase the risk of atypical femur fractures
- **CLINICAL PEARLS:** Bisphosphonates have almost no oral absorption and thus have to be given parenterally or on empty stomach with water. They are also associated with an increased risk of osteonecrosis of the jaw (albeit rare) and an increased risk of stress fractures in the femoral shaft's lateral cortex. These risks are a component of the rationale to limit bisphosphonate therapy to approximately 3-5 years (perhaps even shorter), as the risks begin to outweigh the benefits.

High-Yield Basic Pharmacology

- **Mechanism of Action**
  - Increase sensitivity for calcium-sensing receptor (CaSr) receptor for activation by extracellular calcium, leading to reduced parathyroid hormone secretion and serum calcium concentrations.
- **Corrected Calcium**
  - Serum albumin must be followed to account for falsely low laboratory calcium in the setting of hypoalbuminemia.

Primary Net Benefit

- Pharmacologic interventions for secondary hyperparathyroidism in patients on dialysis, additional indications for cinacalcet in the management of parathyroid carcinoma, and primary hyperparathyroidism where parathyroidectomy cannot be performed.

Calcimimetics - Drug Class Review			
High-Yield Med Reviews			
Mechanism of Action: *Increase sensitivity for calcium-sensing receptor (CaSr) receptor for activation by extracellular calcium, leading to reduced parathyroid hormone secretion and serum calcium concentrations.*			
Class Effects: QT prolongation, GI bleed, hypocalcemia			
Generic Name	**Brand Name**	**Indication(s) or Uses**	**Notes**

Cinacalcet	Sensipar	• Hyperparathyroidism (primary and secondary)
		• Parathyroid carcinoma
			• **Dosing (Adult):**
			  – Oral 30 to 120 mg q6-24h
			• **Dosing (Peds):**
			  – Oral 0.2 mg/kg/dose daily titrated q4weeks to target intact parathyroid hormone 100-300 pg/mL
			    • Maximum 180 mg/day or 2.5 mg/kg/dose, whichever is lower
			• **CYP450 Interactions:** Substrate CYP1A2, 2D6, 3A4; Inhibits CYP2D6
			• **Renal or Hepatic Dose Adjustments:**
			  – Child-Pugh class B or C - Close monitoring
			• **Dosage Forms:** Oral (tablet)

Etelcalcetide	Parsabiv	• Hyperparathyroidism (secondary)	• **Dosing (Adult):**
			  – IV 5 mg IV three times per week
			    • Adjusted up to 15 mg three times weekly
			• **Dosing (Peds):**
			  – Not routinely used
			• **CYP450 Interactions:** None
			• **Renal or Hepatic Dose Adjustments:** None
			• **Dosage Forms:** IV (solution)

High-Yield Clinical Knowledge

- **Drug Interactions**
    - Cinacalcet is a substrate of CYP1A2, 2D6, 3A4, and inhibits CYP2D6.
    - Numerous narrow therapeutic agents, including amitriptyline, flecainide, thioridazine, and vinblastine, are at risk of reduced elimination and toxicities combined with cinacalcet.
    - Etelcalcetide is not a substrate or inhibitor of CYP 450.
- **Baseline Calcium**
    - Cinacalcet and etelcalcetide cannot be started without first assessing a baseline serum calcium.
    - Serum calcium must be 8.4 mg/dL or above to safely initiate cinacalcet.

High-Yield Fast-Facts

- **Food Effect**
    - The bioavailability of cinacalcet is increased significantly when taken with food, and patients should always be educated to take cinacalcet with food.
- **Dose Titration**
    - Cinacalcet must be started at a dose of 30 mg daily and titrated every 2 to 4 weeks to either a maximum of 180 mg/day or goal PTH level is reached.
    - Etelcalcetide follows a simpler titration and is administered at the end of dialysis (three times weekly) as it is removed by dialysis.

HIGH-YIELD BOARD EXAM ESSENTIALS
- **CLASSIC AGENTS:** Cinacalcet, etelcalcetide
- **DRUG CLASS:** Calcimimetics
- **INDICATIONS:** Hyperparathyroidism (primary and secondary), parathyroid carcinoma
- **MECHANISM:** Increase sensitivity for CaSr receptor for activation by extracellular calcium, leading to reduced parathyroid hormone secretion and serum calcium concentrations
- **SIDE EFFECTS:** QT prolongation, GI bleed, hypocalcemia
- **CLINICAL PEARLS:** Cinacalcet is a substrate of CYP1A2, 2D6, 3A4, and inhibits CYP2D6. Numerous narrow therapeutic agents, including amitriptyline, flecainide, thioridazine, and vinblastine, are at risk of reduced elimination and toxicities combined with cinacalcet.

High-Yield Basic Pharmacology

- **Mechanism of Action**
  - It inhibits osteoclast resorption and reduces renal calcium and phosphate (as well as sodium, potassium, and magnesium) reabsorption.
- **Endogenous Calcitonin**
  - Calcitonin is normally secreted by the thyroid gland, specifically from the parafollicular cells.
  - It consists of a single-chain peptide with 32 amino acids, with specific attention to the disulfide bond between positions 1 and 7, necessary for its biologic activity.

Primary Net Benefit

- Lowers serum calcium and phosphate through actions on both the bone and kidneys.

Calcitonin - Drug Class Review			
High-Yield Med Reviews			
Mechanism of Action: *Inhibits osteoclast resorption and reduces renal calcium and phosphate (as well as sodium, potassium, and magnesium) reabsorption.*			
Class Effects: Lowers serum calcium and phosphate, risk for tachyphylaxis, allergy (cross sensitivity to Salmon allergy)			
Generic Name	**Brand Name**	**Indication(s) or Uses**	**Notes**

Calcitonin	Miacalcin	• Hypercalcemia
		• Osteogenesis imperfecta
		• Osteoporosis
		• Paget disease
			• **Dosing (Adult):**
			  – IM/SQ 4 to 8 units/kg q12h
			  – IM/SQ 100 units daily
			  – Intranasal 200 units in one nostril daily
			• **Dosing (Peds):**
			  – IM/SQ 2 units/kg/dose three times weekly
			• **CYP450 Interactions:** None
			• **Renal or Hepatic Dose Adjustments:** None
			• **Dosage Forms:** Injection solution, Nasal solution

High-Yield Clinical Knowledge

- **Osteoporosis**
  - The current role of calcitonin for postmenopausal osteoporosis is limited and reserved for salvage therapy.
  - Compared to other therapies, calcitonin only reduces the risk of vertebral fractures.
- **Intranasal Formulation**
  - Calcitonin is only available in an IV formulation or an intranasal formulation.
  - Patients report low satisfaction with and do not prefer intranasal administration, but it has a limited role for short-term relief of vertebral fracture pain.
- **Tachyphylaxis**
  - Salmon calcitonin is associated with the development of antibodies, leading to tachyphylaxis with use beyond four months.

High-Yield Fast-Facts

- **British Medical Research Council**
  - Although calcitonin is a relatively small single-chain peptide, it can be present in heterogeneous forms and sizes.

- As a result of this heterogeneity, calcitonin's activity is compared to a standard maintained by the British Medical Research Council, which expresses calcitonin activity in MRC units.
- **Salmon Calcitonin**
  - Salmon calcitonin, the commonly used product, has a much longer half-life of 50 minutes than human calcitonin (half-life of 10 minutes).

HIGH-YIELD BOARD EXAM ESSENTIALS

- **CLASSIC AGENTS:** Calcitonin
- **DRUG CLASS:** Calcitonin
- **INDICATIONS:** Hypercalcemia, osteogenesis imperfecta, osteoporosis, Paget disease
- **MECHANISM:** It inhibits osteoclast resorption and reduces renal calcium and phosphate (as well as sodium, potassium, and magnesium) reabsorption.
- **SIDE EFFECTS:** Hypocalcemia, tachyphylaxis, allergy (cross sensitivity to Salmon allergy)
- **CLINICAL PEARLS:**
  - The IM or SQ (not intranasal) dosage formulation is used for hypercalcemia of malignancy after failure of IV fluids to reduce calcium.
  - The current role of intranasal calcitonin for postmenopausal osteoporosis is limited and reserved for salvage therapy. Compared to other therapies, calcitonin only reduces the risk of vertebral fractures.

High-Yield Basic Pharmacology

- **Mechanism of Action**
  - Calcium is an essential element necessary for a range of physiologic functions, including neuromuscular activity, endocrine regulation, coagulation, bone metabolism, and cardiac conduction.
- **Calcium Distribution**
  - The vast majority (about 99%) of the body's calcium stores are located in the bone.
  - Factors affecting calcium concentrations include the parathyroid hormone, phosphorus, vitamin D, and calcitonin.

Primary Net Benefit

- Calcium is the most abundant mineral in the body, required for normal functioning, but less than 1% of the total body calcium is located outside the bone.

Calcium Salts - Drug Class Review			
High-Yield Med Reviews			
Mechanism of Action: *Calcium is an essential element necessary for a range of physiologic functions, including neuromuscular activity, endocrine regulation, coagulation, bone metabolism, and cardiac conduction.*			
Class Effects: Increase serum calcium, risk for bloating, constipation.			
Generic Name	**Brand Name**	**Indication(s) or Uses**	**Notes**

Calcium acetate	Calphron Eliphos PhosLo Phoslyra	- Hyperphosphatemia	- **Dosing (Adult):**
			  - Oral 1,334 to 2,668 mg qmeal
			- **Dosing (Peds):**
			  - Oral 667 to 1,000 mg qmeal
			- **CYP450 Interactions:** None
			- **Renal or Hepatic Dose Adjustments:** None
			- **Dosage Forms:** Oral (capsule, solution, tablet)

Calcium carbonate	Antacid Cal-Carb Caltrate Florical Maalox Oysco Tums	- Antacid
		- Calcium supplementation
		- Hyperphosphatemia
		- Hypoparathyroidism
			- **Dosing (Adult):**
			  - Oral 500 to 8,000 mg per day
			    - Maximum for CKD 2,000 mg/day
			- **Dosing (Peds):**
			  - Oral 375 to 7,500 mg/day
			    - Maximum for CKD 2,000 mg/day
			- **CYP450 Interactions:** None
			- **Renal or Hepatic Dose Adjustments:** None
			- **Dosage Forms:** Oral (capsule, powder, suspension, tablet)

Calcium chloride	Calciject	- Cardiac arrest
		- Hyperkalemia
		- Hypocalcemia
		- Hypermagnesemia
			- **Dosing (Adult):**
			  - IV 20 mg/kg, maximum 1 to 2 g/dose q10-20minutes
			- **Dosing (Peds):**
			  - IV 20 mg/kg, max 1 g/dose q10-20minutes
			  - IV 0.5 to 2 mEq/kg/day
			- **CYP450 Interactions:** None
			- **Renal or Hepatic Dose Adjustments:** None
			- **Dosage Forms:** IV (solution)

Calcium Salts - Drug Class Review
High-Yield Med Reviews

Generic Name	Brand Name	Indication(s) or Uses	Notes

Calcium citrate	Calcitrate	• Hypoparathyroidism	• **Dosing (Adult):**
			  – Oral 200 to 1,000 mg q8-12h
			• **Dosing (Peds):**
			  – Oral (elemental calcium) 45 to 65 mg/kg/day in 4 divided doses
			• **CYP450 Interactions:** None
			• **Renal or Hepatic Dose Adjustments:** None
			• **Dosage Forms:** Oral (tablet)

Calcium glubionate	Calcionate	• Dietary supplement	• **Dosing (Adult):**
			  – Oral 345 mg q6-8h
			• **Dosing (Peds):**
			  – Oral 115 to 345 mg q4-8h
			    • Extra info if needed
			• **CYP450 Interactions:** None
			• **Renal or Hepatic Dose Adjustments:** None
			• **Dosage Forms:** Oral (syrup)

Calcium gluconate	Cal-Glu	• Cardiac arrest
		• Hyperkalemia
		• Hypocalcemia
		• Hypermagnesemia
			• **Dosing (Adult):**
			  – IV 60 mg/kg q10-20minutes as needed or 60 to 120 mg/kg/hour infusion
			  – IV 1,500 to 3,000 mg IV over 2-5 minutes
			  – IV 1,000 to 4,000 mg over 2-4 hours
			  – Oral 500 to 4,000 mg/day
			• **Dosing (Peds):**
			  – IV 0.5 to 4 mEq/kg/day (TPN)
			  – IV IV 60 mg/kg (maximum 3,000 mg/dose) q10-20minutes as needed
			  – Oral 500 mg/kg/day divided in 4 doses (maximum 1,000 mg/dose)
			• **CYP450 Interactions:** None
			• **Renal or Hepatic Dose Adjustments:** None
			• **Dosage Forms:** IV (solution), Oral (capsule, tablet)

Calcium lactate	Cal-Lac	• Dietary supplementation	• **Dosing (Adult):**
			  – Oral 252 mg daily
			• **Dosing (Peds):**
			  – Oral (elemental calcium) 45 to 65 mg/kg/day in 4 divided doses
			• **CYP450 Interactions:** None
			• **Renal or Hepatic Dose Adjustments:** None
			• **Dosage Forms:** Oral (capsule, tablet)

High-Yield Clinical Knowledge

- **Serum Calcium Correction**
  - In patients with hypoalbuminemia (albumin less than 4.0), a corrected serum calcium calculation must account for changes in free or active calcium concentrations.
  - Corrected calcium = measured calcium (mg/dL) + 0.8 x [4.0 - albumin {g/dL}].

- This calculation must be correlated clinically as the hypocalcemia may exist in the critically ill, despite normal albumin.
- **Dietary Requirements**
  - Most healthy adults require between 1,000 to 1,200 mg of calcium daily, which should be combined with
  - The elemental calcium in calcium salts must be taken into consideration when determining the daily intake of calcium.
- **GI Complaints**
  - The most common adverse event with oral calcium intake is bloating and constipation but selecting an alternative calcium salt may alleviate these effects.
  - Calcium carbonate is associated with the highest likelihood of constipation.

High-Yield Fast-Facts

- **Fluoride Exposure**
  - Calcium chloride or calcium gluconate can be used topically for the treatment of hydrofluoric acid burns.
- **Thiazides and Lithium**
  - Thiazide diuretics and lithium can cause an increased renal tubular reabsorption of calcium.
- **Drug-Induced Hypocalcemia**
  - Numerous medications may chelate calcium or increase renal elimination, lowering serum levels.
    - Furosemide (and other loop diuretics) increase calcium elimination, while sodium phosphate, EDTA, and foscarnet are common causes of chelation.
  - Agents used for osteoporosis or parathyroid disease can also decrease serum calcium.
    - Calcitonin, cinacalcet, bisphosphonates, and denosumab.
  - Aminoglycosides are a rare cause of hypocalcemia as a secondary effect due to their hypomagnesemic effects.

HIGH-YIELD BOARD EXAM ESSENTIALS
- **CLASSIC AGENTS:** Calcium chloride, calcium gluconate, calcium acetate, calcium carbonate, calcium citrate, calcium glubionate, calcium lactate
- **DRUG CLASS:** Calcium salts
- **INDICATIONS:** Antacid, cardiac arrest, calcium supplementation, hyperphosphatemia, hypoparathyroidism, hypocalcemia, hypermagnesemia
- **MECHANISM:** Calcium is an essential element necessary for a range of physiologic functions, including neuromuscular activity, endocrine regulation, coagulation, bone metabolism, and cardiac conduction.
- **SIDE EFFECTS:** Bloating, constipation
- **CLINICAL PEARLS:**
  - Ca chloride has 3 times the amount of elemental calcium and should mainly be given by central line (or IO in cardiac arrest) whereas Ca gluconate has less elemental Ca can be given by peripheral IV.
  - In patients with hypoalbuminemia (albumin less than 4.0), a corrected serum calcium calculation must account for changes in free or active calcium concentrations. Corrected calcium = measured calcium (mg/dL) + 0.8 x [4.0 - albumin {g/dL}].

High-Yield Basic Pharmacology

- **Mechanism of Action**
  - Mimic the effects of endogenous parathyroid hormone (PTH), causing an anabolic effect and increasing bone resorption.
- **Synthetic PTHrP Analog**
  - As a synthetic analog of parathyroid hormone-related protein (PTHrP), abaloparatide exerts a PTH mimicking effect and exerts an increased anabolic effect.

Primary Net Benefit

- Alternate therapies for osteoporosis that reduce the risk of vertebra but not hip fractures.

Parathyroid Hormone Analogs - Drug Class Review High-Yield Med Reviews			
Mechanism of Action: *Mimic the effects of endogenous parathyroid hormone (PTH), causing an anabolic effect and increasing bone resorption.*			
Class Effects: Improve bone density, risk for discontinuation effect, osteosarcoma, orthostatic hypotension.			
Generic Name	**Brand Name**	**Indication(s) or Uses**	**Notes**
Abaloparatide	Tymlos	• Osteoporosis	• **Dosing (Adult):** – SQ 80 mcg once daily • **Dosing (Peds):** – Not routinely used • **CYP450 Interactions:** None • **Renal or Hepatic Dose Adjustments:** text • **Dosage Forms:** Subcutaneous Pen-injector
Parathyroid Hormone	Natpara	• Hypoparathyroidism	• **Dosing (Adult):** – SQ 25 to 100 mcg once daily • **Dosing (Peds):** – Not routinely used • **CYP450 Interactions:** None • **Renal or Hepatic Dose Adjustments:** text • **Dosage Forms:** Subcutaneous cartridge
Teriparatide	Forteo	• Osteoporosis	• **Dosing (Adult):** – SQ 20 mcg once daily • **Dosing (Peds):** – Not routinely used • **CYP450 Interactions:** None • **Renal or Hepatic Dose Adjustments:** text • **Dosage Forms:** Subcutaneous Pen-injector

High-Yield Clinical Knowledge

- **Discontinuation Effect**
  - The parathyroid hormone analogs must be continued to reduce the risk of vertebral and nonvertebral fractures in postmenopausal women.

- If these agents are discontinued for any reason, alternative antiresorptive therapy should be started to maintain a reduced fracture risk.
- **Osteosarcoma Risk**
  - Teriparatide and abaloparatide therapy is limited to 2 years of (cumulative) treatment to reduce the risk of osteosarcoma.
- **Orthostatic Hypotension**
  - The parathyroid hormone analogs are all administered parenterally and may cause orthostatic hypotension after administration.
  - Patients should be educated to administer the first number of doses while sitting or lying down until their patient-specific response can be appreciated.

High-Yield Fast-Facts

- **Fracture Repair**
  - Teriparatide has been used to aid in the repair of fractures and for the treatment of fracture nonunions.
  - Numerous professional athletes have used teriparatide off-label for this use and to speed recovery from fractures.

HIGH-YIELD BOARD EXAM ESSENTIALS
- **CLASSIC AGENTS:** Abaloparatide, parathyroid hormone, teriparatide
- **DRUG CLASS:** Parathyroid hormone analogs
- **INDICATIONS:** Hypoparathyroidism, osteoporosis
- **MECHANISM:** Mimic the effects of endogenous parathyroid hormone (PTH), causing an anabolic effect and increasing bone resorption.
- **SIDE EFFECTS:** Discontinuation effect, osteosarcoma, orthostatic hypotension
- **CLINICAL PEARLS:**
  - Although the parathyroid hormone analogs do not have a direct CYP450 effect, but there exist clinically relevant pharmacodynamic interactions, specifically with digoxin.
  - Abaloparatide and teriparatide are associated with a high incidence (3.4 to 6.4%) of hypercalcemia, leading to toxic effects of digoxin.

High-Yield Basic Pharmacology

- **Mechanism of Action**
  - Human monoclonal antibody (MAB) that binds to and inhibits the ability of RANKL from binding to the RANK receptor, preventing the activity and maturation of osteoclasts.
- **Rapid Onset**
  - Denosumab is administered as a subcutaneous injection once every six months.
  - However, its onset of action is relatively rapid and occurs within 12 hours of administration, with a peak effect after ten days.

Primary Net Benefit

- Used as a first-line agent management of osteoporosis in men and women who are at a high risk of fracture to decrease the risk of vertebral, hip, and nonvertebral fractures.

<table>
<tr><td colspan="4">RANKL Inhibitor - Drug Class Review
High-Yield Med Reviews</td></tr>
<tr><td colspan="4">Mechanism of Action: Human monoclonal antibody (MAB) that binds to and inhibits the ability of RANKL from binding to the RANK receptor, preventing the activity and maturation of osteoclasts.</td></tr>
<tr><td colspan="4">Class Effects: Increase bone density, risk for hypocalcemia, bone fractures, osteonecrosis.</td></tr>
<tr><td>Generic Name</td><td>Brand Name</td><td>Indication(s) or Uses</td><td>Notes</td></tr>
<tr>
<td>Denosumab</td>
<td>Xgeva</td>
<td>
<ul>
<li>Bone metastases from solid tumors</li>
<li>Giant cell tumor of bone</li>
<li>Hypercalcemia of malignancy</li>
<li>Multiple myeloma</li>
</ul>
</td>
<td>
<ul>
<li>Dosing (Adult):
  <ul><li>SQ 120 mg q4weeks
    <ul><li>During the first month, administer an additional 120 mg on days 8 and 15</li></ul>
  </li></ul>
</li>
<li>Dosing (Peds):
  <ul><li>Adolescents over 45 kg, use adult dosing</li></ul>
</li>
<li>CYP450 Interactions: None</li>
<li>Renal or Hepatic Dose Adjustments: None</li>
<li>Dosage Forms: Subcutaneous solution</li>
</ul>
</td>
</tr>
<tr>
<td>Denosumab</td>
<td>Prolia</td>
<td>
<ul><li>Osteoporosis</li></ul>
</td>
<td>
<ul>
<li>Dosing (Adult):
  <ul><li>SQ 60 mg q6months</li></ul>
</li>
<li>Dosing (Peds):
  <ul><li>Not routinely used</li></ul>
</li>
<li>CYP450 Interactions: None</li>
<li>Renal or Hepatic Dose Adjustments: None</li>
<li>Dosage Forms: Subcutaneous solution, prefilled syringe</li>
</ul>
</td>
</tr>
</table>

High-Yield Clinical Knowledge

- **Hypocalcemia**
  - Before starting denosumab, serum calcium (corrected) levels must be above the lower limit of normal, as denosumab may cause severe, life-threatening hypocalcemia.
  - Risk factors for severe hypocalcemia, aside from pre-existing hypocalcemia, includes renal impairment.
- **Duration of Therapy**
  - Denosumab has been studied for use in patients for up to 10 years in duration.

- Compared to other osteoporosis treatment agents, such as bisphosphonates that are limited to 5 years cumulative therapy, denosumab offers a long-term treatment strategy.
- **Fractures and Osteonecrosis**
  - Although denosumab also carries warnings for atypical femoral fractures and osteonecrosis of the jaw, there is limited high-quality evidence suggesting an unacceptable risk.
    - Bisphosphonates are associated with an increased risk of osteonecrosis of the jaw and an increased risk of stress fractures in the femoral shaft's lateral cortex.

High-Yield Fast-Facts

- **SQ Administration**
  - If patients are not comfortable or otherwise unable to administer denosumab, pharmacists in some states can administer denosumab to patients.

HIGH-YIELD BOARD EXAM ESSENTIALS
- **CLASSIC AGENTS:** Denosumab
- **DRUG CLASS:** RANKL inhibitor
- **INDICATIONS:** Bone metastases from solid tumors, giant cell tumor of bone, hypercalcemia of malignancy, multiple myeloma, osteoporosis
- **MECHANISM:** Human monoclonal antibody (MAB) that binds to and inhibits the ability of RANKL from binding to the RANK receptor, preventing the activity and maturation of osteoclasts.
- **SIDE EFFECTS:** Hypocalcemia, bone fractures, osteonecrosis
- **CLINICAL PEARLS:**
  - Before starting denosumab, serum calcium (corrected) levels must be above the lower limit of normal, as denosumab may cause severe, life-threatening hypocalcemia.
  - Risk of developing osteonecrosis is present.

High-Yield Basic Pharmacology

- **Mechanism of Action**
  - A humanized monoclonal antibody binds to sclerostin, thereby increasing bone formation and reducing bone resorption.
- **Anabolic Agent**
  - Romosozumab is considered an anabolic agent but works primarily by binding sclerostin, promoting Wnt signaling mediated gene transcription and increased osteoblast formation, differentiation, and bone matrix growth.

Primary Net Benefit

- Significantly reduces the risk of fracture in postmenopausal women at high risk of fractures compared to alendronate alone.

Sclerostin Inhibitor - Drug Class Review			
High-Yield Med Reviews			
Mechanism of Action: *A humanized monoclonal antibody binds to sclerostin, increasing bone formation and reducing bone resorption.*			
Class Effects: Increased risk of CV events, osteonecrosis of the jaw, hypocalcemia, increased risk of fractures.			
Generic Name	**Brand Name**	**Indication(s) or Uses**	**Notes**

Romosozumab	Evenity	• Osteoporosis	• **Dosing (Adult):**
			  – SQ 210 mg as two 105 mg injections once monthly for 12 months
			• **Dosing (Peds):**
			  – Not routinely used
			• **CYP450 Interactions:** None
			• **Renal or Hepatic Dose Adjustments:** None
			• **Dosage Forms:** Subcutaneous prefilled syringe

High-Yield Clinical Knowledge

- **Cardiovascular Risk**
  - Romosozumab was associated with a higher risk of cardiovascular vents, as observed in the ARCH trial (details below) and BRIDGE trial.
    - Of note, there was no such observation in terms of cardiovascular events in the FRAME trial that compared romosozumab to placebo.
  - Romosozumab is contraindicated in patients who have had a stroke or MI within the past year.
- **Osteonecrosis of The Jaw**
  - Romosozumab has also been associated with an increased risk of osteonecrosis of the jaw; an effect also linked to bisphosphonate therapy.

High-Yield Fast-Facts

- **Limited Treatment**
  - According to the FDA-approved indication, romosozumab is currently limited to a one-year (or 12 months) treatment course.

- **Adverse Events**
    - Other relevant adverse events associated with romosozumab include hypocalcemia, an increased risk of femoral fractures, and off-target TNF-alfa mediated aggravation of arthritis.

HIGH-YIELD BOARD EXAM ESSENTIALS
- **CLASSIC AGENTS:** Romosozumab
- **DRUG CLASS:** Sclerostin Inhibitor
- **INDICATIONS:** Osteoporosis
- **MECHANISM:** A humanized monoclonal antibody binds to sclerostin, thereby increasing bone formation and reducing bone resorption.
- **SIDE EFFECTS:** Increased risk of CV events, osteonecrosis of the jaw, hypocalcemia, increased risk of fractures
- **CLINICAL PEARLS:** According to the FDA-approved indication, romosozumab is currently limited to a one-year (or 12 months) treatment course.

High-Yield Basic Pharmacology

- **Mechanism of Action**
  - Competitive and partial agonist inhibitor (mixed agonist/antagonist effects) of estradiol at the estrogen receptor.
  - **Tamoxifen Metabolites**
    - Tamoxifen is metabolized by CYP2D6 to its more active component, endoxifen.
  - **Raloxifene Selectivity**
    - Raloxifene is also a mixed agonist/antagonist of estrogen but has selective activity on lipids and bone, but not on the endometrium or breast tissue.

Primary Net Benefit

- SERMs are used in palliative therapy in breast cancer and in breast cancer prevention in high-risk postmenopausal women.

Selective Estrogen Receptor Modulators - Drug Class Review			
High-Yield Med Reviews			
Mechanism of Action: *Competitive and partial agonist inhibitor (mixed agonist/antagonist effects) of estradiol at the estrogen receptor.*			
Class Effects: Increased risk of DVT/PE, endometrial carcinoma, visual disturbances, hot flashes			
Generic Name	**Brand Name**	**Indication(s) or Uses**	**Notes**

Clomiphene	Clomid Serophene	• Ovulation induction	• **Dosing (Adult):**
			  – 50 mg daily x 5 days, followed by 100 mg x 5 days only if ovulation does not occur
			    • Maximum 100 mg/day for 5 doses up to 6 cycles
			• **Dosing (Peds):**
			  – Not routinely used
			• **CYP450 Interactions:** None
			• **Renal or Hepatic Dose Adjustments:**
			  – Hepatic disease or dysfunction - Contraindicated
			• **Dosage Forms:** Oral (tablet)

Bazedoxifene and Estrogens (conjugated, equine)	Duavee	• Osteoporosis
		• Vasomotor symptoms associated with menopause
			• **Dosing (Adult):**
			  – Oral bazedoxifene/estrogens 20mg/0.45 mg
			• **Dosing (Peds):**
			  – Not routinely used
			• **CYP450 Interactions:** Substrate CYP1A2, 2A6, 2B6, 2C19, 2C9, 2D6, 2E1, 3A4; Inhibits CYP1A2
			• **Renal or Hepatic Dose Adjustments:**
			  – Hepatic disease or dysfunction - Contraindicated
			• **Dosage Forms:** Oral (tablet)

Selective Estrogen Receptor Modulators - Drug Class Review
High-Yield Med Reviews

Generic Name	Brand Name	Indication(s) or Uses	Notes

Fulvestrant	Faslodex	• Breast cancer treatment	• **Dosing (Adult):**
			  – IM 500 mg on days 1, 15, then once monthly
			• **Dosing (Peds):**
			  – IM 4 mg/kg once monthly
			• **CYP450 Interactions:** Substrate 3A4
			• **Renal or Hepatic Dose Adjustments:** None
			• **Dosage Forms:** IM solution

Ospemifene	Osphena	• Dyspareunia
		• Vaginal dryness
			• **Dosing (Adult):**
			  – Oral 60 mg daily
			• **Dosing (Peds):**
			  – Not routinely used
			• **CYP450 Interactions:** Substrate CYP2C19, 2C9, 3A4
			• **Renal or Hepatic Dose Adjustments:**
			  – Child-Pugh class C - use not recommended
			• **Dosage Forms:** Oral (tablet)

Raloxifene	Evista	• Osteoporosis
		• Risk reduction for invasive breast cancer in postmenopausal females
			• **Dosing (Adult):**
			  – Oral 60 mg daily
			• **Dosing (Peds):**
			  – Not routinely used
			• **CYP450 Interactions:** None
			• **Renal or Hepatic Dose Adjustments:**
			  – GFR less than 50 mL/minute - use with caution
			  – Hepatic disease or dysfunction - use with caution
			• **Dosage Forms:** Oral (tablet)

Tamoxifen	Soltamox	• Breast cancer risk reduction
		• Breast cancer treatment
			• **Dosing (Adult):**
			  – Oral 20 to 40 mg daily
			• **Dosing (Peds):**
			  – Oral 20 mg daily
			• **CYP450 Interactions:** Substrate CYP2A6, 2B6, 2D6, 2C9, 2C19, 2E1 3A4; Inhibits CYP2C9
			• **Renal or Hepatic Dose Adjustments:** None
			• **Dosage Forms:** Oral (solution, tablet)

Toremifene	Fareston	• Metastatic breast cancer	• **Dosing (Adult):**
			  – Oral 60 to 180 mg daily, until disease progression
			• **Dosing (Peds):**
			  – Not routinely used
			• **CYP450 Interactions:** Substrate CYP1A2, CYP3A4
			• **Renal or Hepatic Dose Adjustments:** None
			• **Dosage Forms:** Oral (tablet)

High-Yield Clinical Knowledge

- **Tamoxifen and CYP2D6**
    - In patients taking potent CYP2D6 inhibitors (such as citalopram, escitalopram, paroxetine, fluoxetine, venlafaxine, and desvenlafaxine), there is a potential for therapeutic failure of tamoxifen.
        - If tamoxifen is indicated, the affecting CYP2D6 inhibitor should be discontinued or changed.
    - Polymorphisms of CYP2D6 can also impact the efficacy and safety of tamoxifen use.
- **Lipid Effects and Thrombosis**
    - Tamoxifen and raloxifene therapy decreases total cholesterol, LDL, and LPA but does not affect HDL or triglycerides.
    - However, despite this cardiovascular benefit, tamoxifen and raloxifene are associated with a significantly increased risk of DVT/PE.
- **Cancer Risk**
    - Tamoxifen increases the risk of endometrial carcinoma.
    - Raloxifene has been associated with a significant reduction in estrogen-receptor-positive breast cancer.

High-Yield Fast-Facts

- **Clomiphene Visual Disturbances**
    - Clomiphene may increase the incidence of "afterimages" and hallucinations, which are self-limiting.
    - Activities such as driving are not recommended in patients experiencing this adverse event or before knowing whether it occurs in a given patient.

HIGH-YIELD BOARD EXAM ESSENTIALS
- **CLASSIC AGENTS:** Clomiphene, bazedoxifene, fulvestrant, ospemifene, raloxifene, tamoxifen, toremifene
- **DRUG CLASS:** Selective estrogen receptor modulators
- **INDICATIONS:** Breast cancer risk reduction, breast cancer treatment, dyspareunia, osteoporosis, ovulation induction, risk reduction for invasive breast cancer in postmenopausal females, vasomotor symptoms, associated with menopause, vaginal dryness
- **MECHANISM:** Competitive and partial agonist inhibitor (mixed agonist/antagonist effects) of estradiol at the estrogen receptor.
- **SIDE EFFECTS:** Increased risk of DVT/PE, endometrial carcinoma, visual disturbances, hot flashes
- **CLINICAL PEARLS:**
    - In patients taking potent CYP2D6 inhibitors (such as citalopram, escitalopram, paroxetine, fluoxetine, venlafaxine, and desvenlafaxine), there is a potential for therapeutic failure of tamoxifen.
    - If tamoxifen is indicated, the affecting CYP2D6 inhibitor should be discontinued or changed.

High-Yield Basic Pharmacology

- **Mechanism of Action**
  - Active forms of vitamin D, acting on vitamin D receptors in the GI, stimulating intestinal calcium absorption and transport, and actions in the bone, renal tissue, and parathyroid glands.
- **Final Hydroxylation**
  - For the final conversion of calcitriol to active vitamin D in renal tissue, 1-alpha-hydroxylase activity is required. However, with progressing chronic kidney disease, the activity of 1-alpha-hydroxylase is gradually lost, leading to a decline in calcitriol activation.

Primary Net Benefit

- Precursors or active vitamin D support a range of physiologic functions, considering its nature as a fat-soluble vitamin with the potential for over-exposure and subsequent toxicities.

Vitamin D - Drug Class Review			
High-Yield Med Reviews			
Mechanism of Action: *Active forms of vitamin D, acting on vitamin D receptors in the GI, stimulating intestinal calcium absorption and transport, as well as actions in the bone, renal tissue, and parathyroid glands.*			
Class Effects: Increase serum calcium or risk for hypercalcemia, hyperphosphatemia, headache, polydipsia			
Generic Name	**Brand Name**	**Indication(s) or Uses**	**Notes**

Calcifediol	Rayaldee	- Secondary hyperparathyroidism	- **Dosing (Adult):**
			  - Oral 30 to 60 mcg at bedtime
			- **Dosing (Peds):**
			  - Not routinely used
			- **CYP450 Interactions:** None
			- **Renal or Hepatic Dose Adjustments:** None
			- **Dosage Forms:** Oral (capsule)

Calcipotriene	Calcitrene
	Dovonex
	Sorilux
		- Plaque psoriasis	- **Dosing (Adult):**
			  - Topically applied to affected area once to twice daily
			- **Dosing (Peds):**
			  - Topically applied to affected area once to twice daily
			- **CYP450 Interactions:** None
			- **Renal or Hepatic Dose Adjustments:** None
			- **Dosage Forms:** Topical (cream, foam, ointment, solution)

Calcitriol	Rocaltrol	- Hypoparathyroidism
		- Secondary hyperparathyroidism
			- **Dosing (Adult):**
			  - Oral 0.25 to 2 mcg/day
			  - IV 0.5 to 4 mcg three times weekly
			- **Dosing (Peds):**
			  - Oral 0.05 to 2 mcg daily, adjusted to corrected calcium, phosphorus, and iPTH levels
			- **CYP450 Interactions:** Substrate CYP3A4
			- **Renal or Hepatic Dose Adjustments:** None
			- **Dosage Forms:** Oral (capsule, solution), IV (solution)

Vitamin D - Drug Class Review			
High-Yield Med Reviews			
Generic Name	**Brand Name**	**Indication(s) or Uses**	**Notes**

Cholecalciferol	Aqueous Vitamin D
	D3 Vitamin
	Decara
		• Hypoparathyroidism
		• Osteoporosis
		• Vitamin D deficiency
			• **Dosing (Adult):**
			  – Oral 800 to 7,000 units/day
			    • Alternatively 50,000 units weekly
			• **Dosing (Peds):**
			  – Oral 400 to 10,000 units/day
			    • Up to 50,000 units weekly
			• **CYP450 Interactions:** None
			• **Renal or Hepatic Dose Adjustments:** None
			• **Dosage Forms:** Oral (capsule, liquid, sublingual, tablet)

Doxercalciferol	Hectorol	• Secondary hyperparathyroidism	• **Dosing (Adult):**
			  – Not on dialysis
			    • Oral 1 mcg daily
			  – On dialysis
			    • Oral 10 to 20 mcg three times weekly
			    • IV 4 to 6 mcg three times weekly
			• **Dosing (Peds):**
			  – Not routinely used
			• **CYP450 Interactions:** None
			• **Renal or Hepatic Dose Adjustments:** None
			• **Dosage Forms:** Oral (capsule), IV (solution)

Ergocalciferol	Calcidol
	Calciferol
	Drisdol
	Ergocal
		• Osteoporosis
		• Vitamin D deficiency
			• **Dosing (Adult):**
			  – Oral 800 to 7,000 units/day
			    • Alternatively 50,000 units weekly
			• **Dosing (Peds):**
			  – Oral 400 to 10,000 units/day
			    • Up to 50,000 units weekly
			• **CYP450 Interactions:** None
			• **Renal or Hepatic Dose Adjustments:** None
			• **Dosage Forms:** Oral (capsule, liquid, tablet)

Generic Name	Brand Name	Indication(s) or Uses	Notes
Vitamin D - Drug Class Review High-Yield Med Reviews			

Paricalcitol	Zemplar	▪ Secondary hyperparathyroidism	▪ **Dosing (Adult):**
			– On dialysis
			  ▪ IV 0.04 to 0.1 mcg/kg with dialysis, adjusted to iPTH level
			    ● Maximum 0.24 mg/kg/day
			  ▪ Oral dose based on iPTH level divided by 80
			– Predialysis
			  ▪ Oral 1 - 2 mcg daily or 2 - 4 mcg three times weekly
			▪ **Dosing (Peds):**
			– Children between 10 and 16 years
			  ▪ Oral dose based on iPTH level divided by 120
			– IV through HD access 0.04 to 0.08 mcg/kg/dose
			– Predialysis
			  ▪ Oral 1 - 2 mcg daily or 2 - 4 mcg three times weekly
			▪ **CYP450 Interactions:** Substrate CYP3A4
			▪ **Renal or Hepatic Dose Adjustments:** None
			▪ **Dosage Forms:** Oral (capsule), IV (solution)

High-Yield Clinical Knowledge

- **Vitamin D2 or D3**
  - Plant-derived vitamin D (vitamin D2) and vitamin D3 are present in the typical American diet and supplemented through fortification of various foods.
  - Vitamin D2, or ergocalciferol, requires activation, whereas cholecalciferol is in the active vitamin D3 format.
  - Ergocalciferol is also less avidly bound to transport proteins, is not as well absorbed, and has a shorter half-life than cholecalciferol.
- **Active Vitamin D**
  - In patients with chronic kidney disease, they cannot renally convert vitamin D to its active form of 1,25-hydroxyvitamin D (1,25(OH)D).
  - Without sufficient 1,25(OH)D, dysregulation of parathyroid hormone release allows for calcium excretion and diminished bone resorption.

High-Yield Fast-Facts

- **Sunshine**
  - Active vitamin D requires the conversion of 7-dehydrocholesterol to cholecalciferol (aka Vitamin D) by sunlight,
  - Cholecalciferol is then hydroxylated in the liver to form 25-OH-D and then converted to 1,25(OH)-D in the kidneys.
- **Secondary Hyperparathyroidism**
  - Paricalcitol is a synthetic form of vitamin D2 that specifically reduces serum PTH levels without affecting serum calcium or phosphorus.
  - This advantage is of clinical use and importance in patients with CKD, who are at risk of hyperphosphatemia and hypercalcemia.

HIGH-YIELD BOARD EXAM ESSENTIALS

- **CLASSIC AGENTS:** Calcifediol, calcipotriene, calcitriol, cholecalciferol, doxercalciferol, ergocalciferol, paricalcitol
- **DRUG CLASS:** Vitamin D analogs
- **INDICATIONS:** Hypoparathyroidism (calcitriol, cholecalciferol), plaque psoriasis (calcipotriene), secondary hyperparathyroidism (calcifediol, calcitriol, doxercalciferol, paricalcitol), vitamin D deficiency, osteoporosis (ergocalciferol)
- **MECHANISM:** Active forms of vitamin D, acting on vitamin D receptors in the GI, stimulating intestinal calcium absorption and transport, and actions in the bone, renal tissue, and parathyroid glands.
- **SIDE EFFECTS:** Hypercalcemia, hyperphosphatemia, headache, polydipsia, UTI
- **CLINICAL PEARLS:**
  - Calcitriol is the active form of vitamin D and thus does not require activation.
  - The synthetic analogs, doxercalciferol and paricalcitol, are used in place of calcitriol as they are less likely to cause hypercalcemia when lowering PTH.

High-Yield Basic Pharmacology

- ▪ **Acetylcholinesterase Inhibition**
    - – The method of acetylcholinesterase inhibition differs between these agents:
        - – **Donepezil**
            - – Is a *reversible, noncompetitive inhibitor* of central acetylcholinesterase.
        - – **Galantamine**
            - – Is *selective, competitive, reversible* acetylcholinesterase inhibition that also improves acetylcholine interaction at nicotinic receptors in the CNS.
        - – **Rivastigmine**
            - – Is a *reversible inhibitor of acetylcholinesterase as well as butyrylcholinesterase.*
    - – Despite these variances by which acetylcholinesterase inhibition occurs, the clinical relevance is unknown

Primary Net Benefit

- ▪ Slow the cognitive dysfunction of patients with Alzheimer's disease, with significant safety improvement compared with the tacrine's historical use.

Alzheimer's Pharmacotherapy - Drug Class Review			
High-Yield Med Reviews			
Mechanism of Action: *Inhibitors of acetylcholinesterase, counteracting the loss of cholinergic neurons in Alzheimer's disease.*			
Class Effects: Slow the cognitive dysfunction of patients with Alzheimer's disease, with significant safety improvement compared with the tacrine's historical use.			
Generic Name	**Brand Name**	**Indication(s) or Uses**	**Notes**

Donepezil	Aricept	▪ Alzheimer disease	▪ **Dosing (Adult):**
			  – Oral 5 to 23 mg daily
			▪ **Dosing (Peds):**
			  – Not routinely used
			▪ **CYP450 Interactions:** Substrate of CYP2D6, 3A4
			▪ **Renal or Hepatic Dose Adjustments:** None
			▪ **Dosage Forms:** Oral (tablet, disintegrating tablet)

Galantamine	Razadyne	▪ Alzheimer disease	▪ **Dosing (Adult):**
			  – Oral IR 4 to 24 mg q12h
			  – Oral ER 8 to 24 mg daily
			▪ **Dosing (Peds):**
			  – Not routinely used
			▪ **CYP450 Interactions:** Substrate of CYP2D6, 3A4
			▪ **Renal or Hepatic Dose Adjustments:**
			  – GFR 9 to 59 mL/minute OR Child-Pugh class B - Maximum 16 mg/day
			  – GFR less than 9 mL/minute OR Child-Pugh class C - Not recommended
			▪ **Dosage Forms:** Oral (capsule, solution, tablet)

		Alzheimer's Pharmacotherapy - Drug Class Review	
		High-Yield Med Reviews	
Generic Name	**Brand Name**	**Indication(s) or Uses**	**Notes**

Memantine	Namenda	▪ Alzheimer disease	▪ **Dosing (Adult):**
			  – Oral 5 to 28 mg/day
			▪ **Dosing (Peds):**
			  – Not routinely used
			▪ **CYP450 Interactions:** None
			▪ **Renal or Hepatic Dose Adjustments:**
			  – GFR 5 to 29 mL/minute - Maximum 5 mg q12h IR, or 14 mg/day ER
			  – GFR less than 5 or Child-Pugh class C - Not recommended
			▪ **Dosage Forms:** Oral (capsule, solution, tablet)

Rivastigmine	Exelon	▪ Alzheimer disease	▪ **Dosing (Adult):**
			  – Oral 1.5 to 6 mg q12h
			  – Transdermal patch 4.6 to 13.3 mg q24h
			▪ **Dosing (Peds):**
			  – Not routinely used
			▪ **CYP450 Interactions:** None
			▪ **Renal or Hepatic Dose Adjustments:**
			  – Child-Pugh class A or B - Maximum dose of 1.5 mg oral daily, or 4.6 mg daily transdermal
			  – Child-Pugh class C - Not recommended
			▪ **Dosage Forms:** Oral (capsule), Transdermal patch

High-Yield Clinical Knowledge

- **Disease-Modifying**
  - Currently, available pharmacotherapy for Alzheimer's does not modify the disease process but rather diminishes symptoms related to cognitive decline and the rate of cognitive decline.
  - However, some experts argue that pharmacotherapy combined with non-pharmacotherapy interventions possesses a disease-modifying effect of a sustained cognitive decline reduction.
- **Combination Therapy**
  - The combination of donepezil with memantine has been shown to slow the rate of cognitive and functional decline in patients with Alzheimer's disease, compared to monotherapy or no treatment.
- **Drug Interactions**
  - Trimethoprim (part of sulfamethoxazole/trimethoprim aka Bactrim) may increase the risk of memantine's adverse effects, namely myoclonus, and delirium.
    - The proposed mechanism is competition for renal elimination via active tubular secretion.
  - In elderly patients where UTIs are frequent, careful selection of antimicrobials should take place to limit the risk of drug-interactions.
- **Donepezil Dose**
  - The dosing of donepezil includes a 23 mg preparation, differing from the other 5 and 10 mg strengths.
  - There is a small improvement in cognitive function to the additional odd-numbered dosage form, which is counterbalanced by an increase in GI-related adverse effects.
- **Neurodegenerative Diseases**
  - Donepezil, galantamine, memantine, and rivastigmine can also be used for other neurodegenerative diseases where cholinergic effects play a role, including patients with Lewy bodies and vascular dementia.

- **Withdrawal**
  - If drug therapy changes or discontinuation of drug therapy occur, there is a risk of an acute withdrawal syndrome that manifests as a combination of worsening cognitive decline or excessive acetylcholinesterase effect (anticholinergic effect).

High-Yield Fast-Facts

- **NaMenDA**
  - The brand name of memantine reflects its mechanism of action, NMDA competitive inhibition.
- **Physostigmine Alternatives**
  - Donepezil, galantamine, or rivastigmine are possible alternatives to physostigmine in patients who are experiencing anticholinergic delirium.

HIGH-YIELD BOARD EXAM ESSENTIALS
- **CLASSIC AGENTS:** Donepezil, galantamine, memantine, rivastigmine
- **DRUG CLASS:** Alzheimer's pharmacotherapy
- **INDICATIONS:** Alzheimer's dementia
- **MECHANISM:** Inhibitors of acetylcholinesterase, counteracting the loss of cholinergic neurons in Alzheimer's disease (donepezil, galantamine, rivastigmine); noncompetitive inhibitor of NMDA receptor (memantine)
- **SIDE EFFECTS:** Diarrhea, insomnia, nausea.
- **CLINICAL PEARLS:** Currently, available pharmacotherapy for Alzheimer's does not modify the disease process but rather diminishes symptoms related to cognitive decline and the rate of cognitive decline. However, some experts argue that pharmacotherapy combined with non-pharmacotherapy interventions possesses a disease-modifying effect of a sustained cognitive decline reduction. Donepezil owns the majority of the market for its most inclusive indications for all severity levels, once-a-day administration, easy dosing titration, and tolerability profile.

High-Yield Basic Pharmacology

- **Mechanism of Action**
  - Reversible inhibition of voltage-gated sodium channels causing a failure to initiate and propagate action potentials.
  - Analgesic properties are attributed to the inhibition of axonal transmission of nerve impulses caused by pain or temperature.

Primary Net Benefit

- Local anesthetics provide isolated pain relief without affecting mental status, respiratory rate, heart rate, or blood pressure at normal therapeutic doses.

Local Anesthetics - Drug Class Review			
High-Yield Med Reviews			
Mechanism of Action: *Reversible inhibition of voltage-gated sodium channels causing a failure to initiate and propagate action potentials*			
Class Effects: Local anesthetic, at high doses cardiac and seizures, benzocaine spray can cause methemoglobinemia			
Generic Name	**Brand Name**	**Indication(s) or Uses**	**Notes**

Articaine and Epinephrine	Articadent Orabloc Septocaine Zorcaine	• Dental anesthesia	• **Dosing (Adult):**
			  – Infiltrate 20 to 204 mg (max 7 mg/kg)
			• **Dosing (Peds):**
			  – Infiltrate 20 to 204 mg (max 7 mg/kg)
			• **CYP450 Interactions:** None
			• **Renal or Hepatic Dose Adjustments:** None
			• **Dosage Forms:** Injection solution

Benzocaine	Anacaine Anbesol Cepacol HurriCaine	• Topical anesthesia
		• Poison ivy/sumac
			• **Dosing (Adult):**
			  – Topically applied to affected area up to 4 times daily
			  – Lozenge - allow to dissolve slowly in the mouth every 2 hours as needed
			• **Dosing (Peds):**
			  – Topically applied to affected area up to 4 times daily
			  – Lozenge - allow to dissolve slowly in the mouth every 2 hours as needed
			• **CYP450 Interactions:** None
			• **Renal or Hepatic Dose Adjustments:** None
			• **Dosage Forms:** Topical (aerosol, gel, liquid, lozenge, ointment, solution, stick, strip, swab)

Benzocaine, Butamben, and Tetracaine	Cetacaine	• Topical anesthesia	• **Dosing (Adult):**
			  – Topically spray for less than 1 second
			  – Gel/liquid 200 mg applied topically
			• **Dosing (Peds):**
			  – Not recommended
			• **CYP450 Interactions:** None
			• **Renal or Hepatic Dose Adjustments:** None
			• **Dosage Forms:** Topical (aerosol, gel, liquid)

Local Anesthetics - Drug Class Review
High-Yield Med Reviews

Generic Name	Brand Name	Indication(s) or Uses	Notes

Bupivacaine	Marcaine Sensorcaine	• Local anesthesia
		• Regional anesthesia
			• **Dosing (Adult):**
			  – Infiltration 5 to 50 mL once
			    ▪ Available as 0.25%, 0.5%, or 0.75%
			    ▪ Maximum 400 mg/24 hours
			• **Dosing (Peds):**
			  – Infiltration 0.3 to 0.6 mL/kg
			    ▪ Maximum volume of 20 mL/dose
			    ▪ Maximum dose 3 mg/kg or 200 mg, whichever is less
			• **CYP450 Interactions:** SubCYP1A2, 2C19, 2D, 3A4
			• **Renal or Hepatic Dose Adjustments:** None
			• **Dosage Forms:** Implant, Solution for injection

Bupivacaine and epinephrine	Marcaine E Sensorcaine/e pinephrine	• Local anesthesia	• **Dosing (Adult):**
			  – Infiltration 2 to 50 mL once
			    ▪ Available as 0.25%, 0.5%, or 0.75%
			    ▪ Maximum 400 mg/24 hours
			• **Dosing (Peds):**
			  – See adult dosing
			• **CYP450 Interactions:** SubCYP1A2, 2C19, 2D, 3A4
			• **Renal or Hepatic Dose Adjustments:** None
			• **Dosage Forms:** Solution for injection

Bupivacaine (liposomal)	Exparel	• Local anesthesia • Regional anesthesia	• **Dosing (Adult):** – Infiltration 7 to 30 mL • **Dosing (Peds):** Not routinely used • **CYP450 Interactions:** Sub CYP1A2, 2C19, 3A4 • **Renal or Hepatic Dose Adjustments:** None • **Dosage Forms:** Suspension for injection

Chloroprocaine	Clorotekal Nesacaine	• Local anesthesia	• **Dosing (Adult):**
			  – Infiltration 0.5 to 10 mL once
			    ▪ Max dose 800 mg
			• **Dosing (Peds):**
			  – Infiltration 0.5 to 10 mL once
			    ▪ Max dose 11 mg/kg
			• **CYP450 Interactions:** None
			• **Renal or Hepatic Dose Adjustments:** None
			• **Dosage Forms:** Solution for injection

Cocaine	Goprelto Numbrino	• Local anesthesia	• **Dosing (Adult):**
			  – Insert 2 cocaine solution cottonoid pledgets in each affected nostril for up to 20 minutes
			    ▪ Max 4 pledgets, 160 mg or 3 mg/kg
			• **Dosing (Peds):**
			  – Same as adult; but max 2 pledgets, or 3 mg/kg
			• **CYP450 Interactions:** Substrate CYP3A4
			• **Renal or Hepatic Dose Adjustments:** None
			• **Dosage Forms:** Topical (solution)

Local Anesthetics - Drug Class Review
High-Yield Med Reviews

Generic Name	Brand Name	Indication(s) or Uses	Notes

Dibucaine	Nupercainal	• Topical anesthesia	• **Dosing (Adult):**
			   – Apply to affected area up to 4 times daily
			• **Dosing (Peds):**
			   – Apply to affected area up to 4 times daily
			• **CYP450 Interactions:** None
			• **Renal or Hepatic Dose Adjustments:** None
			• **Dosage Forms:** Ointment

Lidocaine	Xylocaine	• Topical anesthesia
		• Local anesthesia
		• Regional anesthesia
			• **Dosing (Adult):**
			   – Infiltration 2 to 50 mL
			     • Max 4.5 mg/kg/dose
			   – IV 1.5 mg/kg or 100 mg once
			     • Max 3 mg/kg
			   – IV infusion 1 to 4 mg/minute
			• **Dosing (Peds):**
			   – Infiltration 2 to 50 mL
			     • Max 4.5 mg/kg/dose
			   – IV 1.5 mg/kg or 100 mg once
			     • Max 3 mg/kg
			   – IV infusion 1 to 4 mg/minute
			• **CYP450 Interactions:** Sub CYP1A2, 2A6, 2B6, 2C9, 3A4
			• **Renal or Hepatic Dose Adjustments:**
			   – GFR < 30 mL/min or hepatic impairment - lower maintenance infusion dose
			• **Dosage Forms:** Solution for injection, Topical (aerosol, gel, liquid, ointment)

Lidocaine with epinephrine	Xylocaine with epinephrine	• Local anesthesia	• **Dosing (Adult):**
			   – Infiltration 1 to 5 mL/dose (max 7 mg/kg)
			• **Dosing (Peds):**
			   – Infiltration 1 to 5 mL/dose (max 7 mg/kg)
			• **CYP450 Interactions:** Substrate CYP1A2, 2A6, 2B6, 2C9, 3A4
			• **Renal or Hepatic Dose Adjustments:**
			   – GFR < 30 mL/minute or hepatic impairment - lower maintenance dose
			• **Dosage Forms:** Solution for injection

Mepivacaine	Carbocaine Polocaine	• Local anesthesia
		• Regional anesthesia
			• **Dosing (Adult):**
			   – Infiltration 5 to 40 mL
			     • Max 400 mg, or 500 mg with epinephrine
			• **Dosing (Peds):**
			   – Infiltration 5 to 6 mg/kg
			     • Max dose: 270 mg
			• **CYP450 Interactions:** None
			• **Renal or Hepatic Dose Adjustments:** None
			• **Dosage Forms:** Solution for injection

Local Anesthetics - Drug Class Review
High-Yield Med Reviews

Generic Name	Brand Name	Indication(s) or Uses	Notes

Prilocaine	Citanest Plain Dental	• Dental anesthesia	• **Dosing (Adult):**
			  – Infiltration of 400 mg or 6 mg/kg
			    • Max dose: 400 mg
			• **Dosing (Peds):**
			  – Infiltration 1 mL of 4% solution for single tooth procedures
			• **CYP450 Interactions:** None
			• **Renal or Hepatic Dose Adjustments:** None
			• **Dosage Forms:** Solution for injection

Proparacaine	Alcaine	• Topical anesthesia	• **Dosing (Adult):**
			  – Ophthalmic 1 to 2 drops per eye every 5 to 10 minutes for up to 7 doses
			• **Dosing (Peds):**
			  – Ophthalmic 1 to 2 drops per eye every 5 to 10 minutes for up to 7 doses
			• **CYP450 Interactions:** None
			• **Renal or Hepatic Dose Adjustments:** None
			• **Dosage Forms:** Ophthalmic solution

Ropivacaine	Naropin	• Local anesthesia
		• Regional anesthesia
			• **Dosing (Adult):**
			  – Infiltration 5 to 50 mL; Max 3 mg/kg
			    • Available as 0.5%, 0.75%, 1%
			• **Dosing (Peds):**
			  – Infiltration 0.5 to 50 mL; Max 3 mg/kg
			    • Available as 0.5%, 0.75%, 1%
			• **CYP450 Interactions:** Sub CYP1A2, 2B6, 2D6, 3A4
			• **Renal or Hepatic Dose Adjustments:** None
			• **Dosage Forms:** Solution for injection

Tetracaine	Altacaine
	Tetcaine
		• Topical anesthesia	• **Dosing (Adult):**
			  – Ophthalmic instill 1 to 2 drops in the affected eye as needed q3-5minutes up to 3 doses
			• **Dosing (Peds):**
			  – Ophthalmic instill 1 to 2 drops in the affected eye prn q3-5min up to 3 doses
			• **CYP450 Interactions:** None
			• **Renal or Hepatic Dose Adjustments:** None
			• **Dosage Forms:** Ophthalmic solution

High-Yield Clinical Pharmacology

- **Amide or Ester**
  - Local anesthetics can be grouped into two structural classes: amino amides or amino esters.
  - Amino esters typically have one "i" in their drug name and are mostly all metabolized by plasma cholinesterase to a toxic metabolite para-aminobenzoic acid (PABA).
    - Patients with altered plasma cholinesterase function, hepatic impairment, or decreased hepatic blood flow are at risk of amino ester toxicity.
  - Patients with allergies to amino esters are likely to have cross-sensitivity to other amino ester anesthetics.
    - However, patients with amino ester allergies can safely receive amino amide anesthetics.

- **Epinephrine coformulation**
  - Many local anesthetics are co-formulated with dilute epinephrine (either 1:100,000 or 1:200,000), which is intended to limit bleeding, increase the anesthetic effect duration, and further limit systemic exposure to the drug.
    - These co-formulated products must not be administered IV and can only be administered for local infiltration.
- **Maximum doses**
  - Local anesthetics should be dosed with the awareness of a maximum dose for each agent.
  - Lidocaine, for local anesthetic purposes, should not be given at doses exceeding 4.5 mg/kg.
    - When co-formulated with epinephrine, this maximum dose increases to 7 mg/kg.
  - Bupivacaine doses should not exceed 2.5 mg/kg, but epinephrine can be given at doses up to 3 mg/kg.
  - Mepivacaine's maximum dose is 5 mg/kg, but can be given up to 7 mg/kg when formulated with epi.
  - Ropivacaine has a maximum dose of 3 mg/kg.
- **Lidocaine Metabolites**
  - When used for cardiac indications, lidocaine can be given as a continuous infusion and monitored therapeutically using lidocaine plasma levels.
  - One of the toxic metabolites of lidocaine, monoethylglycinexylidide (MEGX), should also be monitored alongside lidocaine due to the risk of seizures.
- **Benzocaine and Methemoglobin**
  - Benzocaine is metabolized to the toxic oxidizing metabolites phenylhydroxylamine and nitrobenzene.
  - Standard doses of benzocaine have been associated with clinically relevant methemoglobinemia.
  - Increased risk of methemoglobin exists when local anesthetics are administered in excessive doses or a breakdown of mucosal barriers to systemic absorption.
- **Cardiac and Central Effects**
  - Local anesthetics may cause cardiac or central nervous system adverse events.
  - As the local anesthetics are sodium channel blockers, they can act on cardiac tissue as antiarrhythmics or cause arrhythmias.
    - Lidocaine is classified as a Vaughn Williams 1B antiarrhythmic.
    - Bupivacaine is also thought to affect mitochondrial function, limiting cardiac cellular energy production from carbohydrates and precipitating cardiac arrest.
  - Seizures can occur with excessive exposure to local anesthetics, which can often be preceded by tinnitus.

High-Yield Fast-Facts

- **Methylene Blue**
  - If methemoglobinemia occurs due to local anesthetics, methylene blue should be considered.
  - However, methylene blue itself can induce methemoglobin.
- **Liposomal Bupivacaine**
  - Bupivacaine is available as a liposomal encapsulation that permits sustained release of bupivacaine, extending its local anesthesia duration.

HIGH-YIELD BOARD EXAM ESSENTIALS
- **CLASSIC AGENTS:** Benzocaine, bupivacaine, lidocaine, proparacaine, tetracaine
- **DRUG CLASS:** Local anesthetics
- **INDICATIONS:** Local (bupivacaine, lidocaine) & Topical analgesia (benzocaine, proparacaine, tetracaine)
- **MECHANISM:** Inhibit nerve impulses for pain by blocking Na+ channels in nerve axons
- **SIDE EFFECTS:** At high doses cardiac and seizures. Benzocaine spray can cause methemoglobinemia.
- **CLINICAL PEARLS:** Amino esters typically have one "i" in their drug name and amides have two "i"s. Max dose of lidocaine WITHOUT epi is 4.5 mg/kg, but WITH epi is 7 mg/kg.

High-Yield Basic Pharmacology

- **Mechanism of Action**
  - Acetaminophen possesses numerous actions that contribute to its analgesic and antipyretic effects.
    - Indirectly inhibits prostaglandin production by reducing heme on the peroxidase portion of prostaglandin H_2.
  - Its prostaglandin synthesis inhibition occurs where prostaglandin synthesis and arachidonic acid are low.
    - Macrophages and platelets are present when arachidonic acid and prostaglandin synthesis are high; therefore, acetaminophen is minimally affected during normal therapeutic uses.
    - Conversely, the CNS where peroxide tone (a.k.a., arachidonic acid synthesis) is low

Primary Net Benefit

- An analgesic and antipyretic that is commonly used in all age groups, safe in pregnancy, associated with almost not drug interactions, present alone or in combination with various products, available OTC, and relatively cheap.

Acetaminophen - Drug Class Review			
High-Yield Med Reviews			
Mechanism of Action: *Central indirect inhibitor of COX-2, selectively decreasing PGE_2 synthesis when prostaglandin and arachidonic acid concentrations are low.*			
Class Effects: <ul><li>Over the counter, analgesic (but no antiinflammatory) effects, and antipyretic are commonly used and present alone or in combination in a variety of different products. Safe in pregnancy. No major drug interactions.</li><li>Toxic single dose: 200 mg/kg. Toxicity risk: liver damage from metabolite NAPQI. Per Rumack-Matthew Nomogram the first drug level check is at 4 hours (if time of overdose is known).</li></ul>			
Generic Name	**Brand Name**	**Indication(s) or Uses**	**Notes**

Acetaminophen	Ofirmev, Tylenol	• Fever
		• Pain
			• **Dosing (Adult):**
			   – Oral 325 to 1000 mg q4-6hours, maximum 3,000 mg/day (OTC) or 4,000 mg/day (Rx)
			   – IV 12.5 mg/kg or 650 mg q4-6hours, maximum 75 mg/kg/day or 4,000 mg/day
			   – Rectal 325 to 650 mg q4-6h, maximum 3,900 mg/day
			• **Dosing (Peds):**
			   – Oral 10 to 15 mg/kg/dose q4-6hours, maximum 75 mg/kg/day or 4,000 mg/day
			   – IV 12.5 mg/kg q4-6hours, maximum 75 mg/kg/day or 4,000 mg/day
			   – Rectal 10 to 15 mg/kg/dose q4-6hours, maximum 75 mg/kg/day or 3,900 mg/day
			• **CYP450 Interactions:** Substrate mainly CYP2E1, but also 1A2, 2A6, 2C9, 2D6, 2E1, 3A4
			• **Renal or Hepatic Dose Adjustments:**
			   – Child-Pugh class B or C - maximum 3,000 mg/day
			• **Dosage Forms:** Oral (capsule, elixir, liquid, powder, solution, suspension, syrup, tablet), IV (solution; Ofirmev)

High-Yield Clinical Knowledge

- **Metabolism**
  - Acetaminophen normally undergoes hepatic glucuronidation and sulfation at normal therapeutic doses.
  - If glucuronidation or sulfation capacity is exceeded, either in overdose or hepatic dysfunction, the acetaminophen oxidation pathway is induced where CYP2E1 metabolized the drug.
    - CYP2E1 metabolism of acetaminophen yields a toxic metabolite, N-acetyl-p-benzoquinone imine (NAPQI), which is then complexed with glutathione and safely eliminated.
    - When glutathione capacity is exceeded, NAPQI can accumulate, causing hepatic centrilobular necrosis and hepatic failure.
- **Maximum Dose**
  - Acetaminophen has maximum dose differences, depending on whether the drug is used on a prescription or nonprescription (over-the-counter) basis.
  - For OTC use of acetaminophen, the maximum daily dose is 3,000 mg/day.
  - For prescription use of acetaminophen, the maximum daily dose is 4,000 mg/day.
    - Close attention must be paid to combination products that contain acetaminophen, as the omission of this quantity from the daily dose calculation will lead to overdosing.
- **N-Acetylcysteine**
  - A weight-based dose of 150 mg/kg or greater than 12,000 mg ingested over a single 4-hour period is considered a toxic dose.
  - If acetaminophen toxicity is suspected, a four-hour post-ingestion level should be drawn and plotted on the Rumack-Matthew Nomogram.
    - An acetaminophen level greater than 150 mcg/mL at 4 hours warrants N-acetylcysteine therapy.
- **Delayed Peak**
  - Acetaminophen is rapidly absorbed after oral administration within 2 hours, but peak plasma concentrations occur approximately 4 hours after ingestion.
    - For acetaminophen level screening in possible or confirmed overdose, a 4-hour level is recommended to account for this delay.

High-Yield Fast-Facts

- **Paracetamol**
  - In other parts of the world, acetaminophen is known as paracetamol.
- **Non-Linear Elimination**
  - Although the common graphic representation of the Rumack-Matthew nomogram appears linear, it is actually a log-linear graph, representing the non-linear elimination of acetaminophen.
- **Antipyretic Effects**
  - Antipyresis from acetaminophen is a result of its inhibition of endogenous pyrogens at the hypothalamic thermoregulatory center.

HIGH-YIELD BOARD EXAM ESSENTIALS
- **CLASSIC AGENTS:** Acetaminophen (Tylenol)
- **DRUG CLASS:** Non-opioid analgesic
- **INDICATIONS:** Fever, Pain
- **MECHANISM:** Antipyresis is a result of its inhibition of endogenous pyrogens (i.e., prostaglandins) at the hypothalamic thermoregulatory center.
- **SIDE EFFECTS:** None unless toxicity occurs from doses exceeding 4,000 mg/d from NAPQI formation.
- **CLINICAL PEARLS:** No antiinflammatory effects like NSAIDS. Safe in pregnancy. No major drug interactions.

High-Yield Basic Pharmacology

- **Mechanism of Action**
  - Inhibit the conversion of arachidonic acid to prostaglandins by inhibition of COX-1 and/or COX-2 either reversibly (NSAIDs).
  - NSAIDs differ in the degree of inhibition of COX1:COX2. NSAIDs that have more inhibition of COX-2 over COX-1 are thought to be "COX-2 selective" (e.g., celecoxib, etodolac, meloxicam) and thus cause less gastritis and/or risk of bleeding.
  - NSAIDs are unlike aspirin which has irreversible inhibition of preferentially COX-1.

Primary Net Benefit

- NSAIDs produce dose-dependent analgesia, anti-inflammatory, and antiplatelet effects, which are devoid of CNS effects but are associated with GI bleeding, adverse cardiac effects (other than aspirin), and may be nephrotoxic.

NSAIDs - Drug Class Review			
High-Yield Med Reviews			
Mechanism of Action: *Inhibit the conversion of arachidonic acid to prostaglandins by inhibition of COX-1 and/or COX-2 either reversibly (NSAIDs) or irreversibly (aspirin).*			
Class Effects: NSAIDs produce dose-dependent analgesia, anti-inflammatory, and antiplatelet effects, which are devoid of CNS effects but are associated with GI bleeding, adverse cardiac effects (other than aspirin), and may be nephrotoxic.			
Generic Name	**Brand Name**	**Indication(s) or Uses**	**Notes**

Aspirin	Bayer Aspirin	• Analgesia
		• Antipyresis
		• Anti-inflammatory
		• Cardiovascular disease primary and secondary prevention
		• Ischemic stroke or transient ischemic attack
			• **Dosing (Adult):**
			  – Oral 81 to 1000 mg q4-24h
			  – Rectal 300 to 600 mg q4-24h
			• **Dosing (Peds):**
			  – Oral 1 to 15 mg/kg/dose q4-6h
			    • Maximum 4000 mg/day or 100 mg/kg/day, whichever is less
			• **CYP450 Interactions:** Substrate of CYP2C9
			• **Renal or Hepatic Dose Adjustments:**
			  – None
			• **Dosage Forms:** Oral (caplet, capsule, suppository, tablet chewable, tablet delayed release, tablet enteric coated)

Celecoxib	Celebrex	• Analgesia	• **Dosing (Adult):**
			  – Oral 100 to 200 mg q12-24h
			    • Maximum 400 mg/day
			• **Dosing (Peds):**
			  – Oral 50 to 100 mg q12h
			• **CYP450 Interactions:** Substrate CYP2C9, 3A4; Inhibits CYP2D6
			• **Renal or Hepatic Dose Adjustments:**
			  – GFR less than 30 mL/minute – Avoid use
			  – Child-Pugh class B – Reduce dose by 50%
			  – Child-Pugh class C – Avoid the use
			• **Dosage Forms:** Oral (capsule)

NSAIDs - Drug Class Review
High-Yield Med Reviews

Generic Name	Brand Name	Indication(s) or Uses	Notes

Diclofenac	Cambia
	Cataflam
	Zipsor
	Zorvolex
		▪ Analgesia
		▪ Dysmenorrhea
			▪ **Dosing (Adult):**
			  – Oral 25 to 75 mg q8-12h
			  – IV 37.5 mg q6h as needed, maximum 150 mg/day
			▪ **Dosing (Peds):**
			    ▪ Not routinely used
			▪ **CYP450 Interactions:** Substrate CYP1A2, 2B6, 2C19, 2C9, 2D6, 3A4; Inhibits UGT 1A6
			▪ **Renal or Hepatic Dose Adjustments:**
			  – GFR less than 30 mL/minute – Avoid use
			  – Child-Pugh class B or C – Avoid use
			▪ **Dosage Forms:** Oral (capsule, packet, solution, tablet)

Diflunisal	Dolobid	▪ Analgesia	▪ **Dosing (Adult):**
			  – Oral 250 to 750 mg q12h
			    ▪ Maximum 1,500 mg/day
			▪ **Dosing (Peds):**
			  – Oral 250 to 750 mg q12h
			    ▪ Maximum 1,500 mg/day
			▪ **CYP450 Interactions:** None
			▪ **Renal or Hepatic Dose Adjustments:**
			  – GFR < 50 mL/minute – reduce dose by 50%
			▪ **Dosage Forms:** Oral (tablet)

Etodolac	Lodine	▪ Acute pain
		▪ Arthritis
			▪ **Dosing (Adult):**
			  – Oral 200 to 400 mg q6-12h
			    ▪ Maximum 1,000 mg/day
			▪ **Dosing (Peds):**
			  – Oral 7.5 to 10 mg/kg/dose q12h
			    ▪ Maximum 1,000 mg/day
			▪ **CYP450 Interactions:** None
			▪ **Renal or Hepatic Dose Adjustments:**
			  – GFR less than 37 mL/minute – Avoid use
			▪ **Dosage Forms:** Oral (capsule, tablet)

Fenoprofen	Fenortho
	Nalfon
		▪ Analgesia
		▪ Arthritis
			▪ **Dosing (Adult):**
			  – Oral 400 to 600 mg q6-8h
			    ▪ Maximum 3,200 mg/day
			▪ **Dosing (Peds):** Not routinely used
			▪ **CYP450 Interactions:** None
			▪ **Renal or Hepatic Dose Adjustments:** None
			▪ **Dosage Forms:** Oral (capsule, tablet)

Flurbiprofen		▪ Arthritis	▪ **Dosing (Adult):** – Oral 50 to 100 mg q6-12h ▪ **Dosing (Peds):** Not routinely used ▪ **CYP450 Interactions:** Substrate CYP2C9 ▪ **Renal or Hepatic Dose Adjustments:** None ▪ **Dosage Forms:** Oral (tablet)

NSAIDs - Drug Class Review
High-Yield Med Reviews

Generic Name	Brand Name	Indication(s) or Uses	Notes
Ibuprofen	Caldolor Motrin	• Analgesia • Antipyresis • Anti-inflammatory	• **Dosing (Adult):** – Oral 200 to 800 mg q6-8h; Max: 3,200 mg/day – IV 200 to 800 mg q4-6h PRN pain; Max 2,400 mg/day • **Dosing (Peds):** – Oral 4 to 10 mg/kg/dose q6-8h; Max 400 mg/dose – IV 10 mg/kg/dose q4-6h PRN; Max: 2,400 mg/day • **CYP450 Interactions:** Substrate CYP2C9/19 • **Renal or Hepatic Dose Adjustments:** – GFR < 30 mL/minute - not recommended • **Dosage Forms:** IV (solution), oral (capsule, kit, suspension, tablet)
Indomethacin	Indocin Tivorbex	• Analgesia • Antipyresis • Anti-inflammatory • Closure of patent ductus arteriosus (infants only)	• **Dosing (Adult):** – Oral/Rectal 20 to 75 mg q12-24h; Max 150 mg/day • **Dosing (Peds):** – Oral/Rectal 1 to 2 mg/kg/day divided q6-12h • Max 4 mg/kg/day or 200 mg/day, whichever is less – IV 0.2 mg/kg then 0.1 to 0.25 mg/kg for 2 doses • **CYP450 Interactions:** Substrate CYP2C19, 2C9 • **Renal or Hepatic Dose Adjustments:** – GFR less than 30 mL/minute – Avoid use • **Dosage Forms:** Oral (capsule, suppository, suspension), IV (solution)
Ketoprofen	Anafen Ketoprofen	• Analgesia • Anti-inflammatory	• **Dosing (Adult):** – Oral 25 to 100 mg q6-12h • Maximum 300 mg/day • **Dosing (Peds):** Not routinely used • **CYP450 Interactions:** Substrate & inhibitor of OAT1/3 • **Renal or Hepatic Dose Adjustments:** – GFR less than 30 mL/minute – Avoid use • **Dosage Forms:** Oral (capsule)
Ketorolac	Toradol	• Analgesia • Anti-inflammatory	• **Dosing (Adult):** – Oral 10 mg q4-6h PRN; • Max 40 mg/day x 5 days – IV 15 to 30 mg once q6h PRN or IM 30 to 60 mg once q6h PRN; Max 120 mg/day for 5 days • **Dosing (Peds):** – IV 0.5 mg/kg/dose q6-8h • Maximum 30 mg/dose for 5 days – Oral 1 mg/kg/dose q4-6h; Max 10 mg/dose x5 days • **CYP450 Interactions:** None • **Renal or Hepatic Dose Adjustments:** – GFR 10 to 50 mL/min - reduce dose 50% – GFR less than 10 mL/minute – avoid use • **Dosage Forms:** Oral (tablet), IV (solution)

NSAIDs - Drug Class Review
High-Yield Med Reviews

Generic Name	Brand Name	Indication(s) or Uses	Notes

Meclofenamate	Meclomen	• Analgesia
		• Anti-inflammatory
		• Primary dysmenorrhea
			• **Dosing (Adult):**
			  – Oral 50 mg to 100 mg q4-6h
			    ▪ Maximum 400 mg/day
			• **Dosing (Peds):** Not routinely used
			• **CYP450 Interactions:** None
			• **Renal or Hepatic Dose Adjustments:**
			  – GFR less than 30 mL/minute – Avoid use
			• **Dosage Forms:** Oral (capsule)

Mefenamic acid	Ponstel	• Analgesia
		• Anti-inflammatory
		• Primary dysmenorrhea
			• **Dosing (Adult):**
			  – Oral 500 mg once, then 250 mg q6h for 3 days
			• **Dosing (Peds):** Not routinely used
			• **CYP450 Interactions:** Substrate of CYP2C9
			• **Renal or Hepatic Dose Adjustments:**
			  – GFR less than 30 mL/minute – Avoid use
			• **Dosage Forms:** Oral (capsule)

Meloxicam	Anjeso
	Mobic
	Vivlodex
		• Analgesia
		• Antipyresis
		• Anti-inflammatory
			• **Dosing (Adult):**
			  – Oral 5 to 15 once daily
			  – IV 30 mg daily
			• **Dosing (Peds):**
			  – Oral 0.125 mg/kg daily; Max: 7.5 mg/day
			• **CYP450 Interactions:** Substrate CYP2C9, 3A4
			• **Renal or Hepatic Dose Adjustments:**
			  – GFR less than 30 mL/minute – Avoid use
			  – Child-Pugh class C – Avoid use
			• **Dosage Forms:** Oral (capsule, tablet), IV (solution)

Nabumetone	Relafen	• Analgesia	• **Dosing (Adult):**
			  – Oral 1,000 to 2,000 mg daily
			• **Dosing (Peds):**
			  – Not routinely used
			• **CYP450 Interactions:** None
			• **Renal or Hepatic Dose Adjustments:**
			  – GFR 30 to 49 mL/minute – maximum 1,500 mg/day
			  – GFR less than 30 mL/minute – maximum 1,000 mg/day
			• **Dosage Forms:** Oral (tablet)

Naproxen	Aleve
	Naprosyn
		• Analgesia
		• Antipyresis
		• Anti-inflammatory
			• **Dosing (Adult):**
			  – Oral 250 to 1,000 mg q12-24h
			    ▪ Maximum 1,500 mg/day
			• **Dosing (Peds):**
			  – Oral 5 to 10 mg/kg/dose q12h
			    ▪ Maximum 1,000 mg/day
			• **CYP450 Interactions:** Substrate CYP1A2, 2C9
			• **Renal or Hepatic Dose Adjustments:**
			  – GFR less than 30 mL/minute – Avoid use
			• **Dosage Forms:** Oral (capsule, suspension, tablet)

		NSAIDs - Drug Class Review	
		High-Yield Med Reviews	
Generic Name	**Brand Name**	**Indication(s) or Uses**	**Notes**

Oxaprozin	Daypro	▪ Analgesia	▪ **Dosing (Adult):**
			  – Oral 1,200 mg daily
			    ▪ Maximum 1,800 mg/day or 26 mg/kg/day, whichever is less
			▪ **Dosing (Peds):**
			  – Oral 10 to 20 mg/kg/dose
			    ▪ Maximum 1,200 mg/day
			▪ **CYP450 Interactions:** None
			▪ **Renal or Hepatic Dose Adjustments:**
			  – GFR less than 30 mL/minute – Avoid use
			▪ **Dosage Forms:** Oral (tablet)

Piroxicam	Feldene	▪ Analgesia	▪ **Dosing (Adult):**
			  – Oral 20 mg daily
			▪ **Dosing (Peds):**
			  – Oral 0.2 to 0.4 mg/kg/day
			    ▪ Maximum 20 mg/day
			▪ **CYP450 Interactions:** Substrate CYP2C9
			▪ **Renal or Hepatic Dose Adjustments:**
			  – GFR less than 30 mL/minute – Avoid use
			▪ **Dosage Forms:** Oral (capsule)

Sulindac	Clinoril
	Sulin
		▪ Analgesia
		▪ Anti-inflammatory
			▪ **Dosing (Adult):**
			  – Oral 150 to 200 mg q12h for 7 to 14 days
			▪ **Dosing (Peds):**
			  – Oral 2 to 6 mg/kg/day divided q12h
			    ▪ Maximum 400 mg/day
			▪ **CYP450 Interactions:** None
			▪ **Renal or Hepatic Dose Adjustments:**
			  – GFR less than 30 mL/minute – Avoid use
			▪ **Dosage Forms:** Oral (tablet)

High-Yield Clinical Knowledge

- **Cardiovascular Risk**
  - Inhibition of COX-2 by NSAIDs produces an inhibition of endothelial-derived prostacyclin I2 and lack of potent TXA2 inhibitory effect on platelets, leading to an increased risk of cardiovascular adverse events.
  - COX-2 selective inhibitors were originally developed to reduce the risk of GI and cardiac adverse events, but rofecoxib and valdecoxib were removed from the market due to their association with increased cardiac events.
    - Celecoxib remains in the market but carries a black boxed warning concerning this cardiovascular risk.
  - Aspirin is the exception to this class effect, as it has a net clinical benefit in reducing cardiovascular morbidity and mortality.
- **GI Bleeds**
  - Inhibition of COX-1 by NSAIDs prevents the production of PGE2 and PGI2, which leads to a decline in the production of the protective mucous lining in the GI mucosal lining, exposing the underlying tissue to gastric acid.

- Normal coagulation may be impaired due to NSAIDs due to their inhibition of TXA2 and direct cytotoxic and irritating effects.
- The most common ulcers formed by NSAIDs are located in the duodenum.
- **Kidney Injury**
  - Renal perfusion and glomerular filtration rate are partially regulated by COX-1 and PGI2, PGE2, and PGD2.
  - Inhibition of COX-1 can decrease renal blood flow and counteract renal hemodynamics by causing increased sodium reabsorption and decreased renin synthesis.
    - This can lead to increased plasma volume which could cause an increase in BP and heart failure exacerbation in patients with underlying HFrEF.
- **Selective Vs. Non-Selective NSAIDs**
  - Selective COX-2 inhibitors (celecoxib, etodolac, meloxicam) maintain the antiinflammatory properties of non-selective COX inhibition, potentially reducing the risk of GI and kidney adverse effects, as well as modification of platelet function.
    - However, prostacyclin synthesis is inhibited, which still may cause adverse cardiovascular effects.
    - COX-2 inhibitors have also been historically controversial as rofecoxib was removed from the market as it was associated with an increased risk of cardiovascular events.
- **Closing Patent Ductus Arteriosus**
  - Ibuprofen and indomethacin can be used intravenously in preterm infants for the closure of patent ductus arteriosus.
    - Other parenteral NSAIDs include ketorolac and meloxicam, although these are only used in adult patients.
- **NSAIDs in Pregnancy**
  - The use of NSAIDs during pregnancy is associated with premature closure of the ductus arteriosus which impairs fetal circulation in utero.
    - This was observed among patients who were given indomethacin for the purposes of terminating preterm labor.
- **Indomethacin Indications**
  - Indomethacin may be particularly useful in gouty arthritis as it may reduce neutrophil migration but comes with a relatively high risk of GI bleeding.
- **NSAIDs and Methotrexate**
  - Although patients with Rheumatoid Arthritis may take both, NSAIDs may increase the serum levels of methotrexate, potentially leading to toxicity.
  - NSAIDs are believed to decrease the renal excretion of methotrexate by inhibiting its renal transport and a decreased renal perfusion.
- **Adverse Events**
  - In addition to GI, renal, and cardiovascular adverse events, NSAIDs may also cause hematologic adverse events (thrombocytopenia, neutropenia, aplastic anemia), hepatic dysfunction, drug-induced asthma, and drug-induced rashes.

HIGH-YIELD BOARD EXAM ESSENTIALS

- **CLASSIC AGENTS:** Ibuprofen, Ketorolac, Meloxicam, Naproxen
- **DRUG CLASS:** Non-opioid analgesic NSAID
- **INDICATIONS:** Fever, Pain, Inflammation, Closure of patent ductus arteriosus (indomethacin only; infants)
- **MECHANISM:** Inhibition of COX decreases the production of not just prostaglandins but also thromboxane and prostacyclin that regulate inflammation and platelet activation.
- **SIDE EFFECTS:** Gastritis, nausea, bleeding, renal effects (AKI, ATN, Interstitial nephritis), increase risk of CVD.
- **CLINICAL PEARLS:** Avoid in pregnancy. Drug interactions with ACE inhibitors/ARBs, other anticoagulants, antiplatelet agents, and lithium, methotrexate.

High-Yield Basic Pharmacology

- **Mechanism of Action**
  - Irreversible inhibition of cyclooxygenase 1 and 2 (COX-1, COX-2) decreasing prostaglandin precursors, inhibition of thromboxane A2.
- **Non-Acetylated Salicylates**
  - The non-acetylated salicylates, including choline magnesium trisalicylate, methyl salicylate, salsalate, and trolamine, possess antiinflammatory properties but lack any antiplatelet properties.
    - Their use is limited but may be options in patients with asthma with sensitivity to aspirin for anti-inflammatory indications.

Primary Net Benefit

- Salicylates are not routinely used for analgesic properties where better-tolerated alternatives exist, but aspirin is widely used for cardiovascular benefits.

<table>
<tr><td colspan="4">Salicylates - Drug Class Review
High-Yield Med Reviews</td></tr>
<tr><td colspan="4">Mechanism of Action: Irreversible inhibition of cyclooxygenase 1 and 2 (COX-1, COX-2) decreasing prostaglandin precursors, inhibition of thromboxane A2.</td></tr>
<tr><td colspan="4">Class Effects: Analgesia, antipyretic effect, dyspepsia, GI bleed, rash, and in overdose mixed acid-base disorder</td></tr>
<tr><td>Generic Name</td><td>Brand Name</td><td>Indication(s) or Uses</td><td>Notes</td></tr>
<tr>
<td>Aspirin</td>
<td>Bayer Aspirin</td>
<td>
<ul>
<li>Analgesic</li>
<li>Antiinflammatory</li>
<li>Antipyretic</li>
<li>Ischemic cardiac disease</li>
<li>Ischemic stroke or transient ischemic attack</li>
<li>Kawasaki disease</li>
<li>Myocardial infarction</li>
<li>Rheumatic fever</li>
</ul>
</td>
<td>
<ul>
<li>Dosing (Adult):
  <ul>
  <li>Oral 81 to 325 mg daily</li>
  <li>Oral 325 to 1,000 mg q4-6h, maximum 4,000 mg/day</li>
  <li>Rectal 300 to 600 mg/day</li>
  </ul>
</li>
<li>Dosing (Peds):
  <ul>
  <li>Oral/Rectal 10 to 15 mg/kg/dose q4-6h
    <ul><li>Maximum 90 mg/kg/day or 4,000 mg/day</li></ul>
  </li>
  </ul>
</li>
<li>CYP450 Interactions: None</li>
<li>Renal or Hepatic Dose Adjustments:
  <ul><li>Severe hepatic disease - Avoid use</li></ul>
</li>
<li>Dosage Forms: Oral (caplet, capsule, tablet), Rectal (suppository)</li>
</ul>
</td>
</tr>
<tr>
<td>Choline Magnesium Trisalicylate</td>
<td>Trilisate</td>
<td><ul><li>Analgesia</li></ul></td>
<td>
<ul>
<li>Dosing (Adult):
  <ul><li>Oral 1,500 to 3,000 mg q8-24h</li></ul>
</li>
<li>Dosing (Peds):
  <ul><li>Oral 25 mg/kg/dose q12h</li></ul>
</li>
<li>CYP450 Interactions: None</li>
<li>Renal or Hepatic Dose Adjustments: None</li>
<li>Dosage Forms: Oral (Liquid)</li>
</ul>
</td>
</tr>
<tr>
<td>Magnesium Salicylate</td>
<td>Doan's Pills</td>
<td><ul><li>Analgesia</li></ul></td>
<td>
<ul>
<li>Dosing (Adult):
  <ul><li>Oral 1 - 2 tablet q4-6h as needed for pain</li></ul>
</li>
<li>Dosing (Peds):
  <ul><li>Not routinely used</li></ul>
</li>
<li>CYP450 Interactions: None</li>
<li>Renal or Hepatic Dose Adjustments: None</li>
<li>Dosage Forms: Oral (tablet)</li>
</ul>
</td>
</tr>
</table>

Salicylates - Drug Class Review
High-Yield Med Reviews

Generic Name	Brand Name	Indication(s) or Uses	Notes

Methyl salicylate	Bengay Icy Hot Salonpas Thera-Gesic	• Analgesia	• **Dosing (Adult):**
			  – Topically apply to affected area q6-8h as needed
			  – Topical patch applied to affected area q6-8h as needed
			• **Dosing (Peds):**
			  – Not routinely used
			• **CYP450 Interactions:** None
			• **Renal or Hepatic Dose Adjustments:** None
			• **Dosage Forms:** Topical (balm, cream, foam, spray, stick)

Salsalate	N/A	• Analgesia	• **Dosing (Adult):**
			  – Oral 1 g q8h
			• **Dosing (Peds):**
			  – Not routinely used
			• **CYP450 Interactions:** None
			• **Renal or Hepatic Dose Adjustments:** None
			• **Dosage Forms:** Oral (tablet)

Trolamine	Arthricream Asper-flex Myoflex	• Analgesia	• **Dosing (Adult):**
			  – Topically apply to affected area q6-8h as needed
			• **Dosing (Peds):**
			  – Topically apply to affected area q6-8h as needed
			• **CYP450 Interactions:** None
			• **Renal or Hepatic Dose Adjustments:** None
			• **Dosage Forms:** Topical (cream, lotion)

High-Yield Clinical Knowledge

- **Analgesic Properties**
  - Upon tissue injury and the accompanying inflammation contributing pain is caused by the release of prostaglandins by cytokines such as bradykinin.
  - Local or systemic COX inhibition and prostaglandins by salicylates contribute to analgesia, combined with other pain management strategies.
- **Antipyresis**
  - The physiologic process by which fever is produced is mediated by inflammatory cytokines (IL-1, IL-6, TNF-alpha), which increase the synthesis of prostaglandin E2, triggering the hypothalamic response to elevate the body temperature set point.
  - Inhibition of prostaglandins using salicylates can contribute to an antipyretic of salicylates.
  - The antipyretic dose range of aspirin is much higher than that for cardiovascular indications, 324 to 1,000 mg by mouth q4-6h.
    - The maximum daily dose for adults is 4 g.
- **Antiplatelet Effects**
  - The covalent modification of COX-1 and COX-2 by aspirin leads to irreversible platelet function for the duration of the platelet's life as these cells are not capable of independently generating COX-1.

- **GI Bleeds**
  - Inhibition of COX-1 by salicylates prevents PGE2 and PGI2 production, which leads to a decline in the production of the protective mucous lining in the GI mucosal lining, exposing the underlying tissue to gastric acid.
  - As aspirin possesses a potent antiplatelet effect, normal coagulation may be impaired due to its inhibition of TXA2 and direct cytotoxic and irritating effects.
  - The most common ulcers formed by NSAIDs are located in the duodenum.
- **Aspirin in Pediatrics**
  - High doses of aspirin may be given to children with Kawasaki disease in combination with IV immune globulin.
    - Kawasaki disease is a vasculitis syndrome that may lead to heart disease in children, including coronary artery dilation and coronary aneurysms.
  - This is an essential distinction from over-the-counter aspirin use in children for analgesia and antipyresis recovering from chickenpox or influenza, which may develop Reye syndrome.

- **Niacin Flushing**
  - Patients who take high-dose niacin for cholesterol modulating effects can experience intense facial flushing due to the release of prostaglandin D2.
  - This prostaglandin-mediated flushing reaction can be blunted with concomitant aspirin use.
- **Hypersensitivity and Cross-Reactivity**
  - Patients who report an allergy to aspirin or NSAIDs may experience cross-sensitivity to other NSAIDs or aspirin.
  - Aspirin is contraindicated in patients with a history of hypersensitivity to NSAIDs.
    - In some clinical scenarios where aspirin is still necessary, desensitization protocols permit aspirin's safe use, but these must occur in an acute-care setting.

High-Yield Fast-Facts

- **Resistance**
  - Genetic variants of COX can lead to alternative pathways, and ultimately clinical failure of aspirin, referred to as aspirin resistance.
- **Salicylate Toxicity**
  - Salicylate overdose is a potentially life-threatening toxicity that can be fatal within hours of a massive overdose.
  - This mechanism involves the uncoupling of oxidative phosphorylation and the inability to form ATP from glucose.

HIGH-YIELD BOARD EXAM ESSENTIALS
- **CLASSIC AGENTS:** Aspirin, choline magnesium trisalicylate, methyl salicylate, salsalate, trolamine
- **DRUG CLASS:** Salicylates
- **INDICATIONS:** Analgesic, antiinflammatory, antipyretic, ischemic cardiac disease, ischemic stroke or transient ischemic attack, Kawasaki disease, myocardial infarction, rheumatic fever
- **MECHANISM:** Irreversible inhibition of cyclooxygenase 1 and 2 (COX-1, COX-2) decreasing prostaglandin precursors, inhibition of thromboxane A2.
- **SIDE EFFECTS:** Dyspepsia, GI bleed, rash
- **CLINICAL PEARLS:** High doses of aspirin may be given to children with Kawasaki disease in combination with IV immune globulin. Kawasaki disease is a vasculitis syndrome that may lead to heart disease in children, including coronary artery dilation and coronary aneurysms.

High-Yield Basic Pharmacology

- **Baclofen**
  - GABA-B agonist acts at the spinal cord level to inhibit transmission of reflexes resulting in skeletal muscle relaxation.
- **Botulinum toxin type A & B**
  - Inhibits synaptic exocytosis through clipping of vesicle fusion proteins in the presynaptic nerve terminal
- **Carisoprodol/Meprobamate**
  - Inhibits NMDA receptors and directly opens GABA-A receptors, similar to barbiturates.
- **Chlorzoxazone**
  - GABA-A and GABA-B agonists, as well as voltage-gated calcium channel antagonists.
- **Cyclobenzaprine**
  - Structurally similar to tricyclic antidepressants, producing antimuscarinic effects and skeletal muscle relaxation.
- **Dantrolene**
  - Ryanodine calcium channel receptor blocker, preventing increases in myoplasmic calcium and inhibition.
- **Metaxalone & Methocarbamol**
  - Inhibitions acetylcholinesterase, producing anticholinergic effects at the spinal cord level and within the CNS.
- **Orphenadrine**
  - Central and spinal antimuscarinic effects, producing analgesia and skeletal muscle relaxation.
- **Riluzole**
  - Inhibits the release of glutamate and inactivates voltage-dependent sodium channels.
- **Tizanidine**
  - Spinal alpha-2 receptor agonist.

Primary Net Benefit

- Skeletal muscle relaxants provide relief of muscle spasms and can be combined with other analgesics but can be associated with an anticholinergic adverse event of particular concern in the elderly.

Skeletal Muscle Relaxants - Drug Class Review			
High-Yield Med Reviews			
Mechanism of Action: *See agents above*			
Class Effects: Skeletal muscle relaxants provide relief of muscle spasms and can be combined with other analgesics but can be associated with an anticholinergic adverse event of particular concern in the elderly.			
Generic Name	**Brand Name**	**Indication(s) or Uses**	**Notes**

Abobotulinumto xinA	Dysport	• Cervical dystonia
		• Skeletal muscle relaxant
			• **Dosing (Adult):**
			  – IM 100 to 1,000 units divided among affected areas
			• **Dosing (Peds):**
			  – Not routinely used
			• **CYP450 Interactions:** None
			• **Renal or Hepatic Dose Adjustments:** None
			• **Dosage Forms:** IV (solution)

Skeletal Muscle Relaxants - Drug Class Review
High-Yield Med Reviews

Generic Name	Brand Name	Indication(s) or Uses	Notes

Baclofen	Gablofen
	Lioresal
	Ozobax
		• Skeletal muscle relaxant	• **Dosing (Adult):**
			  – Oral 5 to 10 mg TID, maximum 120 mg/day
			  – Intrathecal 50 mcg test dose followed by incremental doses to determine maintenance dose range.
			• **Dosing (Peds):**
			  – Oral 2.5 to 10 mg TID, maximum 60 mg/day
			  – Intrathecal 25 mcg test dose followed by incremental doses to determine maintenance dose range.
			• **CYP450 Interactions:** None
			• **Renal or Hepatic Dose Adjustments:**
			  – GFR 50 to 80 mL/minute - 5 mg q12h
			  – GFR 30 to 50 mL/minute - 2.5 mg q8h
			  – GFR less than 30 mL/minute - avoid use
			• **Dosage Forms:** Oral (solution, tablet), Intrathecal solution

Carisoprodol	Soma
	Vanadom
		• Skeletal muscle relaxant	• **Dosing (Adult):**
			  – Oral 250 to 350 mg TID, maximum 3 weeks
			• **Dosing (Peds):**
			  – Oral 250 to 350 mg TID, maximum 3 weeks
			    • Maximum 1,400 mg/day
			• **CYP450 Interactions:** Substrate CYP2C19
			• **Renal or Hepatic Dose Adjustments:** None
			• **Dosage Forms:** Oral (tablet)

Chlorzoxazone	Lorzone
	Parafon Forte
		• Skeletal muscle relaxant	• **Dosing (Adult):**
			  – Oral 250 to 750 mg q6-8h
			• **Dosing (Peds):**
			  – Oral 20 mg/kg/day in 3-4 divided doses
			    • Maximum 750 mg/dose
			• **CYP450 Interactions:** Substrate CYP1A2, 2A6, 2D6, 2E1, 3A4; Inhibits CYP3A4
			• **Renal or Hepatic Dose Adjustments:** None
			• **Dosage Forms:** Oral (tablet)

Cyclobenzaprine	Amrix,
	Fexmid,
	Flexeril
		• Skeletal muscle relaxant	• **Dosing (Adult):**
			  – Oral 5 to 15 mg q8-24h
			• **Dosing (Peds):**
			  – Oral 5 to 10 mg q8h
			• **CYP450 Interactions:** Substrate CYP1A2, 2D6, 3A4
			• **Renal or Hepatic Dose Adjustments:**
			  – Child-Pugh class B or C - use not recommended
			• **Dosage Forms:** Oral (tablet)

Skeletal Muscle Relaxants - Drug Class Review
High-Yield Med Reviews

Generic Name	Brand Name	Indication(s) or Uses	Notes

Dantrolene	Dantrium Revonto Ryanodex	▪ Skeletal muscle relaxant
		▪ Malignant hyperthermia
			▪ **Dosing (Adult):**
			  – Oral 25 to 100 mg q8-24h
			    ▪ Maximum 400 mg/day
			  – IV 2.5 mg/kg once followed by 1 mg/kg as needed to a maximum of 10 mg/kg
			▪ **Dosing (Peds):**
			  – Oral 4 to 8 mg/kg/day in 3 to 4 divided doses
			  – IV 2.5 mg/kg once followed by 1 mg/kg as needed to a maximum of 10 mg/kg
			▪ **CYP450 Interactions:** Substrate CYP3A4
			▪ **Renal or Hepatic Dose Adjustments:** None
			▪ **Dosage Forms:** Oral (capsule), IV (solution, suspension)

IncobotulinumtoxinA	Xeomin	▪ Blepharospasm
		▪ Skeletal muscle relaxant
			▪ **Dosing (Adult):**
			  – IM 25 to 100 units divided among affected areas
			▪ **Dosing (Peds):**
			  – IM 4 to 22.5 units to the parotid or submandibular gland
			  – IM 0.5 to 3 units/kg divided among affected areas
			    ▪ Maximum 50 units/dose
			▪ **CYP450 Interactions:** None
			▪ **Renal or Hepatic Dose Adjustments:** None
			▪ **Dosage Forms:** IV (solution)

Meprobamate	N/A	▪ Anxiety	▪ **Dosing (Adult):**
			  – Oral 1,200 to 1,600 mg/day in 3-4 divided doses
			    ▪ Maximum 2,400 mg/day
			▪ **Dosing (Peds):**
			  – Oral 200 to 600 mg/day in 2-3 divided doses
			▪ **CYP450 Interactions:** None
			▪ **Renal or Hepatic Dose Adjustments:**
			  – GFR 10 to 50 mL/minute - q9-12h
			  – GFR less than 10 mL/minute - q12-18h
			▪ **Dosage Forms:** Oral (tablet)

Metaxalone	Skelaxin	▪ Skeletal muscle relaxant	▪ **Dosing (Adult):**
			  – Oral 400 to 800 mg q6-8h
			▪ **Dosing (Peds):**
			  – Oral 400 to 800 mg q6-8h
			▪ **CYP450 Interactions:** Substrate CYP1A2, C19, 2C8, 2C9, 2D6, 2E1, 3A4
			▪ **Renal or Hepatic Dose Adjustments:** None
			▪ **Dosage Forms:** Oral (tablet)

Skeletal Muscle Relaxants - Drug Class Review
High-Yield Med Reviews

Generic Name	Brand Name	Indication(s) or Uses	Notes

Methocarbamol	Robaxin	▪ Skeletal muscle relaxant	▪ **Dosing (Adult):**
			  – Oral 1.5 g q6-8h for 3 days
			  – IM/IV 1 g q8h prn for muscle spasm
			▪ **Dosing (Peds):**
			  – Oral 1.5 g q6-8h for 3 days
			  – IM/IV 15 mg/kg/dose q6-8h prn for muscle spasm
			▪ **CYP450 Interactions:** None
			▪ **Renal or Hepatic Dose Adjustments:** None
			▪ **Dosage Forms:** Oral (tablet), IV (solution)

OnabotulinumtoxinA	Botox	▪ Axillary hyperhidrosis
		▪ Cervical dystonia
		▪ Chronic migraine
		▪ Neurogenic detrusor overactivity
		▪ Overactive bladder
		▪ Skeletal muscle relaxant
		▪ Urinary incontinence
			▪ **Dosing (Adult):**
			  – IM 5 to 75 units (total dose)
			    ▪ Maximum 400 units/3 months or cumulative dose of 6 units/kg
			▪ **Dosing (Peds):**
			  – Not routinely used
			▪ **CYP450 Interactions:** None
			▪ **Renal or Hepatic Dose Adjustments:** None
			▪ **Dosage Forms:** IV (solution)

Orphenadrine	Norflex	▪ Skeletal muscle relaxant	▪ **Dosing (Adult):**
			  – Oral 100 mg BID
			  – IM/IV 60 mg q12h
			▪ **Dosing (Peds):**
			  – Not routinely used
			▪ **CYP450 Interactions:** Substrate CYP1A2, 2B6, 2D6, 3A4
			▪ **Renal or Hepatic Dose Adjustments:** None
			▪ **Dosage Forms:** Oral (tablet), IV (solution)

PrabotulinumtoxinA	Nuceiva	▪ Glabellar lines	▪ **Dosing (Adult):**
			  – IM 4 units to up to 5 sites, or total dose of 20 units q3months
			▪ **Dosing (Peds):**
			  – Not routinely used
			▪ **CYP450 Interactions:** None
			▪ **Renal or Hepatic Dose Adjustments:** None
			▪ **Dosage Forms:** IV (solution)

Riluzole	Rilutek
	Tiglutik
		▪ Amyotrophic lateral sclerosis (ALS)	▪ **Dosing (Adult):**
			  – Oral 50 mg BID
			▪ **Dosing (Peds):**
			  – Not routinely used
			▪ **CYP450 Interactions:** Substrate CYP1A2
			▪ **Renal or Hepatic Dose Adjustments:** None
			▪ **Dosage Forms:** Oral (suspension, tablet)

Skeletal Muscle Relaxants - Drug Class Review
High-Yield Med Reviews

Generic Name	Brand Name	Indication(s) or Uses	Notes

RimabotulinumtoxinB	Myobloc	• Cervical dystonia	• **Dosing (Adult):**
			  – IM 2,00 to 5,000 units divided to affected areas
			• **Dosing (Peds):**
			  – Not routinely used
			• **CYP450 Interactions:** None
			• **Renal or Hepatic Dose Adjustments:** None
			• **Dosage Forms:** IV (solution)

Tizanidine	Zanaflex	• Skeletal muscle relaxant	• **Dosing (Adult):**
			  – Oral 2 to 4 mg q6-12h
			    • Maximum 24 mg/day
			• **Dosing (Peds):**
			  – Oral 1 to 4 mg at bedtime
			• **CYP450 Interactions:** Substrate CYP1A2
			• **Renal or Hepatic Dose Adjustments:**
			  – GFR less than 25 mL/minute - Reduce dose by 50%
			• **Dosage Forms:** Oral (capsule, tablet)

High-Yield Clinical Knowledge

- **Baclofen Toxicity and Withdrawal**
  - Baclofen in supratherapeutic doses can produce profound CNS depression, seizures, and respiratory depression in the setting of an overdose or baclofen infusion pump dysfunction.
  - Conversely, baclofen withdrawal presents similarly with altered mental status and seizures.
  - Patients on chronic baclofen therapy, particularly those who receive it through an implanted infusion device, must be educated on the signs and symptoms of baclofen toxicity or withdrawal.
- **Tizanidine and CYP1A2**
  - Concomitant use of tizanidine with either ciprofloxacin or fluvoxamine is contraindicated as a result of the risk of significant tizanidine toxicity from CYP1A2 inhibition.
- **Abuse Potential**
  - Carisoprodol and meprobamate are schedule IV drugs, as they pose a significant abuse potential risk due to their sedating properties.
    - Although sedative properties are concerning, so too is acute or abrupt discontinuation of chronic therapy, which can precipitate an acute withdrawal syndrome consisting of anxiety, tremors, muscle spasms, insomnia, and hallucinations.
  - Although other agents in this group also carry an abuse potential, no other agents are currently scheduled controlled substances.
- **Dantrolene Use**
  - Oral dantrolene is used to manage chronic spasticity in patients with spinal cord injuries, cerebral palsy, multiple sclerosis, or previous stroke.
  - Parenteral dantrolene is reserved for use in malignant hyperthermia cases, which is most often encountered as a result of anesthetic gases or succinylcholine.
  - Anesthetic gases in some patients are associated with unregulated calcium release from the sarcoplasmic reticulum, causing a potentially fatal cascade of excessive muscle contraction, ATP depletion, oxidative stress, and hyperthermia.
  - The ryanodine calcium channel is specifically identified in the pathophysiologic course of malignant hyperthermia.

- Its inhibition by dantrolene can be helpful in conjunction with invasive cooling, benzodiazepines, and supportive care.
- **Botulinum Toxin**
  - OnabotulinumtoxinA, the pharmacological product of botulinum toxin, and is derived from Clostridium botulinum.
  - Toxin A inhibits the presynaptic calcium-dependent release of acetylcholine, causing muscle inactivation until new fibrils grow and new junctions are formed.
  - Other botulinum toxin products include abobotulinumtoxinA, incobotulinumtoxinA, prabotulinumtoxinA, and rimabotulinumtoxinB.
    - Toxin B cleaves synaptic VAMPs, preventing docking and fusion of the synaptic vesicle to the presynaptic membrane, thus preventing neurotransmitter release.

HIGH-YIELD BOARD EXAM ESSENTIALS
- **CLASSIC AGENTS:** AbobotulinumtoxinA, baclofen, carisoprodol, chlorzoxazone, cyclobenzaprine, dantrolene
- incobotulinumtoxinA, metaxalone, methocarbamol, meprobamate, onabotulinumtoxinA, orphenadrine, prabotulinumtoxinA, rimabotulinumtoxinB, riluzole, tizanidine
- **DRUG CLASS:** Skeletal Muscle Relaxants
- **INDICATIONS:** Anxiety, blepharospasm, cervical dystonia, malignant hyperthermia,
- **MECHANISM:** Baclofen - GABA-B agonist; Onabotulinumtoxin A & B - Inhibits synaptic exocytosis of acetylcholine; Carisoprodol/Meprobamate - Inhibits NMDA receptors and directly opens GABA-A receptors; Chlorzoxazone - GABA-A and GABA-B agonists; Cyclobenzaprine - Antimuscarinic effects and skeletal muscle relaxation; Dantrolene - Ryanodine calcium channel receptor blocker; Metaxalone & Methocarbamol - Inhibitions acetylcholinesterase; Orphenadrine - Central and spinal antimuscarinic effects; Riluzole - Inhibits the release of glutamate and inactivates voltage-dependent sodium channels; Tizanidine - Spinal alpha-2 receptor agonist.
- **SIDE EFFECTS:** Abuse potential, CNS depression, seizures, and respiratory depression.
- **CLINICAL PEARLS:** Concomitant use of tizanidine with either ciprofloxacin or fluvoxamine is contraindicated as a result of the risk of significant tizanidine toxicity from CYP1A2 inhibition.

High-Yield Basic Pharmacology

- **Mechanism of Action**
  - Opioid receptor agonists blunt the perception and response to pain through inhibition of ascending pain pathways.
- **Unique Opioid (Methadone)**
  - Methadone is a racemic mixture of R- and S-methadone.
  - S-methadone is a substrate of CYP3A4 and 2D6 and associated with the QT-prolonging effects of methadone.
    - R-methadone is available in Europe, which is devoid of QT-prolonging effects.

Primary Net Benefit

- Long-acting opioid agonists are a component of chronic pain management but are associated with opioid dependence, which can lead to the need for methadone, a key element in treating opioid use disorder.

Opioid Analgesics, Long-Acting - Drug Class Review			
High-Yield Med Reviews			
Mechanism of Action: *Opioid receptor agonists blunt the perception and response to pain by inhibiting ascending pain pathways.*			
Class Effects: Constipation, altered mental status, respiratory depression, euphoria, abuse potential, QT prolongation (methadone).			
Generic Name	**Brand Name**	**Indication(s) or Uses**	**Notes**

Diphenoxylate and Atropine	Lomotil	• Diarrhea	• **Dosing (Adult):**
			  – Oral 5 mg 4 times daily until control achieved; Maximum 20 mg/day
			• **Dosing (Peds):**
			  – Oral 1.5 to 5 mL (2.5mg/5mL) 4 times daily until control achieved
			• **CYP450 Interactions:** None
			• **Renal or Hepatic Dose Adjustments:** None
			• **Dosage Forms:** Oral (liquid, tablet)

Fentanyl (buccal tablets, lozenges, sublingual spray, transdermal)	Actiq, Duragesic, Lazanda, Subsys	• Analgesia	• **Dosing (Adult):**
			  – Transmucosal lozenge 200 mcg over 15 min for 2 doses
			  – Buccal tablet 100 mcg followed by 100 mcg 30 minutes later, maximum 2 doses
			  – Sublingual spray/tablet 100 mcg followed by 100 mcg 30 minutes later, max 2 doses
			• **Dosing (Peds):**
			  – Intranasal 1.5 mcg/kg/dose; Max 100 mcg/dose
			• **CYP450 Interactions:** Substrate CYP3A4
			• **Renal or Hepatic Dose Adjustments:**
			  – Transdermal patch
			    • GFR 10 to 50 mL/minute - Reduce dose by 25%
			    • GFR < 10 mL/minute - Reduce dose by 50%
			    • Child-Pugh class C - Not recommended
			• **Dosage Forms:** Oral (liquid, lozenge, tablet), Nasal solution, Transdermal patch

Opioid Analgesics, Long-Acting - Drug Class Review
High-Yield Med Reviews

Generic Name	Brand Name	Indication(s) or Uses	Notes

Levorphanol	Dromoran	▪ Analgesia	▪ **Dosing (Adult):**
			  – Oral 1 to 4 mg q6-8h
			▪ **Dosing (Peds):**
			  – Not routinely used
			▪ **CYP450 Interactions:** None
			▪ **Renal or Hepatic Dose Adjustments:** None
			▪ **Dosage Forms:** Oral (tablet)

Loperamide	Diamode
	Imodium A-D
		▪ Diarrhea	▪ **Dosing (Adult):**
			  – Oral 4 mg followed by 2 mg after each loose stool
			    ▪ Maximum 16 mg/day
			▪ **Dosing (Peds):**
			  – Oral 1 to 4 mg with the first loose stool followed by 1 to 2 mg after each loose stool
			    ▪ Maximum dose by age
			      – Age 2-5; 3 mg/day
			      – Age 6-8; 4 mg/day
			      – Age 9-11; 6 mg/day
			▪ **CYP450 Interactions:** Substrate CYP2B6, 2C8, 2D6, 3A4, P-gp
			▪ **Renal or Hepatic Dose Adjustments:** None
			▪ **Dosage Forms:** Oral (capsule, liquid, suspension, tablet)

Methadone	Dolophine	▪ Analgesia
		▪ Opioid use disorder
			▪ **Dosing (Adult):**
			  – Oral 10 to 100 mg daily (opioid use disorder)
			  – Oral 2.5 to 10 mg q8-12h (analgesia)
			▪ **Dosing (Peds):**
			  – IV/SQ 0.025 mg/kg/dose 4-8h
			  – Oral 0.025 to 0.2 mg/kg/dose q4-8h
			▪ **CYP450 Interactions:** Substrate CYP2B6, 2C19, 2C9, 2D6, 3A4, P-gp; Inhibits CYP2D6
			▪ **Renal or Hepatic Dose Adjustments:** None
			▪ **Dosage Forms:** Oral (concentrate, tablet), IV (solution)

Opioid Analgesics, Long-Acting - Drug Class Review
High-Yield Med Reviews

Generic Name	Brand Name	Indication(s) or Uses	Notes

Morphine (sustained-release)	Duramorph Infumorph MS Contin	▪ Analgesia	▪ **Dosing (Adult):**
			  – Oral ER administer total oral morphine daily dose in two divided doses
			▪ **Dosing (Peds):**
			  – Oral ER 0.3 to 0.6 mg/kg/dose q12h
			▪ **CYP450 Interactions:** Substrate of P-gp
			▪ **Renal or Hepatic Dose Adjustments:**
			  – GFR 30 - 60 mL/min - Reduce dose by 50%
			  – GFR 15 - 30 mL/min - Reduce dose by 75%
			  – GFR < 15 mL/minute - Not recommended
			▪ **Dosage Forms:** Oral (capsule, solution, tablet), Suppository, IV solution

Oxycodone (With or without acetaminophen)	<u>Without acetaminophen</u> Oxycontin
	
	<u>With acetaminophen</u> Percocet
		▪ Analgesia	▪ **Dosing (Adult):**
			  – Oral ER 10 to 20 mg q12-24h
			▪ **Dosing (Peds):**
			  – Oral IR 0.1 to 0.2 mg/kg/dose q4-6h
			    ▪ Maximum 10 mg/dose
			▪ **CYP450 Interactions:** Substrate CYP2C6, CYP3A4
			▪ **Renal or Hepatic Dose Adjustments:**
			  – GFR < 30 mL/minute - Reduce dose by 50%
			  – Child-Pugh class C - Reduce dose by 50%
			▪ **Dosage Forms:** Oral (capsule, tablet)

Tapentadol	Nucynta	▪ Analgesia	▪ **Dosing (Adult):**
			  – Oral IR 50 to 100 mg q4-6h
			    ▪ Maximum 600 mg/day
			  – Oral ER 50 to 250 mg q12h
			▪ **Dosing (Peds):**
			  – Not routinely used
			▪ **CYP450 Interactions:** text
			▪ **Renal or Hepatic Dose Adjustments:**
			  – GFR less than 30 mL/minute - use not recommended
			  – Child-Pugh class B - IR start q8h; ER start q24h
			  – Child-Pugh class C - Not recommended
			▪ **Dosage Forms:** Oral (tablet immediate release, extended-release)

Opioid Analgesics, Long-Acting - Drug Class Review
High-Yield Med Reviews

Generic Name	Brand Name	Indication(s) or Uses	Notes

Tramadol	Ultram	▪ Analgesia	▪ **Dosing (Adult):**
			– Oral IR 50 to 100 mg q4-6h
			   ▪ Maximum 400 mg/day
			– Oral ER 100 - 300 mg daily
			▪ **Dosing (Peds):**
			– Extra info if needed
			   ▪ Extra info if needed
			▪ **CYP450 Interactions:** text
			▪ **Renal or Hepatic Dose Adjustments:**
			– GFR less than 30 mL/minute - IR q12h; ER use not recommended
			– Child-Pugh class C - Not recommended
			▪ **Dosage Forms:** Oral (tablet immediate release, extended-release)

High-Yield Clinical Knowledge

- **Methadone QT and Hepatic Oxidation**
  - Methadone is associated with dose-dependent prolongation of the QT interval.
  - It is also a major substrate of CYP 3A4 and 2B6 and a minor substrate of CYP 2C19, 2C9, and 2D6.
  - Numerous drug interactions may increase the risk of respiratory depression as well as QT-prolonging effects.
- **Diphenoxylate and Loperamide**
  - Diphenoxylate and loperamide are over-the-counter opioids that are structurally similar to meperidine.
  - These agents are not absorbed systemically and used for self-care of diarrhea.
  - Diphenoxylate is co-formulated with atropine to deter abuse, as massive doses of it or loperamide may overcome P-glycoprotein in the gut, which produces sufficient systemic levels to cause CNS opioid effects.
    - Alternatively, co-ingestion with a P-glycoprotein inhibitor, such as clarithromycin, colchicine, diltiazem, erythromycin, omeprazole, or duloxetine, can also produce a systemic opioid agonist effect at standard dosing of diphenoxylate or loperamide.
- **Opioid Cross-Reactivity**
  - Patients who report allergies to opioids may have cross-reactivity to other similar opioid structural classes but may safely take opioids in different structural classes.
  - For example, patients with reported allergies to the phenanthrenes (codeine, morphine, heroin, hydrocodone, oxycodone) should not receive any agent within this class.
    - However, cross-reactivity risk is lower in distinct structural classes such as the phenylpiperidines (fentanyl, meperidine).
  - Opioid cross-reactivity may also refer to laboratory detection of opioids or opiates.
    - Like allergies, opioids with structural similarities (for example, morphine and oxycodone) may result in cross-reactivity on opioid screening assays.
- **Tapentadol and Tramadol Seizures**
  - Seizures at regular doses or supratherapeutic doses have been observed with tapentadol and tramadol use.
  - These seizures should not be managed with naloxone as it has been associated with worsening seizures.
  - Benzodiazepines should be considered first-line agents for the management of drug-induced seizures.
- **Diminished Analgesic Effects**
  - Conversely to precipitating withdrawal, patients taking mixed opioid receptor agents may experience diminished responses to opioid analgesics, commonly in the post-surgical environment.
  - In these situations, patients may receive repeated doses, or high doses, to achieve analgesia; however, respiratory depression may be unaffected by this effect and can occur without other opioid-like products.

- **Fentanyl Transdermal Disposal**
  - Patients must be counseled on appropriate disposal of used fentanyl patches, as these patches, although therapeutically no longer beneficial, still contain significant quantities of fentanyl.
  - Surreptitious removal of the remaining fentanyl reservoir is a common method of acquisition of illicit fentanyl.
    - Once removed from the patch, this fentanyl can be smoked or injected.
  - Used patches must be folded with the adhesive ends together, disposed of in a biohazard container, and returned to the patient's pharmacy.
  - Like the transdermal disposal, fentanyl buccal tablets, lozenges, sublingual spray, or other dosage forms that are not used must also be disposed of properly to avoid diversion.

High-Yield Fast-Facts

- **Kratom Use**
  - Kratom is an extract from the plant *Mitragyna speciosa* that exhibits partial mu-opioid receptor agonist effects.
- **Neonatal Abstinence Syndrome**
  - Methadone or morphine is used to treat neonatal abstinence syndrome in neonates born to mothers who are chronically taking therapeutic opioids or illicit use of opioids.
- **Precipitating Acute Withdrawal**
  - Administration of an opioid agonist combined with a partial agonist or mixed agonist/antagonists (buprenorphine, butorphanol, nalbuphine, or pentazocine) may precipitate acute opioid withdrawal.

HIGH-YIELD BOARD EXAM ESSENTIALS
- **CLASSIC AGENTS:** Diphenoxylate, fentanyl, levorphanol, loperamide, methadone, morphine, oxycodone, tapentadol, tramadol
- **DRUG CLASS:** Opioid Analgesics, Long-Acting
- **INDICATIONS:** Analgesia, opioid-use disorder
- **MECHANISM:** Opioid receptor agonists blunt the perception and response to pain by inhibiting ascending pain pathways.
- **SIDE EFFECTS:** Constipation, altered mental status, respiratory depression, euphoria, abuse potential, QT prolongation (methadone)
- **CLINICAL PEARLS:** Diphenoxylate and loperamide are over-the-counter opioids that are structurally similar to meperidine. These agents are not absorbed systemically and used for self-care of diarrhea.

High-Yield Basic Pharmacology

- **Mechanism of Action**
  - Opioid receptor agonists blunt the perception and response to pain through inhibition of ascending pain pathways.
- **Mu Receptors**
  - Opioid agonist effects on the mu-1 receptors located in the CNS are the primary therapeutic target of opioids for analgesia.
    - Central mu-1 receptors are also partially responsible for the euphoric effects associated with opioid use.
  - Mu-2 receptors are also located in the CNS, but when stimulated, they cause a diminished sensitivity if the medullary chemoreceptors to hypercapnia, which decreases the ventilatory response to hypoxia.
    - An alternative nomenclature of opioid receptors has been proposed, which would rename mu receptors OP3 receptors.

Primary Net Benefit

- Rapid-acting analgesics have been a cornerstone of pain management, but the benefits must be balanced with the risk of dependence or abuse.

<table>
<tr><td colspan="4"> Opioid Analgesics, Short-Acting - Drug Class Review
High-Yield Med Reviews </td></tr>
<tr><td colspan="4">Mechanism of Action: Opioid receptor agonists blunt the perception and response to pain by inhibiting ascending pain pathways.</td></tr>
<tr><td colspan="4">Class Effects: Constipation, rash, flushing, erythema, respiratory depression, hypotension (with IV push).</td></tr>
<tr><td>Generic Name</td><td>Brand Name</td><td>Indication(s) or Uses</td><td>Notes</td></tr>
<tr>
<td>Alfentanil</td>
<td>Alfenta</td>
<td>
<ul><li>Analgesia</li><li>Anesthesia</li></ul>
</td>
<td>
<ul>
<li>Dosing (Adult):
  <ul><li>IV induction 8 to 235 mg/kg</li>
  <li>IV maintenance 0.5 to 1.5 mcg/kg/min</li></ul></li>
<li>Dosing (Peds):
  <ul><li>IV induction 8 to 235 mg/kg</li>
  <li>IV maintenance 0.5 to 1.5 mcg/kg/min</li></ul></li>
<li>CYP450 Interactions: Substrate CYP3A4</li>
<li>Renal or Hepatic Dose Adjustments: None</li>
<li>Dosage Forms: IV (solution)</li>
</ul>
</td>
</tr>
<tr>
<td>Codeine</td>
<td>N/A</td>
<td>
<ul><li>Analgesia</li><li>Cough</li></ul>
</td>
<td>
<ul>
<li>Dosing (Adult):
  <ul><li>IM/SQ 30 to 60 mg q406h as needed for pain</li>
  <li>Oral 15 to 60 mg q4h as needed for pain
    <ul><li>Extra info if needed</li></ul></li></ul></li>
<li>Dosing (Peds):
  <ul><li>Use with caution
    <ul><li>Oral 0.5 to 1 mg/kg/dose q4-6h</li></ul></li></ul></li>
<li>CYP450 Interactions: Substrate CYP2D6, 3A4</li>
<li>Renal or Hepatic Dose Adjustments:
  <ul><li>GFR 10 to 50 mL/minute - Reduce dose by 25%</li>
  <li>GFR less than 10 mL/minute - Reduce dose by 50%</li></ul></li>
<li>Dosage Forms: Oral (tablet)</li>
</ul>
</td>
</tr>
</table>

Opioid Analgesics, Short-Acting - Drug Class Review
High-Yield Med Reviews

Generic Name	Brand Name	Indication(s) or Uses	Notes

Dihydrocodeine-Aspirin-Caffeine	Synalgos-DC	▪ Analgesia	▪ **Dosing (Adult):**
			  – Oral two capsules q4h as needed for pain
			▪ **Dosing (Peds):** [same as adult]
			  – Extra info if needed
			    ▪ Extra info if needed
			▪ **CYP450 Interactions:** Substrate CYP 2D6, 3A4
			▪ **Renal or Hepatic Dose Adjustments:**
			  – GFR less than 10 mL/minute - Not recommended
			  – Child-Pugh class C - Not recommended
			▪ **Dosage Forms:** Oral (capsule)

Fentanyl	Actiq, Duragesic, Lazanda, Subsys	▪ Analgesia	▪ **Dosing (Adult):**
			  – IV loading 1 to 2 mcg/kg
			  – IV 0.35 to 0.5 mcg/kg q30-60min or 25 to 200 mcg/hour
			  – IM 50 to 100 mcg q1-2hours
			  – Intranasal 100 mcg once
			  – Transmucosal lozenge 200 mcg over 15 min for 2 doses
			  – Buccal tablet 100 mcg followed by 100 mcg 30 minutes later, maximum 2 doses
			  – Sublingual spray/tablet 100 mcg followed by 100 mcg 30 minutes later, maximum 2 doses
			▪ **Dosing (Peds):**
			  – IV loading 1 to 2 mcg/kg
			  – IV/IM 0.35 to 0.5 mcg/kg q30-60min
			  – Intranasal 1.5 mcg/kg/dose
			    ▪ Maximum 100 mcg/dose
			▪ **CYP450 Interactions:** Substrate CYP3A4
			▪ **Renal or Hepatic Dose Adjustments:**
			  – Transdermal patch
			    ▪ GFR 10 to 50 mL/minute - Reduce dose by 25%
			    ▪ GFR less than 10 mL/minute - Reduce dose by 50%
			    ▪ Child-Pugh class C - Not recommended
			▪ **Dosage Forms:** IV (solution), Oral (liquid, lozenge, tablet), Nasal solution, Transdermal patch

Opioid Analgesics, Short-Acting - Drug Class Review
High-Yield Med Reviews

Generic Name	Brand Name	Indication(s) or Uses	Notes

Hydrocodone (With or without acetaminophen)	<u>With Acetaminophen</u>
	Lorcet, Lortab, Norco, Vicodin, Xodol
	
	<u>Without Acetaminophen</u>
	Hysingla ER Zohydro
		▪ Analgesia	▪ **Dosing (Adult):**
			  – Oral IR 5 to 10 mg q4-6h as needed for pain
			  – Oral ER 10 to 20 mg q12-24h
			▪ **Dosing (Peds):**
			  – Oral IR 0.1 to 0.2 mg/kg/dose q4-6h
			    ▪ Maximum 10 mg/dose
			▪ **CYP450 Interactions:** Substrate CYP2C6, CYP3A4
			▪ **Renal or Hepatic Dose Adjustments:**
			  – GFR less than 30 mL/minute - Reduce dose by 50%
			  – Child-Pugh class C - Reduce dose by 50%
			▪ **Dosage Forms:** Oral (capsule, tablet)

Hydromorphone	Dilaudid Exalgo	▪ Analgesia	▪ **Dosing (Adult):**
			  – Oral 2.5 to 10 mg q4-6h as needed for pain
			  – IV 0.2 to 1 mg q2-3h as needed for pain
			  – IM/SQ 1 to 2 mg q2-3h as needed for pain
			▪ **Dosing (Peds):**
			  – Oral 0.03 to 0.06 mg q4-6h as needed for pain
			  – IV 0.015 mg/kg/dose q2-3h as needed for pain
			  – IM/SQ 0.8 to 1 mg q2-3h as needed for pain
			▪ **CYP450 Interactions:** None
			▪ **Renal or Hepatic Dose Adjustments:**
			  – GFR 30 to 60 mL/minute - Reduce dose by 50%
			  – GFR less than 30 mL/minute - Reduce dose by 75%
			  – Child-Pugh class C - Not recommended
			▪ **Dosage Forms:** Oral (liquid, tablet), Suppository, IV (solution)

Meperidine	Demerol	▪ Analgesia	▪ **Dosing (Adult):**
			  – IM/SQ 12.5 to 150 mg q3-4h
			    ▪ Extra info if needed
			▪ **Dosing (Peds):**
			  – IM/IV/SQ 0.2 to 1 mg/kg/dose q2-3hours
			  – Oral 0.5 to 4 mg/kg/dose q3-4h
			▪ **CYP450 Interactions:** None
			▪ **Renal or Hepatic Dose Adjustments:**
			  – GFR less than 30 mL/minute - not recommended
			  – Child-Pugh class B or C - not recommended
			▪ **Dosage Forms:** Oral (tablet, solution), IV (solution)

Opioid Analgesics, Short-Acting - Drug Class Review
High-Yield Med Reviews

Generic Name	Brand Name	Indication(s) or Uses	Notes
Morphine	Duramorph Infumorph MS Contin	▪ Analgesia	▪ **Dosing (Adult):** – Oral IR/Rectal 10 to 30 mg q4h as needed for pain – IV 0.01 mg/kg or 1 to 4 mg q1-4 hours – SQ 2 to 5 mg q3-4h as needed for pain ▪ **Dosing (Peds):** – IM/IV/SQ 0.05 to 0.2 mg/kg/dose – Infusion 0.01 to 0.04 mg/kg/hour – Oral IR 0.2 to 0.5 mg/kg/dose q3-4h as needed for pain ▪ **CYP450 Interactions:** Substrate of P-gp ▪ **Renal or Hepatic Dose Adjustments:** – GFR 30 to 60 mL/minute - Reduce dose by 50% – GFR 15 to 30 mL/minute - Reduce dose by 75% – GFR less than 15 mL/minute - Not recommended ▪ **Dosage Forms:** Oral (capsule, solution, tablet), Suppository, IV solution
Oxycodone (With or without acetaminophen)	<u>Without acetaminophen</u> Oxycontin <u>With acetaminophen</u> Percocet	▪ Analgesia	▪ **Dosing (Adult):** – Oral IR 5 to 15 mg q4-6h as needed for pain – Oral ER 10 to 20 mg q12-24h ▪ **Dosing (Peds):** – Oral IR 0.1 to 0.2 mg/kg/dose q4-6h ▪ Maximum 10 mg/dose ▪ **CYP450 Interactions:** Substrate CYP2C6, CYP3A4 ▪ **Renal or Hepatic Dose Adjustments:** – GFR less than 30 mL/minute - Reduce dose by 50% – Child-Pugh class C - Reduce dose by 50% ▪ **Dosage Forms:** Oral (capsule, tablet)
Oxymorphone	Opana	▪ Analgesia	▪ **Dosing (Adult):** – IM/SQ 1 to 1.5 mg q4-6h – IV 0.5 to 1 mg – Oral IR 5 to 10 mg q4-6h as needed for pain – Oral ER 5 mg q12h ▪ **Dosing (Peds):** – Not routinely used ▪ **CYP450 Interactions:** text ▪ **Renal or Hepatic Dose Adjustments:** text ▪ **Dosage Forms:** Oral (tablet), IV solution

Opioid Analgesics, Short-Acting - Drug Class Review
High-Yield Med Reviews

Generic Name	Brand Name	Indication(s) or Uses	Notes

Remifentanil	Ultiva	• Analgesia
		• Anesthesia
			• **Dosing (Adult):**
			  – IV 0.25 to 2 mg/kg/minute
			• **Dosing (Peds):**
			  – IV 0.15 to 2 mg/kg/minute
			• **CYP450 Interactions:** None
			• **Renal or Hepatic Dose Adjustments:** None
			• **Dosage Forms:** IV (solution)

Sufentanil	Dsuvia	• Analgesia
		• Anesthesia
			• **Dosing (Adult):**
			  – SL 30 mcg q1h as needed for pain, maximum 360 mg/day
			  – IV 1 to 2 mcg/kg initially followed by 10 to 25 mcg as needed, maximum 1 mcg/kg/hour
			• **Dosing (Peds):**
			  – IV 5 to 25 mcg/kg initially followed by 1 to 5 mcg/kg/dose up to 50 mcg/dose as needed
			• **CYP450 Interactions:** Substrate CYP3A4
			• **Renal or Hepatic Dose Adjustments:** None
			• **Dosage Forms:** Oral (sublingual tablet), IV (solution)

High-Yield Clinical Knowledge

- **Opioid-Induced Constipation**
  - Constipation associated with opioid use is mediated by mu-2 receptor stimulation in the intestinal wall.
  - Bowel regimens including fiber, stool softeners, and laxatives should be considered in patients taking opioid agonists.
    - Oral naloxone doses between 2 and 6 mg can be administered to help relieve opioid-induced constipation.
    - Doses of oral naloxone above 6 mg should be avoided to reduce the risk of sufficient systemic absorption to produce acute opioid withdrawal.
- **Histamine Release**
  - Parenteral administration of some opioids induces mast cell-mediated histamine release, producing pruritus.
  - Meperidine and morphine are most likely to cause clinically relevant histamine release, whereas fentanyl is least likely associated with histamine release.
- **Respiratory Depression**
  - Opioid agonists who act on mu-2 receptors are associated with a dose-dependent decrease in the hypercapnia's ventilatory response.
  - Respiratory depression observed due to opioids is more closely related to decreased tidal volume and not necessarily respiratory rate.
- **Opioid Hyperalgesia**
  - The phenomena of opioid hyperalgesia is an increased innate response to pain after exposure to opioid agents.
    - This can be confused with opioid tolerance as patients may require higher doses to achieve an appropriate analgesic response.
  - Opioid hyperalgesia was first observed in patients in methadone maintenance programs but has been contemporarily described in surgical and critical care populations.

- **Fentanyl Rigid Chest Syndrome**
  - The rapid administration of fentanyl, mainly when doses are above 300 mcg, can produce an intercostal muscle spasm and a "rigid chest syndrome."
    - This intercostal muscle spasm impairs respiratory accommodation and diminishes spontaneous ventilation.
  - This is thought to be a non-opioid receptor effect caused by dopamine receptor antagonist effects in the basal ganglia but can be reversed with naloxone.
- **Codeine In Pediatrics**
  - The use of codeine in children under the age of 18 is discouraged as they are at higher risk of clinically relevant opioid toxicity in the setting of undiagnosed CYP2D6 polymorphisms.
  - As codeine is a prodrug, which is metabolized by CYP2D6 to morphine and by CYP3A4 to norcodeine.
    - In patients with polymorphism leading to CYP2D6 overexpression, patients may unpredictably produce significant quantities of morphine.
- **Meperidine Neurotoxicity**
  - Meperidine is an opioid agonist as well as a presynaptic serotonin reuptake inhibitor.
  - In patients with concomitant serotonergic agents, the use of meperidine carries a risk of serotonin syndrome characterized by muscle rigidity, hyperthermia, and altered mental status.
  - Meperidine's active metabolite, normeperidine, is also neurotoxic and potentially induces delirium, tremor, myoclonus, and seizures.

High-Yield Fast-Facts

- **Runner's High**
  - The physiologic basis for the euphoria experienced after running or intense exercise has been observed to be reversed by naloxone and thought to result from endogenous opioid release.
- **Opioid Vs. Opiate**
  - Opiates refer to natural opium derivatives (codeine, heroin, morphine, hydromorphone), whereas opioids are synthetic derivatives of opiates (fentanyl, methadone).
- **Heroin and Cocaine**
  - The combination of heroin and cocaine, known as a speedball, causes competition for their shared metabolic pathway via plasma cholinesterase and liver carboxylesterases.
  - The result is an increased physiologic response to one or both of these agents.

HIGH-YIELD BOARD EXAM ESSENTIALS
- **CLASSIC AGENTS:** Alfentanil, codeine, dihydrocodeine, fentanyl, heroin, hydrocodone, hydromorphone, meperidine, morphine, oxycodone, oxymorphone, remifentanil, sufentanil
- **DRUG CLASS:** Opioid analgesics, short-acting
- **INDICATIONS:** Analgesia
- **MECHANISM:** Opioid receptor agonists blunt the perception and response to pain through inhibition of ascending pain pathways
- **SIDE EFFECTS:** Constipation, rash, flushing, erythema, respiratory depression, hypotension
- **CLINICAL PEARLS:** Constipation associated with opioid use is mediated by mu-2 receptor stimulation in the intestinal wall. Bowel regimens including fiber, stool softeners, and laxatives should be considered in patients taking opioid agonists.

High-Yield Basic Pharmacology

- **Mechanism of Action**
  - Competitive opioid receptor (including mu, kappa, and delta) antagonists.
- **Oral Bioavailability**
  - At normal dose ranges, naloxone is minimally absorbed orally (bioavailability approximately 2%).
    - For acute opioid overdose, this route is not appropriate, and naloxone must be given parenterally or intranasally.
    - For opioid-induced constipation, oral administration of naloxone is possible, as it exerts a local effect on the GI.
  - Naltrexone, on the other hand, has a wide range of bioavailability due to first-pass metabolism between 5 and 60%.
  - Naloxegol is a pegylated derivative of naloxone, which increases oral bioavailability, and reduces penetration into the CNS.

Primary Net Benefit

- Naloxone is a life-saving intervention in opioid intoxicated patients, but it and other opioid antagonists can be used for local opioid withdrawal effects, primarily constipation.

Opioid Antagonists - Drug Class Review			
High-Yield Med Reviews			
Mechanism of Action: *Competitive opioid receptor (including mu, kappa, and delta) antagonists.*			
Class Effects: Reversal of opioids, risk for acute opioid withdrawal, diarrhea, and ARDS with rapid reversal.			
Generic Name	**Brand Name**	**Indication(s) or Uses**	**Notes**
Alvimopan	Entereg	• Postoperative ileus	• **Dosing (Adult):** – Oral 12 mg 30 minutes to 5 hours before surgery, then 12 mg q12h for a maximum of 7 days • **Dosing (Peds):** – Not routinely used • **CYP450 Interactions:** None • **Renal or Hepatic Dose Adjustments:** – ESRD - Not recommended – Child-Pugh class C - Not recommended • **Dosage Forms:** Oral (capsule)
Naldemedine	Symproic	• Opioid-induced constipation	• **Dosing (Adult):** – Oral 0.2 mg once daily • **Dosing (Peds):** – Not routinely used • **CYP450 Interactions:** Substrate CYP3A4, P-gp • **Renal or Hepatic Dose Adjustments:** – Child-Pugh class C - Not recommended • **Dosage Forms:** Oral (tablet)

Opioid Antagonists - Drug Class Review
High-Yield Med Reviews

Generic Name	Brand Name	Indication(s) or Uses	Notes

Naloxegol	Movantik	▪ Opioid-induced constipation	▪ **Dosing (Adult):**
			  – Oral 12.5 to 25 mg daily
			▪ **Dosing (Peds):**
			  – Not routinely used
			▪ **CYP450 Interactions:** Substrate CYP3A4, P-gp
			▪ **Renal or Hepatic Dose Adjustments:**
			  – GFR less than 60 mL/minute - initial dose of 12.5 mg
			  – Child-Pugh class C - Not recommended
			▪ **Dosage Forms:** Oral (tablet)

Naloxone	Narcan	▪ Opioid overdose
		▪ Opioid-induced constipation or pruritus
			▪ **Dosing (Adult):**
			  – IV/IM/SQ 0.04 to 2 mg repeated as needed q2-3minutes
			  – Intranasal 2 mg, repeated as needed q2-3minutes
			  – IV infusion 0.25 to 3 mcg/kg/hour
			▪ **Dosing (Peds):**
			  – IV/IM/SQ 0.04 to 2 mg repeated as needed q2-3minutes
			  – IV 0.1 mg/kg/dose repeated as needed
			  – Intranasal 2 mg, repeated as needed q2-3minutes
			  – IV infusion 0.25 to 3 mcg/kg/hour
			▪ **CYP450 Interactions:** None
			▪ **Renal or Hepatic Dose Adjustments:** None
			▪ **Dosage Forms:** Nasal (liquid), IV (solution)

Naltrexone	Vivitrol	▪ Alcohol use disorder
		▪ Opioid use disorder
			▪ **Dosing (Adult):**
			  – Oral 50 to 100 mg/day
			  – IM 380 mg q4weeks
			▪ **Dosing (Peds):**
			  – Not routinely used
			▪ **CYP450 Interactions:** None
			▪ **Renal or Hepatic Dose Adjustments:** None
			▪ **Dosage Forms:** Oral (tablet), Suspension for intramuscular injection

Methylnaltrexone	Relistor	▪ Opioid-induced constipation	▪ **Dosing (Adult):**
			  – IM 8 to 12 mg once
			  – IM 0.15 mg/kg if less than 38 kg or greater than 114 kg
			  – Oral 450 mg once daily
			▪ **Dosing (Peds):**
			  – Not routinely used
			▪ **CYP450 Interactions:** Substrate CYP2D6
			▪ **Renal or Hepatic Dose Adjustments:**
			  – GFR less than 60 mL/minute - reduce dose by 50%
			▪ **Dosage Forms:** Solution for injection, Oral (Tablet)

High-Yield Clinical Knowledge

- **Naloxone Dose-Response**
  - Low doses of naloxone (0.04 mg IV) are typically sufficient for most adult patients with opioid-related respiratory depression.
    - As opioids decrease the central respiratory response to hypoxia, this low dose of naloxone competitively inhibits opioid receptors in sufficient quantity to restore normal respiratory performance.
    - In opioid-naive patients, 1 mg of naloxone occupies 50% of available opioid receptors.
  - However, the duration of effect of most opioids (including heroin) is longer than naloxone; thus, the diminished response to hypoxia will return.
    - Additional doses of naloxone may be appropriate or as an infusion; however, airway, breathing, and ventilation support should also be utilized.
- **Bystander Naloxone Administration**
  - Naloxone distribution programs aim to provide opioid reversal via intranasal administration to lay individuals, bystanders, and medical professionals in non-acute care settings (such as pharmacies).
  - Patients, family members, and medical professionals should be educated on the role of naloxone and its administration and the importance of contacting 911 after administration.
- **Opioid-Induced Constipation**
  - Chronic opioid therapy decreases GI motility and frequently causes constipation.
  - Opioid antagonists, including those that act locally in the GI, can relieve constipation by causing a local opioid competitive inhibition without causing a systemic opioid withdrawal.
  - Methylnaltrexone is parenterally administered but does not cross the blood-brain barrier, thus causing peripheral opioid withdrawal and constipation relief.
    - Opioid antagonists are contraindicated in patients with bowel obstructions, as the risk of GI perforation is high in this setting.
  - Naldemedine and naloxegol are orally administered opioid antagonists that act locally on the GI to resolve constipation and are minimally absorbed.
- **Naloxone And ARDS**
  - Naloxone use for emergent reversal of opioid respiratory depression in opioid-dependent patients is at risk of secondary acute respiratory distress syndrome.
    - However, this is not proposed to be attributed directly to naloxone, but rather naloxone uncovers ARDS previously induced by the offending opioid.
- **Alvimopan And Recent Opioid Use**
  - Alvimopan is contraindicated in patients who have taken opioids for more than seven consecutive days.
    - This is due to the risk of systemic opioid withdrawal, despite alvimopan being minimally absorbed.
- **Naltrexone for Alcohol Abstinence**
  - Naltrexone is available as an IM depot injection as adjunctive therapy in ethanol abstinence.
  - Opioid antagonism by naltrexone is proposed to inhibit central opioid-mediated ethanol craving, reduces ethanol intake and incidence of relapse.

HIGH-YIELD BOARD EXAM ESSENTIALS
- **CLASSIC AGENTS:** Alvimopan, naldemedine, naloxegol, naloxone, naltrexone, methylnaltrexone
- **DRUG CLASS:** Opioid antagonists
- **INDICATIONS:** Opioid-induced constipation, opioid overdose (naloxone), post-operative ileus
- **MECHANISM:** Competitive opioid receptor (including mu, kappa, and delta) antagonists.
- **SIDE EFFECTS:** Acute opioid withdrawal, diarrhea, ARDS
- **CLINICAL PEARLS:** Low doses of naloxone (0.04 mg IV) are typically sufficient for most adult patients with opioid-related respiratory depression.

High-Yield Basic Pharmacology

- **Mechanism of Action**
  - Carbonic anhydrase inhibitors at type II and type IV isoforms exist in the CNS, decreasing intracellular pH and causing a shift of potassium to the extracellular compartment, ultimately leading to hyperpolarization of cells, increasing seizure threshold.
    - Additional antiepileptic effects have been attributed to inhibition of voltage-gated sodium channels, GABA-A agonist activity, and AMPA/kinate receptor inhibition.

Primary Net Benefit

- It can be used to treat specific epilepsies, but its benefits must be weighed against adverse effects of carbonic anhydrase inhibition.

Brain Carbonic Anhydrase Inhibitor - Drug Class Review			
High-Yield Med Reviews			
Mechanism of Action: *Decrease intracellular pH and cause hyperpolarization of cells, increasing seizure threshold. Inhibition of voltage-gated sodium channels, GABA-A agonist activity, and AMPA/kinate receptor inhibition.*			
Class Effects: Acid-base disturbances (metabolic acidosis), risk of acute closed-angle glaucoma; weight loss with topiramate			
Generic Name	**Brand Name**	**Indication(s) or Uses**	**Notes**

Acetazolamide	Diamox	• Acute altitude/mountain sickness
		• Glaucoma/Elevated intraocular pressure
		• Edema
		• Epilepsy
			• **Dosing (Adult):**
			  – Oral 125 to 500 mg once to four times per day
			    • Maximum 30 mg/kg/day
			  – IV 500 mg once
			• **Dosing (Peds):**
			  – Oral 2.5 to 30 mg/kg/dose q12h
			    • Maximum 1000 mg/day
			• **CYP450 Interactions:** None
			• **Renal or Hepatic Dose Adjustments:**
			  – Contraindicated in severe renal impairment
			  – Contraindicated in patients with cirrhosis or marked liver disease
			• **Dosage Forms:** IV solution, oral (extended-release capsule, immediate-release tablet)

Topiramate	Topamax	• Migraine prophylaxis
		• Seizures
			• **Dosing (Adult):**
			  – Oral 15 to 25 mg daily slowly titrating up to 100 to 400 mg/day
			• **Dosing (Peds):**
			  – Oral 0.5 to 20 mg/kg/day following slow titration
			    • Maximum 400 mg/day
			• **CYP450 Interactions:** Possible CYP3A4 induction
			• **Renal or Hepatic Dose Adjustments:**
			  – GFR less than 70 mL/minute - reduce dose by 50%, slower titration
			• **Dosage Forms:** Oral (capsule, extended-release, sprinkle, tablet)

Brain Carbonic Anhydrase Inhibitor - Drug Class Review
High-Yield Med Reviews

Generic Name	Brand Name	Indication(s) or Uses	Notes
Zonisamide	Zonegran	• Focal seizures	• **Dosing (Adult):** – Oral 25 mg/day slowly titrating up to 100 to 600 mg/day • **Dosing (Peds):** – Oral 1 to 2 mg/kg/day slowly titrating up to 5 to 8 mg/kg/day • Maximum 12 mg/kg/day • **CYP450 Interactions:** Substrate of CYP2C19, CYP3A4 • **Renal or Hepatic Dose Adjustments:** – GFR less than 50 mL/minute - use not recommended • **Dosage Forms:** Oral (capsule)

High-Yield Clinical Knowledge

- **Sulfonamide Derivatives**
    - There is a theoretical risk of cross-reactivity in patients with a history of sulfonamide hypersensitivity.
        - As a result of its sulfonamide structure, carbonic anhydrase inhibitors carry a risk of bone marrow depression, Stevens-Johnson Syndrome, and sulfonamide-like kidney injury.
    - Acetazolamide and methazolamide may cause a diversion of ammonia from urine into the systemic circulation, which can worsen existing hepatic encephalopathy
- **Hyperchloremic Metabolic Acidosis**
    - Carbonic anhydrase inhibitors block the excretion of hydrogen ions accumulating in the plasma.
        - In normal healthy kidneys reabsorb bicarbonate and offsets the accumulation of hydrogen and ensuing acidosis.
        - With impaired renal function, high doses, or otherwise altered metabolic function, renal tubules' capacity to reabsorb bicarbonate is impaired, which ultimately leads to an increasing acidosis.
            - The acidosis typically resolves upon discontinuation of the carbonic anhydrase inhibitor.
- **Topiramate Cognitive Impairment**
    - Patients taking topiramate may experience cognitive effects in a dose-dependent manner, including impaired expressive language function, impaired verbal memory, and slowed cognitive processing.
    - These cognition changes typically occur without a change in mental status, without sedation, or mood changes.
        - Doses above 400 mg/day significantly increase the incidence of adverse cognitive effects.
- **Topiramate and Oral Contraceptives**
    - Topiramate causes a dose-dependent induction of CYP3A4 metabolism of progestins, potentially decreasing the efficacy of birth control.
    - Substituting other contraceptive methods or changing to an ethinyl estradiol-based birth control with doses above 50 mcg/day may be reasonable.
- **Topiramate Paresthesias**
    - Therapeutic dosing of topiramate has been associated with paresthesias, occurring with more frequency early after initiation of treatment or at high doses.
    - Paresthesias may resolve spontaneously with continued treatment and without therapy modification.
- **Hyperthermia/Oligohydrosis**
    - Oligohydrosis may occur during topiramate therapy, potentially causing hyperthermia, particularly during exposure to hot weather.
    - Exposure to hot weather, participating in strenuous exercise, or patients concomitantly taking carbonic anhydrase or anticholinergic agents.

- **Weight Loss**
  - Topiramate is used off-label for weight loss after observation from clinical trials consistently found this effect in patients receiving the drug.
  - Weight loss from topiramate is gradual, peaking at 12 to 18 months after the initiation of treatment.
  - Additional benefits include improvement in lipid profiles, glucose control, and blood pressure improvement.

High-Yield Fast-Facts

- **Topical Carbonic Anhydrase Inhibition**
  - The ophthalmologic carbonic anhydrase inhibitors (brinzolamide and dorzolamide) are key components of glaucoma management.
- **Skin Reactions**
  - Topiramate and zonisamide are associated with the rare occurrence of Stevens-Johnson syndrome and toxic epidermal necrolysis.
- **Eating Disorders**
  - Topiramate and zonisamide should be used with caution in patients with a history of eating disorders. These disorders may be acutely worsened or manifest in patients without a history of such disorders.

HIGH-YIELD BOARD EXAM ESSENTIALS
- **CLASSIC AGENTS:** Acetazolamide, topiramate, zonisamide
- **DRUG CLASS:** Brain carbonic anhydrase inhibitor
- **INDICATIONS:** Acute altitude/mountain sickness, glaucoma/elevated intraocular pressure, edema, epilepsy, migraine prophylaxis, seizures
- **MECHANISM:** Decrease intracellular pH and cause hyperpolarization of cells, increasing seizure threshold.
- Inhibition of voltage-gated sodium channels, GABA-A agonist activity, and AMPA/kinate receptor inhibition.
- **SIDE EFFECTS:** Hyperchloremic metabolic acidosis, cognitive impairment, paresthesia, hyperthermia/oligohidrosis
- **CLINICAL PEARLS:**
  - Acetazolamide is also for the outpatient management of pseudotumor cerebri in some patients to reduce the pressures applied to the eye and optic nerve.
  - Topiramate causes a dose-dependent induction of CYP3A4 metabolism of progestins, potentially decreasing the efficacy of birth control. Substituting other contraceptive methods or changing to an ethinyl estradiol-based birth control with doses above 50 mcg/day may be reasonable.

High-Yield Basic Pharmacology

- **Mechanism of Action**
  - Binds to the alpha-2-delta-1 subunit of the N-type calcium channel, reducing the frequency of calcium fusion of synaptic vesicles to membranes, thereby reducing glutamate exocytosis
- **No GABA**
  - Although their names may suggest it, neither gabapentin nor pregabalin functionally acts as GABA.
  - These agents are amino acid-like structures that were first synthesized as analogs of GABA but were not observed to have any GABA related action.

Primary Net Benefit

- Gabapentin and pregabalin can be used to treat focal seizures but are more routinely used to treat neuropathic pain and certain anxiety disorders.

Gabapentinoids - Drug Class Review				
High-Yield Med Reviews				
Mechanism of Action: *Binds to the alpha-2-delta-1 subunit of the N-type calcium channel, reducing the frequency of calcium fusion of synaptic vesicles to membranes and reducing glutamate exocytosis.*				
Class Effects: Adjuncts to focal seizures, mainly used for neuropathic pain, require renal dose adjustments, cause sedation				
Generic Name	**Brand Name**	**Indication(s) or Uses**	**Notes**	

Gabapentin	Neurontin	• Focal seizures
		• Postherpetic neuralgia
			• **Dosing (Adult):**
			  – Oral 100 to 300 mg q8-12h
			    ▪ Up to 3,600 mg/day has been used
			• **Dosing (Peds):**
			  – Oral 10 to 15 mg/kg/day divided into 3 doses
			    ▪ Maximum 3,600 mg/day
			• **CYP450 Interactions:** None
			• **Renal or Hepatic Dose Adjustments:**
			  – GFR 30 to 49 mL/minute - Max 900 mg/day
			  – GFR 15 to 29 mL/minute - Max 600 mg/day
			  – GFR < 15 mL/minute - Max 300 mg/day
			• **Dosage Forms:** Oral (capsule, solution, tablet)	

Pregabalin	Lyrica	▪ Fibromyalgia
		▪ Focal seizures
		▪ Neuropathic pain
		▪ Postherpetic neuralgia
			• **Dosing (Adult):**
			  – Oral 75 to 150 mg q12-24h
			• **Dosing (Peds):**
			  – Oral 2.5 to 3.5 mg/kg/day divided q8h
			    ▪ Maximum 14 mg/kg/day
			• **CYP450 Interactions:** None
			• **Renal or Hepatic Dose Adjustments:**
			  – GFR 30 to 60 mL/minute - Maximum 300 mg/day
			  – GFR 15 to 29 mL/minute - Maximum 150 mg/day
			  – GFR less than 15 mL/minute - Maximum 75 mg/day
			• **Dosage Forms:** Oral (capsule, solution, tablet)	

High-Yield Clinical Knowledge

- **Pregabalin CV**
  - Pregabalin is a federally controlled substance in schedule V (or C-V), whereas gabapentin is not federally scheduled.
- **Withdrawal**
  - Abrupt discontinuation of gabapentin is not recommended as a clinical withdrawal syndrome has been observed.
  - Gabapentin withdrawal manifests as agitation, confusion, tachycardia, and seizures.
  - Withdrawal should be managed by re-starting and then tapering gabapentin as benzodiazepines are not effective for this purpose.
- **Renal Dose Adjustment**
  - The primary elimination route of the gabapentinoids is renal, with dose adjustments beginning when GFR falls below 50-60 mL/minute.
- **Gabapentin Absorption**
  - Gabapentin displays a saturable oral absorption with decreasing absorption, thus penetrating the CNS, as doses increase.
    - This absorption of gabapentin is dependent on L-amino acid transport located exclusively in the upper small intestine.
    - Pregabalin displays more consistent absorption, with no observed saturation as it is absorbed by mechanisms other than L-amino acid transport.
  - At doses of 900 mg/day, bioavailability is approximately 60%, falling to 33% at 3,600 mg/day.
- **TDM**
  - Gabapentin and pregabalin can be monitored using therapeutic drug monitoring of serum levels but are not routinely recommended due to these agents' large therapeutic window and safety.
    - Gabapentin therapeutic range of 2 to 20 mg/L.
    - Pregabalin therapeutic range of 2.8 to 8.3 mg/L.
- **Pregabalin Safety**
  - Pregabalin has been associated with cardiac adverse events, including third-degree atrioventricular block, QT prolongation, as well as encephalopathy, and respiratory failure.
  - Like gabapentin, pregabalin can lead to peripheral edema, weight gain, and decompensated congestive heart failure.
  - Both gabapentinoids can cause weight gain and peripheral edema.

High-Yield Fast-Facts

- **Seizures in OD**
  - Gabapentin overdose has been associated with the development of seizures.
  - Other antiepileptic agents that cause seizures in overdose include carbamazepine, topiramate, valproic acid, and zonisamide.

HIGH-YIELD BOARD EXAM ESSENTIALS
- **CLASSIC AGENTS:** Gabapentin, pregabalin
- **DRUG CLASS:** Gabapentinoids
- **INDICATIONS:** Fibromyalgia, focal seizures, neuropathic pain, postherpetic neuralgia
- **MECHANISM:** Binds to the alpha-2-delta-1 subunit of the N-type calcium channel, reducing the frequency of calcium fusion of synaptic vesicles to membranes, thereby reducing glutamate exocytosis.
- **SIDE EFFECTS:** Altered mental status, headache, withdrawal
- **CLINICAL PEARLS:**
  - Gabapentin is more commonly used for neuropathy than as an adjunct for seizures.
  - Gabapentin and pregabalin are both renally cleared and need to be adjusted especially once the CrCl < 60 ml/min.
  - Pregabalin has been associated with cardiac adverse events, including third-degree atrioventricular block, QT prolongation, as well as encephalopathy, and respiratory failure.

High-Yield Basic Pharmacology

- **Mechanism of Action**
  - Increase synaptic availability of GABA, decreasing neuronal excitation.
- **Paradoxical GABA-A Inhibition**
  - Vigabatrin is a GABA analog that prevents GABA breakdown by inhibiting GABA transaminase.
  - However, it may lead to a paradoxical inhibition of synaptic GABA-A receptors and prolong the activation of extrasynaptic GABA-A receptors.

Primary Net Benefit

- Antiepileptic agents are reserved for refractory patients intolerant to other agents due to significant toxicities.

GABA Uptake Inhibitors and GABA Transaminase Inhibitor - Drug Class Review High-Yield Med Reviews			
Mechanism of Action: *Increase synaptic availability of GABA, decreasing neuronal excitation.*			
Class Effects: Potential to worsen seizures, cause changes in mental status, reserved for refractory cases only			
Generic Name	**Brand Name**	**Indication(s) or Uses**	**Notes**

Tiagabine	Gabitril	• Focal seizures	• **Dosing (Adult):**
			  – Oral 4 mg daily titrating to 32 to 56 mg/day
			• **Dosing (Peds):**
			  – Oral 4 mg daily titrating to 32 mg/day
			    • Maximum 32 mg/day
			• **CYP450 Interactions:** Substrate of CYP3A4
			• **Renal or Hepatic Dose Adjustments:** None
			• **Dosage Forms:** Oral (tablet)

Vigabatrin	Sabril	• Infantile spasms
		• Refractory complex partial seizures
			• **Dosing (Adult):**
			  – Oral 500 mg BID up to 1,500 mg BID
			• **Dosing (Peds):**
			  – Oral 25 mg/kg/dose q12h
			    • Maximum 150 mg/kg/day
			• **CYP450 Interactions:** None
			• **Renal or Hepatic Dose Adjustments:**
			  – GFR 50 to 80 mL/minute - decrease by 25%
			  – GFR 30 to 50 mL/minute - decrease by 50%
			  – GFR 10 to 30 mL/minute - decrease by 75%
			• **Dosage Forms:** Oral (packet, tablet)

High-Yield Clinical Knowledge

- **Irreversible Vision Loss**
  - Vigabatrin is associated with irreversible vision loss, causing it to be reserved for patients intolerant or not responding to other treatments.
    - Vision loss can occur within weeks of starting or may not manifest for months to years after initiation.
- **Agitation and Psychosis**
  - Vigabatrin is associated with new-onset or worsening of existing agitation, confusion, and psychosis.
  - In patients with a history of psychiatric illness, alternative antiepileptic agents should be sought.

- **Worsening Seizures**
  - Tiagabine can paradoxically worsen myoclonic seizures and pose a risk of causing nonconvulsive status epilepticus, including among patients without a history of epilepsy.
    - Myoclonic seizure activity may be a result of the activation of extrasynaptic GABA-A receptors by tiagabine.
  - Seizures caused by tiagabine or vigabatrin may respond to benzodiazepines, barbiturates or propofol.
- **Lennox-Gastaut Syndrome**
  - Vigabatrin may decrease seizures refractory to valproic acid in patients with Lennox-Gastaut syndrome.

High-Yield Fast-Facts

- **Tiagabine and Valproic Acid**
  - Tiagabine may decrease therapeutic concentrations of valproic acid; however, it may not lead to clinically relevant changes in response to valproic acid.
- **Endogenous GHB**
  - Vigabatrin may lower excessive endogenous gamma-hydroxybutyrate (GHB) in patients with genetic GABA metabolism deficiencies.
  - There is no effect on GHB from exogenous sources.

HIGH-YIELD BOARD EXAM ESSENTIALS
- **CLASSIC AGENTS:** Tiagabine, vigabatrin
- **DRUG CLASS:** GABA uptake inhibitors and GABA transaminase inhibitor
- **INDICATIONS:** Focal seizures, infantile spasms, refractory complex partial seizures
- **MECHANISM:** Increase synaptic availability of GABA, decreasing neuronal excitation.
- **SIDE EFFECTS:** Agitation, irreversible vision loss, seizures, psychosis
- **CLINICAL PEARLS:** Tiagabine can paradoxically worsen myoclonic seizures and pose a risk of causing nonconvulsive status epilepticus, including among patients without a history of epilepsy. Myoclonic seizure activity may be a result of the activation of extrasynaptic GABA-A receptors by tiagabine.

High-Yield Basic Pharmacology

- **Mechanism of Action**
  - Selective use-dependent block of certain NMDA receptors, and GABA-A activation independent of GABA.
- **GABA-A**
  - In addition to its effects on the NMDA receptor, felbamate causes a weak inhibition of GABA-A receptors in a fashion similar to barbiturates.
  - Felbamate also possesses voltage-gated sodium channel blocking and calcium channel blocking properties.

Primary Net Benefit

- Limited role in focal seizure/Lennox-Gastaut seizure management as a result of toxicities, including aplastic anemia.

NMDA Receptor Antagonist - Drug Class Review			
High-Yield Med Reviews			
Mechanism of Action: *Selective use-dependent block of certain NMDA receptors, and GABA-A activation independent of GABA.*			
Class Effects: Limited role in focal seizure/Lennox-Gastaut; associated with risk of aplastic anemia, liver toxicity, and drug interactions with other anticonvulsants.			
Generic Name	**Brand Name**	**Indication(s) or Uses**	**Notes**

Felbamate	Felbatol	• Focal seizures	• **Dosing (Adult):**
			  – Oral 1,200 mg/day divided q8-12h titrated up to 3,600 mg/day
			• **Dosing (Peds):**
			  – Oral 15 mg/kg/day divided q8-12h titrated to maximum 45 mg/kg/day or 3,600 mg/day, whichever is less
			• **CYP450 Interactions:** Substrate of CYP 2E1, 3A4
			• **Renal or Hepatic Dose Adjustments:**
			  – GFR less than 50 mL/minute - reduce dose by 50%
			• **Dosage Forms:** Oral (suspension, tablet)

High-Yield Clinical Knowledge

- **Aplastic Anemia**
  - Felbamate-related aplastic anemia was observed after FDA approval and through post-marketing research.
    - There is no evidence to suggest this is a dose-dependent effect.
  - Patients experiencing aplastic anemia had a history of allergies or toxicity to other antiepileptic drugs, a history of cytopenias, or a history of immune diseases.
- **Hepatic Failure**
  - Like aplastic anemia, felbamate associated hepatic failure was noted first in post-marketing data, not in initial phase III research.
  - Patients with symptoms of jaundice, fatigue, and/or GI complaints should seek immediate medical care.

High-Yield Fast-Facts

- **Phenytoin**
  - As a result of inhibition of CYP2C19, felbamate decreases the clearance of phenytoin, possibly leading to high therapeutic levels and potential toxicity.
- **Valproic Acid**
  - Valproic acid levels may increase in the presence of felbamate due to an inhibition of valproic acid beta-oxidation.
- **Carbamazepine**
  - Although felbamate may reduce carbamazepine levels, but increase 10,11, epoxide concentrations potentially leading to neurotoxic sequelae.

HIGH-YIELD BOARD EXAM ESSENTIALS
- **CLASSIC AGENTS:** Felbamate
- **DRUG CLASS:** NMDA receptor antagonist
- **INDICATIONS:** Focal seizures
- **MECHANISM:** Selective use-dependent block of certain NMDA receptors, and GABA-A activation independent of GABA.
- **SIDE EFFECTS:** Aplastic anemia, hepatic failure
- **CLINICAL PEARLS:** As a result of inhibition of CYP2C19, felbamate decreases the clearance of phenytoin, possibly leading to high therapeutic levels and potential toxicity.

High-Yield Basic Pharmacology

- **Mechanism of Action**
  - Inhibition of sodium channels by reducing their capacity for recovery from activation.
- **Michaelis-Menten**
  - Michaelis-Menten pharmacokinetics (pk) describes pk properties of phenytoin.
  - This pk model describes a process where at low plasma concentrations, phenytoin exhibits first-order (or linear) pharmacokinetics, but as plasma levels increase, it shifts to non-linear kinetics.
  - There is wide patient-to-patient variability concerning the plasma level where this "switch" occurs, making phenytoin a medication requiring close therapeutic drug monitoring, particularly during initiation, dosing adjustments, or additions/subtraction of medications interacting with phenytoin.

Primary Net Benefit

- The broad antiepileptic activity can be used acutely for seizures or status epilepticus and therapeutic drug monitoring but balanced by significant dose-dependent and dose-independent toxicities.

<table>
<tr><td colspan="4" align="center">Sodium Channel Blocking Drugs - Drug Class Review
High-Yield Med Reviews</td></tr>
<tr><td colspan="4">Mechanism of Action: Inhibition of sodium channels by reducing their capacity for recovery from activation.</td></tr>
<tr><td colspan="4">Class Effects: Broad antiepileptic activity, risk of drug interactions due to CYP induction, rashes, risk of teratogenicity in pregnancy</td></tr>
<tr><td>Generic Name</td><td>Brand Name</td><td>Indication(s) or Uses</td><td>Notes</td></tr>
<tr>
<td>Carbamazepine</td>
<td>Carbatrol
Equetro
Tegretol</td>
<td>• Bipolar disorder
• Seizures</td>
<td>

- **Dosing (Adult):**
  - Oral 100 to 400 mg/day titrating based on therapeutic drug monitoring
- **Dosing (Peds):**
  - Oral 10 to 20 mg/kg/day divided q6-8h, adjusted to therapeutic levels
- **CYP450 Interactions:** Substrate of CYP2C8, 3A4; Induces CYP1A2, 2B6, 2C9, 3A4, P-gp
- **Renal or Hepatic Dose Adjustments:** Monitor 10,11-carbamazepine epoxide levels closely
- **Dosage Forms:** Oral (capsule, suspension, tablet)

</td>
</tr>
<tr>
<td>Eslicarbazepine</td>
<td>Aptiom</td>
<td>• Seizures</td>
<td>

- **Dosing (Adult):**
  - Oral 400 mg daily titrated to 1,600 mg daily
- **Dosing (Peds):**
  - Oral 200 mg/day titrated to weight-based maximum between 600 and 1,200 mg/day
- **CYP450 Interactions:** Inhibits CYP2C19; Induces CYP3A4
- **Renal or Hepatic Dose Adjustments:**
  - GFR less than 50 mL/minute - reduce initial dose by 50%, slow titration
- **Dosage Forms:** Oral (tablet)

</td>
</tr>
</table>

Sodium Channel Blocking Drugs - Drug Class Review
High-Yield Med Reviews

Generic Name	Brand Name	Indication(s) or Uses	Notes
Oxcarbazepine	Oxtellar Trileptal	▪ Seizures	▪ **Dosing (Adult):** – Oral 150 to 300 mg q12h, titrated to a maximum of 2,400 mg/day ▪ **Dosing (Peds):** – Oral 8 to 10 mg/kg/day, divided q12h ▪ Maximum 2,400 mg/day ▪ **CYP450 Interactions:** Induces CYP3A4 ▪ **Renal or Hepatic Dose Adjustments:** – GFR less than 30 mL/minute - slower titration ▪ **Dosage Forms:** Oral (suspension, tablet)

Phenytoin	Dilantin Phenytek	▪ Seizures
		 ▪ Status epilepticus
			▪ **Dosing (Adult):**
			 – IV 15 to 20 mg/kg infused no faster than 50 mg/minute
			 – IV maintenance 4 to 7 mg/kg/day, or 100 mg q8h
			 – Oral 4 to 7 mg/kg/day divided q8h, or 100 mg q8h
			   ▪ Target level 10 to 20 mg/L (total), or 1 to 2 mg/L (free)
			 ▪ **Dosing (Peds):**
			 – IV 15 to 20 mg/kg infused no faster than 50 mg/minute
			 – IV maintenance 4 to 7 mg/kg/day
			 – Oral 4 to 7 mg/kg/day divided q8h
			   ▪ Target level 10 to 20 mg/L (total), or 1 to 2 mg/L (free)
			 ▪ **CYP450 Interactions:** Substrate of CYP2C19, 2C9, 3A4; Induces CYP1A2, 2B6, 3A4, P-gp
			 ▪ **Renal or Hepatic Dose Adjustments:**
			 – No empiric adjustments, follow drug levels
			 ▪ **Dosage Forms:** Oral (suspension, tablet); As sodium salt: Oral (capsule), IV (solution)

Rufinamide	Banzel	▪ Lennox-Gastaut syndrome	▪ **Dosing (Adult):** – Oral 200 to 400 q12h, titrated to a maximum 1,600 mg/day ▪ **Dosing (Peds):** – Oral 5 mg/kg/dose q12h, titrated to target of 22.5 mg/kg/dose q12h ▪ Maximum 1,600 mg/dose ▪ **CYP450 Interactions:** Induces CYP3A4 ▪ **Renal or Hepatic Dose Adjustments:** None ▪ **Dosage Forms:** Oral (suspension, tablet)

High-Yield Clinical Knowledge

- **HLA-B*1502**
    - Before initiation of carbamazepine, eslicarbazepine, oxcarbazepine, or phenytoin, screening for HLA-B*1502 allele is strongly recommended, particularly in patients Asian or South Asian ancestry.
    - Patients with positive screening have a significantly higher risk of severe cutaneous adverse events, including DRESS (drug reactions with eosinophilia and systemic symptoms), Stevens-Johnson syndrome, or toxic epidermal necrolysis.
- **Phenytoin Binding Kinetics**
    - Numerous comorbidities or patient characteristics can alter phenytoin pk parameters, particularly distribution and protein binding.
        - Patients with renal failure, pregnant, neonates, or critical care patients may have altered phenytoin binding kinetics.
- **CYP Inducer**
    - Carbamazepine, eslicarbazepine, oxcarbazepine, phenytoin, and rufinamide are inducers of CYP 450 enzymes and contribute to numerous clinically significant drug interactions.
    - Carbamazepine is unique as it is an inducer of hepatic metabolism and an autoinducer - as it induces its own metabolism.
        - As opposed to inhibition, hepatic induction occurs over a period of time; in the case of carbamazepine occurs over approximately 96 hours.
            - Dose adjustments should occur shortly after initiation and therapeutic drug monitoring of both the parent carbamazepine and 10,11-epoxide metabolite concentration.
- **Phenytoin IV Administration**
    - When phenytoin is administered intravenously, specific precautions must be taken to avoid phlebitis, tissue necrosis (purple-glove syndrome), vasodilation, and cardiac toxicity.
    - The maximum infusion rate for phenytoin is 50 mg/minute, but patients rarely tolerate rates greater than 20 mg/minute.
    - Phenytoin must be diluted in sodium chloride 0.9% and administered with an in-line filter.
    - Phenytoin should not be administered via IM injection; however, fosphenytoin may be administered IM.
        - However, the volume for a typical adult loading dose of fosphenytoin is around 10 mL, limiting IM sites to the gluteal tissue, but is still not ideal.
- **Fosphenytoin Administration**
    - Fosphenytoin may be administered at a rate up to 150 mg/minute, diluted in either sodium chloride 0.9% or D5W, and does not require an in-line filter.
        - Fosphenytoin may still cause cardiac arrhythmias and has been associated with rate-dependent pruritus.
    - Although fosphenytoin can be administered three-times faster than phenytoin, it has the same time to one of activity due to the time required for dephosphorylation to occur.
        - Fosphenytoin is dosed in "phenytoin-equivalents," which may lead to confusion and hypothetical dosing errors.
            - However, the clinical use of any dosing other than "phenytoin-equivalents" is infrequent.
- **Phenytoin Therapeutic Range & Toxicity**
    - Phenytoin has a narrow therapeutic range, and unique characteristics of toxicities occur when plasma levels exceed normal upper limits (total - 20 mg/L)
        - Nystagmus is one of the first signs of toxicity as phenytoin levels increase to between 20 and 30 mg/L.
        - If phenytoin levels continue to rise to between 30 and 40 mg/L, cerebellar ataxia and dysequilibrium predominate where nystagmus may no longer be appreciated.
        - With phenytoin levels between 40 to 50 mg/L, confusion, altered mental status predominate.
        - As levels extend beyond 50 mg/L, patients may experience dystonias, depressed deep tendon reflexes.

- It is currently controversial whether phenytoin toxicity can produce seizures in overdose/toxicity but is more likely attributed to the propylene glycol content of the IV phenytoin product.
- **Carbamazepine Adverse Toxicity**
  - Carbamazepine has a broad toxicity profile, ranging from teratogenic effects in pregnant patients to respiratory failure, seizures, or anticholinergic toxicity.
  - Blood dyscrasias have occurred during normal carbamazepine therapeutic use, including leukocytosis, leukopenia, eosinophilia, thrombocytopenia, pancytopenia to agranulocytosis, aplastic anemia, and bone marrow depression.
  - Carbamazepine has been known to cause hyponatremia and inappropriate antidiuretic hormone (SIADH), occurring in from 1 to 40% of patients throughout chronic therapy.
  - Other notable toxicities include QRS/QT prolongation, hypotension, nystagmus, diplopia, ataxia, dystonic reactions, or choreoathetosis.

High-Yield Fast-Facts

- **Carbamazepine Alternatives**
  - Eslicarbazepine and oxcarbazepine are structurally and mechanistically related to carbamazepine but have improved safety and pharmacokinetic profile, as they are not autoinducer agents.
  - However, CYP induction is still an action of these agents.
- **Phenytoin Cardiology**
  - Phenytoin acts as a Vaughn Williams classification 1B antiarrhythmic, which was once used for digoxin toxicities.
- **Carbamazepine TCA**
  - Carbamazepine structurally resembles a tricyclic antidepressant and shares many clinical and toxicology effects, namely cardia sodium channel blockade and anticholinergic effects.

HIGH-YIELD BOARD EXAM ESSENTIALS
- **CLASSIC AGENTS:** Carbamazepine, eslicarbazepine, fosphenytoin, oxcarbazepine, phenytoin, rufinamide, topiramate
- **DRUG CLASS:** Sodium channel blocking drugs
- **INDICATIONS:** Bipolar disorder, seizures
- **MECHANISM:** Inhibition of sodium channels by reducing their capacity for recovery from activation.
- **SIDE EFFECTS:** Hepatotoxicity, dose-dependent toxicities (phenytoin), anticholinergic effects (carbamazepine)
- **CLINICAL PEARLS:**
  - Before initiation of carbamazepine, eslicarbazepine, oxcarbazepine, or phenytoin, screening for HLA-B*1502 allele is strongly recommended, particularly in patients Asian or South Asian ancestry.
  - Avoid the use of phenytoin or fosphenytoin in a patient with TCA-induced seizure as it could worsen the seizure since both can inhibit sodium channels.
  - Fosphenytoin is the prodrug to phenytoin which can be given IM or IV whereas phenytoin should only be given IV or by mouth.
  - The administration rate of IV phenytoin is 50 mg/min due to the presence of propylene glycol whereas fosphenytoin is 150 mg/min and does NOT have propylene glycol.
  - Phenytoin initially exhibits first-order elimination kinetics, but at a certain dose it can convert to zero order elimination and result toxicity rapidly.

High-Yield Basic Pharmacology

- **Mechanism of Action**
  - Selectively bind to the SV2A receptor in synaptic vesicles, reducing the release of glutamate during high-frequency activity.
    - SV2A is a synaptic vesicle essential to membrane proteins as it functions to recycle synaptic vesicles through vesicle endocytosis.

Primary Net Benefit

- Broad antiepileptic activity with wide therapeutic window and relatively safe adverse event profile compared to other antiepileptic drugs.

SV2AProtein-Ligand - Drug Class Review			
High-Yield Med Reviews			
Mechanism of Action: *Selectively bind to the SV2A receptor in synaptic vesicles, reducing glutamate during high-frequency activity.*			
Class Effects: Overall well tolerated; good oral bioavailability; need renal dose adjustments, lower overall risk for drug interactions via CYP450.			
Generic Name	**Brand Name**	**Indication(s) or Uses**	**Notes**

Brivaracetam	Briviact	• Partial onset seizures	• **Dosing (Adult):**
			  – Oral/IV 25 to 100 mg q12h
			• **Dosing (Peds):**
			  – Oral/IV 0.5 to 1.25 mg/kg/dose q12h
			    • Maximum 5 mg/kg/day or 200 mg/day, whichever is less
			• **CYP450 Interactions:** Substrate CYP2C19
			• **Renal or Hepatic Dose Adjustments:**
			  – Child-Pugh class A, B, or C - Initial 25 mg q12h to maximum 75 mg q12h
			• **Dosage Forms:** Oral (solution, tablet), IV (solution)

Levetiracetam	Keppra	• Seizures
		• Status epileptics
			• **Dosing (Adult):**
			  – Oral/IV 500 to 2,000 mg q12-24h
			  – IV 60 mg/kg once, maximum 4,500 mg
			• **Dosing (Peds):**
			  – Oral/IV 7 to 21 mg/kg/dose q12h
			    • Maximum 3,000 mg/day
			  – IV 60 mg/kg once
			    • Maximum 4,500 mg
			• **CYP450 Interactions:** None
			• **Renal or Hepatic Dose Adjustments:**
			  – GFR 30 to 50 mL/minute - 250 to 750 mg q12h
			  – GFR 15 to 30 mL/minute - 250 to 500 mg q12h
			  – Less than 15 mL/minute - 250 to 500 mg q24h
			• **Dosage Forms:** Oral (solution, tablet), IV (solution)

High-Yield Clinical Knowledge

- **Adverse Events**
  - Levetiracetam has a wide therapeutic range but may cause CNS depression and ataxia at high drug levels.
  - Agitation is a common adverse event in pediatric patients prescribed levetiracetam.
- **Brivaracetam and Carbamazepine**
  - Brivaracetam may decrease the elimination of 10,11-carbamazepine epoxide, the active metabolite of carbamazepine.
    - The 10,11-carbamazepine epoxide is associated with neurologic toxicities and can be therapeutically monitored with a normal range of 1 to 10 mg/L.
- **Appropriate Levetiracetam Dosing**
  - Although conventional dosing of levetiracetam is typically between 500 to 1000 mg per dose, the recent ESETT, ConSEPT, and EcLiPSE trials used higher weight-based doses of 40 to 60 mg/kg per dose, with a maximum of 4,500 mg.
    - When considering the results suggesting similar effects to phenytoin, it's important to remember levetiracetam was studied at these doses, whereas phenytoin was used at doses more familiar to clinical practice.
- **Rapid IV Administration**
  - Levetiracetam may be administered via IV slow push, allowing for delivery of therapeutic dosing rapidly.
  - This contrasts with alternative agents used for acute seizures, such as phenytoin, which must be infused slowly over at a maximum rate of 50 mg/minute but rarely tolerated at rates above 20 mg/minute.
- **Controlled Substance**
  - Unlike levetiracetam, which is not controlled, brivaracetam is a scheduled C-V medication.

High-Yield Fast-Fact

- **Controlled Substance**
  - Unlike levetiracetam, which is not controlled, brivaracetam is a scheduled C-V medication.

HIGH-YIELD BOARD EXAM ESSENTIALS
- **CLASSIC AGENTS:** Brivaracetam, levetiracetam
- **DRUG CLASS:** SV2A Protein-Ligand
- **INDICATIONS:** Seizures, status epileptics
- **MECHANISM:** Selectively bind to the SV2A receptor in synaptic vesicles, reducing the release of glutamate during high-frequency activity.
- **SIDE EFFECTS:** Ataxia, CNS depression
- **CLINICAL PEARLS:**
  - Brivaracetam may decrease the elimination of 10,11-carbamazepine epoxide, the active metabolite of carbamazepine. The 10,11-carbamazepine epoxide is associated with neurologic toxicities and can be therapeutically monitored with a normal range of 1 to 10 mg/L.
  - The oral bioavailability of both agents is the same as IV (or close enough) to allow for easier dosing where the oral and IV dose are the same.
  - Levetiracetam needs to be renally dose adjusted.

High-Yield Basic Pharmacology

- **Ethosuximide, Lamotrigine, Valproic Acid**
  - Inhibition of voltage-gated T-type calcium channels, decreasing thalamic neuronal transmission.
- **Lamotrigine, Valproic acid**
  - Inhibition of sodium channels by reducing their capacity for recovery from activation.
    - Valproic acid has broad effects on both CNS and spinal cord neurons by reducing repetitive depolarizations.
    - The primary actions are attributed to valproic acid's voltage-gated sodium channel blocking activity, inhibition of T-type calcium channels, stimulation of GABA synthesis, and inhibition of GABA degradation.

Primary Net Benefit

- Antiepileptics with calcium channel blocking properties useful for absence seizure treatment, with notable toxicities related to dose titration (lamotrigine) or hyperammonemia (valproic acid).

	**Voltage-Gated Calcium Channel Blockers - Drug Class Review** High-Yield Med Reviews
	**Mechanism of Action:** *See agents above.*
	**Class Effects:** Useful for absence seizures, notable toxicities related to dose titration (lamotrigine) or hyperammonemia (valproic acid), rash (lamotrigine), hypotension, respiratory depression, pancreatitis, hepatotoxicity
Generic Name	**Brand Name**	**Indication(s) or Uses**	**Notes**

Ethosuximide	Zarontin	• Absence seizures	• **Dosing (Adult):**
			  – Oral 500 to 1,500 mg/day in divided doses
			• **Dosing (Peds):**
			  – Oral 10 mg/kg/day divided q12h
			    • Maximum 60 mg/kg/day or 2,000 mg/day
			• **CYP450 Interactions:** Substrate CYP3A4
			• **Renal or Hepatic Dose Adjustments:** None
			• **Dosage Forms:** Oral (capsule, solution)

Lamotrigine	Lamictal
	Subvenite
		• Bipolar disorder
		• Focal seizures
			• **Dosing (Adult):**
			  – Oral 25 mg/day with slow titration to 100 to 200 mg/day target dose
			• **Dosing (Peds):**
			  – Oral 0.15 mg/kg/day with slow titration to target maintenance of 5.1 mg/kg/day
			    • Maximum 5.1 mg/kg/day or 200 mg/day, whichever is less
			• **CYP450 Interactions:** None
			• **Renal or Hepatic Dose Adjustments:**
			  – Child-Pugh class B or C without ascites - reduce dose by 25%
			  – Child-Pugh class B or C with ascites - reduce dose by 50%
			• **Dosage Forms:** Oral (kit, tablet, chewable tablet, orally disintegrating tablet)

Voltage-Gated Calcium Channel Blockers - Drug Class Review			
High-Yield Med Reviews			
Generic Name	Brand Name	Indication(s) or Uses	Notes

Valproic acid	Depacon Depakene Depakote	• Bipolar disorder
		• Focal seizures
		• Migraine
			• **Dosing (Adult):**
			  – Oral 10 to 60 mg/kg/day, adjusted to therapeutic levels
			  – IV 20 to 40 mg/kg administered 10 mg/kg/minute, maximum dose of 3,000 mg
			• **Dosing (Peds):**
			  – Oral 10 to 60 mg/kg/day, adjusted to therapeutic levels
			  – IV 20 to 40 mg/kg administered 10 mg/kg/minute, maximum dose of 2,000 mg
			• **CYP450 Interactions:** Substrate of CYP2A6, 2B6, 2C19, 2C9, 2E1
			• **Renal or Hepatic Dose Adjustments:**
			  – Hepatic impairment - use not recommended.
			• **Dosage Forms:** Oral (capsule, solution, tablet), IV (solution)

High-Yield Clinical Knowledge

- **Lamotrigine Titration**
  - Lamotrigine dose titration must follow a strict schedule with close monitoring of the patient for severe hypersensitivity signs and symptoms.
  - If patients who will be started on lamotrigine but are currently taking valproic acid, the initial dose titration should be slower, with a lower target maximum dose.
    - Starting with 25 mg q48h for 2 weeks, then increase to 25 mg q24h for 2 weeks, after which doses can be increased by 25 to 50 mg/day every 1-2 weeks up to a maintenance dose of 100-150 mg/day divided into 2 doses.
  - For patients on lamotrigine inducers (carbamazepine, estrogens, phenytoin) may start at higher initial doses.
- **Pregnant Patients**
  - Valproic acid has indication dependent use in patients who are pregnant.
    - Valproic acid is contraindicated in pregnant women since it is associated with neural tube defects in children born to mothers taking valproic acid during pregnancy.
    - For patients with bipolar disorder or seizure disorders who are stable on chronic valproic acid therapy and become pregnant, a risk-benefit discussion must occur with providers to determine whether or not valproic acid should be continued.
      - Patients with bipolar disorder or seizure disorders but are not currently taking valproic acid should not be started while pregnant if alternatives exist.
- **Ethosuximide Adverse Events**
  - Although the most common adverse events with ethosuximide therapy are GI complaints, there is a risk of CNS effects, including Parkinson-like symptoms, behavioral effects in patients with a history of psychiatric disorders, Stevens-Johnson syndrome, lupus erythematosus, and leukopenia, thrombocytopenia, pancytopenia, and aplastic anemia.
- **Valproic Acid Adverse Events**
  - Valproic acid is associated with concentration-dependent toxicities inducing hypotension, respiratory depression, pancreatitis, hepatotoxicity, and coma.
  - Byproducts of valproic acid metabolism, including ketoacids, carboxylic acid, and propionic acid, can cause an anion-gap metabolic acidosis.
  - Chronic toxicities that can occur at normal therapeutic dosing include hepatic steatosis and hyperammonemia with encephalopathy.

- **L-Carnitine**
  - L-carnitine is the treatment of choice for valproic acid hyperammonemia or hepatotoxicity and should be given in the IV dosage form as oral absorption is limited.
    - Oral L-carnitine can be an alternative in select patients in whom ammonia levels are elevated, but the patients are otherwise asymptomatic.
- **Bipolar Disorder**
  - Lamotrigine, and valproic acid, may be used to treat bipolar mood disorders or migraine prophylaxis.

High-Yield Fast-Facts

- **Hemodialysis**
  - Severe valproic acid toxicity can be managed with hemodialysis, particularly when the levels are above 900 mg/L, requiring mechanical ventilation, pH less than 7.1, or coma.
- **Many Names of Valproic Acid**
  - Valproic acid may be referred to by many different names, including valproate, divalproex (a compound of sodium valproate and valproic acid).

HIGH-YIELD BOARD EXAM ESSENTIALS

- **CLASSIC AGENTS:** Ethosuximide, lamotrigine, valproic acid
- **DRUG CLASS:** Voltage-gated calcium channel blockers
- **INDICATIONS:** Absence seizures, bipolar disorder, focal seizures, migraine
- **MECHANISM:** Inhibition of voltage-gated T-type calcium channels, decreasing thalamic neuronal transmission (ethosuximide, lamotrigine, valproic acid); Inhibition of sodium channels by reducing their capacity for recovery from activation (lamotrigine, valproic acid)
- **SIDE EFFECTS:** Rash (lamotrigine), hypotension, respiratory depression, pancreatitis, hepatotoxicity, and coma.
- **CLINICAL PEARLS:** Lamotrigine dose titration must follow a strict schedule with close monitoring of the patient for severe hypersensitivity signs and symptoms. If patients who will be started on lamotrigine but are currently taking valproic acid, the initial dose titration should be slower, with a lower target maximum dose.

High-Yield Basic Pharmacology

- **Eptinezumab, Erenumab, Galcanezumab, Fremanezumab**
  - Human monoclonal antibodies bind to and inhibit the CGRP receptor function.
- **Rimegepant, Ubrogepant**
  - Small molecule antagonist of the CGRP receptor
- **CGRP and Migraines**
  - CGRP is a neuropeptide that has a strong association with migraine and cluster headache.
  - CGRP levels are acutely elevated in the cerebral circulation during a migraine and decrease in response to triptans, dihydroergotamine, or onabotulinumtoxinA.

Primary Net Benefit

- Acute and chronic migraine pharmacotherapy that applies novel therapeutic targets and improves safety and efficacy compared to existing antimigraine therapeutics.

Calcitonin Gene-Related Peptide Receptor Antagonist - Drug Class Review			
High-Yield Med Reviews			
Mechanism of Action: *See agents above*			
Class Effects: Prevention of migraines, risk of neutralizing antibody formation due to being MABs.			
Generic Name	**Brand Name**	**Indication(s) or Uses**	**Notes**

Eptinezumab	Vyepti	▪ Migraine prophylaxis	▪ **Dosing (Adult):**
			  – IV 100 to 300 mg q3months
			▪ **Dosing (Peds):**
			  – Not routinely used
			▪ **CYP450 Interactions:** None
			▪ **Renal or Hepatic Dose Adjustments:** None
			▪ **Dosage Forms:** IV (solution)

Erenumab	Aimovig	▪ Migraine prophylaxis	▪ **Dosing (Adult):**
			  – SQ 70 to 140 mg q1month
			▪ **Dosing (Peds):**
			  – Not routinely used
			▪ **CYP450 Interactions:** None
			▪ **Renal or Hepatic Dose Adjustments:** None
			▪ **Dosage Forms:** Subcutaneous (solution)

Fremanezumab	Ajovy	▪ Migraine prophylaxis	▪ **Dosing (Adult):**
			  – SQ 225 or 675 mg q3months
			▪ **Dosing (Peds):**
			  – Not routinely used
			▪ **CYP450 Interactions:** None
			▪ **Renal or Hepatic Dose Adjustments:** None
			▪ **Dosage Forms:** Subcutaneous (solution)

Calcitonin Gene-Related Peptide Receptor Antagonist - Drug Class Review
High-Yield Med Reviews

Generic Name	Brand Name	Indication(s) or Uses	Notes

Galcanezumab	Emgality	• Migraine prophylaxis	• **Dosing (Adult):**
			  – SQ 120 to 300 mg q1months
			• **Dosing (Peds):**
			  – Not routinely used
			• **CYP450 Interactions:** None
			• **Renal or Hepatic Dose Adjustments:** None
			• **Dosage Forms:** Subcutaneous (solution)

Rimegepant	Nurtec	• Migraine prophylaxis	• **Dosing (Adult):**
			  – Oral 75 mg every other day
			  – Oral 75 mg once for migraine treatment
			• **Dosing (Peds):**
			  – Not routinely used
			• **CYP450 Interactions:** None
			• **Renal or Hepatic Dose Adjustments:**
			  – GFR less than 15 mL/minute - Avoid use
			  – Child-Pugh class C - Avoid use
			• **Dosage Forms:** Oral (tablet disintegrating)

Ubrogepant	Ubrelvy	• Migraine prophylaxis	• **Dosing (Adult):**
			  – Oral 50 to 100 mg x 1, may repeat once
			    • Maximum 200 mg/day
			• **Dosing (Peds):**
			  – Not routinely used
			• **CYP450 Interactions:** None
			• **Renal or Hepatic Dose Adjustments:**
			  – GFR less than 15 to 29 mL/minute - Maximum 100 mg/day
			  – GFR less than 15 mL/minute - Avoid use
			  – Child-Pugh class C - Maximum 100 mg/day
			• **Dosage Forms:** Oral (tablet)

High-Yield Clinical Knowledge

- **Combination Therapy**
  - The anti-CGRP agents are novel advances in migraine therapy that, in addition to an established efficacy, can be combined with other existing migraine pharmacotherapy, including triptans.
  - This offers multimodal pharmacotherapy intervention in patients with treatment-resistant migraines and avoids other drug therapies such as valproic acid, tricyclic antidepressants, or opioids.
- **Preventative Therapy**
  - Anti-CGRP pharmacotherapy is an alternative to topiramate for the prevention of episodic migraine.
  - Although there are no prospective head-to-head trials, anti-CGRP agents are associated with relatively mild adverse events, including upper respiratory tract infection and injection site pain.
    - Topiramate has been associated with anorexia, fatigue, memory problems, and paresthesias.
- **Safety**
  - Compared to existing antimigraine pharmacotherapy, the anti-CGRP agents do not risk serotonin syndrome, diminished sexual function and drive, or complicating existing coronary artery disease, angina, history of stroke, transient ischemic attack, or ischemic bowel disease.

- **-Umabs and -Zumabs**
  - Of the CGRP-mab agents, erenumab is a fully human monoclonal antibody, whereas eptinezumab, galcanezumab, and fremanezumab are humanized murine or yeast antibodies.
- **Molecule Size**
  - The monoclonal antibodies are too large to cross the blood-brain barrier and exert their antimigraine activity outside the CNS at the trigeminal nerve ending.
  - Conversely, the small molecule CGRP antagonists rimegepant and ubrogepant can work both within and outside the CNS.
- **Safety**
  - Compared to existing antimigraine pharmacotherapy, the anti-CGRP agents do not risk serotonin syndrome, diminished sexual function and drive, or complicating existing coronary artery disease, angina, history of stroke, transient ischemic attack, or ischemic bowel disease.

HIGH-YIELD BOARD EXAM ESSENTIALS
- **CLASSIC AGENTS:** Eptinezumab, erenumab, fremanezumab, galcanezumab, rimegepant, ubrogepant
- **DRUG CLASS:** CGRP Receptor Antagonist
- **INDICATIONS:** Migraine treatment/prophylaxis
- **MECHANISM:** Human monoclonal antibodies bind to, and inhibit the CGRP receptor function (eptinezumab, erenumab, galcanezumab, fremanezumab); Small molecule antagonist of the CGRP receptor (rimegepant, ubrogepant)
- **SIDE EFFECTS:** Neutralizing antibody formation
- **CLINICAL PEARLS:**
  - Compared to existing antimigraine pharmacotherapy, the anti-CGRP agents do not risk serotonin syndrome, diminished sexual function and drive, or complicating existing coronary artery disease, angina, history of stroke, transient ischemic attack, or ischemic bowel disease.
  - The agents ending with "-mab" are all biologic agents (i.e., monoclonal antibodies) that we require parenteral administration but have longer half-lives.

High-Yield Basic Pharmacology

- **Mechanism of Action**
  - Selective agonists of the 5HT-5HT-1D/1B (triptans) or non-selective 5HT-1D/1B agonists mediating cerebral vessel dilation, blocking the release of substance P and calcitonin gene-related peptide (CGRP) from the trigeminal nucleus caudalis).
  - **Excess Serotonin Effects**
    - In addition to the beneficial therapeutic effects, SSRIs increase serotonergic tone throughout the body, causing various, specifically gastrointestinal distress, early after initiation but resolving after one week of treatment.

Primary Net Benefit

- Triptans evolved the care of migraine by maintaining abortive efficacy and improving safety vs. ergot derivatives.

Antimigraine Agents - Drug Class Review High-Yield Med Reviews			

Mechanism of Action: *Selective agonists of the 5HT-5HT-1D/1B (triptans) or non-selective 5HT-1D/1B agonists mediating cerebral vessel dilation, blocking the release of substance P and calcitonin gene-related peptide (CGRP) from the trigeminal nucleus caudalis)*

Class Effects: Acute migraine treatment, risk of hypertension, ergotism, serotonin syndrome.

Generic Name	Brand Name	Indication(s) or Uses	Notes

Almotriptan	Axert	• Migraine	• **Dosing (Adult):**
			   – Oral 6.25 to 12.5 mg once; Max 25 mg/day
			 • **Dosing (Peds):**
			   – Oral 6.25 to 12.5 mg once; Max 25 mg/day
			 • **CYP450 Interactions:** Substrate of CYP2D6, 3A4
			 • **Renal or Hepatic Dose Adjustments:**
			   – GFR less than 30 mL/minute - Maximum 12.5 mg/day
			 • **Dosage Forms:** Oral (Tablet)

Dihydro-ergotamine	D.H.E, Migranal	• Migraine	• **Dosing (Adult):**
			   – IM/SQ 1 mg at the first sign of headache then q1h as needed
			     • Maximum 3 mg/day or 6 mg/week
			   – IV 1 mg at the first sign of headache then q1h as needed
			     • Maximum 2 mg/day or 6 mg/week
			   – Intranasal 1 spray per nostril once, repeat in 15 minutes for a total of 4 sprays.
			     • Maximum 6 sprays/24 hours or 8 sprays/week
			 • **Dosing (Peds):**
			   – IV 0.1 to 0.2 mg/dose q6h
			     • Maximum 8 doses per episodes
			 • **CYP450 Interactions:** Substrate CYP3A4
			 • **Renal or Hepatic Dose Adjustments:**
			   – Severe renal or hepatic impairment - contraindicated
			 • **Dosage Forms:** Injection solution, Nasal solution

Antimigraine Agents - Drug Class Review
High-Yield Med Reviews

Generic Name	Brand Name	Indication(s) or Uses	Notes
Eletriptan	Relpax	• Migraine	• **Dosing (Adult):** – Oral 20 to 40 mg once, may repeat in 2 hours • Maximum 80 mg/day • **Dosing (Peds):** – Not routinely used • **CYP450 Interactions:** Substrate CYP3A4 • **Renal or Hepatic Dose Adjustments:** – Severe hepatic impairment - contraindicated • **Dosage Forms:** Oral (tablet)

Ergotamine	Ergomar	• Migraine	• **Dosing (Adult):**
			– SL 2 mg at first sign of migraine, then 2 mg q30minutes as needed
			  • Maximum 6 mg/24 hours, 10 mg/week
			• **Dosing (Peds):**
			– SL 2 mg at first sign of migraine, then 2 mg q30minutes as needed
			  • Maximum 6 mg/24 hours, 10 mg/week
			• **CYP450 Interactions:** Substrate CYP3A4
			• **Renal or Hepatic Dose Adjustments:**
			– Severe renal or hepatic impairment - contraindicated
			• **Dosage Forms:** Oral (sublingual tablet)

Frovatriptan	Frova	• Migraine	• **Dosing (Adult):** – Oral 2.5 mg, may repeat after 2 hours • Maximum 7.5 mg/day • **Dosing (Peds):** – Not routinely used • **CYP450 Interactions:** Substrate CYP1A2 • **Renal or Hepatic Dose Adjustments:** – Severe hepatic impairment - use with caution • **Dosage Forms:** Oral (tablet)
Lasmiditan	Reyvow	• Migraine	• **Dosing (Adult):** – Oral 50 to 200 mg once • **Dosing (Peds):** – Not routinely used • **CYP450 Interactions:** Substrate P-gp • **Renal or Hepatic Dose Adjustments:** – Child-Pugh class C - not recommended • **Dosage Forms:** Oral (tablet)

Antimigraine Agents - Drug Class Review
High-Yield Med Reviews

Generic Name	Brand Name	Indication(s) or Uses	Notes

Naratriptan	Amerge	• Migraine	• **Dosing (Adult):**
			  – Oral 1 to 2.5 mg once, may repeat in 4 hours
			    • Maximum 5 mg/24 hours
			• **Dosing (Peds):**
			  – Extra info if needed
			    • Extra info if needed
			• **CYP450 Interactions:** text
			• **Renal or Hepatic Dose Adjustments:**
			  – GFR less than 15 mL/minute - contraindicated
			  – Child-Pugh class C - contraindicated
			• **Dosage Forms:** Oral (tablet)

Rizatriptan	Maxalt	• Migraine	• **Dosing (Adult):**
			  – Oral 5 to 10 mg once, may repeat in 2 hours
			    • Maximum 30 mg/24 hours
			• **Dosing (Peds):**
			  – Oral 5 to 10 mg once
			• **CYP450 Interactions:** None
			• **Renal or Hepatic Dose Adjustments:** None
			• **Dosage Forms:** Oral (tablet)

Sumatriptan	Imitrex, Onzetra, Sumavel, Tosymra, Zembrace	• Cluster headache
		• Cyclic vomiting syndrome
		• Migraine
			• **Dosing (Adult):**
			  – Oral 50 to 100 mg once, may repeat in 2 hours
			    • Maximum 100 mg/dose or 200 mg/24 hours
			  – SQ 3 to 6 mg once
			    • Maximum 6 mg/dose or 12 mg/24 hours
			  – Nasal 20 mg once in a single nostril contralateral to the side of headache
			    • Maximum 40 mg/24 hours
			• **Dosing (Peds):**
			  – Oral 50 to 100 mg once, may repeat in 2 hours
			    • Maximum 100 mg/dose or 200 mg/24 hours
			  – SQ 3 to 6 mg once
			    • Maximum 6 mg/dose or 12 mg/24 hours
			  – Nasal 20 mg once in a single nostril contralateral to the side of headache
			    • Maximum 40 mg/24 hours
			• **CYP450 Interactions:** None
			• **Renal or Hepatic Dose Adjustments:**
			  – Severe hepatic impairment - use with caution
			• **Dosage Forms:** Oral (tablet), Nasal (powder, solution), subcutaneous solution

Antimigraine Agents - Drug Class Review			
High-Yield Med Reviews			
Generic Name	Brand Name	Indication(s) or Uses	Notes

Zolmitriptan	Zomig	▪ Migraine	▪ **Dosing (Adult):**
			  – Nasal 2.5 to 10 mg at the onset of migraine
			  – Oral 1.25 to 5 mg at the onset of migraine
			▪ **Dosing (Peds):**
			  – Nasal 2.5 to 5 mg at the onset of migraine
			▪ **CYP450 Interactions:** Substrate CYP1A2
			▪ **Renal or Hepatic Dose Adjustments:**
			  – Child-Pugh class B or C - not recommended
			▪ **Dosage Forms:** Oral (tablet), Nasal (solution)

High-Yield Clinical Knowledge

- **Migraine Treatment**
  - The triptans are effective in managing acute migraines and should not be used for the prevention of migraines.
  - Triptans must be administered as soon as possible after the onset of migraine signs and symptoms for maximum abortive efficacy.
- **Coronary Artery Disease**
  - All triptans are contraindicated in patients with coronary artery disease, angina, history of stroke, transient ischemic attack, or ischemic bowel disease.
  - Additional contraindications exist for specific triptans, including
    - Eletriptan, frovatriptan, and naratriptan are contraindicated in patients with peripheral vascular disease.
    - Eletriptan and naratriptan are contraindicated in patients with severe renal or hepatic impairment.
    - Patients with Wolff-Parkinson-White syndrome should not receive zolmitriptan.
- **Serotonin Syndrome**
  - Serotonin syndrome is the combination of a rapid onset of altered mental status, autonomic instability, hyperthermia, and hyperreflexia/myoclonus.
  - Triptans, dihydroergotamine, and ergotamine have been implicated in serotonin syndrome and other antidepressants, including MAO inhibitors, contribute to serotonin toxicity.
  - To reduce the likelihood of serotonin syndrome, most triptans may only be administered once or twice (depending on the agent) in 24 hours and cannot be combined with ergot derivatives.
  - Treatment of serotonin syndrome involves the management of hyperthermia through invasive or noninvasive cooling, skeletal muscle relaxation using benzodiazepines, and airway support.
    - Dantrolene and cyproheptadine have been suggested as adjuncts for managing serotonin syndrome but are of questionable patient-oriented benefit.
- **Ergotism**
  - Excessive ergot alkaloid use, or administration may produce ergotism, characterized by the extremities' intense burning sensation, hemorrhagic vesiculation, gangrene, pruritus, formication, nausea, and vomiting.
  - Convulsive ergotism includes additional central effects such as headache, fixed miosis, hallucinations, delirium, cerebrovascular ischemia, and seizures.
  - Although excessive doses can cause ergotism, interactions with CYP3A4 inhibitors can also lead to ergotism.
- **Triptan Duration**
  - In many patients, the duration of the migraine is longer than the duration of effect for triptans.
  - All triptans except for almotriptan and lasmiditan can be administered twice in acute migraine episodes.
    - Almotriptan and lasmiditan may only be administered once.

HIGH-YIELD BOARD EXAM ESSENTIALS

- **CLASSIC AGENTS:** Almotriptan, dihydroergotamine, eletriptan, ergotamine, frovatriptan, lasmiditan, naratriptan, rizatriptan, sumatriptan, zolmitriptan
- **DRUG CLASS:** Antimigraine agents
- **INDICATIONS:** Migraine
- **MECHANISM:** Selective agonists of the 5HT-5HT-1D/1B (triptans) or non-selective 5HT-1D/1B agonists mediating cerebral vessel dilation, blocking the release of substance P and calcitonin gene-related peptide (CGRP) from the trigeminal nucleus caudalis).
- **SIDE EFFECTS:** Hypertension, ergotism, serotonin syndrome
- **CLINICAL PEARLS:**
    - The triptans are effective in managing acute migraines and should not be used for the prevention of migraines because they can worsen the frequency of migraines.
    - Triptans must be administered as soon as possible after the onset of migraine signs and symptoms for maximum abortive efficacy.
    - Injectable options can sometimes cause chest pain (discomfort or pressure sensation). Use with caution in patients with moderate to severe ischemic heart disease.

High-Yield Basic Pharmacology

- **Mechanism of Action**
  - Barbiturates bind to a specific barbiturate site on the GABA-A receptor, increasing the receptor's mean open time, increasing the influx of chloride intracellularly.
- **Direct GABA-A Opening**
  - Differ from benzodiazepines because barbiturates open GABA-A receptors independent of GABA.
  - This effect generally occurs at high concentrations and is coupled with other CNS inhibitory effects including blocking AMPA/kainate receptors and inhibition of glutamate release.

Primary Net Benefit

- Dose-dependent CNS effects ranging from anxiolysis to sedation to coma and ultimately brain-death at dosing extremes. Benzodiazepines have largely replaced use with improved safety and efficacy.

<table>
<tr><td colspan="4">Barbiturates - Drug Class Review
High-Yield Med Reviews</td></tr>
<tr><td colspan="4">Mechanism of Action: Barbiturates bind to a specific barbiturate site on the GABA-A receptor, increasing the mean open time of the receptor, thus increasing the influx of chloride intracellularly.</td></tr>
<tr><td colspan="4">Class Effects: Anxiolysis, risk of respiratory depression, altered mental status, hypotension, decreased cardiac output, & drug interactions (inducer of CYP450).</td></tr>
<tr><td>Generic Name</td><td>Brand Name</td><td>Indication(s) or Uses</td><td>Notes</td></tr>
<tr>
<td>Amobarbital</td>
<td>Amytal Sodium</td>
<td>• Sedative/hypnotic</td>
<td>
• Dosing (Adult):]
  – IM/IV 30 to 200 mg q8-24h
    • Maximum 1,000 mg/dose
• Dosing (Peds):
  – IM/IV 2 to 3 mg/kg/dose
    • Maximum 500 mg/dose
• CYP450 Interactions: CYP Inducer
• Renal or Hepatic Dose Adjustments: None
• Dosage Forms: IV (solution)
</td>
</tr>
<tr>
<td>Butalbital</td>
<td>Butisol (others in combination: Fioricet Fiorinal Esgic</td>
<td>• Sedative/hypnotic
• Tension headache</td>
<td>
• Dosing (Adult):
  – Oral 15 to 100 mg q6-24h
• Dosing (Peds):
  – Oral 2 to 6 mg/kg/dose before surgery
    • Maximum 100 mg/dose
• CYP450 Interactions: CYP Inducer
• Renal or Hepatic Dose Adjustments: None
• Dosage Forms: Oral (capsule, tablet)
</td>
</tr>
<tr>
<td>Methohexital</td>
<td>Brevital</td>
<td>• Anesthesia
• Sedative/hypnotic
•
•</td>
<td>
• Dosing (Adult):
  – IV 0.5 to 1.5 mg/kg q2-5 minutes as needed
• Dosing (Peds):
  – IM - 6.6 to 25 mg/kg/dose
    • Maximum 500 mg/dose
  – IV 0.5 to 2 mg/kg/dose
    • Maximum 500 mg/dose
• CYP450 Interactions: CYP Inducer
• Renal or Hepatic Dose Adjustments: None
• Dosage Forms: IV (solution)
</td>
</tr>
</table>

Barbiturates - Drug Class Review
High-Yield Med Reviews

Generic Name	Brand Name	Indication(s) or Uses	Notes

Phenobarbital	Luminal	• Anesthesia
		• Sedative/hypnotic
		• Seizures
			• **Dosing (Adult):**
			  – Oral/IM/IV 30 to 260 mg/kg q6-12h
			    • Maximum 400 mg/day
			  – IV 15 to 20 mg/kg IV
			• **Dosing (Peds):**
			  – Oral - 2 to 5 mg/kg/dose
			    • Maximum 500 mg/dose
			  – IV 10 to 20 mg/kg/dose
			    • Maximum 1000 mg/dose
			• **CYP450 Interactions:** CYP Inducer (CYP 1A2, 2A6, 2B6, 2C9, 3A4); Substrate of CYP2C19, 2C9, 2E1
			• **Renal or Hepatic Dose Adjustments:**
			  – GFR less than 10 mL/minute - Decrease to q12-16hours
			• **Dosage Forms:** Oral (elixir, tablet, solution), IV (solution)

Pentobarbital	Nembutal	• Anesthesia
		• Barbiturate coma
		• Sedative/hypnotic
			• **Dosing (Adult):**
			  – IM 150 to 200 mg x1
			  – IV bolus 5 to 15 mg/kg
			  – IV infusion 0.5 to 5 mg/kg/hour
			• **Dosing (Peds):**
			  – IM 2 to 6 mg/kg/dose
			    • Maximum 100 mg/dose
			  – IV 1 to 15 mg/kg infusion
			    • Maximum 6 mg/kg or 100 mg/dose
			• **CYP450 Interactions:** CYP inducer
			• **Renal or Hepatic Dose Adjustments:** None
			• **Dosage Forms:** IV (solution)

Primidone	Mysoline	• Seizures
		• Essential tremor
			• **Dosing (Adult):**
			  – Oral 100 to 1500 mg q6-24h
			• **Dosing (Peds):**
			  – Oral 10 to 25 mg/kg/day divided q8-12h
			    • Maximum 500 mg/dose
			• **CYP450 Interactions:** CYP Inducer (CYP 1A2, 2A6, 2B6, 2C9, 3A4); Substrate of CYP2C19, 2C9, 2E1
			• **Renal or Hepatic Dose Adjustments:**
			  – GFR 10 to 50 mL/minute - Administer q12-24h
			  – GFR less than 10 mL/minute - Administer q24h
			• **Dosage Forms:** Oral (tablet)

High-Yield Clinical Knowledge

- **Selective Antiepileptic Action**
  - Not all barbiturates possess antiepileptic properties at clinically used doses.
    - Only those containing a 5-phenyl substituent (phenobarbital, pentobarbital) possess this action as conventionally used.

- **Hypnotic Dose Range**
  - As with other CNS effects, the hypnotic effects of barbiturates are dose-dependent in nature.
  - Generally, barbiturates extend the total sleep time, modify sleep stages, decrease the number of awakenings, and decrease REM sleep duration.
  - Tolerance also develops with repetitive use, where a reduction of total sleep time can be cut in half after 2 weeks.
    - Conversely, upon abrupt discontinuation, rebound effects on sleep manifesting as acute worsening of sleep parameters.
- **Tolerance, Abuse, and Dependence**
  - Barbiturates exhibit both pharmacokinetic and pharmacodynamic tolerance, each of which occurs at different time frames relative to drug therapy initiation.
  - The clinical implications of tolerance include narrowing the therapeutic index towards toxic ranges and cross-tolerance to other CNS depressant drugs.
    - Pharmacokinetic tolerance (equilibration of absorption, distribution, metabolism, and elimination) occurs rapidly after therapy initiation, achieving a peak within 3 to 7 days.
    - Pharmacodynamic tolerance to the euphoric, sedative, and hypnotic effects occurs rapidly but develops over the course of weeks to months.
- **CYP Inhibition-Induction**
  - Although barbiturates are known to cause induction of CYP 450 enzymes, acutely, they inhibit numerous CYP isoenzymes (1A2, 2C9, 2C19, 3A4), affecting both numerous medications and endogenous steroids.
  - With chronic administration, barbiturates cause numerous hepatic functions including CYP 450 oxidation (namely 1A2, 2C9, 2C19, 2E1, 3A4).
    - Just as with inhibition, induction of hepatic oxidation also increases the metabolism of numerous drugs and endogenous substances, including steroids, hormones, cholesterol, and vitamin K.
- **Respiratory Depression**
  - Barbiturates possess many respiratory depressant effects, including decreasing respiratory drive, hypoxic drive, chemoreceptor drive, and protective reflexes.
    - In the CNS, the respiratory drive is fully suppressed at three times normal anesthetic doses.
- **Cardiovascular System**
  - Barbiturates can cause vasodilation during rapid IV administration and decrease reflex responses via partial inhibition of ganglionic transmission.
    - Compensatory mechanisms are thus impaired, particularly in patients with heart failure, hypovolemic shock, and acute stroke (dependent on cerebral blood flow).

High-Yield Fast-Facts

- **Primidone (2-desoxyphenobarbital)**
  - Primidone is a prodrug releasing phenobarbital after metabolism.

HIGH-YIELD BOARD EXAM ESSENTIALS
- **CLASSIC AGENTS:** Amobarbital, butalbital, methohexital, phenobarbital, pentobarbital, primidone
- **DRUG CLASS:** Barbiturates
- **INDICATIONS:** Alcohol withdrawal treatment, headache/migraine, sedation, seizure treatment
- **MECHANISM:** Bind to a specific barbiturate site on the GABA-A receptor, increasing the mean open time of the receptor, thus increasing the influx of chloride intracellularly
- **SIDE EFFECTS:** Respiratory depression, altered mental status, hypotension, decreased cardiac output
- **CLINICAL PEARLS:** Although barbiturates are known to cause induction of CYP 450 enzymes, acutely, they inhibit numerous CYP isoenzymes (1A2, 2C9, 2C19, 3A4), affecting both numerous medications and endogenous steroids. With chronic administration, barbiturates cause numerous hepatic functions including CYP 450 oxidation (namely 1A2, 2C9, 2C19, 2E1, 3A4).

High-Yield Basic Pharmacology

- **GABAergic Effects**
  - Benzodiazepines appear to increase GABAergic synaptic inhibition efficiency by binding to the alpha-1 subunit of GABA-A receptors containing a gamma-2 subunit.
  - **GABA-A Receptor**
    - The GABA-A receptor most commonly contains a 5-subunit complex with alpha, beta, and gamma subunits.
    - The non-benzodiazepine sedative hypnotic "z-drugs" also bind to the alpha-1 subunit in a fashion similar to benzodiazepines.

Primary Net Benefit

- Achieve CNS depressant activity related to barbiturates, but improved safety with sedative "ceiling" effect when used alone, and no direct negative cardiovascular or respiratory effects.
- Useful to prevent alcohol withdrawal and seizures with many dosage formulations and routes of administration.

Benzodiazepines - Drug Class Review			
High-Yield Med Reviews			
Mechanism of Action: *Benzodiazepines increase the frequency of GABA-A channel opening, potentiating GABAergic inhibition of neurotransmission.*			
Class Effects: Improved safety with sedative "ceiling" effect when used alone vs barbiturates, and no direct negative cardiovascular or respiratory effects, anxiolysis, altered mental status, withdrawal (abrupt discontinuation from chronic use), risk of abuse or physical dependence with repeated use, contraindicated in pregnancy.			
Generic Name	**Brand Name**	**Indication(s) or Uses**	**Notes**

Alprazolam	Xanax	• Anxiety
		• Chemotherapy nausea and vomiting
		• Vertigo
			• **Dosing (Adult):**
			  – Oral 0.25 to 1 mg q8-12h
			    • Maximum 10 mg/day
			• **Dosing (Peds):**
			  – 0.005 to 0.02 mg/kg/dose q8h
			    • Maximum 10 mg/day
			• **CYP450 Interactions:** Substrate CYP3A4; Inhibits CYP3A4
			• **Renal or Hepatic Dose Adjustments:**
			  – Child-Pugh class C - 0.25 mg q8-12h
			• **Dosage Forms:** Oral (concentrate, disintegrating tablet, tablet IR, tablet XR)
			•

Chlordiazepoxide	Librium	• Alcohol withdrawal
		• Anxiety
			• **Dosing (Adult):**
			  – Oral 25 to 100 mg q6-24h
			• **Dosing (Peds):**
			  – Oral 5 to 10 mg q6-12h
			• **CYP450 Interactions:** Substrate CYP3A4
			• **Renal or Hepatic Dose Adjustments:**
			  – GFR less than 10 mL/minute - administer 50% of the dose
			• **Dosage Forms:** Oral (capsule)

Benzodiazepines - Drug Class Review
High-Yield Med Reviews

Generic Name	Brand Name	Indication(s) or Uses	Notes

Clobazam	Onfi	• Lennox-Gastaut syndrome	• **Dosing (Adult):**
			  – Oral 5 mg daily, up to 20 mg q12h
			• **Dosing (Peds):**
			  – 0.2 to 1 mg/kg/day divided q12h
			    • Maximum 40 mg/day
			• **CYP450 Interactions:** Substrate of CYP2B6, 2C19, 3A4, P-gp; Inhibits CYP2D6; Induces CYP3A4
			• **Renal or Hepatic Dose Adjustments:** None
			• **Dosage Forms:** Oral (film, suspension, tablet)

Clorazepate	Tranxene-T	• Alcohol withdrawal
		• Anxiety disorders
		• Seizures
			• **Dosing (Adult):**
			  – Oral 30 mg/day in divided doses
			    • Maximum 90 mg/day
			• **Dosing (Peds):**
			  – Oral 0.3 to 1 mg/kg/day divided q8-24h
			    • Maximum 90 mg/day
			• **CYP450 Interactions:** Substrate CYP3A4
			• **Renal or Hepatic Dose Adjustments:** None
			• **Dosage Forms:** Oral (tablet)

Diazepam	Diastat, Valium, Valtoco	• Alcohol withdrawal
		• Anxiety disorders
		• Muscle spasms
		• Sedation
		• Seizures
			• **Dosing (Adult):**
			  – IV/IN 0.2 mg/kg as needed
			    • Maximum 20 mg/dose
			• **Dosing (Peds):**
			  – IV/IN 0.2 mg/kg as needed
			    • Maximum 20 mg/dose
			  – Rectal 0.2 to 0.5 mg/kg
			    • Maximum 20 mg/dose
			• **CYP450 Interactions:** Substrate CYP1A2, 2C19, 2C9, 3A4
			• **Renal or Hepatic Dose Adjustments:** None
			• **Dosage Forms:** Oral (concentrate, solution, tablet), Rectal (gel), IV (solution)

Estazolam	Prosom	• Insomnia	• **Dosing (Adult):** – Oral 1 mg at bedtime • **Dosing (Peds):** Not routinely used • **CYP450 Interactions:** Substrate CYP3A4 • **Renal or Hepatic Dose Adjustments:** None • **Dosage Forms:** Oral (tablet)

Flurazepam	Som-Pam	• Insomnia	• **Dosing (Adult):**
			  – Oral 15 to 30 mg at bedtime
			• **Dosing (Peds):**
			  – Oral 15 mg at bedtime
			• **CYP450 Interactions:** Substrate CYP3A4
			• **Renal or Hepatic Dose Adjustments:** None
			• **Dosage Forms:** Oral (tablet)

Benzodiazepines - Drug Class Review
High-Yield Med Reviews

Generic Name	Brand Name	Indication(s) or Uses	Notes

Lorazepam	Ativan	• Anxiety disorders
		• Sedation
		• Seizures
			• **Dosing (Adult):**
			  – IM/IV 0.25 to 4 mg q3-5minutes to q3-6hours
			  – Oral 0.5 to 2 mg q6-24hours
			• **Dosing (Peds):**
			  – Oral 0.05 mg/kg/dose q4-8hours
			    ▪ Maximum 2 mg/dose
			  – IV 0.1 mg/kg up to 2 doses
			    ▪ Maximum 5 mg/dose
			• **CYP450 Interactions:** None
			• **Renal or Hepatic Dose Adjustments:** None
			• **Dosage Forms:** Oral (concentrate, solution, tablet), IV (solution)

Midazolam	Versed	• Sedation
		• Seizures
			• **Dosing (Adult):**
			  – IN/IM/IV 0.5 to 10 mg q3-5minutes
			  – IV 0.05 to 2 mg/kg/hour infusion
			• **Dosing (Peds):**
			  – Oral/Rectal 0.25 to 0.5 mg/kg/dose
			    ▪ Maximum 10 mg/dose
			  – IN/IM/IV 0.1 to 0.5 mg/kg/dose
			    ▪ Maximum 10 mg/dose
			  – IV infusion 0.05 to 2mg/kg/hour
			• **CYP450 Interactions:** Substrate CYP2B6, 3A4
			• **Renal or Hepatic Dose Adjustments:**
			  – No specific adjustments, but continuous administration will lead to the accumulation of midazolam and metabolites.
			• **Dosage Forms:** Oral (syrup), IV (solution)

Oxazepam	Oxpam	• Alcohol withdrawal
		• Anxiety
			• **Dosing (Adult):**
			  – Oral 10 to 30 mg q6-24h
			• **Dosing (Peds):**
			  – Oral 10 to 30 mg q6-24h
			• **CYP450 Interactions:** None
			• **Renal or Hepatic Dose Adjustments:** None
			• **Dosage Forms:** Oral (capsule)
			•

Quazepam	Doral	• Insomnia	• **Dosing (Adult):** – Oral 7.5 mg at bedtime • **Dosing (Peds):** Not routinely used • **CYP450 Interactions:** Substrate CYP3A4 • **Renal or Hepatic Dose Adjustments:** None • **Dosage Forms:** Oral (tablet) •
Remimazolam	Byfavo	• Sedation	• **Dosing (Adult):** – IV 1.25 to 5 mg as needed • **Dosing (Peds):** Not routinely used • **CYP450 Interactions:** None known • **Renal or Hepatic Dose Adjustments:** None • **Dosage Forms:** IV (solution)

Benzodiazepines - Drug Class Review
High-Yield Med Reviews

Generic Name	Brand Name	Indication(s) or Uses	Notes
Temazepam	Restoril	• Insomnia	• **Dosing (Adult):** – Oral 7.5 to 30 mg at bedtime • **Dosing (Peds):** Not routinely used • **CYP450 Interactions:** Substrate CYP2B6, 2C19, 2C9, 3A4 • **Renal or Hepatic Dose Adjustments:** None • **Dosage Forms:** Oral (capsule) •

Triazolam	Halcion	• Insomnia	• **Dosing (Adult):**
			  – Oral 0.125 to 0.25 mg at bedtime
			• **Dosing (Peds):**
			  – Oral 0.125 to 0.25 mg at bedtime
			• **CYP450 Interactions:** Substrate CYP3A4
			• **Renal or Hepatic Dose Adjustments:** None
			• **Dosage Forms:** Oral (tablet)
			•

High-Yield Clinical Knowledge

- **Metabolism**
  - All benzodiazepines are metabolized hepatically but differ in hepatic metabolism, undergoing either oxidation (phase 1) or glucuronidation (phase 2).
  - The "LOT" agents, lorazepam, oxazepam, and temazepam, are benzodiazepines that undergo glucuronidation.
  - Most other benzodiazepines (i.e., chlordiazepoxide, diazepam, midazolam, etc.) undergo hepatic oxidation by the CYP450 system.
    - Oxidation often produces metabolites that can accumulate with prolonged administration, leading to excessive sedation.
- **ICU Sedation**
  - Sedation of mechanically ventilated patients should be accomplished using propofol or dexmedetomidine, with benzodiazepines reserved for cases where either of the aforementioned agents cannot be used.
    - Benzodiazepine use for sedation of mechanically ventilated patients is associated with ICU delirium and the accumulation of metabolites (diazepam and midazolam), potentially prolonging mechanical ventilation.
  - If used, lorazepam is preferred over diazepam or midazolam as an agent for sedation of mechanically ventilated patients and should be administered using an intermittent push rather than continuous infusion.
- **Withdrawal**
  - As a result of chronic administration, followed by downregulation of GABA-A receptors, or GABA, abrupt discontinuation of benzodiazepines can cause a neurologic excitatory withdrawal syndrome, sharing many similarities with an alcohol withdrawal syndrome.
  - The management of benzodiazepine withdrawal involves providing appropriate doses of diazepam in a symptom-triggered fashion.
  - Benzodiazepine withdrawal is potentially fatal.
- **Chlordiazepoxide Metabolites**
  - CYP3A4 oxidizes chlordiazepoxide to numerous active metabolites including nordiazepam, and oxazepam.
  - For the management of alcohol withdrawal, this property is ideal. It permits self-titration and, when combined with symptom-triggered dosing(rather than a scheduled dose), allows for less drug to be used and fewer excessive sedation episodes.

- **Anesthesia**
  - Beyond sedation and hypnosis, some benzodiazepines (diazepam, lorazepam, and midazolam) are used clinically to achieve anesthesia.
  - If used alone, respiratory depression is unlikely to occur, but if combined with other agents (opioids, anesthetic gases, propofol, etc.), clinically relevant respiratory depression may occur.
    - In patients who are otherwise not chronically taking benzodiazepines, flumazenil is routinely used to reverse respiratory depressant effects that may occur.
- **Anticonvulsant**
  - Diazepam, lorazepam, and midazolam are routinely used as an essential component for the acute management of seizures.
    - However, additional antiepileptic agents are necessary as this effect is short-lived with benzodiazepines.
  - Diazepam is the most lipophilic of the available agents used to treat seizures, which permits rapid entry to the CNS, terminating seizures. However, this also leads to rapid redistribution of the CNS to other tissues, allowing for recurrent seizures.
    - However, diazepam is still used but is limited to outpatient use in the Dia-Stat rectal dosage form intended for parents/guardians to use on their dependents' seizure activity.
- **Flumazenil**
  - Flumazenil is a competitive antagonist of benzodiazepine binding to the GABA-A receptor, which can reverse unwanted effects of benzodiazepines, namely respiratory depression or excessive sedation.
  - In patients with chronic use of benzodiazepines, flumazenil may induce acute withdrawal. Still, given that the duration of action of flumazenil is much shorted than most offending benzodiazepines, this is a short-lived event.
    - Furthermore, acute withdrawal seizures can be treated using non-benzodiazepine agents, including propofol.
  - In benzodiazepine-naive patients, flumazenil is routinely used in the OR/PACU setting to speed the time to recovery from anesthesia.

HIGH-YIELD BOARD EXAM ESSENTIALS
- **CLASSIC AGENTS:** Clobazam, clorazepate, diazepam, lorazepam, midazolam, remimazolam
- **DRUG CLASS:** Benzodiazepines
- **INDICATIONS:** Alcohol withdrawal, anxiety disorders, sedation, seizures, Lennox-Gastaut syndrome, muscle spasms
- **MECHANISM:** Increase the frequency of GABA-A channel opening, potentiating GABAergic inhibition of neurotransmission.
- **SIDE EFFECTS:** Altered mental status, withdrawal (abrupt discontinuation from chronic use), risk of physical dependence with repeated/chronic use.
- **CLINICAL PEARLS:**
  - Achieve CNS depressant activity related to barbiturates, but improved safety with sedative "ceiling" effect when used alone, and no direct negative cardiovascular or respiratory effects.
  - Avoid mixing with use of alcohol due to increase CNS depression.
  - Benzodiazepines are considered contraindicated in pregnancy.
  - Diazepam and lorazepam the drugs of choice in cocaine-induced MI and alcohol withdrawal.
  - Long infusions of lorazepam in the ICU can result in an anion gap metabolic acidosis due to conversion of propylene glycol to lactic acid.

High-Yield Basic Pharmacology

- **Amphetamines:**
  - Stimulate the release of biogenic amines, particularly dopamine, norepinephrine, and serotonin.
- **Methylphenidate:**
  - Inhibits the reuptake of biogenic amines, particularly dopamine, norepinephrine, and serotonin.
    - This is the same mechanism as cocaine!

Primary Net Benefit

- Stimulants are effective drug treatment options for attention-deficit/hyperactivity disorder (ADHD) and can be applied to other stimulant indications, including narcolepsy.

<table>
<tr><td colspan="4">Amphetamines - Drug Class Review
High-Yield Med Reviews</td></tr>
<tr><td colspan="4">Mechanism of Action: Stimulate the release of biogenic amines, particularly dopamine, norepinephrine, and serotonin.</td></tr>
<tr><td colspan="4">Class Effects: Effective for ADHD, can stunt growth velocity, risk of mental/mood disturbances, severe anxiety, tachycardia, abuse or diversion potential high.</td></tr>
<tr><td>Generic Name</td><td>Brand Name</td><td>Indication(s) or Uses</td><td>Notes</td></tr>
<tr>
<td>Amphetamine</td>
<td>Adzenys, Dyanavel, Eveko</td>
<td><ul><li>Attention-deficit/hyperactivity disorder</li></ul></td>
<td><ul><li>Dosing (Adult):<ul><li>Oral ER 12.5 to 30 mg daily</li><li>Oral IR 10 to 60 mg daily</li></ul></li><li>Dosing (Peds):<ul><li>Oral IR 2.5 to 40 mg/day in 1-2 divided doses</li><li>Oral ER 3.1 to 18.8 mg daily</li></ul></li><li>CYP450 Interactions: Substrate CYP2D6</li><li>Renal or Hepatic Dose Adjustments: None</li><li>Dosage Forms: Oral (suspension, tablet, ODT)</li></ul></td>
</tr>
<tr>
<td>Armodafinil</td>
<td>Nuvigil</td>
<td><ul><li>Narcolepsy</li><li>Obstructive sleep apnea</li><li>Shift-work disorder</li></ul></td>
<td><ul><li>Dosing (Adult):<ul><li>Oral 150 to 250 mg daily</li></ul></li><li>Dosing (Peds):<ul><li>Not routinely used</li></ul></li><li>CYP450 Interactions: Substrate CYP3A4; Inhibits CYP2C19; Induces CYP3A4</li><li>Renal or Hepatic Dose Adjustments:<ul><li>Child-Pugh class C - use reduced dose</li></ul></li><li>Dosage Forms: Oral (tablet)</li></ul></td>
</tr>
<tr>
<td>Dexmethyl-phenidate</td>
<td>Focalin</td>
<td><ul><li>Attention-deficit/hyperactivity disorder</li></ul></td>
<td><ul><li>Dosing (Adult):<ul><li>Oral IR 2.5 to 10 mg BID</li><li>Oral ER 10 to 40 mg daily</li></ul></li><li>Dosing (Peds):<ul><li>Oral IR 2.5 to 10 mg BID</li><li>Oral ER 10 to 40 mg daily</li></ul></li><li>CYP450 Interactions: None</li><li>Renal or Hepatic Dose Adjustments: None</li><li>Dosage Forms: Oral (capsule, tablet)</li></ul></td>
</tr>
</table>

Amphetamines - Drug Class Review
High-Yield Med Reviews

Generic Name	Brand Name	Indication(s) or Uses	Notes

Dextroamphetamine	Dexedrine, ProCentra, Zenzedi	• Narcolepsy	• **Dosing (Adult):**
			  – Oral IR/ER 10 to 60 mg daily
			• **Dosing (Peds):**
			  – Oral IR 2.5 to 40 mg daily divided q4-6h
			  – Oral ER 5 to 40 mg daily in 2 divided doses
			• **CYP450 Interactions:** Substrate CYP2D6
			• **Renal or Hepatic Dose Adjustments:** None
			• **Dosage Forms:** Oral (capsule, solution, tablet)

Lisdexamfetamine	Vyvanse	• Attention-deficit/hyperactivity disorder	• **Dosing (Adult):**
			  – Oral 30 to 70 mg daily
			• **Dosing (Peds):**
			  – Oral 20 to 70 mg daily
			• **CYP450 Interactions:** Substrate CYP2D6
			• **Renal or Hepatic Dose Adjustments:**
			  – GFR 15 to 30 mL/minute - maximum 50 mg/day
			  – GFR less than 15 mL/minute - maximum 30 mg/day
			• **Dosage Forms:** Oral (capsule, tablet)

Methamphetamine	Desoxyn	• Narcolepsy	• **Dosing (Adult):**
			  – Oral 20 to 60 mg within 1 hour of awakening
			• **Dosing (Peds):**
			  – Oral 5 to 25 mg daily
			• **CYP450 Interactions:** Substrate CYP2D6
			• **Renal or Hepatic Dose Adjustments:** None
			• **Dosage Forms:** Oral (tablet)

Methylphenidate	Adhansia, Aptensio, Concerta, Cotempla, Daytrana, Jornay, Metadate, Methylin, QuilliChew, Quillivant, Relexxii, Ritalin	• Attention-deficit/hyperactivity disorder	• **Dosing (Adult):**
			  – Oral ER 10 to 100 mg/day
			  – Oral SR 20 to 100 mg/day
			  – Oral IR 10 to 60 mg/day in 2-3 divided doses
			  – Transdermal 10 mg applied 2 hours before the effect is needed, and removed after 9 hours
			• **Dosing (Peds):**
			  – Oral ER 10 to 100 mg/day
			  – Oral SR 20 to 100 mg/day
			  – Oral IR 2.5 to 60 mg/day in 2-3 divided doses
			  – Transdermal 10 mg applied 2 hours before the effect is needed, and removed after 9 hours
			• **CYP450 Interactions:** None
			• **Renal or Hepatic Dose Adjustments:** None
			• **Dosage Forms:** Oral (capsule, solution, suspension, tablet), Transdermal patch

		Amphetamines - Drug Class Review	
		High-Yield Med Reviews	
Generic Name	**Brand Name**	**Indication(s) or Uses**	**Notes**

Modafinil	Provigil	▪ Narcolepsy
		▪ Obstructive sleep apnea
		▪ Shift-work disorder
			▪ **Dosing (Adult):**
			  – Oral 100 to 400 mg daily
			▪ **Dosing (Peds):**
			  – Oral 100 to 400 mg daily
			▪ **CYP450 Interactions:** Substrate CYP3A4; Inhibits CYP2C19; Induces CYP3A4
			▪ **Renal or Hepatic Dose Adjustments:**
			  – Child-Pugh class C - reduce dose by 50%
			▪ **Dosage Forms:** Oral (tablet)

High-Yield Clinical Knowledge

- **Psychiatric Adverse Events**
  - The FDA applied warnings to all ADHD and amphetamine stimulant medications regarding the increased risk of acute psychiatric adverse events, including psychosis, mood disturbances, and severe anxiety.
  - The MTA study (described below) found no statistically significant difference in the incidence of psychosis among children receiving stimulant medication for ADHD.
- **Height and Weight**
  - Amphetamine ADHD medications are strongly associated with growth deficits of approximately 1 to 1.4 cm/year and weight gain deficits of 3 kg in the first year of therapy.
  - However, long-term follow-up of patients taking amphetamines has revealed that patients generally achieve their predicted growth potential upon discontinuation.
- **Cardiac Events**
  - Stimulant medication is associated with a 3 to 10 beat per minute increase in heart rate and changes in systolic blood pressure of approximately 12 mmHg.
  - These changes are not associated with significant changes in cardiovascular events among children but may be relevant in adolescents and adults who continue taking these medications.
- **Dosage Forms**
  - As many of these agents are used in children, a wide range of formulations exist to enhance pharmacokinetics but also ease of administration and to encourage compliance.
  - Numerous products feature oral dosage forms, including immediate, delayed, and extended-release preparations and oral liquids or orally disintegrating tablets.
    - Disadvantages to immediate-release forms are a short duration of action, requiring multiple doses per day.
  - Methylphenidate is available as a transdermal patch, which may be used if oral administration is not suitable or other compliance issues have been identified.
- **Dependence, Tolerance, and Abuse**
  - With chronic use, patients may become psychologically dependent on amphetamines, but tolerance does develop to the anorexigenic effects of amphetamines and mood changes.
  - However, these agents have a high potential for abuse due to their stimulant, hallucinogenic, and adaptogenic properties.
- **Non-amphetamines**
  - Compared to amphetamines for treating ADHD, non-amphetamine stimulants such as atomoxetine, clonidine, and guanfacine, are not as effective but can be used adjunctively in selected patients.

HIGH-YIELD BOARD EXAM ESSENTIALS

- **CLASSIC AGENTS:** Amphetamine, armodafinil, dexmethylphenidate, dextroamphetamine, lisdexamfetamine, methamphetamine, methylphenidate, modafinil
- **DRUG CLASS:** Amphetamines
- **INDICATIONS:** ADHD (amphetamine, dexmethylphenidate, lisdexamfetamine, methylphenidate), narcolepsy (armodafinil, dextroamphetamine, methamphetamine, modafinil), obstructive sleep apnea (armodafinil, modafinil), shift work sleep disorder (armodafinil, modafinil)
- **MECHANISM:** Stimulate the release of biogenic amines, particularly dopamine, norepinephrine, and serotonin.
- **SIDE EFFECTS:** Psychosis, mood disturbances, severe anxiety, tachycardia
- **CLINICAL PEARLS:**
    - Amphetamines (and derivatives) increase the release of norepinephrine (NE) and dopamine (DA) whereas methylphenidate agents inhibit the re-uptake of NE and DA.
    - Amphetamine ADHD medications are strongly associated with growth deficits of approximately 1 to 1.4 cm/year and weight gain deficits of 3 kg in the first year of therapy. However, long-term follow-up of patients taking amphetamines has revealed that patients generally achieve their predicted growth potential upon discontinuation.
    - Lisdexamfetamine is a pro-drug that must be taken by mouth to facilitate conversion to active form which can help prevent abuse if attempting to use it by another route of administration.

High-Yield Basic Pharmacology

- **Mechanism of Action**
  - Binds to acetylcholine receptors of the motor endplate, causing an initial depolarization but causes a persistent effect resistant to acetylcholinesterase.
  - **Phase 1 to 2 Block**
    - With excessive doses or prolonged exposure, the initial depolarizing neuromuscular blockade of succinylcholine can transition to a phase 2 block that is a competitive inhibition of acetylcholine.

Primary Net Benefit

- Rapid onset and short duration of paralysis facilitating endotracheal intubation, but with potentially clinically relevant hyperkalemia and other neuromuscular adverse effects.

Depolarizing Neuromuscular Blocker - Drug Class Review			
High-Yield Med Reviews			
Mechanism of Action: *Binds to acetylcholine receptors of the motor endplate, causing an initial depolarization but causes a persistent effect resistant to acetylcholinesterase.*			
Class Effects: Rapid onset; short duration of paralysis, Hyperkalemia, rhabdomyolysis, malignant hyperthermia, fasciculations			
Generic Name	**Brand Name**	**Indication(s) or Uses**	**Notes**

Succinylcholine	Anectine Quelicin	• Neuromuscular blockade for endotracheal intubation, surgery, or mechanical ventilation	• **Dosing (Adult):**
			  – IV 1.0 to 1.5 mg/kg
			  – IM 3 to 4 mg/kg
			• **Dosing (Peds):**
			  – IV 1.0 to 3 mg/kg
			  – IM 4 to 5 mg/kg
			• **CYP450 Interactions:** None
			• **Renal or Hepatic Dose Adjustments:** None
			• **Dosage Forms:** IV (solution)

High-Yield Clinical Knowledge

- **Short Duration**
  - Succinylcholine is rapidly metabolized by butyrylcholinesterase, with a duration of action of approximately 10 minutes.
- **Dose-Dependent Effect**
  - Neuromuscular blockers exert a dose-dependent effect on motor endplate function, ranging from muscle weakness to complete flaccid paralysis.
- **Fasciculation**
  - Succinylcholine, by nature of its mechanism, causes an initial depolarization before paralysis.
  - The physical manifestation of this depolarization appears as fasciculations that are typically appreciated in the mandible.
    - Small doses of non-depolarizing neuromuscular blockers (10% of a standard dose) can be administered shortly before succinylcholine to blunt fasciculations.
    - The clinical role of this intervention is questionable and has mostly fallen out of favor.
- **Hyperkalemia**
  - Succinylcholine causes an increase in serum potassium, possibly as a result of its depolarizing action.
    - The magnitude of this increase can vary but is clinically estimated to be 0.5 mEq/L.

- Patients with pre-existing renal disease are at increased risk of hyperkalemia due to succinylcholine.; however, the magnitude of these changes occurs within the normal range of pressures.
  - Furthermore, these studies were conducted in a neurosurgical population with existing intracranial pressure monitors, which is not consistent with the physiology of many emergency or critical care patients requiring intubation.
- **Prolonged Effect or Response**
  - Patients with a history of neuromuscular disease (ex., myasthenia gravis, multiple sclerosis, etc.) may have a prolonged and unpredictable paralysis duration.
- **Malignant hyperthermia**
  - Succinylcholine has been associated with malignant hyperthermia.
    - The proposed mechanism is via stimulation of ryanodine calcium channels of the sarcoplasmic reticulum leading to an uncontrolled calcium-dependent calcium release causing excessive muscle contraction, leading to energy depletion, generation of free-radicals, and thermal energy.

HIGH-YIELD BOARD EXAM ESSENTIALS

- **CLASSIC AGENTS:** Succinylcholine
- **DRUG CLASS:** Depolarizing neuromuscular blocker
- **INDICATIONS:** Neuromuscular blockade for endotracheal intubation, surgery, or mechanical ventilation
- **MECHANISM:** Binds to acetylcholine receptors of the motor endplate, causing an initial depolarization but causes a persistent effect resistant to acetylcholinesterase.
- **SIDE EFFECTS:** Hyperkalemia, rhabdomyolysis, malignant hyperthermia, fasciculations
- **CLINICAL PEARLS:**
  - The only neuromuscular blocker that you can use as IM injection although not preferred over IV.
  - Has a quick onset of action within 1 minute and short duration.
  - Patients with a history of neuromuscular disease (ex., myasthenia gravis, multiple sclerosis, etc.) may have a prolonged and unpredictable paralysis duration.
  - Traditionally avoided in patients with known hyperkalemia or at increased risk of hyperkalemia as the depolarizing effect can cause muscles to release intracellular potassium during muscle fasciculations.

High-Yield Basic Pharmacology

- **Mechanism of Action**
  - Competitively inhibit acetylcholine at the skeletal muscle motor endplate. No fasciculations seen.
  - **Atracurium and Cisatracurium Metabolite**
    - Atracurium is metabolized to laudanosine, which can cross the blood-brain barrier and placental barrier leading to neuroexcitation without any neuromuscular blocking effects.
      - Laudanosine is a GABA antagonist and an antagonist of nicotinic acetylcholine receptors and opioid receptor antagonists.
    - Patients receiving prolonged infusions or liver disease, biliary obstruction, or renal impairment are at high risk of laudanosine accumulation.

Primary Net Benefit

- Produce a dose-dependent neuromuscular blockade without initial fasciculations or many other adverse events related to succinylcholine.

Non-Depolarizing Neuromuscular Blocker - Drug Class Review			
High-Yield Med Reviews			
Mechanism of Action: *Competitively inhibit acetylcholine at the skeletal muscle motor endplate.*			
Class Effects: Dose-dependent neuromuscular blockade WITHOUT initial fasciculations, small risk of anaphylaxis, persistent muscle weakness (especially if used repeatedly like in the ICU or with corticosteroids).			
Generic Name	**Brand Name**	**Indication(s) or Uses**	**Notes**

Atracurium	Tracrium	• Neuromuscular blockade for endotracheal intubation, surgery, or mechanical ventilation	• **Dosing (Adult):**
			  – IV 0.4 to 0.5 mg bolus
			  – IV infusion 4 to 20 mcg/kg/minute
			• **Dosing (Peds):**
			  – IV 0.3 to 0.5 mg bolus
			  – IV infusion 4 to 20 mcg/kg/minute
			• **CYP450 Interactions:** None
			• **Renal or Hepatic Dose Adjustments:** None
			• **Dosage Forms:** IV (solution)

Cisatracurium	Nimbex	• Neuromuscular blockade for endotracheal intubation, surgery, or mechanical ventilation	• **Dosing (Adult):**
			  – IV 0.1 to 0.2 mg/kg followed by 1 to 3 mcg/kg/minute
			• **Dosing (Peds):**
			  – IV 0.1 to 0.2 mg/kg followed by 1 to 3 mcg/kg/minute
			• **CYP450 Interactions:** None
			• **Renal or Hepatic Dose Adjustments:** None
			• **Dosage Forms:** IV (solution)

Non-Depolarizing Neuromuscular Blocker - Drug Class Review
High-Yield Med Reviews

Generic Name	Brand Name	Indication(s) or Uses	Notes

Mivacurium	Mivacron	• Neuromuscular blockade for endotracheal intubation, surgery, or mechanical ventilation	• **Dosing (Adult):**
			  – IV 0.15 to 0.25 mg/kg
			  – IV 5 to 10 mcg/kg/minute
			• **Dosing (Peds):**
			  – IV 0.15 to 0.25 mg/kg
			  – IV 1 to 10 mcg/kg/minute
			• **CYP450 Interactions:** None
			• **Renal or Hepatic Dose Adjustments:**
			  – GFR less than 30 mL/minute - maximum bolus 0.15 mg/kg, reduce infusion rates by 50%
			• **Dosage Forms:** IV (solution)

Pancuronium	Pavulon	• Neuromuscular blockade for endotracheal intubation, surgery, or mechanical ventilation	• **Dosing (Adult):**
			  – IV 0.04 to 0.1 mg/kg
			  – IV 0.8 to 2 mcg/kg/minute
			• **Dosing (Peds):**
			  – IV 0.04 to 0.1 mg/kg
			  – IV 0.8 to 2 mcg/kg/minute
			• **CYP450 Interactions:** None
			• **Renal or Hepatic Dose Adjustments:**
			  – GFR 10 to 50 mL/minute - Reduce by 50%
			  – GFR less than 10 mL/minute - Avoid use
			  – Hepatic impairment - can have increased or decreased response
			• **Dosage Forms:** IV (solution)

Rocuronium	Zemuron	• Neuromuscular blockade for endotracheal intubation, surgery, or mechanical ventilation	• **Dosing (Adult):**
			  – IV 0.6 to 1.2 mg/kg x 1
			  – IV 8 to 12 mcg/kg/minute
			• **Dosing (Peds):**
			  – IV 0.6 to 1.8 mg/kg x 1
			  – IV 8 to 12 mcg/kg/minute
			• **CYP450 Interactions:** None
			• **Renal or Hepatic Dose Adjustments:**
			  – Hepatic impairment - no specific guidance, but may require higher doses
			• **Dosage Forms:** IV (solution)

Vecuronium	Norcuron	• Neuromuscular blockade for endotracheal intubation, surgery, or mechanical ventilation	• **Dosing (Adult):**
			  – IV 0.08 to 0.1 mg/kg
			  – IV 0.8 to 1.2 mcg/kg/minute
			• **Dosing (Peds):**
			  – IV 0.08 to 0.1 mg/kg
			  – IV 0.8 to 1.2 mcg/kg/minute
			• **CYP450 Interactions:** None
			• **Renal or Hepatic Dose Adjustments:** None
			• **Dosage Forms:** IV (solution)

High-Yield Clinical Knowledge

- **Muscarinic Effects**
  - Pancuronium may cause dose-dependent and rate-dependent muscarinic effects including tachycardia, and hypertension.
    - This effect is caused by a parasympathetic response from activation of muscarinic receptors by pancuronium.
- **Anaphylaxis**
  - Anaphylaxis may occur with a high incidence among patients receiving rocuronium that can be difficult to treat.
  - Although standard management of anaphylaxis should be a cornerstone of therapy, the reversal agent sugammadex can treat anaphylaxis due to either rocuronium or vecuronium.
- **Limited Contraindications**
  - Compared with succinylcholine and its long list of contraindications and warnings, the non-depolarizing neuromuscular blockers have few contraindications.
    - These contraindications consist of a history of allergy or hypersensitivity to a neuromuscular blocker.
- **Persistent Weakness**
  - Non-depolarizing neuromuscular blockers that are administered as IV infusions for greater than 48 hours pose a risk of prolonged neuromuscular blockade even after discontinuation of the drug.
  - Risk factors for prolonged paralysis include patients with sepsis, ARDS, multiorgan failure, hyperglycemia, systemic corticosteroids, muscle injury, and thermal injury.
- **Pancuronium Adjustment**
  - Pancuronium is primarily renally excreted and requires dose adjustments for patients with impaired renal function.
  - Accumulation of pancuronium and its active metabolite, 3-desacetyl-pancuronium, can lead to prolonged paralysis even after drug discontinuation.
- **Reversal**
  - Non-depolarizing neuromuscular blocking agents can be reversed using one of two strategies: sugammadex or cholinergic competitive inhibition.
    - Sugammadex encapsulates rocuronium or vecuronium in a 1:1 ratio and prevents further binding to the nicotinic receptors.
    - Neostigmine or pyridostigmine inhibits plasma cholinesterase, increasing acetylcholine at the neuromuscular junction to overcome the competitive inhibition caused by paralytics.

High-Yield Fast-Fact

- **Sugammadex Allergy**
  - Patients experiencing an allergic response to sugammadex should receive rocuronium, which forms a complex and interrupts antigenic activity of sugammadex itself.

HIGH-YIELD BOARD EXAM ESSENTIALS
- **CLASSIC AGENTS:** Atracurium, cisatracurium, mivacurium, pancuronium, rocuronium, vecuronium
- **DRUG CLASS:** Non-depolarizing neuromuscular blocker
- **INDICATIONS:** Neuromuscular blockade for endotracheal intubation, surgery, or mechanical ventilation
- **MECHANISM:** Competitively inhibit acetylcholine at the skeletal muscle motor endplate.
- **SIDE EFFECTS:** Anaphylaxis, persistent muscle weakness
- **CLINICAL PEARLS:** Pancuronium is primarily renally excreted and requires dose adjustments for patients with impaired renal function. Accumulation of pancuronium and its active metabolite, 3-desacetyl-pancuronium, can lead to prolonged paralysis even after drug discontinuation.

High-Yield Basic Pharmacology

- **Neostigmine, Pyridostigmine**
  - Inhibits acetylcholinesterase at the neuromuscular junction, thereby increasing acetylcholine.
  - **Tertiary Vs. Quaternary Ammonium**
    - Neostigmine and pyridostigmine are quaternary ammonium compounds and do not readily cross the blood-brain barrier at normal therapeutic doses.
      - Physostigmine, a similar cholinergic agent, is an example of a tertiary ammonium compound that does cross the blood-brain barrier causing a central cholinergic effect.
- **Sugammadex**
  - Binds to steroid-based neuromuscular blockers (rocuronium, vecuronium), forming a 1:1 complex that prevents the neuromuscular blocker's binding to its nicotinic receptor site.

Primary Net Benefit

- Reversal agents for neuromuscular blocking agents improve recovery time from paralysis but are not associated with any patient-oriented benefits.

Neuromuscular Blocker Reversal - Drug Class Review High-Yield Med Reviews			
Mechanism of Action: *See agents above.*			
Class Effects: Reversal of neuromuscular blocking agents to improve recovery time from paralysis, risk of cholinergic effects (neostigmine, pyridostigmine), allergy/hypersensitivity (sugammadex)			
Generic Name	**Brand Name**	**Indication(s) or Uses**	**Notes**

Glycopyrrolate	Cuvposa	• Reversal of nondepolarizing neuromuscular
		• Reduction of secretions
			• **Dosing (Adult):**
			  – IV 0.2 mg for each 1 mg of neostigmine or 5 mg of pyridostigmine
			• **Dosing (Peds):**
			  – IV 0.2 mg for each 1 mg of neostigmine or 5 mg of pyridostigmine
			• **CYP450 Interactions:** None
			• **Renal or Hepatic Dose Adjustments:** None
			• **Dosage Forms:** IV (solution), Oral (tablet)

Neostigmine	Bloxiverz	• Myasthenia gravis
		• Reversal of nondepolarizing neuromuscular
			• **Dosing (Adult):**
			  – IV 0.03 to 0.07 mg/kg
			    • Maximum 5 mg
			• **Dosing (Peds):**
			  – IV 0.03 to 0.07 mg/kg
			    • Maximum 5 mg
			• **CYP450 Interactions:** None
			• **Renal or Hepatic Dose Adjustments:**
			  – GFR 10 to 50 mL/minute - Reduce dose by 50%
			  – GFR less than 10 mL/minute - Reduce dose by 75%
			• **Dosage Forms:** IV (solution)

Neuromuscular Blocker Reversal - Drug Class Review
High-Yield Med Reviews

Generic Name	Brand Name	Indication(s) or Uses	Notes
Pyridostigmine	Mestinon Regonol	▪ Myasthenia gravis Reversal of nondepolarizing neuromuscular	▪ **Dosing (Adult):** – IV 0.1 to 0.25 mg/kg ▪ **Dosing (Peds):** – IV 0.1 to 0.25 mg/kg ▪ **CYP450 Interactions:** None ▪ **Renal or Hepatic Dose Adjustments:** None ▪ **Dosage Forms:** IV (solution), Oral (tablet)
Sugammadex	Bridion	▪ Reversal of rocuronium or vecuronium	▪ **Dosing (Adult):** – IV 4 to 16 mg/kg once ▪ **Dosing (Peds):** – IV 2 mg/kg once ▪ **CYP450 Interactions:** None ▪ **Renal or Hepatic Dose Adjustments:** – GFR less than 30 mL/minute - not recommended ▪ **Dosage Forms:** IV (solution)

High-Yield Clinical Knowledge

▪ **Paralytic Encapsulation**
   – Sugammadex is a modified cyclodextrin compound with a hydrophilic outer surface and a lipophilic central cavity that encapsulates both rocuronium and vecuronium.
   – This encapsulation creates a concentration gradient by which rocuronium or vecuronium leaves the neuromuscular junction for the plasma and then subsequently bound by sugammadex.

▪ **Killer B's**
   – The administration of neostigmine or pyridostigmine carries a risk of bradycardia, bronchospasm, and bronchorrhea - otherwise known as the killer b's of cholinergic toxicity.
   – The coadministration of an antimuscarinic agent can manage these effects.

▪ **Atropine Vs. Glycopyrrolate**
   – To counterbalance the cholinergic effects (primarily bradycardia) of neostigmine or pyridostigmine, these agents are often administered with an anticholinergic agent, either atropine or glycopyrrolate.
   – Being a quaternary ammonium, glycopyrrolate does not cross the blood-brain barrier, thus does not possess central anticholinergic effects, causing confusion, delirium, or altered mental status.

▪ **Dose-Dependent Time to Reversal**
   – Sugammadex exhibits a dose-dependent time to reversal paralysis, with the shortest time to reversal achieved using the 16 mg/kg dose.
   – At a typical surgical reversal dose of 4 mg/kg, the median time to reach the train of four ratios of 0.9 is 2.4 minutes after rocuronium or 3.4 minutes for vecuronium compared to 49 minutes using neostigmine.

▪ **Sugammadex Allergy**
   – Some patients may experience an acute allergic reaction to sugammadex that can be treated by administering rocuronium or vecuronium.
   – By establishing the sugammadex-rocuronium/vecuronium complex, the antigen-antibody reaction is halted.

▪ **Decreased Hormonal Contraceptive Effectiveness**
   – Sugammadex may bind with progesterone, decreasing its concentrations.
   – Thus, in women taking progesterone-based hormonal contraceptives, this birth control's effectiveness may be diminished for up to 7 days following sugammadex administration.

HIGH-YIELD BOARD EXAM ESSENTIALS

- **CLASSIC AGENTS:** Neostigmine, pyridostigmine, sugammadex
- **DRUG CLASS:** Neuromuscular blocker reversal
- **INDICATIONS:** Reversal of nondepolarizing neuromuscular, reduction of secretions, myasthenia gravis
- **MECHANISM:** Inhibits acetylcholinesterase at the neuromuscular junction, thereby increasing acetylcholine (neostigmine, pyridostigmine); Binds to steroid-based neuromuscular blockers (rocuronium, vecuronium), forming a 1:1 complex that prevents the neuromuscular blocker's binding to its nicotinic receptor site (sugammadex)
- **SIDE EFFECTS:** Cholinergic effects (neostigmine, pyridostigmine), allergy/hypersensitivity (sugammadex)
- **CLINICAL PEARLS:** Sugammadex exhibits a dose-dependent time to reversal paralysis, with the shortest time to reversal achieved using the 16 mg/kg dose. At a typical surgical reversal dose of 4 mg/kg, the median time to reach the train of four ratios of 0.9 is 2.4 minutes after rocuronium or 3.4 minutes for vecuronium compared to 49 minutes using neostigmine.

High-Yield Basic Pharmacology

- **Mechanism of Action**
  - Inhibits excess acetylcholine at muscarinic and nicotinic receptor sites, decreasing parasympathetic nervous system activity to improve motor movements.
  - **Anticholinergic Effect**
    - The anticholinergic agents counteract diminished levels of dopamine by stimulating parasympathetic activity and relative hyperactivity of acetylcholine.

Primary Net Benefit

- Replaced mainly with safer alternatives, anticholinergic agents may reduce tremor and alleviate rigidity associated with Parkinson's diseases but lack bradykinesic effects.

Anticholinergics - Drug Class Review			
High-Yield Med Reviews			
Mechanism of Action: *Inhibits excess acetylcholine at muscarinic and nicotinic receptor sites, decreasing parasympathetic nervous system activity.*			
Class Effects: Helps with resting tremors mainly, risk Dry mucus membranes, tachycardia, altered mental status, or orthostatic hypotension.			
Generic Name	**Brand Name**	**Indication(s) or Uses**	**Notes**

Benztropine	Cogentin	• Drug-induced extrapyramidal symptoms
		• Parkinson's disease
			• **Dosing (Adult):**
			  – IM/IV/Oral 0.5 to 2 mg q8-12h
			    • Maximum 6 mg/day
			• **Dosing (Peds):**
			  – IM/IV/Oral 0.02 to 0.05 mg/kg/dose q8-24h
			    • Maximum 6 mg/day
			• **CYP450 Interactions:** Substrate of CYP2D6
			• **Renal or Hepatic Dose Adjustments:** None
			• **Dosage Forms:** Oral (tablet), IV (solution)

Procyclidine	Kemadrin	• Parkinson's disease	• **Dosing (Adult):**
			  – Oral 2.5 mg three times daily after meals
			    • Maximum 20 mg/day
			• **Dosing (Peds):**
			  – Not routinely used
			• **CYP450 Interactions:** None
			• **Renal or Hepatic Dose Adjustments:** None
			• **Dosage Forms:** Oral (elixir, tablet)

Trihexyphenidyl	Artane, Parkin	• Drug-induced extrapyramidal symptoms
		• Parkinson's disease
			• **Dosing (Adult):**
			  – Oral 1 mg/day titrated to 15 mg/day in 3-4 divided doses
			• **Dosing (Peds):**
			  – Oral 0.1 to 0.2 mg/kg/day divided in 2-3 doses
			    • Maximum 2.6 mg/kg/day
			• **CYP450 Interactions:** None
			• **Renal or Hepatic Dose Adjustments:** None
			• **Dosage Forms:** Oral (tablet, solution)

High-Yield Clinical Knowledge

- **Dopaminergic Pathway**
  - The breakdown of dopaminergic neurons in the nigrostriatal pathway results in the depletion of dopamine-related to Parkinson's disease.
- **Abrupt Discontinuation**
  - Abrupt discontinuation of anticholinergic agents must be avoided as this may precipitate acute exacerbations of parkinsonisms.
  - Careful tapering of doses should take place if changes in the drug regimen are warranted.
- **Elderly Patients**
  - The use of anticholinergic drugs in elderly patients significantly increases their risk of falls and other adverse events that impact comorbidities such as dry mucus membranes, tachycardia, altered mental status, or orthostatic hypotension.
  - Since many patients with Parkinson's disease are elderly, the use of alternative agents (i.e., dopamine agonists) should be strongly considered to minimize these risks.
  - Furthermore, anticholinergic agents in this population have been associated with an increased incidence of dementia.
- **Dopaminergic Agents Vs. Anticholinergic**
  - Dopaminergic agents, such as bromocriptine or ropinirole, are similarly effective in managing Parkinson's tremor as the anticholinergic agents, without the risk of anticholinergic effects.
- **Blind As A Bat...**
  - Common adverse anticholinergic effects that lead to discontinuation include visual changes, confusion, constipation, xerostomia, altered mental status, hyperthermia/flushing, and urinary retention.

High-Yield Fast-Facts

- **Acute Dystonic Reactions**
  - As an alternative to benzodiazepines, benztropine may be used to manage acute dystonic reactions secondary to antipsychotic drugs.
- **Abuse Potential**
  - Anticholinergic drugs possess an abuse potential via dopaminergic effects, which resemble similar results from sympathomimetic abuse.

HIGH-YIELD BOARD EXAM ESSENTIALS
- **CLASSIC AGENTS:** Benztropine, procyclidine, trihexyphenidyl
- **DRUG CLASS:** Anticholinergics
- **INDICATIONS:** Drug-induced extrapyramidal symptoms, Parkinson disease
- **MECHANISM:** Inhibits excess acetylcholine at muscarinic and nicotinic receptor sites, decreasing parasympathetic nervous system activity.
- **SIDE EFFECTS:** Dry mucus membranes, tachycardia, altered mental status, or orthostatic hypotension.
- **CLINICAL PEARLS:**
  - Abrupt discontinuation of anticholinergic agents must be avoided as this may precipitate acute exacerbations of parkinsonisms. Careful tapering of doses should take place if changes in the drug regimen are warranted.
  - Benztropine is a common treatment for acute dystonic reactions associated with antipsychotics.

High-Yield Basic Pharmacology

- **Levodopa**
  - A precursor to dopamine that providing supplemental concentrations to the central nervous system.
- **Carbidopa**
  - Inhibits peripheral conversion of levodopa to dopamine
  - **Carbidopa Rationale**
    - Carbidopa reduces the premature conversion of levodopa to dopamine in the peripheral circulation by inhibiting dopa decarboxylase.
    - Coformulation with levodopa reduces its daily dose by 75%, and the suppression of dopa decarboxylase typically requires a dose of 75 mg/day of carbidopa.

Primary Net Benefit

- Nearly all patients with Parkinson's disease will require carbidopa/levodopa and likely develop fluctuations and dyskinesias due to the drug combination.

Carbidopa-Levodopa Drug Class Review			
High-Yield Med Reviews			
Mechanism of Action: *Levodopa - Precursor to dopamine that providing supplemental concentrations to the central nervous system.* *Carbidopa - Inhibits peripheral conversion of levodopa to dopamine.*			
Class Effects: Improvements in motor movements, risk of dyskinesias, "wearing-off effect", GI side effects (constipation, nausea), orthostatic hypotension, psychosis (hallucinations).			
Generic Name	**Brand Name**	**Indication(s) or Uses**	**Notes**

Carbidopa-Levodopa	Duopa Rytary Sinemet	• Parkinson disease
		• Restless leg syndrome
			• **Dosing (Adult):**
			  – IR/ODT tablets carbidopa/levodopa 12.5 mg/50 mg BID to TID.
			    ▪ Titrated by 1 tablet or up to 25 mg/ 100 mg every 1-2 days
			  – CR tablet 50 mg/200 mg BID
			    ▪ Titrated no faster than q3days to maximum levodopa dose of 2,400 mg/day
			  – ER 23.75 mg/95 mg TID
			    ▪ Titrated q3days to maximum levodopa dose of 2,450 mg/day
			• **Dosing (Peds):** Not routinely used
			• **CYP450 Interactions:** None
			• **Renal or Hepatic Dose Adjustments:** None
			• **Dosage Forms:** Oral (IR, CR, ER, ODT tablet, suspension)

Carbidopa-Levodopa-Entacapone	Stalevo	• Parkinson disease	• **Dosing (Adult):**
			  – Oral initial dose is dependent on carbidopa/levodopa target
			    ▪ All Stalevo products contain entacapone 200 mg
			• **Dosing (Peds):** Not routinely used
			• **CYP450 Interactions:** None
			• **Renal or Hepatic Dose Adjustments:**
			  – Severe hepatic impairment - avoid use
			• **Dosage Forms:** Oral (tablet)

High-Yield Clinical Knowledge

- **Alternative Metabolism**
  - As dopa decarboxylase is inhibited by carbidopa, peripheral metabolism may still occur by catechol-O-methyltransferase (COMT).
  - This secondary metabolic pathway can be inhibited using COMT inhibitors such as entacapone or tolcapone.
- **Continuous Administration**
  - Novel methods to reduce dose fluctuations of levodopa have employed a continuously administered solution of carbidopa-levodopa intraduodenally.
  - These drug delivery systems appear to reduce fluctuations in central dopamine concentrations and may reduce the development of dyskinesias.
- **Dyskinesias**
  - The development of dyskinesias from levodopa is dose-dependent but generally occurs in upwards of 80% of patients after 10 years of continuous therapy.
    - The most common dyskinesias observed is choreoathetosis of the face and distal extremities.
    - Intraduodenal or intrajejunal continuous administration of carbidopa-levodopa has been suggested to reduce or slow the development of dyskinesias by reducing the chronic pulsatile stimulation dopamine receptors leading to dopaminergic denervation.

High-Yield Fast-Facts

- **Response Fluctuation Effects**
  - Long term therapy with levodopa is associated with dyskinesias shortly after oral doses (peak effect) and an end of dose motor fluctuation termed "wearing-off effect."
    - These effects can manifest after inappropriately high dose initiation or long-term therapy as the approximate risk of developing these effects is 10% per year of levodopa therapy.
  - Substituting immediate-release for controlled-release formulations does not reduce the development of these movement disorders.
    - The addition of COMT inhibitors or MAO-B inhibitors may play a role and should be considered.
- **Numerous Formulations**
  - Combinations of carbidopa-levodopa are formulated as immediate-release, controlled-release, and extended-release preparations.
  - Doses are not interchangeable as bioavailabilities differ between these agents.
- **Acute On/Off Management**
  - After titration of levodopa and regimen modification with MAO-B inhibitors or COMT inhibitors, apomorphine has been used to manage acute off episodes.

HIGH-YIELD BOARD EXAM ESSENTIALS
- **CLASSIC AGENTS:** Carbidopa/levodopa, carbidopa/levodopa/entacapone
- **DRUG CLASS:** Anti-Parkinson's
- **INDICATIONS:** Parkinson disease, restless leg syndrome
- **MECHANISM:** Levodopa - Precursor to dopamine that providing supplemental concentrations to the central nervous system; Carbidopa - Inhibits peripheral conversion of levodopa to dopamine.
- **SIDE EFFECTS:** Dyskinesias, "wearing-off effect", GI side effects (constipation, nausea), orthostatic hypotension, psychosis (hallucinations)
- **CLINICAL PEARLS:**
  - The development of dyskinesias from levodopa is dose-dependent but generally occurs in upwards of 80% of patients after 10 years of continuous therapy.
  - Controlled and extended release formulations should not be used as initial therapy and are also not interchangeable on a dose to dose basis. Adjustments in dosing are necessary when switching between agents.

High-Yield Basic Pharmacology

- **Mechanism of Action**
  - Inhibits catechol-O-methyltransferase (COMT), preventing premature metabolism of levodopa in the peripheral circulation.
    - COMT directly increases plasma levels of 3-O-methyldopa (3-OMD), which competes with levodopa for transport in the intestine, or across the blood-brain-barrier.
    - Thus, inhibiting COMT, decreases 3-OMD, allowing for better drug absorption and penetration into the CNS.

Primary Net Benefit

- COMT inhibitors can improve clinical response to levodopa/carbidopa therapy and reduce adverse events associated with excessive levodopa dosing.

<table>
<tr><td colspan="4">COMT Inhibitors - Drug Class Review
High-Yield Med Reviews</td></tr>
<tr><td colspan="4">Mechanism of Action: Inhibits catechol-O-methyltransferase (COMT), preventing levodopa's levodopa metabolism in the peripheral circulation.</td></tr>
<tr><td colspan="4">Class Effects: improve "on time" of levodopa therapy, risk of hepatotoxicity, NMS.</td></tr>
</table>

Generic Name	Brand Name	Indication(s) or Uses	Notes

Entacapone	Comtan	• Parkinson disease	• **Dosing (Adult):**
			  – Oral 200 mg with each levodopa/carbidopa dose
			    ▪ Maximum 1600 mg/day
			• **Dosing (Peds):** Not routinely used
			• **CYP450 Interactions:** None
			• **Renal or Hepatic Dose Adjustments:**
			  – Severe hepatic impairment - use with caution.
			• **Dosage Forms:** Oral (tablet)

Opicapone	Ongentys	• Parkinson disease	• **Dosing (Adult):**
			  – Oral 50 mg daily at bedtime
			• **Dosing (Peds):** Not routinely used
			• **CYP450 Interactions:** Substrate of P-gp
			• **Renal or Hepatic Dose Adjustments:**
			  – Child-Pugh class B - 25 mg at bedtime
			  – Child-Pugh class C - avoid use
			• **Dosage Forms:** Oral (capsule)

Tolcapone	Tasmar	• Parkinson disease	• **Dosing (Adult):**
			  – Oral 100 mg TID with levodopa/carbidopa
			• **Dosing (Peds):** Not routinely used
			• **CYP450 Interactions:** None
			• **Renal or Hepatic Dose Adjustments:**
			  – GFR less than 25 mL/minute - use with caution
			• **Dosage Forms:** Oral (tablet)

- **COMT Addition**
  - A COMT inhibitor should be added to levodopa/carbidopa therapy once maximum daily doses are met, or the need for frequent dosing throughout the day.
  - Alternatively, to COMT inhibitors, MAO-B inhibitors such as rasagiline may be used.
- **No Monotherapy**
  - On their own, COMT inhibitors do not affect Parkinson's disease and must be used in conjunction with levodopa/carbidopa.
- **Hepatotoxicity**
  - Tolcapone, which can be administered less frequently than entacapone, is not preferred due to unclear clinical benefit but an increased risk of hepatotoxicity.
    - This effect is a black boxed warning for tolcapone.
- **Improved "on" Time**
  - COMT inhibitors, when added to levodopa/carbidopa therapy, improve the duration of therapeutic "on" time by approximately 1 to 2 hours per day.
- **Daily Doses**
  - Opicapone is a relative newcomer to the COMT inhibitor class and offers the advantage of once-daily dosing.
  - Although clinical experience is developing, there does not appear to be an excessive risk of hepatotoxicity.
- **Neuroleptic Malignant Syndrome**
  - If abrupt discontinuation of COMT inhibitors occurs for any reason, patients can experience acute and profound worsening of Parkinson's symptoms, including rigidity, altered mental status, and hyperthermia characteristic of NMS.
    - NMS can be life-threatening.

HIGH-YIELD BOARD EXAM ESSENTIALS
- **CLASSIC AGENTS:** Entacapone, opicapone, tolcapone
- **DRUG CLASS:** COMT inhibitor
- **INDICATIONS:** Parkinson disease
- **MECHANISM:** Inhibits catechol-O-methyltransferase (COMT), preventing levodopa's levodopa metabolism in the peripheral circulation.
- **SIDE EFFECTS:** Hepatotoxicity, NMS
- **CLINICAL PEARLS:** A COMT inhibitor should be added to levodopa/carbidopa therapy once maximum daily doses are met, or the need for frequent dosing throughout the day. Alternatively, to COMT inhibitors, MAO-B inhibitors such as rasagiline may be used.

High-Yield Basic Pharmacology

- **Amantadine**
  - Enhances dopamine release from presynaptic terminals and inhibits NMDA receptors.
- **Apomorphine and bromocriptine**
  - Dopamine-2 (D2) receptor agonist, activating postsynaptic dopamine receptors in the tuberoinfundibular and nigrostriatal pathways.
- **Pramipexole and ropinirole**
  - Possess D2 agonist properties and D3 and D4 agonist effects stimulating dopaminergic activity in the striatum and substantia nigra.
- **Rotigotine**
  - D2 agonist effects stimulating dopaminergic activity in the striatum and substantia nigra.
- **Ergot Vs. Non-ergot Agonist**
  - The dopamine agonists can be grouped into either ergot derived agonists, such as bromocriptine, or non-ergot agonists such as apomorphine, pramipexole, ropinirole, and rotigotine.
  - Non-ergot agents provide similar efficacy with improved safety compared to bromocriptine.

Primary Net Benefit

- First-line agents for Parkinson's disease because of a lower incidence of response fluctuations and prolongs time to levodopa therapy, which spares some long-term adverse events, including dyskinesias.

Dopamine Agonists - Drug Class Review			
High-Yield Med Reviews			
Mechanism of Action: *See agents above*			
Class Effects: Improves motor movements, risk for compulsive behaviors, delusions, hallucinations, psychosis, and sudden unexpected sleep episodes.			
Generic Name	**Brand Name**	**Indication(s) or Uses**	**Notes**

Amantadine	Gocovri, Osmolex ER	• Drug-induced parkinsonism
		• Parkinson disease
			• **Dosing (Adult):**
			  – Oral 100 to 200 mg q12-24h
			• **Dosing (Peds):**
			  – Oral 5 mg/kg/day divided q12h; Max 150 mg/day
			• **CYP450 Interactions:** Substrate CYP3A4, Pgp
			• **Renal or Hepatic Dose Adjustments:**
			  – GFR 30 to 59 mL/min - 200 mg x1 then 100 mg/day
			  – GFR 15 to 29 mL/min - 200 mg x1 then 100 mg q24h
			  – GFR less than15 mL/minute - contraindicated
			• **Dosage Forms:** Oral (capsule, tablet, syrup)

Apomorphine	Apokyn, Kynmobi	• Parkinson disease	• **Dosing (Adult):**
			  – SL film 10 mg as needed by at most q2h
			    • Maximum 5 doses/day
			  – SQ 2 to 6 mg as needed
			    • Maximum 20 mg/day
			• **Dosing (Peds):** Not routinely used
			• **CYP450 Interactions:** Substrate of CYP1A2, CYP2C19, CYP3A4
			• **Renal or Hepatic Dose Adjustments:**
			  – GFR less than 30 mL/minute - avoid use
			• **Dosage Forms:** Sublingual film or kit

Dopamine Agonists - Drug Class Review
High-Yield Med Reviews

Generic Name	Brand Name	Indication(s) or Uses	Notes

Bromocriptine	Cycloset, Parlodel	• Diabetes mellitus, type 2
		• Hyperprolactinemia
		• Parkinson disease
		• Neuroleptic malignant syndrome
			• **Dosing (Adult):**
			  – Oral 0.8 to 15 mg/day
			    • Up to 100 mg/day for Parkinsonism
			• **Dosing (Peds):**
			  – Oral 0.8 to 15 mg/day
			• **CYP450 Interactions:** Substrate CYP3A4
			• **Renal or Hepatic Dose Adjustments:** None
			• **Dosage Forms:** Oral (capsule, tablet)

Pramipexole	Mirapex	• Parkinson disease
		• Restless leg syndrome
			• **Dosing (Adult):**
			  – Oral 0.125 to 1.5 mg TID to QD
			• **Dosing (Peds):**
			  – Not routinely used
			• **CYP450 Interactions:** None
			• **Renal or Hepatic Dose Adjustments:**
			  – GFR 30 to 50 mL/minute - maximum 0.75 mg TID
			  – GFR 15 to 29 mL/minute - IR maximum 1.5 mg daily; ER not recommended
			  – GFR less than 15 - not recommended
			• **Dosage Forms:** Oral (tablet)

Ropinirole	Requip	• Parkinson disease
		• Restless leg syndrome
			• **Dosing (Adult):**
			  – Oral IR 0.25 to 8 mg TID
			  – Oral ER 2 to 24 mg daily
			• **Dosing (Peds):**
			  – Not routinely used
			• **CYP450 Interactions:** Substrate CYP1A2, 3A4
			• **Renal or Hepatic Dose Adjustments:**
			  – GFR less than 30 mL/minute - use with caution
			• **Dosage Forms:** Oral (tablet)

Rotigotine	Neupro	• Parkinson disease
		• Restless leg syndrome
			• **Dosing (Adult):**
			  – Transdermal patch - 2 to 16 mg/24hour applied daily
			• **Dosing (Peds):**
			  – Not routinely used
			• **CYP450 Interactions:** None
			• **Renal or Hepatic Dose Adjustments:** None
			• **Dosage Forms:** Transdermal patch

High-Yield Clinical Knowledge

- **Dopaminergic Vs. Levodopa**
  - Dopamine agonists may provide a lower incidence of dopamine fluctuations to the CNS; their use is often limited by lower degrees of Parkinson's related symptom relief and more cognitive adverse events, fatigue, and edema.
  - The use of dopamine agonists may be best as additive therapy to existing regimens with levodopa/carbidopa.

- **Adverse Events**
  - When initiating dopamine agonists, slow dose titration is required to avoid the onset of nausea and vomiting.
  - Patients may also develop compulsive behaviors, delusions, hallucinations, psychosis, and sudden unexpected sleep episodes.
- **Prior Psychiatric or Cardiac Disease**
  - Patients with a history of psychiatric illnesses, recent myocardial infarctions, or active peptic ulcers cannot receive dopamine agonists as they are contraindicated in these populations.
- **Withdrawal**
  - If dopamine agonists are to be discontinued, they must be slowly tapered off to avoid a withdrawal syndrome that manifests as anxiety, agitation, depression, panic attacks, fatigue, orthostatic hypotension, nausea and vomiting, diaphoresis, and drug cravings.
  - This withdrawal syndrome may be resistant to levodopa titration or other dopaminergic agents and can persist for months.
- **Erythromelalgia**
  - This is a unique syndrome associated with ergot derivatives, including bromocriptine, that manifests as painful, red, and swollen feet and/or hands that resolve after discontinuation of the offending drug.
- **Sleep Attacks**
  - Pramipexole or ropinirole have been associated with sleep attacks, which are more commonly observed if dopaminergic agents are abruptly stopped.
  - Should sleep attacks occur during pramipexole or ropinirole therapy, they should be discontinued.

HIGH-YIELD BOARD EXAM ESSENTIALS
- **CLASSIC AGENTS:** Amantadine, apomorphine, bromocriptine, pramipexole, ropinirole, rotigotine
- **DRUG CLASS:** Dopamine agonists
- **INDICATIONS:** Diabetes mellitus type 2, hyperprolactinemia, neuroleptic malignant syndrome, drug-induced parkinsonism, Parkinson disease
- **MECHANISM:** Enhances dopamine release (amantadine); D2 agonist (apomorphine and bromocriptine); D2 agonist properties, but also has D3 and D4 agonist effects (pramipexole and ropinirole); D2 agonist effects (rotigotine)
- **SIDE EFFECTS:** Compulsive behaviors, delusions, hallucinations, psychosis, and sudden unexpected sleep episodes
- **CLINICAL PEARLS:** Pramipexole or ropinirole have been associated with sleep attacks, which are more commonly observed if dopaminergic agents are abruptly stopped. Should sleep attacks occur during pramipexole or ropinirole therapy, they should be discontinued.

High-Yield Basic Pharmacology

- **Mechanism of Action**
  - Inhibition of monoamine oxidase B prevents the metabolism of dopamine in the CNS.
- **Reversible Vs. Irreversible**
  - Rasagiline and selegiline are irreversible inhibitors of MAO-B, sometimes referred to as "suicide inhibition."
  - Safinamide reversibly inhibits MAO-B.

Primary Net Benefit

- MAO-B inhibition may slow Parkinson's disease progression and can be combined with levodopa to enhance its dose-response relationship.

MAO-B Inhibitors - Drug Class Review			
High-Yield Med Reviews			
Mechanism of Action: *Inhibition of monoamine oxidase B prevents the metabolism of dopamine in the CNS.*			
Class Effects: May slow Parkinson's disease progression and can be combined with levodopa, risk for hypertension, headache, serotonin syndrome.			
Generic Name	**Brand Name**	**Indication(s) or Uses**	**Notes**

Rasagiline	Azilect	• Parkinson disease	• **Dosing (Adult):**
			  – Oral 0.5 to 1 mg daily
			• **Dosing (Peds):**
			  – Not routinely used
			• **CYP450 Interactions:** Substrate CYP1A2
			• **Renal or Hepatic Dose Adjustments:**
			  – Child-Pugh Class C - Not recommended
			• **Dosage Forms:** Oral (tablet)

Safinamide	Xadago	• Parkinson disease	• **Dosing (Adult):**
			  – Oral 50 to 100 mg daily
			• **Dosing (Peds):**
			  – Not routinely used
			• **CYP450 Interactions:** Substrate CYP3A4
			• **Renal or Hepatic Dose Adjustments:**
			  – Child-Pugh Class C - Not recommended
			• **Dosage Forms:** Oral (tablet)

Selegiline	Emsam
	Zelapar
		• Depression
		• Parkinson disease
			• **Dosing (Adult):**
			  – Oral 1.25 to 5 mg BID
			  – Transdermal 6 to 12 mg/24 hour patch
			• **Dosing (Peds):**
			  – Not routinely used
			• **CYP450 Interactions:** Substrate of CYP1A2, 2A6, 2B6, 2D6, 3A4
			• **Renal or Hepatic Dose Adjustments:**
			  – GFR less than 30 mL/minute - Use not recommended
			  – Child-Pugh Class C - Not recommended
			• **Dosage Forms:** Oral (capsule, tablet), Transdermal patch

High-Yield Clinical Knowledge

- **MAO-A Vs. MAO-B**
  - MAO-A normally functions to metabolize monoamines, including norepinephrine, serotonin, and dopamine, in the CNS and outside the CNS.
  - MAO-B selectively functions to metabolize dopamine in the CNS but may also exist peripherally.
- **Amphetamine Metabolites**
  - Selegiline undergoes hepatic first-pass metabolism, which produces amphetamine and methamphetamine.
  - These metabolites produce similar effects to their illicit counterparts, leading to insomnia, agitation, and hallucinations.
  - The orally disintegrating and transdermal dosage form of selegiline largely by-passes the first-pass circulation and can minimize the amount of amphetamine and methamphetamine produced.
- **Serotonin Syndrome**
  - Serotonin syndrome associated with MAO-B inhibitors is rare; however, it is still a hypothetical risk.
  - MAO-B inhibitors should not be used with tramadol, methadone, dextromethorphan, cyclobenzaprine, or St. John's wort.
    - The risk of serotonin syndrome with MAO-A inhibitors is substantially higher.
- **Neuroprotection Properties**
  - MAO-B inhibitors are postulated to provide disease-modifying benefits in Parkinson's disease as inhibition of this dopamine pathway diverts it to alternative routes (COMT), which do not produce free radicals.
- **Benefits and Risks**
  - The addition of selegiline may provide up to 1 hour of additional "on" time for patients wearing off phenomena.
  - Conversely, selegiline may increase a levodopa peak effect, further worsening dyskinesias or delusions associated with levodopa therapy.

HIGH-YIELD BOARD EXAM ESSENTIALS
- **CLASSIC AGENTS:** Rasagiline, safinamide, selegiline
- **DRUG CLASS:** MAO-B Inhibitors
- **INDICATIONS:** Depression, Parkinson disease
- **MECHANISM:** Inhibition of monoamine oxidase B prevents the metabolism of dopamine in the CNS.
- **SIDE EFFECTS:** Hypertension, headache, serotonin syndrome
- **CLINICAL PEARLS:**
  - MAO-B inhibitors are postulated to provide disease-modifying benefits in Parkinson's disease as inhibition of this dopamine pathway diverts it to alternative routes (COMT), which do not produce free radicals.
  - The transdermal formulation of selegiline is indicated for major depressive disorder not Parkinson's disease.

High-Yield Basic Pharmacology

- **Melatonin, Ramelteon, Tasimelteon**
  - Melatonin receptor agonists produce sleepiness and influence night-day circadian synchronization.
- **Suvorexant**
  - Orexin receptor antagonist, enhancing REM and non-REM sleep.
- **Endogenous Melatonin**
  - Melatonin is usually produced in the pineal gland from the metabolism of serotonin.
  - The release of melatonin from the pineal gland follows a normal circadian rhythm and influences the sleep-wake behavior of humans.

Primary Net Benefit

- Non-benzodiazepine sleep aids improve the sleep-wake cycle in patients and are an alternative to patients unable to take benzodiazepines.

Melatonin, Ramelteon, Tasimelteon & Suvorexant - Drug Class Review			
High-Yield Med Reviews			
Mechanism of Action: *Melatonin, Ramelteon, Tasimelteon - Melatonin receptor agonists produce sleepiness and influence night-day circadian synchronization.* *Suvorexant - Orexin receptor antagonist, enhancing REM and non-REM sleep.*			
Class Effects: Improve the sleep-wake cycle, risk for abnormal dreams & abuse potential.			
Generic Name	**Brand Name**	**Indication(s) or Uses**	**Notes**
Melatonin	Melatonin	• Insomnia	• **Dosing (Adult):** – Oral 0.3 to 20 mg before bedtime • **Dosing (Peds):** – Use under direction of physicians 0.1 to 6 mg before bedtime • **CYP450 Interactions:** Substrate CYP1A2, 2B6, 2C19, 3A4 • **Renal or Hepatic Dose Adjustments:** – Severe renal or hepatic impairment - OTC not recommended • **Dosage Forms:** Oral (capsule, tablet
Ramelteon	Rozerem	• Insomnia	• **Dosing (Adult):** – Oral 8 mg within 30 minutes of bedtime • **Dosing (Peds):** – Not routinely used • **CYP450 Interactions:** Substrate CYP1A2, 2C19, 3A4 • **Renal or Hepatic Dose Adjustments:** – Severe hepatic impairment - not recommended • **Dosage Forms:** Oral (tablet)

Melatonin, Ramelteon, Tasimelteon & Suvorexant - Drug Class Review
High-Yield Med Reviews

Generic Name	Brand Name	Indication(s) or Uses	Notes

Suvorexant	Belsomra	• Insomnia	• **Dosing (Adult):**
			  – Oral 10 to 20 mg 30 minutes before bedtime
			• **Dosing (Peds):**
			  – Oral 5 to 20 mg at bedtime
			    ▪ Maximum 20 mg/day
			• **CYP450 Interactions:** Substrate CYP2C19, 3A4
			• **Renal or Hepatic Dose Adjustments:**
			  – Severe hepatic impairment - not recommended
			• **Dosage Forms:** Oral (tablet)

Tasimelteon	Hetlioz	• Non-24-hour sleep-wake disorder	• **Dosing (Adult):**
			  – Oral 20 mg at the same time daily before bedtime
			• **Dosing (Peds):**
			  – Not routinely used
			• **CYP450 Interactions:** Substrate CYP1A2, 3A4
			• **Renal or Hepatic Dose Adjustments:**
			  – Severe hepatic impairment - not recommended
			• **Dosage Forms:** Oral (capsule)

High-Yield Clinical Knowledge

- **Jet Lag**
  - Melatonin is widely used as a food supplement for the treatment or prevention of jet lag.
  - When regularly taken at nighttime, melatonin can reduce subjective daytime fatigue while improving mood and faster recovery to regular sleep-wake cycles in a patient's home time zone.
- **Sleep Metric Improvement**
  - Suvorexant is an effective means to improve specific sleep metrics such as decreased time to persistent sleep and increased total sleep time.
  - Melatonin receptor agonists improve persistent sleep without other sleep architecture influences and are mainly devoid of withdrawal symptoms.
- **Drug Interactions**
  - Melatonin, ramelteon, and tasimelteon are metabolized by and may inhibit or induce CYP1A2, potentially leading to clinically relevant drug interactions with many antidepressants, including SSRIs, fluvoxamine, and ciprofloxacin.
  - Additive hypnotic effects can occur when any of these agents are combined with non-benzodiazepine "Z-drugs" such as zileuton.
  - Melatonin may independently decrease prothrombin time and may affect warfarin therapy.
  - As a CYP3A4 substrate, suvorexant is subject to numerous drug interactions from potent CYP3A4 inhibitors such as azole antifungals, macrolides, and non-dihydropyridine calcium channel blockers.
- **Reproductive Function**
  - Melatonin receptors have been identified in both female and male reproductive organs, raising speculative therapeutic targets.
  - In women, melatonin may be an adjunct to infertility treatment during in vitro fertilization and otherwise appears to be safe in pregnancy.
  - Melatonin may improve sperm function in men in whom poor sperm motility and early apoptosis.
- **Surgical Anxiolysis**
  - Melatonin may be similarly effective to midazolam in reducing preoperative anxiety among adult patients.

- However, post-operative melatonin for anxiolysis is not as effective compared to other interventions, including benzodiazepines.
- **Abnormal Dreams**
  - Although ramelteon and tasimelteon are effective hypnotic agents, their use has increased the frequency and intensity of nightmares or abnormal dreams.
  - Other common adverse events include headache, dizziness, and fatigue.
- **Controlled Substance**
  - Suvorexant is a scheduled IV medication.
  - Conversely, melatonin is available over-the-counter, and ramelteon and tasimelteon are non-scheduled prescription agents.
- **Minimum 7 hours**
  - Suvorexant should be taken within thirty minutes before sleep, only if there are at least seven hours of projected sleep time before waking.
  - Increased daytime sleepiness, sudden onset of sleep, or worsening of depression and suicidal ideation are possible.

HIGH-YIELD BOARD EXAM ESSENTIALS

- **CLASSIC AGENTS:** Melatonin, ramelteon, suvorexant, tasimelteon
- **DRUG CLASS:** Hypnotic
- **INDICATIONS:** Insomnia
- **MECHANISM:**
  - Melatonin receptor agonists produce sleepiness and influence night-day circadian synchronization (melatonin, ramelteon, tasimelteon)
  - Orexin receptor antagonist, enhancing REM and non-REM sleep (suvorexant).
- **SIDE EFFECTS:** Abnormal dreams, abuse potential, decreased PT (melatonin)
- **CLINICAL PEARLS:** Melatonin, ramelteon, and tasimelteon are metabolized by and may inhibit or induce CYP1A2, potentially leading to clinically relevant drug interactions with many antidepressants, including SSRIs, fluvoxamine, and ciprofloxacin.

High-Yield Basic Pharmacology

- **Mechanism of Action**
  - Bind to GABA-A receptors containing the alpha-1 subunit, increasing the GABA-A channel opening frequency and potentiating GABAergic inhibition of neurotransmission
    - The GABA-A receptor most commonly contains a five-subunit complex with alpha, beta, and gamma subunits.
    - The non-benzodiazepine sedative hypnotic "z-drugs" also bind to the alpha-1 subunit in a fashion similar to benzodiazepines.

Primary Net Benefit

- Potent hypnotic agents that, although function similarly to benzodiazepines, are less disruptive to sleep stages and lack relevant antiepileptic properties.

Non-Benzodiazepine Hypnotics - Drug Class Review			
High-Yield Med Reviews			
Mechanism of Action: *Bind to GABA-A receptors containing the alpha-1 subunit, increasing the frequency of GABA-A channel opening and potentiating GABAergic inhibition of neurotransmission.*			
Class Effects: Decrease disruption in sleep, risk for abuse potential, daytime sleepiness, somnambulism ("sleepwalking")			
Generic Name	**Brand Name**	**Indication(s) or Uses**	**Notes**
Eszopiclone	Lunesta	▪ Insomnia	▪ **Dosing (Adult):** 　– Oral 1 to 3 mg immediately before bedtime ▪ **Dosing (Peds):** 　– Not routinely used ▪ **CYP450 Interactions:** Substrate CYP2E1, 3A4 ▪ **Renal or Hepatic Dose Adjustments:** 　– Child-Pugh class C - maximum 2 mg ▪ **Dosage Forms:** Oral (tablet)
Zaleplon	Sonata	▪ Insomnia	▪ **Dosing (Adult):** 　– Oral 10 to 20 mg immediately before bedtime ▪ **Dosing (Peds):** 　– Not routinely used ▪ **CYP450 Interactions:** Substrate CYP3A4 ▪ **Renal or Hepatic Dose Adjustments:** 　– Child-Pugh class A or B - maximum 5 mg 　– Child-Pugh class C - not recommended ▪ **Dosage Forms:** Oral (capsule)

Non-Benzodiazepine Hypnotics - Drug Class Review
High-Yield Med Reviews

Generic Name	Brand Name	Indication(s) or Uses	Notes

Zolpidem	Ambien, Edluar, Intermezzo, Zolpimist	• Insomnia	• **Dosing (Adult):**
			  – Oral IR/Spray/SL 5 to 10 mg immediately before bedtime
			  – Oral ER 6.25 to 12.5 mg immediately before bedtime
			• **Dosing (Peds):**
			  – Oral 0.25 mg/kg before bedtime
			    • Maximum 10 mg/dose
			• **CYP450 Interactions:** Substrate CYP2E1, 3A4
			• **Renal or Hepatic Dose Adjustments:**
			  – Child-Pugh class C - maximum 2 mg
			• **Dosage Forms:** Oral (tablet, ER, sublingual)

High-Yield Clinical Knowledge

- **Somnambulism**
    - The Z drug compounds are frequently associated with somnambulism, otherwise known as 'sleepwalking,' a transient anterograde global amnesia.
    - Some reports have described 'sleep-eating where patients have consumed food while asleep, which has led to significant weight gain.
- **Sleep Apnea**
    - Although not explicitly stated in the prescribing information, z-drugs should be used with extreme caution or be avoided entirely in patients with sleep apnea.
- **Withdrawal**
    - Unlike benzodiazepines, z-drug associated withdrawal syndrome is relatively mild and not associated with significant morbidity or mortality.
        - Benzodiazepine withdrawal shares similar physiology to alcohol withdrawal with a potentially complicated course, including delirium tremens, seizures, and death.
- **Overdose**
    - Overdoses of z-drugs are associated with normal vital signs coma and rarely lead to clinically significant manifestations if taken alone.
    - Zopiclone has been linked to methemoglobinemia, although rare.
    - Flumazenil, a GABA-A antagonist, may reverse the hypnotic effects of z-drugs.
- **Hypnosis**
    - Eszopiclone, zaleplon, and zolpidem induce sleep without significantly affecting sleep architecture.
    - Benzodiazepines, on the other hand, will decrease the onset of sleep, increase non-REM sleep duration, reduce the time of REM sleep, and stage 4 non-REM sleep.
- **Drug Interactions**
    - Eszopiclone, zaleplon, and zopiclone are metabolized by CYP3A4 and subject to increased therapeutic effect in the presence of potent CYP3A4 inhibitors, including azole antifungals, macrolides, protease inhibitors, and non-dihydropyridine calcium channel blockers.
- **Tolerance**
    - Non-benzodiazepine hypnotic use is associated with the development of a decreased clinical effect following continuous exposure.
        - Cross-tolerance can be a feature of this effect, including other sedative-hypnotics (barbiturates), benzodiazepines, or ethanol.
    - Tolerance is thought to develop from the downregulation of GABA-A receptors as a counterregulatory response to excessive inhibition.

HIGH-YIELD BOARD EXAM ESSENTIALS

- **CLASSIC AGENTS:** Eszopiclone, zaleplon, zolpidem
- **DRUG CLASS:** Non-benzodiazepine hypnotics
- **INDICATIONS:** Insomnia
- **MECHANISM:** Bind to GABA-A receptors containing the alpha-1 subunit, increasing the frequency of GABA-A channel opening and potentiating GABAergic inhibition of neurotransmission.
- **SIDE EFFECTS:** Abuse potential, daytime sleepiness, somnambulism
- **CLINICAL PEARLS:** Eszopiclone, zaleplon, and zopiclone are metabolized by CYP3A4 and subject to increased therapeutic effect in the presence of potent CYP3A4 inhibitors, including azole antifungals, macrolides, protease inhibitors, and non-dihydropyridine calcium channel blockers.

High-Yield Basic Pharmacology

- **Synthetic estrogen**
  - Alters hypothalamic gonadotropin secretion of follicle stimulating hormone and luteinizing hormone
- **Progestin (synthetic progesterone)**
  - Suppresses luteinizing hormone, thickens cervical mucus, thin endometrial lining
- **Copper**
  - Prompts endometrium to release leukotrienes and prostaglandins yielding a non-favorable environment for implantation

Primary Net Benefit

- Prevents ovulation reducing chance of conception
- Prevents/treats conditions associated with abnormal menstruation and hormonal imbalance

Non-Oral Contraceptives Drug Class Review			
High-Yield Med Reviews			
Mechanism of Action: *suppression of follicle-stimulating hormone and luteinizing hormone prevent ovulation and decrease chance of conception (except for copper IUD)*			
Pediatric Dosing: [use after menarche; dose same as adult]			
Generic Name	**Brand Name**	**Main Indication(s) or Uses**	**Notes**
Ethinyl estradiol + norelgestromin transdermal patch	Xulane (previously marketed as Ortho-Evra)	▪ Combined Hormonal Transdermal Contraceptive	▪ **Dosing (Adult):** apply 1 patch once weekly x 3 weeks, follow with a patch-free week ▪ **CYP450 Interactions:** CYP3A4 inhibitors and inducers ▪ **Renal or Hepatic Dose Adjustments:** contraindicated in hepatic impairment ▪ If patch is inadvertently removed $\geq$48 hours, efficacy is compromised ▪ Contraindicated in women with BMI $\geq$30 kg/m^2 due to increased risk of VTE; consider alternative contraceptive in women weighing >90 kg
Ethinyl estradiol + etonogestrel vaginal ring	EluRyng NuvaRing	▪ Combined Hormonal Vaginal Contraceptive	▪ **Dosing (Adult):** insert 1 ring vaginally continuously x 3 weeks, follow with a ring-free week – New ring inserted each cycle ▪ **CYP450 Interactions:** CYP3A4 inhibitors and inducers ▪ **Renal or Hepatic Dose Adjustments:** contraindicated in hepatic impairment ▪ If ring is inadvertently removed > 3 hours, efficacy is compromised

Non-Oral Contraceptives Drug Class Review
High-Yield Med Reviews

Mechanism of Action: *suppression of follicle-stimulating hormone and luteinizing hormone prevent ovulation and decrease chance of conception (except for copper IUD)*

Generic Name	Brand Name	Main Indication(s) or Uses	Notes
Ethinyl estradiol + segesterone acetate vaginal ring	Annovera	▪ Combined Hormonal Vaginal Contraceptive	▪ **Dosing (Adult):** insert 1 ring vaginally continuously x 3 weeks, follow with a ring-free week – Each ring provides efficacy x 1 year ▪ **CYP450 Interactions:** CYP3A4 inhibitors and inducers ▪ **Renal or Hepatic Dose Adjustments:** contraindicated in hepatic impairment ▪ If ring is inadvertently removed > 2 hours, efficacy is compromised

Medroxyprog-esterone injection	Depo-Provera
	Depo-SubQ Provera 104
	Provera
		▪ Progestin Injection	▪ **Contraception Dosing (Adult):** injection every 3 months
			  – Intramuscular: 150 mg
			  – Subcutaneous: 104 mg
			▪ **CYP450 Interactions:** CYP3A4 inhibitors and inducers
			▪ **Renal or Hepatic Dose Adjustments:** contraindicated in hepatic impairment

Levonorgestrel intrauterine device (IUD)	Kyleena
	Liletta
	Mirena
	Skyla
		▪ Progestin IUD	▪ **Dosing (Adult):** inserted into uterine cavity
			  – Kyleena, Mirena: 5 years
			  – Liletta: 6 years
			  – Skyla: 3 years
			▪ **CYP450 Interactions:** CYP3A4 inhibitors and inducers
			▪ **Renal or Hepatic Dose Adjustments:** contraindicated in hepatic impairment

Etonogestrel implant	Nexplanon	▪ Progestin Implant	▪ **Dosing (Adult):** inserted into inner, upper arm – 3 years duration ▪ **CYP450 Interactions:** none ▪ **Renal or Hepatic Dose Adjustments:** contraindicated in hepatic failure ▪ Consider an alternative contraceptive in women that weigh >130% of ideal body weight (possibly less effective)
Copper IUD	Paragard	▪ Non-hormonal IUD	▪ **Dosing (Adult):** inserted into uterine cavity – 10 years duration ▪ **CYP450 Interactions:** none ▪ **Renal or Hepatic Dose Adjustments:** none

High-Yield Clinical Knowledge

- Additional contraception is *NOT* required following initiation of
    - Copper IUD
    - Progestin IUD (if within 7 days or menstruation start)
    - Progestin implant (if within 5 days of menstruation start)
    - Progestin injection (if within 7 days of menstruation start)
- Estrogen-containing versus progestin-only versus non-hormonal safety and efficacy should be considered when selecting a non—oral contraceptive agent for a woman
    - The most weight-offensive agents include the progestin injection followed by progestin implant
    - The progestin injection has the longest return to fertility after discontinuation (up to 10 months)
    - Estrogen-free products are preferred in breast-feeding women
    - The non-hormonal IUD is associated with the most pain dysmenorrhea and menorrhagia
- **Product Selection Considerations**
    - Estrogen-containing products should be avoided/used cautiously in women:
        - With vascular disease history/risk factors (ie. tobacco use) given estrogen increases risk of MI, stroke and VTE
        - That are breastfeeding given estrogen decreases milk production
        - That are within 21 days post-partum high risk of VTE
        - A history of breast cancer given potential increased risk especially with higher dose formulations
        - With migraines with aura given estrogen increases risk of exacerbations
        - With hepatic failure given estrogen increases risk of further hepatic damage
    - More than half of women with a hormonal IUD experience amenorrhea or oligomenorrhea after two years of use
    - Progestin injections have a maximum recommended duration of two years given loss of bone mineral density, however, difference in fracture frequency has not been demonstrated.

HIGH-YIELD BOARD EXAM ESSENTIALS
- **CLASSIC AGENTS:** Ethinyl estradiol (EE) +/- progestin
- **DRUG CLASS:** Non-oral Contraceptives
- **INDICATIONS:** Contraception, hot flashes, endometriosis
- **MECHANISM:** Suppression of follicle-stimulating hormone and luteinizing hormone prevent ovulation and decrease chance of conception (except for copper IUD).
- **SIDE EFFECTS:** Vaginal spotting or amenorrhea, DVT/PE, decreased milk production (estrogen)
- **CLINICAL PEARLS:** Avoid estrogen containing IUDs post-partum in patients who are breast-feeding as it can decrease milk production. Avoid estrogen containing agents in patients with known hypercoagulable disorders, CAD, or history of VTE due to the increase risk of forming clots.

High-Yield Basic Pharmacology

- **Synthetic estrogen**
  - Alters hypothalamic gonadotropin secretion of follicle stimulating hormone and luteinizing hormone
- **Progestin (synthetic progesterone)**
  - Suppresses luteinizing hormone, thickens cervical mucus, thin endometrial lining

Primary Net Benefit

- Prevents ovulation reducing chance of conception
- Prevents/treats conditions associated with abnormal menstruation and hormonal imbalance

Oral Hormonal Contraceptives - Drug Class Review			
High-Yield Med Reviews			
Mechanism of Action: *suppression of follicle-stimulating hormone and luteinizing hormone prevent ovulation and decrease chance of conception*			
Dosing: EE < 35 mcg in women with pre-existing conditions that increase risk of VTE, higher doses of EE can be considered with women with histories of non-adherence			
Pediatric Dosing: [use after menarche; dose same as adult]			
CYP450 Interactions: CYP3A4 inhibitors and inducers			
Renal or Hepatic Dose Adjustments: contraindicated in hepatic failure			
Generic Name	**Brand Name**	**Main Indication(s) or Uses**	**Notes**
EE + progestin (drospirenone, norethindrone acetate, levonorgestrel, desogestrel, ethynodiol diacetate)	Brand Name more than 50 branded preparations	▪ Monophasic COC	▪ **Dosing (Adult):** Same amount of EE:progestin in active pills ▪ 4 or 7 hormone-free days per 28 day cycle ▪ **Additional Components:** ferrous fumarate, levomefolate calcium in select preparations
EE + progestin (desogestrel, norethindrone)	Brand Name Azurette Bekyree Kariva Kimidess Mircette Necon 10/11 Pimtrea Viorele Volnea	▪ Biphasic COC	▪ **Dosing (Adult):** two different EE:progestin ratios in active pills – 2 or 7 hormone-free days per 28 days cycle

Oral Hormonal Contraceptives - Drug Class Review
High-Yield Med Reviews

Generic Name	Brand Name	Main Indication(s) or Uses	Notes

EE + progestin (norethindrone, desogestrel, norgestimate, levonorgestrel)	Brand Name Alyacen 7/7/7 Aranelle Caziant Cesia Cyclessa Cyclafem 7/7/7 Dasetta 7/7/7 Enpresse Estrostep Fe Leena Levonest Ortho-Novum 7/7/7 Ortho Tri-Cyclen Ortho Tri-Cyclen Lo Myzilra Necon 7/7/7 Nortrel 7/7/7 Tilia Fe Tri-Estarylla Tri-Legest Fe Tri-Linyah TriNessa Tri-Norinyl Tri-Previfem Tri-Sprintec Trivora Velivet	▪ Triphasic COC	▪ **Dosing (Adult):** three different EE:progestin ratios in active pills
			  – 7 hormone-free days per 28-day cycle
			    ▪ Extra info if needed

Estradiol valerate + dienogest	Natazia	▪ Four phasic COC	▪ **Dosing (Adult):** four different estradiol valerate:dienogest ratios in active pills – 2 hormone-free days per 28 day cycle

Ethinyl estradiol + norethindrone	Lo Loestrin Fe	▪ Multiphasic COC	▪ **Dosing (Adult):** EE + progestin day 1-24, EE day 25-26
			  – 2 hormone-free days per 28 day cycle
			    ▪ Extra info if needed
			▪ **Additional Component:** ferrous fumarate day 27-28

EE + levonorgestrel	Amethyst Introvale Jolessa Quasense Seasonale	▪ Extended cycle COC	▪ **Dosing (Adult):**
			  – EE + progestin x 365 days, no hormone-free interval
			  – EE + progestin x 84 days, 7 hormone-free days (4 times annually)

Oral Hormonal Contraceptives - Drug Class Review
High-Yield Med Reviews

Generic Name	Brand Name	Main Indication(s) or Uses	Notes
EE + levonorgestrel	Amethia Amethia Lo Camrese Camrese Lo Jaimiess Lo Jaimiess LoSeasonique Quartette Seasonique	▪ Extended cycle multiphasic COC	▪ **Dosing (Adult):** EE + progestin x 84 − EE + progestin x 84 days, EE x 7 days − Four different EE:progestin ratios per 91 day cycle − No hormone-free interval
Drospirenone	Slynd	▪ Contraception (POP; Progestin-only-Pill)	▪ **Dosing (Adult):** progestin day 1-24, 4 hormone-free days per 28-day cycle ▪ **Missed doses:** only POP that has a 24-hour intake window ▪
Norethindrone	Camila Deblitane Errin Heather Jencycla Jolivette Lyza Nor-QD Nora-BE Norlyroc Ortho Micronor Sharobel	▪ Contraception (POP; Progestin-only-Pill)	▪ **Dosing (Adult):** progestin x 365 days, no hormone-free interval

High-Yield Clinical Knowledge

- Women should use additional contraception measures or abstain from sexual intercourse until one week of therapy has been completed for the majority of oral contraception preparations
- Missed doses should be managed according to the package insert of each specific preparation as there are numerous product-specific considerations. In general:
    - If one dose is missed, a patient can take two doses the following day and then resume the regular one dose daily schedule thereafter without compromising efficacy
    - If two or more doses are missed, a patient can take two doses for two days and then resume the one dose daily schedule thereafter, but efficacy may be compromised requiring additional contraception or abstinence for seven days. Emergency contraception may be considered in cases of two of more missed doses
- Adverse effects such as bloating, irritability and breakthrough bleeding often subside after three months of therapy
    - The use of COCs or POPs is not associated with subsequent ability to conceive after discontinuation.
- **Oral Hormonal Contraction Considerations**
    - There is no difference in the efficacy or safety of monophasic versus multiphasic COCs. Extended-cycle preparations may be safer compared to standard 28-day pill preparations.
    - Women with hirsutism, acne and oily skin should be prescribed COCs with low androgenic affinity.
    - The estrogen component of COCs increase the risk of VTE. Breast cancer data is less affirmative with low estrogen dose preparations hypothesized to carry little/no risk of breast cancer compared to higher estrogen dose preparations.

- Contraindications/strong caution for COC use:
  - Breast cancer
  - Breastfeeding or within 21 days post-partum
  - Hepatic impairment
  - Active VTE or history of VTE, increased risk of VTE
  - Uncontrolled hypertension
  - Vascular disease, heart disease, cerebrovascular disease
  - Current tobacco use
  - Migraine with aura

HIGH-YIELD BOARD EXAM ESSENTIALS

- **CLASSIC AGENTS:** Ethinyl estradiol (EE) +/- progestin
- **DRUG CLASS:** Oral Contraceptives
- **INDICATIONS:** Acne, contraception, hirsutism, hot flashes, endometriosis
- **MECHANISM:** Suppression of follicle-stimulating hormone and luteinizing hormone prevent ovulation and decrease chance of conception. They can also thicken cervical mucous to prevent sperm migration.
- **SIDE EFFECTS:** Vaginal spotting or amenorrhea, DVT/PE, decreased milk production (estrogen)
- **CLINICAL PEARLS:** Avoid estrogen containing IUDs post-partum in patients who are breast-feeding as it can decrease milk production. Avoid estrogen containing agents in patients with known hypercoagulable disorders, CAD, or history of VTE due to the increase risk of forming clots.

High-Yield Basic Pharmacology

- **Agonist vs Antagonist**
  - Degarelix, a GnRH antagonist, can achieve a much more rapid therapeutic antiandrogenic effect in 7 days, compared to 28 days for other GnRH agonists.

Primary Net Benefit

- GnRH agonists are associated with an increased risk of cardiovascular death but are associated with a lower risk of prostate cancer-specific mortality and all-cause mortality.

Gonadotropin-Releasing Hormone Agonists and Antagonist - Drug Class Review **High-Yield Med Reviews**			
Mechanism of Action: *GnRH Agonists - Reversibly inhibiting follicle-stimulating hormone and luteinizing hormone secretion.* *GnRH Antagonist - Reversibly inhibits GnRH receptors on the pituitary gland, reducing the production of testosterone.*			
Class Effects: GnRH agonists are associated with an increased risk of cardiovascular death but are associated with a lower risk of prostate cancer-specific mortality and all-cause mortality.			
Generic Name	**Brand Name**	**Indication(s) or Uses**	**Notes**

Cetrorelix	Cetrotide	• Controlled ovarian stimulation	• **Dosing (Adult):**
			  – SQ 0.25 mg of stimulation day 5 or 6 and continued daily until hCG administration
			• **Dosing (Peds):**
			  – Not routinely used
			• **CYP450 Interactions:** None
			• **Renal or Hepatic Dose Adjustments:**
			  – Severe renal impairment - contraindicated
			• **Dosage Forms:** SQ kit

Degarelix	Firmagon	• Prostate cancer	• **Dosing (Adult):**
			  – SQ 240 mg, then 80 mg q28days
			• **Dosing (Peds):**
			  – Not routinely used
			• **CYP450 Interactions:** None
			• **Renal or Hepatic Dose Adjustments:** None
			• **Dosage Forms:** SQ solution

Ganirelix	Antagon	• Controlled ovarian stimulation	• **Dosing (Adult):**
			  – SQ 250 mcg on day 2 or 3 of the cycle, continued until hCG administration
			• **Dosing (Peds):**
			  – Not routinely used
			• **CYP450 Interactions:** None
			• **Renal or Hepatic Dose Adjustments:** None
			• **Dosage Forms:** SQ kit

Gonadotropin-Releasing Hormone Agonists and Antagonist - Drug Class Review
High-Yield Med Reviews

Generic Name	Brand Name	Indication(s) or Uses	Notes

Elagolix	Orilissa	• Endometriosis	• **Dosing (Adult):**
			  – Oral 150 mg daily for a maximum of 24 months
			• **Dosing (Peds):**
			  – Not routinely used
			• **CYP450 Interactions:** Substrate CYP3A4, P-gp; Inhibits CYP2C19, P-gp; Induces CYP3A4
			• **Renal or Hepatic Dose Adjustments:** None
			• **Dosage Forms:** Oral (tablet)

Goserelin	Zoladex	• Breast cancer
		• Endometriosis
		• Endometriosis
		• Prostate cancer
			• **Dosing (Adult):**
			  – SQ (females) 3.6 mg q28days (duration indication dependent)
			  – SQ (males) 3.6 mg q28days or 10.8 mg q12weeks
			• **Dosing (Peds):**
			  – Not routinely used
			• **CYP450 Interactions:** None
			• **Renal or Hepatic Dose Adjustments:** None
			• **Dosage Forms:** SQ Implant

Histrelin	Supprelin LA
	Vantas
		• Central precocious puberty
		• Prostate cancer
			• **Dosing (Adult):**
			  – SQ 50 mg implant q12months
			• **Dosing (Peds):**
			  – SQ 50 mg implant q12months
			• **CYP450 Interactions:** None
			• **Renal or Hepatic Dose Adjustments:** None
			• **Dosage Forms:** SQ kit

Leuprolide	Eligard,
	Fensolvi,
	Lupron
		• Central precocious puberty
		• Endometriosis
		• Prostate cancer
		• Uterine leiomyomata
			• **Dosing (Adult):**
			  – IM/SQ (depot) 7.5 mg qmonth; 22.5 mg q12weeks; 30 mg q16weeks; 45 mg q24weeks
			  – IM 3.75 mg q1month for 6 months or 11.25 mg q3months for 6 months
			• **Dosing (Peds):**
			  – IM (depot) initial 7.5 to 15 mg qmonth, titrated by 3.75 mg q4weeks
			  – SQ 45 mg q6months
			  – IM 3.75 mg q1month for 6 months or 11.25 mg q3months for 6 months
			• **CYP450 Interactions:** None
			• **Renal or Hepatic Dose Adjustments:** None
			• **Dosage Forms:** SQ kit, Injection kit

Gonadotropin-Releasing Hormone Agonists and Antagonist - Drug Class Review
High-Yield Med Reviews

Generic Name	Brand Name	Indication(s) or Uses	Notes

Nafarelin	Synarel	• Central precocious puberty
		• Endometriosis
			• **Dosing (Adult):**
			  – Intranasal 200 mcg (1 spray) in each nostril BID starting between days 2 and 4 of the menstrual cycle
			    • Up to 4 total sprays for no more than 6 months
			• **Dosing (Peds):**
			  – Intranasal 400 mcg (2 sprays) per nostril BID
			    • Maximum 3 sprays TID (1,800 mcg/day)
			• **CYP450 Interactions:** None
			• **Renal or Hepatic Dose Adjustments:** None
			• **Dosage Forms:** Nasal solution

Triptorelin	Trelstar Mixject, Triptodur	• Central precocious puberty
		• Prostate cancer
			• **Dosing (Adult):**
			  – IM 3.75 mg q4weeks or 11.25 mg q12weeks or 22.5 mg q24weeks
			• **Dosing (Peds):**
			  – IM 22.5 mg q24weeks
			• **CYP450 Interactions:** None
			• **Renal or Hepatic Dose Adjustments:** None
			• **Dosage Forms:** IM suspension

High-Yield Clinical Knowledge

- **Long Duration Dosage Forms**
    - Many GnRH agonists are available in parenteral long-acting dosage forms, including leuprolide depot injection or leuprolide implant, triptorelin depot or implant, and goserelin acetate implant.
- **Comparable Efficacy and Safety**
    - The available evidence suggests no significant differences in either efficacy or toxicity among the GnRH agonists and orchiectomy.
    - Many experts consider the choice of pharmacologic intervention a patient-specific and patient-physician shared decision-making process.
- **Central precocious puberty**
    - Central precocious puberty is the onset of puberty before 7 or 8 years in girls or before the age of 9 in boys.
    - Before GnRH agonist therapy, a test dose must be administered or have a positive gonadotropin response to GnRH.
- **Gonadotropic Flare**
    - Upon initiation of GnRH agonists, a short-lived gonadotropic flare occurs as long-term receptor downregulation develops.
    - Pain that may accompany this phase can be alleviated by the addition of combined hormonal contraceptives or progestin for up to three weeks.
- **Hypoestrogenic Effects**
    - GnRH agonists' common adverse effects relate to their hypoestrogenic effect but dissipate with long-term use beyond six months.
    - These effects include loss of bone mineral density and vasomotor symptoms.

- **Add-Back Therapy**
  - Add-back therapy of estrogens, progestin alone, and progestins plus bisphosphonates are commonly used in combination with GnRH agonists to minimize bone mineral density loss, and symptomatic relieve vasomotor symptoms.
    - Doses of estrogen must be low enough to avoid neutralizing the anti-estrogenic effects of GnRH agonist therapy.
- **GnRH Suppression in Women**
  - GnRH gonadal suppression with continuous use of GnRH agonists is a component of the management of advanced breast cancer and ovarian cancer.

HIGH-YIELD BOARD EXAM ESSENTIALS

- **CLASSIC AGENTS:** Degarelix, goserelin, histrelin, leuprolide, nafarelin, triptorelin
- **DRUG CLASS:** Gonadotropin-releasing hormone agonists and antagonist
- **INDICATIONS:** Breast cancer (goserelin), central precocious puberty (histrelin, leuprolide, nafarelin, triptorelin), controlled ovarian stimulation (cetrorelix, ganirelix), endometriosis (elagolix, goserelin, leuprolide, nafarelin), prostate cancer (goserelin, histrelin, leuprolide, triptorelin), uterine leiomyomata (leuprolide)
- **MECHANISM:** Reversibly inhibiting follicle-stimulating hormone and luteinizing hormone secretion (GnRH Agonists). Reversibly inhibits GnRH receptors on the pituitary gland, reducing the production of testosterone (GnRH Antagonist).
- **SIDE EFFECTS:** Gonadotropic flare, loss of bone mineral density and vasomotor symptoms.
- **CLINICAL PEARLS:** Upon initiation of GnRH agonists, a short-lived gonadotropic flare occurs as long-term receptor downregulation develops.

High-Yield Basic Pharmacology

- **Flutamide, Bicalutamide, Nilutamide**
  - Nonsteroidal antiandrogen that inhibits androgen uptake and inhibits binding of androgen in target tissues
- **Abiraterone**
  - Selectively and irreversibly inhibits CYP17 an enzyme required for androgen biosynthesis and inhibits the formation of testosterone
- **Apalutamide**
  - Nonsteroidal androgen receptor inhibitor
- **Enzalutamide**
  - Pure androgen receptor signaling inhibitor.

Primary Overall Net Benefit

- Monotherapy with antiandrogens is less effective than GNRH agonist therapy and is not currently recommended to be used alone (unless patient had orchiectomy)

Anti-Androgens Drug Class Review			
High-Yield Med Reviews			
Mechanism of Action: *See agents above*			
Class Effects: Diarrhea, Hematuria, Disulfiram-like reaction (nilutamide), hypertension, hypokalemia, edema, LFT elevations, fatigue, hot flashes, cardiovascular disorders			
Generic Name	**Brand Name**	**Indication(s) or Uses**	**Notes**
Flutamide	N/A	▪ Prostate Cancer	▪ **Dosing (Adult):** Oral 250 mg every 8 hours in combination with an GNRH agonist ▪ **Dosing (Peds):** Not used in pediatrics ▪ **CYP450 Interactions:** Substrate of CYP1A2 (minor), CYP3A4 (minor) ▪ **Renal or Hepatic Dose Adjustments:** Severe hepatic impairment: Use is contraindicated. ▪ **Dosage Forms:** 125 mg oral capsule

Anti-Androgens Drug Class Review
High-Yield Med Reviews

Generic Name	Brand Name	Indication(s) or Uses	Notes
Abiraterone acetate	Yonsa; Zytiga	▪ Prostate Cancer	▪ **Dosing (Adult):** Zytiga: oral 1,000 mg once daily (in combination with prednisone 5 mg twice daily). Yonsa (micronized formulation): oral 500 mg once daily (in combination with methylprednisolone 4 mg twice daily) ▪ **Dosing (Peds):** Not used in pediatrics ▪ **CYP450 Interactions:** Substrate of CYP3A4 (major); Inhibits CYP2C8 (weak), CYP2D6 (moderate) ▪ **Renal or Hepatic Dose Adjustments:** ALT and/or AST >5 times ULN or total bilirubin >3 times ULN: Withhold treatment until liver function tests return to baseline then reinitiate at 750 mg once daily (Zytiga) or 375 mg once daily (Yonsa). Recurrent hepatotoxicity on 750 mg/day (Zytiga) or 375 mg/day (Yonsa): Withhold treatment until liver function tests return to baseline then reinitiate at 500 mg once daily (Zytiga) or 250 mg once daily (Yonsa). Recurrent hepatotoxicity on 500 mg once daily (Zytiga) or 250 mg once daily (Yonsa): Discontinue treatment. ▪ **Dosage Forms:** 125 mg, 250 mg 500 mg oral tablet
Apalutamide	Erleada	▪ Prostate Cancer	▪ **Dosing (Adult):** 240 mg once daily (in combination with continuous androgen deprivation therapy) ▪ **Dosing (Peds):** Not used in pediatrics ▪ **CYP450 Interactions:** Substrate of CYP2C8 (major), CYP3A4 (minor); Induces BCRP/ABCG2, CYP2C19 (strong), CYP2C9 (weak), CYP3A4 (strong), OATP1B1/1B3 (SLCO1B1/1B3), P-glycoprotein/ABCB1 ▪ **Renal or Hepatic Dose Adjustments:** Has not been studied in severe hepatic impairment ▪ **Dosage Forms:** 60 mg oral tablet
Bicalutamide	Casodex	▪ Prostate Cancer	▪ **Dosing (Adult):** Oral 50 mg once daily (in combination with an GNRH agonist) or 150 mg once daily as monotherapy ▪ **Dosing (Peds):** Not used in pediatrics ▪ **CYP450 Interactions:** Inhibits CYP3A4 (weak) ▪ **Renal or Hepatic Dose Adjustments:** Hepatic impairment during treatment: ALT >2 times ULN or development of jaundice: Discontinue immediately ▪ **Dosage Forms:** 50 mg oral tablet

Anti-Androgens Drug Class Review
High-Yield Med Reviews

Generic Name	Brand Name	Indication(s) or Uses	Notes
Enzalutamide	Xtandi	▪ Prostate Cancer	▪ **Dosing (Adult):** Oral 160 mg once daily ▪ **Dosing (Peds):** Not used in pediatrics ▪ **CYP450 Interactions:** Substrate of CYP2C8 (major), CYP3A4 (major); Inhibits MRP2; Induces CYP2C19 (moderate), CYP2C9 (moderate), CYP3A4 (strong) ▪ **Renal or Hepatic Dose Adjustments:** Has not been studied in renal impairment ▪ **Dosage Forms:** 40 mg, 80 mg oral tablet
Nilutamide	Nilandron	▪ Prostate Cancer	▪ **Dosing (Adult):** Oral 300 mg once daily for 30 days, followed by 150 mg once daily ▪ **Dosing (Peds):** Not used in pediatrics ▪ **CYP450 Interactions:** None Known ▪ **Renal or Hepatic Dose Adjustments:** Severe hepatic impairment: Use is contraindicated. Hepatotoxicity during treatment: ALT >2 times ULN or jaundice: Discontinue treatment. ▪ **Dosage Forms:** 150 mg oral tablet

High-Yield Clinical Knowledge

- **Anti-Androgen Monotherapy**
  - Monotherapy with antiandrogens is less effective than GNRH agonist therapy and is not currently recommended to be used alone (unless patient had orchiectomy)
- **Efficacy of the antiandrogens is similar**
  - Flutamide has a response rate of 50% to 87%
  - Bicalutamide has a response rate of 54% to 70%
  - Nilutamide has a response rate of approximately 40%
  - Bicalutamide is generally preferred due to better toxicity profile.
- **Abiraterone and Prednisone**
  - Abiraterone acetate is approved for treatment of patients with metastatic castration-resistant prostate cancer in combination with prednisone or prednisolone 5 mg twice daily. Co-administration with the recommended dose of prednisone compensates for abiraterone-induced reductions in serum cortisol and blocks the compensatory increase in adrenocorticotropic hormone seen with abiraterone.
- **Enzalutamide**
  - Requires dose adjustments for strong CYP2C8 inhibitors and CYP3A4 inducers

High-Yield Fast-Facts

- **Combination Therapy**
  - For advanced prostate cancer, all currently available antiandrogens are indicated only in combination with androgen-ablation therapy.
    - Flutamide and bicalutamide are used in combination with an GNRH agonists and nilutamide is used in combination with orchiectomy

HIGH-YIELD BOARD EXAM ESSENTIALS

- **CLASSIC AGENTS:** Abiraterone acetate, apalutamide, bicalutamide, enzalutamide, flutamide, nilutamide
- **DRUG CLASS:** Anti-androgens
- **INDICATIONS:** Prostate cancer
- **MECHANISM:**
  - **Flutamide, Bicalutamide, Nilutamide:** Nonsteroidal antiandrogen that inhibits androgen uptake and inhibits binding of androgen in target tissues.
  - **Abiraterone:** selectively and irreversibly inhibits CYP17 an enzyme required for androgen biosynthesis and inhibits the formation of testosterone.
  - **Apalutamide:** Nonsteroidal androgen receptor inhibitor.
  - **Enzalutamide:** Pure androgen receptor signaling inhibitor.
- **SIDE EFFECTS:** Headache, peripheral edema, hot flashes, gynecomastia, secondary infections
- **CLINICAL PEARLS:** Monotherapy with antiandrogens is less effective than GNRH agonist therapy and is not currently recommended to be used alone (unless patient had orchiectomy).

High-Yield Basic Pharmacology

- **Mechanism of Action**
  - Interferes with the normal function of DNA by alkylation and cross-linking the strands of DNA preventing cell division and decreasing DNA synthesis
  - All of these alkylating agents are hepatically metabolized
    - Ifosfamide/cyclophosphamide are converted into active metabolites and acrolein

Primary Net Benefit

- Interferes with the normal function of DNA by alkylation and cross-linking the strands of DNA preventing cell division and decreasing DNA synthesis

Alkylating Agents Drug Class Review			
High-Yield Med Reviews			
Mechanism of Action: *Interferes with the normal function of DNA by alkylation and cross-linking the strands of DNA preventing cell division and decreasing DNA synthesis*			
Class Effects: Myelosuppression, alopecia, nausea/vomiting, mucositis, rash (bendamustine), hemorrhagic cystitis/renal toxicity (ifosfamide/cyclophosphamide), neurotoxicity (ifosfamide)			
Generic Name	**Brand Name**	**Indication(s) or Uses**	**Notes**

Bendamustine	Belrapzo; Bendeka; Treanda	▪ Chronic lymphocytic leukemia
		▪ Non-Hodgkin lymphoma
		▪ Hodgkin lymphoma
			▪ **Dosing (Adult):** Dosing varies per indication
			  – Typical range 70-120 mg/m^2
			    ▪ Extra info if needed
			▪ **Dosing (Peds):** Not often used in pediatrics
			▪ **CYP450 Interactions:** BCRP/ABCG2 substrate, CYP1A2 substrate (minor), P-glycoprotein/ABCB1 substrate (minor)
			▪ **Renal or Hepatic Dose Adjustments:** CrCl <30 mL/minute or moderate-severe hepatic impairment: Use is not recommended
			▪ **Dosage Forms:** 100 mg/4 mL solution for IV injection

Busulfan	Busulfex; Myleran	▪ Hematopoietic stem cell transplant (HSCT)
		▪ Polycythemia vera (PCV)
		▪ Essential thrombocythemia (ET)
			▪ **Dosing (Adult):** Dosing varies per indication
			  – HSCT: 0.8 mg/kg/dose IV every 6 hours for 4 days (will vary per regimen)
			  – PCV/ET: 2-4 mg orally once daily
			▪ **Dosing (Peds):** Same as adult
			▪ **CYP450 Interactions:** None known
			▪ **Renal or Hepatic Dose Adjustments:** No renal or hepatic dose adjustments (has not been studied)
			▪ **Dosage Forms:** 6 mg/mL solution for IV injection, 2 mg oral tablet

Alkylating Agents Drug Class Review
High-Yield Med Reviews

Generic Name	Brand Name	Indication(s) or Uses	Notes
Cyclophosphamide	N/A	<ul><li>Acute lymphoblastic leukemia</li><li>Breast cancer*</li><li>Ewing sarcoma*</li><li>Graft-vs-host disease prophylaxis*</li><li>Hematopoietic stem cell transplant (HSCT)*</li><li>Hodgkin lymphoma*</li><li>Multiple myeloma*</li><li>Non-Hodgkin lymphoma*</li><li>Osteosarcoma*</li><li>Rhabdomyosarcoma*</li><li>Small cell lung cancer*</li></ul>	<ul><li>**Dosing (Adult):** Dosing varies per indication<ul><li>Typical range 75 mg/m^2 - 1500 mg/m^2</li></ul></li><li>**Dosing (Peds):** Same as adult</li><li>**CYP450 Interactions:** Substrate of CYP2A6 (minor), CYP2B6 (major), CYP2C19 (minor), CYP2C9 (minor), CYP3A4 (minor)</li><li>**Renal or Hepatic Dose Adjustments:** CrCl 10 to 29 mL/minute: Administer 75% of normal dose. CrCl <10 mL/minute: Administer 50% of normal dose. Serum bilirubin 3.1 to 5 mg/dL or transaminases >3 times ULN: Administer 75% of dose. Serum bilirubin >5 mg/dL: Avoid use.</li><li>**Dosage Forms:** 1 g/5 mL solution for IV injection, 500 mg/2.5 mL solution for IV injection, 25 mg oral capsule, 50 mg oral capsule</li></ul>
Ifosfamide	Ifex	<ul><li>Testicular cancer</li><li>Bladder cancer*</li><li>Cervical cancer*</li><li>Ewing sarcoma*</li><li>Hodgkin lymphoma*</li><li>Non-Hodgkin lymphomas*</li><li>Osteosarcoma*</li><li>Ovarian cancer*</li><li>Soft tissue sarcoma*</li></ul>	<ul><li>**Dosing (Adult):** Dosing varies per indication<ul><li>Typical range 1000 mg/m^2- 5000 mg/m^2</li></ul></li><li>**Dosing (Peds):** Same as adult</li><li>**CYP450 Interactions:** Substrate of CYP2B6 (minor), CYP2C19 (minor), CYP2C8 (minor), CYP2C9 (minor), CYP3A4 (minor)</li><li>**Renal or Hepatic Dose Adjustments:** CrCl <10 mL/minute: Administer 75% of dose. Bilirubin >3 mg/dL: Administer 25% of dose.</li><li>**Dosage Forms:** 1 g/20 mL solution for IV injection, 3 g/60 mL mL solution for IV injection</li></ul>
Melphalan	Alkeran; Evomela	<ul><li>Multiple myeloma</li><li>Hematopoietic stem cell transplant (HSCT)</li></ul>	<ul><li>**Dosing (Adult):** Dosing varies per indication<ul><li>HSCT: 140-200 mg/m^2 IV</li><li>Multiple Myeloma: 4-9 mg/m2/day for 4-7 days every 4 weeks</li></ul></li><li>**Dosing (Peds):** Not often used in pediatrics</li><li>**CYP450 Interactions:** None known</li><li>**Renal or Hepatic Dose Adjustments:** Consider a reduced dose for poor renal function (dependent on indication), no hepatic adjustment necessary</li><li>**Dosage Forms:** 50 mg solution for IV injection, 2 mg oral tablet</li></ul>
*Off label use			

Emetic Potential

- **Moderate emetic risk (30-90% frequency of emesis)**
  - Cyclophosphamide $\leq$ 1500 mg/m^2
  - Ifosfamide < 2g/m^2
  - Melphalan < 140 mg/m^2
  - Busulfan
  - Bendamustine
- **High emetic risk (> 90% frequency of emesis)**
  - Cyclophosphamide >1500 mg/m^2
  - Ifosfamide > 2g/m^2
  - Melphalan $\geq$140 mg/m^2

Extravasation Risk

- **Bendamustine**
  - Irritant with vesicant-like properties
  - If extravasation occurs, stop infusion immediately. Gently aspirate extravasated solution and elevate extremity. Apply dry cold compresses for 20 minutes 4 times daily. Consider sodium thiosulfate, injecting 2 mL subcutaneously for each mg of drug suspected to have extravasated.

High-Yield Clinical Knowledge

- **Mucositis**
  - Mucositis is a common side of the alkylating agents, but it is most common/severe with melphalan. This can range from oral mouth sores to irritation of the GI tract leading to severe diarrhea.
    - Oral mucositis can be reduced by having patients chew on ice chips during their melphalan infusion.
- **Hemorrhagic Cystitis**
  - Ifosfamide and cyclophosphamide can cause hemorrhagic cystitis (irritation and bleeding in the bladder). This is due to accumulation of the toxic metabolite acrolein in the bladder.
    - Mesna is a bladder protectant given to bind acrolein and help prevent this complication
    - Vigorous hydration is used as both prevention and treatment of hemorrhagic cystitis
- **Neurotoxicity**
  - Ifosfamide can rarely cause neurotoxicity. Symptoms generally resolve within 3 days of treatment discontinuation and can be managed with supportive care or methylene blue.

High-Yield Fast-Facts

- **Hepatic Veno-Occlusive Disease/Sinusoidal Obstructive Syndrome**
  - High dose busulfan (used in bone marrow transplant) can lead to veno-occlusive disease (VOD)/Sinusoidal Obstructive Syndrome (SOS). Higher busulfan area under the curve increases risk of developing VOD.
  - Patients receiving high dose busulfan conditioning regimens often have pharmacokinetics monitored in order to adjust the dose and target a specific area under the curve.
  - Patients who received high dose busulfan stem cell conditioning should be closely monitored for signs of hepatic dysfunction, unexplained weight gain, edema, abdominal pain and jaundice.
  - Treatment options of SOS/VOD can range from supportive care to defibrotide.
- **History of Alkylating Agents**
  - Alkylating agents were the first anticancer drugs used, and they remain a cornerstone of anticancer therapy
  - Mustard gas (an alkylating agent) was one of a number of weaponized poison gasses used during World War I. Two doctors at Yale University noticed that many of the soldiers affected by mustard gas had a

surprisingly low number of white blood cells. They speculated that if mustard gas can destroy healthy white blood cells that it could also destroy cancerous white blood cells leading to the use of alkylating agents as chemotherapy for the treatment of lymphoma and other cancers.

HIGH-YIELD BOARD EXAM ESSENTIALS
- **CLASSIC AGENTS:** Bendamustine, busulfan, cyclophosphamide, ifosfamide, melphalan
- **DRUG CLASS:** Alkylating agents
- **INDICATIONS:** ALL, breast cancer, Ewing sarcoma, graft-vs-host disease prophylaxis, HSCT, Hodgkin lymphoma, multiple myeloma, non-Hodgkin lymphoma, osteosarcoma, rhabdomyosarcoma, small cell lung cancer
- **MECHANISM:** Interferes with the normal function of DNA by alkylation and cross-linking the strands of DNA preventing cell division and decreasing DNA synthesis.
- **SIDE EFFECTS:** Mucositis, hemorrhagic cystitis, neurotoxicity, hepatic veno-occlusive disease/sinusoidal obstructive syndrome
- **CLINICAL PEARLS:** Mucositis is a common side of the alkylating agents, but it is most common/severe with melphalan. This can range from oral mouth sores to irritation of the GI tract leading to severe diarrhea. Oral mucositis can be reduced by having patients chew on ice chips during their melphalan infusion

High-Yield Basic Pharmacology

- **Mechanism of Action**
  - Inhibits synthesis of DNA and binds to DNA leading to single- and double-strand breaks

Primary Net Benefit

- Inhibits synthesis of DNA and binds to DNA leading to single- and double-strand breaks

Anti-Tumor Antibodies Drug Class Review			
High-Yield Med Reviews			
Mechanism of Action: *inhibits synthesis of DNA; binds to DNA leading to single- and double-strand breaks*			
Class Effects: Pulmonary toxicity, Idiosyncratic reaction (hypotension, mental confusion, fever, chills, and wheezing), anaphylactic reaction, skin reactions, hair loss, nausea/vomiting, mucositis, radiation recall,			
Generic Name	**Brand Name**	**Indication(s) or Uses**	**Notes**
Bleomycin	N/A	<ul><li>Hodgkin lymphoma</li><li>Testicular cancer</li><li>Ovarian germ cell cancer*</li></ul>	<ul><li>**Dosing (Adult):** Dosing varies per indication – 5 units/m² to 30 units/dose</li><li>**Dosing (Peds):** Same as adult</li><li>**CYP450 Interactions:** None known</li><li>**Renal or Hepatic Dose Adjustments:** text</li><li>**Dosage Forms:** 15 unit solution for IV injection, 30 unit solution for IV injection</li></ul>
***Off Label Indication**			

Emetic Potential

- Minimal emetic risk (<10% frequency of emesis)

Extravasation Risk

- None

High-Yield Clinical Knowledge

- **Bleomycin pulmonary toxicity**
  - Bleomycin is deactivated by bleomycin hydrolase. Bleomycin hydrolase is not found in the lungs and lung toxicity may occur with bleomycin use.
  - Interstitial pneumonitis is the most common form of bleomycin pulmonary toxicity but it can also progress to pulmonary fibrosis which is irreversible and potentially fatal.
  - Pulmonary function tests, including DLCO (diffusing capacity of the lung for carbon monoxide) should be followed routinely during bleomycin therapy. Bleomycin should be discontinued for significant changes in pulmonary function, including a decrease in DLCO of 40-60%.
  - The risk for pulmonary toxicity increases with age >70 years and cumulative lifetime dose of >400 units
- **Role of granulocyte colony stimulating factor (GCSF) use**
  - Several retrospective reviews evaluating risk of pulmonary toxicity in patients with Hodgkin lymphoma receiving bleomycin found use of GCSF as risk factor for the development of pulmonary toxicity
    - Guidelines do not recommend the routine use of growth factors during bleomycin therapy when used for the treatment of lymphoma especially since ABVD can be safely given at full dose intensity without GCSF use.

- No increased risk of pulmonary toxicity has been found with the use of GCSF and bleomycin-containing regimens in the treatment of testicular cancer
    - In testicular cancer, use of GCSF is acceptable (although not recommended as primary prophylaxis)
- **Dropping bleomycin in Hodgkin Lymphoma patients with a good response**
    - Studies have shown that in patients with a positive response (Deauville 1 or 2) on interim PET scan after 2 cycles of ABVD for Hodgkin lymphoma can drop the bleomycin and continue with AVD for the remaining cycles of chemotherapy. In these patients who are responding well to therapy, it is safer than continuing with ABVD (from a pulmonary toxicity standpoint) but no less effective.

High-Yield Fast-Facts

- **Idiosyncratic reactions**
    - A severe idiosyncratic reaction consisting of hypotension, mental confusion, fever, chills, and wheezing has been reported in approximately 1% of lymphoma patients treated with bleomycin
- **Test dose for lymphoma patients**
    - Due to the possibility of an anaphylactoid reaction, the manufacturer recommends administering bleomycin 2 units or less before the first 2 doses; if no acute reaction occurs, then the regular dosage schedule may be followed. Monitor carefully, particularly following the first 2 doses

---

HIGH-YIELD BOARD EXAM ESSENTIALS
- **CLASSIC AGENTS:** Bleomycin
- **DRUG CLASS:** Anti-tumor antibodies
- **INDICATIONS:** Hodgkin lymphoma, testicular cancer, ovarian germ cell cancer
- **MECHANISM:** Inhibits synthesis of DNA; binds to DNA leading to single- and double-strand breaks
- **SIDE EFFECTS:** Pulmonary toxicity, hypotension, mental confusion, fever, chills, and wheezing
- **CLINICAL PEARLS:** Due to the possibility of an anaphylactoid reaction, the manufacturer recommends administering bleomycin 2 units or less before the first 2 doses; if no acute reaction occurs, then the regular dosage schedule may be followed. Monitor carefully, particularly following the first 2 doses

---

High-Yield Basic Pharmacology

- **Mechanism of Action**
  - Inhibits DNA and RNA synthesis by intercalation between DNA base pairs by inhibition of topoisomerase II and by steric obstruction. The direct binding to DNA (intercalation) and inhibition of DNA repair (topoisomerase II inhibition) result in blockade of DNA and RNA synthesis and fragmentation of DNA.

Primary Net Benefit

- Inhibits DNA and RNA synthesis by intercalation between DNA base pairs by inhibition of topoisomerase II and by steric obstruction. The direct binding to DNA (intercalation) and inhibition of DNA repair (topoisomerase II inhibition) result in blockade of DNA and RNA synthesis and fragmentation of DNA.

ANTHRACYCLINE Drug Class Review			
High-Yield Med Reviews			
Mechanism of Action: *Inhibits DNA and RNA synthesis by intercalation between DNA base pairs by inhibition of topoisomerase II and steric obstruction*			
Class Effects: Cytopenias, Nausea/Vomiting, Alopecia, Cardiotoxicity, Body Fluid Discoloration, tissue necrosis if extravasated, mucositis, fatigue			
Generic Name	**Brand Name**	**Indication(s) or Uses**	**Notes**
Daunorubicin	N/A	▪ Acute Lymphoblastic Leukemia ▪ Acute Myeloid Leukemia	▪ **Dosing (Adult):** Dosing varies per indication and regimen – Typical range 20-90 mg/m^2 ▪ **Dosing (Peds):** Same as adult ▪ **CYP450 Interactions:** Substrate of P-glycoprotein/ABCB1 (minor) ▪ **Renal or Hepatic Dose Adjustments:** Serum bilirubin 1.2 to 3 mg/dL: Administer 75% of dose. Serum bilirubin 3.1 to 5 mg/dL: Administer 50% of dose. Serum bilirubin >5 mg/dL: Avoid use ▪ **Dosage Forms:** 20 mg/4 mL solution for IV injection
Doxorubicin	Adriamycin	▪ Acute Lymphoblastic Leukemia* ▪ Bladder Cancer* ▪ Breast Cancer ▪ Hodgkin Lymphoma* ▪ Non-Hodgkin Lymphoma* ▪ Osteosarcoma* ▪ Soft Tissue Sarcomas	▪ **Dosing (Adult):** Dosing varies per indication ▪ Typically range 20-75 mg/m^2 ▪ **Dosing (Peds):** Same as adult ▪ **CYP450 Interactions:** Substrate of CYP2D6 (minor), CYP3A4 (major), P-glycoprotein/ABCB1 (major) ▪ **Renal or Hepatic Dose Adjustments:** Serum bilirubin 1.2 to 3 mg/dL: Administer 50% of dose. Serum bilirubin 3.1 to 5 mg/dL: Administer 25% of dose. Severe hepatic impairment (Child-Pugh class C or bilirubin >5 mg/dL): Use is contraindicated. ▪ **Dosage Forms:** 2 mg/mL solution for IV injection

ANTHRACYCLINE Drug Class Review
High-Yield Med Reviews

Generic Name	Brand Name	Indication(s) or Uses	Notes
Doxorubicin Liposomal	Doxil	▪ Kaposi Sarcoma ▪ Breast Cancer* ▪ Ovarian Cancer	▪ **Dosing (Adult):** Dosing varies per indication. Doxorubicin liposomal is NOT interchangeable with conventional doxorubicin – Typical range 20-50 mg/m^2 ▪ **Dosing (Peds):** Not routinely used in pediatrics ▪ **CYP450 Interactions:** Substrate of CYP2D6 (minor), CYP3A4 (major) ▪ **Renal or Hepatic Dose Adjustments:** Bilirubin 1.2 to 3 mg/dL: Reduce dose to 50% of normal dose. Bilirubin >3 mg/dL: Reduce dose to 25% of normal dose ▪ **Dosage Forms:** 2 mg/mL solution for IV injection

Idarubicin	Idamycin	▪ Acute Myeloid Leukemia	▪ **Dosing (Adult):** Dosing varies per regimen
			  – Typical range 6-12 mg/m^2
			▪ **Dosing (Peds):** Same as adult
			▪ **CYP450 Interactions:** text
			  ▪ **Renal or Hepatic Dose Adjustments:** CrCl 10 to 50 mL/minute: Administer 75% of dose. CrCl <10 mL/minute: Administer 50% of dose. Bilirubin 2.6 to 5 mg/dL: Administer 50% of dose. Bilirubin >5 mg/dL: Avoid use
			▪ **Dosage Forms:** 5 mg/5mL, 10 mg/10mL, 20 mg/20mL solution for IV injection

*Off Label Use			

Emetic Potential

- **Low Emetic Risk (10-30% frequency of emesis)**
  - Doxorubicin Liposomal
- **Moderate Emetic Risk (30-90% frequency of emesis)**
  - Doxorubicin <60 mg/m^2
  - Daunorubicin
  - Idarubicin
- **High Emetic Risk (>90% frequency of emesis)**
  - Doxorubicin ≥60 mg/m2

Extravasation Risk

- Vesicants; may cause severe local tissue necrosis if extravasation occurs
  - For intravenous administration only through a free flowing central IV line; not for intramuscular or subcutaneous administration.
  - If extravasation occurs, stop infusion immediately and gently aspirate extravasated solution. Give antidote (dexrazoxane or dimethyl sulfate [DMSO]). Apply dry cold compresses for 20 minutes 4 times daily for 1 to 2 days.
    - Dexrazoxane: 1,000 mg/m^2 IV (administer in a large vein remote from site of extravasation) over 1 to 2 hours days 1 and 2, then 500 mg/m^2 IV over 1 to 2 hours day 3
    - DMSO: Apply topically to a region covering twice the affected area every 8 hours for 7 days

High-Yield Clinical Knowledge

- **Cardiac Toxicity**
    - Anthracycline therapy is associated with an increase in the risk for developing heart failure with significant associated morbidity and mortality. Anthracyclines appear to affect cardiac function mainly through mechanisms that involve reactive oxygen species formation, induction of apoptosis, DNA damage through interaction with topoisomerase II, and inhibition of protein synthesis.
    - Risk factors for anthracycline cardiac toxicity include older age (>65 years) or very young age (<4 years old), female gender, preexisting cardiovascular disorders, hypertension, smoking, hyperlipidemia, obesity, diabetes, and high cumulative anthracycline exposure.
    - Cumulative anthracycline exposure seems to be the most consistent risk factor for cardiotoxicity. It is recommended that patients do not exceed a maximum lifetime dose of 450-550 mg/m^2 of doxorubicin equivalents.
    - Baseline cardiac imaging (generally by echocardiogram) to assess left ventricular ejection fraction (LVEF) should be performed prior to initiation of anthracycline therapy. A history and cardiac exam should be performed prior to every cycle of chemotherapy and patients who develop symptoms or signs of heart failure should have repeat echocardiography performed. The optimum frequency of cardiac surveillance in patients receiving anthracycline-based chemotherapy without signs or symptoms of heart failure is unclear.
    - Dexrazoxane is indicated for the prevention of doxorubicin cardiomyopathy. It is given IV in a 10:1 ratio of dexrazoxane:doxorubicin. Doxorubicin must be administered within 30 minutes of the completion of the dexrazoxane infusion.
        - Its FDA labeled indication is to reduce the incidence and severity of cardiomyopathy associated with doxorubicin administration in women with metastatic breast cancer who have received a cumulative doxorubicin dose of 300 mg/m2 and will continue to receive doxorubicin to maintain tumor control but it may also be used in some pediatric protocols.
        - It is not recommended for use with initial doxorubicin therapy.
- **Vesicant**
    - All of the anthracyclines are potent vesicants and can cause severe tissue necrosis. They are recommended to be given only through a free-flowing central line. In the event of extravasation, IV dexrazoxane or topical dimethyl sulfate can be administered. Patients should be counselled to immediately alert their healthcare team if they notice any pain, redness or swelling at the anthracycline injection site.
- **Body Fluid Discoloration**
    - Most of the anthracyclines are bright red in color and can also cause a red discoloration of a patients urine, tears, sweat and saliva.
        - This discoloration is harmless and will resolve 1-2 days after the anthracycline dose
        - Patients should be counselled that urine discoloration from an anthracycline will be painless, but if they have red urine with symptoms such as urgency, frequency or discomfort, they should be evaluated by their healthcare provider as those could be signs of blood in the urine.

High-Yield Fast-Facts

- **The Red Devil**
    - Doxorubicin earned its infamous nickname, "the red devil", due on its bright red color, vesicant properties, and side-effect profile.
- **Dexrazoxane**
    - Dexrazoxane is marketed under two different brand names (Totect and Zinecard), however they are not interchangeable. Totect is indicated for the treatment of anthracycline extravasations, whereas generic dexrazoxane and Zinecard are indicated for reducing doxorubicin-induced cardiomyopathy.

HIGH-YIELD BOARD EXAM ESSENTIALS

- **CLASSIC AGENTS:** Daunorubicin, doxorubicin, doxorubicin liposomal, idarubicin
- **DRUG CLASS:** Anthracycline
- **INDICATIONS:** ALL, AML, bladder cancer, breast cancer, Hodgkin lymphoma, non-Hodgkin lymphoma, osteosarcoma, soft tissue sarcomas
- **MECHANISM:** Inhibits DNA and RNA synthesis by intercalation between DNA base pairs by inhibition of topoisomerase II and by steric obstruction. The direct binding to DNA (intercalation) and inhibition of DNA repair (topoisomerase II inhibition) result in blockade of DNA and RNA synthesis and fragmentation of DNA.
- **SIDE EFFECTS:** Cardiac toxicity, vesicant, red discoloration of a patient urine, tears, sweat and saliva.
- **CLINICAL PEARLS:** For intravenous administration only through a free flowing central IV line; not for intramuscular or subcutaneous administration. If extravasation occurs, stop infusion immediately and gently aspirate extravasated solution. Give antidote (dexrazoxane or dimethyl sulfate [DMSO]). Apply dry cold compresses for 20 minutes 4 times daily for 1 to 2 days.

High-Yield Basic Pharmacology

- **Mechanism of Action**
  - Folate antimetabolites inhibit DNA synthesis, repair, and cellular replication. They do so by binding to and inhibiting dihydrofolate reductase, inhibiting the formation of reduced folates, and thymidylate synthetase, resulting in inhibition of purine and thymidylic acid synthesis, thus interfering with DNA synthesis, repair, and cellular replication.

Primary Net Benefit

- Plays a key role in treatment of numerous cancers including ALL, bladder cancer, graft vs host disease, head and neck cancer, non-Hodgkin lymphoma, osteosarcoma, and soft tissue sarcoma.

Folate Antagonists Drug Class Review			
High-Yield Med Reviews			
Mechanism of Action: *Inhibits dihydrofolate reductase and the formation of folate resulting in inhibition of DNA synthesis, repair, and cellular replication.*			
Class Effects: Bone marrow suppression, renal dysfunction, mucositis, cutaneous reactions, decreased appetite, diarrhea, nausea and vomiting, alopecia, skin photosensitivity			
Generic Name	**Brand Name**	**Indication(s) or Uses**	**Notes**

Methotrexate	Otrexup; Rasuvo; RediTrex; Trexall; Xatmep	• Acute Lymphoblastic Leukemia
		• Bladder Cancer*
		• Graft vs Host Disease*
		• Head and Neck Cancer
		• Non-Hodgkin Lymphoma
		• Osteosarcoma
		• Soft Tissue Sarcoma
			• **Dosing (Adult):** Dosing varies per indication
			  – Intrathecal: 6-15 mg flat dose
			  – Oral: 15-40 mg/m^2
			  – IV: 100-8,000 mg/m^2
			• **Dosing (Peds):** Same as adult
			• **CYP450 Interactions:** Substrate of BCRP/ABCG2, OAT1/3, OATP1B1/1B3 (SLCO1B1/1B3), P-glycoprotein/ABCB1 (minor)
			• **Renal or Hepatic Dose Adjustments:** CrCl >50 mL/minute: No dose adjustment necessary. CrCl 10 to 50 mL/minute: Administer 50% of dose. CrCl <10 mL/minute: Avoid use. Bilirubin 3.1 to 5 mg/dL or transaminases >3 times ULN: Administer 75% of dose. Bilirubin >5 mg/dL: Avoid use
			Dosage Forms: 1 g/40mL, 50 mg/2 mL, 250 mg/10 mL solution for IV injection. 2.5mg, 5 mg, 7.5 mg, 10 mg, 15 mg oral tablet

Pemetrexed	Alimta	• Bladder Cancer* • Mesothelioma • Non-Small Cell Lung Cancer	• **Dosing (Adult):** Dosing varies per indication – Typical dose 500 mg/m^2 • **Dosing (Peds):** Not routinely used in pediatrics • **CYP450 Interactions:** Substrate of OAT1/3 • **Renal or Hepatic Dose Adjustments:** CrCl <45 mL/minute: Use is not recommended by the manufacturer • **Dosage Forms:** 100 mg, 500 mg solution for IV injection
***Off Label Use**			

Emetic Potential

- **Minimal Emetic Risk (<10% frequency of emesis)**
  - Methotrexate <50 mg/m^2
- **Low Emetic Risk (10-30% frequency of emesis)**
  - Methotrexate 50-250 mg/m^2
  - Pemetrexed
- **Moderate Emetic Risk (30-90% frequency of emesis)**
  - Methotrexate ≥ 250 mg/m^2

Extravasation Risk

- None

High-Yield Clinical Knowledge

- **Leucovorin Rescue with Methotrexate**
  - Methotrexate doses >500 mg/m2 <u>require</u> leucovorin "rescue". Leucovorin is folinic acid or an active form of folate that does not need to be processed by dihydrofolate reductase. It is given to rescue healthy cells from the toxicity of methotrexate and replenish the supply of folate metabolites depleted by methotrexate.
    - Leucovorin is usually started 12-24 hours post methotrexate and given until serum methotrexate levels are below a certain threshold (often 0.05 mM). Dosing varies per protocol but oral absorption is saturable at doses >25 mg, so doses >25 mg are often given IV.
    - Typically, dosing frequency is every 6 hours, although dose and frequency may be increased if a patient is experiencing methotrexate toxicity
- **High Dose Methotrexate**
  - High dose methotrexate (Doses >500-1000 mg/m^2) require inpatient monitoring and levels to ensure appropriate methotrexate clearance. Methotrexate levels are drawn daily per regimen or institutional protocol but are typically checked daily for 3-4 days following methotrexate but may continue until the drug is no longer detected in the patient's blood. Depending on the methotrexate level, supportive care may be altered to aid in methotrexate clearance (increasing fluid rate or increasing leucovorin dose).
  - Methotrexate is almost entirely eliminated in the urine and its excretion is pH dependent. Methotrexate clearance is improved when the urine is alkalized, and most methotrexate protocols will require the urine pH to be >7 before starting methotrexate. Alkalization protocols vary per institution but often use IV fluids, sodium bicarbonate (either IV or oral) and/or acetazolamide. Patient should have their urine pH routinely monitored (1-2 time per day) and their alkalization regimen adjust if urine pH is <7.
  - High dose methotrexate may "third space" or accumulate in fluid collections leading to prolonged methotrexate clearance and increased toxicity. Patients with ascites, pericardial effusions, pleural effusions or other fluid collections should not receive high dose methotrexate until those have been drained.
  - In patients with toxic methotrexate levels (toxic threshold depends on the protocol used), glucarpidase is an enzyme that is an antidote to methotrexate. Glucarpidase hydrolyzes the methotrexate into inactive metabolites rapidly reducing the methotrexate concentration. The typical dose is 50 units/kg and it should ideally be given within 48-60 hours of methotrexate infusion (beyond this point, life threating toxicities may not be preventable).
- **Drug Interactions**
  - Methotrexate has many drug interactions which can cause delayed clearance leading to toxicities like renal dysfunction, bone marrow suppression or mucositis. Patients' medications should be carefully screened prior to high dose methotrexate and they should be counseled on over the counter medications to avoid. Medications that must be stopped prior to high dose methotrexate include Bactrim, proton pump inhibitors, penicillin's, salicylates, probenecid, NSAIDs, tetracyclines, and ciprofloxacin.
    - Many of these agents can be stopped 1-2 days prior to high dose methotrexate and can be resumed after adequate clearance.

- Intrathecal methotrexate or low oral doses of methotrexate do not have the same drug interaction concerns.
- **Folic Acid/Vitamin B12**
  - Patients receiving pemetrexed require vitamin supplementation. Start vitamin supplements 1 week before initial pemetrexed dose: Folic acid 400 to 1,000 mcg orally once daily (begin 7 days prior to treatment initiation; continue daily during treatment and for 21 days after last pemetrexed dose) and vitamin B12 1,000 mcg IM 7 days prior to treatment initiation and then every 3 cycles.
- **Cutaneous reactions**
  - Serious and occasionally fatal dermatologic toxicity may occur with pemetrexed; pretreatment with dexamethasone 4 mg orally twice daily for 3 days is necessary to reduce the incidence and severity of cutaneous reactions.

High-Yield Fast-Facts

- **Oral methotrexate dosing frequency**
  - When checking doses on oral methotrexate, only oncologic indications will have daily dosing options. If a prescription for lupus, psoriasis, arthritis, etc. is written for daily (instead of weekly) it's likely an error!
- **Pemetrexed and Ibuprofen**
  - Patients with a CrCl 45 to 79 mL/minute must avoid ibuprofen for 2 days before, the day of, and for 2 days following a dose of pemetrexed. Monitor more frequently for myelosuppression, renal, and GI toxicities if concomitant ibuprofen administration cannot be avoided.

HIGH-YIELD BOARD EXAM ESSENTIALS
- **CLASSIC AGENTS:** Methotrexate, pemetrexed
- **DRUG CLASS:** Folate antagonists
- **INDICATIONS:** ALL, bladder cancer, graft vs host disease, head and neck cancer, non-Hodgkin lymphoma, osteosarcoma, soft tissue sarcoma
- **MECHANISM:** Inhibits dihydrofolate reductase and the formation of folate resulting in inhibition of DNA synthesis, repair, and cellular replication.
- **SIDE EFFECTS:** Mucositis, hepatitis, myelosuppression, renal injury, ocular injury, rash
- **CLINICAL PEARLS:** Methotrexate doses >500 mg/m2 require leucovorin "rescue." Leucovorin is folinic acid or an active form of folate that does not need to be processed by dihydrofolate reductase. It is given to rescue healthy cells from the toxicity of methotrexate and replenish the supply of folate metabolites depleted by methotrexate.

High-Yield Basic Pharmacology

- **Mechanism of Action**
  - Methylation of tumor suppressor genes can contribute to the growth and survival of the cancer. Hypomethylating agents decrease the amount of cellular DNA methylation allowing for tumor suppressor gene expression preventing cancer growth.

Primary Net Benefit

- Methylation of tumor suppressor genes can contribute to the growth and survival of the cancer. Hypomethylating agents decrease the amount of cellular DNA methylation allowing for tumor suppressor gene expression preventing cancer growth.

Hypomethylators Drug Class Review			
High-Yield Med Reviews			
Mechanism of Action: *Methylation of tumor suppressor genes can contribute to the growth and survival of the cancer. Hypomethylating agents decrease the amount of cellular DNA methylation allowing for tumor suppressor gene expression preventing cancer growth.*			
Class Effects: Bone marrow suppression, nausea/vomiting			
Generic Name	**Brand Name**	**Indication(s) or Uses**	**Notes**

Azacitidine	Vidaza	• Acute Myeloid Leukemia*
		 • Myelodysplastic Syndrome
			• **Dosing (Adult):** Dosing varies per formulation
			   – Oral 300 mg once daily on days 1 to 14 of a 28-day treatment cycle
			   – IV/SQ 75 mg/m^2 on days 1 to 7 of a 28-day treatment cycle
			 • **Dosing (Peds):** Same as adult
			 • **CYP450 Interactions:** None Known
			 • **Renal or Hepatic Dose Adjustments:** None
			 • **Dosage Forms:** 100 mg solution for IV injection; 200mg, 300 mg oral tablet.

Decitabine	Dacogen	• Acute Myeloid Leukemia*
		 • Myelodysplastic Syndrome
			• **Dosing (Adult):** Dosing varies per indication
			   – Typical dose range IV 15-20 mg/m^2 on days 1-5 or 1-10 of a 28-day treatment cycle
			   – Oral decitabine 35 mg/cedazuridine 100 mg once daily on days 1 to 5 of each 28-day treatment cycle
			 • **Dosing (Peds):** Same as adult
			 • **CYP450 Interactions:** None Known
			 • **Renal or Hepatic Dose Adjustments:** None
			 • **Dosage Forms:** 50 mg solution for IV injection; 35-100 mg oral tablet

*Off Label Use			

Emetic Potential

- **Minimal Emetic Risk (<10% frequency of emesis)**
  - Decitabine
- **Moderate Emetic Risk (30-90% frequency of emesis)**

- Azacitidine

Extravasation Risk

- None

High-Yield Clinical Knowledge

- **Time to response**
  - When used as single agent therapy, hypomethylators have a median response time of 3-4 months. These agents are typically well tolerated and are a good choice of therapy for older/frail patients who may not be able to tolerate intensive chemotherapy.
- **Bone Marrow Suppression**
  - Bone marrow suppression is the major side effect of the hypomethylators, however it can be difficult to determine if the cytopenias are from the chemotherapy or the patient's disease. In many cases, we will treat through cytopenias for the first few cycles of therapy (due to the long time to response of hypomethylators) but patients with cytopenias after 3-4 months of therapy may need a bone marrow biopsy to rule out relapsed disease.

High-Yield Fast-Facts

- **Combination Therapy**
  - Recent data has shown that patients have improved response rates when combining hypomethylators with venetoclax (an oral BCL2 inhibitor). This combination also increases toxicity but preferentially used in patients who can tolerate it.

HIGH-YIELD BOARD EXAM ESSENTIALS
- **CLASSIC AGENTS:** Azacitidine, decitabine
- **DRUG CLASS:** Hypomethylators
- **INDICATIONS:** AML, myelodysplastic syndrome
- **MECHANISM:** Methylation of tumor suppressor genes can contribute to the growth and survival of the cancer. Hypomethylating agents decrease the amount of cellular DNA methylation allowing for tumor suppressor gene expression preventing cancer growth.
- **SIDE EFFECTS:** Bone marrow suppression, nausea/vomiting
- **CLINICAL PEARLS:** When used as single agent therapy, hypomethylators have a median response time of 3-4 months. These agents are typically well tolerated and are a good choice of therapy for older/frail patients who may not be able to tolerate intensive chemotherapy.

High-Yield Basic Pharmacology

- **Mechanism of Action**
  - Alkylating agents which covalently binds to DNA and interfere with the function of DNA by producing interstrand DNA cross-links. They preferentially bind to the N-7 position of guanine

Primary Net Benefit

- Alkylating agents which covalently binds to DNA and interfere with the function of DNA by producing interstrand DNA cross-links. They preferentially bind to the N-7 position of guanine.

Platinum Agents Drug Class Review			
High-Yield Med Reviews			
Mechanism of Action: *Alkylating agents which covalently binds to DNA and interfere with the function of DNA by producing interstrand DNA cross-links.*			
Class Effects: Myelosuppression, nephrotoxicity, ototoxicity, hypersensitivity, peripheral neuropathy (cold induced neuropathy with oxaliplatin), nausea/vomiting,			
Generic Name	**Brand Name**	**Indication(s) or Uses**	**Notes**
Carboplatin	Paraplatin	▪ Anal Cancer* ▪ Bladder Cancer* ▪ Breast Cancer* ▪ Esophageal Cancer* ▪ Gastric Cancer* ▪ Head and Neck Cancer* ▪ Hodgkin Lymphoma* ▪ Non-Hodgkin Lymphoma* ▪ Non-Small Cell Lung Cancer* ▪ Gynecologic Cancers* ▪ Small Cell Lung Cancer* ▪ Testicular Cancer*	▪ **Dosing (Adult):** Dosing varies per regimen, based on area under the curve (AUC) with the Calvert Formula – Typical range AUC 2-6 – Total dose (mg) = Target AUC x (GFR + 25) ▪ **Dosing (Peds):** Dosing varies per regimen, may be based on mg/m^2, mg/kg or AUC ▪ **CYP450 Interactions:** None known ▪ **Renal or Hepatic Dose Adjustments:** Dose determination with Calvert formula uses GFR and inherently adjusts for renal dysfunction. ▪ **Dosage Forms:** 50 mg/5 mL, 150 mg/15 mL, 450 mg/45 mL, 600 mg/60 mL, 1000 mg/100 mL solution for IV injection
Cisplatin	N/A	▪ Anal Cancer* ▪ Bladder Cancer* ▪ Breast Cancer* ▪ Esophageal Cancer* ▪ Gastric Cancer* ▪ Head and Neck Cancer* ▪ Hodgkin Lymphoma* ▪ Non-Hodgkin Lymphoma* ▪ Non-Small Cell Lung Cancer* ▪ Gynecologic Cancers* ▪ Small Cell Lung Cancer* ▪ Testicular Cancer*	▪ **Dosing (Adult):** Dosing varies per regimen – Typical range $20\ mg/m^2$ - $100\ mg/m^2$ ▪ **Dosing (Peds):** Same as adult ▪ **CYP450 Interactions:** None known ▪ **Renal or Hepatic Dose Adjustments:** CrCl 46 to 60 mL/minute: Administer 75% of dose. CrCl 31 to 45 mL/minute: Administer 50% of dose. CrCl ≤30 mL/minute: use is not recommended ▪ **Dosage Forms:** 50 mg/50 mL, 100 mg/100 mL, 200 mg/200 mL solution for IV injection

<table>
<tr><th colspan="4" style="text-align:center">Platinum Agents Drug Class Review
High-Yield Med Reviews</th></tr>
<tr><th>Generic Name</th><th>Brand Name</th><th>Indication(s) or Uses</th><th>Notes</th></tr>
<tr>
<td>Oxaliplatin</td>
<td>N/A</td>
<td><ul><li>Biliary adenocarcinoma*</li><li>Colorectal cancer</li><li>Esophageal Cancer*</li><li>Gastric Cancer*</li><li>Non-Hodgkin Lymphoma*</li><li>Pancreatic Cancer*</li><li>Testicular Cancer*</li></ul></td>
<td><ul><li>Dosing (Adult): Dosing varies per regimen<ul><li>Typical range 85 mg/m^2 - 130 mg/m^2</li></ul></li><li>Dosing (Peds): Same as adult</li><li>CYP450 Interactions: None Known</li><li>Renal or Hepatic Dose Adjustments: CrCl <30 mL/minute: Reduce initial dose from 85 mg/m2 to 65 mg/m2</li><li>Dosage Forms: 50 mg/10 mL, 100 mg/20 mL, 200 mg/40 mL solution for IV injection</li></ul></td>
</tr>
<tr><td colspan="4">*Off label use</td></tr>
</table>

Emetic Potential

- **High emetic risk (>90% frequency of emesis)**
  - Cisplatin (commonly regarded as the most emetogenic of all chemotherapies)
  - Carboplatin AUC > 4
- **Moderate emetic risk (30-90% frequency of emesis)**
  - Carboplatin AUC < 4
  - Oxaliplatin

Extravasation Risk

- Oxaliplatin
  - Irritant with vesicant-like properties
  - If extravasation occurs, stop infusion immediately and aspirate extravasated solution. Data conflicts regarding use of warm or cold compresses, old compresses could potentially precipitate or exacerbate peripheral neuropathy

High-Yield Clinical Knowledge

- **Carboplatin Dosing**
  - Dosing is based on area under the curve (AUC) instead of BSA (mg/m2). The typical dosing range is an AUC of 2-6.
  - Dosing is done using the Calvert formula that automatically takes into account a patient's renal function
    - Total dose (mg) = Target AUC x (GFR + 25)
    - If estimating GFR instead of a measured GFR, protocols typically cap GFR at a maximum of 125 mL/minute to avoid potential toxicity (although this does vary per indication)
- **Peripheral Neuropathy**
  - Peripheral neuropathy is a major side effect of the platinums. This can be broken down into two types of neuropathy: acute and chronic
    - Chronic peripheral neuropathy mimics traditional peripheral neuropathy with numbness/tingling in the fingers and toes. This can occur >14 days after the dose. This neuropathy can be persistent and interfere with daily activities like writing or walking. These symptoms may improve in some patients upon discontinuing treatment.
    - Acute peripheral neuropathy is unique to oxaliplatin and presents as cold-induced neuropathy. This often occurs within hours of the oxaliplatin infusion and resolves within 7 days. Symptoms may include transient paresthesia, dysesthesia, and hypoesthesia in the hands, feet, perioral area, or throat; jaw spasm, abnormal tongue sensation, or a feeling of chest pressure. Patients should be counseled to avoid ice chips, exposure to cold temperatures, and cold food/beverages during or within hours after oxaliplatin infusion.

- **Nephrotoxicity**
  - All of the platinum agents have the potential to cause nephrotoxicity.
    - Patients should receive aggressive pre and post platinum hydration with normal saline, ideally targeting urine output of 100 mL/hour prior to the chemotherapy infusion.
    - Patients also should receive potassium and magnesium replacement as these agents (especially cisplatin) can cause electrolyte wasting.
- **Ototoxicity**
  - Cisplatin may cause cumulative and severe ototoxicity. Ototoxicity is manifested by tinnitus, high-frequency (4,000 to 8,000 Hz) hearing loss, and/or decreased ability to hear normal conversational tones. Ototoxicity may occur during or after treatment and may be unilateral or bilateral.
    - Ototoxicity is more common in children and the prevalence of hearing loss in pediatric patients treated with cisplatin is estimated to be 40% to 60%
    - Consider audiometric and vestibular testing, particularly in all pediatric patients receiving cisplatin.
- **Hypersensitivity Reactions**
  - Platinum agents are the second most common source of hypersensitivity reactions among chemotherapy agents (following asparaginase products).
    - Carboplatin: The incidence of carboplatin hypersensitivity reactions is between 1-44%. Reactions to carboplatin are most common after 6-8 doses but patients with mild-moderate reactions can be desensitized and may continue to receive infusions
    - Oxaliplatin: The incidence of acute reactions is between 12-25% of patients receiving oxaliplatin with up to 30% of those being severe infusion reactions. Reactions may occur within minutes of drug administration and with any cycle of therapy. Similar to carboplatin, the risk of hypersensitivity reaction is higher with multiple cycles of therapy. Patients with mild reactions may be re-challenged.

High-Yield Fast-Fact

- **Structure**
  - As the class name suggests, all of these agents have a platinum molecule at the center of their molecular structure

---

HIGH-YIELD BOARD EXAM ESSENTIALS
- **CLASSIC AGENTS:** Carboplatin, cisplatin, oxaliplatin
- **DRUG CLASS:** Platinum analogs
- **INDICATIONS:** Anal cancer, bladder cancer, breast cancer, esophageal cancer, gastric cancer, head and neck cancer, Hodgkin lymphoma, non-Hodgkin lymphoma, non-small cell lung cancer, gynecologic cancers, small cell lung cancer, testicular cancer
- **MECHANISM:** Alkylating agents which covalently binds to DNA and interfere with the function of DNA by producing interstrand DNA cross-links
- **SIDE EFFECTS:** Peripheral neuropathy, neurotoxicity, ototoxicity, nephrotoxicity, hypersensitivity
- **CLINICAL PEARLS:** Platinum agents are a common source of hypersensitivity reactions among chemotherapy agents. Reactions to carboplatin are most common after 6-8 doses but patients with mild-moderate reactions can be desensitized and may continue to receive infusions

High-Yield Basic Pharmacology

- **Mechanism of Action**
  - Purine antagonists inhibit DNA and RNA synthesis by acting as false metabolite. The anti-metabolite is incorporated into DNA and RNA, eventually inhibiting their synthesis. They are specific for the S phase of the cell cycle.

Primary Net Benefit

- Purine antagonists inhibit DNA and RNA synthesis by acting as false metabolite. The anti-metabolite is incorporated into DNA and RNA, eventually inhibiting their synthesis. They are specific for the S phase of the cell cycle.

Purine Antagonists Drug Class Review			
High-Yield Med Reviews			
Mechanism of Action: *Purine antagonists inhibit DNA and RNA synthesis by acting as false metabolite. The anti-metabolite is incorporated into DNA and RNA, eventually inhibiting their synthesis.*			
Class Effects: Cytopenias, nausea/vomiting, fatigue, poor appetite, rash, diarrhea, liver toxicity (6-MP)			
Generic Name	**Brand Name**	**Indication(s) or Uses**	**Notes**
Fludarabine	N/A	<ul><li>Chronic Lymphocytic Leukemia</li><li>Acute Myeloid Leukemia*</li><li>Hematopoietic Stem Cell Transplant*</li><li>Non-Hodgkin Lymphoma*</li></ul>	<ul><li>**Dosing (Adult):** Dosing varies per indication<ul><li>Typical dose range IV 25-40 mg/m^2</li></ul></li><li>**Dosing (Peds):** Same as adult<ul><li>Limited data available for use in pediatrics</li></ul></li><li>**CYP450 Interactions:** None Known</li><li>**Renal or Hepatic Dose Adjustments:** CrCl 50 to 79 mL/minute: Reduce dose to 20 mg/m2. CrCl 30 to 49 mL/minute: Reduce dose to 15 mg/m2. CrCl <30 mL/minute: Use is not recommended.</li><li>**Dosage Forms:** 50 mg solution for IV injection</li></ul>
6-Mercaptopurine	Purixan (Also known as 6-MP)	<ul><li>Acute Lymphoblastic Leukemia</li></ul>	<ul><li>**Dosing (Adult):** Dosing varies per indication<ul><li>Typical dose range oral 50-70 mg/m^2</li><li>Doses are often titrated based on blood counts</li></ul></li><li>**Dosing (Peds):** Same as adult</li><li>**CYP450 Interactions:** None Known</li><li>**Renal or Hepatic Dose Adjustments:** Hepatotoxicity during treatment: Withhold therapy</li><li>**Dosage Forms:** 50 mg oral tablet, 2000 mg/100mL oral solution</li></ul>
*Off Label Use			

Emetic Potential

- Minimal Emetic Risk (<10% frequency of emesis)
  - Fludarabine
- Minimal - Low Emetic Risk (<30% frequency of emesis)
  - 6-Mercaptopurine

Extravasation Risk

- None

High-Yield Clinical Knowledge

- **Genotyping and Dosing 6-mercaptopurine**
  - 6-MP doses for acute lymphoblastic leukemia are typically titrated to maintain an absolute neutrophil count (ANC) between 500-1500 cells/mcL. Methods of dose titration will vary per study/institution protocol but typically involve adjusting doses every 4-8 weeks.
  - In patients with abnormally low CBC unresponsive to dose reduction, severe bone marrow toxicities or repeated myelosuppressive episodes consider genotyping of NUDT15 and TPMT. NUDT15 and TPMT genotyping or phenotyping may assist in identifying patients at risk for developing toxicity and those who may needs empiric dose reductions due to decreased metabolism of 6-MP.

HIGH-YIELD BOARD EXAM ESSENTIALS

- **CLASSIC AGENTS:** 6-MP, fludarabine
- **DRUG CLASS:** Purine antagonists
- **INDICATIONS:** ALL, AML, CLL, HSCT, non-Hodgkin lymphoma
- **MECHANISM:** Purine antagonists inhibit DNA and RNA synthesis by acting as false metabolite. The anti-metabolite is incorporated into DNA and RNA, eventually inhibiting their synthesis.
- **SIDE EFFECTS:** Bone marrow toxicity, hepatotoxicity
- **CLINICAL PEARLS:** 6-MP doses for acute lymphoblastic leukemia are typically titrated to maintain an absolute neutrophil count (ANC) between 500-1500 cells/mcL. Methods of dose titration will vary per study/institution protocol but typically involve adjusting doses every 4-8 weeks.

High-Yield Basic Pharmacology

- **Mechanism of Action**
  - It interferes with DNA and RNA synthesis due to structural similarity to pyrimidine, the antimetabolite is substituted for normal building blocks of RNA/DNA and interferes with enzyme activity causing cell death
  - Capecitabine is an orally administered prodrug of 5-FU.

Primary Net Benefit

- It interferes with DNA and RNA synthesis due to structural similarity to pyrimidine, the antimetabolite is substituted for normal building blocks of RNA/DNA and interferes with enzyme activity causing cell death.

<table>
<tr>
<td colspan="4">Pyrimidine Antagonists Drug Class Review
High-Yield Med Reviews</td>
</tr>
<tr>
<td colspan="4">Mechanism of Action: Interferes with DNA and RNA synthesis due to structural similarity to pyrimidine, the antimetabolite is substituted for normal building blocks of RNA/DNA and interferes with enzyme activity causing cell death.</td>
</tr>
<tr>
<td colspan="4">Class Effects: Myelosuppression, fatigue, decreased appetite, hand/foot syndrome (5-FU/capecitabine), diarrhea, nausea/vomiting, skin reactions, mouth sores, hair loss/thinning</td>
</tr>
<tr>
<td>Generic Name</td>
<td>Brand Name</td>
<td>Indication(s) or Uses</td>
<td>Notes</td>
</tr>
<tr>
<td>Capecitabine</td>
<td>Xeloda</td>
<td>
<ul>
<li>Anal Cancer*</li>
<li>Breast Cancer</li>
<li>Colorectal Cancer</li>
<li>Esophageal and Gastric Cancers*</li>
<li>Head and Neck Cancers*</li>
<li>Pancreatic Cancer*</li>
</ul>
</td>
<td>
<ul>
<li>Dosing (Adult): Dosing varies per indication
  <ul><li>Typical range 650-1250 mg/m^2 twice daily on Days 1-14 of a 21-day cycle</li></ul>
</li>
<li>Dosing (Peds): Not routinely used in pediatrics</li>
<li>CYP450 Interactions: Inhibits CYP2C9 (weak)</li>
<li>Renal or Hepatic Dose Adjustments: CrCl 30 to 50 mL/minute: Initial: Reduce dose to 75% of usual dose. CrCl <30 mL/minute: Use is contraindicated. Hyperbilirubinemia, grade 3 or 4: Interrupt treatment until bilirubin ≤3 times ULN</li>
<li>Dosage Forms: 150 mg, 500 mg oral tablet</li>
</ul>
</td>
</tr>
<tr>
<td>Fluorouracil</td>
<td>N/A</td>
<td>
<ul>
<li>Anal Cancer*</li>
<li>Breast Cancer</li>
<li>Colorectal Cancer</li>
<li>Esophageal and Gastric Cancers</li>
<li>Head and Neck Cancers* Pancreatic Cancer</li>
</ul>
</td>
<td>
<ul>
<li>Dosing (Adult): Dosing varies per indication
  <ul><li>Typical range 200-1000 mg/m^2</li></ul>
</li>
<li>Dosing (Peds): Limited data available for use in pediatrics</li>
<li>CYP450 Interactions: text</li>
<li>Renal or Hepatic Dose Adjustments: Bilirubin >5 mg/dL: Avoid use</li>
<li>Dosage Forms: 1 g/20 mL, 2.5 gm/50 mL, 5 g/100 mL, 500 mg/10 mL solution for IV injection</li>
</ul>
</td>
</tr>
</table>

Pyrimidine Antagonists Drug Class Review
High-Yield Med Reviews

Generic Name	Brand Name	Indication(s) or Uses	Notes
Gemcitabine	Gemzar; Infugem	▪ Bladder Cancer* ▪ Breast Cancer* ▪ Head and Neck Cancer* ▪ Hodgkin Lymphoma* ▪ Non-Hodgkin Lymphoma* ▪ Non-Small Cell Lung Cancer ▪ Pancreatic Cancer* ▪ Small Cell Lung Cancer*	▪ **Dosing (Adult):** Dosing varies per indication – Typical dose 1000 mg/m^2 ▪ **Dosing (Peds):** Same as adult ▪ **CYP450 Interactions:** None known ▪ **Renal or Hepatic Dose Adjustments:** Serum bilirubin >1.6 mg/dL: Use initial dose of 800 mg/m^2; may escalate if tolerated ▪ **Dosage Forms:** 1 g/10 mL, 1 g/26.3 mL, 1.5 g/15 mL, 2 g/20 mL, 2 g/52.6 mL, 200 mg/2 mL, 200 mg/5.26 mL solution for IV injection
*Off Label Use			

Emetic Potential

- **Low Emetic Risk (10-30% frequency of emesis)**
  - Capecitabine
  - Gemcitabine
  - Fluorouracil

Extravasation Risk

- Fluorouracil may be an irritant, avoid extravasation.

High-Yield Clinical Knowledge

- **Continuous infusion 5-Flurourocil/Leucovorin**
  - 5-FU is given as a 46-hour continuous infusion with some chemotherapy regimens. In these cases, leucovorin is often given to enhance the mechanism of 5-FU by adding additional inhibition of thymidylate synthase. This leads to increased cancer cell death but can also cause increased toxicities.
  - In patients who are poorly tolerating their 5-FU/leucovorin containing regimens, you may consider dropping the leucovorin (instead of decreasing the 5-FU dose)
- **Oral Capecitabine**
  - Capecitabine is an orally administered prodrug of 5-FU. It can be used as an oral alternative to IV fluorouracil in many regimens.
  - Oral capecitabine has many drug interactions to be aware of; including proton pump inhibitors (which can decrease efficacy) and warfarin (increased INR).
  - It is often given in divided doses, 12 hours apart for 2 weeks on, 1 week off. It should be taken with food.
  - Oral administration is similar to continuous infusion 5-FU in terms of toxicity
- **Hand/Foot Syndrome**
  - Hand-foot syndrome is also called palmar-plantar erythrodysesthesia and is a common side effect of capecitabine/5-FU. Patients can experience redness, swelling, and pain on the palms of the hands and/or the soles of the feet.
  - It is thought to be caused by damage to the deep capillaries, leading to COX inflammatory-type reactions or related to enzymes involved in 5-FU metabolism
  - Hand/Foot syndrome can be prevented by avoiding friction causing activities (lifting weights, running), avoiding hot water or other sources of heat, and using lotions or creams to keep skin moist.
  - Hand/Foot syndrome is treated by holding chemotherapy and applying topical or oral anti-inflammatory agents and analgesics.

HIGH-YIELD BOARD EXAM ESSENTIALS

- **CLASSIC AGENTS:** Capecitabine, 5-fluorouracil (5-FU), gemcitabine
- **DRUG CLASS:** Pyrimidine antagonists
- **INDICATIONS:** Anal cancer, breast cancer, colorectal cancer, esophageal and gastric cancers, head and neck cancers, pancreatic cancer
- **MECHANISM:** Interferes with DNA and RNA synthesis due to structural similarity to pyrimidine, the antimetabolite is substituted for normal building blocks of RNA/DNA and interferes with enzyme activity causing cell death.
- **SIDE EFFECTS:** Extravasation, hand-foot syndrome, myelosuppression
- **CLINICAL PEARLS:** 5-FU is given as a 46-hour continuous infusion with some chemotherapy regimens. In these cases, leucovorin is often given to enhance the mechanism of 5-FU by adding additional inhibition of thymidylate synthase. This leads to increased cancer cell death but can also cause increased toxicities.

High-Yield Basic Pharmacology

- **Mechanism of Action**
  - Taxanes inhibit the mitotic spindle. They bind to the microtubules and prevent their depolymerization, therefore inhibiting mitosis and inducing apoptosis in cells undergoing the division process. These drugs are cell-cycle specific in the M-phase.
  - Primarily hepatic metabolism by CYP2C8 (Paclitaxel and Nab-Paclitaxel) and CYP3A4 (Docetaxel). Therefore, dose adjustments are recommended in patients with hepatic impairment

Primary Net Benefit

- Taxanes inhibit the mitotic spindle. They bind to the microtubules and prevent their depolymerization, therefore inhibiting mitosis and inducing apoptosis in cells undergoing the division process. These drugs are cell-cycle specific in the M-phase.

Taxanes Drug Class Review			
High-Yield Med Reviews			
Mechanism of Action: *Taxanes inhibit the mitotic spindle. They bind to the microtubules and prevent their depolymerization, therefore inhibiting mitosis and inducing apoptosis in cells undergoing the division process.*			
Class Effects: Myelosuppression, alopecia, peripheral neuropathy, myalgias, hypersensitivity reactions (paclitaxel), peripheral edema (docetaxel), diarrhea			
Generic Name	**Brand Name**	**Indication(s) or Uses**	**Notes**
Docetaxel	Taxotere	<ul><li>Breast Cancer</li><li>Esophageal Cancer*</li><li>Gastric Cancer</li><li>Head and Neck Cancer</li><li>Non-Small Cell Lung Cancer</li><li>Ovarian Cancer*</li><li>Prostate Cancer</li><li>Small Cell Lung Cancer*</li></ul>	<ul><li>**Dosing (Adult):** Dosing varies per indication<ul><li>Typical dose range 65-100 mg/m^2</li></ul></li><li>**Dosing (Peds):** Same as adult</li><li>**CYP450 Interactions:** Substrate of CYP3A4 (major), P-glycoprotein/ABCB1 (minor)</li><li>**Renal or Hepatic Dose Adjustments:** Total bilirubin > ULN or AST and/or ALT >1.5 times ULN concomitant with alkaline phosphatase >2.5 times ULN: Avoid docetaxel use. Transaminases 1.6 to 6 times ULN: Administer 75% of dose. Transaminases >6 times ULN: Use clinical judgment.</li><li>**Dosage Forms:** 20 mg/mL, 80 mg/4 mL, 160 mg/8 mL solution for IV injection</li></ul>
Paclitaxel	Taxol	<ul><li>Anal Cancer*</li><li>Bladder Cancer*</li><li>Breast Cancer</li><li>Cervical Cancer*</li><li>Endometrial Cancer*</li><li>Esophageal Cancer*</li><li>Gastric Cancer*</li><li>Head and Neck Cancer*</li><li>Kaposi Sarcoma</li><li>Non-Small Cell Lung Cancer</li><li>Ovarian Cancer</li><li>Small Cell Lung Cancer</li></ul>	<ul><li>**Dosing (Adult):** Dosing varies per indication<ul><li>Typical dose range 80-175 mg/m^2</li></ul></li><li>**Dosing (Peds):** Not routinely used in pediatrics</li><li>**CYP450 Interactions:** Substrate of CYP2C8 (major), CYP3A4 (major), P-glycoprotein/ABCB1 (minor)</li><li>**Renal or Hepatic Dose Adjustments:** Transaminases <10 times ULN and bilirubin level ≤1.25 times ULN: 175 mg/m^2. Transaminases <10 times ULN and bilirubin level 1.26 to 2 times ULN: 135 mg/m^2. Transaminases <10 times ULN and bilirubin level 2.01 to 5 times ULN: 90 mg/m^2. Transaminases ≥10 times ULN or bilirubin level >5 times ULN: Avoid use</li><li>**Dosage Forms:** 30 mg/5 mL, 100 mg/16.7 mL, 150 mg/25mL, 300 mg/50 mL solution for IV injection</li></ul>

Taxanes Drug Class Review			
High-Yield Med Reviews			
Generic Name	Brand Name	Indication(s) or Uses	Notes
Nab-Paclitaxel	Abraxane	▪ Biliary Cancer* ▪ Bladder Cancer* ▪ Breast Cancer ▪ Cervical Cancer* ▪ Non-Small Cell Lung Cancer ▪ Ovarian Cancer* ▪ Pancreatic Cancer	▪ **Dosing (Adult):** Dosing varies per indication – Typical dose range 100-150 mg/m^2 ▪ **Dosing (Peds):** Not routinely used in pediatrics ▪ **CYP450 Interactions:** Substrate of CYP2C8 (major), CYP3A4 (major), P-glycoprotein/ABCB1 (minor) ▪ **Renal or Hepatic Dose Adjustments:** Hepatic dose adjustments dependent on indication, reference package insert ▪ **Dosage Forms:** 100 mg suspension for IV injection
*Off Label Use			

Emetic Potential

- **Low Emetic Risk (10-30% frequency of emesis)**
  - Docetaxel
  - Paclitaxel
  - Nab-Paclitaxel

Extravasation Risk

- Irritant with vesicant-like properties
  - Paclitaxel extravasation: Consider the use of hyaluronidase. Administer 1 to 6 mL (150 units/mL) into existing IV line; usual dose is 1 mL for each 1 mL of extravasated drug.

High-Yield Clinical Knowledge

- **Infusion reactions with Paclitaxel**
  - Paclitaxel has poor water solubility. In order to be made into an IV solution it must be formulated with a polyethoxylated castor oil (Cremophor EL). This viscous solution is likely to cause hypersensitivity reactions, but these reactions are due to the cremophor (not the paclitaxel).
  - In order to prevent these reactions, patients should be premedicated with antihistamines and corticosteroids. Typically, patients receive dexamethasone 10-20 mg oral 12 and 6 hours prior to the paclitaxel infusion, plus diphenhydramine 50 mg IV and ranitidine 50 mg IV 30 minutes prior to the infusion.
- **Docetaxel peripheral edema**
  - Docetaxel has a black box warning for severe fluid retention. This is characterized by pleural effusions (requiring immediate drainage), ascites with pronounced abdominal distention, peripheral edema, dyspnea at rest, cardiac tamponade, and/or generalized edema.
  - Premedication with corticosteroids for 3 days, beginning the day before docetaxel administration, is recommended to prevent pulmonary/peripheral edema. Patients typically receive dexamethasone 8mg oral twice daily 1 day prior to docetaxel and continuing for 2 days after.
  - Unlike paclitaxel, docetaxel does not contain Cremophor, so it has a much lower risk of hypersensitivity reactions.

- **Paclitaxel vs Nab-Paclitaxel**
  - There are multiple paclitaxel formulations, including conventional paclitaxel and Nab-Paclitaxel (also called protein pound paclitaxel or Abraxane). Nab-Paclitaxel is not interchangeable with other paclitaxel formulations and cannot be substituted for conventional paclitaxel.

High-Yield Fast-Facts

- **History of taxanes**
  - They were discovered in 1971 by NCI researchers during a plant screening program. A crude extract with anti-tumor activity was isolated from the bark of the Pacific Yew, *Taxus brevifolia*. However, the amount of paclitaxel in yew bark was small and extracting it was complicated and expensive. The collection of Pacific Yew bark also became restricted for environmental reasons. This led to production of semi-synthetic form of paclitaxel derived from the needles of the Himalayan yew tree, *Taxus bacatta*.

HIGH-YIELD BOARD EXAM ESSENTIALS
- **CLASSIC AGENTS:** Docetaxel, paclitaxel, nab-paclitaxel
- **DRUG CLASS:** Taxanes
- **INDICATIONS:** anal cancer, bladder cancer, breast cancer, cervical cancer, endometrial cancer, esophageal cancer, gastric cancer, head and neck cancer, Kaposi sarcoma, non-small cell lung cancer, ovarian cancer, small cell lung cancer
- **MECHANISM:** Taxanes inhibit the mitotic spindle. They bind to the microtubules and prevent their depolymerization, therefore inhibiting mitosis and inducing apoptosis in cells undergoing the division process.
- **SIDE EFFECTS:** Infusion reactions, edema, pulmonary edema
- **CLINICAL PEARLS:** Paclitaxel has poor water solubility. In order to be made into an IV solution it must be formulated with a polyethoxylated castor oil (Cremophor EL). This viscous solution is likely to cause hypersensitivity reactions, but these reactions are due to the cremophor (not the paclitaxel). In order to prevent these reactions, patients should be premedicated with antihistamines and corticosteroids.

High-Yield Basic Pharmacology

- **Mechanism of Action**
  - Topoisomerase is an essential enzyme found in all nucleated cells and is responsible for the regulation of DNA topology. DNA is wound around basic proteins called histones and supercoiled however; DNA must be relaxed before it can be copied. Topoisomerases introduce single (topoisomerase I) or double stranded nicks (topoisomerase II) into DNA to allow DNA relaxation. In the presence of topoisomerase inhibitors, these nicks remain, and the DNA is damaged causing cell death
    - Irinotecan: in patients with hepatic function impairment clearance is decreased and exposure to the active metabolite (SN-38) is increased proportional to the degree of hepatic impairment.
    - Etoposide: in renal function impairment, total body clearance is reduced, AUC is increased, and V_d is lower.

Primary Net Benefit

- Damage DNA in cancer cells leading to their death but unfortunately other cells die along with them.

Topoisomerase Inhibitors Drug Class Review			
High-Yield Med Reviews			
Mechanism of Action: *Topoisomerases introduce single (topoisomerase I) or double stranded nicks (topoisomerase II) into DNA to allow DNA relaxation. In the presence of topoisomerase inhibitors, these nicks remain and the DNA is damaged causing cell death.*			
Class Effects: Dose limiting diarrhea (irinotecan), Myelosuppression, Alopecia, Mucositis, risk of secondary malignancies, hypotension (etoposide), nausea/vomiting			
Generic Name	**Brand Name**	**Indication(s) or Uses**	**Notes**
Etoposide	Toposar, VePesid, (Also known by the acronym VP-16)	▪ Breast Cancer* ▪ Hematopoietic Stem Cell Transplant* ▪ Hemophagocytic lymphohistiocytosis* ▪ Hodgkin Lymphoma* ▪ Non-Hodgkin Lymphoma* ▪ Non-Small Cell Lung Cancer* ▪ Small Cell Lung Cancer ▪ Testicular Cancer*	▪ **Dosing (Adult):** Dosing varies per indication – Typical dose range 50-200 mg/m^2 IV, 50 mg/m^2 oral ▪ **Dosing (Peds):** Same as adult ▪ **CYP450 Interactions:** Substrate of CYP1A2 (minor), CYP2E1 (minor), CYP3A4 (major), P-glycoprotein/ABCB1 (major). ▪ **Renal or Hepatic Dose Adjustments:** CrCl 10 to 50 mL/minute: Administer 75% of dose. CrCl <10 mL minute: Administer 50% of dose. Bilirubin 1.5 to 3 mg/dL or AST >3 times ULN: Administer 50% of dose. ▪ **Dosage Forms:** 1 gm/50 mL, 100 mg/5 mL, 500 mg/25 mL solution for IV injection. 50 mg oral capsule.

		Topoisomerase Inhibitors Drug Class Review	
		High-Yield Med Reviews	
Generic Name	**Brand Name**	**Indication(s) or Uses**	**Notes**
Irinotecan	Camptosar	<ul><li>Colorectal Cancer</li><li>Esophageal Cancer*</li><li>Gastric Cancer*</li><li>Non-Small Cell Lung Cancer*</li><li>Pancreatic Cancer*</li><li>Small Cell Lung Cancer*</li></ul>	<ul><li>**Dosing (Adult):** Dosing varies per indication<ul><li>Typical dose range 50-165 mg/m^2</li></ul></li><li>**Dosing (Peds):** Limited data available for use in pediatrics.</li><li>**CYP450 Interactions:** Substrate of BCRP/ABCG2, CYP3A4 (major), OATP1B1/1B3 (SLCO1B1/1B3), P-glycoprotein/ABCB1 (minor), UGT1A1</li><li>**Renal or Hepatic Dose Adjustments:** Bilirubin >ULN to ≤2 mg/dL: Consider reducing initial dose by one dose level. Bilirubin >2 mg/dL: Use is not recommended</li><li>**Dosage Forms:** 40 mg/2 mL, 100 mg/5 mL, 300 mg/15 mL, 500 mg/25 mL solution for IV injection</li></ul>
Topotecan	Hycamtin	<ul><li>Cervical Cancer*</li><li>CNS Malignancy*</li><li>Ewing Sarcoma*</li><li>Ovarian Cancer</li><li>Rhabdomyosarcoma*</li><li>Small Cell Lung Cancer</li></ul>	<ul><li>**Dosing (Adult):** Dosing varies per indication<ul><li>Typical dose range IV: 0.75-1.5 mg/m^2, Oral: 0.8-2.3 mg/m^2</li></ul></li><li>**Dosing (Peds):** Same as adult</li><li>**CYP450 Interactions:** Substrate of BCRP/ABCG2, P-glycoprotein/ABCB1 (major)</li><li>**Renal or Hepatic Dose Adjustments:** CrCl 46 to 60 mL/minute: Administer 80% of usual dose. CrCl 31 to 45 mL/minute: Administer 75% of usual dose. CrCl ≤30 mL/minute: Administer 70% of usual dose.</li><li>**Dosage Forms:** 4 mg/mL solution for IV injection. 0.25 mg, 1 mg oral capsule.</li></ul>
*Off Label Use			

Emetic Potential

- **Low Emetic Risk (10-30% frequency of emesis)**
  - Etoposide
  - Topotecan
- **Moderate Emetic Risk (30-90% frequency of emesis)**
  - Irinotecan

Extravasation Risk

- Irritants

High-Yield Clinical Knowledge

- **Irinotecan Induced Diarrhea**
  - Irinotecan induced diarrhea occurs in two phases, early onset and late onset.
  - Early-onset diarrhea occurs during or within 24 hours of infusion. This is caused by direct inhibition of acetylcholinesterase by irinotecan and is accompanied with cholinergic symptoms such as cramps, diaphoresis, flushing, salivation, visual disturbances, and lacrimation. Acute diarrhea is treated with

atropine 0.25-1 mg SQ or IV. Patients may also be given atropine as secondary prophylaxis after experiencing acute diarrhea in previous chemotherapy cycles.

- Late-onset diarrhea is the dose limiting toxicity of irinotecan and typically occurs >24 hours after drug administration (median time to onset is 6 days). This is thought to occur due to secretory processes caused by the active metabolite of irinotecan. Late onset diarrhea is treated with high dose loperamide and supportive care including fluids if needed. Patient should be instructed to take loperamide 4 mg at first sign of diarrhea, followed by 2 mg every 2 hours (4 mg every 4 hours at night) until 12 hours following last bowel movement up to 24 mg/day. Exceeding the daily limit of loperamide 16 mg/day is recommended for treatment of irinotecan-associated diarrhea in adults. Atropine has no role in the treatment of late onset diarrhea.

- **Race and its effect on Topotecan exposure**
  - Following oral topotecan administration in patients with normal renal function, the AUC of topotecan lactone and total topotecan was 30% higher in Asian patients as compared to white patients.

- **UGT1A1 Genotyping with Irinotecan**
  - Patients homozygous for the UGT1A1*28 allele are at increased risk of neutropenia. Heterozygous carriers of the UGT1A1*28 allele may also be at increased neutropenic risk; however, most patients have tolerated normal starting doses.
  - A test is available for genotyping of UGT1A1; however, use of the test is not widely accepted as dose reductions are already recommended in patients who have experienced toxicity regardless of genotype.

HIGH-YIELD BOARD EXAM ESSENTIALS

- **CLASSIC AGENTS:** Etoposide, irinotecan, topotecan
- **DRUG CLASS:** Topoisomerase inhibitors
- **INDICATIONS:** Breast cancer, colorectal cancer, hematopoietic stem cell transplant, hemophagocytic lymphohistiocytosis, Hodgkin lymphoma, non-Hodgkin lymphoma, non-small cell lung cancer, small cell lung cancer, testicular cancer
- **MECHANISM:** Topoisomerases introduce single (topoisomerase I) or double stranded nicks (topoisomerase II) into DNA to allow DNA relaxation. In the presence of topoisomerase inhibitors, these nicks remain and the DNA is damaged causing cell death.
- **SIDE EFFECTS:** Diarrhea
- **CLINICAL PEARLS:**
  - Early-onset diarrhea occurs during or within 24 hours of infusion. This is caused by direct inhibition of acetylcholinesterase by irinotecan and is accompanied with cholinergic symptoms such as cramps, diaphoresis, flushing, salivation, visual disturbances, and lacrimation.
  - Acute diarrhea is treated with atropine 0.25-1 mg SQ or IV. Patients may also be given atropine as secondary prophylaxis after experiencing acute diarrhea in previous chemotherapy cycles.
  - Patients homozygous for the UGT1A1*28 allele are at increased risk of neutropenia

High-Yield Basic Pharmacology

- **Mechanism of Action**
  - Binds to tubulin and inhibits microtubule formation stopping cell growth by disrupting the formation of the mitotic spindle. These drugs specifically target the M and S phases of the cell cycle.

Primary Net Benefit

- Disrupt cancerous cells from further division.

VINCA ALKLOIDS Drug Class Review				
High-Yield Med Reviews				
Mechanism of Action: *Binds to tubulin and inhibits microtubule formation stopping cell growth by disrupting the formation of the mitotic spindle*				
Class Effects: peripheral and autonomic neuropathy, GI disturbances, myelosuppression (except vincristine)				
Generic Name	**Brand Name**	**Indication(s) or Uses**		**Notes**
Vincristine	Vincasar	<ul><li>Acute lymphoblastic leukemia</li><li>Non-Hodgkin lymphoma</li><li>Rhabdomyosarcoma</li><li>Central nervous system tumors*</li><li>Chronic lymphocytic leukemia/small lymphocytic leukemia*</li><li>Ewing sarcoma*</li><li>Hodgkin lymphoma*</li></ul>		<ul><li>**Dosing (Adult):** Dosing varies per regimen<ul><li>Doses are often capped at 2 mg/dose</li></ul></li><li>**Dosing (Peds):** Dosing varies per regimen<ul><li>Children <30kg are often dosed based on mg/kg/dose</li></ul></li><li>**CYP450 Interactions:** Major substrate of CYP3A4</li><li>**Renal or Hepatic Dose Adjustments:** Administer 50% of dose if bilirubin is 1.5-3 mg/dL and hold for bilirubin >3 mg/dL.</li><li>**Dosage Forms:** 1 mg/mL solution for IV injection</li></ul>
Vinblastine	N/A	<ul><li>Soft Tissue Sarcoma</li><li>Hodgkin lymphoma</li><li>Testicular cancer</li><li>Kaposi Sarcoma</li><li>Bladder cancer*</li><li>Non-small cell lung cancer*</li></ul>		<ul><li>**Dosing (Adult):** Dosing varies per regimen<ul><li>Typical range 3 mg/m^2 - 6 mg/m^2</li></ul></li><li>**Dosing (Peds):** same as adult</li><li>**CYP450 Interactions:** Major CYP3A4 substrate, minor CYP2D6 substrate, Minor P-glycoprotein substrate</li><li>**Renal or Hepatic Dose Adjustments:** Administer 50% of dose if bilirubin is 1.5-3 mg/dL and hold for bilirubin >3 mg/dL.</li><li>**Dosage Forms:** 1 mg/mL solution for IV injection</li></ul>

VINCA ALKLOIDS Drug Class Review
High-Yield Med Reviews

Generic Name	Brand Name	Indication(s) or Uses	Notes

Vinorelbine	Navelbine	■ Non-small cell lung cancer
		■ Breast cancer*
		■ Cervical cancer*
		■ Hodgkin lymphoma*
		■ Mesothelioma*
		■ Ovarian cancer*
		■ Small cell lung cancer*
		■ Soft tissue sarcoma*
			■ **Dosing (Adult):** Dosing varies per regimen
			  – Typical range 15 mg/m^2 - 30 mg/m^2
			■ **Dosing (Peds):** Same as adult
			  – Dosing may be based on BSA (mg/m^2) or weight (mg/kg), use caution when checking doses
			■ **CYP450 Interactions:** Major CYP3A4 substrate, minor CYP2D6 substrate
			■ **Renal or Hepatic Dose Adjustments:** Administer 50% of dose if bilirubin is 2.1-3 mg/dL and 25% of dose if bilirubin is >3 mg/dL. For patients on hemodialysis reduce dose to 20 mg/m^2 once a week
			■ **Dosage Forms:** 10 mg/mL and 50 mg/5 mL solution for IV injection

*Off-label Indication			

Emetic Potential

- Minimal (<10% frequency of emesis)

Extravasation Risk

- Vesicants - avoid extravasation
    - If extravasation occurs, stop infusion immediately and gently aspirate extravasated solution (do not flush the line). Initiate hyaluronidase antidote and apply warm dry compresses for 20 minutes four times a day for 1-2 days.

High-Yield Clinical Knowledge

- **These agents are for IV use only and are FATAL if administered intrathecally**
    - The Institute for Safe Mediation Practices (ISMP) recommends dispensing vinca alkaloids in a mini-bag (**not** a syringe) to prevent inadvertent intrathecal administration.
    - Vincristine is commonly used in the treatment of adult and pediatric ALL which also includes frequent administration of intrathecal chemotherapy. ISMP has reported 135 fatalities worldwide due to inadvertent intrathecal administration of vincristine, all of which were dispensed in a syringe.
- **Myelosuppression**
    - When used as a single agent, Vincristine does not typically cause myelosuppression. Vinorelbine and vinblastine however can both cause cytopenias.
- **Neuropathy**
    - The most common dose limiting side effect of the vinca alkaloids is neuropathy. This can not only affect the peripheral nerves (leading to numbness and tingling in the extremities) but it can also affect the autonomic nerves leading to constipation.
    - Patient should be on an aggressive bowel regimen while receiving vinca alkaloids and be evaluated for neuropathy at every visit. The presence of peripheral neuropathy may require a dose reduction or omission of the vinca alkaloid.
- **Hepatotoxicity**
    - All of the vinca alkaloids are hepatically metabolized and require hepatic dose adjustments. The only exception is based on clinical judgement if the liver dysfunction is known to be due to disease.

High-Yield Fast-Facts

- **History of Vinca Alkaloids**
    - They are derived from the Madagascar periwinkle plant, Vinca rosea. This plant was said to be useful in the treatment of diabetes. Attempts to verify the antidiabetic properties of the plants extracts in the 1950's led instead to the discovery and isolation of vinblastine.
    - Scientists first observed vinblastine's anticancer properties in a lab in 1962 with the observation of regression of lymphocytic leukemia in rats.

HIGH-YIELD BOARD EXAM ESSENTIALS

- **CLASSIC AGENTS:** Vincristine, vinorelbine, vinblastine
- **DRUG CLASS:** Vinca alkaloids
- **INDICATIONS:** ALL, non-Hodgkin lymphoma, rhabdomyosarcoma, CNS tumors, chronic lymphocytic leukemia/small lymphocytic leukemia, Ewing sarcoma, Hodgkin lymphoma
- **MECHANISM:** Binds to tubulin and inhibits microtubule formation stopping cell growth by disrupting the formation of the mitotic spindle
- **SIDE EFFECTS:** Neuropathy, myelosuppression, hepatotoxicity
- **CLINICAL PEARLS:** The most common dose limiting side effect of the vinca alkaloids is neuropathy. This can not only affect the peripheral nerves (leading to numbness and tingling in the extremities) but it can also affect the autonomic nerves leading to constipation.

High-Yield Basic Pharmacology

- **Mechanism of Action**
  - Inhibits aromatase which is the enzyme responsible for the conversion of androgens to estrogens, this leads to a significant decrease in circulating estrogen.
- **Metabolism**
  - Primarily hepatic
- **Onset of Action**
  - 70% estradiol reduction after 24 hours; 80% after 2 weeks of therapy

Primary Net Benefit

- Reduce estrogen mediated stimulation of breast cancer tissue.

Aromatase Inhibitors Drug Class Review			
High-Yield Med Reviews			
Mechanism of Action: *Inhibits aromatase which is the enzyme responsible for the conversion of androgens to estrogens, this leads to a significant decrease in circulating estrogen*			
Class Effects: Hot flashes, arthralgias/myalgias, mild headache, diarrhea, bone loss (osteoporosis, fractures), vaginal dryness, cardiovascular events			
Generic Name	**Brand Name**	**Main Indication(s) or Uses**	**Notes**
Anastrozole	Arimidex	▪ Breast Cancer	▪ **Dosing (Adult):** 1mg orally daily ▪ **Dosing (Peds):** Not used in pediatrics ▪ **CYP450 Interactions:** None known ▪ **Renal or Hepatic Dose Adjustments:** None ▪ **Dosage Forms:** 1mg oral tablet
Exemestane	Femara	▪ Breast Cancer	▪ **Dosing (Adult):** 2.5 mg orally daily ▪ **Dosing (Peds):** Not used in pediatrics ▪ **CYP450 Interactions:** Substrate of CYP2A6 (minor), CYP3A4 (minor) ▪ **Renal or Hepatic Dose Adjustments:** Severe hepatic impairment: 2.5 mg every other day ▪ **Dosage Forms:** 2.5 mg oral tablet
Letrozole	Aromasin	▪ Breast Cancer	▪ **Dosing (Adult):** 25 mg orally daily ▪ **Dosing (Peds):** Not used in pediatrics ▪ **CYP450 Interactions:** Substrate of CYP3A4 (major) ▪ **Renal or Hepatic Dose Adjustments:** None ▪ **Dosage Forms:** 25 mg oral tablet
*Off Label Use			

Emetic Potential

- N/A

Extravasation Risk

- N/A

High-Yield Clinical Knowledge

- **Non-steroidal vs steroidal**
  - Anastrazole and letrozole are non-steroidal aromatase inhibitors, they decrease estrogen synthesis without compromising adrenal steroid synthesis
  - Exemestane is a steroidal aromatase inhibitor, it has a similar structure to androgen and irreversibly binds to aromatase
- **Use in premenopausal women**
  - Aromatase inhibitors work in the peripheral fat to decrease estrogen synthesis. In pre-menopausal women, estrogen is also being produced by the ovaries, so aromatase inhibitors are NOT effective therapy for pre-menopausal women. This includes women who are experiencing therapy-induced amenorrhea. Some sort of ovarian suppression must be used in pre-menopausal women receiving AIs.
  - An AI is the preferred adjuvant treatment of post-menopausal women, although tamoxifen is an acceptable alternative for women who are intolerant of AIs.
- **Musculoskeletal side effects**
  - AIs are commonly associated with musculoskeletal side effects. These include carpal tunnel, arthralgias, joint stiffness, and/or bone pain. In up to 1/3 of patients these symptoms can be severe and may be the cause of treatment discontinuation in 10-20% of patients on AIs. The best strategy for managing these adverse effects includes exercise and nonsteroidal anti-inflammatory drugs.
- **Duration of therapy**
  - ASCO guidelines for Adjuvant Endocrine Therapy of Hormone Receptor-Positive Breast Cancer recommend a maximum duration of 5 years of aromatase inhibitor therapy for postmenopausal women. AIs may be combined with tamoxifen for a total duration of up to 10 years of endocrine therapy.

High-Yield Fast-Fact

- **Risk reduction**
  - Aromatase inhibitors are currently being studied as risk reduction agents in post-menopausal women at a high risk for breast cancer

---

HIGH-YIELD BOARD EXAM ESSENTIALS
- **CLASSIC AGENTS:** Anastrozole, exemestane, letrozole
- **DRUG CLASS:** Aromatase inhibitors
- **INDICATIONS:** Breast cancer
- **MECHANISM:** Inhibits aromatase which is the enzyme responsible for the conversion of androgens to estrogens, this leads to a significant decrease in circulating estrogen.
- **SIDE EFFECTS:** Carpal tunnel, arthralgias, joint stiffness, and/or bone pain
- **CLINICAL PEARLS:** Aromatase inhibitors work in the peripheral fat to decrease estrogen synthesis. In pre-menopausal women, estrogen is also being produced by the ovaries, so aromatase inhibitors are NOT effective therapy for pre-menopausal women. An AI is the preferred adjuvant treatment of postmenopausal women, although tamoxifen is an acceptable alternative for women who are intolerant of AIs.

High-Yield Basic Pharmacology

- **Mechanism of Action**
  - Binds to estrogen receptors on tumors and other tissue targets inhibiting estrogens effects
- **Metabolism**
  - Primarily hepatic
- **Bioavailability of tamoxifen**
  - Tamoxifen oral solution is bioequivalent to tamoxifen tablets

Primary Net Benefit

- Prevent the growth of cancer cells with estrogen receptors.

Estrogen Receptors Antagonists Drug Class Review High-Yield Med Reviews			
Mechanism of Action: *Binds to estrogen receptors on tumors and other tissue targets inhibiting estrogens effects*			
Class Effects: Hot flashes, vaginal dryness/discharge, irregular menses, endometrial thickening, thromboembolism, endometrial/uterine cancer (rare)			
Generic Name	**Brand Name**	**Indication(s) or Uses**	**Notes**
Tamoxifen	Soltamox	▪ Breast Cancer	▪ **Dosing (Adult):** 20 mg orally daily ▪ **Dosing (Peds):** Not used in pediatrics ▪ **CYP450 Interactions:** Substrate of CYP2A6 (minor), CYP2B6 (minor), CYP2C9 (minor), CYP2D6 (major), CYP2E1 (minor), CYP3A4 (major); Inhibits CYP2C9 (weak) ▪ **Renal or Hepatic Dose Adjustments:** None ▪ **Dosage Forms:** 10 mg, 20 mg oral tablet. 10 mg/5mL oral solution.
Fulvestrant	Faslodex	▪ Breast Cancer	▪ **Dosing (Adult):** IM: Initial: 500 mg on days 1, 15, and 29; Maintenance: 500 mg once monthly ▪ **Dosing (Peds):** Not used in pediatrics ▪ **CYP450 Interactions:** Substrate of CYP3A4 (minor) ▪ **Renal or Hepatic Dose Adjustments:** Moderate hepatic impairment: Reduce initial and maintenance doses: Initial: 250 mg on days 1, 15, and 29; Maintenance: 250 mg once monthly. ▪ **Dosage Forms:** 250 mg/5 mL solution for intramuscular injection

Emetic Potential

- N/A

Extravasation Risk

- N/A

- **Management of Hot Flashes**
  - Chemotherapy and tamoxifen can cause more frequent and severe hot flashes than natural menopause, which often results in decreased quality of life and may affect medication adherence. They are thought to be due to a central nervous system antiestrogenic effects causing thermoregulatory dysfunction. 80% of women prescribed tamoxifen complain of hot flashes, with 30% of those having severe symptoms. Premenopausal women, polymorphisms in drug metabolizing enzymes, co-administration of drugs that inhibit the activity of CYP2D6, and specific estrogen receptor genotypes may increase the risk of developing hot flashes.
  - Venlafaxine 75 mg orally daily has been shown to be more effective in managing hot flashes when compared to placebo, clonidine and gabapentin. Data also supports the use of paroxetine, fluoxetine, sertraline, and citalopram to manage hot flashes.
- **Place in therapy**
  - Tamoxifen is the endocrine agent of choice for the adjuvant treatment of premenopausal women with breast cancer and for postmenopausal women who are not candidates for an aromatase inhibitor for whatever reason.
- **Thromboembolism**
  - Tamoxifen is associated with an increased rate of thromboembolism and that there is a significant procoagulant effect when tamoxifen is added to chemotherapy. The relative risks of venous thromboembolism are increased 2-3-fold in older women receiving tamoxifen and this elevated risk continues as long as the patient takes the drug.
- **Bone Loss Prevention**
  - Unlike the aromatase inhibitors, tamoxifen may help prevent bone loss and lowers total cholesterol
- **Drug interactions with Tamoxifen**
  - Tamoxifen is converted to its active metabolites by CYP2D6 and UGT2B7. Drugs that inhibit CYP2D6 (fluoxetine and paroxetine) may potentially alter the metabolism of tamoxifen.

HIGH-YIELD BOARD EXAM ESSENTIALS
- **CLASSIC AGENTS:** Fulvestrant, tamoxifen
- **DRUG CLASS:** ER antagonists
- **INDICATIONS:** Breast cancer
- **MECHANISM:** Binds to estrogen receptors on tumors and other tissue targets inhibiting estrogens effects
- **SIDE EFFECTS:** VTE, hot flashes
- **CLINICAL PEARLS:** Tamoxifen is converted to its active metabolites by CYP2D6 and UGT2B7. Drugs that inhibit CYP2D6 (fluoxetine and paroxetine) may potentially alter the metabolism of tamoxifen.

High-Yield Basic Pharmacology

- **Mechanism of Action:**
  - Agonist analog of gonadotropin releasing hormone (GnRH) and causes suppression of ovarian and testicular steroidogenesis due to decreased levels of LH and FSH with subsequent decrease in testosterone (male) and estrogen (female) levels.
- **Onset of action**
  - Following a transient increase, testosterone suppression occurs in ~2 to 4 weeks of continued therapy

Primary Net Benefit

- Prevent cancerous tissue growth due to androgen stimulation.

<table>
<tr><td colspan="4">GNRH Agonists Drug Class Review
High-Yield Med Reviews</td></tr>
<tr><td colspan="4">Mechanism of Action: Agonist analog of gonadotropin releasing hormone (GnRH) and causes suppression of ovarian and testicular steroidogenesis due to decreased levels of LH and FSH with subsequent decrease in testosterone (male) and estrogen (female) levels</td></tr>
<tr><td colspan="4">Class Effects: Tumor flare, gynecomastia, hot flashes, erectile dysfunction, edema, injection site reactions</td></tr>
<tr>
<th>Generic Name</th>
<th>Brand Name</th>
<th>Indication(s) or Uses</th>
<th>Notes</th>
</tr>
<tr>
<td>Triptorelin</td>
<td>Trelstar Mixject; Triptodur</td>
<td>
<ul>
<li>Prostate Cancer</li>
<li>Endometrial stromal sarcoma*</li>
</ul>
</td>
<td>
<ul>
<li>Dosing (Adult): IM 3.75 mg once every 4 weeks or 11.25 mg once every 12 weeks or 22.5 mg once every 24 weeks</li>
<li>Dosing (Peds): Not used in pediatric cancer treatment</li>
<li>CYP450 Interactions: None known</li>
<li>Renal or Hepatic Dose Adjustments: None</li>
<li>Dosage Forms: 3.75 mg, 11.25 mg, 22.5 mg suspension for IM injection, 22.5 mg ER suspension for IM injection</li>
</ul>
</td>
</tr>
<tr>
<td>Goserelin</td>
<td>Zoladex</td>
<td>
<ul>
<li>Breast Cancer</li>
<li>Prostate Cancer</li>
<li>Prevention of early menopause during chemotherapy*</li>
</ul>
</td>
<td>
<ul>
<li>Dosing (Adult): Dosing varies per indication
<ul><li>Typical dose range SQ 3.6 mg every 28 days or 10.8 mg every 12 weeks.</li></ul>
</li>
<li>Dosing (Peds): Not used in pediatrics</li>
<li>CYP450 Interactions: None known</li>
<li>Renal or Hepatic Dose Adjustments: None</li>
<li>Dosage Forms: 3.6 mg, 10.8 mg subcutaneous implant</li>
</ul>
</td>
</tr>
</table>

<table>
<tr><td colspan="4" align="center">**GNRH Agonists Drug Class Review**
High-Yield Med Reviews</td></tr>
<tr><th>Generic Name</th><th>Brand Name</th><th>Indication(s) or Uses</th><th>Notes</th></tr>
<tr>
<td>**Leuprolide**</td>
<td>Brand Name (if available)</td>
<td>
• Breast Cancer*
• Prostate Cancer
• Prevention of early menopause during chemotherapy*
</td>
<td>
• **Dosing (Adult):** Dosing varies per indication
  – Typical dose range IM: 7.5 mg every month or 22.5 mg every 12 weeks or 30 mg every 16 weeks or 45 mg every 24 weeks. SQ: 7.5 mg monthly or 22.5 mg every 3 months or 30 mg every 4 months or 45 mg every 6 months
• **Dosing (Peds):** Not used in pediatric cancer treatment
• **CYP450 Interactions:** None known
• **Renal or Hepatic Dose Adjustments:** None
• **Dosage Forms:** 7.5 mg, 22.5 mg, 30 mg, 45 mg subcutaneous injection; 3.75 mg, 7.5 mg, 22.5 mg, 30 mg, 45 mg intramuscular depot injection
</td>
</tr>
<tr><td colspan="4">*Off Label Use</td></tr>
</table>

Emetic Potential

- N/A

Extravasation Risk

- N/A

High-Yield Clinical Knowledge

- **Goal of therapy**
    - The goal of therapy with prostate cancer, is to induce castrate levels of testosterone. This can be accomplished by surgical castration (orchiectomy) or medical/chemical castration (GNRH agonists or antagonists).
    - When using GNRH agonists, the goal serum testosterone level is <50 ng/dl after 1 month of therapy
- **Long term adverse effects**
    - Long term use of GNRH agonists can cause adverse effects related to decreased testosterone levels including: osteoporosis, bone fractures, obesity, insulin resistance, hyperlipidemia, increased risk of diabetes and cardiovascular events.
- **Disease flare**
    - Disease flare with GNRH agonists is thought to be caused by initial induction of luteinizing hormone (LH) and follicle stimulating hormone (FSH) by the GNRH agonist. This can manifest as increased bone pain or increased urinary symptoms. Antiandrogen therapy should be started before beginning a GNRH agonist and be continued in combination for at least 7 days for patients with metastasis to help reduce tumor flare. This flare reaction usually resolves after 2 weeks and has a similar onset and duration pattern between the depot and regular acting GNRH agonists.

High-Yield Fast-Facts

- **Alternative names**
    - Gonadotropin-releasing hormone (GnRH) agonists are also referred to as luteinizing hormone-releasing hormone (LHRH) agonists

- **Efficacy**
  - GNRH agonists are a reversible method of androgen ablation and are as effective as orchiectomy in treating prostate cancer

---

HIGH-YIELD BOARD EXAM ESSENTIALS

- **CLASSIC AGENTS:** Goserelin, leuprolide, triptorelin
- **DRUG CLASS:** GNRH agonists
- **INDICATIONS:** Breast cancer, prostate cancer, prevention of early menopause during chemotherapy
- **MECHANISM:** Agonist analog of gonadotropin releasing hormone (GnRH) and causes suppression of ovarian and testicular steroidogenesis due to decreased levels of LH and FSH with subsequent decrease in testosterone (male) and estrogen (female) levels
- **SIDE EFFECTS:** Tumor flare, gynecomastia, hot flashes, erectile dysfunction, edema, injection site reactions
- **CLINICAL PEARLS:** Long term use of GNRH agonists can cause adverse effects related to decreased testosterone levels including: osteoporosis, bone fractures, obesity, insulin resistance, hyperlipidemia, increased risk of diabetes and cardiovascular events.

High-Yield Basic Pharmacology

- **Mechanism of Action**
  - Immune checkpoint inhibitors remove inhibitory signals of T-cell activation, which enables tumor-reactive T cells to overcome regulatory mechanisms and mount an effective antitumor response.
    - Specific targets: Atezolizumab - Anti-PD-L1, Ipilimumab - Anti-CTLA4, Nivolumab - Anti-PD-1, Pembrolizumab - Anti-PD-1

Primary Net Benefit

- Causes tumor cells to take longer to respond to growth allowing.

<table>
<tr><td colspan="4">Immunotherapy Drug Class Review
High-Yield Med Reviews</td></tr>
<tr><td colspan="4">Mechanism of Action: Immune checkpoint inhibitors remove inhibitory signals of T-cell activation, which enables tumor-reactive T cells to overcome regulatory mechanisms and mount an effective antitumor response.</td></tr>
<tr><td colspan="4">Class Effects: Fatigue, rash, diarrhea, decreased appetite, cough, flu like symptoms, increased serum creatine, increased liver function tests, hypothyroidism, electrolyte abnormalities</td></tr>
<tr><td>Generic Name</td><td>Brand Name</td><td>Indication(s) or Uses</td><td>Notes</td></tr>
<tr>
<td>Atezolizumab</td>
<td>Tecentriq</td>
<td>
• Breast Cancer
• Hepatocellular Carcinoma
• Melanoma
• Non-Small Cell Lung Cancer
• Small Cell Lung Cancer
• Urothelial Carcinoma
</td>
<td>
• Dosing (Adult): Dosing varies per indication
  – Typical dose IV 840 mg flat dose every 2 weeks or 1200 mg flat dose every 3 weeks
• Dosing (Peds): Not routinely used in pediatrics
• CYP450 Interactions: None Known
• Renal or Hepatic Dose Adjustments: Hold for renal or hepatoxicity
• Dosage Forms: 840 mg/14 mL, 1200 mg/20 mL solution for IV injection
</td>
</tr>
<tr>
<td>Ipilimumab</td>
<td>Yervoy</td>
<td>
• Colorectal Cancer
• Hepatocellular Carcinoma
• Melanoma
• Non-Small Cell Lung Cancer
• Renal Cell Carcinoma
</td>
<td>
• Dosing (Adult): Dosing varies per indication
  – Typical dose range IV 1-3 mg/kg every 3-12 weeks
• Dosing (Peds): Same as adult
• CYP450 Interactions: None Known
• Renal or Hepatic Dose Adjustments: Hold for renal or hepatoxicity
• Dosage Forms: 50 mg/10 mL, 200 mg/40 mL solution for IV injection
</td>
</tr>
<tr>
<td>Nivolumab</td>
<td>Opdivo</td>
<td>
• Colorectal Cancer
• Esophageal Cancer
• Head and Neck Cancer
• Hepatocellular Carcinoma
• Hodgkin Lymphoma
• Melanoma
• Non-Small Cell Lung Cancer
• Renal Cell Carcinoma
• Urothelial Carcinoma
</td>
<td>
• Dosing (Adult): Dosing varies per indication
  – Typical dose range IV 240 mg once every 2 weeks, 480 mg once every 4 weeks, 3 mg/kg every 2-3 weeks
• Dosing (Peds): Same as adult
• CYP450 Interactions: None Known
• Renal or Hepatic Dose Adjustments: Hold for renal or hepatoxicity
• Dosage Forms: 40 mg/4 mL, 100 mg/10 mL, 240mg/24mL solution for IV injection
</td>
</tr>
</table>

Immunotherapy Drug Class Review			
High-Yield Med Reviews			
Generic Name	Brand Name	Indication(s) or Uses	Notes
Pembrolizumab	Keytruda	<ul><li>Breast Cancer</li><li>Cervical Cancer</li><li>Colorectal Cancer</li><li>Endometrial Cancer</li><li>Esophageal Cancer</li><li>Gastric Cancer</li><li>Head and Neck Cancer</li><li>Hepatocellular Carcinoma</li><li>Hodgkin Lymphoma</li><li>Melanoma</li><li>Microsatellite instability-high or mismatch repair-deficient cancer</li><li>Non-Small Cell Lung Cancer</li><li>Renal Cell Carcinoma</li><li>Small Cell Lung Cancer</li><li>Urothelial Carcinoma</li></ul>	<ul><li>**Dosing (Adult):** Dosing varies per indication<ul><li>IV 200 mg once every 3 weeks or 400 mg once every 6 weeks</li></ul></li><li>**Dosing (Peds):** Dosing varies per indication<ul><li>IV 2 mg/kg/dose; maximum dose: 200 mg/dose; once every 3 weeks</li></ul></li><li>**CYP450 Interactions:** None Known</li><li>**Renal or Hepatic Dose Adjustments:** Hold for renal or hepatoxicity</li><li>**Dosage Forms:** 100 mg/4 mL solution for IV injection</li></ul>

Emetic Potential

- **Minimal Emetic Risk (<10% frequency of emesis)**
    - Nivolumab
    - Pembrolizumab
    - Atezolizumab
    - Ipilimumab

Extravasation Risk

- None

High-Yield Clinical Knowledge

- **Managing Immune Related Adverse Effects**
    - Immunotherapy works by upregulating the immune system to attack the cancer; however, an overactive immune system can also start attacking the body's own tissue causing immune related adverse events (irAEs). These irAEs can affect any organ/tissue in the body (skin, GI tract, lungs, liver, thyroid, etc.).
        - The most common irAEs with immunotherapy are rash, pruritus, diarrhea, colitis, elevated liver enzymes/bilirubin, hepatitis, hypophysitis, and hypothyroidism.
    - Patients should be educated on the mechanism of action of immunotherapy and when a new side effect occurs, there should be a high suspicion for it being treatment related.
    - Though treatment interruption may be needed for some irAEs depending on severity, dose adjustments are not recommended after restarting therapy following toxicity
    - Toxicity Management (except hypothyroidism)
        - Grade 1 toxicity: Continue immunotherapy with close monitoring
        - Grade 2 toxicity: Hold immunotherapy (may resume when toxicity < grade 1), Prednisone 0.5-1 mg/kg/day or equivalent may be administered
        - Grade 3 toxicity: Hold immunotherapy (may resume when toxicity < grade 1), Start prednisone 1-2 mg/kg/day or methylprednisolone IV 1-2 mg/kg/day with taper over > 4-6 weeks. If no improvement after 48-72 hours, then consider infliximab
        - Grade 4 toxicity: Permanently discontinue immunotherapy

- Hypothyroidism management
  - Thyroid supplementation in symptomatic patients with TSH levels > 10 mIU/L, monitor every 6-8 weeks while titrating
- **Drug interactions**
  - As steroids are known to reduce the immune response (and are used to treat immune related adverse events), they may diminish the therapeutic effect of Immune Checkpoint Inhibitors. Carefully consider the need for corticosteroids during the initiation of immune checkpoint inhibitor therapy. Generally, doses of a prednisone-equivalent of 10 mg or less per day are permitted.

High-Yield Fast-Facts

- **Pembrolizumab and Microsatellite Instability (MSI)**
  - Pembrolizumab was one of the first oncology drugs approved for a specific genetic marker (tumors with high microsatellite instability) regardless of cancer type or tissue diagnosis. Meaning that any patient whose tumor is MSI high is eligible to receive pembrolizumab!

HIGH-YIELD BOARD EXAM ESSENTIALS
- **CLASSIC AGENTS:** Atezolizumab, ipilimumab, nivolumab, pembrolizumab
- **DRUG CLASS:** Immunotherapy
- **INDICATIONS:** Breast cancer, colorectal cancer, esophageal cancer, head and neck cancer, hepatocellular carcinoma, Hodgkin lymphoma, melanoma, non-small cell lung cancer, renal cell carcinoma, urothelial carcinoma
- **MECHANISM:** Immune checkpoint inhibitors remove inhibitory signals of T-cell activation, which enables tumor-reactive T cells to overcome regulatory mechanisms and mount an effective antitumor response.
- **SIDE EFFECTS:** irAEs: rash, pruritus, diarrhea, colitis, elevated liver enzymes/bilirubin, hepatitis, hypophysitis, and hypothyroidism
- **CLINICAL PEARLS:** Patients should be educated on the mechanism of action of immunotherapy and when a new side effect occurs, there should be a high suspicion for it being treatment related.

High-Yield Basic Pharmacology

- **Mechanism of Action**
  - The mechanism of action is still under investigation, but it is believed to exert direct cytotoxic effects on the tumor cells causing apoptosis. However, may also be due to augmentation of the immune system and inhibition of angiogenesis.

Primary Net Benefit

- Prevention of tumor growth through disruption through a few mechanisms.

Immune Modulators Drug Class Review			
High-Yield Med Reviews			
Mechanism of Action: *The mechanism of action is still under investigation, but it is believed to exert direct cytotoxic effects on the tumor cells causing apoptosis*			
Class Effects: Hematologic toxicities, diarrhea, neuropathy, fatigue, rash, nausea/vomiting,			
Generic Name	**Brand Name**	**Indication(s) or Uses**	**Notes**
Lenalidomide	Revlimid	<ul><li>Multiple Myeloma</li><li>Non-Hodgkin Lymphoma</li><li>Myelodysplastic Syndrome</li><li>CLL*</li></ul>	<ul><li>**Dosing (Adult):** Dosing varies per indication<ul><li>Typical dose range oral 10-25 mg daily</li></ul></li><li>**Dosing (Peds):** Not used in pediatrics</li><li>**CYP450 Interactions:** Substrate of P-glycoprotein/ABCB1 (minor)</li><li>**Renal or Hepatic Dose Adjustments:** Requires renal dose adjustment, specific adjustment depends on indication for therapy</li><li>**Dosage Forms:** 2.5 mg, 5 mg, 10 mg, 15 mg, 20 mg, 25 mg oral capsule</li></ul>
Pomalidomide	Pomalyst	<ul><li>Multiple myeloma</li><li>Kaposi Sarcoma</li></ul>	<ul><li>**Dosing (Adult):** Dosing varies per indication<ul><li>Typical dose range 4-5 mg once daily on days 1 to 21 of 28-day cycles</li></ul></li><li>**Dosing (Peds):** Not used in pediatrics</li><li>**CYP450 Interactions:** Substrate of CYP1A2 (major), CYP2C19 (minor), CYP2D6 (minor), CYP3A4 (minor), P-glycoprotein/ABCB1 (minor)</li><li>**Renal or Hepatic Dose Adjustments:** Requires renal and hepatic dose adjustments, specific adjustment depends on indication for therapy</li><li>**Dosage Forms:** 1 mg, 2 mg, 3 mg, 4 mg oral capsule</li></ul>
Thalidomide	Thalomid	<ul><li>Multiple myeloma</li></ul>	<ul><li>**Dosing (Adult):** Dosing varies per indication<ul><li>Typical dose 200 mg once daily</li></ul></li><li>**Dosing (Peds):** Limited data for use in pediatrics</li><li>**CYP450 Interactions:** None known</li><li>**Renal or Hepatic Dose Adjustments:** None</li><li>**Dosage Forms:** 50 mg, 100 mg, 150 mg, 200 mg oral capsule</li></ul>
*Off Label Use			

Emetic Potential

- **Minimal-Low Emetic Risk (<30% frequency of emesis)**
    - Lenalidomide
    - Pomalidomide
    - Thalidomide

Extravasation Risk

    - N/A

High-Yield Clinical Knowledge

- **Risk of birth defects**
    - These medications have the risk of causing birth defects to the fetus. Women of childbearing potential need to be on effective contraception for at least 4 weeks prior to starting therapy, during therapy and for at least 4 weeks after discontinuing therapy.
    - Pregnancy screening: prior to initiating therapy pregnancy must be excluded by 2 negative pregnancy tests. During the first month of therapy patients are required to undergo weekly pregnancy
    - tests and then monthly thereafter in women with regular menstrual cycles or every 2 weeks for women with irregular menstrual cycles while they remain on treatment. If pregnancy does occur, IMID therapy must be discontinued.
    - Male patients are required to use condoms during any sexual contact with females of childbearing potential while on treatment and for up to 28 days after receiving therapy, as the drug is present in semen. Male patients taking an IMID must not donate sperm.
- **Thromboembolism**
    - IMIDs also increase the risk for thromboembolism, including venous thromboembolism, pulmonary embolism, myocardial infarction and stroke. All patients receiving an IMID need some sort of VTE prophylaxis. The SAVED score takes into account: recent surgeries, race, VTE history, age and dexamethasone dosing to estimate risk of VTE while taking an IMID. Patients at low risk for VTE (per the SAVED score) can receive aspirin 81 mg once daily. High risk patients should receive full dose warfarin (target INR 2-3), enoxaparin 40 mg daily, Dalteparin 5,000 units daily, or apixaban 2.5 mg every 12 hours. Patient can also receive full dose anticoagulation if indicated for another medical condition.
- **REMS program**
    - The IMID's REMS program has a restricted distribution program for prescribing and dispensing these agents due to the risk of fetal toxicity. Patients, providers and pharmacies must all be enrolled in the REMS program, and there are strict record keeping requirements and restrictions, including limited approved dispensing pharmacies and restricted refills on prescriptions.
- **Stem cell collection**
    - Collect stem cells within first 4 cycles of lenalidomide if deemed transplant eligible (this increases the likelihood of a successful collection)

High-Yield Fast-Facts

- **Thalidomide Babies**
    - Thalidomide was first marketed in 1957 in Europe as an over the counter medication. It was said to help with anxiety, trouble sleeping, and morning sickness. While it was initially thought to be safe in pregnancy, concerns regarding birth defects arose in 1961 and the medication was removed from the market. It is estimated that 10,000 embryos were affected by the use of thalidomide during pregnancy of which 40% died at the time of birth. Those who survived had limb, eye, urinary tract, and heart problems.

- This led to public support for stronger drug laws in the united states and the creation of the Kefauver-Harris drug amendment

---

HIGH-YIELD BOARD EXAM ESSENTIALS
- **CLASSIC AGENTS:** Lenalidomide, pomalidomide, thalidomide
- **DRUG CLASS:** IMIDs
- **INDICATIONS:** CLL, Kaposi sarcoma, multiple myeloma, myelodysplastic syndrome, non-Hodgkin lymphoma
- **MECHANISM:** The mechanism of action is still under investigation, but it is believed to exert direct cytotoxic effects on the tumor cells causing apoptosis
- **SIDE EFFECTS:** Fetal toxicity, thromboembolism, diarrhea, neuropathy, fatigue, rash, nausea/vomiting,
- **CLINICAL PEARLS:** These medications have the risk of causing birth defects to the fetus. Women of childbearing potential need to be on effective contraception for at least 4 weeks prior to starting therapy, during therapy and for at least 4 weeks after discontinuing therapy.

High-Yield Basic Pharmacology

- **Mechanism of Action**
  - Monoclonal antibodies as a class bind to specific targets (immune cells, cell receptors, tumor molecules, etc.) to exert anti-tumor effects. The specific target varies per antibody
- **Half-life Elimination**
  - Monoclonal antibodies typically have a long half-life (many are >15 days), this also often leads to a slower onset of actions (many antibodies can take at least a several weeks before a meaningful effect is achieved)
- **Molecular Size**
  - Monoclonal antibodies are very large proteins (molecular weight of ~146 000 Da) and therefore have poor CNS penetration

Primary Net Benefit

- Monoclonal antibodies as a class bind to specific targets (immune cells, cell receptors, tumor molecules, etc.) to exert anti-tumor effects. The specific target varies per antibody.
- Very specific anti-tumor effects using biologic agents.

Monoclonal Antibodies – General Drug Class Review			
High-Yield Med Reviews			
Mechanism of Action: *Monoclonal antibodies as a class bind to specific targets (immune cells, cell receptors, tumor molecules, etc.) to exert anti-tumor effects. The specific target varies per antibody.*			
Class Effects: Infusion reactions, injection site reactions, dermatologic, gastrointestinal, endocrine, and other inflammatory reactions, Undesired effects related to the target antigen, Cytokine release syndrome, Interference with laboratory or blood bank testing, Cardiac dysfunction (trastuzumab/pertuzumab), Hypertension (bevacizumab), Hepatitis B reactivation (rituximab)			
Generic Name	**Brand Name**	**Indication(s) or Uses**	**Notes**
Trastuzumab (Targets HER-2)	Herceptin; Herzuma; Kanjinti; Ogivri; Ontruzant; Trazimera	▪ Breast Cancer ▪ Gastric Cancer	▪ **Dosing (Adult):** Dosing varies per indication – Typical dose range IV 2-8 mg/kg ▪ **Dosing (Peds):** Not used in pediatrics ▪ **CYP450 Interactions:** None known ▪ **Renal or Hepatic Dose Adjustments:** None ▪ **Dosage Forms:** 150mg, 420 mg solution for IV injection
Cetuximab (Targets EGFR)	Erbitux	▪ Colorectal Cancer ▪ Head and Neck Cancer	▪ **Dosing (Adult):** Dosing varies per indication – Typical dose range IV 250-500 mg/m^2 ▪ **Dosing (Peds):** Not used in pediatrics ▪ **CYP450 Interactions:** None known ▪ **Renal or Hepatic Dose Adjustments:** None ▪ **Dosage Forms:** 100 mg/50 mL, 200 mg/100 mL solution for IV injection
Panitumumab (Targets EGFR)	Vectibix	▪ Colorectal Cancer	▪ **Dosing (Adult):** Dosing varies per indication – Typical dose IV 6 mg/kg ▪ **Dosing (Peds):** Not used in pediatrics ▪ **CYP450 Interactions:** None Known ▪ **Renal or Hepatic Dose Adjustments:** None ▪ **Dosage Forms:** 100 mg/5 mL, 400 mg/20 mL solution for IV injection

Monoclonal Antibodies Drug Class Review
High-Yield Med Reviews

Generic Name	Brand Name	Indication(s) or Uses	Notes
Pertuzumab (Targets HER-2)	Perjeta	▪ Breast Cancer	▪ **Dosing (Adult):** Dosing varies per indication – Typical dose IV 840 mg followed by a maintenance dose of 420 mg ▪ **Dosing (Peds):** Not used in pediatrics ▪ **CYP450 Interactions:** None Known ▪ **Renal or Hepatic Dose Adjustments:** None ▪ **Dosage Forms:** 420 mg/14 mL solution for IV injection
Bevacizumab (Targets VEGF)	Avastin; Mvasi; Zirabev	▪ Cervical Cancer ▪ Colorectal Cancer ▪ Glioblastoma ▪ Hepatocellular Carcinoma ▪ Non-small cell lung cancer ▪ Ovarian cancer ▪ Renal cell carcinoma	▪ **Dosing (Adult):** Dosing varies per indication – Typical dose range IV 5-15 mg/kg/dose ▪ **Dosing (Peds):** Same as adult, limited data for use in pediatrics ▪ **CYP450 Interactions:** None known ▪ **Renal or Hepatic Dose Adjustments:** None ▪ **Dosage Forms:** 100 mg/4 mL, 400 mg/16 mL solution for IV injection
Daratumumab (Targets CD-38)	Darzalex	▪ Multiple Myeloma	▪ **Dosing (Adult):** Dosing varies per regimen – Typical dose IV 16 mg/kg ▪ **Dosing (Peds):** Not used in pediatrics ▪ **CYP450 Interactions:** None Known ▪ **Renal or Hepatic Dose Adjustments:** None ▪ **Dosage Forms:** 100 mg/5 mL, 400 mg/20 mL solution for IV injection
Rituximab (Targets CD-20)	Riabni; Rituxan; Ruxience; Truxima	▪ Chronic Lymphocytic Leukemia ▪ Non-Hodgkin Lymphoma	▪ **Dosing (Adult):** Dosing varies per regimen – Typical dose IV 375 mg/m^2 ▪ **Dosing (Peds):** Same as adult ▪ **CYP450 Interactions:** None Known ▪ **Renal or Hepatic Dose Adjustments:** None ▪ **Dosage Forms:** 100 mg/10 mL, 500 mg/50 mL solution for IV injection

Emetic Potential

- **Minimal Emetic Risk (<10% frequency of emesis)**
  - Trastuzumab
  - Cetuximab
  - Panitumumab
  - Pertuzumab
  - Bevacizumab
  - Daratumumab
  - Rituximab

Extravasation Risk

- None

High-Yield Clinical Knowledge

- **Infusion Reactions**
    - Infusion reactions occur due to the immunogenicity of monoclonal antibodies, this can lead to the development of anti-monoclonal antibodies, which can cause acute hypersensitivity reactions. The risk of reaction varies depending on the species whose proteins forms the base of the molecule. Even fully humanized antibodies can cause allergic reactions.
    - Infusion reactions typically occur in the first 1-2 hours of starting an infusion. They can affect any organ system and range from mildly irritating injection-site reactions, fever or itching/rash, to potentially life-threatening anaphylaxis. Mild reactions are common. Many patients will receive premedication with acetaminophen and diphenhydramine prior to their infusion.
    - In the event of an infusion reaction, always stop the infusion as soon as possible. From there, treatment depends on the severity of the reaction. After a mild reaction (slight rash or itching), the infusion can often be continued after temporarily stopping it with a slower infusion rate or additional doses of antipyretics or antihistamines. More severe reactions (like anaphylaxis) can be managed with epinephrine and may require permeant discontinuation of the drug.

High-Yield Fast-Facts

- **Humanization of recombinant antibodies**
    - Humanized antibodies are produced by merging the DNA that encodes the binding protein of a monoclonal mouse antibody with human antibody producing DNA, this can reduce the risk of hypersensitivity reactions.
- **Naming of antibodies**
    - Chimeric monoclonal antibodies contain "-xi-" (ex. Cetuximab)
    - Humanized monoclonal antibodies contain "-zu-" (ex. Trastuzumab)
    - Fully human antibodies contain "-u-" (ex. Panitumumab)

HIGH-YIELD BOARD EXAM ESSENTIALS
- **CLASSIC AGENTS:** Bevacizumab, cetuximab, daratumumab, panitumumab, pertuzumab, rituximab, trastuzumab
- **DRUG CLASS:** Monoclonal antibodies
- **INDICATIONS:** Cervical cancer, colorectal cancer, glioblastoma, hepatocellular carcinoma, non-small cell lung cancer, ovarian cancer, renal cell carcinoma
- **MECHANISM:** Monoclonal antibodies as a class bind to specific targets (immune cells, cell receptors, tumor molecules, etc.) to exert anti-tumor effects. The specific target varies per antibody.
- **SIDE EFFECTS:** Infusion reactions
- **CLINICAL PEARLS:** Humanized antibodies are produced by merging the DNA that encodes the binding protein of a monoclonal mouse antibody with human antibody producing DNA, this can reduce the risk of hypersensitivity reactions.

High-Yield Basic Pharmacology

- **Mechanism of Action**
  - Mimics natural somatostatin by inhibiting serotonin release and the secretion of gastrin, VIP, insulin, glucagon, secretin, motilin, and pancreatic polypeptide

Primary Net Benefit

- Somatostatin analogues control symptoms that result from release of peptides and neuroamines from neuroendocrine tumors and help control the disease itself.

Somatostatin Analogs Drug Class Review			
High-Yield Med Reviews			
Mechanism of Action: *Mimics natural somatostatin by inhibiting serotonin release and the secretion of gastrin, VIP, insulin, glucagon, secretin, motilin, and pancreatic polypeptide*			
Class Effects: Nausea, abdominal cramps, diarrhea, steatorrhea, flatulence, hyperglycemia, cholelithiasis/biliary sludging, and injection site pain			
Generic Name	**Brand Name**	**Indication(s) or Uses**	**Notes**

Octreotide	Bynfezia Pen; SandoSTATIN; SandoSTATIN LAR Depot	• Carcinoid Crisis*
		• Carcinoid Syndrome
		• Neuroendocrine Tumors*
			• **Dosing (Adult):** Dosing varies per indication
			  – Typical dose range IM 10-30 mg every 4 weeks
			  – Typical dose range SQ 100 to 600 mcg/day in 2 to 4 divided doses
			• **Dosing (Peds):** Not routinely used in pediatrics
			• **CYP450 Interactions:** None Known
			• **Renal or Hepatic Dose Adjustments:** Consider reduced starting IM injection doses in patients with severe renal or hepatic impairment
			• **Dosage Forms:** 50 mcg/mL, 100 mcg/mL, 200 mcg/mL, 500 mcg/mL, 1000 mcg/mL solution for IV/SQ injection. 10 mg, 20 mg, 30 mg long acting IM injection

Lanreotide	Somatuline Depot	• Carcinoid Syndrome • Neuroendocrine Tumors	• **Dosing (Adult):** SQ 120 mg every 4 weeks • **Dosing (Peds):** Not routinely used in pediatrics • **CYP450 Interactions:** None Known • **Renal or Hepatic Dose Adjustments:** Consider reduced starting doses in patients with severe renal or hepatic impairment • **Dosage Forms:** 60 mg/0.2 mL, 90 mg/0.3 mL, 120 mg/0.5 mL SQ depot solution
*Off Label Use			

Emetic Potential

- N/A

Extravasation Risk

- N/A

High-Yield Clinical Knowledge

- **Carcinoid Syndrome**
    - Carcinoid syndrome primary occurs in patients with well differentiated metastatic neuroendocrine tumors. Signs and symptoms include diarrhea and flushing. Serotonin is thought to be the most important factor in the etiology of carcinoid syndrome diarrhea.
    - Long acting somatostatin analogs are highly active for the control of flushing/diarrhea as well as long term disease control. Short acting analogs can be used for immediate effect in patients with uncontrolled carcinoid syndrome. Short-acting octreotide can also be added to octreotide long-acting release for the treatment of breakthrough symptoms.

High-Yield Fast-Facts

- **Duration of action**
    - Octreotide
        - SubQ: 6 to 12 hours
        - IM (LAR depot suspension): Following a single injection, a steady concentration is achieved within 2 to 3 weeks and maintained for an additional 2 to 3 weeks; steady-state levels are achieved after 3 injections administered at 4-week intervals.

HIGH-YIELD BOARD EXAM ESSENTIALS
- **CLASSIC AGENTS:** Lanreotide, octreotide
- **DRUG CLASS:** Somatostatin Analogs
- **INDICATIONS:** Carcinoid crisis, carcinoid syndrome, neuroendocrine tumors
- **MECHANISM:** Mimics natural somatostatin by inhibiting serotonin release and the secretion of gastrin, VIP, insulin, glucagon, secretin, motilin, and pancreatic polypeptide
- **SIDE EFFECTS:** Bradycardia, edema, hyperglycemia
- **CLINICAL PEARLS:** Somatostatin analogues control symptoms that result from release of peptides and neuroamines from neuroendocrine tumors and help control the disease itself.

High-Yield Basic Pharmacology

- **Mechanism of Action**
  - Inhibits BCR-ABL tyrosine kinase, the abnormal gene product of the Philadelphia chromosome in chronic myeloid leukemia.

Primary Net Benefit

- Oral chemotherapeutic agent that Inhibits the cells that promote CML.

BCR-ABL Tyrosine Kinase Inhibitors Drug Class Review			
High-Yield Med Reviews			
Mechanism of Action: *Inhibits BCR-ABL tyrosine kinase, the abnormal gene product of the Philadelphia chromosome in chronic myeloid leukemia*			
Class Effects: Hematologic toxicities, rash, hypertension, fluid retention, nausea, hepatic toxicity			
Generic Name	**Brand Name**	**Indication(s) or Uses**	**Notes**
Bosutinib	Bosulif	▪ CML	▪ **Dosing (Adult):** Dosing varies – Typical dose range oral 400-500 mg daily ▪ **Dosing (Peds):** Not used in pediatrics ▪ **CYP450 Interactions:** Substrate of CYP3A4 (major) ▪ **Renal or Hepatic Dose Adjustments:** Preexisting hepatic impairment: Reduce initial dose to 200 mg once daily. CrCl 30 to 50 mL/minute: Reduce dose to 300 mg once daily. CrCl <30 mL/minute: Reduce dose to 200 mg once daily. ▪ **Dosage Forms:** 100 mg, 400 mg, 500 mg oral tablet
Dasatinib	Sprycel	▪ ALL ▪ CML ▪ GIST*	▪ **Dosing (Adult):** Dosing varies per indication – Typical dose range oral 100 mg-140 mg daily ▪ **Dosing (Peds):** Dosing varies per indication and patient weight – Typical dose range oral 40 mg- 120 mg daily ▪ **CYP450 Interactions:** Substrate of CYP3A4 (major) ▪ **Renal or Hepatic Dose Adjustments:** None ▪ **Dosage Forms:** 20 mg, 50 mg, 70 mg, 80 mg, 100 mg, 140 mg oral tablet

BCR-ABL Tyrosine Kinase Inhibitors Drug Class Review
High-Yield Med Reviews

Generic Name	Brand Name	Indication(s) or Uses	Notes
Imatinib	Gleevec	▪ ALL ▪ CML ▪ GIST	▪ **Dosing (Adult):** Dosing varies per indication − Typical dose range oral 400-800 mg daily ▪ **Dosing (Peds):** 340 mg/m^2/day administered once daily or in 2 divided doses ▪ **CYP450 Interactions:** Substrate of CYP1A2 (minor), CYP2C19 (minor), CYP2C8 (minor), CYP2C9 (minor), CYP2D6 (minor), CYP3A4 (major), P-glycoprotein/ABCB1 (minor); Inhibits CYP3A4 (moderate) ▪ **Renal or Hepatic Dose Adjustments:** CrCl 40 to 59 mL/minute: Maximum recommended dose: 600 mg. CrCl 20 to 39 mL/minute: Decrease recommended starting dose by 50%; dose may be increased as tolerated; maximum recommended dose: 400 mg. CrCl <20 mL/minute: Use caution. Severe hepatic impairment: Reduce dose by 25% ▪ **Dosage Forms:** 100 mg, 400 mg oral tablet
Nilotinib	Tasigna	▪ CML ▪ ALL* ▪ GIST*	▪ **Dosing (Adult):** Dosing varies per indication − Typical dose range oral 300-400 mg twice daily ▪ **Dosing (Peds):** 230 mg/m^2/dose twice daily ▪ **CYP450 Interactions:** Substrate of CYP3A4 (major), P-glycoprotein/ABCB1 (minor); Inhibits CYP3A4 (moderate) ▪ **Renal or Hepatic Dose Adjustments:** Hepatic impairment: Initial: 200 mg twice daily; may increase to 300 mg twice daily based on patient tolerability ▪ **Dosage Forms:** 50 mg, 150 mg, 200 mg oral tablets
Ponatinib	Iclusig	▪ ALL ▪ CML	▪ **Dosing (Adult):** Dosing varies per indication − Typical dose oral 45 mg daily ▪ **Dosing (Peds):** Not used in pediatrics ▪ **CYP450 Interactions:** Substrate of BCRP/ABCG2, CYP2C8 (minor), CYP2D6 (minor), CYP3A4 (major), P-glycoprotein/ABCB1 (minor); Inhibits BSEP/ABCB11 ▪ **Renal or Hepatic Dose Adjustments:** Hepatic impairment: Reduce initial dose to 30 mg once daily. ▪ **Dosage Forms:** 10 mg, 15 mg, 30 mg, 45 mg oral tablet
***Off Label Use**			

Emetic Potential

- **Minimal-Low Emetic Risk (<30% frequency of emesis)**
    - Imatinib <400 mg/day
    - Bosutinib <400 mg/day
    - Ponatinib
    - Dasatinib
    - Nilotinib
- **Moderate-High Emetic Risk (>30% frequency of emesis)**
    - Imatinib >400 mg/day
    - Bosutinib >400 mg/day

Extravasation Risk

- N/A

High-Yield Clinical Knowledge

- **Choice of therapy**
    - Neither dasatinib, nilotinib or bosutinib have shown improved overall survival or progression free survival rates compared to imatinib, so choice of first-line therapy should be individualized. The following should be considered when choosing an agent: toxicity profile of the TKI, patient's age and ability to tolerate therapy, adherence, comorbid conditions, drug interactions, cost, ease of administration, and feasibility of treatment discontinuation.
    - In patients with disease progression, the selection of an alternative TKI is based on prior therapy, concurrent disease states and/or mutational testing.
- **TKI discontinuation**
    - The management of CML as a chronic disease requires long-term therapy which can cause both adverse effects and a financial burden. Discontinuation of TKI <u>may</u> be feasible in selected patients and with careful monitoring. Discontinuation of TKI therapy may be considered only in patients who met all of the following criteria: Chronic phase -CML with no history of accelerated phase or blast crisis, have been inn TKI therapy for at least 3 years with no history of resistance, and had a Stable molecular response for >2 years on at least 4 tests performed at least 3 months apart.
    - Patients who do quality for TKI discontinuation must have monthly molecular monitoring for the first year following discontinuation, then every 6 weeks during the second year, and quarterly thereafter if still in a major molecular response. If a patient loses their molecular response, they must have prompt resumption of TKI within 4 weeks.
- **Resistance to TKIs**
    - Point mutations in the ABL kinase domain are the most frequent mechanism of secondary resistance to TKI therapy. Among mutations in the ABL domain, the presence of the T315I mutation is the most common and displays resistance to all currently available TKIs except ponatinib. T315I mutation is also associated with disease progression and poorer survival.
    - Consider performing BCR-ABL kinase domain mutational analysis in patients who failure to achieve the response milestones, patients with any loss of response or patients who experience disease progression to accelerated phase-CML or blast crisis-CML.
- **Drug Interactions**
    - Dasatinib, Bosutinib, and Ponatinib require an acidic environment for absorption. Avoid the use of proton pump inhibitors and separate H2-antagonists from the TKI by at least two hours.

High-Yield Fast-Facts

- **CNS Penetration**
    - Of available BCR-ABL inhibitors, dasatinib crosses blood-brain barrier to greatest extent

HIGH-YIELD BOARD EXAM ESSENTIALS

- **CLASSIC AGENTS:** Bosutinib, dasatinib, imatinib, nilotinib, ponatinib
- **DRUG CLASS:** BCR-ABL tyrosine kinase inhibitors
- **INDICATIONS:** AML, CLL, GIST
- **MECHANISM:** Inhibits BCR-ABL tyrosine kinase, the abnormal gene product of the Philadelphia chromosome in chronic myeloid leukemia
- **SIDE EFFECTS:** Edema, thrombocytopenia, neutropenia, bleeding
- **CLINICAL PEARLS:** Neither dasatinib, nilotinib or bosutinib have shown improved overall survival or progression free survival rates compared to imatinib, so choice of first-line therapy should be individualized. The following should be considered when choosing an agent: toxicity profile of the TKI, patient's age and ability to tolerate therapy, adherence, comorbid conditions, drug interactions, cost, ease of administration, and feasibility of treatment discontinuation.

High-Yield Basic Pharmacology

- **Mechanism of Action**
  - Selectively targets BRAF kinase and interferes with the mitogen-activated protein kinase (MAPK) signaling pathway that regulates the proliferation and survival of melanoma cells

Primary Net Benefit

- Mainly to prevent melanoma growth and survival.

		BRAF Inhibitors Drug Class Review **High-Yield Med Reviews**	

Mechanism of Action: *Selectively targets BRAF kinase and interferes with the mitogen-activated protein kinase (MAPK) signaling pathway that regulates the proliferation and survival of melanoma cells*			
Class Effects: rash, photosensitivity, hair loss, joint pain, dermatologic effects (keratoacanthoma and cutaneous squamous cell cancer), gastrointestinal effects, fatigue, hand-foot syndrome, hyperglycemia, anemia, arthralgia, QTc prolongation			
Generic Name	**Brand Name**	**Indication(s) or Uses**	**Notes**
Dabrafenib	Tafinlar	▪ Melanoma (with BRAF V600E or BRAF V600K mutation) ▪ Non-small cell lung cancer (with BRAF V600E mutation) ▪ Thyroid cancer (with BRAF V600E mutation)	▪ **Dosing (Adult):** Oral 150 mg twice daily ▪ **Dosing (Peds):** Not routinely used in pediatrics ▪ **CYP450 Interactions:** Substrate of BCRP/ABCG2, CYP2C8 (major), CYP3A4 (major), P-glycoprotein/ABCB1 (minor), Induces CYP2C9 (weak), CYP3A4 (moderate) ▪ **Renal or Hepatic Dose Adjustments:** None ▪ **Dosage Forms:** 50 mg, 75 mg oral tablet
Encorafenib	Braftovi	▪ Colorectal cancer (with BRAF V600E mutation) ▪ Melanoma (with BRAF V600E or BRAF V600K mutation)	▪ **Dosing (Adult):** Dosing varies per indication – Typical dose range Oral 300-450 mg daily ▪ **Dosing (Peds):** Not routinely used in pediatrics ▪ **CYP450 Interactions:** Substrate of CYP2C19 (minor), CYP2D6 (minor), CYP3A4 (major), P-glycoprotein/ABCB1 (minor) ▪ **Renal or Hepatic Dose Adjustments:** Hold therapy for grade 3/4 LFT elevations and resume encorafenib at a reduced dose once resolved ▪ **Dosage Forms:** 75 mg oral capsule
Vemurafenib	Zelboraf	▪ Erdheim-Chester disease (with BRAF V600 mutation) ▪ Melanoma (with BRAF V600E or BRAF V600K mutation) ▪ Non-small cell lung cancer (with BRAF V600E mutation)	▪ **Dosing (Adult):** Oral 960 mg every 12 hours ▪ **Dosing (Peds):** Not routinely used in pediatrics ▪ **CYP450 Interactions:** Substrate of BCRP/ABCG2, CYP3A4 (major), P-glycoprotein/ABCB1 (minor); Inhibits CYP1A2 (moderate), CYP2D6 (weak), P-glycoprotein/ABCB1; Induces CYP3A4 (weak) ▪ **Renal or Hepatic Dose Adjustments:** None ▪ **Dosage Forms:** 240 mg oral tablet
***Off Label Use**			

Emetic Potential

- **Minimal - Low Emetic Risk (<30% frequency of emesis)**
  - **Vemurafenib**
- **Moderate - High Emetic Risk (>30% frequency of emesis)**
  - Dabrafenib
  - Encorafenib

Extravasation Risk

- N/A

High-Yield Clinical Knowledge

- **Choosing therapy in metastatic melanoma**
  - All metastatic tumors should be evaluated for the V600 mutation. In V600E or V600K mutated tumors, the initial selection between BRAF inhibitors and immunotherapy is commonly done based on the aggressive nature of the tumor. Rapidly growing tumors that are symptomatic are treated with BRAF-directed therapy because it generates a higher rate of response that occurs quicker, while asymptomatic or more indolent tumors may be treated with immunotherapy.
- **Resistance to BRAF inhibitors**
  - Though the BRAF inhibitors were initially evaluated as single agents, combination therapy with a MEK inhibitor is now the recommended treatment regimen.
  - This is due to the development of resistance to the single agent BRAF inhibitors after 6-7 months
  - Combination therapy with both BRAF and MEK inhibitors may suppress the downstream resistance mechanism
- **Cutaneous squamous cell cancers and keratoacanthomas**
  - Secondary skin cancers are the result of compensatory RAF signaling seen with BRAF inhibition. The risk of these additional cancers is decreased with the addition of a MEK inhibitor. These cancers are typically localized and easily treated with surgical excision or topical fluorouracil cream. Regular skin assessments should be done throughout therapy with BRAF inhibitors.

High-Yield Fast-Facts

- **ABCDE**
  - Symptoms of melanoma include ABCDE: asymmetry, border, color, diameter and evolving
    - Asymmetry: melanomas are often asymmetrical
    - Border: melanomas often have an irregular boarder
    - Color: melanomas often have more than one color or shade in the mole
    - Diameter: melanomas are often larger than 6mm, or the size of a pencil eraser
    - Evolving: melanomas tend to change over time while benign moles do not

---

HIGH-YIELD BOARD EXAM ESSENTIALS
- **CLASSIC AGENTS:** Dabrafenib, encorafenib, vemurafenib
- **DRUG CLASS:** BRAF inhibitors
- **INDICATIONS:** Specific cancers with BRAF V600E or BRAF V600K mutation
- **MECHANISM:** Selectively targets BRAF kinase and interferes with the mitogen-activated protein kinase (MAPK) signaling pathway that regulates the proliferation and survival of melanoma cells
- **SIDE EFFECTS:** Secondary skin cancer, QT prolongation (vemurafenib)
- **CLINICAL PEARLS:** Though the BRAF inhibitors were initially evaluated as single agents, combination therapy with a MEK inhibitor is now the recommended treatment regimen.

High-Yield Basic Pharmacology

- **Mechanism of Action**
  - EGFR inhibitors are highly selective tyrosine kinase inhibitors that covalently bind to epidermal growth factor receptors and irreversibly inhibit tyrosine kinase phosphorylation and downregulate EGFR signaling preventing cell growth

Primary Net Benefit

- Prevent growth of cancerous cells derived from epidermis.

EGFR Inhibitors Drug Class Review			
High-Yield Med Reviews			
Mechanism of Action: *highly selective tyrosine kinase inhibitors that covalently bind to epidermal growth factor receptors and irreversibly inhibit tyrosine kinase phosphorylation and downregulate EGFR signaling preventing cell growth.*			
Class Effects: Acneiform rash, diarrhea, skin/nail changes, dry mouth, nausea, vomiting, decreased appetite, hepatic dysfunction			
Generic Name	**Brand Name**	**Indication(s) or Uses**	**Notes**
Afatinib	Gilotrif	▪ Non-Small Cell Lung Cancer with EGFR mutation	▪ **Dosing (Adult):** 40 mg oral once daily ▪ **Dosing (Peds):** Not routinely used in pediatrics ▪ **CYP450 Interactions:** Substrate of BCRP/ABCG2, P-glycoprotein/ABCB1 (major) ▪ **Renal or Hepatic Dose Adjustments:** GFR 15 to 29 mL/minute/1.73 m2: Reduce starting dose to 30 mg once daily. Withhold therapy for ≥ grade 3 hepatic dysfunction. Upon improvement to baseline or ≤ grade 1, resume therapy at 10 mg per day less than previous dose. ▪ **Dosage Forms:** 20 mg, 30 mg, 40 mg oral tablet

EGFR Inhibitors Drug Class Review
High-Yield Med Reviews

Generic Name	Brand Name	Indication(s) or Uses	Notes

Erlotinib	Tarceva	▪ Non-Small Cell Lung Cancer with EGFR mutation
		▪ Pancreatic Cancer
			▪ **Dosing (Adult):** Dosing varies per indication
			  – 100-150 mg oral once daily
			  – Avoid tobacco smoking if possible. If unavoidable, increase dose at 2-week intervals in 50 mg increments to a maximum dose of 300 mg (with careful monitoring); immediately reduce erlotinib dose to recommended starting dose (based on indication) upon smoking cessation.
			▪ **Dosing (Peds):** Not routinely used in pediatrics
			▪ **CYP450 Interactions:** Substrate of CYP1A2 (major), CYP3A4 (major)
			▪ **Renal or Hepatic Dose Adjustments:** Grades 3/4 renal toxicity: Withhold treatment and consider discontinuing. If treatment is resumed, reinitiate with a 50 mg dose reduction after toxicity has resolved to baseline or ≤ grade 1. Total bilirubin >3 times ULN and/or transaminases >5 times ULN: Interrupt therapy and consider discontinuing. If treatment is resumed, reinitiate with a 50 mg dose reduction after bilirubin and transaminases return to baseline.
			▪ **Dosage Forms:** 25 mg, 100 mg, 150 mg oral tablet

Gefitinib	Iressa	▪ Non-Small Cell Lung Cancer with EGFR mutation	▪ **Dosing (Adult):** 250 mg oral once daily ▪ **Dosing (Peds):** Not routinely used in pediatrics ▪ **CYP450 Interactions:** Substrate of BCRP/ABCG2, CYP2D6 (minor), CYP3A4 (major) ▪ **Renal or Hepatic Dose Adjustments:** ALT and/or AST elevations (grade 2 or higher): Withhold treatment for up to 14 days; may resume treatment when fully resolved or improved to grade 1. ▪ **Dosage Forms:** 250 mg oral tablet
Osimertinib	Brand Name (if available)	▪ Non-Small Cell Lung Cancer with EGFR mutation ▪ Non-Small Cell Lung Cancer with T790M EGFR-mutation positive ▪ Non-small cell lung cancer with brain or leptomeningeal metastases	▪ **Dosing (Adult):** Dosing varies per indication – 80-160 mg oral once daily ▪ **Dosing (Peds):** Not routinely used in pediatrics ▪ **CYP450 Interactions:** Substrate of BCRP/ABCG2, CYP3A4 (major), P-glycoprotein/ABCB1 (minor) ▪ **Renal or Hepatic Dose Adjustments:** Has not been studied in renal or hepatic impairment ▪ **Dosage Forms:** 40 mg, 80 mg oral tablet
*Off Label Use			

Emetic Potential

- **Minimal- Low Emetic Risk (<30% frequency of emesis)**
  - Afatinib

- Erlotinib
- Gefitinib
- Osimertinib

Extravasation Risk

- N/A

High-Yield Clinical Knowledge

- **T790M Mutation**
  - The T790M mutation is the most common EGFR resistance mechanism (seen in 50-60% of patients) and can be present at diagnosis or develop during treatment. This mutation increases affinity of kinase to ATP and decreases affinity to erlotinib and gefitinib.
  - Patients with the T790M mutation should be switched to osimertinib. Osimertinib is a third-generation EGFR-TKI that is selective for both EGFR-TKI-sensitizing and T790M resistance mutations.
- **Therapy after progression on an EGFR inhibitor**
  - For patients with asymptomatic progression on a TKI, continuation of EGFR-TKI therapy can be considered
    - For patients who have not received osimertinib, recommend testing for the T790M mutation at time of progression. If positive, osimertinib therapy is indicated.
  - For patients with symptomatic progression, options include: continuing with an EGFR inhibitor, switching to osimertinib if T790M mutation positive or switching to systemic chemotherapy
- **Acneiform Rash**
  - Development of an acneiform rash is the most common side effect of EGFR inhibitors. EGFR is expressed in many different tissues, including epithelial tissue, skin, hair follicles, and the gastrointestinal tract. During treatment with EGFR inhibitors cutaneous adverse events occur in 65-90% of patients. This rash usually develops in the first 1-2 weeks, peaks at 3-4 weeks of therapy, and its intensity decreases after 2 weeks but can often persist over some months.
  - Management
    - Mild Rash: patients may not require any form of intervention. Consider topical hydrocortisone cream or clindamycin gel.
    - Moderate Rash: hydrocortisone cream or clindamycin gel plus doxycycline 100 mg oral twice daily or minocycline 100 mg oral twice daily.
  - Studies have found that the development of a rash seems to be associated with an increased likelihood of tumor response and/or survival in NSCLC.
- **Disease flare on EGFR inhibitor discontinuation**
  - Some patients with EGFR mutations have accelerated disease progression after discontinuation of TKI. Patients who develop these disease flares after stopping an EGFR-TKI have shorter post-TKI survival and poorer overall survival.

High-Yield Fast-Facts

- **Lung Cancer Mutations**
  - EGFR mutations lead to increased cell proliferation, motility, and invasion. They are present in 10-15% of non-small cell lung cancers. They typically occur more commonly in women, Asian ethnicity and never-smokers.
  - K-ras and EGFR mutations are mutually exclusive. Meaning that if a patient has a K-ras mutation, they will not respond to EGFR inhibitors.

HIGH-YIELD BOARD EXAM ESSENTIALS

- **CLASSIC AGENTS:** Afatinib, erlotinib, gefitinib, osimertinib
- **DRUG CLASS:** EGFR inhibitors
- **INDICATIONS:** Cancers with T790M EGFR-mutation, or EGFR mutation
- **MECHANISM:** Highly selective tyrosine kinase inhibitors that covalently bind to epidermal growth factor receptors and irreversibly inhibit tyrosine kinase phosphorylation and downregulate EGFR signaling preventing cell growth.
- **SIDE EFFECTS:** Acneiform rash, diarrhea, skin/nail changes, dry mouth, nausea, vomiting, decreased appetite, hepatic dysfunction
- **CLINICAL PEARLS:** The T790M mutation is the most common EGFR resistance mechanism (seen in 50-60% of patients) and can be present at diagnosis or develop during treatment. This mutation increases affinity of kinase to ATP and decreases affinity to erlotinib and gefitinib

High-Yield Basic Pharmacology

- **Mechanism of Action**
  - Binds to VEGF and other endothelial growth factors receptors on endothelial cells blocking signals that promote the growth and survival of new blood vessels.

Primary Net Benefit

- Inhibition of tumor growth by suppressing its vascular supply. Unfortunately, this can also lead to vascular related complications.

<table>
<tr><td colspan="4" align="center">VEGF Inhibitors Drug Class Review
High-Yield Med Reviews</td></tr>
<tr><td colspan="4">Mechanism of Action: Binds to VEGF and other endothelial growth factors receptors on endothelial cells blocking signals that promote the growth and survival of new blood vessels</td></tr>
<tr><td colspan="4">Class Effects: Rash, hand-foot syndrome, nausea, vomiting, diarrhea, GI perforation, myelosuppression, hepatic dysfunction, hypertension, hypothyroidism</td></tr>
<tr><td>Generic Name</td><td>Brand Name</td><td>Indication(s) or Uses</td><td>Notes</td></tr>
<tr>
<td>Axitinib</td>
<td>Inlyta</td>
<td>
<ul>
<li>Renal Cell Carcinoma</li>
<li>Thyroid Cancer*</li>
</ul>
</td>
<td>
<ul>
<li>Dosing (Adult): Dosing varies per indication
  <ul><li>Typical dose range oral 2-10 mg twice daily</li></ul>
</li>
<li>Dosing (Peds): Not routinely used in pediatrics</li>
<li>CYP450 Interactions: Substrate of CYP1A2 (minor), CYP2C19 (minor), CYP3A4 (major), UGT1A1</li>
<li>Renal or Hepatic Dose Adjustments: Hepatic dose adjustments required with hepatic impairment, refer to specific protocol for recommended adjustment</li>
<li>Dosage Forms: 1 mg, 5 mg oral tablet</li>
</ul>
</td>
</tr>
<tr>
<td>Cabozantinib</td>
<td>Cabometyx; Cometriq</td>
<td>
<ul>
<li>Hepatocellular Carcinoma</li>
<li>Renal Cell Carcinoma</li>
<li>Thyroid Cancer</li>
</ul>
</td>
<td>
<ul>
<li>Dosing (Adult): Dosing varies per indication
  <ul><li>Typical dose range oral 40-140 mg once daily</li></ul>
</li>
<li>Dosing (Peds): Not routinely used in pediatrics</li>
<li>CYP450 Interactions: Substrate of CYP2C9 (minor), CYP3A4 (major)</li>
<li>Renal or Hepatic Dose Adjustments: Hepatic dose adjustments required with hepatic impairment, refer to specific protocol for recommended adjustment</li>
<li>Dosage Forms: 20 mg, 40 mg, 60 mg oral tablet, 20 mg, 80 mg oral capsule</li>
</ul>
</td>
</tr>
<tr>
<td>Lenvantinib</td>
<td>Lenvima</td>
<td>
<ul>
<li>Endometrial Cancer</li>
<li>Hepatocellular Carcinoma</li>
<li>Renal Cell Carcinoma</li>
<li>Thyroid Cancer</li>
</ul>
</td>
<td>
<ul>
<li>Dosing (Adult): Dosing varies per indication
  <ul><li>Typical dose range oral 8mg -24 mg daily</li></ul>
</li>
<li>Dosing (Peds): Not routinely used in pediatrics</li>
<li>CYP450 Interactions: Substrate of BCRP/ABCG2, CYP3A4 (minor), P-glycoprotein/ABCB1 (minor)</li>
<li>Renal or Hepatic Dose Adjustments: Hepatic and renal dose adjustments required, refer to specific protocol for recommended adjustment</li>
<li>Dosage Forms: 4 mg, 10 mg oral capsule</li>
</ul>
</td>
</tr>
</table>

VEGF Inhibitors Drug Class Review
High-Yield Med Reviews

Generic Name	Brand Name	Indication(s) or Uses	Notes
Vandetanib	Caprelsa	• Thyroid Cancer	• **Dosing (Adult):** Oral 300 mg once daily • **Dosing (Peds):** Not routinely used in pediatrics • **CYP450 Interactions:** Substrate of CYP3A4 (major), Inhibits OCT2 • **Renal or Hepatic Dose Adjustments:** CrCl <50 mL/minute: Reduce initial dose to 200 mg once daily. Moderate and severe hepatic impairment: Use is not recommended • **Dosage Forms:** 100 mg, 300 mg oral tablet
Pazopanib	Votrient	• Soft tissue sarcoma • Renal Cell Carcinoma • Desmoid Tumors* • Thyroid Cancer*	• **Dosing (Adult):** Oral 800 mg once daily • **Dosing (Peds):** Not routinely used in pediatrics • **CYP450 Interactions:** Substrate of BCRP/ABCG2, CYP1A2 (minor), CYP2C8 (minor), CYP3A4 (major), P-glycoprotein/ABCB1 (major); Inhibits CYP2C8 (weak), CYP3A4 (weak), UGT1A1 • **Renal or Hepatic Dose Adjustments:** Isolated ALT elevations >8 times ULN: Interrupt pazopanib treatment until improvement to grade 1 or baseline. If potential therapy benefit outweighs the risk of hepatotoxicity, resume pazopanib at a reduced dose. ALT >3 times ULN concurrently with bilirubin >2 times ULN: Permanently discontinue pazopanib • **Dosage Forms:** 200 mg oral tablet
Regorafenib	Stivarga	• Colorectal Cancer • GI Stromal Tumors • Hepatocellular Carcinoma • Osteosarcoma*	• **Dosing (Adult):** Dosing varies per indication – Typical dose range oral 80-160 mg daily on days 1-21 of a 28-day cycle • **Dosing (Peds):** Not routinely used in pediatrics • **CYP450 Interactions:** Substrate of CYP3A4 (major), UGT1A9; Inhibits BCRP/ABCG2, UGT1A1 • **Renal or Hepatic Dose Adjustments:** Grade 3 AST and/or ALT elevation: Withhold dose until recovery. If benefit of treatment outweighs toxicity risk, resume therapy at a reduced dose of 120 mg once daily. AST or ALT >20 times ULN: Discontinue permanently. • **Dosage Forms:** 40 mg oral tablet

VEGF Inhibitors Drug Class Review
High-Yield Med Reviews

Generic Name	Brand Name	Indication(s) or Uses	Notes
Sorafenib	NexAVAR	▪ Hepatocellular Carcinoma ▪ Renal Cell Carcinoma ▪ Thyroid Cancer ▪ Angiosarcoma* ▪ GI Stromal Tumors*	▪ **Dosing (Adult):** oral 400 mg twice daily ▪ **Dosing (Peds):** Not routinely used in pediatrics ▪ **CYP450 Interactions:** Substrate of CYP3A4 (major), UGT1A9; Inhibits BCRP/ABCG2, UGT1A1 **Renal or Hepatic Dose Adjustments:** CrCl 40 to 59 mL/minute: 400 mg twice daily. CrCl 20 to 39 mL/minute: 200 mg twice daily. Mild hepatic dysfunction (bilirubin >1 to ≤1.5 times ULN and/or AST >ULN): 400 mg twice daily. Moderate hepatic dysfunction (bilirubin >1.5 to ≤3 times ULN; any AST): 200 mg twice daily. Severe hepatic dysfunction and Albumin <2.5 g/dL (any bilirubin and any AST): 200 mg once daily ▪ **Dosage Forms:** 200 mg oral tablet

Sunitinib	Brand Name (if available)	▪ Soft tissue sarcoma*
		▪ Renal Cell Carcinoma
		▪ Thyroid Cancer*
		▪ Pancreatic Neuroendocrine Tumors
		▪ GI Stromal Tumors
			▪ **Dosing (Adult):** Dosing varies per indication
			  – Typical dose range
			▪ **Dosing (Peds):** Same as adult
			  – Extra info if needed
			    ▪ Extra info if needed
			▪ **CYP450 Interactions:** Substrate of CYP3A4 (major)
			▪ **Renal or Hepatic Dose Adjustments:** text
			▪ **Dosage Forms:** 12.5 mg, 25 mg, 37.5 mg, 50 mg oral tablet

*Off Label Use			

Emetic Potential

- **Minimal - Low Emetic Risk (<30% frequency of emesis)**
  - Axitinib
  - Cabozantinib
  - Lenvatinib <12 mg/day
  - Vandetanib
  - Pazopanib
  - Regorafenib
  - Sorafenib
  - Sunitinib
- **Moderate - High Emetic Risk (>30 frequency of emesis)**
  - Lenvatinib >12 mg/day

Extravasation Risk

- N/A

High-Yield Clinical Knowledge

- **Hypertension**

- VEGF plays a role in nitric oxide production and vasodilation. When the VEGF-signaling pathway is inhibited, hypertension may occur secondary to the decrease in nitric oxide production. Pre-existing hypertension, obesity, and older age increase the risk of developing VEGF inhibitor induced hypertension
- Hypertension secondary to VEGF-signaling pathway inhibitors should be managed similarly to hypertension in the general population. There are no formal guidelines for managing VEGF-signaling pathway inhibitor–induced hypertension, so it is recommended to follow the Joint National Committee hypertension guidelines for these patients. A common BP goal is <140/90 mmHg. Patients should have their BP monitored (and well controlled) prior to starting therapy and then checked at least every 2 to 3 weeks for the duration of treatment.

- **Proteinuria**
  - Proteinuria is a common adverse side effect of the anti-angiogenic agents. VEGF is critical to the maintenance of normal renal function, and under-expression of VEGF can disrupt normal glomerular function leading to proteinuria.
  - Patients should have their urine checked for protein on a regular basis during VEGF inhibitor therapy. Frequency may vary per institutional protocol but it is often checked every 1-2 cycles of chemotherapy. The presence of protein typically requires interruption of anti-VEGF therapy. In the majority of cases, proteinuria resolves or significantly improves with removal of VEGF inhibitors.

- **Bleeding/Thrombotic Events**
  - The VEGF- inhibitors are associated with bleeding events (epistaxis, hemoptysis, hematemesis, gastrointestinal bleeding) and an increased risk of arterial thromboembolic events (stroke, transient ischemic attack, myocardial infarction). Thrombotic events are more likely to occur in patients over 65 years of age or those with a history of thromboembolic events. Gastrointestinal perforation is also an infrequent but potentially life-threatening event during anti-VEGF therapy.
  - This predisposition to thrombosis and bleeding after inhibition of VEGF signaling reflects the multitude of actions VEGF has on vascular walls and the coagulation system.

- **Impaired Wound Healing**
  - Vascular endothelial growth factor receptor inhibitors are associated with impaired wound healing due to decreased angiogenesis. Therapy should typically be held for at least 1 month prior to surgery and only resumed when adequate wound healing has occurred.

- **Hepatotoxicity**
  - The VEGF inhibitors undergo hepatic metabolism and many of them can cause hepatotoxicity. In fact, many of the TKIs have a black boxed warning for hepatotoxicity. Depending on the level of AST/ALT elevations, you may need to hold or dose reduce the VEGF inhibitor.

High-Yield Fast-Facts

- **Skin/hair changes with Sunitinib**
  - Sunitinib can cause yellowing of the skin and hair
  - Think "shine like the sun" to help you remember
- **Cabozantinib Dosage Forms**
  - Cabozantinib is used to treat multiple disease states. However, the tablets and capsules are NOT interchangeable. The tablets are used for renal cell carcinoma and the capsules are used for thyroid cancer.

HIGH-YIELD BOARD EXAM ESSENTIALS
- **CLASSIC AGENTS:** Axitinib, cabozantinib, lenvatinib, vandetanib, pazopanib, regorafenib, sorafenib, sunitinib
- **DRUG CLASS:** VEGF inhibitors
- **INDICATIONS:** Endometrial cancer, hepatocellular carcinoma, renal cell carcinoma, thyroid cancer
- **MECHANISM:** Binds to VEGF and other endothelial growth factors receptors on endothelial cells blocking signals that promote the growth and survival of new blood vessels
- **SIDE EFFECTS:** Bleeding/thrombotic events, hypertension, proteinuria, impaired wound healing, hepatotoxicity
- **CLINICAL PEARLS:** The VEGF inhibitors undergo hepatic metabolism and many of them can cause hepatotoxicity. In fact, many of the TKIs have a black boxed warning for hepatotoxicity. Depending on the level of AST/ALT elevations, you may need to hold or dose reduce the VEGF inhibitor.

High-Yield Basic Pharmacology

- **Mechanism of Action**
  - Tretinoin: binds one or more nuclear receptors and decreases proliferation and induces differentiation of APL cells
  - Arsenic trioxide: induces apoptosis in APL cells via DNA fragmentation and damages the fusion protein promyelocytic leukemia (PML)-retinoic acid receptor (RAR) alpha
  - Hydroxyurea: antimetabolite that selectively inhibits ribonucleoside diphosphate reductase and interferes with DNA repair. In sickle cell anemia, hydroxyurea increases hemoglobin F levels

Primary Overall Net Benefit

- N/A.

Miscellaneous Hematology Agents Drug Class Review			
High-Yield Med Reviews			
Mechanism of Action: *Arsenic trioxide: induces apoptosis in APL cells via DNA fragmentation and damages the fusion protein promyelocytic leukemia (PML)-retinoic acid receptor (RAR) alpha. Tretinoin: binds one or more nuclear receptors and decreases proliferation and induces differentiation of APL cells. Hydroxyurea: antimetabolite that selectively inhibits ribonucleoside diphosphate reductase and interferes with DNA repair. In sickle cell anemia, hydroxyurea increases hemoglobin F levels.*			
Class Effects: Nausea/Vomiting, diarrhea, fatigue, differentiation syndrome (ATO, ATRA), QTc prolongation (ATO), myelosuppression (hydroxyurea), hair thinning (hydroxyurea), skin/nail changes (hydroxyurea), birth defects (hydroxyurea, ATRA)			
Generic Name	**Brand Name**	**Indication(s) or Uses**	**Notes**
All-Trans Retinoic Acid (ATRA, Tretinoin)	N/A	▪ Acute Promyelocytic Leukemia	▪ **Dosing (Adult):** Oral 45 mg/m²/day in 2 equally divided doses ▪ **Dosing (Peds):** Oral 25 mg/m²/day in 2 divided doses ▪ **CYP450 Interactions:** Substrate of CYP2A6 (minor), CYP2B6 (minor), CYP2C8 (minor), CYP2C9 (minor), Induces CYP2E1 (weak) ▪ **Renal or Hepatic Dose Adjustments:** Has not been studied ▪ **Dosage Forms:** 10 mg oral capsule
Arsenic Trioxide (ATO)	Trisenox	▪ Acute Promyelocytic Leukemia	▪ **Dosing (Adult):** Dosing varies per protocol – Typical dose range IV 0.15-0.3 mg/kg daily ▪ **Dosing (Peds):** Same as adult ▪ **CYP450 Interactions:** None Known ▪ **Renal or Hepatic Dose Adjustments:** Hold therapy for hepatotoxicity during treatment. When total bilirubin <1.5 times ULN and AST/AP <3 times ULN, resume treatment with the dose(s) reduced by 50%. ▪ **Dosage Forms:** 10 mg/10 mL, 12 mg/6 mL solution for IV injection

Miscellaneous Hematology Agents Drug Class Review			
High-Yield Med Reviews			
Generic Name	Brand Name	Indication(s) or Uses	Notes
Hydroxyurea	Droxia; Hydrea; Siklos	▪ Chronic Myeloid Leukemia ▪ Head and Neck Cancer ▪ Sickle Cell Anemia ▪ Cytoreduction in hematologic malignancies* ▪ Essential Thrombocythemia* ▪ Polycythemia Vera*	▪ **Dosing (Adult):** Dosing varies per indication − Typical dose range oral 15-100 mg/kg/day ▪ **Dosing (Peds):** Same as adult ▪ **CYP450 Interactions:** None known ▪ **Renal or Hepatic Dose Adjustments:** Cl <60 mL/minute: Reduce initial dose by 50% ▪ **Dosage Forms:** 200 mg, 300 mg, 400 mg, 500 mg oral capsule; 100 mg, 1000 mg oral tablet
*Off Label Use			

Emetic Potential

- **Minimal to Low Emetic Risk (<30% frequency of emesis)**
  - Hydroxyurea
  - Tretinoin
- **Low Emetic Risk (10-30% frequency of emesis)**
  - Arsenic Trioxide

Extravasation Risk

- None

High-Yield Clinical Knowledge

- **Differentiation Syndrome**
  - While acute promyelocytic leukemia (APL) is highly treatable, differentiation syndrome (DS) is potentially fatal complication of APL treatment. DS occurs in approximately 25% of patients who are treated for APL and typically presents in the first 7-12 days of treatment. The pathogenesis of DS is incompletely understood, but in APL, treatment can induce maturation of promyelocytes and promote tissue infiltration which is linked to the production of inflammatory cytokines. Patients are started on APL induction therapy in the hospital to closely monitor for DS.
  - Typical clinical findings of DS include dyspnea, fever, peripheral edema, hypotension, weight gain, pleuro-pericardial effusion, acute renal failure, musculoskeletal pain, and hyperbilirubinemia
  - Treatment of DS includes prompt steroid treatment and holding agents that can cause DS (ATRA and ATO) until signs and symptoms resolve. These agents are typically restarted at a lower dose before slowly titrating back up to full dose.
  - Both ATRA and ATO have black boxed warnings for DS
- **QTc Prolongation and Electrolyte Replacement**
  - Arsenic trioxide has a black box warning for QTc interval prolongation, complete atrioventricular block, and torsade de pointes, which can be fatal.
  - Before administering arsenic trioxide, assess the QTc interval, correct preexisting electrolyte abnormalities (Potassium >4 and magnesium >2), and consider discontinuing drugs known to prolong QTc interval. EKGs should be checked at baseline and 1-2 times per week during therapy. QTc is calculated using the Framingham formula (QTc = QT interval + 154 x (1 - RR interval)) and QTc elevation is considered to be >450 msec.
  - Withhold arsenic trioxide until resolution and resume at reduced dose for QTc prolongation.
- **Pregnancy risk**
  - There is a high risk that a severely deformed infant will result if tretinoin is administered during pregnancy. Within 1 week prior to starting tretinoin therapy, collect blood or urine from the patient for

a serum or urine pregnancy test with a sensitivity of at least 50 milliunits/mL. When possible, delay tretinoin therapy until a negative result from this test is obtained.

- **Dose Titration of Hydroxyurea**
  - Hydroxyurea can be used for cytoreduction (urgently brining down a high white blood cell count) in newly diagnosed hematologic malignancy patients or as maintenance therapy for patients with essential thrombocythemia, sickle cell disease and chronic myeloid leukemia. Regardless of indication, doses are typically titrated to specific white blood cell or platelet counts (that vary depending on indication).
  - When titrating doses for cytoreduction, doses are typically adjusted every few days, while as doses for maintenance indications are typically titrated every few weeks.

High-Yield Fast-Facts

- **Hydroxyurea in sickle cell disease**
  - Hydroxyurea was the first drug FDA approved for the treatment of sickle cell disease back in 1998, it was nearly 20 years before another drug was approved for sickle cell disease in 2017! Since then there have been 3 new drug approvals and more therapies being investigated.

HIGH-YIELD BOARD EXAM ESSENTIALS

- **CLASSIC AGENTS:** Hydroxyurea, all-trans retinoic acid (ATRA, Tretinoin), arsenic trioxide (ATO)
- **DRUG CLASS:** Miscellaneous hematology agents
- **INDICATIONS:** APL, CML, head and neck cancer, sickle cell anemia, cytoreduction in hematologic malignancies, essential thrombocythemia, polycythemia vera
- **MECHANISM:** Arsenic trioxide: induces apoptosis in APL cells via DNA fragmentation and damages the fusion protein promyelocytic leukemia (PML)-retinoic acid receptor (RAR) alpha. Tretinoin: binds one or more nuclear receptors and decreases proliferation and induces differentiation of APL cells. Hydroxyurea: antimetabolite that selectively inhibits ribonucleoside diphosphate reductase and interferes with DNA repair. In sickle cell anemia, hydroxyurea increases hemoglobin F levels.
- **SIDE EFFECTS:** Nausea/Vomiting, diarrhea, fatigue, differentiation syndrome (ATO, ATRA), QTc prolongation (ATO), myelosuppression (hydroxyurea), hair thinning (hydroxyurea), skin/nail changes (hydroxyurea), birth defects (hydroxyurea, ATRA)
- **CLINICAL PEARLS:** Arsenic trioxide has a black box warning for QTc interval prolongation, complete atrioventricular block, and torsade de pointes, which can be fatal.

High-Yield Basic Pharmacology

- **Mechanism of Action**
  - Commonly used antihistamines are inverse agonists of H1 receptors.
  - This is a distinction from H1 antagonists, which are competitive antagonists of histamine at the H1 receptor.

Primary Net Benefit

- Over-the-counter agents for managing common allergy-related complaints and acute care use of specific agents for numerous indications that are extensions of their central and peripheral antihistamine effect.

Antihistamine (Nasal/Ophthalmic) - Drug Class Review			
High-Yield Med Reviews			
Mechanism of Action:			
Antihistamines - Inverse agonist at H1 receptors that compete with histamine for binding sites and stabilizes the receptor's inactive state.			
Anticholinergic - Competitive inhibitor of acetylcholine receptors			
Class Effects: Dry mucous membranes, sedation.			
Generic Name	**Brand Name**	**Indication(s) or Uses**	**Notes**

Alcaftadine	Lastacaft	• Allergic conjunctivitis	• **Dosing (Adult):**
			  – Ophthalmic 1 drop in each eye daily
			• **Dosing (Peds):**
			  – Ophthalmic 1 drop in each eye daily
			• **CYP450 Interactions:** None
			• **Renal or Hepatic Dose Adjustments:** None
			• **Dosage Forms:** Ophthalmic solution

Atropine	Isopto Atropine	• Amblyopia
		• Mydriasis
			• **Dosing (Adult):**
			  – Ophthalmic 1 drop in each eye 40 minutes prior to maximal dilation time
			  – Ophthalmic -apply a small amount in the conjunctival sac 1-2 times daily
			• **Dosing (Peds):**
			  – Ophthalmic 1 drop in each eye 40 minutes prior to maximal dilation time
			• **CYP450 Interactions:** None
			• **Renal or Hepatic Dose Adjustments:** None
			• **Dosage Forms:** Ophthalmic (solution, ointment)

Antihistamine (Nasal/Ophthalmic) - Drug Class Review
High-Yield Med Reviews

Generic Name	Brand Name	Indication(s) or Uses	Notes

Azelastine	Astepro	▪ Allergic conjunctivitis
		▪ Allergic rhinitis
		▪ Vasomotor rhinitis
			▪ **Dosing (Adult):**
			  – Nasal 1 to 2 sprays per nostril twice daily
			  – Ophthalmic 1 drop in affected eye(s) twice daily
			▪ **Dosing (Peds):**
			  – Nasal 1 to 2 sprays per nostril twice daily
			  – Ophthalmic 1 drop in affected eye(s) twice daily
			▪ **CYP450 Interactions:** None
			▪ **Renal or Hepatic Dose Adjustments:** None
			▪ **Dosage Forms:** Ophthalmic solution, Nasal solution

Bepotastine	Bepreve	▪ Allergic conjunctivitis	▪ **Dosing (Adult):**
			  – Ophthalmic 1 drop in affected eye(s) twice daily
			▪ **Dosing (Peds):**
			  – Ophthalmic 1 drop in affected eye(s) twice daily
			▪ **CYP450 Interactions:** None
			▪ **Renal or Hepatic Dose Adjustments:** None
			▪ **Dosage Forms:** Ophthalmic solution

Cetirizine	Zyrtec, Zyrtec-D (with pseudoephedrine), Zerviate, Quzyttir	▪ Allergic rhinitis	▪ **Dosing (Adult):**
			  – Ophthalmic 1 drop in affected eye(s) twice daily
			▪ **Dosing (Peds):**
			  – Ophthalmic 1 drop in affected eye(s) twice daily
			▪ **CYP450 Interactions:** Substrate CYP3A4, P-gp
			▪ **Renal or Hepatic Dose Adjustments:**
			  – GFR 11 to 30 mL/minute - 5 mg daily
			  – GFR less than 10 mL/minute - not recommended
			  – Child-Pugh class A, B or C - 5 mg daily
			▪ **Dosage Forms:** Oral (liquid, tablet), Ophthalmic solution, IV (solution)

Emedastine	Emadine	▪ Allergic conjunctivitis	▪ **Dosing (Adult):**
			  – Ophthalmic 1 drop in affected eye(s) up to 4 times daily
			▪ **Dosing (Peds):**
			  – Ophthalmic 1 drop in affected eye(s) up to 4 times daily
			▪ **CYP450 Interactions:** None
			▪ **Renal or Hepatic Dose Adjustments:** None
			▪ **Dosage Forms:** Ophthalmic solution

Antihistamine (Nasal/Ophthalmic) - Drug Class Review
High-Yield Med Reviews

Generic Name	Brand Name	Indication(s) or Uses	Notes

Epinastine	Elestat	• Allergic conjunctivitis	• **Dosing (Adult):**
			  – Ophthalmic 1 drop in affected eye(s) twice daily
			• **Dosing (Peds):**
			  – Ophthalmic 1 drop in affected eye(s) twice daily
			• **CYP450 Interactions:** None
			• **Renal or Hepatic Dose Adjustments:** None
			• **Dosage Forms:** Ophthalmic solution

Glycopyrrolate	Qbrexza	• Primary axillary hyperhidrosis	• **Dosing (Adult):**
			  – Topically apply to each underarm q24h
			• **Dosing (Peds):**
			  – Children over 9 years - Topically apply to each underarm q24h
			• **CYP450 Interactions:** None
			• **Renal or Hepatic Dose Adjustments:** None
			• **Dosage Forms:** Ophthalmic solution

Ketotifen	Zaditor	• Allergic conjunctivitis	• **Dosing (Adult):**
			  – Ophthalmic 1 drop in affected eye(s) twice daily
			• **Dosing (Peds):**
			  – Ophthalmic 1 drop in affected eye(s) twice daily
			• **CYP450 Interactions:** None
			• **Renal or Hepatic Dose Adjustments:** None
			• **Dosage Forms:** Ophthalmic solution

Olopatadine	Patanase, Pataday	• Allergic conjunctivitis
		• Allergic rhinitis
			• **Dosing (Adult):**
			  – Ophthalmic 1 drop in affected eye(s) once to twice daily
			  – Nasal 2 sprays in each nostril BID
			• **Dosing (Peds):**
			  – Ophthalmic 1 drop in affected eye(s) once to twice daily
			  – Nasal 1 to 2 sprays in each nostril BID
			• **CYP450 Interactions:** None
			• **Renal or Hepatic Dose Adjustments:** None
			• **Dosage Forms:** Ophthalmic solution, Nasal solution

High-Yield Clinical Knowledge

- **Contact Lens Insertion**
  - Patients must be instructed to remove contact lenses before ophthalmic administration.
  - Patients should wait at least 10 minutes after the administration of ophthalmic antihistamines before inserting contact lenses.
- **Multiple Ophthalmic Agent Administration**
  - If the patient has more than one ophthalmic medication, they should be spaced at least five minutes.

- **Oral Ingestion of Topical Products**
  - Accidental ingestion may result in significant morbidity and mortality. Keep out of reach of children since there is no child protection cap after initial use.
- **Symptomatic Management**
  - These agents are not effective at treating the underlying cause of ophthalmic redness, such as allergic conjunctivitis.
  - Corticosteroids are more appropriate for addressing the underlying cause but are not always indicated as allergic conjunctivitis or rhinitis may be self-limiting.
- **Antihistamine Combinations**
  - Additive antihistamine effects and increased risk of adverse events can occur in patients taking over-the-counter topical antihistamines who may also be taking oral antihistamines.
- **Topical Dryness**
  - Azelastine topical nasal products have been associated with mucous membrane drying effects, headache, and decreased clinical response with long-term use.

High-Yield Fast-Fact

- **Atropine and Glycopyrrolate**
  - Although atropine and glycopyrrolate possess antihistamine effects, they are not used as OTC anticholinergics.

HIGH-YIELD BOARD EXAM ESSENTIALS
- **CLASSIC AGENTS:** Alcaftadine, azelastine, bepotastine, cetirizine, clemastine, emedastine, epinastine, ketotifen, olopatadine
- **DRUG CLASS:** Antihistamine
- **INDICATIONS:** Allergic conjunctivitis, allergic rhinitis, vasomotor rhinitis
- **MECHANISM:** Inverse agonists at H1 receptors that compete with histamine for binding sites and stabilizes the receptor's inactive state.
- **SIDE EFFECTS:** Dry mucous membranes, sedation
- **CLINICAL PEARLS:** Patients must be instructed to remove contact lenses before ophthalmic administration. Patients should wait at least 10 minutes after the administration of ophthalmic antihistamines before inserting contact lenses.

High-Yield Basic Pharmacology

- **Mechanism of Action**
  - Enhance normal and uveoscleral outflow of aqueous humor and decrease the production of aqueous humor.
- **Pre- and Postsynaptic Alpha-2**
  - Apraclonidine and brimonidine possess both pre- and postsynaptic alpha-2 agonist properties.
  - Presynaptic agonist actions on the alpha-2 receptor reduce the quantity of sympathetic neurotransmitter release.
  - Postsynaptic alpha-2 agonist actions lead to a reduction in aqueous humor production.

Primary Net Benefit

- Considered second line intraocular pressure (IOP) lowering agents for glaucoma.

Alpha Agonists - Drug Class Review			
High-Yield Med Reviews			
Mechanism of Action: *Enhance normal and uveoscleral outflow of aqueous humor and decrease the production of aqueous humor.*			
Class Effects: Lower intraocular pressure (IOP), risk for rebound elevation in IOP, CNS depression, apnea			
Generic Name	**Brand Name**	**Indication(s) or Uses**	**Notes**

Apraclonidine	Iopidine	• Elevated intraocular pressure	• **Dosing (Adult):**
			  – Ophthalmic - 1 to 2 drops into affected eye(s) 3 times daily
			• **Dosing (Peds):**
			  – Not routinely used
			• **CYP450 Interactions:** None
			• **Renal or Hepatic Dose Adjustments:** None
			• **Dosage Forms:** Ophthalmic solution

Brimonidine	Alphagan P, Lumify	• Elevated intraocular pressure	• **Dosing (Adult):**
			  – Ophthalmic - 1 drop into affected eye(s) q8-12h
			• **Dosing (Peds):**
			  – Ophthalmic - 1 drop into affected eye(s) q8-12h
			• **CYP450 Interactions:** None
			• **Renal or Hepatic Dose Adjustments:** None
			• **Dosage Forms:** Ophthalmic solution

High-Yield Clinical Knowledge

- **Rebound Effects**
  - The alpha-2 agonists are associated with vasoconstriction-vasodilation rebound effects that can cause eye redness.
  - This effect of brimonidine extends to its use as a topical skin agent for the treatment of rosacea.
  - The red discoloration often responds to lowering the dose or conversion to an alternative agent.

- **Children Younger Than 2**
  - Apraclonidine and brimonidine are contraindicated in children younger than 2 because of the risk of CNS depression and apnea.
- **Ophthalmic Drop Administration**
  - Before administering any ophthalmic product, patients should be reminded to wash their hands and remove any contact lenses.
  - Most administrations should begin with 1 drop of solution in the affected eye.
  - No more than 1 drop should be administered at a time, and multiple drops should be separated by at least 1 minute since the aqueous chamber cannot hold the given volume.
  - If drops and ointments are to be given, the drop should be administered first, followed by the ointment.
- **Monitoring Intraocular Pressure**
  - Some patients with glaucoma may only affect individual eyes rather than a bilateral effect.
  - For the purposes of monitoring intraocular pressure changes throughout drug therapy, an initial pressure in the affected should be used as a baseline for monitoring rather than using the unaffected eye intraocular pressure.
  - This results from the possibility of ophthalmic agents that are applied to a single eye, affecting both eyes.
- **Intraocular Pressure Goals**
  - An acute reduction of 20 to 30% in the IOP is the initial goal of drug therapy, as well as monitoring visual fields, and examination of the optic disk.
  - If goal pressures are not achieved with an initial agent, switching to a new agent rather than additional add-on agents is recommended.

High-Yield Fast-Fact

- **Oral Ingestion**
  - Oral ingestion of alpha-agonist ophthalmic products can produce profound diarrhea but may also lead to severe, life-threatening hemodynamic compromise similar to a massive clonidine overdose.
  - Ingestion of small amounts of ophthalmic products by a child is considered a medical emergency.

HIGH-YIELD BOARD EXAM ESSENTIALS
- **CLASSIC AGENTS:** Apraclonidine, brimonidine
- **DRUG CLASS:** Alpha agonists
- **INDICATIONS:** Elevated intraocular pressure
- **MECHANISM:** Enhance normal and uveoscleral outflow of aqueous humor and decrease the production of aqueous humor.
- **SIDE EFFECTS:** Rebound elevation in IOP, CNS depression, apnea
- **CLINICAL PEARLS:** Apraclonidine and brimonidine are contraindicated in children younger than 2 because of the risk of CNS depression and apnea.

High-Yield Basic Pharmacology

- **Mechanism of Action**
  - Beta-2 antagonists decrease intraocular pressure (IOP) decreases aqueous humor production.
- **Beta-1 Selectivity**
  - The ophthalmic beta-antagonists are all non-selective beta-1 and beta-2 agents, except for betaxolol, a beta-1 selective antagonist.
  - The proposed benefit is a reduced likelihood of bronchospasm from systemically absorbed betaxolol.

Primary Net Benefit

- Intraocular pressure (IOP) lowering agents with established safety and efficacy for ophthalmic care.

Beta Antagonists - Drug Class Review			
High-Yield Med Reviews			
Mechanism of Action: *Beta-2 antagonists decrease intraocular pressure (IOP) decreases aqueous humor production.*			
Class Effects: Reduction in intraocular pressure (IOP), risk for eye discomfort, blurry vision, keratitis			
Generic Name	**Brand Name**	**Indication(s) or Uses**	**Notes**

Betaxolol	Betoptic-S	• Elevated intraocular pressure	• **Dosing (Adult):**
			  – Ophthalmic - 1 to 2 drops into affected eye(s) q12h
			• **Dosing (Peds):**
			  – Ophthalmic - 1 drop into affected eye(s) q12h
			• **CYP450 Interactions:** Substrate CYP1A2, 2D6
			• **Renal or Hepatic Dose Adjustments:** None
			• **Dosage Forms:** Ophthalmic (solution, suspension)

Carteolol	Ocupress	• Elevated intraocular pressure	• **Dosing (Adult):**
			  – Ophthalmic - 1 drops into affected eye(s) q12h
			• **Dosing (Peds):**
			  – Not routinely used
			• **CYP450 Interactions:** Substrate CYP2D6
			• **Renal or Hepatic Dose Adjustments:** None
			• **Dosage Forms:** Ophthalmic (solution)

Levobunolol	Betagan	• Elevated intraocular pressure	• **Dosing (Adult):**
			  – Ophthalmic - 1 to 2 drops into affected eye(s) q24h
			• **Dosing (Peds):**
			  – Not routinely used
			• **CYP450 Interactions:** None
			• **Renal or Hepatic Dose Adjustments:** None
			• **Dosage Forms:** Ophthalmic (solution)

Beta Antagonists - Drug Class Review			
High-Yield Med Reviews			
Generic Name	**Brand Name**	**Indication(s) or Uses**	**Notes**
Timolol	Betimol, Istalol, Timoptic	▪ Elevated intraocular pressure	▪ **Dosing (Adult):** – Ophthalmic - 1 drops into affected eye(s) q12h ▪ **Dosing (Peds):** – Ophthalmic - 1 drop into affected eye(s) q12h ▪ **CYP450 Interactions:** Substrate CYP2D6 ▪ **Renal or Hepatic Dose Adjustments:** None ▪ **Dosage Forms:** Ophthalmic (gel forming solution, solution)

High-Yield Clinical Knowledge

- **Alpha and Beta Effects**
  - Levobunolol is a mixed alpha and beta receptor antagonist that may have a specific benefit in controlling IOP after cataract surgery.
- **Timolol Formulations**
  - Although most ophthalmic beta-antagonists are administered multiple times daily, timolol is available in a gel-forming solution permitting once-daily administration.
- **Systemic Effects**
  - Ophthalmic beta-antagonists are systemically absorbed and are expected to lead to common beta-antagonist adverse events, including bronchospasm, bradycardia, masking of sympathetic response to hypoglycemia, and sexual dysfunction.
    - Ophthalmic beta-antagonists should be used with caution in patients with reactive pulmonary disease, symptomatic bradycardia, heart failure, and diabetes.
  - Furthermore, patients who are already taking systemic beta-antagonists experience a lower IOP reduction from ophthalmic beta-antagonist therapy.
- **Monitoring Intraocular Pressure**
  - Some patients with glaucoma may only affect individual eyes rather than a bilateral effect.
  - To monitor intraocular pressure changes throughout drug therapy, an initial pressure in the affected should be used as a baseline for monitoring rather than using the unaffected eye intraocular pressure.
  - This results from the possibility of ophthalmic agents that are applied to a single eye, affecting both eyes.
- **Intraocular Pressure Goals**
  - An acute reduction of 20 to 30% in the IOP is the initial goal of drug therapy, as well as monitoring visual fields and examination of the optic disk.
  - If goal pressures are not achieved with an initial agent, it is recommended to switch to a new agent rather than add additional agents.
- **Ophthalmic Drop Administration**
  - Before administering any ophthalmic product, patients should be reminded to wash their hands and remove any contact lenses.
  - Most administrations should begin with 1 drop of solution in the affected eye.
  - No more than 1 drop should be administered at a time, and multiple drops should be separated by at least 1 minute since the aqueous chamber cannot hold the given volume.
  - If drops and ointments are to be given, the drop should be administered first, followed by the ointment.

HIGH-YIELD BOARD EXAM ESSENTIALS

- **CLASSIC AGENTS:** Betaxolol, carteolol, levobunolol, metipranolol, timolol
- **DRUG CLASS:** Beta antagonists
- **INDICATIONS:** Elevated intraocular pressure
- **MECHANISM:** Beta-2 antagonists decrease intraocular pressure (IOP) decreases aqueous humor production.
- **SIDE EFFECTS:** Eye discomfort, blurry vision, keratitis
- **CLINICAL PEARLS:** An acute reduction of 20 to 30% in the IOP is the initial goal of drug therapy, as well as monitoring visual fields and examination of the optic disk.

High-Yield Basic Pharmacology

- **Mechanism of Action**
  - Inhibit carbonic anhydrase causing a reduction in intraocular fluid transport from a reduction in the formation of bicarbonate.
- **Other Systemic Effects**
  - Inhibition of carbonic anhydrase blunts the reabsorption of sodium bicarbonate, promoting diuresis.
  - Carbonic anhydrase is responsible for converting carbonic acid to carbon dioxide at the renal luminal membrane and rehydration of carbon dioxide to the carbonic acid in the cytoplasm.
  - By blocking these processes, carbonic anhydrase inhibitors promote a reduction of hydrogen secretion, increased renal excretion of sodium, potassium, bicarbonate, and water.

Primary Net Benefit

- Reserved for second-line or combination therapy for the management of elevated intraocular pressure. Considerations of clinically relevant systemic absorption include patients with renal impairment.

<table>
<tr><td colspan="4" align="center">**Carbonic Anhydrase Inhibitors - Drug Class Review**
High-Yield Med Reviews</td></tr>
<tr><td colspan="4">**Mechanism of Action:** *Inhibit carbonic anhydrase, causing a reduction in intraocular fluid transport from a reduction in bicarbonate formation.*</td></tr>
<tr><td colspan="4">**Class Effects:** Reduction in intraocular pressure, minimal side effects topically</td></tr>
<tr><th>Generic Name</th><th>Brand Name</th><th>Indication(s) or Uses</th><th>Notes</th></tr>
<tr>
<td>Brinzolamide</td>
<td>Azopt</td>
<td>- Elevated intraocular pressure</td>
<td>

- **Dosing (Adult):**
  - Ophthalmic - 1 drop into affected eye(s) q8h
- **Dosing (Peds):**
  - Not routinely used
- **CYP450 Interactions:** Substrate CYP3A4
- **Renal or Hepatic Dose Adjustments:**
  - GFR less than 30 mL/minute - use not recommended
- **Dosage Forms:** Ophthalmic solution
</td>
</tr>
<tr>
<td>Dorzolamide</td>
<td>Trusopt</td>
<td>- Elevated intraocular pressure</td>
<td>

- **Dosing (Adult):**
  - Ophthalmic - 1 drop into affected eye(s) q8h
- **Dosing (Peds):**
  - Ophthalmic - 1 drop into affected eye(s) q8h
- **CYP450 Interactions:** Substrate CYP2C9, 3A4
- **Renal or Hepatic Dose Adjustments:**
  - GFR less than 30 mL/minute - use not recommended
- **Dosage Forms:** Ophthalmic solution
</td>
</tr>
</table>

High-Yield Clinical Knowledge

- **Systemic Vs. Topical Carbonic Anhydrase Inhibitors**
  - The topical carbonic anhydrase inhibitors are primarily preferred to oral agents and reduce the incidence of fatigue, depression, paresthesias, and nephrolithiasis associated with the systemic route.
- **Sulfonamide Derivatives**
  - There is a theoretical risk of cross-reactivity in patients with a history of sulfonamide hypersensitivity.
  - As a result of its sulfonamide structure, carbonic anhydrase inhibitors carry a risk of bone marrow depression, Stevens-Johnson Syndrome, and sulfonamide-like kidney injury.
  - The ophthalmic carbonic anhydrase inhibitors are systemically absorbed and may pose a risk in patients with sulfonamide hypersensitivity.
- **Renal Impairment**
  - Unlike other topical ophthalmic agents, brinzolamide and dorzolamide should be avoided in patients with GFR less than 30 mL/minute as the risk of hyperchloremic acidosis is higher among this population.
- **Systemic Carbonic Anhydrase Inhibition**
  - The combination of systemic and topical carbonic anhydrase inhibitors is not recommended.
  - Although systemic CAIs reduce IOP by up to 40%, they should be reserved for third-line agents, as the frequency and severity of systemic adverse events limit their use.
    - These systemic effects range from fatigue, nausea, and altered taste to depression, nephrolithiasis, increased uric acid, and blood dyscrasias.
- **Hyperchloremic Metabolic Acidosis**
  - Carbonic anhydrase inhibitors block the excretion of hydrogen ions accumulating in the plasma.
    - In normal healthy kidneys, reabsorb bicarbonate and offsets the accumulation of hydrogen and ensuing acidosis.
    - With impaired renal function, high doses, or otherwise altered metabolic function, renal tubules' capacity to reabsorb bicarbonate is impaired, which ultimately leads to an increasing acidosis.
      - The acidosis typically resolves upon discontinuation of the carbonic anhydrase inhibitor.
- **Ophthalmic Drop Administration**
  - Before administering any ophthalmic product, patients should be reminded to wash their hands and remove any contact lenses.
  - Most administrations should begin with 1 drop of solution in the affected eye.
  - No more than 1 drop should be administered at a time, and multiple drops should be separated by at least 1 minute since the aqueous chamber cannot hold the given volume.
  - If drops and ointments are to be given, the drop should be administered first, followed by the ointment.

HIGH-YIELD BOARD EXAM ESSENTIALS

- **CLASSIC AGENTS:** Brinzolamide, dorzolamide
- **DRUG CLASS:** Carbonic anhydrase inhibitors
- **INDICATIONS:** Elevated intraocular pressure
- **MECHANISM:** Inhibit carbonic anhydrase, causing a reduction in intraocular fluid transport from a reduction in bicarbonate formation.
- **SIDE EFFECTS:** Very low risk for hyperchloremic acidosis, fatigue, depression, paresthesias, and nephrolithiasis when used topically.
- **CLINICAL PEARLS:** The topical carbonic anhydrase inhibitors are primarily preferred to oral agents and reduce the incidence of fatigue, depression, paresthesias, and nephrolithiasis associated with the systemic route.

High-Yield Basic Pharmacology

- **Mechanism of Action**
  - Lower intraocular pressure (IOP) through ciliary muscle contraction, causing an opening of the trabecular meshwork and an increase in aqueous humor trabecular outflow.
- **Pseudocholinesterase Vs Cholinesterase**
  - Pseudocholinesterase is otherwise known as serum cholinesterase.
  - On the other hand, acetylcholinesterase is considered "true cholinesterase" and is located in erythrocytes, pulmonary tissue, spleen, and the CNS/PNS.

Primary Net Benefit

- Pilocarpine is the preferred cholinergic component of the combination treatment approach to primary open-angle glaucoma.

Cholinergic Agents - Drug Class Review			
High-Yield Med Reviews			
Mechanism of Action: *Lower intraocular pressure (IOP) through ciliary muscle contraction, causing an opening of the trabecular meshwork and an increase in aqueous humor trabecular outflow.*			
Class Effects: Reduction in intraocular pressure, small risk of headache, eyelid twitching, and conjunctival irritation.			
Generic Name	**Brand Name**	**Indication(s) or Uses**	**Notes**
Acetylcholine	Michol-E	• Induce Miosis	• **Dosing (Adult):** – Intraocular 0.5 to 2 mL to affected eye(s) • **Dosing (Peds):** – Intraocular 0.5 to 2 mL to affected eye(s) • **CYP450 Interactions:** None • **Renal or Hepatic Dose Adjustments:** None • **Dosage Forms:** Ophthalmic solution
Carbachol	Miostat	• Elevated intraocular pressure • Induce Miosis	• **Dosing (Adult):** – Ophthalmic - 1 to 2 drops to affected eye(s) up to 3 times/day • **Dosing (Peds):** – Ophthalmic - 1 to 2 drops to affected eye(s) up to 3 times/day • **CYP450 Interactions:** None • **Renal or Hepatic Dose Adjustments:** None • **Dosage Forms:** Ophthalmic solution
Echothiophate iodide	Phospholine Iodide	• Accommodative esotropia • Elevated intraocular pressure	• **Dosing (Adult):** – Ophthalmic - 1 drop to affected eye(s) up to twice daily • **Dosing (Peds):** – Ophthalmic - 1 drop up to into both eyes at bedtime • **CYP450 Interactions:** None • **Renal or Hepatic Dose Adjustments:** None • **Dosage Forms:** Ophthalmic solution

Cholinergic Agents - Drug Class Review			
High-Yield Med Reviews			
Generic Name	Brand Name	Indication(s) or Uses	Notes

Pilocarpine	Isopto Carpine	• Elevated intraocular pressure
		• Induce Miosis
			• **Dosing (Adult):**
			  – Ophthalmic - 1 drop to affected eye(s) up to 4 times/day
			• **Dosing (Peds):**
			  – Ophthalmic - 1 drop to affected eye(s) up to 4 times/day
			• **CYP450 Interactions:** None
			• **Renal or Hepatic Dose Adjustments:** None
			• **Dosage Forms:** Ophthalmic solution

High-Yield Clinical Knowledge

- **Cholinergic Ophthalmic Complications**
    - Pilocarpine is associated with miosis and an associated decrease in vision in low light settings or among patients with central cataracts.
    - Other common adverse events associated with pilocarpine include headache, eyelid twitching, and conjunctival irritation.
- **Systemic Cholinergic Effects**
    - With continued use, cholinergic ophthalmic agents disrupt the blood-aqueous humor barrier and acutely worsen ophthalmic inflammatory conditions.
    - This can also lead to systemic cholinergic manifestations, including bradycardia, bronchospasm, bronchorrhea, diaphoresis, flushing, nausea/vomiting/diarrhea, urinary retention, and altered mental status.
    - As a result of a high likelihood of serious systemic cholinergic effects, the use of echothiophate is minimal.
- **Eyelid Closure**
    - After the administration of pilocarpine, patients may be instructed to close their eyes, which may improve clinical response and decrease pilocarpine administration frequency.
    - Eyelid closure has also been associated with reduced systemic adverse effects related to echothiophate.
    - For optimal response, patients should be instructed to gently close their eyes for 5 minutes following drug administration.
    - The proposed mechanism is a decreased nasolacrimal drainage and increased nasopharyngeal mucosal absorption of the drug.
- **Echothiophate and Cataracts**
    - The use of echothiophate is limited to selected patients with either aphakia or pseudophakia (without lenses or artificial lenses), as it is known to induce the formation of cataracts.
    - Echothiophate has also been associated with numerous adverse ophthalmic structural changes, including fibrinous iritis.
    - The hydrolysis of succinylcholine is slowed by echothiophate, which may significantly prolong paralysis and possibly worsen the associated hyperkalemia.
- **Carbachol**
    - Carbachol is more resistant to cholinesterase hydrolysis than pilocarpine, providing it a longer half-life.
    - While patients who do not adequately respond to pilocarpine can receive carbachol, it is associated with more systemic and ophthalmic adverse events.

High-Yield Fast-Fact

- **Pilocarpine Dose and Eye Color**
    - It has been observed that patients with darkly pigmented eyes require higher pilocarpine concentrations to elicit a reduction in IOP.

HIGH-YIELD BOARD EXAM ESSENTIALS

- **CLASSIC AGENTS:** Acetylcholine, carbachol, echothiophate iodide, pilocarpine
- **DRUG CLASS:** Cholinergic agents
- **INDICATIONS:** Accommodative esotropia, elevated intraocular pressure
- **MECHANISM:** Lower intraocular pressure (IOP) through ciliary muscle contraction, causing an opening of the trabecular meshwork and an increase in aqueous humor trabecular outflow.
- **SIDE EFFECTS:** Systemic cholinergic effects (lacrimation, urination, GI distress, altered mental status).
- **CLINICAL PEARLS:** Pilocarpine is associated with miosis and an associated decrease in vision in low light settings or among patients with central cataracts.

High-Yield Basic Pharmacology

- **Mechanism of Action**
  - Inhibit ophthalmic edema formation, capillary dilation, leukocyte migration, and scar formation.
- **Implants/Injections**
  - Dexamethasone and fluocinolone are available as ophthalmic implants for the treatment of noninfectious uveitis or macular edema.

Primary Net Benefit

- Ophthalmic glucocorticoids exert a wide range of effects from ocular allergies and external eye inflammation to anterior uveitis and intravitreal injections to treat diabetic retinopathy and cystoid macular edema.

Glucocorticoids - Drug Class Review			
High-Yield Med Reviews			
Mechanism of Action: *Inhibit ophthalmic edema formation, capillary dilation, leukocyte migration, and scar formation.*			
Class Effects: Reduction in inflammation, risk of posterior subcapsular cataracts.			
Generic Name	**Brand Name**	**Indication(s) or Uses**	**Notes**
Dexamethasone	Dextenza, Dexycu, Maxidex, Ozurdex	• Inflammatory ocular conditions	• **Dosing (Adult):** – Ophthalmic - apply to inside of lower lid of affected eye(s) every 3 or 4 hours – Ophthalmic - instill 1 to 2 drops to affected eye(s) q1hour during the day and every other hour at night – Ophthalmic - instill 1 to 2 drops to affected eye(s) q4-6h • **Dosing (Peds):** – Ophthalmic - instill 1 to 2 drops to affected eye(s) q1hour during the day and every other hour at night – Ophthalmic - instill 1 to 2 drops to affected eye(s) q4-6h • **CYP450 Interactions:** None • **Renal or Hepatic Dose Adjustments:** None • **Dosage Forms:** Ophthalmic (ointment, solution, suspension)
Difluprednate	Durezol	• Endogenous anterior uveitis	• **Dosing (Adult):** – Ophthalmic - instill 1 to 2 drops to affected eye(s) 4 times daily for 14 days, then taper • **Dosing (Peds):** – Ophthalmic - instill 1 to 2 drops to affected eye(s) 4 times daily for 14 days, then taper • **CYP450 Interactions:** None • **Renal or Hepatic Dose Adjustments:** None • **Dosage Forms:** Ophthalmic emulsion

Glucocorticoids - Drug Class Review
High-Yield Med Reviews

Generic Name	Brand Name	Indication(s) or Uses	Notes

Fluocinolone	Iluvien, Retisert, Yutiq	• Diabetic macular edema	• **Dosing (Adult):**
			   – Intravitreal injected implant in affected eye for 30 to 36 months
			• **Dosing (Peds):**
			   – Children over 12 years, use adult dosing
			• **CYP450 Interactions:** None
			• **Renal or Hepatic Dose Adjustments:** None
			• **Dosage Forms:** Intravitreal implant

Fluorometholone	Flarex, FML, Forte	• Inflammatory ocular conditions	• **Dosing (Adult):**
			   – Ophthalmic - apply to inside of lower lid of affected eye(s) every 1 to 3 times daily
			   – Ophthalmic - instill 1 to 2 drops to affected eye(s) 2 to 4 times daily
			• **Dosing (Peds):**
			   – Ophthalmic - apply to inside of lower lid of affected eye(s) every 1 to 3 times daily
			   – Ophthalmic - instill 1 to 2 drops to affected eye(s) 2 to 4 times daily
			• **CYP450 Interactions:** None
			• **Renal or Hepatic Dose Adjustments:** None
			• **Dosage Forms:** Ophthalmic (ointment, suspension)

Hydrocortisone, Bacitracin, Neomycin, Polymyxin B	Neo-Polycin HC	• Inflammatory ocular conditions	• **Dosing (Adult):**
			   – Ophthalmic - apply to inside of lower lid of affected eye(s) every 3 or 4 hours
			• **Dosing (Peds):**
			   – Ophthalmic - apply to inside of lower lid of affected eye(s) every 3 or 4 hours
			• **CYP450 Interactions:** None
			• **Renal or Hepatic Dose Adjustments:** None
			• **Dosage Forms:** Ophthalmic ointment

Hydrocortisone, Neomycin, Polymyxin B	Brand Name (if available)	• Inflammatory ocular conditions	• **Dosing (Adult):**
			   – Ophthalmic - apply to inside of lower lid of affected eye(s) every 3 or 4 hours
			• **Dosing (Peds):**
			   – Ophthalmic - apply to inside of lower lid of affected eye(s) every 3 or 4 hours
			• **CYP450 Interactions:** None
			• **Renal or Hepatic Dose Adjustments:** None
			• **Dosage Forms:** Ophthalmic ointment

Glucocorticoids - Drug Class Review
High-Yield Med Reviews

Generic Name	Brand Name	Indication(s) or Uses	Notes

Loteprednol	Alrex, Eysuvis, Inveltys, Lotemax	• Inflammatory ocular conditions	• **Dosing (Adult):**
			  – Ophthalmic - instill 1 to 2 drops to affected eye(s) 4 times daily
			  – Ophthalmic - apply ½ inch ribbon to inside of lower lid of affected eye(s) 4 times daily
			• **Dosing (Peds):**
			  – Ophthalmic - instill 1 to 2 drops to affected eye(s) 4 times daily
			• **CYP450 Interactions:** None
			• **Renal or Hepatic Dose Adjustments:** None
			• **Dosage Forms:** Ophthalmic (gel, ointment, suspension)

Prednisolone	Omnipred, Pred Forte, Pred Mild	• Inflammatory ocular conditions	• **Dosing (Adult):**
			  – Ophthalmic - instill 1 to 2 drops to affected eye(s) 2 to 4 times daily
			• **Dosing (Peds):**
			  – Ophthalmic - instill 1 to 2 drops to affected eye(s) 2 to 4 times daily
			• **CYP450 Interactions:** None
			• **Renal or Hepatic Dose Adjustments:** None
			• **Dosage Forms:** Ophthalmic ointment

Triamcinolone	Triesence	• Inflammatory ocular conditions	• **Dosing (Adult):**
			  – Intravitreal 1 to 4 mg once
			• **Dosing (Peds):**
			  – Intravitreal 1 to 4 mg once
			• **CYP450 Interactions:** None
			• **Renal or Hepatic Dose Adjustments:** None
			• **Dosage Forms:** Ophthalmic suspension

High-Yield Clinical Knowledge

- **Cataracts**
    - The use of glucocorticoids is limited by the development of posterior subcapsular cataracts that arise with long-term or high-dose therapy.
- **Secondary Open-Angle Glaucoma**
    - Ophthalmic glucocorticoids may also increase the risk of secondary open-angle glaucoma, with a high risk among patients with a positive family history of glaucoma.
    - Loteprednol carries the lowest risk of elevated IOP.
- **Eye Drop Administration**
    - Nasolacrimal occlusion can reduce the systemic absorption of ophthalmic agents, including glucocorticoids.
    - Patients should be instructed first to wash their hands, followed by gently pulling down the lower eyelid to form a pocket.
    - Holding the drug bottle and bracing their hand with the side of their nose, the tip of the bottle should be placed close to the eye.
    - With their head tilted back, place the prescribed number of drips in the eyelid pocket, then close their eye and immediately press their finger gently against the inside corner of the eye for 1 to 3 minutes.

- **Intraocular Pressure Measurement**
  - Tonometry is the measurement of intraocular pressure and can be conducted with specialized devices known as tonometers.
  - Hand-held tonometers are often used in emergency departments, whereas larger tonometers are found elsewhere.

High-Yield Fast-Fact

- **Eye Drops in the Ear**
  - For some indications, ophthalmic products may be administered ophthalmically and tend to be both more widely available and less expensive than otic preparations of the same drug.
  - Otic products should never be administered ophthalmically.

HIGH-YIELD BOARD EXAM ESSENTIALS
- **CLASSIC AGENTS:** Dexamethasone, difluprednate, fluorometholone, hydrocortisone, loteprednol, prednisolone, triamcinolone
- **DRUG CLASS:** Glucocorticoids
- **INDICATIONS:** Inflammatory ocular conditions, endogenous anterior uveitis, diabetic macular edema
- **MECHANISM:** Inhibit ophthalmic edema formation, capillary dilation, leukocyte migration, and scar formation
- **SIDE EFFECTS:** Posterior subcapsular cataracts
- **CLINICAL PEARLS:**
  - Ophthalmic glucocorticoids may also increase the risk of secondary open-angle glaucoma, with a high risk among patients with a positive family history of glaucoma.
  - Ocular glucocorticoids should never be given to a patient with herpes keratitis unless an ophthalmologist is in involved and managing the patient.

High-Yield Basic Pharmacology

- **Mechanism of Action**
  - Inhibit mast cell degranulation, preventing the release of histamine and inflammatory leukotrienes.
- **Onset of Effect**
  - For mast cell stabilizers to exert their maximal effect, they should be initiated one week before anticipated allergen exposure.

Primary Net Benefit

- More effective alternatives have primarily replaced ophthalmic mast cell stabilizers but may play a role in allergic conjunctivitis.

Mast Cell Stabilizer - Drug Class Review			
High-Yield Med Reviews			
Mechanism of Action: *Inhibit mast cell degranulation, preventing the release of histamine and inflammatory leukotrienes.*			
Class Effects: Reduction in itchy, watery eyes from allergies; risk for burning sensation, eye discomfort, blurry vision.			
Generic Name	**Brand Name**	**Indication(s) or Uses**	**Notes**
Cromolyn	Intal	• Allergic conjunctivitis	• **Dosing (Adult):** – Ophthalmic 1 to 2 drops in affected eye(s) 4 to 6 times daily • **Dosing (Peds):** – Ophthalmic 1 to 2 drops in affected eye(s) 4 to 6 times daily • **CYP450 Interactions:** None • **Renal or Hepatic Dose Adjustments:** None • **Dosage Forms:** Ophthalmic solution
Lodoxamide	Alomide	• Allergic conjunctivitis	• **Dosing (Adult):** – Ophthalmic 1 to 2 drops in affected eye(s) 4 times daily • **Dosing (Peds):** – Ophthalmic 1 to 2 drops in affected eye(s) 4 times daily • **CYP450 Interactions:** None • **Renal or Hepatic Dose Adjustments:** None • **Dosage Forms:** Ophthalmic solution
Nedocromil	Alocril	• Allergic conjunctivitis	• **Dosing (Adult):** – Ophthalmic 1 to 2 drops in affected eye(s) twice daily • **Dosing (Peds):** – Ophthalmic 1 to 2 drops in affected eye(s) twice daily • **CYP450 Interactions:** None • **Renal or Hepatic Dose Adjustments:** None • **Dosage Forms:** Ophthalmic solution

Mast Cell Stabilizer - Drug Class Review
High-Yield Med Reviews

Generic Name	Brand Name	Indication(s) or Uses	Notes

Pemirolast	Alamast	• Allergic conjunctivitis	• **Dosing (Adult):**
			  – Ophthalmic 1 to 2 drops in affected eye(s) 4 times daily
			• **Dosing (Peds):**
			  – Ophthalmic 1 to 2 drops in affected eye(s) 4 times daily
			• **CYP450 Interactions:** None
			• **Renal or Hepatic Dose Adjustments:** None
			• **Dosage Forms:** Ophthalmic solution

High-Yield Clinical Knowledge

- **Symptomatic Management**
  - These agents are not effective at treating the underlying cause of ophthalmic redness, such as allergic conjunctivitis.
  - Corticosteroids are more appropriate for addressing the underlying cause but are not always indicated as allergic conjunctivitis or rhinitis may be self-limiting.

High-Yield Fast-Facts

- **Contact Lens Insertion**
  - Patients must be instructed to remove contact lenses before ophthalmic administration.
  - Patients should wait at least 10 minutes after the administration of ophthalmic antihistamines before inserting contact lenses.
- **Multiple Ophthalmic Agent Administration**
  - If the patient has more than one ophthalmic medication, they should be spaced at least five minutes.
- **Alternative Properties**
  - Nedocromil is proposed to possess weak antihistamine properties.

HIGH-YIELD BOARD EXAM ESSENTIALS
- **CLASSIC AGENTS:** Cromolyn, lodoxamide, nedocromil, pemirolast
- **DRUG CLASS:** Mast cell stabilizer
- **INDICATIONS:** Allergic conjunctivitis
- **MECHANISM:** Inhibit mast cell degranulation, preventing the release of histamine and inflammatory leukotrienes.
- **SIDE EFFECTS:** Burning sensation, eye discomfort, blurry vision
- **CLINICAL PEARLS:** These agents are not effective at treating the underlying cause of ophthalmic redness, such as allergic conjunctivitis.

High-Yield Basic Pharmacology

- **Mechanism of Action**
  - Inhibit the conversion of arachidonic acid to prostaglandins by inhibition of COX-1 and/or COX-2 either reversibly (NSAIDs).
- **Analgesic Properties**
  - Upon tissue injury and the accompanying inflammation contributing pain is caused by the release of prostaglandins by cytokines such as bradykinin.
  - Local or systemic inhibition of COX and prostaglandins by salicylates contribute to analgesia, which may be combined with other pain management strategies.

Primary Net Benefit

- Provide local anti-inflammatory and analgesic effects and may be a component of therapy after ophthalmic surgery.

<table>
<tr><td colspan="4">Ophthalmic NSAIDS - Drug Class Review
High-Yield Med Reviews</td></tr>
<tr><td colspan="4">Mechanism of Action: Inhibit the conversion of arachidonic acid to prostaglandins by inhibition of COX-1 and/or COX-2 either reversibly (NSAIDs)</td></tr>
<tr><td colspan="4">Class Effects: Local anti-inflammatory and analgesic effects; increased risk of sterile corneal melts and perforations.</td></tr>
<tr><td>Generic Name</td><td>Brand Name</td><td>Indication(s) or Uses</td><td>Notes</td></tr>
<tr>
<td>Bromfenac</td>
<td>BromSite, Prolensa</td>
<td>
- Postoperative ocular inflammation or pain
</td>
<td>
- Dosing (Adult):
  - Ophthalmic 1 to 2 drops in affected eye(s) once to twice daily
- Dosing (Peds):
  - Not routinely used
- CYP450 Interactions: None
- Renal or Hepatic Dose Adjustments: None
- Dosage Forms: Ophthalmic solution
</td>
</tr>
<tr>
<td>Diclofenac</td>
<td>Voltarol Ophtha</td>
<td>
- Postoperative ocular inflammation or pain
- Ocular pain
</td>
<td>
- Dosing (Adult):
  - Ophthalmic 1 to 2 drops in affected eye(s) 4 times daily
- Dosing (Peds):
  - Not routinely used
- CYP450 Interactions: None
- Renal or Hepatic Dose Adjustments: None
- Dosage Forms: Ophthalmic solution
</td>
</tr>
<tr>
<td>Flurbiprofen</td>
<td>Ocufen</td>
<td>
- Intraoperative miosis
</td>
<td>
- Dosing (Adult):
  - Ophthalmic 1 drop in affected eye(s) q30minutes beginning 2 hours prior to surgery
- Dosing (Peds):
  - Not routinely used
- CYP450 Interactions: None
- Renal or Hepatic Dose Adjustments: None
- Dosage Forms: Ophthalmic solution
</td>
</tr>
</table>

Ophthalmic NSAIDS - Drug Class Review
High-Yield Med Reviews

Generic Name	Brand Name	Indication(s) or Uses	Notes

Ketorolac	Acular, Acuvail	• Postoperative ocular inflammation or pain
		• Seasonal allergic conjunctivitis
			• **Dosing (Adult):**
			  – Ophthalmic 1 drop in affected eye(s) four times daily
			• **Dosing (Peds):**
			  – Ophthalmic 1 drop in affected eye(s) four times daily
			• **CYP450 Interactions:** None
			• **Renal or Hepatic Dose Adjustments:** None
			• **Dosage Forms:** Ophthalmic solution

Nepafenac	Ilevro, Nevanac	• Postoperative ocular inflammation or pain	• **Dosing (Adult):**
			  – Ophthalmic 1 drop in affected eye(s) three times daily
			• **Dosing (Peds):**
			  – Ophthalmic 1 drop in affected eye(s) three times daily
			• **CYP450 Interactions:** None
			• **Renal or Hepatic Dose Adjustments:** None
			• **Dosage Forms:** Ophthalmic solution

High-Yield Clinical Knowledge

- **Ocular Surface Disease**
  - The use of either topical and systemic NSAIDs, particularly in the elderly, has been associated with an increased risk of sterile corneal melts and perforations.
- **Surgical Adjunct**
  - Ophthalmic ketorolac is available in combination with phenylephrine for the purposes of preventing miosis and reducing postoperative pain in patients undergoing cataract or intraocular lens replacement surgery.
- **Prostaglandin Products**
  - NSAID inhibition of cyclooxygenase decreases the production of not just prostaglandins but also thromboxane and prostacyclin.
    - Prostaglandin H2 typically produces prostacyclin, Prostaglandin D, E, and F, as well as thromboxanes.
  - Thromboxanes stimulate platelet aggregation and decrease renal blood flow.
    - Thus, inhibition of thromboxane (typically TXA2) by NSAIDs decreases platelet aggregation and may augment renal blood flow.
  - Prostaglandin inhibition may also produce vasoconstriction and bronchoconstriction.
- **Central Vs. Peripheral Prostaglandin Inhibition**
  - The anti-inflammatory properties of NSAIDs are attributed to their inhibition of peripherally located prostaglandins.
  - The analgesic properties of NSAIDs are a result of inhibition of prostaglandins located in the CNS.

HIGH-YIELD BOARD EXAM ESSENTIALS

- **CLASSIC AGENTS:** Bromfenac, diclofenac, flurbiprofen, ketorolac, nepafenac
- **DRUG CLASS:** NSAIDs
- **INDICATIONS:** Postoperative ocular inflammation or pain (bromfenac, diclofenac, flurbiprofen, ketorolac, nepafenac), seasonal allergic conjunctivitis (ketorolac)
- **MECHANISM:** Inhibit the conversion of arachidonic acid to prostaglandins by inhibition of COX-1 and/or COX-2 either reversibly (NSAIDs)
- **SIDE EFFECTS:** Increased risk of sterile corneal melts and perforations
- **CLINICAL PEARLS:** The anti-inflammatory properties of NSAIDs are attributed to their inhibition of peripherally located prostaglandins. The analgesic properties of NSAIDs are a result of inhibition of prostaglandins located in the CNS.

High-Yield Basic Pharmacology

- **Mechanism of Action**
  - Alpha-1 agonist in the conjunctiva and nasal mucosa producing vasoconstriction.

Primary Net Benefit

- Over-the-counter agents for managing common allergy-related complaints and acute care use of specific agents for numerous indications that are extensions of their central and peripheral antihistamine effect.

Imidazoline (Nasal/Ophthalmic) - Drug Class Review			
High-Yield Med Reviews			
Mechanism of Action: *Alpha-1 agonist in the conjunctiva and nasal mucosa producing vasoconstriction.*			
Class Effects: Reduction in itching, watery eyes; risk of blurred vision, lacrimation, irritation, hypersensitivity.			
Generic Name	**Brand Name**	**Indication(s) or Uses**	**Notes**
Naphazoline	<u>With pheniramine</u> Naphcon-A, Opcon-A, Visine, Visine-A	• Allergic conjunctivitis	• **Dosing (Adult):** − Ophthalmic 1 drop in affected eye(s) up to 4 times daily • **Dosing (Peds):** − Ophthalmic 1 drop in affected eye(s) up to 4 times daily • **CYP450 Interactions:** None • **Renal or Hepatic Dose Adjustments:** None • **Dosage Forms:** Ophthalmic solution

Oxymetazoline	Afrin, Dristan Spray, Mucinex Nasal Spray, Neo-Synephrine 12 hour spray, Vicks Sinex	• Allergic conjunctivitis
		• Allergic rhinitis
			• **Dosing (Adult):**
			 − Intranasal 2 to 3 sprays into each nostril twice daily
			  ▪ Maximum 3 days of therapy and no more than 2 doses per 24 hours
			• **Dosing (Peds):**
			 − Intranasal 2 to 3 sprays into each nostril twice daily
			  ▪ Maximum 3 days of therapy and no more than 2 doses per 24 hours
			• **CYP450 Interactions:** None
			• **Renal or Hepatic Dose Adjustments:** None
			• **Dosage Forms:** Nasal solution

Imidazoline (Nasal/Ophthalmic) - Drug Class Review
High-Yield Med Reviews

Generic Name	Brand Name	Indication(s) or Uses	Notes
Tetrahydrozoline	Visine, Opticlear, Tyzine	<ul><li>Allergic conjunctivitis</li><li>Allergic rhinitis</li></ul>	<ul><li>**Dosing (Adult):**<ul><li>Intranasal 2 to 3 sprays into each nostril q3-4h as needed</li><li>Ophthalmic 1 drop in affected eye(s) up to 4 times daily</li></ul></li><li>**Dosing (Peds):**<ul><li>Intranasal 2 to 3 drops of 0.05% each nostril q3h as needed</li></ul></li><li>**CYP450 Interactions:** None</li><li>**Renal or Hepatic Dose Adjustments:** None</li><li>**Dosage Forms:** Nasal solution, Ophthalmic solution</li></ul>

High-Yield Clinical Knowledge

- **Narrow-Angle Glaucoma**
  - Do not use in patients with narrow-angle glaucoma. Use with caution in patients with cardiovascular disease, diabetes, hyperthyroidism, or infection.
  - Contains benzalkonium chloride, which may cause corneal damage and be absorbed by soft contact lenses.
- **Contact Lens Insertion**
  - Patients must be instructed to remove contact lenses before ophthalmic administration.
  - Patients should wait at least 10 minutes after the administration of ophthalmic antihistamines before inserting contact lenses.
- **Masking of Corneal Injury**
  - Naphazoline contains benzalkonium chloride, which may cause corneal damage and be absorbed by soft contact lenses.
- **Multiple Ophthalmic Agent Administration**
  - If the patient has more than one ophthalmic medication, they should be spaced at least five minutes.
- **Symptomatic Management**
  - These agents are not effective at treating the underlying cause of ophthalmic redness, such as allergic conjunctivitis.
  - Corticosteroids are more appropriate for addressing the underlying cause but are not always indicated as allergic conjunctivitis or rhinitis may be self-limiting.
- **No More Than Three Days**
  - Imidazolines should not use for more than three days due to rebound congestion.
  - Use with caution in patients with cardiovascular disease, diabetes, hyperthyroidism, or infection.
- **Common Adverse Events**
  - Common adverse events of ophthalmic imidazolines include blurred vision, lacrimation, irritation, hypersensitivity.

HIGH-YIELD BOARD EXAM ESSENTIALS
- **CLASSIC AGENTS:** Naphazoline, oxymetazoline, tetrahydrozoline
- **DRUG CLASS:** Imidazoline
- **INDICATIONS:** Allergic conjunctivitis, allergic rhinitis
- **MECHANISM:** Alpha-1 agonist in the conjunctiva and nasal mucosa producing vasoconstriction.
- **SIDE EFFECTS:** Blurred vision, lacrimation, irritation, hypersensitivity
- **CLINICAL PEARLS:** Do not use in patients with narrow-angle glaucoma. Use with caution in patients with cardiovascular disease, diabetes, hyperthyroidism, or infection.

High-Yield Basic Pharmacology

- **Latanoprostene**
  - The prodrug of latanoprost, latanoprostene, is activated through a nitric oxide donating process, which adds to its antiglaucoma effects by further increasing aqueous humor outflow.
- **Benzalkonium Chloride**
  - The common preservative in many ophthalmic preparations, benzalkonium chloride, has been associated with worsening dry eyes and should be avoided, if possible.

Primary Net Benefit

- First-line intraocular pressure (IOP) lowering agents that can often be administered once daily with sustained IOP control for up to 24-hours.

Prostaglandin Analogs - Drug Class Review			
High-Yield Med Reviews			
Mechanism of Action: *Synthetic analogs of prostaglandin F2-alpha (PGF2a) are hydrolyzed to PGF2a, which modifies ciliary muscle tension, and improves aqueous humor outflow tracts.*			
Class Effects: Reduction in intraocular pressure (IOP); risk for punctate corneal erosion and conjunctival hyperemia			
Generic Name	**Brand Name**	**Indication(s) or Uses**	**Notes**
Bimatoprost	Latisse, Lumigan	• Elevated intraocular pressure • Hypotrichosis of the eyelashes	• **Dosing (Adult):** – Ophthalmic 1 drop in affected eye(s) once daily – Ophthalmic - place one drop on the applicator and apply evenly along the skin of upper eyelid at the base of eyelashes at bedtime • **Dosing (Peds):** – Ophthalmic 1 drop in affected eye(s) four times daily • **CYP450 Interactions:** None • **Renal or Hepatic Dose Adjustments:** None • **Dosage Forms:** Ophthalmic solution
Latanoprost	Xalatan, Xelpros	• Elevated intraocular pressure	• **Dosing (Adult):** – Ophthalmic 1 drop in affected eye(s) once daily • **Dosing (Peds):** – Ophthalmic 1 drop in affected eye(s) four times daily • **CYP450 Interactions:** None • **Renal or Hepatic Dose Adjustments:** None • **Dosage Forms:** Ophthalmic (emulsion, solution)

Prostaglandin Analogs - Drug Class Review
High-Yield Med Reviews

Generic Name	Brand Name	Indication(s) or Uses	Notes

Latanoprostene	Vyzylta	• Elevated intraocular pressure	• **Dosing (Adult):**
			  – Ophthalmic 1 drop in affected eye(s) once daily
			• **Dosing (Peds):**
			  – Ophthalmic 1 drop in affected eye(s) four times daily
			• **CYP450 Interactions:** None
			• **Renal or Hepatic Dose Adjustments:** None
			• **Dosage Forms:** Ophthalmic solution

Tafluprost	Zioptan	• Elevated intraocular pressure	• **Dosing (Adult):**
			  – Ophthalmic 1 drop in affected eye(s) once daily
			• **Dosing (Peds):**
			  – Not routinely used
			• **CYP450 Interactions:** None
			• **Renal or Hepatic Dose Adjustments:** None
			• **Dosage Forms:** Ophthalmic solution

Travoprost	Travatan Z	• Elevated intraocular pressure	• **Dosing (Adult):**
			  – Ophthalmic 1 drop in affected eye(s) once daily
			• **Dosing (Peds):**
			  – Ophthalmic 1 drop in affected eye(s) four times daily
			• **CYP450 Interactions:** None
			• **Renal or Hepatic Dose Adjustments:** None
			• **Dosage Forms:** Ophthalmic solution

Unoprostone	Rescula	• Elevated intraocular pressure	• **Dosing (Adult):**
			  – Ophthalmic 1 drop in affected eye(s) twice daily
			• **Dosing (Peds):**
			  – Not routinely used
			• **CYP450 Interactions:** None
			• **Renal or Hepatic Dose Adjustments:** None
			• **Dosage Forms:** Ophthalmic solution

High-Yield Clinical Knowledge

- **Diurnal Effect**
  - The diurnal IOP lowering effect of prostaglandin analogs allows for consistent control of IOP throughout the day, including at night when IOP is the highest during sleep.
- **Iris Pigmentation**
  - With long-term administration of prostaglandin analogs, iris pigmentation is likely to occur in patients with mixed-color irises.
  - The transition of eye color to brown occurs gradually over 3 to 12 months of continued use and is irreversible upon discontinuation.
  - Hyperpigmentation may also occur around the lids and lashes but is reversible with drug discontinuation.

- **Hypertrichosis**
  - Most prostaglandin analogs may cause hypertrichosis, or lengthening of eyelashes, with continued use.
  - Bimatoprost specifically carries this indication for cosmetic purposes.
- **Ophthalmic Drop Administration**
  - Before administering any ophthalmic product, patients should be reminded to wash their hands and remove any contact lenses.
  - Most administrations should begin with 1 drop of solution in the affected eye.
  - No more than 1 drop should be administered at a time, and multiple drops should be separated by at least 1 minute since the aqueous chamber cannot hold the given volume.
  - If drops and ointments are to be given, the drop should be administered first, followed by the ointment.
- **Adverse Events**
  - Rare but serious adverse events associated with prostaglandin analogs include punctate corneal erosion and conjunctival hyperemia.
- **Combination Therapy**
  - If an inadequate IOP response to an initial agent occurs, the combination with another class often leads to a less than additive further IOP reduction.
  - Furthermore, increasing the dose (i.e., number of drops) per agent rarely leads to a further improvement in IOP lowering effect.
  - Conversion to a new IOP lowering agent is often necessary if an inadequate response occurs.
- **Acute Angle-Closure Crisis**
  - Acute angle-closure crisis is a medical emergency that requires administration of one or more topical ophthalmic agents and may include systemic interventions.
  - Pilocarpine is often added to induce miosis to pull the peripheral iris wavy from its meshwork but may worsen angle closure and should not be used alone.
  - Oral glycerin or IV mannitol can be used in combination with prostaglandin analogs, beta-antagonists, alpha-agonists, or carbonic anhydrase inhibitors.

HIGH-YIELD BOARD EXAM ESSENTIALS
- **CLASSIC AGENTS:** Bimatoprost, latanoprost, latanoprostene, tafluprost, travoprost
- **DRUG CLASS:** Prostaglandin analog
- **INDICATIONS:** Elevated intraocular pressure, hypotrichosis of the eyelashes
- **MECHANISM:** Synthetic analogs of PGF2a are hydrolyzed to PGF2a, which modifies ciliary muscle tension, and improves aqueous humor outflow tracts.
- **SIDE EFFECTS:** Punctate corneal erosion and conjunctival hyperemia
- **CLINICAL PEARLS:** If an inadequate IOP response to an initial agent occurs, the combination with another class often leads to a less than additive further IOP reduction. Furthermore, increasing the dose (i.e., number of drops) per agent rarely leads to a further improvement in IOP lowering effect.

High-Yield Basic Pharmacology

- **Carbamide peroxide**
  - Softens cerumen by its foaming action from the release of hydrogen peroxide.
- **Dexamethasone, Fluocinolone, Hydrocortisone**
  - Suppress polymorphonuclear leukocytes migration, and decrease capillary permeability, thereby reducing inflammation.

Primary Net Benefit

- Otic steroids provide a local anti-inflammatory effect to relieve pain from otitis externa, and carbamide may be used as a ceruminolytic but has questionable efficacy.

Anti-inflammatories and Cerumenolytics - Drug Class Review			
High-Yield Med Reviews			
Mechanism of Action:			
Carbamide peroxide - Softens cerumen by its foaming action from the release of hydrogen peroxide. *Dexamethasone, Fluocinolone, Hydrocortisone - Suppress polymorphonuclear leukocytes migration, and decrease capillary permeability, reducing inflammation.*			
Class Effects: Local cerumenolytic effect, local irritation			
Generic Name	**Brand Name**	**Indication(s) or Uses**	**Notes**

Carbamide peroxide	Auro, Mollifene, Debrox	- Ear wax removal	- **Dosing (Adult):**
			  - Otic 5 to 10 drops twice daily for up to 4 days
			- **Dosing (Peds):**
			  - Otic 1 to 10 drops twice daily for up to 4 days
			- **CYP450 Interactions:** None
			- **Renal or Hepatic Dose Adjustments:** None
			- **Dosage Forms:** Otic (solution)

Dexamethasone (with ciprofloxacin)	Ciprodex	- Acute otitis externa	- **Dosing (Adult):**
			  - Otic 4 drops into affected ear(s) twice daily for 7 days
			- **Dosing (Peds):**
			  - Otic 4 drops into affected ear(s) twice daily for 7 days
			- **CYP450 Interactions:** None
			- **Renal or Hepatic Dose Adjustments:** None
			- **Dosage Forms:** Otic (suspension)

Fluocinolone	DermOtic Oil, Flac	- Chronic eczematous external otitis	- **Dosing (Adult):**
			  - Otic 5 drops into affected ear(s) twice daily for 7 days
			- **Dosing (Peds):**
			  - Otic 5 drops into affected ear(s) twice daily for 7 days
			- **CYP450 Interactions:** None
			- **Renal or Hepatic Dose Adjustments:** None
			- **Dosage Forms:** Otic (oil)

Anti-inflammatories and Cerumenolytics - Drug Class Review
High-Yield Med Reviews

Generic Name	Brand Name	Indication(s) or Uses	Notes

Hydrocortisone (with ciprofloxacin; neomycin/poly myxin b; acetic acid; colistin, neomycin, thonzonium)	Cipro HC, PRamox-HC, Vosol HC, Cortisporin Otic, Casporyn HC, Coly-Mycin S, Cort-Biotic, Cortane-B	• Otic infections	• **Dosing (Adult):**
			  – Otic 2-5 drops into affected ear two to four times daily for 7 days
			• **Dosing (Peds):**
			  – Otic 2-5 drops into affected ear two to four times daily for 7 days
			• **CYP450 Interactions:** None
			• **Renal or Hepatic Dose Adjustments:** None
			• **Dosage Forms:** Otic (suspension, solution)

High-Yield Clinical Knowledge

- **Ceruminolytic Age Restriction**
  - Carbamide peroxide should not be used in children younger than three years, in patients with tympanostomy tubes, or in patients with perforated tympanic membranes.
- **Corticosteroids for Acute Otitis Media**
  - The addition of corticosteroids to antimicrobials for acute otitis media may improve pain, swelling, and redness, but the evidence is lacking to support the combination treatment definitively.
- **Docusate**
  - As an alternative ceruminolytic, docusate capsules can be opened, with their contents emptied into the ear to attempt to loosen impacted ear wax.
- **Ear Irrigation**
  - In patients who fail cerumenolytics, these patients can undergo irrigation and manual removal.
  - Irrigation should use body-temperature water that may be combined with hydrogen peroxide administered gently to aid in removing wax.
  - Carbamide peroxide may be used as an adjunct to attempt to soften wax, facilitating removal by irrigation.
- **Adrenal suppression**
  - Although systemic corticosteroids are associated with adrenal suppression, otic preparations are rarely absorbed systemically in concentrations relevant to cause HPA suppression effects.
  - Yet, adrenal suppression is a warning in the prescribing information for otic corticosteroids.

High-Yield Fast-Fact

- **Cost and Ophthalmic Agents**
  - Otic preparations are often more expensive than the same drug in an ophthalmic preparation.
  - Pharmacists can help reduce the cost of care by recommending ophthalmic preparations for otic administration.
  - However, otic medications should never be administered ophthalmically.

HIGH-YIELD BOARD EXAM ESSENTIALS
- **CLASSIC AGENTS:** Carbamide peroxide, dexamethasone, fluocinolone, hydrocortisone
- **DRUG CLASS:** Anti-inflammatories and cerumenolytics
- **INDICATIONS:** Ear wax removal
- **MECHANISM:** Carbamide peroxide - Softens cerumen by its foaming action from the release of hydrogen peroxide. Dexamethasone, Fluocinolone, Hydrocortisone - Suppress polymorphonuclear leukocytes migration, and decrease capillary permeability, reducing inflammation.
- **SIDE EFFECTS:** Local irritation
- **CLINICAL PEARLS:** Otic steroids provide a local anti-inflammatory effect to relieve pain from otitis externa, and carbamide may be used as a ceruminolytic but has questionable efficacy.

High-Yield Basic Pharmacology

- **Colistin, Polymyxin B**
  - Act as cationic detergents that interact strongly with phospholipids and disrupt bacterial cell membranes' structure, leading to bacterial cell lysis.
  - **Polymyxins Binding Site**
    - Gram-negative bacteria sensitivity to the polymyxins is related to the phospholipids' content in the given bacterial cell wall.
      - The polymyxins' spectrum is limited to gram-negatives as their binding site to the lipopolysaccharide of the outer membrane of gram-negative bacteria inactivating it.
- **Ciprofloxacin, Neomycin, Ofloxacin**
  - Inhibit DNA gyrase and topoisomerase IV, exerting a bactericidal effect on susceptible pathogens

Primary Net Benefit

- Topical antimicrobials may help resolve the infection and relieve pain from otitis externa.

Antimicrobials - Drug Class Review			
High-Yield Med Reviews			
Mechanism of Action: *See agents above.*			
Class Effects: Topical antimicrobials may help resolve the infection and relieve pain from otitis externa.			
Generic Name	**Brand Name**	**Indication(s) or Uses**	**Notes**

Ciprofloxacin	Cetraxal, Otiprio, Vosol	• Acute otitis externa	• **Dosing (Adult):**
			  – Otic instill 0.2 or 0.25 mL into affected ear twice daily
			• **Dosing (Peds):**
			  – Otic instill 0.2 or 0.25 mL into affected ear twice daily
			• **CYP450 Interactions:** None
			• **Renal or Hepatic Dose Adjustments:** None
			• **Dosage Forms:** Otic (solution, suspension)

Ofloxacin	Floxin	• Acute otitis externa	• **Dosing (Adult):**
			  – Otic instill 0.2 or 0.25 mL into affected ear twice daily
			• **Dosing (Peds):**
			  – Otic instill 0.2 or 0.25 mL into affected ear twice daily
			• **CYP450 Interactions:** None
			• **Renal or Hepatic Dose Adjustments:** None
			• **Dosage Forms:** Otic (solution, suspension)

Neomycin, colistin, hydrocortisone, thonzonium	Coly-Mycin, Cortisporin-TC	• Acute otitis externa	• **Dosing (Adult):**
			  – Otic instill 5 drops into affected ear 3-4 times daily
			• **Dosing (Peds):**
			  – Otic instill 4 drops into affected ear 3-4 times daily
			• **CYP450 Interactions:** None
			• **Renal or Hepatic Dose Adjustments:** None
			• **Dosage Forms:** Otic (suspension)

Antimicrobials - Drug Class Review
High-Yield Med Reviews

Generic Name	Brand Name	Indication(s) or Uses	Notes

Neomycin, polymyxin B, hydrocortisone	Odan-Spor-HC	• Acute otitis externa	• **Dosing (Adult):**
			  – Otic instill 4 drops into affected ear 3-4 times daily
			• **Dosing (Peds):**
			  – Otic instill 3 drops into affected ear 3-4 times daily
			• **CYP450 Interactions:** None
			• **Renal or Hepatic Dose Adjustments:** None
			• **Dosage Forms:** Otic (solution, suspension)

High-Yield Clinical Knowledge

- **Ototoxicity**
  - Topical fluoroquinolones are not believed to cause ototoxicity when the tympanic membranes are intact.
- **Ruptured Tympanic Membranes**
  - Ototoxic topical drugs may penetrate the inner ear structures in the setting of ruptured TMs and exert their damaging effects.
  - The ototoxic drugs that are most concerning are the aminoglycosides that are thought to be vestibulotoxic (gentamicin) or cochleotoxic (amikacin, neomycin, and tobramycin), or both, acetic acid altering PH and affecting cochlear function and polymyxin B with an unknown mechanism.
  - In the setting of known or suspected TM perforation, including tympanostomy tube, non-ototoxic topical preparations are preferred.
- **Neomycin hypersensitivity**
  - Neomycin is associated with acute hypersensitivity reactions (believed to be contact dermatitis) in up to 15% of patients, including those using a topical otic dosage form.
- **Ophthalmic Preparations**
  - The difference between ophthalmic products and otic products is that ophthalmic products are sterile and buffered to a neutral pH.
  - Since otic preparations are often more expensive than the same medication and concentration as an ophthalmic preparation, clinicians may substitute an otic antibiotic for an ophthalmic product.
  - However, otic medications must never be used in the eye.

HIGH-YIELD BOARD EXAM ESSENTIALS
- **CLASSIC AGENTS:** Ciprofloxacin, neomycin/colistin/hydrocortisone/thonzonium, neomycin/polymyxin B/hydrocortisone, ofloxacin
- **DRUG CLASS:** Otic antimicrobials
- **INDICATIONS:** Acute otitis externa
- **MECHANISM:** Colistin, Polymyxin B - Act as cationic detergents that interact strongly with phospholipids and disrupt bacterial cell membranes' structure, leading to bacterial cell lysis. Ciprofloxacin, Neomycin, Ofloxacin - Inhibit DNA gyrase and topoisomerase IV, exerting a bactericidal effect on susceptible pathogens.
- **SIDE EFFECTS:** Hypersensitivity, ototoxicity
- **CLINICAL PEARLS:** Ototoxic topical drugs may penetrate the inner ear structures in the setting of ruptured TMs and exert their damaging effects.

High-Yield Basic Pharmacology

- **Mechanism of Action**
  - Binds to the positive allosteric modulation site on the alpha subunit of GABA-A receptors, increasing receptor efficiency and potency.
- **Endogenous Target**
  - Brexanolone was designed to replace the endogenous compound allopregnanolone.
  - Allopregnanolone is a major metabolite of progesterone.

Primary Net Benefit

- Single infusion management of acute postpartum depression.

Allosteric GABA-A Modulator - Drug Class Review			
High-Yield Med Reviews			
Mechanism of Action: *Binds to the positive allosteric modulation site on the alpha subunit of GABA-A receptors, increasing receptor efficiency and potency.*			
Class Effects: Single infusion management of acute postpartum depression; risk for sudden loss of consciousness			
Generic Name	**Brand Name**	**Indication(s) or Uses**	**Notes**
Brexanolone	Zulresso	• Postpartum depression	• **Dosing (Adult):** – IV 60-hour continuous infusion • **Dosing (Peds):** – Not routinely used • **CYP450 Interactions:** None • **Renal or Hepatic Dose Adjustments:** – GFR less than 15 mL/minute - not recommended • **Dosage Forms:** IV (solution)

High-Yield Clinical Knowledge

- **Single Indication**
  - Brexanolone is only indicated for use in postpartum depression.
- **Sudden Loss of Consciousness**
  - As this drug is a GABA-A modulator with possible CNS depression, a black-boxed warning exists for the risk of excessive sedation or sudden loss of consciousness.
  - Time to complete recovery following a sudden loss of consciousness can range from 15 minutes to 60 minutes, during which airway and breathing support may be necessary.
- **IV Administration**
  - The administration of brexanolone is an IV infusion, with the single-dose administered over a 60-hour continuous infusion with variable rate changes through this timeframe.
  - Brexanolone must be administered in an inpatient setting.

High-Yield Fast-Fact

- **Postpartum Management**
  - Other antidepressants or benzodiazepines can be used alone or after brexanolone; however, specific considerations must be made for infant exposure via breast milk.

HIGH-YIELD BOARD EXAM ESSENTIALS

- **CLASSIC AGENTS:** Brexanolone
- **DRUG CLASS:** Allosteric GABA-A modulator
- **INDICATIONS:** Postpartum depression
- **MECHANISM:** Binds to the positive allosteric modulation site on the alpha subunit of GABA-A receptors, increasing receptor efficiency and potency.
- **SIDE EFFECTS:** Sudden loss of consciousness
- **CLINICAL PEARLS:** As this drug is a GABA-A modulator with possible CNS depression, a black-boxed warning exists for the risk of excessive sedation or sudden loss of consciousness.

High-Yield Basic Pharmacology

- **Mechanism of Action**
  - Dopamine antagonist action at D2 receptors, blocking excess signaling in the mesolimbic and mesocortical pathways.
- **Dopamine Receptors**
  - Although the principle pathophysiology of schizophrenia involves the D2 receptor pathway, other dopamine receptors (D1 through D5) have been identified.
  - The D2 like receptors include the D3 and D4 receptors, whereas the D1 receptors are closely related to D5 receptors.
    - Dopamine receptors other than D2 do not appear to play a significant role in the current understanding of schizophrenia pathophysiology.

Primary Net Benefit

- Useful in managing schizophrenia but offset by adverse effects leading to intolerance or permanent neurologic and psychiatric dysfunction.

Antipsychotics First Generation - Drug Class Review **High-Yield Med Reviews**			
Mechanism of Action: *Dopamine antagonist action at D2 receptors, blocking excess signaling in the mesolimbic and mesocortical pathways.*			
Class Effects: Effective for positive symptoms of psychosis, risk for acute dystonia, parkinsonism, akathisia, QT prolongation.			
Generic Name	**Brand Name**	**Indication(s) or Uses**	**Notes**

Chlorpromazine	Thorazine	• Agitation
		 • Bipolar disorder
		 • Hiccups
		 • Hyperactivity
		 • Nausea, vomiting
		 • Schizophrenia
		 • Tetanus
			• **Dosing (Adult):**
			  – Oral 10 to 75 mg/day divided 3 to 4 times daily
			   • Up to 800 mg/day
			  – IM/IV 25 mg q4-6h, up to 300 mg/day
			 • **Dosing (Peds):**
			  – Oral 0.55 to 1 mg/kg/dose q6h
			   • Maximum 40 to 75 mg/day
			 • **CYP450 Interactions:** Substrate CYP1A2, 2D6, 3A4
			 • **Renal or Hepatic Dose Adjustments:** None
			 • **Dosage Forms:** Oral (tablet), IV (solution)

Droperidol	Inapsine	• Agitation
		 • Nausea, vomiting
			• **Dosing (Adult):**
			  – IM/IV 0.625 to 1.25 mg once
			 • **Dosing (Peds):**
			  – IM/IV 0.01 to 0.015 mg/kg/dose
			   • Maximum 0.1 mg/kg/dose
			 • **CYP450 Interactions:** None
			 • **Renal or Hepatic Dose Adjustments:** None
			 • **Dosage Forms:** IV (solution)

Antipsychotics First Generation - Drug Class Review
High-Yield Med Reviews

Generic Name	Brand Name	Indication(s) or Uses	Notes

Fluphenazine	Prolixin	▪ Psychosis	▪ **Dosing (Adult):**
			  – Oral 1 to 20 mg/day divided q6-24h
			  – IM 1.25 mg as needed, maximum 10 mg/day
			▪ **Dosing (Peds):**
			  – Oral 0.5 to 1 mg daily
			    ▪ Maximum dose 24 mg/day
			▪ **CYP450 Interactions:** Substrate of CYP2D6
			▪ **Renal or Hepatic Dose Adjustments:** None
			▪ **Dosage Forms:** Oral (concentrate, elixir, tablet), IV (solution)

Haloperidol	Haldol	▪ Agitation
		▪ Bipolar disorder
		▪ Hiccups
		▪ Hyperactivity
		▪ Nausea, vomiting
		▪ Schizophrenia
			▪ **Dosing (Adult):**
			  – Oral 2 to 10 mg q6h as needed up to 30 mg/day
			  – IM/IV 2 to 20 mg q0.5-6h as needed
			▪ **Dosing (Peds):**
			  – Oral 0.5 to 15 mg/day or 0.05 to 0.075 mg/kg/day divided q8-12h
			    ▪ Maximum 15 mg/day
			  – IM/IV 0.025 to 0.1 mg/kg/dose q0.5-6h
			▪ **CYP450 Interactions:** Substrate of CYP1A2, 2D6, 3A4
			▪ **Renal or Hepatic Dose Adjustments:** None
			▪ **Dosage Forms:** Oral (concentrate, elixir, tablet), IV (solution), IM decanoate

Loxapine	Adasuve	▪ Agitation
		▪ Bipolar disorder
		▪ Schizophrenia
			▪ **Dosing (Adult):**
			  – Oral 60 to 100 mg/day divided q6-12h
			    ▪ Maximum 250 mg/day
			  – Inhalation 10 mg once daily
			▪ **Dosing (Peds):**
			  – Not routinely used
			▪ **CYP450 Interactions:** Substrate of CYP1A2, 2D6, 3A4
			▪ **Renal or Hepatic Dose Adjustments:** None
			▪ **Dosage Forms:** Oral (capsule), Aerosol

Perphenazine	Trilafon	▪ Nausea, vomiting
		▪ Schizophrenia
			▪ **Dosing (Adult):**
			  – Oral 8 to 64 mg/day divided q6-12h
			▪ **Dosing (Peds):**
			  – Oral 8 to 64 mg/day divided q6-12h
			▪ **CYP450 Interactions:** Substrate of CYP1A2, 2C9, 2C19, 2D6, 3A4
			▪ **Renal or Hepatic Dose Adjustments:** None
			▪ **Dosage Forms:** Oral (tablet)

Antipsychotics First Generation - Drug Class Review
High-Yield Med Reviews

Generic Name	Brand Name	Indication(s) or Uses	Notes
Prochlorperazine	Compazine	• Nausea, vomiting	• **Dosing (Adult):** – IM/IV/Oral 2.5 to 10 mg q6-8h, maximum 40 mg/day – Rectal 25 mg q12h • **Dosing (Peds):** – IM/IV/Oral 0.1 to 0.15 mg/kg/dose q3-4h ▪ Maximum 10 mg/dose and 40 mg/day • **CYP450 Interactions:** None • **Renal or Hepatic Dose Adjustments:** None • **Dosage Forms:** Oral (tablet), IV (solution), Suppository
Thioridazine	Mellaril	• Schizophrenia	• **Dosing (Adult):** – Oral 50 800 mg/day divided q6-12h • **Dosing (Peds):** – Oral 0.5 to 3 mg/kg/day divided q6-12h • **CYP450 Interactions:** Substrate of CYP2C19, 2D6; Inhibits CYP2D6 • **Renal or Hepatic Dose Adjustments:** None • **Dosage Forms:** Oral (tablet)
Thiothixene	Navane	• Schizophrenia	• **Dosing (Adult):** – Oral 2 to 20 mg q8h, maximum 60 mg/day • **Dosing (Peds):** – Oral 2 to 20 mg q8h, maximum 60 mg/day • **CYP450 Interactions:** Substrate of CYP1A2 • **Renal or Hepatic Dose Adjustments:** None • **Dosage Forms:** Oral (capsule)
Trifluoperazine	Stelazine	• Schizophrenia	• **Dosing (Adult):** – Oral 2 to 25 mg q12h, maximum 50 mg/day • **Dosing (Peds):** – Oral 2 to 25 mg q12h, maximum 40 mg/day • **CYP450 Interactions:** None • **Renal or Hepatic Dose Adjustments:** None • **Dosage Forms:** Oral (tablet)

High-Yield Clinical Knowledge

- **Extrapyramidal Symptoms (EPS)**
  - EPS consists of acute dystonia, parkinsonism, akathisia, and the more severe tardive dyskinesia and neuroleptic malignant syndrome.
  - Antipsychotic agents that are more selective for the mesolimbic system are less likely to cause EPS effects.
  - High-potency antipsychotics are more likely to cause EPS but less likely to possess anticholinergic activity.
  - Conversely, low-potency antipsychotics are less likely to cause EPS but possess more anticholinergic and alpha-adrenergic antagonist activity.

- **CYP2D6**
  - Most antipsychotics are hepatically metabolized by CYP2D6, potentially leading to clinically relevant drug metabolism changes in patients with polymorphisms causing dysfunction in this oxidation pathway.
  - Numerous agents, including chlorpromazine, fluphenazine, haloperidol, loxapine, perphenazine, and thioridazine (as well as some atypical agents), are metabolized CYP2D6.
  - Among Caucasian patients, up to 25% have overexpression of CYP2D6, and 7% have functionally absent.
  - Genomic testing is suggested before starting these agents.
  - Drug-interactions may also cause CYP2D6 inhibition, including commonly co-prescribed agents such as SSRI (fluoxetine, paroxetine) and bupropion.

- **Nausea and Vomiting**
  - Antipsychotics are commonly used in the acute treatment of nausea and vomiting, as dopamine receptors are present in the post trauma area of the medulla, where the chemoreceptor trigger zone is located.
  - Other adverse effects of D2 antagonism in other areas of the brain include gynecomastia and galactorrhea (hypothalamic D2 antagonism) and parkinsonism (nigrostriatal D2 antagonism).

- **Cardiac Conduction**
  - Phenothiazine antipsychotics can cause cardiac sodium channel blockade and potassium channel blockade.
  - Although not typically relevant at standard therapeutic dosing, these effects may cause QRS and/or QT prolongation in the above therapeutic dosing or the presence of drug interactions.
    - On the one hand, the anticholinergic effects may be protective in the setting of QT prolongation, as tachycardia reduces the risk of torsade de pointes; however, it may exacerbate QRS prolongation related arrhythmias.

- **Sub-Classifications**
  - Antipsychotics are further subclassified according to their affinity for the D2 receptor, divided into low potency or high potency agents.
    - Low potency antipsychotics include chlorpromazine, thioridazine.

HIGH-YIELD BOARD EXAM ESSENTIALS
- **CLASSIC AGENTS:** Chlorpromazine, droperidol, fluphenazine, haloperidol, loxapine, perphenazine, prochlorperazine, thioridazine, thiothixene, trifluoperazine
- **DRUG CLASS:** Antipsychotics first generation
- **INDICATIONS:** Agitation, bipolar disorder, hiccups, hyperactivity, nausea, vomiting, schizophrenia, tetanus
- **MECHANISM:** Dopamine antagonist action at D2 receptors, blocking excess signaling in the mesolimbic and mesocortical pathways.
- **SIDE EFFECTS:** Acute dystonia, parkinsonism, akathisia, QT prolongation
- **CLINICAL PEARLS:** Antipsychotics are commonly used in the acute treatment of nausea and vomiting, as dopamine receptors are present in the post trauma area of the medulla, where the chemoreceptor trigger zone is located.

High-Yield Basic Pharmacology

- **Mechanism of Action**
  - Dopamine antagonist action at D2 receptors, blocking excess signaling in the mesolimbic and mesocortical pathways.
- **Serotonin Antagonists**
  - Serotonin antagonist effects at the 5HT2 (5HT2A and 5HT2C receptors) cause dopamine release and increase sympathetic outflow from the locus coeruleus.
  - Antagonism of the 5HT2 receptors provided improved effectiveness in treating negative schizophrenia symptoms and significantly lowers EPS incidence.
    - Higher relative 5HT2 antagonist effects with weaker D2 antagonism is associated with a lower incidence of EPS symptoms, characteristic of the second-generation or atypical antipsychotics.
  - Other serotonin receptors have been identified as targets for antipsychotics, including the 5HT1, 5HT3, and 5-HT6 receptors.

Primary Net Benefit

- Atypical antipsychotic therapy may improve safety compared to "typical" antipsychotics and aims to reduce psychiatric disease symptoms while enhancing the quality of life and daily functioning.

Antipsychotics Second Generation (Atypical Antipsychotics) - Drug Class Review			
High-Yield Med Reviews			
Mechanism of Action: *Dopamine antagonist action at D2 receptors, blocking excess signaling in the mesolimbic and mesocortical pathways.*			
Class Effects: Good efficacy against positive symptoms of psychosis and some negative symptoms; risk of NMS, anticholinergic effects, agranulocytosis (clozapine), weight gain with some agents, worsening glucose, galactorrhea; risk of EPS is lower than first generation.			
Generic Name	**Brand Name**	**Indication(s) or Uses**	**Notes**
Aripiprazole	Abilify	<ul><li>Autistic disorder irritability</li><li>Bipolar disorder</li><li>Major depressive disorder</li><li>Schizophrenia</li><li>Tourette disorder</li></ul>	<ul><li>**Dosing (Adult):**<ul><li>Oral 2 to 30 mg daily</li><li>IM 400 mg qmonth</li></ul></li><li>**Dosing (Peds):**<ul><li>Oral 1.25 to 15 mg daily</li></ul></li><li>**CYP450 Interactions:** Substrate of CYP2D6, 3A4</li><li>**Renal or Hepatic Dose Adjustments:** None</li><li>**Dosage Forms:** Oral (solution, tablet), IM suspension</li></ul>
Asenapine	Saphris	<ul><li>Bipolar disorder</li><li>Schizophrenia</li></ul>	<ul><li>**Dosing (Adult):**<ul><li>SL 5 to 10 mg BID</li><li>Patch 3.8 mg/24hours daily to maximum 7.6 mg/24hour</li></ul></li><li>**Dosing (Peds):**<ul><li>SL 2.5 to 10 mg BID</li></ul></li><li>**CYP450 Interactions:** Substrate of CYP1A2, 2D6, 3A4</li><li>**Renal or Hepatic Dose Adjustments:**<ul><li>Child-Pugh class C - Use contraindicated</li></ul></li><li>**Dosage Forms:** Oral (sublingual tablet), Transdermal patch</li></ul>

Antipsychotics Second Generation (Atypical Antipsychotics) - Drug Class Review
High-Yield Med Reviews

Generic Name	Brand Name	Indication(s) or Uses	Notes

Brexpiprazole	Rexulti	• Major depressive disorder
		• Schizophrenia
			• **Dosing (Adult):**
			  – Oral 0.25 to 4 mg daily
			• **Dosing (Peds):**
			  – Not routinely used
			• **CYP450 Interactions:** Substrate of CYP2D6, 3A4
			• **Renal or Hepatic Dose Adjustments:**
			  – GFR less than 60 mL/minute - maximum 3 mg/day
			  – Child-Pugh class C - maximum 3 mg/day
			• **Dosage Forms:** Oral (tablet)

Cariprazine	Vraylar	• Bipolar disorder
		• Schizophrenia
			• **Dosing (Adult):**
			  – Oral 1.5 to 12 mg daily
			• **Dosing (Peds):**
			  – Not routinely used
			• **CYP450 Interactions:** Substrate of CYP2D6, 3A4
			• **Renal or Hepatic Dose Adjustments:**
			  – GFR less than 30 mL/minute - use not recommended
			  – Child-Pugh class C - use not recommended
			• **Dosage Forms:** Oral (capsule)

Clozapine	Clozaril	• Schizophrenia	• **Dosing (Adult):**
			  – Oral 6.25 to 900 mg/day
			• **Dosing (Peds):**
			  – Oral 6.25 to 400 mg/day
			• **CYP450 Interactions:** Substrate of CYP1A2, 2D6, 3A4
			• **Renal or Hepatic Dose Adjustments:** None
			• **Dosage Forms:** Oral (suspension, tablet)

Iloperidone	Fanapt	• Schizophrenia	• **Dosing (Adult):**
			  – Oral 1 to 12 mg BID
			• **Dosing (Peds):**
			  – Not routinely used
			• **CYP450 Interactions:** Substrate of CYP2D6, 3A4; Inhibits CYP3A4
			• **Renal or Hepatic Dose Adjustments:**
			  – Child-Pugh class C - use not recommended
			• **Dosage Forms:** Oral (tablet)

Lumateperone	Caplyta	• Schizophrenia	• **Dosing (Adult):**
			  – Oral 42 mg daily
			• **Dosing (Peds):**
			  – Not routinely used
			• **CYP450 Interactions:** Substrate of CYP1A2, 2D6, 3A4
			• **Renal or Hepatic Dose Adjustments:**
			  – Child-Pugh class B or C - use not recommended
			• **Dosage Forms:** Oral (capsule)

Antipsychotics Second Generation (Atypical Antipsychotics) - Drug Class Review
High-Yield Med Reviews

Generic Name	Brand Name	Indication(s) or Uses	Notes

Lurasidone	Latuda	• Bipolar disorder
		• Schizophrenia
			• **Dosing (Adult):**
			  – Oral 20 to 160 mg/day
			• **Dosing (Peds):**
			  – Oral 20 to 160 mg/day
			• **CYP450 Interactions:** Substrate and Inhibitor of CYP3A4
			• **Renal or Hepatic Dose Adjustments:**
			  – GFR less than 50 mL/minute - maximum 80 mg/day
			  – Child-Pugh class B or C - use not recommended
			• **Dosage Forms:** Oral (tablet)

Olanzapine	Zyprexa	• Agitation
		• Bipolar disorder
		• Major depressive disorder
		• Schizophrenia
			• **Dosing (Adult):**
			  – Oral 2.5 to 10 mg daily
			  – IM/IV 2.5 to 10 mg x1 followed by two additional as needed doses of 1.25 to 5 mg
			• **Dosing (Peds):**
			  – Oral 0.625 to 10 mg daily
			  – IM/IV 1.25 to 10 mg x1 followed by two additional as needed doses of 1.25 to 5 mg
			• **CYP450 Interactions:** Substrate of CYP1A2, 2D6, 3A4
			• **Renal or Hepatic Dose Adjustments:** None
			• **Dosage Forms:** Oral (tablet), IV solution, IM suspension

Paliperidone	Invega	• Schizophrenia	• **Dosing (Adult):**
			  – Oral 6 to 12 mg daily
			  – IM 234 mg x1 then 156 mg monthly
			    • Extra info if needed
			• **Dosing (Peds):** [same as adult]
			  – Extra info if needed
			    • Extra info if needed
			• **CYP450 Interactions:** Substrate of P-gp
			• **Renal or Hepatic Dose Adjustments:**
			  – GFR 50 to 79 mL/minute - maximum 6 mg; IM 156 mg followed by 117 mg, then 78 mg qmonth
			  – GFR 10 to 49 mL/minute - maximum 3 mg/day; IM use not recommended
			  – GFR less than 10 mL/minute - oral not recommended
			• **Dosage Forms:** Oral (tablet), IM suspension

Antipsychotics Second Generation (Atypical Antipsychotics) - Drug Class Review
High-Yield Med Reviews

Generic Name	Brand Name	Indication(s) or Uses	Notes

Pimavanserin	Nuplazid	• Parkinson's disease	• **Dosing (Adult):**
			  – Oral 34 mg daily
			• **Dosing (Peds):**
			  – Not routinely used
			• **CYP450 Interactions:** Substrate of CYP3A4
			• **Renal or Hepatic Dose Adjustments:** None
			• **Dosage Forms:** Oral (capsule, tablet)

Quetiapine	Seroquel	• Bipolar disorder
		• Major depressive disorder
		• Schizophrenia
			• **Dosing (Adult):**
			  – Oral 50 to 1,200 mg/day
			• **Dosing (Peds):**
			  – Oral 50 to 1,200 mg/day
			    • Children 10 years or older
			• **CYP450 Interactions:** Substrate CYP2D6, 3A4
			• **Renal or Hepatic Dose Adjustments:**
			  – Hepatic impairment - slower titration
			• **Dosage Forms:** Oral (tablet)

Risperidone	Risperdal	• Autistic disorder irritability
		• Bipolar disorder
		• Major depressive disorder
		• Schizophrenia
			• **Dosing (Adult):**
			  – Oral 0.5 to 6 mg/day
			  – IM 25 to 50 mg q2weeks
			  – SQ 90 to 120 mg qmonth
			• **Dosing (Peds):**
			  – Oral 0.25 to 3 mg/day
			• **CYP450 Interactions:** Substrate CYP2D6, 3A4, P-gp
			• **Renal or Hepatic Dose Adjustments:**
			  – Renal or hepatic impairment - slower dose titration
			• **Dosage Forms:** Oral (solution, tablet), IM suspension

Ziprasidone	Geodon	• Agitation
		• Bipolar disorder
		• Schizophrenia
			• **Dosing (Adult):**
			  – IM 10 mg q2h or 20 mg q4h, maximum 40 mg/day
			  – Oral 20 to 120 mg BID
			• **Dosing (Peds):** [same as adult]
			  – IM 10 mg q2h or 20 mg q4h, maximum 40 mg/day
			  – Oral 20 to 80 mg BID
			• **CYP450 Interactions:** Substrate CYP1A2, 3A4
			• **Renal or Hepatic Dose Adjustments:** None
			• **Dosage Forms:** Oral (capsule), IM solution

High-Yield Clinical Knowledge

- **Clozapine Toxicity**
  - Clozapine is restricted to patients who have failed to respond to other antipsychotics as it carries a significant risk of agranulocytosis and seizures.
  - Although only 1-2% of patients on clozapine develop agranulocytosis, this potentially fatal effect necessitates weekly CBC during the first six months of therapy.
  - Seizures are another complication of clozapine therapy as it is an antagonist of GABA-A receptors.
    - Chlorpromazine also is a similarly potent GABA antagonist but often overlooked in clinical practice.

- **Neuroleptic Malignant Syndrome**
  - NMS results from abrupt reductions in dopamine neurotransmission in the hypothalamus and striatum, leading to modifying the body's core temperature regulation and autonomic dysfunction.
  - Manifestations of NMS include "lead-pipe" rigidity, hyperthermia, and altered mental status.
  - NMS is more likely to occur during dose adjustment of D2 antagonist agents, at the start of therapy, in the presence of dopaminergic agents or idiosyncratic.
  - High potency antipsychotics and depot formulations of antipsychotics (including atypical agents) have also been associated with NMS onset.
  - Treatment of NMS is primarily focused on reducing hyperthermia by administering benzodiazepines to facilitate muscle relaxation and possibly bromocriptine or dantrolene, which are of questionable benefit.
    - For acutely hyperthermic patients, ice-baths, extravascular and/or intravascular cooling may be required.

- **Reduced EPS**
  - The atypical antipsychotics are less likely to cause EPS than first-generation agents as they are less selective for the mesolimbic system and are less likely to cause EPS effects.
  - The atypical agents are also less likely to impact prolactin concentrations, thus have a relatively lower risk of gynecomastia.

- **Acute Agitation**
  - The parenteral atypical antipsychotics olanzapine and ziprasidone offer a clinical tool for the management of acutely agitated patients.
  - Although these agents may have a slightly longer onset of action than haloperidol, their use is associated with marginally improved behavioral responses.
  - Ziprasidone shared similar dose-dependent QT prolongation with haloperidol and extended, or high doses should prompt ECG measurement.

- **Parkinsonism**
  - Like the underlying pathophysiology of Parkinson's disease, antipsychotics may cause a blockade of nigrostriatal D2 receptors, which is the cause of the movement disorders associated with antipsychotic therapy.

- **Overdose**
  - Overdoses of antipsychotic agents are relatively common, given the underlying psychiatric disease.
  - Underlying toxicologic management principles are consistent in these patients with assessment, GI decontamination, and supportive care.
  - Patients should have serial ECGs following the QRS and QT intervals with aggressive treatment with sodium bicarbonate for QRS more significant than 100 ms and adequate replacement of serum potassium and magnesium in patients with QT prolongation.
  - The potential use of physostigmine for the management of anticholinergic delirium is possible but should be guided by expert toxicologic consultation.

High-Yield Fast-Facts

- ▪ **Risperidone Derivative**
    - – Some agents are derivative metabolites of parent compounds, such as paliperidone, which is the active metabolite of risperidone.
- ▪ **Lipid Emulsion**
    - – Some overdoses of antipsychotics can be treated with intravenous lipid emulsion to partition the offending agent into the lipid rather than in the CNS or cardiac tissue.

HIGH-YIELD BOARD EXAM ESSENTIALS

- **CLASSIC AGENTS:** Aripiprazole, asenapine, brexpiprazole, cariprazine, clozapine, iloperidone, lumateperone, lurasidone, olanzapine, paliperidone, pimavanserin, quetiapine, risperidone, ziprasidone
- **DRUG CLASS:** Atypical antipsychotics
- **INDICATIONS:** Autistic disorder irritability, bipolar disorder, major depressive disorder, schizophrenia, Tourette disorder
- **MECHANISM:** Dopamine antagonist action at D2 receptors, blocking excess signaling in the mesolimbic and mesocortical pathways.
- **SIDE EFFECTS:** Parkinsonism, NMS, anticholinergic effects, agranulocytosis (clozapine)
- **CLINICAL PEARLS:** The atypical antipsychotics are less likely to cause EPS than first-generation agents as they are less selective for the mesolimbic system and are less likely to cause EPS effects.

High-Yield Basic Pharmacology

- **Bupropion**
  - Inhibits the reuptake of dopamine and norepinephrine, prolonging norepinephrine and serotonergic neurotransmission.
- **Mirtazapine**
  - Central alpha-2 adrenergic inhibitor, causing increased serotonergic and norepinephrine neurotransmission.
- **Nefazodone, Trazodone, and Vilazodone**
  - Serotonin 2A and 2C (5HT2A and 5HT2C) receptor antagonists, partial 5-HT1 receptor agonist, and serotonin reuptake inhibition.

Primary Net Benefit

- Adjunctive antidepressants with or as an alternative to SSRI therapy; bupropion may specifically help smoking cessation, and nefazodone carries a high risk of hepatic injury.

Atypical Antidepressants - Drug Class Review			
High-Yield Med Reviews			
Mechanism of Action: *Bupropion* - Inhibits the reuptake of dopamine and norepinephrine, prolonging norepinephrine and serotonergic neurotransmission. *Mirtazapine* - Central alpha-2 adrenergic inhibitor, causing increased serotonergic and norepinephrine neurotransmission. *Nefazodone, Trazodone, and Vilazodone* - Serotonin 2A and 2C (5HT2A and 5HT2C) receptor antagonists, partial 5-HT1 receptor agonist, and serotonin reuptake inhibition.			
Class Effects: Adjunctive antidepressants with or as an alternative to SSRI therapy; bupropion may specifically help smoking cessation, and nefazodone carries a high risk of hepatic injury.			
Generic Name	**Brand Name**	**Indication(s) or Uses**	**Notes**

Bupropion	Aplenzin
	Forfivo
	Wellbutrin
	Zyban
		• Major depressive disorder
		• Seasonal affective disorder
		• Smoking cessation
			• **Dosing (Adult):**
			  – Oral 100 to 450 mg daily
			• **Dosing (Peds):**
			  – Oral 3 mg/kg/day in 2-3 divided doses
			    • Maximum 6 mg/kg/day or single dose 150 mg
			• **CYP450 Interactions:** Substrate CYP1A2, 2A6, 2B6, 2C9, 2D6, 2E1, 3A4; Inhibits CYP2D6
			• **Renal or Hepatic Dose Adjustments:**
			  – Child-Pugh class C - reduce dose by 50%
			• **Dosage Forms:** Oral (tablet)

Mirtazapine	Remeron	• Major depressive disorder
		• Migraine prophylaxis
		• Panic disorder
			• **Dosing (Adult):**
			  – Oral 15 to 60 mg/day
			• **Dosing (Peds):**
			  – Not routinely used
			• **CYP450 Interactions:** text
			• **Renal or Hepatic Dose Adjustments:**
			  – GFR less than 30 mL/minute - use an initial dose of 7.5 mg
			  – Child-Pugh class C - reduce dose by 50%
			• **Dosage Forms:** Oral (tablet)

Atypical Antidepressants - Drug Class Review
High-Yield Med Reviews

Generic Name	Brand Name	Indication(s) or Uses	Notes

Nefazodone	Serzone	▪ Major depressive disorder	▪ **Dosing (Adult):**
			  − Oral 50 to 600 mg in 2 divided doses
			▪ **Dosing (Peds):**
			  − Not routinely used
			▪ **CYP450 Interactions:** Substrate CYP2D6, 3A4; Inhibits CYP3A4
			▪ **Renal or Hepatic Dose Adjustments:** None
			▪ **Dosage Forms:** Oral (tablet)

Trazodone	Desyrel	▪ Aggression associated with dementia
		▪ Insomnia
		▪ Major depressive disorder
			▪ **Dosing (Adult):**
			  − Oral 25 to 400 mg/day
			▪ **Dosing (Peds):**
			  − Oral 0.75 to 6.9 mg/kg/day
			    ▪ Maximum 150 mg/dose
			▪ **CYP450 Interactions:** Substrate CYP2D6, 3A4
			▪ **Renal or Hepatic Dose Adjustments:** None
			▪ **Dosage Forms:** Oral (tablet)

Vilazodone	Viibryd	▪ Major depressive disorder	▪ **Dosing (Adult):**
			  − Oral 10 to 40 mg daily
			▪ **Dosing (Peds):**
			  − Not routinely used
			▪ **CYP450 Interactions:** Substrate CYP2C19, 2D6, 3A4
			▪ **Renal or Hepatic Dose Adjustments:** None
			▪ **Dosage Forms:** Oral (tablet)

High-Yield Clinical Knowledge

▪ **Nefazodone Hepatotoxicity**
  − Nefazodone is rarely used clinically as it is associated with a high risk of hepatotoxicity, which can lead to numerous physiologic effects, including jaundice, hepatitis, and hepatic necrosis.
  − Nefazodone is also a potent CYP3A4 inhibitor, contributing to numerous clinically relevant drug interactions.
▪ **Serotonin Syndrome**
  − Serotonin syndrome is the combination of a rapid onset of altered mental status, autonomic instability, hyperthermia, and hyperreflexia/myoclonus.
  − Although some atypical antidepressants have been implicated in serotonin syndrome, other antidepressants, including MAO inhibitors, are more likely to contribute to serotonin toxicity.
    − Treatment of serotonin syndrome involves the management of hyperthermia through invasive or noninvasive cooling, skeletal muscle relaxation using benzodiazepines, and airway support.
      − Dantrolene and cyproheptadine have been suggested as adjuncts for managing serotonin syndrome but are of questionable patient-oriented benefit.
▪ **Bupropion Seizures**
  − Although bupropion has numerous benefits, including smoking cessation characteristics, minor sexual dysfunction, and fatigue than other antidepressants, it can be more troublesome in overdose.
  − The risk of seizures increases if chronic doses are above 450 mg/day or ingest a large overdose.
  − Additional findings from bupropion overdose include hypertension, agitation, QRS, and QT prolongation.
    − The onset of these symptoms can be delayed between 10 and 24 hours following an overdose, with seizures lasting up to 48 hours after exposure.

- The active metabolite hydroxybupropion may cause seizures by acting as a GABA antagonist and as an NMDA agonist.
- **Trazodone Priapism**
    - In addition to CNS depression, orthostatic hypotension, and QT prolongation, trazodone is associated with the development of priapism.
        - Possible mechanisms of this effect pertain to paradoxical alpha vasoconstriction in the penis, limiting blood flow.
- **Mirtazapine for Anxiety**
    - Due to its favorable adverse event profile with fewer GI complaints compared to other agents, mirtazapine can be added to antianxiety regimens, particularly taking advantage of its antihistamine mediated sedative effect.
- **Drug Discontinuation Syndrome**
    - Abrupt discontinuation of any atypical antidepressant can cause a sharp worsening of psychiatric symptoms, which can be worse than pre-treatment psychiatric disturbances.
    - Slow tapering is necessary to avoid this withdrawal syndrome, but agents with prolonged half-lives and active metabolites (such as fluoxetine) may have a lower likelihood due to a self-tapering effect.

High-Yield Fast-Fact

- **No Immediate Effects**
    - Whenever patients are started on antidepressants, they should be informed the maximal effects are not immediate; however, recent evidence suggests that improvements in physical symptoms can occur within the first two weeks of treatment.

HIGH-YIELD BOARD EXAM ESSENTIALS
- **CLASSIC AGENTS:** Bupropion, Mirtazapine, Nefazodone, Trazodone, Vilazodone
- **DRUG CLASS:** Atypical antidepressants
- **INDICATIONS:** Major depressive disorder, migraine prophylaxis, panic disorder
- **MECHANISM:** Bupropion - Inhibits the reuptake of dopamine and norepinephrine, prolonging norepinephrine and serotonergic neurotransmission. Mirtazapine - Central alpha-2 adrenergic inhibitor, causing increased serotonergic and norepinephrine neurotransmission. Nefazodone, Trazodone, and Vilazodone - Serotonin 2A and 2C (5HT2A and 5HT2C) receptor antagonists, partial 5-HT1 receptor agonist, and serotonin reuptake inhibition.
- **SIDE EFFECTS:** Hepatotoxicity (nefazodone), priapism (trazodone), serotonin syndrome
- **CLINICAL PEARLS:** Abrupt discontinuation of any atypical antidepressant can cause a sharp worsening of psychiatric symptoms, which can be worse than pre-treatment psychiatric disturbances.

High-Yield Basic Pharmacology

- **Mechanism of Action**
  - Complex pharmacology without unified agreement on its underlying mechanism.
    - Involves interaction with dopamine, norepinephrine, and serotonin neurotransmission, as well as secondary signaling systems.

Primary Net Benefit

- This monovalent cation has been used for decades for Bipolar Disorder despite a narrow therapeutic index, chronic toxicities, and unclear mechanism of action.

Lithium - Drug Class Review			
High-Yield Med Reviews			
Mechanism of Action: *Complex pharmacology without unified agreement on its underlying mechanism.*			
Class Effects: Mood stabilizer; risk of GI disturbances (primarily diarrhea), nephrogenic DI, hypothyroidism.			
Generic Name	**Brand Name**	**Indication(s) or Uses**	**Notes**

Lithium	Lithobid	• Bipolar disorder
		• Major depressive disorder
			• **Dosing (Adult):**
			  – Oral 600 to 900 mg/day divided into 2-3 doses
			    • Target therapeutic levels between 0.6 and 1.2 mEq/L
			• **Dosing (Peds):**
			  – Oral 8 to 40 mEq/day adjusted to target level between 0.6 to 1.2 mEq/L
			    • Maximum 40 mg/kg/day
			• **CYP450 Interactions:** None
			• **Renal or Hepatic Dose Adjustments:**
			  – GFR less than 30 mL/minute - avoid use
			• **Dosage Forms:** Oral (capsule, solution, tablet)

High-Yield Clinical Knowledge

- **Bipolar Disorder**
  - Lithium remains an essential therapy and first-line treatment for acute mania, acute bipolar depression, and a core component of pharmacotherapeutic maintenance of bipolar type 1 and 2 disorders.
  - As a result of prolonged time to onset of effects and close titration to therapeutic levels, alternative agents, including modern antipsychotic agents, have been used more frequently with similar outcomes.
- **Adverse Events**
  - Lithium therapy is associated with numerous acute and chronic toxicities that may not correlate with serum levels.
  - Common adverse events early on in therapy include GI disturbances (primarily diarrhea) and mild CNS effects.
    - Diarrhea is often managed by slowing dose titration; using liquid rather than tablet or capsule products can alleviate these symptoms.
    - Hand tremors may also develop, which can respond to slower titration, lower doses, or the addition of propranolol.
  - Nephrogenic diabetes insipidus occurs in up to 50% of patients on lithium but is often reversible upon discontinuation.

- Thyroid effects, primary hypothyroidism can occur and can be managed with supplemental thyroid hormone replacement.
- **Lithium Toxicity**
    - Acute overdoses of lithium rarely have toxic CNS concentration s and do not acutely cause neurologic dysfunction.
    - Chronic lithium toxicity is associated with intravascular volume depletion, negative water balance and further worsens lithium toxicity.
        - Additionally, concomitant drugs such as ACE inhibitors or angiotensin receptor blockers (ARBs) that decrease renal blood flow or thiazide diuretics that increase lithium reabsorption can contribute to chronic lithium toxicity.
    - However, in acute-on-chronic or lithium toxicity where serum levels are above 5 mEq/L, or above 4 mEq/L in patients with renal dysfunction, hemodialysis may be required to assist the management of altered mental status, seizures, or cardiac arrhythmias.
    - Risk factors for lithium toxicity include sodium restriction, dehydration, vomiting, diarrhea, patients over the age of 50, or those with concomitant heart failure or cirrhosis.
- **Broad Neuroprotection**
    - Lithium has also been associated with neuroprotective effects owing to its downregulation of the protein p53 from modulation of the bcl-2 gene, limiting apoptosis of CNS tissue.
- **Drug-Interactions**
    - Although lithium does not directly impact hepatic oxidation, there are several clinically relevant drug interactions.
    - ACE inhibitors/ARBs, thiazide diuretics, and NSAIDs affect lithium's renal clearance increasing lithium exposure.
    - Caffeine and theophylline conversely increase lithium renal elimination, lowering lithium exposure.
    - Numerous other clinically relevant drug interactions should prompt further review in other resources.
- **SILENT**
    - Chronic lithium therapy is associated with a syndrome of irreversible neurologic and neuropsychiatric sequelae known as the syndrome of irreversible lithium-effectuated neurotoxicity, or SILENT.
    - SILENT is a new neurologic dysfunction in the absence of prior neurologic illness and persists for at least two months after lithium cessation.
    - These effects are often attributed to other agents these patients may be taking but have occurred in patients after discontinuing these other drugs or lithium monotherapy.

High-Yield Fast-Fact

- **7-Up**
    - Lithium was once found in the soda drink 7-Up, and the "7" in its name has been attributed to the atomic weight of elemental lithium.
- **Batteries**
    - Lithium is a common component of batteries, including the ones powering eclectic vehicles and cell phones.

HIGH-YIELD BOARD EXAM ESSENTIALS
- **CLASSIC AGENTS:** Lithium
- **DRUG CLASS:** Lithium
- **INDICATIONS:** Bipolar disorder, major depressive disorder
- **MECHANISM:** Complex pharmacology without unified agreement on its underlying mechanism.
- **SIDE EFFECTS:** GI disturbances (primarily diarrhea), nephrogenic DI, hypothyroidism
- **CLINICAL PEARLS:** Has a narrow therapeutic index. Although lithium does not directly impact hepatic oxidation, there are several clinically relevant drug interactions. ACE inhibitors/ARBs, thiazide diuretics, and NSAIDs affect lithium's renal clearance increasing lithium exposure.

High-Yield Basic Pharmacology

- **Mechanism of Action**
    - Irreversibly bind to and inhibit monoamine oxidase-A and monoamine oxidase-B, preventing the presynaptic degradation of epinephrine, norepinephrine, dopamine, and serotonin.
- **MAO-A Vs. MAO-B**
    - MAO-A normally functions to metabolize monoamines, including norepinephrine, serotonin, and dopamine, in the CNS and outside the CNS.
        - MAO-A is concentrated in the liver and intestine.
    - MAO-B selectively functions to metabolize dopamine in the CNS, primarily in the basal ganglia, but may also exist peripherally.
    - Selegiline is a selective MAO-B inhibitor, whereas isocarboxazid, phenelzine, and tranylcypromine are nonselective MAO-A and MAO-B inhibitors.

Primary Net Benefit

- MAO inhibitors are reserved for refractory depression not adequately responsive to other antidepressants and when the threat of psychiatric disease outweighs the risks of MAO inhibition.

Monoamine Oxidase Inhibitor - Drug Class Review **High-Yield Med Reviews**			
Mechanism of Action: *Irreversibly bind to and inhibit monoamine oxidase-A and monoamine oxidase-B, preventing the metabolism of epinephrine, norepinephrine, dopamine, and serotonin.*			
Class Effects: Risk of orthostatic or postural hypotension, weight gain, decreased libido, and anorgasmia.			
Generic Name	**Brand Name**	**Indication(s) or Uses**	**Notes**

Isocarboxazid	Marplan	- Major depressive disorder	- **Dosing (Adult):**
			   – Oral 10 to 20 mg twice daily
			 - **Dosing (Peds):**
			   – Not routinely used
			 - **CYP450 Interactions:** None
			 - **Renal or Hepatic Dose Adjustments:** None
			 - **Dosage Forms:** Oral (tablet)

Phenelzine	Nardil	- Major depressive disorder	- **Dosing (Adult):**
			   – Oral 15 mg TID
			     - Maximum 90 mg/day
			 - **Dosing (Peds):**
			   – Not routinely used
			 - **CYP450 Interactions:** None
			 - **Renal or Hepatic Dose Adjustments:**
			   – Child-Pugh class C - contraindicated
			 - **Dosage Forms:** Oral (tablet)

Monoamine Oxidase Inhibitor - Drug Class Review
High-Yield Med Reviews

Generic Name	Brand Name	Indication(s) or Uses	Notes

Selegiline	Emsam
	Zelapar
		• Major depressive disorder
		• Parkinson disease
			• **Dosing (Adult):**
			  – Oral 1.25 to 5 mg BID
			  – Transdermal 6 to 12 mg/24 hour patch
			• **Dosing (Peds):**
			  – Not routinely used
			• **CYP450 Interactions:** Substrate of CYP1A2, 2A6, 2B6, 2D6, 3A4
			• **Renal or Hepatic Dose Adjustments:**
			  – GFR less than 30 mL/minute - Use not recommended
			  – Child-Pugh Class C - Not recommended
			• **Dosage Forms:** Oral (capsule, tablet), Transdermal patch

Tranylcypromine	Parnate	• Major depressive disorder	• **Dosing (Adult):**
			  – Oral 10 to 60 mg/day
			• **Dosing (Peds):**
			  – Not routinely used
			• **CYP450 Interactions:** None
			• **Renal or Hepatic Dose Adjustments:** None
			• **Dosage Forms:** Oral (tablet)

High-Yield Clinical Knowledge

- **Serotonin Syndrome**
  - Serotonin syndrome is the combination of a rapid onset of altered mental status, autonomic instability, hyperthermia, and hyperreflexia/myoclonus.
  - MAO inhibitors are associated with the highest risk of serotonin syndrome among antidepressants.
  - Treatment of serotonin syndrome involves the management of hyperthermia through invasive or noninvasive cooling, skeletal muscle relaxation using benzodiazepines, and airway support.
    - Dantrolene and cyproheptadine have been suggested as adjuncts for managing serotonin syndrome but are of questionable patient-oriented benefit.
- **Hypertensive Crisis**
  - Although drug interactions contribute to serotonin syndrome, certain foods with high tyramine content can precipitate a similar effect, including hypertensive crisis.
  - MAO-A, located in the gut, is usually metabolized tyramine before absorption. But with MAO inhibition, tyramine becomes absorbed and can exert its vasoconstrictor effects.
- **Non-MAOI with MAOI Properties**
  - Numerous other medications possess varying degrees of MAO inhibition, and if combined, can produce hypertensive crisis and or serotonin syndrome.
  - Common examples include linezolid, procarbazine, and methylene blue.
- **St. John's Wort**
  - This common herbal that is cited among many adverse events and drug interactions possesses weak MAO inhibitor activity, attributed to its major components, hypericin, and hyperforin.
- **Adverse Events**
  - MAO inhibitors, particularly phenelzine, are frequently associated with orthostatic or postural hypotension, weight gain, decreased libido, and anorgasmia.
  - Tranylcypromine and selegiline conversely can cause CNS stimulation and insomnia.
- **Not Just MAO Inhibition**
  - Other enzymes are inhibited by MAO inhibitors, notably including alcohol dehydrogenase.

— Patients taking tranylcypromine should avoid alcohol due to this effect.

High-Yield Fast-Facts

- **Hydrazines**
  — Isocarboxazid and phenelzine are hydrazine compounds, similar to the hydrazine isoniazid that can cause seizures.
- **Ayahuasca**
  — Ayahuasca is a hallucinogenic drink prepared by Peruvian and other South American natives, which employs a MAO inhibitor (the plan Banisteriopsis caapi) that permits dimethyltryptamine to be absorbed orally.

HIGH-YIELD BOARD EXAM ESSENTIALS

- **CLASSIC AGENTS:** Isocarboxazid, phenelzine, selegiline, tranylcypromine
- **DRUG CLASS:** MAO inhibitor
- **INDICATIONS:** Major depressive disorder, Parkinson disease
- **MECHANISM:** Irreversibly bind to, and inhibit, monoamine oxidase-A and monoamine oxidase-B, preventing the metabolism of epinephrine, norepinephrine, dopamine, and serotonin.
- **SIDE EFFECTS:** Orthostatic or postural hypotension, weight gain, decreased libido, and anorgasmia.
- **CLINICAL PEARLS:** Numerous other medications possess varying degrees of MAO inhibition, and if combined, can produce hypertensive crisis and or serotonin syndrome. Common examples include linezolid, procarbazine, and methylene blue.

High-Yield Basic Pharmacology

- **S-Ketamine**
  - Ketamine is a racemic mixture, and the s-enantiomer (esketamine) has been identified to possess the antidepressant properties of ketamine.
  - Noncompetitive inhibition of n-methyl-d-aspartate (NMDA) receptor

Primary Net Benefit

- Ketamine is a widely used dissociative anesthetic with many effects, including acute management of depression where its S-enantiomer, esketamine, is uniquely indicated.

<table>
<tr><td colspan="4" align="center">NMDA Antagonist - Drug Class Review
High-Yield Med Reviews</td></tr>
<tr><td colspan="4">Mechanism of Action: Noncompetitive inhibition of n-methyl-d-aspartate (NMDA) receptor.</td></tr>
<tr><td colspan="4">Class Effects: Dissociative anesthetic effects, antidepressant effects, risk for emergence psychosis, abuse risk.</td></tr>
<tr><td>Generic Name</td><td>Brand Name</td><td>Indication(s) or Uses</td><td>Notes</td></tr>
<tr>
<td>Esketamine</td>
<td>Spravato</td>
<td>
<ul>
<li>Major depressive disorder</li>
<li>Treatment-resistant depression</li>
</ul>
</td>
<td>
<ul>
<li>Dosing (Adult):
  <ul>
  <li>Induction: IN 56 mg twice weekly or 84 mg twice weekly</li>
  <li>Maintenance: Decrease frequency to once weekly</li>
  </ul>
</li>
<li>Dosing (Peds):
  <ul>
  <li>Not routinely used</li>
  </ul>
</li>
<li>CYP450 Interactions: text</li>
<li>Renal or Hepatic Dose Adjustments:
  <ul>
  <li>Child-Pugh class C - not recommended</li>
  </ul>
</li>
<li>Dosage Forms: Nasal solution</li>
</ul>
</td>
</tr>
<tr>
<td>Ketamine</td>
<td>Ketalar</td>
<td>
<ul>
<li>Analgesia</li>
<li>Anesthesia</li>
<li>Agitation</li>
<li>Treatment-resistant depression</li>
<li>Sedation</li>
<li>Status epilepticus</li>
</ul>
</td>
<td>
<ul>
<li>Dosing (Adult):
  <ul>
  <li>IV 0.5 to 2 mg/kg bolus
    <ul><li>IV infusion 0.05 to 2 mg/kg/hour</li></ul>
  </li>
  <li>IM/IN 1 to 4 mg/kg</li>
  <li>Oral 0.5 mg/kg/day, maximum 500 mg/day</li>
  </ul>
</li>
<li>Dosing (Peds):
  <ul>
  <li>IV 0.5 to 2 mg/kg bolus
    <ul><li>IV infusion 0.05 to 2 mg/kg/hour</li></ul>
  </li>
  <li>IM/IN 1 to 4 mg/kg</li>
  <li>Oral 0.5 mg/kg/day, maximum 500 mg/day</li>
  </ul>
</li>
<li>CYP450 Interactions: Substrate of CYP2B6, 2C9, 3A4</li>
<li>Renal or Hepatic Dose Adjustments: None</li>
<li>Dosage Forms: IV (solution)</li>
</ul>
</td>
</tr>
</table>

High-Yield Clinical Knowledge

- **Antidepressant Effect**
  - The use of esketamine or ketamine is primarily reserved for patients with depression that has not responded to conventional antidepressants.

- These agents possess advantages over continuing antidepressant treatment or further increasing doses, including rapid onset within 24 hours of administration.
  - However, these antidepressant effects may not last beyond seven days.
- **Esketamine Preparation**
  - Esketamine is only available as an intranasal preparation and retains many of the pharmacokinetic characteristics of ketamine and the antidepressant effects (onset within 24 hours, duration of approximately seven days).
- **Dissociation**
  - Ketamine causes a unique dose-dependent dissociation, where the patient cannot pain, visual or auditory neurotransmission signals to the brain, but the outgoing sympathetic and parasympathetic output front the CNS is not directly affected.
  - This effect occurs at an approximate weight-based dose of 0.5 to 1 mg/kg.
  - Analgesic effects of ketamine occur lower in the dose range, approximately between 0.1 to 0.3 mg/kg.
- **Additional Actions**
  - Esketamine and ketamine each have opioid agonist properties, as well as increasing dopaminergic activity inhibition of dopamine reuptake, cholinergic effects, and voltage-sensitive calcium channel blocking effects.
- **Blood Pressure, Intracranial Pressure, Intraocular Pressure**
  - Ketamine and esketamine are thought to increase blood pressure, intracranial pressure, intraocular pressure but do not do so in a clinically relevant manner.
    - Thus ketamine is not contraindicated specifically because of elevated blood pressure, intracranial pressure, or intraocular pressure.
- **Abuse Potential**
  - Esketamine and ketamine have high abuse potential and can lead to chronic dependence and tolerance.
  - Long-term effects of ketamine abuse can lead to neurogenic bladder or worsening underlying psychiatric disease.

High-Yield Fast-Fact

- **Nothing New**
  - Although recently approved for use in treatment-resistant depression, esketamine has been in use since the early 1960s.

HIGH-YIELD BOARD EXAM ESSENTIALS
- **CLASSIC AGENTS:** Esketamine, ketamine
- **DRUG CLASS:** NMDA antagonists
- **INDICATIONS:** Analgesia, anesthesia, agitation, treatment-resistant depression, sedation, status epilepticus
- **MECHANISM:** Noncompetitive inhibition of n-methyl-d-aspartate (NMDA) receptor.
- **SIDE EFFECTS:** Emergence psychosis, abuse risk
- **CLINICAL PEARLS:** Ketamine and esketamine are thought to increase blood pressure, intracranial pressure, intraocular pressure but do not do so in a clinically relevant manner.

High-Yield Basic Pharmacology

- **Mechanism of Action**
  - **SNRI:** Inhibits the reuptake of both norepinephrine and serotonin, prolonging norepinephrine, and serotonergic neurotransmission.
  - **Buspirone:** Acts as a serotonin (5HT1a) receptor partial agonist
- **Active Metabolites**
  - The active metabolite of venlafaxine, desvenlafaxine, is commercially available as an alternative SNRI.
  - Similarly, levomilnacipran is the single-isomer of milnacipran.

Primary Net Benefit

- First or second-line pharmacotherapy for depression and improved safety compared to conventional antidepressants, including TCA and MAO-inhibitors.

Serotonin-Norepinephrine Reuptake Inhibitors & Buspirone - Drug Class Review			
High-Yield Med Reviews			
Mechanism of Action: *SNRI - Inhibits the reuptake of both norepinephrine and serotonin, prolonging norepinephrine, and serotonergic neurotransmission.* *Buspirone - Acts as a serotonin (5HT1a) receptor partial agonist.*			
Class Effects: Dose-dependent effects on elevation of blood pressure (with venlafaxine).			
Generic Name	**Brand Name**	**Indication(s) or Uses**	**Notes**

Buspirone	Buspirone	• General anxiety	• **Dosing (Adult):**
			  – Oral 10 to 20 mg/day divided in 2-3 doses
			    • Maximum 60 mg/day
			• **Dosing (Peds):**
			  – Oral 5 mg daily to 30 mg twice daily
			    • Maximum 60 mg/day
			• **CYP450 Interactions:** Substrate CYP2D6, 3A4
			• **Renal or Hepatic Dose Adjustments:**
			  – Severe hepatic or renal impairment - not recommended
			• **Dosage Forms:** Oral (tablet)

Desvenlafaxine	Pristiq	• Major depressive disorder	• **Dosing (Adult):**
			  – Oral 50 to 150 mg daily
			• **Dosing (Peds):**
			  – Oral 50 to 150 mg daily
			• **CYP450 Interactions:** Substrate CYP3A4
			• **Renal or Hepatic Dose Adjustments:**
			  – GFR 30 to 50 mL/minute - Maximum 50 mg daily
			  – GFR less than 30 mL/minute - Maximum 25 mg daily
			  – Child-Pugh class B or C - Maxim 100 mg daily
			• **Dosage Forms:** Oral (tablet)

Serotonin-Norepinephrine Reuptake Inhibitors & Buspirone - Drug Class Review
High-Yield Med Reviews

Generic Name	Brand Name	Indication(s) or Uses	Notes

Duloxetine	Cymbalta	• Fibromyalgia
		• Generalized anxiety disorder
		• Major depressive disorder
		• Musculoskeletal pain
		• Neuropathic pain
			• **Dosing (Adult):**
			  – Oral 20 to 120 mg daily
			• **Dosing (Peds):**
			  – Oral 20 to 120 mg daily
			• **CYP450 Interactions:** Substrate CYP1A2, 2D6; Inhibits CYP2D6
			• **Renal or Hepatic Dose Adjustments:**
			  – GFR less than 30 mL/minute - Maximum 60 mg daily
			  – Hepatic impairment - avoid use
			• **Dosage Forms:** Oral (capsule)

Levomilnacipran	Fetzima	• Major depressive disorder	• **Dosing (Adult):**
			  – Oral 20 to 120 mg daily
			• **Dosing (Peds):**
			  – Not routinely used
			• **CYP450 Interactions:** Substrate CYP2C19, 2C8, 2D6, 3A4, P-gp
			• **Renal or Hepatic Dose Adjustments:**
			  – GFR 30 to 59 mL/minute - Maximum 80 mg/day
			  – GFR 15 to 29 mL/minute - Maximum 40 mg daily
			• **Dosage Forms:** Oral (capsule)

Milnacipran	Savella	• Fibromyalgia
		• Major depressive disorder
			• **Dosing (Adult):**
			  – Oral 50 to 100 mg BID
			• **Dosing (Peds):**
			  – Not routinely used
			• **CYP450 Interactions:** None
			• **Renal or Hepatic Dose Adjustments:**
			  – GFR less than 30 mL/minute - Maximum 50 mg BID
			• **Dosage Forms:** Oral (tablet)

Venlafaxine	Effexor	• Generalized anxiety disorder
		• Major depressive disorder
		• Panic disorder
		• Social anxiety disorder
			• **Dosing (Adult):**
			  – Oral 37.5 to 375 mg daily
			• **Dosing (Peds):**
			  – Oral 12.5 to 75 mg daily
			    • Maximum 75 mg/day
			• **CYP450 Interactions:** Substrate CYP2C19, 2C9, 2D6, 3A4; Inhibits CYP2D6
			• **Renal or Hepatic Dose Adjustments:**
			  – GFR less than 30 mL/minute - Maximum 150 mg/day
			• **Dosage Forms:** Oral (capsule, tablet)

High-Yield Clinical Knowledge

- **Overdose Risk**
  - Venlafaxine and desvenlafaxine appear to cause more morbidity and mortality after overdose than other SSRIs and other SNRIs.
  - Owing to its sodium and potassium channel blocking properties, desvenlafaxine, and venlafaxine may prolong the QRS and QT interval, possibly attributing to their overdose mortality.
- **SNRI Adverse Effects**
  - Although many adverse events with the SNRIs are similar to the SSRIs (GI complaints and sexual dysfunction), hyperhidrosis is a common adverse event unique to SNRIs.
  - All SNRIs may also cause increases in blood pressure, with more pronounced effects due to venlafaxine and levomilnacipran.
- **Drug Discontinuation Syndrome**
  - Like SSRIs, SNRIs should not be abruptly discontinued due to the risk of a sudden worsening of psychiatric symptoms, which can be worse than pre-treatment psychiatric disturbances.
    - Slow tapering is necessary to avoid this withdrawal syndrome, but agents with prolonged half-lives and active metabolites (such as fluoxetine) may have a lower likelihood due to a self-tapering effect.
- **Fibromyalgia**
  - Although an SNRI, milnacipran is only FDA approved for treating fibromyalgia and is not routinely used to treat depression.
- **Serotonin Syndrome**
  - Similar to SSRIs, SNRIs carry a risk of serotonin syndrome.
  - Serotonin syndrome is the rapid onset of altered mental status, autonomic instability, hyperthermia, and hyperreflexia/myoclonus.
  - Other antidepressants, including MAO inhibitors, are more likely to contribute to serotonin toxicity.
- **SIADH**
  - Venlafaxine and desvenlafaxine are associated with a higher risk of SIADH compared to other SNRIs and SSRIs.

High-Yield Fast-Fact

- **Duloxetine Jaundice**
  - Duloxetine can cause biliary obstruction with chronic use or excessive use, leading to hyperbilirubinemia and jaundice.

HIGH-YIELD BOARD EXAM ESSENTIALS
- **CLASSIC AGENTS:** Buspirone, desvenlafaxine, duloxetine, levomilnacipran, milnacipran, venlafaxine
- **DRUG CLASS:** SNRI
- **INDICATIONS:** Fibromyalgia, generalized anxiety disorder, major depressive disorder, musculoskeletal pain, neuropathic pain, panic disorder, social anxiety disorder
- **MECHANISM:** SNRI - Inhibits the reuptake of both norepinephrine and serotonin, prolonging norepinephrine, and serotonergic neurotransmission. Buspirone - Acts as a serotonin (5HT1a) receptor partial agonist.
- **SIDE EFFECTS:** SIADH, serotonin syndrome, QRS/QT prolongation (venlafaxine)
- **CLINICAL PEARLS:** Duloxetine can cause biliary obstruction with chronic use or excessive use, leading to hyperbilirubinemia and jaundice.

High-Yield Basic Pharmacology

- **Mechanism of Action**
  - Inhibits the reuptake of serotonin by the serotonin transporter, prolonging serotonergic neurotransmission.
- **First-Line Antidepressants**
  - SSRIs are considered first-line agents for treating major depression due to their improved tolerability and safety, particularly after an overdose, compared to conventional antidepressants (tricyclic antidepressants or monoamine oxidase inhibitors).
  - There is no definitive therapeutic difference between the SSRIs, but agent selection is based upon drug interactions, pharmacokinetic properties, and patient clinical response.

Primary Net Benefit

- First-line pharmacotherapy for depression and improved safety compared to conventional antidepressants including TCA and MAO-inhibitors.

Selective Serotonin Reuptake Inhibitors - Drug Class Review			
High-Yield Med Reviews			
Mechanism of Action: *Inhibits the reuptake of serotonin by the serotonin transporter, prolonging serotonergic neurotransmission.*			
Class Effects: SIADH, QT prolongation (citalopram, escitalopram), sexual dysfunction (e.g., decreased libido, inability to orgasm, etc).			
Generic Name	**Brand Name**	**Indication(s) or Uses**	**Notes**

Citalopram	Celexa	• Major depressive disorder	• **Dosing (Adult):**
			   – Oral 10 to 40 mg daily
			     • Maximum 20 mg/day for poor CYP2C19 metabolizers, presence of inhibitors, hepatic impairment, or over 60 yrs old
			• **Dosing (Peds):**
			   – Oral 5 to 40 mg daily
			• **CYP450 Interactions:** Substrate CYP2C19, 2D6, 3A4; Inhibits CYP2D6
			• **Renal or Hepatic Dose Adjustments:**
			   – GFR less than 20 mL/minute - use caution
			   – Child-Pugh class B or C - Maximum 20 mg/day
			• **Dosage Forms:** Oral (solution, tablet)

Escitalopram	Lexapro	• Generalized anxiety disorder
		• Major depressive disorder
			• **Dosing (Adult):**
			   – Oral 5 to 30 mg daily
			• **Dosing (Peds):**
			   – Oral 2.5 to 30 mg daily
			• **CYP450 Interactions:** Substrate CYP2C19, 3A4; Inhibits CYP2D6
			• **Renal or Hepatic Dose Adjustments:**
			   – GFR less than 20 mL/minute - use caution
			   – Child-Pugh class B or C - Maximum 10 mg/day
			• **Dosage Forms:** Oral (solution, tablet)

Selective Serotonin Reuptake Inhibitors - Drug Class Review
High-Yield Med Reviews

Generic Name	Brand Name	Indication(s) or Uses	Notes

Fluoxetine	Prozac
	Sarafem
		▪ Bipolar major depression
		▪ Bulimia nervosa
		▪ Major depressive disorder
		▪ Obsessive-compulsive disorder
		▪ Panic disorder
		▪ Premenstrual dysphoric disorder
		▪ Treatment-resistant depression
			▪ **Dosing (Adult):**
			  – Oral 10 to 80 mg daily
			▪ **Dosing (Peds):**
			  – Oral 0.25 mg/kg/dose or 5 mg/dose
			    ▪ Maximum 20 mg/day
			▪ **CYP450 Interactions:** Substrate CYP1A2, 2B6, 2C19, 2C9, 2D6, 2E1, 3A4; Inhibits CYP2C19, 2D6
			▪ **Renal or Hepatic Dose Adjustments:**
			  – Cirrhosis or Chronic Liver Disease - Decrease dose by 50%
			▪ **Dosage Forms:** Oral (capsule, solution, tablet)

Fluvoxamine	Luvox	▪ Bulimia nervosa
		▪ Major depressive disorder
		▪ Panic disorder
		▪ Post-traumatic stress disorder
		▪ Social anxiety disorder
			▪ **Dosing (Adult):**
			  – Oral 50 to 300 mg daily
			▪ **Dosing (Peds):**
			  – Oral 25 to 300 mg daily
			▪ **CYP450 Interactions:** Substrate CYP1A2, 2D6; Inhibits CYP1A2, 2C19, 2C9, 2D6, 3A4
			▪ **Renal or Hepatic Dose Adjustments:**
			  – Cirrhosis or Chronic Liver Disease - Decrease dose by 50%
			▪ **Dosage Forms:** Oral (capsule, tablet)

Paroxetine	Paxil	▪ Generalized anxiety disorder
		▪ Major depressive disorder
		▪ Obsessive-compulsive disorder
		▪ Panic disorder
		▪ Posttraumatic stress disorder
		▪ Premenstrual dysphoric disorder
		▪ Social anxiety disorder
		▪ Vasomotor symptoms of menopause
			▪ **Dosing (Adult):**
			  – Oral 10 to 100 mg daily
			▪ **Dosing (Peds):**
			  – Oral 5 to 60 mg daily
			    ▪ Maximum 60 mg/day
			▪ **CYP450 Interactions:** Substrate CYP2D6; Inhibits CYP2D6
			▪ **Renal or Hepatic Dose Adjustments:**
			  – Child-Pugh class C or GFR less than 30 mL/minute - maximum 40 mg/day
			▪ **Dosage Forms:** Oral (capsule, suspension, tablet)

Sertraline	Zoloft	▪ Major depressive disorder
		▪ Obsessive-compulsive disorder
		▪ Panic disorder
		▪ Posttraumatic stress disorder
		▪ Premenstrual dysphoric disorder
		▪ Social anxiety disorder
			▪ **Dosing (Adult):**
			  – Oral 25 to 200 mg daily
			▪ **Dosing (Peds):**
			  – Oral 12.5 to 200 mg daily
			▪ **CYP450 Interactions:** Substrate CYP2B6, 2C19, 2C9, 2D6, 3A4; Inhibits CYP2D6
			▪ **Renal or Hepatic Dose Adjustments:**
			  – Child-Pugh class A or B - reduce dose by 50%
			  – Child-Pugh class C - Not recommended
			▪ **Dosage Forms:** Oral (concentrate, tablet)

Selective Serotonin Reuptake Inhibitors - Drug Class Review
High-Yield Med Reviews

Generic Name	Brand Name	Indication(s) or Uses	Notes

Vortioxetine	Trintellix	▪ Major depressive disorder	▪ **Dosing (Adult):**
			  – Oral 5 to 20 mg daily
			▪ **Dosing (Peds):**
			  – Not routinely used
			▪ **CYP450 Interactions:** Substrate CYP2D6, 2B6, 2C19, 2C8, 2C9, 2D6, 3A4
			▪ **Renal or Hepatic Dose Adjustments:**
			  – None
			▪ **Dosage Forms:** Oral (tablet)

High-Yield Clinical Knowledge

- **Dose-Dependent QT Prolongation**
  - Citalopram and escitalopram are associated with a dose-dependent increase in the QT interval.
  - To reduce Torsade de Pointes' risk, citalopram should be limited to a maximum of 20 mg/day for poor CYP2C19 metabolizers, presence of inhibitors, hepatic impairment, or over 60 years old.
- **Serotonin Syndrome**
  - Serotonin syndrome is the combination of a rapid onset of altered mental status, autonomic instability, hyperthermia, and hyperreflexia/myoclonus.
  - Although SSRIs have been implicated in serotonin syndrome, other antidepressants, including MAO inhibitors, are more likely to contribute to serotonin toxicity.
    - Treatment of serotonin syndrome involves the management of hyperthermia through invasive or noninvasive cooling, skeletal muscle relaxation using benzodiazepines, and airway support.
      - Dantrolene and cyproheptadine have been suggested as adjuncts for managing serotonin syndrome but are of questionable patient-oriented benefit.
- **Antiplatelet Effect**
  - As SSRIs increase available serotonin activity, the excess serotonin acts to inhibit platelet secretory response, platelet aggregation, and platelet plug formation.
- **Movement Disorders**
  - SSRI use and its effect on serotonin and dopamine activity have been associated with the development of parkinsonism like effects, including akathisia, dystonia, and also myoclonus.
- **Drug Discontinuation Syndrome**
  - Abrupt discontinuation of SSRIs can cause an abrupt worsening of psychiatric symptoms, which can be worse than pre-treatment psychiatric disturbances.
  - Slow tapering is necessary to avoid this withdrawal syndrome, but agents with prolonged half-lives and active metabolites (such as fluoxetine) may have a lower likelihood due to a self-tapering effect.

High-Yield Fast-Facts

- **SIADH**
  - SSRIs have been associated with the syndrome of inappropriate antidiuretic hormone, which often requires drug discontinuation.
- **CYP2D6 and CYP2C19 Polymorphisms**
  - Most SSRIs are substrates of CYP2D6 and/or CYP2C19 and are subject to pharmacogenomic variability, leading to drug exposure changes.

HIGH-YIELD BOARD EXAM ESSENTIALS

- **CLASSIC AGENTS:** Citalopram, escitalopram, fluoxetine, fluvoxamine, paroxetine, sertraline, vortioxetine, viladozone
- **DRUG CLASS:** SSRI
- **INDICATIONS:** Bipolar major depression, generalized anxiety disorder, major depressive disorder, obsessive-compulsive disorder, panic disorder, premenstrual dysphoric disorder, social anxiety disorder, treatment-resistant depression, vasomotor symptoms of menopause
- **MECHANISM:** Inhibits the reuptake of serotonin by the serotonin transporter, prolonging serotonergic neurotransmission.
- **SIDE EFFECTS:** SIADH, QT prolongation (citalopram, escitalopram), sexual dysfunction (e.g., decreased libido, inability to orgasm, etc).
- **CLINICAL PEARLS:**
    - With the exception of citalopram which can cause dose dependent increases in the QT interval, this drug class has a large therapeutic index.
    - The onset of clinical benefit can take up to 4-6 weeks.
    - Use lower doses in patients with underlying general anxiety disorder and titrate slowly to avoid exacerbating their condition.
    - Paroxetine use during pregnancy has been classically associated with causing persistent pulmonary hypertension of the newborn (PPHN).
    - Paroxetine and fluoxetine are strong inhibitors of CYP2D6 and can lead to clinically relevant drug interactions of substrates of CYP2D6.
    - Serotonin syndrome is the combination of a rapid onset of altered mental status, autonomic instability, hyperthermia, and hyperreflexia/myoclonus.

High-Yield Basic Pharmacology

- **Mechanism of Action**
  - Inhibit presynaptic reuptake of norepinephrine or serotonin, increasing their concentration at CNS receptors.
- **Secondary or Tertiary Amine**
  - The presence or absence of a methyl group on the amine sidechain of tricyclic antidepressants classifies them as either a secondary or tertiary amine.
    - Tertiary amines include amitriptyline, clomipramine, doxepin, imipramine, trimipramine.
    - Secondary amines include amoxapine, desipramine, nortriptyline, protriptyline.

Primary Net Benefit

- Some of the first pharmacologic interventions for depression are now primarily reserved for resistant depression or alternative uses, including neuropathic pain, migraines, and attention deficit hyperactivity disorder.

Tricyclic Antidepressants - Drug Class Review			
High-Yield Med Reviews			
Mechanism of Action: *Inhibit presynaptic reuptake of norepinephrine or serotonin, increasing their concentration at CNS receptors.*			
Class Effects: Sedation, orthostatic hypotension, weight gain, QRS/QT prolongation, seizures.			
Generic Name	**Brand Name**	**Indication(s) or Uses**	**Notes**
Amitriptyline	Elavil	<ul><li>Fibromyalgia</li><li>Major depressive disorder</li><li>Migraine prophylaxis</li><li>Neuropathic pain</li></ul>	<ul><li>**Dosing (Adult):**<ul><li>Oral 10 to 300 mg daily</li></ul></li><li>**Dosing (Peds):**<ul><li>Oral 1 to 1.5 mg/kg/day in 3 divided doses</li><li>Oral 10 to 200 mg/day</li></ul></li><li>**CYP450 Interactions:** Substrate CYP1A2, 2B6, 2C19, 2C9, 2D6, 3A4</li><li>**Renal or Hepatic Dose Adjustments:** None</li><li>**Dosage Forms:** Oral (tablet)</li></ul>
Amoxapine	Asendin	<ul><li>Major depressive disorder</li></ul>	<ul><li>**Dosing (Adult):**<ul><li>Oral 25 to 600 mg/day<ul><li>Outpatient maximum 400 mg/day</li><li>Inpatient maximum 600 mg/day</li></ul></li></ul></li><li>**Dosing (Peds):** Not routinely used</li><li>**CYP450 Interactions:** Substate of CYP2D6</li><li>**Renal or Hepatic Dose Adjustments:**<ul><li>Hepatic impairment - reduce dose by 50%</li></ul></li><li>**Dosage Forms:** Oral (tablet)</li></ul>
Clomipramine	Anafranil	<ul><li>Obsessive-compulsive disorder</li><li>Major depressive disorder</li><li>Panic disorder</li></ul>	<ul><li>**Dosing (Adult):**<ul><li>Oral 25 to 250 mg/day</li></ul></li><li>**Dosing (Peds):**<ul><li>Oral 3 mg/kg/day or 100 mg/day, whichever is less</li></ul></li><li>**CYP450 Interactions:** Substrate CYP1A2, 2C19, 2D6, 3A4</li><li>**Renal or Hepatic Dose Adjustments:**<ul><li>Hepatic impairment - reduce dose by 50%</li></ul></li><li>**Dosage Forms:** Oral (capsule)</li></ul>

Tricyclic Antidepressants - Drug Class Review
High-Yield Med Reviews

Generic Name	Brand Name	Indication(s) or Uses	Notes

Desipramine	Norpramin	• Major depressive disorder	• **Dosing (Adult):**
			  – Oral 25 to 300 mg/day
			• **Dosing (Peds):**
			  – Oral 1.5 mg/kg/day divided q12h
			    ▪ Maximum 3.5 mg/kg/day or 150 mg/day
			• **CYP450 Interactions:** Substrate CYP1A2, 2D6
			• **Renal or Hepatic Dose Adjustments:** None
			• **Dosage Forms:** Oral (tablet)

Doxepin	Silenor	• Insomnia
		• Major depressive disorder
			• **Dosing (Adult):**
			  – Oral 3 to 50 mg/day
			• **Dosing (Peds):**
			  – Oral 1 to 3 mg/kg/day
			    ▪ Maximum 300 mg/day
			• **CYP450 Interactions:** Substrate CYP1A2, 2C19, 2D6, 3A4
			• **Renal or Hepatic Dose Adjustments:**
			  – Hepatic impairment - reduce dose by 50%
			• **Dosage Forms:** Oral (capsule, concentrate, tablet)

Imipramine	Tofranil	• Major depressive disorder
		• Neuropathic pain
		• Panic disorder
			• **Dosing (Adult):**
			  – Oral 25 to 300 mg/day
			• **Dosing (Peds):**
			  – Oral 1 to 4 mg/kg/day or maximum 200 mg/day
			• **CYP450 Interactions:** Substrate CYP1A2, 2B6, 2C19, 2D6, 3A4
			• **Renal or Hepatic Dose Adjustments:**
			  – Hepatic impairment - reduce dose by 50%
			• **Dosage Forms:** Oral (capsule, tablet)

Nortriptyline	Pamelor	• Major depressive disorder
		• Neuropathic pain
			• **Dosing (Adult):**
			  – Oral 25 to 150 mg/day
			• **Dosing (Peds):**
			  – Oral 0.5 to 2 mg/kg/day or 100 mg/day, whichever is less
			• **CYP450 Interactions:** Substrate CYP1A2, 2C19, 2D6, 3A4
			• **Renal or Hepatic Dose Adjustments:**
			  – Hepatic impairment - reduce dose by 50%
			• **Dosage Forms:** Oral (capsule, solution)

Tricyclic Antidepressants - Drug Class Review			
High-Yield Med Reviews			
Generic Name	**Brand Name**	**Indication(s) or Uses**	**Notes**

Protriptyline	Vivactil	▪ Major depressive disorder	▪ **Dosing (Adult):**
			  – Oral 10 to 60 mg/day in 3-4 divided doses
			▪ **Dosing (Peds):**
			  – Oral 5 to 60 mg/day in 3-4 divided doses
			▪ **CYP450 Interactions:** Substrate CYP2D6
			▪ **Renal or Hepatic Dose Adjustments:**
			  – Hepatic impairment - reduce dose by 50%
			▪ **Dosage Forms:** Oral (tablet)

Trimipramine	Surmontil	▪ Major depressive disorder	▪ **Dosing (Adult):**
			  – Oral 25 to 300 mg/day
			▪ **Dosing (Peds):**
			  – Oral 25 to 200 mg/day
			▪ **CYP450 Interactions:** Substrate of CYP2C19, 2D6
			▪ **Renal or Hepatic Dose Adjustments:**
			  – Hepatic impairment - reduce dose by 50%
			▪ **Dosage Forms:** Oral (capsule)

High-Yield Clinical Knowledge

- **Sodium Channel Block**
  - TCAs inhibit the cardiac fast sodium channels, slowing the phase 0 depolarization, which manifests as QRS prolongation.
  - This QRS prolongation represents a slowing of the propagation of ventricular depolarization, leading to ventricular dysrhythmias.
  - This effect is similar to the Vaughn Williams class 1A antiarrhythmic agents.
- **Characteristic Adverse Events**
  - Compared to SSRIs, TCAs are more likely to cause antimuscarinic adverse events, sedation, orthostatic hypotension, and weight gain.
  - Antimuscarinic effects of TCAs can acutely worsen memory or cause delirium in elderly patients.
- **Sudden Cardiac Death**
  - As a result of sodium channel blockade and potential QT prolongation, TCAs may lead to sudden cardiac death.
    - An FDA warning on desipramine specifically exists regarding this increased risk of cardiac death.
- **Amoxapine**
  - Amoxapine is technically a cyclic antidepressant but is derived from the antipsychotic loxapine and acts as a norepinephrine reuptake inhibitor and dopamine antagonists.
- **Alternative Mechanisms**
  - TCAs possess numerous other actions that may contribute to their actions but largely contribute to adverse events and toxicity.
  - TCAs possess antimuscarinic effects, peripheral alpha-1 antagonist properties, histamine-1 antagonist, cardiac sodium channel blockade, and GABA-A receptor antagonists.
- **Sodium Bicarbonate Use for Weak Bases?**
  - For TCA overdose or toxicity where clinically relevant ECG changes (QRS prolongation more significant than 100 ms), sodium bicarbonate is recommended.
  - Since TCAs are weak bases, this could hypothetically decrease their renal elimination, but the sodium is needed to overcome cardiac sodium channel blockade.
  - However, altering the plasma's pH to approximately 7.5 promotes the TCA movement away from the cardiac sodium channel and into the lipid membrane.

− If patients are alkalemic or are hypercarbic without appropriate ventilation, hypertonic sodium chloride can also be used as an alternative to sodium bicarbonate.

High-Yield Fast-Facts

▪ **Neurologic Toxicity**
  − Although cardiac toxicity is more prevalent, TCAs may cause seizures in large exposures.
  − When the QRS is above 120 ms, the risk of seizures from TCAs is exceptionally high.
▪ **Drug Discontinuation Syndrome**
  − Like SSRIs and SNRIs, TCAs are associated with a drug discontinuation syndrome if therapy is abruptly halted.
  − Symptoms can range from GI disturbance to psychosis and mania.

HIGH-YIELD BOARD EXAM ESSENTIALS
- **CLASSIC AGENTS:** Amitriptyline, amoxapine, clomipramine, desipramine, doxepin, imipramine, nortriptyline, protriptyline, trimipramine
- **DRUG CLASS:** TCA
- **INDICATIONS:** Fibromyalgia, major depressive disorder, migraine prophylaxis, neuropathic pain, obsessive-compulsive disorder, panic disorder
- **MECHANISM:** Inhibit presynaptic reuptake of norepinephrine or serotonin, increasing their concentration at CNS receptors.
- **SIDE EFFECTS:** Sedation, orthostatic hypotension, weight gain, QRS/QT prolongation, seizures,
- **CLINICAL PEARLS:** TCAs inhibit the cardiac fast sodium channels, slowing the phase 0 depolarization, which manifests as QRS prolongation.

High-Yield Basic Pharmacology

- **Bupropion**
  - Inhibits the reuptake of dopamine and norepinephrine, prolonging their neurotransmission.
- **Clonidine**
  - Centrally acting alpha-2 agonist.
- **Nicotine**
  - Agonists of central nicotinic-cholinergic receptors.
- **Nortriptyline**
  - Inhibit presynaptic reuptake of norepinephrine or serotonin, increasing their concentration at CNS.
- **Varenicline**
  - Partial nicotinic receptor agonist, preventing nicotinic stimulation of mesolimbic dopaminergic activity.

Primary Net Benefit

- Complementary interventions for smoking cessation with over-the-counter nicotine replacement therapy with or without additional prescription agents.

Smoking Cessation - Drug Class Review			
High-Yield Med Reviews			
Mechanism of Action: *See agents above.*			
Class Effects: Complementary interventions for smoking cessation with over-the-counter nicotine replacement therapy with or without additional prescription agents.			
Generic Name	**Brand Name**	**Indication(s) or Uses**	**Notes**

Bupropion	Aplenzin Forfivo Wellbutrin Zyban	• Major depressive disorder
		• Seasonal affective disorder
		• Smoking cessation
			• **Dosing (Adult):**
			  – Oral 100 to 450 mg daily
			• **Dosing (Peds):**
			  – Oral 3 mg/kg/day in 2-3 divided doses
			    • Max 6 mg/kg/day or 150 mg
			• **CYP450 Interactions:** Substrate CYP1A2, 2A6, 2B6, 2C9, 2D6, 2E1, 3A4; Inhibits CYP2D6
			• **Renal or Hepatic Dose Adjustments:**
			  – Child-Pugh class C - reduce dose by 50%
			• **Dosage Forms:** Oral (tablet)

Clonidine	Catapres Kapvay	• Hypertension
		• Smoking cessation
			• **Dosing (Adult):**
			  – Oral: Initial: 0.1 mg twice daily, > 0.6 mg/day not recommended.
			  – TD Patch: 0.1 mg/24-hour patch once every 7 days
			• **Dosing (Peds):**
			  – ≤45 kg: Initial: 0.05 mg at bedtime
			  – >45 kg: Initial: 0.1 mg at bedtime.
			  – Max is based on patient weight:
			    • 27 to 40.5 kg: 0.2 mg/day
			    • 40.5 to 45 kg: 0.3 mg/day
			    • > 45 kg: 0.4 mg/day
			• **CYP450 Interactions:** None
			• **Renal or Hepatic Dose Adjustments:** None
			• **Dosage Forms:** Topical (transdermal patch), Oral (tablet, IR and ER)

Smoking Cessation - Drug Class Review
High-Yield Med Reviews

Generic Name	Brand Name	Indication(s) or Uses	Notes

Nicotine	Habitrol, NicoDerm, Nicorette, Nicotine, Nicotrol, Thrive	• Smoking cessation	• **Dosing (Adult):**
			  – Gum chew 1 piece q1-8hours (maximum 24 pieces/day)
			  – Inhalation - 6 to 16 cartridges/day
			  – Lozenge - 1 lozenge q1-8hours (maximum 20 lozenges/day)
			  – Nasal spray 1 to 10 doses/hour (maximum 80 sprays/day)
			  – Transdermal 7 to 21 mg/day
			• **Dosing (Peds):**
			  – Not routinely used
			• **CYP450 Interactions:** Substrate CYP1A2, 2A6, 2B6, 2C19, 2C9, 2D6, 2E1, 3A4
			• **Renal or Hepatic Dose Adjustments:** None
			• **Dosage Forms:** Oral (gum, inhalation, lozenge), Nasal spray, Transdermal patch

Nortriptyline	Pamelor	• Major depressive disorder
		• Neuropathic pain
			• **Dosing (Adult):**
			  – Oral 25 to 150 mg/day
			• **Dosing (Peds):**
			  – Oral 0.5 to 2 mg/kg/day or 100 mg/day, whichever is less
			• **CYP450 Interactions:** Substrate CYP1A2, 2C19, 2D6, 3A4
			• **Renal or Hepatic Dose Adjustments:**
			  – Hepatic impairment - reduce dose by 50%
			• **Dosage Forms:** Oral (capsule, solution)

Varenicline	Chantix	• Smoking cessation	• **Dosing (Adult):**
			  – Oral 0.5 mg daily on days 1 to 3; 0.5 mg BID days 4 to 7; 1 mg BID for at least 11 weeks
			• **Dosing (Peds):**
			  – Not routinely used
			• **CYP450 Interactions:** None
			• **Renal or Hepatic Dose Adjustments:**
			  – GFR less than 30 mL/minute - maximum 0.5 mg BID
			  – ESRD - 0.5 mg daily
			• **Dosage Forms:** Oral (tablet)

High-Yield Clinical Knowledge

- **Varenicline Neuropsychiatric Effects**
  - While patients with a history of depression or other neuropsychiatric illnesses may receive varenicline (although this is still controversial), bupropion is an agent that is both effective for smoking cessation and may help treat certain disorders such as depression.
  - The prescribing information for varenicline no longer lists neuropsychiatric adverse events as a black-boxed warning.

- This change was based on a large randomized controlled trial (EAGLES study further described below).
  - Varenicline is first-line pharmacotherapy for smoking cessation in patients with CVD.
- **Nicotine Replacement Therapy (NRT)**
  - NRT consists of numerous different dosage forms of nicotine and may be added to varenicline in patients who do not adequately respond to varenicline alone.
  - Combination NRT is defined as a continuous nicotine dose (ex. nicotine patch) with the addition of as-needed nicotine for break-through cravings (gum, lozenge, or spray).
  - NRT should be used in patients with cardiovascular disease (CVD). NRT has NOT been associated with increased adverse CVD events.
- **NRT Gum Instructions**
  - Patients who smoke more than 25 cigarettes per day should start with 4 mg gum (rather than the 2 mg gum).
    - A new piece of gum should be used every 2 hours at a fixed schedule for the first 1 to 3 months of use.
  - Patients should be counseled to chew the gum slowly until a peppery or minty taste emerges, at which point, the gum should be "parked" between cheek and gums to facilitate nicotine absorption through the oral mucosa.
  - While using the gum, acidic beverages (coffee, soft drinks, etc.) should be avoided since they may reduce the amount of nicotine absorbed.
- **Sudden Cardiac Death**
  - As a result of sodium channel blockade and potential QT prolongation, TCAs may lead to sudden cardiac death.
    - An FDA warning on desipramine specifically exists regarding this increased risk of cardiac death.
- **Alternative Mechanisms**
  - TCAs possess numerous other actions that may contribute to their actions but largely contribute to adverse events and toxicity.
  - TCAs possess antimuscarinic effects, peripheral alpha-1 antagonist properties, histamine-1 antagonist, cardiac sodium channel blockade, and GABA-A receptor antagonists.
- **Bupropion Seizures**
  - Although bupropion has numerous benefits, including smoking cessation characteristics, minor sexual dysfunction, and fatigue than other antidepressants, it can be more troublesome in overdose.
  - The risk of seizures increases if chronic doses are above 450 mg/day or ingest a large overdose.
  - Additional findings from bupropion overdose include hypertension, agitation, QRS, and QT prolongation.
    - The onset of these symptoms can be delayed between 10 and 24 hours following an overdose, with seizures lasting as long as 48 hours after exposure.
  - The active metabolite hydroxybupropion may cause seizures by acting as a GABA antagonist and as an NMDA agonist.

HIGH-YIELD BOARD EXAM ESSENTIALS
- **CLASSIC AGENTS:** Bupropion, clonidine, nicotine, nortriptyline, varenicline
- **DRUG CLASS:** Smoking cessation agents
- **INDICATIONS:** Smoking cessation
- **MECHANISM:** Bupropion - Inhibits the reuptake of dopamine and norepinephrine, prolonging norepinephrine and serotonergic neurotransmission. Clonidine - Centrally acting alpha-2 agonist. Nicotine - Agonists of central nicotinic-cholinergic receptors, as well as at neuromuscular junctions and adrenal medulla. Nortriptyline - Inhibit presynaptic reuptake of norepinephrine or serotonin, increasing their concentration at CNS. Varenicline - Partial nicotinic receptor agonist, preventing nicotinic stimulation of mesolimbic dopaminergic activity.
- **SIDE EFFECTS:** Neuropsychiatric effects (varenicline), hypertension (bupropion), hypotension (clonidine), QRS prolongation (nortriptyline)
- **CLINICAL PEARLS:** While patients with a history of depression or other neuropsychiatric illnesses may receive varenicline (although this is still controversial), bupropion is an agent that is both effective for smoking cessation and may help treat certain disorders such as depression.

High-Yield Basic Pharmacology

- **Mechanism of Action**
  - Nonselective antimuscarinic at M1, M2, and M3 receptors.
- **M2 Effect**
  - Ipratropium's inhibitory effect on M2 receptors can be counterproductive as antagonism of these receptors causes bronchoconstriction.
    - Some have argued that the paradoxical bronchoconstriction from ipratropium results from the administration of a hypotonic nebulized solution or benzalkonium chloride.
- **Quaternary Ammonium**
  - Both tiotropium and ipratropium are quaternary ammonium structures, which prevent their absorption to the CNS across the blood-brain barrier.
  - This limits the central antimuscarinic potential of these drugs.
  - Ipratropium is poorly absorbed from the respiratory tract itself and further limits systemic antimuscarinic effects

Primary Net Benefit

- Rapid-acting bronchodilator used in combination with albuterol in patients with acute severe asthma or COPD.

Short-Acting Muscarinic Antagonists - Drug Class Review			
High-Yield Med Reviews			
Mechanism of Action: *Nonselective antimuscarinic at M1, M2, and M3 receptors.*			
Class Effects: Bronchodilation, increased risk of sinusitis, headache, UTI, dyspepsia			
Generic Name	**Brand Name**	**Indication(s) or Uses**	**Notes**

Ipratropium	Atrovent, Atrovent Nasal, Ipravent	• Allergic rhinitis
		• Asthma
		• Chronic obstructive pulmonary disease
			• **Dosing (Adult):**
			  – Intranasal - two sprays in each nostril 2-4 times daily
			  – MDI - 2 inhalations (34 mcg) 4 times daily
			  – Nebulization - 0.5 mg q20minutes for three doses, OR 0.5 mg q6-8h
			• **Dosing (Peds):**
			  – Intranasal - two sprays in each nostril 2-4 times daily
			  – MDI - 1 to 2 inhalations (34 mcg) 4 times daily
			    • Maximum 12 inhalations/day
			  – Nebulization - 0.25 to 0.5 mg q20minutes for three doses, OR 0.25 to 0.5 mg q6-8h
			• **CYP450 Interactions:** None
			• **Renal or Hepatic Dose Adjustments:** None
			• **Dosage Forms:** Nasal solution, Inhalation (aerosol, solution)

High-Yield Clinical Knowledge

- ▪ **Adjunctive Therapy**
  - – Ipratropium is used primarily in combination with albuterol for acute severe asthma either empirically or with an incomplete response to albuterol alone.
  - – An additional 15% improvement in FEV1 can be observed when ipratropium is combined with albuterol in emergency department management of acute severe asthma.
- ▪ **Nebulized Administration**
  - – Ipratropium is commonly administered via nebulization.
  - – For this administration route, a tight-fitting mouthpiece is recommended to reduce the exposure of the eyes to ipratropium which may cause a local antimuscarinic effect (pupillary dilation, diminished accommodation).
    - – For this reason, ipratropium should be used with caution in patients with glaucoma.
- ▪ **Maximum Frequency**
  - – In patients with acute severe asthma, ipratropium should be administered at a dose of 0.5 mg q20minutes for a maximum of three doses.
    - – Continued dosing beyond three doses in one hour produces no additional bronchodilatory effect but can prolong the dose-dependent duration of effect and adverse effects beyond eight hours.
- ▪ **Maximum Dose**
  - – If patients take ipratropium chronically for COPD, they may respond to higher doses but be administered at the same frequency (q6-8h).
  - – Ipratropium can be administered as six puffs up to q6h.

High-Yield Fast-Fact

- ▪ **Ipratropium Poor Taste**
  - – Ipratropium is described as having a bitter taste that limits chronic compliance with this therapy.

HIGH-YIELD BOARD EXAM ESSENTIALS
- • **CLASSIC AGENTS:** Ipratropium
- • **DRUG CLASS:** SAMA
- • **INDICATIONS:** Allergic rhinitis, asthma, COPD
- • **MECHANISM:** Nonselective antimuscarinic at M1, M2, and M3 receptors.
- • **SIDE EFFECTS:** Sinusitis, headache, UTI, dyspepsia
- • **CLINICAL PEARLS:** Ipratropium is used primarily in combination with albuterol for acute severe asthma either empirically or with an incomplete response to albuterol alone. An additional 15% improvement in FEV1 can be observed when ipratropium is combined with albuterol in emergency department management of acute severe asthma.

High-Yield Basic Pharmacology

- **Mechanism of Action**
  - Selectively inhibit muscarinic receptors, M1 and M3, with slow dissociation from M3 providing a prolonged bronchodilatory effect.
- **Quaternary Ammonium**
  - LAMAs are quaternary ammonium structures, which prevent their absorption to the CNS across the blood-brain barrier.
  - This limits the central antimuscarinic potential of these drugs.
  - Glycopyrrolate is structurally similar to atropine, except for its quaternary amine core structure.

Primary Net Benefit

- LAMAs improve lung function and COPD symptoms and may reduce the risk of COPD exacerbations, but their role in asthma is reserved for severe uncontrolled asthma.

Long-Acting Muscarinic Antagonists - Drug Class Review			
High-Yield Med Reviews			
Mechanism of Action: *Selectively inhibit muscarinic receptors, M1 and M3, with slow dissociation from M3 providing a prolonged bronchodilatory effect.*			
Class Effects: Bronchodilation; increased risk of xerostomia, secondary pneumonia, tachycardia.			
Generic Name	**Brand Name**	**Indication(s) or Uses**	**Notes**

Aclidinium	Tudorza Pressair	• Chronic obstructive pulmonary disease	• **Dosing (Adult):**
			  – Oral Inhalation 400 mcg (1 inhalation) twice daily
			• **Dosing (Peds):**
			  – Not routinely used
			• **CYP450 Interactions:** Substrate CYP2D6, 3A4
			• **Renal or Hepatic Dose Adjustments:** None
			• **Dosage Forms:** Aerosol powder

Glycopyrrolate	Lonhala Magnair, Seebri Neohaler	• Chronic obstructive pulmonary disease	• **Dosing (Adult):**
			  – DPI - 1 capsule (15.6 mcg) BID
			  – Nebulization - 25 mcg BID
			• **Dosing (Peds):**
			  – Not routinely used
			• **CYP450 Interactions:** None
			• **Renal or Hepatic Dose Adjustments:** None
			• **Dosage Forms:** Inhalation (capsule, solution)

Revefenacin	Yupelri	• Chronic obstructive pulmonary disease	• **Dosing (Adult):**
			  – Nebulization - 175 mcg daily
			• **Dosing (Peds):**
			  – Not routinely used
			• **CYP450 Interactions:** Inhibits P-gp
			• **Renal or Hepatic Dose Adjustments:**
			  – Hepatic impairment - not recommended
			• **Dosage Forms:** Inhalation (solution)

Long-Acting Muscarinic Antagonists - Drug Class Review
High-Yield Med Reviews

Generic Name	Brand Name	Indication(s) or Uses	Notes

Tiotropium	Spiriva	• Asthma
		• Chronic obstructive pulmonary disease
			• **Dosing (Adult):**
			  – Oral inhalation (Respimat) - Two inhalations (2.5 mcg) once daily
			  – Oral inhalation (DPI) - contents of 1 capsule inhaled once daily
			  – Oral inhalation (Soft-mist inhaler) - Two inhalations (5 mcg) once daily
			• **Dosing (Peds):**
			  – Oral inhalation (Respimat) - Two inhalations (1.25 mcg) once daily
			  – Oral inhalation (Soft-mist inhaler) - Two inhalations (5 mcg) once daily
			• **CYP450 Interactions:** Substrate CYP2D6, 3A4
			• **Renal or Hepatic Dose Adjustments:** None
			• **Dosage Forms:** Inhalation (aerosol, capsule)

Umeclidinium	Incruse Ellipta	• COPD	• **Dosing (Adult):**
			  – DPI - 1 (62.5 mcg) inhalation daily
			• **Dosing (Peds):**
			  – Not routinely used
			• **CYP450 Interactions:** Substrate CYP2D6, P-gp
			• **Renal or Hepatic Dose Adjustments:** None
			• **Dosage Forms:** Inhalation aerosol

High-Yield Clinical Knowledge

- **High Risk for Exacerbation**
  - In patients at high risk of COPD exacerbation, tiotropium is preferred as it has the most evidence supporting a more significant reduction in the frequency of exacerbations compared to LABA.
    - Other LAMAs may be used for this benefit; the largest amount of data supports tiotropium.
- **Long Term Benefit**
  - Evidence exists to support the long-term use of tiotropium in patients with COPD by reducing the frequency of COPD exacerbations.
  - There was also no evidence of an increased risk of cardiovascular adverse events associated with long-term use of tiotropium.
  - However, tiotropium did not have a significant impact in slowing lung function decline with long-term therapy.
- **Dosing**
  - There is no dose titration of LAMA agents, as their commercially available dosage forms are the appropriate starting dose and effective for nearly all adult patients.
- **Asthma Use**
  - LAMAs are reserved for the treatment of uncontrolled severe asthma.
    - Alternatives for uncontrolled severe asthma include high-dose inhaled corticosteroids plus LABA, LAMA plus biologic therapy, or oral corticosteroids.
  - Tiotropium decreases the frequency of severe exacerbations and reduces the need for oral corticosteroids in asthma.
- **Capsules**
  - Glycopyrrolate and tiotropium are available in capsules that are intended to have their contents inhaled.
  - Patients must be adequately educated to avoid ingesting these capsules, which will have no therapeutic benefit, increasing their exacerbation risk.

- **Less Pneumonia**
  - Compared to inhaled corticosteroids, LAMAs are associated with a lower risk of secondary pneumonia, with a similar reduction in exacerbation rates.

High-Yield Fast-Fact

- **Glycopyrrolate Uses**
  - Glycopyrrolate has numerous other uses, including ophthalmologic indications, and parenteral uses including recovery from anesthesia and drying of mucous membranes associated with palliative care.

HIGH-YIELD BOARD EXAM ESSENTIALS

- **CLASSIC AGENTS:** Aclidinium, glycopyrrolate, revefenacin, tiotropium, umeclidinium
- **DRUG CLASS:** LAMA
- **INDICATIONS:** Asthma, COPD
- **MECHANISM:** Selectively inhibit muscarinic receptors, M1 and M3, with slow dissociation from M3 providing a prolonged bronchodilatory effect.
- **SIDE EFFECTS:** Xerostomia, secondary pneumonia, tachycardia
- **CLINICAL PEARLS:** In patients at high risk of COPD exacerbation, tiotropium is preferred as it has the most evidence supporting a more significant reduction in the frequency of exacerbations compared to LABA.

High-Yield Basic Pharmacology

- **Mechanism of Action**
  - Activation of beta-2 adrenergic receptors, decreasing intracellular entry of calcium, leading to smooth muscle relaxation.
- **Racemic Mixture**
  - Albuterol is a racemic mixture of R-albuterol and S-albuterol.
  - R-albuterol is available separately as levalbuterol, which is metabolized more rapidly than S-albuterol, and may lack the pro-inflammatory effects that could diminish the bronchodilatory effect.

Primary Net Benefit

- Inhaled SABAs are used for the as-needed treatment of acute bronchospasm, providing a dose-dependent bronchodilatory effect. Systemic SABAs are no longer recommended due to extrapulmonary adverse events.

Short-Acting Beta-2 Agonist - Drug Class Review			
High-Yield Med Reviews			
Mechanism of Action: *Activation of beta-2 adrenergic receptors, decreasing intracellular entry of calcium, leading to smooth muscle relaxation.*			
Class Effects: Bronchodilation; increased risk of tachycardia, tremor, hypokalemia (mainly larger, repeated doses).			
Generic Name	**Brand Name**	**Indication(s) or Uses**	**Notes**
Albuterol	ProAir, Proventil, Ventolin	• Asthma • Bronchospasm • Chronic obstructive pulmonary disease	• **Dosing (Adult):** – MDI/DPI - 2 inhalations q4-6h as needed • Up to 8 to 10 inhalations q20minutes for 3 doses, repeated as necessary – Nebulization 2.5 mg q4-6h as needed • Up to 15 mg/hour via continuous nebulization over 1 hour • **Dosing (Peds):** – MDI/DPI - 1 to 2 inhalations q4-6h as needed • Up to 8 to 10 inhalations q20minutes for 3 doses, repeated as necessary – Nebulization 2.5 mg q4-6h as needed • Up to 15 mg/hour via continuous nebulization over 1 hour • **CYP450 Interactions:** None • **Renal or Hepatic Dose Adjustments:** None • **Dosage Forms:** Inhalation (aerosol, nebulization solution, solution), Oral (syrup, tablet)

Short-Acting Beta-2 Agonist - Drug Class Review
High-Yield Med Reviews

Generic Name	Brand Name	Indication(s) or Uses	Notes
Levalbuterol	Xopenex	• Asthma • Bronchospasm	• **Dosing (Adult):** 　– MDI - 2 inhalations (90 mcg) q4-6h as needed 　　• Up to 4 to 8 inhalations q20minutes for 3 doses, repeated as necessary 　– Nebulization 0.63 to 1.25 mg q6-8h as needed 　　• Up to 2.5 mg q20minutes, then 1.25 to 5 mg q1-4hours as needed • **Dosing (Peds):** 　– MDI/DPI - 1 inhalation q4-6h as needed 　　• Up to 4 to 8 inhalations q20minutes for 3 doses, repeated as necessary 　– Nebulization 0.31 to 1.25 mg q4-6h as needed 　　• Up to 2.5 mg q20minutes, then 1.25 to 5 mg q1-4hours as needed • **CYP450 Interactions:** None • **Renal or Hepatic Dose Adjustments:** None • **Dosage Forms:** Inhalation (aerosol, nebulization solution)
Metaproterenol	Alupent	• Asthma	• **Dosing (Adult):** 　– Oral 20 mg q6-8h • **Dosing (Peds):** 　– Oral 1.3 to 2.6 mg/kg/day divided q6-8h 　　• Maximum 10 mg/dose • **CYP450 Interactions:** None • **Renal or Hepatic Dose Adjustments:** None • **Dosage Forms:** Oral (syrup, tablet)
Racemic epinephrine	Racepi	• Bronchospasm	• **Dosing (Adult):** 　– MDI - 1 (0.125 mg) inhalations q4-6h as needed 　　• Up to 8 inhalations/24 hours 　– Nebulization 2.25% mg q4-6h as needed 　　• Up to 12 inhalations/24 hours • **Dosing (Peds):** 　– MDI - 1 (0.125 mg) inhalations q4-6h as needed 　　• Up to 8 inhalations/24 hours 　– Nebulization 2.25% mg q4-6h as needed 　　• Up to 12 inhalations/24 hours • **CYP450 Interactions:** None • **Renal or Hepatic Dose Adjustments:** None • **Dosage Forms:** Inhalation (solution)

Short-Acting Beta-2 Agonist - Drug Class Review			
High-Yield Med Reviews			
Generic Name	**Brand Name**	**Indication(s) or Uses**	**Notes**

Terbutaline	Bricanyl	▪ Asthma/Bronchospasm
		▪ Extravasation management
		▪ Premature labor
			▪ **Dosing (Adult):**
			  – Oral 2.5 to 5 mg q8h
			  – SQ 0.25 mg/dose q20minutes for 3 doses
			  – IV 2.5 to 5 mcg/minute, increased gradually q20-30min to maximum 25 mcg/minute
			▪ **Dosing (Peds):**
			  – IV infusion 0.2 to 0.4 mcg/kg/minute, maximum 5 mcg/kg/minute
			  – Oral 2.5 mg q8h
			  – SQ 0.01 mg/kg/dose q20minutes x 3 doses
			▪ **CYP450 Interactions:** None
			▪ **Renal or Hepatic Dose Adjustments:** None
			▪ **Dosage Forms:** IV (solution), Oral (tablet)

High-Yield Clinical Knowledge

- **Acute Bronchospasm**
  - Inhaled short-acting beta-2 agonists are the drugs of choice for acute bronchodilation and in the management of acute severe asthma.
- **Maximum Dose**
  - Although the prescribing information of albuterol describes upper limits of recommended doses for MDI and nebulization treatments, there is no maximum clinical dose.
  - The drug information cited maximum doses should be used as surrogates for pharmacologic failure.
  - In acute bronchospasm, albuterol should be administered continuously until sufficient bronchodilatory effect is achieved or advanced airways are necessary (i.e., endotracheal intubation).
- **Hypokalemia**
  - High doses of SABAs may produce potassium shifting intracellularly, potentially leading to conduction delays in cardiac tissue.
  - Patients with acute severe asthma or COPD exacerbations receiving SABA therapy should have their potassium closely monitored and kept above the lower limit of normal (typically above 3.5 mEq/L, but some recommend above 4.0 mEq/L.
  - This effect is used proactively in the acute treatment of hyperkalemia.
- **Levalbuterol Dose**
  - Levalbuterol is commonly cited to produce less tachycardia and extrapulmonary effects than albuterol; however, this was only demonstrated when levalbuterol was administered at a dose of 0.63 mg q8h was compared to albuterol 2.5 mg and has not been able to be reproduced in other clinical studies.
- **Dose-Dependent Adverse Events**
  - High dose SABA therapy can produce elevations in glucose, lactate, as these agents augment glycolysis and cause an anaerobic metabolic shift.
    - Hyperlactemia is not necessarily harmful in all clinical situations, provided patients have sufficient oxidative capacity, hydration, and renal function.
  - Tachycardia is another common adverse event related to SABA therapy; however, it should not prevent the use of SABAs (albuterol) or an indication to lower the dose empirically.
- **Metaproterenol/Terbutaline**
  - Terbutaline use is limited to pediatrics, as its use in adults is accompanied by unacceptably high rates of systemic adverse events.
  - Similarly, metaproterenol is rarely used for bronchodilatory effects.

High-Yield Fast-Fact

- **NCAA Performance Enhancing**
    - Albuterol is considered a performance-enhancing drug, according to the NCAA.
    - Pharmacists should be aware that student-athletes with asthma are required to possess proof for a medical exemption so that they can continue to take albuterol and compete within the NCAA regulations.

HIGH-YIELD BOARD EXAM ESSENTIALS
- **CLASSIC AGENTS:** Albuterol, levalbuterol, metaproterenol, racemic epinephrine, terbutaline
- **DRUG CLASS:** SABA
- **INDICATIONS:** Asthma, bronchospasm, COPD
- **MECHANISM:** Activation of beta-2 adrenergic receptors, decreasing intracellular entry of calcium, leading to smooth muscle relaxation.
- **SIDE EFFECTS:** Tachycardia, tremor, hypokalemia
- **CLINICAL PEARLS:** Although the prescribing information of albuterol describes upper limits of recommended doses for MDI and nebulization treatments, there is no maximum clinical dose.

High-Yield Basic Pharmacology

- **Mechanism of Action:**
  - Activation of beta-2 adrenergic receptors, decreasing intracellular entry of calcium, leading to smooth muscle relaxation.
- **Lipid-Soluble**
  - LABAs are characteristically more lipid-soluble than SABA agents, allowing penetration into the cell membrane's outer phospholipid layer, conferring a longer time of action.

Primary Net Benefit

- Long-acting beta-2 agonists (LABA) provide selective bronchodilation and are a core component for asthma and play a role in COPD therapy, but emerging evidence suggests long-acting muscarinic antagonists (LAMA) may be preferred.

Long-Acting Beta-2 Agonist - Drug Class Review			
High-Yield Med Reviews			
Mechanism of Action: *Activation of beta-2 adrenergic receptors, decreasing intracellular entry of calcium, leading to smooth muscle relaxation.*			
Class Effects: Bronchodilation; small risk of tachycardia, hypokalemia, hyperglycemia, hyperlactemia (but less than short acting agents)			
Generic Name	**Brand Name**	**Indication(s) or Uses**	**Notes**

Arformoterol	Brovana	• Chronic obstructive pulmonary disease	• **Dosing (Adult):**
			  – Nebulization 15 mcg BID
			    • Maximum 30 mcg/day
			• **Dosing (Peds):**
			  – Not routinely used
			• **CYP450 Interactions:** None
			• **Renal or Hepatic Dose Adjustments:** None
			• **Dosage Forms:** Nebulization solution

Formoterol	Perforomist	• Chronic obstructive pulmonary disease	• **Dosing (Adult):**
			  – Nebulization 20 mcg BID
			    • Maximum 40 mcg/day
			• **Dosing (Peds):**
			  – Not routinely used
			• **CYP450 Interactions:** Substrate CYP2C9
			• **Renal or Hepatic Dose Adjustments:** None
			• **Dosage Forms:** Nebulization solution

Indacaterol	Arcapta Neohaler	• Chronic obstructive pulmonary disease	• **Dosing (Adult):**
			  – DPI - 1 capsule (75 mcg) inhaled twice daily
			• **Dosing (Peds):**
			  – Not routinely used
			• **CYP450 Interactions:** Substrate CYP2D6, 3A4, P-gp
			• **Renal or Hepatic Dose Adjustments:** None
			• **Dosage Forms:** Inhalation capsule

		Long-Acting Beta-2 Agonist - Drug Class Review	
		High-Yield Med Reviews	
Generic Name	**Brand Name**	**Indication(s) or Uses**	**Notes**

Olodaterol	Striverdi Respimat	• Chronic obstructive pulmonary disease	• **Dosing (Adult):**
			  – Oral inhalation - two inhalations once daily
			• **Dosing (Peds):**
			  – Not routinely used
			• **CYP450 Interactions:** Substrate CYP2C8, 2C9, 3A4
			• **Renal or Hepatic Dose Adjustments:** None
			• **Dosage Forms:** Inhalation (aerosol)

Salmeterol	Serevent Diskus	• Asthma
		• Chronic obstructive pulmonary disease
		• Exercise-induced bronchospasm
			• **Dosing (Adult):**
			  – DPI - 50 mcg daily
			• **Dosing (Peds):**
			  – DPI - 50 mcg daily
			• **CYP450 Interactions:** Substrate CYP3A4
			• **Renal or Hepatic Dose Adjustments:** None
			• **Dosage Forms:** Inhalation (aerosol)

Vilanterol	Only available in combo: Breo Ellipta, Anoro Ellipta, Trelegy Ellipta	• Asthma
		• Chronic obstructive pulmonary disease
			• **Dosing (Adult):**
			  – Oral inhalation 25 mcg daily
			• **Dosing (Peds):**
			  – Not routinely used
			• **CYP450 Interactions:** Substrate CYP3A4
			• **Renal or Hepatic Dose Adjustments:** None
			• **Dosage Forms:** Inhalation (aerosol)

High-Yield Clinical Knowledge

- **LABA Role**
  - In the treatment of asthma, LABAs are preferred to inhaled corticosteroids (ICS).
  - Combinations of ICS and LABA increase asthma control, reduce the frequency of exacerbations, and do so to a more considerable degree than increasing ICS dose alone.
- **Beta-2 Selectivity**
  - LABAs are generally more beta-2 selective compared to albuterol, owing to their increased time in lung tissue.
- **Dose-Response Curve**
  - The ability of beta-2 agonists to provide bronchodilation is dependent on the baseline degree of bronchoconstriction.
  - With increasing bronchoconstriction, the dose-response curve of beta-2 agonists experiences a rightward shift, with a corresponding decrease in duration of effect.
    - Patients with increasing bronchoconstriction will require higher, more frequent doses of beta-2 agonists of both short- and long-acting forms.
- **Chronic Bronchodilation**
  - LABAs must not be used for the acute management of severe asthma.
  - Although salmeterol has a rapid onset of less than 30 minutes, albuterol is the drug of choice as it is almost immediately effective.
- **Long Vs. Ultra-Long**
  - Formoterol and salmeterol are considered long-acting agents, with a 12-hour duration of effect.
  - The ultra-long-acting beta-2 agonists include indacaterol, olodaterol, and vilanterol, can be administered once daily, as their effects last 24-hours.

- **Downregulation**
  - With long-term administration of beta-2 agonists, a decreasing number of beta-2 receptors and decreased binding affinity occurs.
    - Desensitization of beta-2 agonist effects also occurs in cardiac tissue (as well as other extrapulmonary sites), reducing systemic adverse events from chronic high dose LABA therapy.
  - The addition of systemic corticosteroids, not inhaled corticosteroids, can partially reverse this effect and prevent its occurrence.
  - The duration of bronchodilation is primarily affected, with less of a change in the peak response.

High-Yield Fast-Fact

- **Boxed Warning Removal**
  - The FDA removed the boxed warning for increased asthma-related deaths with ICS/LABA combinations as more robust evidence failed to show this relationship.

HIGH-YIELD BOARD EXAM ESSENTIALS
- **CLASSIC AGENTS:** Arformoterol, formoterol, indacaterol, olodaterol, salmeterol, vilanterol
- **DRUG CLASS:** LABA
- **INDICATIONS:** Asthma, COPD
- **MECHANISM:** Activation of beta-2 adrenergic receptors, decreasing intracellular entry of calcium, leading to smooth muscle relaxation.
- **SIDE EFFECTS:** Tachycardia, hypokalemia, hyperglycemia, hyperlactemia
- **CLINICAL PEARLS:** With long-term administration of beta-2 agonists, a decreasing number of beta-2 receptors and decreased binding affinity occurs.

High-Yield Basic Pharmacology

- **Corticosteroid Effects**
  - Inhaled corticosteroids increase the number of beta-2 receptors in lung tissue, thus improving SABA or LABA therapy responsiveness.
  - ICS also deduce pulmonary hypersecretion, reducing airway edema and exudation.
- **Quaternary Ammonium**
  - LAMAs are quaternary ammonium structures, which prevent their absorption to the CNS across the blood-brain barrier.
  - This limits the central antimuscarinic potential of these drugs.
  - Glycopyrrolate is structurally like atropine, except for its quaternary amine core structure.
- **Beta-2 Selectivity**
  - LABAs are generally more beta-2 selective compared to albuterol, owing to their increased time in lung tissue.

Primary Net Benefit

- Combination inhalers of bronchodilators or inhaled corticosteroids improve drug delivery to the pulmonary sites of action and improve compliance.

Combination Products - Drug Class Review			
High-Yield Med Reviews			
Mechanism of Action: *See specific drug class Rapid Reviews.*			
Class Effects: Combination inhalers of bronchodilators or inhaled corticosteroids improve drug delivery to the pulmonary sites of action and improve compliance.			
Generic Name	**Brand Name**	**Main Indication(s) or Uses**	**Notes**

Aclidinium, formoterol	Duaklir Pressair	• Chronic obstructive pulmonary disease	• **Dosing (Adult):**
			  – Oral Inhalation 1 inhalation twice daily
			• **Dosing (Peds):**
			  – Not routinely used
			• **CYP450 Interactions:** Substrate CYP2C9, 2D6, 3A4
			• **Renal or Hepatic Dose Adjustments:** None
			• **Dosage Forms:** Aerosol powder

Combination Drugs - Drug Class Review
High-Yield Med Reviews

Generic Name	Brand Name	Indication(s) or Uses	Notes

Albuterol, ipratropium	Combivent Respimat, DuoNeb	▪ Asthma
		▪ Chronic obstructive pulmonary disease
			▪ **Dosing (Adult):**
			  – COPD
			    ▪ Oral Inhalation 1 inhalation 4 times daily
			  – Asthma
			    ▪ Oral inhalation 8 inhalations q20minutes as needed for up to 3 hours
			    ▪ Nebulization 3 mL q20minutes for 3 doses or q4-6hours
			▪ **Dosing (Peds):**
			  – Nebulization 1.5 to 3 mL q20minutes for 3 doses
			▪ **CYP450 Interactions:** None
			▪ **Renal or Hepatic Dose Adjustments:** None
			▪ **Dosage Forms:** Solution for nebulization, Solution for oral inhalation

Formoterol, Budesonide	Symbicort	▪ Asthma
		▪ Chronic obstructive pulmonary disease
			▪ **Dosing (Adult):**
			  – MDI - 2 inhalations once to twice daily
			▪ **Dosing (Peds):**
			  – MDI - 2 inhalations once to twice daily
			▪ **CYP450 Interactions:** None
			▪ **Renal or Hepatic Dose Adjustments:** None
			▪ **Dosage Forms:** Symbicort 160/4.5, Symbicort 80/4.5

Formoterol, Glycopyrrolate	Bevespi Aerosphere	▪ Chronic obstructive pulmonary disease	▪ **Dosing (Adult):**
			  – MDI - 2 inhalations twice daily
			▪ **Dosing (Peds):**
			  – Oral Inhalation
			▪ **CYP450 Interactions:** None
			▪ **Renal or Hepatic Dose Adjustments:** None
			▪ **Dosage Forms:** Inhalation aerosol

Formoterol, Budesonide, Glycopyrrolate	Breztri Aerosphere	▪ Chronic obstructive pulmonary disease	▪ **Dosing (Adult):**
			  – MDI - 2 inhalations twice daily
			▪ **Dosing (Peds):**
			  – Oral Inhalation
			▪ **CYP450 Interactions:** None
			▪ **Renal or Hepatic Dose Adjustments:** None
			▪ **Dosage Forms:** [e.g., basic info]

Formoterol, Mometasone	Dulera	▪ Asthma
		▪ Chronic obstructive pulmonary disease
			▪ **Dosing (Adult):**
			  – MDI - 2 inhalations twice daily
			▪ **Dosing (Peds):**
			  – MDI - 2 inhalations twice daily
			▪ **CYP450 Interactions:** Substrate CYP2C9, 3A4
			▪ **Renal or Hepatic Dose Adjustments:** None
			▪ **Dosage Forms:** Dulera (50/5; 100/5; 200/5)

Combination Drugs - Drug Class Review
High-Yield Med Reviews

Generic Name	Brand Name	Indication(s) or Uses	Notes

Indacaterol, Glycopyrrolate	Utibron Neohaler	▪ Chronic obstructive pulmonary disease	▪ **Dosing (Adult):**
			  – DPI - 1 capsule inhaled twice daily
			▪ **Dosing (Peds):**
			  – Not routinely used
			▪ **CYP450 Interactions:** Substrate CYP2D6, 3A4, P-gp
			▪ **Renal or Hepatic Dose Adjustments:** None
			▪ **Dosage Forms:** [e.g., basic info]

Salmeterol, fluticasone	Advair HFA, Advair Diskus, AirDuo, Wixela Inhub	▪ Asthma
		▪ Chronic obstructive pulmonary disease
			▪ **Dosing (Adult):**
			  – DPI - 1 inhalation twice daily
			  – MDI - 2 inhalations twice daily
			▪ **Dosing (Peds):**
			  – DPI - 1 inhalation twice daily
			  – MDI - 1 to 2 inhalations twice daily
			▪ **CYP450 Interactions:** Substrate CYP3A4
			▪ **Renal or Hepatic Dose Adjustments:** None
			▪ **Dosage Forms:** Advair (45/21 mcg; 115/21 mcg; 230;21 mcg), Advair Diskus (100/50; 250/50; 500/50), AirDuo (55/14; 113/14; 232/14), Wixela Inhub (100/50; 250/50; 500/50)

Tiotropium, olodaterol	Stiolto Respimat	▪ Chronic obstructive pulmonary disease	▪ **Dosing (Adult):**
			  – Oral Inhalation - two inhalations once daily
			▪ **Dosing (Peds):**
			  – Oral Inhalation
			▪ **CYP450 Interactions:** Substrate CYP2C8, 2C9, 2D6, 3A4
			▪ **Renal or Hepatic Dose Adjustments:** None
			▪ **Dosage Forms:** Stiolo Respimat 2.5 mg and 2.5 mg olodaterol

Vilanterol, fluticasone	Breo Ellipta	▪ Asthma
		▪ Chronic obstructive pulmonary disease
			▪ **Dosing (Adult):**
			  – DPI - 1 inhalation once daily
			▪ **Dosing (Peds):**
			  – Not routinely used
			▪ **CYP450 Interactions:** Substrate CYP3A4
			▪ **Renal or Hepatic Dose Adjustments:** None
			▪ **Dosage Forms:** Breo Ellipta (25/100; 25/200)

Combination Drugs - Drug Class Review
High-Yield Med Reviews

Generic Name	Brand Name	Indication(s) or Uses	Notes

Vilanterol, umeclidinium	Anoro Ellipta	• Chronic obstructive pulmonary disease	• **Dosing (Adult):**
			  – DPI - 1 inhalation daily
			• **Dosing (Peds):**
			  – Oral Inhalation
			• **CYP450 Interactions:** Substrate CYP2D6, P-gp
			• **Renal or Hepatic Dose Adjustments:** None
			• **Dosage Forms:** Anoro Ellpita (62.5/25 mcg)

Vilanterol, umeclidinium, fluticasone	Trelegy Ellipta	• Asthma
		• Chronic obstructive pulmonary disease
			• **Dosing (Adult):**
			  – DPI - 1 inhalation once daily
			• **Dosing (Peds):**
			  – Not routinely used
			• **CYP450 Interactions:** Substrate CYP2D6, 3A4, P-gp
			• **Renal or Hepatic Dose Adjustments:** None
			• **Dosage Forms:** [e.g., basic info]

High-Yield Clinical Knowledge

- **Asthma Vs. COPD**
    - ICS therapy is central to asthma by providing anti-inflammatory effects that improve long-term morbidity and mortality.
    - However, for patients with COPD, ICS are not preferred as they carry a higher risk of bacterial pneumonia and are limited to patients with severe airflow obstruction, concomitant asthma, or a history of frequent exacerbations.
- **Drug Interactions**
    - Protease inhibitors may significantly reduce the metabolism of inhaled corticosteroids, potentially increasing the risk of toxicity and adrenal suppression.
    - Fluticasone should not be used in patients taking protease inhibitors; however, beclomethasone is the best option as it is not a substrate of CYP3A4.
- **Adjunctive Therapy**
    - Ipratropium is used primarily in combination with albuterol for acute severe asthma either empirically or with an incomplete response to albuterol alone.
    - An additional 15% improvement in FEV1 can be observed when ipratropium is combined with albuterol in emergency department management of acute severe asthma.
- **High Risk for Exacerbation**
    - In patients at high risk of COPD exacerbation, tiotropium is preferred as it has the most evidence supporting a more significant reduction in the frequency of exacerbations compared to LABA.
        - Other LAMAs may be used for this benefit; the largest amount of data supports tiotropium.
- **LABA Role**
    - In the treatment of asthma, LABAs are preferred to inhaled corticosteroids (ICS).
    - Combinations of ICS and LABA increase asthma control, reduce the frequency of exacerbations, and do so to a more considerable degree than increasing ICS dose alone.
- **Chronic Bronchodilation**
    - LABAs must not be used for the acute management of severe asthma.
    - Although salmeterol has a rapid onset of less than 30 minutes, albuterol is the drug of choice as it is almost immediately effective.

HIGH-YIELD BOARD EXAM ESSENTIALS

- **CLASSIC AGENTS:** Aclidinium, albuterol, budesonide, formoterol, glycopyrrolate, indacaterol, ipratropium, mometasone, salmeterol, tiotropium, olodaterol, umeclidinium, vilanterol.
- **DRUG CLASS:** Anticholinergic bronchodilators, beta-2 agonists, corticosteroids, corticosteroids
- **INDICATIONS:** Asthma, COPD
- **MECHANISM:** See specific drug class reviews
- **SIDE EFFECTS:** See specific drug class reviews
- **CLINICAL PEARLS:**
  - Chronic use of ICS in pediatric patients is associated with growth suppression and occurs with low to medium dose ICS.
  - n patients at high risk of COPD exacerbation, tiotropium is preferred as it has the most evidence supporting a more significant reduction in the frequency of exacerbations compared to LABA.
  - With long-term administration of beta-2 agonists, a decreasing number of beta-2 receptors and decreased binding affinity occurs.

High-Yield Basic Pharmacology

- **Mechanism of Action**
  - Ivacaftor
    - Improve lung mucus viscosity and clearance by potentiating the activity of the cystic fibrosis transmembrane conductance regulator (CFTR) protein, prolonging chloride channel opening.
  - Elexacaftor, lumacaftor, tezacaftor
    - Enhance the performance of mutant CFTR protein processing at the cell surface
- **Specific CFTR Targets**
  - Ivacaftor functions to potentiate CFTR, but elexacaftor, lumacaftor, and tezacaftor have slightly different targets.
  - Elexacaftor, lumacaftor, and tezacaftor improve cellular processing and trafficking of normal and mutant CFTR forms, including the mutant F508del-CFTR.

Primary Net Benefit

- Novel disease-modifying therapy for cystic fibrosis through targeted therapy aimed at partially restoring the function of mutated CFTR.

CFTR Modulator - Drug Class Review High-Yield Med Reviews			
Mechanism of Action: *Ivacaftor - Improve lung mucus viscosity and clearance by potentiating the CFTR protein activity, prolonging chloride channel opening.* *Elexacaftor, lumacaftor, tezacaftor - Enhance the performance of mutant CFTR protein processing at the cell surface.*			
Class Effects: Hepatotoxicity, conjunctivitis, cataracts, upper respiratory tract infection.			
Generic Name	**Brand Name**	**Indication(s) or Uses**	**Notes**

Elexacaftor, tezacaftor, ivacaftor	Trikafta	• Cystic Fibrosis	• **Dosing (Adult):**
			  – Oral 2 packet q12h
			• **Dosing (Peds):**
			  – Children over 12 years, use adult dose
			• **CYP450 Interactions:** Substrate CYP3A4, P-gp; Inhibits CYP3A4, P-gp
			• **Renal or Hepatic Dose Adjustments:**
			  – Child-Pugh class B - Day 1: 2 tablets in AM, Day 2: 1 tablet in AM, then alternate day 1/2
			  – Child-Pugh class C - not recommended
			• **Dosage Forms:** Oral (packet)

Ivacaftor	Kalydeco	• Cystic Fibrosis	• **Dosing (Adult):**
			  – Oral 150 mg q12h
			• **Dosing (Peds):**
			  – Oral 25 to 150 mg q12h
			• **CYP450 Interactions:** Substrate CYP3A4; Inhibits CYP3A4, P-gp
			• **Renal or Hepatic Dose Adjustments:**
			  – Child-Pugh class B or C - 150 mg daily
			• **Dosage Forms:** Oral (packet, tablet)

CFTR Modulator - Drug Class Review
High-Yield Med Reviews

Generic Name	Brand Name	Indication(s) or Uses	Notes

Lumacaftor, ivacaftor	Orkambi	▪ Cystic Fibrosis	▪ **Dosing (Adult):**
			  – Oral 2 packet q12h
			▪ **Dosing (Peds):**
			  – Oral 1 to 2 packet q12h
			▪ **CYP450 Interactions:** Substrate CYP3A4; Inhibits CYP3A4, P-gp
			▪ **Renal or Hepatic Dose Adjustments:**
			  – Child-Pugh class B - 2 packets in AM, 1 tablet PM
			  – Child-Pugh class C - 1 packet q12h
			▪ **Dosage Forms:** Oral (packet)

Tezacaftor, ivacaftor	Symdeko	▪ Cystic Fibrosis	▪ **Dosing (Adult):**
			  – Oral 2 packet q12h
			▪ **Dosing (Peds):**
			  – Oral 1 to 2 packet q12h
			▪ **CYP450 Interactions:** Substrate CYP3A4; Inhibits CYP3A4, P-gp
			▪ **Renal or Hepatic Dose Adjustments:**
			  – Child-Pugh class B - 2 packets in AM, 1 tablet PM
			  – Child-Pugh class C - 1 packet q12h
			▪ **Dosage Forms:** Oral (packet)

High-Yield Clinical Knowledge

- **Correctors and Potentiators**
    - Combining both correctors of CFTR protein activity (elexacaftor, lumacaftor, tezacaftor) and potentiators (ivacaftor) are used in patients with Phe508del CFTR mutation.
- **FEV1 Improvements**
    - CFTR modulator therapy significantly improves FEV1 in patients with CF when added to background therapy.
- **CFTR Locations**
    - CFTR proteins are expressed not only in the lung tissue and in sweat glands and in the GI tract (including intestines, pancreas, and bile duct).
- **Mutations**
    - As the cause of cystic fibrosis has been identified to be a result of mutations in the gene encoding the CFTR proteins, most have at least one copy of the Phe508del CFTR mutation.
    - Patients with homozygous mutations of the Phe508del mutation have demonstrated a clinical response to CFTR modulator therapy.

HIGH-YIELD BOARD EXAM ESSENTIALS

- **CLASSIC AGENTS:** Elexacaftor, tezacaftor, ivacaftor, lumacaftor
- **DRUG CLASS:** CFTR modulator
- **INDICATIONS:** Cystic fibrosis
- **MECHANISM:** Ivacaftor - Improve lung mucus viscosity and clearance by potentiating the CFTR protein activity, prolonging chloride channel opening. Elexacaftor, lumacaftor, tezacaftor - Enhance the performance of mutant CFTR protein processing at the cell surface.
- **SIDE EFFECTS:** Hepatotoxicity, conjunctivitis, cataracts, upper respiratory tract infection
- **CLINICAL PEARLS:** As the cause of cystic fibrosis has been identified to be a result of mutations in the gene encoding the CFTR proteins, most have at least one copy of the Phe508del CFTR mutation.

High-Yield Basic Pharmacology

- **Mechanism of Action**
  - Combines with intracellular glucocorticoid receptors and acts as a gene transcription factor, increasing the production of anti-inflammatory mediators, suppression of inflammatory cytokines, and inflammatory cell activation/recruitment/infiltration, and decreases vascular permeability.
- **Onset of Action**
  - The bronchodilatory effects of ICS are not sufficiently rapid enough for acute management of severe asthma, where parenteral corticosteroids are more appropriate.
  - The time to maximal response for ICS therapy is approximately 4 to 8 weeks.

Primary Net Benefit

- ICS are a core component for chronic asthma care but have a limited role in COPD. Numerous combination inhaler products improve compliance and administration of other controller agents, but patients must be educated on proper oral care to reduce the risk of oropharyngeal complications.

Inhaled Corticosteroids - Drug Class Review High-Yield Med Reviews			
Mechanism of Action: *Combines with intracellular glucocorticoid receptors and acts as a gene transcription factor, increasing the production of anti-inflammatory mediators, suppression of inflammatory cytokines, and inflammatory cell activation/recruitment/infiltration, and decreases vascular permeability.*			
Class Effects: Increased risk of thrush, include osteoporosis, ophthalmologic complications (glaucoma, cataracts)			
Generic Name	**Brand Name**	**Indication(s) or Uses**	**Notes**

Beclomethasone	Qvar	• Asthma
		• Chronic obstructive pulmonary disease
			• **Dosing (Adult):**
			  – Oral inhalation 40 to 400 mcg BID
			• **Dosing (Peds):**
			  – Oral inhalation 40 to 320 mcg BID
			• **CYP450 Interactions:** None
			• **Renal or Hepatic Dose Adjustments:** None
			• **Dosage Forms:** Aerosol powder, Inhalation solution

Budesonide	Pulmicort	• Asthma
		• Chronic obstructive pulmonary disease
			• **Dosing (Adult):**
			  – DPI - 360 to 720 mg BID
			  – Nebulization 2 mg q6h
			• **Dosing (Peds):**
			  – Nebulization 0.25 mg BID or 0.5 mg daily
			  – DPI - 180 to 360 mg BID
			• **CYP450 Interactions:** Substrate CYP3A4
			• **Renal or Hepatic Dose Adjustments:** None
			• **Dosage Forms:** Aerosol powder, Inhalation suspension

Ciclesonide	Alvesco	• Asthma	• **Dosing (Adult):**
			  – Oral inhalation 80 to 320 mcg BID
			• **Dosing (Peds):**
			  – Oral inhalation 80 to 320 mcg BID
			• **CYP450 Interactions:** Substrate CYP3A4
			• **Renal or Hepatic Dose Adjustments:** None
			• **Dosage Forms:** Inhalation aerosol solution

Inhaled Corticosteroids - Drug Class Review
High-Yield Med Reviews

Generic Name	Brand Name	Indication(s) or Uses	Notes

Fluticasone	ArmonAir, Arnuity, Flovent	• Asthma
		• COPD
			• **Dosing (Adult):**
			  – DPI (ArmonAir) - 55 to 232 mcg BID
			  – DPI (Arnuity) - 100 to 200 mcg daily
			  – MDI/DPI (Flovent) - 100 to 1,000 mcg BID
			• **Dosing (Peds):**
			  – MDI/DPI (Flovent) - 100 to 1,000 mcg BID
			• **CYP450 Interactions:** Substrate CYP3A4
			• **Renal or Hepatic Dose Adjustments:** None
			• **Dosage Forms:** Inhalation (aerosol, aerosol powder)

Mometasone	Asmanex	• Asthma	• **Dosing (Adult):**
			  – MDI - 200 to 400 mcg BID
			  – DPI - 220 to 440 mcg Daily
			• **Dosing (Peds):**
			  – MDI - 100 to 400 mcg BID
			  – DPI - 110 to 440 mcg Daily
			• **CYP450 Interactions:** Substrate CYP3A4
			• **Renal or Hepatic Dose Adjustments:** None
			• **Dosage Forms:** Inhalation aerosol

High-Yield Clinical Knowledge

- **Corticosteroid Effects**
  - Inhaled corticosteroids increase the number of beta-2 receptors in lung tissue, thus improving SABA or LABA therapy responsiveness.
  - ICS also deduce pulmonary hypersecretion, reducing airway edema and exudation.
- **Asthma Vs. COPD**
  - ICS therapy is central to asthma by providing anti-inflammatory effects that improve long-term morbidity and mortality.
  - However, for patients with COPD, ICS are not preferred as they carry a higher risk of bacterial pneumonia and are limited to patients with severe airflow obstruction, concomitant asthma, or a history of frequent exacerbations.
- **Mouth Rinsing**
  - Patients on ICS must be educated to rinse and spit their mouths after administration to reduce the agent's oral bioavailability and reduce the risk of oral or esophageal candidiasis.
- **Systemic Steroid Effects**
  - ICS may be systemically absorbed, producing numerous adverse events similar to oral or parenteral corticosteroids.
  - These adverse events include osteoporosis, ophthalmologic complications (glaucoma, cataracts), adrenal suppression, delayed wound healing, hyperglycemia, hypertension, and psychiatric disturbances.
- **Systemic Absorption**
  - ICS are all absorbed systemically but can be rapidly metabolized via the first-pass metabolism if absorbed orally.
  - However, systemic absorption through lung tissue bypasses first-pass hepatic circulation, increasing systemic exposure to the corticosteroid.
  - Poor inhaler technique can result in enteral absorption of ICS but in the case of beclomethasone and ciclesonide, which are prodrugs, further limiting bioavailability.

- **Pediatric Growth Velocity**
  - Chronic use of ICS in pediatric patients is associated with growth suppression and occurs with low to medium dose ICS.
  - This effect is transient, and growth velocity returns to normal after 6 to 24 months of therapy and does not affect maximal growth potential.

High-Yield Fast-Fact

- **Dysphonia**
  - Up to 20% of patients taking ICS experience a steroid-induced myopathy of the vocal cords, producing dysphonia.
  - Proper inhaler technique and the use of a spacer device can reduce the risk of thrush, candidiasis, and dysphonia.

HIGH-YIELD BOARD EXAM ESSENTIALS
- **CLASSIC AGENTS:** Beclomethasone, budesonide, ciclesonide, fluticasone, mometasone
- **DRUG CLASS:** Inhaled corticosteroids
- **INDICATIONS:** Asthma, COPD
- **MECHANISM:** Combines with intracellular glucocorticoid receptors and acts as a gene transcription factor, increasing the production of anti-inflammatory mediators, suppression of inflammatory cytokines, and inflammatory cell activation/recruitment/infiltration, and decreases vascular permeability.
- **SIDE EFFECTS:** Thrush, include osteoporosis, ophthalmologic complications (glaucoma, cataracts)
- **CLINICAL PEARLS:** Chronic use of ICS in pediatric patients is associated with growth suppression and occurs with low to medium dose ICS.

High-Yield Basic Pharmacology

- **Mechanism of Action**
  - Methylxanthines nonselectively inhibit phosphodiesterases, increasing intracellular cAMP leading to smooth muscle relaxation.
- **Di- and Trimethylxanthine**
  - Theophylline's chemical name is 1,3-dimethylxanthine, whereas caffeine is 1,3,7-trimethylxanthine.
    - Theobromine is 3,7-dimethylxanthine.
- **Alternative Mechanisms**
  - Methylxanthines may provide bronchodilation through inhibition of adenosine's action on airway smooth muscle.
  - Adenosine has been associated with increased airway smooth muscle release of histamine

Primary Net Benefit

- Once used as first-line agents for asthma, methylxanthines have been relegated to add-on therapy in patients who have otherwise failed alternative bronchodilators and inhaled corticosteroids.

		Methylxanthines - Drug Class Review	
		High-Yield Med Reviews	
Mechanism of Action: *Methylxanthines nonselectively inhibit phosphodiesterases, increasing intracellular cAMP leading to smooth muscle relaxation.*			
Class Effects: Tachycardia, CNS excitation, headache, seizures, diuresis; will need to check levels of theophylline.			
Generic Name	**Brand Name**	**Indication(s) or Uses**	**Notes**

Aminophylline	Norphyl	• Asthma	• **Dosing (Adult):**
			  – IV Loading Dose: 5.7 mg/kg
			  – IV Infusion 0.25 to 0.51 mg/kg/hour
			    ▪ Age over 60 years: Maximum 507 mg/day
			    ▪ Age 60 years or younger: Maximum 1,139 mg/day
			• **Dosing (Peds):**
			  – IV Loading Dose: 5.7 mg/kg
			  – IV Infusion 0.25 to 0.51 mg/kg/hour
			• **CYP450 Interactions:** Substrate CYP1A2, 2C9, 2D6, 2E1, 3A4
			• **Renal or Hepatic Dose Adjustments:**
			  – Hepatic impairment - Maximum 507 mg/day
			• **Dosage Forms:** IV (solution)

Caffeine	NA	• Apnea of prematurity	• **Dosing (Adult):**
			  – IV 250 to 1,000 mg caffeine base over 1 hour
			  – Oral 100 to 200 mg q3-4h as needed
			• **Dosing (Peds):**
			  – Oral 100 to 200 mg q3-4h as needed
			• **CYP450 Interactions:** Substrate CYP1A2, 2C9, 2D6, 2E1, 3A4; Inhibits CYP1A2
			• **Renal or Hepatic Dose Adjustments:** text
			• **Dosage Forms:** IV (solution), Oral (solution, tablet)

Methylxanthines - Drug Class Review
High-Yield Med Reviews

Generic Name	Brand Name	Indication(s) or Uses	Notes

Theophylline	Elixophyllin Theo-Dur	• Bradycardia
		• Reversible airflow obstruction
			• **Dosing (Adult):**
			  – Oral IR 150 to 600 mg/day divided q6-8h
			  – Oral ER 300 to 600 mg/day divided q12h (for 12-hour formulation) or q24h (for 24-hour formulation)
			  – IV 4.6 mg/kg, followed by 0.3 to 0.4 mg/kg/hour
			    • Age over 60 years: Maximum 400 mg/day
			    • Age 60 years or younger: Maximum 900 mg/day
			• **Dosing (Peds):**
			  – IV 4.6 mg/kg, followed by 0.3 to 0.4 mg/kg/hour
			  – IV 0.7 to 1.5 mg/kg/hour
			  – Oral IR 12 to 20 mg/kg/day divided q4-6h
			    • Maximum 400 mg/day
			  – Oral ER 12 to 20 mg/kg/day divided q12-24h
			    • Maximum 400 mg/day
			• **CYP450 Interactions:** Substrate CYP1A2, 2E1, 3A4
			• **Renal or Hepatic Dose Adjustments:**
			  – Hepatic impairment - IV initial dose of 0.2 mg/kg/hour; maximum 400 mg/day
			• **Dosage Forms:** IV (solution), Oral (capsule, elixir, solution, tablet)

High-Yield Clinical Knowledge

- **Methylxanthines and Pulmonary Disease**
  - Theophylline is an effective bronchodilator that was once widely used for asthma.
  - As a result of the development of inhaled bronchodilators, the risks of theophylline due to its narrow therapeutic index outweighed any benefit when compared to other available agents.
- **Apnea of Prematurity**
  - Caffeine is still routinely used in neonates for the treatment of apnea of prematurity.
  - Administered via IV infusion, caffeine is an effective respiratory stimulant.
- **Aminophylline and Theophylline**
  - Aminophylline is a water-soluble theophylline-ethylenediamine complex that is suitable for IV administration.
  - These two agents are otherwise pharmacologically and kinetically similar.
- **CNS Effect**
  - All methylxanthines cross the blood-brain barrier and can exert a mild excitatory effect.
  - Caffeine is widely consumed for its cortical arousal abilities; however, for bronchodilatory effects, the dose is larger, up to 1,000 mg.
    - The potentially fatal caffeine dose is approximately 100 mg/kg, but patients can experience tachycardia and neuropsychiatric effects at much smaller doses.
- **Caffeine Citrate Vs. Sodium Benzoate**
  - Caffeine sodium benzoate should not be used in neonates as benzoate may displace bilirubin.
  - Caffeine citrate is preferred in neonatal apnea.

- Diuresis
  - Methylxanthines promote diuresis by increasing GFR and reduced tubular sodium reabsorption.
  - However, the diuretic effect is not sufficient to allow for its use clinically as a diuretic.
- **Therapeutic Drug Monitoring**
  - Theophylline should be titrated to a target trough of between 8 and 15 mcg/mL.
  - Patients who are consistently within the target range can be monitored once or twice yearly, unless new drug interactions occur, toxicity is suspected, or the patient's disease worsens.
  - Risk factors for theophylline toxicity include elderly patients, pneumonia, heart failure, or liver dysfunction.
  - Common drug interactions include potent CYP inhibitors such as cimetidine, macrolides, fluoroquinolones, and CYP inducers, including smoking (tobacco and marijuana), phenytoin, phenobarbital, or rifampin.
- **CYP1A2**
  - The methylxanthines are metabolized by CYP1A2 and are subject to considerable pharmacokinetics in patients with CYP1A2 genetic polymorphisms.

High-Yield Fast-Fact

- **Pentoxifylline**
  - Pentoxifylline, although used for peripheral arterial disease, is a methylxanthine. It lacks bronchodilatory effects at normal therapeutic dosing.

HIGH-YIELD BOARD EXAM ESSENTIALS
- **CLASSIC AGENTS:** Aminophylline, caffeine, theophylline
- **DRUG CLASS:** Methylxanthines
- **INDICATIONS:** Asthma, COPD
- **MECHANISM:** Methylxanthines nonselectively inhibit phosphodiesterases, increasing intracellular cAMP leading to smooth muscle relaxation.
- **SIDE EFFECTS:** Tachycardia, CNS excitation, headache, seizures, diuresis
- **CLINICAL PEARLS:** Caffeine is still routinely used in neonates for the treatment of apnea of prematurity. Administered via IV infusion, caffeine is an effective respiratory stimulant.

High-Yield Basic Pharmacology

- **Benralizumab**
  - IL-5 receptor antagonist, preventing eosinophilic binding to the IL-5 receptor on airway tissue.
- **Dupilumab**
  - IL-4-alpha receptor antagonist that reduces IgE mediated inflammatory response by disrupting IL-4 and IL-13 signaling pathways.
- **Mepolizumab, reslizumab**
  - Inhibit interleukin-5 (IL-5), reducing the differentiation, recruitment, and activation of eosinophils to the airway.
- **Omalizumab**
  - A recombinant anti-IgE antibody, preventing IgE binding to its receptor on mast cells and basophils.

Primary Net Benefit

- Biologic therapeutics reserved for patients with moderate to severe persistent asthma.

Anti-Asthma Monoclonal Antibody - Drug Class Review			
High-Yield Med Reviews			
Mechanism of Action: _See agents above._			
Class Effects: Injection site reaction, headaches.			
Generic Name	**Brand Name**	**Indication(s) or Uses**	**Notes**

Benralizumab	Fasenra	• Asthma	• **Dosing (Adult):**
			  – SQ 30 mg q4weeks for 3 doses, then q8weeks
			• **Dosing (Peds):**
			  – SQ 30 mg q4weeks for 3 doses, then q8weeks
			• **CYP450 Interactions:** None
			• **Renal or Hepatic Dose Adjustments:** None
			• **Dosage Forms:** Subcutaneous auto-injector or prefilled syringe

Dupilumab	Dupixent	• Asthma
		• Rhinosinusitis
			• **Dosing (Adult):**
			  – SQ 400 to 600 mg once followed by 200 to 300 mg every other week
			• **Dosing (Peds):**
			  – SQ 400 to 600 mg once followed by 200 to 300 mg every other week
			• **CYP450 Interactions:** None
			• **Renal or Hepatic Dose Adjustments:** None
			• **Dosage Forms:** Subcutaneous auto-injector or prefilled syringe

Anti-Asthma Monoclonal Antibody - Drug Class Review
High-Yield Med Reviews

Generic Name	Brand Name	Indication(s) or Uses	Notes

Mepolizumab	Nucala	• Asthma
		• Eosinophilic granulomatosis with polyangiitis
			• **Dosing (Adult):**
			  – SQ 100 to 300 mg q4weeks
			• **Dosing (Peds):**
			  – SQ 40 to 300 mg q4weeks
			• **CYP450 Interactions:** None
			• **Renal or Hepatic Dose Adjustments:** None
			• **Dosage Forms:** Subcutaneous auto-injector or prefilled syringe

Omalizumab	Xolair	• Asthma
		• Chronic idiopathic urticaria
		• Nasal polyps
			• **Dosing (Adult):**
			  – Patient-specific dosing based on serum IgE
			    ▪ SQ 150 to 600 mg q4weeks
			    ▪ SQ 225 to 600 mg q2weeks
			• **Dosing (Peds):**
			  – Patient-specific dosing based on serum IgE
			    ▪ SQ 75 to 300 mg q4weeks
			    ▪ SQ 225 to 375 mg q2weeks
			• **CYP450 Interactions:** None
			• **Renal or Hepatic Dose Adjustments:** None
			• **Dosage Forms:** Subcutaneous auto-injector or prefilled syringe

Reslizumab	Cinqair	• Asthma	• **Dosing (Adult):**
			  – IV 3 mg/kg q4weeks
			• **Dosing (Peds):**
			  – Not routinely used
			• **CYP450 Interactions:** None
			• **Renal or Hepatic Dose Adjustments:** None
			• **Dosage Forms:** IV (solution)

High-Yield Clinical Knowledge

- **Anaphylaxis**
  - Despite a relatively low risk of anaphylaxis (less than 1%), benralizumab, mepolizumab, and reslizumab are parenterally administered in a healthcare setting prepared to respond anaphylaxis.
  - Omalizumab carries a warning of anaphylaxis that can occur at any time during therapy.
- **Herpes Zoster**
  - Patients 50 years or older who are to receive mepolizumab should receive recombinant zoster vaccination four weeks before the first dose of mepolizumab.
- **Reduced Oral Corticosteroids**
  - Benralizumab, dupilumab, mepolizumab, and omalizumab have been observed to reduce the frequency of exacerbations and oral corticosteroid use in patients with severe asthma.
- **Omalizumab and Asthma Exacerbations**
  - Omalizumab may prevent asthma exacerbation in patients with frequent exacerbations by increasing the expression of type 1 interferons which improve antiviral immunity.

HIGH-YIELD BOARD EXAM ESSENTIALS

- **CLASSIC AGENTS:** Benralizumab, dupilumab, mepolizumab, omalizumab, reslizumab
- **DRUG CLASS:** 5-Lipoxygenase Inhibitor
- **INDICATIONS:** Asthma (benralizumab, dupilumab, mepolizumab, omalizumab, reslizumab), chronic idiopathic urticaria (omalizumab), eosinophilic granulomatosis with polyangiitis (mepolizumab), nasal polyps (omalizumab), rhinosinusitis (dupilumab)
- **MECHANISM:** Benralizumab - IL-5 receptor antagonist, preventing eosinophilic binding to the IL-5 receptor on airway tissue. Dupilumab - IL-4-alpha receptor antagonist that reduces IgE mediated inflammatory response by disrupting IL-4 and IL-13 signaling pathways. Mepolizumab, reslizumab - inhibit interleukin-5 (IL-5), reducing the differentiation, recruitment, and activation of eosinophils to the airway. Omalizumab - recombinant anti-IgE antibody, preventing IgE binding to its receptor on mast cells and basophils.
- **SIDE EFFECTS:** Injection site reaction, headache
- **CLINICAL PEARLS:** Despite a relatively low risk of anaphylaxis (less than 1%), benralizumab, mepolizumab, and reslizumab are parenterally administered in a healthcare setting prepared to respond anaphylaxis. Omalizumab carries a warning of anaphylaxis that can occur at any time during therapy.

High-Yield Basic Pharmacology

- **Acetylcysteine**
  - Reduces disulfide bridges that bind glycoproteins to other proteins, including albumin and IgA.
- **Dornase alfa**
  - Cleaves extracellular DNA, thereby decreasing the viscosity of mucus.
- **Hypertonic saline, Mannitol**
  - Hydrates mucous membranes and facilitates ciliary clearance of mucus.

Primary Net Benefit

- Mucolytics are a core anti-obstructive therapy for cystic fibrosis patients and should be combined with anti-inflammatory and antibiotic interventions.

		Mucolytics - Drug Class Review	
		High-Yield Med Reviews	
Mechanism of Action: **Acetylcysteine:** Reduces disulfide bridges that bind glycoproteins to other proteins, including albumin and IgA. **Dornase alfa:** Cleaves extracellular DNA, thereby decreasing the viscosity of mucus. **Hypertonic saline, Mannitol:** Hydrates mucous membranes and facilitates ciliary clearance of mucus.			
Class Effects: Unpleasant odor (acetylcysteine), cough (dornase alfa).			
Generic Name	**Brand Name**	**Indication(s) or Uses**	**Notes**

Acetylcysteine	Acetadote
	 Mucomyst
	 Cetylev
		- Acetaminophen overdose
		 - Mucolytic
			- **Dosing (Adult):**
			   – Oral 140 mg/kg once (maximum 15 g) followed by 70 mg/kg (maximum 7.5g/dose) q4h for 17 doses
			   – IV 150 mg/kg/hour for one hour (maximum 15 g), followed by 12.5 mg/kg/hour for 4 hours (maximum 5 g/dose), followed by 6.25 mg/kg/hour (maximum 10 g/dose) for 16 hours
			   – Nebulized 6 to 10 mL (10%) or 3 to 5 mL (20%) q1-6h
			 - **Dosing (Peds):**
			   – Oral 140 mg/kg once (maximum 15 g) followed by 70 mg/kg (maximum 7.5g/dose) q4h for 17 doses
			   – IV 150 mg/kg/hour for one hour (maximum 15 g), followed by 12.5 mg/kg/hour for 4 hours (maximum 5 g/dose), followed by 6.25 mg/kg/hour (maximum 10 g/dose) for 16 hours
			   – Nebulized 6 to 10 mL (10%) or 3 to 5 mL (20%) q1-6h
			 - **CYP450 Interactions:** None
			 - **Renal or Hepatic Dose Adjustments:** None
			 - **Dosage Forms:** Inhalation solution, IV (solution), Oral (Tablet)

Mucolytics - Drug Class Review
High-Yield Med Reviews

Generic Name	Brand Name	Indication(s) or Uses	Notes

Dornase alfa	Pulmozyme	• Cystic fibrosis
		•
			• **Dosing (Adult):**
			  – Inhalation 2.5 mg daily
			  – Intrapleural 5 mg twice daily
			• **Dosing (Peds):**
			  – Inhalation 2.5 mg daily
			  – Intrapleural 5 mg twice daily
			• **CYP450 Interactions:** None
			• **Renal or Hepatic Dose Adjustments:** None
			• **Dosage Forms:** Inhalation solution
			•

Hypertonic saline	HyperSal	• Cystic fibrosis
		•
			• **Dosing (Adult):**
			  – Inhalation NaCl 7% 4mL BID
			• **Dosing (Peds):**
			  – Inhalation NaCl 3% to 7% 4mL BID
			• **CYP450 Interactions:** None
			• **Renal or Hepatic Dose Adjustments:** None
			• **Dosage Forms:** Inhalation solution
			•

Mannitol	Aridol
	Bronchitol
		• Assessment of bronchial hyperresponsiveness
		• Cystic fibrosis
			• **Dosing (Adult):**
			  – Inhalation 400 mg BID
			• **Dosing (Peds):**
			  – Inhalation 400 mg BID
			• **CYP450 Interactions:** None
			• **Renal or Hepatic Dose Adjustments:** None
			• **Dosage Forms:** Inhalation capsule, inhalation kit
			•

High-Yield Clinical Knowledge

- **CF Treatment**
  - Bronchodilators (including albuterol), dornase alfa, and hypertonic saline should be used in patients with cystic fibrosis who are six years of age and older.
- **Dornase Alfa Cough**
  - The most common complaint with dornase alfa therapy is the development of cough.
  - In small children, the PARI-BABY nebulizer facemask can aid in drug delivery but is associated with a higher incidence of cough.
  - However, dornase alfa can reduce the risk of CF exacerbations by nearly 30%, reduce mortality, and improved sustained lung function.
- **NAC Effects**
  - Nebulized N-acetylcysteine can be used as a mucolytic but has not been shown to reduce disease progression or prevent exacerbations in COPD patients.
- **Acetylcysteine Taste/Odor**
  - Acetylcysteine has an unpleasant odor that patients will complain of if they are receiving nebulized treatments.
  - The taste is similar to rotten eggs and challenging to mask when being administered via nebulization.
- **Hypertonic Saline**
  - The use of hypertonic saline in CF increases mucus clearance at 1 hour and 24 hours, compared to baseline.
  - Hypertonic saline may induce bronchospasm and should be preceded by a bronchodilator.

- **B-HAPII**
  - The core components of treatment for CF include bronchodilators, hypertonic saline, airway clearance, Pulmozyme (dornase alfa), inhaled corticosteroids, and inhaled antibiotics.
  - Airway clearance methods include manual chest percussion, vest physiotherapy, and positive expiratory pressure ventilation.
  - Commonly used inhaled antibiotics for CF include tobramycin, aztreonam, and colistimethate.

HIGH-YIELD BOARD EXAM ESSENTIALS

- **CLASSIC AGENTS:** Acetylcysteine, dornase alfa, hypertonic saline, mannitol
- **DRUG CLASS:** Mucolytics
- **INDICATIONS:** Cystic fibrosis, mucolytic
- **MECHANISM:** Acetylcysteine - Reduces disulfide bridges that bind glycoproteins to other proteins, including albumin and IgA. Dornase alfa - cleaves extracellular DNA, thereby decreasing the viscosity of mucus. Hypertonic saline, Mannitol - Hydrates mucous membranes and facilitates ciliary clearance of mucus.
- **SIDE EFFECTS:** Unpleasant odor (acetylcysteine), cough (dornase alfa)
- **CLINICAL PEARLS:** In small children, the PARI-BABY nebulizer facemask can aid in drug delivery but is associated with a higher incidence of cough. However, dornase alfa can reduce the risk of CF exacerbations by nearly 30%, reduce mortality, and improved sustained lung function.

High-Yield Basic Pharmacology

- **Mechanism of Action**
  - Selective inhibition of phosphodiesterase-4 (PDE4) leads to decreased intracellular cAMP and decreased pro-inflammatory cytokines.
- **Site-Specific PDE4 Inhibition**
  - Roflumilast's actions as a PDE4 inhibitor cause airway smooth muscle tissue relaxation and decreases inflammatory mediators that promote COPD disease progression.

Primary Net Benefit

- Roflumilast is reserved for select severe COPD patients; apremilast may be effective in patients with dermatologic conditions but carry a risk of neuropsychiatric events. Crisaborole does not have a warning for neuropsychiatric effects as it is not systemically absorbed.

Phosphodiesterase-4 Inhibitors - Drug Class Review High-Yield Med Reviews			
Mechanism of Action: *Selective phosphodiesterase-4 (PDE4) inhibition leads to decreased intracellular cAMP and decreased pro-inflammatory cytokines.*			
Class Effects: GI events (nausea, diarrhea), decreased appetite, weight loss, headache, insomnia, anxiety, new or worsening depression.			
Generic Name	**Brand Name**	**Indication(s) or Uses**	**Notes**
Apremilast	Otezla	▪ Behcet disease ▪ Psoriasis ▪ Psoriatic arthritis	▪ **Dosing (Adult):** – Oral 30 mg BID ▪ Titration from 10 mg once to target dose over 6 days ▪ **Dosing (Peds):** – Not routinely used ▪ **CYP450 Interactions:** Substrate CYP3A4, P-gp ▪ **Renal or Hepatic Dose Adjustments:** – GFR less than 30 mL/minute - slower titration and maximum 30 mg once daily ▪ **Dosage Forms:** Oral (capsule)
Crisaborole	Eucrisa	▪ Atopic dermatitis	▪ **Dosing (Adult):** – Topical application to the affected area BID ▪ **Dosing (Peds):** – Topical application to the affected area BID ▪ **CYP450 Interactions:** None ▪ **Renal or Hepatic Dose Adjustments:** None ▪ **Dosage Forms:** Ointment
Roflumilast	Daliresp	▪ COPD	▪ **Dosing (Adult):** – Oral 250 mcg daily x 4 weeks, then 500 mcg daily ▪ **Dosing (Peds):** – Not routinely used ▪ **CYP450 Interactions:** Substrate CYP1A2, 3A4 ▪ **Renal or Hepatic Dose Adjustments:** – Child-Pugh class B or C - contraindicated ▪ **Dosage Forms:** Oral (tablet)

High-Yield Clinical Knowledge

- **COPD Treatment**
  - Roflumilast is reserved for severe COPD patients with chronic cough, sputum production, and a history of frequent exacerbations.
  - Roflumilast, although providing anti-inflammatory properties, does not produce meaningful bronchodilation.
- **CYP3A4 Substrates**
  - Apremilast and roflumilast are substrates of CYP3A4 and subject to numerous drug interactions.
  - In patients taking CYP3A4 inducers (carbamazepine, phenytoin, phenobarbital, rifampin) should not begin apremilast or roflumilast as their effectiveness will be substantially diminished.
  - Potent CYP3A4 inhibitors may be combined with apremilast or roflumilast; however, increased monitoring (neuropsychiatric) should occur.
- **Roflumilast Safety**
  - Common adverse events associated with roflumilast therapy include GI events (nausea, diarrhea), decreased appetite and weight loss, and headache.
  - Neuropsychiatric events including insomnia, anxiety, new or worsening depression, and suicidal thoughts are rare but concerning effects associated with roflumilast.
    - Roflumilast should be avoided in patients with a history of depression or suicidality.
- **CYP1A2 and Smoking**
  - Although generally recommended to avoid and provide smoking cessation education, roflumilast AUC may be significantly lower in active smokers.
  - Cigarette smoke contains polycyclic aromatic hydrocarbons that induce CYP1A2.

HIGH-YIELD BOARD EXAM ESSENTIALS

- **CLASSIC AGENTS:** Apremilast, crisaborole, roflumilast
- **DRUG CLASS:** Phosphodiesterase-4 inhibitors
- **INDICATIONS:** Atopic dermatitis (crisaborole), Behcet disease (apremilast), psoriasis (apremilast), psoriatic arthritis (apremilast), COPD (roflumilast)
- **MECHANISM:** Selective phosphodiesterase-4 (PDE4) inhibition leads to decreased intracellular cAMP and decreased pro-inflammatory cytokines.
- **SIDE EFFECTS:** GI events (nausea, diarrhea), decreased appetite, weight loss, headache, insomnia, anxiety, new or worsening depression, and suicidal thoughts
- **CLINICAL PEARLS:**
  - Roflumilast is not a first-line agent for COPD; instead is an adjunctive treatment to existing therapy. It is also orally administered which may be initially counter-intuitive for COPD.
  - Although generally recommended to avoid and provide smoking cessation education, roflumilast AUC may be significantly lower in active smokers. Cigarette smoke contains polycyclic aromatic hydrocarbons that induce CYP1A2.

High-Yield Basic Pharmacology

- **Mechanism of Action**
  - Antagonists of endothelin-A and endothelin-B receptors, preventing endothelin-induced vasoconstriction of these vessels.
- **ETa Selectivity**
  - Ambrisentan is highly selective for ETa, whereas bosentan is non-selective between ETa and ETb.

Primary Net Benefit

- Endothelin receptor antagonists improve exercise capacity in most patients and impact functional class and time to clinical worsening. All agents require participation in prescription monitoring programs due to significant toxicities.

Endothelin Receptor Antagonist - Drug Class Review			
High-Yield Med Reviews			
Mechanism of Action: *Antagonists of endothelin-A and endothelin-B receptors, preventing endothelin-induced vasoconstriction of these vessels.*			
Class Effects: Hypotension, tachycardia, flushing, and headaches.			
Generic Name	**Brand Name**	**Indication(s) or Uses**	**Notes**

Ambrisentan	Letairis	• Pulmonary arterial hypertension	• **Dosing (Adult):**
			  – Oral 5 to 10 mg daily
			• **Dosing (Peds):**
			  – Not routinely used
			• **CYP450 Interactions:** Substrate CYP2C19, 3A4, P-gp
			• **Renal or Hepatic Dose Adjustments:**
			  – Child-Pugh class C - Not recommended
			  – AST/ALT above 5x upper limit of normal OR 2x upper limit of normal with hepatic injury - discontinue therapy
			• **Dosage Forms:** Oral (tablet)

Bosentan	Tracleer	• Pulmonary arterial hypertension	• **Dosing (Adult):**
			  – Oral 62.5 to 125 mg BID
			• **Dosing (Peds):**
			  – Oral 1 mg/kg/dose twice daily
			  – Oral 3 to 64 mg twice daily
			• **CYP450 Interactions:** Substrate CYP2C9, 3A4; Induces CYP2C9, 3A4
			• **Renal or Hepatic Dose Adjustments:**
			  – Child-Pugh class B or C - Not recommended
			  – AST/ALT above 8x upper limit of normal OR 3x upper limit of normal with hepatic injury - discontinue therapy
			• **Dosage Forms:** Oral (tablet)

Endothelin Receptor Antagonist - Drug Class Review
High-Yield Med Reviews

Generic Name	Brand Name	Indication(s) or Uses	Notes
Macitentan	Opsumit	• Pulmonary arterial hypertension	• **Dosing (Adult):** – Oral 10 mg daily • **Dosing (Peds):** – Not routinely used • **CYP450 Interactions:** Substrate CYP2C9, 3A4; Induces CYP2C9, 3A4 • **Renal or Hepatic Dose Adjustments:** – AST/ALT above 3x upper limit of normal - discontinue therapy – Child-Pugh class B or C - Not recommended • **Dosage Forms:** Oral (tablet)

High-Yield Clinical Knowledge

- **Endothelin Activity**
  - Endothelin has broad effects throughout the body, but concerning pulmonary arterial hypertension, it causes dose-dependent vasoconstriction in vascular beds.
  - These effects are counterbalanced by prostacyclin and nitric oxide, which are also other therapeutic targets in pulmonary hypertension.
- **Hepatic Injury**
  - The use of bosentan is associated with an increased risk of hepatotoxicity, initially manifesting as increases in hepatic enzymes.
  - This occurs due to bile salt retention and its resulting cytotoxic action on hepatocytes due to its competition with bosentan for biliary excretion of bile salts.
  - Baseline and monthly liver enzyme and liver function tests are required during bosentan therapy.
- **Teratogens**
  - All endothelin receptor antagonists are teratogens and are contraindicated in pregnancy.
  - Female patients must participate in a prescription monitoring program (REMS) to receive macitentan.
  - Documentation of a negative pregnancy test is required before initiation, and compliance with two forms of contraception is necessary while taking endothelin receptor antagonists.
- **Dose-Dependent Effects**
  - The endothelin receptor antagonists all exhibit a dose-dependent effect on functional capacity, and patients should be titrated to maximum tolerable doses.
  - Common dose-limiting adverse events include hypotension, tachycardia, flushing, and headaches.
- **Drug Interactions**
  - Bosentan and macitentan are inducers of CYP2C9 and 3A4, leading to numerous drug interactions, including necessary concomitant medications for pulmonary hypertension patients, including oral contraceptives (these agents are teratogens), warfarin, cyclosporine, and glyburide.

HIGH-YIELD BOARD EXAM ESSENTIALS
- **CLASSIC AGENTS:** Ambrisentan, bosentan, macitentan
- **DRUG CLASS:** Endothelin receptor antagonist
- **INDICATIONS:** Pulmonary arterial hypertension
- **MECHANISM:** Antagonists of endothelin-A and endothelin-B receptors, preventing endothelin-induced vasoconstriction of these vessels.
- **SIDE EFFECTS:** Hypotension, tachycardia, flushing, and headaches.
- **CLINICAL PEARLS:** All endothelin receptor antagonists are teratogens and are contraindicated in pregnancy. Female patients must participate in a prescription monitoring program (REMS) to receive macitentan.

High-Yield Basic Pharmacology

- **Mechanism of Action**
  - Sensitizes soluble guanylate cyclase (sGC) to endogenous nitric oxide and directly stimulates sGC independent from nitric oxide.
- **Cigarette Smoke**
  - The metabolism of riociguat and its M1 metabolite is accomplished, in part, by CYP1A1.
  - Polycyclic aromatic hydrocarbons, a component of cigarette smoke, are potent inducers of CYP1A1 and may induce the metabolism of riociguat.
  - Although patients with pulmonary arterial hypertension should not smoke, those regularly exposed to secondhand smoke may also experience induction of CYP1A1.

Primary Net Benefit

- Riociguat is an alternative agent for select patients with pulmonary arterial hypertension, whereas vericiguat has been associated with reductions in heart-failure-associated hospitalizations.

Guanylate Cyclase Stimulator - Drug Class Review			
High-Yield Med Reviews			
Mechanism of Action: *Sensitizes soluble guanylate cyclase (sGC) to endogenous nitric oxide and directly stimulates sGC independent from nitric oxide.*			
Class Effects: Significant hypotension can result from either agent, and they are contraindicated in pregnant women or with PDE5 inhibitors.			
Generic Name	**Brand Name**	**Indication(s) or Uses**	**Notes**

Riociguat	Adempas	• Pulmonary arterial hypertension	• **Dosing (Adult):**
			  – Oral 0.5 to 2.5 mg TID
			• **Dosing (Peds):**
			  – Not routinely used
			• **CYP450 Interactions:** Substrate CYP2C8, 3A4, P-gp
			• **Renal or Hepatic Dose Adjustments:**
			  – GFR less than 15 mL/minute - Not recommended
			  – Child-Pugh class C - Not recommended
			• **Dosage Forms:** Oral (Tablet)

Vericiguat	Verquvo	• Heart failure with reduced ejection fraction	• **Dosing (Adult):**
			  – Oral 2.5 to 10 mg daily
			• **Dosing (Peds):**
			  – Not routinely used
			• **CYP450 Interactions:** Substrate P-gp
			• **Renal or Hepatic Dose Adjustments:** None
			• **Dosage Forms:** Oral (tablet)

High-Yield Clinical Knowledge

- **Pregnancy**
  - Riociguat is contraindicated in pregnancy as teratogenic effects have been observed.
  - Female patients in whom riociguat is considered must go through a medication safety monitoring program (REMS program) to receive the drug.

- **Adverse Events**
  - Common adverse events associated with riociguat therapy include palpitations, headache, dysphagia, epistaxis, abdominal distension, nausea/vomiting/diarrhea, and anemia.
- **Continued Compliance**
  - Strict compliance with riociguat is required, as patients who miss therapy for three or more days must restart at a lower dose.
  - The hazard of skipping doses is the excess risk of symptomatic hypotension.
- **Vericiguat In Heart Failure**
  - Vericiguat has been investigated for use in patients with heart failure and reduced ejection fraction (HFrEF) through the same mechanism of action to riociguat.
  - HFrEF is associated with dysregulation of the nitric oxide-sGC-cGMP pathway, leading to impairment in diastole and microvascular dysfunction.
  - The VICTORIA trial described below demonstrated a vericiguat associated reduction in the composite endpoint of cardiovascular death or hospitalization compared to placebo.
    - This observed benefit was driven by the reduction in hospitalizations for heart failure.
- **Drug Interactions**
  - Riociguat and vericiguat should not be used combined with nitroglycerin or PDE5 inhibitors (sildenafil, tadalafil) as severe hypotension may occur.
  - The concomitant use of vericiguat and nitrates is unclear as limited clinical experience with this drug exists, but it would be anticipated to lead to excess symptomatic hypotension.

HIGH-YIELD BOARD EXAM ESSENTIALS
- **CLASSIC AGENTS:** Riociguat, vericiguat
- **DRUG CLASS:** Guanylate cyclase stimulator
- **INDICATIONS:** HFrEF, pulmonary arterial hypertension
- **MECHANISM:** Sensitizes soluble guanylate cyclase (sGC) to endogenous nitric oxide and directly stimulates sGC independent from nitric oxide.
- **SIDE EFFECTS:** Palpitations, headache, dysphagia, epistaxis, abdominal distension, nausea/vomiting/diarrhea, and anemia
- **CLINICAL PEARLS:** Vericiguat has been investigated for use in patients with heart failure and reduced ejection fraction (HFrEF) through the same mechanism of action to riociguat.

High-Yield Basic Pharmacology

- **Mechanism of Action**
    - **Epoprostenol, Iloprost, Treprostinil**
        - Prostacyclin (PGI2) synthetic analogs induce pulmonary vascular smooth muscle relaxation, vasodilation, and inhibition of platelet aggregation.
    - **Selexipag**
        - Selective prostacyclin IP receptor agonist, increasing cAMP and relaxation of vascular smooth muscle causing pulmonary vasodilation
- **PGI2 Physiology**
    - Prostacyclin analogs and agonists directly modify this process by providing vascular vasodilation and inhibition of platelet aggregation, anti-inflammatory properties, and cytoprotective actions.

Primary Net Benefit

- Prostacyclin analogs and agonists induce pulmonary vasodilation, counteracting the physiology of pulmonary arterial hypertension, but due to administration complications and toxicities, are generally reserved for WHO functional class II or higher.

Synthetic Prostacyclin & Prostacyclin IP Receptor Agonist - Drug Class Review High-Yield Med Reviews			
Mechanism of Action: *See agents above.*			
Class Effects: Myalgias, jaw pain, nausea, diarrhea, abdominal pain, headaches, flushing, dizziness, and hypotension.			
Generic Name	**Brand Name**	**Indication(s) or Uses**	**Notes**

Epoprostenol	Flolan, Veletri	- Pulmonary arterial hypertension	- **Dosing (Adult):**
			  - IV initial 2 nanogram/kg/minute, titrated by 1-2 ng/kg/minute q15minutes until dose-limiting adverse events occur
			    - Target 25 to 40 ng/kg/minute
			  - Inhalation 20,000 ng/mL solution nebulized at 8mL/hour, titrating down q30min to q4h to 10,000 ng/mL, then 5,000 ng/mL, then 2,500 ng/mL
			- **Dosing (Peds):**
			  - IV initial 2 nanogram/kg/minute, titrated by 1-2 ng/kg/minute q15minutes until dose-limiting adverse events occur
			    - Target 25 to 40 ng/kg/minute
			  - Continuous nebulization 20 to 50 ng/kg/minute
			- **CYP450 Interactions:** None
			- **Renal or Hepatic Dose Adjustments:** None
			- **Dosage Forms:** IV (solution)

Synthetic Prostacyclin & Prostacyclin IP Receptor Agonist - Drug Class Review
High-Yield Med Reviews

Generic Name	Brand Name	Indication(s) or Uses	Notes

Iloprost	Ventavis	▪ Pulmonary arterial hypertension	▪ **Dosing (Adult):**
			  – Inhalation 2.5 mcg/dose, increased to 5 mcg/dose administered 6 to 9 times daily no sooner than q2h while awake
			    ▪ Maximum 45 mcg/day
			▪ **Dosing (Peds):**
			  – Inhalation 2.5 mcg/dose, increased to 5 mcg/dose administered 6 to 9 times daily no sooner than q2h while awake
			    ▪ Maximum 45 mcg/day
			  – Inhalation 0.5 mcg/kg over 10 minutes, increased q10minutes to 2 mcg/kg
			▪ **CYP450 Interactions:** None
			▪ **Renal or Hepatic Dose Adjustments:**
			  – Child-Pugh class B or C - Increase dosing interval to q3-4h
			▪ **Dosage Forms:** Inhalation solution

Treprostinil	Orenitram
	Remodulin
	Tyvaso
		▪ Pulmonary arterial hypertension	▪ **Dosing (Adult):**
			  – Inhalation 18 mcg QID while awake, titrated by 18 mcg q1-2weeks to maximum 54 mcg/dose QID while awake
			  – Oral 0.125 mg q8h, titrated by 0.125 mg/dose q3-4days to target 8 mg TID
			  – Oral 0.25 mg q12h, titrated by 0.25 or 0.5 mg/dose q3-4days to target 8 mg TID
			  – IV/SQ 1.25 nanogram/kg/minute, titrated by 1.25 nanogram/kg/minute q1week for 4 weeks, then 2.5 nanogram/kg/minute q1week to target dose of 40 to 80 ng/kg/minute
			▪ **Dosing (Peds):**
			  – Not routinely used
			▪ **CYP450 Interactions:** Substrate CYP2C8, 2C9
			▪ **Renal or Hepatic Dose Adjustments:**
			  – Oral dosage form only -
			    ▪ Child-Pugh class B - Avoid use
			    ▪ Child-Pugh class C - Contraindicated
			▪ **Dosage Forms:** Inhalation solution, IV solution

Selexipag	Uptravi	▪ Pulmonary arterial hypertension	▪ **Dosing (Adult):**
			  – Oral 200 to 1,600 mcg BID
			▪ **Dosing (Peds):**
			  – Not routinely used
			▪ **CYP450 Interactions:** Substrate CYP2C8, 3A4
			▪ **Renal or Hepatic Dose Adjustments:**
			  – Child-Pugh class B - Administer once daily
			  – Child-Pugh class C - Avoid use
			▪ **Dosage Forms:** Oral (tablet)

High-Yield Clinical Knowledge

- **Epoprostenol Administration**
  - Epoprostenol requires continuous IV infusion, including as outpatients.
  - After initiation and dose titration in an acute care setting, patients are discharged home with a central venous catheter and pump.
- **Short Half-Life**
  - The synthetic PGI2 epoprostenol has a very short half-life of 3 to 5 minutes, necessitating continuous IV infusion, including as outpatients.
  - Patients must have backup supplies of medication cartridges to prevent administration gaps, which can lead to potentially life-threatening rebound pulmonary vasoconstriction.
  - Treprostinil has a longer half-life permitting subcutaneous administration, which can be limited due to injection site reactions.
    - In patients who cannot tolerate subcutaneous site reaction, IV administration of treprostinil is permissible.
    - However, transitioning between dosage forms must be conducted under expert observation, as acute decompensations and rebound pulmonary vasoconstriction are possible adverse events.
- **Inhalation Administration**
  - In contrast to the other prostacyclin analogs, iloprost and treprostinil may be administered via inhalation.
  - Iloprost must be administered six to up to 9 times per day, each taking up to 10 minutes to administer, and with each administration approximately 2 hours apart over the waking hours.
  - Treprostinil is administered using three inhalations four times daily during waking hours.
    - Similar to the other prostacyclin analogs, gaps in administration can lead to acute decompensations and rebound pulmonary vasoconstriction.
- **Dose Titration**
  - The prostacyclin analogs and agonists must be slowly titrated to the maximum tolerable doses to achieve the therapeutic benefits.
- **Class Adverse Events**
  - Common adverse events observed with each of these agents include myalgias, jaw pain, nausea, diarrhea, abdominal pain, headaches, flushing, dizziness, and hypotension.
  - These effects are dose-dependent but dissipate over time with continued exposure and administration.
- **Conventional PAH Therapy**
  - The conventional therapeutic approach to managing pulmonary arterial hypertension includes oral anticoagulation, diuresis, digoxin, and supplemental oxygen therapy.
  - Calcium channel blockers may be appropriate in selected patients where a positive acute vasoreactivity test is observed.
  - Combination drug therapy targeting numerous physiologic pathways is a common approach in managing pulmonary arterial hypertension and is associated with reduced time to clinical failure and hospitalizations.

HIGH-YIELD BOARD EXAM ESSENTIALS

- **CLASSIC AGENTS:** Epoprostenol, iloprost, treprostinil, selexipag
- **DRUG CLASS:** Synthetic prostacyclin & prostacyclin IP receptor agonist
- **INDICATIONS:** Pulmonary arterial hypertension
- **MECHANISM:** Epoprostenol, Iloprost, Treprostinil - Prostacyclin (PGI2) synthetic analogs induce pulmonary vascular smooth muscle relaxation, vasodilation, and inhibition of platelet aggregation. Selexipag - Selective prostacyclin IP receptor agonist, increasing cAMP and vascular smooth muscle relaxation causing pulmonary vasodilation.
- **SIDE EFFECTS:** Myalgias, jaw pain, nausea, diarrhea, abdominal pain, headaches, flushing, dizziness, and hypotension.
- **CLINICAL PEARLS:** In contrast to the other prostacyclin analogs, iloprost and treprostinil may be administered via inhalation. Iloprost must be administered six to up to 9 times per day, each taking up to 10 minutes to administer, and with each administration approximately 2 hours apart over the waking hours. Treprostinil is administered using three inhalations four times daily during waking hours.

High-Yield Basic Pharmacology

- Herb specific with many uncertain mechanisms that would be tested on a board exam.

Primary Overall Net Benefit

- A wide variety of herbal products patients may take for various indications often require detailed patient discussion to uncover their use. Essential considerations for disease and drug-interactions that are prevalent throughout herbal supplement use.

<table>
<tr><td colspan="4" align="center">**Herbals - Drug Class Review**
High-Yield Med Reviews</td></tr>
<tr><td colspan="4">**Mechanism of Action:** *Various mechanisms that have been described, for further details, reference accompanying text.*</td></tr>
<tr><td colspan="4">**Class Effects:** There exist a wide variety of herbal products patients may take for various indications that often require detailed patient discussion to uncover their use. Essential considerations for disease and drug-interactions that are prevalent throughout herbal supplement use.</td></tr>
<tr><td>**Generic Name**</td><td>**Brand Name**</td><td>**Indication(s) or Uses**</td><td>**Notes**</td></tr>
<tr>
<td>**Coenzyme Q10**</td>
<td>Acitve Q, H2Q, Q-Gel</td>
<td>- Bone and joint health</td>
<td>
- **Dosing (Adult):**
  – Oral 300 mg/day
- **Dosing (Peds):**
  – Not routinely used
- **CYP450 Interactions:** None
- **Renal or Hepatic Dose Adjustments:** None
- **Dosage Forms:** Oral (capsule, liquid)
</td>
</tr>
<tr>
<td>**Echinacea**</td>
<td>Numerous branded products</td>
<td>- Prophylaxis for common cold</td>
<td>
- **Dosing (Adult):**
  – Oral one capsule daily
- **Dosing (Peds):**
  – Not routinely used
- **CYP450 Interactions:** Substrate CYP3A4, a possible inducer of CYP3A4
- **Renal or Hepatic Dose Adjustments:** None
- **Dosage Forms:** Oral (capsule, liquid)
</td>
</tr>
<tr>
<td>**Garlic**</td>
<td>N/A</td>
<td>- Various indications including cancer, diabetes, dyslipidemia, hypertension, heart failure, liver disease, osteoarthritis and peripheral vascular disease</td>
<td>
- **Dosing (Adult):**
  – Oral 2 to 5 g fresh garlic
  – Oral 300 to 2,400 mg dried garlic, or garlic extract
- **Dosing (Peds):**
  – Not routinely used
- **CYP450 Interactions:** Substrate of CYP3A4, P-gp
- **Renal or Hepatic Dose Adjustments:** None
- **Dosage Forms:** Oral (capsule, extract)
</td>
</tr>
</table>

Herbals - Drug Class Review
High-Yield Med Reviews

Generic Name	Brand Name	Indication(s) or Uses	Notes

Ginkgo	Quercetin	• Various indications including heart disease, stroke, depression, dementia, and schizophrenia	• **Dosing (Adult):**
			  – Oral 120 to 240 mg
			• **Dosing (Peds):**
			  – Not routinely used
			• **CYP450 Interactions:** Inhibits CYP3A4; Induces CYP2C19
			• **Renal or Hepatic Dose Adjustments:** None
			• **Dosage Forms:** Oral (capsule, liquid)

Ginseng	N/A	• Various indications including adaptogenic, immunomodulation, antineoplastic, CNS, endocrine, ergogenic effects.	• **Dosing (Adult):**
			  – Oral 300 to 3,000 mg daily
			• **Dosing (Peds):**
			  – Not routinely used
			• **CYP450 Interactions:** None
			• **Renal or Hepatic Dose Adjustments:** None
			• **Dosage Forms:** Oral (capsule, liquid)

Glucosamine	Numerous brand products	• Osteoarthritis	• **Dosing (Adult):**
			  – Oral 1,500 mg daily
			• **Dosing (Peds):**
			  – Not routinely used
			• **CYP450 Interactions:** None
			• **Renal or Hepatic Dose Adjustments:** None
			• **Dosage Forms:** Oral (capsule, liquid)

Milk Thistle	Legalon SIL	• Suspected amatoxin poisoning	• **Dosing (Adult):**
			  – IV 5 mg/kg infused over 1 hour, followed by 20 mg/kg/day continuous infusion
			  – Oral 200 to 420 mg/day
			• **Dosing (Peds):**
			  – IV 5 mg/kg infused over 1 hour, followed by 20 mg/kg/day continuous infusion
			• **CYP450 Interactions:** Substrate CYP2C19, 2D6, 2E1, 3A4, P-gp
			• **Renal or Hepatic Dose Adjustments:** None
			• **Dosage Forms:** Oral (capsule, liquid), IV (solution)

St. John's Wort	Quercetin	• Depression	• **Dosing (Adult):**
			  – Oral 200 to 1,800 mg/day
			• **Dosing (Peds):**
			  – Not routinely used
			• **CYP450 Interactions:** Induces CYP1A2, 2C9, 2C19, 2E1, 3A4, P-gP
			• **Renal or Hepatic Dose Adjustments:** None
			• **Dosage Forms:** Oral (capsule, liquid)

Saw Palmetto	Numerous brand names	• Benign prostatic hyperplasia	• **Dosing (Adult):**
			  – Oral 320 mg/day
			• **Dosing (Peds):**
			  – Not routinely used
			• **CYP450 Interactions:** None
			• **Renal or Hepatic Dose Adjustments:** None
			• **Dosage Forms:** Oral (capsule, liquid)

High-Yield Clinical Knowledge

- **Coenzyme Q10**
    - Ubiquinone, otherwise known as coenzyme Q10, is a fundamental component of the electron transport chain, with complex II being the ubiquinone oxidoreductase enzyme.
    - Ubiquinone is an essential component of mitochondrial respiration and is found in tissues throughout the body, including the heart, kidney, liver, and skeletal muscle.
    - Coenzyme Q10 has been proposed to manage hypertension, heart failure, ischemic heart disease and reduce statin-associated myopathy.
- **Echinacea**
    - Echinacea describes formulations containing numerous components, including flavonoids, alkamides, polyacetylenes, water-soluble polysaccharides, and caffeoyl conjugates.
    - These components' relative content is not regulated and can range depending on the product, species of plant used, and manufacturing method.
    - Echinacea is well tolerated but often associated with a rash, particularly among pediatric patients, but resolves upon drug discontinuation.
    - The proposed uses of echinacea are to enhance immune system function and provide anti-inflammatory effects.
    - Echinacea may improve cold prevention but does not appear to shorten the cold duration.
- **Garlic**
    - The organic sulfur compounds of garlic, including S-allylcysteine, of which many products contain a standardized content.
    - Allicin-related compounds found in garlic are proposed to inhibit HMG-CoA reductase, as well as provide antioxidant properties.
    - Garlic may also provide a mild reduction in systolic and diastolic blood pressure.
    - Garlic possesses antiplatelet properties through its inhibition of thromboxane synthesis and stimulation of nitric oxide synthesis.
- **Ginkgo**
    - Ginkgo Biloba is produced as an extract from the ginkgo tree leaves and contains flavone glycosides, terpenoids, and bilobalide.
    - Ginkgo may promote tissue perfusion by decreasing blood viscosity and causing vasodilation by enhancing nitric oxide and the inhibition of platelet-activating factors.
    - There is limited high-quality data to support ginkgo use in this setting as meta-analysis shows no benefit compared to placebo.
    - Ginkgo supplementation is associated with significant improvements in cognitive performance and daily living activities among patients with dementia.
- **Glucosamine**
    - Glucosamine is a substrate in the production of articular cartilage and helps support cartilage function.
    - Supplementation of glucosamine is proposed to increase the available supply of glycosaminoglycan, necessary for forming new cartilage.
    - This is particularly important in diseases such as osteoarthritis, where the rate of production of new cartilage is exceeded by the speed of degradation of existing cartilage.
    - Glucosamine sulfate should be used, as the hydrochloride formulation has not been shown to provide any benefit.
- **Ginseng**
    - Ginseng and ginsenosides derived from species of Panax plants are used to improve immune function, mood improvements, antioxidant and anti-inflammatory effects, and improved insulin sensitivity.
    - The effects of ginseng in lowering postprandial glucose may be beneficial in some patients; however, evidence to support its use in other applications is limited.
    - Ginseng should be avoided or used with caution in patients with a psychiatric history and avoided in combination with lithium and other neuroleptics.
- **Milk Thistle**
    - Silymarin which is a component of the fruit and seeds of milk thistle plants is used for liver health and has some supportive chemotherapeutic effects.

- The primary use of silymarin compounds, namely silibinin, is to treat hepatotoxic mushroom ingestion (mainly Amanita phalloides mushrooms) but has also been used as an adjunct to acetaminophen, radiation, and ethanol associated hepatic injury.
- **St. John's Wort**
  - Hypericin is the active constituent of St. John's wort and may play a role in patients with mild to moderate depression as it possesses MAO-A and MAO-B inhibitor properties but also affects the reuptake of serotonin, norepinephrine, and dopamine.
  - Concomitant use of SSRIs and other antidepressants may lead to serotonin syndrome and should be used cautiously in depressed patients and concurrent drug therapy.
  - St. John's wort is associated with photosensitivity; thus, patients should be instructed to wear sunscreen and eye protection while in the sun.
  - Drug interactions are prevalent as St. John's wort is an inducer of CYP1A2, 2C9, and 3A4 and should be used with caution among patients taking warfarin, protease inhibitors, as well as digoxin and cyclosporine due to its p-glycoprotein induction.
- **Saw Palmetto**
  - Plant phytosterols and other aliphatic, polyphonic, and flavonoids found in saw palmetto may benefit patients with benign prostatic hyperplasia through inhibition of the enzymatic conversion of testosterone to dihydrotestosterone.

High-Yield Fast-Facts

- **Kratom**
  - Kratom, otherwise known as Mitragyna speciosa, is a popular herbal supplement that has opioid agonist properties. Its use is associate with characteristic opioid effects including analgesia, but also can be habit-forming and associated with an opioid withdrawal syndrome.

HIGH-YIELD BOARD EXAM ESSENTIALS
- **CLASSIC AGENTS:** Coenzyme Q10, echinacea, garlic, ginkgo, ginseng, glucosamine, milk thistle, St. John's Wort, saw palmetto
- **DRUG CLASS:** Herbals
- **INDICATIONS:** Bone and joint health (Coenzyme Q10), prophylaxis for the common cold (echinacea), various indications including cancer, diabetes, dyslipidemia, hypertension, heart failure, liver disease, osteoarthritis, and peripheral vascular disease (garlic), various indications including heart disease, stroke, depression, dementia, and schizophrenia (ginkgo), various indications including adaptogenic, immunomodulation, antineoplastic, cns, endocrine, ergogenic effects. (ginseng), osteoarthritis (glucosamine), suspected amatoxin poisoning (milk thistle), depression (St. John's Wort), benign prostatic hyperplasia (saw palmetto)
- **MECHANISM:** Various mechanisms that have been described, for further details, reference accompanying text.
- **SIDE EFFECTS:** Hypersensitivity, hepatotoxicity
- **CLINICAL PEARLS:** A wide variety of herbal products patients may take for various indications often require detailed patient discussion to uncover their use. Essential considerations for disease and drug-interactions that are prevalent throughout herbal supplement use.

High-Yield Basic Pharmacology

- **Vitamin A**
  - Retinoids are an essential component of normal morphogenesis, growth, and cell differentiation.
- **Cholecalciferol, Ergocalciferol**
  - Active forms of vitamin D, acting on vitamin D receptors in the GI, stimulating intestinal calcium absorption and transport, and actions in the bone, renal tissue, and parathyroid glands.
- **Vitamin E**
  - Tocopherols and tocotrienols primarily function as peroxyl radical scavengers and protect LDL and polyunsaturated fats from oxidation.
- **Phytonadione**
  - Provides exogenous vit K to allow gamma-carboxylation (activation) of coagulation factors (II, VII, IX, X)

Primary Net Benefit

- Fat-soluble vitamins are essential for a wide range of developmental and physiologic functions but are associated with clinically relevant toxicities with excessive dosing.

Fat-Soluble Vitamins - Drug Class Review High-Yield Med Reviews			
Mechanism of Action: *See agents above*			
Class Effects: Varies by agent.			
Generic Name	**Brand Name**	**Indication(s) or Uses**	**Notes**

Vitamin A	A-25, AFirm, Aquasol A, Gordons-Vite A, Vitamin A Fish	• Cystic fibrosis supplementation
		• Dietary supplement
			• **Dosing (Adult):**
			  – Oral - 3,000 to 6,000 units per day for 2 months
			  – IM 100,000 units daily for 3 days, then 50,000 units daily for 2 weeks
			• **Dosing (Peds):**
			  – Oral 1,500 to 10,000 units/day
			• **CYP450 Interactions:** None
			• **Renal or Hepatic Dose Adjustments:** None
			• **Dosage Forms:** Oral (capsule, tablet), Intramuscular (solution)

Vitamin A and D	A&D Jr., D-Natural-5	• Dietary supplement	• **Dosing (Adult):**
			  – Oral - One capsule daily
			• **Dosing (Peds):**
			  – Not routinely used
			• **CYP450 Interactions:** None
			• **Renal or Hepatic Dose Adjustments:** None
			• **Dosage Forms:** Oral (capsule, tablet)

Fat-Soluble Vitamins - Drug Class Review
High-Yield Med Reviews

Generic Name	Brand Name	Indication(s) or Uses	Notes

Cholecalciferol	Aqueous Vitamin D
	D3 Vitamin
	Decara
		• Hypoparathyroidism
		• Osteoporosis
		• Vitamin D deficiency
			• **Dosing (Adult):**
			  – Oral 800 to 7,000 units/day
			    ▪ Alternatively 50,000 units weekly
			• **Dosing (Peds):**
			  – Oral 400 to 10,000 units/day
			    ▪ Up to 50,000 units weekly
			• **CYP450 Interactions:** None
			• **Renal or Hepatic Dose Adjustments:** None
			• **Dosage Forms:** Oral (capsule, liquid, sublingual, tablet)

Ergocalciferol	Calcidol
	Calciferol
	Drisdol
	Ergocal
		• Osteoporosis
		• Vitamin D deficiency
			• **Dosing (Adult):**
			  – Oral 800 to 7,000 units/day
			    ▪ Alternatively, 50,000 units weekly
			• **Dosing (Peds):**
			  – Oral 400 to 10,000 units/day
			    ▪ Up to 50,000 units weekly
			• **CYP450 Interactions:** None
			• **Renal or Hepatic Dose Adjustments:** None
			• **Dosage Forms:** Oral (capsule, liquid, tablet)

Vitamin E	Alph-E,
	Aqueous Vitamin E, E-400, E-Max, E-Pherol, Formula E, Natural Vitamin E, SoluVitaE
		• Dietary supplement	• **Dosing (Adult):**
			  – Oral - One capsule daily
			• **Dosing (Peds):**
			  – Not routinely used
			• **CYP450 Interactions:** None
			• **Renal or Hepatic Dose Adjustments:** None
			• **Dosage Forms:** Oral (capsule, tablet)

Phytonadione	Mephyton	• Hypoprothrombinemia
		• Vitamin K deficiency bleeding (newborn)
		• Warfarin reversal
			• **Dosing (Adult):**
			  – Oral/SQ/IV 2.5 to 10 mg once
			• **Dosing (Peds):**
			  – Oral 0.3 to 5 mg daily
			  – IV 10 mcg/kg/day
			• **CYP450 Interactions:** None
			• **Renal or Hepatic Dose Adjustments:** None
			• **Dosage Forms:** Injection aqueous colloidal, Oral (tablet, solution)

High-Yield Clinical Knowledge

- **Retinoids**
  - The active form of vitamin A, retinaldehyde, is a retinoid that is required for normal vision.
  - Retinoic acid is an essential component of normal morphogenesis, growth, and cell differentiation.
  - Beta-carotene is a major dietary source of provitamin A, whereas preformed vitamin A is found in liver fish, and eggs.
- **Vitamin D Sources**
  - The major source of vitamin D is skin exposure to ultraviolet B radiation from sunlight.

- Plant-derived vitamin D (vitamin D2) and vitamin D3 are present in the typical American diet and supplemented through fortification of various foods.
  - Vitamin D2, or ergocalciferol, requires activation, whereas cholecalciferol is in the active vitamin D3 format.
- Ergocalciferol is also less avidly bound to transport proteins, is not as well absorbed, and has a shorter half-life than cholecalciferol.

- **Vitamin E**
  - All stereoisomers of tocopherols and tocotrienols are classified as vitamin E that primarily function as peroxyl radical scavengers and protect LDL and polyunsaturated fats from oxidation.
  - Vitamin E deficiency is extremely rare but associated with severe and prolonged malabsorptive diseases such as celiac disease or after bariatric surgery.
  - High doses of vitamin E may reduce platelet aggregation and interfere with vitamin K metabolism and should not be used with concomitant warfarin, aspirin, or thienopyridines.

- **Vitamin K**
  - Vitamin K exists in two natural forms: vitamin K1 (phytonadione) and vitamin K2 (menaquinones).
  - Dietary sources of vitamin K included green leafy vegetables, as well as liver and vegetable oils.
  - Newborn infants are susceptible to vitamin K deficiency and increased risk of hemorrhage due to low vitamin K fat stores and low vitamin K content in breast milk.
  - Vitamin K is routinely given prophylactically at delivery to newborn infants.

- **Vitamin A Deficiency**
  - In North America, vitamin A deficiency is rare, but when present, it can lead to vision issues and blindness, compromise barriers, innate and acquired immune function, and protection against infections.

- **Vitamin A Toxicity**
  - Acute vitamin A toxicity causing increased intracranial pressure, vertigo, diplopia, seizures, exfoliative dermatitis, and bulging fontanels in children can result from excessive vitamin A intake.
    - Vitamin A toxicity was first documented by explorers of the Arctic who consumed polar bear liver.
  - Chronic vitamin A toxicity can also occur due to excessive intake and can also lead to intracranial pressure elevations, hyperlipidemia, hypercalcemia, bone demineralization, lymph node enlargement, dry skin, cheilosis, glossitis, vomiting, and alopecia.
  - High doses of beta-carotene have been associated with an increased risk of lung cancer in smokers.

- **Active Vitamin D**
  - Patients with chronic kidney disease cannot renally convert vitamin D to its active form of 1,25-hydroxyvitamin D (1,25(OH)D).
  - Without sufficient 1,25(OH)D, dysregulation of parathyroid hormone release allows for calcium excretion and diminished bone resorption.

- **Rickets**
  - Vitamin D deficiency can manifest as Rickets, consisting of muscle soreness, weakness, and bone pain.

- **Phytonadione IV Administration**
  - Phytonadione must be diluted and administered slowly over 1 hour.
  - Slow IV infusion is required to reduce the risk of an anaphylactoid reaction.
  - Subcutaneous administration should be limited to use when IV administration is unnecessary, but patients cannot tolerate oral phytonadione.
  - IM should be avoided in patients with coagulopathies due to the risk of hematoma and bleeding.

High-Yield Fast Facts

- **IV Suspension**
  - Parenteral phytonadione is an aqueous colloidal suspension of a castor oil derivative, dextrose, and benzyl alcohol.
  - These excipients have been attributed to the risk of anaphylactoid reactions associated with phytonadione use.

- **Sunshine**
  - Active vitamin D requires the conversion of 7-dehydrocholesterol to cholecalciferol (aka Vitamin D) by sunlight,
  - Cholecalciferol is then hydroxylated in the liver to form 25-OH-D and then converted to 1,25(OH)-D in the kidneys

---

HIGH-YIELD BOARD EXAM ESSENTIALS
- **CLASSIC AGENTS:** Vitamin A, Cholecalciferol, Ergocalciferol (Vitamin D), Vitamin E, Vitamin K (phytonadione)
- **DRUG CLASS:** Fat-soluble vitamins
- **INDICATIONS:** Hypoprothrombinemia (phytonadione), Vitamin K deficiency bleeding (newborn) (phytonadione), Warfarin reversal (phytonadione), Cystic fibrosis supplementation (vitamin A), Dietary supplement (vitamin A, vitamin A, and D, cholecalciferol, vitamin E), Hypoparathyroidism (cholecalciferol), Osteoporosis (cholecalciferol), Vitamin D deficiency (cholecalciferol)
- **MECHANISM:**
  - **Vitamin A** - Retinoids are an essential component of normal morphogenesis, growth, and cell differentiation.
  - **Cholecalciferol, Ergocalciferol** - Active forms of vitamin D, acting on vitamin D receptors in the GI, stimulating intestinal calcium absorption and transport, and actions in the bone, renal tissue, and parathyroid glands.
  - **Vitamin E** - Tocopherols and tocotrienols primarily function as peroxyl radical scavengers and protect LDL and polyunsaturated fats from oxidation.
  - **Phytonadione** - Provides exogenous vitamin K to allow gamma-carboxylation (activation) of coagulation factors (II, VII, IX, X).
- **SIDE EFFECTS:** Vertigo, diplopia, seizures, exfoliative dermatitis, and bulging fontanels
- **CLINICAL PEARLS:** All stereoisomers of tocopherols and tocotrienols are classified as vitamin E that primarily function as peroxyl radical scavengers and protect LDL and polyunsaturated fats from oxidation.

High-Yield Basic Pharmacology

- **Thiamine (B1)**
  - Necessary for the combination of thiamine pyrophosphate and ATP in carbohydrate metabolism.
- **Riboflavin (B2)**
  - Functions with flavoprotein enzymes necessary for tissue respiration and activation of pyridoxine activation.
- **Niacin (B3)**
  - Niacin decreases plasma and adipose-free fatty acids, increases lipolysis of triglycerides, and hepatic esterification of triglycerides, promoting chylomicron triglyceride removal from plasma.
  - Increases HDL by reversing cholesterol transport in hepatocytes by apolipoprotein A1.
- **Pantothenic acid (B5)**
  - Essential cofactor of coenzyme A synthesis.
- **Pyridoxine (B6)**
  - Supplementation overcomes inhibition of pyridoxal-5'-phosphate, restoring its action as a coenzyme for L-glutamic acid decarboxylase, facilitating the production of GABA from glutamate.
- **Biotin (B7)**
  - Coenzyme in gluconeogenesis, lipogenesis, and fatty acid synthesis.
- **Folic acid (B9)**
  - Necessary for purine and pyrimidine synthesis, erythropoiesis, and fetal neural tube development.
- **Cyanocobalamin (B12)**
  - Coenzyme for fat and carbohydrate metabolism and protein synthesis.
- **Vitamin C (Ascorbic acid)**
  - Acts as an electron donor used for collagen hydroxylation, carnitine biosynthesis, and amino acid biosynthesis and also required for iron absorption and storage.

Primary Net Benefit

- Water-soluble vitamins are rapidly excreted from the body with no way to store them effectively, thus requiring regular ingestion.

Water-Soluble Vitamins - Drug Class Review			
High-Yield Med Reviews			
Mechanism of Action: *See above*			
Class Effects: Water-soluble vitamins are rapidly excreted from the body with no way to store them effectively, thus requiring regular ingestion.			
Generic Name	**Brand Name**	**Indication(s) or Uses**	**Notes**

Thiamine (B1)	Betaxin, Thimiject	▪ Dietary supplement
		 ▪ Thiamine deficiency
			▪ **Dosing (Adult):**
			   – IV 50 to 500 mg q6-24h
			   – IM 5 to 250 mg q24h
			   – Oral 100 mg daily
			 ▪ **Dosing (Peds):**
			   – IV/IM 10 to 100 mg daily
			   – Oral 0.35 to 0.5 mg/kg/day
			 ▪ **CYP450 Interactions:** None
			 ▪ **Renal or Hepatic Dose Adjustments:** None
			 ▪ **Dosage Forms:** Oral (capsule, solution, tablet)

Water-Soluble Vitamins - Drug Class Review
- ### High-Yield Med Reviews

Generic Name	Brand Name	Indication(s) or Uses	Notes
Riboflavin (B2)	B-2-400	• Dietary supplement	• **Dosing (Adult):** Oral 100 to 400 mg q12-24h • **Dosing (Peds):** Oral 100 to 400 mg q24h • **CYP450 Interactions:** None • **Renal or Hepatic Dose Adjustments:** None • **Dosage Forms:** Oral (capsule, tablet)

Niacin (B3)	Niacor
	Niaspan
		• Dyslipidemia	**Dosing (Adult):**
			  – Oral (regular release) 250 mg daily
			    • Maximum 6 g total daily
			  – Oral (sustained or controlled release) 250 to 750 mg daily.
			  – Oral (extended-release) 500 mg at bedtime
			    • Maximum 2 g daily
			Dosing (Peds): Age over 10 years
			  – Oral (regular release) 100 to 250 mg daily
			    • Maximum 10 mg/kg/day
			  – Oral (sustained or controlled release) 500 to 1500 mg daily
			    • Maximum 10 mg/kg/day
			CYP450 Interactions: None known
			Renal or Hepatic Dose Adjustments: None
			Dosage Forms: Oral (ER capsule, powder, IR tablet, SR tablet, ER tablet)

Pantothenic acid (B5)	Panto-250	• Dietary supplement	• **Dosing (Adult):**
			  – One tablet daily
			• **Dosing (Peds):**
			  – Not routinely used
			• **CYP450 Interactions:** None
			• **Renal or Hepatic Dose Adjustments:** None
			• **Dosage Forms:** Oral (capsule, tablet)

Pyridoxine (B6)	Neuro-K-250,
	Pyri 500
		• Dietary supplement
		• Toxic alcohol poisoning
		• Isoniazid poisoning
		• Peripheral neuropathy
			• **Dosing (Adult):**
			  – IM/IV/Oral 10 to 20 mg/day
			  – IV 5,000 mg infused at 500 to 1,000 mg/minute until seizures stop
			• **Dosing (Peds):**
			  – IM/IV/Oral 5 to 25 mg/day
			  – IV 70 mg/kg infused at 500 to 1,000 mg/minute until seizures stop
			• **CYP450 Interactions:** None
			• **Renal or Hepatic Dose Adjustments:** None
			• **Dosage Forms:** Oral (capsule, solution, tablet)

Biotin (B7)	Biotin Extra Strength,
	Meribin
		• Dietary supplement	• **Dosing (Adult):**
			  – Oral once daily
			• **Dosing (Peds):**
			  – Oral 5 to 20 mg daily
			• **CYP450 Interactions:** None
			• **Renal or Hepatic Dose Adjustments:** None
			• **Dosage Forms:** Oral (capsule, solution, tablet)

Water-Soluble Vitamins - Drug Class Review
High-Yield Med Reviews

Generic Name	Brand Name	Indication(s) or Uses	Notes

Folate (B9)	FA-8	• Dietary supplement
		• Megaloblastic and macrocytic anemia
		• Methanol poisoning
		• Prevention of neural tube defects
			• **Dosing (Adult):**
			  – IV/IM/SQ/Oral 0.4 to 5 mg daily
			  – IV 50 to 70 mg IV q4h
			• **Dosing (Peds):**
			  – IV/IM/SQ/Oral 0.1 to 1 mg daily
			• **CYP450 Interactions:** None
			• **Renal or Hepatic Dose Adjustments:** None
			• **Dosage Forms:** Oral (capsule, tablet), IV (solution)

Cyanocobalamin (B12)	B12 Compliance Injection, Nascobal	• Dietary supplement
		• Pernicious anemia
			• **Dosing (Adult):**
			  – Oral 500 to 2,000 mcg daily
			  – IM/SQ 100 to 1,000 mcg daily to monthly
			• **Dosing (Peds):**
			  – IM/SQ 100 mcg daily to monthly
			  – Oral 500 to 2,000 mcg daily
			• **CYP450 Interactions:** None
			• **Renal or Hepatic Dose Adjustments:** None
			• **Dosage Forms:** Oral (capsule, solution, lozenge, tablet), IV (solution), Nasal (solution)

Vitamin C (ascorbic acid)	Ascocid, Ascor, Fruit C, Ortho-CS, Vita-C	• Dietary supplement
		• Burns
		• Methemoglobinemia
		• Scurvy
			• **Dosing (Adult):**
			  – Oral 100 to 1,500 mg daily
			  – IM/SQ/IV 70 to 1,500 mg q6-24h
			• **Dosing (Peds):**
			  – Oral 100 mg daily
			  – IV 15 to 25 mg/kg/day maximum 80 mg/day
			• **CYP450 Interactions:** None
			• **Renal or Hepatic Dose Adjustments:** None
			• **Dosage Forms:** Oral (capsule, solution, liquid, packet, powder, tablet, wafer), IV (solution)

High-Yield Clinical Knowledge

- **Recommended Daily Allowances**
  - The National Academy of Sciences of the National Research Council initially published to help meet the nutritional needs of 97.5% of healthy individuals in America.
    - Normally recommended dietary intakes are usually higher for pregnant and lactating patients than patients who are otherwise not pregnant.
  - Many water-soluble vitamins can be adequately acquired through normal healthy diets. Patients should attempt dietary modifications prior to supplementation unless they have a compelling indication.
  - RDA for thiamine is between 1.1 and 1.2 mg/day, pyridoxine 1.3 mg/day, folate 400 mcg/day, and cyanocobalamin 2.4 mcg/day.
    - Common nutritional sources of B vitamins include meat, whole grains, cereals, dark-green leafy vegetables, and dairy products.
  - For vitamin C, the RDA is 70 to 90 mg per day.
    - Sources of vitamin C citrus fruits, red pepper, broccoli, and mango.

- **Wernicke Encephalopathy**
  - Wernicke encephalopathy (WE) is the clinical triad of ophthalmoparesis with nystagmus, ataxia, and confusion caused by rapid glucose loading without thiamine.
  - For the treatment of WE, thiamine should be given IV at a dose of 500 mg q8h for three days, followed by 250 mg IV q24h for five days.
- **Isoniazid-Pyridoxine Supplementation**
  - Isoniazid is frequently administered with pyridoxine to limit neurological adverse events associated with its use.
    - Without pyridoxine, the risk of peripheral neuropathies of the hands and feet is approximately 2% but is much higher in patients who are slow acetylators, those with diabetes, or pre-existing anemia.
- **Thiamine**
  - Thiamine is an essential cofactor of numerous steps in the citric acid cycle and the pentose phosphate pathway.
  - Vitamin B1 deficiency is associated with anorexia and weight loss, but severe manifestations include mental status changes and cardiovascular effects.
  - Thiamine deficiency is associated with high output heart failure (also known as wet beriberi) and Wernicke-Korsakoff Syndrome (dry beriberi).
- **Increasing HDL**
  - Niacin is primarily considered to be an add-on agent to increase HDL.
    - The clinical impact of this augmentation has not been significant, and niacin is not generally recommended to be added to lipid pharmacotherapy.
- **Pyridoxine**
  - Vitamin B6 (pyridoxine) is a precursor to pyridoxal essential for the synthesis of GABA and heme.
  - Empiric dosing for suspected hydrazine ingestion is 5 g, which equates to 50 vials.
  - For known isoniazid ingestions, pyridoxine should be dosed 1:1; however, empiric doses of 5 g (70 mg/kg in children) are appropriate.
  - Pyridoxal-5'-phosphate is a cofactor in the detoxification of ethylene glycol toxic metabolites. Doses of 100 mg per day are adequate.
- **Riboflavin**
  - Vitamin B2 (riboflavin) is necessary for normal tissue respiration and the flavoenzymes are important cofactor to activate pyridoxine and conversion of tryptophan to niacin.
- **Niacin**
  - Deficiency of niacin is associated with pellagra which is characterized by appetite loss, weakness, irritability, abdominal pain and vomiting, as well as bright red glossitis, and a characteristic skin rash that is pigmented and scaling.
  - Nicotinamide or nicotinic acid 100-200 mg three times daily for 5 days is an effective treatment of pellagra.
- **Niacin Vs Niacinamide**
  - At appropriate therapeutic doses, niacin is capable of lowering LDL; however, niacinamide has no lipid-lowering effect.
  - Niacinamide is the amide derivative of niacin.
- **Cyanocobalamin**
  - Vitamin B12 (cyanocobalamin) is a coenzyme for fat and carbohydrate metabolism and protein synthesis.
  - Deficiencies of vitamin B12 may result from intrinsic factor deficiency or disruption in the gastric anatomy, such as in patients with gastric bypass surgery.
- **Ascorbic Acid**
  - Vitamin C (ascorbic acid) acts as an electron donor used for collagen hydroxylation, carnitine biosynthesis, and amino acid biosynthesis and is also required for iron absorption and storage.
- **Folic acid**
  - Vitamin B9 (folic acid) necessary for purine and pyrimidine synthesis, erythropoiesis, and fetal neural tube development.
  - Inadequate dietary intake can increase homocysteine and increase risk of cardiovascular events and lead to megaloblastic anemia.

- Folic acid is essential to prevent neural tube defects during fetal development.
    - While folic acid 400 mcg reduces this risk, in patients who've given birth to children with neural tube defects, the dose is increased to 1 to 4 mg/day.
  - Folic acid supplementation is also recommended for therapy with methotrexate, 5-FU, trimethoprim/sulfamethoxazole, sulfasalazine, phenytoin, oral contraceptives for chronic alcoholics.
- **PPIs and B12**
    - Omeprazole, when used chronically, is associated with decreased absorption of vitamin B12.

HIGH-YIELD BOARD EXAM ESSENTIALS

- **CLASSIC AGENTS:** Thiamine (B1), Riboflavin (B2), Niacin (B3), Pantothenic acid (B5), Pyridoxine (B6), Biotin (B7), Folic acid (B9), Cyanocobalamin (B12), Vitamin C
- **DRUG CLASS:** Water-soluble vitamins
- **INDICATIONS:** Burns (vitamin C), Dietary supplement (thiamine, riboflavin, niacin, pantothenic acid, pyridoxine, biotin, folic acid, cyanocobalamin, vitamin C), Dyslipidemia (niacin), Isoniazid poisoning (pyridoxine), Megaloblastic and macrocytic anemia (pyridoxine), Methemoglobinemia (pyridoxine), Peripheral neuropathy (pyridoxine), Pernicious anemia (cyanocobalamin), Prevention of neural tube defects (folic acid), Scurvy (vitamin C), Thiamine deficiency (thiamine), Toxic alcohol poisoning (thiamine, pyridoxine)
- **MECHANISM:**
    - **Thiamine (B1)** - Necessary for the combination of thiamine pyrophosphate and ATP in carbohydrate metabolism.
    - **Riboflavin (B2)** - Functions with flavoprotein enzymes necessary for tissue respiration and activation of pyridoxine activation.
    - **Niacin (B3)** - Niacin decreases plasma and adipose-free fatty acids, increases lipolysis of triglycerides, and hepatic esterification of triglycerides, promoting chylomicron triglyceride removal from plasma. Increases HDL by reversing cholesterol transport in hepatocytes by apolipoprotein A1.
    - **Pantothenic acid (B5)** - Essential cofactor of coenzyme A synthesis.
    - **Pyridoxine (B6)** - Supplementation overcomes inhibition of pyridoxal-5'-phosphate, restoring its action as a coenzyme for L-glutamic acid decarboxylase, facilitating the production of GABA from glutamate.
    - **Biotin (B7)** - Coenzyme in gluconeogenesis, lipogenesis, and fatty acid synthesis.
    - **Folic acid (B9)** - Necessary for purine and pyrimidine synthesis, erythropoiesis, and fetal neural tube development.
    - **Cyanocobalamin (B12)** - Coenzyme for fat and carbohydrate metabolism and protein synthesis.
    - **Vitamin C (Ascorbic acid)** - Acts as an electron donor used for collagen hydroxylation, carnitine biosynthesis, and amino acid biosynthesis, also required for iron absorption and storage.
- **SIDE EFFECTS:** Flushing (niacin)
- **CLINICAL PEARLS:** Thiamine is an essential cofactor of numerous steps in the citric acid cycle and the pentose phosphate pathway.

High-Yield Basic Pharmacology

- **Acamprosate**
  - Modulates the action of glutamate at the NMDA receptor, modulating alcohol cravings.
- **Disulfiram**
  - Inhibits aldehyde dehydrogenase causing an accumulation of acetaldehyde.
- **Naltrexone**
  - Competitive opioid receptor (including mu, kappa, and delta) antagonists

Primary Net Benefit

- Acamprosate and naltrexone are well-tolerated options for alcohol use disorder and have primarily replaced disulfiram.

Alcohol Abuse Deterrents - Drug Class Review High-Yield Med Reviews			
Mechanism of Action: *Acamprosate* - Modulates the action of glutamate at the NMDA receptor, modulating alcohol cravings. *Disulfiram* - Inhibits aldehyde dehydrogenase, causing an accumulation of acetaldehyde. *Naltrexone* - Competitive opioid receptor (including mu, kappa, and delta) antagonists.			
Class Effects: Acamprosate and naltrexone are well-tolerated options for alcohol use disorder and have largely replaced disulfiram.			
Generic Name	**Brand Name**	**Indication(s) or Uses**	**Notes**

Acamprosate	Campral	• Alcohol use disorder	• **Dosing (Adult):**
			  – Oral 666 mg two to three times daily
			• **Dosing (Peds):**
			  – Not routinely used
			• **CYP450 Interactions:** None
			• **Renal or Hepatic Dose Adjustments:**
			  – GFR 30 to 50
			• **Dosage Forms:** Oral (tablet), Suspension for intramuscular injection

Naltrexone	Vivitrol	• Alcohol use disorder
		• Opioid use disorder
			• **Dosing (Adult):**
			  – Oral 50 to 100 mg/day
			  – IM 380 mg q4weeks
			• **Dosing (Peds):**
			  – Not routinely used
			• **CYP450 Interactions:** None
			• **Renal or Hepatic Dose Adjustments:** None
			• **Dosage Forms:** Oral (tablet), Suspension for intramuscular injection

Disulfiram	Antabuse	• Alcohol use disorder	• **Dosing (Adult):**
			  – Oral 125 to 500 mg daily
			• **Dosing (Peds):**
			  – Not routinely used
			• **CYP450 Interactions:** None
			• **Renal or Hepatic Dose Adjustments:** None
			• **Dosage Forms:** Oral (tablet)

High-Yield Clinical Knowledge

- **Disulfiram Like Agents**
    - Numerous medications can produce a disulfiram-like effect, including NMTT cephalosporins (cefazolin, cefotetan), chlorpropamide, griseofulvin, metronidazole, nitrofurantoin, procarbazine, and first-generation sulfonylureas.
- **Metal Chelating and CAD**
    - Disulfiram is metabolized to diethyldithiocarbamate (DDC), which is available in other countries as a chelating agent for nickel or copper chelation.
    - However, DDC is further metabolized to carbon disulfide, which has been associated with pyridoxine deficiency, seizures, atherosclerosis, and heart disease.
- **Alcohol Withdrawal**
    - Naltrexone does not induce alcohol withdrawal but could precipitate opioid withdrawal in patients taking opioids.
        - However, naltrexone should not be initiated in patients suffering from acute alcohol withdrawal.
    - Thorough patient history, including non-prescription/illicit drug use, must be conducted before initiation of naltrexone.
- **Disulfiram Reaction**
    - Disulfiram causes the accumulation of acetaldehyde upon consumption of ethanol due to preventing the function of aldehyde dehydrogenase, but not alcohol dehydrogenase.
    - The characteristic "disulfiram reaction" consists of flushing, headache, nausea/vomiting, chest pain, tachycardia, weakness, blurred vision, and hypotension.
        - As a result, disulfiram should be avoided in patients with a history of heart failure, arrhythmias, recent MI, or CAD risk factors.
        - Disulfiram is also associated with abrupt onset of respiratory depression, seizures, and death.
    - This effect can persist for up to 24 hours after a given dose of disulfiram.
- **Naltrexone for Alcohol Abstinence**
    - Naltrexone is available as an IM depot injection as adjunctive therapy in ethanol abstinence.
    - Opioid antagonism by naltrexone is proposed to inhibit central opioid-mediated ethanol craving, reduces ethanol intake and incidence of relapse.
    - Oral Bioavailability
        - Naltrexone has a wide range of bioavailability due to the first-pass metabolism between 5 and 60%.
        - This differs from other opioid-antagonists, including naloxone, which is minimally absorbed orally (bioavailability approximately 2%).
- **Pharmacogenomic Link**
    - The effectiveness of naltrexone appears to be related to the presence or absence of polymorphisms in the mu-opioid receptor gene, OPRM1.
    - Patients with Asn40Asp polymorphisms may experience a more pronounced response to naltrexone with a lower rate of relapse.

HIGH-YIELD BOARD EXAM ESSENTIALS

- **CLASSIC AGENTS:** Acamprosate, disulfiram, naltrexone
- **DRUG CLASS:** Alcohol abuse deterrents
- **INDICATIONS:** Alcohol use disorder, opioid use disorder (naltrexone)
- **MECHANISM:**
  - **Acamprosate** - Modulates the action of glutamate at the NMDA receptor, modulating alcohol cravings.
  - **Disulfiram** - Inhibits aldehyde dehydrogenase, causing an accumulation of acetaldehyde.
  - **Naltrexone** - Competitive opioid receptor (including mu, kappa, and delta) antagonists.
- **SIDE EFFECTS:** Disulfiram reaction (flushing, headache, nausea/vomiting, chest pain, tachycardia, weakness, blurred vision, and hypotension)
- **CLINICAL PEARLS:** Naltrexone is available as an IM depot injection as adjunctive therapy in ethanol abstinence. Opioid antagonism by naltrexone is proposed to inhibit central opioid-mediated ethanol craving, reduces ethanol intake and incidence of relapse.

High-Yield Basic Pharmacology

- **Atropine**
  - Competitive blockade of central and peripheral muscarinic receptors.
- **Pralidoxime**
  - Reactivated phosphorylated cholinesterases by displacing the offending agent from its binding site.
- **Physostigmine**
  - Inactivates plasma cholinesterases by binding to cholinesterases forming a carbamylated complex and releasing a leaving group. The carbamylated complex is then hydrolyzed, regenerating the enzymatic activity of cholinesterases
  - Duration of Physostigmine
    - The half-life of physostigmine is shorter than the duration of effect of many antimuscarinic xenobiotics. Repeat dosing may be necessary for recurrent antimuscarinic symptoms.
      - This characteristic is similar to flumazenil and naloxone, which have shorter durations of action than their targeted xenobiotics.
    - Atropine should be available at the bedside if cholinergic effects emerge.

Primary Overall Net Benefit

- Acute interventions for cholinergic toxicity (atropine/pralidoxime) or anticholinergic toxicity (physostigmine).

Atropine/Pralidoxime/Physostigmine - Drug Class Review
High-Yield Med Reviews

Mechanism of Action:
Atropine - *Competitive blockade of central and peripheral muscarinic receptors.*
Pralidoxime - *Reactivated phosphorylated cholinesterases by displacing the offending agent from its binding site.*
Physostigmine - *Inactivates plasma cholinesterases by binding to cholinesterases forming a carbamylated complex and releasing a leaving group. The carbamylated complex is then hydrolyzed, regenerating the enzymatic activity of cholinesterases.*

Class Effects: Acute interventions for cholinergic toxicity (atropine/pralidoxime) or anticholinergic toxicity (physostigmine).

Generic Name	Brand Name	Indication(s) or Uses	Notes

Atropine	AtroPen	• Bradycardia
		• Organophosphate or carbamate poisoning
			• **Dosing (Adult):**
			  – IV/IM/IO 0.5 to 1 mg q3-5minutes
			    • Cardiac arrest maximum 3 mg
			  – IV/IM/IO 3 to 5 mg IV repeated by doubling the dose q3-5minutes until clinical response achieved
			• **Dosing (Peds):**
			  – IV/IM/IO 0.02 mg/kg q3-5minutes
			    • Cardiac arrest maximum 3 mg
			  – IV/IM/IO 0.05 to 0.1 mg IV repeated by doubling the dose q3-5minutes until clinical response achieved
			• **CYP450 Interactions:** None
			• **Renal or Hepatic Dose Adjustments:** None
			• **Dosage Forms:** IV solution, Autoinjector kit

Atropine/Pralidoxime/Physostigmine - Drug Class Review
High-Yield Med Reviews

Generic Name	Brand Name	Indication(s) or Uses	Notes

Physostigmine	Antilirium	• Anticholinergic toxicity (except for TCAs)	• **Dosing (Adult):**
			  – IV 1 to 2 mg infused over 10 minutes until 2 mg reached or clinical response observed
			  – IM/IV/IO 0.2 to 2 mg q10-30min as needed
			• **Dosing (Peds):**
			  – IV 0.02 mg/kg infused over 10 minutes until
			    ▪ Maximum 0.5 to 2 mg/dose
			  – IM/IV/IO 0.02 mg/kg q10-30min as needed
			    ▪ Maximum 0.5 to 2 mg/dose
			• **CYP450 Interactions:** None
			• **Renal or Hepatic Dose Adjustments:** None
			• **Dosage Forms:** IV solution

Pralidoxime	2-Pam	• Organophosphate poisoning	• **Dosing (Adult):**
			  – IM 600 mg q15minutes until response or 1,800 mg total dose
			  – IV 30 mg/kg followed by 8 to 10 mg/kg/hour
			• **Dosing (Peds):**
			  – IM 15 mg/kg/dose mg q15minutes until response or 45 mg/kg mg total dose
			  – IV 30 mg/kg (maximum 2,000 mg) followed by 8 to 10 mg/kg/hour
			• **CYP450 Interactions:** None
			• **Renal or Hepatic Dose Adjustments:** None
			• **Dosage Forms:** IV solution, Autoinjector kit

High-Yield Clinical Knowledge

- **Anticholinergic Toxicity**
  - Anticholinergic toxicity can result from numerous drug classes, including antihistamines, antidepressants, antipsychotics, and atropine.
  - Common plant-based causes of anticholinergic toxicity include belladonna alkaloids, Amanita muscaria, Jimson weed, Deadly nightshade, and Mandrake.
- **Anticholinergic Toxidrome**
  - Classic antimuscarinic toxidrome: "Blind as a bat, Dry as a bone, Hot as a hare, Mad as a hatter, Red as a beet."
  - Anticholinergic toxidromes may present in three stages of toxicity:
    - **Induction phase:** peripheral anticholinergic effects.
    - **Stupor phase:** somnolence, restlessness, ataxia hyperthermia, hypertension.
    - **Delirium phase:** amnesia, confusion, hallucinations, incoherent speech.
  - Toxidrome symptoms can overlap with other organic diseases or other toxicities such as sympathomimetics.
- **Cholinergic Toxicity**
  - The organophosphate chemical weapons and pesticides are potential causes of cholinergic toxicity (malathion, parathion, sarin, soman, tabun, VX).
  - Other medications that can produce similar overdose effects include carbamates (donepezil, physostigmine, rivastigmine), cholinomimetics (bethanechol, pilocarpine), and nicotine.

- **Cholinergic Toxidrome**
  - Killer B's: Bronchorrhea, bronchospasm, bradycardia characterize cholinergic toxidrome.
  - SLUDGE: Salivation, lacrimation, urination, defecation, GI upset, emesis - is another mnemonic for signs of cholinergic toxicity.
  - Cholinergic toxicity results from acetylcholinesterase (AChE) inhibition, leading to excess acetylcholine mediated activation of muscarinic and nicotinic receptors.
  - Stages of Toxicity:
    - **Acute exposure:** Bronchorrhea, bronchospasm, bradycardia (Killer B's); Salivation, lacrimation, urination, defecation, GI distress, emesis (SLUDGE); miosis, seizures/fasciculation.
    - **Intermediate syndrome:** recurrent neuromuscular weakness, respiratory depression 24-96 hours after exposure.
    - Neuropathy and neuropsychological sequelae are delayed ranging from 1 week to several months after exposure.
- **Cholinergic Toxidrome Interventions**
  - Pralidoxime therapy can be beneficial in both organophosphate and carbamate exposure.
    - It is most effective in diethyl OP exposure (chlorpyrifos, diazinon).
  - Severe toxicity from carbamate insecticides typically only occurs after oral exposure, not dermal or respiratory exposures.
  - Atropine is a core treatment strategy for cholinergic toxicity and is aggressively dosed to the therapeutic endpoint of dry mucous membranes and resolution of respiratory distress.
    - Total atropine doses of up to 45 to 50 mg are typical for managing patients exposed to chemical weapons.
  - Atropine's tertiary amine structure permits its penetration to the blood-brain barrier.
    - Quaternary amines (glycopyrrolate) do not enter CNS.

High-Yield Fast-Facts

- **Atropine Induced Bradycardia**
  - Low doses, less than 0.5 mg, may cause paradoxical bradycardia.
- **Stockpiled**
  - Pralidoxime is available as an autoinjector, co-formulated with atropine. Atropine and pralidoxime are components of the Strategic National Stockpile.

HIGH-YIELD BOARD EXAM ESSENTIALS
- **CLASSIC AGENTS:** Atropine, pralidoxime, physostigmine
- **DRUG CLASS:** Antidotes
- **INDICATIONS:** Anticholinergic toxicity (physostigmine), cholinergic toxicity (atropine, pralidoxime)
- **MECHANISM:**
  - **Atropine** - Competitive blockade of central and peripheral muscarinic receptors.
  - **Pralidoxime** - Reactivated phosphorylated cholinesterases by displacing the offending agent from its binding site.
  - **Physostigmine** - Inactivates plasma cholinesterases by binding to cholinesterases forming a carbamylated complex and releasing a leaving group. The carbamylated complex is then hydrolyzed, regenerating the enzymatic activity of cholinesterases.
- **SIDE EFFECTS:** Anticholinergic toxicity (atropine), cholinergic toxicity (pralidoxime, physostigmine)
- **CLINICAL PEARLS:** Anticholinergic toxidrome - "Blind as a bat, Dry as a bone, Hot as a hare, Mad as a hatter, Red as a beet." Cholinergic toxicity - SLUDGE: Salivation, lacrimation, urination, defecation, GI upset, emesis - is another mnemonic for signs of cholinergic toxicity.

High-Yield Basic Pharmacology

- **Calcium-Dependent Calcium Release**
  - CCB and BB both ultimately prevent calcium-dependent calcium release from the sarcoplasmic reticulum leading to decreased cardiac contractility.
- **Calcium chloride, Calcium gluconate**
  - Increases calcium concentration gradient, allowing more intracellular calcium entry.
- **Glucagon**
  - Increases intracellular cAMP via specific glucagon binding sites (GTP-Gs) on the beta-adrenergic receptor.
- **Insulin Regular**
  - Shifts cardiac metabolism from fatty acid oxidation to carbohydrate metabolism and increases intracellular calcium by interfering with the sodium-calcium antiporter.
- **Intravenous fat emulsion**
  - Creates a "lipid sink" intravascular lipophilic compartment, which sequesters xenobiotics away from tissue binding sites

Primary Net Benefit

- BB and CCB overdose are associated with significant morbidity and mortality, non-specific reversal agents including calcium, glucagon, insulin, and intravenous fat emulsion may help support these patients' resuscitation.

Beta-Blocker and Calcium Channel Blocker Overdose - Drug Class Review			
High-Yield Med Reviews			
Mechanism of Action: *See above*			
Class Effects: BB and CCB overdose is associated with significant morbidity and mortality, non-specific reversal agents including calcium, glucagon, insulin, and intravenous fat emulsion may help support the resuscitation of these patients.			
Generic Name	**Brand Name**	**Indication(s) or Uses**	**Notes**

Calcium chloride	Calciject	• Cardiac arrest
		• Hyperkalemia
		• Hypocalcemia
		• Hypermagnesemia
			• **Dosing (Adult):**
			  – IV 20 mg/kg, max 1 to 2 g/dose q10-20 min
			• **Dosing (Peds):**
			  – IV 20 mg/kg, max 1 g/dose q10-20 min
			  – IV 0.5 to 2 mEq/kg/day
			• **CYP450 Interactions:** None
			• **Renal or Hepatic Dose Adjustments:** None
			• **Dosage Forms:** IV (solution)

Calcium gluconate	Cal-Glu	• Cardiac arrest
		• Hyperkalemia
		• Hypocalcemia
		• Hypermagnesemia
			• **Dosing (Adult):**
			  – IV 60 mg/kg q10-20 minutes as needed or 60 to 120 mg/kg/hour infusion
			  – IV 1,500 to 3,000 mg IV over 2-5 minutes
			  – IV 1,000 to 4,000 mg over 2-4 hours
			  – Oral 500 to 4,000 mg/day
			• **Dosing (Peds):**
			  – IV 0.5 to 4 mEq/kg/day (TPN)
			  – IV IV 60 mg/kg (maximum 3,000 mg/dose) q10-20minutes as needed
			  – Oral 500 mg/kg/day divided in 4 doses (maximum 1,000 mg/dose)
			• **CYP450 Interactions:** None
			• **Renal or Hepatic Dose Adjustments:** None
			• **Dosage Forms:** IV (solution), Oral (capsule, tablet)

Beta-Blocker and Calcium Channel Blocker Overdose - Drug Class Review
High-Yield Med Reviews

Generic Name	Brand Name	Indication(s) or Uses	Notes

Glucagon	Baqsimi, GlucaGen, Gvoke	▪ Anaphylaxis
		▪ BB or CCB overdose
		▪ Hypoglycemia
			▪ **Dosing (Adult):**
			  – IV Initial dose of 50 mcg/kg (3-5 mg)
			    ▪ Continuous infusion of 2-5 mg/hr is if positive clinical response.
			▪ **Dosing (Peds):**
			  – IV Initial dose of 50 mcg/kg (3-5 mg)
			    ▪ Continuous infusion of 0.05 to 0.1 mg/kg/hr is if positive clinical response.
			▪ **CYP450 Interactions:** None
			▪ **Renal or Hepatic Dose Adjustments:** None
			▪ **Dosage Forms:** IV (solution), Nasal powder

Insulin R	Humulin-R, Novolin-R	▪ BB or CCB overdose
		▪ Hypoglycemia
			▪ **Dosing (Adult):**
			  – IV 1 unit/kg bolus followed by 0.5 to 10 unit/kg/hour
			▪ **Dosing (Peds):**
			  – IV 1 unit/kg bolus followed by 0.5 to 10 unit/kg/hour
			▪ **CYP450 Interactions:** None
			▪ **Renal or Hepatic Dose Adjustments:** None
			▪ **Dosage Forms:** IV (solution)

Intravenous fat emulsion	Intralipid	▪ Local anesthetic systemic toxicity
		▪ Non-local anesthetic toxicity
			▪ **Dosing (Adult):**
			  – IV 1.5 mL/kg bolus followed by 0.25 to 0.5 mL/kg/minute for at least 10 minutes, up to 12 mL/kg in the first 60 minutes.
			▪ **Dosing (Peds):**
			  – See adult dosing
			▪ **CYP450 Interactions:** None
			▪ **Renal or Hepatic Dose Adjustments:** None
			▪ **Dosage Forms:** IV (emulsion)

High-Yield Clinical Knowledge

- **Dihydropyridine Vs. Non-Dihydropyridine Toxicity**
  - Dihydropyridine CCB toxicities are more likely than non-dihydropyridine toxicity to initially present with hypotension and reflex tachycardia.
  - Massive overdoses of dihydropyridine CCBs can mimic non-dihydropyridine toxicity.
  - Characteristic non-dihydropyridine CCB overdose manifests as bradycardia (prolonged PR interval or high-grade AV block), hypotension, and hyperglycemia.
- **Calcium**
  - Calcium chloride has 3x elemental calcium compared to calcium gluconate.
  - Mix with water-based lubricant for hydrofluoric acid dermal exposures.
  - Controversial role in digoxin or digitalis glycoside toxicity
  - Used to manage hypocalcemia from toxins known to form calcium salts: fluoride, citrate in blood products, ethylene glycol, phosphates
- **Glucagon**

- Glucagon has a wide range of acute uses, including hypoglycemia, anaphylaxis refractory to epinephrine, TCA overdose refractory to sodium bicarbonate, and BB overdose.
- In BB toxicity, glucagon can improve both chronotropy, inotropy, and coronary blood flow.
- The initial dose of 50 mcg/kg (3-5 mg) is recommended via slow IV push over 10 minutes.
  - Lower doses can paradoxically worsen bradycardia and hypotension.
  - The slow administration is essential to avoid dose and rate-dependent nausea and vomiting, which may compromise the patient's airway leading to aspiration and require advanced airway support.
- Continuous infusion of 2-5 mg/hr is used if a positive clinical response is observed.
- Tachyphylaxis can occur; increasing the infusion rate may be necessary.
- Administration: Slow IV administration over 10 minutes

- **Insulin**
  - CCBs inhibit pancreatic insulin release and create insulin resistance via GLUT-1 and PIK3 inhibition.
  - High doses of insulin replace the lack of insulin, improve cardiac carbohydrate metabolism, and increase intracellular calcium by interfering with the sodium-calcium antiporter.

- **Lipid**
  - Intralipid (intravenous fat emulsion) is used for local anesthetic systemic toxicity (LAST) and the treatment of numerous lipophilic xenobiotic toxicities.

- **Hyperglycemia or Normoglycemia**
  - Hyperglycemia is more common in CCB overdose and can be used as a predictor of the affecting agent to help guide therapeutic interventions.
    - CCB overdoses presenting with hyperglycemia are associated with higher mortality, and hyperglycemia is a poor prognostic sign.
  - BB toxicity is associated with either slight hypoglycemia or normal glucose.

- **Hyperinsulinemia Euglycemia**
  - An initial bolus of 1 unit/kg followed by infusion of 1 unit/kg/hr of insulin is recommended to treat CCB toxicity.
    - Although insulin's typical kinetics predicts a 15-30 minutes onset, the massive dose administered shortens the onset of action to approximately 2-5 minutes.
  - Continuous infusion of dextrose 10% or dextrose 50% may be necessary for euglycemia.

- **LAST Vs. Non-LAST**
  - Initially used in treating cardiac arrest due to local anesthetic toxicity (bupivacaine, mepivacaine, ropivacaine).
  - Non-local anesthetic (Non-LAST) xenobiotics that may respond to lipid therapy include bupropion, verapamil, propranolol, organic phosphorus compounds, and numerous other lipophilic agents.
  - Non-LAST dosing is lower than LAST with a maximum daily dose of 10 mL/kg.

HIGH-YIELD BOARD EXAM ESSENTIALS

- **CLASSIC AGENTS:** Calcium chloride, calcium gluconate, glucagon, insulin regular, intravenous fat emulsion
- **DRUG CLASS:** Antidotes
- **INDICATIONS:** Beta-blocker and calcium channel blocker overdose
- **MECHANISM:** Calcium chloride, Calcium gluconate - Increases calcium concentration gradient, allowing more intracellular calcium entry. Glucagon - Increases intracellular cAMP via specific glucagon binding sites (GTP-Gs) on the beta-adrenergic receptor. Insulin Regular - Shifts cardiac metabolism from fatty acid oxidation to carbohydrate metabolism and increases intracellular calcium by interfering with the sodium-calcium antiporter. Intravenous fat emulsion - Creates a "lipid sink" intravascular lipophilic compartment, which sequesters xenobiotics away from tissue binding sites.
- **SIDE EFFECTS:** Extravasation/soft tissue injury (calcium), vomiting (glucagon), hypoglycemia (insulin), fat emboli (fat emulsion)
- **CLINICAL PEARLS:** BB and CCB overdose is associated with significant morbidity and mortality, non-specific reversal agents including calcium, glucagon, insulin, and intravenous fat emulsion may help support the resuscitation of these patients.

High-Yield Basic Pharmacology

- **Mechanism of Action**
  - Fab immunoglobulin fragments bind to free digoxin, forming a digoxin-immune fragment complex, which is renally excreted, resulting in a decrease in serum digoxin concentration.
- **Administration**
  - DigiFAB should only be given via IV bolus in cardiac arrest; otherwise, it should be infused over 30 minutes.
- **Duration of Effect**
  - The serum half-life of DigiFAB is approximately 18 hours, which can increase tenfold in patients with impaired renal function.

Primary Overall Net Benefit

- Rapidly binds and neutralizes free digoxin in the plasma, establishing a concentration gradient and removing it from cardiac sites of action.

DigiFAB - Drug Class Review			
High-Yield Med Reviews			
Mechanism of Action: *Fab immunoglobulin fragments bind to free digoxin forming a digoxin-immune fragment complex, which is renally excreted, resulting in decreased serum digoxin concentration.*			
Class Effects: Rapidly binds and neutralizes free digoxin in the plasma, establishing a concentration gradient and removing it from cardiac sites of action.			
Generic Name	**Brand Name**	**Indication(s) or Uses**	**Notes**

Digoxin Immune FAB	DigiFAB	- Digoxin toxicity	- **Dosing (Adult):**
			  - Dose (in # of vials) = (Total digitalis body load in mg) / (0.5 mg of digitalis bound/vial)
			  - Dose (in # of vials) = [(Serum digoxin concentration in ng/mL) X (weight in kg)] / 100
			  - Empiric dosing - 10 to 20 vials
			- **Dosing (Peds):**
			  - Dose (in # of vials) = (Total digitalis body load in mg) / (0.5 mg of digitalis bound/vial)
			  - Dose (in # of vials) = [(Serum digoxin concentration in ng/mL) X (weight in kg)] / 100
			  - Empiric dosing - 10 to 20 vials
			- **CYP450 Interactions:** None
			- **Renal or Hepatic Dose Adjustments:** None
			- **Dosage Forms:** IV (solution)

High-Yield Clinical Knowledge

- **Rechecking Levels**
  - A follow-up digoxin level should NOT be obtained as total serum digoxin concentrations will rise precipitously following administration of DigiFAB.
  - Due to the presence of the Fab-digoxin complex, the bound Fab fragments cannot result in toxicity; this rise has no clinical significance.
  - Digoxin levels should not be ordered for at least 72 hours in patients with normal renal function and > 7 days in patients with severe renal dysfunction.
- **Indications**
  - DigiFAB is indicated in three broad class of digoxin toxicities:
  - Acute toxicity
    - Severe ventricular arrhythmias (ventricular tachycardia or fibrillation)
    - Progressive bradyarrhythmias (ex. atropine resistant symptomatic sinus bradycardia, or second-or-third-degree heart block)
    - Potassium concentration >5 mEq/L in patients with manifestations of severe cardiac glycoside toxicity (described above)
    - Acute ingestion of > 10 mg in an adult and > 4 mg in a child
  - Chronic toxicity / Acute on chronic toxicity
    - Neurologic symptoms (e.g., altered mental status, visual disturbances)
    - SDC ≥ 15 ng/mL at any time or ≥ 10 ng/mL post-distribution (generally 6 to 8 hours post ingestion)
  - Poisoning with a non-digoxin cardioactive steroid
- **DigiFAB Dosing**
  - DigiFab is dosed based on the number of vials, not in a weight metric (i.e., mg, or mcg).
  - Three methods to calculate dose include empiric dosing, dosing based on known ingestion, and dosing based on serum digoxin level.
  - Acute ingestion of a known amount:
    - Dose (in # of vials) = (Total digitalis body load in mg) / (0.5 mg of digitalis bound/vial)
      - IMPORTANT: Multiply total digitalis load in mg by 0.80 if digoxin tablets are involved in accounting for incomplete absorption instead of the injection.
  - Based on steady-state digoxin concentrations:
    - Dose (in # of vials) = [(Serum digoxin concentration in ng/mL) X (weight in kg)] / 100
      - A table located in the prescribing information of DigiFAB provides dosage estimates in the number of vials for adult patients for whom a steady-state serum digoxin concentration is known.
  - Acute ingestion of unknown amount / Cardiac Arrest
    - A DigiFAB dose of 10 vials may be administered, followed by an additional 10 vials as required with close monitoring; for life-threatening symptoms, 20 vials may be given initially.
    - Note: 10-20 vials is rarely needed clinically; please use clinical judgment.
- **Predicting Digoxin Related Mortality**
  - Hyperkalemia (> 5.0 mEq/L) better predictor of mortality compared to serum digoxin level.
- **Reverses Digoxin**
  - Although the intended consequence of DigiFAB administration is to reverse digoxin, its administration may uncover arrhythmias or exacerbate heart failure.
- **Calcium Administration for Digoxin Toxicity**
  - Digoxin toxicity frequently is associated with hyperkalemia.
  - Caution is advised when considering calcium.
    - The basis of this is theoretical: additional calcium with an already increased intracellular concentration of calcium leading to altered contraction of myofibrils delayed conduction and/or altered sarcoplasmic reticulum and mitochondrial functioning.

High-Yield Fast-Facts

- **DigiFAB NOT DigiBIND**
  - DigiFAB is the only available digoxin immune FAB available.
- **Digoxin Drug Interactions - Amiodarone Or Dronedarone**
  - By inhibiting P-gp, amiodarone can potentially double digoxin concentrations; therefore, digoxin dose should be empirically lowered by 50% when amiodarone is started.
    - Similar to amiodarone, dronedarone also inhibits P-gp and can increase digoxin concentrations by about 2.5-fold. The same empiric digoxin dose reduction of 50%

HIGH-YIELD BOARD EXAM ESSENTIALS

- **CLASSIC AGENTS:** Digoxin Immune FAB
- **DRUG CLASS:** Antidote
- **INDICATIONS:** Digoxin toxicity
- **MECHANISM:** Fab immunoglobulin fragments bind to free digoxin forming a digoxin-immune fragment complex, which is renally excreted, resulting in decreased serum digoxin concentration.
- **SIDE EFFECTS:** Uncovering underlying arrhythmias or heart failure.
- **CLINICAL PEARLS:** DigiFab is dosed based on the number of vials, not in a weight metric (i.e., mg, or mcg). Three methods to calculate dose include empiric dosing, dosing based on known ingestion, and dosing based on serum digoxin level.

High-Yield Basic Pharmacology

- **Flumazenil**
  - Competitive antagonist of benzodiazepine receptor on GABA-A chloride channel.
- **Naloxone**
  - Structurally similar to opioids causing a competition and displacement of opioids from the opioid receptor binding site.

Primary Overall Net Benefit

- Naloxone is a life-saving intervention in opioid intoxicated patients.
- Flumazenil can be used for benzodiazepine overdose in naive patients with no other co-ingestants.

Flumazenil/Naloxone - Drug Class Review			
High-Yield Med Reviews			
Mechanism of Action: *Flumazenil - Competitive antagonist of benzodiazepine receptor on GABA-A chloride channel.* *Naloxone - Structurally similar to opioids causing a competition and displacement of opioids from the opioid receptor binding site.*			
Class Effects: Naloxone is a life-saving intervention in opioid intoxicated patients. Flumazenil can be used for benzodiazepine overdose in naive patients with no other co-ingestants.			
Generic Name	**Brand Name**	**Indication(s) or Uses**	**Notes**

Flumazenil	Romazicon	• Benzodiazepine reversal	• **Dosing (Adult):**
			 – IV 0.2 mg over 15-30 seconds, repeated q1minute to a maximum cumulative dose of 1 to 3 mg
			 • **Dosing (Peds):**
			 – IV 0.01 mg/kg over 15-30 seconds, repeated q1minute
			   • Maximum single dose 0.2 mg
			   • Maximum cumulative dose 1 to 3 mg
			 • **CYP450 Interactions:** None
			 • **Renal or Hepatic Dose Adjustments:** None
			 • **Dosage Forms:** IV (solution)

Naloxone	Narcan	• Opioid overdose • Opioid-induced constipation or pruritus	• **Dosing (Adult):** – IV/IM/SQ 0.04 to 2 mg repeated as needed q2-3minutes – Intranasal 2 mg, repeated as needed q2-3minutes – IV infusion 0.25 to 3 mcg/kg/hour • **Dosing (Peds):** – IV/IM/SQ 0.04 to 2 mg repeated as needed q2-3minutes – IV 0.1 mg/kg/dose repeated as needed – Intranasal 2 mg, repeated as needed q2-3minutes – IV infusion 0.25 to 3 mcg/kg/hour • **CYP450 Interactions:** None • **Renal or Hepatic Dose Adjustments:** None • **Dosage Forms:** Nasal (liquid), IV (solution)

High-Yield Clinical Knowledge

- **Bystander Naloxone Administration**
  - Naloxone distribution programs aim to provide opioid reversal via intranasal administration to lay individuals, bystanders, and medical professionals in non-acute care settings (such as pharmacies).
  - Patients, family members, and medical professionals should be educated on the role of naloxone and its administration and the importance of contacting 911 after administration.
- **Naloxone Routes**
  - Can be given IV, IM, IO, SubQ, intranasally, down an endotracheal tube, but NOT orally due to insufficient absorption
- **Flumazenil Alternative Uses**
  - Flumazenil may also play a role in managing paradoxical benzodiazepine-induced agitation that can occur in pediatrics or the elderly.
  - Some have described its role in the management of altered mental status due to hepatic encephalopathy.
- **Acute Benzodiazepine Withdrawal**
  - Flumazenil can precipitate benzodiazepine withdrawal, which can increase patient morbidity and mortality.
  - Flumazenil may also precipitate seizures in patients with a history of seizures and is contraindicated in this population.
  - Other contraindications include ingestion of agents capable of seizures or dysrhythmias, long-term use of benzodiazepines, QRS or QT prolongation, or terminal 40-ms right axis deviation on ECG.
- **Opioid-Induced Constipation**
  - Methylnaltrexone or naloxone can be used to treat opioid-induced constipation.
  - Oral naloxone doses between 2-6 mg are often ideal for this indication, and doses greater than 6 mg should be avoided due to systemic absorption and potential precipitation of acute systemic opioid withdrawal.
- **Flumazenil Effect on Mental Status**
  - Flumazenil primarily improves mental status and does not reverse benzodiazepine-induced respiratory depression.
- **Naloxone Emesis**
  - Unless airway and respirations can be maintained at the bedside, avoid giving rapid IV push, which induces acute opioid withdrawal and emesis risk.
- **Urine Drug Screens**
  - Urine drug screens are not helpful in the acute management of opioid overdose.
  - These tests do not differentiate from acute vs. chronic exposure and have numerous false positives and negatives.
- **Fentanyl Rigid Chest Syndrome**
  - Fentanyl rigid chest syndrome is due to dopamine antagonism but reversed with naloxone.
- **Tramadol Seizures**
  - Tramadol uniquely is associated with seizures that do not respond to and may be made worse with naloxone.

HIGH-YIELD BOARD EXAM ESSENTIALS

- **CLASSIC AGENTS:** Flumazenil, naloxone
- **DRUG CLASS:** Antidotes
- **INDICATIONS:** Benzodiazepine overdose (flumazenil), opioid overdose (naloxone)
- **MECHANISM:** Flumazenil - Competitive antagonist of benzodiazepine receptor on GABA-A chloride channel. Naloxone- Structurally similar to opioids causing a competition and displacement of opioids from the opioid receptor binding site.
- **SIDE EFFECTS:** Benzodiazepine withdrawal seizures (flumazenil), tachycardia, agitation, pulmonary edema (naloxone)
- **CLINICAL PEARLS:** Naloxone distribution programs aim to provide opioid reversal via intranasal administration to lay individuals, bystanders, and medical professionals in non-acute care settings (such as pharmacies).

High-Yield Basic Pharmacology

- **Activated charcoal (AC)**
  - Absorbs susceptible xenobiotics using hydrogen bonding, ion-ion, dipole, and van der Waals forces
- **Polyethylene glycol**
  - Creates a hyperosmotic environment without metabolism, different from lactulose or sorbitol

Primary Net Benefit

- AC decreases absorption of many xenobiotics such as acetaminophen, aspirin, opioids, antidepressants, but no effect on alcohols, acids, alkalis, and metals (iron, lead, lithium, magnesium potassium, sodium).
- Polyethylene glycol is used to accomplish whole bowel irrigation, removing toxins not absorbed by AC.

GI Decontamination - Drug Class Review			
High-Yield Med Reviews			
Mechanism of Action: *Activated charcoal - Absorbs susceptible xenobiotics using hydrogen bonding, ion-ion, dipole, and van der Waals forces. Polyethylene glycol - Creates a hyperosmotic environment without metabolism, different from lactulose or sorbitol.*			
Class Effects: AC decreases absorption of many xenobiotics such as acetaminophen, aspirin, opioids, antidepressants, but no effect on alcohols, acids, alkalis, and metals (iron, lead, lithium, magnesium potassium, sodium). Polyethylene glycol is used to accomplish whole bowel irrigation, removing toxins not absorbed by AC.			
Generic Name	**Brand Name**	**Indication(s) or Uses**	**Notes**

Activated charcoal (with or without sorbitol)	Actidose, Char-flo, EZ Char, Kerr Insta-Char	- GI decontamination	- **Dosing (Adult):**
			  - Oral 25 to 100 g once
			  - Oral 50 to 100 g once then 25 to 50 g q4h
			- **Dosing (Peds):**
			  - Oral 0.5 to 1 g/kg once
			  - Oral 0.5 to 1 g/kg once then 0.25 to 0.5 g/kg q4h
			- **CYP450 Interactions:** None
			- **Renal or Hepatic Dose Adjustments:** None
			- **Dosage Forms:** Oral (liquid, suspension, tablets)

Polyethylene glycol 3350	Gavilax, Gialax, Glycolax, Healthylax, Miralax, PEGylax	- Bowel preparation prior to colonoscopy
		- Whole bowel irrigation
			- **Dosing (Adult):**
			  - Oral 2,000 to 4,000 mL once
			  - Oral 17 g in 240 mL q10minutes until 2,000 mL consumed.
			  - Oral 17g in 240 mL once daily, as needed
			- **Dosing (Peds):**
			  - Oral 1.5 g/kg/day for 4 days
			    - Maximum 100 g/day
			  - Oral 0.2 to 1 g/kg once daily
			    - Maximum 17 g/day
			- **CYP450 Interactions:** None
			- **Renal or Hepatic Dose Adjustments:** None
			- **Dosage Forms:** Oral (kit, packet, powder)

High-Yield Clinical Knowledge

- **Dosage Forms**
  - AC for acute toxicities is primarily used as the oral suspension preparation.
  - AC effervescent tablets are available, but their use in undifferentiated toxicity is not well defined.
- **Storage / Handling**
  - AC should be stored in its original container as it will absorb gases from the air and potentially decrease binding capacity.
- **With or Without Sorbitol**
  - AC with sorbitol is as effective as AC without sorbitol in most toxicities.
    - One exception is AC with sorbitol is preferred for GI decontamination of patients exposed to botulinum-producing spores or botulinum toxin.
  - Sorbitol use is associated with hypotension and electrolyte disturbances.
- **Contraindications**
  - Contraindicated if GI perforation or obstruction present, unprotected airway, or following caustic ingestion.
- **Multiple Dose AC (MDAC)**
  - Can use multiple doses for xenobiotics undergoing enterohepatic recirculation (ex. phenobarbital).
  - AC with sorbitol should only be provided (if at all) with the first dose in an MDAC treatment to avoid salt and water depletion.
- **WBI Indications**
  - WBI is recommended in patients with ingestions of toxins not absorbed by AC, such as iron, lead, and lithium.
  - WBI may also be used to decontaminate foreign body ingestions (including body packers) and ingestion of toxins with slow absorption and high mortality (ex. bupropion extended-release).
- **Salicylate Toxicity**
  - Activated charcoal-aspirin complexes can desorb in an alkaline milieu. AC with sorbitol can decrease intestinal pH and prevent desorption.
- **Common Adverse Events**
  - AC is often associated with constipation, GI obstruction, aspiration, fecal discoloration, dental discoloration.

HIGH-YIELD BOARD EXAM ESSENTIALS
- **CLASSIC AGENTS:** Activated charcoal, polyethylene glycol
- **DRUG CLASS:** GI decontamination
- **INDICATIONS:** GI decontamination
- **MECHANISM:** Activated charcoal - Absorbs susceptible xenobiotics using hydrogen bonding, ion-ion, dipole, and van der Waals forces. Polyethylene glycol - Creates a hyperosmotic environment without metabolism, different from lactulose or sorbitol.
- **SIDE EFFECTS:** Constipation, GI obstruction, aspiration, fecal discoloration, dental discoloration.
- **CLINICAL PEARLS:** Can use multiple doses for xenobiotics undergoing enterohepatic recirculation (ex. phenobarbital). AC with sorbitol should only be provided (if at all) with the first dose in an MDAC treatment to avoid salt and water depletion.

High-Yield Basic Pharmacology

- **Mechanism of Action**
  - Cobalt ion combines with cyanide (CN) to form cyanocobalamin (aka vitamin B12).
- **Molar Absorption**
  - The cobalt ion component of hydroxocobalamin binds to cyanide in an equimolar manner, in a 1:1 ratio, but in common dosage forms, each standard 5 g dose of hydroxocobalamin binds 96 mg of cyanide.

Primary Net Benefit

- Life-saving intervention in cyanide poisoned patients that have a role in resuscitation of patients from fires.

Hydroxocobalamin - Drug Class Review			
High-Yield Med Reviews			
Mechanism of Action: *Cobalt ion combines with cyanide (CN) to form cyanocobalamin (aka vitamin B12).*			
Class Effects: Life-saving intervention in cyanide poisoned patients has a role in the resuscitation of patients from fires.			
Generic Name	**Brand Name**	**Indication(s) or Uses**	**Notes**

Hydroxocobala min	Cyanokit	• Cyanide toxicity	• **Dosing (Adult):**
			  – IV 5 g over 15 minutes, followed by 5 g, depending on clinical response and severity.
			• **Dosing (Peds):**
			  – IV 70 mg/kg over 15 minutes, followed by 70 mg/kg depending on clinical response and severity.
			    • Maximum 5,000 mg/dose
			• **CYP450 Interactions:** None
			• **Renal or Hepatic Dose Adjustments:** None
			• **Dosage Forms:** IV (solution)

High-Yield Clinical Knowledge

- **CN Binding**
  - Binds 1:1 on a molar basis, but an average 5 g dose binds 96 mg of CN.
  - It also binds nitric oxide, causing vasoconstriction and hypertension.
- **Red Discoloration**
  - Turns mucous membranes, secretions, and urine red for up to several days.
  - Red discoloration can also cause false blood leak alarms on hemodialysis machines.
- **Hypertension & Redness**
  - The most common adverse events associated with hydroxocobalamin are hypertension and red discoloration of mucus membranes, skin, and urine.
  - The red discoloration can alter the analysis of some blood samples, including blood gases and CBCs.
  - The degree of increases in blood pressure does not appear to be clinically relevant.
- **Cyanide Treatment**
  - Amyl nitrate, sodium nitrite, and sodium thiosulfate were the components of the old cyanide antidote kit.
    - Amyl nitrate is an inhaled medication, and long with sodium nitrite are indented to induce methemoglobin which has a slightly better oxygen dissociation characteristic than cyanohemoglobin.

- Sodium thiosulfate induces rhodanese and acts as a sulfur donor, ultimately converting cyanide into less toxic thiocyanate.
  - These agents not only induce methemoglobin but may also worsen hypotension, often associated with smoke inhalation.
- **Old and New**
  - Sodium thiosulfate may also be administered with hydroxocobalamin under the guidance of a toxicologist.
  - This additive combination therapy may have a small benefit but must be administered via separate IV access as sodium thiosulfate may inactivate hydroxocobalamin.
- **Sodium Nitroprusside**
  - Sodium nitroprusside is a common iatrogenic cause of cyanide, more specifically thiocyanate, toxicity.
  - The risk of toxicity can be minimized by adding sodium thiosulfate to the same IVPB infusion or through a continuous administration of hydroxocobalamin 25 mg/hour for 10 hours.

High-Yield Fast-Fact

- **Pre-Hospital Hydroxocobalamin**
  - Many urban fire departments carry hydroxocobalamin for pre-hospital administration of fire victims that are in cardiac arrest.

HIGH-YIELD BOARD EXAM ESSENTIALS
- **CLASSIC AGENTS:** Hydroxocobalamin
- **DRUG CLASS:** Antidote
- **INDICATIONS:** Cyanide toxicity
- **MECHANISM:** Cobalt ion combines with cyanide (CN) to form cyanocobalamin (aka vitamin B12).
- **SIDE EFFECTS:** Red discoloration of body fluids, hypertension, tachycardia
- **CLINICAL PEARLS:** The most common adverse events associated with hydroxocobalamin are hypertension and red discoloration of mucus membranes, skin, and urine. The red discoloration can alter the analysis of some blood samples, including blood gases and CBCs.

High-Yield Basic Pharmacology

- **Mechanism of Action**
  - Supplements cysteine as a precursor to glutathione, which is necessary to detoxify N-acetyl-benzoquinoneimine (NAPQI).
  - Increases sulfation capacity of the liver serves as a substitute for glutathione and is a free radical scavenger
- **Oral First Pass**
  - Oral NAC has an extensive first-pass metabolism which produces cysteine and glutathione.
  - However, this is desirable for acetaminophen toxicity, as relatively high glutathione concentrations are delivered to the liver.

Primary Net Benefit

- Reduces the risk of hepatotoxicity (AST greater than 1000 mg/dL) when administered within 8 hours to treat acute acetaminophen overdose.

<table>
<tr><td colspan="4" align="center">N-Acetylcysteine - Drug Class Review
High-Yield Med Reviews</td></tr>
<tr><td colspan="4">Mechanism of Action:
Supplements cysteine as a precursor to glutathione, which is necessary to detoxify NAPQI.
Increases sulfation capacity of the liver serves as a substitute for glutathione and is a free radical scavenger.</td></tr>
<tr><td colspan="4">Class Effects: Reduces the risk of hepatotoxicity (AST greater than 1000 mg/dL) when administered within 8 hours to treat acute acetaminophen overdose.</td></tr>
<tr><td>Generic Name</td><td>Brand Name</td><td>Indication(s) or Uses</td><td>Notes</td></tr>
<tr>
<td>N-Acetylcysteine</td>
<td>Acetadote
Mucomyst
Cetylev</td>
<td>
• Acetaminophen overdose
• Mucolytic
</td>
<td>
• Dosing (Adult):
  – Oral 140 mg/kg once (maximum 15 g) followed by 70 mg/kg (maximum 7.5g/dose) q4h for 17 doses
  – IV 150 mg/kg/hour for one hour (maximum 15 g), followed by 12.5 mg/kg/hour for 4 hours (maximum 5 g/dose), followed by 6.25 mg/kg/hour (maximum 10 g/dose) for 16 hours
  – Nebulized 6 to 10 mL (10%) or 3 to 5 mL (20%) q1-6h
• Dosing (Peds):
  – Oral 140 mg/kg once (maximum 15 g) followed by 70 mg/kg (maximum 7.5g/dose) q4h for 17 doses
  – IV 150 mg/kg/hour for one hour (maximum 15 g), followed by 12.5 mg/kg/hour for 4 hours (maximum 5 g/dose), followed by 6.25 mg/kg/hour (maximum 10 g/dose) for 16 hours
  – Nebulized 6 to 10 mL (10%) or 3 to 5 mL (20%) q1-6h
• CYP450 Interactions: None
• Renal or Hepatic Dose Adjustments: None
• Dosage Forms: Inhalation solution, IV (solution), Oral (Tablet)
</td>
</tr>
</table>

High-Yield Clinical Knowledge

- **Anaphylactoid Reactions**
  - Anaphylactoid reactions from IV administration of NAC are relatively common but have further decreased in frequency with purified NAC formulations.
  - Before the availability of Acetadote, IV NAC administration was accomplished using the respiratory product, which is not pyrogen-free.
  - Slowing the infusion rate does not decrease the risk of infusion reactions.
- **Acetaminophen Absorption**
  - APAP absorption occurs within 2 hours, but levels peak around 4 hours post-ingestion.
  - 4-hour levels plotted on RM nomogram to guide NAC therapy.
- **Rumack-Matthew**
  - Rumack-Matthew (RM) nomogram plots the risk of hepatotoxicity (AST > 1,000 IU/L) as a function of APAP level and time since ingestion.
  - No adjustment is required in the setting of chronic ethanol abuse, presence of CYP inducers, inadequate nutrition, or extended/modified release acetaminophen products.
- **Acetaminophen Hepatotoxicity**
  - NAPQI creates protein adducts and covalently binds and arylates proteins in hepatic cells leading to zone III hepatic cell necrosis.
  - Stages of Toxicity:
    - Stage 1 (0-24 hrs): nonspecific GI upset/distress.
    - Stage 2 (24-36 hrs): onset of hepatic injury (elevation of AST/ALT, INR).
    - Stage 3 (72-96 hrs): Maximal hepatotoxicity (encephalopathy, coma, coagulopathy).
    - Stage 4 (>96 hrs): Recovery, liver transplant, or death.
  - Diagnosis: Acute ingestion: APAP level 4 hours post-ingestion > 150 mcg/mL.
  - NAC is nearly 100% effective if started within 8 hours.
- **Anticipatory Nausea and Vomiting**
  - Oral NAC is frequently associated with nausea, vomiting, flatus, dysgeusia, urticaria.
    - As NAC is administered q4h for 17 doses, patients can develop anticipatory nausea and vomiting due to NAC's horrible taste and smell.

High-Yield Fast-Fact

- **Other NAC Uses**
  - In addition to acetaminophen, NAC can be used to treat toxicity due to certain metals (cadmium, chromium, cobalt, gold, and organic mercury), amatoxin, chloroform, carbon tetrachloride, cyclophosphamide, doxorubicin, eugenol, pulegone, ricin, and zidovudine.

HIGH-YIELD BOARD EXAM ESSENTIALS
- **CLASSIC AGENTS:** N-Acetylcysteine (NAC)
- **DRUG CLASS:** Antidote
- **INDICATIONS:** Acetaminophen toxicity, non-specific hepatotoxicity
- **MECHANISM:** Supplements cysteine as a precursor to glutathione, which is necessary to detoxify NAPQI. Increases sulfation capacity of the liver serves as a substitute for glutathione and is a free radical scavenger.
- **SIDE EFFECTS:** Anaphylactoid reaction, hypotension, sulfur-taste (oral), nausea
- **CLINICAL PEARLS:** NAPQI creates protein adducts and covalently binds and arylates proteins in hepatic cells leading to zone III hepatic cell necrosis.

High-Yield Basic Pharmacology

- **Mechanism of Action**
    - Increases plasma and urine bicarbonate, buffering excess hydrogen ions.
    - Increases sodium and changes the proportion of sodium channel blocking xenobiotic that is ionized, displacing it from binding sites
- **Alkalosis or Acidosis**
    - Sodium bicarbonate is metabolized to CO_2, water, and sodium.
    - In patients with normal minute ventilation, they can sufficiently "blow-off" or eliminate the CO_2 produced by sodium bicarbonate.
    - In patients who are mechanically ventilated with fixed rates or otherwise unable to eliminate CO_2, it may accumulate, leading to respiratory acidosis.

Primary Net Benefit

- Widely used for numerous toxicities from acidosis and sodium channel blockade.

Sodium Bicarbonate - Drug Class Review			
High-Yield Med Reviews			
Mechanism of Action: *Increases plasma and urine bicarbonate, buffering excess hydrogen ions. Increases sodium and changes the proportion of sodium channel blocking xenobiotic that is ionized, displacing it from binding sites.*			
Class Effects: Widely used for numerous toxicities from acidosis and sodium channel blockade.			
Generic Name	**Brand Name**	**Indication(s) or Uses**	**Notes**
Sodium Bicarbonate	Neut	<ul><li>Management of metabolic acidosis</li><li>Sodium channel blocker toxicity</li><li>Urine alkalinization</li></ul>	<ul><li>**Dosing (Adult):**<ul><li>IV/IO 1 mEq/kg/dose repeated as necessary with or without 0.5 to 1 mEq/kg/hour infusion</li></ul></li><li>**Dosing (Peds):**<ul><li>IV/IO 1 mEq/kg/dose repeated as necessary with or without 0.5 to 1 mEq/kg/hour infusion</li></ul></li><li>**CYP450 Interactions:** None</li><li>**Renal or Hepatic Dose Adjustments:** None</li><li>**Dosage Forms:** IV (solution), Oral (powder, tablet)</li></ul>

High-Yield Clinical Knowledge

- **Urine Alkalinization and Hypokalemia**
    - Urine alkalinization, targeting a pH of 8.0, should occur for salicylate, phenobarbital, and methotrexate.
    - The use of sodium bicarbonate will cause hypokalemia, and potassium supplementation is required for ongoing use.
- **Administration: IV bolus or infusion**
    - Although the commonly used 8.4% sodium bicarbonate product is hypertonic (approximately 2000 mOsmol/L), it can be given in emergent scenarios via peripheral IV.
    - The onset of Action: Rapid
- **Salicylate Toxicity**

- Uncouples oxidative phosphorylation by increasing hydrogen in the inner mitochondrial matrix diminishes the electrochemical gradient or forms pores in the membrane permeable to hydrogen.
- This physiologic effect manifests as three stages of toxicity:
  - Early: non-specific GI distress, tachypnea, primary respiratory alkalosis, tinnitus
  - Late: Hypoglycorrhachia, hyperpnea, altered mental status, hyperthermia, coagulopathy, ARDS, severe metabolic acidosis
- Early aggressive treatment with activated charcoal (AC) with sorbitol, sodium bicarbonate, dextrose, and hemodialysis are necessary to reduce mortality.
- Intubation should be avoided due to the risk of carbon dioxide retention, shunting more salicylate into CNS.
- HD indicated for aspirin level > 100 mg/dL or with levels > 90 mg/dL with renal impairment.

- **Signs of Sodium Channel Blockade**
  - Sodium bicarbonate should be administered when QRS is more significant than 100 ms in the setting of a possible sodium channel blocking xenobiotic (cyclic antidepressant, diphenhydramine, antipsychotics, etc.).
  - The appropriate starting dose is 0.5 to 1 mEq/kg of 8.4% sodium bicarbonate.
- **SSRI Ingestion**
  - Sodium bicarbonate should not empirically be administered to patients with SSRI overdose as it may increase renal potassium elimination and risk of QT prolongation.
    - QT prolongation is common among SSRIs, particularly with citalopram and escitalopram.
- **Sodium Bicarbonate Use for Weak Bases?**
  - For TCA overdose or toxicity where clinically relevant ECG changes (QRS prolongation more significant than 100 ms), sodium bicarbonate is recommended.
  - Since TCAs are weak bases, this could hypothetically decrease their renal elimination, but the sodium is needed to overcome cardiac sodium channel blockade.
  - However, altering the plasma's pH to approximately 7.5 promotes the TCA movement away from the cardiac sodium channel and into the lipid membrane.
    - If patients are alkalemic or are hypercarbic without appropriate ventilation, hypertonic sodium chloride can also be used as an alternative to sodium bicarbonate.
- **Contrast-Induced Nephropathy**
  - Sodium bicarbonate is of questionable use in preventing contrast-induced nephropathy, as evidence is inconsistent in diverse populations.

High-Yield Fast-Fact

- **Nebulized Sodium Bicarbonate**
  - Sodium bicarbonate can be nebulized for chlorine gas exposure and does not cause an exothermic response as alveoli are efficient at heat exchange.

HIGH-YIELD BOARD EXAM ESSENTIALS
- **CLASSIC AGENTS:** Sodium bicarbonate
- **DRUG CLASS:** Antidote
- **INDICATIONS:** Management of metabolic acidosis, sodium channel blocker toxicity, urine alkalinization
- **MECHANISM:** Increases plasma and urine bicarbonate, buffering excess hydrogen ions. Increases sodium and changes the proportion of sodium channel blocking xenobiotic that is ionized, displacing it from binding sites.
- **SIDE EFFECTS:** Alkalemia, hypernatremia
- **CLINICAL PEARLS:** Although the commonly used 8.4% sodium bicarbonate product is hypertonic (approximately 2000 mOsmol/L), it can be given in emergent scenarios via peripheral IV.

HIGH-YIELD
MED REVIEWS

PART 3

DISEASE STATE
RAPID REVIEW

ACLS - BRADYCARDIA
- **PATHO:** Altered automaticity and impulse generation (sinus bradycardia and sick sinus syndrome) or conduction disturbance in the atria and ventricles (first-, second-, and third-degree block).
- **CLASSIC PRESENTATION:** May be asymptomatic, or lightheadedness, presyncope or syncope, angina.
- **CLASSIC FINDINGS:** ECG changes consistent with bradyarrhythmia. Pulse < 60 bpm.
- **TREATMENT:**
  - Identify reversible causes.
  - Acute management includes pacing (transcutaneous, transvenous), atropine, or epinephrine.

ACLS - PULSELESS ELECTRICAL ACTIVITY (PEA)
- **PATHO:** Organized or semi-organized cardiac electrical activity and ineffective LV stroke volume, not producing a detectable pulse.
- **CLASSIC PRESENTATION:** Cardiac arrest (unresponsive, no palpable pulse, no spontaneous breathing)
- **CLASSIC FINDINGS:** Pulseless, apneic or agonal respirations, not responding to verbal/painful stimulation.
- **TREATMENT:**
  - ACLS protocol (chest compressions, intubation/ventilation). Epinephrine IV/IO 1 mg q3-5 minutes.
  - Consider treatment of the H's: Hypovolemia, hypoxia, hydrogen (acidosis), hyper/hypokalemia, hyper/hypothermia, hypoglycemia and T's: Trauma, tamponade, tension pneumothorax, thrombus (coronary), thromboembolism (PE), toxins.
  - No defibrillation, use of atropine, lidocaine, or amiodarone.

ACLS - PULSELESS V-TACH/V-FIB
- **PATHO:** Increased automaticity and triggered activity causing ventricular tachycardia (VT), inadequate diastole, and hemodynamic collapse from insufficient cardiac output.
- **CLASSIC PRESENTATION:** Cardiac arrest (unresponsive, no palpable pulse, no spontaneous breathing)
- **CLASSIC FINDINGS:** Pulseless with either monomorphic VT or polymorphic VT.
- **TREATMENT:**
  - ACLS protocol (chest compressions, intubation/ventilation), defibrillation.
  - Epinephrine IV/IO 1 mg q3-5minutes, amiodarone IV/IO 300 mg OR lidocaine IV 1.5 mg/kg.

ACLS - SUSTAINED V-TACH
- **PATHO:** Consecutive beats with a wide QRS and a rate of at least 100 bpm associated with CAD or structural heart disease.
- **CLASSIC PRESENTATION:** Chest pain, palpitations, diaphoresis, nausea/vomiting, altered mental status, and palpable pulses.
- **CLASSIC FINDINGS:** V-tach sustained for at least 30 sec or causing a hemodynamic collapse in < 30 sec.
- **TREATMENT:**
  - Synchronized cardioversion (NOT defibrillation), amiodarone IV 150 mg over 10 minutes.

ACUTE CORONARY SYNDROME – NSTEMI – UNSTABLE ANGINA

- **PATHO:** Coronary artery atherosclerotic plaque causing partial occlusion of a coronary vessel leading to myocardial ischemia.
- **CLASSIC PRESENTATION:** Pressure-like substernal chest pain persisting for more than 10 minutes which occurs with minimal effort or at rest, and that may radiate to either the arm, neck, or jaw.
- **CLASSIC FINDINGS:** Elevations in troponin and ECG findings that may include ST-segment depression, T-wave flattening/inversion, or ST-segment elevation that otherwise does not meet STEMI criteria.
- **TREATMENT:**
    - Delayed PCI may be selected and clinically appropriate.
    - Aspirin, heparin or enoxaparin, oxygen if saturation below 90%, nitroglycerin (if no recent use of type 5 PDE inhibitors, right-sided MI, or SBP < 90 mmHg).

ACUTE CORONARY SYNDROME – STEMI

- **PATHO:** Complete and persistent occlusion of perfusion in the heart due to rupture of coronary atherosclerotic plaque and subsequent platelet adhesion, activation, and aggregation to form a thrombus.
- **CLASSIC PRESENTATION:** Pressure-like substernal chest pain persisting for more than 10 minutes which occurs with minimal effort or at rest, and that may radiate to either the arm, neck, or jaw.
- **CLASSIC FINDINGS:** New ST-segment elevation of at least 0.1 mV in two contiguous leads.
- **TREATMENT:**
    - Primary PCI (either GP IIb/IIIa plus anticoagulation with heparin, enoxaparin, or bivalirudin strategy), aspirin, P2Y12 inhibitor (clopidogrel, prasugrel, ticagrelor), +/- morphine, +/- supplemental O2 (only if pulse ox < 92%).
    - Thrombolytic strategy (alternative if not cath lab available, symptom onset within 12 hrs, and assuming no contraindications).

ACUTE CORONARY SYNDROME – COCAINE-INDUCED

- **PATHO:** Dose-dependent decreased in oxygen supply due to coronary vessel vasoconstriction, induction of prothrombotic states, and accelerating atherosclerosis.
- **CLASSIC PRESENTATION:** Recent cocaine use, usually within 3 hours but may be up to 4 days with pressure-like substernal chest pain.
- **CLASSIC FINDINGS:** ECG showing UA/NSTEMI or STEMI + patient-reported or lab evidence of cocaine use.
- **TREATMENT:** Benzodiazepines (1st line), +/- aspirin and UA/NSTEMI or STEMI management strategies if patient has underlying CAD. NO BETA-BLOCKERS, including carvedilol or labetalol.

AORTIC DISSECTION – STANDFORD A or DeBakey TYPE I & II

- **PATHO:** LV hydrodynamic forces produce stress tears allowing blood to enter the aortic media or, as a result of hemorrhage into the aortic media from the damaged vasa vasorum.
- **CLASSIC PRESENTATION:** Acute chest pain radiating to the back described as tearing or sharp quality, hypertension, pulse deficit, syncope, aortic regurgitation, new murmur
- **CLASSIC FINDINGS:** Dissection of the ascending aorta.
- **TREATMENT:**
    - Negative inotrope and vasodilators titrated to SBP of 100 to 120 mmHg, and HR of < 60 bpm (esmolol plus sodium nitroprusside IV) as fast as possible.
    - STAT consult to CVT surgery for acute surgical intervention (graft replacement of the ascending aorta, aortic valve resuspension, or replacement).

AORTIC DISSECTION – STANDFORD B or DeBAKEY TYPE III
- **PATHO:** LV hydrodynamic forces produce stress tears allowing blood to enter the aortic media or, as a result of hemorrhage into the aortic media from the damaged vasa vasorum.
- **CLASSIC PRESENTATION:** Acute abdominal pain radiating to the back described as tearing or sharp quality, hypertension.
- **CLASSIC FINDINGS:** Dissection of any other part of the aorta that is not the ascending aorta.
- **TREATMENT:**
  - Not commonly surgical emergencies, but rather elective candidates.
  - Negative inotrope and vasodilators titrated to SBP of 100 to 120 mmHg and HR of less than 60 bpm (esmolol plus sodium nitroprusside IV).

AORTIC STENOSIS
- **PATHO:** LV outflow obstruction leading to LV systolic dysfunction with afterload mismatch, diastolic dysfunction, and irreversible myocardial fibrosis.
- **CLASSIC PRESENTATION:** SAD symptoms (syncope, angina, dyspnea), crescendo-decrescendo systolic ejection murmur, displaced point of maximal pulse, diminished carotid pulse with delayed upstroke, and narrowed pulse pressure.
- **CLASSIC FINDINGS:** Patients with symptoms: elevated aortic jet velocity, mean pressure gradient elevation, and decreased aortic valve area.
- **TREATMENT:** Definitive management of aortic stenosis and includes surgical interventions (aortic valve replacement, percutaneous aortic balloon valvuloplasty) plus careful management of hypertension recognizing that these patients can still be preload and afterload dependent where sudden changes can lead to lightheadedness and syncope.

ATRIAL FIBRILLATION (CHRONIC, RATE-CONTROLLED)
- **PATHO:** Local ectopic focus, a single localized re-entry circuit, or multiple functional reentry circuits.
- **CLASSIC PRESENTATION:** Chest palpitations, chest pain, shortness of breath, lightheadedness, and near syncope. Further categorized as either paroxysmal, persistent, long-standing, or permanent.
- **CLASSIC FINDINGS:** 12-lead ECG findings of irregularly irregular rhythm.
- **TREATMENT:**
  - Rate control with either a non-dihydropyridine calcium channel blocker or beta-1 selective antagonist is preferred for most patients. Rhythm control may be used in selected populations.
  - Avoid non-DHP CCB ins patients with AFIB + Wolff-Parkinson-White (WPW) syndrome.

ATRIAL FIBRILLATION (ACUTE; RAPID VENTRICULAR RESPONSE (RVR))
- **PATHO:** Local ectopic focus, a single localized re-entry circuit, or multiple functional reentry circuits.
- **CLASSIC PRESENTATION:** Chest palpitations, chest pain, shortness of breath, lightheadedness, and near syncope.
- **CLASSIC FINDINGS:** ECG findings of irregularly irregular rhythm and hemodynamic instability
- **TREATMENT:**
  - Rate control (hemodynamically stable) with diltiazem, metoprolol, or amiodarone (low dose).
  - Rhythm control (in patients who are hemodynamically unstable) with DC cardioversion.
  - Avoid non-DHP CCB ins patients with AFIB + Wolff-Parkinson-White (WPW) syndrome (it can result in an increase in pulse due to push of action potentials down accessory pathway).

HYPERLIPIDEMIA

- **PATHO:**
  - The primary differentiating factor between the 2 centers around the presence of elevated TGs and, to some degree, the severity of LDL concentrations.
  - **Type IIa**
    - Significant elevations in LDL levels dues to:
      - Alterations in the regulation of LDL production.
      - More commonly, the autosomal dominant genetic defect disorder resulting from a deficiency in LDL receptors that make it difficult to clear LDL cholesterol from the circulating blood.
  - **Type IIb**
    - More commonly seen in patients with metabolic syndrome.
- **CLASSIC FINDINGS:**
  - **Type IIa**
    - Increase incidence of premature CAD, Achilles tendon xanthoma, yellow plaques on the eyelids, tuberous xanthomas.
  - **Type IIb**
    - Patterns of metabolic syndrome with elevated TG and low HDL
- **TREATMENT:**
  - Nutrition and lifestyle modifications PLUS HMG CoA reductase inhibitors (statins)
    - Mainstay of evidence-based treatment for both primary and secondary prevention.
  - Ezetimibe
    - Especially considered in patients for secondary prevention of ASCVD and where high-intensity statin either has not achieved the LDL goal or cannot be tolerated.
  - PCSK9 Inhibitors (Alirocumab & evolocumab)
    - Should be added to existing maximal statin dosing as well as ezetimibe in patients considered very high risk for ASCVD or who have not achieved their desired LDL goals (typically LDLs < 70 mg/dL)

	High-Intensity Statins	**Moderate Intensity**	**Low Intensity**
Primary Prevention	ASCVD Risk of ≥ 20% or "High Risk"	ASCVD Risk of ≥ 7.5% to < 20% or "Intermediate Risk" ASCVD Risk of 5% to < 7.5% or "Borderline Risk" + ASCVD Risk Enhancers	ASCVD Risk of < 5% or "Low Risk"
Secondary Prevention	"Very High Risk" ASCVD	ASCVD + Unable to Tolerate High-Intensity Statins	ASCVD + Unable to Tolerate Moderate-Intensity Statins
Desired LDL-c Lowering	≥ 50%	30% - 49%	< 30%
Statins	▪ Atorvastatin 40 – 80 mg ▪ Rosuvastatin 20 – 40 mg	▪ Atorvastatin 10 – 20 mg ▪ Rosuvastatin 5 – 10 mg ▪ Simvastatin 20 – 40 mg ▪ Pravastatin 40 – 80 mg ▪ Lovastatin 40 – 80 mg ▪ Fluvastatin XL 80 mg ▪ Fluvastatin 40 mg BID ▪ Pitavastatin 1 – 4 mg	▪ Simvastatin 10 mg ▪ Pravastatin 10 – 20 mg ▪ Lovastatin 20 mg ▪ Fluvastatin 20 – 40 mg

HYPERTENSION

- **PATHO:** Elevated peripheral vascular resistance, cardiac output, or both.
- **CLASSIC PRESENTATION:** May be completely asymptomatic.
- **CLASSIC FINDINGS:** The average of two or more appropriately seated BP values from two or more clinical encounters of an SBP > 130 mmHg or DBP > 80 mmHg.
- **TREATMENT:**
  - Selection of initial antihypertensive should be based on compelling indications and the degree of BP elevation.
  - Common first-line agents include ACE-inhibitors, ARBs, CCB, and thiazide diuretics. In black patients, ACE-inhibitors or ARBs as monotherapy may not be as effective but can be added to other agents.
  - Avoid ACE-inhibitors or ARBs during pregnancy.

HEART FAILURE – ACUTE DECOMPENSATED (ADHF)

- **PATHO:** Sustained neurohormonal response to decreased perfusion, inflammatory and oxidative stress causing cardiac tissue hypoxemia, and acute worsening of systemic perfusion and target organ hypoperfusion.
- **CLASSIC PRESENTATION:** Acute pulmonary edema, fatigue, tachycardia, bilateral lower extremity edema, abdominal distension, elevated JVD, hepatojugular reflex, elevated BNP.
- **CLASSIC FINDINGS:** Acute pulmonary edema evident on chest x-ray, ultrasound findings of B-lines, inferior vena cava collapsibility index, left ventricular function, Forrester classification I, II, III, or IV.
- **TREATMENT:**
  - Positive-pressure ventilation, loop diuretics, and vasodilators (nitroglycerin given IV or SL).
  - May require inotropic +/- vasopressor support.

HEART FAILURE – CHRONIC WITH PRESERVED EF or REDUCED (HFpEF & HFrEF)

- **PATHO:** A neurohormonal response to decreased perfusion, increased plasma volume, impaired venous capacitance resulting in impaired contraction or inotropy of the left and or right-side decreased organ perfusion.
- **CLASSIC PRESENTATION:** LV failure: reduced exercise tolerance, dyspnea, orthopnea, paroxysmal nocturnal dyspnea, rales, fatigue, and possible tachycardia and/or elevated BNP. RV failure: weight gain, bilateral lower extremity swelling and edema, abdominal distension, elevated JVD, hepatojugular reflex.
- **CLASSIC FINDINGS:** NYHA class I through IV and AHA/ACC Stages A, B, C, or D.
- **TREATMENT:** Based on AHA/ACC stage and compelling indications, but commonly includes ACE-inhibitors or ARB, sacubitril/valsartan, beta-blockers, and/or diuretics.

HEART FAILURE – HYPERTROPHIC OBSTRUCTIVE CARDIOMYOPATHY (HOCM or HCM)

- **PATHO:** Cardiac ischemia affecting mitral valve systolic anterior motion causing a dynamic outflow obstruction. Patient usually experience sudden cardiac death.
- **CLASSIC PRESENTATION:** Dyspnea, paroxysmal nocturnal, presyncope or syncope, angina, palpitations, peripheral edema, orthopnea. A cause of sudden cardiac death.
- **CLASSIC FINDINGS:** Left ventricular outflow obstruction, mitral valve regurgitation.
- **TREATMENT:**
  - Non-dihydropyridine calcium channel blockers, beta-1 selective antagonists, loop diuretics. Avoid digoxin as it can worsen symptoms due to inotropic effects.
  - Consider ICD placement to prevent SCD.

PERICARDITIS
- **PATHO:** Inflammation of the pericardium from MI, drugs (hydralazine; procainamide), infections (mainly viral), or immune mediated reasons (e.g., SLE or lupus)
- **CLASSIC PRESENTATION:** Chest pain worsened with lying back, improved leaning forward; pericardial friction rub on auscultation of the heart.
- **CLASSIC FINDINGS:** 12-lead ECG: Widespread ST segment elevation or PR depression; ECHO: can show pericardial effusion
- **TREATMENT:**
  - If post-MI (aspirin), if viral or immune mediated (NSAIDs or steroids) x 1-2 weeks. Add on colchicine up 3 months.
  - If pericardial effusion with symptoms & vital sign changes (needs pericardiocentesis).

PERIPHERAL ARTERIAL DISEASE (PAD)
- **PATHO:** Atherosclerosis or thromboembolic processes that alters the normal structure and or function of the aorta, its visceral arterial branches and the arteries of the lower extremities.
- **CLASSIC PRESENTATION:** Sudden onset of ischemic leg symptoms (6 P's), postprandial abdominal pain, nonhealing lower extremity wounds.
- **CLASSIC FINDINGS:** ABI less than or equal to 0.9
- **TREATMENT:**
  - Smoking cessation, management of hypertension, hyperlipidemia, diabetes and or hyperhomocystinemia.
  - Aspirin, ACE-inhibitors with pentoxifylline (ABI < 0.9) or anticoagulation (if ABI < 0.4).

RAYNAUD'S SYNDROME
- **PATHO:** Hematologic and connective tissue changes affecting blood flow through vessels commonly in the fingers and toes.
- **CLASSIC PRESENTATION:** Paroxysmal color changes to the distal aspect of the fingers and toes with a white to blue and eventually red sequence.
- **CLASSIC FINDINGS:** Abnormal cold challenge test.
- **TREATMENT:** Gentle hand/feet warming, topical nitroglycerin, amlodipine or nifedipine. Avoid triggers.

PULMONARY HYPERTENSION
- **PATHO:** Imbalance in endothelial vasoconstrictors versus vasodilators, increasing vascular resistance and pulmonary artery pressures, also facilitates increased risk of thrombosis, increased proliferation of smooth muscle cells and a proptosis of smooth muscle cells.
- **CLASSIC PRESENTATION:** Exertional dyspnea, increased JVP, lower extremity pitting edema in the lower.
- **CLASSIC FINDINGS:** Increased pulmonary artery pressure, pulmonary capillary wedge pressure. ECG- right axis deviation, RV enlargement, right atrial enlargement and RV strain; cardiac ECHO- paradoxical bulging of the interventricular septum into the LV during systole.
- **TREATMENT:**
  - Treatment of the underlying cause of possible or removal of offending agent (if possible) based on one of the five WHO group classifications: CCB (WHO group 1), anticoagulation (usually WHO group 1,4), and WHO group 2,3 consider: ET-1 antagonists, PDE-5 inhibitors (sildenafil or tadalafil), and/or IP receptor agonist therapy (selexipag).

SHOCK - CARDIOGENIC

- **PATHO:** Relates to its precipitating cardiac event, which is most likely an acute MI.
- **CLASSIC PRESENTATION:** Acute pulmonary edema, fatigue, tachycardia, bilateral lower extremity edema, abdominal distension, elevated JVD, hepatojugular reflex, hepatosplenomegaly, elevated BNP.
- **CLASSIC FINDINGS:** SBP < 90 mmHg, evidence of end-organ hypoperfusion.
- **TREATMENT:**
  - Identify and treat the underlying cause (very important this is considered)
  - Airway control, breathing and ventilation assistance, and vasopressor support (e.g., high-dose dopamine, epinephrine, or norepinephrine).

SHOCK - HEMORRHAGIC

- **PATHO:** Volume losses that impair the delivery of adequate oxygen supply to meet the demands of tissue and causing intracellular hypoxia.
- **CLASSIC PRESENTATION:** Acute intravascular volume loss (trauma, surgery, or other hemorrhages).
- **CLASSIC FINDINGS:** SBP < 90 mmHg, evidence of end-organ hypoperfusion.
- **TREATMENT:**
  - Volume replacement with either crystalloid (0.9% NS or LR) or colloid (albumin 5%, Dextran, or blood).
  - Use blood (PRBCs) if traumatic and bleeding or hemorrhage.

SHOCK - HYPOVOLEMIC

- **PATHO:** Volume losses that impair the delivery of adequate oxygen supply to meet the demands of tissue and causing intracellular hypoxia.
- **CLASSIC PRESENTATION:** Acute intravascular volume loss (trauma, surgery, or other hemorrhages).
- **CLASSIC FINDINGS:** SBP < 90 mmHg, evidence of end-organ hypoperfusion.
- **TREATMENT:** Volume replacement with either crystalloid (0.9% NS or LR) or colloid (albumin 5%, Dextran, or blood). Use blood (PRBCs) if traumatic and bleeding or hemorrhage.

SHOCK - NEUROGENIC

- **PATHO:** A loss of vascular tone, loss of sympathetic cardiovascular innervation, and unopposed parasympathetic innervation to the heart.
- **CLASSIC PRESENTATION:** Evidence of end-organ hypoperfusion.
- **CLASSIC FINDINGS:** Spinal cord injury with SBP less than 100 mmHg and HR less than 60 bpm.
- **TREATMENT:**
  - Maintaining tissue perfusion and preventing secondary cord injury from hypoperfusion with "inopressor" therapies:
    - Norepinephrine or phenylephrine that deliver both increases in vascular resistance as well as provide inotropic effects.

SHOCK - SEPTIC

- **PATHO:** Inflammatory response to infectious processes resulting in tissue injury, endothelial dysfunction, and macrophage activation causing a dynamic pro-inflammatory/anti-inflammatory process.
- **CLASSIC PRESENTATION:** Temperature > 38 C or < 36 C; pulse > 90 bpm, respiratory rate > 20 bpm or PaCO2 < 32 mmHg, WBC > 12,000 or < 4,000 or > 10% bands.
- **CLASSIC FINDINGS:** Two or more SIRS/qSOFA score plus hypotension despite adequate fluid resuscitation or a lactate greater than or equal to 2 mmol/L.
- **TREATMENT:**
    - Airway/breathing support, crystalloid volume resuscitation (20-30 cc/kg with 0.9% NS or LR)
    - Initial broad-spectrum antibiotic (after blood and urine cultures).
    - Add norepinephrine (if MAP is still < 65 mmHg after IV fluids and antibiotics)
        - Can consider adding hydrocortisone if MAP < 65 mmHg after IV fluids + norepinephrine.

SUPRAVENTRICULAR TACHYCARDIA (SVT)

- **PATHO:** Abnormal cardiac conduction where two paths of an electrical circuit exist, each with unequal responsiveness, and one pathway has slower conduction.
- **CLASSIC PRESENTATION:** Anxiety, palpitations, chest discomfort, lightheadedness, syncope, exercise intolerance, lightheadedness, dyspnea, hypotension, acute HF, or shock.
- **CLASSIC FINDINGS:** Narrow complex, regular tachycardia with a ventricular rate of 180 to 220 bpm, no detectable P waves on 12-lead ECG.
- **TREATMENT:**
    - Hemodynamically unstable – immediate synchronized cardioversion.
    - Hemodynamically stable – Valsalva maneuvers, or adenosine 6 mg rapid IV push, may repeat once at 6 mg, then 12 mg IVP.

VASCULITIS – KAWASAKI DISEASE (MUCOCUTANESOUS LYMPH NODE SYNDROME)

- **PATHO:** acute febrile vasculitis of small to medium sized arteries in pediatric patients resulting in coronary artery aneurysms, dissection, and or thrombosis.
- **CLASSIC PRESENTATION:** Fever for 5 days or more, and at least 4 of the 5 clinical signs: rash, cervical lymphadenopathy, bilateral conjunctival injection, oral mucosal changes, peripheral extremity changes.
- **CLASSIC FINDINGS:** Elevated ESR, CRP, ischemic changes on ECG, coronary aneurysm & dissection on ECHO.
- **TREATMENT:**
    - IVIG, aspirin (high dose) at least 6 to 8 weeks but for life if coronary aneurysm present.
    - May consider prednisone, infliximab, and warfarin.

VASCULITIS – RAYNAUD'S DISEASES

- **PATHO:** Hematologic and connective tissue changes affecting blood flow through vessels commonly in the fingers and toes.
- **CLASSIC PRESENTATION:** Paroxysmal color changes to the distal aspect of the fingers and toes with a white to blue and eventually red sequence.
- **CLASSIC FINDINGS:** Abnormal cold challenge test.
- **TREATMENT:** Gentle hand/feet warming, topical nitroglycerin, amlodipine or nifedipine. Avoidance of triggers.

VASCULITIS – TEMPORAL (or GIANT CELL) ARTERITIS
- **PATHO:** Vasculitis of moderate to large vessels with multi nucleated giant cells, and a lymphoid infiltrate involving the superficial temporal and ophthalmic arteries. Risk of blindness if not treated early and aggressively.
- **CLASSIC PRESENTATION:** Ipsilateral temporal headache with jaw claudication (pain with chewing due to ischemia), absent temporal pulses, progressive visual changes/loss.
- **CLASSIC FINDINGS:** Elevation in ESR and CRP, temporal artery biopsy showing vasculitis.
- **TREATMENT:**
  - Prednisone 40 to 60 mg/d for at least 1 month but may require taper over 1-2 years plus with or without aspirin.

VENOUS THROMBOEMBOLISM – DEEP VEIN THROMBOSIS (DVT)
- **PATHO:** Virchow's triad of venous stasis, activation of coagulation, and endothelial injury triggers formation of a venous thrombosis that can embolize and travel to other organs (commonly the lungs).
- **CLASSIC PRESENTATION:** Unilateral leg pain, swelling, redness, or warmth.
- **CLASSIC FINDINGS:** Wells score greater than 1; ultrasound findings on imaging consistent with DVT.
- **TREATMENT:**
  - Anticoagulation (primarily with apixaban, dabigatran, rivaroxaban, or enoxaparin at full doses) for 3 months following the first unprovoked DVT (longer if unprovoked; duration is dependent on bleeding and recurrent VTE risk).
  - Alternative agents to these include: warfarin titrated to an INR of 2 - 3 and edoxaban.

VENOUS THROMBOEMBOLISM – PULMONARY EMBOLISM (PE)
- **PATHO:** Previously formed DVT that dislodges, travels to the right ventricle, and lodges in the pulmonary vasculature
- **CLASSIC PRESENTATION:** Focal, sharp, pleuritic chest pain and painful respirations, hypoxia, tachycardia, hypotension.
- **CLASSIC FINDINGS:** PERC Rule, Wells criteria.
- **TREATMENT:**
  - Acute management: Anticoagulation (with unfractionated heparin or enoxaparin) and/or if patients have a submassive or massive PE with evidence of instability or RV dysfunction then consider fibrinolytics (primarily alteplase or tenecteplase) may be used with mechanical thrombectomy, or intravascular directed thrombolysis.
  - Once stabilized, the patient can bridged to oral anticoagulation for 3 months following the first unprovoked event (longer if unprovoked; duration is dependent on bleeding and recurrent VTE risk).

ACNE VULGARIS
- **PATHO:** Enhanced secretion and retention of sebum due to hyperproliferation of the follicular epidermis.
- **CLASSIC PRESENTATION:** May occur on the face, back, upper trunk, or deltoid.
- **CLASSIC FINDINGS:** Dilated follicle with keratin plugs or open comedone.
- **TREATMENT:**
  - Retinoids are the first line for inflammatory acne in combination with benzoyl peroxide.
  - Other non-pharmacologic treatments alone or in combination with topical or systemic drug therapy.
  - Isotretinoin is reserved for severe, recalcitrant nodular acne and females must be a part of the iPLEDGE program.

BURNS - THERMAL
- **PATHO:** Zone of coagulation/necrosis (innermost region), zone of ischemia/stasis, and zone of hyperemia.
- **CLASSIC PRESENTATION:** Discolored skin (pink, red, white, or brown), dry surface (1st & 4th degree), moist surface (2nd & 3rd degree), blistering.
- **CLASSIC FINDINGS:** First through fourth-degree burn to a given region of body surface area.
- **TREATMENT:**
  - Early and aggressive fluid resuscitation using calculated volume (Parkland, among others) in the first 24 hours for 2nd degree burns and greater, followed by albumin and supportive care measures.
  - Also requires wound debridement, nutrition, temperature regulation and wound care/dressings.

CONTACT DERMATITIS
- **PATHO:** Sensitization phase (antigen presentation to CD4 and CD8 T-cells), and elicitation phase (T-cells stimulated recruitment of cytokines, inflammatory mediators, and keratinocyte secretion of IL-4, and IL-8).
- **CLASSIC PRESENTATION:** Inflammation, swelling, urticaria, and pain of the skin.
- **CLASSIC FINDINGS:** Delayed onset of erythema (up to 1-3 days), blisters, edema, vesicles, pustules, weals.
- **TREATMENT:**
  - Decontamination/removal of the affecting irritant, topical corticosteroids (clobetasol, cortisone, hydrocortisone), emollients (aloe vera, ammonium lactate, salicylic acid, urea).
  - Refractory cases can consider addition of topical calcineurin inhibitors (pimecrolimus, tacrolimus).

DRUG-INDUCED HYPERSENSITIVITY SYNDROME
- **PATHO:** Accumulation of arene oxide metabolites causing activation of cell-mediated immunity into the local tissue, proinflammatory environment, and ultimately resulting in cell death.
- **CLASSIC PRESENTATION:** Within the first two months of therapy of a medication associated with DIHS.
- **CLASSIC FINDINGS:** Fever, skin eruption, and internal organ involvement.
- **TREATMENT:**
  - Discontinuation of suspected affecting medication, methylprednisolone IV 30 mg/kg.

ERYTHEMA MULTIFORME

- **PATHO:** Cell-mediated immunity caused by an influx of macrophages and CD8+ T lymphocytes into the local tissue result in a proinflammatory environment, ultimately resulting in cell death.
- **CLASSIC PRESENTATION:** Target lesions followed by a blistering rash on mucosal surfaces, face, trunk, and limbs.
- **CLASSIC FINDINGS:** EM minor (symmetrical lesions in acral disposition without mucosal involvement), EM major (extensive skin lesions covering less than 10% BSA with typical target lesions, and at least two different mucosal sites).
- **TREATMENT:**
  - Treat underlying infection, topical corticosteroids, analgesia.
  - Alternative agents: oral corticosteroids.

HERPES ZOSTER (SHINGLES)

- **PATHO:** VZV reactivation causes viral replication in neuronal cell bodies, resulting in inflammation and blistering of the skin following a centripetal that follows a dermatome.
- **CLASSIC PRESENTATION:** Pre-eruptive, acute eruptive, chronic infection stages.
- **CLASSIC FINDINGS:** Macule formation, turning into painful vesicle development and rupture, ulceration, and crust emergence.
- **TREATMENT:**
  - Immunocompetent patients receive oral antiviral (acyclovir, famciclovir, valacyclovir) or parenteral therapy in immunocompromised patients (acyclovir, foscarnet).
  - Analgesia with multimodal pain management.

ONYCHOMYCOSIS (TOENAIL FUNGAL INFECTION)

- **PATHO:** Dermatophytes penetrate the nail bed, proliferating on the dead corneocytes, and breach the hyponychium, proximal spread of proliferation, causing a dense inflammatory infiltrate, cytokine response, and progression to a chronic nail bed infection. Diabetics at greater risk of complications.
- **CLASSIC PRESENTATION:** Discoloration of nails, onycholysis, subungual hyperkeratosis, thickened nail plate.
- **CLASSIC FINDINGS:** Dermoscopy findings of onychomycosis with a fungal culture.
- **TREATMENT:**
  - Oral antifungals (terbinafine or itraconazole).
  - If Griseofulvin is used, must take for 4-6 months.

PSORIASIS

- **PATHO:** Chronic T-cell mediated inflammatory disease influenced by both genetic & environmental factors.
- **CLASSIC PRESENTATION:** Red patches with white scales on the forearms, shins, navel, and scalp.
- **CLASSIC FINDINGS:** Erythrodermic, guttate, inverse, or plaque in appearance, with positive Auspitz sign.
- **TREATMENT:**
  - Topical agents (Emollients, anthralin, coal tar, salicylic acid, steroids (cortisone, dexamethasone, hydrocortisone), tazarotene) with or without systemic DMARD, biologic DMARDs or corticosteroids.
  - Avoid TNF-alpha inhibitors in patients with NYHA Class 2 or 3 HF or known latent TB not on treatment.

STAPHYLOCOCCAL SCALDING SKIN SYNDROME

- **PATHO:** Skin exfoliation caused by toxins produced by Staphylococcus bacteria targeting the desmoglein 1 complex in the zona granulosa of the epidermis.
- **CLASSIC PRESENTATION:** Irritability, fever, malaise followed by a tender rash 24 to 48 hours later and generation of flaccid blisters and bullae with fluid or frank yellow pus.
- **CLASSIC FINDINGS:** Ranging from mild localized area to exfoliation of the entire body (but NOT mucosal membranes) due to systemic distribution of staphylococcal exotoxins.
- **TREATMENT:** Systemic antimicrobials (cefazolin, nafcillin, vancomycin), topical Aquaphor applied 2-3 times per day.

STEVENS-JOHNSON SYNDROME (SJS) & TOXIC EPIDERMAL NECROLYSIS (TEN)

- **PATHO:** Sensitization (antigen presentation), followed by secondary inflammatory process (T-helper cells, NK cells, TNF-alpha, nitric oxide, and IL-8).
- **CLASSIC PRESENTATION:** Inflammation, swelling, urticaria, and pain of the skin, followed by keratinocyte apoptosis.
- **CLASSIC FINDINGS:** SJS – BSA less than 10%; SJS/TEN overlap – BSA 10-30%; TEN – BSA greater than 30%.
- **TREATMENT:** Treat similar to a 2nd and 3rd degree thermal burn, but may also consider cyclosporine, IVIG, plasmapheresis.

URTICARIA

- **PATHO:** Initial sensitization after allergen exposure, followed by re-exposure to the sensitized allergen stimulates IgE-mediated mast cell degranulation, increasing capillary permeability, vasodilation, smooth muscle contraction, sensory nerve stimulation, myocardial depression, and activation of secondary inflammatory pathways.
- **CLASSIC PRESENTATION:** Intensely pruritic, well-circumscribed wheals with erythematous raised borders and blanched centers that last for less than 24 hours.
- **CLASSIC FINDINGS:** Affects the superficial dermis
- **TREATMENT:** Removal of the offending agent, diphenhydramine, famotidine. For severe, chronic, or unresponsive cases consider prednisone x 5 days.

ANAPHYLAXIS

- **PATHO:** Initial sensitization, followed by re-exposure, IgE mast cell degranulation, causing increased capillary permeability, vasodilation, smooth muscle contraction, sensory nerve stimulation, myocardial depression, and activation of secondary inflammatory pathways.
- **CLASSIC PRESENTATION:** Pruritus, nausea/vomiting/diarrhea, flushing, urticaria, abdominal pain, chest pain, dyspnea, wheezing, respiratory insufficiency and failure, dizziness, syncope, hypotension, angioedema, and shock.
- **CLASSIC FINDINGS:** New onset of cutaneous symptoms, respiratory difficulty, hypotension, or signs of shock.
- **TREATMENT:** Management of anaphylaxis prioritizes airway, breathing, and circulation with early aggressive pharmacotherapy with epinephrine to potentially avoid endotracheal intubation.

ANTICOAGULANT REVERSAL

- **PATHO:** Drug-induced anticoagulation resulting in hemorrhage or other indications for rapid reversal.
- **CLASSIC PRESENTATION:** Fatigue, generalized lethargy, blood in vomit/urine/stool, coffee-ground emesis, hypotension, tachycardia.
- **CLASSIC FINDINGS:** Acute major bleeding - hypotension, altered mental status, end-organ injury, acute hemoglobin decrease of at least 2 g/dL, thrombocytopenia.
- **TREATMENT:** Specific reversal agents including aPCC, andexanet alfa, PCC, idarucizumab, phytonadione, and protamine.

PAIN, AGITATION, DELIRIUM

- **PATHO:** Perception of pain through inflammation and secondary neurotransmission to the brain. Agitation results from sympathetic activity due to pain perception and HPA axis dysregulation. Delirium results from decreased dopaminergic and serotonergic neurotransmission in the brain.
- **CLASSIC PRESENTATION:** Self-reported pain, tachycardia, hypertension, hyperpyrexia, diaphoresis, increased analgesia, and sedation demands.
- **CLASSIC FINDINGS:** Pain – CPOT, BPS; Agitation – RASS, SAS; Delirium – CAM-ICU, ICDSC.
- **TREATMENT:** Treat underlying process and reversible causes, appropriate analgesia, sedation.

RAPID SEQUENCE INTUBATION (RSI)

- **PATHO:** Simultaneous administration of a sedative and an NMB agent to render a patient rapidly unconscious and flaccid to facilitate emergent endotracheal intubation.
- **CLASSIC PRESENTATION:** 7 P's of RSI.
- **CLASSIC FINDINGS:** Altered mental status, hypoxia, poor ventilation or oxygenation despite non-invasive interventions, impending airway obstruction.
- **TREATMENT:** Induction of sedation (etomidate or ketamine), paralysis (succinylcholine, or rocuronium). Common teaching is to avoid ketamine in patients with risk of elevated ICP.

DEFINITIONS
- **Biologic Agents**
    - High-priority agents pose a significant risk to National security because of their ability to be found in natural resources over the environment that can quickly be disseminated and transmitted from 1 person to another, and that carries a high risk of mortality and risk for panic and social disruption.
    - Agents are broken down into categories A, B, and C based on their ability to disseminate and cause significant burden and death.
- **Bioterrorism**
    - The intentional use of biologic agents to in fact, injure and or kill unsuspecting individuals while also causing social disruption and panic.
- **Weaponized**
    - The process of making a naturally occurring biological agent into an easily splittable substance.
- **Emergency preparedness**
    - Plans that can be implemented in the event of a natural or human-made disaster.
    - CDC has specific criteria and emergency preparedness and response recommendations and guidelines.
- **Isolation**
    - Restriction of movement or separation of the sick or infected person with contagious disease. Usually in a hospital setting but can also be at home or in a dedicated isolation facility.
- **Quarantine**
    - Restriction of movement or separation of healthy persons presumed exposed to a contagious disease usually at home but can also be in a dedicated quarantine facility.

GENERAL CONCEPTS OF BIOTERRORISM
- Mass casualty pattern is usually the first indication of terrorism.
- Signs and symptoms of the disease may not be apparent for several days after the attack.
- Greatest risk of expression occurs via inhalation, ingestion, and/or skin contact.
- Many toxins may cause direct pulmonary or systemic toxicity that leads to death if not recognized early.

FACTOR THAT IMPACT OUTCOMES
- Biologic agent of exposure in the amount or dose.
- Early recognition of the exposure to an agent.
- Early management of exposure to an agent.
- Isolation to reduce exposure of others through contact.
- Timely and effective communication.
- Access to essential resources.
- Age and comorbidities present in the patient's exposed.
- Immune system regulation and immune O senescence.

CDC CATEGORIES OF BIOLOGIC AGENTS
Category A Agents
- Can quickly disseminate or be transmitted from person to person.
- Can result in high mortality rates and potential for significant disruption of the public health services.
- Might cause public panic and social disruption.
- Requires special attention and action for public health preparedness.
- Agents included
    - Anthrax (Bacillus anthracis)

- Botulism (Clostridium botulinum toxin)
- Plague (Yersinia pestis)
- Smallpox (Variola major)
- Tularemia (Francisella tularensis)
- Viral Hemorrhagic Fever (mainly outside the US)

Class B Agents
- Moderate to easy dissemination
- Can result in moderate morbidity rates in low mortality rate
- Require specific enhancements of CDC diagnostic capacity and enhanced disease surveillance
- Example agents include
  - Brucellosis
  - Q fever (Coxiella burnetii)
  - Ricin Toxin
  - Typhus
  - Cholera (Water safety concerns)

Class C Agents
- Availability
- Ease of production in
- Potential for high morbidity and mortality rates a major health impact
- Example agents include
  - Nipah virus
  - Hantavirus

ANTHRAX
- **PATHO:** *B. anthracis* spores enter cells releasing edema & lethal toxin, causing multi-organ failure and death. Primary mode of entry is contact with or inhalation of spores. Incubation period of 2 – 60 days.
- **CLASSIC PRESENTATION:** Cutaneous, inhalational, or GI. Chest X-ray shows widened mediastinum +/- pleural effusions
- **CLASSIC FINDINGS:** Edema, redness, and swelling to a blister and then to eschar; flu-like then respiratory failure; oral or esophageal ulcer and bloody diarrhea.
- **TREATMENT:**
  - Ciprofloxacin, doxycycline treatment/prophylaxis.
  - Severe cases require parenteral combination.

BOTULINUM (BOTULISM)
- **PATHO:** Spore-forming bacteria (C. botulinum) produces neurotoxins that cleave SNARE proteins, preventing acetylcholine neurotransmission.
- **CLASSIC PRESENTATION:** Similar to anticholinergic toxidrome with symmetrical descending paralysis.
- **CLASSIC FINDINGS:** Bioassay using mouse neutralization with or without EMG.
- **TREATMENT:**
  - Mechanical ventilation until new neurotransmitters/synapses form, heptavalent botulinum antitoxin, trivalent antitoxin, or infant botulinum antitoxin.

BRUCELLOSIS

- **PATHO:** Brucellae species transmitted to humans via ingestion, inhalation, mucous membranes, or skin abrasion that then attacks the cells of the reticuloendothelial system. Goats and sheep carry the most common form, Brucella melitensis.
- **CLASSIC PRESENTATION:** Arthralgia, fever, fatigue/malaise.
- **CLASSIC FINDINGS:** Enlarged liver or spleen, lymphadenopathy, malodorous perspiration (pathognomic but rare).
- **TREATMENT:** Doxycycline plus streptomycin or gentamicin.

CHOLERA

- **PATHO:** Vibrio cholera infection causing severe acute onset watery diarrhea due to heat labile enterotoxin that inhibits absorption while also enhancing intestinal secretion.
- **CLASSIC PRESENTATION:** Rice water diarrhea, intestinal cramping without abdominal pain or fever.
- **CLASSIC FINDINGS:** Dark field or phase contrast microscopy can show motile vibrio by visualization.
- **TREATMENT:**
  - Primary treatment with oral or parenteral rehydration with salt solution or LR
  - Can consider azithromycin or doxycycline.

Q-FEVER

- **PATHO:** Infection caused by Coxiella burnetii resulting in endocarditis, pericarditis, and myocarditis. Commonly found in cattle, goats, and sheep which can serve as natural reservoirs, thereby putting farmers and slaughterhouse workers at increased risk
- **CLASSIC PRESENTATION:** Flu-like illness with pleuritic chest pain.
- **CLASSIC FINDINGS:** Whole blood or serum PCR examination, mild hepatitis, thrombocytopenia.
- **TREATMENT:** Tetracycline or doxycycline, trimethoprim-sulfamethoxazole.

PLAGUE

- **PATHO:** Transmitted through bites from infected fleas from rodents or inhalation of droplets containing Y. pestis in the Southwestern part of the US.
- **CLASSIC PRESENTATION:** Acute painful lymph nodes or "bubo."
- **CLASSIC FINDINGS:** Bacteremic, CXR showing lobar pneumonia with cavitation
- **TREATMENT:** Fluroquinolones (ciprofloxacin, levofloxacin, moxifloxacin), doxycycline or gentamicin.

RICIN

- **PATHO:** A potent protein lectin that comes from castor beans that are native to India and also grown in the southern United States. It consists of B-chain. facilitating cell binding and entry of A-chain into cells, inhibiting protein synthesis.
- **CLASSIC PRESENTATION:** Ingestion – Severe GI distress, hepatic injury, hemorrhage; inhaled – cough, fever, pulmonary edema and hypoxemia.
- **CLASSIC FINDINGS:** Leukocytosis and fever, similar to other infectious diseases.
- **TREATMENT:** Supportive care, decontamination.

SMALLPOX

- **PATHO:** Infection by Variola virus, resulting in multiple complications including circulating immune complexes, significant viremia, and immune system leading to multiorgan dysfunction.
- **CLASSIC PRESENTATION:** Incubation period followed by prodrome, then variola major or variola minor.
- **CLASSIC FINDINGS:** Fever followed by a papular rash, progressing to vesicular and pustular rash.
- **TREATMENT:** Vaccination within 4 days of exposure with or without cidofovir plus quarantine for 17 days.

TULAREMIA

- **PATHO:** Infection caused by F. tularensis after exposure to rabbits, hares, and some rodents in the south–central and western part of the United States during the summer.
- **CLASSIC PRESENTATION:** Depends on route of exposure – ulceroglandular, glandular, oculoglandular, oral pharyngeal, pneumonia.
- **CLASSIC FINDINGS:** Blood and sputum culture in cysteine enriched medium.
- **TREATMENT:** Gentamicin, tobramycin plus chloramphenicol (for meningitis). Prophylaxis with ciprofloxacin or doxycycline.

ADDISON'S DISEASE
- **PATHO:** Adrenal failure causing reduced cortisol production, followed by aldosterone, eventually causing an elevation of ACTH and MSH due to the loss of negative feedback inhibition.
- **CLASSIC PRESENTATION:** Weakness, weight loss, orthostasis, hyperpigmentation of the skin.
- **CLASSIC FINDINGS:** Decreased cortisol level, increase in K+ but a low Na+
- **TREATMENT:** Treat underlying cause, hydrocortisone +/- fludrocortisone (if additional mineralocorticoid effect needed to correct K+ and Na+ in serum and urine). Non-pharmacological additional support: TED hose.

ADRENAL CRISIS
- **PATHO:** Inadequate concentrations of cortisol leading to systemic and hemodynamic compromise.
- **CLASSIC PRESENTATION:** Due to an acute stressful event such as infection, traumatic injuries, or unexpected surgical interventions.
- **CLASSIC FINDINGS:** Hypotension, weakness, hyperkalemia, and hyponatremia.
- **TREATMENT:** Hydrocortisone by IV infusion with dose ranging from 25 – 100 mg every 6 hours with the dose determined in part by the severity of stress (infection vs trauma). If in the context of sepsis, make sure there is adequate fluid resuscitation and vasopressor use.

CUSHINGS SYNDROME
- **PATHO:** Excess production of corticosteroids most commonly from a pituitary adenoma.
- **CLASSIC PRESENTATION:** Obesity, moon facies, hypertension, hyperglycemia, dyslipidemia, osteoporosis.
- **CLASSIC FINDINGS:** Elevated cortisol, low ACTH, hyponatremia, hypokalemia
- **TREATMENT:** Surgical resection +/- mitotane (or) ketoconazole +/- metyrapone

DIABETES INSIPIDUS
- **PATHO:** Inadequate or absent ADH; Central DI (CDI) secondary to CNS trauma, hypoxic encephalopathy, or a tumor; Nephrogenic DI (NDI) renal failed response to ADH.
- **CLASSIC PRESENTATION:** Polyuria, excess urination, increased thirst (polydipsia).
- **CLASSIC FINDINGS:** POsm > 295 mOsm/kg and UOsm is < 500 mOsm/kg.
- **TREATMENT:** CDI – desmopressin; NDI – treat underlying cause.

DIABETES MELLITUS - GESTATIONAL
- **PATHO:** Pregnancy-related hormone changes resulting in insulin resistance.
- **CLASSIC PRESENTATION:** Asymptomatic but may initially present as DKA or HHNK.
- **CLASSIC FINDINGS:** Positive oral glucose tolerance test.
- **TREATMENT:** Oral (metformin, glyburide), or insulin to target HbA1c 6.5% or lower, FPG less than 95 mg/dL, PPG (1 hour) less than 140 mg/dL, PPG (2 hour) less than 120 mg/dL.

DIABETES MELLITUS – TYPE 1
- **PATHO:** Autoimmune destruction of pancreatic beta-cells resulting in absent or deficient insulin.
- **CLASSIC PRESENTATION:** DKA, but symptoms may have existed for days (polyuria, polydipsia, polyphagia).
- **CLASSIC FINDINGS:** HbA1c 6.5% or higher, FPG 126 mg/dL or above, OGTT 200 mg/dL or above. random plasma glucose 200 mg/dL or above.
- **TREATMENT:** Basal (insulin degludec, glargine, detemir) plus bolus (using insulin aspart, glulisine, lispro, or inhaled) strategy is preferred and initially started with a total daily insulin dose of 0.4-1 units/kg/d divided in approximately a 50/50% ratio between basal to bolus then adjust.

DIABETES MELLITUS – TYPE 2
- **PATHO:** Progressive pancreatic beta-cell destruction coupled with insulin resistance and often is accompanied by concomitant hypertension and dyslipidemia
- **CLASSIC PRESENTATION:** Asymptomatic but may initially present as DKA or HHNK.
- **CLASSIC FINDINGS:** HbA1c 6.5% or higher, FPG 126 mg/dL or above, OGTT 200 mg/dL or above. random plasma glucose 200 mg/dL or above.
- **TREATMENT:** Metformin (generic and well-established); GLP-1 receptor agonists or SGLT2 inhibitor (ASCVD or CKD), SGLT2 inhibitor (HF or CKD), DPP-4 inhibitor, GLP-1 receptor agonists, SGLT2 inhibitor, or thiazolidinediones (No ASCVD or CKD).

DIABETES MELLITUS – DKA & HHS
- **PATHO:** Insulin deficiency/resistance and glucagon excess, resulting in hyperglycemia, dehydration and electrolyte disturbances (DKA); Increased hepatic gluconeogenesis and glycogenolysis, with absent ketosis, resulting in osmotic diuresis and dehydration with impaired renal excretion of glucose (HHNS).
- **CLASSIC PRESENTATION:** AMS, dehydration, hypotension, polyuria, polydipsia, polyphagia.
- **CLASSIC FINDINGS:** Anion gap acidosis, low CO_2, ketones, glucose > 250 (DKA); Glucose > 600, hyperosmolarity (HHNS)
- **TREATMENT:** Crystalloid volume resuscitation, electrolyte replacement (K. Na, Mg, Phos), insulin. Note: Do not start insulin until potassium checked. Can start to feed after anion-gap has closed.

DIABETES MELLITUS - HYPOGLYCEMIA
- **PATHO:** Enhanced insulin secretion (or exogenous insulin/secretagogues), or decreased glucose intake.
- **CLASSIC PRESENTATION:** Behavioral changes, confusion, fatigue, tremor, palpitations, hunger, paresthesias, seizures, coma, death.
- **CLASSIC FINDINGS:** Whipple's triad: Symptoms suggesting hypoglycemia, glucose less than 60-70 mg/L, and resolution of symptoms after administration of glucose.
- **TREATMENT:** Mild cases: 15 g of oral glucose. Mod to Severe: parenteral dextrose 10% to 50% or glucagon.

HYPERALDOSTERONISM
- **PATHO:** Aldosterone release is independent of renin (primary), outside adrenal gland where increases in aldosterone is renin dependent (secondary).
- **CLASSIC PRESENTATION:** Refractory hypertension.
- **CLASSIC FINDINGS:** Hypokalemia, elevated aldosterone, aldosterone:renin.
- **TREATMENT:** If due to adenoma or carcinoma: Surgical resection. If dur to bilateral adrenal hyperplasia: aldosterone antagonist (spironolactone or eplerenone).

INSULINOMA

- **PATHO:** Tumor of the beta islet cells in the pancreas that secretes an increased amount of insulin without regulation resulting in hypoglycemia.
- **CLASSIC PRESENTATION:** Hypoglycemia typically resulting in acute mental status changes.
- **CLASSIC FINDINGS:** 72-hour fast, glucose, serum insulin, and C-peptide followed by tumor identification.
- **TREATMENT:** Diazoxide, everolimus, dietary modification, surgical resection of tumor.

OBESITY

- **PATHO:** Excess caloric intake coupled with decreased energy expenditure.
- **CLASSIC PRESENTATION:** BMI 30 kg/m^2 or greater.
- **CLASSIC FINDINGS:** High BMI + commonly associated with hypertension, hyperlipidemia, and/or diabetes (insulin resistance).
- **TREATMENT:** Dietary modification, exercise, reduction/control of ASCVD risk factors or active processes. May consider phentermine/topiramate, naltrexone/bupropion, liraglutide, or surgical interventions.

PARATHYROID DISORDERS – HYPERPARATHYROIDISM

- **PATHO:** Parathyroid adenomas, hyperplasia, or carcinomas causing increased bone resorption of Ca & P and increased renal Ca & P resorption (primary); secondary response to hypocalcemia and associated with vitamin D deficiency, CDK (secondary).
- **CLASSIC PRESENTATION:** Bones, groans, stones, thrones, and psychic overtones (primary); Chvostek/Trousseau signs, arrhythmia, bronchospasm, paresthesia, AMS, seizures (secondary).
- **CLASSIC FINDINGS:** Persistent hypercalcemia and elevated PTH (primary); Hypocalcemia with elevated PTH (secondary)
- **TREATMENT:** IV crystalloids, bisphosphonates (given by IV infusion; also used for hypercalcemia of malignancy, calcitonin (given subcutaneously or by IM injection; not intranasal), prednisone, HD (primary); IV or PO calcium (secondary).

PHEOCHROMOCYTOMA

- **PATHO:** Adrenal medulla tumor that releases large amounts of catecholamines. Also referred to as a paraganglionoma.
- **CLASSIC PRESENTATION:** Pressure, pain, palpitations, perspiration, pallor.
- **CLASSIC FINDINGS:** Elevated plasma free metanephrines, urine metanephrines, urine VMA.
- **TREATMENT:** Ultimately will need surgical resection but requires control of BP first using: phenoxybenzamine or symptomatic management with clevidipine, nicardipine, doxazosin, terazosin.

SYNDROME OF INAPPROPRIATE ANTIDIURETIC HORMONE (SIADH)

- **PATHO:** Excess secretion of ADH in the presence of decreased plasma osmolality and/or hyponatremia.
- **CLASSIC PRESENTATION:** Anorexia, muscle weakness, nausea
- **CLASSIC FINDINGS:** Hyponatremia, high serum osmolarity, high urine osmolarity, high urine sodium, euvolemia
- **TREATMENT:** Sodium correction (8-12 mEq/L over 24 hours), free water restriction, oral sodium, hypertonic sodium.

THYROID DISORDERS – HYPOTHYROIDISM

- **PATHO:** Decreased production of T4 despite TSH stimulation of the thyroid.
- **CLASSIC PRESENTATION:** Bradycardia, pericardial/pleural effusion, slow DTRs, paresthesia, constipation, dysfunctional uterine bleeding hypothermia, weight gain, weakness.
- **CLASSIC FINDINGS:** Primary – TSH elevation, low free T4; Secondary – Low TSH, low free T4.
- **TREATMENT:** Levothyroxine (i.e., synthetic T4) is drug of choice. Rechecked TSH in 6-7 weeks after initial dose or dose change. Note: Avoid T4/T3 combinations in most patients.

THYROID DISORDERS – HYPERTHYROIDISM

- **PATHO:** Lack of negative feedback response of newly formed T4 & T3 on the hypothalamus and anterior pituitary.
- **CLASSIC PRESENTATION:** Anxiety, agitation, dyspnea, menstrual irregularities, proximal and pelvic girdle weakness, tachycardia, tremor, fever, diffuse goiter, ophthalmopathy, lid retraction or lag.
- **CLASSIC FINDINGS:** High T4 & T3, low TSH; Burch and Wartofsky Diagnostic Criteria score above 25.
- **TREATMENT:** MMI or PTU. For thyrotoxicosis, SSKI or Lugol's plus PTU, +/- propranolol +/- dexamethasone (or) hydrocortisone which helps to reduce peripheral conversion of T4 to T3 in thyroid storm.

CONSTIPATION
- **PATHO:** Occurs due to normal transit, slow transit, or disordered defecation.
- **CLASSIC PRESENTATION:** Intermittent abdominal pain, bloating, nausea/vomiting, difficulty defecating.
- **CLASSIC FINDINGS:** Less than 3 bowel movements per week that require straining, produce small, hard or dry stool, and a feeling of incomplete evacuation.
- **TREATMENT:**
  - Dietary modifications to include fiber should always be considered.
  - Stool softeners and laxatives. Prokinetic agents reserved for non-obstructive, chronic constipation.
  - If related to opioid analgesic use and the above fail, then consider peripherally acting opioid receptor antagonists.

DIARRHEA – NON-INFECTIOUS
- **PATHO:** Disruption in water and electrolyte balance, due to altered GI transit, exudative diarrhea, osmotic diarrhea, or secretory diarrhea.
- **CLASSIC PRESENTATION:** Frequent, non-bloody bowel movements lasting 12 to 72 hours.
- **CLASSIC FINDINGS:** Increased frequency of defecation with at least 3 bowel movements per day.
- **TREATMENT:**
  - Oral rehydration, BRAT diet, bismuth subsalicylate, diphenoxylate/atropine, or loperamide.

DIARRHEA – TRAVELER'S (INFECTIOUS)
- **PATHO:** Fecal-oral transmission of infectious diarrhea-causing organisms from contaminated food or water.
- **CLASSIC PRESENTATION:** Abdominal cramps, nausea/vomiting, fever, fecal urgency, or tenesmus.
- **CLASSIC FINDINGS:** Increased frequency of defecation with at least 3 bowel movements per day
- **TREATMENT:**
  - Oral rehydration, BRAT diet, azithromycin, ciprofloxacin, or rifaximin.
  - Limit use of antidiarrheal agents (e.g., loperamide) to intermittent use to avoid potential retention of infectious agent.

GASTROESOPHAGEAL REFLUX DISEASE
- **PATHO:** Regurgitation of gastric contents into the esophagus, resulting in dyspepsia.
- **CLASSIC PRESENTATION:** Burning pain/discomfort with or after meals, made worse by lying supine, dysphagia.
- **CLASSIC FINDINGS:** Clinical diagnosis based on signs and symptoms.
- **TREATMENT:**
  - Body positioning during sleep, avoid tight clothing, and dietary modifications.
  - Drug therapy: Antacids, H2RA, or PPI. Risk of tolerance or breakthrough acid production with oral and H2RA therapy, not PPI.
  - Overall goal: Prevent or treat to avoid development of Barrett's esophagus which is a pre-cancerous condition while also controlling symptoms.

HEMOCHROMATOSIS
- **PATHO:** Excess deposit of iron in tissues due to hereditary or transfusional causes.
- **CLASSIC PRESENTATION:** Acute: arthralgias, fatigue, lethargy; Chronic: arthritis, dilated cardiomyopathy, skin hyperpigmentation, jaundice, liver cancer & dysfunction, spoon nails (koilonychia), secondary DM, infections.
- **CLASSIC FINDINGS:** Serum ferritin above 300 mcg/L in men, above 200 mcg/L in women or more; Transferrin saturation above 50% in men, above 40% in women.
- **TREATMENT:** Phlebotomy 1-2 times per week until iron normalize +/- chelating agents (e.g., deferoxamine, deferasirox, deferiprone).

IMFLAMMATORY BOWEL DISEASE - CROHN'S DISEASE
- **PATHO:** Transmural inflammation that may occur anywhere from the mouth to the perianal area, but most commonly affects the terminal ileum and right colon.
- **CLASSIC PRESENTATION:** Abdominal pain, bloating, diarrhea, obstruction, hemorrhage, toxic megacolon.
- **CLASSIC FINDINGS:** Ileocolonoscopy findings of cobblestoning mucosa and aphthous or linear ulcers.
- **TREATMENT:** Aminosalicylates, antidiarrheals, steroids, antibiotics, DMARDs, bDMARDs (mainly TNF alpha inhibitors if no TB or class III or IV heart failure).

IMFLAMMATORY BOWEL DISEASE - ULCERATIVE COLITIS
- **PATHO:** Inflammatory process of the colon resulting in ulceration of the intestinal mucosa.
- **CLASSIC PRESENTATION:** Bloody diarrhea, abdominal pain, bloating, diarrhea, flatulence, fever, malabsorption, weight loss.
- **CLASSIC FINDINGS:** Cobblestoning mucosa and aphthous or linear ulcers in the colon.
- **TREATMENT:**
  - Chronic & Mild to Mod Disease: Aminosalicylates (5-ASA agents).
  - Acute Flares or Severe Disease: DMARDs/bDMARDs and TNF alpha inhibitors +/- corticosteroids. Avoid antidiarrheal agents in acute flares due to risk of toxic megacolon.

IRRITABLE BOWEL SYNDROME
- **PATHO:** Altered intestinal somatovisceral and motor dysfunction.
- **CLASSIC PRESENTATION:** Abdominal pain, bloating, diarrhea, constipation.
- **CLASSIC FINDINGS:** ROME IV criteria, Manning criteria
- **TREATMENT:**
  - IBS-C: bulk forming laxatives, or linaclotide, lubiprostone, plecanatide (constipation x 6 months).
  - IBS-D: eluxadoline, loperamide, alosetron.

LIVER DISEASE - ASCITES
- **PATHO:** Hypoalbuminemia and endothelial dysfunction cause mesenteric vessels and liver tissue to leak into the peritoneal cavity especially with increased portal pressures.
- **CLASSIC PRESENTATION:** Abdominal distension, positive fluid wave.
- **CLASSIC FINDINGS:** SAAG > 1.1 g/dL with homogenous freely mobile anechoic collection.
- **TREATMENT:** Salt & water restriction +/- therapeutic paracentesis, spironolactone + furosemide (at a ratio of 100:40).

LIVER DISEASE - ESOPHAGEAL VARICES

- **PATHO:** Dilated submucosal esophageal veins between the portal and systemic circulation and are caused by hepatic venous pressure gradients greater than 10 mmHg due to portal hypertension.
- **CLASSIC PRESENTATION:** Coffee-ground hematemesis, dark tarry stools, dyspepsia, epigastric pain, hypotension, tachycardia, melena, syncope.
- **CLASSIC FINDINGS:** Endoscopic visualization of varices; BUN:Cr of > 30.
- **TREATMENT:** Acute: Endoscopic interventions (banding or sclerotherapy), PPI, octreotide, ceftriaxone (to prevent risk of SBP), tranexamic acid.

LIVER DISEASE - HEPATIC ENCEPHALOPATHY

- **PATHO:** Accumulation of nitrogenous substances due to decreased hepatic function causing CNS depression, and confusion.
- **CLASSIC PRESENTATION:** Presents on a spectrum from stage 1 to 4 with varying changes in mental status.
- **CLASSIC FINDINGS:** New mental status changes +/- elevated ammonia levels.
- **TREATMENT:** Treat underlying problem especially infection (e.g., SBP). Lactulose (titrated to 2-3 loose stools per day; rectal enema if presenting with AMS, +/- rifaximin.

LIVER DISEASE - HEPATORENAL SYNDROME

- **PATHO:** Vasodilation of splanchnic & systemic vessels causing baroreceptor feedback, activating RAAS, SNS, vasopressin release; contributing to systemic and renal vasoconstriction and decreased cardiac output.
- **CLASSIC PRESENTATION:** Decreased appetite, jaundice, fatigue, lethargy, hepatic encephalopathy.
- **CLASSIC FINDINGS:** New renal failure with existing severe hepatic failure, SBP.
- **TREATMENT:** TIPS, HD, transplant; enhanced renal perfusion (albumin, norepinephrine, vasopressin, midodrine, octreotide). Also avoid over diuresis or lactulose induced diarrhea.

LIVER DISEASE - SPONTANEOUS BACTERIAL PERITONITIS

- **PATHO:** Acute ascitic fluid infection attributed to the translocation of gram-negative bacilli from the GI.
- **CLASSIC PRESENTATION:** Diffuse abdominal pain, altered mental status, fever, and chills.
- **CLASSIC FINDINGS:** SAAG > 1.1 g/dL; ascitic fluid ANC > 250 c, protein < 1, glucose > 50, pH < 7.35, ascites-blood pH gradient > 0.1.
- **TREATMENT:**
  - Acute: Ceftriaxone or cefotaxime + albumin at a dose of 1.5 g/kg within 6 hrs of diagnosis, then repeat on Day 3 at 1 mg/kg.
  - Prophylaxis Therapy (debated): Cipro or norfloxacin.

NAUSEA & VOMITING - CANNABINOID HYPEREMESIS SYNDROME

- **PATHO:** Direct stimulation of histamine receptors in the GI tract and dysregulation of TRPV-1 system.
- **CLASSIC PRESENTATION:** Cyclical vomiting that may be relieved by hot showers or baths, and cessation of cannabis.
- **CLASSIC FINDINGS:** History of weekly or daily use of marijuana.
- **TREATMENT:** Reduce marijuana use, diphenhydramine, droperidol, haloperidol, capsaicin cream (applied to the abdomen).

NAUSEA & VOMITING - PREGNANCY
- **PATHO:** Elevated estrogen, progesterone, and hCG during the first 12 weeks of pregnancy.
- **CLASSIC PRESENTATION:** Nausea, vomiting that may occur at any time throughout the day.
- **CLASSIC FINDINGS:** Concerning symptoms include weight loss and signs of volume depletion, and fetal heart tone assessment.
- **TREATMENT:** Oral/IV rehydration, doxylamine plus pyridoxine, antiemetics.

PANCREATITIS
- **PATHO:** pancreatic duct and acinar injury, resulting in auto-digestion and inflammation (acute); repetitive acute pancreatitis causing chronic inflammation and fibrosis (chronic).
- **CLASSIC PRESENTATION:** Persistent right upper quadrant or epigastric pain, nausea/vomiting, abdominal distension, Cullen sign, Turner sign.
- **CLASSIC FINDINGS:** Must have two of the following criteria; abdominal pain consistent with pancreatitis, and lipase three times the upper limit of normal
- **TREATMENT:**
  - Acute: NPO diet, IV fluids (Crystalloids), parenteral analgesia, parenteral or rectal antiemetics, +/- surgical interventions (e.g., ERCP if related to biliary problem such as gallstones).
  - Chronic: Pancrelipase by mouth with meals, gastric acid reduction (H2RA or PPI), and vitamin supplementation (A, D, E, K).

PEPTIC ULCER DISEASE
- **PATHO:** Excess acid secretion in the GI +/- H. pylori causing lesions in the stomach or duodenum
- **CLASSIC PRESENTATION:** Burning epigastric pain, awaken at night or made it worse when lying supine.
- **CLASSIC FINDINGS:** Endoscopic visualization of ulceration, positive H. pylori screening.
- **TREATMENT:** H2RA, PPI, and/or H. pylori eradication regimens.

STRESS ULCER PROPHYLAXIS
- **PATHO:** Increased gastric acid secretion coupled with reduced gastric mucosal blood flow and gastric mucosal oxidative stress.
- **CLASSIC PRESENTATION:** Asymptomatic occurring in critically ill patients, burn patients or trauma patients.
- **CLASSIC FINDINGS:** GI hemorrhage may be the first sign.
- **TREATMENT:** Prophylactic use of H2RA, or PPI.

BENIGN PROSTATIC HYPERPLASIA (BPH)
- **PATHO:** Dysregulation of epithelial and stromal cellular proliferation in the prostate transition zone that results in urethral compression and bladder outflow obstruction.
- **CLASSIC PRESENTATION:** Urinary retention, difficulty initiating urination, nocturia, urinary frequency, weak urinary stream.
- **CLASSIC FINDINGS:** Elevated AUASI of 7 or above with decreased urine flow below 10 mL/second and increased post-void residual volume.
- **TREATMENT:** Surgical interventions (TURP/TUIP, HoLEP, UroLift), 5-alpha reductase inhibitors, alpha-1 antagonists.

PRIAPISM
- **PATHO:** Decreased arterial flow to the corpora cavernosa, trapping venous blood (ischemic), unregulated arterial blood flow to the corpora cavernosa without the trapping of venous blood (non-ischemic).
- **CLASSIC PRESENTATION:** Abnormally long-lasting erection.
- **CLASSIC FINDINGS:** Sustained erection for more than 4 hours in the absence of appropriate stimulation.
- **TREATMENT:** Terbutaline, phenylephrine, or aspiration and irrigation of corpus cavernosum.

URINARY INCONTINENCE
- **PATHO:** Numerous causes including functional, overflow, stress, urge, and mixed urinary incontinence.
- **CLASSIC PRESENTATION:** Urinary incontinence.
- **CLASSIC FINDINGS:** 3 incontinence questions.
- **TREATMENT:** Alpha-1 antagonists, antimuscarinics, and behavioral therapies, pelvic floor muscle strengthening, weight loss, or surgical management.

ANEMIA OF CHRONIC DISEASE
- **PATHO:** RBC hypo-proliferation due to a disorder of iron homeostasis, promoted by the hepatic production of hepcidin and in response to inflammation.
- **CLASSIC PRESENTATION:** Vague symptoms involving generalized fatigue, malaise.
- **CLASSIC FINDINGS:** Normocytic or microcytic anemia pattern, decreased serum iron, TIBC, percent iron saturation, increase in serum ferritin.
- **TREATMENT:** Treat underlying chronic medical condition.

ANEMIA OF CHRONIC KIDNEY DISEASE
- **PATHO:** Absent renal production of EPO.
- **CLASSIC PRESENTATION:** Generalized weakness, malaise or fatigue. If severe can lead to SOB.
- **CLASSIC FINDINGS:** Normochromic and normocytic RBC, "burr cells" on peripheral blood smear, hemoglobin < 10 mg/dL, RI < 2, low EPO < 500 mU/mL.
- **TREATMENT:** Oral or parenteral iron (iron deficiency); ESA agents (to no more than a Hgb of 11 mg/dL).

ANTIPHOSPHOLIPID SYNDROME
- **PATHO:** Thrombosis occurs from increased TF expression and activation of complement, resulting in impaired fibrinolysis and inhibition of protein C.
- **CLASSIC PRESENTATION:** Thrombosis (arterial or venous), fetal loss, thrombocytopenia, microangiopathic hemolytic anemia, livedo reticularis, valvular heart disease. Catastrophic antiphospholipid syndrome.
- **CLASSIC FINDINGS:** At least 1 clinical criterion and 1 laboratory criteria (Revised Sapporo Classification).
- **TREATMENT:** Lifelong anticoagulation (warfarin, enoxaparin).

ANTITHROMBIN DEFICIENCY
- **PATHO:** inherited, autosomal dominant disease caused by mutations in the SERPINC1 gene with variable clinical penetrance determining whether patients with altered genes will develop symptomatic disease.
- **CLASSIC PRESENTATION:** VTE, typically before the age of 40, without other identifiable causes.
- **CLASSIC FINDINGS:** Presence of SERPINC1 gene mutations.
- **TREATMENT:** Warfarin, DTIs, DOACs.

FACTOR V LEIDEN
- **PATHO:** Point mutations eliminate the cleavage site in Factor V, and Va resulting in Factor V Leiden and an increased risk of VTE.
- **CLASSIC PRESENTATION:** Is often asymptomatic and only discovered on laboratory analysis.
- **CLASSIC FINDINGS:** Superficial vein thrombosis, DVT, or PE at a young age (younger than 40).
- **TREATMENT:** Warfarin (historically), apixaban, rivaroxaban, enoxaparin.

G20210A (FACTOR II) MUTATION
- **PATHO:** Overproduction of factor II, resulting in hypercoagulability.
- **CLASSIC PRESENTATION:** Unprovoked arterial or venous thrombosis at an early age (younger than 40).
- **CLASSIC FINDINGS:** Heterozygous prothrombin gene mutation.
- **TREATMENT:** Warfarin, apixaban, rivaroxaban, enoxaparin.

HEMOLYTIC ANEMIA
- **PATHO:** The combination of increased RBC destruction, increased Hb catabolism, low Hb levels, and bone marrow stimulation.
- **CLASSIC PRESENTATION:** Ascites, arrhythmias, anemia, bruising, cholestasis, diarrhea, dyspnea, fatigue, jaundice, hematuria, hepatosplenomegaly, lymphadenopathy, petechiae.
- **CLASSIC FINDINGS:** Haptoglobin (decreased); reticulocyte (elevated; RI > 2); unconjugated bilirubin (elevated); LDH (elevated); peripheral smear (schistocytes present); urinalysis (UA; urobilinogen positive)
- **TREATMENT:** Removal of drugs possibly contributing to hemolytic anemia, transfusion, folic acid, ESAs, hydroxyurea.

HEMOLYTIC UREMIC SYNDROME
- **PATHO:** Microangiographic hemolytic anemia, associated with renal ischemia.
- **CLASSIC PRESENTATION:** Triad of acute renal failure, MAHA, and thrombocytopenia.
- **CLASSIC FINDINGS:** Thrombocytopenia with microangiopathic hemolytic anemia and acute renal injury.
- **TREATMENT:** Eculizumab, plasma exchange, plasmapheresis, hemodialysis.

HEMOPHILIA A & B
- **PATHO:** Hemophilia A – deficiency of factor VIII; hemophilia B – deficiency of factor IX
- **CLASSIC PRESENTATION:** Abnormal bruising, prolonged bleeding, hematoma formation and joint effusions
- **CLASSIC FINDINGS:** Presence of deficient clotting factors IX or VIII
- **TREATMENT:** Hemophilia A – desmopressin (mild), cryoprecipitate (active bleed); hemophilia B – FFP, factor IX.

HEPARIN INDUCED THROMBOCYTOPENIA (HIT)
- **PATHO:** PF4 binds to heparin, inducing antibodies specific to the PF4-heparin complex, which activates platelets to induce further platelet aggregation and thrombin generation resulting in continued PF4 release and ongoing formation of PF4-heparin complex.
- **CLASSIC PRESENTATION:** Thrombocytopenia, timing, thrombosis, and no other cause
- **CLASSIC FINDINGS:** 4 T score above 4, with confirmatory positive PF4 ELISA and SRA.
- **TREATMENT:** D/C heparin or enoxaparin. Antithrombotic treatment with DTI or DOAC.

IMMUNE THROMBOCYTOPENIA PURPURA (ITP)
- **PATHO:** Antiplatelet antibodies resulting in thrombocytopenia, purpura, and bleeding.
- **CLASSIC PRESENTATION:** Epistaxis, GI bleed, gingival bleeding, ICH, menorrhagia, petechiae.
- **CLASSIC FINDINGS:** Platelets below 50,000, exclusion of other causes.
- **TREATMENT:** Prednisone, IVIG, RhoD IG, splenectomy.

MACROCYTIC ANEMIA

- **PATHO:** RBCs larger than normal, due to RBCs not being produced properly (megaloblastic, or normoblastic).
- **CLASSIC PRESENTATION:** Peripheral neuropathy, ataxia, paresthesias (B12 deficiency); chronic atrophic gastritis (pernicious anemia).
- **CLASSIC FINDINGS:** RI < 2, Hgb/HCT are reduced, MCV and MCH are elevated, RBCs are large.
- **TREATMENT:** Cyanocobalamin (B12 deficiency), folic acid (folic acid deficiency).

MICROCYTIC ANEMIA

- **PATHO:** Smaller than normal RBCs due to a defect in hemoglobin synthesis due to anemia of chronic disease, iron deficiency, thalassemia, or sideroblastic anemia.
- **CLASSIC PRESENTATION:** Generalized fatigue or malaise, if severe can result in shortness of breath or dyspnea.
- **CLASSIC FINDINGS:** Reduced hemoglobin, hematocrit, MCV, MCH, MCHC, RI < 2, increased RDW, serum ferritin < 15 mcg/L, TIBC > 400 mcg/dL, iron saturation of < 20%.
- **TREATMENT:** Oral or parenteral iron (iron deficiency).

PROTEIN C & S DEFICIENCY

- **PATHO:** Mutations in PROC gene (abnormal protein C antigen and protein activity), PROS1 gene (abnormal protein S antigen and protein activity).
- **CLASSIC PRESENTATION:** Unprovoked arterial or venous thrombosis at an early age (younger than 40).
- **CLASSIC FINDINGS:** Protein C functional assay, total protein C, PROC1 mutations; total protein S, free protein S, protein S functional assay, PROS1 mutation.
- **TREATMENT:** Warfarin, apixaban, rivaroxaban, enoxaparin.

SICKLE CELL DISEASE

- **PATHO:** Genetic mutations to proteins in the beta subunit because sickle cell trait (HbAS) and sickle cell disease (HbSS).
- **CLASSIC PRESENTATION:** Pain crisis, acute chest syndrome, acute coronary syndrome, avascular necrosis, cholestasis, priapism, pulmonary hypertension, renal failure, retinal detachment and retinopathy, splenic sequestration and infarction, stroke, transient red cell aplasia, traumatic hyphemia.
- **CLASSIC FINDINGS:** Presence of HbAS or HbSS
- **TREATMENT:** Analgesia, L-glutamine, voxelotor.

THROMBOTIC THROMBOCYTOPENIA PURPURA (TTP)

- **PATHO:** Microangiopathic hemolytic anemia due to the absence or decreased function of ADAMTS13, resulting in large vWF multimer accumulation, platelet aggregation, hemolysis, and microthrombi formation.
- **CLASSIC PRESENTATION:** Pentad of fever, MAHA, neurologic dysfunction, renal dysfunction, and thrombocytopenia.
- **CLASSIC FINDINGS:** Thrombocytopenia and the presence of microangiopathic hemolytic anemia.
- **TREATMENT:** Plasma exchange, RBC transfusion, FFP, splenectomy, prednisone.

UREMIC PLATELET DYSFUNCTION

- **PATHO:** Results from and in balance in factors that promote clotting & factors that promote laminar flow.
- **CLASSIC PRESENTATION:** Ecchymosis, epistaxis, gingival bleeding, GI bleeds, prolonged bleeding from puncture sites
- **CLASSIC FINDINGS:** BT > 15 minutes, prolonged PT and aPTT in patients with a CrCl < 10, thrombocytopenia, HCT < 30%
- **TREATMENT:** ESAs, proper HD (prevention); Cryoprecipitate, desmopressin (acute bleeding).

Von Willebrand Disease

- **PATHO:** Deficiency in vWF.
- **CLASSIC PRESENTATION:** Increased risk of bleeding, bruising or ecchymosis.
- **CLASSIC FINDINGS:** Low vWF, increased BT, Ristocetin cofactor activity test, clotting Factor VIII activity test, vWF multimer test.
- **TREATMENT:** Desmopressin, factor VIII concentrates.

ALLERGIC RHINITIS

- **PATHO:** Immune response to an allergen and can be described as IgE mediated early-phase reaction, late phase, or non-IgE mediated hyperresponsiveness.
- **CLASSIC PRESENTATION:** Nasal edema, congestion, rhinorrhea (thin, transparent), pruritis, sneezing.
- **CLASSIC FINDINGS:** Allergen-specific IgE or skin testing for patients not responding to conventional therapy.
- **TREATMENT:** Intranasal steroids, antihistamines.

ANGIOEDEMA (Non-IgE; Hereditary)

- **PATHO:** HAE (both type 1 and 2 HAE) is unregulated bradykinin activation of the complement pathway; RAAS-induced angioedema is caused by increased bradykinin activity; Idiopathic angioedema results from histaminergic or non-histaminergic pathways.
- **CLASSIC PRESENTATION:** Non-pruritic, painful swelling and deformity of the skin. HAE may have a prodrome.
- **CLASSIC FINDINGS:** Angioedema of the GI, abdomen, rarely airway.
- **TREATMENT:** Rule out IgE mediated angioedema; C1-inhibitor, ecallantide, icatibant.

GRAFT-VERSUS-HOST DISEASE

- **PATHO:** Transplantation of immunologically competent cells into an immunocompromised host followed by an immune response between the donor cells/tissue and host.
- **CLASSIC PRESENTATION:** Afferent (Phase 1), efferent (Phase 2), effector (Phase 3).
- **CLASSIC FINDINGS:** Billingham criteria.
- **TREATMENT:** Acute induction (antithymocyte globulin, alemtuzumab, basiliximab); Post transplant (corticosteroids, calcineurin inhibitors, antimetabolites, mTOR inhibitors, costimulation blocker).

ANIMAL BITES
- **PATHO:** Immediate trauma and tissue damage, and secondary infection from mouth or skin flora that inoculates tissue beneath the skin.
- **CLASSIC PRESENTATION:** Bite wounds to the extremities, head, neck, or abdomen.
- **CLASSIC FINDINGS:** Purulent discharge from wounds, decreased range of motion, erythema, swelling, and pain.
- **TREATMENT:** Wound irrigation, and debridement, amoxicillin/clavulanic acid, tetanus prophylaxis, rabies prophylaxis.

APPENDICITIS
- **PATHO:** Obstruction of the appendix from an increased intraluminal and intramural pressure causing small vessel occlusion and lymphatic stasis, leading to ischemia and necrosis of the appendix.
- **CLASSIC PRESENTATION:** Generalized abdominal pain that migrates to the right lower quadrant.
- **CLASSIC FINDINGS:** CT abdomen findings consistent with acute appendicitis.
- **TREATMENT:** Laparoscopic appendectomy, antibiotics (cefoxitin, metronidazole, pip/tazo).

ASCENDING CHOLANGITIS
- **PATHO:** Ascending bacterial infection of the biliary tree, resulting from choledocholithiasis.
- **CLASSIC PRESENTATION:** Fever, jaundice, right upper quadrant pain, may include AMS, hypotension.
- **CLASSIC FINDINGS:** Abnormal liver labs, signs of systemic infection plus endoscopic/surgical evidence of purulent bile.
- **TREATMENT:** ERCP, percutaneous transhepatic cholangiography, endoscopic ultrasonography-guided drainage, or surgical drainage; antibiotics (metronidazole plus ciprofloxacin, pip/tazo).

BACTERIAL MENINGITIS
- **PATHO:** CNS inflammatory from bacterial cell wall components, resulting in edema of the brain and meninges.
- **CLASSIC PRESENTATION:** Purpura, papilledema, altered mental status, fever, focal neurologic deficits, headache, neck stiffness, seizures. Brudzinski's sign and/or Kernig's sign may be present.
- **CLASSIC FINDINGS:** CSF opening pressure > 300, WBC > 1000/mm^3, PMN > 80%, glucose < 40 mg/dL, protein > 200 mg/dL, positive CSF culture.
- **TREATMENT:** Age/risk factor dependent empiric antibiotics, generally beta-lactam (ampicillin, ceftriaxone, cefotaxime) with or without vancomycin. Remember add on ampicillin if < 1 month or > 50 yrs of age.

BACTERIAL VAGINOSIS
- **PATHO:** Overgrowth of normal vaginal flora, resulting in an increased vaginal discharge.
- **CLASSIC PRESENTATION:** Complaints of malodorous vaginal discharge, which may be more pronounced after sexual intercourse. Dysuria, dyspareunia, vaginal pruritus.
- **CLASSIC FINDINGS:** Positive whiff test, wet prep.
- **TREATMENT:** Metronidazole (topical or systemic), clindamycin (topical or systemic).

BRONCHIOLITIS
- **PATHO:** Acute lower respiratory tract viral infection caused by RSV but may also be caused by adenovirus, influenza, or parainfluenza.
- **CLASSIC PRESENTATION:** Fever, increased mucus production and labored breathing.
- **CLASSIC FINDINGS:** Air trapping, atelectasis, decreased ventilation, airway obstruction
- **TREATMENT:** Nebulized hypertonic saline, supplemental oxygen, palivizumab in selected patients.

BRONCHITIS
- **PATHO:** Acute airway epithelial inflammation resulting from infection or environmental factors.
- **CLASSIC PRESENTATION:** Cough (productive/purulent), malaise, and wheezing.
- **CLASSIC FINDINGS:** Difficulty breathing, cough, and wheezing (acute); chronic, productive cough for > 3 consecutive months of the year for 2 consecutive years without other identified etiologies (chronic).
- **TREATMENT:** Chest PT, antipyretics, antitussives, bronchodilators.

CANDIDIASIS
- **PATHO:** C. albicans infection in immunocompromised patients, patients using antibiotics, or other host factors such as coinfection with tuberculosis, hypothyroidism, diabetes, pregnancy, neonates, and the elderly
- **CLASSIC PRESENTATION:** Local mucocutaneous infections or invasive infections, including UTI, endocarditis, meningitis, empyema, mediastinitis, or pericarditis. Systemic candidiasis presents with fever, chills, hypotension, altered mental status.
- **CLASSIC FINDINGS:** Fungal culture.
- **TREATMENT:** Fluconazole, nystatin (mild-moderate); echinocandin antifungals (severe).

CAVERNOUS SINUS THROMBOSIS
- **PATHO:** Embolization of infectious pathogens, causing a secondary thrombin generation and trapping the pathogen within the cavernous sinus.
- **CLASSIC PRESENTATION:** Fever, headache, altered mental status, lethargy, periorbital swelling, ptosis, proptosis, chemosis, eye pain, papilledema, and vision changes or vision loss. Horner syndrome
- **CLASSIC FINDINGS:** CT/MRI with contrast findings of bulging of the cavernous sinus, increased dural enhancement, and absent flow void.
- **TREATMENT:** Vancomycin plus ceftriaxone and metronidazole, antithrombotic therapy.

CELLULITIS
- **PATHO:** Infection that initially affects the epidermis and dermis, spreading within the superficial fascia.
- **CLASSIC PRESENTATION:** Inflammation, erythema, edema of the local area. Fever, malaise, chills, tender lymphadenopathy.
- **CLASSIC FINDINGS:** Non-elevated lesion with poorly defined margins.
- **TREATMENT:** Empiric antibiotics including PCN VK, cephalexin, ceftriaxone, or clindamycin (non-purulent); I&D plus empiric antibiotics including tmp/smx, doxycycline, or vancomycin (purulent).

CERVICITIS AND URETHRITIS
- **PATHO:** Inflammation of the columnar epithelium of the uterine endocervix.
- **CLASSIC PRESENTATION:** Dysuria, pruritus, burning, discharge, although patients may be asymptomatic.
- **CLASSIC FINDINGS:** Identification of causative pathogen (bacterial, HSV, mycoplasma, Trichomoniasis)
- **TREATMENT:** Ceftriaxone or doxycycline (empiric).

CHOLECYSTITIS
- **PATHO:** Gallstones that obstruct the cystic duct or other dysfunctional gallbladder emptying result in acute inflammation of the gallbladder.
- **CLASSIC PRESENTATION:** Right upper quadrant pain with Murphy sign
- **CLASSIC FINDINGS:** Imaging evidence consistent with cholecystitis.
- **TREATMENT:** Laparoscopic cholecystectomy, surgical antibiotics (metronidazole plus ciprofloxacin, ertapenem).

CLOSTRIDOIDES DIFFICILE
- **PATHO:** Clostridial toxins A and B inactivate Rho family protein pathways, damaging colonocytes, and disrupt intercellular tight junctions resulting in colitis.
- **CLASSIC PRESENTATION:** Abdominal pain/discomfort, fever, watery, non-bloody diarrhea.
- **CLASSIC FINDINGS:** C. difficile PCR or enzyme immune assay, leukocytosis (frequently with WBC above 20,000/mm3)
- **TREATMENT:** Vancomycin PO with metronidazole for severe, fulminant infection.

COCCIDIOIDOMYCOSIS
- **PATHO:** Coccidioides mycelia reach the terminal bronchioles, undergo remodeling to form spherical shapes and begin to grow, spreading to other components of lung tissue and alveolar sacs.
- **CLASSIC PRESENTATION:** Often asymptomatic, but severe presentations may include arthralgias, chest pain, erythema nodosum, and fever.
- **CLASSIC FINDINGS:** PCR identification of Coccidiosis with radiologic evidence of pneumonia
- **TREATMENT:** Fluconazole for three months.

COMMUNITY-ACQUIRED PNEUMONIA
- **PATHO:** Infection of the respiratory tract, often caused by S. pneumoniae, S. aureus, H. influenza, M. catarrhalis, K. pneumoniae, or atypical pathogens.
- **CLASSIC PRESENTATION:** Abrupt onset of illness with fever, chills, dyspnea, and productive cough.
- **CLASSIC FINDINGS:** Chest X-ray with dense lobar or segmental infiltrates; mortality risk assessment (CURB-65, or PORT/PSI)
- **TREATMENT:** Empiric antibiotics based on inpatient vs outpatient treatment, risk factors for MDR pathogens, and presence of comorbidities and/or immunosuppression.

CONJUNCTIVITIS
- **PATHO:** Inflammation or infection of the conjunctiva due to infectious pathogens or allergens and irritants resulting in injection or dilation of the conjunctival vessels producing redness, hyperemia, and edema.
- **CLASSIC PRESENTATION:** Unilateral eye redness and crusting but spreads bilaterally within 48 hours (bacterial), single eye affected, producing clear and watery discharge (viral), bilateral eye involvement with cobblestoning, redness, pruritis in a seasonal pattern (allergic).
- **CLASSIC FINDINGS:** Chlamydia and gonorrhea screening.
- **TREATMENT:** Topical ophthalmic antibiotics

CRYPTOSPORIDIOSIS
- **PATHO:** Cryptosporidium oocyst releasees sporozoites that settle in the small intestinal wall where they undergo asexual multiplication producing thin-walled oocytes that cause severe disease in immunocompromised patients by avoiding apoptosis.
- **CLASSIC PRESENTATION:** Chronic watery diarrhea in patients with HIV.
- **CLASSIC FINDINGS:** Positive stool culture and PCR for Cryptosporidium
- **TREATMENT:** Nitazoxanide +/- HAART for HIV patients.

CYTOMEGALOVIRUS
- **PATHO:** Primary CMV infection, or secondary reactivation resulting in various symptoms secondary to viral replication.
- **CLASSIC PRESENTATION:** Retinitis, colitis, esophagitis, ventriculoencephalitis, and pneumonitis.
- **CLASSIC FINDINGS:** CMV inclusion bodies and serologic testing.
- **TREATMENT:** Ganciclovir, CMV Immune Globulin IV (treatment); letermovir, valganciclovir (prophylaxis).

DIABETIC FOOT INFECTIONS
- **PATHO:** Soft tissue infections due to skin breakdown caused by single pathogens or polymicrobial infections.
- **CLASSIC PRESENTATION:** Edema, erythema, warmth, pus, foul-smelling odors, and fever.
- **CLASSIC FINDINGS:** Advanced ulcers with patients unaware due to diabetic neuropathy.
- **TREATMENT:** Surgical debridement and wound irrigation, antibiotics to cover MSSA (MRSA if risk factors present), streptococcus, Enterobacteriaceae, and obligate anaerobes.

DIVERTICULITIS
- **PATHO:** Diverticula fill with feces causing bacterial overgrowth and expansion, affecting local vascular structures leading to microperforations, localized infection, and inflammation
- **CLASSIC PRESENTATION:** Left lower quadrant abdominal pain, change in bowel habits, hypoactive bowel sounds, fever.
- **CLASSIC FINDINGS:** Endoscopic assessment of diverticula, abdominal CT.
- **TREATMENT:** Analgesia, docusate, and antibiotics (amoxicillin-clavulanate; ciprofloxacin plus metronidazole; piperacillin-tazobactam).

ENDOCARDITIS

- **PATHO:** Cardiac endothelial tissue damage promotes turbulent blood flow of the diseased valve or tissue surface, leading to platelet and fibrin deposition, allowing for bacterial pathogens' surface binding and promoting colonization and bacterial growth.
- **CLASSIC PRESENTATION:** Prolonged fever, fatigue, myalgia, arthralgia, headache, chills, nausea, and vomiting, new heart murmur or changing heart murmur, splenomegaly, Roth's, Janeway lesions, Osler, splinter hemorrhages.
- **CLASSIC FINDINGS:** Modified Duke criteria.
- **TREATMENT:** Empiric regimens include vancomycin IV plus cefazolin, ampicillin/sulbactam, or ceftriaxone (native valve), vancomycin plus gentamicin plus cefepime or cefazolin (prosthetic valve), vancomycin plus piperacillin-tazobactam (IV drug abuse). Pathogen directed therapy after culture identification.

ERYSIPELAS AND IMPETIGO

- **PATHO:** Infection of the superficial dermis and may spread rapidly through the lymphatic system.
- **CLASSIC PRESENTATION:** Fever, pruritus, pain around the area of infection.
- **CLASSIC FINDINGS:** Elevated edge and sharply demarcated, painful, erythematous region with fever and leukocytosis (Erysipelas); bullous or non-bullous infection, erythematous plaques that may be itchy or painful (Impetigo).
- **TREATMENT:** Empiric antibiotics including systemic (PCN VK, cephalexin), or topical antibiotics after wound cleaning.

FOLLICULITIS

- **PATHO:** Infection of the hair follicle (bacterial, fungal, or viral), or non-infectious inflammatory causes.
- **CLASSIC PRESENTATION:** Erythematous air follicles, pustules, furuncles.
- **CLASSIC FINDINGS:** Wound/skin cultures.
- **TREATMENT:** Topical antibiotics, but oral or systemic antibiotics may be considered for extensive disease.

GENERAL HIV MANAGEMENT

- **PATHO:** HIV attaches and enters host CD4+ lymphocytes, where it uses reverse-transcription to form DNA, which migrates to the host cell nucleus integrating into the host chromosome, followed by viral proteins and DNA is packaged by viral protease into a budding virion, where a mature virus is formed and able to infect other cells.
- **CLASSIC PRESENTATION:** One of the numerous AIDS-defining illnesses, or fever, fatigue, pharyngitis, a pruritic papular eruption of HIV, headache, and lymphadenopathy.
- **CLASSIC FINDINGS:** HIV ELISA with confirmatory Western Blot
- **TREATMENT:** First-line regimens include bictegravir/emtricitabine/tenofovir AF abacavir/dolutegravir/lamivudine, and dolutegravir/emtricitabine/tenofovir AF.

HEPATITIS B

- **PATHO:** HBV causes an immune-mediated liver disease due to T-cell mediated hepatocellular lysis of HBV infected cells that present HB surface antigen on the cell membranes.
- **CLASSIC PRESENTATION:** Often asymptomatic, but may include fatigue, nausea/vomiting, weight loss, jaundice, right upper quadrant pain, splenomegaly, and fever.
- **CLASSIC FINDINGS:** Acute infection – Positive HBsAg; positive anti-HBc; positive IgM anti-HBc; negative anti-HBs. Chronic infection – Positive HBsAg; positive anti-HBc; negative IgM anti-HBc; negative anti-HBs
- **TREATMENT:** Vaccination, post-exposure prophylaxis. Treatment for HBV directed at viral suppression, not cure.

HEPATITIS C

- **PATHO:** HCV entry into hepatocytes via endocytosis where it is translated into mature peptides which are cleaved by viral and host proteases (NS3-4a serine proteases which are now drug targets) that resides on the endoplasmic reticulum where it establishes a replication complex containing NS5B RNA dependent RNA polymerase (another drug target).
- **CLASSIC PRESENTATION:** May be asymptomatic until evidence of hepatic injury is evident.
- **CLASSIC FINDINGS:** Positive anti-hepatitis C, HCV RNA detected.
- **TREATMENT:** Numerous antiviral regimens: elbasvir and grazoprevir, glecaprevir and pibrentasvir, ombitasvir, paritaprevir, and ritonavir, ombitasvir, paritaprevir, ritonavir, and dasabuvir, sofosbuvir, sofosbuvir and velpatasvir, sofosbuvir and ledipasvir, sofosbuvir, velpatasvir, and voxilaprevir.

HERPES (GENITAL)

- **PATHO:** HSV2 invades epithelial cells on the skin and mucous membranes causing primary infection, followed by dormant phase with viral replication in the peri-axonal sheath of sensory nerves, followed by reactivation.
- **CLASSIC PRESENTATION:** Painful genital ulcers, sores, crusts, tender lymphadenopathy, and dysuria.
- **CLASSIC FINDINGS:** Positive HSV identification on PCR or serology.
- **TREATMENT:** Acyclovir with specific dosing and duration for initial, recurrent, or suppressive treatment.

HISTOPLASMOSIS

- **PATHO:** Replicates and produced a unicellular yeast in alveoli, and induces an immune response forming granulomas that fibrose and calcify. Immunocompromised patients may not mount a sufficient response to initial infection, or reactivation of histoplasmosis may develop causing disseminated histoplasmosis.
- **CLASSIC PRESENTATION:** Flu-like (acute); chronic cough with low-grade fever, weight loss, malaise, night sweats, and hemoptysis, sputum production, and occasionally dyspnea (chronic); lymphadenopathy, hepatosplenomegaly, mucocutaneous ulcers of the mouth, nose, tongue, and GI tract (disseminated).
- **CLASSIC FINDINGS:** Histoplasma antigen (blood or urine), anti-Histoplasma antibodies (CSF).
- **TREATMENT:** Amphotericin B

HOSPITAL AND VENTILATOR-ASSOCIATED PNEUMONIA

- **PATHO:** Infection of the respiratory tract; HAP (occurs 48 hours after admission, hospitalized ≥ 2 days within the past 90 days, nursing home or long-term care facility, home IV antibiotics, dialysis/chronic wound care/chemotherapy, or are otherwise immunocompromised; VAP (> 48 hours after the start of mechanical ventilator).
- **CLASSIC PRESENTATION:** Abrupt onset of illness with fever, chills, dyspnea, tachypnea, productive cough, and chest pain.
- **CLASSIC FINDINGS:** IDSA Severe Pneumonia Criteria (one major, or three or more minor criteria).
- **TREATMENT:** Beta-lactam plus either a macrolide, doxycycline, or respiratory fluoroquinolone plus vancomycin. May consider adding an aminoglycoside.

HUMAN BITES

- **PATHO:** Direct inoculation of mouth flora to joint spaces or tendon sheaths, commonly Eikenella corrodens.
- **CLASSIC PRESENTATION:** Lacerations over the third, fourth, or fifth metacarpophalangeal joints.
- **CLASSIC FINDINGS:** Delayed presentation, poor wound healing, extending pain and swelling, erythema, and reduced range of motion.
- **TREATMENT:** Wound irrigation, and debridement, amoxicillin/clavulanic acid, tetanus prophylaxis.

INFLUENZA

- **PATHO:** Influenza viral hemagglutinin adheres to the respiratory tract's epithelial cells, causing inflammation and allowing the virus to enter host cells.
- **CLASSIC PRESENTATION:** Fever, myalgia, headache, malaise, nausea, vomiting, nonproductive cough, sore throat, and rhinitis.
- **CLASSIC FINDINGS:** Positive influenza PCR or viral culture
- **TREATMENT:** Immunization (prevention), oseltamivir.

LYME DISEASE

- **PATHO:** Initial inflammatory response mediated by TNF-alfa and interferon-gamma, causing further release of inflammatory cytokines and eosinophilia adjacent to the bite site. Inflammation causes collagen fibril injury in the joint spaces, nerves, and heart, leading to a chronic inflammatory response.
- **CLASSIC PRESENTATION:** Erythema migrans (early localized), extension to multiple erythema migrans lesions with arthralgias, myalgia, flu-like symptoms, cranial nerve palsy, myocarditis, pericarditis, ptosis, lymphadenopathy, and lymphocytic meningitis (early disseminated), arthritis affecting large joints (late).
- **CLASSIC FINDINGS:** Positive findings on B. burgdorferi quantitative screening (EIA, IFA or Western blot).
- **TREATMENT:** Amoxicillin, cefuroxime, or doxycycline.

MALARIA

- **PATHO:** Sporozoites rapidly distribute to the liver, invade hepatocytes and replicate, forming merozoites, where the Plasmodium organisms may reenter the blood, infecting erythrocytes, and consume hemoglobin to form immature trophozoites, which then mature and replicate to form schizonts that disrupt the erythrocyte cell membrane's integrity causing cell lysis.
- **CLASSIC PRESENTATION:** Symptoms that matches the Plasmodium lifecycle – rigors followed by fever lasting for hours, then diaphoresis and defervescence to normal body temperature.
- **CLASSIC FINDINGS:** Microscopic evaluation of Giemsa-stained thick and thin smear of a free-flowing venipuncture blood sample.
- **TREATMENT:** Numerous regimens, selected based upon uncomplicated or complicated malaria, and chloroquine-sensitive regions or resistant.

MASTOIDITIS

- **PATHO:** Infection of the mastoid air cells, often as an extension otitis media infection from the middle ear.
- **CLASSIC PRESENTATION:** Onset 2-6 days after AOM, irritability, lethargy, fever, ear pain
- **CLASSIC FINDINGS:** Postauricular erythema, protrusion of the auricle, tenderness, warmth, fluctuance, pus behind the tympanic, and bulging of the external auditory canal's posterosuperior wall.
- **TREATMENT:** Vancomycin plus either ceftriaxone or ampicillin/sulbactam.

MONONUCLEOSIS

- **ATHO:** EBV viral replication in the oropharynx and infects B lymphocytes as the infection spreads throughout the body via lymphatic distribution.
- **CLASSIC PRESENTATION:** Triad of fever, pharyngitis, and posterior chain lymphadenopathy.
- **CLASSIC FINDINGS:** Positive heterophil antibody (monospot) or EBV IgM
- **TREATMENT:** Antipyretics or anti-inflammatory agents

MYCOBACTERIUM AVIUM COMPLEX

- **PATHO:** Produces a persistent bacteremia and pulmonary infections where nodules and cavitary lesions may develop.
- **CLASSIC PRESENTATION:** Productive cough, dyspnea, fever, fatigue, lymphadenitis, night sweats.
- **CLASSIC FINDINGS:** CT findings of multifocal bronchiectasis with multiple small nodules and two or more sputum cultures (or 1 bronchial lavage) of acid-fast bacilli, lung biopsy with granuloma/AFB or culture for NTM, exclusion of other pulmonary diseases.
- **TREATMENT:** Clarithromycin plus ethambutol (treatment); azithromycin (prophylaxis).

NECROTIZING FASCIITIS

- **PATHO:** Rapidly progressing SSTI causing necrosis along the muscle fascia and other subcutaneous tissues, resulting in potentially limb or life-threatening infection.
- **CLASSIC PRESENTATION:** Fever, tachycardia, erythema, very tender skin, skip lesions, hemorrhagic bullae, crepitus, lymphangitis, compartment syndrome.
- **CLASSIC FINDINGS:** LRINEC Score.
- **TREATMENT:** Surgical exploration and debridement plus clindamycin, followed by piperacillin/tazobactam plus vancomycin.

OCCUPATIONAL EXPOSURE OF BLOOD / RISK OF HIV
- **PATHO:** HIV attaches and enters host CD4+ lymphocytes, where a mature virus is formed and able to infect other cells.
- **CLASSIC PRESENTATION:** One of the numerous AIDS-defining illnesses, or fever, fatigue, pharyngitis, a pruritic papular eruption of HIV, headache, and lymphadenopathy.
- **CLASSIC FINDINGS:** HIV ELISA with confirmatory Western Blot
- **TREATMENT:** Raltegravir plus tenofovir/emtricitabine for at least 4 weeks.

OSTEOMYELITIS
- **PATHO:** Hematogenous, contiguous, or direct inoculation of bone by pathogens causing acute infection of bone or bone structures.
- **CLASSIC PRESENTATION:** Acute pain, swelling, redness, decreased range of motion of the affected area, as well as fever, chills, and malaise.
- **CLASSIC FINDINGS:** Positive culture from bone biopsy or MRI evidence consistent with osteomyelitis
- **TREATMENT:** Empiric treatment covering S. aureus, streptococci, Enterobacteriaceae, anaerobes, followed by culture driven therapy.

OTITIS EXTERNA
- **PATHO:** Inflammation of the external ear canal secondary to infection.
- **CLASSIC PRESENTATION:** Ranges from mild discomfort and ear canal edema to occlusion of the external ear with intense pain, lymphadenopathy, and fever.
- **CLASSIC FINDINGS:** Otoscopic findings of the erythematous and edematous ear canal with associated debris, erythematous tympanic membranes.
- **TREATMENT:** Otic antibiotics, analgesia.

OTITIS MEDIA
- **PATHO:** Acute inflammation in the Eustachian tubes, decreasing ventilation, increasing negative pressure in the middle ear, furthering exudate production and accumulation of mucosal secretion, promoting colonization of bacterial and viral pathogens in the middle ear.
- **CLASSIC PRESENTATION:** Otalgia, fever, pulling or tugging at the ear(s), irritability, headache, disturbed sleep, poor feeding, vomiting, diarrhea.
- **CLASSIC FINDINGS:** Otoscopic findings of erythema, bulging and opaque tympanic membranes, air bullae.
- **TREATMENT:** Amoxicillin and analgesia.

PELVIC INFLAMMATORY DISEASE
- **PATHO:** Ascending infection of the upper female genital tract. frequently caused by N. gonorrhoeae or C. trachomatis.
- **CLASSIC PRESENTATION:** Pelvic pain, vaginal discharge, vaginal and post-cotidal bleeding, dysuria, fever, malaise, nausea/vomiting.
- **CLASSIC FINDINGS:** Adnexal tenderness, cervical motion tenderness, mucopurulent cervicitis, right upper quadrant pain. Positive GC/Chlamydia testing.
- **TREATMENT:** Admit to the hospital with surgical GYN consult + Ceftriaxone plus doxycycline with or without metronidazole.

966

PERIORBITAL & ORBITAL CELLULITIS
- **PATHO:** hematogenous spread of bacteria from sinusitis, from direct inoculation of the skin with bacteria, facial trauma, and impetigo.
- **CLASSIC PRESENTATION:** Periorbital swelling, diplopia, reduced visual acuity, impaired or painful extraocular movements, chemosis, proptosis, headache.
- **CLASSIC FINDINGS:** CT of the orbits and sinuses.
- **TREATMENT:** Periorbital cellulitis - amoxicillin; orbital cellulitis – ophthalmology consult + ceftriaxone or ampicillin/sulbactam IV.

PERTUSSIS
- **PATHO:** B. pertussis adheres to ciliated respiratory epithelial cells resulting in a local inflammatory response that disrupts the mucosal lining of the respiratory tract.
- **CLASSIC PRESENTATION:** URI like symptoms (catarrhal phase), fever resolution, whoop and staccato cough with post-tussive emesis (paroxysmal phase), residual cough (convalescent phase).
- **CLASSIC FINDINGS:** High leukocytosis (20 to 60,000 c/mL), PCR for B pertussis.
- **TREATMENT:** Catarrhal phase- macrolide antibiotics; post-exposure prophylaxis for household contacts, and other high-risk individuals; vaccination.

PHARYNGITIS AND PERITONSILAR ABSCESS
- **PATHO:** Acute inflammation of oropharynx mucus membranes from bacterial or viral pathogens. Peritonsillar abscess is the localized collection of pus between the tonsillar capsule and the superior constrictor muscle.
- **CLASSIC PRESENTATION:** Sore throat, dysphonia, dysphagia, fever.
- **CLASSIC FINDINGS:** CENTOR criteria, rapid strep testing.
- **TREATMENT:** Drainage (peritonsillar abscess), PCN VK, amoxicillin.

PNEUMOCYSTIS JIROVECI PNEUMONIA
- **PATHO:** Alveolar attachment results in diffuse alveolar damage resulting in pulmonary tissue injury leading to impaired function, hypoxia, and possibly respiratory failure.
- **CLASSIC PRESENTATION:** Fever, progressive dyspnea, non-productive cough and hypoxia.
- **CLASSIC FINDINGS:** Chest X-ray findings of diffuse, symmetrical bilateral interstitial infiltrates with a characteristic ground-glass appearance.
- **TREATMENT:** Trimethoprim/sulfamethoxazole with or without prednisone (treatment); Trimethoprim/sulfamethoxazole (prophylaxis).

PRE-EXPOSURE PROPHYLAXIS
- **PATHO:** HIV attaches and enters host CD4+ lymphocytes, where it uses reverse-transcription to form DNA, which migrates to the host cell nucleus integrating into the host chromosome, followed by viral proteins and DNA is packaged by viral protease into a budding virion, where a mature virus is formed and able to infect other cells.
- **CLASSIC PRESENTATION:** One of the numerous AIDS-defining illnesses, or fever, fatigue, pharyngitis, a pruritic papular eruption of HIV, headache, and lymphadenopathy.
- **CLASSIC FINDINGS:** HIV ELISA with confirmatory Western Blot.
- **TREATMENT:** Truvada (emtricitabine and tenofovir disoproxil fumarate) PO 1 tablet daily

PROGRESSIVE MULTIFOCAL LEUKOENCEPHALOPATHY

- **PATHO:** consequence of infection by the JC virus resulting in demyelinating disease from a destructive infection of oligodendrocytes.
- **CLASSIC PRESENTATION:** New onset of neurologic symptoms in patients with known immunosuppression.
- **CLASSIC FINDINGS:** Progressive, multifocal, and subacute focal neurological deficits including cognitive impairment, aphasia, ataxia, hemiparesis, and hemianopia.
- **TREATMENT:** No specific treatments.

SARS-COV-2 (COVID)

- **PATHO:** SARS-CoV-2/ACE2 interaction results in pneumonia and pulmonary vascular injury.
- **CLASSIC PRESENTATION:** Ranges from mild pneumonia that is self-limiting, cough, to dyspnea, tachypnea, hypoxia, with findings of lung infiltrates, respiratory failure, shock, and end-organ dysfunction.
- **CLASSIC FINDINGS:** Positive COVID-19 antigen or PCR.
- **TREATMENT:** Evolving therapy based on ventilation, supportive care and prevention, vaccination. Dexamethasone if on oxygen supplementation in the hospital.

SEPSIS

- **PATHO:** Dysregulated host response to infection influenced by the host immune response, inflammatory pathway, and coagulation pathway.
- **CLASSIC PRESENTATION:** Signs of infection plus at least two SIRS criteria, or more than one qSOFA.
- **CLASSIC FINDINGS:** Leukocytosis, tachycardia, tachypnea, hypotension, infection site specific radiologic findings.
- **TREATMENT:** Crystalloid volume resuscitation, hemodynamic support (airway, ventilation, circulation) antibiotics).

SEPTIC ARTHRITIS

- **PATHO:** Bacterial inoculation of joint synovium from hematogenous spread or contiguous spread from adjacent osteomyelitis, resulting in an acute inflammatory response.
- **CLASSIC PRESENTATION:** Warm joint, swelling, pain in the joint with either monoarticular or polyarticular involvement, decreased range of motion, weight loss, fever.
- **CLASSIC FINDINGS:** Synovial fluid with yellow-green discoloration, elevated WBC with 75% or more PMN, glucose 30% of blood.
- **TREATMENT:** Empiric treatment covering S. aureus, streptococci, Enterobacteriaceae, anaerobes, followed by culture driven therapy, and surgical debridement of affected tissue or revision/removal of joint replacement.

SINUSITIS (BACTERIAL)

- **PATHO:** Edema and inflammation of nasal tissue where an overproduction of mucus blocks the paranasal drainage sinuses promoting secondary bacterial overgrowth.
- **CLASSIC PRESENTATION:** Fever, facial pain, pressure, congestion, headache, fatigue, malaise, dental pain, cough, and otalgia.
- **CLASSIC FINDINGS:** Hyposmia, nasal obstruction, or postnasal purulence.
- **TREATMENT:** Decongestants, if symptoms worsening over 10 days: amoxicillin/clavulanic acid (for severe symptoms).

SPOROTRICHOSIS
- **PATHO:** Sporothrix schenckii infection affecting skin with rare dissemination to lungs, bone, joints, and CNS.
- **CLASSIC PRESENTATION:** Papules/pustules and ulcerated nodules with local lymphadenopathy (cutaneous), cough, fever, weight loss (pulmonary), develop lung abscesses, fungemia, and other organ involvement (disseminated).
- **CLASSIC FINDINGS:** Blood/Sputum/Urine culture, direct examination of pus from lesions, tissue biopsy.
- **TREATMENT:** Itraconazole, amphotericin B.

SURGICAL PROPHYLAXIS
- **PATHO:** Introduction of normal flora bacterial pathogens into the given anatomical region the procedure involves.
- **CLASSIC PRESENTATION:** New fever, erythema, wound drainage.
- **CLASSIC FINDINGS:** Acute wound with non-purulent inflammation.
- **TREATMENT:** Appropriate aseptic technique, surgical site specific antimicrobial prophylaxis prior to surgery.

SYPHILIS
- **PATHO:** Spirochetal infection causing syphilis, which is transmitted through sexual vaginal, anogenital, and orogenital contact and vertical transmission.
- **CLASSIC PRESENTATION:** Primary, secondary, tertiary, congenital, or neurosyphilis.
- **CLASSIC FINDINGS:** Dark-field microscopy and serological evidence of T. pallidum.
- **TREATMENT:** Penicillin G benzathine (treatment frequency and duration dependent on stage of syphilis.)

TOXOPLASMOSIS
- **PATHO:** Consumption of T. gondii results in conversion into tachyzoites, which then differentiate by penetrating nucleated cells, eliciting an immune response that stimulates the tachyzoites' conversion to bradyzoites. Reactivation of the bradyzoites to tachyzoites may occur during host immunosuppression.
- **CLASSIC PRESENTATION:** Fever, confusion, headaches, motor weakness, and focal encephalitis.
- **CLASSIC FINDINGS:** T. gondii DNA PCR
- **TREATMENT:** Trimethoprim/sulfamethoxazole (prophylaxis); pyrimethamine plus sulfadiazine plus leucovorin (treatment).

TRICHOMONIASIS
- **PATHO:** Sexually transmitted protozoan that resides in the lumen of the urogenital tract, where it releases cytotoxic proteins that disrupt the epithelial lining.
- **CLASSIC PRESENTATION:** Foul-smelling vaginal discharge that may be yellow or green, dyspareunia, urinary frequency, dysuria, or vulvar pruritus and erythema (women); asymptomatic (men).
- **CLASSIC FINDINGS:** Speculum examination observation of a "strawberry cervix," Nucleic acid amplification tests for T. vaginalis, Whiff test (fishy odor).
- **TREATMENT:** Metronidazole 2,000 mg once, or 500 mg BID x 7 days (HIV-positive, or non-pregnant).

TUBERCULOSIS

- **PATHO:** Primary tuberculosis from initial contact with M. tuberculosis, localizes in the middle portion of the lungs, followed by latent phase, and subsequent reactivation.
- **CLASSIC PRESENTATION:** Productive cough, hemoptysis, dyspnea, pleuritic chest pain, fever, night sweats, malaise, fatigue, weight loss.
- **CLASSIC FINDINGS:** Positive screening test with confirmatory chest X-ray; positive Acid Fast Staining-Ziehl-Neelsen; positive nuclear amplification tests
- **TREATMENT:** Isoniazid, Rifampin, Pyrazinamide, Ethambutol (active TB); Isoniazid (latent TB).

URINARY TRACT INFECTION (UTI)

- **PATHO:** Pathogenic bacteria entering the otherwise sterile environment of the urinary tract by ascending, descending/hematogenous, and lymphatic pathways.
- **CLASSIC PRESENTATION:** Dysuria, urgency, nocturia, suprapubic pain, hematuria (uncomplicated); abdominal pain, altered mental status, weakness, fever (complicated); non-specific symptoms, fever, elevated WBC, or complain of catheter malfunction/poor drainage (catheter-associated).
- **CLASSIC FINDINGS:** Urinalysis (WBC > 5, nitrate positive, leukocyte esterase), urine culture
- **TREATMENT:** Empiric antibiotics including nitrofurantoin, fosfomycin, tmp/smx, fluoroquinolones, or cephalosporins. Culture driven therapy after identification of causative pathogen.

VACCINATIONS

- **PATHO:** Vaccines induce an active immune response to numerous diseases that improve morbidity, mortality, and public health.
- **CLASSIC PRESENTATION:** Available as live attenuated vaccines, inactivated vaccines, subunit vaccines, DNA vaccines, immunoglobulins, and numerous novel mechanisms under development
- **TREATMENT:** Numerous vaccines available.

VIRAL ENCEPHALITIS

- **PATHO:** Viral infection and inflammation of brain parenchyma.
- **CLASSIC PRESENTATION:** Purpura, papilledema, altered mental status, fever, focal neurologic deficits, headache, neck stiffness, seizures.
- **CLASSIC FINDINGS:** CSF opening pressure < 300, WBC < 1000/mm^3, PMN 1 to 5%, glucose > 40 mg/dL, protein < 200 mg/dL. Positive CSF viral culture or absence of bacterial positive culture.
- **TREATMENT:** Acyclovir IV 10 to 15 mg/kg every 8 hours.

CONTRACEPTION
- **PATHO:** Prevent, interrupt, or nullify implantation and growth before or after conception.
- **CLASSIC PRESENTATION:** Estrogens and progestins promote changes in cervical mucus, uterine endometrium, and uterine tubal motility and secretion.
- **CLASSIC FINDINGS:** Routine physical examination prior to hormonal contraception is unnecessary
- **TREATMENT:** Combination oral hormonal contraceptives, implantable, parenteral, or intrauterine devices.

DYSMENORRHEA
- **PATHO:** Hypersecretion of PGF2 alpha and PGF2, increasing uterine tone and inducing high amplitude contractions of the uterus.
- **CLASSIC PRESENTATION:** Constipation, diarrhea, dysuria, dyspareunia, fatigue, headache, nausea, nodular adnexal masses, and vomiting.
- **CLASSIC FINDINGS:** Recurrent pelvic and lower abdominal pain associated with menstruation.
- **TREATMENT:** Analgesia, oral contraceptives, healthy diet, routine physical activity, and local heat applied to relieve pain.

ENDOMETRIOSIS
- **PATHO:** Presence of endometrial glands and stroma in anatomical locations outside the uterine cavity.
- **CLASSIC PRESENTATION:** Abnormal uterine bleeding, chronic fatigue, dyschezia, dysmenorrhea, dyspareunia, and lower back pain.
- **CLASSIC FINDINGS:** Laparoscopic findings consistent with endometriosis.
- **TREATMENT:** Surgical interventions including excision of lesions, cystectomy, oophorectomy; analgesia, oral contraceptives.

INFERTILITY
- **PATHO:** An underlying disorder of ovulation, endometriosis, pelvic adhesions, tubal blockages, tubal/uterine abnormalities, or hyperprolactinemia (female); hypogonadism, infections, primary testicular defects, sperm transport disorders, urogenital abnormalities, genetic, or idiopathic (male).
- **CLASSIC PRESENTATION:** Inability to conceive.
- **CLASSIC FINDINGS:** Unsuccessful pregnancy after 12 months of unprotected regular intercourse.
- **TREATMENT:** Clomiphene (females, males), letrozole (females).

MENOPAUSE
- **PATHO:** Reduction of ovulation secondary to decreased ovarian follicles response to FSH and lack of LH surge.
- **CLASSIC PRESENTATION:** Psychogenic – anger, anxiety, depression, confusion, sleep disturbances (psychogenic), sexual dysfunction, urethral atrophy, vaginal atrophy (urogenital), hot flashes, migraines, night sweats, palpitations (vasomotor).
- **CLASSIC FINDINGS:** Cessation of menses for 12 months.
- **TREATMENT:** Hormonal therapy (estrogen), SERM (bazedoxifene, ospemifene, raloxifene, tamoxifen).

POLYCYSTIC OVARY SYNDROME
- **PATHO:** Commonly due to excess androgen secretion from functional ovarian hyperandrogenism, results in over response of 17-hydroxyprogesterone to gonadotropin stimulation
- **CLASSIC PRESENTATION:** Acne, hirsutism, hair loss, irregular menstruation, seborrhea), oligomenorrhea, anovulation, polycystic ovaries.
- **CLASSIC FINDINGS:** Hyperandrogenism plus anovulation/oligomenorrhea or polycystic ovaries.
- **TREATMENT:** Progestin containing hormonal contraceptives, metformin.

SEXUAL DYSFUNCTION
- **PATHO:** Erectile dysfunction may be due to a disturbance in blood flow from the penis, diabetic-associated vascular and neurogenic effects, decreased testosterone, medication, or psychogenic (male), hypoactive sexual desire, sexual arousal disorder, orgasmic disorder, or sexual pain disorders (female).
- **CLASSIC PRESENTATION:** Patients may not openly disclose sexual dysfunction and should be assessed using open-ended questions.
- **CLASSIC FINDINGS:** Serum testosterone and prolactin for erectile dysfunction
- **TREATMENT:** PDE-5 inhibitors (males; use caution of already on nitrates), estrogen hormonal therapy (females).

BURSITIS

- **PATHO:** Inflammation and irritating process resulting in synovial fluid accumulation resulting in pain or discomfort as tendons and muscle move over bony prominences.
- **CLASSIC PRESENTATION:** Pain on palpation of the bursa, pain limited range of motion (acute), may be painless, large fluid-filled bursa, warmth over the bursa (chronic).
- **CLASSIC FINDINGS:** Aspiration of bursa with culture, cell count, glucose, and crystal analysis.
- **TREATMENT:** RICE therapy, acetaminophen, NSAIDs, local injection of hydrocortisone.

GOUT

- **PATHO:** Uric acid forms monosodium urate crystals that are deposited into the joints and other tissues leading to the activation of the immune system leading to inflammation, tissue destruction, and remodeling.
- **CLASSIC PRESENTATION:** Nocturnal, painful monoarticular arthritis (acute); tophi of the fingers, wrists, knees, Achilles tendon areas (chronic).
- **CLASSIC FINDINGS:** Arthrocentesis of the joint with needle shaped, negatively birefringent crystals, WBC 20-100,000 with greater than 50% PMNs.
- **TREATMENT:** NSAIDs, colchicine, corticosteroids (acute); xanthine oxidase inhibitors (chronic).

GUILLAIN-BARRE SYNDROME

- **PATHO:** An immune-mediated peripheral nerve myelin sheath destruction associated with Campylobacter infections, viral infection (CMV, EBV), or vaccinations.
- **CLASSIC PRESENTATION:** Ascending symmetrical weakness, loss of deep tendon reflexes, paralysis.
- **CLASSIC FINDINGS:** Ascending paralysis eventually affecting the diaphragm
- **TREATMENT:** IVIG, plasmapheresis, +/- intubation with mechanical ventilation.

MYASTHENIA GRAVIS

- **PATHO:** An autoimmune disorder of the neuromuscular junction of the skeletal muscles, often resulting from abnormal thymus function.
- **CLASSIC PRESENTATION:** Fluctuating pattern of disease, extraocular muscle weakness, bulbar muscle weakness, limb weakness.
- **CLASSIC FINDINGS:** Edrophonium test (myasthenic versus cholinergic crisis), Electrophysiologic testing (repetitive nerve stimulation, single-fiber electromyography), anti-AChR antibody, anti-MuSK antibody, anti-LRP4 antibody.
- **TREATMENT:** Pyridostigmine with or without glucocorticoids, azathioprine. Thymectomy

OSTEOARTHRITIS

- **PATHO:** Dysregulation of acute inflammatory responses and bone and joint, influenced by inflammatory cytokines, macrophages, matrix metalloproteinases, cysteine proteinases, and serine proteases.
- **CLASSIC PRESENTATION:** Joint pain (aching, dull, throbbing) that improves with rest.
- **CLASSIC FINDINGS:** Joint crepitus, deformity, instability, limited range of motion, stiffness, swelling, tenderness, Bouchard nodes, Heberden's nodes, and joint deformity.
- **TREATMENT:** Topical or systemic analgesia, and exercise, heat/cold therapy, physical or occupational therapy, weight loss, surgical intervention.

OSTEOPOROSIS

- **PATHO:** The progressive loss of bone mineral density caused by the deterioration of bone microstructure, resulting in a loss of bone strength and increased fracture risk.
- **CLASSIC PRESENTATION:** Commonly asymptomatic until advanced disease is present, or fractures occur.
- **CLASSIC FINDINGS:** DEXA t-score less than –2.5; DEXA z-score less than –1.5.
- **TREATMENT:** Bisphosphonates, calcium, vitamin D; exercise, reduction in smoking and alcohol consumption, dietary modification to include calcium and vitamin D.

PSORIASIS

- **PATHO:** Autoimmune disease caused by T-lymphocyte-induced proliferation of keratinocytes, resulting in dysregulation of cell turnover and formation of epidermal hyperplasia, parakeratosis, and plaques.
- **CLASSIC PRESENTATION:** Plaques on the forearms, shins, navel, and scalp.
- **CLASSIC FINDINGS:** Psoriasis Area Severity Index (PASI).
- **TREATMENT:** Topical Coal tar, corticosteroids, emollients, retinoids, calcipotriene; methotrexate, IL-17 receptor antagonists, IL-23 receptor antagonists, TNF-alpha inhibitors, selective T-cell costimulation blocker.

RHEUMATOID ARTHRITIS

- **PATHO:** Systemic autoimmune disease where synovial space becomes infiltrated by innate immune cells, resulting in the recruitment of inflammatory cytokines to the joint space, causing thickening of the synovial membrane, and small villous projections into the joint space.
- **CLASSIC PRESENTATION:** Polyarthritis, morning stiffness, flexor tenosynovitis, rheumatoid nodules.
- **CLASSIC FINDINGS:** Presence of four of the following criteria for at least 6 weeks: Morning stiffness lasting at least 1 hour, swelling in three or more joints, swelling in the hand or wrist joints, symmetrical arthritis, rheumatoid nodules, positive RF factor, radiologic changes (joint erosions or decalcifications)
- **TREATMENT:** NSAIDs, glucocorticoids, conventional DMARDs, biologic DMARDs.

SCLERODERMA

- **PATHO:** Autoimmune processes, excess fibrosis, or vascular abnormalities resulting in hardening and thickening of the skin that may be localized or systemic.
- **CLASSIC PRESENTATION:** Single or multiple plaques that occur in three phases of edematous, indurated/sclerotic, and atrophic (local); skin manifestations pus it internal organs involvement (systemic).
- **CLASSIC FINDINGS:** Scleroderma-type nail fold capillary pattern, scleroderma selective autoantibodies.
- **TREATMENT:** Topical/systemic steroids, MTX (localized), CCB (Raynaud's), PPI, ursodiol (CREST).

SYSTEMIC LUPUS ERYTHEMATOSUS

- **PATHO:** Initial cell damage resulting in B-cell and T-cell activation evolving into a self-sustained chronic immune response leading to further cytokine release, complement activation, and antibody production.
- **CLASSIC PRESENTATION:**
    - Clinical criteria: acute cute cutaneous lupus, chronic cutaneous lupus, oral ulcers, nonscarring alopecia, synovitis involving two or more joints, serositis, renal, neurologic, hemolytic anemia, leukopenia, thrombocytopenia
    - Immunologic criteria: ANA positive, anti-dsDNA positive, Anti-Smith antibodies, antiphospholipid antibody, low complement, direct Coombs test positive with hemolytic anemia.
- **CLASSIC FINDINGS:** SLICC more than 4 (1 clinical and 1 immunologic) of the 11 criteria required; biopsy proven lupus with positive ANA or anti-dsDNA.
- **TREATMENT:** Antimetabolites, DMARDs, corticosteroids, NSAIDs, cyclophosphamide, belimumab, rituximab.

ACUTE KIDNEY INJURY

- **PATHO:** Numerous pathophysiologic processes, subdivided into pre-renal, renal, and post-renal.
- **CLASSIC PRESENTATION:**
    - Pre-renal – BUN/Scr > 20, FeNa < 1%, high urine osmolarity, high specific gravity, low urine sodium, low fractional excretion of urea
    - Intrinsic – BUN/Scr < 12, FeNa > 1%, low urine osmolarity, low specific gravity, high urine sodium, high fractional excretion of urea. May also see RBCs, casts, tubular epithelial cells, eosinophils
    - Post-renal – BUN/Scr normal, high fractional excretion of sodium, low urine osmolarity
- **CLASSIC FINDINGS:** AKIN/KDIGO (stage 1 – 3), RIFLE
- **TREATMENT:** Dialysis (AEIOU), treat the underlying cause of AKI and removal of offending drugs.

CHRONIC KIDNEY DISEASE

- **PATHO:** From chronic and sustained kidney injury, progressive nephropathies and pathologic fibrosis causing abnormal renal architecture of the interstitial, glomeruli, and tubules.
- **CLASSIC PRESENTATION:** Early CKD may be asymptomatic. Chest pain, dizziness, fatigue, edema, headaches, persistent itching, rash, bruising, decreased urine output, joint pain, muscle cramping.
- **CLASSIC FINDINGS:** KDIGO Staging
- **TREATMENT:** Dialysis (AEIOU), treat the underlying, removal of offending drugs, treat comorbidities (HTN, DM), ESAs, vaccinations.

HYPERCALCEMIA

- **PATHO:** Primarily a result of hyperparathyroidism or malignancies.
- **CLASSIC PRESENTATION:** Bones, groans, stones, thrones, and psychic overtones.
- **CLASSIC FINDINGS:** Calcium above 10.5 mg/dL.
- **TREATMENT:** IV fluids with 0.9% NS, calcitonin (parenteral; not nasal), bisphosphonates (parenteral by IV infusion; not oral), prednisone, reduction in risk factors.

HYPOCALCEMIA

- **PATHO:** Either decreased absorption, increased excretion, endocrine-related, drug-induced, or other causes.
- **CLASSIC PRESENTATION:** Muscle cramps or tetany, increased deep tendon reflexes, bronchospasm, arrhythmias, paresthesia, weakness, confusion/hallucinations, seizures.
- **CLASSIC FINDINGS:** Calcium less than 8.8 mg/dL.
- **TREATMENT:** IV calcium gluconate or calcium chloride (symptomatic); oral calcium, calcitriol (activated form of vit D for deficient patients).

HYPERKALEMIA

- **PATHO:** Either increased potassium intake, intracellular shifts of potassium, or reduced potassium excretion
- **CLASSIC PRESENTATION:** Chest pain, SOB, fatigue, lethargy, muscle weakness, paresthesias, palpitations.
- **CLASSIC FINDINGS:** ECG findings of peaked T waves, wide-complex tachycardia, Serum potassium > 5.0 mEq/L
- **TREATMENT:** IV fluids, plus calcium gluconate or chloride (if ECG changes), insulin with dextrose, albuterol, furosemide, potassium binding resins, and likely will need HD.

HYPOKALEMIA

- **PATHO:** Increased potassium elimination, transcellular shifts in potassium, or decreased potassium intake.
- **CLASSIC PRESENTATION:** Muscle cramps, ileus, hyporeflexia, and weakness.
- **CLASSIC FINDINGS:** Serum potassium < 3.5 mEq/L
- **TREATMENT:** For every potassium chloride 10 mEq, serum potassium should increase by 0.1 mEq/L

HYPERMAGNESEMIA

- **PATHO:** An intra- and extracellular calcium channel blocker, producing smooth muscle relaxation by displacing calcium from actin/myosin, disrupting cardiac conduction, and blocking calcium entry into synapse.
- **CLASSIC PRESENTATION:** Loss of deep tendon reflexes can extend to loss of skeletal and smooth muscle activity, respiratory depression, hypotension, heart block, and cardiac arrest.
- **CLASSIC FINDINGS:** Serum magnesium > 2.2 mg/dL.
- **TREATMENT:** Sodium chloride, loop diuretics, calcium gluconate or calcium chloride.

HYPOMAGNESEMIA

- **PATHO:** Closely related to hypokalemia and hypocalcemia, may contribute to refractory hypokalemia.
- **CLASSIC PRESENTATION:** QT, PR, and QRS prolongation, hyperreflexia, tetany, muscle weakness, tremor, positive Chvostek's sign, positive Trousseau's sign, apathy, dizziness, irritability, papilledema, seizures, coma
- **CLASSIC FINDINGS:** Serum magnesium < 1.7 mg/dL.
- **TREATMENT:** Magnesium oral or parenteral. Caution with oral replacement as leads to diarrhea.

HYPERNATREMIA

- **PATHO:** Decrease in free water, excess water losses, or rarely due to increased total body sodium.
- **CLASSIC PRESENTATION:** Agitation, irritability, lethargy, orthostatic hypotension, poor skin turgor, somnolence coma.
- **CLASSIC FINDINGS:** Serum sodium > 145 mEq/L.
- **TREATMENT:** Gradual correction of sodium, no more than 12 mEq over 24-48 hours.

HYPONATREMIA

- **PATHO:** an absolute decrease in sodium and the rate of sodium decline related to urine osmolality and ADH.
- **CLASSIC PRESENTATION:** Agitation, apathy, confusion, depression, disorientation, psychosis, focal neurological deficits, seizures
- **CLASSIC FINDINGS:** Serum sodium < 135 mEq/L.
- **TREATMENT:** If SIADH, then free water restriction. Gradual correction of sodium, no more than 8 to 12 mEq over 24-48 hours.

HYPERPHOSPHATEMIA

- **PATHO:** An increased phosphate intake, renal reabsorption, decreased excretion, or transcellular shifts.
- **CLASSIC PRESENTATION:** Persistent itching, rash, bruising, joint pain, muscle cramping, SOB, productive cough, confusion, lethargy, sleep disturbances, tremors
- **CLASSIC FINDINGS:** Serum phosphorus > 4.5 mg/dL.
- **TREATMENT:** Treat underlying cause of hyperphosphatemia, IV hydration, phosphate binders.

HYPOPHOSPHATEMIA

- **PATHO:** Inadequate phosphate intake, increased excretion, or as a result of intracellular shifting of phosphate.
- **CLASSIC PRESENTATION:** Asymptomatic (mild), AMS, decreased deep tendon reflexes, heart failure, paresthesias, and weakness (moderate-severe).
- **CLASSIC FINDINGS:** Serum phosphate < 2.5 mg/dL.
- **TREATMENT:** Oral phosphate (mild-moderate); potassium phosphate (severe).

METABOLIC ACIDOSIS

- **PATHO:** Increase in serum hydrogen ion concentration relative to a decreased serum bicarbonate due to an identified or suspected metabolic etiology.
- **CLASSIC PRESENTATION:** Altered mental status, confusion, dehydration, dry mucous membranes, diarrhea, headache, hyperventilation, tachycardia, tachypnea, seizures, coma.
- **CLASSIC FINDINGS:** Serum pH less than 7.35 with a serum bicarbonate less than 24.
- **TREATMENT:** Treat the underlying cause of metabolic acidosis.

METABOLIC ALKALOSIS

- **PATHO:** The excess physiologic base resulting in a serum pH > 7.45 and elevated serum bicarbonate.
- **CLASSIC PRESENTATION:** AMS, arrhythmias, confusion, hypocalcemia, hypokalemia, hypertension muscle weakness, paresthesia, peripheral neuropathies, tremor, volume overload.
- **CLASSIC FINDINGS:** Serum pH > 7.45 with serum bicarbonate > 28.
- **TREATMENT:** Treat the underlying cause.

NEPHROLITHIASIS

- **PATHO:** Physiochemical change in urine resulting in supersaturation producing precipitation, nucleation, and concretions.
- **CLASSIC PRESENTATION:** Acute onset of abdominal pain, flank pain, distal/mid/upper ureter pain, most patients also present with hematuria and nausea/vomiting.
- **CLASSIC FINDINGS:** Hematuria, radiologic evidence of nephrolithiasis.
- **TREATMENT:** Analgesia, antiemetics, expulsion therapy (e.g., tamsulosin).

RESPIRATORY ACIDOSIS
- **PATHO:** A lowering of the serum pH below 7.35; due to insufficient ventilation.
- **CLASSIC PRESENTATION:** AMS, HF, hypercapnia, hypertension, impaired coordination, myoclonus, polycythemia, pulmonary hypertension, stroke like symptoms, seizures.
- **CLASSIC FINDINGS:** Serum pH less than 7.35 with a PCO2 greater than 42.
- **TREATMENT:** Treat the underlying cause.

RESPIRATORY ALKALOSIS
- **PATHO:** A relative decrease in carbon dioxide, either from decreased production, or hyperventilation and increased ventilation of carbon dioxide.
- **CLASSIC PRESENTATION:** Anxiety, chills, confusion, dyspnea, fever, hyperventilation, hemoptysis, peripheral edema, shortness of breath.
- **CLASSIC FINDINGS:** Serum pH > 7.45 with a carbon dioxide < 38
- **TREATMENT:** Treat the underlying issue.

ABSENCE SEIZURE

- **PATHO:** Abnormal oscillatory rhythm of neuronal discharge of T-type calcium channels and/or increased GABA-B activity in the thalamic nucleus reticularis.
- **CLASSIC PRESENTATION:** A sudden onset of a non-convulsive, dissociative state that persists for seconds to minutes before spontaneously terminating.
- **CLASSIC FINDINGS:** EEG: bilateral synchronous and symmetrical 3-Hertz spike-and-wave discharges that begin and terminate spontaneously.
- **TREATMENT:**
  - Ethosuximide (drug of choice for most exams)
  - Other Options: Lamotrigine, topiramate, or valproic acid

ACUTE ISCHEMIC STROKE

- **PATHO:** Cerebral artery occlusion resulting in decreased CBF and infarction of a core area of tissue.
- **CLASSIC PRESENTATION:** Rapidly progressive focal neurologic deficits.
- **CLASSIC FINDINGS:** Measurable neurologic deficit (NIHSS) with no evidence of acute hemorrhage on neuroimaging.
- **TREATMENT:**
  - If presentation within 4.5 hours of the onset of symptoms plus NO contraindications consider alteplase IV 0.09 mg bolus over 1 minute, followed by 0.81 mg/kg over 1 hour.

ALZHEIMER'S DISEASE

- **PATHO:** Gradual progressive neurodegenerative disease from accumulation of neuritic plaques and neurofibrillary tangles.
- **CLASSIC PRESENTATION:** Slow and steady course of delirium, delusions, depression, hallucinations, repetitive behaviors, loss of mental capacity.
- **CLASSIC FINDINGS:** CSF analysis for beta-amyloid 42, Braak and Braak staging.
- **TREATMENT:** Cholinesterase inhibitors (most commonly donepezil), +/- the NMDA antagonist, memantine.

BELL'S PALSY

- **PATHO:** Seventh cranial nerve compression caused by inflammation at the geniculate ganglion resulting in unilateral facial weakness that characteristically includes muscles of the forehead.
- **CLASSIC PRESENTATION:** Acute onset of unilateral facial paralysis peaking in severity at 72 hours.
- **CLASSIC FINDINGS:** House-Brackmann Facial Nerve Grading System
- **TREATMENT:**
  - If eye involvement: Artificial tears q1h while awake
  - Prednisone PO 60 to 80 mg daily x 7 days (best within 72 hours)
  - Antivirals for selected patients within 72 hours of onset of symptoms (if possible)

CLUSTER HEADACHE
- **PATHO:** Cerebrovascular vasodilation and abnormal hypothalamus morphology likely contribute to cluster headaches.
- **CLASSIC PRESENTATION:** Severe unilateral pain, located intraorbitally or supraorbitally.
- **CLASSIC FINDINGS:** Ipsilateral conjunctival injection or lacrimation, nasal congestion/rhinorrhea, eyelid edema, forehead edema, facial edema, miosis, or ptosis.
- **TREATMENT:** Lidocaine intranasal, triptans, prednisone (acute), verapamil ER (prophylaxis).

DRUG-INDUCED SEIZURES
- **PATHO:** Broad classification of seizures due to toxicity, withdrawal, or idiosyncratic mechanisms.
- **CLASSIC PRESENTATION:** Altered mental status, generalized-tonic clonic seizures.
- **CLASSIC FINDINGS:** Evidence of exposure to a drug withdrawal/toxicity or known to cause seizures.
- **TREATMENT:** Benzodiazepines, GI decontamination, urine alkalinization, hemodialysis.

GENERALIZED OR COMPLEX SEIZURE
- **PATHO:** Generalized seizures propagate through both hemispheres of the brain enhanced by excitatory neurotransmission and suppressed inhibitory neurotransmission
- **CLASSIC PRESENTATION:** Clonic, tonic-clonic, myoclonic, or atonic seizures.
- **CLASSIC FINDINGS:** Two or more unprovoked seizures at least 24 hours apart; one unprovoked seizure and at least a 60% risk of two unprovoked seizures occurring over the next ten years.
- **TREATMENT:** Antiepileptic drug selection based on type of epilepsy and patient-specific characteristics.

HEMORRHAGIC STROKE
- **PATHO:** Results in compression of brain tissue caused by the hematoma and increases in intracranial pressure.
- **CLASSIC PRESENTATION:** Headache, vomiting, hypertension, elevations in ICP, seizure, coma.
- **CLASSIC FINDINGS:** Acute hemorrhage on CT head.
- **TREATMENT:**
    - Clevidipine, nicardipine, labetalol (blood pressure); nimodipine (vasospasm)
    - +/- anticoagulant reversal (if applicable)
    - +/- surgical interventions.

HIGH-ALTITUDE SICKNESS
- **PATHO:** Decreased partial pressure of oxygen at high altitudes, ultimately resulting in tissue hypoxia.
- **CLASSIC PRESENTATION:** Anorexia, nausea, vomiting, headache, ataxia, confusion, dizziness, fatigue, weakness, insomnia.
- **CLASSIC FINDINGS:** Lake Louise self-assessment of acute mountain sickness scoring system.
- **TREATMENT:** Terminating ascent or begin the descent, supplemental oxygen, and hyperbaric therapy. May also use acetazolamide, dexamethasone, or ibuprofen as treatment or prophylaxis.

LOW BACK PAIN
- **PATHO:** Secondary to numerous other etiologies.
- **CLASSIC PRESENTATION:** Back pain that may be accompanied by disease specific features.
- **CLASSIC FINDINGS:** No routine workup, however, diagnostic imaging only in the presence of neurological deficits or where serious underlying causes are suspected.
- **TREATMENT:** Acetaminophen, NSAIDs, +/- skeletal muscle relaxants. Physical therapy can also be beneficial.

MIGRAINE HEADACHE
- **PATHO:** Complex physiology of intracranial and extracranial primary neurological impairments that primarily affects trigeminal afferent nerves.
- **CLASSIC PRESENTATION:** Prodrome, aura, migraine (unilateral, with a pulsatile feature that increases in intensity over the first few hours and can last for hours to days), postdrome.
- **CLASSIC FINDINGS:** No routine labs, may use International Classification of Headache Disorders
- **TREATMENT:** Antidepressants/anticonvulsants, BB/CCB, CGRP antagonists (prophylaxis), antiemetics, CGRP antagonists, NSAIDs, triptans, dexamethasone (treatment).

MULTIPLE SCLEROSIS
- **PATHO:** Autoimmune-mediated lymphocytes, macrophages, antibodies, & complement infiltration into CNS.
- **CLASSIC PRESENTATION:** New or recurrent MS symptoms lasting for 24-48 hours, followed by recovery for prolonged periods (relapsing-remitting); gradual progression of symptoms from onset without episodes of relapse (primary progressive); a gradual progression of symptoms that is preceded by an initial relapse-remitting course (secondary progressive); overlapping characteristics of relapse-remitting and secondary progressive MS (progressive-relapsing).
- **CLASSIC FINDINGS:** MRI, McDonald criteria.
- **TREATMENT:** Reduce MRI lesion activity and to prevent secondary progressive MS; DMARDs, interferon-beta, S1P Receptor Modulators.

PARKINSON DISEASE
- **PATHO:** Reduced dopamine neurotransmission involving the substantia nigra and resulting in increased activity of inhibitory GABA employing output nuclei in the basal ganglia, globus pallidus interna, and substantia nigra pars compacta.
- **CLASSIC PRESENTATION:** Tremor at rest, rigidity, akinesia, posture/equilibrium impairment.
- **CLASSIC FINDINGS:** Positron-emission tomography (PET), Single-photon emission computed tomography (SPECT)
- **TREATMENT:** Carbidopa/Levodopa, +/- dopamine agonists or +/- COMT inhibitors or +/- MAO inhibitors.

PERIPHERAL NEUROPATHY
- **PATHO:** Peripheral nerve injury, including segmental demyelination and axonal degeneration in a distinct pattern beginning distally and progressing proximally with a symmetrical polyneuropathy.
- **CLASSIC PRESENTATION:** Atrophy, sensory changes, numbness, or pain beginning in digits and progressing proximally.
- **CLASSIC FINDINGS:** Loss of deep tendon reflexes, stocking-glove pattern of sensory loss, muscle wasting, and weakness.
- **TREATMENT:** Neurologic analgesia.

PSEUDOTUMOR CEREBRI

- **PATHO:** Idiopathic intracranial hypertension, a result of CSF accumulation from a decreased reabsorption and or increased production.
- **CLASSIC PRESENTATION:** Cranial nerve VI palsy, diplopia, headache, photophobia, transient or persistent vision loss, papilledema, pulsatile tinnitus, visual field loss.
- **CLASSIC FINDINGS:** Modified Dandy Criteria
- **TREATMENT:** Acetazolamide, chlorthalidone, topiramate, corticosteroids (dexamethasone, hydrocortisone, methylprednisolone), optic nerve sheath defenestration, and lumbar puncture with drainage or CSF diversion.

RESTLESS LEG SYNDROME

- **PATHO:** Movement disorder associated with central dopaminergic dysfunction and decreased central iron deficiencies.
- **CLASSIC PRESENTATION:** Periodic leg movements that are involuntary and may occur with forceful dorsiflexion of the foot.
- **CLASSIC FINDINGS:** Uncontrollable urge to move the lower extremities with or without uncomfortable sensations; diurnal pattern, worsening in the evenings and at night, making sleep difficult or of poor quality; the urge to move the lower extremities is wholly or partially relieved by ambulation or stretching; symptoms are not attributable to other movement disorders.
- **TREATMENT:** Dopamine agonists at night: Cabergoline, pramipexole, ropinirole, rotigotine transdermal patch.

SECONDARY STROKE PREVENTION

- **PATHO:** Risk reduction of secondary strokes due to the existing underlying pathophysiology of stroke and secondary injury.
- **CLASSIC PRESENTATION:** Long-term antiplatelet therapy, blood pressure management, cholesterol-lowering, diabetes management, and identification of other reversible/modifiable stroke risk factors.
- **CLASSIC FINDINGS:** Evidence of previous stroke/TIA on history or imaging (CT/MRI).
- **TREATMENT:** Antiplatelet agents (aspirin or clopidogrel), secondary stroke prevention.

STAUTS EPILEPTICUS

- **PATHO:** Related to gray matter cell changes causing abnormal potassium conductance, voltage-sensitive sodium or calcium channels, or deficiency ion transport in membrane ATPases.
- **CLASSIC PRESENTATION:** Multiple seizures without recovery between episodes or prolonged, continuous seizure activity of more than 5 minutes.
- **CLASSIC FINDINGS:** May be convulsive, nonconvulsive or refractory.
- **TREATMENT:** Lorazepam or midazolam IM/IV, fosphenytoin (IV/IM), or rectal diazepam.

TENSION HEADACHE

- **PATHO:** Myofascial trigger point abnormalities resulting in excessive pericranial muscle contraction, causing oxidative stress and substance P and nitric oxide release.
- **CLASSIC PRESENTATION:** Headache lasting 0.5-6 hours (up to 7 days) with at least two of the following: bilateral location, pressure or tightening quality, mild to moderate intensity, not aggravated by routine physical activity. May have photophobia or phonophobia, but not both.
- **CLASSIC FINDINGS:** No routine labs
- **TREATMENT:** Acute management: Acetaminophen, NSAIDs; For Prevention: TCA, topiramate, or valproic acid.

TRAUMATIC BRAIN INJURY

- **PATHO:** TBI represents a range of injuries, including blunt, concussive, or penetrating injuries to the brain.
- **CLASSIC PRESENTATION:** AMS, nausea and vomiting, memory loss, paralysis/hemiparesis.
- **CLASSIC FINDINGS:** Cushing's triad, Babinski's sing, decorticate posturing, decerebrate posturing, oculocephalic response (Doll's eyes), oculovestibular response.
- **TREATMENT:** Prevention and reduction in the risk of secondary injury to include 7 days if seizure prophylaxis (with phenytoin or levetiracetam) + concussive precautions.

TRIGEMINAL NEURALGIA

- **PATHO:** Trigeminal nerve compression resulting in neuronal demyelination from ectopic impulse generation resulting in the coupling of adjacent nerve fibers and dysregulated neuronal transmission yielding disproportionate pain responses to light tactile stimulation.
- **CLASSIC PRESENTATION:** Paroxysmal pain response is caused by minimal stimuli that is maximal near the time of onset.
- **CLASSIC FINDINGS:** International Classification of Headache Disorders.
- **TREATMENT:** Baclofen, antiepileptics (especially carbamazepine), botulinum toxins.

ECLAMPSIA & PRE-ECLAMPSIA
- **PATHO:** Reduced blood supply to the placenta resulting in increased uterine arterial resistance, and vasoconstriction producing placental oxidative stress and ischemia.
- **CLASSIC PRESENTATION:** Acute hypertension, abdominal pain, altered mental status, headache, visual changes, generalized tonic-clonic seizures.
- **CLASSIC FINDINGS:** New-onset hypertension after 20 weeks' gestation with proteinuria, liver/renal dysfunction, CNS manifestations, pulmonary edema, or thrombocytopenia (pre-eclampsia); generalized tonic-clonic seizures (eclampsia).
- **TREATMENT:** Delivery of the baby, magnesium sulfate, labetalol.

MASTITIS
- **PATHO:** Skin flora and inadequate milk drainage resulting in organism growth and infection (lactational); associated with autoimmune diseases, hyperprolactinemia, lactation, oral contraception, and trauma (non-lactational).
- **CLASSIC PRESENTATION:** Fever, flu-like symptoms.
- **CLASSIC FINDINGS:** Breast tenderness, chills, erythematous breast tissue.
- **TREATMENT:** Warm compress and massage, analgesia, +/- antibiotics (e.g., cephalexin or dicloxacillin).

NAUSEA AND VOMITING - PREGNANCY
- **PATHO:** Hormone concentration elevations (estrogen or hCG) and esophageal sphincter relaxation.
- **CLASSIC PRESENTATION:** Nausea and vomiting between weeks 4 and 20 of gestation.
- **CLASSIC FINDINGS:** Ketonemia, hypokalemia, volume depletion, or weight loss.
- **TREATMENT:** Pyridoxine, antiemetics PRN.

POSTPARTUM HEMORRHAGE
- **PATHO:** Inadequate contraction of the uterus, abnormal placentation, genital tract lacerations, retained placenta, underlying coagulation disorders, uterine inversion, or uterine inversion.
- **CLASSIC PRESENTATION:** Acute postpartum vaginal hemorrhage, AMS, blurry vision, clammy skin, tachycardia, tachypnea, weakness.
- **CLASSIC FINDINGS:** Estimated loss of blood greater than 1,000 mL with signs and symptoms of hypovolemia within 24 hours of delivery.
- **TREATMENT:** Bimanual uterine message to encourage contractions +/- tranexamic acid, oxytocin, misoprostol, methylergonovine, +/- blood.

DOSE-LIMITING TOXICITIES OF CHEMOTHERAPY

- **Alkylating Agents:** Mucositis, irritant with vesicant-like properties (bendamustine), pulmonary fibrosis, skin hyperpigmentation (busulfan), hemorrhagic cystitis (cyclophosphamide & ifosfamide)
- **Angiogenesis Inhibitors:** Teratogenicity, peripheral neuropathy, BMS, bradycardia, skin reactions (including SJS and TEN), VTE
- **Anthracyclines:** Cardiac toxicity (especially if cumulative doses > 400 mg/m²), extravasation risk, BMS
- **Folate Antagonists:** Mucositis, liver and kidney toxicity or fibrosis (methotrexate), mild to severe dermatologic toxicity (pemetrexed)
- **Platinum analogs:** Nephrotoxicity, peripheral neuropathy
- **Pyrimidine Antagonists:** Severe diarrhea, BMS, hand-foot syndrome (5-FU)
- **Taxanes:** Peripheral neuropathy, edema, BMS, hypersensitivity reactions
- **Topoisomerase Inhibitors:** Severe acute and delayed diarrhea, pulmonary fibrosis, BMS (irinotecan)
- **Vinca Alkaloids:** Peripheral neuropathy (vincristine >> vinblastine=vinorelbine), extravasation risk, BMS (except vincristine)
- **HER-2 inhibitors:** Reduced LVEF/cardiac toxicity, diarrhea, infusion reactions, severe teratogenicity
- **Immunotherapy:** irAEs including rash, pruritus, diarrhea, colitis, elevated liver enzymes and bilirubin, hepatitis, hypothyroidism
- **Tyrosine kinase inhibitors:** Diarrhea, QT prolongation, CYP3A4 substrates; EGFR inhibitors – SJS/TEN, interstitial lung disease, ocular toxicity; VEGF inhibitors – bleeding, wound dehiscence, hypertension, proteinuria

CHEMOTHERAPY-INDUCED NAUSEA & VOMITING

- **PATHO:** Complex physiology involving numerous CNS sites including the CTZ, emetic center, cerebral cortex and peripheral sites.
- **CLASSIC PRESENTATION:** Can be one or mixture of acute, delayed, anticipatory, breakthrough, or refractory.
- **CLASSIC FINDINGS:** No specific lab abnormalities, but dehydration, hyponatremia, hypokalemia may occur due to vomiting.
- **TREATMENT:** Antiemetics targeted to specific type of nausea (antihistamines, benzamides, benzodiazepines, butyrophenones, cannabinoids, phenothiazines, serotonin antagonists, NK1 RA)

CHEMOTHERAPY INDUCED DIARRHEA

- **PATHO:** Commonly associated with irinotecan, tyrosine kinase inhibitors (EGFR inhibitors), 5-FU, and, HER-2 inhibitors.
- **CLASSIC PRESENTATION:** Increased stool frequency, dizziness, abdominal pain, weakness.
- **CLASSIC FINDINGS:** Diarrhea graded as uncomplicated (grade 1 or 2), or complicated (grade 3 or 4).
- **TREATMENT:** Uncomplicated diarrhea treated primarily with loperamide; complicated diarrhea treatment includes loperamide, IV fluid and electrolyte replacement, antibiotics, octreotide.

Copyright: High-Yield Med Reviews
highyieldmedreviews.com

FEBRILE NEUTROPENIA

- **PATHO:** Decreased neutrophil concentration resulting in impaired immunity and increased susceptibility to bacterial, viral, fungal and other infections.
- **CLASSIC PRESENTATION:** Fever, usually weakness or malaise, cough or shortness of breath if the infection involves the lungs
- **CLASSIC FINDINGS:** > 38.3 °C or 101 °F for a single episode or 100.4 for > 1 hour + an absolute neutrophil count < 500 cells/mm3 (or ANC expected to fall < 500 over the next 48 hours)
- **TREATMENT:** IV empiric antibiotic therapy to include monotherapy with an antipseudomonal beta-lactam agent

HYPERURICEMIA / TUMOR LYSIS SYNDROME

- **PATHO:** Rapid and massive cellular breakdown with the subsequent release of cell contents and cytokines into the bloodstream leading to systemic complications including hyperuricemia hyperkalemia, hyperphosphatemia with subsequent hypocalcemia.
- **CLASSIC PRESENTATION:** Nausea vomiting, cardiac dysrhythmias, renal failure
- **CLASSIC FINDINGS:** Presence of 2 or more abnormal labs occurring within 3 days before her up to 7 days after use of cytotoxic chemotherapy for malignancy: Hyperuricemia, hyperkalemia, hyperphosphatemia, hypocalcemia
- **TREATMENT:** Prophylaxis (allopurinol, hydration, rasburicase); treatment (IV hydration, allopurinol, rasburicase, HD)

EXTRAVASATION

- **PATHO:** Accidental complication of chemotherapy administration where the drug deposits outside of the blood vessel and into the tissue at the location of IV insertion thereby damaging the tissue in the surrounding area.
- **CLASSIC PRESENTATION:** Can range from redness with or without pain to blistering and tissue necrosis depending on the timeframe from extravasation and agent used
- **CLASSIC AGENTS:** Bendamustine (Alkylating Agent), Dactinomycin, Daunorubicin, Doxorubicin, & Idarubicin (Anthracyclines), Oxaliplatin (Platinum analog), Paclitaxel (Taxane), Vinblastine, Vincristine, Vinorelbine (Vinca Alkaloids)
- **TREATMENT:** Stop infusion immediately, gently aspirate extravasated solution, elevate extremity, apply dry, cold compress for 20 minutes 4 times daily x 1-2 days; followed by drug (extravasate) specific treatments.

ALLERGIC CONJUNCTIVITIS
- **PATHO:** IgE mediated hypersensitivity reaction where direct contact with an allergen results in mast cell degranulation.
- **CLASSIC PRESENTATION:** Bilateral clear, chemosis, eyelid edema, pruritis, watery discharge.
- **CLASSIC FINDINGS:** Giant papillary conjunctivitis, atopic, and vernal keratoconjunctivitis may additionally present with blurry vision, foreign body sensation, pain, photophobia.
- **TREATMENT:** Ophthalmic topical antihistamines, mast-cell stabilizer, imidazoline.

ANGLE CLOSURE-GLAUCOMA
- **PATHO:** Aqueous humor outflow obstruction, acutely increasing IOP.
- **CLASSIC PRESENTATION:** Acute onset of severe unilateral eye pain, blurry vision, conjunctival injection, fixed pupils, hazy cornea, headache, rigid globe, seeing rings or halos around lights.
- **CLASSIC FINDINGS:** IOP greater than 20 mmHg, mid-dilated nonreactive pupil, shallow anterior chamber with occlusion.
- **TREATMENT:** Acute IOP reduction with acetazolamide IV/PO, mannitol IV, and timolol 1 drop.

CORNEAL ULCERATION
- **PATHO:** Defect in the corneal epithelium permitting infectious pathogens entry into the underlying stroma.
- **CLASSIC PRESENTATION:** Conjunctival redness and swelling, ocular pain.
- **CLASSIC FINDINGS:** Decreased visual acuity, gray/white corneal lesion with fluorescein uptake, photophobia
- **TREATMENT:** Topical antibiotics +/- cyclopentolate (if suspicious for iritis).

NORMAL-TENSION GLAUCOMA
- **PATHO:** Optic disc cupping and peripheral visual-field loss at normal IOP.
- **CLASSIC PRESENTATION:** Often asymptomatic, with abnormal slit-lamp examination findings.
- **CLASSIC FINDINGS:** Focal visual field defects, concomitant systemic vascular conditions.
- **TREATMENT:** Ophthalmic alpha antagonists, beta-blockers, carbonic anhydrase inhibitor, cholinergics, prostaglandin.

OPEN-ANGLE GLAUCOMA
- **PATHO:** Increased IOP due to resistance of the trabecular meshwork to drainage of aqueous outflow from the eye, despite the angle between the cornea and iris remaining open.
- **CLASSIC PRESENTATION:** Early disease is asymptomatic. Peripheral vision loss (tunnel vision), difficulties driving, bumping into things.
- **CLASSIC FINDINGS:** Elevated IOP, optic disk changes, visual field changes.
- **TREATMENT:** Ophthalmic alpha antagonists, beta-blockers, carbonic anhydrase inhibitor, cholinergics, prostaglandin.

SECONDARY GLAUCOMA
- **PATHO:** Preexisting or concomitant ophthalmic disease, injury, or secondary to ophthalmic surgery that results in elevated IOP and optic neuropathy.
- **CLASSIC PRESENTATION:** Early disease is asymptomatic, peripheral vision loss (tunnel vision), difficulties driving, bumping into things.
- **CLASSIC FINDINGS:** Elevated IOP, optic disk changes, visual field changes.
- **TREATMENT:** Identification and treatment of the concomitant or underlying cause of elevated IOP, ophthalmic alpha antagonists, beta-blockers, carbonic anhydrase inhibitor, cholinergics, prostaglandin.

UVEITIS & IRITIS
- **PATHO:** Inflammation of the anterior and posterior chamber and iris.
- **CLASSIC PRESENTATION:** Acute onset of red, painful eye that is made worse with movement, with small, poorly reactive pupils (anterior); visual changes including blind spots, flashing lights, floaters (posterior).
- **CLASSIC FINDINGS:** May be associated with ankylosing spondylitis, rheumatoid arthritis, ulcerative colitis, sarcoidosis, and trauma.
- **TREATMENT:** Prednisolone (ophthalmic) if no concerns for viral etiology and if so after consultation with ophthalmologist, cyclopentolate to treat the photophobia.

ULTRAVIOLET KERATITIS
- **PATHO:** Acute ophthalmic inflammatory response and subsequent desquamation of corneal epithelium, exposing corneal nerve endings from UV light exposure.
- **CLASSIC PRESENTATION:** May be delayed in onset by 6 to 12 hours after exposure and may resolve spontaneously in 48-72 hours.
- **CLASSIC FINDINGS:** Bilateral eye pain, blepharospasm, chemosis, decreased visual acuity, foreign body sensation, photophobia, lacrimation.
- **TREATMENT:** Analgesia, carboxymethylcellulose drops.

ALCOHOL USE DISORDER

- **PATHO:** Attributed to multiple factors, including environmental, genetic, cognitive function, and personality disorders.
- **CLASSIC PRESENTATION:** Intoxication, alcohol ketoacidosis, beer potomania, beriberi, thiamine deficiency, Wernicke-Korsakoff syndrome, alcohol withdrawal
- **CLASSIC FINDINGS:** AUDIT, CAGE
- **TREATMENT:** CBT, Alcoholics Anonymous, abuse deterrents (acamprosate, disulfiram, or naltrexone)

AMPHETAMINES AND DERIVATIVES ABUSE

- **PATHO:** Excitatory neurotransmission and smooth muscle modulation of glycogenolysis, increased fatty acid oxidation, thermogenesis.
- **CLASSIC PRESENTATION:** Mydriasis, tachycardia, tachypnea, hypertension, hyperthermia, psychomotor agitation (early); tissue hypoxia, metabolic acidosis, end-organ dysfunction (myocardial infarction, cerebral ischemia (late).
- **CLASSIC FINDINGS:** Hyperthermia, tachycardia, agitation
- **TREATMENT:**
  - (Acute Management): Benzodiazepines, intra/extravascular cooling
  - (Chronic Management): Requires a slow taper to avoid withdrawal seizures

ATTENTION DEFICIT HYPERACTIVITY DISORDER

- **PATHO:** A dysfunction of diffuse brain deficits, including frontal lobe activity and executive functioning, regulating attention, decision making, and emotional responses.
- **CLASSIC PRESENTATION:** Forgetfulness, hesitation, inattention, procrastination (predominantly inattentive), difficulty paying attention, difficulty controlling behavior, excessive activity (predominantly hyperactive), hyperactivity, impulsiveness, inattention (combined).
- **CLASSIC FINDINGS:** Six or more symptoms must be present for at least six months, significant impairment must be seen in two or more settings, such as at home and school, symptoms must be documented by the parent, teacher, and clinician.
- **TREATMENT:**
  - CBT +/- Stimulants (amphetamine or methylphenidate derivatives)
  - Non-Stimulants (long-acting clonidine or guanfacine)

BIPOLAR DISORDER

- **PATHO:** Excess dopamine and norepinephrine neurotransmission in mania, with depression associated with a deficiency in dopamine, norepinephrine, and serotonin.
- **CLASSIC PRESENTATION:** Manic episodes, hypomanic episodes, major depressive episodes.
- **CLASSIC FINDINGS:** Rapid cycling or at least four episodes of mood disorder in a 12-month period. Presence of psychotic features, mixed features, atypical features, anxious distress, a peripartum onset, or seasonal pattern.
- **TREATMENT:** Lithium, valproic acid, cariprazine, risperidone (mania), SSRI, SNRI (depression).

GENERAL ANXIETY DISORDER
- **PATHO:** Multiple regions of the brain and abnormal neurotransmission of cholecystokinin, corticotropin-releasing factor, dopamine, GABA, norepinephrine, and serotonin.
- **CLASSIC PRESENTATION:** Cognitive and psychosocial symptoms, physical symptoms.
- **CLASSIC FINDINGS:** Excessive anxiety and worry, anxiety results in significant distress or impairment in social and occupational areas, anxiety not attributable to any physical cause.
- **TREATMENT:** CBT, antidepressants (low initial dose with slow titration), +/- buspirone

INSOMNIA
- **PATHO:** Abnormal functioning of orexin-mediated neurotransmission in the wake-promoting function of the ventrolateral preoptic nucleus and inhibition of the sleep-promoting median preoptic nucleus.
- **CLASSIC PRESENTATION:** Sleep disturbances that have been present over a 3-month period (short-term); sleep disturbances at least three times per week and present for the past 3 months (chronic).
- **CLASSIC FINDINGS:** Difficulty initiating sleep, difficulty maintaining sleep, early-morning awakening with inability to return to sleep.
- **TREATMENT:** Non-benzodiazepine hypnotics, melatonin receptor agonists, orexin receptor antagonist, CBT, sleep hygiene, sleep restriction therapy, stimulus control therapy, relaxation therapy.

MAJOR DEPRESSIVE DISORDER
- **ATHO:** Abnormal functioning or a deficiency in dopamine, norepinephrine, and serotonin.
- **CLASSIC PRESENTATION:** Cognitive, emotional, physical, psychomotor symptoms.
- **CLASSIC FINDINGS:** Five of major depressive features of major depression associated with pregnancy or within 4 weeks of delivery, develop over a two-week period, and must include depressed mood or anhedonia.
- **TREATMENT:** Antidepressants, CBT, impersonal therapy, ECT (for resistant cases), transcranial magnetic stimulation, or vagus nerve stimulation.

MARIJUANA & K2 ABUSE
- **PATHO:** THC and delta-9-THC modulate endocannabinoid, GABA, glutamate, and serotonin transmission.
- **CLASSIC PRESENTATION:** Intoxication, withdrawal, cannabinoid hyperemesis syndrome
- **CLASSIC FINDINGS:** Problematic pattern of cannabis use leading to clinically significant impairment or distress
- **TREATMENT:** (Acute Complications Only): Benzodiazepines; capsaicin, haloperidol, lorazepam, hot showers, isopropyl alcohol inhalation (CHS).

OBSESSIVE-COMPULSIVE DISORDER
- **PATHO:** Abnormal function of the cortical-striatal-thalamocortical circuits, particularly the orbitofrontal cortex, the caudate, anterior cingulate cortex, and thalamus.
- **CLASSIC PRESENTATION:** Recurrent images, thoughts, or urges that are unwanted and result in marked distress resulting in attempts to suppress the images, thoughts, or urges with another action or thought (obsession), repetitive behaviors or mental acts that an individual perceives they are driven to perform in response to the obsession, with the specific aim to reduce anxiety or distress, but do not connect in a realistic way with what they are designed to prevent or are noticeably excessive (compulsion).
- **CLASSIC FINDINGS:** Symptoms of another mental disorder do not explain the disturbance.
- **TREATMENT:** Cognitive-behavioral therapy, exposure and response prevention therapy, SSRI.

PANIC DISORDER

- **PATHO:** A lack of appropriate neurochemical mechanisms to counteract elevated serotonergic changes in the fear network model of the autonomic nervous system or as a result of endogenous opioid deficiency resulting in separation anxiety and increased awareness of a perceived threat.
- **CLASSIC PRESENTATION:** Choking sensation, chills, depersonalization, diaphoresis, dyspnea, chest pain, palpitations.
- **CLASSIC FINDINGS:** Recurrent unexpected panic attacks, persistent concern about having additional panic attacks, worry about the implications of the attack or its consequences, a significant change in behavior related to the attacks.
- **TREATMENT:** Benzodiazepines (acute and chronic), SSRI, SNRI (chronic), CBT.

PHENCYCLIDINE (PCP) ABUSE

- **PATHO:** CNS excitation and CNS depression through its actions as a non-competitive NMDA receptor antagonist.
- **CLASSIC PRESENTATION:** Agitation, confusion, delusions, hallucinations, miosis, muscle rigidity, seizures, trauma.
- **CLASSIC FINDINGS:** Hyperthermia, hypertension hypoxia, nystagmus (rotary), tachycardia.
- **TREATMENT:** (Acute Management Only): Benzodiazepines

POST-PARTUM DEPRESSION

- **PATHO:** Multifactorial, related to genetic factors, hormonal, psychological, and social stressors, neuroendocrine pathways, and rapid changes in estradiol, progesterone, oxytocin, and prolactin influencing other neurophysiologic factors.
- **CLASSIC PRESENTATION:** Cognitive, emotional, physical, psychomotor symptoms.
- **CLASSIC FINDINGS:** Five of major depressive features of major depression associated with pregnancy or within 4 weeks of delivery, develop over a two-week period, and must include depressed mood or anhedonia.
- **TREATMENT:** Cognitive-behavioral therapy and SSRI, brexanolone.

POST-TRAUMATIC STRESS DISORDER (PTSD)

- **PATHO:** Occurs due to exposure to an actual or perceived trauma, combat-related trauma, interpersonal conflicts, post-medical illness, or threatened serious injury, sexual assault, or death.
- **CLASSIC PRESENTATION:** Persistently re-experiencing the traumatic event and intense adverse emotional and physiological reaction from exposure to a reminder of the traumatic event.
- **CLASSIC FINDINGS:** Disturbance causes significant functional impairment or distress in various areas of life, such as social or occupational; the disturbance is not attributable due to substance use, medication, or another medical illness.
- **TREATMENT:** SSRI, SNRI, CBT, exposure and response prevention therapy, EMDR, and imaginal exposure.

SCHIZOPHRENIA

- **PATHO:** Excessive D2 activation in the mesolimbic pathway (positive symptoms); low dopamine concentration in the nigrostriatal pathway (negative symptoms).
- **CLASSIC PRESENTATION:** Delusions, disorganized speech, formal thought disorders, hallucinations (positive); anhedonia, alogia, avolition, flattened affect (negative); deficiency in attention, executive functioning, and memory (cognitive); dysphoria, hopelessness, suicidality (mood).
- **CLASSIC FINDINGS:** Two or more symptoms must be present for a significant portion of time during one month (delusions, disorganized speech, grossly disorganized or catatonic behavior, hallucinations, negative symptoms); social and/or occupational dysfunction must also be present; signs of disturbance must persist for at least six months, including at least one month of symptoms.
- **TREATMENT:** Antipsychotics (mainly 2nd generation or atypical agents as first-line), CBT, social skills and resiliency therapy, and adherence therapy.

SMOKING CESSATION

- **PATHO:** Nicotine stimulates the cerebral cortex and limbic system, improving alertness and stimulating reward but neuroadaptation and tolerance develop over time.
- **CLASSIC PRESENTATION:** Decreased dopaminergic transmission causing malaise, difficulty concentrating, irritability, insomnia, and cravings (nicotine withdrawal).
- **CLASSIC FINDINGS:** Substance abuse pattern leading to clinically significant impairment or distress.
- **TREATMENT:** Bupropion, nicotine, varenicline, social and psychological support.

ASTHMA (CHRONIC)
- **PATHO:** Acute reactive airway disease of airflow obstruction characterized by acute airway inflammation and bronchiole hyperresponsiveness in response to an environmental trigger.
- **CLASSIC PRESENTATION:** Chest tightness, cough, shortness of breath, nighttime awakenings, wheeze.
- **CLASSIC FINDINGS:** Reduced FEV1/FVC
- **TREATMENT:**
  - SABA, ICS, LABA (e.g., tiotropium)
  - +/- biologics (benralizumab, dupilumab, mepolizumab, omalizumab, reslizumab) for difficult to control patients.

ASTHMA EXACERBATION (ACUTE)
- **ATHO:** May occur over days or rapidly progress over 1 to 2 hours resulting in severe SOB, respiratory failure.
- **CLASSIC PRESENTATION:** Accessory muscle use, altered mental status, dry cough, hyperinflated chest, tachypnea, tachycardia, prolonged expiration, wheezing.
- **CLASSIC FINDINGS:** FEV1 less than 40% of predicted, hypoxia.
- **TREATMENT:** Non-invasive ventilation (CPAP, BiPAP) or invasive ventilation (intubation), SABA, systemic glucocorticoid, IV magnesium sulfate.

COPD (CHRONIC)
- **PATHO:** Chronic inflammation resulting in the airways, lung parenchyma, and pulmonary vasculature in response to exposure to noxious gases or particles which induce inflammation.
- **CLASSIC PRESENTATION:** Barrel chest, chronic cough, chronic sputum production, dyspnea, tachypnea.
- **CLASSIC FINDINGS:** FEV1/FVC less than 70%, reduced FEV1
- **TREATMENT:**
  - SABA, SAMA, LABA, LAMA
  - +/- ICS for more moderate to severe cases

COPD EXACERBATION (ACUTE)
- **PATHO:** Acute, persistent, and progressive airflow limitation that is not fully reversible and results from ventilation-perfusion mismatch.
- **CLASSIC PRESENTATION:** Altered mental status, accessory muscle use, productive cough, cyanosis, dyspnea, hypercapnia, hypoxemia, hypertension, pursed-lip exhalation, tachycardia, tachypnea.
- **CLASSIC FINDINGS:** May occur secondary to new infections, heart failure, pneumothorax, pulmonary embolism, smoking, beta-blockers, opioids, or cold weather exposure.
- **TREATMENT:**
  - Supplemental oxygen, non-invasive ventilation, SABA, glucocorticoids, magnesium
  - +/- antibiotics (if evidence or concerns for bacterial infection)

CYSTIC FIBROSIS

- **PATHO:** Autosomal recessive genetic disorder that has been identified to be a result of mutations in the gene encoding the CFTR proteins; most have at least one copy of the Phe508del CFTR mutation.
- **CLASSIC PRESENTATION:** Cor pulmonale, type 1 diabetes, chronic diarrhea, and malabsorption of fat-soluble vitamins (A, D, E, and K), neonatal meconium ileus failure, cough, sputum production, pneumonia, aspergillosis, bronchitis, bronchiectasis, pneumothorax, sinusitis, hypokalemia, hypochloremic metabolic acidosis, suppurative parotitis.
- **CLASSIC FINDINGS:** Evidence of CFTR dysfunction – abnormal nasal potential difference, elevated sweat chloride more than 60 mEq/L on two occasions, two disease-causing CFTR mutations.
- **TREATMENT:** Airway clearance therapies, antibiotics, bronchodilators, CFTR modulators, ICS, mucolytics, NSAIDs, pancrelipase, vitamins ADEK supplementation.

ACETAMINOPHEN TOXICITY
- **PATHO:** NAPQI induced liver injury/failure.
- **CLASSIC PRESENTATION:** Four stages, (1) non-specific GI, (2) hepatic injury onset, (3) hepatotoxicity, (4) recover, transplant, or death.
- **CLASSIC FINDINGS:** Elevated acetaminophen level, elevated AST, ALT.
- **TREATMENT:** N-acetylcysteine.

ANTICHOLINERGIC TOXICITY
- **PATHO:** Competitively blocks ACh binding to muscarinic receptors.
- **CLASSIC PRESENTATION:** Blind as a bat, dry as a bone, hot as a hare, mad as a hatter, red as a beet.
- **CLASSIC FINDINGS:** Peripheral anticholinergic effects (induction), somnolence, restlessness, ataxia hyperthermia, hypertension (stupor), delirium phase: amnesia, confusion, hallucinations, incoherent speech. (delirium).
- **TREATMENT:** Physostigmine.

ASPIRIN / SALICYLATE TOXICITY
- **PATHO:** Uncouples oxidative phosphorylation.
- **CLASSIC PRESENTATION:** Non-specific GI distress, tachypnea, primary respiratory alkalosis, tinnitus, progressing to hypoglycorrhachia, hyperpnea, altered mental status, hyperthermia, coagulopathy, ARDS, severe metabolic acidosis.
- **CLASSIC FINDINGS:** Salicylate level > 20 mg/dL, metabolic acidosis with a positive anion gap, hyperthermia, altered mental status
- **TREATMENT:** GI decontamination, sodium bicarbonate, hemodialysis.

BETA-BLOCKERS / CALCIUM CHANNEL BLOCKER TOXICITY
- **PATHO:** Prevents Ca-dependent Ca release from the SR leading to decreased cardiac contractility.
- **CLASSIC PRESENTATION:** Hypotension, bradycardia, hyperglycemia (CCB).
- **CLASSIC FINDINGS:** Prolonged PR interval, hypotension.
- **TREATMENT:** High-dose insulin plus dextrose, glucagon.

CHOLINERGIC TOXICITY
- **PATHO:** AChE inhibition, causing excess activation of muscarinic and nicotinic receptors.
- **CLASSIC PRESENTATION:** Bronchorrhea, bronchospasm, bradycardia (Killer B's); salivation, lacrimation, urination, defecation, GI distress, emesis (SLUDGE).
- **CLASSIC FINDINGS:** RBC AChE, BuChE activity.
- **TREATMENT:** Atropine, pralidoxime, benzodiazepines.

DIGOXIN TOXICITY

- **PATHO:** Inhibits the Na-K- ATPase pump increasing myocardial Ca and causing a positive inotropic effect.
- **CLASSIC PRESENTATION:** Ventricular arrhythmias, bradyarrhythmias, hyperkalemia (acute toxicity); neurologic symptoms (chronic and acute on chronic).
- **CLASSIC FINDINGS:** Serum K > 5 mEq/L, SDC 15 ng/mL or above.
- **TREATMENT:** DigiFAB.

ENVENOMATIONS

- **PATHO:** A complex pool of components that contribute to toxicity.
- **CLASSIC PRESENTATION:** Dependent on snake species, but may include hematologic, neurologic, or myologic effects.
- **CLASSIC FINDINGS:** Clinical signs of envenomation including progressing tissue injury, coagulopathy, neurologic abnormalities.
- **TREATMENT:** Antivenom (Anavip or Crofab).

MALIGNANT HYPERTHERMIA

- **PATHO:** Uncontrolled Ca release from RYR1 causing excessive muscle contraction, metabolic demands, and oxidative stress.
- **CLASSIC PRESENTATION:** Early tachycardia, hypercarbia; diaphoresis.
- **CLASSIC FINDINGS:** Muscle rigidity, hyperthermia, rhabdomyolysis, ventricular fibrillation, DIC.
- **TREATMENT:** Dantrolene, intravascular/extravascular cooling, benzodiazepines.

METHEMEGLOBINEMIA

- **PATHO:** Oxidative stress reduces hemoglobin-bound iron from Fe^{2+} to Fe^{3+}, creating methemoglobin.
- **CLASSIC PRESENTATION:** Cyanosis, dyspnea, dizziness, fatigue, AMS, arrhythmias, coma, death.
- **CLASSIC FINDINGS:** Methemoglobin > 10 %
- **TREATMENT:** Methylene blue, removal of oxidant.

NEUROLEPTIC MALIGNANT SYNDROME

- **PATHO:** Core temperature set point elevation via dopaminergic hypoactivity in the CNS and/or antagonism of the D2 receptor in the hypothalamus and nigrostriatal pathway.
- **CLASSIC PRESENTATION:** Tetrad of altered mental status, fever, muscle rigidity, and autonomic dysfunction.
- **CLASSIC FINDINGS:** Worsening EPS, mental status changes, and rigidity, autonomic dysfunction.
- **TREATMENT:** Discontinue affecting agent, bromocriptine, benzodiazepines.

OPIOID TOXICITY

- **PATHO:** Depresses ventilatory response to hypoxia due to diminished sensitivity of medullary chemoreceptors to hypercapnia.
- **CLASSIC PRESENTATION:** Analgesia, euphoria progressing to altered mental status, hypoxia, coma.
- **CLASSIC FINDINGS:** AMS, hypoventilation and decreased ventilatory response to hypoxia.
- **TREATMENT:** Naloxone.

SEDATIVE – HYPNOTIC TOXICITY

- **PATHO:** Potentiate GABA binding to GABA-A receptor (benzodiazepine); activation of GABA-A chloride channels without the presence of GABA (barbiturate).
- **CLASSIC PRESENTATION:** Slurred speech, hypothermia, ataxia, altered mental status, coma.
- **CLASSIC FINDINGS:** Normal vital sign coma (benzodiazepines), coma progressing to suppression of central respiratory drive (barbiturates).
- **TREATMENT:** Flumazenil (benzodiazepines), sodium bicarbonate (phenobarbital).

SEROTONIN SYNDROME

- **PATHO:** Excessive stimulation of 5-HT1A and/or 5-HT2A receptors.
- **CLASSIC PRESENTATION:** Rapid onset of mydriasis, altered mental status, hyperreflexia, clonus, and diaphoresis.
- **CLASSIC FINDINGS:** Sternbach's or Hunter criteria.
- **TREATMENT:** Cyproheptadine, intravascular/extravascular cooling, benzodiazepines.

SYMPATHOMIMETIC TOXICITY

- **PATHO:** Excitatory neurotransmission and smooth muscle, modulation of glycogenolysis, increased fatty acid oxidation, thermogenesis.
- **CLASSIC PRESENTATION:** Mydriasis, tachycardia, tachypnea, hypertension, hyperthermia, psychomotor agitation.
- **CLASSIC FINDINGS:** Tissue hypoxia, metabolic acidosis, end-organ dysfunction.
- **TREATMENT:** Benzodiazepines.

TOXIC ALCOHOLS

- **PATHO:** Metabolism by ADH and ALDH to toxic metabolites.
- **CLASSIC PRESENTATION:** Intoxication, AMS.
- **CLASSIC FINDINGS:** Osmolar gap and/or anion gap metabolic acidosis.
- **TREATMENT:** Fomepizole, thiamine, pyridoxine, hemodialysis.

CPSIA information can be obtained
at www.ICGtesting.com
Printed in the USA
LVHW110118180222
711336LV00003B/4